Contemporary Authors®
NEW REVISION SERIES

ISSN 0275-7176

REF
Z
1224
.C6
NRS
v.125

Contemporary

Authors®

80891

A Bio-Bibliographical Guide to Current Writers in Fiction, General Nonfiction, Poetry, Journalism, Drama, Motion Pictures, Television, and Other Fields

NEW REVISION SERIES volume 125

GALE®

THOMSON
━━━✦━━━ ™
GALE

Detroit • New York • San Diego • San Francisco • Cleveland • New Haven, Conn. • Waterville, Maine • London • Munich

Contemporary Authors, New Revision Series, Vol. 125

Project Editor
Tracey Watson

Editorial
Katy Balcer, Shavon Burden, Sara Constantakis, Natalie Fulkerson, Michelle Kazensky, Julie Keppen, Joshua Kondek, Jenai A. Mynatt, Lisa Kumar, Mary Ruby, Lemma Shomali, Susan Strickland, Maikue Vang

Research
Michelle Campbell, Tracie A. Richardson, Robert Whaley

Permissions
Margaret Chamberlain, Sue Rudolph

Imaging and Multimedia
Randy Bassett, Dean Dauphinais, Leitha Etheridge-Sims, Lezlie Light, Michael Logusz, Dan Newell, Christine O'Bryan, Kelly A. Quin

Composition and Electronic Capture
Kathy Sauer

Manufacturing
Lori Kessler

LIBRARY OF CONGRESS CATALOG CARD NUMBER 81-640179

ISBN 0-7876-6717-X
ISSN 0275-7176

Printed in the United States of America
10 9 8 7 6 5 4 3 2 1

Contents

Indexing note: All *Contemporary Authors* entries are indexed in the *Contemporary Authors* cumulative index, which is published separately and distributed twice a year.

As always, the most recent Contemporary Authors cumulative index continues to be the user's guide to the location of an individual author's listing.

Preface

Contemporary Authors (*CA*) provides information on approximately 115,000 writers in a wide range of media, including:

- Current writers of fiction, nonfiction, poetry, and drama whose works have been issued by commercial publishers, risk publishers, or university presses (authors whose books have been published only by known vanity or author-subsidized firms are ordinarily not included)

- Prominent print and broadcast journalists, editors, photojournalists, syndicated cartoonists, graphic novelists, screenwriters, television scriptwriters, and other media people

- Notable international authors

- Literary greats of the early twentieth century whose works are popular in today's high school and college curriculums and continue to elicit critical attention

A *CA* listing entails no charge or obligation. Authors are included on the basis of the above criteria and their interest to *CA* users. Sources of potential listees include trade periodicals, publishers' catalogs, librarians, and other users.

How to Get the Most out of *CA*: Use the Index

The key to locating an author's most recent entry is the *CA* cumulative index, which is published separately and distributed twice a year. It provides access to *all* entries in *CA* and *Contemporary Authors New Revision Series* (*CANR*). Always consult the latest index to find an author's most recent entry.

For the convenience of users, the *CA* cumulative index also includes references to all entries in these Gale literary series: *Authors and Artists for Young Adults, Authors in the News, Bestsellers, Black Literature Criticism, Black Literature Criticism Supplement, Black Writers, Children's Literature Review, Concise Dictionary of American Literary Biography, Concise Dictionary of British Literary Biography, Contemporary Authors Autobiography Series, Contemporary Authors Bibliographical Series, Contemporary Dramatists, Contemporary Literary Criticism, Contemporary Novelists, Contemporary Poets, Contemporary Popular Writers, Contemporary Southern Writers, Contemporary Women Poets, Dictionary of Literary Biography, Dictionary of Literary Biography Documentary Series, Dictionary of Literary Biography Yearbook, DISCovering Authors, DISCovering Authors: British, DISCovering Authors: Canadian, DISCovering Authors: Modules* (including modules for Dramatists, Most-Studied Authors, Multicultural Authors, Novelists, Poets, and Popular/Genre Authors), *DISCovering Authors 3.0, Drama Criticism, Drama for Students, Feminist Writers, Hispanic Literature Criticism, Hispanic Writers, Junior DISCovering Authors, Major Authors and Illustrators for Children and Young Adults, Major 20th-Century Writers, Native North American Literature, Novels for Students, Poetry Criticism, Poetry for Students, Short Stories for Students, Short Story Criticism, Something about the Author, Something about the Author Autobiography Series, St. James Guide to Children's Writers, St. James Guide to Crime & Mystery Writers, St. James Guide to Fantasy Writers, St. James Guide to Horror, Ghost & Gothic Writers, St. James Guide to Science Fiction Writers, St. James Guide to Young Adult Writers, Twentieth-Century Literary Criticism, 20th Century Romance and Historical Writers, World Literature Criticism,* and *Yesterday's Authors of Books for Children.*

A Sample Index Entry:

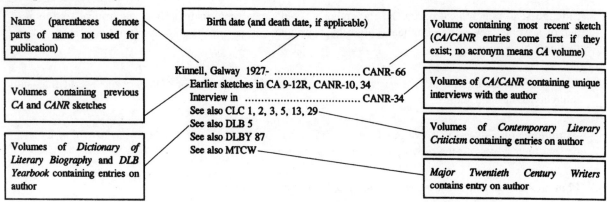

How Are Entries Compiled?

The editors make every effort to secure new information directly from the authors; listees' responses to our questionnaires and query letters provide most of the information featured in *CA*. For deceased writers, or those who fail to reply to requests for data, we consult other reliable biographical sources, such as those indexed in Gale's *Biography and Genealogy Master Index,* and bibliographical sources, including *National Union Catalog, LC MARC,* and *British National Bibliography.* Further details come from published interviews, feature stories, and book reviews, as well as information supplied by the authors' publishers and agents.

An asterisk (*) at the end of a sketch indicates that the listing has been compiled from secondary sources believed to be reliable but has not been personally verified for this edition by the author sketched.

What Kinds of Information Does An Entry Provide?

Sketches in *CA* contain the following biographical and bibliographical information:

- **Entry heading:** the most complete form of author's name, plus any pseudonyms or name variations used for writing

- **Personal information:** author's date and place of birth, family data, ethnicity, educational background, political and religious affiliations, and hobbies and leisure interests

- **Addresses:** author's home, office, or agent's addresses, plus e-mail and fax numbers, as available

- **Career summary:** name of employer, position, and dates held for each career post; resume of other vocational achievements; military service

- **Membership information:** professional, civic, and other association memberships and any official posts held

- **Awards and honors:** military and civic citations, major prizes and nominations, fellowships, grants, and honorary degrees

- **Writings:** a comprehensive, chronological list of titles, publishers, dates of original publication and revised editions, and production information for plays, television scripts, and screenplays

- **Adaptations:** a list of films, plays, and other media which have been adapted from the author's work

- **Work in progress:** current or planned projects, with dates of completion and/or publication, and expected publisher, when known

- **Sidelights:** a biographical portrait of the author's development; information about the critical reception of the author's works; revealing comments, often by the author, on personal interests, aspirations, motivations, and thoughts on writing

- **Interview:** a one-on-one discussion with authors conducted especially for *CA*, offering insight into authors' thoughts about their craft

- **Autobiographical essay:** an original essay written by noted authors for *CA*, a forum in which writers may present themselves, on their own terms, to their audience

- **Photographs:** portraits and personal photographs of notable authors

- **Biographical and critical sources:** a list of books and periodicals in which additional information on an author's life and/or writings appears

- **Obituary Notices** in *CA* provide date and place of birth as well as death information about authors whose full-length sketches appeared in the series before their deaths. The entries also summarize the authors' careers and writings and list other sources of biographical and death information.

Related Titles in the *CA* Series

Contemporary Authors Autobiography Series complements *CA* original and revised volumes with specially commissioned autobiographical essays by important current authors, illustrated with personal photographs they provide. Common topics include their motivations for writing, the people and experiences that shaped their careers, the rewards they derive from their work, and their impressions of the current literary scene.

Contemporary Authors Bibliographical Series surveys writings by and about important American authors since World War II. Each volume concentrates on a specific genre and features approximately ten writers; entries list works written by and about the author and contain a bibliographical essay discussing the merits and deficiencies of major critical and scholarly studies in detail.

Available in Electronic Formats

GaleNet. *CA* is available on a subscription basis through GaleNet, an online information resource that features an easy-to-use end-user interface, powerful search capabilities, and ease of access through the World-Wide Web. For more information, call 1-800-877-GALE.

Licensing. *CA* is available for licensing. The complete database is provided in a fielded format and is deliverable on such media as disk, CD-ROM, or tape. For more information, contact Gale's Business Development Group at 1-800-877-GALE, or visit us on our website at www.galegroup.com/bizdev.

Suggestions Are Welcome

The editors welcome comments and suggestions from users on any aspect of the *CA* series. If readers would like to recommend authors for inclusion in future volumes of the series, they are cordially invited to write the Editors at *Contemporary Authors*, Gale Group, 27500 Drake Rd., Farmington Hills, MI 48331-3535; or call at 1-248-699-4253; or fax at 1-248-699-8054.

Contemporary Authors Product Advisory Board

The editors of *Contemporary Authors* are dedicated to maintaining a high standard of excellence by publishing comprehensive, accurate, and highly readable entries on a wide array of writers. In addition to the quality of the content, the editors take pride in the graphic design of the series, which is intended to be orderly yet inviting, allowing readers to utilize the pages of *CA* easily and with efficiency. Despite the longevity of the *CA* print series, and the success of its format, we are mindful that the vitality of a literary reference product is dependent on its ability to serve its users over time. As literature, and attitudes about literature, constantly evolve, so do the reference needs of students, teachers, scholars, journalists, researchers, and book club members. To be certain that we continue to keep pace with the expectations of our customers, the editors of *CA* listen carefully to their comments regarding the value, utility, and quality of the series. Librarians, who have firsthand knowledge of the needs of library users, are a valuable resource for us. The *Contemporary Authors* Product Advisory Board, made up of school, public, and academic librarians, is a forum to promote focused feedback about *CA* on a regular basis. The seven-member advisory board includes the following individuals, whom the editors wish to thank for sharing their expertise:

- **Anne M. Christensen,** Librarian II, Phoenix Public Library, Phoenix, Arizona.

- **Barbara C. Chumard,** Reference/Adult Services Librarian, Middletown Thrall Library, Middletown, New York.

- **Eva M. Davis,** Youth Department Manager, Ann Arbor District Library, Ann Arbor, Michigan.

- **Adam Janowski, Jr.,** Library Media Specialist, Naples High School Library Media Center, Naples, Florida.

- **Robert Reginald,** Head of Technical Services and Collection Development, California State University, San Bernadino, California.

- **Stephen Weiner,** Director, Maynard Public Library, Maynard, Massachusetts.

International Advisory Board

Well-represented among the 115,000 author entries published in *Contemporary Authors* are sketches on notable writers from many non-English-speaking countries. The primary criteria for inclusion of such authors has traditionally been the publication of at least one title in English, either as an original work or as a translation. However, the editors of *Contemporary Authors* came to observe that many important international writers were being overlooked due to a strict adherence to our inclusion criteria. In addition, writers who were publishing in languages other than English were not being covered in the traditional sources we used for identifying new listees. Intent on increasing our coverage of international authors, including those who write only in their native language and have not been translated into English, the editors enlisted the aid of a board of advisors, each of whom is an expert on the literature of a particular country or region. Among the countries we focused attention on are Mexico, Puerto Rico, Spain, Italy, France, Germany, Luxembourg, Belgium, the Netherlands, Norway, Sweden, Denmark, Finland, Taiwan, Singapore, Malaysia, Thailand, South Africa, Israel, and Japan, as well as England, Scotland, Wales, Ireland, Australia, and New Zealand. The sixteen-member advisory board includes the following individuals, whom the editors wish to thank for sharing their expertise:

- **Lowell A. Bangerter,** Professor of German, University of Wyoming, Laramie, Wyoming.

- **Nancy E. Berg,** Associate Professor of Hebrew and Comparative Literature, Washington University, St. Louis, Missouri.

- **Frances Devlin-Glass,** Associate Professor, School of Literary and Communication Studies, Deakin University, Burwood, Victoria, Australia.

- **David William Foster,** Regent's Professor of Spanish, Interdisciplinary Humanities, and Women's Studies, Arizona State University, Tempe, Arizona.

- **Hosea Hirata,** Director of the Japanese Program, Associate Professor of Japanese, Tufts University, Medford, Massachusetts.

- **Jack Kolbert,** Professor Emeritus of French Literature, Susquehanna University, Selinsgrove, Pennsylvania.

- **Mark Libin,** Professor, University of Manitoba, Winnipeg, Manitoba, Canada.

- **C. S. Lim,** Professor, University of Malaya, Kuala Lumpur, Malaysia.

- **Eloy E. Merino,** Assistant Professor of Spanish, Northern Illinois University, DeKalb, Illinois.

- **Linda M. Rodríguez Guglielmoni,** Associate Professor, University of Puerto Rico—Mayagüez, Puerto Rico.

- **Sven Hakon Rossel,** Professor and Chair of Scandinavian Studies, University of Vienna, Vienna, Austria.

- **Steven R. Serafin,** Director, Writing Center, Hunter College of the City University of New York, New York City.

- **David Smyth,** Lecturer in Thai, School of Oriental and African Studies, University of London, England.

- **Ismail S. Talib,** Senior Lecturer, Department of English Language and Literature, National University of Singapore, Singapore.

- **Dionisio Viscarri,** Assistant Professor, Ohio State University, Columbus, Ohio.

- **Mark Williams,** Associate Professor, English Department, University of Canterbury, Christchurch, New Zealand.

CA Numbering System and Volume Update Chart

Occasionally questions arise about the *CA* numbering system and which volumes, if any, can be discarded. Despite numbers like "29-32R," "97-100" and "217," the entire *CA* print series consists of only 270 physical volumes with the publication of *CA* Volume 218. The following charts note changes in the numbering system and cover design, and indicate which volumes are essential for the most complete, up-to-date coverage.

CA First Revision
- 1-4R through 41-44R (11 books)
  Cover: Brown with black and gold trim.
  There will be no further First Revision volumes because revised entries are now being handled exclusively through the more efficient *New Revision Series* mentioned below.

CA Original Volumes
- 45-48 through 97-100 (14 books)
  Cover: Brown with black and gold trim.
  101 through 218 (118 books)
  Cover: Blue and black with orange bands.
  The same as previous *CA* original volumes but with a new, simplified numbering system and new cover design.

CA Permanent Series
- *CAP*-1 and *CAP*-2 (2 books)
  Cover: Brown with red and gold trim.
  There will be no further Permanent Series volumes because revised entries are now being handled exclusively through the more efficient *New Revision Series* mentioned below.

CA New Revision Series
- CANR-1 through CANR-125 (125 books)
  Cover: Blue and black with green bands.
  Includes only sketches requiring significant changes; **sketches are taken from any previously published CA, CAP, or CANR volume.**

If You Have:	You May Discard:
CA First Revision Volumes 1-4R through 41-44R and *CA Permanent Series* Volumes 1 and 2	*CA* Original Volumes 1, 2, 3, 4 and Volumes 5-6 through 41-44
CA Original Volumes 45-48 through 97-100 and 101 through 218	**NONE:** These volumes will not be superseded by corresponding revised volumes. Individual entries from these and all other volumes appearing in the left column of this chart may be revised and included in the various volumes of the *New Revision Series*.
CA New Revision Series Volumes *CANR*-1 through *CANR*-125	**NONE:** The *New Revision Series* does not replace any single volume of *CA*. Instead, volumes of *CANR* include entries from many previous *CA* series volumes. All *New Revision Series* volumes must be retained for full coverage.

A Sampling of Authors and Media People
Featured in This Volume

Isaac Asimov

Asimov, a prolific writer and titan in the science-fiction genre, was posthumously inducted into the Science Fiction and Fantasy Hall of Fame in 1997. Two of his works from the 1970s, the novel *The Gods Themselves* and the story "The Bicentennial Man," won both the prestigious Hugo and Nebula awards. Asimov also garnered Hugo Awards for 1983's *Foundation's Edge* and his 1995 memoir, *I. Asimov.* Asimov died in 1992, leaving considerable amounts of unpublished writings. His wife organized this manuscript into an autobiography titled *It's Been a Good Life,* which was published in 2002.

Andre Dubus III

Dubus launched his literary career by writing short fiction, but it was his debut novel, *House of Sand and Fog,* that brought him to national prominence upon its publication in 2000. The novel was a National Book Award finalist, a *New York Times* bestseller, and a featured selection in Oprah Winfrey's book club. The positive reception of the novel culminated in its adaptation into a film of the same title that was released to critical acclaim in 2003.

Henry Louis Gates, Jr.

Gates is a distinguished and influential scholar, having taught at Cornell, Duke, and Harvard universities. As the W. E. B. DuBois Professor of the Humanities at Harvard, he expanded the university's African-American Studies program, drawing famous lecturers and sometimes creating controversy. Concurrently, he produced such works as *Black Literature and Literary Theory* and *Colored People: A Memoir.* His most recent publications include *The Trials of Phillis Wheatley* and 2004's *America behind the Color Line.*

Bobbie Ann Mason

Mason is a highly regarded fiction writer whose themes of muted hopes and alienation play out in a rural, western-Kentucky landscape that unsuccessfully resists the intrusion of popular culture and suburban values. Her first published volume of fiction, *Shiloh and Other Stories,* won a PEN-Faulkner Award in 1983. Another collection, *Love Life: Stories,* was widely praised upon its release in 1989. Mason branched out into nonfiction with a memoir, *Clear Springs,* which was a Pulitzer-Prize finalist in 2000 and a short biography of legendary singer Elvis Presley, published in 2003.

Mary Beth Norton

Norton is considered a pioneer in the field of history, as both an educator and author. In 1971 she became the first woman hired in Cornell University's history department, she helped develop the school's women's studies program, and she was a founding member of the International Federation for Research in Women's History. Norton's publications include *Liberty's Daughters, Founding Mothers & Fathers,* which was a finalist for the Pulitzer prize in history in 1997, and *In the Devil's Snare: The Salem Witchcraft Crisis of 1692,* published in 2002.

Andrew A. Rooney

Rooney's trademark dry wit has made his short essay segment on the CBS newsmagazine *60 Minutes* a hit since its debut in 1978. The rants of an ordinary man about the mundane aspects of life have resulted in four Emmy awards for commentating and a syndicated newspaper column. Rooney has also published several collections of his essays, including *A Few Minutes with Andy Rooney, Pieces of My Mind,* and his most recent offering, *Years of Minutes,* published in 2003.

Stephen Sondheim

Composer and lyricist Sondheim's contributions to musical theater—in a career spanning six decades—have earned him a Kennedy Center Honor for Lifetime Achievement. Beginning with *West Side Story,* Sondheim's musicals have drawn appreciative audiences and critical acclaim. He is an eight-time Tony Award winner for such works as *A Little Night Music, Sweeney Todd: The Demon Barber of Fleet Street,* and 2002's revival of *Into the Woods.* Sondheim has also garnered a Pulitzer Prize for drama in 1985 for *Sunday in the Park with George* and an Academy Award in 1990 for his song "Sooner or Later (I Always Get My Man)" from the film *Dick Tracy.*

Quentin Tarantino

Tarantino, a screenplay writer and director, attracted widespread critical attention with the film *Reservoir Dogs.* This film set the tone for Taratino's trademark aesthetic of meshing pop culture, violence, and literary dialogue evident in subsequent motion pictures, including his most notable hit *Pulp Fiction.* Tarantino received several awards for *Pulp Fiction,* including the Academy and Golden Globe Award for best screenplay (with Robert Avary) in 1994. In 2003 Tarantino expanded his creative penchant to fiction writing with the novel *Kill Bill,* which was published almost simultaneously with the film adapted from it *Kill Bill, Vol. 1* released by Miramax.

Acknowledgments

Grateful acknowledgment is made to those publishers, photographers, and artists whose work appear with these authors' essays. Following is a list of the copyright holders who have granted us permission to reproduce material in this volume of *CA*. Every effort has been made to trace copyright, but if omissions have been made, please let us know.

Photographs/Art

Peter Abrahams: Abrahams, photograph by Carl Van Vechten. Reproduced by permission of the Estate of Carl Van Vechten.

Isaac Asimov: Asimov, photograph. AP/Wide World Photos. Reproduced by permission.

David Attenborough: Attenborough, photograph. AP/Wide World Photos. Reproduced by permission.

Bernardo Bertolucci: Bertolucci, photograph. The Kobal Collection. Reproduced by permission.

Roy Blount, Jr.: Blount, photograph. © Roger Ressmeyer/Corbis. Reproduced by permission.

Robert Bly: Bly, photograph by Christopher Felver. Reproduced by permission.

Ray Bradbury: Bradbury, photograph. The Library of Congress.

Asa Briggs: Briggs, photograph. © Christopher Cormack/Corbis. Reproduced by permission.

Andrei Codrescu: Codrescu, photograph. Archive Photos, Inc./Laurence Agron. Reproduced by permission.

Joan Didion: Didion, photograph. © Jerry Bauer. Reproduced by permission.

Annie Dillard: Dillard, photograph. © Jerry Bauer. Reproduced by permission.

Lawrence Ferlinghetti: Ferlinghetti, photograph. AP/Wide World Photos. Reproduced by Permission.

Francis Fukuyama: Fukuyama, November, 1991, photograph by Brad Markel. Brad Markel/Liaison Agency. Reproduced by permission.

Diana Gabaldon: Gabaldon, photograph. © Jerry Bauer. Reproduced by permission.

Henry Louis Gates, Jr.: Gates, photograph by Jerry Bauer. © Jerry Bauer. Reproduced by permission.

Maggie Gee: Gee, photograph. © Rune Hellestad/Corbis. Reproduced by permission.

William Gibson: Gibson, photograph. Archive Photos, Inc. Reproduced by permission.

Herbert Gold: Gold, photograph by Chris Felver. Hulton/Archive by Getty Images. Reproduced by permission.

Arthur Golden: Golden, photograph by Jerry Bauer. © Jerry Bauer. Reproduced by permission.

Bo Goldman: Goldman, 1982, photograph. AP/Wide World Photos. Reproduced by permission.

A

ABERCROMBIE, Nicholas 1944-

PERSONAL: Born April 13, 1944, in Birmingham, England; son of Michael (a university professor) and Jane (a university professor; maiden name, Johnson) Abercrombie; married Brenda Patterson (a publisher), January 2, 1969; children: Robert Benjamin, Joseph Edward. *Ethnicity:* "White." *Education:* Queen's College, Oxford, B.A., 1966; London School of Economics and Political Science, London, M.Sc., 1968; University of Lancaster, Ph.D., 1980. *Politics:* Socialist.

ADDRESSES: Home—1A Derwent Rd., Lancaster LA1 3ES, England. *Office*—Department of Sociology, University of Lancaster, Bailrigg, Lancaster, England; fax: 01524-36841. *E-mail*—n.abercrombie@lancaster.ac.uk.

CAREER: University of London, University College, London, England, research officer in town planning, 1968-70; University of Lancaster, Bailrigg, England, lecturer, 1970-83, senior lecturer, 1983-88, reader, 1988-90, professor of sociology, 1990—, pro-vice chancellor, 1995—. Framework Press, chair. Active in local political organizations and with Campaign for Nuclear Disarmament.

MEMBER: Royal Society of Arts (fellow), British Sociological Association.

AWARDS, HONORS: Morris Ginsberg fellow, London School of Economics and Political Science, University of London, 1983.

WRITINGS:

Class, Structure, and Knowledge, Basil Blackwell (Oxford, England), 1980.

(With Stephen Hill and Bryan S. Turner) *The Dominant Ideology Thesis,* Allen & Unwin (London, England), 1980.

(With John Urry) *Capital, Labour, and the Middle Classes,* Allen & Unwin (London, England), 1983.

(With Stephen Hill and Bryan S. Turner) *The Penguin Dictionary of Sociology,* Penguin (London, England), 1984, 4th edition, 2000.

(With Stephen Hill and Bryan S. Turner) *Sovereign Individuals of Capitalism,* Allen & Unwin (London, England), 1986.

(With Alan Warde, Keith Soothill, and others) *Contemporary British Society,* Polity Press (Cambridge, England), 1988, 3rd edition, 2000.

(Editor, with Stephen Hill and Bryan S. Turner) *Dominant Ideologies,* Unwin Hyman (London, England), 1990.

(Editor, with Russell Keat) *Enterprise Culture,* Routledge (London, England), 1991.

(Editor, with Alan Warde) *Social Change in Contemporary Britain,* Polity Press (Cambridge, England), 1992.

(Editor, with Russell Keat and Nigel Whiteley) *The Authority of the Individual,* Routledge (London, England), 1994.

(Editor, with Alan Warde) *Family, Household, and Life-Course,* Framework Press (Lancaster, England), 1994.

(Editor, with Alan Warde) *Stratification and Inequality,* Framework Press (Lancaster, England), 1994.

(Editor, with Russell Keat and Nigel Whiteley) *The Authority of the Consumer,* Routledge (London, England), 1994.

Television and Society, Polity Press (Cambridge, England), 1996.

(With Brian Longhurst) *Audiences: A Sociological Theory of Performance and Imagination,* Sage Publications (London, England), 1998.

(Editor, with Alan Warde) *The Contemporary British Society Reader,* Polity Press (Cambridge, England), 2000.

Contributor to books, including *The University in an Urban Environment: A Study of Activity Patterns from a Planning Viewpoint,* Sage Publications (London, England), 1973.

WORK IN PROGRESS: An introductory book on sociology as a way of thinking, for Polity Press; further editions of *The Penguin Dictionary of Sociology; Getting and Spending,* a book on money.

SIDELIGHTS: Nicholas Abercrombie once told *CA:* "I am an academic interested in the sociological analysis of culture. My primary interest lies in the impact of cultural values on a society. *The Dominant Ideology Thesis,* for instance, is an examination of the idea that there are dominant beliefs in a society which become widely shared and help to perpetuate the particular social order. My coauthors and I showed, to the contrary, that in historical societies, and contemporary ones, there is either no dominant culture or, if there is, it makes remarkable little impact on subordinate groups, mainly because the machinery for transmitting it is relatively inefficient.

"In other work, past or projected, I examine the relationship of individualistic values to economic life, the impact of television on audiences, particularly in the way that viewers talk about television and the manner in which a consumer culture affects the book publishing industry.

"I also try to write introductory books on sociology, books that are accessible to the general reader. This accessibility is very important to sociology, as is a method of teaching that is student-centered, not teacher-centered. The latter consideration has dictated my involvement with a firm that publishes teaching materials for use in schools in the United Kingdom."

BIOGRAPHICAL AND CRITICAL SOURCES:

PERIODICALS

Times Literary Supplement, September 11, 1981.

*   *   *

ABRAHAMS, Peter (Henry) 1919-

PERSONAL: Born March 19, 1919, in Vrededorp, South Africa; son of James Henry and Angelina (DuPlessis) Abrahams; married Dorothy Pennington, 1942 (marriage dissolved, 1948); married Daphne Elizabeth Miller (an artist), June 1, 1948; children: (second marriage) Anne, Aron, Naomi. *Education:* Attended St. Peter's College and Teacher's Training College. *Hobbies and other interests:* Gardening, tennis, walking, conversation, reading, travel.

ADDRESSES: Home—Red Hills, P. O. Box, St. Andrew, Jamaica, West Indies. *Agent*—Faber & Faber Ltd., 3 Queen Sq., London WC1N 3AU, England; and 50 Cross St., Winchester, MA.

CAREER: Began working as a tinsmith's helper at the age of nine; attended schools between periods of working at jobs such as kitchen helper, dishwasher, porter, and clerk; failed in his attempt to start a school near Capetown for poor Africans; worked for a short time as an editor in Durban; in 1939, to reach England, he took work as a stoker, and spent two years at sea; correspondent in Kenya and South Africa for the London *Observer* and the *New York Herald Tribune* (New York and Paris), 1952-54; commissioned by British Government in 1955 to write a book on Jamaica; immigrated to Jamaica in 1956; regular radio news commentator in Jamaica, 1957—; editor of the *West Indian Economist,* Jamaica, 1958-62, and radio commentator and controller for the "West Indian News" Program, 1958-62; full-time writer, 1964—. Radio Jamaica chairman, set up a new ownership structure, making major interest groups into shareholders, 1978-80.

MEMBER: International PEN, Society of Authors, Authors League.

WRITINGS:

NOVELS

Song of the City, Dorothy Crisp (London, England), 1945.

Peter Abrahams

Mine Boy, Dorothy Crisp (London, England), 1946, Knopf (New York, NY), 1955, reprinted with an introduction by Charles R. Larson, Collier Books (New York, NY), 1970.

The Path of Thunder, Harper (New York, NY), 1948, Chatham Bookseller, 1975.

Wild Conquest (historical fiction), Harper (New York, NY), 1950, Anchor Books, 1970.

A Wreath for Udomo, Knopf (New York, NY), 1956, Collier Books (New York, NY), 1971.

A Night of Their Own, Knopf (New York, NY), 1965.

This Island Now, Faber (London, England), 1966, Knopf (New York, NY), 1967, revised edition, Faber & Faber (London, England), 1985.

The View from Coyaba (historical fiction), Faber & Faber (London, England), 1985.

The Coyaba Chronicles: Reflections on the Black Experience in the 20th Century, Ian Randle (Kingston, Jamaica, West Indies), 2001.

OTHER

Here, Friend: Poems, [Durban, South Africa], 1941.

A Blackman Speaks of Freedom (poetry), Universal Printing Works (Durban, South Africa), 1941.

Dark Testament (short stories), Allen & Unwin (London, England), 1942, Kraus Reprint, 1970.

Return to Goli (autobiography), Faber & Faber (London, England), 1953.

Tell Freedom (autobiography), Knopf (New York, NY), 1954, published as *Tell Freedom: Memories of Africa,* Knopf (New York, NY), 1969, abridged edition, Macmillan (New York, NY), 1970.

Jamaica: An Island Mosaic (travel), Her Majesty's Stationery Office (London, England), 1957.

(Editor) *Souvenir Pictorial Review of the West Indies Federation, 1947-57,* Edna Manley (Kingston, Jamaica), c. 1958.

(With the staff of *Holiday* magazine and others) *The World of Mankind,* Golden Press (New York, NY), 1962.

(With others) *History of the Pan-African Congress,* Hammersmith Bookshop, 1963.

The Black Experience in the 20th Century: An Autobiography and Meditation, Indiana University Press (Bloomington, IN), 2000.

Contributor to *Modern African Prose,* edited by Richard Rive and to *Schwarze Ballade,* edited by Janheinz Jahn. Also author of radio scripts for British Broadcasting Corp. during the 1950s. Contributor to *Holiday* and *Cape Standard.* Abrahams's books have been translated into numerous languages, including French and Russian.

ADAPTATIONS: Abrahams's novel *Mine Boy* was adapted as a play; the novel *Path of Thunder* was made into a movie and a ballet in the Soviet Union.

SIDELIGHTS: Peter Abrahams's writings provide insight into the racial and political troubles of his native country, South Africa. Although the author left South Africa when he was only twenty years old, that country has continued to dominate his imagination and his poetry, prose, and novels.

Abrahams's father was Ethiopian, while his mother was of mixed French and African ancestry. This put him in the legal category "Colored," a term referring to the descendants of blacks and early white settlers. His first book was published at a time when nearly all the novelists in South Africa were white. The Colored people had traditionally remained aloof from blacks, but Abrahams was unusual in that he took political sides with black South Africans. Abrahams also stood apart by being one of South Africa's first non-whites to make a living as a writer. And whether using fiction or autobiography, his focus has remained on the non-whites' struggle for respect and political power. In the book *Peter Abrahams,* Michael Wade wrote that "Peter Abrahams is a novelist of ideas. He writes about the machinery of politics and power, but he uses his considerable grasp of this area of activity to serve his central interest, which is the problem of individual freedom in contemporary affairs."

Abrahams grew up in the slums of Johannesburg, where illiteracy was common. He didn't learn to read until he was nine years old, but thereafter immersed himself in books. He sought out British classics, including Shakespeare, and found works by black American authors in the local library. At the age of eleven, he started writing short stories. His earliest successful poems were published *Bantu World,* a white-owned newspaper aimed at black readers. These poems were later collected in *Here, Friend* and *A Blackman Speaks of Freedom.*

While attending St. Peter's, Abrahams became interested in the Pan-Africanism and the ideas of Marcus Garvey. He also made friends who initiated him into Marxism. For the next few years he wrote short stories, sketches, and poems and engaged in political activity. Abrahams's youthful short stories and sketches, collected under the title *Dark Testament,* "express with uncontrolled emotion the feelings of loneliness and despair of the young writer and intellectual in the context of political struggle," according to a writer for *Dictionary of Literary Biography.* "Given his color and the rarity of left-wing writers of fiction in South Africa in the late 1930s, it is not surprising that Abrahams felt isolated. But another conflict was also palpable: between Abrahams's simultaneous attraction to and distrust of strong ideological frameworks. This tension was to become a distinguishing mark of his literary career."

In addition to his writing, Abrahams worked in trade unions in Johannesburg with the Trotskyite Max Gor-

don, then moved to Cape Town for a while before going on to Durban. There he came under Stalinist-Communist influences. His political activities drew unfavorable attention from the authorities, and Abrahams eventually decided to leave the country. He went into exile by signing on as a crewmember of a freighter bound for England. In his autobiographical *Return to Goli,* he explains, "I had to escape or slip into that negative destructiveness that is the offspring of bitterness and frustration." He later moved to France, and then to Jamaica, which became his permanent home. After immigrating, he only returned to South Africa as a visitor.

Abrahams's early novels were influenced by Marxist thought, and are less concerned with politics than with issues of race and economics. The terrible consequences of urbanization and industrialization are exposed in *Song of the City* and *Mine Boy,* which trace the lives of young black workers as they move from country to city or in the diamond mines. In both novels, whites oppress and mistreat non-whites. *Mine Boy* stands as "the highest achievement" of the early phase of Abrahams's career, suggested the *Dictionary of Literary Biography* writer. "With it he staked his claim to a permanent place in South Africa's literary history on three solid and impressive grounds. First, he presents objective urban reality from a black point of view; second, for the first time in a South African novel, a convincing account of the state of mind of urban blacks is presented; and third, he is the first South African novelist to pose a possible solution to the continuing crisis of black experience in the industrial city." In *The Path of Thunder,* another early novel, Abrahams turns to the theme of interracial love, exploring its impact on a young Colored schoolteacher and an Afrikaner girl. Their passionate affair ends tragically when her community discovers they are lovers.

Two years later Abrahams moved in yet another direction, this time reconstructing the era of the Afrikaner migration or "Great Trek" in *Wild Conquest,* an historical novel in which he makes an effort to be fair to all the major ethnic groups in South Africa—Bantu, Boer and Briton. Abrahams's fiction became more political after these early works, all of which were written in the 1940s. *A Wreath for Udomo,* published just before Ghana attained its independence, was an attempt to predict what might happen when independent black African nations were confronted with the choice between the financial advantages of collaborating with the white regimes in southern Africa and the moral imperative of opposing them by actively supporting black liberation movements.

While Abrahams always felt strongly about the problems of non-whites in Africa, when writing his early works he restrained his anger toward the government. In *Return to Goli,* he explains that he had "purged himself of hatred," since "art and beauty come of love, not hate." Believing that love was necessary to overcome racial prejudice, Abrahams frequently incorporated mixed-race love affairs in his early novels. These relationships and their resulting children represented a new order, where the individual would not be judged by his color. In *An African Treasury,* Abrahams claims that this perception comes from tribal Africa, where "the attitude to colour is healthy and normal. Colour does not matter. Colour is an act of God that neither confers privileges nor imposes handicaps on a man. . . . What does matter to the tribal African, what is important, is the complex pattern of his position within his own group and his relations with the other members of the group. . . . The important things in his life are anything but race and colour until they are forced on him."

And yet at the same time, Abrahams felt that the great influence of African tribalism on contemporary blacks was a handicap. He embraced Western culture, because, as he wrote in an issue of *International Affairs,* "The true motive forces of Western culture are to be found in the first place in the teachings of the Christ who taught a new concept of men's relations with their God and with each other, a concept that cuts across tribal gods and tribal loyalties and embraces all men in all lands offering them a common brotherhood." In his novel *A Night of Their Own,* Abrahams emphasizes the common goals of South African Indians and blacks. Both groups work together to change their tyrannical government. While the setting is fictional, Abrahams tied it to contemporary issues by dedicating the book to imprisoned South African activists Walter Sisulu and Nelson Mandela.

Although critics have frequently praised Abrahams's handling of political issues, his characterizations have not been as well received. In the *New York Times Book Review* critique of *A Night of Their Own,* Martin Levin said, "What is rich in this novel is the complexity of its political climate," but added that "what snarls mat-

ters is the author's tendency to spell out his characters' thinking." In *The Writing of Peter Abrahams,* Kolawole Ogungbesan voiced a similar concern: "The tone of [*A Night of Their Own*] is uncompromisingly noble and determinedly serious, making the characters' gestures as stagey as their dialogues. But the cumulative effect is powerful."

In *This Island Now,* Abrahams turns from his early call for a pluralistic society to insisting that blacks first establish their own identity, socially and politically, as free men. He also stops looking to Western civilization for solutions. The plot concerns a left-wing black leader who rises to power on a fictional island. But according to Ogungbesan, "There is no doubt that the physical terrain of *This Island Now* is largely that of Jamaica as described in [Abrahams's] essay, *The Real Jamaica,* . . . [with] the political terrain of Haiti." *New York Times Book Review* contributor Peter Buitenhuis commented, "As an analysis of this kind of political process, [*This Island Now*] throws light on the motivations of black leaders who have risen to power in recent years in the Caribbean and elsewhere. Unfortunately [Abrahams's] attempt to make this material into a novel has not been too successful. He has tried to embody each interest—political, journalistic, financial, etc.—in a different character, and as a result, the book is overpopulated and over-schematic." But Ogungbesan felt the book's strengths and weaknesses are inseparable, and that it must be regarded as a purely political work. He remarked, "The book is a serious political novel precisely because it avoids the easy banalities that its theme . . . might provoke. . . . Abrahams is so preoccupied with the political conflict that everything else recedes to the background."

The View from Coyaba is the work that reflects Abrahams's thorough disenchantment with what he calls "destructive Westernism." Some critics, however, find Abrahams's work closer to a tract or treatise than a novel. While *Times Literary Supplement* contributor David Wright considered the book "highminded, sincere, committed," he thought that "as a philosophic and humane survey of the history of black emancipation since the British abolition of slavery, his book may be recommended; as a novel, not." Judith Wilson, writing in the *New York Times Book Review,* agreed in finding *The View from Coyaba* "unmistakably didactic fiction." However, she found that "the originality of Mr. Abrahams's message, its global sweep and political urgency exert their own force. . . . Peter Abrahams challenges us to rethink a large chunk of modern history and to question many of our current ideological assumptions." But Andrew Salkey in *World Literature Today* never questioned whether the work is a true novel, as Abrahams has produced, he stated, "the most dramatically resonant writing I have read in many years. . . . It is not only a composite novelistic picture, but also a reverberating metaphor."

Reflecting on Abrahams's prose style, an essayist for *Contemporary Novelists* noted that the author has "always written in a simple, direct prose style which wavers between superior reportage and maudlin romanticizing. He is at his best when transcribing newsworthy events which have a basis in fact; his autobiographical and travel writings, for instance, are superb. However, he has a regrettable tendency to sentimentalize personal relationships between men and women, especially if they are of different races, as they so often are in his novels." Abrahams is better when writing of exciting events, such as intense political debates, savage frontier battles, or impromptu labor strikes, according to the essayist. At such times Abrahams "can carry the reader along swiftly and persuasively, building up a spell-binding momentum."

Abrahams's books do not point to any definite means of eliminating racism, but they do contain hope that conditions will improve. Ogungbesan affirmed, "Himself such an incurable optimist, all his books are open to the future, based on his belief that change is inevitable, a natural process. This is why the image of the day assumes such symbolic significance in his novels. The implication is that although the black people in South Africa are passing through a long night, their ordeal will not last for ever: after the night inevitably comes the dawn. Abrahams thinks that it will be a glorious dawn if the whites and the blacks can cooperate peacefully to work towards that day."

BIOGRAPHICAL AND CRITICAL SOURCES:

BOOKS

Abrahams, Peter, *Return to Goli,* Faber & Faber (London, England), 1953.

Barnett, Ursula A., *A Vision of Order: A Study of Black South African Literature in English (1914-1980),* University of Massachusetts Press (Amherst, MA), 1983.

Bock, Hedwig, and Albert Wertheim, editors, *Essays on Contemporary Post-Colonial Fiction,* Hueber (Munich, Germany), 1986.

Contemporary Literary Criticism, Volume 4, Gale (Detroit, MI), 1975.

Contemporary Novelists, 6th edition, St. James Press (Detroit, MI), 1996.

Dictionary of Literary Biography, Gale (Detroit, MI), Volume 117: *Twentieth-Century Caribbean and Black African Writers,* 1992, Volume 225: *South African Writers,* 2000.

Ensor, Robert, *The Novels of Peter Abrahams and the Rise of Nationalism in Africa,* Verlag Die Blaue Eule (Essen, Germany), 1992.

Gakwandi, Shatto Arthur, *The Novel and Contemporary Experience in Africa,* Africana (New York, NY), 1977.

Heywood, Christopher, editor, *Perspectives on African Literature,* Africana (New York, NY), 1971.

Hughes, Langston, editor, *An African Treasury,* Gollancz, 1961.

Larson, Charles R., *The Emergence of African Fiction,* Indiana University Press (Bloomington, IN), 1972.

Lindfors, Bernth, *Early Nigerian Literature,* Africana Publishing, 1982.

Ogungbesan, Kolawole, *The Writing of Peter Abrahams,* Hodder & Stoughton (London, England), 1979.

Tucker, Martin, *Africa in Modern Literature: A Survey of Contemporary Writing in English,* Ungar (New York, NY), 1967.

Wade, Michael, *Peter Abrahams,* Evans Brothers (London, England), 1971.

PERIODICALS

Black American Literature Forum, spring-summer, 1987, Cynthia Hamilton, "Work and Culture: The Evolution of Consciousness in Urban Industrial Society in the Fiction of William Attaway and Peter Abrahams," pp. 147-163.

Commonwealth Essays and Studies, spring, 1990, Serge Menager, "Peter Abrahams, Icare Metis," pp. 91-100.

Critique: Studies in Modern Fiction, Volume XI, number 1, 1968; December, 1969, Michael Wade, "The Novels of Peter Abrahams," pp. 54-60.

English in Africa, October, 1989, Jean-Philippe Wade, "Peter Abrahams's *The Path of Thunder:* The Crisis of the Liberal Subject," pp. 61-75; November,

1997, Catherine Woeber, "A Long Occupation of the Mind: Peter Abrahams's Perspective on His Education," pp. 87-104.

English Studies, number 50, 1969, Hena Maes-Jelinek, "Race Relationships and Identity in Peter Abrahams's 'Pluralia,'" pp. 106-112.

Entertainment Weekly, April 21, 1995, p. 49.

International Fiction Review, number 13, 1986, Bernth Lindfors, "Exile and Aesthetic Distance: Geographical Influences on Political Commitment in the Works of Peter Abrahams," pp. 76-81.

Journal of Southern African Affairs, Volume 2, number 2, 1977, Chukwudi T. Maduka, "Colonialism, Nation-Building and the Revolutionary Intellectual in Peter Abrahams's *A Wreath for Udomo,*" pp. 245-247.

Library Journal, May 1, 1991, p. 89; July, 1992, p. 119.

Los Angeles Times Book Review, July 14, 1985.

New Statesman, February 22, 1985.

New World Quarterly, Sylvia Wynter, number 3, 1967, "The Instant Novel Now," pp. 78-81.

New Yorker, September 25, 1965.

New York Times Book Review, April 11, 1965; September 24, 1967; April 2, 1972; May 26, 1985.

Observer, February 17, 1985.

Obsidian, numbers 1-2, 1980, Paul A. Scanlon, "Dream and Reality in Abrahams's *A Wreath for Udomo,*" pp. 25-32.

Presence Africaine, 83, number 3, 1972, Kolawole Ogungbesan, "The Political Novels of Peter Abrahams," pp. 33-50.

Pretexts, summer, 1990, Stephen Gray, "The Long Eye of History: Four Autobiographical Texts by Peter Abrahams," pp. 99-115.

Publishers Weekly, September 29, 1989, p. 60; January 10, 1994, p. 43; January 23, 1995, p. 58.

Research in African Literatures, summer, 1980, Kolawole Ogungbesan, "A Long Way from Vrededorp: The Reception of Peter Abrahams's Ideas," pp. 187-205; number 3, 1990, Jean-Phillipe Wade, "*Song of the City* and *Mine Boy:* The 'Marxist' Novels of Peter Abrahams," pp. 89-101.

Southern African Review of Books, June-July, 1989, Cecil Abrahams, "The Long Journey Home: A Portrait of Peter Abrahams," pp. 7-8, Michael Wade, "The View from Pisgah? Peter Abrahams at Seventy," pp. 9-10.

Times Literary Supplement, March 25, 1965; October 20, 1966; March 22, 1985.

Vandag, April, 1947, Oliver Walker, "Peter Abrahams: Coloured Omen," pp. 23-26.

West African Review, March, 1952, Cyprian Ekwensi, "Challenge to West African Writers," pp. 255, 259.

World Literature Today, fall, 1985.

World Literature Written in English, November, 1974, p. 184-190; spring, 1988, Michael Harris, "South Africa Past and Future in Peter Abrahams's *Wild Conquest,*" pp. 1-11.

Zagadnienia Rodzajow Literackich, number 24, 1981, Chukwudi T. Maduka, "Limitation and Possibility: The Intellectual As Hero-Type in Peter Abrahams's *A Wreath for Udomo,*" pp. 51-60.

Zuka, May, 1968, Primila Lewis, "Politics and the Novel: An Appreciation of *A Wreath for Udomo* and *This Island Now* by Peter Abrahams," pp. 41-47.

*   *   *

ADAIR, Gilbert

PERSONAL: Born in Scotland.

ADDRESSES: Agent—c/o Author Mail, HarperCollins, 10 East 53rd St., New York, NY 10022-5299.

CAREER: Freelance author, critic, and journalist.

WRITINGS:

Alice through the Needle's Eye (sequel to Lewis Carroll's *Alice in Wonderland* and *Through the Looking Glass*), illustrated by Jenny Thorne, Dutton (New York, NY), 1984.

(Adaptor) *Alice and Her Friends from Wonderland,* illustrated by Jenny Thorne, Macmillan (London, England), 1986.

Peter Pan and the Only Children (sequel to J. M. Barrie's *Peter Pan*), illustrated by Jenny Thorne, Dutton (New York, NY), 1987.

The Holy Innocents: A Romance (novel), Heinemann (London, England), 1988, Dutton (New York, NY), 1989.

Love and Death on Long Island (novel), Heinemann (London, England), 1990.

The Death of the Author (novel), Heinemann (London, England), 1992.

Surfing the Zeitgeist, Faber & Faber (London, England), 1997.

The Key of the Tower (novel), Secker & Warburg (London, England), 1997.

A Closed Book (novel), Faber & Faber (London, England), 1999.

OTHER

(With Nick Roddick) *A Night at the Pictures: Ten Decades of British Film,* Columbus Books (London, England), 1985.

Myths and Memories: A Dazzling Dissection of British Life and Culture, Fontana (London, England), 1986.

Hollywood's Vietnam: From "The Green Berets" to "Apocalypse Now," Scribners (New York, NY), 1981, published as *Hollywood's Vietnam,* Heinemann (London, England), 1989.

(Translator) François Truffaut, *Correspondence, 1945-1984,* edited by Gilles Jacob and Claude de Givray, foreword by Jean-Luc Godard, Noonday Press (New York, NY), 1988, published as *François Truffaut: Correspondence, 1945-84,* Farrar, Straus (New York, NY) 1990.

The Postmodernist Always Rings Twice: Reflections on Culture in the Nineties (essays), Fourth Estate (London, England), 1992.

Flickers: An Illustrated Celebration of One Hundred Years of Cinema, Faber & Faber, 1995.

(Translator) Georges Perec, *A Void* (novel), Harvill Press (London, England), 1995, HarperCollins (New York, NY), 1995.

(Editor, with Marina Warner) *Wonder Tales: Six French Stories of Enchantment,* illustrated by Sophie Herxheimer, Chatto & Windus (London, England), 1994, Farrar, Straus (New York, NY), 1996.

(Editor) *Movies,* Penguin (New York, NY), 1999.

The Real Tadzio: Thomas Mann's "Death in Venice" and the Boy Who Inspired It, Short Books (London, England), 2001.

(Translator, with Robert Bononno) Michel Ciment, *Kubrick: The Definitive Edition,* Faber & Faber (New York, NY), 2001.

Contributor to periodicals, including *Film Comment* and *Sight and Sound.*

SIDELIGHTS: Gilbert Adair is a versatile writer who has published novels, children's books, criticism, and translations. He is known for the intelligence and play-fulness with which he invests his works, regardless of genre, and for the multiplicity of allusions that are likewise an inevitable aspect of his varied writings. Adair's affinity for allusions is evident in his first novel, 1989's *The Holy Innocents: A Romance,* which evokes Jean Cocteau's film *Les Enfants terrible,* but also includes references to French New Wave masters such as Jean-Luc Godard and Jacques Rivette. This novel concerns the increasingly sordid pastimes enjoyed by a pair of movie-loving twins and their American friend. *Listener* reviewer Gavin Millar noted that the three protagonists' relationship degenerates "from sensuality to perverse eroticism and ends in violent nightmare."

Love and Death on Long Island, Adair's next novel, constitutes another excursion into degradation. Here an aging writer, who long ago rejected much of contemporary culture, finds himself obsessed with a teen idol, whereupon he becomes immersed in homosexual pornography as a means of vicariously gratifying his rampant desires. This novel, which has been perceived by some as a spoof of Thomas Mann's novel *Death in Venice,* was decried by *New Statesman* reviewer Zoe Heller as "mean and demeaning."

Adair's third novel, *The Death of the Author,* derives from a controversy that ensued after the death of admired critic and educator Paul de Man, who was posthumously revealed to be the author of anti-Semitic works from the Nazi era. Leopold Sfax, the novel's protagonist, attempts to obscure his past through the unlikely imposition of his own ambiguous theories on the offensive texts in question. But Sfax's efforts at deception result in further complications that, in turn, continue to jeopardize his eminent standing. *Spectator* reviewer John Spurling noted that "the subject and setting are inescapably Nabokovesque," and he called *The Death of the Author* "a highly polished piece of postmodernist marquetry."

Among Adair's other works of fiction are *Alice through the Needle's Eye,* which serves as a sequel to the noted children's books by Lewis Carroll. In Adair's first book for children, Carroll's world-famous heroine meets a particularly helpful kangaroo and enters a world where it literally rains cats and dogs. John Fuller, writing in the *New York Times Book Review,* contended that *Alice through the Needle's Eye* sometimes lacks "the peculiar tension that exists between the original Alice and the characters she meets." Fuller conceded, however, that the book proves Adair "strong on lexical play and well able to keep the narrative proceeding at a brisk pace."

In *Peter Pan and the Only Children* Adair continues the adventures of British author J. M. Barrie's beloved character. In Adair's update on Barrie's childhood classic, a child hurls herself from a ship and discovers an undersea world in which Pan and his band once again do battle with the evil Captain Hook. Humphrey Carter proclaimed in the *Times Literary Supplement* that Adair "has caught the Barrie manner triumphantly."

In 1999 Adair published *A Closed Book,* a mystery in which he again creatively borrows from other authors: in this instance from Anthony Shaffer's *Sleuth,* wherein the main male characters engage in a power struggle, and Frederick Knott's *Wait until Dark,* in which one of the men has lost his eyesight. In Adair's novel Paul is blinded as a result of an accident and employs Ryder to be his "eyes" and describe the world to him. The mystery develops when the reader no longer knows if Ryder is telling Paul the truth about what Paul is not seeing. As Jonathon Romney pointed out in the *Guardian,* "These uncertainties set us thinking about the precarious nature of truth in fiction." Romney also noted, when discussing Adair's stylistic intentions in *A Closed Book,* that "The effect is to create an unsettling interference between spoken and written word." Isobel Montgomery, also reviewing the novel for the *Guardian,* commented, "Delightfully simple and ever so playful, Adair leads the reader through a mystery with intellectual bite."

The Real Tadzio: Thomas Mann's "Death in Venice" and the Boy Who Inspired It is the title of Adair's nonfiction work based on Thomas Mann's well-known short novel *Death in Venice.* Tadzio is the nickname of Wladyslaw Moes, the young Polish boy on whom Mann based the object of obsession of his central character, a grown man. A central theme in Adair's reflective work is that of beauty being in the eye of the beholder. As Gregory Woods noted in the *Times Literary Supplement,* Adair's "conclusion is that beauty, far from being purely eternal or universal, is subject to the vagaries of social history." *The Real Tadzio* is also a commentary on the state of Poland under communism and the Nazi regime. A critic for the *Guardian* commented that Adair's work is both "charming and fascinating in equal measure."

Although Adair is perhaps best known for his fiction, he has also gained recognition as a film reviewer and

has published several volumes of criticism. In the early 1980s he completed *Hollywood's Vietnam: From "The Green Berets" to "Apocalypse Now,"* in which he decries films such as *The Green Berets, The Deer Hunter,* and *Apocalypse Now* as distortions of the actual Vietnam conflict. *American Film* reviewer Jonathan Rosenbaum praised *Hollywood's Vietnam* for "the gracefulness of its prose style," and the critic added that "Adair is deft in charting the surface of a moral dilemma—America's involvement in Vietnam—that Hollywood has tended either to ignore . . . or distort."

Adair has published several other volumes of film criticism, among them *Flickers: An Illustrated Celebration of One Hundred Years of Cinema,* in which he surveys the history of cinema by concentrating on a specific film for each year. The book includes commentaries on both vaunted classics such as *Battleship Potemkin* and *Citizen Kane* as well as the cult classic *Shock Corridor,* the film *Imitation of Life,* and Jerry Lewis's screwball comedy *The Nutty Professor.* Peter Matthews described *Flickers* in his *New Statesman* critique as "witty and impassioned."

Social criticism by Adair includes *Myths and Memories: A Dazzling Dissection of British Life and Culture* and *The Postmodernist Always Rings Twice: Reflections on Culture in the Nineties.* In these volumes he surveys various aspects of contemporary culture and discusses film, television, and fashion while acknowledging the self-reflexive nature of his enterprise. *Listener* reviewer Colin McCabe deemed *Myths and Memories* "absolutely required reading for anybody who has to endure the dominant representations of our cultural life." In appraising the essays in *The Postmodernist Always Rings Twice,* which focuses on the nature of parody, Robert Hutchison wrote in the *Times Educational Supplement* that Adair is "good on—among other things—the genius of [Berthold Brecht, the reasons why the concentration camp should never be fictionalized in film, and the need for 'a sense of passionate partisanship' in literary criticism."

In 1990 Adair translated French filmmaker François Truffaut's *Correspondence, 1945-1984,* edited by Gilles Jacob and Claude de Givray. Dennis Potter wrote of the work in the *New York Times Book Review* that "The sweet perils of self-invention are almost as tenderly on display in this hefty, well-annotated collection . . . as they are in the shining ironies of [Truffaut's] much-loved films." Potter added that the letters of the late filmmaker are "capably translated" by Adair. Adair also provided the translation of Georges Perec's *A Void,* a novel that does not contain any words featuring the letter "e." Sarah A. Smith noted in *New Statesman* that "Adair's translation is markedly similar to that of his own, rather knowing fiction" and lauded the translation as an achievement as "equally extraordinary" as Perec's French-language original.

BIOGRAPHICAL AND CRITICAL SOURCES:

PERIODICALS

American Film, April 1982, pp. 71-72.
Boston Herald, January 18, 1999, Paul Sherman, "Love and Death Is Original, Warm, Funny," p. 38.
Contemporary Review, January, 1993, pp. 48-50.
Economist, August 15, 1981, p. 73.
Guardian, September 29, 1999, Jonathan Romney, review of *A Closed Book,* p. 22; October 21, 2000, Isobel Montgomery, review of *A Closed Book,* p. 11; January 12, 2002, review of *The Real Tadzio,* p. 9.
Library Journal, August, 2001, p. 110.
Listener, October 2, 1986, pp. 24-25; November 19, 1987, pp. 39-40; October 13, 1988, p. 31.
London Review of Books, September 13, 1990, pp. 18-19; September 10, 1992, p. 22.
New Statesman and Society, July 6, 1990, p. 40; June 2, 1992, pp. 42-43; October 14, 1994, pp. 46-47; October 25, 1999, Vicky Hutchings, review of *A Closed Book,* p. 57.
New Yorker, May 13, 1985, p. 147.
New York Review of Books, October 11, 1990, pp. 14-16.
New York Times Book Review, May 5, 1985, p. 42; May 27, 1990, pp. 1, 25; March 12, 1995, p. 3.
Observer (London, England), September 13, 1992, p. 55.
Publishers Weekly, December 19, 1994, p. 45.
Spectator, December 10, 1988, p. 26; August 29, 1992, p. 30; December 8, 2001, Francis King, review of *The Real Tadzio,* p. 58.
Sunday Times (London, England), November 22, 1998, p. 2; December 9, 2001, Paul Bailey, "Mann's Love Lost," p. 41.
Times (London, England), November 11, 1999, Michael Arditti, "Toward a Greater Evil," p. 48.

Times Educational Supplement, September 18, 1992, p. 9.
Times Literary Supplement, December 4, 1981, p. 1422; January 4, 1985, p. 18; November 20, 1987, p. 1282; September 9, 1988; August 21, 1992, p. 18; December 4, 1992, p. 13; December 18, 1992, pp. 3-4.
Washington Post Book World, August 20, 1995, p. 12.*

*   *   *

ANDERSON, M. T(obin) 1968-

PERSONAL: Born November 4, 1968, in Cambridge, MA; son of Will (an engineer) and Juliana (an Episcopal priest) Anderson. *Ethnicity:* "Caucasian/European." *Education:* Attended Harvard University, 1987; Cambridge University, B.A., 1991; Syracuse University, M.F.A., 1998.

ADDRESSES: Agent—c/o Author Mail, Candlewick Press, 2067 Massachusetts Ave., Cambridge, MA 02140.

CAREER: Writer. Candlewick Press, Cambridge, MA, editorial assistant, 1993-96; *Boston Review,* intern; WCUW-Radio, disc jockey. Vermont College, MFA program in Writing for Children, faculty member, 2000—. Has also worked as sales clerk at a department store.

AWARDS, HONORS: Winner, 2002 *Los Angeles Times* Book Award, and finalist, 2002 National Book Award, for *Feed;* nominee, *Boston Globe-Horn Book* Award in nonfiction category, 2002, for *Handel, Who Knew What He Liked,* and in the novel category, 2003, for *Feed.*

WRITINGS:

Thirsty (horror novel), Candlewick Press (Cambridge, MA), 1997.
Burger Wuss, Candlewick Press (Cambridge, MA), 1999.
Handel, Who Knew What He Liked, illustrated by Kevin Hawkes, Candlewick Press (Cambridge, MA), 2001.

Feed, Candlewick Press (Cambridge, MA), 2002.

Strange Mr. Satie, illustrated by Petra Mathers, Viking (New York, NY), 2003.

The Game of Sunken Places, Scholastic (New York, NY), 2004.

Just Me, All Alone, at the End of the World, illustrated by Kevin Hawkes, Candlewick Press (Cambridge, MA), 2004.

Author of reviews for *Improper Bostonian.*

SIDELIGHTS: M. T. Anderson once commented: "Writing is a kind of weakness, I think. We write because we can't decipher things the first time around. As a reader, I like best those books in which the author, mulling things over for him or herself, enables readers to see a world anew.

"We are so used to the bizarre images, cabals, rituals, and rites that constitute our lives that they seem natural, even invisible, to us. I admire books that facilitate renewed awareness of the way we live, and this is what I'm attempting in my own work: renewed awareness both for myself and, I hope, for my readers. That's my goal, in any case."

Anderson's debut novel, *Thirsty,* set in a small town in Massachusetts, features a high school freshman named Chris who realizes he is on the verge of growing into a vampire—despite his town's very elaborate and ritualistic attempts to fight the dreaded monsters, which seem to reap a steady New England harvest. "Chris's turbulent transformation . . . is paralleled by and inextricable from the changes of adolescence: insatiable appetite, sleepless nights, and a deep sense of insecurity and isolation," noted *Horn Book* reviewer Lauren Adams, who added: "The unusual blend of camp horror and realistic adolescent turmoil and the suspenseful plot affirm a new talent worth watching." A *Kirkus Reviews* critic also praised *Thirsty* as a "startling, savagely funny debut."

Burger Wuss stars Anthony, who gets a job at a burger joint after catching his girlfriend making out with Turner, who works at the same burger place. Bent on revenge, Anthony dreams up a series of plans to get Turner into trouble; these become increasingly absurd as the novel unfolds. *Horn Book* reviewer Peter D. Sieruta wrote, "Anderson has an eye for the dark and demented aspects of everyday life."

In *Handel, Who Knew What He Liked,* Anderson presents anecdotes from the musician's life, such as telling how as a boy Handel smuggled a clavichord past his parents into the attic, and how he created the famous work "Messiah." In addition to these stories, the book also includes a chronology of Handel's life, a discography, and a list of further reading.

Feed presents a chilling view of a future society controlled by "the feed"—an Internet/television-like device implanted in each person's brain. Titus, the book's teenaged narrator, has never questioned the use of this mind-controlling device, or other issues in his society, such as the facts that parents choose the characteristics of their children; corporations control everything; and "School" is a trademarked concept. However, when Titus and his friends go to the Moon on vacation, he meets Violet, who thinks for herself and tells him that the feed is simply a mechanism the corporations are using to control everyone's minds and choices. At the end of each chapter, excerpts from the "feed" show the overwhelming amount of advertising that is barraging everyone in society. According to a *Publishers Weekly* reviewer, the book offers a "scathing indictment" of our culture's emphasis on corporate and media power. Elizabeth Devereaux, writing in *New York Times Book Review,* called the book "subversive, vigorously conceived, painfully situated at the juncture where funny crosses into tragic, *Feed* demonstrates that young-adult novels are live and well and able to deliver a jolt."

BIOGRAPHICAL AND CRITICAL SOURCES:

PERIODICALS

Booklist, November 15, 1999, Jean Franklin, review of *Burger Wuss,* p. 613; December 15, 2001, p. 727.

General Music Today, winter, 2002, Richard Ammon, review of *Handel, Who Knew What He Liked,* p. 31.

Horn Book, May-June, 1997, p. 313; November, 1999, Peter Sieruta, review of *Burger Wuss,* p. 732; September-October, 2002, pp. 564-565.

Kirkus Reviews, January 1, 1997, p. 56; September 15, 2001, review of *Handel, Who Knew What He Liked,* p. 1352; November-December, 2001, p. 767; September 1, 2002, p. 1301.

New York Times Book Review, November 12, 2002, Elizabeth Devereaux, review of *Feed,* p. 47.

Publishers Weekly, January 27, 1997, p. 108; August 2, 1999. review of *Burger Wuss,* p. 86; October 15, 2001, p. 72; July 22, 2002, p. 181.
School Library Journal, December, 2001, Wendy Lukehart, review of *Handel, Who Knew What He Liked,* p. 117; September, 2002, p. 219.

* * *

ARAGONÉS, Sergio 1937-

PERSONAL: Surname accented on fourth syllable; born September 6, 1937, in Castellon, Spain; immigrated to United States, 1962; son of Pascual (a movie producer) and Isabel (Domenech) Aragonés; married Lilio Chomette (a teacher), September 14, 1962. *Education:* Attended the University of Mexico for four years. Studied mime with Marcel Marceau and Alexandro Jodorowsky. *Hobbies and other interests:* Pantomime, model ship building, traveling, sailing, scuba diving.

*ADDRESSES: Home—*Ojai, CA. *Office—Mad,* 1700 Broadway, New York, NY 10019.

CAREER: Freelance cartoonist, 1954—; *Mad* magazine, New York, NY, editor, cartoonist and writer, 1962—. Cartoonist and writer of comic book stories and comic strips for National Periodical Publications, beginning in 1967; has worked as a clown and as a documentary filmmaker. *Military service:* Served in Mexican Navy.

MEMBER: National Cartoonists Society, Academy of Comic Writers Guild of America, American Federation of Television and Radio Artists, Cartoonist Guild, Comic Art Professional Society (vice-president, 1980-81), Academy of Comic Book Arts, Screen Actors Guild.

AWARDS, HONORS: Harvey, Will Eisner Hall of Fame, and Reuben Award from National Cartoonists Society, 1997.

WRITINGS:

ILLUSTRATOR

Woody Gelman, *Sam, the Ceiling Needs Painting,* Kanrom, 1964.

Betty Rollin, *Mothers Are Funnier Than Children,* Doubleday, 1964.
Edward J. Hegarty, *The Seven Secrets of Sales Success,* McGraw-Hill, 1966.
John De Coursey, *Up Your Lexicon,* Kanrom, 1966.
Henry Blankfort, *Henry, the Smiling Dog* (juvenile), Putnam, 1967.
David M., *The World's Best Dirty Limericks,* Lyle Stuart, 1982.
Galactic Phrase Book & Travel Guide: Beeps, Bleats, Boskas, and Other Common Intergalactic Verbiage (Star Wars), by Ben Burtt, Ballantine, 2001.
Mark Evanier, *Comic Books and Other Necessities of Life* (essays) TwoMorrows Publishing, 2002.

SELF-ILLUSTRATED

Viva Mad, New American Library, 1968.
Mad about Mad, New American Library, 1970.
Aunts in Your Pants: Memoirs of a Dirty Old Woman, Kanrom, 1972.
Mad-ly Yours, Warner Books, 1972.
In Mad We Trust, Warner Books, 1974.
Mad Marginals, Warner Books, 1974.
Mad as the Devil, Warner Books, 1975.
Incurably Mad, Warner Books, 1977.
Sergio Aragonés on Parade, edited by Albert B. Feldstein and Jerry De Fuccio, Warner Books, 1978, published as *Mad's Sergio Aragonés on Parade,* Warner Books, 1982.
Mad As a Hatter, Warner Books, 1981.
Mad Menagerie, Warner Books, 1983.

OTHER

More Mad Pant Mines, Warner Books, 1988.
Harvey Kurtzman's Strange Adventures, Epic Comics, 1990.
Groo the Wanderer, Epic Comics, 1991.
The Life of Groo, Epic Comics, 1993.
Sergio Aragones' The Groo Festival, Epic Comics, 1993.
Sergio Massacres Marvel, Volume 1, number 1 (serial), Marvel Comics, June, 1996.
(Editor) *Mad: The Half-Wit and Wisdom of Alfred E. Neuman,* Warner Books, 1997.
(Author of foreword) Tayyar Ozkan, *Cave Man: Evolution, Heck!* Nantier Beall Minoustchine (NBM Publishing), April, 1997.

Louder Than Words, Dark Horse Comics, September 16, 1998.

(With Mark Evanier) *Groo: Most Intelligent Man in the World,* Dark Horse Comics, December 2, 1998.

Groo: Houndbook, Dark Horse Comics, June 9, 1999.

Boogeyman, Dark Horse Comics, June 23, 1999.

Groo: Inferno, Dark Horse Comics, October 27, 1999.

Groo and Rufferto, Dark Horse Comics, April 26, 2000.

Groo: Jamboree, Dark Horse Comics, July 19, 2000.

New Comics and Conversation: Using Humor to Develop Vocabulary and Elicit Conversation, JAG, 2000.

Sergio Aragones' Groo: Library, Dark Horse Comics, 2000.

The Death and Life of Groo, Graphitti Design, 2001.

Groo: Kingdom, Dark Horse Comics, March 14, 2001.

Sergio Aragones' Groo: Mightier Than the Sword, Dark Horse Comics, November 30, 2001.

The Groo Maiden, Dark Horse Comics, March, 2002.

Sergio Aragones' Groo: Nursery, Dark Horse Comics, 2002.

Sergio Aragones' Actions Speak, Dark Horse Comics, May, 2002.

Groo: Death & Taxes, Dark Horse Comics, November 15, 2002.

Groo Odyssey, Dark Horse Comics, February, 2003.

Coauthor of television special "It's a Wacky World." Contributor of cartoons and drawings to Mexican magazines, including *Ja Ja* and *Mantildeana.*

SIDELIGHTS: Widely regarded as one of the greatest living cartoonists, Sergio Aragonés was born in Spain. He and his family moved to Mexico in the early 1940s to escape the Spanish civil war. Once in the Americas, "The young Aragonés became an avid artist, sketching, drawing, and lampooning his way through Catholic school and through four years of architectural studies at the University of Mexico," according to the publisher of *Sergio Aragones' Groo: Library.* In an International Museum of Cartoon Art sketch, Aragonés says he spent most of the time at architecture school "drawing cartoons, doing theatre, pantomime, and being a clown in an aquatic ballet troupe." He began selling comic drawings to humor magazines in 1954.

Although, in his clowning role, he briefly studied pantomime with Alexandro Jodorowsky, he found his niche when he arrived in New York City in 1962 with twenty dollars in his pocket and portfolio in hand. For a while he worked at low-paying jobs, including playing guitar and singing at restaurants. But when he gathered enough courage to show his work to the editors of *MAD* magazine, he was taken on board to produce inspired doodles in the margins of each issue. He has worked with them ever since, being published in every issue but one and becoming an editor. He also branched out into animation for television, including *Laugh-In* and *TV Bloopers and Practical Jokes.* In 1967 he started creating comic books for DC, moving on to Pacific, Eclipse, Marvel/Epic, and Image Comics, three of which have since gone bankrupt. In the early 1980s, it became possible for cartoonists to own their own work—partly because of Aragonés' refusal to give away the copyright to his character Groo. During a legal battle between Steve Gerber and Marvel Comics, Gerber and friends produced a "benefit comic," *Destroyer Duck,* to bolster Gerber's dwindling legal fund, and as part of it, Aragonés gave Groo to the world. In late 1982, the independent publisher, Pacific Comics, produced "Groo the Wanderer," a spoof of barbarian heroes such as Robert E. Howard's Conan. "Groo," with writing by Mark Evanier, has been serialized for twenty years and more than 150 issues at the time of writing. Aragonés has also come up with "Buzz and Bell," "Smoke House Five" and others. Aragonés and Evanier have published over twenty books, among them *Louder Than Words,* and *Boogeyman,* a spoof on the comic-book horror genre, with Dark Horse Comics (since 1998).

Asked on "Ask Sergio," a Web site run by Mark Evanier, how much research he does to produce his cartoons, Aragonés responded, "Research takes a great percentage of my time. For my '*MAD* Look At . . .' articles, I have a few weeks to read about the specific topic. For instance, I just did a piece about videogames and I went to shops that specialized in them and I had the enormous help of Kirby Shaw, who spent a long time after his homework showing me all his video games, what's popular, how to play them, etc. For the graphics, I looked at the magazines and advertisements. Every month, the same process gets repeated with a different subject. For the comics, it's different. Once the story is all solved, I immerse myself in *National Geographics* and memories of my travels to give the characters the proper backgrounds that at the same time is different and appealing to the reader. Weapons take a long time, as do crafts and architecture. The greatest amount of research goes into stories involving known characters, such as the *Star Wars* projects I've done, or when Mark wrote *Sergio Destroys DC* and *Sergio Massacres Marvel.* I had to go through so many comic books in order to faithfully reproduce the characters."

Aragonéss's cartoons are stories without words, which are supplied by Mark Evanier. Groo, "the most intelligent man in the world," is an unsurpassedly brainless barbarian who roams the world with his slightly more intelligent dog, Rufferto. Groo unintentionally creates havoc wherever he goes, mirroring the well-intentioned but disastrous efforts of ordinary human beings everywhere to "manage" the environment, relationships, and life in general. If Groo is the most intelligent man in the world, we are in deep trouble. And, it could be said, we certainly are. In one story, reprinted in *Sergio Aragones' Groo: Nursery,* Groo "lands on a tropical island paradise and attempts to be helpful, disrupting the ecology of the area with each effort," according to a *School Library Journal* review. Randy Lander, in a *4th-Rail* review, pointed out that *Death & Taxes,* which came out in 2002, "is a particularly timely book as it is a commentary on the folly of war and how governments manipulate the facts to turn the enemy into a faceless obstacle to be defeated. Evanier has a particularly cynical take on the force behind this war, a greedy undertaker with plenty of smarts but little to no morals, and though this is a gross exaggeration of the kind of third-party factors that can affect a war effort, that allows it to be funny rather than overly tragic or sad." A *Whole Earth Review* critique of the "Groo" series commented, "Nominally a satire of the hulking-barbarian genre, this title displays the comedic timing of a Keystone Kops film and elevates the device of the running joke to an art form. But the best thing about 'Groo' is its integrity. . . . In graduating to the full-length format, Aragonés has produced one of the most consistently funny comics around."

BIOGRAPHICAL AND CRITICAL SOURCES:

PERIODICALS

Library Journal, January, 2003, p. 80.
School Library Journal, December, 2001, p. 175; December, 2002, p. 176.
Science Fiction Chronicle, February, 1992, p. 33.
Whole Earth Review, summer, 1989, p. 91.

ONLINE

4th-Rail, http://www.thefourthrail.com/ (September 10, 2003), Randy Lander, review of *Death & Taxes.*

Dark Horse Comics, http://www.darkhorse.com/ (September 10, 2003).
Groo the Wanderer Official Homepage, http://www.groo.com/ (September 10, 2003).
International Museum of Cartoon Art, http://www.cartoon.org/aragones.htm/ (September 10, 2003).
POV Online, http://www.povonline.com/Groo/Stuff/htm/ (September 10, 2003), Mark Evanier Web site.
Sergio Aragonés Home Page, http://www.sergio aragones.com/ (September 10, 2003).*

*   *   *

ARNOLD, Eve 1913-

PERSONAL: Born 1913, in Philadephia, PA; married Arnold Arnold (divorced); children: one son. *Education:* Studied medicine; attended New School for Social Research, 1947-48.

ADDRESSES: Home—26 Mount St., London WIY 5RB, England. *Agent*—Magnum Photos, 115 West 25th St., New York, NY 10001; Magnum Photographic Agency, Moreland Buildings, 2nd Floor, 5 Old St., London EC1V 9HL, England.

CAREER: Photojournalist. Magnum Photos (cooperative photography agency), New York, NY, and Paris, France, freelance photographer for advertising agencies and periodicals, including *Life, Stern, Match, Vogue,* London *Sunday Times,* and London *Times,* 1951—. Filmmaker, with films including *Behind the Veil,* 1973. *Exhibitions:* Exhibitions of photographs include "In China," Brooklyn Museum, 1980 and U.S. cities, 1980-82; Knoedler Gallery, London, 1987; "In Retrospect," International Center of Photography, Menil Museum, University of Texas, and Barbican, all 1996; and "Women around the World," Tokyo, 1996.

AWARDS, HONORS: American Library Association Notable Book designation, 1980, for *In China;* Lifetime Achievement Award, American Society of Magazine Photographers, 1980; Royal Photographic Society fellow, 1995; Master Photographer citation, New York's International Center of Photography, 1995.

WRITINGS:

SELF-ILLUSTRATED

The Unretouched Woman, Knopf (New York, NY), 1976.

Flashback!: The '50s, Knopf (New York, NY), 1978, published as *The Fifties,* 1985.

In China, Knopf (New York, NY), 1980.

In America, Knopf (New York, NY), 1983.

Marilyn Monroe: An Appreciation, Borzoi (New York, NY), 1987.

All in a Day's Work, Bantam (New York, NY), 1989.

The Great British, Knopf (New York, NY), 1991, published as *In Great Britain,* Sinclair-Stevenson (London, England), 1991.

In Retrospect, Knopf (New York, NY), 1995.

Eve Arnold: Film Journal, St. Martin's Press (New York, NY), 2002.

PHOTOGRAPHY

(With others) *For God's Sake, Care,* introduction by David Frost, foreword by General Frederick Coutts, Constable (London, England), 1967.

The Opening Ceremony of Cullinan Hall, October 10, 1958, Houston, Texas (photographic essay), text by Hugo V. Neuhaus, Jr., (Houston, TX), 1972.

(With others) *The 1974 Marilyn Monroe Datebook,* commentary by Norman Mailer, Alskog/Simon & Schuster (New York, NY), 1973.

Private View: Inside Baryshnikov's American Ballet Theatre, text by John Fraser, Bantam (New York, NY), 1988.

Arthur Miller, *The Misfits: Story of a Shoot,* Phaidon (London, England), 2000.

Handbook with Footnotes, Bloomsbury, 2003.

Contributor of articles to *Nouveau Photocinema* and *Camera 35.* Some of Arnold's books have been published in France, Spain, Italy, Japan, Germany, Canada, and England.

SIDELIGHTS: Eve Arnold, according to *Guardian* writer Ian Mayes, "comes from a school of photography that is rapidly disappearing. She is a representative of that dwindling band of photojournalists who were given plenty of time to explore their subjects . . . and then left amazingly free from editorial interference while they did so."

One of the twentieth century's most influential women photographers, Arnold did not set out to follow a career in photojournalism. She was studying to become a doctor in the 1940s when her boyfriend presented her with a Rolleicord camera. Arnold soon enrolled in Alexey Brodovitch's photography class at the New School for Social Research in New York City and with one of her first assignments—a fashion show—determined the tenor of her future photographic works. Instead of snapping glossy, high-fashion pictures, Arnold sought to convey the vitality of local shows in Harlem. Brodovitch liked the project so much that he encouraged his student to pursue it for a year and a half; the study eventually culminated in a major article for London's *Picture Post.*

Arnold gave up medicine and joined the prestigious Magnum photography agency in 1951, becoming its first American woman member. During the 1950s she often photographed stories that dealt with women, the aged, the poor, and blacks for popular magazines. She treated her subjects kindly and candidly, attempting to capture honestly the common flow of life. In the 1960s and 1970s Arnold's photographs concentrated on the more political aspects of the civil rights and women's movements, although her photos still retained an emphasis on the individual.

In *Flashback!: The '50s,* Arnold presents a portfolio of her photographs, with personal commentary, from a decade Douglas Davis described in a *Newsweek* review as "the golden age of American postwar photojournalism" in "its last and sweetest phase." Picture magazines like *Life* and *Look* were popular and photographers were encouraged to use extreme measures to capture powerful, memorable images. The life of the photojournalist in that era, Arnold recalls in her book, was "free and adventurous." Because of her affiliation with the Magnum agency, Arnold photographed numerous celebrities and prominent figures, including Dwight D. Eisenhower, Joseph McCarthy, Marilyn Monroe, and Joan Crawford, in addition to her studies of minority and political subjects. She also covered current events, religious gatherings, fads, and fashions. According to Davis the 1950s was the last decade to be defined by photojournalism before television assumed the role, and *Flashback* is "a superb collection of some of the decade's most sharp-eyed pictures." He also maintained that "Arnold's prints are so bound up with the 50s, so faithful to the pace and rhythm of the decade, that they exert an irresistible nostalgic attraction." A critic in the *New Republic* expressed a similar sentiment: "[This] is sharp-eyed, unpretentious photojournalism at its best. Arnold's pictures of the decade of Ike, falsies, McCarthy, Marilyn, and Little

Rock (touchstone words she cites in her graceful account of her work) literally tell the stories. . . . The impact of such pictures is not easy or ephemeral: they stick." *Village Voice* reviewer Eliot Fremont-Smith deemed all the photos in the book "revealing" and some "deeply affecting." He concluded: "This is one of the more rewarding photo books of the year."

In 1973 Arnold made the film *Behind the Veil,* about harems in Arabia and the position of women in Muslim society. In 1976 she expanded on that theme for her second collection, *The Unretouched Woman.* In this collection she examines the humor, incongruities, and pathos of the lives of women around the world. "I am a woman and I wanted to know more about women," Arnold stated in her book. "I realize now that through my work . . . I have been searching for myself, my time, and the world I live in." Taken over a span of nearly twenty-five years, the pictures range from peasant women performing backbreaking daily tasks with great dignity to Hollywood actress Joan Crawford putting on makeup. In *Ms.,* Anita Gottlieb found *The Untouched Woman* an "eloquent, poignant, feast of images." The reviewer added, "Arnold's photographs are formally and technically superb. In the manner of the best art, they move the heart through the balance of the eye. . . . Reality is enhanced by light but never censored or romanticized." *Newsweek* critic Walter Clemons labeled the collection "expert photojournalism."

In 1979 Arnold made two trips to China: the first to the more familiar places; the second to remote regions not usually visited by foreigners. The trip resulted in the book *In China,* a collection of 179 photographs with text under the four headings "Landscape," "People," "Work" and "Living." Fremont-Smith acknowledged that the volume was among "the year's best book 'portraits' of faraway lands," but wondered if the photos were truly representative. "The celebrative factor . . . seems generically to preclude ugliness, poverty, boring routine, anger and landscapes and artifacts that are less than quaintly or arrestingly photogenic," he observed. Beverly Beyette of the *Los Angeles Times Book Review* had a different view, however, noting that Arnold "does not take picture post-cards. She photographs laundry drying on the balconies of a modern apartment house, a dormitory for women oilfield workers, a demonstration by people out of work in Shanghai." A *New York Times Book Review* critic called *In China* "surely one of the handsomest picture

books of the year," showing "the most appealing faces since Steichen's *Family of Man* exhibit."

Arnold followed *In China* with *In America,* a photographic look at her native country, *Newsweek*'s Mark Stevens judged it "an enjoyable melting pot of the many styles and races and characters that make up modern America." Her highest achievement in the collection, he said, is "not a single image, but the composite portrait carried away of a vigorous and varied nation." In the collection *The Great British,* published in England as *In Britain,* Arnold gathers together a wide selection of photographs she has taken of her adopted country. Ranging from portraits of the queen to candid behind-the-scenes looks at film stars, and from nuns to office workers, the photographs reveal an England of many social and economic strata. "This book," wrote Ardys Kozbial in the *Boston Review,* "presents a varied, candid look at the British by a practiced, imaginative eye." According to Quentin Crisp, reviewing the book in the *New York Times Book Review,* "Arnold's camera . . . bestows a keen interest and a kindness on whatever if sees. . . . This is a beautifully produced record, full of sly humor and deep compassion."

"I learned by doing," writes Arnold in her autobiography, *In Retrospect.* "I began to understand how to approach a subject, how to get close to a subject, and how to search out and try to record the essence of a subject in the 125th part of a second." That talent led Arnold to capture the moment in some historic settings: a meeting held by Malcolm X, and a small group of Russian dissidents assembled in a psychiatric ward "undergoing hydrotherapy intended to cure them of their unorthodox views," according to *Guardian* writer Peter Lennon. How did Arnold get access to two such closed environments? "She says she works on 'robber's time,' swiftly grabbing shots, often with the subject realizing it," Lennon commented. In the case of the dissidents, Arnold shot through a window when her Russian escort's back was turned.

In 2002 the photographer published *Eve Arnold: Film Journal,* a collection of images from the 1950s through the 1980s, with many of the photos devoted to the Hollywood stars Arnold was hired to shoot during that era. Indeed, "her list of subjects is long enough to amount to a miniature biographical dictionary of cinema," noted *Sunday Times* reporter Kevin Jackson, citing portraits of Clark Gable, Montgomery Clift, Marilyn Monroe, Richard Burton, and Elizabeth Taylor. "With few exceptions, they are splendidly done, and if the president of your local camera club sniffs haughtily that some of them . . . are unacceptably soft, then vote him out and re-elect someone who understands that masters and mistresses of their craft know just when and how to break the rules." Not every photo is a glamour shot; Arnold includes a picture of "a bone-weary Anne Bancroft on the set of *The Pumpkin Eater*, taken just days after President Kennedy's assassination," according to Stephen Rees in *Library Journal*. In the words of *Houston Chronicle* reviewer Patricia Johnson, "The narrative eloquence of the photos may tell a story of the private person behind the Hollywood glitz."

BIOGRAPHICAL AND CRITICAL SOURCES:

BOOKS

Arnold, Eve, *In Retrospect*, Knopf (New York, NY), 1995.
Contemporary Photographers, 3rd edition, St. James Press (Detroit, MI), 1998.

PERIODICALS

Boston Review, February, 1992, Ardys Kozbial, review of *The Great British*, pp. 29-30.
British Journal of Photography, November 21, 1991, pp. 28-29.
Chicago Tribune Book World, December 7, 1980.
Creative Review, August, 2002, review of *Eve Arnold Film Journal*, p. 59.
Daily Telegraph (London, England), June 29, 2002, Mark Monahan, "Art of Intimacy."
Esquire, August, 1987, p. 120.
Guardian (London, England), May 9, 1996, Ian Mayes, "All about Eve," p. 12; May 5, 1999, Rebecca Smithers, "Photography A-level 'Vital,'" p. 13; November 1, 2000, Peter Lennon, "Moments of Truth," p. 11.
Independent (London, England), October 9, 1997, Mark Irvine, "Eye of Victory," p. S2.
Library Journal, September 15, 1991, p. 53; May 15, 2002, Stephen Rees, review of *Eve Arnold: Film Journal*, p. 99.
Los Angeles Time Book Review, November 30, 1980, Beverly Beyette, review of *In China*.

Ms., June, 1977.
New Republic, December 16, 1978, review of *Flashback!: The '50s*.
New Statesman & Society, November 29, 1991, p. 34.
Newsweek, December 13, 1976; September 25, 1978; December 12, 1983, Mark Stevens, review of *In America*.
New York Times Book Review, November 23, 1980; December 4, 1983; July 21, 1985; p. 22; December 27, 1987, p. 19; December 1, 1991, Quentin Crisp, review of *The Great British*, p. 51; February 11, 1996, Rosemary Ranck, review of *In Retrospect*, p. 23.
Publishers Weekly, September 19, 1980; October 9, 1995, p. 71.
Sunday Times (London, England), October 31, 1999, Beatrice Colin, "Women Who Fired with Magnum," p. 7; July 28, 2002, Kevin Jackson, "Softly, Softly Approach of a Mistress of Image," p. 40.
Times (London, England), September 4, 1987.
Times Educational Supplement, December 6, 1991, p. 27.
Times Literary Supplement, November 14, 1980.
Tribune Books (Chicago, IL), December 3, 1989, p. 7.
U.S. News and World Report, October 6, 1997, "Eve Arnold," p. 64.
Village Voice, December 13, 1976; September 18, 1978; December 10, 1980.
Wall Street Journal, December 3, 1991, p. A12.
Washington Post Book World, November 30, 1980.
You and Your Camera, May 10, 1979.*

*   *   *

ASIMOV, Isaac 1920-1992
(Dr. A, George E. Dale, Paul French)

PERSONAL: Born January 2, 1920, in Petrovichi, USSR; immigrated to United States, 1923, naturalized citizen, 1928; died of complications related to AIDS, April 6, 1992, in New York, NY; son of Judah (a candy store owner) and Anna Rachel (Berman) Asimov; married Gertrude Blugerman, July 26, 1942 (divorced, November 16, 1973); married Janet Opal Jeppson (a psychiatrist), November 30, 1973; children: David, Robyn Joan. *Education:* Columbia University, B.S., 1939, M.A., 1941, Ph.D., 1948.

CAREER: Writer. Boston University School of Medicine, Boston, MA, instructor, 1949-51, assistant professor, 1951-55, associate professor, 1955-79, professor

Isaac Asimov

of biochemistry, 1979-92. Worked as a civilian chemist at U.S. Navy Air Experimental Station, Philadelphia, PA, 1942-45. *Military service:* U.S. Army, 1945-46.

MEMBER: Authors League of America, Science Fiction Writers of America, National Association of Science Writers, American Chemical Society, Zero Population Growth, Population Institute, National Organization of Non-Parents, Sigma Xi, Mensa.

AWARDS, HONORS: Guest of honor, Thirteenth World Science Fiction Convention, 1955; Edison Foundation National Mass Media Award, 1958; Blakeslee Award for nonfiction, 1960; special Hugo Award for distinguished contributions to the field, 1963; special Hugo Award for best all-time science-fiction series, 1966, for *Foundation, Foundation and Empire,* and *Second Foundation;* James T. Grady Award, American Chemical Society, 1965; American Association for the Advancement of Science-Westinghouse award for science writing, 1967; Nebula Award, Science Fiction Writers of America, and Hugo Award for best novel, both

1973, both for *The Gods Themselves;* Nebula Award, and Hugo Award for best short story, both 1977, both for "The Bicentennial Man"; Glenn Seabord Award, International Platform Association, 1979; Hugo Award for best novel, 1983, for *Foundation's Edge;* Science Fiction Writers of America Grand Master Award, 1986; Hugo Award for best nonfiction book, 1995, for *I. Asimov;* inducted into Science Fiction and Fantasy Hall of Fame, 1997.

WRITINGS:

SCIENCE FICTION

Pebble in the Sky (novel; also see below), Doubleday (New York, NY), 1950, reprinted, R. Bentley, 1982.

I, Robot (short stories), Gnome Press, 1950, reprinted, Fawcett (New York, NY), 1970.

The Stars, Like Dust (novel; also see below), Doubleday (New York, NY), 1951, published as *The Rebellious Stars* with *An Earth Gone Mad* by R. D. Aycock, Ace Books (New York, NY), 1954, reprinted under original title, Fawcett (New York, NY), 1972.

Foundation (also see below), Gnome Press, 1951, published as *The 1,000 Year Plan* with *No World of Their Own* by Poul Anderson, Ace Books (New York, NY), 1955, reprinted under original title, Ballantine (New York, NY), 1983.

(Under pseudonym Paul French) *David Starr, Space Ranger* (juvenile; also see below), Doubleday (New York, NY), 1952, reprinted under name Isaac Asimov, Twayne Publishers (Boston, MA), 1978.

Foundation and Empire (also see below), Gnome Press, 1952, reprinted, Ballantine (New York, NY), 1983.

The Currents of Space (novel; also see below), Doubleday (New York, NY), 1952, reprinted, Fawcett (New York, NY), 1971.

Second Foundation (also see below), Gnome Press, 1953, reprinted, Ballantine (New York, NY), 1983.

(Under pseudonym Paul French) *Lucky Starr and the Pirates of the Asteroids* (juvenile; also see below), Doubleday (New York, NY), 1953, reprinted under name Isaac Asimov, Twayne Publishers (Boston, MA), 1978.

The Caves of Steel (novel; also see below), Doubleday (New York, NY), 1954, reprinted, Fawcett (New York, NY), 1972.

(Under pseudonym Paul French) *Lucky Starr and the Oceans of Venus* (juvenile), Doubleday (New York, NY), 1954, reprinted under name Isaac Asimov, Twayne Publishers (Boston, MA), 1978.

The Martian Way and Other Stories (also see below), Doubleday (New York, NY), 1955, reprinted, Ballantine (New York, NY), 1985.

The End of Eternity (novel; also see below), Doubleday (New York, NY), 1955, reprinted, Fawcett (New York, NY), 1971.

(Contributor) Groff Conklin, editor, *Science Fiction Terror Tales by Isaac Asimov and Others,* Gnome Press, 1955.

(Under pseudonym Paul French) *Lucky Starr and the Big Sun of Mercury* (juvenile), Doubleday (New York, NY), 1956, published under name Isaac Asimov as *The Big Sun of Mercury,* New English Library, 1974, reprinted under name Isaac Asimov under original title, Twayne (Boston, MA), 1978.

The Naked Sun (novel; also see below), Doubleday (New York, NY), 1957, reprinted, Fawcett (New York, NY), 1972.

(Under pseudonym Paul French) *Lucky Starr and the Moons of Jupiter* (juvenile), Doubleday (New York, NY), 1957, reprinted under name Isaac Asimov, Twayne (Boston, MA), 1978.

Earth Is Room Enough: Science Fiction Tales of Our Own Planet (also see below), Doubleday (New York, NY), 1957.

The Robot Novels (contains *The Caves of Steel* and *The Naked Sun*; also see below), Doubleday (New York, NY), 1957.

(Under pseudonym Paul French) *Lucky Starr and the Rings of Saturn* (juvenile), Doubleday (New York, NY), 1958, reprinted under name Isaac Asimov, Twayne Publishers (Boston, MA), 1978.

Nine Tomorrows: Tales of the Near Future, Doubleday (New York, NY), 1959.

Triangle: "The Currents of Space," "Pebble In the Sky," and "The Stars, Like Dust," Doubleday (New York, NY), 1961, published as *An Isaac Asimov Second Omnibus,* Sidgwick & Jackson (London, England), 1969.

The Foundation Trilogy: Three Classics of Science Fiction (contains *Foundation, Foundation and Empire,* and *Second Foundation*), Doubleday (New York, NY), 1963, published as *An Isaac Asimov Omnibus,* Sidgwick & Jackson (London, England), 1966, reprinted, Doubleday (New York, NY), 1982.

The Rest of the Robots (short stories and novels; includes *The Caves of Steel* and *The Naked Sun*),

Doubleday (New York, NY), 1964, published as *Eight Stories from the Rest of the Robots,* Pyramid Books, 1966.

Fantastic Voyage (novelization of screenplay by Harry Kleiner), Houghton Mifflin (Boston, MA), 1966.

Through a Glass Clearly, New English Library, 1967.

Asimov's Mysteries (short stories), Doubleday (New York, NY), 1968.

Nightfall and Other Stories, Doubleday, 1969, published in two volumes, Panther Books (London, England), 1969, published as *Nightfall: Twenty SF Stories,* Rapp Whiting, 1971.

The Best New Thing (juvenile), World Publishing (New York, NY), 1971.

The Gods Themselves (novel), Doubleday (New York, NY), 1972.

The Early Asimov; or, Eleven Years of Trying (short stories), Doubleday (New York, NY), 1972.

(Contributor) Groff Conklin, editor, *Possible Tomorrows by Isaac Asimov and Others,* Sidgwick & Jackson (London, England), 1972.

An Isaac Asimov Double: "Space Ranger" and "Pirates of the Asteroids," New English Library (London, England), 1972.

A Second Isaac Asimov Double: "The Big Sun of Mercury" and "The Oceans of Venus," New English Library (London, England), 1973.

The Third Isaac Asimov Double, Times Mirror (New York, NY), 1973.

The Best of Isaac Asimov (short stories), Doubleday (New York, NY), 1974.

Have You Seen These?, NESFA Press, 1974.

Buy Jupiter and Other Stories, Doubleday (New York, NY), 1975.

The Heavenly Host (juvenile), Walker (New York, NY), 1975.

The Bicentennial Man and Other Stories, Doubleday (New York, NY), 1976.

The Collected Fiction of Isaac Asimov, Volume 1: *The Far Ends of Time and Earth* (contains *Pebble in the Sky, Earth Is Room Enough,* and *The End of Eternity*), Doubleday (New York, NY), 1979, Volume 2: *Prisoners of the Stars* (contains *The Stars, Like Dust, The Martian Way and Other Stories,* and *The Currents of Space*), Doubleday (New York, NY), 1979.

Three by Asimov, Targ Editions, 1981.

The Complete Robot (also see below), Doubleday (New York, NY), 1982.

Foundation's Edge (novel), Doubleday (New York, NY), 1982.

The Winds of Change and Other Stories, Doubleday (New York, NY), 1983.

(With wife, Janet Asimov) *Norby, the Mixed-up Robot* (juvenile; also see below), Walker (New York, NY), 1983.

The Robots of Dawn (novel), Doubleday (New York, NY), 1983.

The Robot Collection (contains *The Caves of Steel, The Naked Sun,* and *The Complete Robot*), Doubleday (New York, NY), 1983.

(With Janet Asimov) *Norby's Other Secret* (juvenile; also see below), Walker (New York, NY), 1984.

Isaac Asimov's Magical World's of Fantasy, Crown (New York, NY), 1985.

Robots and Empire (novel), Doubleday (New York, NY), 1985.

(With Janet Asimov) *Norby and the Invaders* (juvenile; also see below), Walker (New York, NY), 1985.

(With Janet Asimov) *Norby and the Lost Princess* (juvenile; also see below), Walker (New York, NY), 1985.

The Best Science Fiction of Isaac Asimov, Doubleday (New York, NY), 1986.

The Alternative Asimovs (contains *The End of Eternity*), Doubleday (New York, NY), 1986.

(With Janet Asimov) *The Norby Chronicles* (contains *Norby, the Mixed-up Robot* and *Norby's Other Secret*), Ace Books (New York, NY), 1986.

Foundation and Earth (novel), Doubleday (New York, NY), 1986.

(With Janet Asimov) *Norby and the Queen's Necklace* (juvenile; also see below), Walker (New York, NY), 1986.

(With Janet Asimov) *Norby: Robot for Hire* (contains *Norby and the Lost Princess* and *Norby and the Invaders*), Ace Books (New York, NY), 1987.

Fantastic Voyage II: Destination Brain, Doubleday (New York, NY), 1987.

(With Janet Asimov) *Norby Finds a Villain* (juvenile; also see below), Walker (New York, NY), 1987.

(With Janet Asimov) *Norby through Time and Space* (contains *Norby and the Queen's Necklace* and *Norby Finds a Villain*), Ace Books (New York, NY), 1988.

Azazel, Doubleday (New York, NY), 1988.

Nemesis, Doubleday (New York, NY), 1988.

Prelude to Foundation, Doubleday (New York, NY), 1988.

(With Theodore Sturgeon) *The Ugly Little Boy/The Widget, the Wadget, and Boff,* Tor Books (New York, NY), 1989.

Franchise (juvenile), Creative Education (Mankato, MN), 1989.

(With Janet Asimov) *Norby down to Earth* (juvenile), Walker (New York, NY), 1989.

All the Troubles of the World (juvenile), Creative Education (Mankato, MN), 1989.

(With Janet Asimov) *Norby and Yobo's Great Adventure* (juvenile), Walker (New York, NY), 1989.

Sally (juvenile), Creative Education (Mankato, MN), 1989.

Robbie (juvenile), Creative Education (Mankato, MN), 1989.

(Editor, with Martin Greenberg) *Visions of Fantasy: Tales from the Masters,* Doubleday (New York, NY), 1989.

The Asimov Chronicles, three volumes, Ace Books (New York, NY), 1990.

Invasions, New American Library (New York, NY), 1990.

(With Janet Asimov) *Norby and the Oldest Dragon* (juvenile), Walker (New York, NY), 1990.

Isaac Asimov: The Complete Stories, Doubleday (New York, NY), 1990.

Robot Visions, New American Library (New York, NY), 1991.

(With Janet Asimov) *Norby and the Court Jester* (juvenile), Walker (New York, NY), 1991.

(With Robert Silverberg) *The Positronic Man,* Doubleday (New York, NY), 1993.

Gold: The Final Science Fiction Collection, HarperPrism (New York, NY), 1995.

Isaac Asimov's I-Bots: History of I-Botics: An Illustrated Novel, HarperPrism (New York, NY), 1997.

Also editor or coeditor of numerous science fiction and fantasy anthologies.

MYSTERY NOVELS

The Death Dealers, Avon Publications (New York, NY), 1958, published as *A Whiff of Death,* Walker (New York, NY), 1968.

Tales of the Black Widowers, Doubleday (New York, NY), 1974.

Murder at the ABA: A Puzzle in Four Days and Sixty Scenes, Doubleday (New York, NY), 1976, published as *Authorised Murder: A Puzzle in Four Days and Sixty Scenes,* Gollancz (London, England), 1976.

More Tales of the Black Widowers, Doubleday (New York, NY), 1976.

The Key Word and Other Mysteries, Walker (New York, NY), 1977.

Casebook of the Black Widowers, Doubleday (New York, NY), 1980.

The Union Club Mysteries, Doubleday (New York, NY), 1983.

Computer Crimes and Capers, Academy Chicago Publishers (Chicago, IL), 1983.

Banquets of the Black Widowers, Doubleday (New York, NY), 1984.

The Disappearing Man and Other Mysteries, Walker (New York, NY), 1985.

The Best Mysteries of Isaac Asimov, Doubleday (New York, NY), 1986.

Puzzles of the Black Widowers, Doubleday (New York, NY), 1990.

(With Martin H. Greenburg, Martin Harry, and Charles Waugh) *Isaac Asimov Presents the Best Crime Stories of the Nineteenth Century,* Barricade (New York, NY), 1995.

Also editor, with others, of numerous mystery anthologies.

ADULT NONFICTION

(With William C. Boyd and Burnham S. Walker) *Biochemistry and Human Metabolism,* Williams Wilkins, 1952, 3rd edition, 1957.

The Chemicals of Life: Enzymes, Vitamins, Hormones, Abelard-Schuman (London, England), 1954.

(With William C. Boyd) *Races and People,* Abelard-Schuman (London, England), 1955.

(With Burnham S. Walker and Mary K. Nicholas) *Chemistry and Human Health,* McGraw (New York, NY), 1956.

Inside the Atom, Abelard-Schuman (London, England), 1956, revised and updated edition, 1966.

Only a Trillion (essays), Abelard-Schuman (London, England), 1958, published as *Marvels of Science: Essays of Fact and Fancy on Life, Its Environment, Its Possibilities,* Collier Books (New York, NY), 1962, reprinted under original title, Ace Books (New York, NY), 1976.

The World of Carbon, Abelard-Schuman (London, England), 1958, revised edition, Collier Books (New York, NY), 1962.

The World of Nitrogen, Abelard-Schuman (London, England), 1958, revised edition, Collier Books (New York, NY), 1962.

The Clock We Live On, Abelard-Schuman (London, England), 1959, revised edition, 1965.

Words of Science and the History behind Them, Houghton Mifflin (Boston, MA), 1959, revised edition, Harrap (London, England), 1974.

Realm of Numbers, Houghton Mifflin (Boston, MA), 1959.

The Living River, Abelard-Schuman (London, England), 1959, published as *The Bloodstream: River of Life,* Collier Books (New York, NY), 1961.

The Kingdom of the Sun, Abelard-Schuman (London, England), 1960, revised edition, 1963.

Realm of Measure, Houghton Mifflin (Boston, MA), 1960.

The Wellsprings of Life, Abelard-Schuman, (London, England), 1960, New American Library (New York, NY), 1961.

The Intelligent Man's Guide to Science, two volumes, Basic Books (New York, NY), 1960, Volume 1 published separately as *The Intelligent Man's Guide to the Physical Sciences,* Pocket Books (New York, NY), 1964, Volume 2 published separately as *The Intelligent Man's Guide to the Biological Sciences,* Pocket Books (New York, NY), 1964, revised edition published as *The New Intelligent Man's Guide to Science,* 1965, published as *Asimov's Guide to Science,* 1972, revised edition published as *Asimov's New Guide to Science,* 1984.

The Double Planet, Abelard-Schuman (London, England), 1960, revised edition, 1967.

Realm of Algebra, Houghton Mifflin (Boston, MA), 1961.

Life and Energy, Doubleday (New York, NY), 1962.

Fact and Fancy (essays), Doubleday (New York, NY), 1962.

The Search for the Elements, Basic Books (New York, NY), 1962.

The Genetic Code, Orion Press (New York, NY), 1963.

The Human Body: Its Structure and Operation (also see below), Houghton Mifflin (Boston, MA), 1963.

View from a Height, Doubleday (New York, NY), 1963.

The Human Brain: Its Capacities and Functions (also see below), Houghton Mifflin (Boston, MA), 1964, revised and expanded edition, Penguin (New York, NY), 1994.

A Short History of Biology, Natural History Press for the American Museum of Natural History, 1964, reprinted, Greenwood Press (Westport, CT), 1980.

Quick and Easy Math, Houghton Mifflin (Boston, MA), 1964.

Adding a Dimension: Seventeen Essays on the History of Science, Doubleday (New York, NY), 1964.

(With Stephen H. Dole) *Planets for Man,* Random House (New York, NY), 1964.

Asimov's Biographical Encyclopedia of Science and Technology, Doubleday (New York, NY), 1964, 2nd revised edition, 1982.

A Short History of Chemistry, Doubleday (New York, NY), 1965.

Of Time and Space and Other Things (essays), Doubleday (New York, NY), 1965.

An Easy Introduction to the Slide Rule, Houghton Mifflin (Boston, MA), 1965.

The Noble Gasses, Basic Books (New York, NY), 1966.

The Neutrino: Ghost Particle of the Atom, Doubleday (New York, NY), 1966.

Understanding Physics, three volumes, Walker (New York, NY), 1966.

The Genetic Effects of Radiation, U.S. Atomic Energy Commission (Washington, DC), 1966.

The Universe: From Flat Earth to Quasar, Walker (New York, NY), 1966, 3rd edition published as *The Universe: From Flat Earth to Black Holes—and Beyond,* 1980.

From Earth to Heaven (essays), Doubleday (New York, NY), 1966.

Environments out There, Abelard-Schuman (London, England), 1967.

Is Anyone There? (essays), Doubleday (New York, NY), 1967.

Science, Numbers and I (essays), Doubleday (New York, NY), 1968.

Photosynthesis, Basic Books (New York, NY), 1968.

Twentieth-Century Discovery (essays), Doubleday (New York, NY), 1969, revised edition, Ace Books (New York, NY), 1976.

The Solar System and Back (essays), Doubleday (New York, NY), 1970.

The Stars in Their Courses (essays), Doubleday (New York, NY), 1971, revised edition, Ace Books (New York, NY), 1976.

The Left Hand of the Electron (essays), Doubleday (New York, NY), 1972.

Electricity and Man, U.S. Atomic Energy Commission (Washington, DC), 1972.

Worlds within Worlds: The Story of Nuclear Energy, three volumes, U.S. Atomic Energy Commission (Washington, DC), 1972.

A Short History of Chemistry, Heinemann (London, England), 1972.

Today and Tomorrow and . . . , Doubleday (New York, NY), 1973.

The Tragedy of the Moon, Doubleday (New York, NY), 1973.

Asimov on Astronomy (essays), Doubleday (New York, NY), 1974.

Our World in Space, foreword by Edwin E. Aldrin, Jr., New York Graphic Society (New York, NY), 1974.

Asimov on Chemistry (essays), Doubleday (New York, NY), 1974.

Of Matters Great and Small, Doubleday (New York, NY), 1975.

Science Past, Science Future, Doubleday (New York, NY), 1975.

Eyes on the Universe: A History of the Telescope, Houghton Mifflin (Boston, MA), 1975.

The Ends of the Earth: The Polar Regions of the World, Weybright Talley, 1975.

Asimov on Physics (essays), Doubleday (New York, NY), 1976.

The Planet That Wasn't (essays), Doubleday (New York, NY), 1976.

The Collapsing Universe, Walker (New York, NY), 1977.

Asimov on Numbers (essays), Doubleday (New York, NY), 1977.

The Beginning and the End (essays), Doubleday (New York, NY), 1977.

Quasar, Quasar, Burning Bright (essays), Doubleday (New York, NY), 1978.

Life and Time, Doubleday (New York, NY), 1978.

The Road to Infinity (essays), Doubleday (New York, NY), 1979.

A Choice of Catastrophes: The Disasters That Threaten Our World, Simon & Schuster (New York, NY), 1979.

The Shaping of England, Houghton Mifflin (Boston, MA), 1969.

Constantinople: The Forgotten Empire, Houghton Mifflin (Boston, MA), 1970.

The Land of Canaan, Houghton Mifflin (Boston, MA), 1970.

Visions of the Universe, preface by Carl Sagan, Cosmos Store, 1981.

The Sun Shines Bright (essays), Doubleday (New York, NY), 1981.

Exploring the Earth and the Cosmos: The Growth and Future of Human Knowledge, Crown (New York, NY), 1982.

Counting the Eons, Doubleday (New York, NY), 1983.

The Roving Mind, Prometheus Books (Amherst, NY), 1983, revised edition, 1997.

The Measure of the Universe, Harper (New York, NY), 1983.

X Stands for Unknown, Doubleday (New York, NY), 1984.

The History of Physics, Walker (New York, NY), 1984.

Isaac Asimov on the Human Body and the Human Brain (contains *The Human Body: Its Structure and Operation* and *The Human Brain: Its Capacities and Functions*), Bonanza Books (New York, NY), 1984.

The Exploding Suns: The Secrets of the Supernovas, Dutton (New York, NY), 1985, updated edition, Plume (New York, NY), 1996.

Asimov's Guide to Halley's Comet, Walker (New York, NY), 1985.

The Subatomic Monster, Doubleday (New York, NY), 1985.

(With Karen Frenkel) *Robots: Machines in Man's Image,* Robot Institute of America, 1985.

Isaac Asimov's Wonderful Worldwide Science Bazaar: Seventy-two Up-to-Date Reports on the State of Everything from Inside the Atom to Outside the Universe, Houghton Mifflin (Boston, MA), 1986.

The Dangers of Intelligence and Other Science Essays, Houghton Mifflin (Boston, MA), 1986.

Far As Human Eye Could See (essays), Doubleday (New York, NY), 1987.

The Relativity of Wrong: Essays on the Solar System and Beyond, Doubleday (New York, NY), 1988.

Asimov on Science: A Thirty-Year Retrospective, Doubleday (New York, NY), 1989.

Asimov's Chronology of Science and Technology: How Science Has Shaped the World and How the World Has Affected Science from 4,000,000 B.C. to the Present, Harper (New York, NY), 1989, updated and illustrated edition, 1994.

The Secret of the Universe, Doubleday (New York, NY), 1989.

The Tyrannosaurus Prescription and One Hundred Other Essays, Prometheus Books (Amherst, NY), 1989.

Out of the Everywhere, Doubleday (New York, NY), 1990.

Atom: Journey across the Subatomic Cosmos, New American Library (New York, NY), 1991.

Frontiers: New Discoveries about Man and His Planet, Outer Space, and the Universe, New American Library (New York, NY), 1991.

Asimov's Chronology of the World, HarperCollins (New York, NY), 1991.

Asimov's Guide to Earth and Space, Random House (New York, NY), 1991.

(With Frederick Pohl) *Our Angry Earth,* Tor Books (New York, NY), 1991.

Frontiers II: More Recent Discoveries about Life, Earth, Space, and the Universe, Truman Valley Books/Dutton (New York, NY), 1993.

Aliens and Extraterrestrials: Are We Alone? (revised and updated edition of *Is There Life on Other Planets?*), Gareth Stevens (Milwaukee, WI), 1995.

JUVENILE NONFICTION

Building Blocks of the Universe, Abelard-Schuman (London, England), 1957, revised and updated edition, 1974.

Breakthroughs in Science, Houghton Mifflin (Boston, MA), 1960.

Satellites in Outer Space, Random House (New York, NY), 1960, revised edition, 1973.

Words from the Myths, Houghton Mifflin (Boston, MA), 1961.

Words in Genesis, Houghton Mifflin (Boston, MA), 1962.

Words on the Map, Houghton Mifflin (Boston, MA), 1962.

Words from Exodus, Houghton Mifflin (Boston, MA), 1963.

The Kite That Won the Revolution (juvenile), Houghton Mifflin (Boston, MA), 1963, revised edition, 1973.

The Greeks: A Great Adventure, Houghton Mifflin (Boston, MA), 1965.

The Roman Republic, Houghton Mifflin (Boston, MA), 1966.

The Moon, Follett (New York, NY), 1966.

To the Ends of the Universe, Walker (New York, NY), 1967, revised edition, 1976.

Mars, Follett (New York, NY), 1967.

The Roman Empire, Houghton Mifflin (Boston, MA), 1967.

The Egyptians, Houghton Mifflin (Boston, MA), 1967.

The Near East: Ten Thousand Years of History, Houghton Mifflin (Boston, MA), 1968.

Asimov's Guide to the Bible, Doubleday (New York, NY), Volume 1: *The Old Testament,* 1968, Volume 2: *The New Testament,* 1969.

The Dark Ages, Houghton Mifflin (Boston, MA), 1968.
Words from History, Houghton Mifflin (Boston, MA), 1968.
Stars, Follett (New York, NY), 1968.
Galaxies, Follett (New York, NY), 1968.
ABC's of Space, Walker (New York, NY), 1969, published as *Space Dictionary,* Scholastic (New York, NY), 1970.
Great Ideas of Science, Houghton Mifflin (Boston, MA), 1969.
ABC's of the Ocean, Walker (New York, NY), 1970.
Light, Follett (New York, NY), 1970.
What Makes the Sun Shine?, Little, Brown (Boston, MA), 1971.
ABC's of the Earth, Walker (New York, NY), 1971.
ABC's of Ecology, Walker (New York, NY), 1972.
Ginn Science Program, Ginn (New York, NY), intermediate levels A, B, and C, 1972, advanced levels A and B, 1973.
Comets and Meteors, Follett (New York, NY), 1972.
The Sun, Follett (New York, NY), 1972.
More Words of Science, Houghton Mifflin (Boston, MA), 1972.
The Story of Ruth, Doubleday (New York, NY), 1972.
The Shaping of France, Houghton Mifflin (Boston, MA), 1972.
The Shaping of North America from Earliest Times to 1763, Houghton Mifflin (Boston, MA), 1973.
Jupiter, the Largest Planet, Lothrop (New York, NY), 1973, revised edition, 1976.
Please Explain, Houghton Mifflin (Boston, MA), 1973.
Earth: Our Crowded Spaceship, John Day (New York, NY), 1974.
The Birth of the United States, 1763-1816, Houghton Mifflin (Boston, MA), 1974.
Our Federal Union: The United States from 1816 to 1865, Houghton Mifflin (Boston, MA), 1975.
The Solar System, Follett (New York, NY), 1975.
Alpha Centauri, the Nearest Star, Lothrop (New York, NY), 1976.
Mars, the Red Planet, Lothrop (New York, NY), 1977.
The Golden Door: The United States from 1865 to 1918, Houghton Mifflin (Boston, MA), 1977.
Animals of the Bible, Doubleday (New York, NY), 1978.
Saturn and Beyond, Lothrop (New York, NY), 1979.
Extraterrestrial Civilizations (speculative nonfiction), Crown (New York, NY), 1979.
Isaac Asimov's Book of Facts, Grosset (New York, NY), 1979.
Venus: Near Neighbor of the Sun, Lothrop (New York, NY), 1981.

In the Beginning: Science Faces God in the Book of Genesis, Crown (New York, NY), 1981.
The Edge of Tomorrow, T. Doherty (New York, NY), 1985.
(With James Burke and Jules Bergman) *The Impact of Science on Society,* National Aeronautics and Space Administration (NASA), 1985.
Futuredays: A Nineteenth-Century Vision of the Year 2000, Holt (New York, NY), 1986.
Beginnings: The Story of Origins—Of Mankind, Life, the Earth, the Universe, Walker (New York, NY), 1987.
Franchise, Creative Education (Mankato, IL), 1988.
All the Troubles of World, Creative Education (Mankato, IL, 1988.
(With Frank White) *Think about Space: Where Have We Been and Where Are We Going?,* Walker (New York, NY), 1989.
Little Treasury of Dinosaurs, Crown (New York, NY), 1989.
Unidentified Flying Objects, Dell (New York, NY), 1990.
(With Frank White) *The March of the Millennia: A Key to Looking at History,* Walker (New York, NY), 1990.
Ancient Astronomy, Dell (New York, NY), 1991.

Also author of volumes in the "How Did We Find Out" series, Walker (New York, NY), beginning 1972.

"NEW LIBRARY OF THE UNIVERSE" SERIES

Ferdinand Magellan: Opening the Door to World Exploration, Gareth Stevens (Milwaukee, WI), 1991.
Henry Hudson: Arctic Explorer and North American Adventurer, Gareth Stevens (Milwaukee, WI), 1991.
A Distant Puzzle: The Planet Uranus (revised edition of *Uranus, the Sideways Planet*), Gareth Stevens (Milwaukee, WI), 1994.
Cosmic Debris: The Asteroids (revised edition of *The Asteroids*), Gareth Stevens (Milwaukee, WI), 1994.
Death from Space: What Killed the Dinosaurs? (revised and updated edition of *Did Comets Kill the Dinosaurs?*), Gareth Stevens (Milwaukee, WI), 1994.
(With Greg Walz-Chojnacki) *The Moon* (revised edition of *Earth's Moon*), Gareth Stevens (Milwaukee, WI), 1994.

(With Francis Reddy) *The Red Planet: Mars* (revised edition of *Mars*), Gareth Stevens (Milwaukee, WI), 1994.

(With Francis Reddy) *Mysteries of Deep Space: Black Holes, Pulsars, and Quasars* (revised edition of *Quasars, Pulsars, and Black Holes*), Gareth Stevens (Milwaukee, WI), 1994.

(With Greg Walz-Chojnacki) *Our Planetary System* (revised edition of *Our Solar System*), Gareth Stevens (Milwaukee, WI), 1994.

(With Francis Reddy) *The Sun and Its Secrets* (revised edition of *Sun*), Gareth Stevens (Milwaukee, WI), 1994.

(With Greg Walz-Chojnacki) *UFOs: True Mysteries or Hoaxes?* (revised edition of *Unidentified Flying Objects*), Gareth Stevens (Milwaukee, WI), 1995.

Astronomy in Ancient Times (revised and updated), Gareth Stevens (Milwaukee, WI), 1995.

The Birth of Our Universe (revised and updated edition of *How Was the Universe Born?*), Gareth Stevens (Milwaukee, WI), 1995.

Discovering Comets and Meteors (revised edition of *Comets and Meteors*), Gareth Stevens (Milwaukee, WI), 1995.

(With Greg Walz-Chojnacki) *Our Vast Home: The Milky Way and Other Galaxies* (revised edition of *Our Milky Way and Other Galaxies*), Gareth Stevens (Milwaukee, WI), 1995.

(With Francis Reddy) *Exploring Outer Space: Rockets, Probes, and Satellites* (revised edition of *Rockets, Probes, and Satellites,* Gareth Stevens (Milwaukee, WI), 1995.

(With Greg Walz-Chojnacki) *Science Fiction: Visions of Tommorow?* (revised edition of *Science Fiction, Science Fact*), Gareth Stevens (Milwaukee, WI), 1995.

(With Greg Walz-Chojnacki) *Pollution in Space* (revised edition of *Space Garbage*), Gareth Stevens (Milwaukee, WI), 1995.

(With Greg Walz-Chojnacki) *Space Colonies* (revised edition of *Colonizing the Planets and Stars*), Gareth Stevens (Milwaukee, WI), 1995.

(With Francis Reddy) *Space Explorers* (revised edition of *Piloted Space Flights*), Gareth Stevens (Milwaukee, WI), 1995.

(With Francis Reddy) *Star Cycles: The Life and Death of Stars* (revised edition of *Birth and Death of Stars*), Gareth Stevens (Milwaukee, WI), 1995.

(With Francis Reddy) *A Stargazer's Guide* (revised edition of *Space Spotter's Guide*), Gareth Stevens (Milwaukee, WI), 1995.

(With Francis Reddy) *Our Planet Earth* (revised edition), Gareth Stevens (Milwaukee, WI), 1995, revised by Richard Hantula as *Earth,* 2002.

(With Francis Reddy) *The Ringed Planet: Saturn* (revised edition of *Saturn*), Gareth Stevens (Milwaukee, WI), 1995.

(With Greg Walz-Chojnacki) *Planet of Extremes—Jupiter* (revised edition of *Jupiter*), Gareth Stevens (Milwaukee, WI), 1995.

(With Francis Reddy) *Nearest Sun: The Planet Mercury* (revised edition of *Mercury*), Gareth Stevens (Milwaukee, WI), 1995.

A Distant Giant: The Planet Neptune (revised edition of *Neptune*), Gareth Stevens (Milwaukee, WI), 1996.

(With Greg Walz-Chojnacki) *A Double Planet?: Pluto and Charon* (revised edition of *Pluto*), Gareth Stevens (Milwaukee, WI), 1996, revised by Richard Hantula, 2002.

(With Francis Reddy) *Earth's Twin: The Planet Venus* (revised edition of *Venus*), Gareth Stevens (Milwaukee, WI), 1996.

(With Francis Reddy) *Global Space Programs* (revised edition of *The World's Space Programs*), Gareth Stevens (Milwaukee, WI), 1996.

(With Francis Reddy) *Folklore and Legend of the Universe* (revised edition of *Mythology and the Universe*), Gareth Stevens (Milwaukee, WI), 1996.

(With Greg Walz-Chojnacki) *The Twenty-first Century in Space* (revised edition of *The Future in Space*), Gareth Stevens (Milwaukee, WI), 1996.

(With Greg Walz-Chojnacki) *Modern Astronomy* (revised edition of *Astronomy Today*), Gareth Stevens (Milwaukee, WI), 1996.

(With Greg Walz-Chojnacki) *Astronomy Projects* (revised edition of *Projects in Astronomy),* Gareth Stevens (Milwaukee, WI), 1996.

Isaac Asimov's New Library of the Universe Index, Gareth Stevens (Milwaukee, WI), 1996.

OTHER

Opus 100 (selections from author's first one hundred books), Houghton Mifflin (Boston, MA), 1969.

Asimov's Guide to Shakespeare, two volumes, Doubleday (New York, NY), 1970, published in one volume, Avenel Books, 1981.

Unseen World (teleplay), American Broadcasting Co. (ABC-TV), 1970.

(Under pseudonym Dr. A) *The Sensuous Dirty Old Man,* Walker (New York, NY), 1971.

Isaac Asimov's Treasury of Humor: A Lifetime Collection of Favorite Jokes, Anecdotes, and Limericks with Copious Notes on How to Tell Them and Why, Houghton Mifflin (Boston, MA), 1971.

(With James Gunn) *The History of Science Fiction from 1938 to the Present* (filmscript), Extramural Independent Study Center, University of Kansas, 1971.

Asimov's Annotated "Don Juan," Doubleday (New York, NY), 1972.

Asimov's Annotated "Paradise Lost," Doubleday (New York, NY), 1974.

Lecherous Limericks, Walker (New York, NY), 1975.

"The Dream," "Benjamin's Dream," and "Benjamin's Bicentennial Blast": Three Short Stories, Printing Week in New York (New York, NY), 1976.

More Lecherous Limericks, Walker (New York, NY), 1976.

Familiar Poems Annotated, Doubleday (New York, NY), 1977.

Still More Lecherous Limericks, Walker (New York, NY), 1977.

Asimov's Sherlockian Limericks, New Mysterious Press, 1978.

(With John Ciardi) *Limericks Too Gross,* Norton (New York, NY), 1978.

Opus 200 (selections from the author's second hundred books), Houghton Mifflin (Boston, MA), 1979.

In Memory Yet Green: The Autobiography of Isaac Asimov, 1920-1954, Doubleday (New York, NY), 1979.

In Joy Still Felt: The Autobiography of Isaac Asimov, 1954-1978, Doubleday (New York, NY), 1980.

The Annotated "Gulliver's Travels," C. N. Potter, 1980.

Asimov on Science Fiction, Doubleday (New York, NY), 1981.

Change!: Seventy-one Glimpses of the Future (forecasts), Houghton Mifflin (Boston, MA), 1981.

(With John Ciardi) *A Grossery of Limericks,* Norton (New York, NY), 1981.

Would You Believe?, Grosset (New York, NY), 1981.

(With Ken Fisher) *Isaac Asimov Presents Superquiz,* Dembner, 1982.

More—Would You Believe?, Grosset (New York, NY), 1982.

(Editor, with George R. Martin) *The Science Fiction Weight-Loss Book,* Crown (New York, NY), 1983.

(Editor, with Martin H. Greenberg and Charles G. Waugh) *Isaac Asimov Presents the Best Horror and Supernatural of the Nineteenth Century,* Beaufort Books, 1983.

(Editor) *Thirteen Horrors of Halloween,* Avon (New York, NY), 1983.

(Editor, with Martin H. Greenberg and George Zebrowski, and author of introduction) *Creations: The Quest for Origins in Story and Science,* Crown (New York, NY), 1983.

(With Ken Fisher) *Isaac Asimov Presents Superquiz 2,* Dembner, 1983.

Opus 300 (selections from the author's third hundred books), Houghton Mifflin (Boston, MA), 1984.

Isaac Asimov's Limericks for Children, Caedmon, 1984.

(Editor) *Living in the Future* (forecasts), Beaufort Books, 1985.

Isaac Asimov, Octopus Books, 1986.

(Editor) *Sherlock Holmes through Time and Space,* Bluejay Books, 1986.

The Alternate Asimovs, Doubleday (New York, NY), 1986.

Other Worlds of Isaac Asimov, edited by Martin H. Greenberg, Avenel, 1986.

Past, Present, and Future, Prometheus Books (Amherst, NY), 1987.

Robot Dreams, edited by Byron Preiss, Berkley (New York, NY), 1987.

(With Janet Asimov) *How to Enjoy Writing: A Book of Aid and Comfort,* Walker (New York, NY), 1987.

Asimov's Annotated Gilbert and Sullivan, Doubleday (New York, NY), 1988.

(Editor, with Jason A. Schulman) *Isaac Asimov's Book of Science and Nature Quotations,* Weidenfeld & Nicolson (London, England), 1988.

Asimov's Galaxy: Reflections on Science Fiction, Doubleday (New York, NY), 1989.

Foundation's Friends: Stories in Honor of Isaac Asimov, edited by Martin H. Greenberg, Tom Doherty (New York, NY), 1989.

(Compiler, with Martin H. Greenberg) *Cosmic Critiques: How and Why Ten Science Fiction Stories Work,* Writer's Digest, 1990.

(Contributor) *The John W. Campbell Letters with Isaac Asimov and A. E. van Vogt,* A. C. Projects, 1991.

Isaac Asimov Laughs Again, HarperCollins (New York, NY), 1991.

I. Asimov: A Memoir, Doubleday (New York, NY), 1994.

I, Robot: The Illustrated Screenplay, Warner (New York, NY), 1994.

Yours, Isaac Asimov: A Lifetime of Letters, Doubleday (New York, NY), 1995.

Magic: The Final Fantasy Collection, HarperPrism (New York, NY), 1996.

The Best of Isaac Asimov's Super Quiz, Barricade (New York, NY), 1996.

Isaac Asimov's I-Bots: History of I-Botics: An Illustrated Novel, HarperPrism (New York, NY), 1997.

Isaac Asimov's Christmas, Ace Books (New York, NY), 1997.

Isaac Asimov's Solar System, Ace Books (New York, NY), 1999.

Isaac Asimov's Father's Day, Ace Books (New York, NY), 2001.

Isaac Asimov's Halloween, Ace Books (New York, NY), 2001.

Isaac Asimov Collected Short Stories, Peterson Publishing (North Mankato, MN), 2001.

It's Been a Good Life, edited by Janet Jeppson Asimov, Prometheus (Amherst, NY), 2002.

Also author of *The Adventures of Science Fiction,* Ameron Ltd. Author of "Science" column in *Magazine of Fantasy and Science Fiction,* 1958-92. Contributor of stories to numerous science-fiction anthologies, and to many science-fiction magazines, including *Astounding Science Fiction, Amazing Stories, Fantastic Adventures, Science Fiction,* and *Future Fiction;* contributor of short story under pseudonym George E. Dale to *Astounding Science Fiction.* Contributor of articles to science journals and periodicals. Editorial director, *Isaac Asimov's Science Fiction Magazine.*

ADAPTATIONS: A sound recording of William Shatner reading the first eight chapters of *Foundation* was produced as *Foundation: The Psychohistorians,* Caedmon, 1976, and of Asimov reading from the same novel was produced as *The Mayors,* Caedmon, 1977; the film *The Ugly Little Boy* was adapted from Asimov's short story of the same title, Learning Corporation of America, 1977.

SIDELIGHTS: Isaac Asimov was "the world's most prolific science writer," according to David N. Samuelson in *Twentieth-Century Science-Fiction Writers,* and he "has written some of the best-known science fiction ever published." Considered one of the three greatest writers of science fiction in the 1940s—along with Robert Heinlein and A. E. van Vogt—Asimov remained throughout his life a potent force in the genre. Stories such as "Nightfall" and "The Bicentennial Man," and novels such as *The Gods Themselves* and *Foundation's Edge* have received numerous honors and are recognized as among the best science fiction

ever written. As one of the world's leading writers on science, explaining everything from nuclear fusion to the theory of numbers, Asimov illuminated for many the mysteries of science and technology. He was a skilled raconteur as well, who enlivened his writing with incidents from his own life. "In his autobiographical writings and comments," stated James Gunn in *Isaac Asimov: The Foundations of Science Fiction,* "Asimov continually invites the reader to share his triumphs, to laugh at his blunders and lack of sophistication, and to wonder, with him, at the rise to prominence of a bright Jewish boy brought to this country from Russia at the age of three and raised in a collection of Brooklyn candy stores."

Asimov's interest in science fiction began when he first noticed several of the early science-fiction magazines for sale on the newsstand of his family's candy store. Although as a boy he read and enjoyed numerous volumes of nonfiction as well as many of the literary "classics," Asimov recalled in his first autobiography, *In Memory Yet Green,* that he still longed to explore the intriguing magazines with their glossy covers. But his father refused, maintaining that fiction magazines are "junk! . . . Not fit to read. The only people who read magazines like that are bums." And bums represented "the dregs of society, apprentice gangsters."

In August of 1929, a new magazine appeared on the scene called *Science Wonder Stories.* Asimov knew that as long as science-fiction magazines had titles like *Amazing Stories,* he would have little chance of convincing his father of their worth. However, the new periodical had the word "science" in its title, and he said, "I had read enough about science to know that it was a mentally nourishing and spiritually wholesome study. What's more, I knew that my father thought so from our occasional talks about my schoolwork." When confronted with this argument, the elder Asimov consented. Soon Isaac began collecting even those periodicals that didn't have "science" in the title. He noted: "I planned to maintain with all the strength at my disposal the legal position that permission for one such magazine implied permission for all the others, regardless of title. No fight was needed, however; my harassed father conceded everything." Asimov rapidly developed into an avid fan.

Asimov first tried writing stories when he was eleven years old. He had for some time been reading stories and then retelling them to his schoolmates, and had also started a book like some of the popular boys' series volumes of the 1920s: "The Rover Boys," "The Bobbsey Twins," and "Pee Wee Wilson." Asimov's story was called "The Greenville Chums at College," patterned after *The Darewell Chums at College,* and it grew to eight chapters before he abandoned it. Asimov, in *In Memory Yet Green,* described the flaw in his initial literary venture: "I was trying to imitate the series books without knowing anything but what I read there. Their characters were small-town boys, so mine were, for I imagined Greenville to be a town in upstate New York. Their characters went to college, so mine did. Unfortunately, a junior high school youngster living in a shabby neighborhood in Brooklyn knows very little about small-town life and even less about college. Even I, myself, was forced eventually to recognize the fact that I didn't know what I was talking about."

Despite initial discouragements, Asimov continued to write. His first published piece appeared in his high school's literary semiannual and was accepted, he once admitted, because it was the only funny piece anyone wrote, and the editors needed something funny. In the summer of 1934 Asimov had a letter published in *Astounding Stories* in which he commented on several stories that had appeared in the magazine. His continuing activities as a fan prompted him to attempt a science fiction piece of his own; in 1937, at the age of seventeen, he began a story titled "Cosmic Corkscrew." The procedure Asimov used to formulate the plot was, he later said, "typical of my science fiction. I usually thought of some scientific gimmick and built a story about that."

By the time he finished the story on June 19, 1938, *Astounding Stories* had become *Astounding Science Fiction.* Its editor was John W. Campbell, who was to influence the work of some of the most prominent authors of modern science fiction, including Arthur C. Clarke, Robert Heinlein, Poul Anderson, L. Sprague de Camp, and Theodore Sturgeon. Since Campbell was also one of the best-known science fiction writers of the thirties and *Astounding* one of the most prestigious publications in its field at the time, Asimov was shocked by his father's suggestion that he submit "Cosmic Corkscrew" to the editor in person: mailing the story would cost twelve cents while subway fare, round trip, was only ten cents. In the interest of economy, therefore, Asimov agreed to make the trip to the magazine's office, fully expecting to leave the manuscript with a secretary.

It was Campbell's habit to invite many young writers to discuss their work with him, and when Asimov arrived he was shown into the editor's office. Campbell talked with him for over an hour and agreed to read the story; two days later Asimov received the manuscript back in the mail. It had been rejected, but Campbell offered extensive suggestions for improvement and encouraged the young man to keep trying. This began a pattern that was to continue for several years, with Campbell guiding Asimov through his formative beginnings as a science-fiction writer.

Asimov's association with the field of science fiction was a long and distinguished one. He has been credited with the introduction of several innovative concepts into the genre, including the formulation of the "Three Laws of Robotics." Asimov maintained that the idea for the laws was given to him by Campbell; Campbell, on the other hand, said that he had merely picked them out of Asimov's early robot stories. In any case, it was Asimov who first formally stated the three laws: "1. A robot may not injure a human being or, through inaction, allow a human being to come to harm. 2. A robot must obey the orders given it by human beings except where such orders would conflict with the First Law. 3. A robot must protect its own existence as long as such protection does not conflict with the First or Second Laws." Asimov said that he used these precepts as the basis for "over two dozen short stories and three novels . . . about robots," and he felt that he was "probably more famous for them than for anything else I have written, and they are quoted even outside the science-fiction world. The very word 'robotics' was coined by me." The three laws gained general acceptance among readers and among other science-fiction writers; Asimov, in his autobiography, wrote that they "revolutionized" science fiction and that "no writer could write a *stupid* robot story if he used the Three Laws. The story might be bad on other counts, but it wouldn't be stupid." The laws became so popular, and seemed so logical, that many people believed real robots would eventually be designed according to Asimov's basic principles.

Also notable among Asimov's science-fiction works is the "Foundation" series. This group of short stories, published in magazines in the 1940s and then collected into a trilogy in the early 1950s, was inspired by Edward Gibbon's *Decline and Fall of the Roman Empire.* It was written as a "future history," a story being told in a society of the distant future which relates events of that society's history. The concept was not invented by Asimov, but there can be little doubt that he became a master of the technique. *Foundation, Foundation and Empire,* and *Second Foundation* have achieved special standing among science-fiction enthusiasts. In 1966 the World Science Fiction Convention honored them with a special Hugo Award as the best all-time science-fiction series. Decades after its original publication Asimov's future-history series remained popular, and in the 1980s Asimov added a new volume, *Foundation's Edge,* and eventually linked the "Foundation" stories with his robot novels in *The Robots of Dawn, Robots and Empire, Foundation and Earth,* and *Prelude to Foundation.*

Asimov's first stories written specifically for a younger audience were his "Lucky Starr" novels. In 1951, at the suggestion of his Doubleday editor, he began working on a series of science-fiction stories that could easily be adapted for television. "Television was here; that was clear," he wrote in *In Memory Yet Green.* "Why not take advantage of it, then? Radio had its successful long-running series, 'The Lone Ranger,' so why not a 'Space Ranger' modeled very closely upon that?" *David Starr: Space Ranger,* published under the pseudonym Paul French, introduced David 'Lucky' Starr, agent of the interplanetary law enforcement agency the Council of Science. Accompanying Lucky on his adventures is sidekick John Bigman Jones, a short, tough man born and raised on the great agricultural farms of Mars. Together the two of them confront and outwit space pirates, poisoners, mad scientists, and interstellar spies—humans from the Sirian star system, who have become the Earth's worst enemies.

Although the "Lucky Starr" series ran to six volumes, the television deal Asimov and his editor envisioned never materialized. "None of us dreamed that for some reason . . . television series would very rarely last more than two or three years," Asimov wrote. "We also didn't know that a juvenile television series to be called *Rocky Jones: Space Ranger* was already in the works." Another problem the series faced was in the scientific background of the stories. "Unfortunately," stated Jean Fiedler and Jim Mele in *Isaac Asimov,* "Asimov had the bad luck to be writing these stories on the threshold of an unprecedented exploration of our solar system's planets, an exploration which has immensely increased our astronomical knowledge. Many of his scientific premises, sound in 1952, were later found to be inaccurate." In subsequent editions of the books Asimov included forewords explaining the situation to new readers.

Asimov's first nonfiction book—the beginning of what would number several hundred works for adults and younger readers—was a medical text titled *Biochemistry and Human Metabolism,* begun in 1950 and written in collaboration with William Boyd and Burnham Walker, two of his colleagues at the Boston University School of Medicine. He had recognized his ability as an explainer early in life, and he enjoyed clarifying scientific principles for his family and friends. He also discovered that he was a most able and entertaining lecturer who delighted in his work as a teacher. He once told *New York Times* interviewer Israel Shenker that his talent lay in the fact that he could "read a dozen dull books and make one interesting book out of them." The result was that Asimov was phenomenally successful as a writer of science books for the general public. Asimov later added: "I'm on fire to explain, and happiest when it's something reasonably intricate which I can make clear step by step. It's the easiest way I can clarify things in my own mind."

Toward the end of his career particularly, Asimov was concerned with a variety of subjects that went far beyond the scientific, and wrote on such diverse topics as the Bible, mythology, William Shakespeare, ecology, and American history. Asimov additionally wrote several volumes of autobiography, beginning with *In Memory Yet Green* in 1979 and culminating in *I. Asimov: A Memoir,* a 1994 work composed of 166 short chapters that discuss key elements which shaped the author's life. Michael Swanwick characterized the work as "quintessential Asimov," and Michael White commented that Asimov "was our era's great artist of explanation, a master of the declarative sentence and the lockstep paragraph, and both his fiction and his nonfiction conspire to convince you that the world makes more sense than you thought it did." In 1995 Stanley Asimov presented a significant contribution to the literary biography of his brother by publishing *Yours, Isaac Asimov: A Lifetime of Letters.* Organized thematically, the volume presents excerpts from thousands of letters and notes written by Isaac Asimov over the course of his life.

The years immediately preceding and following the author's death witnessed the publication of anthologies and collections of Asimov's fictional and prose writings. In 1990, for example, a collection titled *Ro-*

bot Visions appeared, encompassing all of Asimov's short stories and essays concerning robots. In 1995 the posthumous collection *Magic: The Final Fantasy Collection* was published, collecting numerous pieces for the first time. Many of the short stories in the anthology feature the comic adventures of George and the feckless supernatural being Azazel; and the volume additionally contains Asimov's critical writings on such noted fantasy writers as J. R. R. Tolkien, Robert E. Howard, and L. Sprague de Camp.

When Asimov died in 1992 he received numerous tributes highlighting the breadth of his curiosity and acknowledging his profound impact in enlarging the possibilities of the science fiction genre. Over the following decade, Asimov's second wife, Janet Jeppson Asimov, condensed her husband's autobiographies—numbering some 2,000 pages—into a single 300-page volume titled *It's Been a Good Life*, which was published in 2002. Arranged topically rather than chronologically, the work is divided into chapters that treat such topics as education, war, religion, family, writing, sexism, and his own illnesses. In addition to Asimov's words, Jepson Asimov includes excerpts from her correspondence with her husband, an account of his final days alive, and an epilogue in which she explains that he had contracted the AIDS virus from a blood transfusion during an 1983 triple-bypass operation, a fact he kept secret. Among the work's enthusiasts was *Booklist*'s Roland Green, who dubbed it a "good introduction" to Asimov's career, and a *Publishers Weekly* reviewer, who predicted that this "readable and idiosyncratic self-portrait" would likely attract new readers to Asimov's works.

BIOGRAPHICAL AND CRITICAL SOURCES:

BOOKS

Asimov, Isaac, *The Bicentennial Man and Other Stories,* Doubleday (New York, NY), 1976.

Asimov, Isaac, *In Memory Yet Green: The Autobiography of Isaac Asimov, 1920-1954,* Doubleday (New York, NY), 1979.

Asimov, Isaac, *In Joy Still Felt: The Autobiography of Isaac Asimov, 1954-1979,* Doubleday (New York, NY), 1980.

Boerst, William J., *Isaac Asimov: Writer of the Future,* Morgan Reynolds, 1998.

Children's Literature Review, Volume 12, Gale (Detroit, MI), 1987.

Clareson, Thomas D., editor, *Voices for the Future: Essays on Major Science-Fiction Writers,* Popular Press, 1976.

Contemporary Literary Criticism, Gale (Detroit, MI), Volume 1, 1973, Volume 3, 1975, Volume 9, 1978, Volume 19, 1981, Volume 26, 1983.

Dictionary of Literary Biography, Volume 8: *Twentieth-Century American Science-Fiction Writers,* Gale (Detroit, MI), 1981.

Fiedler, Jean, and Jim Mele, *Isaac Asimov,* Ungar, 1982.

Greenberg, Martin H., and Joseph D. Olander, editors, *Isaac Asimov,* Taplinger, 1977.

Gunn, James, *Isaac Asimov: The Foundations of Science Fiction,* Oxford University Press (New York, NY), 1982.

Isaac Asimov: An Annotated Bibliography of the Asimov Collection at Boston University, Greenwood Press (Westport, CT), 1995.

Judson, Karen, *Isaac Asimov: Master of Science Fiction,* Enslow Publishers, 1998.

Miller, Marjorie Mithoff, *Isaac Asimov: A Checklist of Works Published in the United States,* Kent State University Press (Kent, OH), 1972.

Patrouch, Joseph F., Jr., *The Science Fiction of Isaac Asimov,* Doubleday (New York, NY), 1974.

Platt, Charles, *Dream Makers: The Uncommon People Who Write Science Fiction,* Berkley (New York, NY), 1980.

Schweitzer, Darrell, *Science Fiction Voices 5,* Borgo Press (San Bernardino, CA), 1981, pp. 7-14.

Slusser, George E., *Isaac Asimov: The Foundations of His Science Fiction,* Borgo Press (San Bernardino, CA), 1979.

Touponce, William F., *Isaac Asimov,* Twayne (Boston, MA), 1991).

Twentieth-Century Science-Fiction Writers, 2nd edition, St. James Press (Detroit, MI), 1986.

Wollheim, Donald A., *The Universe Makers,* Harper (New York, NY), 1971.

PERIODICALS

Analog: Science Fiction/Science Fact, December 15, 1994, p. 167; May, 1998, review of *Isaac Asimov's I-Bots,* p. 144; September, 1998, Tom Easton, review of *The Roving Mind,* p. 133.

Booklist, July, 1993; January 1, 2000, Mary Ellen Quinn, review of *Asimov's Chronology of Science and Technology,* p. 966; May 1, 2000, Shelle

Rosenfeld, review of *Caves of Steel*, p. 1608; February 15, 2002, Roland Green, review of *It's Been a Good Life*, p. 984.

Books and Bookmen, July, 1968; February, 1969; July, 1973.

Chicago Tribune Book World, March 4, 1979; January 19, 1986.

Chicago Tribune Magazine, April 30, 1978.

Facts on File World News Digest, May 2, 2002, p. 327.

Fantasy Newsletter, April, 1983.

Fantasy Review, September, 1985.

Globe and Mail (Toronto, Ontario, Canada), August 10, 1985.

Hastings Center Report, March, 1998, review of *The Roving Mind*, p. 45.

Isis, March, 2003, Errol Vieth, review of *It's Been a Good Life*, pp. 183-185.

Library Journal, March 1, 2002, Robert L. Kelly, review of *It's Been a Good Life*, p. 98.

Magazine of Fantasy and Science Fiction, October, 1966; September, 1980; July, 1991; February, 1992.

Nation, March 5, 1983.

New Scientist, March 2, 2002, review of *It's Been a Good Life*, p. 46.

New York Review of Books, September 12, 1977; October 24, 1985.

New York Times, October 18, 1969; January 1, 1980; December 17, 1984; February 26, 1985.

New York Times Book Review, November 17, 1968; January 28, 1973; January 12, 1975; May 30, 1976; June 25, 1978; February 25, 1979; December 16, 1979; December 19, 1982; October 20, 1985; May 8, 1994, p. 25.

Publishers Weekly, April 17, 1972; September 2, 1983; March 7, 1994; September 11, 1995, p. 67; January 28, 2002, review of *It's Been a Good Life*, p. 279.

School Library Journal, February, 1992.

Science Books and Films, special edition, 1998, review of *The Caves of Steel*, p. 18.

Science Fiction and Fantasy Book Review, December, 1982; June, 1983; November, 1983; May 8, 1994.

Science Fiction Chronicle, July, 1998, review of *Isaac Asimov's I-Bots*, p. 41.

Science Fiction Review, winter, 1982; spring, 1984; winter, 1985.

Time, February 26, 1979; November 15, 1982.

Times Literary Supplement, October 5, 1967; December 28, 1967.

Washington Post, April 4, 1979.

Washington Post Book World, April 1, 1979; May 25, 1980; September 26, 1982; September 27, 1983; August 25, 1985.

ONLINE

Issac Asimov Home Page, http://www.asimovonline.com/ (April 15, 2003).

OTHER

Isaac Asimov Talks: An Interview (sound recording), Writer's Voice, 1974.

OBITUARIES:

PERIODICALS

Chicago Tribune, April 7, 1992, sec. 1, p. 13.
Detroit Free Press, April 7, 1992, p. 1B.
Los Angeles Tribune, April 7, 1992, p. 1A.
New York Times, April 7, 1992, p. B7.
Times (London, England), April 7, 1992, p. 19.
Washington Post, April 7, 1992.*

*   *   *

ATTENBOROUGH, David (Frederick) 1926-

PERSONAL: Born May 8, 1926, in London, England; son of Frederick Levi and Mary (Clegg) Attenborough; married Jane Elizabeth Oriel, 1950; children: Robert, Susan. *Education:* Clare College, Cambridge, M.A., 1947. *Hobbies and other interests:* Music, tribal art.

ADDRESSES: Home—5 Park Rd., Richmond, Surrey TW10 6NS, England.

CAREER: Editorial assistant in British publishing house, 1949-52; British Broadcasting Corp., London, England, producer, 1952-62, controller of programs for BBC-2, 1965-68, director of programs and member of board of management, 1969-72; independent producer and television series host, 1972—, shows include *Life on Earth*, 1979, *The Living Planet*, 1984, and *The First Eden: The Mediterranean World and Man*, 1987. Member of Nature Conservancy Council, 1973—; trustee of British Museum, 1980—, World Wildlife Fund, 1981—, and Science Museum, 1984—. Has un-

David Attenborough

dertaken numerous zoological, geological, and ethnographic filming expeditions, including Sierra Leone, 1954, New Guinea, 1957, Zambesi, 1964, Borneo, 1973, Solomon Islands, 1975, and the Mediterranean region, 1986. *Military service:* Royal Navy, 1947-49; became lieutenant.

MEMBER: Society of Film and Television Arts (fellow, 1980—).

AWARDS, HONORS: Society of Film and Television Arts special award, 1961; silver medals from Zoological Society of London and Royal Television Society, both 1966; Desmond Davis Award, 1970; Cherry Kearton Award from Royal Geographical Society, 1972; Commander of the Order of the British Empire, 1974; Kalinga Prize from UNESCO and medal from Academy of Natural Sciences, Philadelphia, both 1982; W.H. Smith Book awards, both 2003, in biography/autobiography genre, for *Life on Air,* and in general knowledge genre, for *The Life of Mammals.* Honorary degrees include D.Litt., University of Leicester, 1970, City University (London), 1972, and Birmingham University; D.Sc., University of Liverpool, 1974, Heriot-Watt University, 1978, University of Ulster, Sussex University, University of Bath, Durham University,

and Keele University; honorary fellow, Manchester Polytechnic, 1976; LL.D., University of Bristol and University of Glasgow, both 1977; D.Univ., Open University, 1980.

WRITINGS:

Zoo Quest to Guiana (also see below), Lutterworth (Cambridge, England), 1956, Crowell, 1957, abridged edition, University of London Press (London, England), 1962.

Zoo Quest for a Dragon (also see below), Lutterworth (Cambridge, England), 1957.

Zoo Quest in Paraguay (also see below), Lutterworth (Cambridge, England), 1959.

Quest in Paradise, Lutterworth (Cambridge, England), 1960.

People of Paradise, Harper (New York, NY), 1961.

Zoo Quest to Madagascar, Lutterworth (Cambridge, England), 1961, published as *Bridge to the Past: Animals and People of Madagascar,* Harper (New York, NY), 1962.

Quest under Capricorn, Lutterworth (Cambridge, England), 1963.

(Editor) *My Favorite Stories of Exploration,* Lutterworth (Cambridge, England), 1964.

(With Molly Cox) *David Attenborough's Fabulous Animals,* BBC Publications (London, England), 1975.

The Tribal Eye, Norton (New York, NY), 1976.

Life on Earth: A Natural History, BBC Publications (London, England), 1979, Little, Brown (Boston, MA), 1980.

Journeys to the Past: Travels in New Guinea, Madagascar, and the Northern Territory of Australia, Lutterworth (Cambridge, England), 1981.

Tribal Encounters: An Exhibition of Ethnic Objects Collected by David Attenborough (exhibition catalog), Leicester Museums, Art Galleries, and Records Service, 1981.

Discovering Life on Earth: A Natural History (juvenile), Little, Brown (Boston, MA), 1981.

The Zoo Quest Expeditions: Travels in Guyana, Indonesia, and Paraguay (contains *Zoo Quest to Guiana, Zoo Quest for a Dragon,* and *Zoo Quest in Paraguay*), Penguin (New York, NY), 1982.

The Living Planet: A Portrait of the Earth, Little, Brown (Boston, MA), 1984.

(Author of introduction) *Wildlife through the Camera,* Parkwest Publications (Jersey City, NJ), 1985.

(Author of foreword) Andrew Langley, *The Making of "The Living Planet,"* Little, Brown (Boston, MA), 1985.

The First Eden: The Mediterranean World and Man, Little, Brown (Boston, MA), 1987.

The Atlas of the Living World, Houghton Mifflin (Boston, MA), 1989.

The Trials of Life, Little, Brown (Boston, MA), 1990.

The Private Life of Plants: A Natural History of Plant Behaviour, Princeton University Press (Princeton, NJ), 1995.

The Life of Birds, Princeton University Press (Princeton, NJ), 1998.

The Life of Mammals, Princeton University Press (Princeton, NJ), 2002.

Life on Air: Memoirs of a Broadcaster, Princeton University Press (Princeton, NJ), 2002.

General editor of "New Generation Guide" series, University of Texas Press (Austin, TX), 1987-1989. Also narrator of *Wildlife on One: The Birdman of Afikim* (video cassette), produced by George Inger, series produced by Dilys Breese, written by Peter France, BBC-1, 1989.

SIDELIGHTS: David Attenborough has spent most of his career explaining the wonders of the natural world to public television audiences. As producer and host of such popular series as "Zoo Quest," "Life on Earth," "The Living Planet," and "The First Eden: The Mediterranean World and Man," Attenborough has traveled around the world, and—striding through marshes or cuddling baby mountain gorillas—has communicated his personal enthusiasm for natural phenomena. Attenborough has two aims in his award-winning work: to entertain and to inform. His productions find a balance between the "believe-it-or-not" approach of some animal shows and the complex theoretical approach associated with strict schooling. *Newsweek* contributor Harry F. Waters wrote: "Attenborough, schooled in geology, zoology and biology, possesses a remarkably eclectic scientific range as well as the sensibilities of a poet." According to Timothy S. Green in *Smithsonian,* the naturalist "has a rare talent for describing with great simplicity the complexities of evolution," while he "never underrates the intelligence of his audience." In addition to his television series, Attenborough has authored lavishly illustrated companion volumes that cover the same topics as his films. *New York Times Book Review* correspondent Clifford D. May noted that these books add up to "an outstanding introduc-

tion to natural history and a sobering reminder that the works of man don't amount to a hill of bat guano beside the miracles of nature."

Attenborough was born and raised in London, the son of scholar Frederick Levi Attenborough and the younger brother of actor-director Richard Attenborough. The spirit of intellectual curiosity was paramount in the Attenborough household, and young David was encouraged to pursue his interest in fossils and in the live animals he extracted from the ponds near his home. He admired his father's academic colleagues, and he has praised his father for the educational role he played. He told *Smithsonian:* "My father . . . believed that the way you teach children is to allow them to discover for themselves. . . . I'd find a fossil and show it to my father and he'd say, 'Good, good, tell me all about it.' So I responded and became my own expert." Attenborough attended Clare College, Cambridge, where he majored in geology and zoology and earned a master's degree in 1947. After completing his military service in the Royal Navy, he became an editorial assistant at an educational publishing house. In 1952 he joined the British Broadcasting Corporation, where he was trained to produce television programs.

At first, Attenborough produced BBC shows on a variety of topics, from politics to ballet. In 1954 he and Jack Lester, a curator of the London Zoo, proposed an animal collecting expedition. Attenborough would film what happened for the BBC and Lester would bring back animals for the London Zoo. The resulting series of programs was called "Zoo Quest." Attenborough told *Smithsonian* that his idea was to "combine the benefits" of an up-close studio look at an animal and a field trip to its natural environment. He thought it would be interesting to see an animal in the wild and then show it live in the studio. The first trip, to Sierra Leone in West Africa, resulted in the capture of a great variety of animals, the most famous of which was the bald-headed rock crow (*Picathartes gymnocephalus*). Thereafter Attenborough went to British Guiana, Indonesia, New Guinea, Paraguay, Madagascar, and northern Australia, always in search of largely unknown species of wild animals. Lester was stricken with a fatal illness in 1955, and Attenborough took over as show host as well as producer. Green described Attenborough's unexpected success in front of the cameras: "Clad in shorts and hiking boots, he . . . trekked through jungles and waded across swamps in search of orangutans, birds of paradise, or a spectacular [Indonesian] lizard known as the Komodo dragon. His infectious enthusiasm . . . for every kind of animal he found appealed to armchair travelers who felt that here was a real explorer taking them along and sharing wildlife secrets, gamely brushing discomfort aside." Attenborough's adventures were collected in a series of "Zoo Quest" books, reprinted together in two volumes as *The Zoo Quest Expeditions* (1980) and *Journeys to the Past* (1981).

In 1965 Attenborough was named controller of a second BBC channel that became the first in Europe to offer color programming. The station was established to provide a planned alternative to the BBC's first channel, but Attenborough set out to capture most if not all of Great Britain's nightly audience. He was soon attracting five million viewers with dramatic series such as "Henry the Eighth" and "The Forsyte Saga," and he earned critical acclaim by commissioning Jacob Bronowski's "The Ascent of Man" and Kenneth Clark's "Civilization." Attenborough told *Smithsonian* that his idea for the latter series was to use color television to show "all the loveliest things of this civilization over the last 2,000 years," and do it in a historical sequence. On the strength of his programming capabilities, Attenborough was promoted to director of programs for both BBC channels in 1968. He held the position for four years, then resigned in order to return to the creative work of producing and directing shows. He wanted to do an epic series on natural history in the same style as Clark's "Civilization," but first he produced and hosted a series on art in primitive societies. His seven-part work, "The Tribal Eye," aired in 1975 and drew four million viewers.

The series "Life on Earth" began as a six-page outline tracing life from its origins in the sea to the advent of the human race. Attenborough wanted to produce "not just a natural history but a history of nature," he told *CA*. He did so by exploring the fossil record and by showing footage of living species of animals and plants. The series required a team of more than fifty wildlife photographers, more than a million miles of travel to thirty countries, and the cooperation of major zoos, museums, and universities worldwide. First broadcast in England in 1979, "Life on Earth" quickly became the most popular science series ever put on the air, with twelve million regular viewers each week. It was received with equal enthusiasm when it ran in America early in 1982. *Washington Post* contributor

Bruce Brown called the work "a tour de force: fresh and vivid with incredible variety married to the clear exposition of the mechanisms of evolution." Waters offered a similar opinion in *Newsweek:* "By coupling lyrical rhythms and evocative images, ['Life on Earth'] achieves the emotional power of a cinematic poem." Attenborough also wrote a companion book, *Life on Earth: A Natural History,* that has likewise drawn praise from reviewers. In the *Washington Post Book World,* Joseph Kastner wrote that the volume "is the best kind of spin-off—literate, witty, full of earthly marvels presented without any of the orotund self-consciousness of some cosmic TV guides." Elisabeth Whipp elaborated in *Spectator:* "With a pleasant enthusiasm [Attenborough] effortlessly encompasses 3000 million years in 300 pages, from the very start of life to its most bizarre and intricate manifestations. Using the historical framework of the gradually evolving species, he juxtaposes fossil evidence and comparative anatomy to give a vivid picture of our present understanding of how life came about."

If "Life on Earth" examined the overall history of evolution, "The Living Planet," first broadcast in America in 1984, showed how plants and animals adapt to extreme environments. Once again Attenborough traveled the length and breadth of the globe, filming sequences from the rim of an active volcano, in a mangrove swamp, and in the sweltering heat of Death Valley, among others. Brown wrote of the series: "Natural adaptations are compared and contrasted until—almost by surprise—the reader has acquired a pretty good idea of how life is shaped on the [global] anvil." Another illustrated companion volume, *The Living Planet: Portrait of the Earth,* appeared at the same time the series aired. In his *Newsweek* review, Jim Miller contended that the reader first notices "the arresting images: a hairy sloth hanging upside down, an ocean of brightly tasseled foxtail grass, two albatrosses courting, a beach blanketed with breeding sea turtles, an uncanny ghost crab looking quite like its name. The text almost seems an afterthought—until you begin to read it. Like Attenborough's on-air scripts, it has the lilt and texture of the spoken word and something of the offhand appeal of a face-to-face conversation. The real pleasure of the book, though, lies in Attenborough's old-fashioned skill as a prose stylist."

Attenborough's next series, "The First Eden: The Mediterranean World and Man," focused on the Mediterranean region from the Ice Age to the present. Aired in 1987, the series showed how various sophisticated human cultures developed around the inland sea, some holding nature in reverence and others exploiting it until forests turned into deserts. *Earth Science* contributor Louise J. Fisher noted that the point of "The First Eden" is that nature "has never failed to support people, but people have failed to support nature." The short series and its book of the same title helped to counter a complaint formerly leveled at Attenborough; namely, that he has tended to underplay the devastation humankind is wreaking on the global environment. Attenborough himself told *Earth Science:* "My television programs are just for the wonder of it all. I don't start with a message or preach to people, but try to enrich their lives by showing them our fascinating and delightful planet." He did state, however: "I hope my work has helped people become more aware of nature and the Earth. Understanding the geosciences gives us a sense of time and evolution. . . . I have always thought an education in the natural sciences illuminates your life forever. You can't be a natural scientist without acquiring a profound reverence for nature." Everyone starts with that reverence, he said, "it's just that some of us lose sight of it. We can't let that happen. We would be deprived of so much." Attenborough told Fred Hauptfuhrer of *People* magazine that his unusual career has been a source of constant pleasure for him, no matter what conditions he confronted in his travels. "I'm the luckiest man," he said. "I go to the most marvelous places in the world, and I'm paid for it."

Despite his reputation, Attenborough's proposal for another big project, "The Life of Birds," took a little convincing before BBC would agree to produce it. As he explained to *Los Angeles Times* reporter David Gritten, "I was told birds aren't furry or cuddly. . . . Might ten episodes not be boring? What would they be about? I said, 'Well, we might do one program entirely on the egg.' They said, 'The egg? You must be joking!'" He wasn't, and ultimately he won over the BBC, which aired the ten-part series in 1998. In addition to the egg and the complex mechanics of flight, Attenborough covered the diverse sex lives, migratory patterns, and survival strategies of an amazing variety of birds. His search took him to forty-two countries and every continent, and he uncovered a number of surprises, such as the female hedge sparrows that take a secret lover in addition to their mate, just in case they need extra food in hard times, and the Japanese crows that have learned to let cars smash open particularly hard nuts, timing their feeding ac-

cording to the traffic lights. As *New York Times* reviewer Andrew Revkin noted, "The documentary series is a primer in basic bird biology, but rises beyond rote because of the extraordinarily colorful lives of its subjects. . . . It also draws energy from Sir David, who served as the writer and narrator and who crawls, hikes, peers and probes to get at his subjects in dozens of scenes." Reviewing the companion book of the same title, *Boston Globe* reporter Mark Wilson concluded, "For a sharp kid, this book could foster a lifelong passion. For a jaded adult, *The Life of Birds* might provide fresh eyes. And for anyone, the book proves how watchable birds are."

Attenborough followed up with another in-depth look at an entire class of animals, this time the one that includes our own species, and of course many others. His "Life of Mammals," which aired in 2002, "is six wondrous hours with an astonishing number of the species that thrive today in every corner of the world. The infinite variety of them will amaze you. And wherever they are, Attenborough's right there with them," reported Ann Hodges in the *Houston Chronicle*. At age seventy-seven, Attenborough can be seen swimming with sea otters, climbing rocks with baboons, or watching a leopard slink past his hut in an Indian village. Once again, "the host's curiosity is boundless and infectious, and one is repeatedly reminded that once teeming and scheming humanity is left behind, the Earth can still be a magically amazing place," according to *Washington Post* television critic Tom Shales. The companion book, also titled *The Life of Mammals,* was similarly well received. *Booklist* reviewer Nancy Bent found it "a terrific introduction to the wonders of our hairy, milk-producing relatives."

BIOGRAPHICAL AND CRITICAL SOURCES:

BOOKS

Langley, Andrew, *The Making of "The Living Planet,"* Little, Brown, 1985.

PERIODICALS

Booklist, April 15, 2003, Nancy Bent, review of *Life of Mammals,* p. 1435.
Boston Globe, December 6, 1998, Mark Wilson, review of *Life of Birds,* p. 17.

Earth Science, fall, 1987, Louise J. Fisher, "Sir David Attenborough," p. 11.

Houston Chronicle, May 8, 2003, Ann Hodges, "Animal Magnetism," p. D6.

Los Angeles Times, July 27, 1999, David Gritten, "This Guy Isn't Just Winging It," p. 3.

Newsweek, February 4, 1985, Harry F. Waters, review of "The Living Planet," p. 69; February 11, 1985, Jim Miller, review of *The Living Planet: Portrait of the Earth.*

New York Times, July 18, 1999, Andrew Revkin, "The Things Birds Do after They Fly Away," p. 4.

New York Times Book Review, January 3, 1982, Clifford D. May, review of *Life on Earth,* p. 10.

People, February 8, 1982, Fred Hauptfuhrer, "David Attenborough Stalks Flora and Fauna Worldwide for His Stunning 'Life on Earth,'" p. 105.

Smithsonian, November, 1981, Timothy S. Green, "Stalking the World of Nature with BBC's Superguide," p. 134.

Spectator, March 31, 1979, Elisabeth Whipp, review of *Life on Earth: A Natural History.*

Washington Post, January 12, 1982, Bruce Brown, review of "Life on Earth"; May 8, 2003, Tom Shales, "On Discovery, the Animal Kingdom in All Its Glory," p. C1.

Washington Post Book World, November 8, 1981, Joseph Kastner, review of *Life on Earth: A Natural History.*

ONLINE

Life of Birds Web site, http://www.pbs.org/lifeofbirds/sirdavid/ (November 17, 2003), "Meet Sir David."*

*   *   *

AUSTIN, Carrie
See SEULING, Barbara

B

BANGS, Richard 1950-

PERSONAL: Born August 24, 1950, in New Haven, CT; son of Lawrence Cutler (a psychologist) and Louise (a housewife; maiden name, Morton) Bangs; married Pamela Roberson; children: Walker. *Education:* Northwestern University, B.A., 1972; University of Southern California, M.A., 1975, graduate study, 1975.

ADDRESSES: Home—Montclair, CA. *Office*—Mountain Travel Sobek U.S, 1266 66th Street, Suite 3 and 4 Emeryville, CA 94608. *E-mail*—richardbangs@msn. com.

CAREER: Sobek Expeditions (international adventure travel company), Angels Camp, CA, president, beginning 1973; founding partner of Mountain Travel-Sobek U.S., Montclair, CA; president of Outward Bound U.S. A., 2001.

MEMBER: Explorers Club, Sierra Club, Sobek's International Explorers Society.

AWARDS, HONORS: Lowell Thomas Award for Best Travel Book of 1989 for *Riding the Dragon's Back: The Race to Raft the Upper Yangtze*; Eisner Prize for Literature; Bosner Award for Journalism; National Outdoor Book Award in the literature category for *The Lost River: A Memoir of Life, Death, and Transformation on Wild Water,* 2000.

WRITINGS:

(Contributor, with others) *South America: River Trips,* Bradt Enterprises, 1981.

(With Christian Kallen) *Rivergods: Exploring the World's Great Rivers,* Sierra Club Books, 1985.

(Editor, with Christian Kallen) *Paths Less Travelled: Dispatches from the Front Lines of Exploration,* Atheneum (New York, NY), 1988.

(With Christian Kallen) *Islands of Fire, Islands of Spice: Exploring the Wild Places of Indonesia,* Sierra Club Books (San Francisco, CA), 1988.

(With Christian Kallen) *Riding the Dragon's Back: The Race to Raft the Upper Yangtze,* Atheneum (New York, NY), 1989.

(Editor) *Adventure Vacations: From Trekking in New Guinea to Swimming in Siberia,* Norton (New York, NY), 1990.

Islandgods: Exploring the World's Most Exotic Islands, Taylor Publishing (Dallas, TX), 1991.

Peaks: Seeking High Ground across the Continents, Taylor Publishing (Dallas, TX), 1994.

The Last Wild River Ride, Turner Publishing (Atlanta, GA), 1997.

The Lost River: A Memoir of Life, Death, and Transformation on Wild Water, Sierra Club Books (San Francisco, CA), 1999.

Adventure without End, Mountaineers Books (Seattle, WA), 2001.

WITH SOBEK'S INTERNATIONAL EXPLORERS SOCIETY

The Adventure Book, Frommer-Pasmantier, 1983.

One Thousand Adventures: Journeys to the Rivers, Lands, and Seas of Seven Continents, Harmony Books, 1983.

The Adventure Book II, Sobek's International Explorers Society, 1984.

Sobek's Adventure Vacations, Running Press, 1986.

Also author of *Whitewater Adventure.* Contributing editor of *Outside* and *River Runner* magazines; contributor of articles to periodicals in the United States and abroad. Author of several film scripts; executive producer of film "River of the Red Ape." Columnist for *Mother Lode Weekly,* a local paper; contributor of essays to Expedia.com; producer of "Well-Traveled" column on the Microsoft Network (msn.com).

SIDELIGHTS: Richard Bangs, writer, adventurer, and travel-company executive, told Michael Bowker in *Western's World:* "If I had a million dollars I wouldn't be able to do any more than I'm doing now." His company's books, adventure logs with photographs and accompanying text, take the reader down some of the world's least navigable rivers, such as the Copper in Alaska, the Zaskar in India, the Omo in Ethiopia, and the Bio Bio in Chile; some of the most legendary, including the Indus, Euphrates, and Yangtze; and some of the most foreboding, like the Eater of Men. Bangs—who named his company Sobek, after the crocodile goddess of the Nile—was inspired to take his first raft ride by Mark Twain's *Huckleberry Finn.* Although the debut river ride down the Potomac was foiled by a park ranger, Bangs and his friends were hooked. They proceeded throughout high school to "canoe and raft most of the wild rivers on the Eastern Seaboard," he told Bowker.

Rivergods, written with Christian Kallen, includes photographs in "wild color" of twelve major rivers and provides illustrative text as well, according to David Graber in the *Los Angeles Times Book Review.* He termed the prose "adventure writing" and explained that it tells the story not of the river, its people, or its wildlife, but replays each step of the expedition itself, telling a story of drama and danger in which the lives of the actual explorers and tourists are threatened by rapids and crocodiles. Graber described the book as "big, bold, brash; adrenaline leaking from between the pages." The critic concluded that *Rivergods* "raises the word *vicarious* to new heights."

Bangs hit upon a unique book project in 1988. He recruited a dozen top writers and sent them on all-expenses-paid trips asking only that they write about their adventures. The writers' recollections became the basis for *Paths Less Travelled: Dispatches from the*

Front Lines of Exploration. Such literary figures as Edward Hoagland, Roy Blount, Bobbie Ann Mason and William Broyles served as the commentators. "Upshot?" asked a *Kirkus Reviews* critic. "About the same as picking twelve strangers off the street—a few prove to be first-rate travellers . . . while the rest enjoy themselves and send some pretty postcards." The reviewer singled out Hoagland's "Arabia Felix" and Barry Lopez's "The Resplendent Oryx" as worthy travel essays; Jay McInerney's "Deadly Hazards, Minor Hassles," about a rafting trip in Victoria Falls was deemed "funny [and] sharp-eyed."

Bangs provided reminiscences of his own, most notably *The Lost River: A Memoir of Life, Death, and Transformation on Wild Water* and *Adventure without End.* In *The Lost River,* Bangs "recounts a nearly thirty-year obsession with rafting some of the swiftest, most dangerous waters on earth," according to a *Publishers Weekly* contributor. During one expedition, to the Nile in 1975, Bangs's closest friend, Lee Greenwald, drowned in a freak accident. The final third of the book describes a 1998 expedition in honor of Greenwald to the Tekeze River, one of Africa's deepest. *Adventure without End* collects Bangs's online contributions to Expedia.com, the travel web site. Expeditions to Patagonia, Indonesia, Kalimantan (Borneo) and Morocco are described, leading George Cohen of *Booklist* to say that the author's "madcap experiences are a pleasure to read about."

Bangs once told *CA:* "I write for fellow adventurers—for those who venture beyond the mainstream, who turn the unturned stone and seek the unclimbed summit. My writings are an attempt to share my adventures, knowledge, and love of the outdoors with those who are aware enough to appreciate them.

"I've always enjoyed a good story and have found writing my own to be an extremely rewarding experience."

BIOGRAPHICAL AND CRITICAL SOURCES:

PERIODICALS

Booklist, December 15, 1991, review of *Islandgods: Exploring the World's Most Exotic Islands,* p. 746; October 1, 1994, Alice Joyce, review of *Peaks:*

Seeking High Ground across the Continents, p. 232; February 15, 2002, George Cohen, review of *Adventure without End,* p. 165.

Chicago Tribune, December 1, 1985.

Kirkus Reviews, June 15, 1988, review of *Paths Less Travelled: Dispatches from the Front Lines of Exploration,* p. 867; June 1, 1999, review of *The Lost River: A Memoir of Life, Death, and Transformation on Wild Water,* p. 844.

Library Journal, August, 1989, Roland Person, review of *Riding the Dragon's Back: The Race to Raft the Upper Yangtze,* p. 153; November 1, 1991, Joseph Buelna, review of *Islandgods,* p. 121; July, 1999, Will Hepfer, review of *The Lost River,* p. 100; March 1, 2002, Lonnie Weatherby, review of *Adventure without End,* p. 128.

Los Angeles Times Book Review, December 1, 1985, David Graber, review of *Rivergods;* September 18, 1988, Alex Raksin, review of *Paths Less Travelled.*

National Geographic Traveler, July-August, 1992, Allan Fallow, review of *Islandgods,* p. 130.

Publishers Weekly, August 25, 1989, Genevieve Stuttaford, review of *Riding the Dragon's Back,* p. 54; October 5, 1990, p. 86; July 26, 1999, review of *The Lost River* p. 77.

School Library Journal, June, 1990, Jenni Elliott, review of *Riding the Dragon's Back,* p. 146; December, 1999, Pam Spencer, review of *The Lost River* p. 165.

Sports Afield, October, 1999, review of *The Lost River* p. 58.

Tribune Books (Chicago, IL), December 4, 1994, review of *Peaks,* p. 10.

Western's World, August, 1983.

Whole Earth Review, spring, 1991, J. Baldwin, review of *Adventure Vacations: From Trekking in New Guinea to Swimming in Siberia,* p. 105.

ONLINE

Mountain Travel Sobek, http://mtsobek.com/ (July 20, 2003).

*   *   *

BASKET, Raney
See EDGERTON, Clyde (Carlyle)

BERGEN, David 1957-

PERSONAL: Born 1957, in Manitoba, Canada.

ADDRESSES: Agent—c/o Author Mail, HarperCollins, 10 East 53rd St., 7th Fl., New York, NY 10022-5299.

CAREER: Fiction writer.

WRITINGS:

Sitting Opposite My Brother (short stories), Turnstone (Winnipeg, Manitoba, Canada), 1994.
A Year of Lesser, HarperCollins (New York, NY), 1996.
See the Child, HarperFlamingo Canada (Toronto, Ontario, Canada), 1999, Simon & Schuster (New York, NY), 2002.
The Case of Lena S, McClelland & Stewart (Toronto, Ontario, Canada), 2002.

Contributor to several editions of *The Journey Prize Anthology* (Canada).

SIDELIGHTS: "David Bergen's stories are identifiably, disturbingly, marked 'Bergen,'" wrote P. J. Gerbrecht in a review of *Sitting Opposite My Brother* in *Canadian Literature.* But John Oughton, reviewing the same volume for *Books in Canada,* aligned Bergen with other Manitoban writers who shared a Mennonite heritage, specifically Di Brandt and Patrick Friesen. Thus achieving both individuality and communality, Bergen, at his best, Oughton remarked, "plays skillfully on many levels."

The stories in Bergen's first book, *Sitting Opposite My Brother,* deal with ordinary realistic problems of love and marriage, sibling relationships, alcoholism, mental illness, and religious faith and doubt. Many of them feature a set of recurring family members, including Timothy, a Mennonite missionary, and Thomas, his doubting brother, who serves frequently as narrator. Blending careful observation with occasional philosophic flights, Bergen uses guilt-ridden first-person narrators to portray a dark vision of life in which, according to Pat Bolger in *Canadian Materials,* "religion . . . is a source of pain rather than comfort, and families are unhappy or corrupt."

Both the title story and the story "Where You're From" in *Sitting Opposite My Brother* are narrated by Thomas; other stories cited favorably by Bolger were "The Bottom of the Glass," which concerns a drowned child and its father; "Cousins," a tale about a sexual relationship between cousins; "La Rue Prevette," which depicts three dysfunctional generations in a family; and the very short "The Vote," which ironically portrays a congregation's process of selecting a pastor. In "The Translator," Timothy marries, or at least appears to have married, a Guyanese woman who has emigrated to North America.

Gerbrecht analyzed "The Translator" as an example of the alienation that she found in many of Bergen's stories, particularly in those dealing with the brothers Timothy and Thomas; she speculated that Bergen's Mennonite relatives and friends would not approve of his often-ironic view of that culture. Oughton perceived in Bergen's stories "a common tone—a sense of life as painful and random, yet holding moments of tenderness and beauty." Commenting on his own work—and perhaps also on his working method—in a press release quoted by Oughton, Bergen observed that "only the minute detail will save these characters." Oughton, despite noting some lapses of craftsmanship in the stories, particularly in transitions, asserted, "[Bergen's] work is worth following, both for the complexity and realism of his characters and for the pleasures of lines like, 'He was nothing to her, and nothing was what she was looking for.'"

Bergen's first novel, *A Year of Lesser,* was published by HarperCollins in 1996. It describes a year in the life of one Johnny Fehr, who volunteers at a teen center run by a man named Lesser. Fehr is unhappily married to alcoholic Charlene and is having an affair with the cynical widow Lorraine. *Library Journal* reviewer David A. Beron enjoyed the novel's descriptions, which he called "distinctive," more than its plot and characterizations, claiming that weaknesses in the latter two areas prevented him from feeling deeply about the characters and events.

See the Child, published in 1999, is a story of grief and the search for healing, guilt and attempted absolution, disintegrating family relationships and the process of restoring broken ties. It begins early one morning when small town businessman Paul Unger is roused by the news that his estranged teenaged son, Stephen, has been found dead. Unable to cope with the result-

ing depression and guilt, Unger withdraws from his wife and adult daughter to his remote farm, where he pours his energies into his longtime interest of bee keeping. Nicole, Stephen's promiscuous girlfriend, arrives at the farm with two-year-old Sky, whom she says is Stephen's son. Unger turns to them to assuage his pain, despite the talk his devotion to this new "family" causes among his old family and in his small town. Bergen employs flashbacks to depict Unger's troubled relationship with Stephen and the events that led to his death. A *Publishers Weekly* reviewer called *See the Child* a "plaintive, deeply moving novel," praising Bergen's concise, revealing writing, and particularly noting the strong portrayals of secondary characters. "This authenticity deepens the novel's perspective, allowing this compassionate tale of mourning to be told with graceful honesty," the reviewer reflected. Gillian Engberg, writing in *Booklist,* noted the questions the book raises concerning how one should live and take care of others and oneself. She found it "an uneven whole of beautiful parts." The parts she considered best, "written in Bergen's tender, unflinching, precise, language . . . capture private revelations between people." A *Kirkus Reviews* contributor regarded it to be "emotionally compelling," and concluded, "The novel succeeds brilliantly in showing how people who believe they're solving problems and healing wounds are instead helplessly drifting away from one another."

BIOGRAPHICAL AND CRITICAL SOURCES:

PERIODICALS

Booklist, May 15, 2002, Gillian Engberg, review of *See the Child,* p. 1573.
Books in Canada, February, 1994, review of *Sitting Opposite My Brother,* p. 32; October, 1996, review of *A Year of Lesser,* p. 40.
Canadian Literature, spring, 1996, review of *Sitting Opposite My Brother,* pp. 144-146; summer, 1998, review of *A Year of Lesser,* pp. 138-139; winter, 2000, review of *See the Child,* pp. 177-178.
Canadian Materials, January, 1994, review of *Sitting Opposite My Brother,* p. 15.
Globe and Mail, March 27, 1999, review of *See the Child,* p. D16.
Kirkus Reviews, January 1, 1997, review of *A Year of Lesser,* p. 4; March 15, 2002, review of *See the Child,* p. 356.

Library Journal, February 1, 1997, review of *A Year of Lesser,* p. 104.

New York Times Book Review, December 7, 1994, review of *A Year of Lesser,* p. 64; April 6, 1997, review of *A Year of Lesser,* p. 29; June 1, 1997, review of *A Year of Lesser,* p. 37.

Publishers Weekly, April 8, 2002, review of *See the Child,* p. 203.

Quill & Quire, April, 1999, review of *See the Child,* pp. 26-27.*

* * *

BERTOLUCCI, Bernardo 1940-

PERSONAL: Born March 16, 1940, in Parma, Italy; son of Attilio (a poet, film critic, and teacher) and Ninetta (a teacher) Bertolucci; married Adriana Asti (marriage ended); married Clare Peploe (a director and screenwriter), 1978. *Education:* Attended University of Rome, 1960-62. *Politics:* Communist. *Hobbies and other interests:* Literature, opera.

ADDRESSES: Home—Via del Babuino 51, Rome, Italy. *Agent*—International Creative Management, 8942 Wilshire Blvd., Beverly Hills, CA 90211.

CAREER: Screenwriter and director of motion pictures. Worked as assistant director for Pier Paolo Pasolini on motion picture "Accatone," 1961. Lecturer at Museum of Modern Art, New York, NY, 1969. Director of films, including *La Commare secca, Last Tango in Paris,* and *The Dreamers.*

AWARDS, HONORS: Premio Viareggio, 1962, for *In cerca del mistero;* Critics' Award from Cannes Film Festival and Max Ophuls prize, both 1964, both for *Prima della rivoluzione;* best director award, National Society of Film Critics, and Academy Award nomination for best foreign-language film, Academy of Motion Picture Arts and Sciences, both 1971, both for *Il Conformista;* Raoul Levy Prize and Silver Ribbon, both 1973, both for *Last Tango in Paris;* Academy Award for screenplay based on material from another medium, 1987, for *The Last Emperor;* numerous other filmmaking awards.

WRITINGS:

SCREENPLAYS; AND DIRECTOR

(With Pier Paolo Pasolini and Sergio Citti) *La Commare secca* (title means "The Grim Reaper";

Bernardo Bertolucci

adapted from the story by Pasolini; released by Cinematografica Cervi, 1962), G. Zibetti, 1962.

(With Gianni Amico) *Prima della rivoluzione* (also known as *Before the Revolution*), Iride Cinematografica, 1964.

"Il fico infruttuoso" (title means "The Infertile Fig Tree"), *Vangela 70,* Castoro Films, 1967.

(With Gianni Amico) *Partner* (adapted from *The Double* by Fyodor Dostoevski), Red Films, 1968.

(With Marilu Parolini and Edoardo De Gregorio) *La Strategia del ragno* (also known as *The Spider's Strategy;* adapted from *Theme of the Traitor and the Hero* by Jorge Luis Borges), Red Films, 1970.

Il Conformista (also known as *The Conformist;* adapted from the novel by Alberto Moravia), Mars Film/Marianne Productions/Maran Film, 1970.

(With Franco Arcalli) *Last Tango in Paris* (United Artists, 1973) published as *Bernardo Bertolucci's Last Tango in Paris,* with essays by Pauline Kael and Norman Mailer, Delacorte (New York, NY), 1973.

(With Franco Arcalli and Giuseppe Bertolucci) *La Luna* (title means "The Moon"), Twentieth Century-Fox, 1979.

(With Franco Arcalli and Giuseppe Bertolucci) *Novecento* (two volumes; also known as *1900,* Paramount, 1977), Einaudi (Milan, Italy), 1976.

Tragedio dell uomo ridicuolo (also known as *Tragedy of a Ridiculous Man*), Fiction Cinematografica, 1981.

(With Mark Peploe and Enzo Ungari) *The Last Emperor* (adapted from the autobiography *From Emperor to Citizen* by Pu Yi with Li Wenda), Columbia, 1987.

(With Mark Peploe) *The Sheltering Sky* (adapted from the novel by Paul Bowles), Warner Bros., 1990.

(With Mark Peploe and Rudolph Wurlitzer) *Little Buddha,* Miramax, 1994.

(And author of story) Susan Minot, *Stealing Beauty* (Twentieth Century-Fox, 1996), Grove Press (New York, NY), 1996.

(With wife, Clare Peploe) *Besieged* (also known as *The Siege;* adapted from a story by James Lasdun), Fine Line Cinema, 1998.

"Histoire d'eaux," (short; title means "The History of Water"), in *Ten Minutes Older: The Cello,* 2002.

Also writer and director of teleplays *La Via del petrolio* (contains *Le Origini, I Viaggio,* and *Attraverso l'Europe*), for RAI-TV, 1965-66, and documentary *I Poveri muoino prima,* 1971, and *La Salute e malata,* 1972. Coauthor of screen story for *Once upon a Time in the West,* Rafran-San Marco, 1969. Also author of unproduced screenplay *Red Harvest* (adapted from the book by Dashiell Hammett). Contributor of poems to Italian periodicals.

OTHER

In cerca del mistero (poetry; title means "In Search of Mystery"), Longanesi, 1962.

Agonia (based on "Il Fico infruttuoso"), produced by Living Theatre, 1967.

(With Don Ranvaud and Enzo Ungari) *Bertolucci by Bertolucci,* Plexus (London, England), 1987.

Bertolucci's "The Last Emperor": Multiple Takes, edited by Bruce H. Sklarew and others, Wayne State University Press (Detroit, MI), 1998.

Bernardo Bertolucci: Interviews, University Press of Mississippi, 2000.

Contributor of poems to Italian periodicals; contributor of articles on films and filmmaking to periodicals, including *Cahiers du cinema, Film Comment, Film Quarterly,* and *Rolling Stone.*

SIDELIGHTS: As a self-described autobiographical artist, Italian filmmaker Bernardo Bertolucci creates films that are alternately obscure and overt in their expressions of subconscious fears and anxieties. "Movies are made of the same stuff as dreams," he once contended, adding that it is the act of self-expression that makes "the irrational become lucid." The act of filmmaking then becomes a process of self-liberation for Bertolucci, a process that has found expression in such films as *Il Conformista, The Last Emperor* and *The Sheltering Sky.*

Bertolucci also wants his films to be popular, and he unites the violent with the sentimental and the melodramatic with the realistic in an effort to engage audiences. And because he tries to engage audiences with relevant subjects, he considers his films to be political. His ability to sustain an audience's interest has, according to many critics, largely been dependent on his skill at depicting sexuality, particularly in its most controversial forms, such as lesbianism and incest. In *Il Conformista* lesbianism serves as background to a tale of treachery and murder; *Last Tango in Paris* embraces sadomasochistic elements; *1900* similarly delves into such sexual bizarreness as a menage à trois with a convulsing epileptic, and child molestation; and *Luna* melodramatically renders the psychological implications of mother-son incest. *The Sheltering Sky* portrays the sexual misadventures of a married couple traveling in Algeria to allay their romantic malaise, while *Stealing Beauty* revolves around a young American woman's desire to discover her parentage and to loose her virginity. In *Besieged* an Englishman living in Italy becomes obsessed with his African maid, a refugee who awaits the arrival of her husband.

Such pessimistic depictions have inspired wildly conflicting reactions from Bertolucci's critics. In *Life* Pauline Kael hailed the "primitive force, the . . . thrusting jabbing eroticism" of *Last Tango in Paris* as perhaps "the most liberating movie ever made," while other reviewers characterized the numerous acts of male dominance as a celebration of chauvinism. Similarly, the intimations of incest in *Luna* prompted *Roll-*

ing Stone contributor Jonathan Cott to praise the film-maker for "reawakening . . . the possibilities of the cinema." The same film, however, inspired *New Republic*'s Stanley Kauffmann to declare that Bertolucci is "a clever, cheap exploiter of everything that comes to his hand, including the talent he began with."

Bertolucci's art was largely inspired by his father's own poetry and enthusiasm for films. The father encouraged his son's poetic and filmmaking endeavors. At twelve young Bernardo had already published his poems; at fifteen he completed his second sixteen-millimeter film. When he entered the University of Rome in 1960, Bertolucci was already steeped in film lore culled from viewing as many as four motion pictures per day, and his familiarity with English-language literature included the writers of the "Lost Generation" as well as such poets as Emily Dickinson and Dylan Thomas.

During his second year at the university, Bertolucci met Pier Paolo Pasolini, an eminent writer and friend of Bertolucci's father. Pasolini was preparing to direct *Accatone,* his first film, and he engaged Bertolucci as his assistant director. Working with Pasolini thrilled Bertolucci, and when the film—detailing the actions of pimps and prostitutes in Roman slums—was applauded by critics for its grueling and unflinching style, Bertolucci decided to quit school and direct his own films.

In 1962 Bertolucci visited Paris, where he frequented cinemas featuring the work of "New Wave" directors such as François Truffaut and Jean-Luc Godard. Stimulated by Godard's unconventional techniques, especially the jump-cutting and freewheeling camerawork of *Breathless,* Bertolucci returned to Italy and accepted an offer from Pasolini to direct *The Grim Reaper.* The novice filmmaker overcame severe budget restrictions by completely rewriting Pasolini's original script; then he produced a film that is both a thriller and a tale of budding political consciousness. Reviewers cited Bertolucci's affinity with Godard and praised his disdain for sentimentality. "Bertolucci's style establishes itself as a passionate romanticism," declared *Film Quarterly* reviewer Henry Heifetz; "he uses a restless, widely moving camera, with jump-cuts derived from Godard but without Godard's elegance or his watered emotion." While awaiting the premiere of *The Grim Reaper,* Bertolucci was awarded the prestigious Premio Viareggio for a collection of his poetry, *In Search of*

Mystery, most of which recalled his childhood and life in the Italian countryside. Bertolucci had already abandoned verse, however, in favor of filmmaking, calling cinema "the true poetic language."

Most critics considered Bertolucci's next film, *Before the Revolution,* precisely poetic. It concerns a young intellectual's flirtation with Marxism before succumbing to the bourgeois life, and most reviewers were amazed by twenty-four-year-old Bertolucci's skill in fashioning a film that is both political and intimate. "Astonishingly, he has managed to assimilate a high degree of filmic and literary erudition into a distinctively personal visual approach," contended *New Yorker* reviewer Eugene Archer, who called Bertolucci "a new talent of outstanding promise." John Thomas of *Film Quarterly* held a similar view, noting that "Bertolucci tries something new in every scene; like Godard, [he] often fails; like Godard, [he] sometimes succeeds spectacularly."

After the success of *Before the Revolution* Bertolucci turned to several small projects. He directed a series of short films and documentaries for television, then contributed "The Infertile Fig Tree" to the omnibus *Vangelo 70,* a segmented film that also features shorts by Pasolini and Godard. The influence of these two filmmakers is also evident in *Partner,* which in 1968 marked Bertolucci's return to the feature-length format. The film details the schizophrenic nature of a radical professor whose obsession with Antonin Artaud's *Theatre of Cruelty* compels him towards violence—he drowns a girl in a washing machine—which repulses his passive personality. Most critics expressed dissatisfaction with the use of Godardian devices, such as discontinuity and gyroscopic camerawork, that frequently obscure the narrative. In a review for *New Republic,* Stanley Kauffmann called *Partner* "heavily dated" and added, "cinematically it's redolent of high sixties rhetoric and gesture." Bertolucci was also displeased with the work. He deemed it "sadomasochistic" to the audience and himself and later explained, "In the sixties, when I was making a dolly shot, I used to think the audience had to understand that the camera was on wheels—it was like every movie was asking the great question of what cinema is." He also admitted that he "tried to hide the emotions behind any kind of alibi—like existential characters or political statements."

Bertolucci's next film, *The Spider's Strategy,* marks a departure from the pyrotechnics and explicit politics of his previous work. The film is a meticulously crafted account of a young man's efforts to discover the killers of his martyred, war-hero father. After returning to the site of his father's death, the son learns that his father had actually turned against his fellow anti-fascists during World War II and had consented to his own murder as a means of rectifying his betrayal. The subdued quality of *The Spider's Strategy* impressed critics as an improvement over the flashy technique of *Partner.* A reviewer in *New York* deemed the film Bertolucci's "simplest and most glowing work," and in the *New York Times* Vincent Canby called it "a handsome film."

With *Il Conformista—The Conformist* Bertolucci's other work of 1970, he clinched his separation from the excessive experimentation that had marred *Partner.* *The Conformist* does feature Bertolucci's signature floating camerawork, but most of the work subordinates flashy technique to the plot: young Marcello shoots his sexual assailant, matures into an opportunist willing to murder his old professor to please his fellow fascists, and learns that his assailant from childhood survived the shooting. The film ends with Mussolini's fall, after which Marcello exposes the other fascists to curry favor with the new regime.

Most reviewers hailed *The Conformist* as Bertolucci's finest work, and several critics accorded special attention to his recreation and portrayal of decadent fascist society. Canby called the film "a superior chronicle" and cited "scenes of . . . unusual beauty and vitality," such as Marcello's visit to a mental hospital and a portentous tango between the professor's wife and her lesbian lover. In *Film* Ruth Kreitzman wrote: "From start to finish [*The Conformist*] has been immaculately conceived and constructed. Bertolucci's keen eye for architecture here reaches its most perfect synthesis yet, and each shot is constructed as though traced from a drawing-board." And Bill Nichols, writing in *Cineaste,* cited Bertolucci's fusion of sumptuous cinematography and camerawork with such topics as lesbianism and fascism. "Bertolucci avoids the melodramatic pitfalls that claim many socially conscious films," Nichols declared, "crafting a work of considerable polish and remarkable unity." He added that the film's "greatest value is in the beauty of its own, unique appearance." *The Conformist* was re-released in 1994 with added footage.

The popularity of *The Conformist* at film festivals in Cannes and New York City led Bertolucci to an in-

creased awareness of his purpose as an artist: to be both an experimenter and an entertainer. He intended to fuse both aspects in his next work by exploring the present nature of sexuality. When *Last Tango in Paris* premiered at the New York Film Festival in 1972, audiences were shocked by the fairly explicit sexuality in Bertolucci's tale of two people meeting for brutally sexual purposes. It was Brando's character, Paul, that some observers found particularly outrageous. As a profane American widower whose sole diversion from despair is his position as caretaker of a flophouse, Paul indulges in several monologues on humiliation and cruelty. In many of their encounters, he forces Jeanne, his nubile partner, into unwilling sodomy and other, more psychically jarring, acts. "The excitement of Brando's performance here is in the revelation of how creative screen acting can be," wrote Kael. She attributed much of the film's success to Brando's performance and claimed that both Brando and Bertolucci "have altered the face of an art form."

Despite critical appraisal to the contrary, Bertolucci insisted that *Last Tango in Paris* is not an erotic film, "only a film *about* eroticism," and attributed the film's erotic aspects to the initial sexual nature of the relationship between Paul and Jeanne. In an interview in *Film Quarterly,* he also maintained that *Last Tango in Paris* recalls *Partner* in its intensely cinematic nature. "I find *Tango* very close to *Partner*," he revealed, "because in *Tango* there is a continual enquiry in filmic terms, a research on the use of the camera, an attempt to question the structures of cinema." Kael offered the same view, according particular attention to the cinematography. "The colors in this movie are late-afternoon orange-beige-browns and pink—the pink of flesh drained of blood, corpse blood," she asserted. "They are so delicately modulated . . . that romance and rot are one." She added: "The film is utterly beautiful to look at. The virtuosity of Bertolucci's gliding camera style is such that he can show you the hype of the tango-contest scene . . . by stylizing it . . . and still make it work."

Buoyed by the overwhelming critical and popular success of *Last Tango in Paris,* Bertolucci undertook his then most ambitious project, *1900,* a film intended to portray peasant culture, living from the land. To fashion this epic he procured $5 million from producer Alberto Grimaldi, thus making *1900* one of Italy's most expensive productions.

Once filming began, Bertolucci's original conception of *1900* was replaced by a recounting of events culminating in the rise of communism in Italy in 1945. He persevered with *1900* for more than three years before filming was completed in 1976 and released in a version that cut ninety minutes off the original running time of over five hours. As a tale of two men— landowner Alfredo and one of his peasant workers, Olmo—spanning the first half of the twentieth century, *1900,* according to most viewers, exhausted its appeal in the first two hours. The film begins with Alfredo's birth in 1900, continues with the death of the two men's grandparents, details the conflicts between the peasants and the landowners, completely omits World War I, and concludes its first half with premonitions of fascism. "By the end of 'Act One,'" wrote Jack Kroll in *Newsweek,* "most viewers will be dazzled and excited by two hours of almost relentless beauty and power."

The film's second half, however, was faulted by *Time*'s Frank Rich as a "good-guys v. bad-guys melodrama." The rise of Fascist leader Attila, an employee of Alfredo's family, precipitates several ghoulish murders, including the impaling of a woman on a spiked fence. After Alfredo slaughters several peasants in retaliation for his own public humiliation—they bombarded him with horse manure—Olmo leads a revolt against the Fascists and the wealthy landowners. The action culminates in Alfredo's death and a renunciation of Italy's class society. "The *padrone* is dead," the peasants announce during an elaborate celebration of communism. Rich called the finale a "propagandistic pageant" and asserted, "By the time *1900* reaches its flag-waving Liberation Day climax, the sloganeering and confusion are almost unbearable."

Despite reservations regarding the film's political slant, many reviewers still found much to praise in *1900.* Rich hailed its "voluptuous emotional texture" and conceded, "If Bertolucci irritates as much as he dazzles, he never bores: his extravagant failure has greater staying power than most other directors' triumphs." Kroll acknowledged the acting and cinematography as "marvelous" and contended, "It's a huge work and its faults are the excesses of a huge talent." Perhaps the film's most exuberant acclaim came from Kael. She recognized flaws in some of the characterizations, but charged that "it's like a course to be enrolled in." "The film is appalling," she added, "yet it has the grandeur of a classic visionary folly. Next to it, all other new movies are like something you hold up at the end of a toothpick."

In *Luna,* Bertolucci returned to the sexual sensationalism of *Last Tango in Paris. Luna* follows a potentially incestuous relationship between an opera diva, Caterina, and her son, Joe. Following the death of her second husband, Caterina returns to Italy with Joe, there to resume her musical career. What follows is a harrowing tale of drug addiction and perversity, as Caterina tries to cope with Joe's heroin use. Their relationship culminates in a series of violent encounters: after witnessing Joe's initial withdrawal symptoms, Caterina gives him the necessary heroin but reveals that she has disposed of his syringe. Enraged, Joe tries to pierce his vein with a fork, then collapses against Caterina, who proceeds to suckle and masturbate him. Later, Joe abandons his mother after she has changed a flat tire on their car. They rendezvous at an inn, whereupon Caterina tries to seduce Joe. He resists, however, and begins searching for his father. The quest ends with Joe and his father reunited as they watch Caterina rehearse. Moments before, she had reached an oblique understanding, if not reconciliation, with Joe.

The critical reception for *Luna* was mixed. Rich called it "perfect," and Cott noted its "intensity and cinematic brilliance." But other viewers were appalled by Bertolucci's unabashed exploitation of incest. John Simon deemed it "a dreadfully poseurish film," and Kauffmann called it "ludicrously bad." He added, "When the film isn't being portentously symbolic, it's being empty—one or the other." Kauffmann dubbed Bertolucci "a monstrous and disgusting artist, not a failed authentic one."

In response to the negative reviews, Bertolucci charged critics with "irresponsibility." "I've been through very hard times with critics on *Luna,*" he told an *American Film* writer. "I've read things almost personally offensive, like 'There is not a second in this movie that is acceptable.' It's a very experimental movie." In an interview with Cott, Bertolucci also explained that *Luna* is actually "autobiographical" and that he may have been using the film to psychoanalyze himself. He also conceded that "the movie gravitates between melodrama and psychoanalysis," but both elements are necessary because "the characters are either epical-lyrical or determined by their own subconsciouses."

Bertolucci's style was more subdued in his following film, *The Tragedy of a Ridiculous Man.* Departing from the sensationalized sex and violence that marked *Last Tango in Paris, 1900,* and *Luna,* he fashioned, according to Canby, "a distant meditation on Italian politics" in the manner of *The Spider's Strategy.* The "ridiculous man" of the film's title is Primo, a factory owner faced with ransom demands from his son's kidnappers. After learning of his son's possible murder, Primo nonetheless continues compiling the ransom for business purposes. Canby was especially impressed with Bertolucci's attention to characterization in the film; *The Tragedy of a Ridiculous Man* "is sometimes poetic and warm-hearted, then cooly satiric and finally surreal," Canby observed. "The reality of the characters, however, is never in doubt."

Bertolucci continued to make films of epic grandeur, including the 1987 production *The Last Emperor,* which tells the story of Pu Yi, the final emperor of China before the communist revolution felled the monarchy. The film chronicles Pu Yi's life, from his childhood in the Forbidden City to his old age as an "ordinary man." With permission of the Chinese government, Bertolucci filmed most of the motion picture, based on Pu Yi's autobiography, in the Forbidden City, which had not been seen by outsiders in person or on film in decades. *The Last Emperor* won nine Academy awards, including best picture and best director, giving Bertolucci's lagging directing career new life. In 1998 *The Last Emperor* was re-released with new footage. About the 1998 release, *Variety*'s Godfrey Cheshire commented: "Easily one of the most intelligent and genuinely artistic historical epics in cinema history, . . . [the film] remains extremely impressive on every technical level." Yet John Simon in the *National Review* begged to differ. He likened *The Last Emperor* to "a set of splendid picture postcards whose text side can be ignored" because the screenplay does not "get into the protagonist's inner life, let alone that of any other character."

Upon Bertolucci's request, screenwriter Mark Peploe wrote the script for the 1990 film *The Sheltering Sky,* based on the 1949 book of the same name by Paul Bowles. In this work, which *Time*'s Richard Corliss dubbed "swank, sexy, bleak and very beautiful," viewers follow the Moresby couple's desire for adventure in the hope that it will relieve their ennui, and as Bertolucci explained it to Corliss, "the impossibility of love. It is about the impossibility of being happy within love." Reviews of the film varied dramatically: Stanley Kauffmann, in the *New Republic,* described both the book and film as "vapid and pretentious," while Corliss asserted that the film's "beauty . . . is that it ultimately locates a married couple's humanity."

Returning to the Far East for inspiration, Bertolucci collaborated with Peploe and Rudolph Wurlitzer on the screenplay for *Little Buddha.* Although it is another historical piece, this film is dually plotted in the past—telling the story of Indian prince Siddhartha's rejection of his royal status and transformation into the first Buddha—and the present—telling of Buddhist monks who try to determine which of three children might be the true reincarnation of a Tibetan lama. Several reviewers wrote in lukewarm fashion about *Little Buddha. Entertainment Weekly*'s Owen Gleiberman, for example, complained that Buddhism "gets short shrift" and that "the movie flops egregiously . . . in its parallel contemporary story." Kauffmann found the *Little Buddha* screenplay "flaccid" and suggested that Bertolucci intended that the pictorial exoticism carry the film.

In a departure from his far-reaching historical dramas, Bertolucci's next film, *Stealing Beauty,* is a nostalgic comment on "life lived before the upheavals of sex and loss, before the corruption of innocence," to quote Peter Rainer in *Los Angeles* magazine. With the story focusing on Lucy, a nineteen-year-old American who is summering in Italy with friends of her deceased mother, Bertolucci and American novelist Susan Minot "joined the sensibility of romance schlock fiction with a lament for blasted bourgeois lives. It's Harlequin Chekhov," quipped Rainer. Both Ty Burr in *Entertainment Weekly* and Rainer likened *Stealing Beauty* to soft-core pornography, and Kauffmann went so far as to assert that the middle-aged Bertolucci is simply "infatuated" with star Liv Tyler, who, as Lucy, wants to solve the mystery of her parentage and lose her virginity. "Trying to capture her awakening soul, Bertolucci remains a tourist, his film an album of beautiful snapshots," concluded *Newsweek*'s David Ansen.

Clare Peploe and Bertolucci teamed up to write the screenplay for *Besieged,* based on a short story by James Ladsun, which Peploe had long liked. This tale revolves around the reclusive Kinsky, an Englishman living in an Italian villa, who falls obsessively in love with his maid, Shandurai, an African woman who has fled the chaos of her homeland. When Kinsky professes his love for Shandurai, she retorts that if he really love her, he would help free her husband, who is a political prisoner in Africa. As in the past, some critics were at odds over what to make of the film. Kauffmann found it lacking in "character conviction" and criticized it as poorly constructed and skimpily filmed, while Schickel complained that the many silent moments create a "distancing and annoying" foreboding. The film's ironic ending also elicited comment, with Schickel suggesting that even O. Henry, master of the surprise ending, would have pause about this denouement. In contrast, *Entertainment*'s Lisa Schwarzbaum, who dubbed the work a "deeply felt love story," predicted that O. Henry would have appreciated the "extraordinarily elegant plot spiral" that concludes *Besieged.*

Bertolucci's next film, *The Dreamers,* follows a screenplay by novelist Gilbert Adair, based on Adair's novel *The Holy Innocents. The Dreamers* tells the story of an American college student, Matthew, who becomes involved, both intellectually and romantically, with a fraternal set of French twins, Theo and Isabelle. While the student riots of 1968 take place outside the twins' family's apartment, the students play psychosexual games, their motivation described by *Variety*'s David Rooney as "inaccessible to many audiences." In *Interview* Erika Abeel saw similarities between *The Dreamers* and *Last Tango in Paris,* likening the former to an à trois version of Bertolucci's controversial 1973 motion picture. Rooney noted, "The eroticism and nudity [of *The Dreamers*] are even more explicit here [than in *Last Tango in Paris*], yet somehow oddly repressed for a film set during the sexual revolution. And the issues being addressed seem diluted. In fact, the whole spirit of rebellion, passion and protest that should be a driving force for the characters play more like a cultivated affectation." While Rooney expressed confusion over Bertolucci's intentions with the film, he was certain of its workmanship, calling it "meticulously crafted on all technical levels." After its fall, 2003, premiere in Venice, Italy, *The Dreamers* underwent editing to eliminate much of its frontal nudity in order to make it acceptable to the American movie raters. It was slated to open in North America in March of 2004.

BIOGRAPHICAL AND CRITICAL SOURCES:

BOOKS

Bertolucci, Bernardo, *Bernardo Bertolucci: Interviews,* edited by Fabien S. Gerard, T. Jefferson Kline, and Bruce Sklarew, University Press of Mississippi (Jackson, MS), 2000.

Burgoyne, Robert, *Bertolucci's "1900": A Narrative and Historical Analysis,* Wayne State University Press (Detroit, MI), 1991.

Contemporary Literary Criticism, Volume 16, Gale (Detroit, MI), 1981.

Gelmis, Joseph, *The Film Director As Superstar,* Doubleday (Garden City, NY), 1970.

International Dictionary of Films and Filmmakers, Volume 2: *Directors,* St. James Press (Detroit, MI), 1996.

Kline, T. Jefferson, *Bertolucci's Dream Loom: A Psychoanalytical Study of the Cinema,* University of Massachusetts Press (Amherst, MA), 1987.

Kolker, Robert Philip, *Bernardo Bertolucci,* Oxford University Press (New York, NY), 1985.

Loshitzky, Yosefa, *The Radical Faces of Godard and Bertolucci,* Wayne State University Press (Detroit, MI), 1995.

Mellen, Joan, *Women and Sexuality in the New Film,* New Horizon Press (New York, NY), 1973.

Negri, Livio, and Fabien S. Gerard, editors, *The Sheltering Sky: A Film by Bernardo Bertolucci Based on the Novel by Paul Bowles,* [London, England], 1990.

Sklarew, Bruce H., and others, editors, *Bertolucci's "The Last Emperor": Multiple Takes,* Wayne State University Press (Detroit, MI), 1998.

Tonetti, Claretta, *Bernardo Bertolucci: The Cinema of Ambiguity,* Twayne Publishers (New York, NY), 1995.

Ungari, Enzo, *Bertolucci by Bertolucci,* translated by Donald Ranvaud, Plexus (London, England), 1987.

PERIODICALS

American Film, October, 1986, Don Ranvaud, "After the Revolution," pp. 19-21; November, 1987, John Powers, "Last Tango in Beijing," pp. 34-40; December, 1990, Harlan Kennedy, "Radical Sheik," pp. 30-35, 56.

Boston, July, 1996, Jeffrey Hogrefe, review of *Stealing Beauty,* pp. 96-98.

Chatelaine, February, 1991, Gina Mallet, review of *The Sheltering Sky,* p. 12.

Christian Herald, February, 1988, Harry Cheney, review of *The Last Emperor,* p. 56.

Christianity Today, April 8, 1988, Stefan Ulstein, "Last Emperor, Lost Emperor," pp. 57-58.

Christian Science Monitor, May 21, 1998, Gloria Goodale, review of *Besieged,* p. 18.

Cineaste, spring, 1971; fall, 1999, Bruce Sklarew, "Returning to My Low-Budget Roots" (interview), p. 16.

Cinema Journal, Volume 28, number 3, 1989, Robert Burgoyne, "Temporality As Historical Argument in Bertolucci's *1900.*"

Commonweal, December 23, 1977; December 18, 1987, Tom O'Brien, review of *The Last Emperor,* pp. 747-748.

Detroit Free Press, October 26, 1979; October 30, 1979.

East-West Film Journal, Volume 7, number 2, 1993, Yosefa Loshitzy, "The Tourist/Traveler Gaze: Bertolucci and Bowles' *The Sheltering Sky.*"

Entertainment Weekly, January 28, 1994, p. 76; June 17, 1994, Owen Gleiberman, review of *Little Buddha,* pp. 32-34; November 11, 1994, Kathleen Cromwell, review of *Little Buddha,* p. 89; November 25, 1994, Kenneth M. Chanko, review of *Little Buddha,* p. 101; June 14, 1996, Ken Tucker, review of *Stealing Beauty,* p. 43; August 22, 1997, Ty Burr, review of *Stealing Beauty,* pp. 136-137; May 21, 1999, Lisa Schwarzbaum, review of *Besieged,* p. 52.

Film, spring, 1971, R. Kreitzman, "Bernardo Bertolucci, an Italian Young Master."

Film and History, February, 1980, A. Horton, "History As Myth and Myth As History in Bertolucci's *1900.*"

Film Comment, May-June, 1974; November-December, 1979, P. Schwartzman, "Embarrass Me More!"; November-December, 1987, Tony Rayns, "Model Citizen: Bernardo Bertolucci on Location in China," pp. 31-36; July-August, 1989; May-June, 1991, David Thomson, review of *The Sheltering Sky,* pp. 18-23; July-August, 1994, Robert Horton, "Nonconformist: Bernardo Bertolucci's *Little Buddha,*" pp. 26-28; March, 1999, Dave Kehr, review of *Besieged,* p. 6.

Film Heritage, summer, 1976, D. Lopez, "The Father Figure in *The Conformist* and in *Last Tango in Paris.*"

Film Quarterly, fall, 1966; winter, 1966-67; summer, 1972; spring, 1973; fall, 1975; fall, 1986, Robert Burgoyne, "The Somatization of History in Bertolucci's *1900*"; fall, 1988, review of *Bertolucci on Bertolucci;* winter, 1988, Fatimah Tobing Rony, review of *The Last Emperor,* pp. 47-52.

Films in Review, September-October, 1996, Andy Pawelczak, review of *Stealing Beauty,* pp. 66-67.

Glamour, January, 1988, Joy Gould Boyum, review of *The Last Emperor,* p. 108; July, 1996, Juliann Garvey, review of *Stealing Beauty,* p. 58.

Guardian (London, England), March 14, 1973.

Harper's Bazaar, July, 1994, Polly Frost, review of *Little Buddha,* p. 39.

History and Memory, Volume 3, number 2, 1991, Yosefa Loshitzky, "'Memory of My Own Memory': Processes of Private and Collective Remembering in Bertolucci's *The Spider's Stratagem* and *The Conformist.*"

Hollywood Reporter, 1988, pp. 22, 70.

International Film Guide, 1972.

Interview, May, 1988, pp. 74-78; October, 2003, Erika Abeel, *Eva Green,* p. 66.

Journal of Film and Video, spring, 1998, Vincent Hausmann, reviews of *La Luna* and *The Sheltering Sky,* pp. 20-41.

Jump Cut, November, 1977, W. Aiken, "Bertolucci's Gay Images."

Life, August 13, 1965, Pauline Kael, "Starburst by a Gifted Twenty-Two-Year-Old."

Literature-Film Quarterly, July, 1998, Allan James Thomas, "*The Sheltering Sky* and the Sorrow of Memory," pp. 196-203.

Los Angeles, July, 1996, Peter Rainer, review of *Stealing Beauty,* pp. 114-115; Merrill Shindler, review of *The Sheltering Sky,* p. 121.

Los Angeles Times, July 31, 1991, Kevin Brass, "Bertolucci Film Festival Honors His Early Works," p. F1; June 27, 1994, Karl Springer, review of *Little Buddha,* p. F3; June 21, 1996, Jack Matthews, "Bertolucci's *Beauty* Searches for Identity, '60s Idealism," p. 6; October 18, 1996, Kevin Thomas, "The Filmmaker Looks Back at His Work While Exploring New Realms" (interview), p. 6; May 16, 1999, David Gritten, "Bertolucci's Next: The Opposite of X" (interview), p. 17; May 21, 1999, Kevin Thomas, "Bertolucci Captures the Seductive in *Besieged,*" p. 6.

Maclean's, July 8, 1996, Brian D. Johnson, review of *Stealing Beauty,* p. 49; November, 5, 2001, "The Sheltering Cinema: Bernardo Bertolucci Tries to Bridge Cultural Divides," p. 61.

Massachusetts Review, autumn, 1975.

Millimeter, December, 1981, R. Gentry, "Bertolucci Directs *Tragedy of a Ridiculous Man.*"

Nation, June 24, 1996, Stuart Klawans, review of *Stealing Beauty,* pp. 34-36.

National Review, December 21, 1979; December 18, 1987, John Simon, review of *The Last Emperor,* pp. 54-58; July 15, 1996, John Simon, review of *Stealing Beauty,* pp. 52-53.

New Republic, March 3, 1973; February 9, 1974; October 20, 1979; December 14, 1987, Stanley Kauffmann, review of *The Last Emperor,* pp. 22-23; January 7, 1991, Stanley Kauffmann, review of *The Sheltering Sky,* p. 33; June 13, 1994, Stanley Kauffmann, review of *Little Buddha,* p. 32; June 24, 1996, Stanley Kauffmann, review of *Stealing Beauty,* p. 32; June 21, 1999, Stanley Kauffmann, review of *Besieged,* p. 30.

New Statesman, March, 1988, Georgina Born, review of *The Last Emperor,* pp. 30-31; February 4, 1994, Jonathan Romney, review of *The Conformist,* pp. 41-42; April 29, 1994, Boyd Tonkin, review of *Little Buddha,* pp. 57-58.

Newsweek, November 18, 1974; September 27, 1976; October 17, 1977; October 28, 1979; June 24, 1996, David Ansen, review of *Stealing Beauty,* p. 83; May 24, 1999, review of *Besieged,* p. 74.

New Times, November 11, 1977.

New York, November 30, 1987, David Denby, review of *The Last Emperor,* pp. 76-78; June 6, 1994, David Denby, review of *Little Buddha,* p. 53.

New Yorker, October 28, 1972; October 31, 1972; November 20, 1987, Pauline Kael, review of *The Last Emperor,* pp. 98-104; December 17, 1990, Pauline Kael, review of *The Sheltering Sky,* pp. 118-121; May 30, 1994, Anthony Lane, review of *Little Buddha,* pp. 97-99; June 10, 1996, Anthony Lane, review of *Stealing Beauty,* pp. 90-92.

New York Post, February 3, 1973.

New York Review of Books, May 17, 1973; February 18, 1988, John K. Fairbank, review of *The Last Emperor,* pp. 14-16.

New York Times, September 25, 1964; September 18, 1970; September 19, 1970; October 16, 1972; February 2, 1973; February 11, 1973.

Observer (London, England), January 6, 1980.

People, May 9, 1988, p. 63; June 24, 1996, Leah Rozen, review of *Stealing Beauty,* p. 20.

Premiere, October, 1990, Rob Medich and Sally Weltman, review of *The Sheltering Sky,* p. 78; December, 1990, Kitty Bowe Hearty, review of *The Sheltering Sky,* p. 22; July, 1996, Todd McCarthy, review of *Stealing Beauty,* pp. 35-36.

Rolling Stone, November 15, 1979; January 14, 1988, Lynn Hirschberg, "Romancing the East," p. 33; January 7, 1991, Stuart Klawans, review of *The Sheltering Sky,* p. 22; June 24, 1999, Peter Travers, review of *Besieged,* p. 75.

Sight and Sound, spring, 1971, Richard Roud, "Fathers and Sons"; spring, 1973; fall, 1973, Marsha Kinder and Beverle Houston, "Bertolucci and the Dance of Danger"; spring, 1978; May, 1999, Sally Chatsworth, review of *Besieged,* p. 40.

South Atlantic Quarterly, Volume 91, number 2, 1992, Jody McAuliff, "The Church of the Desert: Reflections on *The Sheltering Sky.*"

Spectator (London, England), April 30, 1988, review of *Bertolucci by Bertolucci,* p. 36.

Time, January 22, 1973; May 24, 1976; October 17, 1977; October 8, 1979; December 3, 1990, Richard Corliss, review of *The Sheltering Sky,* p. 95; May 31, 1999, Richard Schickel, review of *Besieged,* p. 99.

Times Literary Supplement, February 26, 1998, Richard Harris, review of *The Last Emperor,* p. 220.

Variety, November 23, 1998, Godfrey Cheshire, review of *The Last Emperor,* p. 48; May 22, 2000, p. 74; September 8, 2003, David Rooney, review of *The Dreamers,* pp. 31-32.

Video Review, April, 1991, Glenn Kenny, review of *Last Tango in Paris,* pp. 91-92.

Village Voice, October 8, 1979.

Vogue, March, 1994, Joan Juliet Buck, "The Last Romantic."

Washington Post, December 18, 1987, Rita Kempley, "*The Last Emperor*: China Dull," p. G7; January 11, 1991, Hal Hinson, "Bertolucci's Clouded *Sky,*" p. D6; May 25, 1994, Desson Howe, "*Little Buddha*: Bertolucci's Spiritual Glow," p. C1; November 25, 1994, Hal Hinson, "*The Conformist*: Bertolucci at His Best," p. B7; June 11, 1999, Stephen Hunter, review of *Besieged,* p. C5.

Western Humanities Review, Volume 44, number 2, 1990, L. K. Bundtzen, "Bertolucci's Erotic Politics and the Auteur Theory: From *Last Tango in Paris* to *The Last Emperor.*"*

*   *   *

BLOUNT, Roy (Alton), Jr. 1941-
(Noah Sanders, C. R. Ways)

PERSONAL: Surname rhymes with "punt"; born October 4, 1941, in Indianapolis, IN; son of Roy Alton (a savings and loan executive) and Louise (Floyd) Blount; married Ellen Pearson, September 6, 1964 (divorced, March, 1973); married Joan Ackerman, 1976 (separated); children: (first marriage) Ennis Cald-

Roy Blount, Jr.

well, John Kirven. *Education:* Vanderbilt University, B.A. (magna cum laude), 1963; Harvard University, M.A., 1964. *Politics:* "Dated white Southern liberalism, with healthy undertones of redneckery and anarchism; nostalgia for Earl Long." *Religion:* "Lapsed Methodist."

ADDRESSES: Home—Mill River, MA; and New York, NY. *Agent*—c/o Author Mail, Viking, 375 Hudson St., New York, NY 10014.

CAREER: Journalist, author, and broadcaster. *Decatur-DeKalb News,* Decatur, GA, reporter and sports columnist, 1958-59; *Morning Telegraph,* New York, NY, reporter, summer, 1961; *New Orleans Times-Picayune,* New Orleans, LA, reporter, summer, 1963; *Atlanta Journal,* Atlanta, GA, reporter, editorial writer, and columnist, 1966-68; *Sports Illustrated,* New York, NY,

staff writer, 1968-74, associate editor, 1974-75; freelance writer, 1975—. Occasional performer for American Humorists' Series, American Place Theatre, 1986 and 1988, and has appeared on *A Prairie Home Companion, The CBS Morning Show, The Tonight Show, The David Letterman Show, Austin City Limits, All Things Considered, Mark Twain, The Main Stream, Wait Wait Don't Tell Me,* and many other radio and television programs. Instructor at Georgia State College, 1967-68. Member of usage panel, *American Heritage Dictionary.* Has lectured at Manhattan Theatre Club, San Diego Forum, Washington State University, Wyoming Bar Association, and others. *Military service:* U.S. Army, 1964-66; became first lieutenant.

MEMBER: Phi Beta Kappa.

WRITINGS:

About Three Bricks Shy of a Load, Little, Brown (Boston, MA), 1974, revised edition published as *About Three Bricks Shy—and the Load Filled Up: The Story of the Greatest Football Team Ever,* Ballantine (New York, NY), 1989.

Crackers: This Whole Many-Sided Thing of Jimmy, More Carters, Ominous Little Animals, Sad-Singing Women, My Daddy and Me, Knopf (New York, NY), 1980.

One Fell Soup; or, I'm Just a Bug on the Windshield of Life, Little, Brown (Boston, MA), 1982.

What Men Don't Tell Women, Atlantic-Little, Brown (New York, NY), 1984.

Not Exactly What I Had in Mind, Atlantic Monthly Press (New York, NY), 1985.

It Grows on You: A Hair-Raising Survey of Human Plumage, Doubleday (New York, NY), 1986.

Roy Blount's Happy Hour and a Half (one-man show), produced Off-Broadway at American Place Theatre, January 22-February 7, 1986.

Soupsongs/Webster's Ark (double book of verse), Houghton Mifflin (Boston, MA), 1987.

(Contributor) *The Baseball Hall of Fame 50th Anniversary Book,* Prentice Hall Press (Englewood Cliffs, NJ), 1988.

Now, Where Were We?, Villard (New York, NY), 1989.

First Hubby, Villard (New York, NY), 1990.

Camels Are Easy, Comedy's Hard, Villard (New York, NY), 1991.

Roy Blount's Book of Southern Humor, Norton (New York, NY), 1994.

(With Dave Marsh, Kathi Kamen Glodmark, and G. Shields) *The Great Rock 'n' Roll Joke Book,* St. Martin's Press (New York, NY), 1997.

If Only You Knew How Much I Smell You: True Portraits of Dogs, photographed by Valerie Shaff, Bulfinch Press (New York, NY), 1998.

The Wit & Wisdom of the Founding Fathers: Benjamin Franklin, George Washington, John Adams, Thomas Jefferson, edited by Paul M. Zall, Ecco Press (New York, NY), 1998.

Be Sweet: A Conditional Love Story, Knopf (New York, NY), 1998.

(Author of introduction) E.W. Kemble, *Mark Twain's Library of Humor,* Modern Library (New York, NY), 2000.

I Am Puppy, Hear Me Yap: Ages of a Dog, photographs by Valerie Shaff, HarperCollins (New York, NY), 2000.

Am I Pig Enough for You Yet? Voices of the Barnyard, photographs by Valerie Shaff, HarperCollins (New York, NY), 2001.

Robert E. Lee: A Penguin Life, Lipper/Viking (New York, NY), 2003.

Also author of two one-act plays produced at Actors Theater of Louisville, KY, November, 1983, and fall, 1984. Contributor to numerous anthologies, including *The Best of Modern Humor,* 1983, *Laughing Matters,* 1987, *The Norton Book of Light Verse,* 1987, *The Oxford Book of American Light Verse, The Ultimate Baseball Book, Classic Southern Humor,* and *Sudden Fiction.* Author of preface for *New Stories from the South: The Year's Best, 2003.* Columnist, *Atlanta Journal,* 1967-70; for the *Oxford American.* Contributor of articles, short stories, poems, crossword puzzles, and drawings, sometimes under pseudonyms Noah Sanders and C. R. Ways, to numerous periodicals, including *Sports Illustrated, New Yorker, Atlantic, New York Times, Magazine, Esquire, Playboy, Rolling Stone, GQ, Conde Nast Traveler, Spy,* and *Antaeus.* Contributing editor, *Atlantic,* 1983—.

ADAPTATIONS: Now, Where Were We? was adapted for audiocassette by sound Editions (Holmes, PA), 1989.

SIDELIGHTS: Roy Blount, Jr. is an author, humorist, sportswriter, performer, lecturer, dramatist, lyricist, television talking head, film actor, radio panelist, and usage consultant to the *American Heritage Dictionary.* He has entertained the American public not only through his multitudinous magazine publications and his books, but also through other media—he has performed on radio and television shows ranging from Minnesota Public Radio's *A Prairie Home Companion* to TV's *David Letterman Show.* "The unceasing drip-drip-drip of bizarre images, intricate wordplay, droll asides and crazy ideas disorients the reader," stated Patrick F. McManus in the *New York Times Book Review,* "until Mr. Blount finally has him at his mercy."

Blount's books, said Leslie Bennetts in the *New York Times,* "attest to the breadth of his interests, from *One Fell Soup, or I'm Just a Bug on the Windshield of Life* (which is also the name of one of the original songs Mr. Blount sings 'unless I'm forcibly deterred') to *What Men Don't Tell Women* to *It Grows on You,* a volume about hair." His first book, *About Three Bricks Shy of a Load,* "did for the Pittsburgh Steelers roughly what Sherman did for the South," stated Donald Morrison in *Time. New York Times Book Review* contributor Robert W. Creamer called *About Three Bricks Shy of a Load* "a terrific book," and he concluded, "I have never read anything else on pro football, fiction or nonfiction, as good as this."

With his second book, *Crackers: This Whole Many-Sided Thing of Jimmy, More Carters, Ominous Little Animals, Sad-Singing Women, My Daddy and Me,* Blount established his reputation as a humorist. *Crackers* examines the presidency of Jimmy Carter, a Georgian like Blount, and concludes that what the Carter administration needed was a more down-to-earth, redneck approach to the business of governing the country. "If *Crackers* reveals an overarching thesis, it is that contemporary America, like its president, is too emotionally constrained, too given to artifice, too Northern," explained Morrison. The book was a critical success. Blount has also achieved success in collections of his magazine articles, including *One Fell Soup; or, I'm Just a Bug on the Windshield of Life, What Men Don't Tell Women, Not Exactly What I Had in Mind, It Grows on You: A Hair-Raising Survey of Human Plumage,* and *Now, Where Were We?* Gathered from sources as diverse as *Esquire,* the *New Yorker,* and *Eastern Airlines Pastimes,* the collections prove Blount's "ability to be amusing on a diversity of topics," according to Beaufort Cranford of the *Detroit*

News. After all, he asked, "what other source can prove the existence of God by considering the testicle?"

Although some critics—like *Los Angeles Times* contributor Taffy Cannon, who called Blount's stories "considerably funnier in a bar at midnight than spread at meandering and pointless length across the printed page"—found that Blount's later works aren't as successful as his earlier ones, many others celebrated his collections. Ron Givens, writing in *Newsweek,* declared, "It's downright refreshing, then, to read somebody who has taste, intelligence, style and, oh, bless you, wit—qualities that Roy Blount, Jr. . . . [has] in abundance."

Blount has also attracted attention as a versifier and songwriter. Despite his claims to be "singing impaired," Blount has performed both his stories and his verses in his one-man show, *Roy Blount's Happy Hour and a Half,* and on radio programs such as *A Prairie Home Companion.* A collection of the comic's verse, *Soupsongs/Webster's Ark,* "contains odes to beets, chitlins, barbeque sauce, catfish and grease ('I think that I will never cease / To hold in admiration grease')," explained Bennetts, "along with a 'Song against Broccoli' that reads in its entirety: 'The neighborhood stores are all out of broccoli, / Loccoli.'" "Blount's verses may resemble Burma Shave's more than Byron's," declared the *Chicago Tribune*'s Jim Spencer, "but they are bodaciously funny."

Blount continued to strike literary gold with a string of well-reviewed books published in 1989, 1990, and 1991—*Now, Where Were We?, First Hubby,* and *Camels Are Easy, Comedy's Hard,* respectively. The first and most lauded of these, *Now, Where Were We?,* is a collection of the author's previously published essays. "The genre of earnest, plain-spoken bumpkinhood," wrote Deborah Mason in the *New York Times Book Review,* "forms one of the primal pools of American humor. . . . These pieces are brilliantly loopy, reassuringly subversive, and they put Mr. Blount in serious contention for the title of America's most cherished humorist." Indeed, *Washington Post Book World* contributor Jonathan Yardley went so far as to say that "a half dozen [of the essays] are likely to cause guttural eruptions, five are moderately dangerous to one's health—and one may be, for those with weak constitutions, terminally fatal."

Blount's debut novel, *First Hubby,* was generally considered a credible first effort in the longer genre. The story hinges on a major political event: the first female vice-president of the United States becomes president after the elected chief executive is killed by a huge falling fish. The narrator of *First Hubby* is none other than the frustrated writer-husband of the nation's new president, and he expounds upon his life and times with familiar Blountian humor. "Dialogue, internal and external, is Blount's forte," stated Christopher Hitchens in the *Washington Post Book World.*

Blount delights in confounding expectations in his book production as much as he does in magazine markets. He served as an anthologizer and contributor for *Roy Blount's Book of Southern Humor.* Blount chose short southern writings from over one hundred artists—Flannery O'Connor, Edgar Allan Poe, Alice Walker, Lyle Lovett, Davy Crocket, and Louis Armstrong among them—and the resulting volume received warm praise from critics. According to Mark Bautz in *People,* "Some of the best selections are from people you wouldn't expect to find in such a tome." A critic for *Publishers Weekly* thought that this "generous volume" would be a good gift for the "eclectic—or Dixie-minded— reader."

Critics have tried to define with varying success the sources of Blount's sense of humor. One contributing factor, suggested Givens, "derives from his off-center perceptions." Kenneth Turan of *Time* called Blount's work "in the tradition of the great curmudgeons like H. L. Mencken and W. C. Fields." And the comic "is not of the punch-line school of humor writing," declared McManus. "His humor is cumulative in effect, like Chinese water torture. When you can bear it no longer, you collapse into a spasm of mirth, often at a line that taken by itself would provoke no more than a smile."

Reaching his mid-fifties made Blount introspective; in his 1998 memoir *Be Sweet: A Conditional Love Story,* he "plumbs the depths" of his youth in Georgia, according to *People*'s Thomas Fields-Meyer. Such a childhood was greatly informed by his domineering mother, whose continual admonition of "Be sweet" is used as the title of the book. A reviewer for *Publishers Weekly* observed that Blount "lays bare a Mother-complex that seems obsessive." Still, even with such potentially dark material, Blount provides an "achingly funny anecdote" on almost every page, according to Fields-Meyer.

Blount supplied a learned introduction to the year 2000 Modern Library *Mark Twain's Library of Humor,* and then made another change of direction for his 2003 biography, *Robert E. Lee.* Written for the Penguin Life series of concise biographies, the latter book is much like that of the life of Lee himself, noted a contributor for *Publishers Weekly:* "valiant, honorable and surprisingly successful with limited resources." Blount uses the perspective of his own southern heritage to detail the life of the Confederate general from his lonely childhood (abandoned by his once heroic but alcoholic father) to his appointment to West Point, his career under General Winfield Scott in the Mexican War, his Civil War career leading the Confederacy, and the postwar years when Lee, in failing health, was a strong proponent of reconciliation between the former enemy sides. The same reviewer further praised Blount's chronicling of these postwar years as the "most moving part of the book" and went on to comment that *Robert E. Lee* is a "literate and balanced introduction." Nathan Ward, reviewing the biography in *Library Journal,* similarly found it to be a "vibrant introduction." Ward also felt that Blount managed to "humanize his portrait," and found the detailing of Lee's childhood "surprisingly moving." For Ward, Blount "succeeds" in presenting a multifaceted portrait of Lee, a man at once "flawed, brilliant, but recognizable." Chuck Leddy, writing in the *Denver Post,* similarly thought that Blount "largely succeeds in humanizing the man behind the myth" in his biography. Leddy went on to conclude that Blount's book was an "excellent, concise biography." David Walton, in the *New York Times Book Review,* observed that Blount's biography was primarily a "series of speculations and appendixes," but also allowed that the book was "witty, lively and wholly fascinating." Cameron McWhirter, in a review for the *Atlanta Journal-Constitution,* felt that "long after finishing the book, readers will be haunted by Lee." And a critic for *Kirkus Reviews* thought that "Blount honors Lee without slipping into hagiography."

Blount once commented: "Raised in South by Southern parents. Couldn't play third base well enough so became college journalist. Ridiculed cultural enemies. Boosted integration. Decided to write, teach. Went to Harvard Graduate School. Didn't like it. Went back to journalism. Liked it. Got a column. Ridiculed cultural enemies. Wrote limericks. Boosted integration. Wanted to write for magazines. Took writing job at *Sports Illustrated.* Have seen country, met all kinds of people, heard all different kinds of talk. Like it. Ready now to write a novel that sums it all up."

BIOGRAPHICAL AND CRITICAL SOURCES:

BOOKS

Brown, Jerry Elijah, *Roy Blount, Jr.,* Twayne (Boston, MA), 1990.

PERIODICALS

American Heritage, August-September, 2003, review of *Robert E. Lee,* p. 18.
Atlanta Journal, May 18, 2003, Cameron McWhirter, review of *Robert E. Lee,* p. C4.
Chicago Tribune, December 24, 1987, Jim Spencer, "Let Us Now Praise Not-So-Lean Cuisine," p. 3.
Denver Post, May 25, 2003, Chuck Leddy, review of *Robert E. Lee,* p. EE3.
Detroit News, October 17, 1982.
Kirkus Reviews, March 1, 2003, review of *Robert E. Lee,* p. 355.
Library Journal, April 1, 2003, Nathan Ward, review of *Robert E. Lee,* p. 108; May 1, 2003, Nathan Ward, "Reckoning with Robert E. Lee," p. 137.
Los Angeles Times, December 13, 1985, Taffy Cannon, "Even One-Liners Can't Save a Humor Theme," p. 44.
Newsweek, September 17, 1984, Ron Givens, review of *What Men Don't Tell Women,* p. 82.
New York Times, January 25, 1988, Leslie Bennetts, review of *Roy Blount's Happy Hour and a Half,* p. 20.
New York Times Book Review, December 1, 1974, Robert W. Creamer, review of *About Three Bricks Shy of a Load*; November 17, 1985, Patrick F. McManus, review of *Not Exactly What I Had in Mind,* p. 14; April 2, 1989, Deborah Mason, review of *Now, Where Were We?,* p. 9; May 11, 2003, David Walton, review of *Robert E. Lee,* p. 20.
People, November 21, 1994, Mark Bautz, review of *Roy Blount's Book of Southern Humor,* p. 41; June 15, 1998, Thomas Fields-Meyer, review of *Be Sweet: A Conditional Love Story,* p. 49.
Publishers Weekly, September 5, 1994, review of *Roy Blount's Book of Southern Humor,* p. 88; May 1, 1998, review of *Be Sweet,* p. 59; March 10, 2003, review of *Robert E. Lee,* pp. 61-62.
Time, October 20, 1980, Donald Morrison, review of *Crackers: This Whole Many-Sided Thing of Jimmy, More Carters, Ominous Little Animals, Sad-Singing Women, My Daddy and Me,* p. E-2.

Washington Post Book World, February 19, 1989, Jonathan Yardley, review of *Now, Where Were We?,* p. 3; June 17, 1990, Christopher Hitchens, review of *First Hubby,* p. 9.

ONLINE

Atlantic Monthly Online, http://www.theatlantic.com/ unbound/blount/rbbio.htm/ (October, 22, 2003).
Roy Blount, Jr., Web site, http://www.royblountjr.com/ (October, 22, 2003).*

*   *   *

BLY, Robert (Elwood) 1926-

PERSONAL: Born December 23, 1926, in Madison, MN; son of Jacob Thomas (a farmer) and Alice (Aws) Bly; married Carolyn McLean, June 24, 1955 (divorced, June, 1979); married Ruth Counsell, June 27, 1980; children: Mary, Bridget, Noah Matthew Jacob, Micah John Padma. *Ethnicity:* "Caucasion." *Education:* Attended St. Olaf College, 1946-47; Harvard University, A.B., 1950; University of Iowa, M.A., 1956. *Politics:* Democrat. *Religion:* Lutheran.

ADDRESSES: Home—308 First St., Moose Lake, MN 55767. *Office*—1904 Girard Ave. Minneapolis, MN 55403. *Agent*—c/o Author Mail, George Borchardt, 136 East 57th St., New York, NY 10022. *E-mail*—odinhouse@earthlink.net .

CAREER: Poet, translator, and editor. Fifties (became Sixties, Seventies, Eighties, then Nineties) Press, Moose Lake, MN, founder, publisher, and editor, 1958—. Conductor of writing workshops. *Military service:* U. S. Navy, 1944-46.

MEMBER: American Academy and Institute of Arts and Letters, Association of Literary Magazines of America (executive committee), American Poets against the Vietnam War (founding member; co-chairman).

AWARDS, HONORS: Fulbright grant, 1956-57; Amy Lowell travelling fellowship, 1964; Guggenheim fellowship, 1964, 1972; American Academy grant, 1965;

Robert Bly

Rockefeller Foundation fellowship, 1967; National Book Award, 1968, for *The Light around the Body;* nomination for poetry award from *Los Angeles Times,* 1986, for *Selected Poems.*

WRITINGS:

POEMS

(With William Duffy and James Wright), *The Lion's Tail and Eyes: Poems Written Out of Laziness and Silence,* Sixties Press (Madison, MN), 1962.
Silence in the Snowy Fields, Wesleyan University Press (Middletown, CT), 1962.
(Compiler, with David Ray) *A Poetry Reading against the Vietnam War,* Sixties Press (Madison, MN), 1966.
The Light around the Body, Harper (New York, NY), 1967.
Chrysanthemums, Ox Head Press (Menomonie, WI), 1967.

Ducks, Ox Head Press (Menomonie, WI), 1968.

The Morning Glory: Another Thing That Will Never Be My Friend (twelve prose poems), Kayak Books (San Francisco, CA), 1969, revised edition, 1970, complete edition, Harper (New York, NY), 1975.

The Teeth Mother Naked at Last, City Lights (San Francisco, CA), 1971.

(With William E. Stafford and William Matthews) *Poems for Tennessee,* Tennessee Poetry Press, 1971.

Christmas Eve Service at Midnight at St. Michael's, Sceptre Press (Rushden, Northamptonshire, England), 1972.

Water under the Earth, Sceptre Press (Rushden, Northamptonshire, England), 1972.

The Dead Seal Near McClure's Beach, Sceptre Press (Rushden, Northamptonshire, England), 1973.

Sleepers Joining Hands, Harper (New York, NY), 1973.

Jumping Out of Bed, Barre (Barre, MA), 1973.

The Hockey Poem, Knife River Press, 1974.

Point Reyes Poems, Mudra, 1974, new edition, Floating Island (Point Reyes Station, CA), 1989.

Old Man Rubbing His Eyes, Unicorn Press (Greensboro, NC), 1975.

The Loon, Ox Head Press (Marshall, MN), 1977.

This Body Is Made of Camphor and Gopherwood (prose poems), Harper (New York, NY), 1977.

Visiting Emily Dickinson's Grave and Other Poems, Red Ozier Press (Madison, WI), 1979.

This Tree Will Be Here for a Thousand Years, Harper (New York, NY), 1979.

The Man in the Black Coat Turns, Doubleday (New York, NY), 1981.

Finding an Old Ant Mansion, Martin Booth (Knotting, Bedford, England), 1981.

Four Ramages, Barnwood Press, 1983.

The Whole Moisty Night, Red Ozier Press (Madison, WI), 1983.

Out of the Rolling Ocean, Dial Press (New York, NY), 1984.

Mirabai Versions, Red Ozier Press (Madison, WI), 1984.

In the Month of May, Red Ozier Press (Madison, WI), 1985.

A Love of Minute Particulars, Sceptre Press (Rushden, Northamptonshire, England), 1985.

Selected Poems, Harper (New York, NY), 1986.

Loving a Woman in Two Worlds, Perennial/Harper (New York, NY), 1987.

The Moon on a Fencepost, Unicorn Press, 1988.

The Apple Found in the Plowing, Haw River Books, 1989.

Angels of Pompeii, Ballantine (New York, NY), 1991.

What Have I Ever Lost by Dying?: Collected Prose Poems, HarperCollins (New York, NY), 1992.

Gratitude to Old Teachers, BOA Editions (Brockport, NY), 1993.

Meditations on the Insatiable Soul: Poems, HarperPerennial (New York, NY), 1994.

Morning Poems, HarperCollins (New York, NY), 1997.

Holes the Crickets Have Eaten in Blankets: A Sequence of Poems (Boa Pamphlets, No 9), Boa Editions (Rochester, NY), 1997.

Snowbanks North of the House, HarperCollins (New York, NY), 1999.

The Night Abraham Called to the Stars, HarperCollins (New York, NY), 2001.

EDITOR

The Sea and the Honeycomb, Sixties Press (Madison, MN), 1966.

(With David Ray) *A Poetry Reading against the Vietnam War,* Sixties Press (Madison, MN), 1967.

Forty Poems Touching Upon Recent History, Beacon Press (Boston, MA), 1970.

News of the Universe: Poems of Twofold Consciousness, Sierra Books (San Francisco, CA), 1980.

Ten Love Poems, Ally Press (St. Paul, MN), 1981.

(With William Duffy) *The Fifties and the Sixties* (ten volumes), Hobart and William Smith, 1982.

The Winged Life: The Poetic Voice of Henry David Thoreau, Yolla Bolly Press (Covelo, CA), 1986.

(With James Hillman and Michael Meade) *The Rag and Bone Shop of the Heart: Poems for Men,* HarperCollins (New York, NY), 1992.

Leaping Poetry, Beacon Press (Boston, MA), 1975.

David Ignatow, *Selected Poems,* Wesleyan University Press (Middletown, CT), 1975.

Selected from Twentieth-Century American Poetry: An Anthology, New Readers Press, 1991.

William Stafford, *The Darkness around Us Is Deep: Selected Poems of William Stafford,* HarperPerennial (New York, NY), 1993.

(With Roy U. Schenk, John Everingham, and Gershen Kaufman), *Men Healing Shame: An Anthology,* Springer Publishing (New York, NY), 1995.

The Soul Is Here for Its Own Joy: Sacred Poems from Many Cultures, Ecco Press (Hopewell, NJ), 1995.

Eating the Honey of Words: New and Selected Poems, HarperFlamingo (New York, NY), 1999.

The Best American Poetry 1999, Scribner (New York, NY), 1999.

TRANSLATOR

Hans Hvass, *Reptiles and Amphibians of the World,* Grosset (New York, NY), 1960.

(With James Wright) Georg Trakl, *Twenty Poems,* Sixties Press (Madison, MN), 1961.

Selma Lager, *The Story of Gosta Berling,* New American Library (New York, NY), 1962.

(With James Knoefle and James Wright) César Vallejo, *Twenty Poems,* Sixties Press (Madison, MN), 1962.

Knut Hamsun, *Hunger* (novel), Farrar, Straus (New York, NY), 1967.

(With Christina Paulston) Gunnar Ekeloef, *I Do Best Alone at Night,* Charioteer Press (Washington, DC), 1967.

(With Christina Paulston) Gunnar Ekeloef, *Late Arrival on Earth: Selected Poems,* Rapp & Carroll (London, England), 1967.

Wang Hui-ming, *Woodcut* (limited edition), Epoh Studio (Amherst, MA), 1968.

(With James Wright) Pablo Neruda, *Twenty Poems,* Sixties Press (Madison, MN), 1968.

(With others) Yvan Goll, *Selected Poems,* Kayak, 1968.

Issa Kobayashi, *Ten Poems,* privately printed, 1969.

(And editor) Pablo Neruda and César Vallejo, *Selected Poems,* Beacon Press (Boston, MA), 1971.

Kabir, *The Fish in the Sea Is Not Thirsty: Versions of Kabir,* Lillabulero Press (Northwood Narrows, NH), 1971.

Tomas Tranströmer, *Night Vision,* Lillabulero Press (Northwood Narrows, NH), 1971.

Tomas Tranströmer, *Twenty Poems,* Seventies Press (Madison, MN), 1972.

Rainer Maria Rilke, *Ten Sonnets to Orpheus,* Zephyrus Image (San Francisco, CA), 1972.

Basho, *Basho,* Mudra, 1972.

Tomas Tranströmer, *Elegy; Some October Notes* (limited edition), Sceptre Press (Rushden, Northamptonshire, England), 1973.

Federico Garcia Lorca and Juan Ramon Jimenez, *Selected Poems,* Beacon Press (Boston, MA), 1973.

Friends, You Drank Some Darkness: Three Swedish Poets—Martinson, Ekeloef, and Tranströmer, Beacon Press (Boston, MA), 1975.

Kabir, *Grass from Two Years,* Ally Press (Denver, CO), 1975.

Kabir, *Twenty-eight Poems,* Siddha Yoga Dham, 1975.

Kabir, *Try to Live to See This!,* Ally Press (Denver, CO), 1976.

Rainer Maria Rilke, *The Voices,* Ally Press (Denver, CO), 1977.

Kabir, *The Kabir Book: Forty-four of the Ecstatic Poems of Kabir,* Beacon Press (Boston, MA), 1977.

Rolf Jacobsen, *Twenty Poems of Rolf Jacobsen,* Eighties Press (Madison, MN), 1977.

Antonio Machado, *I Never Wanted Fame,* Ally Press (St. Paul, MN), 1979.

Antonio Machado, *Canciones,* Toothpaste Press (West Branch, IA), 1980.

Tomas Tranströmer, *Truth Barriers,* Sierra Books (San Francisco, CA), 1980.

Rainer Maria Rilke, *I Am Too Alone in the World: Ten Poems,* Silver Hands Press (New York, NY), 1980.

(And editor) Rainer Maria Rilke, *Selected Poems of Rainer Maria Rilke: A Translation from the German, and Commentary,* Harper (New York, NY), 1981.

Rumi, Jalal alDin, *Night and Sleep,* Yellow Moon Press (Cambridge, MA), 1981.

Goran Sonnevi, *The Economy Spinning Faster and Faster,* SUN, 1982.

Antonio Machado, *Times Alone: Selected Poems,* Wesleyan University Press (Middletown, CT), 1983.

Windows That Open Inward: Images of Chile, photographs by Milton Rogovin, poems by Pablo Neruda, edited by Dennis Maloney, introduction by Pablo Neruda, White Pine Press (Buffalo, NY), 1985.

Rumi, Jalal al-Din, *When Grapes Turn to Wine,* Yellow Moon Press (Cambridge, MA), 1986.

Olav H. Hauge, *Trusting Your Life to Water and Eternity,* Milkweed Editions (Minneapolis, MN), 1987.

Ten Poems of Francis Ponge, and *Ten Poems of Robert Bly Inspired by the Poems of Francis Ponge,* Owl's Head Press (Riverview, New Brunswick, Canada), 1990.

Lorca and Jimenez: Selected Poems, Beacon Press (Boston, MA), 1997.

(With Sunil Dutta) Ghalib, *The Lightning Should Have Fallen on Ghalib: Selected Poems of Ghalib,* Ecco Press (Hopewell, NJ), 1999.

(With Roger Greenwald and Robert Hedin) *The Roads Have Come to an End Now: Selected and Last Poems of Rolf Jacobsen,* Copper Canyon Press (Port Townsend, WA), 2001.

Tomas Tranströmer, *The Half-Finished Heaven: The Best Poems of Tomas Tranströmer,* Graywolf Press (St. Paul, MN), 2001.

Tomas Tranströmer, *Air Mail: Brev 1964-1990,* Bonnier (Stockholm, Sweden), 2001.

Kabir, *Kabir: Ecstatic Poems,* Beacon Press (Boston, MA), 2004.

The Winged Energy of Delight, HarperCollins (New York, NY), 2004.

Also translator of such volumes as *Forty Poems of Juan Ramon Jimenez,* 1967, and, with Lewis Hyde, *Twenty Poems of Vincente Alexandre,* 1977.

OTHER

A Broadsheet against the New York Times Book Review, Sixties Press (Madison, MN), 1961.

(Contributor) *Ten Songs for Low Man's Voice and Piano,* Mobart (Hillsdale, NY), 1978.

What the Fox Agreed to Do: Four Poems, Croissant (Athens, OH), 1979.

Talking All Morning: Collected Conversations and Interviews, University of Michigan Press (Ann Arbor, MI), 1980.

The Eight Stages of Translation, Rowan Tree (Boston, MA), 1983, 2nd edition, 1986.

The Pillow and the Key: Commentary on the Fairy Tale "Iron John," Ally Press (St. Paul, MN), 1987.

A Little Book on the Human Shadow, edited by William Booth, Harper (New York, NY), 1988.

American Poetry: Wildness and Domesticity, Harper (New York, NY), 1990.

Iron John: A Book about Men, Addison-Wesley (Reading, MA), 1990.

Remembering James Wright, Ally Press (St. Paul, MN), 1991.

(With Jacob Boehme) *Between Two Worlds,* music by John Harbison, G. Schirmer (New York, NY), 1991.

The Spirit Boy and the Insatiable Soul, HarperCollins (New York, NY), 1994.

The Sibling Society, Addison-Wesley Publishers (Reading, MA), 1996.

(With Marion Woodman) *The Maiden King: The Reunion of Masculine and Feminine,* Henry Holt (New York, NY), 1998.

ADAPTATIONS: Bly appears on the recordings *Today's Poets 5,* Folkways, and *For the Stomach: Selected Poems,* Watershed, 1974; Bly appears on the videocassettes *On Being a Man,* 1989, *A Gathering of Men,* 1990, and *Bly and Woodman on Men and Women,* 1992.

WORK IN PROGRESS: The Winged Energy of Delight: Selected Translations, in progress.

SIDELIGHTS: Robert Bly is one of America's most respected and influential poets. Since the 1960s, Bly has practiced a poetry that is nonacademic, based in the natural world, the visionary, and the realm of the irrational. In addition to his verse, he has drawn attention for his theories on the roots of social problems, and his efforts to help men reclaim their masculinity and channel it in a positive direction. Believing that modern man has become lost with his primitive roots, he often focuses on the hidden connections between the natural world and the human mind, and their surreal interactions. Bly's poetry is often categorized as part of the deep image school of writing, in which the poet employs a system of private imagery; however, Bly's wish is not to create a personal mythology, but rather to describe modern American life through powerful metaphors and intense imagery. Two of his major inspirations in this regard have been Spanish-language writers César Vallejo and Federico Garcia Lorca. Hugh Kenner, writing in the *New York Times Book Review,* remarked that "Bly is attempting to write down what it's like to be alive, a state in which, he implies, not all readers find themselves all the time."

Born in western Minnesota, Bly grew up in that state in a community dominated by the culture of Norwegian immigrant farmers. After two years in the Navy, he attended St. Olaf College in Minnesota for one year, then transferred to Harvard University. There he associated with other graduates who went on to make their name as writers, including Donald Hall, Adrienne Rich, John Ashbery, John Hawkes, George Plimpton, and Kenneth Koch. After his graduation in 1950, Bly spent some time in New York City before studying for two years at the University of Iowa Writers Workshop, along with W. D. Snodgrass and Donald Justice. In 1956, he traveled on a Fulbright grant to Norway, where he translated Norwegian poetry into English. Translation would continue to be an important activity for him throughout his career. While in Norway, he discovered the work of many poets who would influence him greatly, including Neruda, Vallejo, and Gunnar Ekeloef. He founded his literary magazine and publishing house, *The Fifties* (which later changed its name to reflect the passing decades), as a forum for translated poetry. Returning to Minnesota, he took up residence on a farm there with his wife and children.

Bly's first widely acclaimed collection was *Silence in the Snowy Fields.* In an author's note, Bly stated that he is "interested in the connection between poetry and simplicity. . . . The fundamental world of poetry is an inward world. We approach it through solitude." He added that the poems in this volume "move toward that world."

In 1966, Bly cofounded American Writers against the Vietnam War and led much of the opposition among writers to that war. After winning the National Book Award for *The Light around the Body,* he contributed the prize money to the antiwar effort. The 1970s were a prolific decade for him, in which he published eleven books of poetry, essays, and translations, celebrating the power of myth, Indian ecstatic poetry, meditation, and storytelling. He was strongly influenced by the work of Robert Graves, and his poetry showed his interest in mythology and pre-Christian religion.

In 1979, Bly and his wife divorced, an event which precipitated a serious crisis of the soul for the poet. His emotional journey through this time eventually led him to begin leading men's seminars, in collaboration with James Hillman and Michael Meade. Participants were encouraged to reclaim their male traits and to express their severely repressed feelings through poetry, stories, and other rites. During these seminars, Bly was quoted as saying in *Newsweek,* the emotions can run high. "On the first night of a seminar," he explained, "I may simply put out a question like, 'Why are you having such trouble in relationships with women, or your father?' And the amount of grief and loneliness that pours out is tremendous. So sometimes by the third day there'll be a lot of weeping."

Bly's work in this area led to the character of "Iron John," based on a fairy tale by the Brothers Grimm; it came to stand for an archetype that could help men connect with their psyches. It is Bly's belief that modern men are greatly damaged by an absence of intergenerational male role models and initiation rituals. In his preface to *Iron John: A Book about Men,* he wrote, "The grief in men has been increasing steadily since the start of the Industrial Revolution and the grief has reached a depth now that cannot be ignored." Some critics found Bly's work in this vein to be antifeminist; he replied by acknowledging and denouncing the dark side of male domination and exploitation. Bly posits a "Wild Man" inside of each male, an archetypical figure who leads men into their full manhood. Not an advocate of machoism or destructive behavior, Bly emphasizes that true masculinity contains such virtues as courage, strength, and wisdom. Still, some feminists continued to argue that Bly was advocating a return to traditional gender roles for both men and women, and other critics assailed what they saw as Bly's indiscriminate, New Age-influenced salad of tidbits from many traditions. Others found great value in the book, stressing its importance to contemporary culture's ongoing redefinition of sexuality. As Deborah Tannen put it in the *Washington Post Book World,* "This rewarding book is an invaluable contribution to the gathering public conversation about what it means to be male—or female." Bly's poetic style comes through in his prose as well. "To be sure, Bly's quirky style of argumentation does not follow a linear model from Point A to Point B," Dan Cryer noted in the *Detroit News.* "When he uses poems to make a point, clarity sometimes suffers. And his metaphorical language no doubt will put off some readers. Once a reader catches on, though, the rewards are plentiful." *Iron John* was at the top of the New York Times best-seller list for ten weeks and stayed on the list for more than a year. A related videocassette, *A Gathering of Men,* was an equally phenomenal success.

Bly put forth more "timely and important" ideas on social ills in his 1997 book *The Sibling Society.* In it, he contends that North Americans are like a race of perpetual adolescents; that young children grow up too quickly, yet never quite finish the process to become full-fledged adults. The result is a world full of people who lack empathy or sympathy, whose lives are self-serving and detrimental to the human race as a whole. The root of these problems, in Bly's opinion, is the erosion of respect for authority of all sorts. As Andres Rodriguez wrote in *National Catholic Reporter,* the poet finds that "consumer capitalism, in other words, has created a savage society where greed and desire extend almost limitlessly on the horizontal plane, while the vertical plane (for example, tradition, religion, devotion) is nearly totally absent." John Bemrose, reviewing *The Sibling Society* in *Maclean's,* remarked that while Bly is not the first person to present the ideas found in his book, "he brings a unique ability to bear on the subject as an interpreter of folktales and great literature," and explains the way "a constant bombardment of advertising keeps the hunger for new goods raging, and as corporations convince politicians that they must be allowed to do what they like (essentially taking over the leadership of society), people succumb to an infantile need for instant gratification." The poet "makes a convincing stab at defining maturity, championing such traditional virtues as self-discipline and a concern for others, as well as less obvious qualities, including a deeper respect for the gifts of the dead to the living. Bly's cranky and often brilliant jeremiad is not going to please apologists for the consumer society. But that alone should be enough to recommend it."

Throughout his career, Bly has maintained his devotion to translating the world's visionary poetry, in part as an effort to furthering multicultural understanding. His collection *The Night Abraham Called to the Stars* reflects his interest in other cultures; the poems in it are stylized versions of a Middle Eastern lyric known as the ghazal. Though traditionally a love-poem, the ghazal also regularly shifts its focus to touch on politics, myth, and philosophy. As such, it was a natural choice for Bly, and his best work in the form is "simple in diction and understated in effect," wrote a *Publishers Weekly* reviewer.

Michiko Kakutani observed in the *New York Times*, "What has remained constant in his work, . . . is Mr. Bly's interest in man's relationship with nature, and his commitment to an idiom built upon simplified diction and the free associative processes of the unconscious mind." Peter Stitt of the *New York Times Book Review* also emphasized the importance of free association in Bly's poetry. "Bly's method," Stitt wrote, "is free association; the imagination is allowed to discover whatever images it deems appropriate to the poem, no matter the logical, literal demands of consciousness." M. L. Rosenberg, writing in *Tribune Books*, noted in Bly's work a blending of European and South American influences with a decidedly American sensibility: "Bly is a genius of the elevated 'high' style, in the European tradition of Rilke and Yeats, the lush magical realism of the South Americans like Lorca and Neruda. Yet Bly's work is truly American, taking its atmosphere of wide empty space from the Midwest, and its unabashed straightforward emotionalism and spiritualism." "The energy with which the Minnesota poet Robert Bly unreservedly gives

himself to his ideas, or in some cases, his prejudices," James F. Mersmann commented in his *Out of the Vietnam Vortex: A Study of Poets and Poetry against the War,* "makes him both one of the most annoying and most exciting poets of his time."

BIOGRAPHICAL AND CRITICAL SOURCES:

BOOKS

Bly, Robert, *Silence in the Snowy Fields,* Wesleyan University Press (Middletown, CT), 1962.

Contemporary Literary Criticism, Gale (Detroit, MI), Volume 1, 1973, Volume 2, 1974, Volume 5, 1976, Volume 10, 1979, Volume 15, 1980, Volume 38, 1986.

Contemporary Poets, St. James Press (Detroit, MI), 2001.

Daniels, Kate and Richard Jones, editors, *On Solitude and Silence: Writings on Robert Bly,* Beacon Press (Boston, MA), 1982, pp. 146-152.

Davis, William V., *Understanding Robert Bly,* University of South Carolina Press (Columbia, SC), 1989.

Davis, William Virgil, *Robert Bly: The Poet and His Critics,* Camden House (Columbia, SC), 1994.

Dictionary of Literary Biography, Volume 5: *American Poets since World War II,* Gale (Detroit, MI), 1980.

Friberg, Ingegard, *Moving Inward: A Study of Robert Bly's Poetry,* Acta University Gothoburgensis, 1977.

Heep, Hartmut, *A Different Poem: Rainer Maria Rilke's American Translators Randall Jarrell, Robert Lowell, and Robert Bly,* Peter Lang (New York, NY), 1996.

Howard, Richard, *Alone with America: Essays on the Art of Poetry in the United States since 1950,* Atheneum (New York, NY), 1969, revised edition, 1980.

Lacey, Paul A., *The Inner War: Forms and Themes in Recent American Poetry,* Fortress Press, 1972.

Lensing, George S., and Ronald Moran, *Four Poets and the Emotive Imagination: Robert Bly, James Wright, Louis Simpson, and William Stafford,* Louisiana State University Press (Baton Rouge, LA), 1976.

Malkoff, Karl, *Escape from the Self: A Study in Contemporary American Poetry and Poetics,* Columbia University Press (New York, NY), 1977.

Mersmann, James F., *Out of the Vietnam Vortex: A Study of Poets and Poetry against the War,* University Press of Kansas (Lawrence, KS), 1974, pp. 113-157.

Molesworth, Charles, *The Fierce Embrace: A Study of Contemporary American Poetry,* University of Missouri Press (Columbia, MO), 1979.

Nelson, Howard, *Robert Bly: An Introduction to the Poetry,* Columbia University Press (New York, NY), 1984.

Newsmakers 1992, Gale (Detroit, MI), 1992.

Ossman, David, *The Sullen Art,* Corinth, 1963.

Peseroff, Joyce, editor, *Robert Bly: When Sleepers Awake,* University of Michigan Press (Ann Arbor, MI), 1984.

Poems for Young Readers, National Council of Teachers of English, for the Houston Festival of Contemporary Poetry, 1966.

Roberson, William H., *Robert Bly: A Primary and Secondary Bibliography,* Scarecrow (Lanham, MD), 1986.

St. James Encyclopedia of Popular Culture, St. James Press (Detroit, MI), 2000.

Shaw, Robert B., editor, *American Poetry since 1960: Some Critical Perspectives,* Dufour, 1974, pp. 55-67.

Smith, Thomas R., editor, *Walking Swiftly: Writings and Images on the Occasion of Robert Bly's 65th Birthday,* Ally Press (St. Paul, MN), 1992.

Stepanchev, Stephen, *American Poetry Since 1945: A Critical Survey,* Harper (New York, NY), 1965, pp. 185-187.

Sugg, Richard P., *Robert Bly,* Twayne (Boston, MA), 1986.

PERIODICALS

America, September 28, 1996, William J. O'Malley, review of *The Sibling Society,* p. 34.

American Dialog, winter, 1968-69.

Antioch Review, summer, 2002, John Taylor, review of *The Roads Have Come to an End Now,* p. 535.

Book, January-February, 2002, Stephen Whited, review of *The Night Abraham Called to the Stars,* p. 70.

Booklist, October 15, 1994, Ray Olson, review of *Meditations on the Insatiable Soul,* p. 395; April 1, 1996, Ray Olson, review of *The Sibling Society,* p. 1322; May 1, 1999, Ray Olson, review of *Eating the Honey of Words: New and Selected Poems,* p. 1573.

Boundary 2, spring, 1976, pp. 677-700, 707-725.

Carleton Miscellany, Volume XVIII, number 1, 1979-80, pp. 74-84.

Chicago Review, Volume 19, number 2, 1967.

Chicago Tribune Book World, May 3, 1981; February 28, 1982, p. 2.

Christian Science Monitor, January 23, 1963.

Commonweal, July 23, 1971, pp. 375-380.

Detroit News, December 5, 1990, p. 3D.

English Studies, April, 1970, pp. 112-137.

Explicator, fall, 1999, Tom Hansen, review of *Surprised by Evening,* p. 53.

Far Point, fall-winter, 1969, pp. 42-47.

Globe and Mail (Toronto, Ontario, Canada), April 4, 1987; December 8, 1990, p. C10.

Harper's Magazine, August, 1968, pp. 73-77; January, 1980, p. 79.

Hollins Critic, April, 1975, pp. 1-15.

Hudson Review, autumn, 1968, p. 553; spring, 1976; spring, 1978; summer, 1987.

Iowa Review, summer, 1972, pp. 78-91; spring, 1973, pp. 111-126; fall, 1976, pp. 135-153.

Lamp in the Spine, number 3, 1972.

Library Journal, October 15, 1994, p. 62; July, 1996, Terry McMaster, review of *The Sibling Society,* p. 140; June 1, 1997, Fred Muratori, review of *Morning Poems,* p. 103; October 1, 1998, Mary Ann Hughes, review of *The Maiden King: The Reunion of Masculine and Feminine,* p. 118; June 1, 1999, Frank Allen, review of *Eating the Honey of Words: New and Selected Poems,* p. 118.

Listener, June 27, 1968.

London, December, 1968.

Los Angeles Times Book Review, May 18, 1980, p. 9; December 29, 1985, p. 11; October 26, 1986, p. 4; November 30, 1986, p. 11; December 2, 1990.

Maclean's, July 22, 1996, John Bemrose, review of *The Sibling Society,* p. 61.

Michigan Quarterly Review, spring, 1981, pp. 144-154.

Minneapolis-St. Paul Magazine, January, 1994, p. 38.

Modern Language Quarterly, March, 2001, Margaret Bruzelius, "The Kind of England . . . Loved to Look upon a Man," p. 19.

Modern Poetry Studies, winter, 1976, pp. 231-240.

Moons and Lion Tailes, Volume II, number 3, 1977, pp. 85-89.

Nation, March 25, 1968, pp. 413-414; November 17, 1979, pp. 503-504; October 31, 1981, pp. 447-448; November 26, 2001, Ian Tromp, review of *Stargazing and Sufi Poetics,* p. 54, review of *The Night Abraham Called to the Stars,* p. 54.

National Catholic Reporter, February 7, 1997, Andres Rodriguez, review of *The Sibling Society,* p. 23.

National Review, May 20, 1996, Florence King, review of *The Sibling Society,* p. 66.

New Republic, November 14, 1970, pp. 26-27; January 3, 1994, p. 31A; September 16, 1996, David Bromwich, review of *The Sibling Society,* p. 31.

New Statesman, November 15, 1996, Kirsty Milne, review of *The Sibling Society,* p. 47.

Newsweek, November 26, 1990, pp. 66-68.

New York Review of Books, June 20, 1968; November 28, 1996, Diane Johnson, review of *The Sibling Society,* p. 22.

New York Times, May 3, 1986; May 16, 1996.

New York Times Book Review, September 7, 1975; January 1, 1978; March 9, 1980, p. 8; April 26, 1981; February 14, 1982, p. 15; January 22, 1984, p. 1; October 13, 1985, p. 15; May 25, 1986, p. 2; February 22, 1987, p. 34; September 30, 1990, p. 29; December 9, 1990, p. 15; May 29, 1994, Richard Tillinghast, review of *The Darkness around Us Is Deep: Selected Poems of William Stafford,* p. 10; December 31, 1995, Bruno Maddox, review of *The Soul Is Here for Its Own Joy: Sacred Poems from Many Cultures,* p. 8; October 11, 1998, Karen Lehrman, review of *The Maiden King: The Reunion of Masculine and Feminine,* p. 11; November 18, 2001, Noah Isenberg, review of *The Half-Finished Heaven,* p. 68.

New York Times Magazine, February 3, 1980, p. 16.

Ohio Review, fall, 1978.

Partisan Review, Volume XLIV, number 2, 1977.

Poetry, June, 1963; March, 1996, Ben Howard, review of *Meditations on the Insatiable Soul,* p. 346; April, 2002, John Taylor, review of *The Night Abraham Called to the Stars,* p. 45.

Prairie Schooner, summer, 1968, pp. 176-178.

Publishers Weekly, May 9, 1980, pp. 10-11; October 12, 1990; March 25, 1996, review of *The Sibling Society,* p. 70; September 14, 1998, review of *The Maiden King,* p. 61; March 29, 1999, review of *Eating the Honey of Words,* p. 97; July 26, 1999, review of *The Best American Poetry 1999,* p. 84; April 23, 2001, review of *The Night Abraham Called to the Stars,* p. 73.

Rocky Mountain Review of Language and Literature, number 29, 1975, pp. 95-117.

San Francisco Review of Books, July-August, 1983, pp. 22-23.

Schist I, fall, 1973.

Sewanee Review, spring, 1974.

Shenandoah, spring, 1968, p. 70.

Star Tribune, December 2, 2001, John Habich, *Weird Elation,* p. E1.

Texas Quarterly, number 19, 1976, pp. 80-94.

Times Literary Supplement, March 16, 1967; February 20, 1981, p. 208.

Tribune Books (Chicago, IL), April 12, 1987, p. 5.

TWA Ambassador, December, 1980.

U.S. News & World Report, June 24, 1996, John Leo, review of *The Sibling Society,* p. 24.

Utne Reader, May-June, 1996, interview with Robert Bly, p. 58.

Virginia Quarterly Review, winter, 1963.

Washington Post, October 23, 1980; February 3, 1991, p. F1.

Washington Post Book World, April 1, 1973, p. 13; January 5, 1986, p. 6; December 14, 1986, p. 9; November 18, 1990, p. 1.

Western American Literature, spring, 1982, pp. 66-68; fall, 1982, pp. 282-284.

Win, January 15, 1973.

Windless Orchard, number 18, 1974, pp. 30-34.

World Literature Today, autumn, 1981, p. 680; spring, 1994, Ashley Brown, review of *Gratitude to Old Teachers,* p. 378; winter, 2000, Michael Leddy, review of *The Best American Poetry, 1999,* p. 172.

ONLINE

Menweb, http://www.menweb.org/ (July 5, 2003), Bert H. Hoff, interview with Robert Bly.

PBS Web site, http://www.pbs.org/ (July 5, 2003), "No Safe Place: Violence against Women" (interview with Robert Bly).

Robert Bly Home Page, http://www.robertbly.com/ (July 5, 2003), Frances Quinn, interview with Robert Bly.*

*   *   *

BOLAND, Bridget 1913-1988

PERSONAL: Born March 13, 1913, in London, England; died January 19, 1988; daughter of John Pius Boland (an Irish MP). *Education:* Oxford University, B.A. (with honors), 1935.

CAREER: Writer, 1937-88. *Military service:* Auxiliary Territorial Force, 1941-46; became senior commander.

AWARDS, HONORS: Co-nominee for award from Writers Guild and winner of Academy Award for best screenplay, both 1969, both for *Anne of the Thousand Days.*

WRITINGS:

PLAYS

The Arabian Nights, first produced in Nottingham, England, 1948.

Cockpit (first produced in London, England, 1948), included in *Plays of the Year 1,* Elek (London, England), 1949.

The Damascus Blade, first produced in Edinburgh, Scotland, 1950.

The Return (three-act; first produced as "*Journey to Earth*" in Liverpool, England, 1952; produced as "*The Return*" in London, 1953), Samuel French (London, England), 1954.

The Prisoner (three-act; first produced in London, 1954), Dramatists Play Service, 1956.

Temple Folly (three-act comedy; first produced in London, 1951), Evans Brothers (London, England), 1958.

Gordon (first produced in Derby, England, 1961), included in *Plays of the Year 25,* Elek (London, England), 1962.

The Zodiac in the Establishment (first produced in Nottingham, England, 1963), M. Evans (London, England), 1963.

A Juan by Degrees (adapted from the play by Pierre Humblot), first produced in London, 1965.

NOVELS

The Wild Geese, Heinemann (London, England), 1938, reprint, 1988.

Portrait of a Lady in Love, Heinemann (London, England), 1942.

Caterina, Souvenir Press, 1975, St. Martin's Press (New York, NY), 1976.

NONFICTION

(With Maureen Boland) *Old Wives' Lore for Gardeners,* Bodley Head (London, England), 1976, Farrar, Straus (New York, NY), 1977.

(With Maureen Boland) *Gardener's Magic and Other Old Wives Lore,* Farrar, Straus (New York, NY), 1977.

At My Mother's Knee, Bodley Head (London, England), 1978.

(Editor, with Muriel St. Clare Byrne) *The Lisle Letters: An Abridgement,* foreword by Hugh Trevor-Roper, University of Chicago Press (Chicago, IL), 1983.

(With Maureen Boland) *Gardener's Lore: Planting, Potions, and Practical Wisdom* (reprint of *Old Wives' Lore for Gardeners* and *Gardener's Magic and Other Old Wives Lore*), Ecco Press (Hopewell, NY), 1998.

SCREENPLAYS

(With A. R. Rawlinson) *Gaslight,* Anglo-American Films, 1940, re-released as *Angel Street,* Commercial Pictures, 1953.

(With A. R. Rawlinson) *This England,* World, 1941.

(With Robert Westerby, King Vidor, Mario Camerini, Ennio De Coneini, and Ivo Perilli) *War and Peace* (adapted from the novel by Leo Tolstoy), Paramount, 1956.

(With Barry Oringer) *Damon and Pythias,* released by Metro-Goldwyn-Mayer, 1962.

(With John Hale) *Anne of the Thousand Days* (adapted from the play by Maxwell Anderson), Universal, 1969.

Also author of *Sheba* (radio play), 1954, and *Beautiful Forever* (teleplay), 1965.

ADAPTATIONS: The Prisoner was released as a film by Columbia, 1955.

SIDELIGHTS: Although Bridget Boland was born March 13, 1913, in London, England, she was the daughter of an Irish politician and thought of herself as Irish. She became an author of plays, screenplays, novels, and nonfiction, trekking the unusual path of a screenwriter who later wrote for the stage. In another departure from custom, Boland wrote about panoramic historical events rather than the domestic themes which many of her female contemporaries treated. Boland was probably best known for her published play *The Prisoner,* about a man's psychiatric degeneration from incarceration and interrogation. Boland also wrote the screenplays for several notable motion pictures, including the 1956 adaptation of Leo Tolstoy's *War and Peace* and the 1969 film *Anne of the Thousand Days,* for which she won an Academy Award for best screenplay.

Boland was ahead of her time in her creative theatrics, such as the staging of the 1948 play *Cockpit,* which deals with displaced persons (D.P.) in Europe during World War II. By using the audience as part of the play as the refugees in a D.P. center she presaged the environmental theater movement that would take place off-Broadway during the 1960s. The audience members suffer discomfort as actors dressed as refugees and soldiers appear and play out their roles. When one of the refugees becomes ill and a Polish professor suggests he is suffering from the plague, soldiers prevent anyone from leaving the D.P. center. Finally the plague is called a false alarm and the audience/actors are allowed to leave from what was certainly a memorable evening.

Boland's play *The Prisoner* deals with the psychological interactions between a prisoner, a Catholic Cardinal, and his Communist party interrogator. It has been suggested that Boland was inspired by the real-life trial of Hungarian Cardinal Mindszenty and *Darkness at Noon,* a novel with a similar theme by Arthur Koestler. Nevertheless, Boland's work presents a new experience of the captor-captive relationship, with its subtle attempts at manipulation by both actors. In 1955 the play was adapted for film which starred Alec Guinness, and it provided the basis for the popular 1960s television series of the same title.

In addition to writing several dozen plays and screenplays, the prolific Boland penned novels and nonfiction works. Among her publications are the novels *The Wild Geese,* a historical tale told through letters, *Portrait of a Lady in Love,* and *Caterina.* She also produced the memoir *At My Mother's Knee* and several volumes about gardening with her sister Maureen Boland: *Old Wives' Lore for Gardeners* and *Gardener's Magic and Other Old Wives Lore.* The gardening book found new life in 1998 with a tandem edition reprint. The last work Boland published before her death in 1988 was a one-book abridgment of a six-volume collection of letters written by Arthur Plantagenet, the maternal uncle of the English king Henry VIII. Thus *The Lisle Letters: An Abridgement,* edited by Boland and Muriel St. Clare Byrne, makes available to researchers and interested readers primary-source letters from Tudor England.

BIOGRAPHICAL AND CRITICAL SOURCES:

PERIODICALS

Library Journal, May 1, 1991, review of *The Wild Geese,* p. 112.
New Statesman, October 18, 1985, Alan Brien, review of *The Lisle Letters: An Abridgment,* pp. 26-27.
Publishers Weekly, August 12, 1983, review of *The Lisle Letters,* p. 61.
Times (London), January 27, 1988.
Times Educational Supplement, July 10, 1981, review of *Old Wives' Lore for Gardeners,* p. 25; May 27, 1988, review of *The Wild Geese,* p. B2.*

*   *   *

BOOT, William
  See STOPPARD, Tom

*   *   *

BRACKEN, Len 1961-

PERSONAL: Born January 5, 1961, in Andrews, MD; son of Tony and Martha (Dobar) Bracken. *Ethnicity:* "Caucasian." *Education:* George Washington University, B.A. *Politics:* "Anarcho-communist." *Hobbies and other interests:* "Agit-prop."

ADDRESSES: Home—P.O. Box 5585, Arlington, VA 22205. *E-mail*—lenbracken@hotmail.com.

CAREER: Black Planet Books, Baltimore, MD, bookseller, beginning 1996; Bureau of National Affairs, copy editor of *Daily Report for Executives,* 2000—.

MEMBER: Washington Psychogeography Association.

WRITINGS:

Freeplay (novel), Backbone, 1990.
The East Is Black (novel), Backbone, 1992.

Secret City (novel), Backbone, 1994.

The Neo-Cataline Conspiracy (nonfiction), Backbone, 1996.

Guy Debord: Revolutionary, Feral House (Portland, OR), 1997.

(Translator) Gianfranco Sanguinetti, *The Real Report on the Last Chance to Save Capitalism in Italy,* Flatland, 1997.

(Translator) Paul Lafargue, *The Right to Be Lazy,* Fifth Season Press, 1999.

The Arch Conspirator, Adventures Unlimited Press, 1999.

The Shadow Government: 9-11 and State Terror, Adventures Unlimited Press, 2002.

SIDELIGHTS: Len Bracken once told *CA:* "I write to develop and clarify my understanding of what it means to be a human in this world of ours and to make it a better place. My influences? My friends and current events top a list that also includes writers as diverse as Picabia and Trifinov. For many years now, my habit has been to rise and write; research and revision wait until later in the day. I was inspired to write about Guy Debord because he set an excellent example of putting his revolutionary theory into practice."

* * *

BRADBURY, Ray (Douglas) 1920-
  (Douglas Spaulding, Leonard Spaulding, pseudonyms)

PERSONAL: Born August 22, 1920, in Waukegan IL; son of Leonard Spaulding and Esther (Moberg) Bradbury; married Marguerite Susan McClure, September 27, 1947 (died, 2003); children: Susan Marguerite, Ramona, Bettina, Alexandra. *Education:* Attended schools in Waukegan, IL, and Los Angeles, CA. *Politics:* Independent. *Religion:* Unitarian Universalist. *Hobbies and other interests:* Painting in oil and water colors, collecting Mexican artifacts.

ADDRESSES: Home—10265 Cheviot Drive, Los Angeles, CA 90064. *Agent*—Don Congdon, 156 Fifth Ave., No. 625, New York, NY 10010.

CAREER: Newsboy in Los Angeles, CA, 1940-43; full-time writer, 1943—.

Ray Bradbury

MEMBER: Writers Guild of America, Screen Writers Guild, Science Fantasy Writers of America, Pacific Art Foundation.

AWARDS, HONORS: O. Henry Prize, 1947 and 1948; Benjamin Franklin Award, 1953-54, for "Sun and Shadow"; gold medal, Commonwealth Club of California, 1954, for *Fahrenheit 451;* National Institute of Arts and Letters award, 1954, for contribution to American literature; Junior Book Award, Boys' Clubs of America, 1956, for *Switch on the Night;* Golden Eagle Award, 1957, for screenwriting; Academy Award nomination for best short film, 1963, for *Icarus Montgolfier Wright;* Mrs. Ann Radcliffe Award, Count Dracula Society, 1965, 1971; Writers Guild Award, 1974; World Fantasy Award, 1977, for lifetime achievement; D.Litt., Whittier College, 1979; Balrog Award, 1979, for best poet; Aviation and Space Writers Award, 1979, for television documentary; Gandalf Award, 1980; Body of Work Award, PEN, 1985; medal for "Distinguished Contribution to American Letters," inducted into the University of Kansas Center for the Study of Science Fiction's Science Fiction and Fantasy Hall of Fame, 1999; National Book Foundation, 2000;

Bram Stoker Award nominee in novel category, Horror Writers Association, 2001, for *From the Dust Returned,* and 2003, for *One More for the Road;* the play version of *The Martian Chronicles* won five Los Angeles Drama Critics Circle Awards; Grand Master Nebula Award, Science Fiction and Fantasy Writers of America; star on Hollywood Walk of Fame.

WRITINGS:

NOVELS

The Martian Chronicles (also see below), Doubleday (Garden City, NY), 1950, revised edition published as *The Silver Locusts,* Hart-Davis (London, England), 1965, anniversary edition published as *The Martian Chronicles: The Fortieth Anniversary Edition,* Doubleday (New York, NY), 1990.

Dandelion Wine (also see below), Doubleday (Garden City, NY), 1957.

Something Wicked This Way Comes (also see below), Simon & Schuster (New York, NY), 1962.

Death Is a Lonely Business, Knopf (New York, NY), 1985.

A Graveyard for Lunatics, Knopf (New York, NY), 1990.

Quicker Than the Eye, Avon (New York, NY), 1996.

Green Shadows, White Whale, Knopf (New York, NY), 1992, published with a new afterword by the author, Perennial (New York, NY), 2002.

Let's All Kill Constance, Morrow (New York, NY), 2003.

STORY COLLECTIONS

Dark Carnival, Arkham (Sauk City, WI), 1947, revised edition, Hamish Hamilton (London, England), 1948.

The Illustrated Man, Doubleday (Garden City, NY), 1951, revised edition, Hart-Davis (London, England), 1952.

Fahrenheit 451 (contains "Fahrenheit 451" [also see below], "The Playground", and "And the Rock Cried Out"), Ballantine (New York, NY), 1953.

The Golden Apples of the Sun (also see below), Doubleday (Garden City, NY), 1953, fortieth anniversary edition with a new foreword by the author, G. K. Hall (Thorndike, ME), 1997.

Fahrenheit 451 (novelette), Ballantine (New York, NY), 1953.

The October Country, Ballantine (New York, NY), 1955.

A Medicine for Melancholy (also see below), Doubleday (Garden City, NY), 1959, revised edition published as *The Day It Rained Forever* (also see below), Hart-Davis (London, England), 1959.

The Ghoul Keepers, Pyramid (New York, NY), 1961.

The Small Assassin, Ace (New York, NY), 1962.

The Machineries of Joy, Simon & Schuster (New York, NY), 1964.

The Vintage Bradbury, Vintage (New York, NY), 1965.

The Autumn People, Ballantine (New York, NY), 1965.

Tomorrow Midnight, Ballantine (New York, NY), 1966.

Twice Twenty-Two (contains *The Golden Apples of the Sun* and *A Medicine for Melancholy*), Doubleday (Garden City, NY), 1966.

I Sing the Body Electric!, Knopf (New York, NY), 1969.

(With Robert Bloch) *Bloch and Bradbury: Ten Masterpieces of Science Fiction,* Tower, 1969 (published as *Fever Dreams and Other Fantasies,* Sphere (London, England), 1970.

(With Robert Bloch) *Whispers from Beyond,* Peacock Press, 1972.

Selected Stories, Harrap (London, England), 1975.

Long after Midnight, Knopf (New York, NY), 1976.

The Best of Bradbury, Bantam (New York, NY), 1976.

To Sing Strange Songs, Wheaton, 1979.

The Stories of Ray Bradbury, Knopf (New York, NY), 1980.

Dinosaur Tales, Bantam (New York, NY), 1983.

A Memory of Murder, Dell (New York, NY), 1984.

The Toynbee, Convector, Random House (New York, NY), 1988.

Quicker Than the Eye, Avon (New York, NY), 1997.

Driving Blind, Avon (New York, NY), 1997.

Ray Bradbury Collected Short Stories, illustrated by Robert Court, Peterson Publishing (North Mankato, MN), 2001.

One More for the Road: A New Short Story Collection, Morrow (New York, NY), 2002.

Bradbury Stories: 100 of His Most Celebrated Tales, Morrow (New York, NY), 2003.

FOR CHILDREN

Switch on the Night, Pantheon (New York, NY), 1955.

R Is for Rocket (story collection), Doubleday (Garden City, NY), 1962.

S Is for Space (story collection), Doubleday (Garden City, NY), 1966.

The Halloween Tree, Knopf (New York, NY), 1972.

The April Witch, Creative Education (Mankato, MN), 1987.

The Other Foot, Creative Education (Mankato, MN), 1987.

The Foghorn (also see below), Creative Education (Mankato, MN), 1987.

The Veldt (also see below), Creative Education (Mankato, MN), 1987.

Fever Dream, St. Martin's Press (New York, NY), 1987.

A Graveyard for Lunatics: Another Tale of Two Cities, Knopf (New York, NY), 1990.

Ahmed and the Oblivion Machines, Avon (New York, NY), 1998.

Something Wicked This Way Comes, Avon (New York, NY), 1999.

You Are Here: The Jerde Partnership International, Phaidon Press Limited (London, England), 1999.

Dandelion Wine: A Novel, Avon (New York, NY), 1999.

Death Is a Lonely Business, Avon (New York, NY), 1999.

The Illustrated Man, Chivers Press (Bath, England), 1999.

The Country, illustrated by Joe Mugnaini, Avon (New York, NY), 1999.

From the Dust Returned: A Family Remembrance, William Morrow (New York, NY), 2001.

PLAYS

The Meadow, produced in Hollywood at the Huntington Hartford Theatre, 1960.

Way in the Middle of the Air, produced in Hollywood at the Desilu Gower Studios, 1962.

The Anthem Sprinters, and Other Antics (play collection produced in Beverly Hills, CA), Dial (New York, NY), 1963.

The World of Ray Bradbury (three one-acts), produced in Los Angeles, CA, at the Coronet Theater, 1964, produced off-Broadway at Orpheum Theatre, 1965.

Leviathan 99 (radio play), British Broadcasting Corp., 1966, produced in Hollywood, 1972.

The New York, NYed Forever (one-act), Samuel French (New York, NY), 1966.

The Pedestrian (one-act), Samuel French (New York, NY), 1966.

Dandelion Wine (based on his novel of same title; music composed by Billy Goldenberg), produced at Lincoln Center's Forum Theatre, 1967.

Christus Apollo (music composed by Jerry Goldsmith), produced in Los Angeles at Royce Hall, University of California, 1969.

The Wonderful Ice-Cream Suit and Other Plays (collection; *The Wonderful Ice-Cream Suit,* produced in Los Angeles at the Coronet Theater, 1965; *The Veldt* [based on his story of same title], produced in London, 1980; includes *To the Chicago Abyss*), Bantam (New York, NY), 1972, published as *The Wonderful Ice-Cream Suit and Other Plays for Today, Tomorrow, and Beyond Tomorrow,* Hart-Davis (London, England), 1973.

Madrigals for the Space Age (chorus and narration; music composed by Lalo Schifrin; performed in Los Angeles, 1976), Associated Music Publishers, 1972.

Pillar of Fire and Other Plays for Today, Tomorrow, and Beyond Tomorrow (*Pillar of Fire,* produced in Fullerton at the Little Theatre, California State College, 1973; *The Foghorn* [based on his story of same title], produced in New York, 1977; includes *Kaleidoscope*), Bantam (New York, NY), 1975.

That Ghost, That Bride of Time: Excerpts from a Play-in-Progress, Squires, 1976.

The Martian Chronicles (based on his novel of same title), produced in Los Angeles, 1977.

Fahrenheit 451 (musical, based on his story of same title), produced in Los Angeles, 1979.

A Device out of Time, Dramatic Publishing (Woodstock, IL), 1986.

Falling Upward (produced in Los Angeles, March, 1988), Dramatic Publishing (Woodstock, IL), 1988.

To the Chicago Abyss, Dramatic Publishing (Woodstock, IL), 1988.

The Day It Rained Forever (musical based on his story of the same title), Dramatic Publishing (Woodstock, IL), 1990.

On Stage: A Chrestomathy of His Plays, Primus (New York, NY), 1991.

SCREENPLAYS

It Came from Outer Space, Universal Pictures, 1953.

The Beast from 20,000 Fathoms (based on his story, "The Foghorn"), Warner Bros., 1953.

Moby Dick, Warner Bros., 1956.

(With George C. Johnson) *Icarus Montgolfier Wright,* Format Films, 1962.

(Author of narration and creative consultant) *An American Journey,* U.S. Government for United States Pavilion at New York World's Fair, 1964.

(Under pseudonym Douglas Spaulding, with Ed Weinberger) *Picasso Summer,* Warner Bros./Seven Arts, 1972.

Something Wicked This Way Comes (based on his novel of same title), Walt Disney, 1983.

Also author of television scripts for *Alfred Hitchcock Presents, Jane Wyman's Fireside Theatre, Steve Canyon, Trouble Shooters, Twilight Zone, Alcoa Premiere,* and *Curiosity Shop* series. Author of television scripts for *Ray Bradbury Television Theatre,* USA Cable Network, 1985-90.

POEMS

Old Ahab's Friend, and Friend to Noah, Speaks His Piece: A Celebration, Roy A. Squires Press (Glendale, CA), 1971.

When Elephants Last in the Dooryard Bloomed: Celebrations for Almost Any Day in the Year (also see below), Knopf (New York, NY), 1973.

That Son of Richard III: A Birth Announcement, Roy A. Squires Press (Glendale, CA), 1974.

Where Robot Mice and Robot Men Run 'Round in Robot Towns (also see below), Knopf (New York, NY), 1977.

Twin Hieroglyphs That Swim the River Dust, Lord John (Northridge, CA), 1978.

The Bike Repairman, Lord John (Northridge, CA), 1978.

The Author Considers His Resources, Lord John (Northridge, CA), 1979.

The Aqueduct, Roy A. Squires Press (Glendale, CA), 1979.

This Attic Where the Meadow Greens, Lord John (Northridge, CA), 1979.

The Last Circus and *The Electrocution,* Lord John (Northridge, CA), 1980.

The Ghosts of Forever (five poems, a story, and an essay), Rizzoli (New York, NY), 1980.

The Haunted Computer and the Android Pope (also see below), Knopf (New York, NY), 1981.

The Complete Poems of Ray Bradbury (contains *Where Robot Mice and Robot Men Run 'Round in Robot Towns, The Haunted Computer and the Android Pope,* and *When Elephants Last in the Dooryard Bloomed*), Ballantine (New York, NY), 1982.

The Love Affair (a short story and two poems), Lord John (Northridge, CA), 1983.

Forever and the Earth, limited edition, Croissant & Co. (Athens, OH), 1984.

Death Has Lost Its Charm for Me, Lord John (Northridge, CA), 1987.

With Cat for Comforter, illustrated by Louise Reinoehl Max, Gibbs Smith (Salt Lake City, UT), 1997.

Dogs Think That Every Day Is Christmas, illustrated by Louise Reinoehl Max, Gibbs Smith (Salt Lake City, UT), 1997.

I Live by the Invisible: New and Selected Poems, Salmon (Dublin, Ireland), 2002.

OTHER

(Editor and contributor) *Timeless Stories for Today and Tomorrow,* Bantam (New York, NY), 1952.

(Editor and contributor) *The Circus of Dr. Lao and Other Improbable Stories,* Bantam (New York, NY), 1956.

Sun and Shadow (short story), Quenian Press (Berkeley, CA), 1957.

(With Lewy Olfson) *Teacher's Guide: Science Fiction,* Bantam (New York, NY), 1968.

Zen and the Art of Writing, Capra Press (Santa Barbara, CA), 1973.

(With Bruce Murray, Arthur C. Clarke, Walter Sullivan, and Carl Sagan) *Mars and the Mind of Man,* Harper (New York, NY), 1973.

The Mummies of Guanajuato, Abrams (New York, NY), 1978.

(Author of text) *About Norman Corwin,* Santa Susana Press (Northridge, CA), 1979.

Beyond 1984: Remembrance of Things Future, Targ (New York, NY), 1979.

(Author of text) *Los Angeles,* Skyline Press, 1984.

The Last Good Kiss: A Poem, Santa Susana Press (Glendale, CA), 1984.

(Author of text) *Orange County,* Skyline Press, 1985.

(Author of text) *The Art of "Playboy,"* Alfred Van der Marck (New York, NY), 1985.

The Dragon, B. Munster (Round Top, NY), 1988.

The Fog Horn, Creative Education (Mankato, MN), 1988.

Yestermorrow: Obvious Answers to Impossible Futures, Joshua O'Dell (New York, NY), 1991.

The Smile, Creative Education (Mankato, MN), 1991.

Journey to Far Metaphor: Further Essays on Creativity, Writing, Literature, and the Arts, Joshua O'Dell (New York, NY), 1994.

A Chapbook for Burnt-Out Priests, Rabbis, and Ministers, 2001.

Conversations with Ray Bradbury, edited by Steven L. Aggelis, University Press of Mississippi (Jackson, MS), 2004.

Work represented in over seven hundred anthologies. Contributor of short stories and articles, sometimes under pseudonyms including Leonard Spaulding, to *Playboy, Saturday Review, Weird Tales, Magazine of Fantasy and Science Fiction, Omni, Life,* and other publications.

ADAPTATIONS: Fahrenheit 451 was filmed by Universal in 1966 and adapted as an opera by Georgia Holof and David Mettere and produced in Fort Wayne, IN, 1988; *The Illustrated Man* was filmed by Warner Bros. in 1969; the story "The Screaming Woman" was filmed for television in 1972; the story "Murderer" was filmed for television by WGBH-TV (Boston, MA), 1976; *The Martian Chronicles* was filmed as a television mini-series in 1980. *Bradbury Theatre* presented adaptations of Bradbury's short stories on the USA Network from 1985-1992. Many of Bradbury's works have also been adapted as sound recordings.

SIDELIGHTS: Ray Bradbury is one of the best-known writers of science fiction, thanks to his numerous short stories, screenplays, and classic books such as *The Martian Chronicles, Dandelion Wine, Fahrenheit 451,* and *Something Wicked This Way Comes.* Ironically, Bradbury does not identify himself as a science-fiction writer and has proclaimed his aversion to much of modern technology: he does not drive a car or own a computer. His fiction reflects this mind-set, for unlike many of his colleagues, Bradbury de-emphasizes gimmicky space hardware and gadgetry in favor of an exploration of the impact of scientific development on human lives. In general, Bradbury warns man against becoming too dependent on science and technology at the expense of moral and aesthetic concerns. Writing in the *Dictionary of Literary Biography,* George Edgar Slusser noted that "to Bradbury, science is the forbidden fruit, destroyer of Eden. . . . In like manner, Bradbury is a fantasist whose fantasies are oddly circumscribed: he writes less about strange things happening to people than about strange imaginings of the human mind. Corresponding, then, to an outer labyrinth of modern technological society is this inner one—fallen beings feeding in isolation on their hopeless dreams."

Bradbury was born in Waukegan, Illinois, in 1920. By the age of eight he was eagerly reading the popular pulp magazines of the time, such as *Amazing Stories.* In 1934 the Bradbury family moved to Los Angeles, California. Bradbury began to work seriously on his writing at that time, his efforts including attendance at a writing class taught by science fiction master Robert Heinlein. His first published story appeared in an amateur fan magazine in 1938. He continued to work hard on honing his writing craft, and by the 1940s he was publishing in the better magazines and receiving national recognition for his work, winning several important awards and being featured in major anthologies.

In 1950 Bradbury published *The Martian Chronicles,* a cycle of stories chronicling the Earth's colonization of, and eventual destruction of, the planet Mars. The portrayal of the Martians ranged from sympathetic to threatening, but the stories really focus on the Earthling colonists. *The Martian Chronicles* was lavishly praised by such literary standouts as Christopher Isherwood, Orville Prescott, and Angus Wilson, bringing its author a standing as a writer of highest merit. "The book owed much to the American tradition of frontier literature, and quickly consolidated Bradbury's reputation as one of science fiction's leading stylists," commented an essayist for *St. James Guide to Science Fiction Writers.*

The Illustrated Man, which appeared the following year, was another story cycle; in this volume, though, each story represents a tattoo that has come alive. The Martian setting of the previous book is revisited in a few of the tales, notably "The Fire Balloons," which probes the question of whether or not an alien life form can receive Christian grace. The amoral tendencies of children is the basis of "The Veldt" and "Zero Hour." In "Kaleidoscope," Bradbury dramatized the fate of a crew of astronauts whose spaceship has exploded, and who are drifting through space to slowly meet their deaths.

The novella *Fahrenheit 451* is, along with *The Martian Chronicles,* Bradbury's most famous work. In this story, "firemen" are those who set forbidden books aflame, rather than those who put out fires. It is a somewhat simple tale, "as much an attack on mass culture as it is a satire of McCarthy-era censorship," remarked the essayist for *St. James Guide to Science Fiction Writers.* The story implies that the government-sanctioned illiteracy is the outgrowth of pandering to special interest groups in the mass media, as well as a result of the rise of television. A society of outcasts is the only bastion of great literature; its members dedicate themselves to memorizing the great books of the world. Many commentators note a disturbing similarity between Bradbury's fictional world and our real one.

After the publication of *Fahrenheit 451,* Bradbury moved away from the science fiction genre with which he had become identified. He published other story collections during the 1950s containing a mix of fantasies, stories set in Mexico (a setting which had a lasting fascination for the author), crime stories, and small-town tales. The repressive future world is so vividly depicted in this work that the novella has become as much a staple of political study as George Orwell's *1984.* In *A Medicine for Melancholy,* Bradbury published his first stories concerning Irish life and character. This interest, sparked during a stay in Ireland in 1954, would be another ongoing concern in his work for years to come.

Something Wicked This Way Comes was Bradbury's first full-length novel, and another of his best-known works. This fantasy concerns a malevolent carnival that disrupts life in a small Midwestern town. The action occurs mostly at night and in the darker parts of humanity. The supernatural powers within the carnival have the power to grant dreams, but also to steal away one's soul. "The merry-go-round, the Hall of Mirrors, the parade and other carnivalesque trappings become truly creepy under Bradbury's skillful pen," noted the writer for *St. James Guide to Science Fiction Writers.*

In the 1960s and 1970s, Bradbury's subject matter became more realistic, and his output slightly less prolific. His themes were frequently rather dark, concerning dysfunctional marriages, fear of aging and death, and more warnings on the dangers of technology. Such stories can be found in *The Machineries of Joy* and *I Sing the Body Electric!* The author also worked on some nonfiction, plays, editing of anthologies, and writing children's stories. In 1985, he published a long-awaited new novel, titled *Death Is a Lonely Business.* Based loosely on his early years as a writer in the pulp-fiction market, it features a protagonist whose optimism works to save him from the strange deaths that are striking down his comrades. *A Graveyard for Lunatics* tells of a writer working in Hollywood during the 1950s, who discovers a body,

frozen in time, in the graveyard next to the studio that employs him. There were autobiographical threads in this story as well; Bradbury wrote for such popular early television shows as *The Twilight Zone* and the *Alfred Hitchcock* series, and his work in Hollywood included writing the award-winning screen adaptation of Herman Melville's *Moby-Dick.* He wrote yet another mystery with a film-noir flavor with *Let's All Kill Constance.* In this, the screenwriter/detective is asked for help by Constance Rattigan, an aging film star who seems to be the prey of a killer. A *Publishers Weekly* reviewer called it a "whirlwind of staccato dialogue, puns and references to old Hollywood," and added that "Bradbury's giddy pleasure is infectious; though he throws in an unexpected conclusion, it's the author's exuberant voice more than the mystery itself that will have readers hooked."

Throughout his career, Bradbury has remained an energetic and insightful writer. Damon Knight observed in his *In Search of Wonder: Critical Essays on Science Fiction:* "His imagery is luminous and penetrating, continually lighting up familiar corners with unexpected words. He never lets an idea go until he has squeezed it dry, and never wastes one. As his talent expands, some of his stories become pointed social commentary; some are surprisingly effective religious tracts, disguised as science fiction; others still are nostalgic vignettes; but under it all is still Bradbury the poet of 20th-century neurosis. Bradbury the isolated spark of consciousness, awake and alone at midnight; Bradbury the grown-up child who still remembers, still believes."

BIOGRAPHICAL AND CRITICAL SOURCES:

BOOKS

Adams, Anthony, *Ray Bradbury,* Harrap (London, England), 1975.

Clareson, Thomas D., editor, *Voices for the Future: Essays on Major Science Fiction Writers,* Volume 1, Bowling Green State University Press (Bowling Green, OH), 1976.

Concise Dictionary of American Literary Biography: Broadening Views, 1968-1988, Gale (Detroit, MI), 1989.

Contemporary Literary Criticism, Gale (Detroit, MI), Volume 1, 1973, Volume 3, 1975, Volume 10, 1979, Volume 15, 1980, Volume 42, 1987.

Contemporary Popular Writers, St. James Press (Detroit, MI), 1997.

Dictionary of Literary Biography, Gale (Detroit, MI), Volume 2: *American Novelists since World War II,* 1978; Volume 8: *Twentieth-Century American Science-Fiction Writers,* 1981.

Ketterer, David, *New Worlds for Old: The Apocalyptic Imagination, Science Fiction, and American Literature,* Indiana University Press (Bloomington, IN), 1974.

Kirk, Russell, *Enemies of the Permanent Things: Observations of Abnormity in Literature and Politics,* Arlington House (New Rochelle, NY), 1969.

Knight, Damon, *In Search of Wonder: Critical Essays on Science Fiction,* 2nd edition, Advent, 1967.

Moskowitz, Sam, *Seekers of Tomorrow: Masters of Modern Science Fiction,* Ballantine (New York, NY), 1967, pp. 351-370.

Nolan, William F., *The Ray Bradbury Companion,* Gale (New York, NY), 1975.

Platt, Charles, *Dream Makers: Science-Fiction and Fantasy Writers at Work,* Ungar (New York, NY), 1987.

St. James Encyclopedia of Popular Culture, St. James Press (Detroit, MI), 2000.

St. James Guide to Horror, Ghost & Gothic Writers, St. James Press (Detroit, MI), 1998.

St. James Guide to Science Fiction Writers, 4th edition, St. James Press (Detroit, MI), 1996.

St. James Guide to Young Adult Writers, 2nd edition, St. James Press (Detroit, MI), 1999.

Slusser, George Edgar, *The Bradbury Chronicles,* Borgo Press (San Bernardino, CA), 1977.

Toupounce, William F., *Ray Bradbury and the Poetics of Reverie: Fantasy, Science Fiction, and the Reader,* UMI Research Press (Ann Arbor, MI), 1984.

Toupounce, William F, *Naming the Unnameable: Ray Bradbury and the Fantastic after Freud,* Starmont House, 1997.

Wollheim, Donald, *The Universe Makers,* Harper (New York, NY), 1971.

World Literature Criticism (New York, NY), Gale (Detroit, MI), 1992.

PERIODICALS

Ad Astra, July-August, 1991.

Analog Science Fiction & Fact, March, 1989, p. 183; July, 1992, p. 311.

Austin American-Statesman, February 16, 2003, Dorman T. Shindler, "Bradbury Has Mystery Noir Down to a Science," p. K5.

Back Stage West, July 25, 2002, Dally Margolies, "Bradbury: Past, Present and Future at the Court Theatre," p. 27; April 3, 2003, Jenelle Riley, "What's Up with Ray Bradbury?," p. 4.

Book, September-October, 2003, Eric Wetzel, review of the 50th anniversary hardcover of *Fahrenheit 451,* p. 34.

Booklist, March 1, 1992, p. 1191; February 1, 1994, p. 989; October 1, 1998, Ray Olson, review of *Ahmed and the Oblivion Machines,* p. 312; August, 2001, Candace Smith, review of *From the Dust Returned,* p. 2049; November 15, 2002, Connie Fletcher, review of *Let's All Kill Constance,* p. 579; July, 2003, Ray Olson, review of *Bradbury Stories: 100 of His Most Celebrated Tales,* p. 1844.

Christianity Today, May 14, 1990.

Coventry Evening Telegraph, May 31, 2003, Michael Wood, review of *One More for the Road,* p. 26.

English Journal, February, 1970, pp. 201-205; 1971, pp. 877-887.

Entertainment Weekly, October 15, 1993.

Extrapolation, December, 1971, pp. 64-74; fall, 1984.

Future, October, 1978.

Journal of Popular Culture, summer, 1973, pp. 227-248.

Kirkus Reviews, June 15, 2003, review of *Bradbury Stories: 100 of His Most Celebrated Tales,* p. 834.

Library Journal, May 1, 1999, Michael Rogers, review of *Death Is a Lonely Business,* p. 118; December, 2002, Devon Thomas, review of *Let's All Kill Constance,* p. 174; August, 2003, A. Berger, review of *Bradbury Stories: 100 of His Most Celebrated Tales,* p. 138; November 15, 2003, Michael Rogers, review of the 50th anniversary hardcover of *Fahrenheit 451,* p. 103.

Magazine of Fantasy and Science Fiction, May, 1963, pp. 7-22.

National Review, April 4, 1967.

Newsweek, July 30, 1990, p. 54.

New York Times, April 24, 1983.

New York Times Book Review, August 8, 1951; December 28, 1969; October 29, 1972; October 26, 1980; December 11, 1988, p. 26; December 9, 2001, Mary Elizabeth Williams, review of *From the Dust Returned: A Family Remembrance,* p. 28; January 26, 2003, Marilyn Stasio, review of *Let's All Kill Constance,* p. 20.

New York Times Magazine, November 5, 2000, Mary Roach, interview with Ray Bradbury, p. 21.

Omni, January, 1989; February, 1989.

Publishers Weekly, December 20, 1991, p. 71; October 26, 1998, review of *Ahmed and the Oblivion Machines,* p. 49; March 19, 2001, review of *A Chapbook for Burnt-Out Priests, Rabbis, and Ministers,* p. 81; August 27, 2001, review of *From the Dust Returned: A Family Remembrance,* p. 60; October 22, 2001, Ben P. Indick, interview with Ray Bradbury, p. 40; September, 2002, review of *I Live by the Invisible: New and Selected Poems,* p. 54; November 11, 2002, review of *Let's All Kill Constance,* p. 40.

Reader's Digest, September, 1986.

School Library Journal, May, 1987.

Time, March 24, 1975; October 13, 1980; May 25, 1992, p. 68.

Washington Post, July 7, 1989.

Washington Post Book World, November 2, 1980, pp. 4-5; November 3, 1985, p. 7.

Winesburg Eagle, summer, 1997.

Writer, December, 2003, "'I Was Never a Science Fiction Writer,' Ray Bradbury Says," p. 11.

Writer's Digest, February, 1967, pp. 40-44, 47, 94-96; March, 1967, pp. 41-44, 87; December, 1974; February, 1976, pp. 18-25.

Writing!, November-December, 2001, Sarah Kizis, "A Virtual Visit to the Veldt," p. 14.

ONLINE

Ray Bradbury Home Page, http://www.raybradbury.com/ (July 11, 2003).

Salon.com, http://www.salon.com/ (July 11, 2003), James Hibberd, "Ray Bradbury Is on Fire!"*

*   *   *

BREECHER, Maury M. 1944-

PERSONAL: Born November 7, 1944, in Jersey City, NJ; son of Maury, Sr. (an owner of a pest control company) and Marie (Martin) Breecher; married; first wife's name Connie (divorced); married Anne Boudreau (divorced, January, 1989); married Rebecca Oxford (a university administrator), February 22, 1991 (divorced, September 30, 1999); children: (first marriage) Martin, Christopher; (second marriage) Michael.

Education: Attended Wichita State University and University of Kansas, between 1963 and 1967; State University of New York, B.S., 1987; University of Alabama—Birmingham, M.P.H., 1990; University of Alabama—Tuscaloosa, Ph.D., 1996. *Religion:* Unitarian-Universalist.

ADDRESSES: Home and office—18350 Hatteras St., No. 110, Tarzana, CA 91356. *E-mail*—lance4hire@nasw.org.

CAREER: Parsons Sun, Parsons, KS, staff member, 1966; *Wichita Beacon,* Wichita, KS, courthouse reporter, 1967-68; *Salina Journal,* Salina, KS, aviation editor, editorial page columnist, and reporter, 1968-71; Illinois State Medical Society, Chicago, IL, writer and executive assistant in Division of Public Relations, 1971-72; West Suburban Hospital, Oak Park, IL, public relations director, 1972-73; GP Group, Lantana, FL, articles editor, 1973-79; Feature Enterprises (syndicate), owner, editor, and chief writer, 1979-90; journalist and author, 1990—. University of Alabama, adjunct instructor, 1991; guest on television and radio programs; public speaker.

MEMBER: American Medical Writers Association, American Society of Journalists and Authors, Association for Education in Journalism and Mass Communication, Authors Guild, Authors League of America, National Association of Science Writers, National Writers Union.

WRITINGS:

(With Robert Johnson and Shirley Linde) *The Charleston Program: The Revolutionary New Way to Lose Weight,* Green Tree Press (Erie, PA), 1988.

(With Shirley Linde) *Healthy Homes in a Toxic World,* Wiley (New York, NY), 1992.

(With James W. Anderson) *Dr. Anderson's Antioxidant, Anti-aging Health Program,* Carroll & Graf (New York, NY), 1996.

(With James E. Anderson) *Live Longer Better: Dr. Anderson's Complete Anti-aging Health Program,* Carroll & Graf Publishers (New York, NY) 1997.

(With Robert Johnson) *The New Charleston Program: The Permanent Weight-Control Solution,* Features Enterprises (Tarzana, CA), 2002.

Ghostwriter of books by other authors. Contributor to books, including *Best Places to Stay in America's Cities: Unique Hotels, City Inns, and Bed and Breakfasts,* edited by Kenneth Hale-Wehmann, Harvard Common Press (Cambridge, MA), 1986. Contributor of more than 1,000 articles to magazines, newspapers, and Internet publications, including *Cooking Light, Dun's Business Month, Ladies' Home Journal, Medical World News, Psychology Today, In Touch, Working Mother, Woman's World, Reader's Digest,* and *Liberty: Magazine of Religious Freedom.* Work distributed by Los Angeles Times Syndicate, News America/Times of London, and New York Times Syndicate. Also worked as articles editor, *National Enquirer.*

SIDELIGHTS: Maury M. Breecher once told *CA:* "I learn best by writing about what I have learned. That's why I chose to become a journalist and author. I wanted to be able to support myself by writing about what I have learned. While attending college I started my freelance career by selling an article about the difficulties encountered by the first female at the University of Kansas to be enrolled in the Army ROTC Program. Even after all these years, I remember thinking, 'Wow, they actually paid me to do this!' I've never gotten over that feeling.

"In the summer of 1966, my first paid job in journalism was on the *Parsons Sun,* a newspaper owned and edited by a feisty old newsman named Clyde Reed. I may have learned a bit about being a maverick from Reed. He felt that the spotlight of publicity was good for 'all that ails government.' I still agree with him.

"The pressure of supporting a family forced me to leave college prematurely during my senior year. I was able to talk my way into a wonderful full-time job, a plum assignment covering the Sedgwick County courthouse for the *Wichita Beacon.* The next year I had an opportunity to obtain a significant raise in salary at the *Salina Journal,* and, later, at the Illinois State Medical Society. I jumped at the chance to be in the medical information loop.

"Working for physicians enlightened me in many ways, both positive and negative. I did good work, especially in ghostwriting a series of articles about the growing problem and treatment of alcoholism in Illinois. I had hoped the society would continue to support such programs, but instead, the leaders decided to battle 'increasing governmental interference in medicine.'

"That's why I accepted a job—at double what I was then making—as one of several articles editors at the *National Enquirer.* My primary responsibility was to produce accurate medical stories. At that time, the *Enquirer's* reputation for accuracy wasn't the best. During my tenure there, I helped to develop an arrangement with the National Cancer Institute and the American Cancer Society to check our stories. I also was one of the editors who successfully lobbied for the creation of a research department to double-check the accuracy of medical stories turned in by freelancers and staff. The *National Enquirer* became the only tabloid newspaper—in fact, the only newspaper I know of—to require that tape recordings of interviews with medical experts be turned in with reporters' copy.

"The job had its satisfactions. Still, I wanted to get back to my own writing. I became a ghostwriter, which afforded me income to complete my bachelor's degree and earn a master's degree. Research pursued during that time led me to write *Healthy Homes in a Toxic World.* It was published in 1991, the same year I began studying for a doctorate in mass communication.

"My educational goal was to learn more about mass communication. What does science know about how effective messages are created, transmitted, and received? I enjoyed myself immensely. At the same time I developed diabetes.

"I hope to do future research and writing in the field of mass communication risk assessment and preventive health. Also, since I have the talent to make complicated medical information understandable, I will continue to write on medical topics."

*   *   *

BRIGGS, Asa 1921-

PERSONAL: Born May 7, 1921, in Keighley, Yorkshire, England; son of William Walker and Jane (Spencer) Briggs; married Susan Anne Banwell, September 1, 1955; children: Katharine, Daniel, Judith, Matthew. *Education:* Sidney Sussex College, Cambridge, B.A. (with first class honors), 1941; University of London, B.Sc. (with first class honors), 1941. *Religion:* Anglican. *Hobbies and other interests:* Travel.

Asa Briggs

ADDRESSES: Home—The Caprons, Keere St., Lewes, E. Sussex, England. *Office*—Humphrey, 26 Ockmede Way, Rigmer, East Sussex, England, BN8 SJL.

CAREER: Writer, historian, academic, and administrator. Oxford University, Oxford, England, fellow of Worcester College, 1945-55, university reader in recent social and economic history, 1950-55; University of Leeds, Leeds, England, professor of modern history, 1955-61; University of Sussex, Sussex, England, dean of School of Social Studies, 1961-65, pro-vice-chancellor, 1961-67, vice-chancellor, 1967-76; Oxford University, Oxford, provost of Worcester College, 1976-91. President, European Institute of Education (Paris, France), 1975-1996; governor, British Film Institute, 1970-77; chairman, Committee on Nursing, 1970-72, Heritage Education Group, 1976-86; vice-chairman, United Nations University Council, 1974-80. Trustee, Civic Trust, 1976-86. Created Life Peer, 1976. OECD consultant on Danish higher education, 1977-78. Open University, Milton Keynes, chancellor, 1979-1995. *Military service:* British Army, Intelligence Corps, 1942-45.

MEMBER: Workers Education Association (president, 1958—), Oxford Union Society (senior treasurer, 1952-55), Royal Historical Society, Royal Economic Society (member of council), Sociological Association (member of council), Victorian Society (member of council, president, 1983), Pavilin Brighton Trust, chairman, 1983—; National Council for Economic and Social Research, Society of Authors, British Social History Society (president), William Morris Society (president, 1989-92), Brorke Society, 1987-96.

AWARDS, HONORS: Marconi Medal, 1975, for communications history; Medaille de Vermeil de la Formation, Fondation de l'Academie de Architecture, 1979; Wolfson History Prize, 2000; honorary doctorates from University of East Anglia, University of Strathclyde, University of Leeds, University of Liverpool, Florida Presbyterian University (now Eckerd College), York University (Canada), University of Cincinnati, Bradford, Sussex University, Open University, and University of London.

WRITINGS:

(With D. Thompson and E. Meyer) *Patterns of Peacemaking,* Routledge & Kegan Paul (London, England), 1945.

History of Birmingham (1865-1938), Oxford University Press (Oxford, England), 1952.

Victorian People, Odhams, 1954, University of Chicago Press (Chicago, IL), 1955, revised and illustrated edition published as *Victorian People: A Reassessment of Persons and Themes,* University of Chicago Press (Chicago, IL), 1973, 3rd revised edition, Folio Society, 1986.

Friends of the People, Batsford (London, England), 1956.

The Age of Improvement, Longmans, Green (London, England), 1959, published as *The Making of Modern England, 1783-1867: The Age of Improvement,* Harper (New York, NY), 1965, published as *The Age of Improvement, 1783-1867,* Longman (London, England), 1979, 2nd edition, 1999.

(Editor) *Chartist Studies,* Macmillan (Londond, England), 1959.

(Editor) *They Saw It Happen: An Anthology of Eyewitnesses' Accounts of Events in British History,* Volume IV: *1897-1940,* Basil Blackwell (London, England), 1960.

The History of Broadcasting in the United Kingdom, Oxford University Press (New York, NY), Volume I: *The Birth of Broadcasting,* 1961, Volume II: *The Golden Age of Wireless,* 1965, Volume III, 1970, Volume IV: *Sound and Vision,* 1979, Volume V: *Competition: 1955-1974,* 1995.

A Study of the Work of Seebohm Rowntree, 1871-1954: Social Thought and Social Action, Longmans, Green (London, England), 1961.

Victorian Cities, Odhams, 1963, revised edition, Folio Society, 1996.

(Editor, with John Saville) *Essays in Labour History: In Memory of G.D.H. Cole,* Macmillan (London, England), 1967.

William Cobbett, Oxford University Press (New York, NY), 1968.

(Editor and contributor) *The Nineteenth Century,* Thames & Hudson (London, England), 1970.

(Editor and author of introduction) *William Morris: Selected Writings and Designs,* Penguin (New York, NY), 1973.

(Editor) *Essays in the History of Publishing: A Celebration of the 250th Anniversary of the House of Longman, 1724-1974,* Longman (London, England), 1974.

Iron Bridge to Crystal Palace: Impact and Images of the Industrial Revolution, Thames & Hudson (London, England), 1979.

The Power of Steam: An Illustrated History of the World's Steam Age, M. Joseph, 1982.

Marx in London: An Illustrated Guide, British Broadcasting Corporation (London, England), 1982.

Karl Marx, the Legacy, British Broadcasting Corp. (London, England), 1983.

Social History and Human Experience, Grace A. Tanner Center for Human Values, 1984.

A Social History of England, Viking Press (New York, NY), 1984.

(With Anne Macartney) *Toynbee Hall: The First Hundred Years,* Routledge & Kegan Paul (London, England), 1984.

(Editor and author of introduction) *Gladstone's Boswell: Late Victorian Conversations,* St. Martin's Press (New York, NY), 1984.

(Consultant editor) Alan Isaacs and Elizabeth Martin, editors, *Longman Dictionary of 20th Century Biography,* Longman (Essex, England), 1985.

(Editor and author of text) *The Nineteenth Century: The Contradictions of Progress,* Bonanza Books (New York, NY), 1985.

The BBC: The First Fifty Years, Oxford University Press (New York, NY), 1985.

The Collected Essays of Asa Briggs, University of Illinois Press (Champaign, IL), 1985.

Wine for Sale: Victoria Wine and the Liquor Trade, 1860-1984, University of Chicago Press (Chicago, IL), 1985.

(Editor, with Julian H. Shelley) *Science, Medicine, and the Community: The Last Hundred Years: Proceedings of the Fifth Boehringer Ingelheim Symposium, Held at Kronberg, Taunus, 8th-11th May 1985,* Excerpta Medica (Princeton, NJ), 1986.

(With Joanna Spicer) *The Franchise Affair: Creating Fortunes and Failures in Independent Television,* Century (London, England), 1986.

Victorian Things, University of Chicago Press (Chicago, IL), 1989, reprinted, Sutton Publishing (Stroud, Gloucestershire, England), 2003.

(With Archie Miles) *A Victorian Portrait: Victorian Life and Values As Seen through the Work of Studio Photographers,* Harper & Row (New York, NY), 1989.

(Consultant editor) *A Dictionary of Twentieth-Century World Biography,* Oxford University Press (New York, NY), 1992.

Victorian Cities, foreword by Andres and Lynn Hollen Lees, University of California Press (Berkeley, CA), 1993.

(Editor, with Daniel Snowman) *Fins de siecle: How Centuries End, 1400-2000,* Yale University Press (New Haven, CT), 1996.

(Editor, with Jonathan Andrews, Roy Porter, Penny Tucker, and Keir Waddington) *The History of Bethlem,* Routledge (London, England), 1997.

(With Patricia Clavin) *Modern Europe 1789-1989,* Longman (London, England), 1997, 2nd edition, 2003.

Chartism (pocket edition), Sutton (Stroud, Gloucestershire, England), 1998.

(Consultant editor) *Who's Who in the Twentieth Century,* Oxford University Press (New York, NY), 1999.

Michael Young: Social Entrepreneur, Palgrave (New York, NY), 2000.

Go to It: Working for Victory on the Home Front, 1939-1945, Beazley (London, England), 2000.

(With Peter Burke) *A Social History of the Media: From Gutenberg to the Internet,* Blackwell (Malden, MA), 2001.

Also author of *Governing the BBC,* London, 1979; *Haut-Brion: An Illustrious Lineage,* Faber & Faber (London, England), 1994; and *The Channel Islands: Occupation and Liberation.*

WORK IN PROGRESS: Additional volumes for *The History of Broadcasting in the United Kingdom;* editing *Social and Economic History of England,* nine volumes, for publication by Longman.

SIDELIGHTS: A quick glance at the considerable oeuvre of British historian Asa Briggs shows his interests are wide, but a closer look determines that his particular interests are Victorian social history and culture—titles include *Victorian People, Victorian Cities,* and *Victorian Things*—and communications history, particularly that of the British Broadcasting Corporation, on which he wrote a five-volume history. He was awarded the Marconi Medal in 1975 for his work in that field. Briggs also has been the consulting editor on several dictionaries and reference books, including the *Longman Dictionary of 20th Century Biography, Who's Who in the Twentieth Century,* and *A Dictionary of Twentieth-Century World Biography,* and has edited collections of essays on a variety of topics, such as *Essays in Labour History: In Memory of G.D.H. Cole, Gladstone's Boswell: Late Victorian Conversations,* and *They Saw It Happen: An Anthology of Eyewitnesses' Accounts of Events in British History, Volume IV: 1897-1940.* He has tackled broad topics: *The Nineteenth Century,* *Social History and Human Experience,* and *Modern Europe 1789-1989,* as well as more narrow ones: *A Victorian Portrait: Victorian Life and Values As Seen through the Work of Studio Photographers, Marx in London: An Illustrated Guide,* and *Michael Young: Social Entrepreneur.*

This body of work was produced by a man born in 1921 in Keighly, Yorkshire, an industrial town on the edge of the moors, to a working class family whose members had neither university education nor interest in history. Briggs, however, attended Sidney Sussex College, Cambridge, earning first-class honors in history in 1941, the year that he also earned first-class honors in economics at the University of London. He has had a distinguished academic career, teaching in English, Australian, and American universities, as well as holding several administrative positions. He was a founder and the first dean of the University of Sussex's School of Social Studies, as well as vice-chancellor, and was chancellor of the Open University beginning in 1979. He was made a Life Peer in 1976 with the title Baron.

A. J. P. Taylor of the *Observer Review* wrote of *The Nineteenth Century,* "The volume edited by Asa Briggs is . . . substantial in every sense," yet warned, "The

book is not suited to bedtime reading." Taylor continued, "Professor Briggs himself, with three essays, is a universal provider, a historian's Marks and Spencer." A *Times Literary Supplement* critic described the book as a "lavish survey" and a "formidable volume which, with certain reservations, is an outstanding achievement in popularization." The reviewer criticized the "fragmented" integration of ideas throughout the essays and would have preferred to see a greater scope of nineteenth-century world history encompassed, yet enjoyed Briggs's comments and supporting evidence.

The Power of Steam: An Illustrated History of the World's Steam Age brings the power of illustrations to an examination of industrial history. Beginning with descriptions of the way steam was used in manufacturing about one hundred years before James Watt invented the steam engine, particularly in textile mills, the book works its way up to modern times and the development of internal combustion and electronics. "The book seeks to 'bridge the gulf' between the pictorial albums and the austere volumes of economic history," commented *Scientific American* reviewer Philip Morrison. "Briggs is a distinguished cultural historian of the period; his text is supple and persuasive, although it is more a fragrant broth than a savory hot pot."

Wine for Sale: Victoria Wine and the Liquor Trade, 1860-1984 recounts the efforts of Victoria Wine company founder W. H. Hughes to market wine to the lower- and middle-class London citizens considered uninterested in wine by other wine sellers. He started the business in 1865; by his death, he controlled ninety-eight shops, and he introduced a variety of innovations, including importing the wine himself to cut out the middleman and hiring women as branch managers because he considered them more reliable. Hughes passed the thriving business to his widow, and it continued its success as an independent company until it was purchased by brewing company Taylor & Walker in 1929. By the mid-1980s, it was a subsidiary of Allied Lyons but still had more than nine hundred stores with the Victoria name. "The development of the Victoria Wine business . . . is traced in terms of British contemporary culture and social history," described *Business History Review* contributor R. P. T. Davenport-Hines. "The company's history is intertwined with the evolution of both national palate and of the British class structure." Concluding his review, Davenport-Hines declared, "Asa Briggs writes with grace and wit: his quotations are felicitous, and every page is luminous. Dour mechanicans in the business history community may despise this book; others will delight in it."

The History of Broadcasting in the United Kingdom, Volume V: Competition is a "splendid book" about the British Broadcasting Corporation (BBC), observed *Business History* contributor Michael Sanderson. The period covered is from 1955-1974, and the competition of the title begins with the development of Independent Television, established by the Television Act of 1954, and the resulting advent of commercial television paid for by advertising. The BBC's radio and television branches both are discussed, and Briggs examines people, such as director general Hugh Carleton Green and his innovations, and technological changes and challenges, such as the hand-held transistor radio in 1956 and color television in 1967. Concluded Sanderson, "At 1,133 pages, the book may initially daunt the reader. Have no fear. It is not only an impressive scholarly achievement but a rich, absorbingly readable story told by a master social historian with driving enthusiasm." Anthony Smith, in *New Statesman & Society,* commended the scholarship Briggs has put into his BBC history. "This volume has both short-term and long-term value. It provides a vast cornucopia of information on people, policies, programmes, and for the patient reader, re-evokes the era during which the BBC turned itself from a self-worshipping monopoly into the responsive apparatus of a national culture. . . . The real long-term value of Briggs's project is the way he outlines the issues emerging from the vast mound of . . . files at the BBC's Caversham archives."

Briggs coedited with Daniel Snowman *Fins de siecles: How Centuries End, 1400-2000.* Experts in each period address the history and the historiography of England in the last ten years of each century. *Historian* contributor Robert W. Butler regarded it the most "well written [and] wonderfully illustrated" of the host of books published on the theme. "There are many strong points to this fascinating book," Butler wrote. "Most significant perhaps, is the sense of change over centuries that it evokes. . . . The book bridges the gap [between centuries] not by means of a plodding narrative, but by creating what are actually short biographies of a nation. . . . The result is a riveting and remarkable achievement." He warns, however, that it

"is not a book for beginners." Arthur Marwick, reviewing the book for *English Historical Review,* was less favorable, but he did allow that "The good news is that there are just over ten absolutely brilliant pages by Briggs opening the penultimate chapter, 'The 1890s: Past, Present and Future in Headlines,' a truly scholarly discussion of the origins of notions about 'centuries,' 'the future,' and 'fin de siecle.'" Commented Francis Fukuyama, a *Foreign Affairs* contributor, "More compelling are the sharp social transitions that occur from one century to the next, and the growth of historical consciousness."

Modern Europe 1789-1989, which Briggs cowrote with Patricia Clavin, is the final portion of an illustrated three-volume series on Europe since the fifth century. Clare Griffiths, in *English Historical Review,* remarked that it "tackles its two centuries relatively efficiently," and "in general, the book presents a fairly conventional and dominantly political approach."

Briggs was a coeditor of *The History of Bethlem,* which was published to commemorate the 750th anniversary of this British mental institution. The many site changes, treatment methods, and the patients through the centuries are examined in different essays. "Asa Briggs takes the reader through the age of reform from 1783 to 1900 with characteristic command and panache," noted reviewer Paul Slack in *English Historical Review.*

New Statesman reviewer John Gray referred to Briggs's *Michael Young: Social Entrepreneur* as "one of the liveliest and most engrossing biographies of a living public figure to have been published for some time." Young, head of the Labour Party's research department in the 1940s, helped develop the Consumer's Association, the Open University (where Briggs was eventually chancellor), the Social Science Research Council, the University of the Third Age, and the School of Social Entrepreneurs, but he is most famous for writing *The Rise of the Meritocracy,* a dystopian satire responsible for making the concept of meritocracy very unpopular in British political circles. Gray noted that Briggs "suggests at several points that Young's attitude to meritocracy may be more complex than most of his readers have supposed."

In *A Social History of the Media: From Gutenberg to the Internet,* Briggs's and coauthor Peter Burke's examination of media history, the authors make comparisons between different ages to show how each has had its concerns over the repercussions of its emerging communication technology—the twenty-first century is worried about the dangers of television and the Internet, the sixteenth century worried about the harmful emotions generated by widespread reading. Reviewing the book for *Library Journal,* Susan M. Colowick commented, "Given [the author's belief in the nonlinear evolution of the media, the text moves dizzyingly back and forth, at times verging on stream of consciousness. . . . A meticulous chronology should help to alleviate confusion."

BIOGRAPHICAL AND CRITICAL SOURCES:

PERIODICALS

American Historical Review, review of *The History of Broadcasting in the United Kingdom,* Volume IV, p. 132.

Booklist, November 1, 1992, review of *Dictionary of 20th Century World Biography,* p. 545.

Books & Bookmen, October, 1984, review of *Gladstone's Boswell: Late Victorian Conversations,* p. 7.

Business History, April, 1996, Michael Sanderson, review of *The History of Broadcasting in the United Kingdom,* Volume V: *Competition: 1955-1974,* pp. 112-113.

Business History Review, winter, 1986, R. P. T. Davenport-Hines, review of *Wine for Sale: Victoria Wine and the Liquor Trade, 1860-1984,* pp. 694-695.

Christian Science Monitor, December 5, 1986, review of *The BBC: The First Fifty Years,* p. B3.

Economic History Review, November, 1989, Harold Perkin, review of *Victorian Things,* pp. 604-605.

Economist, December 21, 1985, review of *Wine for Sale,* p. 116; December 7, 1996, review of *Fins de Siecles: How Centuries End, 1400-2000,* p. S6.

English Historical Review, June, 1998, Clare Griffiths, review of *Modern Europe 1789-1989,* pp. 771-772; September, 1998, Arthur Marwick, review of *Fins de Siecles,* pp. 1044-1045; November, 1998, Paul Slack, review of *The History of Bethlem,* p. 1260.

Foreign Affairs, March-April, 1997, Francis Fukuyama, review of *Fins de Siecles,* p. 174.

Historian, winter, 1999, Robert W. Butler, review of *Fins de Siecles,* p. 485.

History Today, August, 1985, John Burrows, review of *Toynebee Hall: The First Hundred Years,* p. 60; November, 1985, review of *The BBC,* p. 58; May 1993, Ian Bradley, review of *The Collected Essays of Asa Briggs,* Volume 3: *Serious Pursuits, Communications and Education,* pp. 57-58.

Journalism Quarterly, spring, 1987, review of *The Franchise Affair,* p. 242.

Journal of Communications, spring, 1981, review of *Governing the BBC,* p. 212; summer, 1992, review of *Serious Pursuits,* p. 207.

Library Journal, March 15, 1990, Barbara J. Dunlap, review of *Victorian Portrait: Victorian Life and Values As Seen through the Work of Studio Photographs,* p. 88; January, 2002, Susan M. Colowick, review of *A Social History of the Media: From Gutenberg to the Internet,* p. 118.

Literature and History, autumn, 1986, review of *The Collected Essays of Asa Briggs,* Volimes 1 and 2, p. 262.

London Review of Books, June 6, 1985, review of *The Nineteenth Century,* p. 3.

New Scientist, February 2, 1991, Ian Stewart, review of *The Longman Encylopedia,* p. 64.

New Statesman, October 15, 2001, John Gray, "A Reputation of Merit," p. 54.

New Statesman & Society, May 29, 1992, David Widgery, review of *Dictionary of 20th Century World Biography,* p. 38; June 2, 1995, Anthony Smith, review of *The History of Broadcasting in the United Kingdom,* Volume V: *Competition: 1955-1974,* pp. 39-40.

New Yorker, June 18, 1984, review of *A Social History of England,* p. 116.

New York Review of Books, April 3, 1980, review of *Iron Bridge to Crystal Palace: Impact and Images of the Industrial Revolution,* p. 35; February 15, 1990, David Cannadine, review of *Victorian Things,* p. 25.

New York Times, March 15, 1983, R. W. Apple, "London Recalls Marx on Centenary of Death," p. C14; April 1, 1984, R. K. Webb, review of *A Social History of England,* pp. 9-10; April 15, 1984, "On the Medieval Menu," (excerpt from *A Social History of England*), p. 43.

New York Times Book Review, August 21, 1983, review of *The Power of Steam: An Illustrated History of the World's Steam Age,* p. 27.

Observer Review, November 29, 1970, A. J. P. Taylor, review of *The Nineteenth Century.*

Scientific American, March, 1983, Philip Morrison, review of *The Power of Steam,* pp. 39-40.

Social Science Quarterly, December 1983, review of *Essays in Labour History: In Memory of G. D. H. Cole,* p. 820.

Times Educational Supplement, July 12, 1991, Maureen O'Connor, "The History Man," p. 22.

Times Literary Supplement, October 30, 1970, review of *The Nineteenth Century;* April 10, 1981, review of *Iron Bridge to Crystal Palace,* p. 396; May 2, 1986, review of *The Franchise Affair,* p. 471.

Victorian Studies, summer, 1990, R. H. Super, review of *Victorian Things,* pp. 651-652.

Village Voice Literary Supplement, March, 1986, review of *Wine for Sale,* p. 4.

Washington Post Book World, November 28, 1982, review of *The Power of Steam,* p. 13.*

*   *   *

BROCK, Rose
See HANSEN, Joseph

*   *   *

BROOKS, Andrée (Nicole) Aelion 1937-

PERSONAL: Born February 2, 1937, in London, England; daughter of Leon Luis (a business executive) and Lillian (Abrahamson) Aelion; married Ronald J. Brooks (an attorney), August 16, 1959 (divorced, August, 1986); children: Allyson, James. *Education:* Northwest London Polytechnic, journalism certificate, 1958.

ADDRESSES: Home and office—15 Hitchcock Rd., Westport, CT 06880. *Agent*—Diane Cleaver, 55 Fifth Ave., New York, NY 10003.

CAREER: Journalist. *Hampstead News,* London, England, reporter, 1954-58; *Photoplay,* New York, NY, story editor, 1958-60; Australian Broadcasting Co., New York, NY, correspondent, 1961-68; *Ladies' Home Journal,* New York, NY, member of editorial staff,

1957-58; freelance journalist, 1960—. Hertsmere Council, conservative representative from Elstree, 1973-74; Fairfield University, Fairfield, CT, adjunct professor of journalism, 1983-87; parent educator, 1987—; Yale University, New Haven, CT, associate fellow, 1989—. Guest on radio and television programs, including *Donahue* and *Oprah.*

MEMBER: Women in Communications, National Federation of Press Women, American Jewish Committee, Connecticut Press Club, British Schools and Universities Club, Halloween Yacht Club.

AWARDS, HONORS: First place awards for newswriting, Connecticut Press Club, 1980, 1981, 1983, 1985, 1987; outstanding achievement award, National Federation of Press Women (NFPW), 1981; awards for news and feature writing, Fairfield County chapter of Women in Communications, 1982, 1983, 1986, 1987; second-place award in magazine writing, National Association of Home Builders, 1982, 1984; special service award, Connecticut chapter of American Planning Association, 1983; first-place award for magazine writing, NFPW, 1983; journalism award, Connecticut Society of Architects, 1984; named American Jewish Woman of Achievement, 1989; first-place award for nonfiction, NFPW, 1990.

WRITINGS:

Children of Fast-Track Parents: Raising Self-Sufficient and Confident Children in an Achievement-Oriented World (nonfiction), Viking (New York, NY), 1989.

The Woman Who Defied Kings: The Life and Times of Dona Gracia Nasi—A Jewish Leader during the Renaissance, Paragon House (St. Paul, MN), 2002.

Russian Dance (biography), Wiley (Hoboken, NJ), 2004.

Author of weekly real-estate column, *New York Times,* 1978—. Contributor to periodicals, including *New York Times, McCall's, Glamour, Advertising Age, Kappan, Woman's Day,* and *Preservation.*

SIDELIGHTS: Journalist Andrée Aelion Brooks once told *CA:* "My writing has always been aimed at airing an issue or a problem of contemporary life that possibly had been overlooked to the detriment of the public at large. The goal is to improve the quality of our lives by creating a climate where corrective or compassionate action can be taken. Issues that I have helped to bring to the public's awareness (long before they became well-known topics) include the financial and emotional problems of single parents, serial marriages, contaminated well water, the dwindling supply of nurses, insensitive and archaic use of zoning powers in relation to modern lifestyle, and conservation needs."

BIOGRAPHICAL AND CRITICAL SOURCES:

PERIODICALS

Behavior Today, October 10, 1988.
Journal of American Management Association, October, 1989.
Journal of the American Orthopsychiatric Association, September, 1989.
New York Times, November 26, 1989.
Washington Post, July 4, 1989.*

C

CARD, Tim(othy) S. B. 1931-2001

PERSONAL: Born November 19, 1931, in Lichfield, England; died, September 13, 2001; son of A. T. T. (a military officer and schoolteacher) and Monica (Beardsley) Card. *Education:* Attended Trinity College, Cambridge, 1952-55. *Politics:* "Central." *Religion:* Church of England.

CAREER: Eton College, Windsor, England, assistant master, 1955-88, vice-provost, beginning 1988. *Military service:* British Army, Infantry, 1950-52; became second lieutenant.

WRITINGS:

Eton Renewed: A History from 1860 to the Present Day, J. Murray (London, England), 1994.
Eton Established, a History from 1440 to 1860, John Murray (London, England), 2001.

SIDELIGHTS: Tim S. B. Card once told *CA:* "I began writing an up-to-date history of Eton College when my two predecessors as vice-provost died on the job. It seemed sensible for marketing reasons to begin with the more recent history, and then go back to the beginning. Honesty and entertainment were my guiding principles, but I hope to have written with some insight about the education of the young male."

Tim Card's second book *Eton Established, a History from 1440 to 1860,* was reviewed by David Horspool in the *Times Literary Supplement* as a "thorough, well-researched continuation of . . . Henry-Maxwell-Lyte['s] . . . *History of Eton College* . . . to recommend it to the Queen as a model for all schools." However, there is little about the school in 1860, according to Card, that supports the reputation of the institution's educational system. Card's history describes the many reforms that took the school from a disorganized "slum tenement" to the respected institution it is today. C. J. Tyerman related in the *English Historical Review* that "*Eton Established* stands as one of the more distinguished in the long line of traditional public school histories; affectionate; introspective; undemanding; often slightly defensive; indulgently critical, regarding human and institutional faults as peccadilloes; a work of homage as much as revelation."

BIOGRAPHICAL AND CRITICAL SOURCES:

PERIODICALS

Contemporary Review, November, 2001, review of *Eton Established,* pp. 315-316.
English Historical Review, June, 2002, C. J. Tyerman, review of *Eton Established,* pp. 730-732.
Times Educational Supplement, May 27, 1994, Andrew Davies, review of *Eton Renewed,* p. A12.
Times Literary Supplement, July 8, 1994, David Horspool, review of *Eton Renewed,* p. 32.

OBITUARIES:

PERIODICALS

Times, September 28, 2001, p. 23.*

CERULLO, Mary M. 1949-

PERSONAL: Born September 6, 1949, in San Francisco, CA; daughter of George R. (an engineer) and Kathleen (a homemaker; maiden name, Waltz) Moore; married Arthur Cerullo (an attorney), August 19, 1973; children: Christopher, Margaret. *Education:* Tufts University, B.S. (cum laude), 1971; Boston University, M.Ed., 1981. *Hobbies and other interests:* Hiking, biking, camping with family and friends.

ADDRESSES: Home—South Portland, ME. *Agent*— c/o Author Mail, Dutton, 345 Hudson St., New York, NY 10014.

CAREER: RISE (Resources in Science Education), owner and consultant to schools and environmental organizations, 1988—; Maine Mathematics and Science Alliance, communications coordinator.

MEMBER: Gulf of Maine Marine Education Association (president), Maine Writers and Publishers Association.

AWARDS, HONORS: Outstanding Marine Educator of 1992, National Marine Education Association; Outstanding Science Trade Books for Children citation, National Science Teachers Association/Children's Book Council (NSTA/CBC), for *Sharks: Challengers of the Deep* and *Lobsters: Gangsters of the Sea;* Outstanding 1999 Books, *Appraisal* magazine, and Notable Books for Children citation, *Smithsonian* magazine, 1999, both for *Sea Soup: Phytoplankton;* Notable Books for Children citation, *Smithsonian* magazine, 2000, Honor Book, Society of School Librarians International, 2001, and Outstanding Science Trade Books for Children citation, NSTA/CBC, 2002, all for *Sea Soup: Zooplankton;* Lupine Award, Maine State Library Association, 2000, for *The Truth about Great White Sharks.*

WRITINGS:

Sharks: Challengers of the Deep, photographs by Jeffrey L. Rotman, Dutton/Cobblehill (New York, NY), 1993, reprinted as part of the series *Paperback Plus Teacher's Resource. Level 6. Easy,* Houghton Mifflin (Boston, MA), 1996.

Lobsters: Gangsters of the Sea, photographs by Jeffrey L. Rotman, Dutton/Cobblehill (New York, NY), 1994.

Coral Reef: A City That Never Sleeps, Dutton/Cobblehill (New York, NY), 1996.

The Octopus: Phantom of the Sea, photographs by Jeffrey L. Rotman, Dutton (New York, NY), 1997.

Reading the Environment: Children's Literature in the Science Classroom, Heinemann (Portsmouth, NH), 1997.

Dolphins: What They Can Teach Us, photographs by Jeffrey L. Rotman, Scholastic (New York, NY), 1998.

Sea Soup: Phytoplankton, photographs by Bill Curtsinger, Tilbury House (Gardiner, ME), 1999.

The Truth about Great White Sharks, photographs by Jeffrey L. Rotman, illustrated by Michael Wertz, Chronicle Books (San Francisco, CA), 2000.

Ocean Detectives: Solving the Mysteries of the Sea, (with teacher's resource binder, videocassette, and posters), Steck-Vaughn (Austin, TX), 2000.

Sea Soup: Zooplankton, photographs by Bill Curtsinger, Tilbury House (Gardiner, ME), 2001.

The Truth about Dangerous Sea Creatures, photographs by Jeffrey L. Rotman, illustrated by Michael Wertz, Chronicle Books (San Francisco, CA), 2003.

Life under Ice, photographs by Bill Curtsinger, Tilbury House (Gardiner, ME), 2003.

Sea Turtles: Ocean Nomads, photographs by Jeffrey L. Rotman, Dutton (New York, NY), 2003.

SIDELIGHTS: Mary M. Cerullo has made a career of writing books that champion misunderstood or overlooked creatures in the world's oceans. Her texts are well-regarded for being informative, thought-provoking, and well-written, of interest to both report-writers and browsers. While providing information about feeding, mating, and endangerment, Cerullo is credited with keeping her eye upon the intriguing details that often capture children's imaginations. Her science books are generally written in a casual tone, in short bursts of prose that seamlessly interweave facts about her subjects. Though some reviewers have complained that this makes her books difficult to use for some students, others have praised Cerullo's choice as one particularly engaging for reluctant readers.

Introducing youngsters to marine life, the author has written books that help erase some common myths about sea creatures. She once told *CA,* "Although I teach and write about other areas of science, I am most intrigued by ocean life, partly because so little is known about even the most popular (or infamous) animals of the sea, such as sharks, octopuses, dolphins, and whales. I found when I was researching *Sharks: Challengers of the Deep* that scientists couldn't even agree on how many species of sharks there are, let alone about their behavior, how long they live, and their number of offspring. Part of the reason I wrote the book was to dispel some of the prejudices against sharks that portray them as blood-thirsty man-eaters."

Sharks is filled with information about sharks' anatomy, habits, reproduction, survival, and behavior, including the fact that out of 350 species of sharks, only five to ten percent are potential man-eaters. Interestingly, as Cerullo reveals in her book, a large shark produces as many as twenty thousand teeth in a ten year span of time. Recalling her early experiences with actual sharks, Cerullo once told *CA:* "After more than twenty years of writing and teaching about the ocean, I . . . became a certified scuba diver. My first open ocean dive was in the Bahamas, in the company of ten Caribbean reef sharks. I sat on the ocean floor almost breathless as sharks swarmed around a diver handing out fish scraps and then silently glided over my head. At one point, I turned around to discover a shark watching me from ten feet away. I looked at it, it looked at me. It blinked first (with a nictitating membrane) and swam off."

Lobsters: Gangsters of the Sea is a good, early example of Cerullo's approach to her subject. The focus is on the crustacean's relationship with the human world and the behavior revealed as they are farmed, hunted, caught, cooked, and eaten. Cerullo takes her intriguing title from the lobster's reputation for behaving in an excessively aggressive and territorial manner, even toward other lobsters. "Cerullo's style is informal and immediate," remarked Hazel Rochman in *Booklist.* "Scientific discoveries and questions raised about the continued health of the species round out a first-rate presentation," contended Margaret A. Bush in *Horn Book.*

Unlike some of her other titles, *Coral Reef: A City That Never Sleeps* focuses on a wide variety of sea life in its highly-illustrated pages. Keeping the metaphor of the title alive throughout the book, Cerullo brings the densely populated crevices of the coral reef home to young readers who may never see a coral reef

in person. This "intelligently constructed and highly appealing presentation [ends] on a thought-provoking note," remarked Bush in *Horn Book,* referring to the author's essay on destruction of the coral reefs and conservation efforts. And, like Cerullo's other books on sea-life, *Coral Reef* features numerous photographs that bring the world of these creatures alive. The combination of a "fascinatingly fact-filled" text and "clear, bright, well-composed pictures" makes this book "a standout" according to Lisa Wu Stowe in *School Library Journal.*

In *The Octopus: Phantom of the Sea* Cerullo discusses one of the most mysterious sea creatures in existence and one often considered among the most frightening. Here, the author offers an "objective and respectful look" at the life cycle, feeding, and mating habits of this cephalopod, which can regenerate, create camouflage, and swim by jet propulsion, according to Denia Hester in *Booklist.* "This is a spellbinding look at the octopus, up close and personal," remarked Janice M. Del Negro in the *Bulletin of the Center for Children's Books.*

Almost as mysterious and perhaps even more often the subject of nightmares are the so-called man-eating sharks, the subject of Cerullo's book, *The Truth about Great White Sharks.* As in many of her science books for young adults, the focus is on the relationship with humans, and the work of various marine biologists who research great white shark habits, mating, and longevity are prominently featured in these pages.

By contrast, the mammals at the center of Cerullo's *Dolphins: What They Teach Us* have long been a favorite of humanity for their friendliness, intelligence, and usefulness. Here, Cerullo highlights the interplay of humans and dolphins through research in echolocation, hydrodynamics, and deep-diving, as well as therapy programs with sick children. The book is structured by visits to various dolphin research labs and thus is somewhat more difficult to follow than Cerullo's other books, according to some reviewers. However, "this title is a good supplemental source" concluded Arwen Marshall in *School Library Journal,* adding, "it has lots of appeal for casual readers and fans of this popular animal."

In *Sea Turtles: Ocean Nomads,* Cerullo turns her attention to these hard-backed creatures who seem so solid and yet teeter on the brink of extinction. Described as "a first rate choice" by *School Library Journal* critic Susan Oliver, *Sea Turtles* offers readers information about the long-lived turtle, including facts about its physical characteristics, habitat, and endangered status. "The narrative is lively and immediate," claimed *Booklist* contributor Catherine Andronik, who went on to predict that *Sea Turtles* "will please students."

In two related books, Cerullo brings to life the microscopic plants and animals that make the ocean's water a source of sustenance for smaller creatures. In *Sea Soup: Zooplankton* and *Sea Soup: Phytoplankton,* the author uses a question-and-answer format to detail the lives of these tiny flora and fauna. "This is a fascinating look at a watery zoo of creatures," remarked Patricia Manning in a *School Library Journal* review of *Sea Soup: Zooplankton.* Accompanied by a teacher's guide for each volume, written by Betsy Stevens, the book provides "a wonderfully unusual resource that provides many opportunities for students to learn about marine life, ecology, and global warming," concluded a critic, reviewing *Sea Soup: Phytoplankton* in *Appraisal.* The author has also written *Ocean Detectives,* which outlines how oceanographers solve the mysteries of the ocean. For teachers, *Reading the Environment: Children's Literature in the Science Classroom* makes the case for combining science and literature studies for children in order to help them learn about and record the world around them.

Cerullo once told *CA:* "At thirteen, I decided to become an oceanographer because adults were always asking me, 'What do you want to be when you grow up?' If they were asking, I figured I was supposed to have my future planned out. I studied through high school and college preparing for a career in oceanography. I put off six or more years of graduate school and started working at the New England Aquarium in Boston. It was there that I discovered I was really a dilettante, not a scientist, and that I preferred learning a little about a lot of different subjects rather than specializing in one narrow field of study.

"I love collecting children's books on science, both fact and fiction. I keep finding new favorite authors, including Joanna Cole, Patricia Lauber, and Lynne Cherry. One of the things I enjoy most is helping elementary teachers use children's trade books to teach science."

BIOGRAPHICAL AND CRITICAL SOURCES:

PERIODICALS

American Biology Teacher, May, 2002, Mark C. Belk, review of *Sea Soup: Zooplankton,* p. 386.

American Scientist, November, 1994, p. 568.

Appraisal, fall, 1993, p. 14; spring-summer-fall, 2000, review of *Sea Soup: Phytoplankton,* p. 19, and review of *Ocean Detectives: Solving the Mysteries of the Sea,* p. 167.

Booklist, January 15, 1993, p. 887; March 1, 1994, Hazel Rochman, review of *Lobsters: Gangsters of the Sea,* p. 1254; March 1, 1996, Chris Sherman, review of *Coral Reef: A City That Never Sleeps,* p. 1175; February 1, 1997, Denia Hester, review of *The Octopus: Phantom of the Sea,* p. 936; March 15, 2000, Carolyn Phelan, review of *Sea Soup: Phytoplankton,* p. 1372; April 1, 2000, Shelle Rosenfeld, review of *The Truth about Great White Sharks,* p. 1456; July, 2001, Carolyn Phelan, review of *Sea Soup: Zooplankton,* p. 2001; May 15, 2003, Catherine Andronik, review of *Sea Turtles: Ocean Nomads,* p. 1658.

Bulletin of the Center for Children's Books, February, 1997, Janice M. Del Negro, review of *The Octopus,* p. 201; February, 1999, Janice M. Del Negro, review of *Dolphins: What They Can Teach Us,* p. 197.

Faces, October, 2001, review of *Coral Reef,* p. 46.

Horn Book, January-February, 1994, Margaret A. Bush, review of *Lobsters,* p. 87; March-April, 1996, Margaret A. Bush, review of *Coral Reef,* p. 223.

Kirkus Reviews, December 15, 1992, p. 1569; February 15, 1994, review of *Lobsters;* November 15, 1996, review of *The Octopus,* p. 1667; January 1, 1999, review of *Dolphins,* p. 63; May 1, 2003, review of *Sea Turtles,* p. 674.

Plays, May, 1999, review of *Dolphins,* p. 75.

Publishers Weekly, March 20, 2000, "Animal Friends," review of *The Truth about Great White Sharks,* p. 94.

School Library Journal, February, 1993, p. 96; March, 1994, Karey Wehner, review of *Lobsters,* p. 226; January, 1996, Lisa Wu Stowe, review of *Coral Reef,* p. 115; December, 1997, Kathleen McCabe, review of *The Octopus,* p. 134; April, 1998, Edith Ching, review of *Reading the Environment: Children's Literature in the Science Classroom,* p.

47; March, 1999, Arwen Marshall, review of *Dolphins,* p. 218; May, 2000, Nora Jane Natke, review of *Sea Soup: Phytoplankton,* p. 179; July, 2000, Nora Jane Natke, review of *The Truth about Great White Sharks,* p. 92; December, 2000, review of *The Truth about Great White Sharks,* p. 52; August, 2001, Patricia Manning, review of *Sea Soup: Zooplankton,* p. 193; July, 2003, Susan Oliver, review of *Sea Turtles,* p. 138.

Science Books and Films, April, 1993, p. 84; August, 1994, p. 176; December, 1997, Johnes K. Moore, review of *The Octopus,* p. 275.

Wildlife Conservation, September-October, 2001, review of *Sea Soup: Phytoplankton,* p. 68.*

*   *   *

CODRESCU, Andrei 1946-
(Betty Laredo, Marie Parfenie, Urmuz)

PERSONAL: Born December 20, 1946, in Sibiu, Romania; immigrated to the United States, 1966; naturalized U.S. citizen, 1981; son of Julius and Eva (Mantel) Codrescu; married Alice Henderson, 1968; children: Lucian, Tristan. *Education:* Attended University of Bucharest.

ADDRESSES: Agent—Jonathan Lazear, 930 First Ave. N., Suite 416, Minneapolis, MN 55401. *E-mail*—acodrescu@aol.com.

CAREER: Writer, journalist, editor, and translator. Johns Hopkins University, Baltimore, MD, visiting assistant professor, 1979-80; Naropa Institute, Boulder, CO, visiting professor; Louisiana State University, Baton Rouge, professor of English, beginning in 1984. Regular commentator on National Public Radio's *All Things Considered.* Appeared in the Peabody Award-winning documentary film *Road Scholar,* directed by Roger Weisberg, Metro- Goldwyn-Mayer, 1993.

MEMBER: American-Romanian Academy of Arts and Sciences, Modern Language Association of America, American Association of University Professors, Authors League of America, PEN American Chapter.

AWARDS, HONORS: Big Table Younger Poets Award, 1970, for *License to Carry a Gun;* National Endowment for the Arts fellowships, 1973, 1983; Pushcart

Andrei Codrescu

Prize, 1980, for "Poet's Encyclopedia," and 1983, for novella *Samba de Los Agentes;* A.D. Emmart Humanities Award, 1982; National Public Radio fellowship, 1983; Towson University prize for literature, 1983, for *Selected Poems: 1970-1980;* National Endowment for the Arts grants, 1985, 1988; General Electric/CCLM Poetry Award, 1985, for "On Chicago Buildings"; American-Romanian Academy of Arts and Sciences Book Award, 1988; George Foster Peabody Award, Best Documentary Film, San Francisco Film Festival, Best Documentary Film, Seattle Film Festival, Cine Award, and Golden Eagle Award, all for *Road Scholar;* ACLU Civil Liberties Award, 1995; Romanian National Foundation Literature Award, 1996.

WRITINGS:

POETRY

License to Carry a Gun, Big Table/Follett (Chicago, IL), 1970.

A Serious Morning, Capra Press (Santa Barbara, CA), 1973.

The History of the Growth of Heaven, George Braziller (New York, NY), 1973, originally published in limited edition chapbook, Kingdom Kum Press (San Francisco, CA), 1973.

For the Love of a Coat, Four Zoas Press (Boston, MA), 1978.

The Lady Painter, Four Zoas Press (Boston, MA), 1979.

Necrocorrida, Panjandrum (Los Angeles, CA), 1982.

Selected Poems: 1970-1980, Sun Books (New York, NY), 1983.

Comrade Past and Mister Present, Coffee House Press (Minneapolis, MN), 1986, 2nd edition, 1991.

Belligerence, Coffee House Press (Minneapolis, MN), 1991.

Alien Candor: Selected Poems, 1970-1995, Black Sparrow Press (Santa Rosa, CA), 1996.

It Was Today: New Poems by Andrei Codrescu, Coffee House Press (Minneapolis, MN), 2003.

NOVELS

The Repentance of Lorraine, Pocket Books (New York, NY), 1976.

Monsieur Teste in America and Other Instances of Realism, Coffee House Press (Minneapolis, MN), 1987, Romanian edition translated by Traian Gardus and Lacrimioara Stoie, published as *Domnul Teste in America,* Editura Dacia (Cluj, Romania), 1993.

The Blood Countess, Simon & Schuster (New York, NY), 1995.

Messiah, Simon & Schuster (New York, NY), 1999.

Casanova in Bohemia, Free Press (New York, NY), 2002.

ESSAYS

A Craving for Swan, Ohio State University Press (Columbus, OH), 1986.

Raised by Puppets Only to Be Killed by Research, Addison-Wesley (Reading, MA), 1988.

The Disappearance of the Outside: A Manifesto for Escape, Addison-Wesley (Reading, MA), 1990, Romanian edition translated by Ruxandra Vasilescu, published as *Disparitia Lui Afara,* Editura Univers (Bucharest), 1995.

The Muse Is Always Half-Dressed in New Orleans and Other Essays, St. Martin's Press (New York, NY), 1993.

Zombification: Stories from NPR, St. Martin's Press (New York, NY), 1994.

The Dog with the Chip in His Neck: Essays from NPR and Elsewhere, St. Martin's Press (New York, NY), 1996.

Hail Babylon! In Search of the American City at the End of the Millennium, St. Martin's Press (New York, NY), 1998.

Ay, Cuba! A Socio-Erotic Journal, St. Martin's Press (New York, NY), 1999.

The Devil Never Sleeps and Other Essays, St. Martin's Press (New York, NY), 2000.

CHAPBOOKS; LIMITED EDITIONS

Why I Can't Talk on the Telephone (stories), Kingdom Kum Press (San Francisco, CA), 1972.

The Here What Where (poetry), Isthmus Press (San Francisco, CA), 1972.

Grammar and Money (poetry), Arif Press (Berkeley, CA), 1973.

A Mote Suite for Jan and Anselm (poetry), Stone Pose Art (San Francisco, CA), 1976.

Diapers on the Snow (poetry), Crowfoot Press (Ann Arbor, MI), 1981.

RADIO/AUDIO RECORDINGS

Traffic au bout du temps (poetry reading), Watershed Intermedia (Washington, DC), 1980.

American Life with Andrei Codrescu, National Public Radio (Washington, DC), 1984.

New Letters on the Air: Andrei Codrescu (poetry reading and interview), KSUR Radio (Kansas City, KS), 1987.

An Exile's Return, National Public Radio (Washington, DC), 1990.

Common Ground (radio series on world affairs), Stanley Foundation, 1991.

(With Spalding Grey, Linda Barry, Tom Bodett, and others) *First Words* (tape and compact disc; introductory recording to "Gang of Seven" spoken word series), BMG Distribution, 1992.

No Tacos for Saddam (tape and compact disc; "Gang of Seven" spoken word series), BMG Distribution, 1992.

Fax Your Prayers, Dove Audio (Los Angeles, CA), 1995.

Plato Sucks, Dove Audio (Los Angeles, CA), 1996.

Valley of Christmas, Gert Town, 1997.

OTHER

(Editor, with Pat Nolan) *The End over End,* privately printed, 1974.

(Translator) *For Max Jacob* (poetry), Tree Books (Berkeley, CA), 1974.

The Life and Times of an Involuntary Genius (autobiography), George Braziller, 1975.

In America's Shoes (autobiography), City Lights (San Francisco, CA), 1975.

(Editor and contributor) *American Poetry since 1970: Up Late* (anthology), Four Walls Eight Windows (New York, NY), 1987, 2nd edition, 1990.

(Editor) *The Stiffest of the Corpse: An Exquisite Corpse Reader,* City Lights (San Francisco, CA), 1988.

(Translator) Lucian Blaga, *At the Court of Yearning: Poems by Lucian Blaga,* Ohio State University Press (Columbus, OH), 1989.

The Hole in the Flag: A Romanian Exile's Story of Return and Revolution (reportage), Morrow (New York, NY), 1991.

Road Scholar (screenplay), directed by Roger Weisberg, Metro-Goldwyn-Mayer, 1993.

Road Scholar: Coast to Coast Late in the Century (reportage), with photographs by David Graham, Hyperion (New York, NY), 1994.

(Editor) *Reframing America: Alexander Alland, Otto Hagel & Hansel Mieth, John Gutmann, Lisette Model, Marion Palfi, Robert Frank,* University of New Mexico Press (Albuquerque, NM), 1995.

(Editor, with Laura Rosenthal) *American Poets Say Goodbye to the Twentieth Century,* Four Walls Eight Windows (New York, NY), 1996.

(Author of essay) *Walker Evans: Signs,* J. Paul Getty Museum (Los Angeles, CA), 1998.

A Bar in Brooklyn; Novellas & Stories 1970-1978, Black Sparrow Press (Santa Rosa, CA), 1999.

(Author of introduction) Kerri McCaffety, *Obituary Cocktail: The Great Saloons of New Orleans,* 2nd edition, Winter Books (New Orleans, LA), 1999.

(Author of commentary) *Land of the Free: What Makes Americans Different,* photographs by David Graham, Aperture (New York, NY), 1999.

(Editor, with Laura Rosenthal) *Thus Spake the Corpse: An Exquisite Corpse Reader, 1988-1998,* two volumes, Black Sparrow Press (Santa Rosa, CA), 2000.

An Involuntary Genius in America's Shoes and What Happened Afterwards, Black Sparrow Press (Santa Rosa, CA), 2001.

(Author of essay) Walker Evans, *Walker Evans, Cuba,* introduction by Judith Keller, J. Paul Getty Museum (Los Angeles, CA), 2001.

Also author, under pseudonym Betty Laredo, of *Meat from the Goldrush* and *36 Poems by Betty Laredo.* Author of novella *Samba de Los Agentes.* Contributor to anthologies, including *The World Anthology,* Bobbs-Merrill, 1969; *Another World,* Bobbs-Merrill, 1973; *The Fiction Collective Anthology,* Braziller, 1975; *Kaidmeon: An International Anthology,* Athens, 1976; *The Penguin Anthology of British and American Surrealism,* Penguin, 1978; *The Random House Anthology of British and American Surrealism,* Random House, 1979; *Longman Poetry Anthology,* Longman, 1985. Author of columns "La Vie Boheme," 1979-82, and "The Last Word," 1981-85, and a biweekly editorial column, "The Penny Post," all for the Baltimore *Sun*; author of monthly book column "The Last Word," for *Sunday Sun* and *Philadelphia Inquirer,* 1982—; author of weekly column "Caveman Cry," for *Soho Arts Weekly,* 1985-86; author of weekly book column "Melville & Frisby," for the *City Paper* in Baltimore and Washington, DC; author of the column "Actual Size," for *Organica,* and of weekly book review for National Public Radio's *Performance Today.*

Contributor of poetry, sometimes under pseudonyms Urmuz and Marie Parfenie, to periodicals, including *Poetry, Poetry Review, Chicago Review, World, Antaeus, Sun, Confrontation, Isthmus,* and *Editions Change*; also contributor of short stories and book reviews to periodicals, including *Washington Post Book World, New York Times Book Review, American Book Review, Chicago Review, Playboy, Tri-Quarterly, Paris Review, World Press Review, Co-Evolution Quarterly,* and *New Directions Annual.* Poetry editor, *City Paper,* 1978-80, and Baltimore *Sun,* 1979-83; contributing editor, *San Francisco Review of Books,* 1978-83, and *American Book Review,* 1983—; editor, *Exquisite Corpse: A Journal of Books and Ideas,* 1983-1997; contributing editor, *Cover: The Arts,* 1986-88; editor, *American Poetry,* 1970—. Member of advisory board, *Performance Today* and *ARA: Journal of the American Romanian Academy of Arts and Sciences.*

Codrescu's writing has been translated into six languages. A collection of Codrescu's manuscripts is kept at the Hill Memorial Library, Louisiana State University.

ADAPTATIONS: The Blood Countess has been recorded by Simon & Schuster Audio, read by Codrescu and Suzanne Bartish, 1995.

SIDELIGHTS: A Romanian-born poet, fiction writer, editor, and journalist, Andrei Codrescu was expelled from the University of Bucharest for his criticism of the communist government and fled his homeland before he was conscripted into the army. Traveling to Rome, the young writer learned to speak fluent Italian; he then went to Paris and finally to the United States. Arriving in the United States in 1966 without any money or knowledge of English, Codrescu was nonetheless impressed with the social revolution that was occurring around the country. Within four years he had learned to speak colloquial English colorfully and fluently enough to write and publish his first poetry collection, *License to Carry a Gun.* The collection was hailed by many critics who recognized Codrescu to be a promising young poet.

Although Codrescu enjoys the artistic freedoms that exist in the United States, he is still as critical of bureaucracy in his adopted country as he was in his native Romania—a skepticism that is made evident in his poetry and his autobiographies, *The Life and Times of an Involuntary Genius* and *In America's Shoes.* "In Mr. Codrescu's native Transylvania," Bruce Schlain observed in a *New York Times Book Review* article on the author's poetry collection *Comrade Past and Mister Present,* "poets are social spokesmen, and that perhaps explains his fearlessness of treading on the languages of philosophy, religion, politics, science or popular culture. His focus on a pet theme, oppression, is as much concerned with the private as with the public."

Just as *Comrade Past and Mister Present* compares East and West through poetry, in *The Disappearance of the Outside: A Manifesto for Escape* Codrescu discusses the matter in direct prose. He addresses here such subjects as the mind-numbing effects of television and mass marketing, the sexual and political implications that are a part of language, and the use of drugs and alcohol. "In line with his literary modern-

ism," wrote Josephine Woll in the *Washington Post Book World,* "[Codrescu's] tastes run to the whimsical, the surreal (about which he writes with great understanding), even the perverse. He means to provoke, and he does. His ideas are worth thinking about." Codrescu's skill as an observant commentator about life in the United States has been praised by critics.

Codrescu returned to Romania after twenty-five years to observe firsthand the 1989 revolution that shook dictator Nicolai Ceausescu from power. The range of emotions Codrescu experienced during this time, from exhilaration to cynicism, are described in the volume *The Hole in the Flag: A Romanian Exile's Story of Return and Revolution.* Initially enthusiastic over the prospects of a new political system to replace Ceausescu's repressive police state, Codrescu became disheartened as neo-communists, led by Ion Iliescu, co-opted the revolution. Iliescu himself exhorted gangs of miners to beat student activists "who represented to Codrescu the most authentic part of the revolution in Bucharest," according to Alfred Stepan in the *Times Literary Supplement.* "It seemed to him the whole revolution had been a fake, a film scripted by the Romanian communists."

In preparation for the 1993 book and documentary film *Road Scholar: Coast to Coast Late in the Century,* Codrescu drove across the United States in a red Cadillac accompanied by photographer David Graham and a video crew. Encountering various aspects of the American persona in such cities as Detroit and Las Vegas, Codrescu filters his experiences through a distinctively wry point of view. "Codrescu is the sort of writer who feels obliged to satirize and interplay with reality and not just catalogue impressions," observed Francis X. Clines in the *New York Times Book Review,* who compared Codrescu's journey to the inspired traveling of "road novelist" Jack Kerouac and poet Walt Whitman.

The title of Codrescu's 1995 novel *The Blood Countess* refers to Elizabeth Bathory, a sixteenth-century Hungarian noblewoman notorious for bathing in the blood of hundreds of murdered girls. "While during the day she functions as administrator for her and her husband's estates . . . at night, in her private quarters, she rages at, tortures, and frequently kills the endless supply of peasant maidens. . . . Convinced that blood restores the youth of her skin, she installs a cage over her bath, in which young girls are pierced to death," noted Robert L. McLaughlin in the *American Book Review.*

Codrescu tells Bathory's gruesome story in tandem with a contemporary narrative about the countess's descendant, Drake Bathory-Kereshtur, a U.S. reporter working in Budapest. Of royal lineage, Drake is called upon by Hungarian monarchists to become the next king (although the true goal of this group, which Drake soon suspects, is to install a fascist government). During the course of Drake's travels in Hungary, he meets up with various manifestations of Elizabeth and eventually is seduced by her spirit to commit murder. "Pleating the sixteenth century with the twentieth, Codrescu is nervously alert for recurrent patterns of evil and its handmaiden, absolute authority," pointed out *Time* contributor R. Z. Sheppard. "Both Elizabeth's and Drake's Hungarys are emerging from long periods of totalitarian culture," commented McLaughlin in the *American Book Review.* The critic further stated, "These monolithic systems, by tolerating no heresy, were able to establish virtually unquestioned order and stability for a period of time. But when these periods end, the societies are thrown into chaos." During the era of communist repression in Hungary, the violence inextricably linked to the land was dormant. But in the words of Nina Auerbach in the *New York Times Book Review,* "ancient agents of savagery" are roused from sleep in *The Blood Countess* after the fall of communism and during the resultant political upheaval— these evil forces "overwhelm modernity and its representative, the bemused Drake."

While some reviewers commented on the horrific aspects of *The Blood Countess,* Bettina Drew pointed out in the *Washington Post Book World* that "Codrescu has done more than tap into a Western fascination, whipped up by Hollywood Draculas and vampires. . . . He has written a vivid narrative of the sixteenth century . . . [and] has made the history of Hungary and its shifting contemporary situation entertaining and compelling." Although McLaughlin observed in the *American Book Review* that *The Blood Countess*'s "historical foundation is interesting; the incidents of its parallel plots keep one turning the pages; it has much to say about our world." Sheppard observed in *Time* that "*The Blood Countess* offers stylish entertainment," while *Entertainment Weekly* contributor Margot Mifflin found the book "beautifully written and meticulously researched."

Like *Zombification,* the volume of essays that precedes it, *The Dog with the Chip in His Neck: Essays from NPR and Elsewhere* collects Codrescu's commentaries

for National Public Radio's "All Things Considered" along with other essays and addresses that Codrescu has published or presented, as the title suggests, elsewhere. In an interview with *New Orleans Magazine,* Codrescu commented on the experience of writing poetry and fiction and of writing prose: "I write poetry and fiction for pleasure, and nonfiction for money. [Nonfiction] is plenty of fun; it's just sloweddown poetry." In this collection, Codrescu attempts to slow down the motion of mass culture in America. Joanne Wilkinson, writing for *Booklist,* noted that "Codrescu is a very distinctive writer, displaying a formidable command of the language, heady opinions, and a mordant sense of humor. This potent combination makes him perfectly suited to address America's strange brew of high culture and low."

In *Ay Cuba! A Socio-Erotic Journey,* Codrescu addresses another strange brew, this time the mix of exotic sensuality and heavy-handed dogma in Castro's Cuba. Growing out of Codrescu's visit in late 1997 "to see for myself a decomposing ideology," the book "takes the form of an ironic travelogue-cum-report from the front," according to a *Publishers Weekly* contributor. What Codrescu found was an island surviving on a black market catering to Western tourists, including a number of Americans defying the U.S. travel ban, presided over by an aging revolutionary who keeps the faith while turning a blind eye to the hustlers, prostitutes, and illegal entrepreneurs who actually keep the economy from collapsing. But this is not a political exposé. Instead, it is a series of revealing encounters with a wide variety of Cubans, from street people to doctors, bureaucrats, and Santeria practitioners. "The result is a lively, tragicomic look at Cuba, enriched by insights gleaned from Codrescu's own experience with communism," noted *Library Journal* reviewer Boyd Childress. "In the end, it is refreshing to read a Cuban account where the human takes such firm precedence over the political," concluded Henry Shukman in the *New York Times.*

Codrescu returned to the novel with *Casanova in Bohemia,* again fictionalizing a real historical figure and providing an odd connection to modern times. This time his subject is the legendary Giacomo Casanova, but at a time when old age has generally reduced his sexual adventures to voyeurism and storytelling. The stories are told largely to Laura Brock, a maidservant at the castle where Casanova works as librarian to Count Waldstein and completes his fascinating memoirs. "There is no plot to this novel. Rather it follows the ramblings of a nostalgic and learned man as he looks back in delight and forward with dread," noted reviewer Brigitte Weeks in the *Washington Post.* Along with the seductions that have made his very name part of the language, Casanova recounts his travels throughout Europe and his encounters with Benjamin Franklin, Mozart, Marie Antoinette, and other notables from his long and illustrious life. He also muses on a vast range of subjects, reminding the reader that he has authored books on physics, mathematics, and even the history of cheese. "Taking full advantage of the factual eccentricities of his subject, Codrescu succeeds in probing the depths and details of his fictional subject. The reader feels as if he or she has had a close, almost intimate relationship with the elderly roué. Codrescu's imagination is astounding," wrote Weeks.

But of course the sexual escapades, both real and imagined, play a central role throughout the novel, and "Codrescu fans will enjoy this tongue-in-cheek patchwork of bawdy escapades," noted Chicago *Tribune Books* reviewer Brian Bouldrey. "This is ultimately a fun and sexy romp through a libertine's freely fictionalized life," observed a *Kirkus Reviews* contributor. The main character is every bit the rake that has been imagined, but with one major difference: he is not the cold-blooded seducer some have portrayed, eagerly corrupting virgins before moving on to his next victim. "As Codrescu points out, Casanova's image has been reimagined and degraded 'by the likes of Federico Fellini and other unfair or rancorous assassins of his character.' . . . Codrescu's novel is a valuable corrective and a useful piece of pop history. It's also a blast," concluded *Times-Picayune* reviewer Phil Nugent. In the novel, Casanova gets to see that degradation up close, living well past his "official" death in 1798 to see his name dragged down and his works either banned or hopelessly sanitized, until 1960 when a proper French edition of his memoirs is finally published.

Codrescu returns to poetry in *It Was Today,* once again displaying his wide range. In one poem, he imagines a dialogue between two lovers in fourteenth-century China. The collection itself moves between lighter, everyday poems and more serious pieces, harking back to a grim youth in communist Romania and the struggles of a refugee in a foreign land. "No matter which poet is speaking, the effect is arresting," ob-

served *Library Journal* reviewer Rochelle Ratner. For a *Publishers Weekly* contributor, these poems express the wisdom of a radical "whose pop and zing has been mellowed not with age so much as the bodily memory . . . of having seen more than most."

BIOGRAPHICAL AND CRITICAL SOURCES:

PERIODICALS

American Book Review, September-October, 1995, Robert L. McLaughlin, review of *The Blood Countess,* pp. 16, 23.

Booklist, July, 1996, Joanne Wilkinson, review of *The Dog with the Chip in His Neck: Essays from NPR and Elsewhere,* p. 1796.

Entertainment Weekly, September 8, 1995, Margot Mifflin, review of *The Blood Countess,* p. 76.

Kirkus Reviews, January 1, 2002, review of *Casanova in Bohemia,* p. 7.

Library Journal, March 1, 1999, Boyd Childress, review of *Ay Cuba! A Socio-Erotic Journal,* p. 102; August, 2003, Rochelle Ratner, review of *It Was Today,* p. 88.

New Orleans Magazine, October, 1996 (interview), p. 13.

New York Times Book Review, January 25, 1987, Bruce Schlain, review of *Comrade Past and Mister Present,* p. 15; May 9, 1993, Francis X. Clines, review of *Road Scholar: Coast to Coast Late in the Century,* pp. 1, 22-23; July 30, 1995, Nina Auerbach, review of *The Blood Countess,* p. 7; March 28, 1999, Henry Shukman, review of *Ay Cuba!,* p. 19.

Publishers Weekly, January 18, 1999, review of *Ay Cuba!,* p. 19; July 21, 2003, review of *It Was Today,* p. 188.

Time, August 14, 1995, R. Z. Sheppard, "Gothic Whoopee," p. 70.

Times Literary Supplement, October 9, 1992, Alfred Stepan, review of *The Hole in the Flag: A Romanian Exile's Story of Return and Revolution,* p. 26.

Times-Picayune (New Orleans), February 24, 2002, Phil Nugent, "Lover, Come Back," p. D8.

Tribune Books (Chicago), April 14, 2002, Brian Bouldrey, review of *Casanova in Bohemia,* p. 14.

Washington Post Book World, July 29, 1990, Josephine Woll, "Persistence of Memory," p. WBK8; August 6, 1995, Bettina Drew, review of *The Blood Countess,* pp. 3, 10; July 7, 2002, Brigitte Weeks, "Lothario in Winter," p. 13.*

COLLINS, Philip (Arthur William) 1923-

PERSONAL: Born May 28, 1923, in London, England; son of Arthur Henry and Winifred Nellie (Bowmaker) Collins; married Mildred Lowe, November 1, 1952 (divorced, 1963); married Joyce Dickins, August 18, 1965; children: Simon, Rosamund, Marcus. *Education:* Emmanuel College, Cambridge University, M.A., 1947. *Hobbies and other interests:* Amateur theatre actor and producer, especially Shakespeare; music.

ADDRESSES: Home—26 Knighton Dr., Leicester LE2 3HB, England. *Office*—University of Leicester, University Rd., Leicester LE1 7RH, England.

CAREER: Vaughan College, Leicester, England, staff tutor in adult education, 1947-54, warden, 1954-62; University of Leicester, Leicester, England, senior lecturer in English, 1962-64, professor of English literature, 1964-82, chair of Victorian Studies Centre, 1966, head of English department, 1971-76, 1981-82; emeritus professor of English, 1982—. Visiting professor at University of California, Berkeley, 1967, Columbia University, 1969, and Victoria University (New Zealand), 1974; Byron lecturer, University of Nottingham, England, 1969; lecturer, Tennyson Society, Lincoln, England, 1972; Annie Tolbot Cole lecturer, Bowdoin University, 1973. Public orator, 1975-78, 1980-82; has given several international lecture tours, performances, scripts and talks for radio and television; member of drama panel of Arts Council of Great Britain, 1970-75, and board of directors of National Theatre, 1976-82; secretary to board of directors, Leicester Theatre Trust Ltd., 1963-87; research consultant to British Broadcasting Corp. television. *Military service:* British Army, 1942-45; served in Royal Army Ordinance Corps and Royal Norfolk Regiment; became lieutenant.

MEMBER: Drama Panel, Arts Council of Great Britain (1970-75), British American Drama Academy board (1983-97); Tennyson Society (chair, 1984-97), Dickens Fellowship (vice president, 1969; president, 1983-85), Dickens Society (president, 1975), Dickens House Museum (chair, board of trustees, 1984-92), Victorian Society (executive committee), Leicester Film Society, Leicester Poetry Society.

WRITINGS:

James Boswell, Longmans, Green (London, England), 1956.

(Editor) *English Christmas: An Anthology,* Gordon Fraser Gallery (Bedford, England), 1956.

Dickens's Periodicals, [Leicester, England], 1957.

(Editor, with others) *Letters of Charles Dickens,* Volume 1, Pilgrim Edition, Oxford University Press (Oxford, England), 1960-63.

Dickens and Crime, St. Martin's Press (New York, NY), 1962, 3rd edition, 1994.

Dickens and Adult Education, University of Leicester, Department of Adult Education (Leicester, England), 1962.

Dickens and Education, St. Martin's Press (New York, NY), 1963, 2nd edition, 1964.

The Impress of the Moving Age (inaugural lecture), Leicester University Press (Leicester, England), 1965.

Thomas Cooper, the Chartist: Byron and the "Poets of the Poor," University of Nottingham Press (Nottingham, England), 1970.

(Compiler) *A Dickens Bibliography,* Cambridge University Press (Cambridge, England), 1970.

(Editor) *Dickens: The Critical Heritage,* Barnes & Noble (New York, NY), 1971.

(Editor) *A Christmas Carol: The Public Reading Version,* 1971.

A Critical Commentary on Dickens's "Bleak House," Macmillan (London, England), 1971.

Reading Aloud: A Victorian Metier, Tennyson Society (Lincoln, England), 1972.

(Editor) *The Public Readings of Charles Dickens,* Clarendon Press (Oxford, England), 1975.

From Manly Tear to Stiff Upper Lip: The Victorians and Pathos, Victoria University Press (Wellington, England), 1975.

Charles Dickens: David Copperfield, (critical studies), Edward Arnold (London, England), 1977, Dynamic Learning Corp., 1977.

(Contributor) George H. Ford, editor, *Victorian Fiction: A Second Guide to Research,* Modern Language Association (New York, NY), 1978.

(Editor) *Charles Dickens: Hard Times,* 1978.

(Editor) *Dickens: Interviews and Recollections,* two volumes, Barnes & Noble (Totowa, NJ), 1981.

(Editor) *Thackeray: Interviews and Recollections,* two volumes, Barnes & Noble (New York, NY), 1982.

(Editor) *Trollope's London,* 1983.

(Editor and author of introduction and notes) *Sikes and Nancy and Other Public Readings,* Oxford University Press (Oxford, England), 1983.

Tennyson, Poet of Lincolnshire, Tennyson Society (Lincoln, England), 1985.

(Editor, with Edward Giuliano) *The Annotated Dickens,* two volumes, C. N. Potter (New York, NY), 1986.

Dickens and Other Victorians: Essays in Honor of Philip Collins, edited by Joanne Shattock, St. Martin's Press (New York, NY), 1988.

(Editor) *Tennyson: Seven Essays,* St. Martin's Press (New York, NY), 1992.

Also coauthor of *The Canker and the Rose,* performed in London, at Mermaid Theatre, 1964; author of talks and scripts for radio and television; contributor to *Encyclopaedia Britannica;* contributor to journals and periodicals, including *Dickensian, Essays and Studies, Listener, Notes and Queries, Review of English Studies,* and *Times Literary Supplement.* Member of editorial board of *Dickens Studies Annual* and *Victorian Studies.*

SIDELIGHTS: English scholar, educator, and dramatic performer Philip Collins's numerous books on the nineteenth-century English novelist Charles Dickens have "turned [Collins] into something of a one-man Dickens industry," noted Peter Davalle in the London *Times.* Regarding *Dickens: Interviews and Recollections,* a two-volume set of reminiscences by Dickens's contemporaries, an *Economist* reviewer commented, "No better editor than Professor Collins could be found for this compendium: his expertise on Victorian literature and society, on all levels, is unchallengeable. The major testimonies are here, with enlightening and scholarly annotations." Davalle urged readers to "dip into Professor Collins's . . . volumes where you will find some fascinating or half-forgotten tidbit about Dickens [which] beckons to be savoured."

Collins once told *CA:* "I feel almost ashamed to have 'gone on so' about Dickens: but when I started working on him thirty years ago, little scholarly work on him existed, and much still remains to be done. Thus we still lack an adequate study of his politics. Lately, however, I have been diversifying into Tennyson, Thackeray, Trollope and Hardy."

Collins edited *Thackeray: Interviews and Recollections* and *Trollope's London* in 1983. He also edited the 1992 volume *Tennyson: Seven Essays,* which honors the Victorian poet Alfred, Lord Tennyson, on the centennial of his death and acknowledges a renewal of interest in the poet, reaching a peak between 1988 and 1990. The book contains essays on Tennyson's relationships with other writers, such as Coleridge, Wordsworth, Percy Bysshe Shelley, Arthur Hallam, Edward Fitzgerald, and the Cambridge Apostles. Other essays focus on Tennyson and balladic and lyric traditions and on the theme of loss in two of Tennyson's works, "The Lover's Tale" and "In Memoriam." Still another examines ideological influences on "In Memoriam" and "Maud." The essays are written by John Beer, Eric Griffiths, Norman Page, W. W. Robson, Jerome H. Buckley, Aidan Day, and Isobel Armstrong. Rhoda L. Flaxman of *Victorian Studies* enjoyed the volume, saying that Collins "presents us with a straightforward gathering of revised or expanded lectures to the Tennyson Society, published as a single volume toward the general goal of demonstrating 'Tennyson's present value,' using no single critical approach. Most of his essayists contribute mainstream approaches to Tennyson's biography and oeuvre."

BIOGRAPHICAL AND CRITICAL SOURCES:

PERIODICALS

Books & Bookmen, July, 1982, review of *Dickens: Interviews and Recollections,* p. 24.

British Book News, April, 1982, review of *Dickens: Interviews and Recollections,* p. 256; September, 1983, review of *Thackeray: Interviews and Recollections,* p. 577; December, 1984, review of *Charles Dickens: David Copperfield,* p. 714.

Choice, February, 1982, review of *Dickens: Interviews and Recollections,* p. 764; June, 1983, review of *Thackeray: Interviews and Recollections,* p. 1460.

Economist, January 23, 1971; January 16, 1982, review of *Dickens: Interviews and Recollections,* p. 83.

Guardian Weekly, February 14, 1982, review of *Dickens: Interviews and Recollections,* p. 21.

Modern Language Review, October, 1979.

Modern Philology, May, 1985, review of *Thackeray: Interviews and Recollections,* p. 434.

Nineteenth-Century Literature, June, 1993, review of *Tennyson: Seven Essays,* p. 135; December, 1995, review of *Dickens and Crime,* 3rd edition, p. 415.

Observer (London, England), January 10, 1982, review of *Dickens: Interviews and Recollections,* p. 45.

Times (London, England), Peter Davalle, January 28, 1982.

Times Educational Supplement, March 19, 1982, review of *Dickens: Interviews and Recollections,* p. 26.

Times Literary Supplement, March 5, 1971; August 8, 1983; October 7, 1992, review of *Tennyson: Seven Essays,* p. 7.

Victorian Studies, summer, 1983, review of *Dickens: Interviews and Recollections,* p. 469; winter, 1994, Rhoda L. Flaxman, review of *Tennyson: Seven Essays,* p. 358.

*   *   *

COLTON, James
See HANSEN, Joseph

*   *   *

COMSTOCK, Gary D(avid) 1945-

PERSONAL: Born March 12, 1945, in CT; son of John Franklin (a tool and die maker) and Evelyn (a bookkeeper; maiden name, Rawson; present surname, Libby) Comstock; companion of Theodore J. Stein (a professor). *Ethnicity:* "American." *Education:* Union Theological Seminary, Ph.D., 1989.

ADDRESSES: Office—Wesleyan University, 171 Church St., Middletown, CT 06459. *E-mail*—gcomstock@wesleyan.edu.

CAREER: Wesleyan University, Middletown, CT, university Protestant chaplain and visiting professor of sociology, 1990—.

WRITINGS:

Violence against Lesbians and Gay Men, Columbia University Press (New York, NY), 1991.

Gay Theology without Apology, Pilgrim Press (Cleveland, OH), 1993.

Unrepentant, Self-Affirming, Practicing: Lesbian/ Bisexual/Gay People within Organized Religion, Continuum (New York, NY), 1996.

(With Susan E. Henking) *Que(e)rying Religion: A Critical Anthology,* Continuum (New York, NY), 1997.

A Whosoever Church: Welcoming Lesbians and Gay Men into African-American Congregations, Westminster John Knox Press (Louisville, KY), 2001.

The Work of a Gay College Chaplain: Becoming Ourselves in the Company of Others, Harrington Park Press (Binghamton, NY), 2001.

SIDELIGHTS: Gary D. Comstock once told *CA:* "I began research and writing in the field of social ethics to document and advance the lives of lesbians and gay men in contemporary society. My work includes both empirical studies of lesbian, bisexual, and gay people, as well as theological reflection on the quality of our lives. I work as an openly gay man in my scholarship and as a university chaplain and professor. I often draw on my personal experience to select and initiate my research and writing projects."

*   *   *

COOK, Paul 1950-

PERSONAL: Born November 12, 1950, in Tucson, AZ. *Ethnicity:* "White." *Education:* Northern Arizona University, B.A., 1972; Arizona State University, M.A., 1978; University of Utah, Ph.D., 1981.

ADDRESSES: Home—1108 West Cornell, Tempe, AZ 85283. *Office*—Department of English, Arizona State University, Tempe, AZ 85287. *Agent*—Richard Curtis, Richard Curtis Associates, Inc., 171 East 74th St., Suite 2, New York, NY 10021. *E-mail*—pcook@ dancris.com.

CAREER: Arizona State University, Tempe, AZ, senior lecturer in English, 1987—.

WRITINGS:

SCIENCE FICTION

Duende Meadow, Bantam (New York, NY), 1985.
Halo, Bantam (New York, NY), 1986.
On the Rim of the Mandala, Bantam (New York, NY), 1987.
Fortress on the Sun, Penguin (New York, NY), 1997.
Thinking of You, Xlibris (Philadelphia, PA), 2000.

WORK IN PROGRESS: A novel, *The Engines of Dawn.*

SIDELIGHTS: Paul Cook once told *CA:* "I find it difficult to talk about myself and my writing. This is because I've seen too many good people fall victim to the contemplation of their literary immortality to such a degree that their writing is usually its first casualty. It either becomes a reflection of marketplace expediencies or it bows to one of the many specters of political correctness that still haunt our culture. This is true even in the science fiction field, where chest-thumping and ego-yodeling are as loud as in any other field.

"I do know that I am lucky to be publishing at all, given the hundreds of thousands of people trying to get their books into print in any way they can. I am also lucky to have an agent who puts up with my insecurities and an editor who finds my writing worth her time to promote. Writing, though, is something I've always done, and the future has always been my principal focus of interest. When the two come together and produce something—a novel, a short story—that some adult person at a New York publishing house wants to advocate, publish, and distribute to book stores all across the country, then I figure life can't get much better than this. (Actually, it can, but for now I'll settle with what I have and keep my fingers crossed about the rest.)"

*   *   *

COULTON, James
  See HANSEN, Joseph

*   *   *

CRAWFORD, Tad 1946-

PERSONAL: Born August 8, 1946, in New York, NY. *Education:* Tufts University, B.A., economics; Columbia University Law School, J.D.

ADDRESSES: Home—New York, NY. *Office*—10 East 23rd St., Ste. 400, New York, NY 10010. *Agent*—Jean V. Naggar, Jean V. Naggar Literary Agency, 216 East 75th St., New York, NY 10021. *E-mail*—crawford@allworth.com.

CAREER: Writer and lecturer. Attorney, New York, NY, 1971-86; School of Visual Arts, New York, NY, instructor in humanities, 1973-98; Allworth Press, New

York, NY, founder and president, 1989—. Served as general counsel for Graphic Artists Guild; has served as counsel for the Copyright Justice Coalition; regular columnist and editor for Legal Affairs, *Communication Arts* magazine; has appeared as guest on television and radio programs, including *The O'Reilly Report, Fox on Money, Good Day, It's Only Money, Wake Up,* and *New York & Company;* lecturer on business practices for artists.

MEMBER: Small Press Advisory Committee.

AWARDS, HONORS: Body, Mind, Spirit Award of Excellence for *The Secret Life of Money: How Money Can Be Food for the Soul,* 1997.

WRITINGS:

(With Kay Murray) *The Writer's Legal Guide,* Hawthorn Books (New York, NY), 1977, 2nd edition, Allworth Press (New York, NY), 1999, 3rd edition, Allworth Press and Authors Guild (New York, NY), 2002.
Legal Guide for the Visual Artist, Hawthorn Books (New York, NY), 1977, 4th edition, 1999.
The Visual Artist's Guide to the New Copyright Law, Graphic Artists Guild (New York, NY), 1978.
(With Arie Kopelman) *Selling Your Photography: The Complete Marketing, Business, and Legal Guide,* St. Martin's Press (New York, NY), 1980.
(With Arie Kopelman) *Selling Your Graphic Design and Illustration: The Complete Marketing, Business, and Legal Guide,* St. Martin's Press (New York, NY), 1981.
(With Susan Mellon) *The Artist-Gallery Partnership: A Practical Guide to Consignment,* American Council of Arts (New York, NY), 1981, 2nd edition published as *The Artist-Gallery Partnership: A Practical Guide to Consigning Art,* Allworth Press (New York, NY), 1998.
Legal Guide for the Visual Artist, revised edition, Madison Square Press (New York, NY), 1985.
Business and Legal Forms for Fine Artists, Allworth Press (New York, NY), 1990, fourth edition, 1999.
Business and Legal Forms for Authors and Self-Publishers, Allworth Press (New York, NY), 1990, 4th revised edition, 2000.
Business and Legal Forms for Illustrators, Allworth Press (New York, NY), 1990, revised edition, 1998.

(With Eva Doman Bruck) *Business and Legal Forms for Graphic Designers,* Allworth Press (New York, NY), 1990, 3rd edition, 2003.

Business and Legal Forms for Photographers, Allworth Press (New York, NY), 1991, 3rd edition, 2002.

The Secret Life of Money: Teaching Tales of Spending, Receiving, Saving, and Owing, Putnam (New York, NY), 1994, published as *The Secret Life of Money: How Money Can Be Food for the Soul,* Allworth Press (New York, NY), 1996.

Business and Legal Forms for Crafts, Allworth Press (New York, NY), 1998.

(Editor) *AIGA Professional Practices in Graphic Design,* American Institute of Graphic Arts and Allworth Press (New York, NY), 1998.

(With Eva Doman Bruck) *Business and Legal Forms for Interior Designers,* Allworth Press (New York, NY), 2001.

The Money Mentor: A Tale of Finding Financial Freedom, Allworth Press (New York, NY), 2001.

(With Kay Murray) *The Writer's Legal Guide: An Authors Guild Desk Reference,* Allworth Press and Authors Guild (New York, NY), 2002.

Starting Your Career As a Freelance Photographer, Allworth Press (New York, NY), 2003.

Also author of play, *Cradle Me,* produced in Woodstock, NY, at Little Theatre Off the Green. Contributor to art and literary journals and magazines, including *Art in America, Art and Artists, Art Workers News, Communication Arts, Central Park, Family Circle, Harper's Bazaar, Glamour, Lapis, New Age Journal, Self, Nation, National Review, The Writer,* and *Writer's Digest.*

SIDELIGHTS: New York City attorney, economist, publisher, and supporter of the arts and artists, Tad Crawford has written books on marketing and selling an array of artistic works, from interior design to novels, providing the necessary legal forms for making a career in the arts successful. In 1989 he founded Allworth Press, which continues to publish new books on the business of the arts and new editions of Crawford's standard works, in addition to general-interest nonfiction and a series of critical essays on fine art and design. Also an economist, Crawford has published two books on personal finance, *The Secret Life of Money* and *The Money Mentor.* In an interview with Calvin Reid of *Publishers Weekly* on the tenth anniversary of Allworth Press's founding, Crawford

said that his mission is the same as when he started the company: "To serve the creative community by generating content for them."

Crawford's best-selling title, *Legal Guide for the Visual Artist,* was published in a fourth edition in 1999. The book devotes five chapters to copyright issues and also covers studio and gallery contracts, sales, licensing, disputes with clients, reproduction and publishing, taxes and estate planning, leases, and even moral rights. It also contains model contracts and a listing of artists' organizations and legal assistance for artists. In the preface, Crawford states, "Artists should never feel intimidated, helpless, or victimized." A reviewer for *American Artist* wrote, "Artists now have the information they need to protect their artwork and reputation—all in one source." A companion book, *The Artist-Gallery Partnership: A Practical Guide to Consigning Art,* deals in detail with the artist-gallery relationship, covering such topics as pricing and commissions, insurance coverage, transportation of artwork, and promotion of consigned work.

A related book is *AIGA Professional Practices in Graphic Design.* It includes standard forms of the American Institute for Graphic Arts (AIGA) and covers topics that include contracts; fees; audits; insurance; Internet and print marketing; relationships with employees, suppliers, and clients; copyright, trademarks, and licensing; and ethical standards. A reviewer for *Independent Publisher* referred to the book as having "exacting and up-to-date legal precision and ethical thoughtfulness."

Crawford's successful *Business and Legal Forms* series—with actual sample forms and a computer CD-ROM for customizing and printing the forms—provides much-needed guidance for others in the arts. Ivan E. Johnson and Jerome J. Hausman of *Arts & Activities* found that *Business and Legal Forms for Illustrators* offers "much more" information about art and design itself than other computer-based legal manuals. Gayle A. Williamson of *Library Journal* "highly recommended" *Business and Legal Forms for Interior Designers,* written by Crawford and coauthor Eva Doman Bruck, a professional designer. *Business and Legal Forms for Crafts* contains twenty-three forms, including invoices, sales and consignment contracts, copyright and trademark applications, licensing contracts, gallery agreements, exhibition loans, and many others. *Business and Legal Forms for Photogra-*

phers contains a complete set of forms and checklists for all types of photographers. The third edition covers photography in relation to the Internet as well as video photography.

Crawford turns his attention to the literary arts in *Business and Legal Forms for Authors and Self-Publishers,* a field in which his expertise allows him to provide information on negotiating with publishers. In addition to sample publishing contracts, the book contains forms for agreements with agents and collaborators, contracts with printers, copyright forms, and licensing agreements. A contributor to *Writers Write* called the book "a valuable reference for any writer who wants to understand contracts and maximize potential revenue." In 2002 Crawford and coauthor Kay Murray published the third edition of *The Writer's Legal Guide,* containing the latest information on electronic publishing rights, changes in copyright law, and the Freedom of Information Act, plus information on fair use and permissions, agency contracts, collaboration agreements, and more.

Crawford's *The Secret Life of Money: Teaching Tales of Spending, Receiving, Saving and Owing*—published in 1996 as *The Secret Life of Money: How Money Can Be Food for the Soul*—takes money and all its accoutrements to a deeper level after analyzing surface points like debt, the stock market, credit cards, and consumerism. Crawford uses philosophy and classic tales to bring home his theory that money represents life forces and energy. A *Publishers Weekly* contributor commented that the book will "enlighten those who tend to view money only in the most literal terms." In a second money book, *The Money Mentor: A Tale of Finding Financial Freedom,* Crawford follows the story of a fictitious but typical 23-year-old woman and her money woes. An injured and unemployed dancer, the young "Iris" is burdened with credit card debt, so common among young Americans in the twenty-first century. As Crawford follows Iris through her steps to financial freedom, he speaks to persons of any age. Anyone with a similar situation can apply the financial advice he presents within the engaging tale.

BIOGRAPHICAL AND CRITICAL SOURCES:

PERIODICALS

Afterimage, January, 1999, review of *The Artist-Gallery Partnership: A Practical Guide to Consigning Art,* p. 19.

American Artist, June, 1981, review of *Selling Your Photography: The Complete Marketing, Business, and Legal Guide,* p. 21; July, 1986, review of *Legal Guide for the Visual Artist,* p. 10; August, 1999, review of *Legal Guide for the Visual Artist,* 4th eition, p. 80.

American Reference Books Annual, 1998, review of *Business and Legal Forms for Authors and Self-Publishers,* 2nd edition, p. 261; 1999, review of *Business and Legal Forms for Crafts,* p. 357, review of *Business and Legal Forms for Photographers,* revised edition, p. 359.

Art Direction, October, 1981, review of *Selling Your Photography,* and *Selling Your Graphic Design and Illustration: The Complete Marketing, Business, and Legal Guide,* p. 84; February, 1986, review of *Legal Guide for the Visual Artist,* p. 88; November, 1989, review of *Legal Guide for the Visual Artist,* p. 95.

Arts & Activities, May, 2002, Ivan E. Johnson; Jerome J. Hausman, review of *Business and Legal Forms for Illustrators,* p. 56.

Bloomsbury Review, May, 1990, review of *Business and Legal Forms for Authors and Self-Publishers,* p. 14.

Booklist, June 15, 1981, review of *Selling Your Graphic Design and Illustration,* p. 1327.

Bookwatch, September, 1995, review of *Business and Legal Forms for Graphic Designers,* p. 11; November, 1996, review of *The Secret Life of Money: Teaching Tales of Spending, Receiving, Saving, and Owing,* p. 7; March, 1999, review of *The Writer's Legal Guide,* 2nd edition, p. 3.

Ceramics Monthly, June-August, 1998, review of *Business and Legal Forms for Crafts,* p. 34; October, 1998, review of *The Artist-Gallery Partnership: A Practical Guide to Consigning Art,* p. 30; June, 1999, review of *Legal Guide for the Visual Artist,* p. 32.

Choice, September, 1999, H. Leskovac, review of *The Writer's Legal Guide,* 2nd edition, p. 103.

Communication Arts, November, 1991, Byron Ferris, review of *Business and Legal Forms for Graphic Designers,* p. 240.

Independent Publisher, September-October, 1998, review of *AIGA Professional Practices in Graphic Design.*

Kliatt Paperback Book Guide, fall, 1980, review of *Legal Guide for the Visual Artist,* p. 61.

Library Journal, June 1, 1981, review of *Selling Your Graphic Design and Illustration,* p. 1214; November 1, 1990, review of *Business and Legal Forms for Authors and Self-Publishers,* p. 45; November 15, 1994, Joseph Barth, review of *The Secret Life of Money,* p. 74; July, 1997, review of *Business and Legal Forms for Authors and Self-Publishers,* 2nd edition, p. 50; June 1, 2001, review of *Business and Legal Forms for Photographers,* p. 109; January, 2002, Gayle A. Williamson, review of *Business and Legal Forms for Interior Designers,* p. 99.

Modern Photography, April, 1987, review of *Legal Guide for the Visual Artist,* p. 7.

Petersen's Photographic, September, 1991, review of *Business and Legal Forms for Photographers,* p. 34.

Publishers Weekly, November 7, 1994, review of *The Secret Life of Money,* p. 56; November 15, 1999, Calvin Reid, "Allworth Press: Ten Years of Arts Business Titles," p. 20; March 19, 2001, review of *The Money Mentor: A Tale of Finding Financial Freedom,* p. 94.

School Library Journal, September, 1981, review of *Selling Your Graphic Design and Illustration,* p. 149.

Small Press, June, 1990, review of *Business and Legal Forms for Authors and Self-Publishers,* p. 11.

Writer, November, 1999, review of *The Writer's Legal Guide,* 2nd edition, p. 47; June, 2003, Stephanie Dickison, review of *The Writer's Legal Guide: An Authors Guild Desk Reference,* p. 45.

ONLINE

Allworth Press Web site, http://www.allworth.com/ (August 5, 2002), "Tad Crawford," reviews of *The Writer's Legal Guide,* 3rd edition, and *The Secret Life of Money.*

Writers Write: The Internet Writing Journal Web site, http://www.writerswrite.com/ (March, 2000), review of *Business and Legal Forms for Authors and Self-Publishers.**

*   *   *

CRONE, Moira 1952-

PERSONAL: Born August 10, 1952, in Goldsboro, NC; daughter of James Clarence (an accountant) and Ethel (an executive assistant; maiden name, Donnelly) Crone; married Rodger L. Kamentz (a poet and writer), October 14, 1979; children: Anya Miriam, Kezia Vida.

Ethnicity: "Caucasian." *Education:* Smith College, B.A. (with high honors), 1974; Johns Hopkins University, M.A., 1977.

ADDRESSES: Office—Department of English, Louisiana State University, Allen Hall, Baton Rouge, LA 70808. *E-mail*—moiracrpme@aol.com.

CAREER: Enoch Pratt Free Library, Baltimore, MD, tutor in reading and English as a second language, 1977-78; Goucher College, Towson, MD, lecturer in English, 1979-81; Louisiana State University, Baton Rouge, LA, instructor, 1981-83, assistant professor, 1983-86, associate professor, beginning 1986, currently professor of English and director of M.F.A. program in creative writing. Johns Hopkins University, lecturer, 1979-81; Prague Summer Seminars, faculty member, 2000-02. Bethesda Writers' Center, member of board of directors, 1981; Fiction Collective, New York, NY, member of board of directors.

MEMBER: Authors Guild, Associated Writing Programs of America, Society for the Study of the Short Story in English, Phi Kappa Phi.

AWARDS, HONORS: Fellow at Mary Ingraham Bunting Institute, Radcliffe College, 1987-88; Collin C. Diboll award, Pirates Alley Faulkner Society, 1993, for *Dream State: Stories;* Ragdale Foundation fellow, 1995.

WRITINGS:

The Winnebago Mysteries and Other Stories, Fiction Collective (New York, NY), 1982.

The Life of Lucy Fern (novel), *Part One* and *Part Two,* Adult Fiction (Cambridge, NY), 1983.

A Period of Confinement (novel), Putnam (New York, NY), 1986.

Dream State: Stories, University Press of Mississippi (Jackson, MS), 1995.

Work represented in anthologies, including *American Made,* Fiction Collective (New York, NY), 1986; *New Stories by Southern Women,* University of South California Press (Columbia, SC), 1990; and *New Best Stories from the South,* Algonquin Books (Chapel Hill, NC), 1996. Contributor of short stories to magazines, including *New Yorker, Gettysburg Review, North American Review, Negative Capability, Boston Sunday Globe Magazine, American Voice, Mademoiselle, Western Humanities Review,* and *Southern Review.* Coeditor, *City Lit,* 1980; founder and editor of *New Delta Review,* 1983-86.

SIDELIGHTS: In her stories and novels, Moira Crone "emphasizes that most people are scared of human relationships because so much can and does go wrong," as Paul A. Doyle wrote in *Contemporary Novelists.* Crone's stories tell of a college-aged daughter who leaves school to wander the country in a Winnebago, of a woman whose father has abandoned the family only to call for help whenever he is broke and drunk, and of a young father cheating on his wife with a teenaged girl.

"The strength of Crone's short fiction," wrote a critic for *Publishers Weekly,* "is the realism that the author grants to her characters and their situations." Although, as Gary Krist wrote in the *New York Times Book Review,* "many of Ms. Crone's characters are . . . adrift, as confused as they are self-aware, as uncertain of what they want to say as they are forthcoming," Crone "presents her characters and themes with much sensitivity and perception," according to Doyle. "Even when we become exasperated with a character's behavior, we usually understand the reasons—often totally illogical and perverse—for the actions," commented Doyle.

In *Dream State: Stories,* Crone sets her stories in the Deep South of Louisiana, writing of the Cajuns, Creoles and French Quarter characters in what Krist described as "arguably . . . patronizing" and reminiscent of "well-meaning anthropology." Still, Krist believed, the collection "successfully presents a fresh version of the Deep South, one that is exotic without being either grotesque or romanticized."

Crone once told *CA:* "I was born in the tobacco country of North Carolina in 1952. My father was a native of the region, and my mother was from Brooklyn, New York. I spent my childhood in the same house where my father was born, with frequent visits to New York City to visit my grandmother and other relatives. In 1970 I entered Smith College, where I worked with V. S. Pritchett.

"After graduation, I lived in Boston and studied with another British author, Penelope Mortimer. In 1976 I was offered a fellowship for the Johns Hopkins Writing Seminars, where John Barth and Leslie Epstein taught. From 1977 to 1980 I worked as a teacher of English as a second language to Spanish-speaking adults in the Fells Point section of Baltimore and as a fiction workshop teacher. I also began publishing in literary magazines. Since 1981 I have lived in Louisiana, with extended stays out of the country—in France in 1983 and Jerusalem in 1986.

"My first book, *The Winnebago Mysteries and Other Stories,* was accepted for publication in 1980. It is a novella and a collection of stories I wrote during the late seventies. The strong reception of my book of stories helped me find a place for my novel, *A Period of Confinement,* a book about pregnancy and motherhood, and art.

"My next book is about the way a second generation absorbs the intentional and unintentional inflictions they receive as children and how their parents' losses and disappointments are transmuted into their own. It is a coming-of-age novel, concerning the attachments that threaten people and the need for separation, and for betrayal, as well as for forgiveness.

"My primary concerns as a writer have always been the questions of separation—questions about difference and individuation. I am centrally obsessed with motherhood and the conundrum of identity motherhood presents to mothers and children."

More recently, Crone wrote: "My writing process involves the gathering of, and the editing or re-visioning of, ideas, impressions, anecdotes. I often rewrite a story a hundred times, trying out new points of view, new angles, new approaches. A good ending is a discovery, first for the writer, and eventually for the reader. I usually work backwards from the ending, once I have uncovered it. The final discovery in a story, for me, is the motivation of the narrator, the character of the narrator, whether that narrator speaks in third or first person. The story process ends when I know the answer to these questions: 'Who is telling us this? Why does he want us to know it?'"

BIOGRAPHICAL AND CRITICAL SOURCES:

BOOKS

Contemporary Novelists, 6th edition, St. James Press (Detroit, MI), 1996.

PERIODICALS

Kirkus Reviews, July 15, 1995, review of *Dream State: Stories,* p. 965.

New York Times Book Review, October 29, 1995, Gary Krist, review of *Dream State,* p. 35.

Publishers Weekly, August 28, 1995, review of *Dream State,* p. 103.

Short Story, fall, 1995, review of *Dream State,* pp. 81-90.

* * *

CUNNINGHAM, Hugh 1942-

PERSONAL: Born January 8, 1942, in Cheltenham, England; married Diane Le May (a psychotherapist), 1969; children: Petra, Kirsty, Gemma. *Education:* Cambridge University, B.A., 1963, M.A., 1966; University of Sussex, D.Phil., 1969.

ADDRESSES: Office—School of History, Rutherford College, University of Kent—Canterbury, Canterbury, Kent CT2 7NX, England; fax: 01227-827258. *E-mail*—H.Cunningham@ukc.ac.uk.

CAREER: University of Sierra Leone, Freetown, Sierra Leone, lecturer in history, 1963-66; University of Kent—Canterbury, Canterbury, England, lecturer, 1969-84, senior lecturer, 1984-91, professor of social history, 1991—.

WRITINGS:

The Volunteer Force: A Political and Social History, 1859-1908, Croom Helm, 1975.

Leisure in the Industrial Revolution, Croom Helm, 1980.

The Children of the Poor: Representations of Childhood since the Seventeenth Century, Basil Blackwell, 1991.

Children and Childhood in Western Society since 1500, Longman (White Plains, NY), 1996.

(Editor) *Child Labour in Historical Perspective: 1800-1985: Case Studies from Europe, Japan, and Colombia,* UNICEF: Istituto degli Innocenti (Florence, Italy), 1996.

(Editor, with Joanna Innes) *Charity, Philanthropy, and Reform: From the 1690s to 1850,* St. Martin's Press (New York, NY), 1998.

The Challenge of Democracy: Britain 1932-1918, Longman (White Plains, NY), 2001.

WORK IN PROGRESS: Research on English national identity.

D

DALE, George E.
   See ASIMOV, Isaac

*   *   *

DAS, Lama Surya 1950-

PERSONAL: Born Jeffrey Miller, December 26, 1950, in Brooklyn, NY; son of Harold (a certified public accountant) and Joyce (a teacher; maiden name, Rothouse) Miller; married Kathleen Peterson, May 12, 2001. *Education:* State University of New York at Buffalo, degree in creative education (summa cum laude), 1971; studied with spiritual teachers in India and Nepal, 1971-77; studied Zen and haiku, Kyoto, Japan, 1973-74; Vipassana meditation courses, beginning in the 1970s; completed two traditional lama-training retreats at Nyingmapa Retreat Center, Dordogne, France, 1980-88. *Politics:* Democrat. *Religion:* Buddhist. *Hobbies and other interests:* Sports, poetry, dogs.

ADDRESSES: Office—Dzogchen Foundation, P.O. Box 400734, Cambridge, MA 02140. *Agent*—Susan Lee Cohen, Riverside Literary Agency, 1052 Weatherhead Hollow, Guilford, VT 05301. *E-mail*—surya@surya. org.

CAREER: College English teacher, Kyoto, Japan, 1974-75; Karma Triyana Dharma Chakra monastery, Woodstock, NY, founder, 1977, director, 1977-80; Lama in Non-Sectarian Practice Lineage of Tibetan Buddhism, 1988—. Meditation workshop and retreat teacher in Dzogchen, Vajrayana, and Mahayana Buddhism; charity worker with Tibetan refugee communities and Cambodian and Vietnamese boat people; organizer of Western Buddhist Teachers Network with the Dalai Lama, Dharamsala, India; founding board member of the Seva Foundation international health projects; Dzogchen Foundation, Cambridge, MA, founder and spiritual director, 1999—. Established Dzogchen Center and Meditation Gardens outside Austin, TX, 2002—.Talks by Lama Surya Das have been recorded on audio cassettes and released by the Dzogchen Foundation.

MEMBER: International Padmakara Translation Committee, Western Buddhist Teachers Network (president, 1993-99), SEVA Service Foundation (board member, 1978-80), Phi Beta Kappa.

AWARDS, HONORS: Short poetry award, Library of Congress; First Buddhist Web site award; Spiritual Broadcaster Service award, Inner Dimensions Radio Foundation, Infinity Foundation Spirituality Award.

WRITINGS:

The Snow Lion's Turquoise Mane: Wisdom Tales from Tibet, HarperSanFrancisco (San Francisco, CA), 1992.
(With Nyoshul Khenpo Rinpoche, and translator) *Natural Great Perfection: Dzogchen Teachings and Vajra Songs,* Snow Lion Publications (Ithaca, NY), 1995.
Dancing with Life: Dzogchen View, Meditation, and Action, Dzogchen Foundation (Cambridge, MA), 1996.

Awakening the Buddha Within: Eight Steps to Enlightenment, Broadway Books (New York, NY), 1997.

Awakening to the Sacred: Creating a Spiritual Life from Scratch, Broadway Books (New York, NY), 1999.

Awakening the Buddhist Heart: Integrating Love, Meaning and Connection into Every Part of Your Life, Broadway Books (New York, NY), 2000.

Letting Go of the Person You Used to Be: Lessons on Change, Loss, and Spiritual Transformation, Broadway-Doubleday (New York, NY), 2002.

Also author of *The Facts of Life from a Buddhist Perspective;* author of "Ask the Lama" Web column, www.wurya.org. Appears on sound recording *Chants to Awaken the Buddhist Heart,* Inner Peace Music (Ashland, OR), 2001. Translator, editor, and publisher of Buddhist works. Contributor of articles and poetry to periodicals.

WORK IN PROGRESS: New Dharma Talks: Buddhism for Today and Tomorrow.

SIDELIGHTS: Lama Surya Das, an American-born lama (Tibetan Buddhist priest and teacher) and meditation master, is a well-known spiritualist. The author/teacher described by *Boston Herald* writer Christopher Cox as a "nice Jewish boy named Jeffrey Miller who lettered in three sports at Valley Stream Central High and bar mitzvahed at Temple Gates of Zion" found his spiritual calling in college. That's when the young man's good friend, Allison Krause, was one of four Kent State University students shot to death by the Ohio National Guard during a 1970 antiwar demonstration. As Surya Das put it in an interview with Guy Spiro, "Another kid I knew, Jeffery Miller, my namesake from Long Island, was shot and killed that day." Miller finished his American education at the State University of New York, then traveled to Asia—looking "to find peace and become peace," as he told Spiro in *Monthly Aspectarian.*

Miller trained as a Tibetan Buddhist monk for ten years, earning his Sanskrit name (which means "servant of the sun") and eventually becoming a lama; after that Surya Das entered into the first of two meditative cloistered periods, a "three-year, three-month retreat that is a formal Lama training," as he noted to Spiro. Buddhism, he told Cox, "is not so much a reli-

gion as an ethical, psychological philosophy of awakening. There's no dogma, no theology, no God, no fixed rules. It's much more a way of life."

Returning to the United States, Surya Das sought to share that way of life through his writings and teachings. He established the Dzogchen Foundation, in Cambridge, Massachusetts, where he teaches meditation; according to the *Ann Online* Web site, Surya Das says he conducts "two dozen retreats in ten different countries" each year. He also began to publish books. In the preface to his bestselling and widely translated *Awakening the Buddha Within: Eight Steps to Enlightenment,* Surya Das states that he seeks to make Buddhism's Eightfold Path to enlightenment available to American readers by offering "an essential, Western Buddhism: pragmatic, effective, and experiential, rather than theoretical or doctrinal." In addition to explaining Buddhist concepts, the book lays out meditation exercises for readers to follow as they undertake the "heroic journey" along the Eightfold Path. A contributor to *Publishers Weekly* praised the book's "elegantly written short essays," presented in an approachable manner for both beginning and advanced Buddhist practitioners.

In a 1999 volume, *Awakening to the Sacred: Creating a Spiritual Life from Scratch,* Surya Das, according to *Booklist*'s Donna Seaman, combines tradition from the East and the West to "[guide] readers toward an understanding of what a spiritual practice consists of and how to establish one that meets their personal needs." Indeed, the author does not downplay his American cultural upbringing, referring to himself as a "player-coach" in the guide to enlightenment, according to a *Publishers Weekly* reviewer; the critic added that Surya Das provides an "affable, conversational tour of spiritual ideas." One aspect of traditional Buddhist practice, meditation, is discussed in the book. Surya Das maintains that mediation does not necessarily entail sitting for hours on end. "That's just one way and may not even be the best way," he told Spiro. "I like to jokingly say that sitting so long and solemnly is positively un-American. Chanting and walking meditation and eating meditation and yoga meditation and things like gardening and ocean-gazing and star-gazing can be meditation." "While flexibility is the hallmark of Buddhism," commented Cox, "the lama acknowledges the dangers of cafeteria-style dilettantism. However, he says, 'the upside is we can find out what works for us and have a tailor-made spiritual life . . . not just a one-size-fits-all curriculum that we inherit.'"

Surya Das's philosophy embraces self-discovery. "If you can't love yourself, how can you love and respect others?" as he put it in a 2001 *Share Guide* interview with Dennis Hughes. "We have to learn not just mentally but physically, such as with yoga. And we have to learn emotionally through attitude transformation or therapy or other kinds of spiritual work to see through our self-illusions and our limited self-concepts and find out who we truly are through self-inquiry and introspection. This can help us a lot."

"At heart I am a poet, and write poems almost daily," Surya Das told *CA.* "Haiku and mystic poetry deeply influenced me in my formative years, and during my year in Kyoto, Japan, during the seventies. Dreams, mediation experiences, insights, visions and nature are all important to my work. My mission is to further the transmission of authentic transformative spiritual practices here in America today, and to help awaken the atmosphere of contemporary spirituality. I have discovered that it is all within, innate in each of us. What we seek, we *are.*"

BIOGRAPHICAL AND CRITICAL SOURCES:

BOOKS

Das, Lama Surya, *Awakening the Buddha Within: Eight Steps to Enlightenment,* Broadway Books, 1997.

PERIODICALS

Booklist, April 1, 1999, Donna Seaman, *Awakening to the Sacred: Creating a Spiritual Life from Scratch,* p. 1363.
Boston Herald, June 10, 1999, Christopher Cox, "A Thoroughly Modern Monk," p. O69.
Bulletin with Newsweek, July 3, 2001, Gillian Mears, review of *Awakening the Buddhist Heart,* p. 86.
Houston Chronicle, January 20, 2001, review of *Awakening the Buddhist Heart: Integrating Love, Meaning and Connection into Every Part of Your Life,* p. 1.
Library Journal, May 15, 1999, David Bourquin, review of *Awakening to the Sacred,* p. 100; October 15, 2000, James Kuhlman, review of *Awakening the Buddhist Heart,* p. 76.

Los Angeles Times Book Review, June 19, 1999, Peter Clothier, review of *Awakening to the Sacred,* p. 2.
Publishers Weekly, July 14, 1997, review of *Awakening the Buddha Within,* p. 80; April 26, 1999, review of *Awakening to the Sacred,* p. 73.
Share Guide, March, 2001, Dennis Hughes, "An Interview with Lama Surya Das," p. 14.

ONLINE

Ann Online, http://www.annonline.com/ (June 18, 2002), "Biography."
Dzogchen Organization, http://www.dzogchen.org/ (November 17, 1997).
Lama Surya Das Home Page, http://www.surya.org/ (September 23, 2003).
Monthly Aspectarian, http://www.lightworks.com/ (June 18, 2002), Guy Spiro, "A Conversation with Lama Surya Das."

*   *   *

DAVIES, J. Clarence III 1937- (Terry Davies)

PERSONAL: Born November 16, 1937, in New York, NY; son of J. Clarence, Jr. (a real estate consultant) and Helen (Wolfe) Davies; married Barbara Schonfeld, December 20, 1959; children: Elizabeth, Eric. *Ethnicity:* "White." *Education:* Dartmouth College, B.A. (cum laude), 1959; Columbia University, Ph.D., 1965.

ADDRESSES: Home—8650 Burning Tree Rd., Bethesda, MD 20817. *Office*—Resources for the Future, 1616 P St. NW, Washington, DC 20036; fax: 202-939-3460.

CAREER: Bowdoin College, Brunswick, ME, instructor in government and director of Bureau for Research in Municipal Government, 1963-65; Executive Office of the President, Bureau of the Budget, Washington, DC, chief examiner for environmental and consumer protection, 1965-67; Princeton University, Princeton, NJ, assistant professor of politics and public affairs, 1967-70; Executive Office of the President, Council on Environmental Quality, Washington, DC, senior staff member, 1970-73; Resources for the Future, Inc., Washington, DC, assistant director of Institutions and

Public Decisions Divisions, 1973-76; Conservation Foundation, Washington, DC, executive vice president, 1976-89; U.S. Environmental Protection Agency, Washington, DC, assistant administrator for policy, planning, and evaluation, 1989-91; National Commission on the Environment, Washington, DC, executive director, 1991-92; Resources for the Future, Inc., director of Center for Risk Management, 1992-2000, senior fellow, 1992—. National Academy of Sciences, chair of Committee on Principles of Decision Making for Regulating Chemicals in the Environment, 1974-75, member of Environmental Studies Board, 1983-85; Environmental Protection Agency, member at large of executive committee, Science Advisory Board 1976-81; National Safety Council, member of board of governors, Environmental Health and Safety Institute, 1986-89; Wildlife Habitat Enhancement Council, member of board of directors, 1987-89; Institute for Cooperation in Environmental Management, member of board of directors, 1991-95; RESOLVE, Inc., chair of board of directors, 1993-2002.

MEMBER: Phi Beta Kappa.

WRITINGS:

Neighborhood Groups and Urban Renewal, Columbia University Press (New York, NY), 1966.

The Politics of Pollution, Bobbs-Merrill (Indianapolis, IN), 1970, 2nd edition, 1975.

(Coeditor) *Business and Environment: Toward Common Ground,* Conservation Foundation (Washington, DC), 1977.

(Coauthor) *Determining Unreasonable Risk under the Toxic Substances Control Act,* Conservation Foundation (Washington, DC), 1979.

(Coauthor) *Training for Environmental Groups,* Conservation Foundation (Washington, DC), 1984.

(Coeditor) *Risk Communication,* Conservation Foundation (Washington, DC), 1987.

(Editor) *Comparing Environmental Risks: Tools for Setting Government Priorities,* Resources for the Future (Washington, DC), 1996.

(With Jan Mazurek) *Regulating Pollution: Does the U.S. System Work?,* Resources for the Future (Washington, DC), 1997.

(With Jan Mazurek) *Pollution Control in the United States: Evaluating the System,* Resources for the Future (Washington, DC), 1998.

Reforming Permitting, Resources for the Future (Washington, DC), 2001.

Contributor to books, including *Growing against Ourselves: The Energy-Environment Tangle,* Lexington Books (Boston, MA), 1974; *Strategies for Public Health,* Van Nostrand (New York, NY), 1981; *Pollutants in a Multimedia Environment,* Plenum (New York, NY), 1986; *Integrated Pollution Control in Europe and North America,* Conservation Foundation (Washington, DC), 1990; and *Keeping Pace with Science and Engineering: Case Studies in Environmental Regulation,* National Academy of Engineering (Washington, DC), 1993. Contributor to periodicals, sometimes under name Terry Davies. Member of editorial board, *Toxic Substances Journal,* 1979-89, and *APP AM Journal,* 1996-2000; member of editorial advisory board, *Risk: Health, Safety, and Environment,* 1996-99.

BIOGRAPHICAL AND CRITICAL SOURCES:

PERIODICALS

Best Sellers, July 15, 1970.
Environment, November, 1996, p. 30.

*   *   *

DAVIES, Terry
    See DAVIES, J. Clarence III

*   *   *

DIDION, Joan 1934-

PERSONAL: Born December 5, 1934, in Sacramento, CA; daughter of Frank Reese and Eduene (Jerrett) Didion; married John Gregory Dunne (a writer), January 30, 1964; children: Quintana Roo (daughter). *Education:* University of California, Berkeley, B.A., 1956.

ADDRESSES: Agent—Lynn Nesbit, Janklow & Nesbit, 445 Park Ave., Floor 13, New York, NY 10022.

CAREER: Writer. *Vogue,* New York, NY, 1956-63, began as promotional copywriter, became associate feature editor. Visiting regents lecturer in English, University of California—Berkeley, 1976.

Joan Didion

AWARDS, HONORS: First prize, *Vogue*'s Prix de Paris, 1956; Bread Loaf fellowship in fiction, 1963; National Book Award nomination in fiction, 1971, for *Play It As It Lays*; Morton Dauwen Zabel Award, National Institute of Arts and Letters, 1978; National Book Critics Circle Prize nomination in nonfiction, 1980, and American Book Award nomination in nonfiction, 1981, both for *The White Album*; *Los Angeles Times* Book Prize nomination in fiction, 1984, for *Democracy*; Edward MacDowell Medal, 1996.

WRITINGS:

NOVELS

Run River, Obolensky (New York, NY), 1963.
Play It As It Lays (also see below), Farrar, Straus (New York, NY), 1970.
A Book of Common Prayer, Simon & Schuster (New York, NY), 1977.
Democracy, Simon & Schuster (New York, NY), 1984.
The Last Thing He Wanted, Knopf (New York, NY), 1996.

SCREENPLAYS; WITH HUSBAND, JOHN GREGORY DUNNE

Panic in Needle Park (based on James Mills's book of the same title), Twentieth Century-Fox, 1971.
Play It As It Lays (based on Didion's book of the same title), Universal, 1972.
(With others) *A Star Is Born,* Warner Bros., 1976.
True Confessions (based on John Gregory Dunne's novel of the same title), United Artists, 1981.
Hills Like White Elephants (based on Ernest Hemingway's short story), HBO, 1990.
Broken Trust (based on the novel *Court of Honor* by William Wood), TNT, 1995.
Up Close and Personal, Touchstone, 1996.

NONFICTION

Slouching toward Bethlehem, Farrar, Straus (New York, NY), 1968.
The White Album, Simon & Schuster (New York, NY), 1979.
Salvador, Simon & Schuster (New York, NY), 1983.
Joan Didion: Essays & Conversations, Ontario Review Press (Princeton, NJ), 1984.
Miami, Simon & Schuster (New York, NY), 1987.
Robert Graham: The Duke Ellington Memorial in Progress, Los Angeles County Museum of Art (Los Angeles, CA), 1988.
After Henry, Simon & Schuster (New York, NY), 1992, published in England as *Sentimental Journeys,* HarperCollins (London, England), 1993.
Political Fictions, Knopf (New York, NY), 2001.
Where I Was From, Knopf (New York, NY), 2003.
Fixed Ideas: America since 9.11, New York Review of Books (New York, NY), 2003.
Vintage Didion, Vintage Books (New York, NY), 2004.

Author of introduction, Robert Mapplethorpe, *Some Women,* Bulfinch Press (Boston, MA), 1992. Author of column, with John Gregory Dunne, "Points West," *Saturday Evening Post,* 1967-69, and "The Coast," *Esquire,* 1976-77; former columnist, *Life.* Contributor of short stories, articles, and reviews to periodicals, including *Vogue, Saturday Evening Post, Holiday, Harper's Bazaar,* and *New York Times Book Review, New Yorker,* and *New York Review of Books.* Former contributing editor, *National Review.*

SIDELIGHTS: Throughout her long literary career, Joan Didion has distinguished herself with her highly polished style, her keen intelligence, and her provocative social commentary. Although her work frequently criticizes trends in the contemporary world, which she sees as increasingly chaotic, "her moral courage and tenacious search for truth deeply honor American values. No literary journalist currently writing is better able to shape the shards of American disorder into a living history of this time," commended Paul Ashdown in *Dictionary of Literary Biography.* The author of novels, essays, and screenplays, Didion has always identified herself as being more interested in images than in ideas, and she is noted for her use of telling details. In addition to being "a gifted reporter," according to *New York Times Magazine* contributor Michiko Kakutani, Didion "is also a prescient witness, finding in her own experiences parallels of the times. The voice is always precise, the tone unsentimental, the view unabashedly subjective. She takes things personally." Didion has written a great deal about her native state, California, a place which seemed to supply her with ample evidence of the disorder in society. Her theme has remained essentially unchanged, but as the years have passed she has found new ways to express it, writing about troubles of Latin America, Southeast Asia, and the American political scene.

After graduating from the University of California at Berkeley in 1956, Didion took a job at *Vogue* magazine's New York office, where she remained for eight years, rising from promotional copywriter to associate feature editor. During this period, she met John Gregory Dunne and, after several years of friendship, they married, becoming not just matrimonial partners but writing collaborators as well. While still at *Vogue,* Didion began her first novel, *Run River,* which was published in 1963. The story concerns two families prominent in the Sacramento Valley, the Knights and the McClellans. Everett and Lily are children of these two prosperous families who elope. Before long they have two children, but their marriage slides into danger when Everett must leave home to serve in the armed forces during World War II. In his absence, Lily has an affair, which leads to her pregnancy. Everett returns and convinces Lily to abort the child, but their marriage can never recover; they live out their lives engaged in mutual recrimination, eventually ending in violence. "The novel depicts the social fragmentation of California that results from the dashed dreams of people drawn to the state by its promise of prosperity," mused Mark Royden in another *Dictionary of Literary Biography* essay. "What is finally ennobling about Lily's western experience, Didion seems to be saying, is not the dream that gave it birth, but the life force that enables her to survive the failure of that dream."

In 1964, Didion and Dunne moved back to the West Coast, where she was determined to earn a living as a freelance reporter. Working on a series of magazine columns about California for the *Saturday Evening Post,* the couple earned a meager $7,000 in their first year. But their writing did attract widespread attention, and when Didion's columns were collected and published in 1968 as *Slouching toward Bethlehem,* her reputation as an essayist soared. The collection takes its theme from William Butler Yeats's poem "The Second Coming," which reads: "Things fall apart; the center cannot hold; / Mere anarchy is loosed upon the world." For Didion those words sum up the chaos of the 1960s, a chaos so far-reaching that it affected her ability to perform. Convinced "that writing was an irrelevant act, that the world as I had understood it no longer existed," Didion, as she states in the book's preface, realized, "If I was to work again at all, it would be necessary for me to come to terms with disorder." She went to Haight-Ashbury to explore the hippie movement and out of that experience came the title essay. Most critics reserved high praise for *Slouching toward Bethlehem.* Writing in the *Christian Science Monitor,* Melvin Maddocks suggested that Didion's "melancholy voice is that of a last survivor dictating a superbly written wreckage report onto a tape she doubts will ever be played." And while *Best Sellers* reviewer T. O'Hara argued that "the devotion she gives to America-the-uprooted-the-lunatic-and-the-alienated is sullied by an inability to modulate, to achieve a respectable distance," most critics applauded her subjectivity. "Nobody captured the slack-jawed Haight-Ashbury hippies any better," acknowledged *Saturday Review* contributor Martin Kasindorf.

In 1970 Didion published *Play It As It Lays,* a best-selling novel that received a National Book Award nomination and, at the same time, created enormous controversy with its apparently nihilistic theme. The portrait of a woman on what *New York Times Book Review* contributor Lore Segal called a "downward path to wisdom," *Play It As It Lays* tells the story of Maria Wyeth's struggle to find meaning in a meaningless world. "The setting is the desert; the cast, the careless hedonists of Hollywood; the emotional climate, bleak as the surroundings," Kakutani reported in the *New York Times Magazine.* Composed of eighty-four brief chapters, some less than a page in length, the book possesses a cinematic quality and such technical precision that Richard Shickel remarked in *Harper's* that it is "a rather cold and calculated fiction—more a problem in human geometry . . . than a novel that truly lives."

A Book of Common Prayer continues the author's theme of social disintegration with the story of Charlotte Douglas, a Californian "immaculate of history, innocent of politics." Until her daughter Marin abandoned home and family to join a group of terrorists, Charlotte was one who "understood that something was always going on in the world but believed that it would turn out all right." When things fall apart, Charlotte takes refuge in Boca Grande, a fictitious Central American country embroiled in its own domestic conflicts. There she idles away her days at the airport coffee shop, futilely waiting for her daughter to surface and eventually losing her life in a military coup.

Because Charlotte's story is narrated by Grace, an American expatriate and long-time Boca Grande resident, the book presented several technical problems. "The narrator was not present during most of the events she's telling you about. And her only source is a woman incapable of seeing the truth," Didion explained to Diehl. In her *New York Times Book Review* article, Joyce Carol Oates speculated that Didion employs this technique because Grace permits Didion "a free play of her own speculative intelligence that would have been impossible had the story been told by Charlotte. The device of an uninvolved narrator is a tricky one, since a number of private details must be presented as if they were within the range of the narrator's experience. But it is a measure of Didion's skill as a novelist that one never questions [Grace's] near omniscience in recalling Charlotte's story." Christopher Lehmann-Haupt, on the other hand, maintained in the *New York Times* that Didion "simply asks too much of Charlotte, and overburdened as she is by the pitiless cruelty of the narrator's vision, she collapses under the strain."

After *A Book of Common Prayer,* Didion published *The White Album,* a second collection of magazine essays similar in tone to *Slouching towards Bethlehem.* "I don't have as many answers as I did when I wrote *Slouching,*" Didion explained to Kakutani. She called the book *The White Album* in consideration of a famous Beatles album that captured for her the disturbing ambiance of the sixties. "I am talking here about a time when I began to doubt the premises of all the stories I had ever told myself," Didion writes in the title essay. "This period began around 1966 and continued until 1971." During this time, says Didion, "all I knew was what I saw: flash pictures in variable sequence, images with no 'meaning' beyond their temporary arrangement, not a movie but a cuttingroom experience."

Salvador stands as one of Didion's most successful reportorial works. Originally published as two articles in the *New York Review of Books,* it was also nominated for a Pulitzer Prize. The piece was based on a two-week visit Didion and Dunne made to the embattled Republic of El Salvador in June, 1982. A repressive military regime had taken hold there and horrific violence was a daily occurrence. Like Joseph Conrad's *Heart of Darkness, Salvador* "contemplates the meaning of existence when one confronts absolute evil," stated Ashman. "Taken only as a short, impressionistic report on the war, *Salvador* would be a slight work. Something much more is intended, however, than telling the facts about El Salvador. Like Conrad's tale, *Salvador* is a journey into the interior of the human soul." Although highly acclaimed for its literary merits, *Salvador* did generate criticism as well as praise. *Newsweek* reviewer Gene Lyon, for example, allowed that "Didion gets exactly right both the ghastliness and the pointlessness of the current killing frenzy in El Salvador," but then suggested that "ghastliness and pointlessness are Didion's invariable themes wherever she goes. Most readers will not get very far in this very short book without wondering whether she visited that sad and tortured place less to report than to validate the Didion world view."

A year after *Salvador* was published, Didion produced *Democracy.* The book was to have been the story of a family of American colonialists whose interests were firmly entrenched in the Pacific at a time when Hawaii was still a territory, but Didion abandoned this idea. The resulting novel features Inez Christian and her family. In the spring of 1975—at the time the United States completed its evacuation of Vietnam and Cambodia—Inez's father is arrested for a double murder with political and racial overtones. "The Christians and their in-laws are the emblems of a misplaced confidence," according to John Lownsbrough in Toronto's *Globe & Mail,* "the flotsam and jetsam of a Manifest Destiny no longer so manifest. Their disintegration as a family in the spring of 1975 . . . is paralleled by the fall of Saigon a bit later that year and the effective disintegration of the American expansionist dream in all its ethnocentric optimism." Somehow, her family's tragedy enables Inez to break free of her marriage to a self-serving politician and escape to Malaysia with Jack Lovett, a freelance CIA agent and the man she has always loved. Though he dies abruptly, Inez holds on to her freedom, choosing to remain in Kuala Lumpur where she works among the Vietnamese refugees.

New York Review of Books critic Thomas R. Edwards believed *Democracy* "finally earns its complexity of form. It is indeed 'a hard story to tell' and the presence in it of 'Joan Didion' trying to tell it is an essential part of its subject. Throughout one senses the author struggling with the moral difficulty that makes the story hard to tell—how to stop claiming what Inez finally relinquishes, 'the American exemption' from having to recognize that history records not the victory of personal wills over reality . . . but the 'undertow of having and not having, the convulsions of a world largely unaffected by the individual efforts of anyone in it.'"

Miami once again finds Didion on the literary high wire, in a work of nonfiction that focuses on the cultural, social, and political impact the influx of Cuban exiles has had upon the city of Miami and, indeed, upon the entire United States. Culminating in an indictment of American foreign policy from the presidential administrations of John F. Kennedy through Ronald Reagan, *Miami* "is a thoroughly researched and brilliantly written meditation on the consequences of power, especially on power's self-addictive delusions," according to *Voice Literary Supplement* reviewer Stacey D'Erasmo. The book explores the thirty-year history of the community of Cuban immigrants which now comprises over half the population of that city. Didion paints these émigrés as existing within a country that threatens their political agenda, and a city full of enemies. "The shadowy missions, the secret fundings, the conspiracies beneath conspiracies, the deniable support by parts of the U.S. government and active discouragement by other parts," Richard Eder wrote in the *Los Angeles Times Book Review,* paraphrasing Didion's argument, "all these things have fostered a tensely paranoid style in parts of our own political life. . . . Miami is us." While noting that Didion's intricate—if journalistic—style almost overwhelms her argument, Eder compared *Miami* to a luxury hunting expedition: "You may look out the window and see some casually outfitted huntsman trudging along. You may wonder whether his experience is more authentic than yours. Didion's tour is overarranged, but that is a genuine lion's carcass strapped to our fender."

After Henry, published in the United Kingdom as *Sentimental Journeys,* is a collection of twelve essays organized loosely around three geographical areas that Didion has focused on throughout her writing career: Washington, D.C., California, and New York City. "For her they are our Chapels Perilous," declared Robert Dana in the *Georgia Review,* "where power and dreams fuse or collide." The title essay is a tribute to Didion's friend and mentor Henry Robbins, who served as her editor prior to his death in 1979.

Politics are discussed in the section titled "Washington." The essay "In the Realm of the Fisher King" is an analysis of the years of the Reagan presidency. "Her difficulty with politics is that she really doesn't know it as well as she imagines," stated Jonathan Yardley in the *Washington Post Book World,* "and brings to it no especially useful insights." However, reviewer Hendrik Hertzberg lauded "Inside Baseball," Didion's essay on the 1988 presidential campaign, in the *New York Times Book Review:* "Her cool eye sees sharply when it surveys the rich texture of American public folly. . . . What she has to say about the manipulation of images and the creation of pseudo-events makes familiar territory new again." But, Hertzberg added, Didion's "focus on the swirl of 'narratives' is useful as a way of exploring political image-mongering, but surprisingly limited as a way of describing the brute political and social realities against which candidates and ideas must in the end be measured."

Included among the remaining works in *After Henry* is "Sentimental Journeys," a three-part "attack on New York City and the sentimentality that distorts and obscures much of what is said and done there, and which has brought the city to the edge of bankruptcy and collapse," according to Dana. One section explores the way in which the highly publicized 1990 rape of a white investment banker jogging in New York City's Central Park—and the trial that followed—was transformed by the media into what Didion terms a "false narrative." Combined with her illuminating discussion of the many rapes occurring in the city that are not given such intensive press coverage and the decreasing competitive edge possessed by the city when viewed in real terms, "Didion's portrait is one of a city drugged nearly to death on the crack of its own myths," according to Dana, "its own 'sentimental stories told in defense of its own lazy criminality.'"

After a twelve-year hiatus, Didion returned to fiction with *The Last Thing He Wanted.* Set in 1984, the year *Democracy* was published, it contains some of the same elements, but this time in a different outpost of American foreign-policy gamesmanship, Central America. Told from the viewpoint of a "not quite omniscient" narrator, it is the story of Elena McMahon, a writer who walks away from a job covering the presidential campaign and returns to Florida and her widowed father. A shady wheeler-dealer fading into senility, her father sees a chance to turn a huge profit by supplying arms to Nicaragua's anticommunist *contras,* and Elena flies to Costa Rica to close the deal. Before long, she is caught in a web of gunrunners, CIA operatives, and a conspiracy that stretches from the JFK assassination to the Iran-Contra scandal. Some reviewers criticized the narrator, and by extension the novel, as too vague and unreal. "The problem of *The Last Thing He Wanted,*" according to *New Republic* critic James Wood, "is not that our author is 'not quite omniscient.' It is that our narrator is not quite a person." Michiko Kakutani, writing in the *New York Times,* found the novel equally unconvincing: "Despite Ms. Didion's nimble orchestration of emotional and physical details, despite her insider's ear for lingo, her conspiratorial view of history never feels terribly persuasive. . . . In the end, what's meant to be existential angst feels more like self-delusion; what's meant to be disturbing feels more like paranoia." Other critics, however, found this "unreality" oddly appropriate. For example, John Weir wrote in the *New Yorker:* "A dream is disorienting but it adheres to its own particular logic. By contrast, the real life events on which novels are traditionally based have lately taken on a quality that almost defies their being retold. 'This is something different,' Didion's narrator writes about the story she's driven to tell. The result is entrancing—a dream without the logic of a dream, the way we live now."

Didion published another collection of her essays in 2001. *Political Fictions* is made up of pieces previously printed in the *New York Review of Books.* Her central theme is that political life in the United States has become increasingly inauthentic, designed for and shaped by the media, and controlled by a small elite class that shows complete disregard for the majority of the electorate. She is acerbic in her criticism of the media's part in this state of affairs, claiming that they are willing accomplices with the political powers that be. Her time frame begins with the rivalry between Michael Dukakis and George Bush, Sr., continues through the years of the Clinton administration and on to the bitter battle of the presidential campaign in 2000. Again and again she reaches the conclusion that democracy in modern America is "not a system of majority rule or an expression of voter choice; it is a cheap spectacle acted out by the craven officials and smug journalists of Washington's 'political class,'"

explained Sean McCann in *Book.* McCann found some of the author's conclusions "questionable," but added that the "anger and beauty of Didion's work" is so great that "while one reads, it is hard not to nod one's head in assent." A *Publishers Weekly* writer stated that "at her best, Didion is provocative, persuasive and highly entertaining." Noting that Democrats, Republicans, and political reporters all come under fire from Didion, the writer added: "Didion's willingness to skewer nearly everyone is one of the pleasures of the book."

Didion published two books in 2003: *Where I Was From* and *Fixed Ideas: America since 9.11.* The first returned to one of her favorite subjects, the state of California. She had actually started the book in the 1970s, but found it so difficult to write that she set it aside for many years. The death of her mother finally provided the impetus for her to finish it. Her aim was to explore the vast gap between the reality of California and the popular image of the state. Coming from a long line of Californians, Didion explored many family stories in the course of her narrative. The picture she paints of modern-day California is not flattering; she sees "greed, acquisitiveness and wasteful extravagance lurking beneath the state's eternal sunshine," wrote a *Publishers Weekly* reviewer. Even in its earlier days, now greatly romanticized, California was in fact a place where bigotry and other forms of inhumanity flourished. While many people might find her opinions debatable, "the book is a remarkable document precisely because of its power to trigger a national debate that can heighten awareness and improve conditions on the West Coast and throughout the country," concluded the reviewer. Terren Ilana Wein, a writer for *Library Journal,* defined *Where I Was From* as "a complex and challenging memoir, difficult to enter into but just as difficult to put down. . . . Those who have long admired the clarity and precision of her prose will not be disappointed with this partly autobiographical, partly historical, but fully engrossing account."

Didion critiqued the political aftermath of the September 11, 2001, destruction of the World Trade Center towers in her book *Fixed Ideas: America since 9.11.* "In times of national crisis, the public turns to such proven, clear-eyed observers of American society to place events within a historical and political context," stated Donna Seaman in *Booklist.* She noted, however, that meaningful discussion as to the roots of the tragedy was difficult because those who tried to initiate it were "instantly branded as traitors" by the Bush administration. Didion dissects the administration's tactics and strategies for managing the public perception of the terrorist attacks and the war on Iraq that followed. Her analysis proves her to be a "shrewd, seasoned, and superbly articulate interpreter of the machinations of American politics, particularly the art of spin." The author was quoted by Chauncey Mabe, a contributor to the *South Florida Sun-Sentinel,* as saying: "My immediate thought after 9/11 was that it would alter everything. . . . But whatever did change doesn't seem to include the political process. I knew this as soon as President Bush made his first speech to the nation, and all the commentators were analyzing how it played, how it was an 'up thing' that took attention off the economy. That was pretty discouraging." Discouraged or not, Didion stands as a significant witness to the modern world. "Her prose is a literary seismograph," claimed Dana, "on which are clearly registered the tremors and temblors that increasingly shake the bedrock of the American social dream."

BIOGRAPHICAL AND CRITICAL SOURCES:

BOOKS

Concise Dictionary of American Literary Biography: Broadening Views, 1968-1988, Gale (Detroit, MI), 1989.

Contemporary Literary Criticism, Gale (Detroit, MI), Volume 1, 1973, Volume 3, 1975, Volume 8, 1978, Volume 14, 1980.

Contemporary Novelists, St. James Press (Detroit, MI), 2001.

Dictionary of Literary Biography, Gale (Detroit, MI), Volume 2: *American Novelists since World War II,* 1978; Volume 173: *American Novelists since World War II,* fifth series, 1996; Volume 185: *American Literary Journalists, 1945-1995,* first series, 1997.

Dictionary of Literary Biography Yearbook, Gale (Detroit, MI), 1981, 1986.

Friedman, Ellen G., editor, *Joan Didion: Essays and Conversations,* Ontario Review Press (Princeton, NJ), 1984.

Henderson, Katherine, *Joan Didion,* Ungar (New York, NY), 1981.

Loris, Michelle, *Innocence, Loss, and Recovery in the Art of Joan Didion,* Peter Lang (New York, NY), 1989.

St. James Encyclopedia of Popular Culture, St. James Press (Detroit, MI), 2000.

Winchell, Mark, *Joan Didion,* Twayne (Boston, MA), 1980.

PERIODICALS

America, April 5, 1997, Lewis A. Turlish, review of *The Last Thing He Wanted,* p. 28.

American Prospect, February 25, 2002, Ronald Brownstein, review of *Political Fictions,* p. 33.

American Scholar, winter, 1970-71.

American Spectator, September, 1992.

Atlantic Monthly, April, 1977.

Belles Lettres, fall, 1992, p. 14.

Book, September, 2001, Sean McCann, review of *Political Fictions,* p. 75.

Booklist, March 1, 1992; July, 1996, Donna Seaman, review of *The Last Thing He Wanted,* p. 1779; October 15, 1998, Mary Carroll, review of *The Last Thing He Wanted,* p. 397; August, 2001, Donna Seaman, review of *Political Fictions,* p. 2075; May 15, 2003, Donna Seaman, review of *Fixed Ideas: America since 9.11,* p. 1621.

Boston Globe, May 17, 1992, p. 105.

Boston Magazine, September, 1996, Sven Birkerts, review of *The Last Thing He Wanted,* p. 124.

Chicago Tribune, June 12, 1979.

Chicago Tribune Book World, July 1, 1979; April 3, 1983; April 15, 1984.

Chicago Tribune Magazine, May 2, 1982.

Christian Science Monitor, May 16, 1968; September 24, 1970; July 9, 1979; June 1, 1992, p. 13.

Commentary, June, 1984, pp. 62-67; October, 1996, Elizabeth Powers, review of *The Last Thing He Wanted,* p. 70.

Commonweal, November 29, 1968; October 23, 1992.

Critique, spring, 1984, pp. 160-170.

Detroit News, August 12, 1979.

Dissent, summer, 1983.

Economist, August 22, 1992.

Entertainment Weekly, September 20, 1996, Vanessa V. Friedman, review of *The Last Thing He Wanted,* p. 75.

Esquire, March, 1996, p. 36.

Georgia Review, winter, 1992, pp. 799-802.

Globe and Mail (Toronto, Ontario, Canada), April 28, 1984.

Harper's, August, 1970; December, 1971.

Harper's Bazaar, September, 1996, Philip Weiss, review of *The Last Thing He Wanted,* p. 124.

Harvard Advocate, winter, 1973.

Interview, September, 1996, Mark Marvel, interview with Joan Didion, p. 84; November, 2001, Amy Spindler, interview with Joan Didion, p. 80.

Library Journal, July, 1996, Barbara Hoffert, review of *The Last Thing He Wanted,* p. 156; October 1, 2001, Cynthia Harrison, review of *Political Fictions,* p. 124; June 15, 2003, Terren Ilana Wein, review of *Where I Was From,* p. 72.

London Review of Books, December 10, 1987, pp. 3, 5-6; October 21, 1993, pp. 12-13.

Los Angeles, September, 2001, Tom Carson, review of *Political Fictions,* p. 137; March, 1996, Peter Rainer, review of *Up Close and Personal,* p. 145.

Los Angeles Times, May 9, 1971; July 4, 1976.

Los Angeles Times Book Review, March 20, 1983; September 27, 1987, pp. 3, 6.

Maclean's, March 4, 1996, Brian D. Johnson, review of *Up Close and Personal,* p. 79.

Miami Herald, December 2, 1973.

Ms., February, 1977.

Nation, September 26, 1979; September 30, 1996, John Leonard, review of *The Last Thing He Wanted,* p. 23.

National Review, June 4, 1968; August 25, 1970; October 12, 1979; November 23, 1987; June 22, 1992, pp. 53-54.

New Republic, June 6, 1983; April 9, 1984; November 23, 1987; October 14, 1996.

Newsweek, August 3, 1970; December 21, 1970; March 21, 1977; June 25, 1979; March 28, 1983; April 16, 1984; March 4, 1996, David Ansen, review of *Up Close and Personal,* p. 70; September 9, 1996, Laura Shapiro, review of *The Last Thing He Wanted,* p. 68.

New York, February 15, 1971; June 13, 1979; March 4, 1996, David Denby, review of *Up Close and Personal,* p. 66; September 2, 1996, Linda Hall, interview with Joan Didion, p. 28.

New Yorker, June 20, 1977; April 18, 1983; January 25, 1988, p. 112; March 11, 1996, James Wolcott, review of *Up Close and Personal,* p. 107; September 16, 1996.

New York Observer, September 17, 2001, Susan Faludi, review of *Political Fictions,* p. 14.

New York Review of Books, October 22, 1970; May 10, 1984; December 20, 2001, Joseph Lelvveld, review of *Political Fictions,* p. 8.

New York Times, July 21, 1970; October 30, 1972; March 21, 1977; June 10, 1979; June 5, 1979; March 11, 1983; April 6, 1984; September 14, 1984; February 8, 1987; September 3, 1996; September 30, 2001, review of *Political Fictions,* p. 22.

New York Times Book Review, July 21, 1968; August 9, 1970; April 3, 1977; June 17, 1979; March 13, 1983; April 22, 1984; October 25, 1987, p. 3; May 17, 1992, pp. 3, 39; September 8, 1996, Michael Wood, review of *The Last Thing He Wanted,* p. 10; September 20, 2001, review of *Political Fictions,* p. 22; October 7, 2001, review of *Political Fictions,* p. 26; October 6, 2002, Scott Veale, review of *Political Fictions,* p. 36.

Observer (London, England), March 27, 1988, p. 43; January 24, 1993, p. 53; January 12, 2003, Jemima Hunt, "The Didion Bible," p. 3.

People, October 28, 1996, Paula Chin, review of *The Last Thing He Wanted,* p. 40.

Plain Dealer (Cleveland, OH), September 30, 2001, John Freeman, review of *Political Fictions,* p. J9.

Publishers Weekly, June 24, 1996, review of *The Last Thing He Wanted,* p. 43; August 6, 2001, review of *Political Fictions,* p. 72; October 15, 2001, Natasha Wimmer, interview with Joan Didion, p. 41; June 30, 2003, Joel Hirschhorn, review of *Where I Was From,* p. 68.

Quill and Quire, December, 1987, p. 30.

St. Louis Post-Dispatch, September 25, 2002, Jane Henderson, "Fans May Be Stuck in the '60s, but . . . Didion Has Moved on," p. D1.

San Francisco Chronicle, September 25, 2001, John M. Hubbell, "A Sharp Eye on Politics," p. B1.

San Francisco Review of Books, May, 1977.

Saturday Review, August 15, 1970; March 5, 1977; September 15, 1979; April 1982.

Sewanee Review, fall, 1977.

South Florida Sun-Sentinel, November 20, 2002, Chauncey Mabe, review of *Political Fictions.*

Star-Ledger (Newark, NJ), September 30, 2001, Jonathan Schell, review of *Political Fictions,* p. 5; October 14, 2001, Deborah Jerome-Cohen, review of *Political Fictions,* p. 5.

Time, August 10, 1970; March 28, 1977; August 20, 1979; April 4, 1983; May 7, 1984; June 29, 1992; March 4, 1996, Richard Corliss, review of *Up Close and Personal,* p. 63; September 9, 1996, Paul Gray, review of *The Last Thing He Wanted,* p. 69.

Times Literary Supplement, February 12, 1970; March 12, 1971; July 8, 1977; November 30, 1979; June 24, 1983; January 29, 1993, p. 10; November 5, 1993, p. 28.

Tribune Books (Chicago, IL), May 10, 1992, pp. 3, 7.

Variety, March 4, 1996, Leonard Klady, review of *Up Close and Personal,* p. 72.

Village Voice, February 28, 1977; June 25, 1979; May 26, 1992, pp. 74-76.

Vogue, April, 2002, Susan Orlean, interview with Joan Didion, p. 281.

Voice Literary Supplement, October 1987, pp. 21-22.

W, October, 2001, James Reginato, "Joan of Arch," p. 110.

Washington Post, April 8, 1983.

Washington Post Book World, June 17, 1979; March 13, 1983; April 15, 1984; May 10, 1992, p. 3.

Writer, March, 1999, Lewis Burke Frumkes, interview with Joan Didion, p. 14.

ONLINE

Metroactive, http://www.metroactive.com/ (July 10, 2003), "Why Ask Why?"

Salon.com, http://www.salon.com/ (July 10, 2003), interview with Joan Didion.*

*   *   *

Annie Dillard

DILLARD, Annie 1945-

PERSONAL: Born April 30, 1945, in Pittsburgh, PA; daughter of Frank and Pam (Lambert) Doak; married Richard Dillard (a professor and writer), June 5, 1964 (divorced); married Gary Clevidence (a writer), April 12, 1980 (divorced); married Robert D. Richardson, Jr. (a professor and writer), 1988; children: (second marriage) Cody Rose; Carin, Shelly (stepchildren). *Education:* Hollins College, B.A., 1967, M.A., 1968. *Religion:* Roman Catholic.

ADDRESSES: Agent—Timothy Seldes, Russell and Volkening, 50 West 29th St., New York, NY 10001.

CAREER: Writer and educator. *Harper's Magazine,* editor, 1973-85; Western Washington University, Bellingham, scholar-in-residence, 1975-79; Wesleyan University, Middletown, CT, distinguished visiting professor, 1979-81, full adjunct professor, 1983-98, writer-in-residence, 1987-98; professor emeritus, 1999—. Member of U.S. cultural delegation to China, 1982. Board member for various organizations, including,

Western States Arts Foundation, Milton Center, and Key West Literary Seminar; Wesleyan Writers' Conference, board member and chair, 1991—. Member, New York Public Library national literacy committee, National Committee for U.S.-China relations, and Catholic Commission on Intellectual and Cultural Affairs. Member of usage panel, *American Heritage Dictionary*; member of McNair Mentors Program; has served as a juror for various writing prizes, including Yale University Bollingen Prize, Pulitzer Prize in general nofiction, and PEN Martha Albrand Award in nonfiction.

MEMBER: International PEN, Poetry Society of America, Society of American Historians, National Association for the Advancement of Colored People, National Citizens for Public Libraries, Phi Beta Kappa.

AWARDS, HONORS: Pulitzer Prize in general nonfiction, 1975, for *Pilgrim at Tinker Creek;* New York Press Club Award for Excellence, 1975, for "Innocence in the Galapagos"; Washington State Governor's

Award for Literature, 1977; grants from National Endowment for the Arts, 1982-83, and Guggenheim Foundation, 1985-86; *Los Angeles Times* Book Prize nomination, 1982, for *Living by Fiction;* honorary degrees from Boston College, 1986, and Connecticut College, and University of Hartford, both 1993; National Book Critics Circle Award nomination, 1987, for *An American Childhood*; Appalachian Gold Medallion, University of Charleston, 1989; St. Botolph's Club Foundation Award, 1989; English-Speaking Union Ambassador Book Award, 1989, for *The Writing Life; Teaching a Stone to Talk* named a Best Book of the 1980s, *Boston Globe*; Best Foreign Book Award (France), 1990, for *Pilgrim at Tinker Creek,* and 2002, for *For the Time Being*; History Maker Award, Historical Society of Western Pennsylvania, 1993; Connecticut Governor's Arts Award, 1993; Campion Medal, *America* magazine, 1994; Milton Prize, 1994; inducted into Connecticut Women's Hall of Fame, 1997; Academy Award in Literature, American Academy of Arts and Letters, 1998; fellow, American Academy of Arts and Letters, 1999.

WRITINGS:

Tickets for a Prayer Wheel (poems), University of Missouri Press (Columbia, MO), 1974.

Pilgrim at Tinker Creek (also see below), Harper's Magazine Press (New York, NY), 1974.

Holy the Firm (also see below), Harper (New York, NY), 1977.

The Weasel, Rara Avis Press (Claremont, CA), 1981.

Living by Fiction (also see below), Harper (New York, NY), 1982.

Teaching a Stone to Talk: Expeditions and Encounters (also see below), Harper (New York, NY), 1982.

Encounters with Chinese Writers, Wesleyan University Press (Middletown, CT), 1984.

(Contributor) *Inventing the Truth: The Art and Craft of Memoir,* edited by William Zinsser, Houghton (Boston, MA), 1987.

An American Childhood (also see below), Harper (New York, NY), 1987.

(Editor, with Robert Atwan) *The Best American Essays, 1988,* Houghton Mifflin (Boston, MA), 1988.

The Annie Dillard Library (contains *Living by Fiction, An American Childhood, Holy the Firm, Pilgrim at Tinker Creek,* and *Teaching a Stone to Talk*), Harper (New York, NY), 1989.

The Writing Life, Harper (New York, NY), 1989.

Three by Annie Dillard (contains *Pilgrim at Tinker Creek, An American Childhood,* and *The Writing Life*), Harper (New York, NY), 1990.

The Living (novel), HarperCollins (New York, NY), 1992.

The Annie Dillard Reader, HarperCollins (New York, NY), 1994.

(Editor, with Cort Conley) *Modern American Memoirs,* HarperCollins (New York, NY), 1995.

Mornings Like This: Found Poems, HarperCollins (New York, NY), 1995.

For the Time Being, Knopf (New York, NY), 1999.

Columnist, *Living Wilderness,* 1973-75. Contributing editor, *Harper's,* 1974-81, and 1983-85. Contributor of fiction, essays, and poetry to numerous periodicals and anthologies, including *Atlantic Monthly, American Scholar, Poetry, Mill Mountain Review, Black Warrior Review, Esquire, Ploughshares, Yale Review, American Heritage, Antioch Review, Carolina Quarterly, Tri-Quarterly, North American Review, New York Times Magazine, New York Times Book Review, Chicago Review, The Lure of Tahiti, The Norton Reader,* and *Incarnation*

ADAPTATIONS: Several of Dillard's writings have been adapted as plays, or as readings to accompany music and art.

SIDELIGHTS: Annie Dillard has carved a unique niche for herself in the world of American letters. Over the course of her career, Dillard has written essays, a memoir, poetry, literary criticism—even a western novel. In whatever genre she works, Dillard distinguishes herself with her carefully wrought language, keen observations, and original, metaphysical insights. Her first significant publication, 1974's *Pilgrim at Tinker Creek,* drew numerous comparisons to Henry David Thoreau's *Walden;* in the years since, Dillard's name has come to stand for excellence in writing.

Tickets for a Prayer Wheel was Dillard's first publication. This slim volume of poetry—which expresses the author's yearning for a hidden God—was praised by reviewers. Within months of its appearance, however, Dillard's debut work was completely overshadowed by the release of her second, *Pilgrim at Tinker Creek.*

Dillard lived quietly on Tinker Creek in Virginia's Roanoke Valley, observing the natural world, taking notes, and reading voluminously in a wide variety of disciplines, including theology, philosophy, natural science, and physics. Following the progression of seasons, in *Pilgrim at Tinker Creek* she probes the cosmic significance of the beauty and violence coexisting in the natural world.

"One of the most pleasing traits of the book is the graceful harmony between scrutiny of real phenomena and the reflections to which that gives rise," noted a *Commentary* reviewer of *Pilgrim at Tinker Creek.* "Anecdotes of animal behavior become so effortlessly enlarged into symbols by the deepened insight of meditation. Like a true transcendentalist, Miss Dillard understands her task to be that of full alertness." Other critics found fault with Dillard's work, however, calling it self-absorbed or overwritten. Charles Deemer of the *New Leader,* for example, claimed that "if Annie Dillard had not spelled out what she was up to in this book, I don't think I would have guessed. . . . Her observations are typically described in overstatement reaching toward hysteria." A more charitable assessment came from Muriel Haynes of *Ms.* While finding Dillard to be "susceptible to fits of rapture," Haynes asserted that the author's "imaginative flights have the special beauty of surprise."

Dillard's next book delves into the metaphysical aspects of pain. *Holy the Firm* was inspired by the plight of one of her neighbors, a seven-year-old child who was badly burned in a plane crash. As Dillard reflects on the maimed child and on a moth consumed by flame, she struggles with the problem of reconciling faith in a loving God with the reality of a violent world. Only seventy-six pages long, *Holy the Firm* overflows with "great richness, beauty and power," according to Frederick Buechner in the *New York Times Book Review. Atlantic* reviewer C. Michael Curtis concurred, adding that "Dillard writes about the ferocity and beauty of natural order with . . . grace."

Elegant writing also distinguishes *Living by Fiction,* Dillard's fourth book, in which the author analyzes the differences between modernist and traditional fiction. "Everyone who timidly, bombastically, reverently, scholastically—even fraudulently—essays to live 'the life of the mind' should read this book," advised Carolyn See in the *Los Angeles Times.* See went on to describe *Living by Fiction* as "somewhere between scholarship, metaphysics, an acid trip and a wonderful conversation with a most smart person." "Whether the field of investigation is nature or fiction, Annie Dillard

digs for ultimate meanings as instinctively and as determinedly as hogs for truffles," remarked *Washington Post Book World* contributor John Breslin. "The resulting upheaval can be disconcerting . . . still, uncovered morsels are rich and tasty."

Dillard returns again to reflecting on nature and religion in *Teaching a Stone to Talk: Expeditions and Encounters.* In minutely detailed descriptions of a solar eclipse, visits to South America and the Galapagos Islands, and other, more commonplace events and locations, she continues "the pilgrimage begun at Tinker Creek with an acuity of eye and ear that is matched by an ability to communicate a sense of wonder," according to Beaufort Cranford in the *Detroit News. Washington Post Book World* contributor Douglas Bauer was similarly pleased with the collection, judging Dillard's essays to be "almost uniformly splendid." In his estimation, Dillard's "art . . . is to move with the scrutinous eye through events and receptions that are random on their surfaces and to find, with grace and always-redeeming wit, the connections."

Dillard looked deeply into her past to produce another best-seller, *An American Childhood.* On one level, *An American Childhood* details the author's upbringing in an idiosyncratic, wealthy family; in another sense, the memoir tells the story of a young person's awakening to consciousness. In the words of *Washington Post* writer Charles Trueheart, Dillard's "memories of childhood are like her observations of nature: they feed her acrobatic thinking, and drive the free verse of her prose." Critics also applauded Dillard's keen insight into the unique perceptions of youth, as well as her exuberant spirit. "Loving and lyrical, nostalgic without being wistful, this is a book about the capacity for joy," stated *Los Angeles Times Book Review* contributor Cyra McFadden, while Noel Perrin of the *New York Times Book Review* observed that "Dillard has written an autobiography in semimystical prose about the growth of her own mind, and it's an exceptionally interesting account."

The activity that has occupied most of Dillard's adulthood serves as the subject of *The Writing Life.* With regard to content, *The Writing Life* is not a manual on craft nor a guide to getting published; rather, it is a study of a writer at work and the processes involved in that work. Among critics, the book drew mixed reaction. "Dillard is one of my favorite contemporary authors," Sara Maitland acknowledged in the *New York Times Book Review*. "Dillard is a wonderful writer and *The Writing Life* is full of joys. These are clearest to me when she comes at her subject tangentially, talking not of herself at her desk but of other parallel cases—the last chapter, a story about a stunt pilot who was an artist of air, is, quite simply, breathtaking. There are so many bits like this. . . . Unfortunately, the bits do not add up to a book." *Washington Post Book World* contributor Wendy Law-Yone voiced similar sentiments, finding the book "intriguing but not entirely satisfying" and "a sketch rather than a finished portrait." Nevertheless, the critic wondered, "Can anyone who has ever read Annie Dillard resist hearing what she has to say about writing? Her authority has been clear since *Pilgrim at Tinker Creek*—a mystic's wonder at the physical world expressed in beautiful, near-biblical prose."

Dillard ventured into new territory with her 1992 publication, *The Living,* a sprawling historical novel set in the Pacific Northwest. Reviewers hailed the author's first novel as masterful. "Her triumph is that this panoramic evocation of a very specific landscape and people might as well have been settled upon any other time and place—for this is, above all, a novel about the reiterant, precarious, wondrous, solitary, terrifying, utterly common condition of human life," exclaimed Molly Gloss in a review for the *Washington Post Book World.* Dillard's celebrated skill with words is also much in evidence here, according to Gloss, who noted that the author "uses language gracefully, releasing at times a vivid, startling imagery." Carol Anshaw concurred in the *Los Angeles Times Book Review:* "The many readers who have been drawn in the past to Dillard's work for its elegant and muscular language won't be disappointed in these pages."

Following the 1994 publication of *The Annie Dillard Reader,* a collection of poems, stories, and essays that prompted a *Publishers Weekly* reviewer to term Dillard "a writer of acute and singular observation," Dillard produced two works during 1995. *Modern American Memoirs,* which she edited with Cort Conley, is a collection of thirty-five pieces excerpted from various writers' memoirs. Authors whose work appears here include Ralph Ellison, Margaret Mead, Reynolds Price, Kate Simon, and Russell Baker. "Many of these memoirs are striking and memorable despite their brevity," commented Madeline Marget in a *Commonweal* review of the collection.

Mornings Like This: Found Poems, Dillard's other 1995 publication, is an experimental volume of verse. To create these poems, Dillard culled lines from other writers' prose works—Vincent Van Gogh's letters and a Boy Scout Handbook, for example—and "arranged" the lines "in such a way as to simulate a poem originating with a single author," explained John Haines in the *Hudson Review.* While commenting that Dillard's technique works better with humorous and joyful pieces than with serious ones, a *Publishers Weekly* critic added that "these co-op verses are never less than intriguing." Haines expressed concern over the implications of Dillard's experiment: "What does work like this say about the legitimacy of authorship?" He concluded, however, that "on the whole the collection has in places considerable interest."

In 1999 Dillard produced another book of theological musings that has been praised as a worthy successor to her earlier works in the genre. *For the Time Being* specifically addresses the questions of cruelty and suffering. In this volume, Dillard displays a fascination with statistics, quoting facts about the number of dead people in the earth versus the number of living; how many suicides take place each day; what percentage of the population is mentally retarded; and how many people die each day. She describes in clinical detail various birth defects, the wholesale slaughter of enemies practiced by rulers throughout history, and the ritual burial of thousands of living soldiers and concubines with deceased Chinese rulers. As Jean Bethke Elshtain put it in the *Journal of Religion,* the author "does this through a variety of genres that are not often on display in a single text. Weaving together poetry, vignette, ethnography, autobiography, history, theology, Dillard provides multiple entry points into the mysteries of time, history, natural calamity, and the possibility of grace." *For the Time Being* "is, among other things, an impressionist picture of [a] tempest-tossed world. . . ," remarked Michael J. Farrell in *National Catholic Reporter.* "The book is a gradual unveiling of the world as Dillard is obsessed by it, which also, of course, is a gradual unveiling of the author." Maggie Mortimer noted in the *National Post* that *For the Time Being* "embodies the cryptic and the insightful," and that "*For the Time Being* sometimes reaches heights that can only be deemed inspirational."

"Few writers depict what's wrong with the world as vividly as Dillard," concluded Farrell. "At the end of the most brutal century in human history, we, weary, search desperately for the happy ending, the escape, while Dillard urges us not to turn away, coaxes us instead to look Life in the eye. . . . Relentlessly. Her books are one tour de force after another." Andre La Sana, critiquing *For the Time Being* in *First Things*, concurred, describing Dillard's work as "a valuable attempt to cut us loose from a complacent acceptance of life's enigmas."

BIOGRAPHICAL AND CRITICAL SOURCES:

BOOKS

Anderson, Chris, *Literary Nonfiction: Theory, Criticism, Pedagogy,* Southern Illinois University Press (Carbondale, IL), 1989.

Carnes, Mark C., *Novel History: Historians and Novelists Confront America's Past (and Each Other),* Simon & Schuster (New York, NY), pp. 109-118.

Contemporary Literary Criticism, Gale (Detroit, MI), Volume 9, 1978, Volume 60, 1990.

Detweiler, Robert, *Breaking the Fall: Religious Readings of Contemporary Fiction,* Harper (New York, NY), 1989.

Dictionary of Literary Biography Yearbook: 1980, Gale (Detroit, MI), 1981.

Elder, John, *Imagining the Earth: Poetry and the Vision of Nature,* University of Illinois Press (Chicago, IL), 1985.

Fritzell, Peter A., *Nature Writing and America: Essays on a Cultural Type,* Iowa State University Press (Ames, IA), 1990.

Hassen, Ihab, *Selves at Risk: Patterns of Quest in Contemporary American Letters,* University of Wisconsin Press (Madison, WI), 1991.

Johnson, Sandra Humble, *The Space Between: Literary Epiphany in the Works of Annie Dillard,* Kent State University Press (Kent, OH), 1992.

Lohafer, Susan, and Jo Ellyn Clarey, editors, *Short Story Theory at a Crossroads,* Louisiana State University Press (Baton Rouge, LA), 1989.

Parrish, Nancy C., *Lee Smith, Annie Dillard, and the Hollins Group: A Genesis of Writers,* Louisiana State University Press (Baton Rouge, LA), 1998.

Rainwater, Catherine, and William J. Scheick, editors, *Contemporary American Women Writers: Narrative Strategies,* University Press of Kentucky (Lexington, KY), 1985.

Slovac, Scott, *Seeking Awareness in American Nature Writing: Henry Thoreau, Annie Dillard, Edward Abbey, Wendell Berry, Barry Lopez,* University of Utah Press (Salt Lake City, UT), 1992.

Smith, Linda, *Annie Dillard,* Twayne (Boston, MA), 1991.

PERIODICALS

America, April 20, 1974; February 11, 1978, pp. 363-364; May 6, 1978, pp. 363-364; April 16, 1988, p. 411; November 25, 1989, p. 1; November 19, 1994, p. 2.

American Heritage, December, 1993, p. 104.

American Literature, March, 1987.

American Scholar, summer, 1990, p. 445.

Atlantic, December, 1977; October, 1984, p. 126.

Best Sellers, December, 1977.

Booklist, February 15, 1992, p. 1066; August, 1993, p. 2081; November 1, 1994, p. 530; November 15, 1994, p. 572; February 15, 1995, p. 1104; June 1, 1995, p. 1721; October 1, 1995, p. 245; February 1, 1999, p. 939.

Chicago Tribune, October 1, 1987.

Christian Century, November 14, 1984, p. 1062; June 7, 1989, p. 592; November 15, 1989, p. 1063; October 7, 1992, p. 871; June 4, 1997, p. 569.

Christianity Today, May 5, 1978, pp. 14-19, 30-31; January 5, 1983, p. 23; May 18, 1983, p. 483; July 15, 1983, p. 50; December 11, 1987, p. 58; April 8, 1988, p. 30; September 14, 1992, p. 46.

Commentary, October, 1974.

Commonweal, October 24, 1975, pp. 495-496; February 3, 1978; December 3, 1982, p. 668; November 6, 1987, p. 636; March 9, 1990, p. 151; April 5, 1996, p. 32.

Cross Currents, fall, 2000, Peggy Rosenthal, "Joking with Jesus in the Poetry of Kathleen Norris and Annie Dillard," p. 383.

Denver Quarterly, fall, 1985, Mary Davidson McConahay, "Into the Bladelike Arms of God: The Quest for Meaning through Symbolic Language in Thoreau and Annie Dillard," pp. 103-116.

Detroit News, October 31, 1982, p. 2H.

English Journal, April, 1989, p. 90; May 1, 1989, p. 69; December, 1989, Joan Bischoff, "Fellow Rebels: Annie Dillard and Maxine Hong Kingston," pp. 62-67.

Entertainment Weekly, August 7, 1992, p. 54.

Esquire, August, 1985, p. 123.

Fifty Plus, December, 1982, p. 56.

First Things, April, 2000, Andre LaSana, review of *For the Time Being,* p. 74.

Globe and Mail (Toronto, Ontario, Canada), November 28, 1987.

Hudson Review, winter, 1996, p. 666.

Library Journal, March 15, 1982, p. 638; September 1, 1982, p. 1660; November 15, 1984, p. 2150; September 1, 1987, p. 177; May 1, 1989, p. 69; March 1, 1992, p. 136; March 15, 1992, p. 124; July, 1992, p. 146; March 1, 1994, p. 138; April 1, 1994, p. 150; December, 1994, p. 155; May 15, 1995, p. 76; October 1, 1995, p. 83; April 1, 1999, p. 103.

Los Angeles Times, April 27, 1982; November 19, 1982.

Los Angeles Times Book Review, October 31, 1982, p. 2; November 18, 1984, p. 11; July 6, 1986, p. 10; September 20, 1987, pp. 1, 14; May 31, 1992, pp. 1, 7.

Mosaic, spring, 1989, Susan M. Felch, "Annie Dillard: Modern Physics in a Contemporary Mystic," pp. 1-14.

Ms., August, 1974; June, 1985, p. 62; December, 1985, p. 80; October, 1987, p. 78.

Nation, November 20, 1982, pp. 535-536; October 16, 1989, pp. 435-436; May 25, 1992, p. 692.

National Catholic Reporter, November 3, 1989, p. 14; May 11, 1990, p. 28; May 7, 1999, p. 29.

National Post, May 20, 2000, Maggie Mortimer, "Imparting New Meaning to the Personal Narrative," p. B8.

New Leader, June 24, 1974; November 2, 1987, p. 17; August 10, 1992, p. 17.

New Republic, April 6, 1974.

New Statesman, June 10, 1988, p. 42; December 23, 1988, p. 30; November 9, 1990, p. 34.

Newsweek, June 8, 1992, p. 57.

New Yorker, May 17, 1982, p. 140; February 14, 1983, p. 118; December 25, 1989, p. 106; July 6, 1992, p. 80.

New York Times, September 21, 1977; March 12, 1982, p. C18; November 25, 1982, p. C18.

New York Times Book Review, March 24, 1974, pp. 4-5; September 25, 1977, pp. 12, 40; July 1, 1979, p. 21; May 9, 1982, pp. 10, 22-23; July 4, 1982, p. 38; November 28, 1982, pp. 13, 19; December 5, 1982, p. 34; January 1, 1984, p. 32; September 23, 1984, p. 29; September 27, 1987, p. 7; September 17, 1989, p. 15; April 26, 1992, p. 34; May 3, 1992, p. 9; March 28, 1999, p. 9.

New York Times Magazine, April 26, 1992, p. 34.

Old Northwest, winter, 1989-90, Eugene H. Pattison, "The Great Lakes Childhood: The Experience of William Dean Howells and Annie Dillard," pp. 311-329.

People, October 19, 1987, p. 99; July 20, 1992, p. 27.

Progressive, June, 1982, p. 61; December, 1987, p. 31.

Publishers Weekly, January 29, 1982, p. 60; July 20, 1984, p. 73; July 24, 1987, p. 180; September 23, 1988, p. 70; July 14, 1989, p. 62; September 1, 1989, pp. 67-68; February 24, 1992, p. 41; July 6, 1992, p. 22; April 4, 1994, p. 15; October 31, 1994, p. 45; April 24, 1995, p. 65.

Reason, April, 1990, p. 56.

Religion and Literature, summer, 1985, David Lavery, review of *Living by Fiction, Teaching a Stone to Talk,* and *Encounters with Chinese Writers,* pp. 61-68.

Saturday Review, March, 1982, p. 64; April, 1986, p. 64; May-June, 1986, p. 23.

School Library Journal, April, 1988, p. 122.

Smithsonian, November, 1982, p. 219.

South Atlantic Quarterly, spring, 1986, pp. 111-122.

Studia Mystica, fall, 1983, Joseph Keller, "The Function of Paradox in Mystical Discourse."

Theology Today, July, 1986, Eugene H. Peterson, "Annie Dillard: With Her Eyes Open," pp. 178-191.

Threepenny Review, summer, 1988.

Time, March 18, 1974; October 10, 1977.

Tribune Books (Chicago), September 12, 1982, p. 7; September 13, 1987, pp. 1, 12; November 21, 1982, p. 5; December 18, 1988, p. 3; August 27, 1989, p. 6.

U.S. Catholic, September, 1992, p. 48.

Village Voice, July 13, 1982, pp. 40-41.

Virginia Quarterly Review, autumn, 1974, pp. 637-40; spring, 1996, p. 57.

Washington Post, October 28, 1987.

Washington Post Book World, October 16, 1977, p. E6; April 4, 1982, p. 4; January 2, 1983, p. 6; September 9, 1984, p. 6; July 6, 1986, p. 13; September 6, 1987, p. 11; August 14, 1988, p. 12; August 27, 1989, p. 6; September 24, 1989, p. 4, May 3, 1992, pp. 1-2.

Writer's Digest, April, 1989, p. 53.

Yale Review, October, 1992, p. 102.*

* * *

DOLIN, Sharon (Julie) 1956-

PERSONAL: Born July 25, 1956, in Brooklyn, NY; daughter of Irving and Selma (Fellerman) Dolin; married Barry Magid, October 18, 1995. *Education:* Cornell University, B.A., 1977, Ph.D., 1990; attended

University of Edinburgh, 1977; studied in Perugia, Italy, 1979; University of California—Berkeley, M.A., 1982.

ADDRESSES: Home—New York, NY. *Agent*—c/o Author Mail, Marsh Hawk Press, P.O. Box 206, East Rockaway, NY 11518. *E-mail*—sdolin@earthlink.net.

CAREER: Poet, editor and educator. Rebus, Inc., New York, NY, executive editor, 1988-90. Cooper Union, instructor in humanities, beginning 1988; New School for Social Research, instructor in poetry, beginning 1997; also taught at New York University; Ninety-Second Street Young Men's Christian Association, teacher of poetry workshops at Unterberg Poetry Center; Center for Book Arts, coordinator and member of panel of judges for annual Letterpress Poetry Chapbook Competition.

MEMBER: Modern Language Association of America, Poetry Society of America, Associated Writing Programs, PEN, Poets House.

AWARDS, HONORS: Fulbright scholar in Bologna, Italy, 1985-86; Gordon Barber Memorial Award, Poetry Society of America, 1990.

WRITINGS:

POETRY

Mind Lag, Turtle Watch Press, 1982.
Heart Work, Sheep Meadow Press (Riverdale-on-Hudson, NY), 1995.
Climbing Mount Sinai, Dim Gray Bar Press (New York, NY), 1996.
Mistakes (chapbook), Poetry New York (New York, NY), 1999.
The Seagull (chapbook), Center for Book Arts (New York, NY), 2001.
Serious Pink (ekphrastic poems), Marsh Hawk Press (East Rockaway, NY), 2003.

Contributor of poetry to literary journals, including *Poetry, Boulevard, Threepenny Review, Salamander, Kenyon Review, Ploughshares, American Voice,* and *Tikkun.*

WORK IN PROGRESS: Realm of the Possible, for Four Way Books.

SIDELIGHTS: Poet, editor, and educator Sharon Dolin has always had a particular interest in the city of Brooklyn, New York. Born there in 1956, Dolin has included various aspects of the city in much of her poetry. Although she has had many of her poems published in literary journals, Dolin is best known for her collection of poems titled *Heart Work. Heart Work,* wrote *Choice* contributor L. Berk, "creates a sophisticated, cosmopolitan atmosphere" and "weaves moments of feeling against a rich, heavily allusive field of literary presence." *American Book Review* critic Judy Michaels called the collection "challenging," explaining that in some of the poems Dolin takes an approach that is "too self-consciously Keatsian in their approach to art, nature, and love," and stating that "the dynamic of self-discovery is lacking, so the reader is walled in along with the poet." Berk concluded that it would be worthwhile to add the book to contemporary poetry collections.

Dolin's 2003 release *Serious Pink* presents a series of "ekphrastic" poems, or poetry about paintings. Mark Doty explained that "*Serious Pink* is playful, high-spirited, and deeply serious, and in it Sharon Dolin has done a seemingly impossible thing: her poems have the presence of paintings, a vivid materiality. Her fields of color vibrate . . . and the language of which they are made involves us in a deeply individual, engaging sensibility." The book also received mention in *Publisher's Weekly* as a good read: "'Periwinkle drowns pentimenti-almost/ could be a headline,' notes the speaker of *Serious Pink,* Sharon Dolin's collection of poems written from art work by Richard Diebenkorn, Joan Mitchell and others: 'Rosettes/ are not poppies/ but moments of attention/ burned into the wall.'"

BIOGRAPHICAL AND CRITICAL SOURCES:

PERIODICALS

American Book Review, Judy Michaels, review of *Heart Work,* April-May, 1996, p. 26.
Choice, June, 1996, L. Berk, review of *Heart Work,* p. 1641.

Publishers Weekly, May 19, 2003, "Poetry Notes," review of *Serious Pink.**

*   *   *

DR. A
  See ASIMOV, Isaac

*   *   *

DUBUS, Andre III 1959-

PERSONAL: Born September 11, 1959, in Oceanside, CA; son of Andre II (a fiction writer and educator) and Patricia (a social worker; maiden name, Lowe) Dubus; married Fontaine Dollas (a dancer), June 25, 1989. *Education:* Bradford College, A.A., 1979; University of Texas at Austin, B.A. (sociology), 1981; attended Vermont College. *Politics:* Liberal Democrat. *Religion:* Roman Catholic.

ADDRESSES: Home—Newburyport, MA. *Agent*—Philip G. Spitzer Literary Agency, 788 Ninth Ave., New York, NY 10019.

CAREER: Fiction writer. Boulder Community Treatment Center, Boulder, CO, counselor, 1982-83; worked variously as a bartender, bounty hunter, prison counselor, and actor, c. 1980s; carpenter, 1988—. Part-time writing instructor at Emerson College, Boston, MA.

MEMBER: International Sociology Honor Society, Authors Guild, Authors League, Alpha Kappa Delta.

AWARDS, HONORS: National Magazine Award for Fiction, 1985; American Library Association Notable Book selection, and finalist for National Book Award, *Los Angeles Times* book award, L. L. Winship/PEN New England Award, and Booksense Book of the Year award, all 2000, all for *House of Sand and Fog.*

WRITINGS:

The Cage Keeper and Other Stories, Dutton (New York, NY), 1989.

House of Sand and Fog, Norton (New York, NY), 1999.
Bluesman, Norton (New York, NY), 2001.

Contributor of stories and reviews to periodicals, including *Playboy, Crazyhorse Quarterly,* and *Crescent Review.*

House of Sand and Fog has been translated into over twenty-two languages.

ADAPTATIONS: House of Sand and Fog was adapted as a motion picture directed by Vadim Perelman, Dreamworks, 2003. The novel was also adapted as an audiobook read by Dubus and his wife, Fontaine Dubus, HarperAudio, 2001.

SIDELIGHTS: Andre Dubus III is the son of the late famed short-fiction writer of the same name. Dubus III has also had success with the short-story form, but he is perhaps best known for his acclaimed 2000 novel, *House of Sand and Fog. House of Sand and Fog*—which took Dubus four years to write and which was turned down by over twenty publishers before being accepted by Norton—follows the collision course of an ex-Iranian colonel named Behrani and Kathy Nicolo, a young former drug addict whose modest bungalow Behrani purchases during a bank foreclosure auction. Complicating the plot is one of the officers who evicts Kathy, who then starts dating her and helping her fight to get her house back. Although the novel did well after publication, moving to the top of the *New York Times* bestseller list, it became a publishing phenomenon after being chosen by talk show personality Oprah Winfrey as an *Oprah* Book Club selection.

Reviewers of *House of Sand and Fog* had unqualified praise for Dubus's debut novel. Donna Seaman, writing in *Booklist,* noted that the book's characters "are headed for a resolution of stunningly tragic dimensions." Liz Keuffer, discussing *House of Sand and Fog* for *BookReporter,* praised the novel as well, concluding that Dubus "chronicles the clash of cultures between the Americans and the Iranians while keeping the humanity of everyone involved at the forefront." Reflecting also on the culture clash that is at the core of Dubus's novel, Joanna Burkhardt commented in *Library Journal* that "the frustration and anger are visceral, the tension intense." *House of Sand and Fog* "captures the hope, confusion, resolve, and uncertainty" of a cast of compelling characters.

Dubus told *CA:* "Every one of us needs to express himself in some way. I feel very fortunate that creative writing has tapped me on the shoulder."

BIOGRAPHICAL AND CRITICAL SOURCES:

PERIODICALS

Booklist, February 1, 1999, Donna Seaman, review of *House of Sand and Fog,* p. 961.

Library Journal, January, 1989, Starr E. Smith, review of *The Cage Keeper and Other Stories,* p. 101; May 15, 1993, Charles Michaud, review of *Bluesman,* p. 96; March 1, 1999, Reba Leiding, review of *House of Sand and Fog,* p. 108; May 1, 2001, Joanna Burkhardt, review of *House of Sand and Fog,* p. 145.

Macclean's, May 14, 2001, "House That Oprah Built," p. 53.

New York Times Book Review, February 5, 1989, Deborah Solomon, review of *The Cage Keeper and Other Stories,* p. 24; April 25, 1999, Bill Sharp, review of *House of Sand and Fog,* p. 104.

People, March 12, 2001, "Blood Knot: Bestselling Novelist Andre Dubus III Knew One Thing Growing Up—He Wouldn't Be a Writer Like His Father," p. 75.

Publishers Weekly, October 21, 1988, review of *The Cage Keeper and Other Stories,* p. 48; November 1, 1999, review of *House of Sand and Fog,* p. 45.

Times Literary Supplement, April 7, 2000, Henry Hitchings, review of *House of Sand and Fog,* p. 28.

ONLINE

BookReporter, http://www.bookreporter.com/ (May 1, 2003).

House of Sand and Fog Official site, http://www.dreamworks.com/houseofsandandfog/ (January 14, 2004).*

E

EBERHART, Richard (Ghormley) 1904-

PERSONAL: Born April 5, 1904, in Austin, MN; son of Alpha La Rue and Lena (Lowenstein) Eberhart; married Helen Elizabeth Butcher (a teacher), August 29, 1941; children: Richard, Gretchen. *Education:* Attended University of Minnesota, 1922-23; Dartmouth College, B.A., 1926; St. John's College, Cambridge, B.A., 1929, M.A., 1933; attended Harvard University, 1932-33. *Politics:* Democrat. *Religion:* Episcopal. *Hobbies and other interests:* Swimming, sailing.

ADDRESSES: Home—80 Lyme Rd., #161, Hanover, NH 03755-1230.

CAREER: Poet. Worked in a slaughterhouse, 1929; private tutor in Florida, and then for the son of King Prajadhipok of Siam (now Thailand), 1930-31; St. Mark's School, Southboro, MA, master in English, 1933-41; Cambridge School, Kendal Green, MA, English teacher, 1941-42; Butcher Polish Co., Boston, MA, assistant manager to vice president, 1946-52, then honorary vice president and member of board of directors; University of Washington, Seattle, poet-in-residence, 1952-53; University of Connecticut, Storrs, professor of English, 1953-54; Wheaton College, Norton, MA, professor of English and poet-in-residence, 1954-55; Princeton University, Princeton, NJ, Christian Gauss Lecturer and resident fellow, 1955-56; Dartmouth College, Hanover, NH, professor of English and poet-in-residence, 1956-68, Class of 1925 professor, 1968-71, professor emeritus, 1971—. Elliston Lecturer, University of Cincinnati, 1961. Visiting professor, University of Washington, Seattle, 1952-53, 1967, 1972, Wheaton College, 1954-55, and University of Florida, 1974-80; adjunct professor, Columbia University, spring, 1975; regents professor, University of California, Davis, fall, 1975. Phi Beta Kappa poet at Tufts University, 1941, Brown University, 1957, Swarthmore College, 1963, Trinity College, 1963, College of William and Mary, 1963, University of New Hampshire, 1964, and Harvard University, 1967. Yaddo Corp., member, beginning 1955, director, 1964. Founder and president, The Poets' Theatre, Inc., 1950. Member of advisory committee on the arts, John F. Kennedy Memorial Theatre, beginning 1959. Library of Congress, Washington, DC, consultant in poetry, 1959-61, honorary consultant in American letters, 1963-69. *Military service:* U.S. Naval Reserve, 1942-46; personnel officer; became lieutenant commander.

MEMBER: Poetry Society of America (honorary president, 1972—), Academy of American Poets (fellow), American Academy and Institute of Arts and Letters, American Academy of Arts and Sciences, Phi Beta Kappa, Century Club (New York), Signet Club, Bucks Harbor Yacht Club (Maine).

AWARDS, HONORS: Harriet Monroe Memorial Prize, 1950; New England Poetry Club award, 1950; Shelley Memorial Award, 1952; Harriet Monroe Poetry Award, 1955; National Institute of Arts and Letters grant in literature, 1955; Bollingen Prize in Poetry (shared with John Hall Wheelock), Yale University, 1962; Pulitzer Prize, 1966, for *Selected Poems, 1930-1965;* Academy of American Poets fellowship, 1969; National Book Award, 1977, for *Collected Poems, 1930-1976;* President's Medallion, University of Florida, 1977; appointed poet laureate of the State of New

Hampshire, 1979-84; Sarah Josepha Hale Award, Newport, NH Library, 1982; Richard Eberhart Day proclaimed by governor of Rhode Island and Dartmouth College, 1982; named Florida ambassador of arts, 1984; St. John's College honorary fellow, 1986; Poetry Society of America Robert Frost Medal, 1986; Presidential Medal for Outstanding Leadership and Achievement, Dartmouth College, 1990; Gold medal for poetry, Dartmouth College, 1992. D.Litt. from Dartmouth College, 1954, Skidmore College, 1966, College of Wooster, 1969, and Colgate University, 1974; D.H.L. from Franklin Pierce College, 1978, St. Lawrence University, 1985, and Plymouth State College, 1987.

WRITINGS:

POETRY

A Bravery of Earth, J. Cape (London, England), 1930, Cape & Smith (New York, NY), 1931.

Reading the Spirit, Chatto & Windus (London, England), 1936, Oxford University Press (New York, NY), 1937.

Song and Idea, Chatto & Windus (London, England), 1940, Oxford University Press (New York, NY), 1942.

A World-View, Tufts College Press (Medford, MA), 1941.

Poems, New and Selected, New Directions (Norfolk, CT), 1944.

Burr Oaks, Oxford University Press (New York, NY), 1947.

Brotherhood of Men, Banyan Press (Pawlet, VT), 1949.

An Herb Basket, Cummington Press (Cummington, MA), 1950.

Selected Poems, Oxford University Press (New York, NY), 1951.

Undercliff: Poems, 1946-1953, Chatto & Windus (London, England), 1953, Oxford University Press (New York, NY), 1954.

Great Praises, Oxford University Press (New York, NY), 1957.

The Oak: A Poem, Pine Tree Press (Hanover, NH), 1957.

Collected Poems, 1930-1960, Oxford University Press (New York, NY), 1960.

The Quarry: New Poems, Oxford University Press (New York, NY), 1964.

The Vastness and Indifference of the World, Ferguson Press (Cambridge, MA), 1965.

Fishing for Snakes, privately printed, 1965.

Selected Poems, 1930-1965, New Directions (New York, NY), 1965.

Thirty-one Sonnets, Eakins (New York, NY), 1967.

Shifts of Being: Poems, Oxford University Press (New York, NY), 1968.

The Achievement of Richard Eberhart: A Comprehensive Selection of His Poems, edited by Bernard F. Engle, Scott, Foresman (Glenview, IL), 1968.

Three Poems, Pym Randall (Cambridge, MA), 1968.

Fields of Grace, Oxford University Press (New York, NY), 1972.

The Groundhog Revisiting, Pomegranate Press (Cambridge, MA), 1972.

Two Poems, Aralia Press (Westchester, PA), 1975.

Collected Poems, 1930-1976, Oxford University Press (New York, NY), 1976.

Poems to Poets, Penmaen Press (Lincoln, MA), 1976.

Hour, Gnats, Putah Creek Press (Davis, CA), 1977.

Survivors, BOA Editions (Northport, NY), 1979.

Ways of Light: Poems, 1972-1980, Oxford University Press (New York, NY), 1980.

New Hampshire: Nine Poems, Pym Randall (Rosedale, MA), 1980.

Four Poems, Palaemon (Winston-Salem, MA), 1980.

Florida Poems, Konglomerati (Gulfport, FL), 1981.

The Long Reach: New and Uncollected Poems, 1948-1984, New Directions (New York, NY), 1984.

Snowy Owl, Palaemon (Winston-Salem, MA), 1984.

Throwing Yourself Away, Stone House (New York, NY), 1984.

Spite Fence, Mountain State (Charleston, WV), 1984.

Collected Poems, 1930-1986, Oxford University Press (New York, NY), 1988.

Maine Poems, Oxford University Press (New York, NY), 1989.

New and Selected Poems, 1930-1990, Blue Moon (New York, NY), 1990.

Poetry represented in anthologies, including *Moment of Poetry,* Johns Hopkins Press (Baltimore, MD), 1962. Contributor of poetry and reviews to journals in United States and other countries.

PLAYS

The Apparition (also see below), first produced in Cambridge, MA, 1951.

The Visionary Farms (also see below), first produced in Cambridge, MA, 1952.

Triptych (also see below), first produced in Chicago, IL, 1955.

Devils and Angels (first produced by Poets' Theatre, 1956; also see below), Poets' Theatre (Cambridge, MA), 1956.

The Mad Musician, and Devils and Angels (also see below), first produced in Cambridge, MA, 1962.

Collected Verse Plays (contains *The Apparition, The Visionary Farms, Triptych, The Mad Musician,* and *Devils and Angels*), University of North Carolina Press (Chapel Hill, NC), 1962.

(Adapter) Lope de Vega, *The Bride from Mantua,* first produced in Hanover, New Hampshire, 1964.

Chocorua (limited edition), Nadja (New York, NY), 1981.

OTHER

(Editor, with others) *Free Gunner's Handbook,* revised edition, 1944.

(Editor, with Selden Rodman) *War and the Poet: An Anthology of Poetry Expressing Man's Attitude to War from Ancient Times to the Present,* Devin-Adair, 1945, reprinted, Greenwood Press (Westport, CT), 1974.

Poetry As a Creative Principle, Wheaton College (Norton, MA), 1952.

(Editor and contributor) *Dartmouth Poems,* twelve volumes, Dartmouth Publications (Hanover, NH), 1958-59, 1962-71.

(Editor) *To Eberhart from Ginsberg: A Letter about "Howl," 1956,* Penmaen Press (Lincoln, MA), 1976.

Of Poetry and Poets (criticism), University of Illinois Press (Urbana, IL), 1979.

Also author of *Dream Journey of the Head and Heart,* 1962. Contributor to *The Arts Anthology: Dartmouth Verse 1925,* Mosher Press (Portland, ME), 1925; *Cambridge Poetry, 1929,* Hogarth Press (London, England), 1929; *New Signatures,* edited by Michael Roberts, Hogarth Press (London, England), 1932; *War and the Poet,* edited by Eberhart and Selden Rodman, Devin-Adair (New York, NY), 1945; and *After This Exile,* edited by Manuel A. Viray, Phoenix House (London, England), 1965

SIDELIGHTS: One of the most prominent American poets of the twentieth century, Pulitzer Prize-winner Richard Eberhart emerged out of the 1930s as a modern stylist with romantic sensibilities. Sometimes labeled a nature poet, he often writes about death, most notably in his famous poem "The Groundhog," but his themes also include a preoccupation with such things as the tension between childhood and adulthood, innocence and experience. Praised for the honest emotions of his verses, he has been criticized for occasionally sloppy writing that contains at times too many clichéd or overwrought phrases. However, when his poetry avoids such flaws, his verses are widely admired. As Ralph J. Mills, Jr. put it in a *Parnassus* review of *Fields of Grace,* the poet's sometimes awkward phrasing and meter might be attributed to the fact that he writes in the spur of the moment: "the uniqueness of his poetry resides in [his] visionary intensity that throws caution to the winds in order to seize the given insight."

Eberhart's happy childhood was marked by tragedy by the time he was a teenager; subsequently there followed a long period where he could not find acceptance as a writer, which lasted until he reached his forties. This pattern led *Dictionary of Literary Biography* contributor Joel Roache to speculate that the poet's blend of romanticism and preoccupation with death might very well be a result of his early experiences. Eberhart's father was vice president of the Hormel Meat Packing Company, a position that allowed his family to be comfortably well off financially. The future poet also enjoyed having a devoted mother who helped foster the boy's love of reading. But two tragedies soon turned the family's world upside down: one of his father's employees embezzled a fortune from the company, causing Hormel's stock to fall and seriously damaging the family's assets. An argument at the company later caused his father to quit, and the family never regained its fortunes fully. Eberhart would later base his verse play *The Visionary Farms* on this time in his life. His poem "Orchard" is also based on a real-life tragedy, the death of his mother from lung cancer when he was eighteen. "Eberhart himself has said that the death of his mother made him a poet," reported Roache.

While attending college in both America and England, Eberhart worked on his poetry, contributing verses to magazines and anthologies and attending lectures, debates, and parties featuring such luminaries as George Bernard Shaw, C. P. Snow, William Butler Yeats, and G. K. Chesterton. His first book, *A Bravery of Earth,* published while he was still at Cambridge University, was received with some stark criticism. "There is plenty—a too great plenty—of bad writing in this one-hundred-and-twenty-page poem," wrote Harriet Monroe in *Poetry*. However, critics saw much promise in Eberhart. As Monroe continued, "I prefer to credit this young poet, not only with sincerity and enthusiasm . . . but also with an outreaching imagination, and an authentic talent." R. P. Blackmur, writing in *Partisan Review*, also saw promise in the young writer, saying that what he lacked at the time was an abiding philosophy to go with his poems: "He so far lacks a theme adequate to his ambition as he sees it, or perhaps it would be more accurate to put it that he has never so felt a theme as to require his consistent utmost in craft." Roache, on the other hand, felt that *A Bravery of Earth* marks the beginning of "his lifelong exploration of the parallel dichotomy between the human being's life-seeking, order-creating spirit, and the death-dealing chaos of the exterior, 'objective' world, a dichotomy that finds its only, albeit temporary, resolution in art."

After completing his second bachelor's degree at Cambridge, Eberhart spent a couple years working non-academic jobs. He was employed at a slaughterhouse in 1929, and from 1930 to 1931 he was a tutor, one of his students being the son of the King of Siam. With some money saved up, he returned to his studies, completing a master's degree at Cambridge and attending Harvard University for a time. He then became a teacher in Massachusetts, all the while working on his poetry but achieving little recognition for his efforts. The Great Depression led to a year-and-a-half of unemployment for the struggling poet, but according to Roache this proved to be "an important transitional moment in Eberhart's life. His long search for a new position, a livelihood, underscored the sharpness of his struggle throughout the 1930s to continue writing and to gain some degree of literary recognition."

Success briefly reared its head in 1934, when Eberhart's poem "The Groundhog" was first published in the *Listener* and was roundly praised by literary critics. The poem concerns the thoughts of the narrator as he views the dead body of a groundhog in four different stages of decay over time. The first time he sees the body it is filled with surging swarms of maggots that denote a force of life even as they feed off death; the decomposition of the groundhog continues for three more visits until every last trace of it has disappeared. The final lines of the poem express both

a sense of tragic loss and acceptance. "Even in this vision of death," explained Peter L. Thorslev, Jr. in *Poets in Progress: Critical Prefaces to Thirteen Modern American Poets,* "a kind of fierce mystic joy is possible, an impassioned acceptance of the impersonal, of death and decay. This attitude is more than mere resignation: it is the affirmation which comes to the heart of tragedy." *Scrutiny* critic W. H. Mellers noted that "The Groundhog," which was first collected in Eberhart's *Sound and Idea,* is a perfect example of the kind of writing that makes the poet's voice distinctive. A sense of nervous anguish, according to Mellers, "seems to me to be the impetus behind all of Mr. Eberhart's best verse." Mellers continued, "In a rather patent fashion one can see this in 'The Groundhog' where some characteristic reflections on death and decay are woven into more complex and far-reaching emotions; more subtly it is manifested in the comparatively balanced movement—a tranquility as it were poised over the most agile and alert conflict of feelings."

"The themes of ['The Groundhog']," commented Roache, "life and death, man and nature, mortality and immortality, mind and body, concreteness and transcendence, recur throughout Eberhart's career, and they draw upon the central dilemma of his work," which is the struggle between "the innocence of childhood" and "the adult world of experience, limitation, and delusion." The "intensity of childhood," as a contributor to *Contemporary Poets* described it, is particularly well highlighted in Eberhart's poem "If I Could Only Live at the Pitch That Is Near Madness." Although the experiences of childhood seems more vivid to the poet, "the grown man accepts and indeed delights in the obligations of adulthood," explained the *Contemporary Poets* writer, who continued: "Age brings with it . . . the awareness of human cruelty, and many of Eberhart's poems treat the varieties of human suffering that grow out of social, political, and family strife."

The instability in Eberhart's life was eased considerably by his marriage to Helen Butcher in 1941 and a teaching job at the Cambridge School. During World War II, the poet joined the U.S. Navy and was an aerial gunnery instructor at several bases throughout the United States. Although up until this point his poems had successfully avoided addressing current events in favor of broader themes, the enormity of the war could not be entirely avoided, and he wrote about it in such verses as "The Fury of Aerial Bombardment" and "An Airman Considers His Power."

After the war Eberhart joined his wife's family's company, the Butcher Polish Company, in Boston, eventually becoming vice president. The late 1940s and early 1950s were also a time of great prolificness for the poet, who swerved into some experimentation when he joined the Poets' Theatre in Cambridge and began writing verse dramas. More poetry than drama, these plays typically involve spectators of a scene who comment on what is happening, or are dialogues between two or three characters. One of these works, *The Visionary Farms,* involves an embezzler whose theft of corporate funds ruins his company's manager and the manager's family in a plot reflecting Eberhart's own childhood experiences. The verse plays, however, were only an aside that occupied the poet's time during the 1950s before he abandoned them to return to his regular poetic works.

After leaving his company job in 1952, Eberhart embarked on a long academic career and finally began to find satisfaction on a professional level. He taught at a number of universities before joining the faculty at Dartmouth College in 1956, where he remained for the rest of his active career, becoming professor emeritus in 1971. As a professor, Eberhart found a sense of security and recognition that obviously pleased him. One can see this reflected in his later poems, which, as Roache pointed out, express a characteristic "serenity of tone." The highlights of his poetic career came with the 1966 Pulitzer Prize-winning *Selected Poems, 1930-1965* and the 1977 National Book Award-winning *Collected Poems, 1930-1976,* along with many other honors and prizes. Even though his more recent poems have a "serenity" and a "greater clarity and firmer mastery of [the] medium" in them than did earlier verses, Eberhart's preoccupations have remained the same, according to Roache, and are apparent in such collections as *Fields of Grace* and *Ways of Light.* "His vision has always been rooted in the ancient confrontation between innocence and experience, between the drive for order and the awareness of reality, a confrontation that seems unresolvable in the actual world," wrote Roache.

Eberhart's romantic spirit has been compared to that of such giants as William Blake and Walt Whitman. *Nation* critic Hayden Carruth labeled him "a misplaced eighteenth-century sentimentalist," yet characterized the poet's style as thoroughly modern. "However much of his poems share common themes with other Romantic poets," said Thorslev, "Eberhart's style and idiom are nevertheless always his own. His lines are short, his rhymes oblique or infrequent, and his rhythms intentionally irregular, but within these limits he shows a quite extraordinary range." One of the few poets to arise from the 1930s and remain relevant decades later, Eberhart retains appeal to contemporary readers due to his "oddly affecting naiveté," as Jay Parini described it in a *Times Literary Supplement* review of *Ways of Light.* "He is unabashedly vatic, believing in 'inspiration' as innocently as any poet ever has." Kenneth Rexroth, writing in the *Saturday Review,* argued that the poet's resilience is due to three things: "Innocence. Wisdom. A pure heart." While others of his generation wrote on narrow topics that addressed the concerns of the day, Eberhart stuck to the big questions about life, making him, in the opinion of Rexroth and many others, "the most profound poet of his time."

Eberhart once told *CA:* "Consciousness is still a vast reservoir of spirit which we only partially perceive. If we could see or feel beyond the human condition is it possible to think that we could feel or think the unthinkable? The Greeks had aspiration to ideas of immortality. We twentieth-century Americans live closer to materialism than to idealism so we are more nearly measurers, like Aristotle, than dreamers of immortal types, like Plato. I am on Plato's side rather than on Aristotle's. However, our highest imaginations are ungraspable and we are constantly thrown back into the here and now, into materialistic reality. I think that poetry is allied to religion and to music. It helps us to live because it expresses our limitations, our mortality, while exciting us to a beyond which may or not be there, therefore death poems can be written in fullness of spirit, inviting contemplation of ultimate mysteries. Death poems are as good as life poems because they are also life poems, written in flesh and blood. Poetry embraces the moment as it flies."

Eberhart has been the subject of two films, one directed by Samuel Mandelbaum for Tri-Prix in 1972 and the other directed by Irving Broughton for the University of Washington in 1974.

BIOGRAPHICAL AND CRITICAL SOURCES:

BOOKS

Contemporary Literary Criticism, Gale (Detroit, MI), Volume 3, 1975, Volume 11, 1979, Volume 19, 1981, Volume 56, 1989.

Contemporary Poets, 7th edition, St. James Press (Detroit, MI), 2001.

Dictionary of Literary Biography, Volume 48: *American Poets, 1880-1940, Second Series,* Gale (Detroit, MI), 1986, pp. 148-159.

Dillard, R. H. W., George Garrett, and John Rees Moore, editors, *The Sounder Few,* University of Georgia Press (Athens, GA), 1971.

Donoghue, Denis, *The Third Voice,* Princeton University Press (Princeton, NJ), 1964, pp. 194-195, 223-235.

Engle, Bernard F., *Richard Eberhart,* Twayne (New York, NY), 1972.

Mills, Ralph J., Jr., *Contemporary American Poetry,* Random House (New York, NY), 1965, pp. 9-31.

Mills, Ralph J., Jr., *Richard Eberhart,* University of Minnesota Press, 1966.

Modern American Literature, Volume 1, St. James Press (Detroit, MI), 1999.

Nemerov, Howard, editor, *Poets on Poetry,* Basic Books (New York, NY), 1966.

Poets in Progress (series), Northwestern University Press, 1962, pp. 73-91, 1967.

Reference Guide to American Literature, 4th edition, St. James Press (Detroit, MI), 2000.

Roache, Joel, *Richard Eberhart: The Progress of an American Poet,* Oxford University Press (New York, NY), 1971.

PERIODICALS

Book Week, August 2, 1964.

Christian Science Monitor, December 22, 1960; July 23, 1968; December 3, 1996, p. 13.

Commonweal, December 30, 1960; May 14, 1971.

Forum, spring, 1969.

Furioso, summer, 1941, John Crowe Ransom, "Lyrics Important, Sometimes Rude," pp. 68-70.

Hollins Critic, October, 1964, pp. 1-12.

Nation, January 21, 1961, Hayden Carruth, "The Errors of Excellence," pp. 63-64; August 10, 1964.

New Republic, July 9, 1930, Edith H. Walton, review of *A Bravery of Earth,* p. 214; April 2, 1945, p. 452; November 20, 1976.

New Statesman, October 15, 1960; September 25, 1964.

New York Herald Tribune, December 4, 1960.

New York Herald Tribune Books, February 27, 1938, Muriel Rukeyser, "Straight through to Life," p. 17.

New York Times Book Review, November 22, 1953; January 8, 1961; September 6, 1964; January 12, 1969; January 1, 1978; July 8, 1979.

Northwestern University Tri-Quarterly, winter, 1960.

Paris Review, autumn, 1953, pp. 113-119.

Parnassus, spring/summer, 1973, Ralph J. Mills, Jr., review of *Fields of Grace,* pp. 215-216.

Partisan Review, February, 1938, R. P. Blackmur, review of *Reading the Spirit,* pp. 52-56.

Poetry, September, 1930, Harriet Monroe, "Brave Youth," pp. 343-346; December, 1942; May, 1945, David Daiches, "Towards the Proper Spirit," pp. 92-95; January, 1949, Arthur Mizener, "The Earnest Victorian," pp. 226-228; November, 1954, Reuel Denney, "The Idiomatic Kingdom," pp. 102-105; November, 1954, Byron Vazakas, "Eberhart: A Negative Report," pp. 106-108; October, 1957; February, 1970.

Publishers Weekly, April 29, 1968; February 12, 1979.

Saturday Review, December, 1957, Kenneth Rexroth, "Finest of the Last," pp. 15-16; February 11, 1961; December 6, 1962; March 6, 1971.

Scrutiny, December, 1940, W. H. Mellers, "Cats in Air-Pumps (or Poets in 1940)," pp. 298-300.

Sewanee Review, spring, 1952, Howard Nemerov, "The Careful Poets and the Reckless Ones," pp. 318-329.

Shenandoah, summer, 1964, pp. 62-69.

South Atlantic Review, November, 1985, Cleanth Brooks, "A Tribute to Richard Eberhart," pp. 21-33.

Southern Review, October, 1977.

Spectator, September 30, 1960.

Times Literary Supplement, October 29, 1964; September 26, 1980, Jay Parini, review of *Ways of Light,* p. 1060.

Virginia Quarterly Review, winter, 1965.

Western Review, summer, 1954, James Hall, "Richard Eberhart: The Sociable Naturalist," pp. 315-321.

Yale Review, March, 1961.

ONLINE

Academy of American Poets Web site, http://www.poets.org/ (April 17, 2002).*

*   *   *

EDGERTON, Clyde (Carlyle) 1944-
(Raney Basket)

PERSONAL: Born May 20, 1944, in Durham, NC; son of Ernest Carlyle (in insurance sales) and Susan Truma (a homemaker; maiden name, Warren) Edgerton; married, June 21, 1975 (marriage ended); married Kristina Jones, December 22, 2001; children: Catherine, Nathan. *Education:* University of North Carolina—Chapel Hill, B.A., 1966, M.A.T., 1972, Ph.D., 1977.

ADDRESSES: Office—Creative Writing Program, University of North Carolina—Wilmington, 601 College Rd., Wilmington, NC 28403. *Agent*—Liz Darhansoff, 1220 Park Ave., New York, NY 10128. *E-mail*—cedgerton@earthlink.net.

CAREER: Southern High School, Durham, NC, English teacher, 1972-73; English Teaching Institute, Chapel Hill, NC, codirector, 1976; Campbell University, Buies Creek, NC, assistant professor, 1977-82, associate professor of education and psychology, 1982-85; St. Andrews Presbyterian College, Laurinburg, NC, associate professor of English and education, 1985-89; full-time writer, 1989-98; University of North Carolina—Wilmington, Wilmington, NC, distinguished visiting professor, 1998-2002, professor of creative writing, 2002—. North Carolina Central University, visiting lecturer, 1977; Agnes Scott College, visiting writer in residence, 1991; Duke University, visiting professor, 1992; Millsaps College, Eudora Welty Visiting Professor and Eudora Welty cochair of southern studies, 1996; lecturer at conferences and workshops. Guest on television and radio programs, including *Today, Sunday Weekend Edition,* National Public Radio, *Morning Edition,* and *Good Evening with Noah Adams.* Musician; member of Rank Strangers Band. *Military service:* U.S. Air Force, 1966-71, pilot for reconnaissance and forward air control missions in Southeast Asia; received Distinguished Flying Cross.

AWARDS, HONORS: Publishers Weekly named *The Floatplane Notebooks* one of the best books of 1988; Guggenheim fellow, 1989; Lyndhurst fellow, 1991; honorary doctorate, University of North Carolina—Asheville, 1993; D.H.L., St. Andrews Presbyterian College, 1994; Ragan-Rubin Award, 1995; award from Fellowship of Southern Writers, 1997; five "notable book" citations from *New York Times;* North Carolina Award for Literature, 1997.

WRITINGS:

Raney (novel), Algonquin Books (Chapel Hill, NC), 1985.

Walking across Egypt (novel; Book-of-the-Month Club featured "discovery" selection), Algonquin Books (Chapel Hill, NC), 1987.

Understanding the Floatplane (chapbook), Mud Puppy Press (Chapel Hill, NC), 1987.

The Floatplane Notebooks (novel; Book-of-the-Month Club alternate selection), Algonquin Books (Chapel Hill, NC), 1988.

Cold Black Peas (chapbook), Mud Puppy Press (Chapel Hill, NC), 1990.

Killer Diller (novel; Book-of-the-Month Club alternate selection), Algonquin Books (Chapel Hill, NC), 1991.

In Memory of Junior: A Novel, Algonquin Books (Chapel Hill, NC), 1992.

Redeye: A Western, Algonquin Books (Chapel Hill, NC), 1995.

Where Trouble Sleeps: A Novel, Algonquin Books (Chapel Hill, NC), 1997.

Lunch at the Piccadilly, Algonquin Books (Chapel Hill, NC), 2003.

Contributor to *Family Portraits: Remembrances by Twenty Distinguished Writers,* edited by Carolyn Anthony, Doubleday (New York, NY), 1989; work represented in other anthologies, including *Weymouth: An Anthology of Poetry,* edited by Sam Ragan, St. Andrews Press (Laurinburg, NC), 1987; *New Stories from the South: The Year's Best, 1990,* edited by Shannon Ravenel, Algonquin Books (Chapel Hill, NC), 1990; *Best American Short Stories,* 1997, and *New Stories from the South: The Year's Best,* 2000. Contributor of short stories, essays, and reviews to periodicals, including *Chattahoochee Review, Descant, Daily Tar Heel, Atlanta Journal and Constitution, Just Pulp, Leader, Lyricist, Mid-Atlantic Country, Old Hickory Review,* and *New York Times;* some periodical articles appeared under the pseudonym Raney Basket. Work available on sound recordings, including *Walking across Egypt: Songs and Readings from the Books "Raney" and "Walking across Egypt,"* music performed by Edgerton and other members of the Tarwater Band, Flying Fish Records, 1987; *Clyde Edgerton Reads "The Floatplane Notebooks,"* Random House Audiobooks, 1989; and *The "Killer Diller" Tapes.*

ADAPTATIONS: Walking across Egypt was adapted by John Justice for a play of the same title, first produced in 1989; it was also adapted as a screenplay, 1999. *Raney* was adapted by John Justice for a play of the same title, first produced in Fayetteville, NC, in

1990. *Killer Diller* was adapted for the screen as *Bottleneck*, 2003. *Lunch at the Piccadilly* and *Killer Diller* were also adapted for the stage.

SIDELIGHTS: "If I can get a handle on a good character," commented novelist Clyde Edgerton in the *Huntsville Times,* "then everything else follows, including plot." The author's works, set in the small towns of North Carolina, have been hailed for vivid characters that are drawn with insight, compassion, and humor. "When you finish one of his novels," wrote *Times* critic Ann Martin, "you feel as if you have a new friend." A product of North Carolina himself, Edgerton draws inspiration from such respected Southern writers as Eudora Welty and Flannery O'Connor. He doesn't mind being called a "Southern" writer as long as onlookers remember that "regional" writing can have widespread significance. "Shakespeare's works," he told the *Milwaukee Journal,* "were quite regional."

Edgerton didn't grow up expecting to be a writer. Only years later did he realize that his childhood, immersed in the storytelling traditions of the rural South, had been a fine preparation for the job. "Some of us grew up in a South in the 1950s that most people think disappeared after the 1930s," he told the *Atlanta Journal.* "I'm aware that [novelist] Walker Percy said people don't sit on the front porch and tell stories anymore. But I did, and [people in my family] did." Lacking the distractions of big cities and mass communication, rural Americans traditionally stayed in touch with their relatives and regaled each other with stories—particularly family stories—as a form of entertainment. "It's a kind of ancestor worship," Edgerton told the *Washington Post Book World.* "You get a picture of these people, and they're part of you, and you're very proud."

As a student at the University of North Carolina in the 1960s, Edgerton wrote only a few unfinished short stories and a smattering of poems, including a verse condemning those who opposed America's entry into the Vietnam war. He was more interested in flying, and after graduation he joined the U.S. Air Force and piloted reconnaissance and forward air control flights over Vietnam as the conflict there continued. Though Edgerton's missions generally kept him high above the combat raging on the ground, his wartime experiences were enough to leave him a changed man, haunted by concerns that he would need years to express. His

choice of presidential candidates changed at once. "In 1964, I worked for [conservative Republican] Barry Goldwater," he told R. K. Underwood of the *Augusta Chronicle.* "In 1970, I went to Southeast Asia. In 1972, I worked for [liberal Democrat] George McGovern." Soon thereafter Edgerton married Susan Ketchin, with whom he shared an interest in teaching and bluegrass music. He became an professor of education at Campbell University, a Baptist-affiliated school in the small town of Buies Creek, North Carolina. The couple expected a quiet, conventional life.

But writing gradually unsettled their plans. It began innocuously at Christmas, 1977, when Edgerton became curious about a soft spot in his kitchen floor, entered the crawlspace under his house, and found an old well. He became inspired to write a short story about a boy named Meredith who breaks through a kitchen floor and drops into the well beneath. As he polished the story a few months later, Edgerton experienced a literary conversion of sorts while watching Eudora Welty read one of her short stories on public television. The story, "Why I Live at the P.O.," shows an absurd quarrel in a small-town Southern family that ends when one of the grown children stomps off to live in the back room of the post office. Authors like Welty and O'Connor, Edgerton recalled in *Publishers Weekly,* "were writing about people and situations and places that earlier I might have thought not worthy of literature." By the day after the broadcast—May 15, 1978—Edgerton had decided that writing was his true vocation.

He began by writing more short stories. Between 1979 and 1983 "I sent out 12 or 13 stories and got back 202 rejections," he told the *Augusta Chronicle.* "I knew that writers were supposed to get rejected, but it seemed like a year of rejections would be enough." Eventually six of his stories were accepted, half of them by friends. The stories had an unexpected dividend, though; two of them featured a character that Edgerton liked well enough to use as the basis of a novel. She was Raney Bell Shepherd: a small-town Free Will Baptist, narrow-minded, unapologetic, fiercely loyal to her family, but somehow loveable because of her bouncy personality and commonsense approach to life. Raney, Edgerton realized, was a strong character—strong enough to be the narrator of her own book—because she was a voice from his childhood, where women were the principal storytellers. "I just had the voice," he recalled in the

Milwaukee Journal. "Because in my family women talked a lot, and because I was an only child . . . I've been around talking women. I had to have a woman tell the story." The book, naturally, was also called *Raney.*

Edgerton spent two years writing and rewriting *Raney* and gathering rejections from New York publishers. Finally his wife suggested that he send the manuscript to Louis Rubin, a former professor of hers at the University of North Carolina. Rubin liked the novel so much that he offered to publish it as part of his new venture, Algonquin Books. He sent the manuscript on to Algonquin editor Shannon Ravenel, who also edited the renowned annual *Best American Short Stories.* As *Publishers Weekly* reported, Edgerton found his new partnership with Ravenel "to be an essential element in the success of his books." The two spent several months reworking *Raney,* which sold more than 200,000 copies after it was published by Algonquin in 1985.

Raney depicts the title character's tumultuous first two years of married life. The marriage is a Southern cultural mismatch. Raney's husband, Charles Shepherd, is a slightly stuffy librarian from Atlanta who has settled in Raney's small town to enjoy tranquility and bluegrass music. Love of music, in fact, seems to be the only thing the couple has in common. Charles is irked by Raney's strong family ties, and Raney is shocked that Charles considers a black man to be his best friend. The couple proceeds to clash about everything from sex to religion to the importance of the world outside Bethel, North Carolina, and Raney finally leaves home. She soon returns, however—a bit more tolerant and mature—and even engages Charles in some after-hours lovemaking in the back of her father's general store.

Reviewers discovered Edgerton's first novel with delight. In the *Sewanee Review,* editor George Core observed: "*Raney*'s effectiveness stems from its wonderfully sustained tone, the sound of Raney Bell's voice as she narrates [her] deliciously funny story." The book, Core told readers of the *Washington Post Book World,* was something that humorist James Thurber "might have written had he lived in North Carolina rather than Connecticut." "What really distinguishes this novel," wrote Chuck Moss in the *Detroit News,* "is its warmth and amused tolerance. This could easily be a wicked satire, slashing at ignorant Crackers

or the primly liberal bourgeoisie. Instead, Edgerton draws all his people with sympathy, acceptance and comic affection. His is a free country, even if what you're doing plainly doesn't make sense at all and never did."

Edgerton's toughest audience seems to have been his own bosses at Campbell University, where he was still an associate professor of education. *Raney* was published in January of 1985, shortly before it was time to renew the author's contract to teach. Instead of the contract, Edgerton received an invitation to a meeting with the administration. At first he thought his bosses might offer him tenure; instead, they wanted to discuss *Raney.* "They gave me [several] specific problems they had with the book," he recalled in *Publishers Weekly.* "One, that it was a demeaning characterization of the Baptist Church. Second, that it showed a clash between the old and the new, with the new replacing the old." Moreover, Edgerton told *CA,* the administration complained that the book "showed alcohol used as a "catalyst."" They challenged Edgerton to explain how *Raney* would further the mission of the university—and he refused to answer. After several tense weeks the author finally received a contract offer, but it was missing the customary raise. Contending that his academic freedom had been violated, Edgerton made a fruitless appeal to his bosses for an impartial hearing, then quit his job. "Once I resigned," he told the *Milwaukee Journal,* "I realized I should have been gone long before." He went to another church-related school in North Carolina, St. Andrews Presbyterian College, where he resumed his teaching career and received unqualified support for his writing.

Edgerton's next novel, *Walking across Egypt,* was inspired by some family storytelling. One day Edgerton's mother, while entertaining him and his aunts, admitted that she had sat down in a seatless rocking chair the day before and remained stuck for fifteen minutes. "Well, we thought that was the funniest thing we had ever heard," he recalled in *Publishers Weekly,* "and I wondered how I could use it in a story. Then I said, 'This *is* a story!' So I went home and wrote about twenty pages in no time." The woman in the rocking chair became Mattie Rigsbee, a feisty, warmhearted, devoutly Christian widow who may or may not resemble Edgerton's mother. (His mother did pose for the photograph on the cover of the hardback edition.) The title of the novel ostensibly refers to one of Mattie's favorite hymns, but in reality, suggested

Chuck Moss, the title reflects Mattie's "personal creed of endurance." Mattie endures despite her age and her loneliness, waiting for someone she can love and cook for. Since she has no grandchildren, she finds one on her own: Wesley Benfield, a hapless juvenile delinquent in need of some good parenting. "*Walking across Egypt* is a book that teeters on the very edge of terminal cuteness," wrote Carolyn See in the *Los Angeles Times*, "but the longer you read it, the dearer it gets. Mattie is so brave (and resigned) in her loneliness that you have to like her." "I can't think of anything I've read quite like [this book]," said Donald McCaig in the *Washington Post*. "Not many writers have dealt, fondly, with the life of an ordinary Christian believer." He concluded: "Clyde Edgerton's book is brilliant, brief and kind."

So far Edgerton's books had shown a certain pattern: strong women as central characters, and what Kathryn Morton of the *New York Times Book Review* called a "penchant for picturesque farce." But Edgerton was already experimenting by the time he wrote his second novel. "I admired other writers who would write from an omniscient point of view and move from inside one head to another," he said in the *Milwaukee Journal*, "so when I started *Walking across Egypt*, I said I think I'll try that." His third novel—*The Floatplane Notebooks*—represented a far larger challenge, for it was his first effort to confront his concerns about the Vietnam war.

The Floatplane Notebooks, Edgerton told the *Atlanta Journal,* "is a book about what wars do to people, and about persistence, the lingering of a family through generations." The novel is a glimpse into the saga of the Copeland family, descendants of slaveowners who spend the 1950s and 1960s as ordinary members of the American middle class until one of their own is horribly maimed during the Vietnam War. Using a far broader canvas than in his earlier works, Edgerton tells his story through the eyes of many different characters. In an unusual move, the history of the Copelands is recited by an old wisteria vine that has grown next to the family graveyard since slave owning days. The twentieth century arrives with Albert Copeland, father of the family, who fills endless notebooks with observations about his experimental water-launched "floatplane." The youngest generation of Copelands includes Thatcher, a plain but reliable construction worker, and Bliss, his wife; Noralee, a hippie with black friends; Mark, a ladies' man who

becomes a glamorous Air Force pilot in the Vietnam War; and Meredith, whose high-spirited youth comes to an end when he becomes a footsoldier in that same war and emerges so badly wounded that he cannot walk or speak.

Albert and his bizarre floatplane, observers suggest, represent the capacity of the Copeland clan to survive their many changes of fortune. Albert spends decades trying to perfect his ungainly craft, lying to himself about its shortcomings in order to find an excuse to go on. After years of trying to describe the impact of Vietnam by writing philosophical discussions or lengthy accounts of combat, Edgerton found his symbol of haphazard human endurance when he met an inventor during a fishing trip. "It was like stumbling upon the Wright brothers," Edgerton told the *St. Paul Pioneer Press-Dispatch.* "When I saw that red floatplane—the primal ambition that had to be part of it, the man in his blue football helmet and orange life vest—what it symbolized for me I could not express. Whatever that floatplane stands for is a little clearer after writing the novel—a certain kind of courage, a certain kind of obsession."

With its panoramic sweep and tragic climax, *The Floatplane Notebooks* clearly marked a new direction for Edgerton as a writer. Reviewers differed sharply about the success of the effort. "*The Floatplane Notebooks* shows laudable ambitions but fulfills few of them very satisfactorily," wrote Maude McDaniel in Chicago *Tribune Books.* "Maybe the ambitions are part of the problem. Both [of Edgerton's] earlier books were modest in intent, but *Floatplane* takes on a whole family . . . and presents their story in fifty-two increments. . . . The characters are believable, but the episodic style focuses on them only in passing—as though one were looking out the window of a train." By contrast, Frank Levering of the *Los Angeles Times Book Review* hailed what he called a new "depth of feeling" and "hard edge" in Edgerton's work. "The last third of the book, in which Meredith and Mark go off to war . . . , is among the wisest, most heartfelt writing to emerge from the South in our generation," Levering stated. "Meredith Copeland's first-person account of his Vietnam experience, homecoming and physical paralysis in North Carolina is breathtakingly stark, full and real." "Unlike the clumsy, earthbound craft of its title," wrote novelist Barbara Kingsolver in the *New York Times Book Review, The Floatplane Notebooks* "easily lifts itself and soars."

Edgerton returned to the small-town human comedy of his earlier works with his next novel, *Killer Diller.* The book came about after he moved with his family to Durham, North Carolina, and realized that his neighbors included a diet center and a halfway house for soon-to-be-released convicts. "I called the zoning commission," Edgerton recalled in the *Washington Post Book World,* "and said, 'Do you have any problems with the halfway house?' And the guy said, 'We have more problems with the diet house.' Two doors down, meanwhile, was a Baptist church. I said to myself, 'This is a novel.'" *Killer Diller* centers on Wesley Benfield of *Walking across Egypt,* who at the age of twenty-four is trying to leave his criminal past behind by living in the Back on Track Again center for reformed criminals. The center is one of several well-publicized ventures of the Baptist-affiliated Ballard University; another is Nutrition House, home of Wesley's new love—heavyweight dieter Phoebe Trent. Over the course of the novel, Wesley makes many comical efforts to reconcile his carnal desire for Phoebe with his desire to become a good Christian. "Edgerton's handling of [the couple's] erratic love affair," wrote Michael Upchurch in the *Washington Post Book World,* "is ruefully funny."

The meaning of being a good Christian, reviewers suggested, is one of the serious issues explored by *Killer Diller*'s comic plot. Wesley may seem ludicrously self-serving as he uses spicy scenes from the Bible to justify his sexual passion, but far more sinister are Ted and Ned Sears, who as Ballard's chief administrators spend their time steadily enlarging the school's Christian financial empire. "Edgerton has no mercy for the Sears twins," wrote Upchurch, "whose reluctance to run a halfway house is overcome not by a sense of Christian duty but by the favorable media attention and federal grants the project will bring." Wesley, by comparison, seems a model of Christian charity: he visits every Sunday with Mattie Rigsbee, now the frustrated resident of a nursing home, and he uses one of Ballard's outreach programs to become the protector of a retarded teenage boy. At the end of the novel, observed a writer for *Kirkus Reviews,* Wesley may be "just outside the law" but he's "well on the path to true goodness." "There's an affecting story, authenticity of voice and moral complexity here," wrote *New York Times Book Review* contributor Lisa Koger, who felt the novel had "a broader, more accomplished feel than either *Walking across Egypt* or *Raney.*" "*Killer Diller* is Edgerton's fourth novel," wrote Upchurch, "and it may be his best."

With *Redeye: A Western,* Edgerton turned to the American West of the 1890s for the setting of his story. The novel tells the story of a Colorado rancher who discovers Indian cliff dwellings on his property and who, despite his best efforts, succumbs to the inevitable barrage of tourists, archeologists, and curiosity-seekers by writing and selling a souvenir booklet to the site. "Artfully using a kaleidoscopic sequence of first-person vignettes and shifting the narrative voice . . . , Edgerton larks along from one outrageous incident to another," according to the reviewer for *Publishers Weekly.* Mae Miller, writing in *America,* found that "Edgerton's genius lies in his depiction of essential human truths."

Where Trouble Sleeps: A Novel is set in the North Carolina of 1950 and tells the story of a stranger coming to a small town and the resulting havoc his visit causes. "Once more," wrote Wade Hall in the *Lexington Herald-Leader,* Edgerton "creates a wonderful gallery of comic characters." Laurie Parker in *BookPage* praised Edgerton's characters, who are "all too human, . . . and we love them for it." She concluded that *Where Trouble Sleeps* is "one of Edgerton's finest, funniest and warmest novels yet."

As Edgerton's writing career has blossomed, he has spent less time in the classroom. But admirers shouldn't imagine that they've narrowly missed the chance to take a writing class from him—as an education professor, teaching about teaching was always his main interest. "I'm uncomfortable teaching creative writing," he once told the *Milwaukee Journal.* "I can see how it would make me conscious of technique. I'm sure that this has happened: writers who started teaching and thinking about what they're doing consequently have become not able to do it." The author might, however, be found outside Durham in the old Edgerton family graveyard, which he visits regularly—sometimes to share family stories with his young daughter. "Finally she said, 'Will you just stop telling me these stories?,'" he confessed in the *Washington Post Book World.* "I was hitting her with one after another, and I guess she got a little overwhelmed."

BIOGRAPHICAL AND CRITICAL SOURCES:

BOOKS

Contemporary Literary Criticism, Volume 39, Gale (Detroit, MI), 1986.

PERIODICALS

America, November 4, 1995, Mae Miller, review of *Redeye: A Western,* p. 35.

Arts Journal, November, 1988, p. 36.

Atlanta Journal, May 10, 1985; May 12, 1987; October 23, 1988.

Augusta Chronicle, December 11, 1988, article by R. K. Underwood.

BookPage, September, 1997, Laurie Parker, review of *Where Trouble Sleeps: A Novel.*

Denver Post, March 10, 1991.

Detroit News, March 31, 1985, Chuck Moss, review of *Raney;* June 14, 1987.

Durham Herald-Sun, April 14, 1991, p. E1.

Excursus: A Review of Religious Studies, March, 1989, p. 18.

Greensboro News and Record, February 17, 1991, p. B5.

Houston Post, November 18, 1990, p. C7.

Huntsville Times, March 25, 1990, article by Ann Martin.

Kirkus Reviews, December 15, 1990, review of *Killer Diller,* p. 1693.

Lexington Herald-Leader, September 21, 1997, Wade Hall, review of *Where Trouble Sleeps.*

Los Angeles Times, March 30, 1987, Carolyn See, review of *Walking across Egypt.*

Los Angeles Times Book Review, June 23, 1985, p. 3; November 6, 1988, Frank Levering, review of *The Floatplane Notebooks,* p. 3.

Milwaukee Journal, August 28, 1988.

Newsweek, February 25, 1985, p. 86.

New York Times Book Review, June 23, 1985, p. 20; March 29, 1987, p. 17; October 9, 1988, Barbara Kingsolver, review of *The Floatplane Notebooks,* p. 10; February 10, 1991, Lisa Koger, review of *Killer Diller,* p. 1.

Oxford Review, February, 1991, p. 1.

Poets and Writers, November-December, 1987, p. 8.

Publishers Weekly, September 16, 1988, p. 58; March 20, 1995, review of *Redeye,* p. 43.

Rocky Mountain News, February 20, 1991.

St. Paul Pioneer Press-Dispatch, October 16, 1988.

Sewanee Review, spring, 1985, George Core, review of *Raney,* p. xxxix.

Tribune Books (Chicago, IL), November 6, 1988, Maude McDaniel, review of *The Floatplane Notebooks,* p. 5.

Washington Post, June 2, 1987, Donald McCaig, review of *Walking across Egypt.*

Washington Post Book World, June 30, 1985, George Core, review of *Raney,* p. 11; November 20, 1988, p. 6; February 24, 1991, pp. 3, 15.

Washington Times, February 13, 1991, Michael Upchurch, review of *Killer Diller,* p. E1.

*   *   *

EKWENSI, C. O. D.
   See EKWENSI, Cyprian (Odiatu Duaka)

*   *   *

EKWENSI, Cyprian (Odiatu Duaka) 1921-
(C. O. D. Ekwensi)

PERSONAL: Born September 26, 1921, in Minna, Nigeria; son of Ogbuefi David Duaka and Uso Agnes Ekwensi; married Eunice Anyiwo; children: five. *Education:* Attended Achimota College, Ghana, and Ibadan University; received B.A.; further study at Chelsea School of Pharmacy, London, and University of Iowa. *Hobbies and other interests:* Hunting, swimming, photography, motoring, weightlifting.

ADDRESSES: Home—12 Hillview, Independence Layout, P.O. Box 317, Enugu, Anambra, Nigeria. *Agent*—David Bolt Associates, 12 Heath Drive, Send, Surrey GU23 7EP, England.

CAREER: Novelist and writer of short stories and stories for children. Igbodi College, Lagos, Nigeria, lecturer in biology, chemistry, and English, 1947-49; School of Pharmacy, Lagos, lecturer in pharmacognosy and pharmaceutics, 1949-56; pharmacist superintendent for Nigerian Medical Services, 1956-57; head of features, Nigerian Broadcasting Corporation, 1957-61; Federal Ministry of Information, Lagos, director of information, 1961-66; chair of Bureau for External Publicity during Biafran secession, 1967-69, and director of an independent Biafran radio station; chemist for plastics firm in Enugu, Nigeria; managing director of Star Printing and Publishing Co. (publishers of *Daily Star*), 1975-79; managing director of Niger Eagle Publishing Company, 1980-81; managing director of Ivory Trumpet Publishing Co. Ltd., 1981-83. Owner of East Niger Chemists and East Niger Trading Company; chair of East Central State Library Board, 1972-75;

newspaper consultant to *Weekly Trumpet* and *Daily News* of Anambra State and to *Weekly Eagle* of Imo State, 1980-83; consultant on information to the executive office of the president; consultant to Federal Ministry of Information; public relations consultant; visiting lecturer at Iowa University.

MEMBER: PEN, Society of Nigerian Authors, Nigerian Arts Council, Pharmaceutical Society of Great Britain, Pharmaceutical Society of Nigeria, Institute of Public Relations (London), Institute of Public Relations (Nigeria; fellow).

AWARDS, HONORS: Dag Hammarskjold International Prize for Literary Merit, 1969; Association of Nigerian Authors Solidra Prize for the Arts, 1992.

WRITINGS:

NOVELS

People of the City, Andrew Dakers (London, England), 1954, Northwestern University Press (Evanston, IL), 1967, revised edition, Fawcett (New York, NY), 1969.
Jagua Nana, Hutchinson (London, England), 1961, Fawcett (New York, NY), 1969.
Burning Grass: A Story of the Fulani of Northern Nigeria, Heinemann (London, England), 1962, East African Educational Publishers, 1998.
Beautiful Feathers, Hutchinson (London, England), 1963.
Iska, Hutchinson (London, England), 1966, Spectrum Books (Ibadan, Nigeria), 1981.
Survive the Peace, Heinemann (London, England), 1976.
Divided We Stand, Fourth Dimension Publishers (Enugu, Nigeria), 1980.
For a Roll of Parchment, Heinemann (London, England), 1987.
Jagua Nana's Daughter, Spectrum (Ibadan, Nigeria), 1987.

JUVENILE

(Under name C. O. D. Ekwensi) *Ikolo the Wrestler and Other Ibo Tales,* Thomas Nelson (London, England), 1947.

(Under name C. O. D. Ekwensi) *The Leopard's Claw,* Thomas Nelson (London, England), 1950.
The Drummer Boy, Cambridge University Press (Cambridge, England), 1960.
The Passport of Mallam Ilia, Cambridge University Press (Cambridge, England), 1960.
An African Night's Entertainment (folklore), African Universities Press (Lagos, Nigeria), 1962, revised edition, 1986.
Yaba Roundabout Murder (short novel), Tortoise Series Books (Lagos, Nigeria), 1962.
The Great Elephant-Bird, Thomas Nelson (London, England), 1965.
Juju Rock, African Universities Press (Lagos, Nigeria), 1966.
The Boa Suitor, Thomas Nelson (London, England), 1966.
Trouble in Form Six, Cambridge University Press (Cambridge, England), 1966.
Coal Camp Boy, Longman Nigeria (Ibadan, Nigeria), 1971.
Samankwe in the Strange Forest, Longman Nigeria (Ibadan, Nigeria), 1973.
The Rainbow-Tinted Scarf and Other Stories (collection), illustrated by Gay Galsworthy, Evans Africa Library (London, England), 1975.
Samankwe and the Highway Robbers, Evans Africa Library (London, England), 1975.
Motherless Baby (novella), Fourth Dimension Publishers (Enugu, Nigeria), 1980.
Behind the Convent Wall, Evans (London, England), 1990.
Murder Mile Two, Evans (London, England), 1990.
Gone to Mecca, Heinemann (Ibadan, Nigeria), 1991.
Masquerade Time, Heinemann Educational Books (London, England), 1992.
King Forever!, Heinemann Educational Books (London, England), 1992.
The Red Flag, Heinemann (London, England), 1993.

OTHER

(Under name C. O. D. Ekwensi) *When Love Whispers* (novella), Tabansi Bookshop (Onitsha, Nigeria), 1947.
The Rainmaker and Other Short Stories (short story collection), African Universities Press (Lagos, Nigeria), 1965, revised edition, 1971.
Lokotown and Other Stories (short story collection), Heinemann (London, England), 1966.

The Restless City and Christmas Gold, with Other Stories Heinemann (London, England), 1975.

(Editor) *Festac Anthology of Nigerian New Writing,* Festac (Lagos, Nigeria), 1977.

Cyprian Ekwensi of Nigeria (sound recording), Voice of America (Washington, DC), 1975-1979.

Nigerian Writer Cyprian Ekwensi Reading from His Works (sound recording), recorded for the Archive of World Literature on Tape, 1988.

Also author of "No Escape from S.A.P.," published on the Internet. Writer of plays and scripts for BBC radio and television, Radio Nigeria, and other communication outlets. Contributor of stories, articles, and reviews to magazines and newspapers in Nigeria and England, including *West African Review, London Times, Black Orpheus, Flamingo,* and *Sunday Post.* Several of Ekwensi's novels have been translated into other languages, including Russian, Italian, German, Serbo-Croatian, Danish, and French. His novellas have been used primarily in schools as supplementary readers.

SIDELIGHTS: "Cyprian Ekwensi is the earliest and most prolific of the socially realistic Nigerian novelists," according to Martin Tucker in his *Africa in Modern Literature: A Survey of Contemporary Writing in English.* "His first writings were mythological fragments and folk tales. From these African materials he turned to the city and its urban problems, which he now feels are the major issues confronting his people." Reviewing Cyprian Ekwensi's *Beautiful Feathers* in *Critique: Studies in Modern Fiction,* John F. Povey wrote: "The very practice of writing, the developing professionalism of his work, makes us find in Ekwensi a new and perhaps important phenomenon in African writing. . . . Other Nigerian novelists have sought their material from the past, the history of missionaries and British administration as in Chinua Achebe's books and the schoolboy memoirs of Onuora Nzekwu. Ekwensi faces the difficult task of catching the present tone of Africa, changing at a speed that frighteningly destroys the old certainties. In describing this world, Ekwensi has gradually become a significant writer."

Born in Northern Nigeria in 1921, Ekwensi grew up in various cities and had ample opportunity to observe what one critic called the "urban politics" of Nigeria. He went to schools in Ibadan, Lagos, and the Gold Coast, excelling in English, mathematics, and science;

a high school record indicates that only his temper and occasional sullen moods kept him from being the ideal student. In the early 1940s he enrolled at the School of Forestry in Western Nigeria; successfully completing his degree requirements in 1944, he began his work as a forestry officer. According to biographer Ernest Emenyonu, "It was . . . while wandering in the domains of animals and trees that Ekwensi decided to become a writer. Taking advantage of his wild and lonely environment he began to create adventure stories with forest backgrounds." Among his early works are the short stories "Banana Peel," "The Tinted Scarf," and "Land of Sani," which he published together with a collection of Igbo folk tales under the title *Ikolo the Wrestler and Other Ibo Tales* in 1947. Other early works include *When Love Whispers* and *The Leopard's Claw;* he also published several adventure stories for children. In addition to being a professional writer, Ekwensi has worked as a pharmacist and a teacher. He has been involved with the Nigerian Broadcasting Corporation and various newspaper and publishing organizations.

Despite his popularity as a folklorist and writer of children's literature, Ekwensi's fans frequently cite his urban novels as their favorites. *People of the City, Jagua Nana, Beautiful Feathers,* and *Iska* are all set in the city of Lagos, and according to Juliet Okonkwo, Ekwensi "revels in the excitement of city life and loves to expose its many faces of modernity. He writes about . . . its criminals, prostitutes, band-leaders, ministers of state, businessmen, civil servants, professionals, policemen on duty, thugs, thieves, and many other types that are found in the city. . . . Employing a naturalistic narrative technique reminiscent of Emile Zola, Ekwensi has been able to capture both the restless excitement and the frustrations of life in the city." *Burning Grass: A Story of the Fulani of Northern Nigeria* and *Survive the Peace* are exceptions to his "city novels." The former centers on Mai Sunsaye, a Fulani cattleman living on the grassy plains of Nigeria, and the latter on James Oduga, a radio journalist who tries to rebuild his life after a war.

Of Ekwensi's city novels, *Jagua Nana* is considered his best work. It focuses on Jagua Nana, an aging prostitute who thrives on Lagos nightlife—"They called her Jagua because of her good looks and stunning fashions. They said she was Ja-gwa, after the famous British prestige car." When the novel opens, she is in love with Freddie Namme, an ambitious young teacher. She continues to sleep with other men for money, to Freddie's dismay, because she wants to "wear fine cloth." Ekwensi goes on to explain that Jagua "loved Freddie well, but his whole salary would not buy that dress. He must understand that taking money from the Syrian did not mean that she loved him less." Freddie claims to despise Jagua's lifestyle but doesn't refuse the luxuries that her income provides. Seeking consolation, Freddie has an affair with a younger woman, but before Jagua can unleash her jealous rage, he leaves for England. When Jagua and Freddie meet again, Freddie is running for office against Uncle Taiwo, a large, crass, power-hungry politician "who has chosen to absorb and use all that is worst in European ways," according to critic John Povey. The novel ends with Freddie and Uncle Taiwo both murdered and Jagua fleeing Lagos for her life. "Through Jagua, her career, her pursuits and her fluctuating fortune," Okonkwo observed, "Ekwensi reveals the common wickedness, squalor, materialism and immorality of the city, together with its crimes and violence." Since its publication in 1961, *Jagua Nana* has attracted bitter controversy. Church organizations and women's groups vehemently attacked it, prompting some schools to ban it from their libraries. The Nigerian Parliament refused an Italian studio's request to film the book. Some readers called it "obscene" and "pornographic," while others praised it as a masterpiece. Similarly, literary critics were equally divided in their opinions: some were impressed with *Jagua Nana,* particularly by Ekwensi's use of language and depth of characterization, but others dismissed it as another "whore-with-a-heart-of-gold" story commonly found in bad American movies and books.

Controversy appears to follow all of Ekwensi's fiction; while *Jagua Nana* has received the most attention, his other books have also been scrutinized. Assessing Ekwensi as a writer, critic Bernth Lindfors declared: "Not one [of his works] is entirely free of amateurish blots and blunders, not one could be called the handiwork of a careful, skilled craftsman." Ekwensi's supporters, most notably Povey, have argued otherwise. Acknowledging Ekwensi's weaknesses as a writer, Povey explained: "He often dangerously approaches the sentimental, the vulgar and melodramatic. Behind his work stands a reading of American popular fiction and paperback crime stories. Yet Ekwensi's writing cannot be dismissed with such assertions. . . . Ekwensi is interesting because he is concerned with the present, with the violence of the new Lagos slums, the dishonesty of the new native politicians. . . . Only

Ekwensi has dared to approach the contemporary scene with critical satire."

Ekwensi states that his life in government and quasi-government organizations like the Nigerian Broadcasting Corporation has prevented him from expressing any strong political opinions, but adds, "I am as much a nationalist as the heckler standing on the soap-box, with the added advantage of objectivity." During the late-1960s Biafran war, in which the eastern region of Biafra seceded temporarily from the rest of Nigeria, Ekwensi visited the United States more than once to help raise money for Biafra and to purchase radio equipment for the independent Biafran radio station he served as director. He has also traveled in western Europe. Later in his career, Ekwensi spoke out against the difficulties facing writers of fiction in Nigeria and elsewhere in Africa. In an interview with Charles R. Larson for *World and I,* he maintained that the Nigerian publishing "system fails to provide regular income for the writer." Larson explained further that "Nigerian writers typically have to sign contracts loaded in favor of the publisher—such as control of world rights. . . . Authors seldom receive royalties from their books without demanding them." Ekwensi told Larson: "I have yet to know of an African author living in Africa who died a wealthy man from his writing. The rich ones all live abroad."

J. O. J. Nwachukwu-Agbada, in *World Literature Today,* described Ekwensi as the "Nigerian Defoe," because "Ekwensi has been writing fiction since the 1940s. He is prolific and versatile, especially in the subject matter of his works, which can range from sex to science. . . . The 'new' work [*For a Roll of Parchment*] also reveals considerable artistic development, particularly in language and descriptive power." Though published relatively late in Ekwensi's oeuvre, 1986's *For a Roll of Parchment* is based on the author's own experience as a pharmacy student in London during the 1950s. The fictional protagonist, however, seeks a law degree rather than one in pharmacy. According to Emenyonu, writing in the *Concise Dictionary of World Literary Biography,* "The plot tells of mental torture, disorientation, unrequited love, and the degradation to which the hero is subjected in the British social and political environment because of his skin color." Emenyonu went on to note that the novel "is a revealing imaginative documentary of race relations and color prejudice in England during the 1950s. It is also an evocative tale filled with pathos and narrated with candor, its acrimonious undertones notwithstanding."

In a later issue of *World Literature Today,* Nwachukwu-Agbada talked of "Cyprian Ekwensi's Rabelaisian jeu d'esprit whose obscene flavor sparked considerable outrage among Nigerian readers of the sixties [upon the release of *Jagua Nana* in 1961]. The new novel's [*Jagua Nana's Daughter*] bawdiness twenty-five years later has not attracted similar attention, probably due to the increased permissiveness and decreased influence of tradition in modern-day Nigeria." The title character of *Jagua Nana's Daughter* is Lizza, the result of an illicit union Jagua had as a teenager. She is raised in Jagua's hometown, unknown to her grandparents, while Jagua pursues her life in the big city of Lagos. When Jagua returns at the end of the events portrayed in *Jagua Nana* to look for her daughter, "she is led to believe that Lizza has since died," in the words of Emenyonu in the *Concise Dictionary of World Literary Biography.* "Later events reveal that Lizza is alive and prosperous," Emenyonu continued. The critic summed up *Jagua Nana's Daughter* as "the story of a dual search—daughter for mother, and mother for daughter," which "later develops into a moving account of international border clashes and migrant labor."

According to the *St. James Guide to Children's Writers,* "Ekwensi is an acknowledged pioneer in writing Nigerian youth literature. He is nearly unique among African writers in publishing stories for children as early as the 1940s . . . before children's literature was emphasized, and in continuing to write for children after becoming an internationally known novelist." The entry on the author went on to state that "Ekwensi's fiction includes the same elements he enjoyed reading as a youth: truth, poetic justice, heroism, romance, folkloric mystery, and adventure. His stories, most of which are about the adventures of boys and men, reflect real experiences, such as going to school in the colonial and post-colonial eras, poverty in urban areas, and the aftermath of the Nigerian Civil War, as well as fictional experiences prominent in the mass media, such as capturing thieves and searching for lost treasure." Comparing Ekwensi's writing for children to his writing for adults, Emenyonu in the *Concise Dictionary of World Literary Biography* noted that in his adult-oriented works the author "catered for the ravishing tastes and appetites of reckless youths in the newly emergent bubbling urban centers." As a

children's author, however, Emenyonu saw Ekwensi as "a grandfather-artist" who "seems concerned with . . . shaping . . . the future of young readers, some of them his grandchildren." The critic went on to explain that Ekwensi's "themes emphasize disciplined adventurism, heroic enterprises, friendship across cultures, gallantry, humanitarianism, truth, honesty, integrity in human relations, healthy competition and rivalry, the dignity of labor, building and producing things, and the search for and the acquisition of moral and spiritual endowments." Emenyonu singled out 1992's *King for Ever!* as "a well-crafted parable on the nature and fate of military dictators and self-proclaimed absolute rulers for life," because the tale centers on Sinanda, a man who wrests power from a legitimate king but is in turn deposed and killed himself, despite killing almost everyone he once loved in an effort to hang onto the throne. Ekwensi's fellow African writer Kole Omotoso remarked in an article for the online *Bellagio Publishing Network* that one of Ekwensi's works for children had a great influence on him. *The Yaba Roundabout Murders* "taught me the importance of space in fiction writing," Omotoso stated. "Ekwensi was putting on paper my environment and it was so delightful!"

Ekwensi's stature as a novelist is still debated. Emenyonu believes that Ekwensi's commitment "to portray the naked truth about the life of modern man" is the reason for the existing controversy over *Jagua Nana* and all of Ekwensi's fiction. "When one looks at his works over the past three decades," he observed, "one sees the deep imprints of a literature of social awareness and commitment, and this is Ekwensi's greatest achievement in the field of modern African writing."

BIOGRAPHICAL AND CRITICAL SOURCES:

BOOKS

Concise Dictionary of World Literary Biography, Volume 3, Gale (Detroit, MI), 1999.
Contemporary Black Biography, Volume 37, Gale (Detroit, MI), 2003.
Contemporary Literary Criticism, Volume 4, Gale (Detroit, MI), 1975.
Emenyonu, Ernest N., *The Essential Ekwensi: A Literary Celebration of Cyprian Ekwensi's Sixty-fifth Birthday,* Heinemann, 1987.

St. James Guide to Children's Writers, 5th edition, St. James Press (Detroit, MI), 1999.

Tucker, Martin, *Africa in Modern Literature: A Survey of Contemporary Writing in English,* Ungar, 1967.

PERIODICALS

Books Abroad, autumn, 1967.

Critique: Studies in Modern Fiction, October, 1965.

Times Literary Supplement, June 4, 1964.

World and I, October, 2000, Charles R. Larson, "Fame and Poverty: The Career of Nigerian Novelist Cyprian Ekwensi Exemplifies the Plight of the African Writer," p. 254.

World Literature Today, autumn, 1988; winter, 1989.

ONLINE

Bellagio Publishing Network, http://www.bellagiopublishingnetwork.org/newsletter29/omotoso.htm/ (May 2, 2003), "What Cyprian Ekwensi Meant to Me."*

*　　*　　*

ELLENBECKER, Todd S. 1962-

PERSONAL: Born August 12, 1962, in Merril, WI; son of Sidney (a pharmacist) and Karen (a homemaker; maiden name, Meyer) Ellenbecker; married Gail Haertel, May 3, 1986. *Ethnicity:* "White." *Education:* University of Wisconsin—LaCrosse, B.S. (with honors), 1985; Arizona State University, M.S., 1989. *Hobbies and other interests:* Tennis, running, travel.

ADDRESSES: Home—Scottsdale, AZ. *Office*—Physiotherapy Associates, Scottsdale Sports Clinic, 9449 North 90th St., Suite 100, Scottsdale, AZ 85258.

CAREER: Lincoln Institute for Athletic Medicine, Phoenix, AZ, staff physical therapist, 1986-89; Healthsouth Sports Medicine and Rehabilitation, Scottsdale, AZ, clinical director of sports medicine and coordinator of clinical education, 1989-95; Physiotherapy Associates, Scottsdale, AZ, clinic director, 1995—. Pre-

senter of seminars and training courses; past consultant to San Francisco Giants, Milwaukee Brewers, Oakland Athletics, and Hygenic Corp.

MEMBER: U.S. Tennis Association (life member; member of sports science committee, 1988—), American Physical Therapy Association (chair of Shoulder Special Interest Group, 1996-2002), American College of Sports Medicine, National Strength and Conditioning Association (certified strength and conditioning specialist), U.S. Professional Tennis Association (certified tennis teaching professional).

AWARDS, HONORS: Grant from U.S. Tennis Association, 1988; Joe Bergin Memorial Award, outstanding clinician of the year, Healthsouth Corp., 1991; Clinical Education Award, Sports Physical Therapy Section, American Physical Therapy Association, 1999.

WRITINGS:

The Elbow in Sport: Mechanism of Injury, Evaluation, and Treatment, Human Kinetics (Champaign, IL), 1996.

(With Paul Roetert) *Complete Conditioning for Tennis,* Human Kinetics (Champaign, IL), 1998.

Knee Ligament Rehabilitation, Churchill Livingstone (New York, NY), 2000.

(With George J. Davies) *Closed Kinetic Chain Exercise: A Comprehensive Guide to Multiple Joint Exercise,* Human Kinetics (Champaign, IL), 2001.

Contributor to books, including *Physical Rehabilitation of the Injured Athlete,* edited by Gary L.Harrelson, Kevin E. Wilk, and James R. Andrews, W. B. Saunders (Philadelphia, PA), 1997; *Isokinetic Performance Enhancement,* edited by Lee Brown, Human Kinetics (Champaign, IL). Contributor to professional journals, including *American Journal of Sports Medicine, Journal of Orthopaedic and Sports Physical Therapy, Journal of Strength and Conditioning,* and *Isokinetics and Exercise Science.*

WORK IN PROGRESS: Knee Ligament Rehabilitation, 2nd edition, for W. B. Saunders (Philadelphia, PA).

ENGEL, Matthew (Lewis) 1951-

PERSONAL: Born June 11, 1951, in Northampton, England; son of Max David (a lawyer) and Betty Ruth (a homemaker; maiden name, Lesser) Engel; married Hilary Davies (a publisher), October 27, 1990; children: Laurence Gabriel, Victoria Betty. *Education:* Victoria University of Manchester, B.A. (with honors), 1972.

ADDRESSES: Home—Fair Oak, near Bacton, Herefordshire HR2 OAT, England. *Office*—*Guardian,* 119 Farringdon Rd., London EC1R 3ER, England. *E-mail*—matthewengel@ndirect.co.uk.

CAREER: Northampton Chronicle and Echo, Northampton, England, journalist, 1972-75; Reuters News Agency, journalist, 1977-79; *Guardian,* London, England, feature writer, 1979—, cricket correspondent, 1982-87, sports columnist and occasional political, foreign, and war correspondent, 1987-2001; columnist, 1998—; Washington correspondent, 2001-2003.

AWARDS, HONORS: Named sports journalist of the year by *What the Papers Say,* 1985, and by British Press Awards, 1991; runner-up, reporter of the year, 1997.

WRITINGS:

Ashes '85, Pelham Books (London, England), 1986.
The Guardian Book of Cricket, Pavilion Books (London, England), 1986.
Tickle the Public: One Hundred Years of the Popular Press, Gollancz (London, England), 1996.
(Editor) *The Bedside Years: The Best Writing from the Guardian, 1951-2000,* Atlantic Books (London, England), 2001.

Editor, *Sportspages Almanac,* Simon & Schuster, 1989-91, and *Wisden Cricketers' Almanack,* John Wisden, 1992-2000, 2004—. Engel's humorous column "Engel in America" for the *Guardian Unlimited* reports on the U.S. sports scene from Washington, D.C., 2001—.

SIDELIGHTS: "Even the most cynical hacks are usually sentimental souls at heart," wrote Francis Wheen in a 1996 *Observer* article, "and Matthew Engel is no

exception." A sports and feature writer in England, Engel has, "for some years . . . been one of the most consistently readable performers in journalism," according to *Spectator* writer Alan Watkins. "He is an ornament to the profession." Engel looked back on the British newspaper industry with *Tickle the Public: One Hundred Years of the Popular Press.* The author examines what Boyd Tonkin called "every dominant title" among the British papers, including the venerated *Times,* plus its competitors the *Daily Telegraph,* the *Daily Mail,* the *Daily Express,* the *Daily Mirror,* and the *Sun.* Tonkin, writing for *New Statesman & Society,* added that the book ends with the *Sun* "soaring away into scandal and TV gossip."

The history of Fleet Street is a colorful one, characterized by what Wheen described as the "late-night thunder of the presses and the hubbub in the pubs." "One of the interesting points [Engel] makes about the 19th century is that literacy was more common in the earlier half than we had been led to believe," commented Watkins. But for all the romance that seems to have gone the way of the cell phone and the Internet, Engel resists "the conclusion that the mass-circulation newspapers of the past were somehow nobler or more imaginative than their modern counterparts," said Wheen. "If anything, he errs in the other direction, by arguing that popular journalism is an endlessly recurring cycle." Watkins thought Engel was mistaken in writing that the "shabby" journalistic practices that began in the 1980s—such as the *Sun*'s "simply inventing stories"—were "always part of popular journalism. This may be because [the author] has himself been a national journalist only since 1979." But overall, Watkins praised *Tickle the Public* as "possibly the best and certainly the most entertaining account of British newspapers since Francis Williams' *Dangerous Estate.*"

BIOGRAPHICAL AND CRITICAL SOURCES:

PERIODICALS

Books, June, 1996, review of *Tickle the Public: One Hundred Years of the Popular Press,* p. 21.
London Review of Books, July 18, 1996, review of *Tickle the Public,* p. 13.
New Statesman, April 26, 1999, p. 46; January 28, 2002, Richard Gott, "The Lost Magic of Manchester," p. 49.

New Statesman & Society, May 3, 1996, Boyd Tonkin, review of *Tickle the Public,* p. 41.

Observer (London, England), April 28, 1996, Francis Wheen, "Yesterday's News," p. 15.

Spectator (London, England), May 18, 1996, Alan Watkins, "Goodness Had Little to Do with It," p. 38.

Times Educational Supplement, December 27, 1996, review of *Tickle the Public,* p.16.

Times Literary Supplement, July 26, 1996, Michael Davie, review of *Tickle the Public,* p. 27; February 15, 2002, review of *The Bedside Years: The Best Writing from the Guardian, 1951-2000,* p. 31.

*   *   *

ESTY, Daniel C. 1959-

PERSONAL: Born June 6, 1959, in MA; son of John (an educator) and Katherine (a management consultant) Esty; married Elizabeth Henderson (a lawyer), October 20, 1984; children: Sarah, Thomas, Jonathan. *Education:* Harvard University, B.A., 1981; Oxford University, M.A., 1983; Yale University, J.D., 1986. *Religion:* United Church of Christ. *Hobbies and other interests:* Ice hockey.

ADDRESSES: Home—Cheshire, CT. *Office*—Center for Environmental Law and Policy, Yale University, P.O. Box 208215, New Haven, CT 06520-8215.

CAREER: Arnold & Porter, Washington, DC, attorney, 1986-89; U.S. Environmental Protection Agency, Washington, DC, special assistant to the administrator, 1989-90, deputy chief of staff, 1990-91, deputy assistant administrator for policy, 1991-93; Institute for International Economics, Washington, DC, senior fellow, 1993-94; Yale University, New Haven, CT, professor of law and director of Center for Environmental Law and Policy, 1994—, associate dean of School of Forestry and Environmental Studies, 1998-2002. American Farmland Trust, board member; U.S. Trade Representative-Public Advisory Committee, member. Planning and Zoning Commission, Cheshire, CT, member, 1995-99.

MEMBER: American Bar Association, Council on Foreign Relations.

AWARDS, HONORS: Rhodes scholar in England, 1981-83; U.S. Environmental Protection Agency, Fitzhugh Green Award, 1992, and New England regional merit award, 1997; named among the "world's one hundred most influential environmental leaders" by *Earth Times,* 1998.

WRITINGS:

Greening the GATT, Institute for International Economics (Washington, DC), 1994.

(Editor, with Simon S. C. Tay) *Asian Dragons and Green Trade: Environment, Economics and International Law,* Times Academic Press (Singapore), 1996.

(Editor, with Marian R. Chertow) *Thinking Ecologically: The Next Generation of Environmental Policy,* Yale University Press (New Haven, CT), 1997.

(With André Duci) *Sustaining the Asia Pacific Miracle,* Institute for International Economics (Washington, DC), 1997.

(Editor, with Damien Geradin) *Regulatory Competition and Economic Integration: Comparative Perspectives,* Oxford University Press (New York, NY), 2000.

(Editor, with Peter Cornelius) *Environmental Performance Management: The Global Report, 2001-2002,* Oxford University Press (New York, NY), 2002.

(Editor, with Carolyn L. Deere) *Greening the Americas: NAFTA's lessons for Hemispheric Trade,* MIT Press (Cambridge, NY), 2002.

(Editor, with Maria H. Ivanova) *Global Environmental Governance: Options and Opportunities,* School of Forestry and Environmental Studies, Yale University (New Haven, CT), 2002.

WORK IN PROGRESS: Research on environmental protection in the information age, trade and the environment, environmental performance measurement, and global environmental governance.

F

FAIRBAIRN, Brett 1959-

PERSONAL: Born April 29, 1959, in Winnipeg, Manitoba, Canada; son of Clarence Bertram (a journalist) and Eva Evelyn (a journalist, legal secretary, and homemaker; maiden name, Hurlbert) Fairbairn; married Norma Braul (a businessperson), August 20, 1983; children: Catherine Naomi, Elena Kirstin, David Thomas. *Ethnicity:* "Canadian." *Education:* University of Saskatchewan, B.A., 1981; Oxford University, B.A. (with first class honors), 1984, D.Phil., 1988. *Politics:* Social Democrat. *Religion:* Christian.

ADDRESSES: Home—Saskatoon, Saskatchewan, Canada. *Office*—Centre for the Study of Co-operatives, University of Saskatchewan, 101 Diefenbaker Pl., Saskatoon, Saskatchewan S7N 5B8, Canada; fax: 306-966-8517. *E-mail*—brett.fairbairn@usask.ca.

CAREER: University of Saskatchewan, Saskatoon, began as assistant professor, became professor of history, 1986—, director of graduate studies in history, 1996-99, director of Centre for the Study of Co-operatives, 2000—. Community Health Services Association of Saskatoon; president, 1991-92; Government of Saskatchewan, special advisor to department of post-secondary education, 1996; Saskatchewan Archives Board, chair, 1997—.

MEMBER: Canadian Historical Association, German Studies Association, Canadian Association for Studies in Co-operation (president, 1991-92), Saskatchewan Environmental Society (member of board of directors, 1994-96).

AWARDS, HONORS: Alexander von Humboldt fellow, 1998.

WRITINGS:

Building a Dream: The Co-operative Retailing System in Western Canada, 1928-1988, Prairie Books (Saskatoon, Saskatchewan, Canada), 1989.

(With June Bold, Murray Fulton, and others) *Co-operatives and Community Development: Economics in Social Perspective,* Centre for the Study of Co-operatives, University of Saskatchewan (Saskatoon, Saskatchewan, Canada), 1991.

(Editor, with Harold Baker and James Draper) *Dignity and Growth: Citizen Participation in Social Change,* Detselig Press (Calgary, Alberta, Canada), 1991.

Democracy in the Undemocratic State: The German Reichstag Elections of 1898-1903, University of Toronto Press (Toronto, Ontario, Canada), 1997.

(Editor, with Ian MacPherson and Nora Russell) *Canadian Co-operatives in the Year 2000: Memory, Mutual Aid, and the Millennium,* Centre for the Study of Co-operatives (Saskatoon, Saskatchewan, Canada), 2000.

Editor, *Canadian Journal of History,* 1988-95; member of editorial cooperative, *NeWest Review,* 1988-98.

WORK IN PROGRESS: A profile of Federated Co-operatives Ltd., research on cooperatives and social cohesion in Canada; research on the history of the cooperative movement in Germany.

SIDELIGHTS: Brett Fairbairn once told *CA:* "Most of my research is inspired by the desire to understand historical roots of democracy, popular participation, and social movements. In addition I am active in extension education, consulting, and policy development regarding cooperatives and community development, which further informs my research."

* * *

FERLINGHETTI, Lawrence (Monsanto) 1919-

PERSONAL: Born Lawrence Ferling, March 24, 1919, in Yonkers, NY; original family name of Ferlinghetti restored, 1954; son of Charles S. (an auctioneer) and Clemence (Mendes Monsanto) Ferling; married Selden Kirby-Smith, April, 1951 (divorced, 1976); children: Julie, Lorenzo. *Education:* University of North Carolina, A.B., 1941; Columbia University, M.A., 1947; Sorbonne, University of Paris, doctorat (with honors), 1949. *Politics:* "Now an enemy of the State." *Religion:* "Catholique manque."

ADDRESSES: Home—San Francisco, CA. *Office*—City Lights Books, 261 Columbus Ave., San Francisco, CA 94133.

CAREER: Poet, playwright, editor, and painter; worked for *Time,* New York, NY, post-World War II; taught French in an adult education program, San Francisco, CA, 1951-52; City Lights Pocket Bookshop (now City Lights Books), San Francisco, co-owner, 1953—, founder, publisher, and editor of City Lights Books, 1955—. Participant in literary conferences, art exhibitions, and poetry readings. *Military service:* U.S. Naval Reserve, 1941-45; became lieutenant commander; was commanding officer during Normandy invasion.

AWARDS, HONORS: National Book Award nomination, 1970, for *The Secret Meaning of Things;* Notable Book of 1979 citation, *Library Journal,* 1980, for *Landscapes of Living and Dying;* Silver Medal for poetry, Commonwealth Club of California, 1986, for *Over All the Obscene Boundaries;* poetry prize, City of Rome, 1993; San Francisco street named in his honor, 1994; named first poet laureate of San Francisco, 1998; *Los Angeles Times* Robert Kirsch Award, 2001, for body of work; PEN Center West Literary Award, 2002, for lifetime achievement.

Lawrence Ferlinghetti

WRITINGS:

(Translator) Jacques Prevert, *Selections from "Paroles,"* City Lights (San Francisco, CA), 1958.

Her (novel), New Directions (New York, NY), 1960.

Howl of the Censor (trial proceedings), edited by J. W. Ehrlich, Nourse Publishing, 1961.

(With Jack Spicer) *Dear Ferlinghetti,* White Rabbit Press, 1962.

The Mexican Night: Travel Journal, New Directions (New York, NY), 1970.

A World Awash with Fascism and Fear, Cranium Press, 1971.

A Political Pamphlet, Anarchist Resistance Press, 1976.

Northwest Ecolog, City Lights (San Francisco, CA), 1978.

(With Nancy J. Peters) *Literary San Francisco: A Pictorial History from the Beginning to the Present,* Harper (New York, NY), 1980.

The Populist Manifestos (includes "First Populist Manifesto"), Grey Fox Press, 1983.

Seven Days in Nicaragua Libre (journal), City Lights (San Francisco, CA), 1985.

Leaves of Life: Fifty Drawings from the Model, City Lights (San Francisco, CA), 1985.

(Translator with others) Nicanor Parra, *Antipoems: New and Selected,* New Directions (New York, NY), 1985.

(Translator, with Francesca Valente) Pier Paolo Pasolini, *Roman Poems,* City Lights (San Francisco, CA), 1986.

Love in the Days of Rage (novel), Dutton (New York, NY), 1988.

(With Alexis Lykiard) *The Cool Eye: Lawrence Ferlinghetti Talks to Alexis Lykiard,* Stride, 1993.

(With Christopher Felver) *Ferlinghetti: Portrait,* Gibbs Smith, 1998.

What Is Poetry?, Creative Arts (Berkeley, CA), 2000.

(Translator, with others) Homero Aridjis, *Eyes to See Otherwise,* New Directions (New York, NY), 2002.

Life Studies, Life Stories: Drawings, City Lights (San Francisco, CA), 2003.

POETRY

Pictures of the Gone World, City Lights (San Francisco, CA), 1955, enlarged edition, 1995.

Tentative Description of a Dinner Given to Promote the Impeachment of President Eisenhower, Golden Mountain Press, 1958.

A Coney Island of the Mind, New Directions (New York, NY), 1958.

Berlin, Golden Mountain Press, 1961.

One Thousand Fearful Words for Fidel Castro, City Lights (San Francisco), 1961.

Starting from San Francisco (with recording), New Directions (New York, NY), 1961, revised edition (without recording), 1967.

(With Gregory Corso and Allen Ginsberg) *Penguin Modern Poets 5,* Penguin (New York, NY), 1963.

Thoughts of a Concerto of Telemann, Four Seasons Foundation, 1963.

Where Is Vietnam?, City Lights (San Francisco), 1965.

To F—- Is to Love Again, Kyrie Eleison Kerista; or, The Situation in the West, Followed by a Holy Proposal, F—- You Press, 1965.

Christ Climbed Down, Syracuse University (Syracuse, NY), 1965.

An Eye on the World: Selected Poems, MacGibbon & Kee, 1967.

Moscow in the Wilderness, Segovia in the Snow, Beach Books, 1967.

After the Cries of the Birds, Dave Haselwood Books, 1967.

Fuclock, Fire Publications, 1968.

Reverie Smoking Grass, East 128, 1968.

The Secret Meaning of Things, New Directions (New York, NY), 1969.

Tyrannus Nix?, New Directions (New York, NY), 1969.

Back Roads to Far Places, New Directions (New York, NY), 1971.

Love Is No Stone on the Moon, ARIF Press, 1971.

The Illustrated Wilfred Funk, City Lights (San Francisco, CA), 1971.

Open Eye, Open Heart, New Directions (New York, NY), 1973.

Director of Alienation: A Poem, Main Street, 1976.

Who Are We Now? (also see below), City Lights (San Francisco, CA), 1976.

Landscapes of Living and Dying (also see below), New Directions (New York, NY), 1979.

Mule Mountain Dreams, Bisbee Press Collective, 1980.

A Trip to Italy and France, New Directions (New York, NY), 1980.

Endless Life: Selected Poems (includes "Endless Life"), New Directions (New York, NY), 1984.

Over All the Obscene Boundaries: European Poems and Transitions, New Directions (New York, NY), 1985.

Inside the Trojan Horse, Lexikos, 1987.

Wild Dreams of a New Beginning: Including "Landscapes of Living and Dying" and "Who Are We Now?," New Directions (New York, NY), 1988.

When I Look at Pictures, Peregrine Smith Books, 1990.

These Are My Rivers: New and Selected Poems, 1955-1993, New Directions (New York, NY), 1993.

A Far Rockaway of the Heart, New Directions (New York, NY), 1997.

San Francisco Poems, City Lights (San Francisco, CA), 2001.

How to Paint Sunlight: Lyric Poems and Others, 1997-2000, New Directions (New York, NY), 2001.

PLAYS

Unfair Arguments with Existence: Seven Plays for a New Theatre (contains *The Soldiers of No Country* [produced in London, England, 1969], *Three Thousand Red Ants* [produced in New York, NY, 1970; also see below], *The Alligation* [produced in San Francisco, 1962; also see below], *The Victims of*

Amnesia [produced in New York, NY, 1970; also see below], *Motherlode, The Customs Collector in Baggy Pants* [produced in New York, NY, 1964], and *The Nose of Sisyphus*), New Directions (New York, NY), 1963.

Routines (includes *The Jig Is Up, His Head, Ha-Ha,* and *Non-Objection*), New Directions (New York, NY), 1964.

Three by Ferlinghetti: Three Thousand Red Ants, The Alligation, [and] *The Victims of Amnesia,* produced in New York, NY, 1970.

EDITOR

Beatitude Anthology, City Lights (San Francisco, CA), 1960.

Pablo Picasso, *Hunk of Skin,* City Lights (San Francisco, CA), 1969.

Charles Upton, *Panic Grass,* City Lights (San Francisco, CA), 1969.

City Lights Anthology, City Lights (San Francisco, CA), 1974, reprinted, 1995.

City Lights Pocket Poets Anthology, City Lights (San Francisco, CA), 1995.

RECORDINGS

(With Kenneth Rexroth) *Poetry Readings in "The Cellar,"* Fantasy, 1958.

Tentative Description of a Dinner to Impeach President Eisenhower, and Other Poems, Fantasy, 1959.

Tyrannus Nix? and Assassination Raga, Fantasy, 1971.

(With Gregory Corso and Allen Ginsberg) *The World's Greatest Poets 1,* CMS, 1971.

OTHER

Author of narration, *Have You Sold Your Dozen Roses?* (film), California School of Fine Arts Film Workshop, 1957. Contributor to numerous periodicals, including *San Francisco Chronicle, Nation, Evergreen Review, Liberation, Chicago Review, Transatlantic Review,* and *New Statesman.* Editor, *Journal for the Protection of All Beings, Interim Pad,* and *City Lights Journal.*

Ferlinghetti's manuscripts are collected at Columbia University, New York, NY.

ADAPTATIONS: Ferlinghetti's poem "Autobiography" was choreographed by Sophie Maslow, 1964. *A Coney Island of the Mind* was adapted for the stage by Steven Kyle Kent, Charles R. Blaker, and Carol Brown and produced at the Edinburgh Festival, Scotland, 1966; poem was adapted for television by Ted Post on *Second Experiment in Television,* 1967.

SIDELIGHTS: As poet, playwright, publisher, and spokesman, Lawrence Ferlinghetti helped to spark the San Francisco literary renaissance of the 1950s and the subsequent "Beat" movement. Ferlinghetti was one of a group of writers—labeled the "Beat Generation"—who felt strongly that art should be accessible to all people, not just a handful of highly educated intellectuals. His career has been marked by a constant challenge to the status quo in art; his poetry engages readers, defies popular political movements, and reflects the influence of American idiom and modern jazz. In *Lawrence Ferlinghetti: Poet-at-Large,* Larry Smith noted that the author "writes truly memorable poetry, poems that lodge themselves in the consciousness of the reader and generate awareness and change. And his writing sings, with the sad and comic music of the streets."

Ferlinghetti performed numerous functions essential to the establishment of the Beat movement while also creating his own substantial body of work. His City Lights bookstore provided a gathering place for the fertile talents of the San Francisco literary renaissance, and the bookstore's publishing arm offered a forum for publication of Beat writings. He also became "America's best-selling poet of the twentieth century," according to Paul Varner in *Western American Literature.* As Smith noted in the *Dictionary of Literary Biography,* "What emerges from the historical panorama of Ferlinghetti's involvement is a pattern of social engagement and literary experimentation as he sought to expand the goals of the Beat movement." Smith added, however, that Ferlinghetti's contribution far surpasses his tasks as a publisher and organizer. "Besides molding an image of the poet in the world," the critic continued, "he created a poetic form that is at once rhetorically functional and socially vital." *Dictionary of Literary Biography* essayist Thomas Mc-Clanahan likewise contended that Ferlinghetti "became the most important force in developing and publicizing antiestablishment poetics."

Ferlinghetti was born Lawrence Monsanto Ferling, the youngest of five sons of Charles and Clemence Ferling.

His father, an Italian immigrant, had shortened the family name upon arrival in America. Only years later, when he was a grown man, did Ferlinghetti discover the lengthier name and restore it as his own.

A series of disasters struck Ferlinghetti as a youngster. Before he was born, his father died suddenly. When he was only two, his mother suffered a nervous breakdown that required lengthy hospitalization. Separated from his brothers, Lawrence went to live with his maternal uncle, Ludovic Monsanto, a language instructor, and Ludovic's French-speaking wife, Emily. The marriage disintegrated, and Emily Monsanto returned to France, taking Lawrence with her. During the following four years, the youngster lived in Strasbourg and spoke only French.

Ferlinghetti's return to America began with a stay in a state orphanage in New York; he was placed there by his aunt while she sought work in Manhattan. The pair were reunited when the aunt found a position as governess to the wealthy Bisland family in Bronxville. Young Ferlinghetti endeared himself to the Bislands to such an extent that when his aunt disappeared suddenly, he was allowed to stay. Surrounded by fine books and educated people, he was encouraged to read and learn fine passages of literature by heart. His formal education proceeded first in the elite Riverdale Country Day School and later in Bronxville public schools. As a teenager he was sent to Mount Hermon, a preparatory academy in Massachusetts.

Ferlinghetti enrolled at the University of North Carolina in 1937. There he majored in journalism and worked with the student staff of the *Daily Tarheel*. He earned his bachelor's degree in the spring of 1941 and joined the U.S. Navy that fall. His wartime service included patrolling the Atlantic coast on submarine watch and commanding a ship during the invasion of Normandy. After his discharge Ferlinghetti took advantage of the G.I. Bill to continue his education. He did graduate study at Columbia University, receiving his master's degree in 1948, and he completed his doctoral degree at the University of Paris in 1951.

Ferlinghetti left Paris in 1951 and moved to San Francisco. For a short time he supported himself by teaching languages at an adult education school and by doing freelance writing for art journals and for the *San Francisco Chronicle*. In 1953 he joined with Peter

D. Martin to publish a magazine, *City Lights,* named after a silent film starring actor Charlie Chaplin. In order to subsidize the magazine, Martin and Ferlinghetti opened the City Lights Pocket Book Shop in a neighborhood on the edge of Chinatown.

Before long the City Lights Book Shop was a popular gathering place for San Francisco's avant-garde writers, poets, and painters. "We were filling a big need," Ferlinghetti told the *New York Times Book Review.* "City Lights became about the only place around where you could go in, sit down, and read books without being pestered to buy something. That's one of the things it was supposed to be. Also, I had this idea that a bookstore should be a center of intellectual activity; and I knew it was a natural for a publishing company too."

In addition to his new career as an entrepreneur, Ferlinghetti was busy creating his own poetry, and in 1955 he launched the City Lights Pocket Poets publishing venture. First in the "Pocket Poets" series was a slim volume of his own, *Pictures of the Gone World.* In *Lawrence Ferlinghetti,* Smith observed that, from his earliest poems onwards, the author writes as "the contemporary man of the streets speaking out the truths of common experience, often to the reflective beat of the jazz musician. As much as any poet today he . . . sought to make poetry an engaging oral art." McClanahan wrote: "The underlying theme of Ferlinghetti's first book is the poet's desire to subvert and destroy the capitalist economic system. Yet this rather straightforward political aim is accompanied by a romantic vision of Eden, a mirror reflecting the Whitmanesque attempts to be free from social and political restraints."

These sentiments found an appreciative audience among young people of the mid-twentieth century, who were agonizing over the nuclear arms race and cold war politics. By 1955 Ferlinghetti counted among his friends such poets as Kenneth Rexroth, Allen Ginsberg, and Philip Whalen, as well as the novelist Jack Kerouac. Ferlinghetti was in the audience at the watershed 1955 poetry reading "Six Poets at the Six Gallery," at which Ginsberg unveiled his poem *Howl.* Ferlinghetti immediately recognized *Howl* as a classic work of art and offered to publish it in the "Pocket Poets" series. The first edition of *Howl and Other Poems* appeared in 1956 and sold out quickly. A second shipment was ordered from the publisher's British printer, but U.S. customs authorities seized it on the grounds of alleged obscenity. When federal authorities declined to pursue the case and released the books, the San Francisco Police Department arrested Ferlinghetti on charges of printing and selling lewd and indecent material.

Ferlinghetti engaged the American Civil Liberties Union for his defense and welcomed his court case as a test of the limits to freedom of speech. Not only did he win the suit on October 3, 1957, he also benefitted from the publicity generated by the case. In the *Dictionary of Literary Biography,* Smith wrote: "The importance of this court case to the life and career of Ferlinghetti as well as to the whole blossoming of the San Francisco renaissance in poetry and the West Coast Beat movement is difficult to overestimate. Ferlinghetti and Ginsberg became national as well as international public figures leading a revolution in thinking as well as writing. The case solidified the writing into a movement with definite principles yet an openness of form."

For Ferlinghetti, these "principles" included redeeming poetry from the ivory towers of academia and offering it as a shared experience with ordinary people. He began reading his verses to the accompaniment of experimental jazz and reveled in an almost forgotten oral tradition in poetry. In 1958 New York's New Directions press published Ferlinghetti's *A Coney Island of the Mind,* a work that has since sold well over one million copies in America and abroad. In his *Dictionary of Literary Biography* piece, Smith called *A Coney Island of the Mind* "one of the key works of the Beat period and one of the most popular books of contemporary poetry. . . . It launched Ferlinghetti as a poet of humor and satire, who achieves an open-form expressionism and a personal lyricism." Walter Sutton offered a similar assessment in *American Free Verse: The Modern Revolution in Poetry.* Sutton felt that the general effect of the book "is of a kaleidoscopic view of the world and of life as an absurd carnival of discontinuous sensory impressions and conscious reflections, each with a ragged shape of its own but without any underlying thematic unity or interrelationship." Sutton added, "To this extent the collection suggests a Surrealistic vision. But it differs in that meanings and easily definable themes can be found in most of the individual poems, even when the idea of meaninglessness is the central concern."

In *Lawrence Ferlinghetti,* Smith suggested that the poems in *A Coney Island of the Mind* demonstrate the direction Ferlinghetti intended to go with his art. The poet "enlarged his stance and developed major themes of anarchy, mass corruption, engagement, and a belief in the surreality and wonder of life," to quote Smith. "It was a revolutionary art of dissent and contemporary application which jointly drew a lyric poetry into new realms of social—and self-expression. It sparkles, sings, goes flat, and generates anger or love out of that flatness as it follows a basic motive of getting down to reality and making of it what we can." Smith concluded: "Loosely, the book forms a type of 'Portrait of the Artist as a Young Poet of Dissent.' There are some classic contemporary statements in this, Ferlinghetti's—and possibly America's—most popular book of modern poetry. The work is remarkable for its skill, depth, and daring."

If certain academics grumbled about Ferlinghetti's work, others found it refreshing for its engagement in current social and political issues and its indebtedness to a bardic tradition. "Ferlinghetti has cultivated a style of writing visibly his own," claimed Linda Hamalian in the *American Book Review.* "He often writes his line so that it approximates the rhythm and meaning of the line. He also has William Carlos Williams' gift of turning unlikely subjects into witty poems. . . . He introduces the unexpected, catching his readers open for his frequently sarcastic yet humorous observations." *Poetry* contributor Alan Dugan maintained that the poet "has the usual American obsession, asking, 'What is going on in America and how does one survive it?' His answer might be: By being half a committed outsider and half an innocent Fool. He makes jokes and chants seriously with equal gusto and surreal inventiveness, using spoken American in a romantic, flamboyant manner."

Two collections of Ferlinghetti's poetry provide insight into the development of the writer's overarching style and thematic approach: *Endless Life: Selected Poems* and *These Are My Rivers: New and Selected Poems, 1955-1993.* Ferlinghetti chose selections from among his eight books of poetry and his work in progress, written over twenty-six years, for inclusion in *Endless Life.* The poems reflect the influences of e. e. cummings, Kenneth Rexroth, and Kenneth Patchen and are concerned with contemporary themes, such as the antiwar and antinuclear movements. Some critics have dismissed Ferlinghetti "as either sentimental or the literary entrepreneur of the Beat generation," noted John Trimbur in *Western American Literature,* the critic adding that he feels such labels are unjustified. Ferlinghetti writes a "public poetry to challenge the guardians of the political and social status quo for the souls of his fellow citizens," Trimbur maintained, noting that the poet does so while "risking absurdity." In *World Literature Today,* J. Martone acknowledged that while Ferlinghetti has produced heralded poetry, some of that poetry is stagnant. "Ferlinghetti never moves beyond—or outgrows—the techniques of [his] early poems," maintained Martone, adding that "his repertoire of devices (deliberately casual literary allusion, self-mockery, hyperbole) becomes a bit tedious with repetition." However, Joel Oppenheimer praised the poet in the *New York Times Book Review,* contending that Ferlinghetti "learned to write poems, in ways that those who see poetry as the province of the few and the educated had never imagined."

Ferlinghetti focuses on current political and sexual matters in *These Are My Rivers.* As Rochelle Ratner noted in *Library Journal,* the poems are experimental in technique, often lacking common poetic devices such as stanza breaks, and they appear in unusual ways on the page, "with short lines at the left margin or moving across the page as hand follows eye." Yet, despite its visual effect, Ashley Brown commented in *World Literature Today,* "Ferlinghetti writes in a very accessible idiom; he draws on pop culture and sports as much as the modern poets whom he celebrates." Ratner averred that "Ferlinghetti is the foremost chronicler of our times." Indeed, the collection shows "Ferlinghetti still speaking out against academic poetry just as he did when the Beat Movement began," remarked Varner in *Western American Literature.* "Ferlinghetti, always the poet of the topical now, still sees clearly the 1990s," the critic added.

Drama has also proved a fertile ground for Ferlinghetti. He carried his political philosophies and social criticisms into experimental plays, many of them short and surrealistic. In *Lawrence Ferlinghetti,* Smith contended that the writer's stint as an experimental dramatist "reflects his stronger attention to irrational and intuitive analogy as a means of suggesting the 'secret meaning' behind life's surface. Though the works are provocative, public, and oral, they are also more cosmic in reference, revealing a stronger influence from Buddhist philosophy." In *Dialogue in American Drama,* Ruby Cohn characterized the poet's plays as "brief sardonic comments on our contemporary lifestyle. . . . The themes may perhaps be resolved into a

single theme—the unfairness of industrial, consumer-oriented, establishment-dominated existence—and the plays are arguments against submission to such existence."

In 1960 Ferlinghetti's first novel, *Her,* was published. An autobiographical, experimental work that focuses on the narrator's pursuit of a woman, the novel received very little critical comment when it was published. According to Smith in the *Dictionary of Literary Biography, Her* "is an avant-garde work that pits character and author in a battle with the subjective relativity of experience in a quest for ideals; a surrealistic encounter with the subconscious—filled with phallic symbols and prophetic visions of desire. At once existential, absurd, symbolic, expressionistic, cinematic and surrealistic in vision and form, *Her* is controlled, as all of Ferlinghetti's work is, by a drive toward expanded consciousness." Smith concluded, "The book is truly a spirited, though somewhat self-mocking, projection of the optimistic goals the Beat and San Francisco poetry movements placed on a grand imaginative scale."

Ferlinghetti published another novel in 1988, *Love in the Days of Rage.* This chronicles a love affair between an expatriate American painter named Annie, and a Parisian banker of Portuguese extraction named Julian. Their relationship takes place against the backdrop of 1968 Paris, during the student revolution that took place during that year. Though at first Annie thinks Julian is conservative, because of his clothing style and occupation, he eventually reveals his involvement in a subversive plot—which she supports him in. Alex Raksin, discussing *Love in the Days of Rage* in the *Los Angeles Times Book Review,* praised the work as an "original, intense novel" in which Ferlinghetti's "sensitivity as a painter . . . is most apparent." Patrick Burson, critiquing for the *San Francisco Review of Books,* explained that "*Love in the Days of Rage* challenges the reader on several stylistic levels as it attemps to mirror the anarchistic uprising of '68 which briefly united intellectuals, artists, and proletariats in common cause." Burson went on to conclude that the book is "an uneven ride, at times maddeningly confused, but noble in intent and final effect."

Ferlinghetti, who continues to operate the City Lights bookstore, travels frequently to give poetry readings. His paintings and drawings have been exhibited in San Francisco galleries; his plays have been performed in experimental theaters. He also continues to publish new poetry, including the 1997 collection *A Far Rockaway of the Heart,* which is to some degree a follow-up to *A Coney Island of the Mind.* In 2001 readers saw the arrival of two books by Ferlinghetti: *How to Paint Sunlight: Lyric Poems and Others, 1997-2000* and *San Francisco Poems.* As Smith observed in the *Dictionary of Literary Biography,* Ferlinghetti's life and writing "stand as models of the existentially authentic and engaged. . . . His work exists as a vital challenge and a living presence to the contemporary artist, as an embodiment of the strong, anticool, compassionate commitment to life in an absurd time." *New York Times Book Review* correspondent Joel Oppenheimer cited Ferlinghetti's work for "a legitimate revisionism which is perhaps our best heritage from those raucous [Beat] days—the poet daring to see a different vision from that which the guardians of culture had allowed us." As *New Pages* contributor John Gill concluded, reading a work by Ferlinghetti "will make you feel good about poetry and about the world—no matter how mucked-up the world may be."

BIOGRAPHICAL AND CRITICAL SOURCES:

BOOKS

Cherkovski, Neeli, *Ferlinghetti: A Biography,* Doubleday (New York, NY), 1979.

Cohn, Ruby, *Dialogue in American Drama,* Indiana University Press, 1971.

Contemporary Literary Criticism, Gale (Detroit, MI), Volume 2, 1974, Volume 6, 1976, Volume 10, 1979, Volume 27, 1984, Volume 111, 1998.

Contemporary Poets, 7th edition, St. James Press (Detroit, MI), 2001.

Dictionary of Literary Biography, Volume 16: *The Beats: Literary Bohemians in Post-War America,* Gale (Detroit, MI), 1983.

Parkinson, Thomas, *Poets, Poems, Movements,* UMI Research Press, 1987.

Poetry Criticism, Volume 1, Gale (Detroit, MI), 1991.

Rexroth, Kenneth, *American Poetry in the Twentieth Century,* Herder & Herder, 1971.

Rexroth, Kenneth, *Assays,* New Directions (New York, NY), 1961.

Silesky, Barry, *Ferlinghetti: The Artist in His Time,* Warner Books (New York, NY), 1990.

Smith, Larry, *Lawrence Ferlinghetti: Poet-at-Large,* Southern Illinois University Press (Carbondale, IL), 1983.

Sutton, Walter, *American Free Verse: The Modern Revolution in Poetry,* New Directions (New York, NY), 1973.

PERIODICALS

American Book Review, March-April, 1984.

American Poetry Review, September-October, 1977.

Arizona Quarterly, autumn, 1982.

Booklist, November 15, 1995, p. 532; May 15, 1997, p. 1557.

Chicago Tribune, May 19, 1986; September 13, 1988.

Chicago Tribune Book World, February 28, 1982.

Critique, Volume 19, number 3, 1978.

Explicator, winter, 2001, Marilyn Ann Fontane, "Ferlinghetti's 'Constantly Risking Absurdity,'" p. 106.

Georgia Review, winter, 1989.

Guardian, April 16, 1998, p. T20.

Library Journal, November 15, 1960; October 1, 1993, p. 98; March 15, 1998, p. 107.

Life, September 9, 1957.

Listener, February 1, 1968.

Los Angeles Times, July 20, 1969; March 18, 1980; September 27, 1985.

Los Angeles Times Book Review, August 24, 1980; October 19, 1980; March 24, 1985; September 4, 1988, Alex Raksin, review of *Love in the Days of Rage,* p. 4.

Midwest Quarterly, autumn, 1974.

Minnesota Review, July, 1961.

Nation, October 11, 1958.

New Pages, spring-summer, 1985.

New York Times, April 14, 1960; April 15, 1960; April 16, 1960; April 17, 1960; February 6, 1967; February 27, 1967; September 13, 1970.

New York Times Book Review, September 2, 1956; September 7, 1958; April 29, 1962; July 21, 1968; September 8, 1968; September 21, 1980; November 1, 1981; November 6, 1988; November 6, 1994.

Observer (London, England), November 1, 1959; April 9, 1967.

Parnassus, spring-summer, 1974.

Poetry, November, 1958; July, 1964; May, 1966.

Prairie Schooner, fall, 1974; summer, 1978.

Publishers Weekly, September 26, 1994, p. 59; November 27, 1995, p. 67; March 31, 1997, p. 69; September 28, 1998, p. 24.

Punch, April 19, 1967.

San Francisco Chronicle, March 5, 1961.

San Francisco Review of Books, September, 1977; fall, 1988, Patrick Burnson, "Passionate Spring," p. 44.

Saturday Review, October 5, 1957; September 4, 1965.

Sewanee Review, fall, 1974.

Sunday Times (London, England), June 20, 1965.

Times (London, England), October 27, 1968.

Times Literary Supplement, April 27, 1967; November 25, 1988.

Virginia Quarterly Review, autumn, 1969; spring, 1974.

Washington Post Book World, August 2, 1981.

West Coast Review, winter, 1981.

Western American Literature, spring, 1982, p. 79; winter, 1995, p. 372.

Whole Earth, summer, 1999, Lawrence Ferlinghetti, "A Far Rockaway of the Heart," p. 38.

World Literature Today, summer, 1977; spring, 1982, p. 348; autumn, 1994, p. 815; winter, 1998, p. 138.

ONLINE

City Lights Web site, http://www.citylights.com/ (May 3, 2003), "Lawrence Ferlinghetti."*

*   *   *

FERRIGNO, Robert 1948(?)-

PERSONAL: Born c. 1948, in Florida; married; wife's name Jody; children: Jake, Dani. *Education:* Received B.A.; Bowling Green State University, M.F.A., 1971.

ADDRESSES: Agent—Sandra Dijkstra, 1155 Camino del Mar, No. 515, Del Mar, CA 92014.

CAREER: Writer. Instructor in English and literature in Seattle, WA, 1971-73; feature writer for *Orange County Register,* until 1988; instructor in journalism at California State University, Fullerton.

WRITINGS:

NOVELS

The Horse Latitudes, Morrow (New York, NY), 1990.
The Cheshire Moon, Morrow (New York, NY), 1993.

Dead Man's Dance, Putnam (New York, NY), 1995.
Dead Silent, Putnam (New York, NY), 1996.
Heartbreaker, Pantheon (New York, NY), 1999.
Flinch, Pantheon (New York, NY), 2001.
Scavenger Hunt, Pantheon (New York, NY), 2003.

Contributor to periodicals, including *California* and *Women's Sports and Fitness.*

SIDELIGHTS: Robert Ferrigno drew critical attention with the 1990 publication of his first novel, *The Horse Latitudes.* The author began the book after his wife survived a difficult pregnancy and gave birth to their son, Jake. "Even though they both pulled out of it, and they're both fine, it gave me a very powerful sense that life is fleeting," Ferrigno told Dennis McLellan in the *Los Angeles Times.* "It made me realize I had been talking and thinking about writing a book for a long time, but should probably not count on having the rest of my life to finish it." Ferrigno started *The Horse Latitudes* while working as a feature writer for the *Orange County Register,* rising at four each morning to write. But after about eighteen months, his heavy schedule began to take its toll, and with his wife's encouragement, Ferrigno quit his job at the newspaper to work on his novel full time.

Ferrigno's gamble proved to be a profitable one, as William Morrow and Company bought the rights to his unfinished novel for $150,000 in 1988. Set in southern California, *The Horse Latitudes* concerns Danny DiMedici, a former marijuana dealer who lost his taste for the outlaw life after killing a man. DiMedici's amoral wife Lauren, a corporate motivational psychologist, left him after he reformed, explaining that "God hates a coward." As the novel opens, DiMedici is attempting to come to terms with his recent divorce: "There were nights when Danny missed Lauren so bad that he wanted to take a fat man and throw him through a plate-glass window." He is soon visited by the police, who inform him that Lauren has disappeared and that her current lover, a scientist who has discovered a way to use fetal tissue to preserve youth, has been murdered at her beach house. A suspect in the killing, DiMedici searches for Lauren and is pursued himself by a pair of police officers and several other eccentric characters.

Some reviewers of *The Horse Latitudes* compared Ferrigno to Elmore Leonard and Raymond Chandler. Chicago *Tribune Books* contributor Gary Dretzka commented that "the chases, kidnappings, beatings, black-mail and extortion attempts that result after this crazy California salad is tossed are imaginatively rendered and make for a quick, chilling, often humorous read." Though he found *The Horse Latitudes* to be unoriginal, Michael Dirda acknowledged in the *Washington Post* that "Ferrigno does possess some genuine storytelling skills. He can make you afraid, he can make you laugh. . . . and he can make you keep turning his pages." Dirda also observed that *The Horse Latitudes* reads like a film script, "which may be fine if you were expecting a movie, but not so good if you were hoping for a novel." *Time* contributor Margaret Carlson was more enthusiastic, calling *The Horse Latitudes* "a work of *noir* literature that is the most memorable fiction debut of the season. With a magic all his own, [Ferrigno] has written an illuminating novel that never fails to entertain but also, surprisingly, makes us feel."

The seamy underworld Ferrigno depicts in *The Horse Latitudes* is similar to one the author experienced firsthand. Dissatisfied with the job of teaching English and literature he had landed after graduate school, Ferrigno quit and spent the next six years playing poker for a living. He resided in a high-crime area of downtown Seattle, where one of his neighbors was a heroin dealer. Ferrigno turned to writing after taking a freelance assignment for an alternative weekly newspaper. "There is an intensity in coming home at 4 in the morning and throwing a couple of thousand dollars on your bed and throwing it in the air [and saying], I won all of it!," he told McLellan. "But that wasn't even close to getting $10 for an article with your name on it."

Ferrigno followed *The Horse Latitudes* with *The Cheshire Moon,* published in 1993. In this novel a reporter, Quinn, and his photographer sidekick, Jen Takamura, pursue the murderer of Quinn's best friend, Andy. Andy had witnessed a killing, and the murderer found it necessary to dispose of Andy as well, making his death appear a suicide. The killer is Emory Roy Liston, a "crazed rhinoceros of a former pro football player," according to Christopher Lehmann-Haupt in the *New York Times.* Liston, who attends night school, polishes his football trophies regularly, and is a frequent cable shopping-channel customer, "provides the spice" of the novel, wrote Michael Anderson in the *New York Times Book Review.* "Despite the conventionality of its plot, Mr. Ferrigno develops the qualities he showed off with such promise in his first

novel," commented Lehmann-Haupt, who particularly noted Ferrigno's "black wit embellished with images of violence." The reviewer concluded that *The Cheshire Moon* is "a lot of fun to read, and Mr. Ferrigno certainly knows how to lay contrasting colors on his canvas."

Ferrigno continued to set his novels in rich-for-exploitation southern California. His 1995 novel, *Dead Man's Dance,* features investigative reporter Quinn attempting to uncover the brutal murder of his southern California judge stepfather and untangling a massive web of deceit in the process. "A slick, sleek story that races to a slam-bankg ending" is how *Booklist* contributor Emily Melton described it. *Dead Silent* has at its lurid core the decadent world of the music business as independent music producer Nick Carbonne investigates how the naked, dead bodies of his wife and best friend ended up in his hot tub. As Joe Gores commented in the *San Francisco Chronicle,* "Set in the glitter and grit of the southern California dreamtime, *Dead Silent* probes, with almost despairing violence, lives of such amorality that few of us can imagine them."

A *Publisher Weekly* contributor called Ferrigno's *Heartbreaker* "his best novel in years. . . . a cinematic thriller . . . populated by mean drug dealers, beautiful surfers, 'trust fund babies,' 'thugs on commission' and murderers for hire." Val Duran, an ex-undercover cop escaping his past, leaves Miami for a quiet life as a stuntman in Los Angeles only to find himself enmeshed in the psychodrama of his girlfriend's scheming family while attempting to avoid the vengeful drug dealer who killed his partner. "As usual with Ferrigno's novels," stated Scott Veale in the *New York Times Book Review,* "the southern California atmospherics and razor-sharp dialogue are first-rate, and the villains quirky and memorable."

Featured in Ferrigno's next two thrillers is tabloid journalist Jimmy Gage. In *Flinch,* this cool and engaging antihero "stumbles on evidence which may link his absurdly competitive brother to a serial killer," explained a contributor to the *Booklist* list of the best crime novels of 2002. And a *Publishers Weekly* reviewer praised *Flinch* for its "expansive canvas, spot-on characterizations, excellent prose and incisive dialogue."

Gage reappears in *Scavenger Hunt,* Ferrigno's seventh novel. In this thriller, Gage is enlisted to write an article about the tell-all script of Hollywood director

Garrett Walsh, recently released from prison for a murder he was falsely accused of committing. Soon Walsh is dead and Gage risks his life against a cast of crooked and powerful Hollywood characters in order to set the record straight about Walsh's innocence. J. Kingston Pierce of *January Magazine* reflected that Ferrigno's "tale of ambition and guilt is driven by what for him is particularly dense, circuitous plotting, buttressed by clever dialogue."

BIOGRAPHICAL AND CRITICAL SOURCES:

BOOKS

Contemporary Literary Criticism, Volume 65, Gale (Detroit, MI), 1991, pp. 47-50.
Ferrigno, Robert, *The Horse Latitudes,* Morrow (New York, NY), 1990.

PERIODICALS

Booklist, April 15, 1995, Emily Melton, review of *Dead Man's Dance,* p. 1452; p. 1452; October 15, 2001, Joanne Wilkinson, review of *Flinch,* p. 386; May 1, 2002.
Kirkus Reviews, August 15, 2001, review of *Flinch,* p. 1166.
Library Journal, May 1, 1995, Stacie Browne Chandler, review of *Dead Man's Dance,* p. 130; October 1, 2001, Emily Doro, review of *Flinch,* p. 140; December, 2002, Susan Clifford Braun, review of *Scavenger Hunt,* p. 177.
Los Angeles Times, March 2, 1990.
Los Angeles Times Book Review, April 8, 1990, pp. 2, 8; June 20, 1999, p. 16; November 13, 2001, Michael Harris, review of *Flinch,* p. E1.
New Yorker, February 22, 1993, review of *The Cheshire Moon,* p. 183.
New York Times, March 19, 1990, p. C20; February 25, 1993, review of *The Cheshire Moon,* p. B2.
New York Times Book Review, February 7, 1993, p. 22; July 15, 1995, Marilyn Stasio, review of *Dead Man's Dance,* p. 16; September 8, 1996, Marilyn Stasio, review of *Dead Silent,* p. 26.
Publishers Weekly, January 5, 1990, Sybil Steinberg, review of *The Horse Latitudes,* p. 62; August 2, 1993, review of *Cheshire Moon,* p. 30; June 17, 1996, review of *Dead Silent,* p. 45; March 15, 1999, review of *Heartbreaker,* p. 44; August 13, 2001, review of *Flinch,* p. 282; December 16, 2002, review of *Scavenger Hunt,* p. 47.
San Francisco Chronicle, August 27, 1996, Joe Gores, review of *Dead Silent,* p. B3.
Time, March 26, 1990, p. 78; March 15, 1993, review of *The Cheshire Moon,* p. 75.
Tribune Books (Chicago, IL), March 11, 1990, pp. 6-7.
Village Voice, April 3, 1990, p. 76.
Wall Street Journal, March 9, 1990, p. A11.
Washington Post, March 16, 1990; February 18, 1993, Tom Nolan, review of *The Cheshire Moon,* p. A16.

ONLINE

January Magazine, http://www.januarymagazine.com/ (February 15, 2003), J. Kingston Pierce, review of *Scavenger Hunt.**

*   *   *

FINLEY, Michael 1950-

PERSONAL: Born July 4, 1950, in Flint, MI; son of Paul (a sales engineer) and Mary (a business owner; maiden name, Konik) Finley; married Rachel Frazin, June 25, 1981; children: Daniele, Jonathan. *Ethnicity:* "Irish-American." *Education:* Attended College of Wooster, 1967-69; University of Minnesota—Twin Cities, B.A., 1972.

ADDRESSES: Home—1841 Dayton Ave., St. Paul, MN 55104. *Agent*—Andrea Pedolsky, Altair Literary Agency, 141 Fifth Ave., Suite 8-N, New York, NY. *E-mail*—mfinley@mfinley.com.

CAREER: University of Minnesota—Twin Cities, Minneapolis, MN, editor, 1973-78; *Worthington Daily Globe,* Worthington, MN, editor, 1978-80; On the Edge (writing and consulting business), owner, 1980—.

AWARDS, HONORS: Wisconsin arts fellow, 1986; Global Business Book Award, *Financial Times,* 1995; named "wizard of the wired world," Financial Times Press, 1999; named "American reporter correspondent of the year," 1999.

WRITINGS:

Techno-Crazed, Peterson, 1995.

(With Harvey Robbins) *Why Teams Don't Work,* Peterson, 1995, new edition published as *The New Why Teams Don't Work,* Berrett Koehler (San Francisco, CA), 2000.

(With Harvey Robbins) *Why Change Doesn't Work,* Peterson, 1996.

(With Harvey Robbins) *Transcompetition,* McGraw-Hill (New York, NY), 1998.

Author, with Harvey Robbins, of the book *Turf Wars.* Author of "On the Edge," a weekly column in *St. Paul Pioneer Press.* Author of an Internet journal, *Michael Finley's Future Shoes.*

WORK IN PROGRESS: The Accidental Leader, with Harvey Robbins.

SIDELIGHTS: Michael Finley once told *CA:* "I'm your basic late-blooming writer, though I've been hacking weeds now for thirty years. I've worked as a security guard, soda pop bottler, storefront minister, talk show host, aerial photographer, Fuller Brush man, rock critic, fashion designer, and worse, but I was always writing. I began at the apex, writing surrealistic poetry (eight books), but quickly descended into disreputable genres: book reviews, fiction, essays. Then I went further down into television, public relations copy, and ghostwriting. I didn't hit rock bottom, writing about business and technology, until the last ten years.

"For several years I worked with psychologist Harvey Robbins on a series of books lampooning business fads and fashions: *Turf Wars, Why Teams Don't Work, Why Change Doesn't Work,* and our summa opus, *Transcompetition.*

"We're disgusted at the blindness with which so many organizations, from social groups to businesses to governments, consistently achieve the opposite of what they want, because they are unwilling to understand what the other side is after. Our books are the antidote for the happy nonsense that passes for business journalism in this age."

BIOGRAPHICAL AND CRITICAL SOURCES:

ONLINE

Michael Finley's Future Shoes, http://mfinley.com/ (September 10, 2003).

FRANCK, Dan 1952-

PERSONAL: Born 1952, in Paris, France. *Education:* Studied sociology at the University of Paris, Sorbonne, 1970.

ADDRESSES: Agent—c/o Author Mail, Random House, 1745 Broadway, New York, NY 10019.

CAREER: Novelist and screenwriter. Actor in films, including *En compagnie d'Antonin Artaud* (also known as *My Life and Times with Antonin Artaud*).

AWARDS, HONORS: Prix du Premier Roman, 1980, for *Les calendes grecques: Roman;* prix litteraire Renaudot, 1991, for *La separation: Roman.*

WRITINGS:

Les Calendes grecques: Roman, Calmann-Lévy (Paris, France), 1980.

Le Petit livre de l'orchestre et de ses instruments, illustrated by Anne Victoire, Mazarine (Paris, France), 1981.

Apolline, Stock (Paris, France), 1982.

Les Têtes de l'art, B. Grasset (Paris, France), 1983.

La Dame du soir: Roman, Mercure de France (Paris, France), 1984.

Les Adieux: Roman, Flammarion (Paris, France), 1987.

Le Cimetiere des fous: Roman, Flammarion (Paris, France), 1989.

La Separation: Roman, Editions du Seuil (Paris, France), 1991, translation by Jon Rothschild published as *Separation: A Novel,* Knopf (New York, NY), 1994.

Une Jeune fille: Roman, Editions du Seuil (Paris, France), 1994, translation by Jon Rothschild published as *My Russian Love,* Nan A. Talese/Doubleday (Garden City, NY), 1997.

Tabac: Recit, Editions du Seuil (Paris, France), 1995.

Nu couché, Editions du Seuil (Paris, France), 1998.

Bohèmes (nonfiction), Calmann-Lévy (Paris, France), 1998, translation by Cynthia Hope Liebow published in the U.S. as *Bohemian Paris: Picasso, Modigliani, Matisse, and the Birth of Modern Art,* Grove (New York, NY), 2001, published in England as *The Bohemians: The Birth of Modern Art, Paris, 1900-1930,* Weidenfeld & Nicolson (London, England), 2001.

(Author of text) *Le Carnet de la Californie: Dessins 1.11.1955-14.1.1956 / Picasso et Promenade,* Cercle d'art (Paris, France), 1999.

"LES AVENTURES DE BORO" SERIES; WITH JEAN VAUTRIN

La Dame de Berlin: Les Aventures de Boro, reporter-photographe, Fayard & Balland (Paris, France), 1987.
Les Temps des cerises, Fayard (Paris, France), 1990.
Les Noces de Guernica, Fayard (Paris, France), 1994.

SCREENPLAYS

(Author of dialogue, with Jacques Deray) *Netchaieev est de retour* (also known as *Netchaieev Is Back*), Les Films d'Ecluse/Italmedia Film/TF1 Films Productions, 1991.
(With Christian Vincent) *La Separation* (also known as *The Separation*), C.M.V. Productions/Canal+ Productions/France 2 Cinema/D.A. Films/Renn Productions, 1994.
(With Enki Bilal) *Tykho Moon,* Salome/Schlemmer Film, 1996.

SIDELIGHTS: French-language author/screenwriter Dan Franck has been known since the 1980s particularly for his novels. These works, which include *La Dame du soir, Les Adieux,* and *La Separation,* have been favorably compared to the works of other prominent writers in the French language such as Marcel Proust, Samuel Beckett, and Marguerite Duras. Franck's reputation was further cemented when his novel *Les Calendes grecques* won the distinguished Prix du Premier Roman in 1980. Reviewer John J. Lakich, writing in *World Literature Today,* praised this story of an old man's slow mental and physical decay as he chronicles his last few days while dying of cancer and called it "highly readable; it is one of those books that hold a reader's attention to the very end and is hard to put down," and declared that it "has a force and originality of its own."

Another of Franck's novels, *La Separation,* chronicles the eroding marriage of a well-to-do French couple. It received the 1991 Prix litteraire Renaudot and received much praise from French critics. However, *New York Times* contributor Michiko Kakutani wrote that "the

lack of detail in *Separation* makes for a vague, disembodied narrative and characters who feel more like illustrations in a psychology textbook than flesh-and-blood human beings." Kakutani added that "though some of Mr. Franck's descriptions of the couple's slow dance toward divorce are genuinely moving, his narrative bogs down in increasingly strained and sentimental images." Writing in the *Review of Contemporary Fiction,* Renee Kingcaid declared that *La Separation* is reminiscent of *thirtysomething,* a popular "yuppie melodrama" broadcast on American television in the 1980s, and that "the novel's *thirtysomething*ness" reflects "Franck's attempt to speak for a generation of heartbroken idealists."

Other reviewers praised the novel for its attempt to present the pain of rejection. Marian Winik, writing in the *Washington Post Book World,* commented that in *La Separation,* Franck creates "an emotional resonance that goes beyond generation or gender and a depiction of heartbreak so sharp that anyone recently separated, divorced or dumped should approach the book with care." *New York Times Book Review* contributor Elizabeth Benedict maintained that the author "is enormously skillful at conveying the wild swings of emotion in a marriage under siege" and deemed *La Separation* "a powerful story." Richard Eder declared in the *Los Angeles Times Book Review* that the novel "is a very precisely delineated slice not of life but of life's pain," but added that "Franck has not written a tragedy. Without our quite realizing it, perhaps, he has given us something more like comedy. It is the comedy of pain, and it gives his book its distinctiveness."

My Russian Love, an English translation of *Une Jeune fille,* is another Franck novel that garnered extensive criticism. In *My Russian Love,* a filmmaker named Luca sees a woman while leaving Moscow on a train. She reminds him of a Russian girl with whom he had an affair years before. They met while they were both students in France, but the affair ended when the girl, Anna, returned to Russia to help her parents who were imprisoned for their pro-Western beliefs. Writing in the *New York Times,* Richard Bernstein noted that "*My Russian Love* is the work of a skilled writer, a man of refined sensibility and a keen dramatic sense, but it needs a less well-worn theme and a deeper exploration of character than the author provides to make it fully realized." According to a *Publishers Weekly* contributor, "Franck certainly knows how to structure a story, and his short vignette-like chapters slip by at a brisk pace." Reviewing *My Russian Love* in the *New York Times Book Review*, Zofia Smardz said that Franck "has written a book as spare as a screenplay but fully novelistic in its language, imagery and psychological insight."

Departing from fiction, Franck produced *Bohèmes*, a French-language volume that in translation went under two titles. Known in the United Kingdom as *The Bohemians: The Birth of Modern Art, Paris, 1900-1930*, the book illustrates, noted *Spectator* critic William Feaver, "how notoriety arises, how legend develops, [and] how youthful poverty degenerates, with success, into tedious affluence." The great names of the Belle Époque—Pablo Picasso, Jean Cocteau, Alfred Jarry, Max Jacob—are intertwined in Franck's book. Published in the United States as *Bohemian Paris: Picasso, Modigliani, Matisse, and the Birth of Modern Art*, the work came under the scrutiny of a *Publishers Weekly* reviewer, who observed that the author seemingly wants to "lighten up . . . with a series of nonfiction anecdotes rife with novelistic invented dialogue" and saw "little conventionally grounded history among these yarns of brawls, food-fights [and] drunken disputes." *Library Journal* contributor Carol Binkowski, on the other hand, found more to like in the "marvelous and informative" *Bohemian Paris*. Binkowski remarked that the author is "especially good" at showing "how all these artists interacted while allowing them to remain individuals."

BIOGRAPHICAL AND CRITICAL SOURCES:

PERIODICALS

Booklist, February 1, 1994, p. 994; February 15, 1997, pp. 1002-1003.
French Review, April, 1986, pp. 812-813.
Library Journal, January, 2002, Carol Binkowski, review of *Bohemian Paris: Picasso, Modigliani, Matisse, and the Birth of Modern Art*, p. 94.
Los Angeles Times Book Review, December 26, 1993, Richard Eder, review of *La Separation*, pp. 3, 7.
New York Times, January 21, 1994, Michiko Kakutani, review of *La Separation*, p. C27; March 21, 1997, Richard Bernstein, review of *My Russian Love*, p. B30.
New York Times Book Review, January 23, 1994, Elizabeth Benedict, review of *La Separation*, p. 10; March 9, 1997, Zofia Smardz, review of *My Russian Love*, p. 19.

Publishers Weekly, November 1, 1993, p. 66; December 30, 1996, review of *My Russian Love*, pp. 55-56; November 26, 2001, review of *Bohemian Paris*, p. 46.
Review of Contemporary Fiction, fall, 1992, Renee Kingcaid, review of *La Separation*, pp. 211-212.
Spectator, December 21, 1991, p. 80; October 20, 2001, William Feaver, review of *The Bohemians: The Birth of Modern Art, Paris, 1900-1930*, p. 54.
Washington Post Book World, February 13, 1994, Marian Winik, review of *La Separation*, p. 9.
World Literature Today, summer, 1981, John J. Lakich, review of *Les Calendes grecques*, p. 425.

ONLINE

e.Peak, http://www.peak.sfu.ca/ (December 30, 1997).
Standard Times, http://www.s-t.com/ (December 30, 1997).*

*   *   *

FREEMAN, Castle (William), Jr. 1944-

PERSONAL: Born November 26, 1944, in San Antonio, TX; son of Castle William (a business executive) and Janet (a homemaker; maiden name, Cunningham) Freeman; married Alice Chaffee (an artist and designer), July 12, 1969; children: Alexander C., Sarah S. *Ethnicity:* "White." *Education:* Columbia University, B.S. (cum laude), 1968. *Hobbies and other interests:* American and European history, natural history (especially botany and entomology).

ADDRESSES: Agent—Christina Ward, Christina Ward Literary Agency, P.O. Box 505, North Scituate, MA 02060.

CAREER: Franklin Institute, Philadelphia, PA, technical writer, 1970-72; Stephen Greene Press, Brattleboro, VT, editor, 1976-80; *Country Journal*, copy editor, Manchester, VT, 1981-87; freelance writer and editor, 1987—. New Brook Fire Department, Newfane, VT, member.

MEMBER: Phi Beta Kappa.

AWARDS, HONORS: Award for New England Writers, St. Botolph's Club Foundation, 1993.

WRITINGS:

The Bride of Ambrose (short stories), Soho Press (New York, NY), 1987.

Spring Snow (essays), Houghton Mifflin (Boston, MA), 1996.

Judgment Hill (novel), University Press of New England (Hanover, NH), 1997.

My Life and Adventures (novel), St. Martin's Press (New York, NY), 2002.

Author of the column "Farmer's Calendar," *Old Farmer's Almanac*, 1981—. Contributor of articles and stories to periodicals, including *New England Review, Ontario Review, Southwest Review, Yankee, Harrowsmith, Atlantic Monthly, Harvard, Massachusetts Review,* and *Shenandoah.*

ADAPTATIONS: Two of the author's writings have been adapted for the Puppet Theater.

WORK IN PROGRESS: A collection of short stories "unified by common characters, setting, and themes."

SIDELIGHTS: Castle Freeman, Jr. told *CA:* "*My Life and Adventures* is the fictional reminiscences of the narrator, Mark Noon, as he takes up his inheritance: a derelict hill farm in an isolated community in rural Vermont. Time is the late sixties and early seventies. Noon recounts how he got to make the township his home, got to know its people, its nature, its history, its lore; how he found work, friends, love.

"The story is told by way of Noon's reflections on a range of topics having to do with Vermont and present-day America in general—topics personal, political, historical, literary, philosophical. It is also told in alternation with three kinds of other matter: entries from the diary of the predecessor on Noon's property, a busted hill farmer; tabular and statistical content (made up) about the economy, population, geography, and fauna of the vicinity; and Noon's recollections of his career before he came to Vermont, in particular his darkly comic account of a disastrous year working on behalf of shadowy forces in a forbidding, chaotic, Latin American port city (unnamed)."

BIOGRAPHICAL AND CRITICAL SOURCES:

PERIODICALS

Booklist, July 1, 2002, Joanne Wilkinson, review of *My Life and Adventures,* p. 1820.

Kirkus Reviews, July 15, 1997, review of *Judgment Hill,* p. 1049; June 1, 2002, review of *My Life and Adventures,* p. 756.

Library Journal, September 15, 1997, Barbara Maslekoff, review of *Judgment Hill,* p. 101; June 15, 1998, review of *Judgment Hill,* p. 132; September 1, 2002, Cheryl L. Conway, review of *My Life and Adventures,* p. 211.

New York Times Book Review, February 1, 1998, Martha E. Stone, review of *Judgment Hill,* p. 18.

Publishers Weekly, July 8, 2002, review of *My Life and Adventures,* p. 31.

World and I, January, 1998, review of *Judgment Hill,* p. 282.*

*   *   *

FRENCH, Paul
See ASIMOV, Isaac

*   *   *

FUKUYAMA, Francis 1952-

PERSONAL: Born October 27, 1952, in Chicago, IL; son of Yoshio (a Congregationalist minister and educator) and Toshiko (a potter; maiden name, Kawata) Fukuyama; married Laura Holmgren (a homemaker), September 8, 1986; children: Julia, David, John. *Education:* Cornell University, B.A., 1974; graduate studies at Yale University, 1974-75; Harvard University, Ph.D. (political science), 1981. *Religion:* Protestant.

ADDRESSES: Home—McLean, VA. *Office*—Paul H. Nitze School of Advanced International Studies, 1740 Massachusetts Avenue NW, Rome 732, Washington, DC 20036. *Agent*—Esther Newberg, International Creative Management, 40 West 57th St., New York, NY 10019. *E-mail*—fukuyam@jhu.edu.

CAREER: Pan Heuristics, Inc., Los Angeles, CA, consultant, 1978-79; RAND Corporation, Santa Monica, CA, associate social scientist, 1979-81, senior staff

Francis Fukuyama

member of political science department, 1983-89, consultant, 1990-94, senior social scientist, 1995-96; U.S. Department of State, Policy Planning Staff, Washington, DC, member of U.S. delegation to Egyptian-Israeli talks on Palestinian autonomy, 1981-82, deputy director, 1989-90, consultant, 1990—; Johns Hopkins University, Paul H. Nitze School of Advanced International Studies (SAIS), Washington, DC, fellow of foreign policy institute and director of SAIS Telecommunications Project, 1994-96, currently dean of SAIS and Bernard L. Schwartz Professor of Political Economy; George Mason University, Institute of Public Policy, Fairfax, VA, Omer L. and Nancy Hirst Professor of Public Policy, beginning 1996. University of California, Los Angeles, visiting lecturer in political science, 1986 and 1989. Member of Council on Foreign Relations and President's Council on Bioethics; founding member, Pacific Council on International Policy. Member of advisory boards, National Endowment for Democracy and New American Foundation.

MEMBER: American Association for the Advancement of Slavic Studies, Sierra Club.

AWARDS, HONORS: Premio Capri International Award and *Los Angeles Times* Book Critics Award in current interest category, both 1992, both for *The End of History and the Last Man;* received Medal of the Presidency of the Italian Republic, 1993; Connecticut College, honorary doctorate, 1995; Excellence 2000 Award, U.S. Pan-Asian American Chamber of Commerce, 1995.

WRITINGS:

(Editor, with Andrzej Korbonski) *The Soviet Union and the Third World: The Last Three Decades,* Cornell University Press (Ithaca, NY), 1987.
A Look at "The End of History?," edited by Kenneth M. Jensen, U.S. Institute of Peace (Washington, DC), 1990.
The End of History and the Last Man, Free Press (New York, NY), 1992.
Trust: The Social Virtues and the Creation of Prosperity, Free Press (New York, NY), 1995.
(With Peter Breuer and David Chandler) *Transit: Passagen globaler Kooperation = Passages of Global Cooperation,* photographs by Peter Bialobrzeski and Henrik Spohler, Edition Braus (Heidelberg, Germany), 1997.
The Great Disruption: Human Nature and the Reconstitution of Social Order, Free Press (New York, NY), 1999.
Our Posthuman Future: Consequences of the Biotechnology Revolution, Farrar, Straus (New York, NY), 2002.

Author of numerous documents for the RAND Corporation, including *Soviet Threats to Intervene in the Middle East, 1956-1973,* 1980; *Escalation in the Middle East and Persian Gulf,* 1984; *Moscow's Post-Brezhnev Reassessment of the Third World,* 1986; *Soviet Civil-Military Relations and the Power Projection Mission,* 1987; *Gorbachev and the New Soviet Agenda in the Third World,* 1989; *The U.S.-Japan Security Relationship after the Cold War,* 1993; and (with Abram N. Shulsky) *The "Virtual Corporation" and Army Organization,* 1997; and (with Caroline S. Wagner, Richard Schum, and Danilo Pelletiere) *Information and Biological Revolutions: Global Governance Challenges: Summary of a Study Group,* 2000. Contributor to books, including *U.S. Strategic Interests in Southwest Asia,* edited by Shirin Tahir-Kheli, Praeger, 1982; *Hawks, Doves, and Owls,* edited by Graham Allison, Albert Carnesale, and Joseph Nye, Norton, 1985; and *The Future of the Soviet Empire,* edited by Henry Rowen and Charles Wolf, St. Martin's Press, 1987.

Book review editor, *Foreign Affairs;* advisory board member, *Journal of Democracy* and *National Interest.* Contributor to periodicals, including *American Spectator, Commentary, Current History, Foreign Affairs, Guardian, Journal of Democracy, Middle East Contemporary Survey, National Interest, New Republic, Orbis,* and *Political Science Quarterly.*

The End of History and the Last Man has been translated into Danish, Dutch, Finnish, French, German, Greek, Hebrew, Italian, Japanese, Korean, Portuguese, Spanish, and Swedish.

SIDELIGHTS: Following a stint as senior staff member of the political science department of the RAND Corporation, Francis Fukuyama captured attention worldwide in 1989 after penning an essay on the current state of history. Called "The End of History?," the sixteen-page article appeared in the foreign policy journal *National Interest* and became the topic of considerable debate. In his thesis, Fukuyama, who was then working as deputy director of the U.S. State Department's policy planning staff, contended that history had evolved to its logical end: that of liberal democracy. Fukuyama's notion of "history," as explained by Toronto *Globe and Mail* contributor Jeffrey Simpson, is "the struggle for universal acceptance of the most effective and just organization of human society."

Based in part on the ideologies of German philosopher Georg Wilhelm Friedrich Hegel, Fukuyama's argument centers on the fact that one form of government will ultimately win out over all others. Fukuyama maintains that his assertion that liberal democracy has been victorious has been validated by the reunification of Germany and the collapse of Communism. According to James Atlas in the *New York Times Magazine,* Fukuyama suggests that "history is a protracted struggle to realize the idea of freedom latent in human consciousness. In the 20th century, the forces of totalitarianism have been decisively conquered by the United States and its allies, which represent the final embodiment of this idea." The end result, predicts Fukuyama, will be "a very sad time," as people turn to solving technological troubles rather than fighting ideological battles.

Fukuyama's essay, which he later expanded into the 1992 book *The End of History and the Last Man,* would continue to be the subject of much debate in the years following its hardbound publication. While some commentators have agreed with the author's delineations, others argue that liberal democracy certainly will be challenged by Third World countries and religious fundamentalists. Some critics pointed to the problems of drugs and poverty in U.S. society as further evidence that liberal democracy may not be the key ideology. In response to such debate, Fukuyama told Atlas: "The last thing I want to be interpreted as saying is that our society is a utopia, or that there are no more problems." He added, "I simply don't see any competitors to modern democracy."

In his 1995 book *Trust: The Social Virtues and the Creation of Prosperity,* Fukuyama argues that "economical success depends only partly on the factors customarily emphasized by economists: markets, competition, technology and skills," according to a contributor to the *Economist.* George Weigel explained in *Commentary* that "Fukuyama has come to agree that there is life after history" and that the results of this "post-historical" period will be determined by civil society; "'a complex welter of intermediate institutions, including businesses, voluntary associations, educational institutions, clubs, unions, media, charities, and churches,' of which the most crucial is the family," according to Weigel. The detailed case studies in *Trust* illustrate how "the level of 'trust' in a society or nation is the key variable determining its capacity to compete in the modern world."

Many critics praised *Trust* for its interesting thesis and engaging style, but faulted Fukuyama for his book's omissions and for failing to prove his thesis. An *Economist* contributor remarked that "despite the plausibility of its opening argument, despite Mr. Fukuyama's clear writing and hard work, *Trust* is not convincing." According to Norman Stone in *Management Today,* the book has serious "mis-statements" and "several . . . huge omissions." In the *New Republic,* Robert M. Solow called the book's central thesis "interesting, even plausible, but not very original." Within the book's argument, Solow maintained, "there are too many escape hatches, too many spineless terms, too many ways to rationalize exceptions," and concluded that while "the sorts of things that Fukuyama wants to talk about are more important than my colleagues in economics are willing to admit. . . . I would rather they were discussed imprecisely than not discussed at all." Solow concluded that "imprecision is not a virtue, a 'for example' is not an argument."

In *New Statesman & Society,* Anthony Giddens echoed Solow's belief that *Trust* lacked a convincing argument for its thesis; Giddens nevertheless described the book as "a work of considerable intellectual substance, engagingly written and ambitious in content." In a *Forbes* review, Steve Forbes described the book as "fascinating, disturbing, well-researched . . . [and] timely." "Fukuyama is not particularly alarmist in his book," summarized Perry Pascarella in *Industry Week:* "The quiet man leads us to see that unrestrained individualism harms society, the economy, and ultimately, the individual. He convinces us that we will have to settle for a less viable society and less productive economy until we find a way to rebalance individualism with community."

Fukuyama builds on the themes of his previous books in 1999's *The Great Disruption: Human Nature and the Reconstitution of Social Order.* He examines the "Great Disruption" of the social order that began in the 1960s with rising rates of social distrust, crime, illegitimacy, and divorce; explores their causes; and proposes that human nature will lead to a reversal of this trend. He points out that it is not government policies, but rather social and technological changes—like the sexual revolution caused by the birth control pill and the change from a manufacturing to an information economy—that have led to social upheaval. "Simply put, he contends that the social order responds to change in a pattern of decay and adaptive reconstitution," as Stephen Schneck summarized it in the *Review of Metaphysics.* "On this basis, Fukuyama argues that the great disruption is not linked to the triumph of democracy and capitalism. In fact, the biological and rational resources of human nature will work and are presently working to reconstitute morality and social order."

As with Fukuyama's previous books, *The Great Disruption* engendered much debate among critics, with some agreeing with the author's conclusions and others finding flaws in his methodology. Alan Wolfe, for instance, found a contradiction between Fukuyama's discussion of the Great Disruption's past (Part I of the book) and his speculation about its future resolution (Part II): "The precise and carefully qualified language of Part I gives rise to vagueness and guesswork in Part

II," the critic observed in the *New Republic.* "Yet even as Fukuyama speculates, he also speaks with great certainty. . . . Part I seeks parsimonious explanations of complicated realities. Part II offers baroque accounts of relatively uncomplicated realities." Geoffrey E. Schneider, Winston H. Griffith, and Janet T. Knoedler similarly wrote in the *Journal of Economic Issues* that "*The Great Disruption* offers a few interesting insights into the evolution of contemporary institutions. As fascinating as the topic is—the evolution of cultural norms and values in response to technological changes, the relationship between biology and human institutions—Fukuyama's insights amount to little more than standard sociology with a smattering of game theory, infused with conservative ideology." The critics added, "It is a frustrating book that oscillates between an evolutionary approach to social science and biological determinism." Charles Murray, however, observed in *Commentary* that "*The Great Disruption* takes on questions that go to the heart of social policy writ large," and concluded: "It is written with never-failing lucidity, brings together vast and disparate literatures, and makes one think in new ways about the prospects of post-industrial society. That is quite enough for one book."

Fukuyama, who sits on the President's Council on Bioethics, "is sometimes a philosopher, sociologist, social psychologist, anthropologist, or economist," Richard J. Coleman observed in the *Christian Century.* "But preeminently he is a social scientist interested in what makes us tick as social beings and in what political consequences our actions bring." In his 2002 work, *Our Posthuman Future: Consequences of the Biotechnology Revolution,* the author reassesses his theory that history has ended—not because liberal democracy has failed, but because "there can be no end of history without an end of modern natural science and technology." The author examines the origins and development of the biotechnology revolution, considering general trends in the field and their potential social ramifications. He argues that new biotechnologies have the potential to destabilize society by creating a "genetic arms race," as wealthy parents use genetic manipulation to give their children advantages of health, intelligence, and beauty. By creating such "posthumans," there is a risk of changing the human behaviors that are the basis for modern society and government. The way to prevent this, the author suggests, is through government intervention. "In clear, thoughtful, and at times elegant prose," a *Virginia Quarterly Review* critic noted, "Fukuyama makes a case for preemptive regulation of biotechnological advances in a series of steps."

Critics have praised the author's detailed exploration of the issues surrounding biotechnology, although many disagree with his arguments for government restrictions. Coleman, for instance, remarked that "one of Fukuyama's strengths is that he is continually asking what the political implications of the new technology are and how can we prepare for them," although the critic added that "many will be disappointed with the thinness of Fukuyama's understanding of those [moral] behaviors and characteristics that are uniquely human." *Guardian* critic Steven Poole, however, found *Our Posthuman Future* a "pseudish slab of alarmo-futurism," filled with "repetitive criticism." While Dan W. Brock wrote in *American Scientist* that "the book's central argument against employing this new biotechnology is seriously flawed," he added that *Our Posthuman Future* "is a well-written and accessible discussion" of biotechnological advances and issues. In recommending the book, Fredrick R. Abrams noted in the *Journal of the American Medical Association* that Fukuyama "explores diverse viewpoints and cites a variety of arguments to support or refute them." The critic concluded that by reading this book, "the researcher, politician, ethicist, and theologian would broaden their horizons in a subject that will affect all our futures."

BIOGRAPHICAL AND CRITICAL SOURCES:

BOOKS

Bertram, Christopher, and Andrew Chitty, *Has History Ended? Fukuyama, Marx, Modernity,* Avebury (Brookfield, VT), 1994.

Burns, Timothy, *After History? Francis Fukuyama and His Critics,* Rowman & Littlefield (Lanham, MD), 1994.

Fukuyama, Francis, *Our Posthuman Future: Consequences of the Biotechnology Revolution,* Farrar, Straus (New York, NY), 2002.

PERIODICALS

American Scientist, September-October, 2002, Dan W. Brock, "Messing with Mother Nature," p. 479.

Books & Culture, July-August, 2002, Michael Cromartie, "Our Posthuman Future: An Interview with Francis Fukuyama," p. 9.

British Medical Journal, June 15, 2002, Trevor Jackson, "Future Imperfect: Francis Fukuyama Is Back," p. 1462.

Christian Century, July 26, 2003, Richard J. Coleman, review of *Our Posthuman Future,* p. 36.

Commentary, October, 1995, George Weigel, review of *Trust: The Social Virtues and the Creation of Prosperity,* pp. 34-38; July, 1999, Charles Murray, review of *The Great Disruption,* p. 80.

Commonweal, June 19, 1992, Patrick J. Deneen, review of *The End of History and the Last Man,* pp. 25-26.

Economist, September 2, 1995, review of *Trust,* pp. 79-80.

Forbes, September 25, 1995, Steve Forbes, review of *Trust,* p. 24.

Globe and Mail (Toronto), April 4, 1992, Jeffrey Simpson, review of *The End of History and the Last Man,* p. C6.

Guardian (London), April 12, 2003, Steven Poole, review of *Our Posthuman Future,* p. 31.

Industry Week, November 6, 1995, Perry Pascarella, review of *Trust,* pp. 32-36.

Journal of Economic Issues, December, 2000, Geoffrey E. Schneider, Winston H. Griffith, and Janet T. Knoedler, review of *The Great Disruption,* p. 997.

Journal of the American Medical Association, January 22-29, 2003, Fredrick R. Abrams, review of *Our Posthuman Future,* p. 488.

Management Today, January, 1996, Norman Stone, review of *Trust,* p. 25.

National Review, October 27, 1989, John Gray, "The End of History—or of Liberalism?," p. 33; November 24, 1989, William F. Buckley, Jr., "The End of History," p. 62.

New Republic, September 11, 1995, Robert M. Solow, review of *Trust,* pp. 36-39; August 2, 1999, Alan Wolfe, "The Shock of the Old," p. 42.

New Statesman, June 14, 1999, Bryan Gould, review of *The Great Disruption,* p. 46.

New Statesman & Society, October 13, 1995, Anthony Giddens, review of *Trust,* p. 30.

New York Times Book Review, January 26, 1992, William H. McNeill, review of *The End of History and the Last Man,* p. 14.

New York Times Magazine, October 22, 1989, James Atlas, "What Is Fukuyama Saying?," p. 38.

Quarterly Review of Biology, March, 2003, Evan Selinger, review of *Our Posthuman Future,* p. 76.

Review of Metaphysics, September, 2000, Stephen Schneck, review of *The Great Disruption,* p. 139.

Spectator, June 1, 2002, Robert Macfarlane, "Danger: Men at Work," p. 35.

Time, September 4, 1989, John Elson, "Has History Come to an End? A Provocative Case: Democracy Has Outlived Communism," p. 57; September 11, 1989, Strobe Talbott, "The Beginning of Nonsense," p. 39.

Times (London), February 20, 1992, p. 4.

Times Literary Supplement, April 24, 1992, John Dunn, review of *The End of History and the Last Man,* p. 6.

Virginia Quarterly Review, summer, 2003, review of *Our Posthuman Future,* p. 95.

Wall Street Journal, February 6, 1992, Robert Reich, review of *The End of History and the Last Man,* p. A12.

Washington Monthly, July, 1999 Steven Waldman, review of *The Great Disruption,* p. 44.

ONLINE

Merrill Lynch Forum, http://www.ml.com/ (October 24, 2003).

School of Advanced International Studies, Johns Hopkins University, http://www.sais-jhu.edu/ (November 3, 2003).*

G

GABALDON, Diana 1952-

PERSONAL: Surname pronounced "*GAB*-uhl-dohn"; born January 11, 1952, in AZ; daughter of Jacqueline (Sykes) Gabaldon; married Douglas Watkins (in construction and real estate), c. 1977; children: Laura Juliet, Samuel Gordon, Jennifer Rose. *Education:* Arizona State University, B.S. (zoology), 1973, Ph.D. (behavioral ecology), 1978; University of California, San Diego, M.S. (marine biology), 1975.

ADDRESSES: Home—P.O. Box 584, Scottsdale, AZ 85252-0584. *E-mail*—dgabaldon@aol.com; 76530. 523@compuserve.com.

CAREER: Northern Arizona University, laboratory technician, 1972-73; University of Pennsylvania, researcher, 1978-79; University of California, Los Angeles, researcher, 1979-80; Center for Environmental Studies, Arizona State University, Tempe, AZ, from field ecologist to assistant professor of research, 1980-92; full-time freelance writer, 1992—. Founder and editor of *Science Software* magazine during 1980s and 1990s.

AWARDS, HONORS: Best First Novel Award from B. Dalton book stores, and Best Book of the Year Award from the Romance Writers of America, both 1991, for *Outlander; Voyager* was chosen as a main selection of both the Literary Guild and the Doubleday Book Club, 1994.

WRITINGS:

"OUTLANDER" SERIES; HISTORICAL NOVELS

Outlander, Delacorte (New York, NY), 1991.
Dragonfly in Amber, Delacorte (New York, NY), 1992.

Diana Gabaldon

Voyager, Delacorte (New York, NY), 1994.
Drums of Autumn, Delacorte (New York, NY), 1997.
The Outlandish Companion: In Which Much Is Revealed Regarding Claire and Jamie Fraser, Their Lives and Times, Antecedents, Adventures, Companions, and Progeny, with Learned Commentary (and Many Footnotes), Delacorte (New York, NY), 1999.

158

The Fiery Cross, Delacorte (New York, NY), 2001.
Lord John and the Private Matter, Doubleday Canada, 2003.

Also author of software reviews for *Byte* magazine; contributor of articles to scholarly journals; author of comic book scripts for Walt Disney Productions.

WORK IN PROGRESS: Two more books in the "Outlander" series; a mystery novel.

SIDELIGHTS: Diana Gabaldon is a former biologist and university professor who has become the bestselling writer of the "Outlander" series of historical novels. Gabaldon's writing career began with two unlikely endeavors, considering the eventual direction of her career. While she was an assistant professor at Arizona State University in the 1980s, she became an expert in the use of software programs for scientific research. This led to her founding the scholarly journal *Science Software,* which she ran and edited. While this experience gave her a good deal of background in writing, she credits her freelance work writing comics about Mickey Mouse, Donald Duck, and Uncle Scrooge for Walt Disney Productions from 1979 to 1980 for teaching her "most of what I know about the mechanics of storytelling," as she states on her Web site.

The Disney work and other freelance assignments provided Gabaldon with additional income for her family, and she began to believe that she could succeed as a full-time writer. "From the late 70's to the early 90's, I wrote anything anybody would pay me for," she said. "This ranged from articles on how to clean a longhorn cow's skull for living-room decoration to manuals on elementary math instruction on the Apple II . . . to a slew of software reviews and application articles done for the computer press." When her contract expired at the university in 1992, Gabaldon decided she was ready to take the plunge and become a full-time writer. But instead of continuing to write nonfiction, she started to write a historical novel set in eighteenth-century Scotland. Using her knowledge of computers, she joined discussion forums, where she eventually found an encouraging audience for her forays into fiction. She also made contacts online that helped her finish her first novel, *Outlander,* and find an agent and publisher.

Outlander was published in 1991. Its protagonist, English nurse Claire Randall, visits Scotland in 1945, hoping to rekindle a marriage stressed by separation during World War II. Occupying herself by collecting plant samples while her husband studies history, she accidentally touches a stone in an ancient circle similar to Stonehenge, and she is transported to the year 1743. The novel then recounts events leading to the Second Jacobite Rising through her modern eyes. While in the 1700s, Claire marries outlaw Scotsman Jamie Fraser, and she eventually must choose between returning to her husband in the twentieth century and remaining with Jamie. *Outlander* garnered awards from both the Romance Writers of America and B. Dalton book stores in the year of its publication. A *Publishers Weekly* reviewer hailed *Outlander* as "absorbing and heartwarming"; and Cynthia Johnson of *Library Journal* lauded the book as "a richly textured historical novel with an unusual and compelling love story."

Gabaldon followed *Outlander* with *Dragonfly in Amber.* This novel recounts Claire and Jamie's desperate attempt to alter history by preventing Charles Stuart from actually starting the Jacobite uprising that led to the slaughter of the Scots at the battle of Culloden. When they fail at this, they use Claire's knowledge of history to prepare Jamie's family and clan for this disaster as best they can. However, *Dragonfly in Amber* also deals with a second story in a different timeline—Claire's trip to Scotland with her daughter Brianna in 1968 to tell her about her real father, Jamie Fraser. A *Publishers Weekly* critic commended Gabaldon's "fresh and offbeat historical view" and asserted that *Dragonfly in Amber* is "compulsively readable."

The third volume in the saga, *Voyager,* appeared on the *Publishers Weekly* hardcover bestsellers list in January 1994. In this installment, having discovered that Jamie did not die at the battle of Culloden, Claire returns to the eighteenth century to be with him. The years spent apart are recounted, and adventures lead the couple to America in pursuit of Jamie's kidnapped nephew. Roland Green, reviewing *Voyager* in *Booklist,* praised its "highly appealing characters" and "authentic feel." *Locus* contributor Carolyn Cushman felt that Gabaldon "masterfully interweaves" plot elements separated by two centuries, "crossing time periods with abandon but never losing track of the story."

Though a *Publishers Weekly* reviewer labeled *Voyager* a "triumphant conclusion" to the story of Claire and Jamie, Gabaldon was preparing a fourth book that would carry the characters through the American

Revolution. *Drums of Autumn* leapt onto the bestseller lists as soon as it appeared in 1997. Set in the New World, the novel finds the two lovers building a life as the Americans set about building a nation. Jamie and Claire first arrive at Charleston, then join other Scottish exiles along the Cape Fear River in North Carolina. Troubled by events there, the couple moves inland to the mountains in search of tranquility. The couple's attempts at avoiding conflict and an impending war give the book an epic quality. In the view of one *Booklist* contributor, "Gabaldon is clearly trying to write on the same scale as Margaret Mitchell, and in terms of length and of thoroughness of research, largely succeeds." A reviewer for *Maclean's* noted that "the meticulous period detail is in contrast to the serendipitous development of the central premise: the love story of a modern woman somehow flung into the past."

This quality of *Drums of Autumn* reflects its author's approach to all of the books in the series. In an interview published in *Heart to Heart*, Gabaldon discussed some of her feelings about the series she began with *Outlander:* "Part of my purpose in my books has been to tell the complete story of a relationship and a marriage; not just to end with 'happily ever after,' leaving the protagonists at the altar or in bed. . . . I wanted to show some of the complicated business of actually living a successful marriage." Concerning the history depicted in the first four novels, Gabaldon revealed that she "wanted to show the changing face of the world at that time, moving from the ancient feudal system of Highland clans to the violent upheavals of democracy in the New World." She further noted that with "Claire's perspective as a time-traveler, we see the events of that time through a modern eye, and can fully appreciate their significance to the future that will come."

Four years after *Drums of Autumn*, Gabaldon completed the next installment of Claire and Jamie's adventures in colonial America with *The Fiery Cross*. Taking place in the years 1771 and 1772, the novel tells how Jamie, who is now a landowner, is asked by the governor of North Carolina to form a militia in preparation for what looks like the upcoming war against the British. Reluctant at first to comply, Jamie is convinced by Claire, who knows the Revolution is inevitable, that this is the right thing to do. Although the initial crisis is averted and the militia is dispersed, Claire and readers know that war still lies ahead. *Fiery*

Cross received a range of reviews. *People* contributor Bella Stander claimed that new readers to the series will not know "who the characters are, how they got to the colonies and why we should care." On the other hand, Johnson praised the novel in *Library Journal*, asserting that the writing "is superb—lush, evocative, and sensual, with a wealth of historic detail and a good deal of humor."

Originally, Gabaldon had intended *Fiery Cross* to follow Claire and Jamie up to the beginning of the American Revolution, but she ended far short of this mark. Therefore, she revealed on her Web site that she intends to write at least two more "Outlander" books to cover the time through the Revolution and tie up some plot threads. Because her series has grown into quite a complex tale, she also recently completed *The Outlandish Companion: In Which Much Is Revealed Regarding Claire and Jamie Fraser, Their Lives and Times, Antecedents, Adventures, Companions, and Progeny, with Learned Commentary (and Many Footnotes)*, which answers many of her fans questions, including how time travel works in her books, plot synopses, character backgrounds, and even information about her personal life.

BIOGRAPHICAL AND CRITICAL SOURCES:

PERIODICALS

Booklist, November 15, 1993, Roland Green, review of *Voyager;* November 15, 1996, review of *Drums of Autumn.*

Heart to Heart, September-October, 1994, review of *Voyager,* pp. 3, 8-9.

Library Journal, July, 1991, Cynthia Johnson, review of *Outlander,* p. 134; January, 2002, Cynthia Johnson, review of *The Fiery Cross,* p. 152.

Locus, January, 1994, Carolyn Cushman, review of *Voyager,* p. 29.

Maclean's, February 17, 1997, review of *Drums of Autumn,* p. 71; August 9, 1999, "Tying Up Loose Ends: A Best-selling Novelist Pens a Reference Book to Answer Her Fans' Queries," p. 21; January 14, 2002, "Over and Under Achievers: Teaching the Ropes of the Rock," p. 6.

People, April 14, 1997, review of *Drums of Autumn,* p. 64; December 24, 2001, Bella Stander, review of *The Fiery Cross,* p. 39.

Publishers Weekly, May 31, 1991, review of *Outlander,* p. 59; June 22, 1992, review of *Dragonfly in Amber,* p. 49; December 20, 1993, p. 52; January 17, 1994, p. 2; January 6, 1997, p. 50; January 13, 1997, p. 18; November 19, 2001.
Time, January 20, 1997, p. 79.*

ONLINE

Diana Gabaldon, http://www.cco.caltech.edu/~gatti/gabaldon/ (November 11, 2002).

*   *   *

GATES, Henry Louis, Jr. 1950-

PERSONAL: Born September 16, 1950, in Keyser, WV; son of Henry Louis and Pauline Augusta (Coleman) Gates; married Sharon Lynn Adams (a potter), September 1, 1979; children: Maude Augusta Adams, Elizabeth Helen-Claire. *Education:* Yale University, B.A. (summa cum laude), 1973; Clare College, Cambridge, M.A., 1974, Ph.D., 1979. *Religion:* Episcopalian. *Hobbies and other interests:* Jazz, pocket billiards.

ADDRESSES: Office—Department of Afro-American Studies, Harvard University, 12 Quincy St., Cambridge, MA 02138. *Agent*—Carl Brandt, Brandt & Brandt Literary Agents, Inc., 1501 Broadway, New York, NY 10036.

CAREER: Anglican Mission Hospital, Kilimatinde, Tanzania, general anesthetist, 1970-71; John D. Rockefeller gubernatorial campaign, Charleston, WV, director of student affairs, 1971, director of research, 1972; *Time,* London Bureau, London, England, staff correspondent, 1973-75; Yale University, New Haven, CT, lecturer, 1976-79, assistant professor, 1979-84, associate professor of English and Afro-American Studies, 1984-85, director of undergraduate Afro-American studies, 1976-79; Cornell University, Ithaca, NY, professor of English, comparative literature, and African studies, 1985-88, W. E. B. DuBois Professor of Literature, 1988-90; Duke University, Durham, NC, John Spencer Bassett Professor of English and Literature, 1990—; Harvard University, Cambridge, MA, W. E. B. DuBois Professor of the Humanities, professor of

Henry Louis Gates, Jr.

English, chair of Afro-American studies, and director of W. E. B. DuBois Institute for Afro-American Research, 1991—. Virginia Commonwealth, visiting professor, 1987; visiting scholar, Princeton University, Institute for Advanced Study, 2003-2004. Created the Public Broadcasting Service (PBS) television series *The Image of the Black in the Western Imagination,* 1982, and *Wonders of the African World with Henry Louis Gates, Jr.,* 1999.

MEMBER: Council on Foreign Relations, American Antiquarian Society, Union of Writers of the African Peoples, Association for Documentary Editing, African Roundtable, African Literature Association, Afro-American Academy, American Studies Association, Trans-Africa Forum Scholars Council, Association for the Study of Afro-American Life and History (life member), Caribbean Studies Association, College Language Association (life member), Modern Language Association, Stone Trust, Zora Neale Hurston Society, Cambridge Scientific Club, American Civil Liberties Union National Advisory Council, German American Studies Association, National Coalition against Censorship, American Philosophical Society, Saturday Club, New England Historic Genealogical Society, Phi Beta Kappa.

AWARDS, HONORS: Carnegie Foundation Fellowship for Africa, 1970- 71; Phelps Fellowship, Yale University, 1970-71; Mellon fellowships, Cambridge University, 1973-75, and National Humanities Center, 1989-90; grants from Ford Foundation, 1976-77 and 1984-85, and National Endowment for the Humanities, 1980-86; A. Whitney Griswold Fellowship, 1980; Rockefeller Foundation fellowships, 1981 and 1990; MacArthur Prize Fellowship, MacArthur Foundation, 1981-86; Yale Afro-American teaching prize, 1983; award from Whitney Humanities Center, 1983-85; Princeton University Council of the Humanities lectureship, 1985; Award for Creative Scholarship, Zora Neale Hurston Society, 1986; associate fellowship from W. E. B. DuBois Institute, Harvard University, 1987-88 and 1988-89; John Hope Franklin Prize honorable mention, American Studies Association, 1988; Woodrow Wilson National Fellow, 1988-89 and 1989-90; Candle Award, Morehouse College, 1989; American Book Award and Anisfield-Wolf Book Award for Race Relations, both 1989, both for *The Signifying Monkey: Towards a Theory of Afro-American Literary Criticism;* recipient of honorary degrees from many universities, including Dartmouth College, 1989, University of West Virginia, 1990, University of Rochester, 1990, Pratt Institute, 1990, University of Bridgeport, 1991 (declined), University of New Hampshire, 1991, Bryant College, 1992, Manhattan Community College, 1992, George Washington University, 1993, University of Massachusetts at Amherst, 1993, Williams College, 1993, Emory University, 1995, Colby College, 1995, Bard College, 1995, and Bates College, 1995; Richard Wright Lecturer, Center for the Study of Black Literature and Culture, University of Pennsylvania, 1990; Potomac State College Alumni Award, 1991; Bellagio Conference Center Fellowship, 1992; Clarendon Lecturer, Oxford University, 1992; Best New Journal of the Year award (in the humanities and the social sciences), Association of American Publishers, 1992; elected to the American Academy of Arts and Sciences, 1993; Golden Plate Achievement Award, 1993; African-American Students Faculty Award, 1993; George Polk Award for Social Commentary, 1993; Heartland Prize for Nonfiction, 1994, for *Colored People: A Memoir;* Lillian Smith Book Award, 1994; West Virginian of the Year, 1995; Humanities Award, West Virginia Humanities Council, 1995; Ethics Award, Tikkun (magazine), 1996; Distinguished

Editorial Achievement, *Critical Inquiry,* 1996; voted one of the twenty-five most influential Americans, *Time* magazine, 1997; National Humanities Medal, 1998; elected to American Academy of Arts and Letters, 1999; named honorary citizen of Benin, 2001; W. D. Weatherford Award.

WRITINGS:

Figures in Black: Words, Signs, and the Racial Self, Oxford University Press (New York, NY), 1987.

The Signifying Monkey: Towards a Theory of Afro-American Literary Criticism, Oxford University Press (New York, NY), 1988.

Loose Canons: Notes on the Culture Wars (essays), Oxford University Press (New York, NY), 1992.

Colored People: A Memoir, Knopf (New York, NY), 1994.

Speaking of Race, Speaking of Sex: Hate Speech, Civil Rights, and Civil Liberties, New York University Press (New York, NY), 1995.

(With Cornel West) *The Future of the Race,* Knopf (New York, NY), 1996.

Thirteen Ways of Looking at a Black Man, Random House (New York, NY), 1997.

Wonders of the African World, Knopf (New York, NY), 1999.

(With Cornel West) *The African-American Century: How Black Americans Have Shaped Our Country,* Free Press (New York, NY), 2000.

(Author of text) *Come Sunday: Photographs by Thomas Roma,* Museum of Modern Art (New York, NY), 2002.

Back to Africa, Duke University Press (Durham, NC), 2002.

The Trials of Phillis Wheatley: America's First Black Poet and Her Encounters with the Founding Fathers, BasicCivitas Books (New York, NY), 2003.

America behind the Color Line: Dialogues with African Americans, Warner (New York, NY), 2004.

EDITOR

(And author of introduction) *Black Is the Color of the Cosmos: Charles T. Davis's Essays on Afro-American Literature and Culture, 1942-1981,* Garland Publishing (New York, NY), 1982.

(And author of introduction) Harriet E. Wilson, *Our Nig; or, Sketches from the Life of a Free Black,* Random House (New York, NY), 1983.

(And author of introduction) *Black Literature and Literary Theory,* Methuen (New York, NY), 1984.

(And author of introduction, with Charles T. Davis) *The Slave's Narrative: Texts and Contexts,* Oxford University Press (New York, NY), 1986.

(Editor, with James Gibbs and Ketu H. Katrak) *Wole Soyinka: A Bibliography of Primary and Secondary Sources,* Greenwood Press (Westport, CT), 1986.

(And author of introduction) *"Race," Writing, and Difference,* University of Chicago Press (Chicago, IL), 1986.

(And author of introduction) *The Classic Slave Narratives,* New American Library (New York, NY), 1987.

(And author of introduction) *In the House of Oshugbo: A Collection of Essays on Wole Soyinka,* Oxford University Press (New York, NY), 1988.

(Series editor) *The Oxford-Schomburg Library of Nineteenth-Century Black Women Writers,* thirty volumes, Oxford University Press (New York, NY), 1988.

W. E. B. DuBois, *The Souls of Black Folk,* Bantam Books (New York, NY), 1989.

James Weldon Johnson, *The Autobiography of an Ex-Coloured Man,* Vintage (New York, NY), 1989.

Three Classic African-American Novels, Vintage (New York, NY), 1990.

Zora Neale Hurston, *Their Eyes Were Watching God,* introduction by Mary Helen Washington, Harper (New York, NY), 1990.

Zora Neale Hurston, *Jonah's Gourd Vine,* introduction by Rita Dove, Harper (New York, NY), 1990.

Zora Neale Hurston, *Tell My Horse,* introduction by Ishmael Reed, Harper (New York, NY), 1990.

Zora Neale Hurston, *Mules and Men,* introduction by Arnold Rampersad, Harper (New York, NY), 1990.

Reading Black, Reading Feminist: A Critical Anthology, Meridian Book (New York, NY), 1990.

Voodoo Gods of Haiti, introduction by Ishmael Reed, Harper (New York, NY), 1991.

The Schomburg Library of Nineteenth-Century Black Women Writers, ten-volume supplement, Oxford University Press (New York, NY), 1991.

(With Randall K. Burkett and Nancy Hall Burkett) *Black Biography, 1790-1950: A Cumulative Index,* Chadwyck-Healey (Teaneck, NJ), 1991.

(With George Bass) Langston Hughes and Zora Neale Hurston, *Mulebone: A Comedy of Negro Life,* HarperPerennial (New York, NY), 1991.

Bearing Witness: Selections from African-American Autobiography in the Twentieth Century, Pantheon Books (New York, NY), 1991.

(With Anthony Appiah) *Gloria Naylor: Critical Perspectives Past and Present,* Amistad (New York, NY), 1993.

(With Anthony Appiah) *Alice Walker: Critical Perspectives Past and Present,* Amistad (New York, NY), 1993.

(With Anthony Appiah) *Langston Hughes: Critical Perspectives Past and Present,* Amistad (New York, NY), 1993.

(With Anthony Appiah) *Richard Wright: Critical Perspectives Past and Present,* Amistad (New York, NY), 1993.

(With Anthony Appiah) *Toni Morrison: Critical Perspectives Past and Present,* Amistad (New York, NY), 1993.

(With Anthony Appiah) *Zora Neale Hurston: Critical Perspectives Past and Present,* Amistad (New York, NY), 1993.

The Amistad Chronology of African-American History from 1445-1990, Amistad (New York, NY), 1993.

(And annotations) *Frederick Douglass: Autobiographies,* Library of America, 1994.

(With Anthony Appiah) *The Dictionary of Global Culture,* Knopf (New York, NY), 1995.

The Complete Stories of Zora Neale Hurston, HarperCollins (New York, NY), 1995.

(With Anthony Appiah) *Identities,* University of Chicago (Chicago, IL), 1996.

(With N. Y. McKay) *The Norton Anthology of African-American Literature,* Norton (New York, NY), 1996.

Ann Petry: Critical Perspectives Past and Present, Amistad (New York, NY), 1997.

Chinua Achebe: Critical Perspectives Past and Present, Amistad (New York, NY), 1997.

Harriet A. Jacobs: Critical Perspectives Past and Present, Amistad (New York, NY), 1997.

Ralph Ellison: Critical Perspectives Past and Present, Amistad (New York, NY), 1997.

Wole Soyinka: Critical Perspectives Past and Present, Amistad (New York, NY), 1997.

Frederick Douglass: Critical Perspectives Past and Present, Amistad (New York, NY), 1997.

The Essential Soyinka: A Reader, Pantheon (New York, NY), 1998.

(Coeditor) *Pioneers of the Black Atlantic: Five Slave Narratives from the Enlightenment, 1772-1815,* Civitas (Washington, DC), 1998.

(Coeditor) *Black Imagination and the Middle Passage,* Oxford University Press (New York, NY), 1999.

(Coeditor) *The Civitas Anthology of African-American Slave Narratives,* Civitas/Counterpoint (Washington, DC), 1999.

Wonders of the African World, Random House (New York, NY), 1999.

Slave Narratives, Library of America (New York, NY), 2000.

Harvard Guide to African-American History, Harvard University Press (Cambridge, MA), 2001.

Schomburg Library of Nineteenth-Century Black Women Writers, Oxford University Press (New York, NY), 2002.

Hannah Crafts, *The Bondwoman's Narrative,* Warner (New York, NY), 2002.

(With Anthony Appiah) *Africana: The Encyclopedia of the African and African- American Experience,* Running Press (New York, NY), 2003.

In the House of Oshugbo: Critical Essays on Wole Soyinka, Oxford University Press (New York, NY), 2003.

(With Anthony Appiah) *Transition 96,* Soft Skull Press, 2004.

(With Anthony Appiah) *Transition 97/98,* Soft Skull Press, 2004.

(With Evelyn Brooks Higginbotham) *African-American Lives,* Oxford University Press (New York, NY), 2004.

Also editor, with Anthony Appiah, of "Amistad Critical Studies in African-American Literature" series, 1993, and editor of the Black Periodical Literature Project. Advisory editor of "Contributions to African and Afro-American Studies" series for Greenwood Press (Westport, CT), "Critical Studies in Black Life and Culture" series for Garland Press, and "Perspectives on the Black World" series for G. K. Hall (Boston, MA). General editor of *A Dictionary of Cultural and Critical Theory; Middle-Atlantic Writers Association Review.* Coeditor of *Transition.* Associate editor of *Journal of American Folklore.* Member of editorial boards including, *Critical Inquiry, Studies in American Fiction, Black American Literature Forum, PMLA, Stanford Humanities Review,* and *Yale Journal of Law and Liberation.*

SIDELIGHTS: Henry Louis Gates, Jr. is one of the best-known humanities professors in the United States, and one of the most respected and controversial scholars in the field of African-American studies. Educated at Yale and a professor at Harvard, he had a humble start in Keyser, West Virginia, where the majority of the population worked for a paper mill. The town was a strictly segregated community in his youth, but Gates remembered its strong sense of community in a mostly positive light in his memoir *Colored People.* Gates's father worked as a loader at the mill, and also as a janitor for the telephone company. Young Gates excelled in school, where integration occurred relatively smoothly. During the tumultuous 1960s, Gates was a young student who was gaining an awareness of Africa from studying current events. In 1968, he graduated as the class valedictorian, delivering a commencement address with a militant tone. He moved on to Potomac State College of West Virginia University the following autumn, with the thought of going on to medical school. A professor named Duke Anthony Whitmore saw the spark of genius in Gates, however, and encouraged him to apply to top-tier schools. Gates was soon accepted at Yale University, where he graduated summa cum laude in 1973. He then traveled to Cambridge University to earn a master of arts degree. He began his teaching career at Yale, and distinguished himself early on by discovering and reissuing an 1859 novel written by a black woman, titled *Our Nig; or, Sketches from the Life of a Free Black.* Publication of this work sparked considerable interest in recovering other works by early black women writers.

Gates moved on to take a post at Cornell University, and during his tenure there he published the multi-volume *Schomburg Library of Nineteenth-Century Black Women Writers,* a landmark work that showed black women had written their own stories more than had ever been previously acknowledged. In 1988, he became the W. E. B. DuBois Professor of Literature at Cornell, becoming the first African-American man to hold an endowed chair at that institution. His star continued to rise as he moved on to a position at Duke and then to Harvard University, where he was W. E. B. DuBois Professor of the Humanities at Harvard and head of its Afro-American Studies program. Gates breathed new life and enthusiasm into the program, which at the time of his arrival had very few students and only one full-time professor. He hired high-profile lecturers such as film director Spike Lee and authors Jamaica Kincaid and Wole Soyinka. Under Gates's leadership, the number of students in the program tripled within a few years.

Gates had detractors as well as admirers, however. Some of his colleagues found him to be insufficiently Afro-centric. He engaged in certain high-profile activities that were regarded by some as inappropriate self-promotion, for example, publicly testifying at the obscenity trial of rap group 2 Live Crew, stating that their extreme lyrics were merely part of an African oral tradition. Still, even those who objected to Gates's flashy public activities rarely argued with his credentials, or denied his many important contributions to Afro-American scholarship, as he has written and edited numerous books of literary and social criticism. According to James Olney in the *Dictionary of Literary Biography,* Gates's mission is to reorder and reinterpret "the literary and critical history of Afro-Americans in the context of a tradition that is fully modern but also continuous with Yoruba modes of interpretation that are firmly settled and at home in the world of black Americans."

In his approach to literary criticism, Gates is avowedly eclectic and defines himself as a centrist who rejects extreme positions on either end of the spectrum. Neither the white, Western tradition nor the African tradition is superior; they should coexist and inform each other, in Gates's view. Like the American novelist Ralph Ellison, Gates sees the fluid, indeed porous, relationship between black and white culture in the United States. Gates argues that our conception of the literary canon needs to be enlarged accordingly.

Black Literature and Literary Theory, which Gates edited, is considered by many reviewers to be an important contribution to the study of black literature. Calling it "an exciting, important volume," Reed Way Dasenbrock wrote in *World Literature Today:* "It is a collection of essays . . . that attempts to explore the relevance of contemporary literary theory, especially structuralism and poststructuralism, to African and Afro-American literature. . . . Anyone seriously interested in contemporary critical theory, in Afro-American and African literature, and in black and African studies generally will need to read and absorb this book." R. G. O'Meally wrote in *Choice* that in *Black Literature and Literary Theory* Gates "brings together thirteen superb essays in which the most modern literary theory is applied to black literature of Africa and the U.S. . . . For those interested in [the] crucial issues—and for those interested in fresh and challenging readings of key texts in black literature— this book is indispensable." Finally, Terry Eagleton remarked in the *New York Times Book Review* that "the most thought-provoking contributions to [this] collection are those that not only enrich our understanding of black literary works but in doing so implicitly question the authoritarianism of a literary 'canon.'"

One of Gates's best-known works is *Loose Canons: Notes on the Culture Wars,* in which he discusses gen-

der, literature, and multiculturalism and argues for greater diversity in American arts and letters. Writing in the *Virginia Quarterly Review,* Sanford Pinsker noted that according to Gates "the cultural right . . . is guilty of 'intellectual protectionism,' of defending the best that has been thought and said within the Western Tradition because they are threatened by America's rapidly changing demographic profile; while the cultural left 'demands changes to accord with population shifts in gender and ethnicity.' *Loose Canons* makes it clear that Gates has problems with both positions." "The society we have made," Gates argues in *Loose Canons,* "simply won't survive without the values of tolerance. And cultural tolerance comes to nothing without cultural understanding. . . . If we relinquish the ideal of America as a plural nation, we've abandoned the very experiment that America represents." Writing in the *Los Angeles Times,* Jonathan Kirsch praised the humor and wit that infused Gates's arguments. *Loose Canons,* Kirsch concluded, is "the work of a man who has mastered the arcane politics and encoded language of the canon makers; it's an arsenal of ideas in the cultural wars. But it is also the outpouring of a humane, witty and truly civilized mind."

Colored People: A Memoir played to a wider audience than did *Loose Canons.* In it, Gates recalls his youth in Piedmont, West Virginia, at a time when the town was becoming integrated. It "explores the tension between the racially segregated past and the integrated modernity that the author himself represents," commented David Lionel Smith in *America.* While affirming the progress brought by desegregation, Gates also laments the loss of the strong, united community feeling that segregation created among blacks—a feeling epitomized in the annual all-black picnic sponsored by the paper mill that provided jobs to most of Piedmont's citizens. Numerous reviewers pointed out the gentle, reminiscent tone of Gates's narrative, but some considered this a weakness in light of the momentous changes Gates lived through. Smith remarked: "From an author of Gates's sophistication, we expect more than unreflective nostalgia." Comparing it to other recent African-American memoirs and autobiographies, he concluded, "Some of them address social issues more cogently and others are more self-analytical, but none is more vivid and pleasant to read than *Colored People.*" *Los Angeles Times Book Review* contributor Richard Eder affirmed that *Colored People* was an "affecting, beautifully written and morally complex memoir," and Joyce Carol Oates, in her *London*

Review of Books assessment, described it as an "eloquent document to set beside the grittier contemporary testimonies of black male urban memoirists; in essence a work of filial gratitude, paying homage to such virtues as courage, loyalty, integrity, kindness; a pleasure to read and, in the best sense, inspiring."

Gates wrote *The Future of the Race* with Cornel West, a professor of Afro-American studies at Harvard University. This work contains an essay by Gates, an essay by West, and two essays by black intellectual W. E. B. DuBois, the latter of which are preceded by a foreword by Gates. Writing in the *New York Times Book Review,* Gerald Early noted: "The question . . . that the authors wish to answer—what is their duty to the lower or less fortunate class of blacks?—indicates the black bourgeoisie's inability to understand precisely what their success means to themselves or blacks generally." Early also observed that while "the pieces seem hastily written," Gates's essay is "engagingly witty and journalistic" as well as "charming and coherent."

Gates offers insight into the position of the black male in American society in *Thirteen Ways of Looking at a Black Man.* Through a series of discussions recorded over several years and documented in various magazine articles, Gates brings a broad cross-section of African-American hopes and ideals to the reader's attention. Interviewees include such major black American figures as James Baldwin, Harry Belafonte, Colin Powell, and Bill T. Jones. Writing in *Library Journal,* Michael A. Lutes referred to *Thirteen Ways of Looking at a Black Man* as a "riveting commentary on race in America."

A belief that tolerance proceeds from education and familiarity led Gates to devote himself to working with a variety of media and corporate resources to enlighten the general public about African-American heritage and contributions to society. His efforts in this realm range from writing a set of booklets about black history, distributed at McDonald's restaurants, to creating multi-part television documentaries on black heritage for the Public Broadcasting System (PBS). He also worked with a team of other scholars to fulfil a dream of the late W. E. B. DuBois: to create an answer to the *Encyclopedia Britannica,* called *Encyclopedia Africana* that would take into consideration African influences and contributions to the world. Working with Microsoft, Gates helped to create the CD-ROM

version of the *Encyclopedia Africana,* and he also launched *Africana.com,* a Web site that was later sold to AOL Time Warner.

Gates also brought his message to the masses with his PBS television series, *Wonders of the African World with Henry Louis Gates, Jr.* In this program, Gates took viewers on a journey through Africa that illustrated the remains of the great cultures that once flourished on that continent. Contemporary Africa was also explored, and Gates shared his personal experience of the journey. In making the series, Gates hoped to "debunk the myths of Africa being this benighted continent civilized only when white people arrived," as Lorraine Eaton of the *Virginia Pilot* quoted him as saying. He continued: "In fact, Africans had been creators of culture for thousands of years before. These were very intelligent, subtle and sophisticated people, with organized societies and great art."

Gates continued to bring forth newly discovered works by African Americans of early generations, such as *The Bondwoman's Narrative,* a melodramatic story of a slave's life written by Hannah Crafts. More significant than the literary content of the book are the facts and attitudes it reveals within the slaves' world, and the fact that its author was most likely an escaped slave herself. He looked into the life and work of Phillis Wheatley, the first published black poet in the United States, in *The Trials of Phillis Wheatley: America's First Black Poet and Her Encounters with the Founding Fathers.* Reviewing the volume for *Booklist,* Vanessa Bush commented, "Gates brings scholarly insight and a love of black literature to this examination of how Wheatley, the first published African-American poet, has survived the judgment of past and contemporary critics." When first published in 1773, Wheatley's poems stirred up questions of their authenticity among those who could not believe a black person could create poetry. When their authenticity was established, Wheatley's work was attacked on other grounds. "In this slim, lively volume, Gates extols Wheatley's enduring literary significance and Jefferson's contribution to spurring a tradition of black literature that was first aimed at proving equality and came to signify a black aesthetic," concluded Bush.

The stellar make-up of Harvard's African-American studies department was diminished when Anthony Appiah and Cornel West, two of the department's top scholars, announced they would be moving to other universities after disagreements with Harvard's leadership on the direction of the program. Gates chose to remain at Harvard to continue to try to keep the program vital and forward-looking. He was instrumental in restructuring the department, adding five new faculty members, including an African scholar, a linguist, and even an expert on hip-hop. Gates did, however, take a year's leave from Harvard to join the Institute for Advanced Study in Princeton, New Jersey—a so-called "think tank" most famous for its association with Albert Einstein.

BIOGRAPHICAL AND CRITICAL SOURCES:

BOOKS

Contemporary Black Biography, Gale (Detroit, MI), 2003.

Contemporary Southern Writers, St. James Press (Detroit, MI), 1999.

Dictionary of Literary Biography, Volume 67: *Modern American Critics since 1955,* Gale (Detroit, MI), 1988.

Notable Black American Men, Gale (Detroit, MI), 1998.

PERIODICALS

America, December 31, 1994, p. 24.

American Spectator, April-May, 1994, p. 69.

Atlanta Journal-Constitution, November 21, 1999, Michael Skube, "Harvard Don on a Mission to Show Africa in All Its Glory," p. K1; December 6, 2000, John Head, interview with Henry Louis Gates, Jr., p. D1.

Black Issues Book Review, November-December, 2003, Herb Boyd, review of *The Trials of Phillis Wheatley: America's First Black Poet and Her Encounters with the Founding Fathers,* p. 66.

Black Issues in Higher Education, January 17, 2002, "Rift between Harvard Scholars, President Makes National News," p. 14; February 28, 2002, "Gates Ponders Move to Princeton," p. 17; June 5, 2003, "Harvard's Gates to be Visiting Scholar at Princeton Think Tank," p. 14.

Booklist, September 1, 2000, Vanessa Bush, review of *The African-American Century: How Black Americans Have Shaped Our Country,* p. 3; February 15, 2001, Nora Harris, review of *The Norton An-thology of African-American Literature,* p. 1172; November 15, 2001, Candace Smith, review of *Wonders of the African World,* p. 588; June 1, 2003, Vanessa Bush, review of *The Trials of Phillis Wheatley,* p. 1728.

Boston Globe, October 20, 1990, p. 3; May 12, 1991, p. 12; April 23, 1992, p. 70; November 7, 1992, p. 15; December 1, 1992, p. 23; April 29, 1993, p. 53; May 29, 1994, p. A13; April, 2002, Greg Lalas, review of *The Bondwoman's Narrative,* p. 161.

Boston Herald, April 9, 2002, Dana Bisbee, review of *The Bondwoman's Narrative,* p. 45.

Callaloo, spring, 1991.

Chicago Tribune, February 18, 1993, section 5, p. 3; November 18, 1993, section 1, p. 32; July 17, 1994, section 14, p. 3; August 24, 1994, section 5, p. 1.

Choice, May, 1985; March, 1995, p. 1059.

Christian Century, January 19, 1994, pp. 53-54.

Christian Science Monitor, April 10, 1992, p. 11; June 7, 1994, p. 13.

Commonweal, December 18, 1992, pp. 22-23.

Criticism, winter, 1994, pp. 155-161.

Emerge, November, 1990, p. 76.

Guardian (London, England), July 6, 2002, Maya Jaggi, "Henry the First," p. 20.

Humanities Magazine, July-August, 1991, pp. 4-10; March-April, 2002, interview with Henry Louis Gates, Jr., p. 6.

International Herald Tribune, July 17, 2003, Sara Rimer, "Harvard Refocuses Afro-American Unit," p. 7.

Jet, August 27, 2001, *Henry Louis Gates, Jr. Named Honorary Citizen of Benin,* p. 31; January 21, 2002, "Harvard University President Meets with Black Scholars to Mend Rift There," p. 36.

Journal of American Ethnic History, fall, 2000, Donald R. Wright, review of *Black Imagination and the Middle Passage,* p. 78.

Kirkus Reviews, October 1, 2003, review of *America behind the Color Line: Dialogues with African Americans,* p. 1207.

Library Journal, February, 1997; November 1, 2000, review of *The African-American Century,* p. 102; November 15, 2000, Thomas J. Davis, review of *The African-American Century,* p. 80; June 1, 2002, Roger A. Berger, review of *The Bondwoman's Narrative,* p. 147.

London Review of Books, July 21, 1994, pp. 22-23; January 12, 1995, p. 14.

Los Angeles Times, October 29, 1990, p. A20; March 25, 1992, p. E2; June 3, 1994, p. E1; February 6, 2000, review of *Africana,* p. E1.

Los Angeles Times Book Review, May 8, 1994, pp. 3, 12.

New Leader, September 12, 1994, pp. 12-13.

New Literary History, autumn, 1991.

New Republic, July 4, 1994, p. 33; June 16, 1997.

New Statesman & Society, February 10, 1995, p. 43.

New York Review of Books, November 2, 2000, George M. Frederickson, review of *Slave Narratives,* p. 61.

New York Times, December 6, 1989, p. B14; April 1, 1990, section 6, p. 25; June 3, 1992, p. B7; May 16, 1994, p. C16; May 8, 2003, Karen W. Arenson, "Harvard Scholar to Visit Princeton Institute," p. A26; July 16, 2003, Sara Rimer, "Harvard Scholar Rebuilds African Studies Department," p. A16.

New York Times Book Review, December 9, 1984; August 9, 1992, p. 21; June 19, 1994, p. 10; April 21, 1996, p. 7; February 9, 1997; May 12, 2002, Mia Bay, review of *The Bondwoman's Narrative,* p. 30.

New York Times Magazine, April 1, 1990.

Plain Dealer (Cleveland, OH), July 28, 2002, Margaret Bernstein, review of *The Bondwoman's Narrative,* p. J11.

Publishers Weekly, October 16, 2000, review of *The African-American Century,* p. 57; April 1, 2002, review of *The Bondwoman's Narrative,* p. 53.

Rocky Mountain News, May 10, 2002, review of *The Bondwoman's Narrative,* p. 29D.

San Francisco Chronicle, May 20, 2002, Steven Winn, review of *The Bondwoman's Narrative,* p. D1.

Seattle Times, May 5, 2002, John Gamino, review of *The Bondwoman's Narrative,* p. K9.

Spectator, February 18, 1995, pp. 31-32.

Time, April 22, 1991, pp. 16, 18; May 23, 1994, p. 73.

Times Literary Supplement, May 17, 1985; February 24, 1995, p. 26.

Tribune Books (Chicago, IL), July 17, 1994, pp. 3, 5; October 9, 1994, p. 11.

U. S. News and World Report, March, 1992; September 18, 2000, Matthew Benjamin, "Africana Dot Sold," p. 64.

Village Voice, July 5, 1994, p. 82.

Virginian Pilot, January 23, 2000, "Gates Refuses to Yield to Popular Opinions," p. E2.

Virginia Quarterly Review, summer, 1993, pp. 562-568.

Voice Literary Supplement, June, 1985.

Washington Post, October 20, 1990, p. D1; August 11, 1992, p. A17.

Washington Post Book World, July 3, 1983; June 7, 1992, p. 6; May 15, 1994, p. 3.

Washington Times, January 2, 2002, Julia Duin, "Cultural Critic Gates named NEH Lecturer," p. 2.

World Literature Today, summer, 1985.

ONLINE

Salon.com, http://www.salon.com/ (June 16, 1999), Craig Offman, "The Making of Henry Louis Gates, CEO.*"

*   *   *

GEE, Maggie (Mary) 1948-

PERSONAL: Born November 2, 1948, in Poole, Dorset, England; daughter of Victor Valentine and Aileen Mary (Church) Gee; married Nicholas Winton Rankin, August 6, 1983; children: one daughter. *Education:* Somerville College, Oxford, M.A., 1970, M.Litt., 1973; Wolverhampton Polytechnic, Ph.D., 1980.

ADDRESSES: Home—London, England. *Agent*—c/o David Godwin Associates, 55 Monmouth St., London WC2H 9DG, England.

CAREER: Elsevier International Press, Oxford, England, editor, 1972-74; research assistant at Wolverhampton Polytechnic, 1975-79; Northern Arts writer in residence, 1996; Sussex University, visiting fellow, 1986—; writer.

MEMBER: Society of Authors, Campaign for Nuclear Disarmament.

AWARDS, HONORS: Eastern Arts Writing Fellow, University of East Anglia, 1982; named among best young British novelists, 1983; Royal Society of Literature fellow, 1994—; shortlist, Orange Prize for Fiction, 2002, for *The White Family.*

WRITINGS:

Dying, in Other Words (novel), Harvester (Brighton, England), 1981, Faber (Boston, MA), 1984.

Maggie Gee

(Editor) *Anthology of Writing against War: For Life on Earth,* University of East Anglia (Norwich, England), 1982.

The Burning Book (novel), St. Martin's (New York, NY), 1983.

Light Years (novel), St. Martin's (New York, NY), 1985.

Grace (novel), Heinemann (London, England), 1988, Weidenfeld & Nicolson (New York, NY), 1989.

Where Are the Snows (novel), Heinemann (London, England), 1991, published as *Christopher and Alexandra,* Ticknor & Fields (New York, NY), 1992.

Lost Children (novel), Flamingo (London, England), 1994.

How May I Speak in My Own Voice? Language and the Forbidden (text of lecture), Birkbeck College (London, England), 1996.

The Ice People (novel), Richard Cohen Books (London, England), 1998.

The White Family (novel), Saqi Books (London, England), 2002.

Also author of several short stories and a radio play, "Over and Out," 1984. Contributor to *Diaspora City: The London New Writing Anthology,* Arcadia Books, 2003. Contributor to periodicals, including *Daily Telegraph, Sunday Times* (London), and *Times Literary Supplement.*

WORK IN PROGRESS: The Flood, for Saqi Books.

SIDELIGHTS: Maggie Gee has a reputation as an original and versatile voice in British literature. Her writings have earned comparisons to those of such acclaimed authors as Virginia Woolf, Vladimir Nabokov, and Samuel Beckett, whom she considers her "chief twentieth-century models," she told *Contemporary Novelists.* Gee's work has not been confined to any single genre; she has used the conventions of crime novels and science fiction, for instance, and has established herself as a technically adept experimentalist whose works are introspective, dark, and wryly humorous.

"Gee's importance as a novelist rests on her stylistic innovations and choices of subject matter, which is often political: Gee is, for example, a fierce opponent of nuclear armament," reported Martha Genn in the *Dictionary of Literary Biography.* Gee is also concerned with the environment, race and gender relations, and distinctions between the rich and the poor. Genn noted that Gee is "inventive and artful in the construction of narrative" and that her novels "vary in genre and yet frequently share concerns, including most notably the lasting, profound, and unpredictable effects of the actions and events of individual lives on surrounding persons and sequences of events."

Gee's debut novel, *Dying, in Other Words,* is an unusual thriller populated by a vast array of eccentric characters, including a murderous milkman. Published in 1981, the book begins with a disclaimer by Gee in which she denies that the work is "a serious novel." *Dying, in Other Words* centers on the mysterious death of young writer Moira Penny. Moira's naked body is found outside the window of her Oxford flat—she has apparently committed suicide. As an inordinate number of the dead woman's acquaintances also die under strange circumstances, authorities begin to suspect foul play in Moira's case. An ensuing investigation reveals the true and unexpected nature of Moira's death.

"Penny's suicide is dropped, as it were, into the pool of lives around her and the ripples spread and impinge on the lives of others and, what makes the novel remarkable, on the continuum of the past and present of those lives," related a contributor to *Contemporary Novelists.* Commenting in the *Times Literary Supplement* on the frequent manipulation of narrative prose and monologue in *Dying, in Other Words,* Stoddard Martin remarked, "Some of the surrealistic scenery is vivid, but the thickets surrounding are impenetrable." While some other critics pointed to the novel's extreme self-consciousness and fragmentation as a source of obscurity, they also thought that Gee's first work had brought a provocative new twist to the thriller genre. In a review for the Toronto *Globe and Mail,* Douglas Hill wrote that *Dying, in Other Words* possesses "a cosmic implication, the death of a planet, the extinction of humanity as the reality of everyday imagination. Death and fiction, for Gee, are inseparable."

Gee continues her thematic exploration of death in her 1983 work, an apocalyptic novel titled *The Burning Book,* which uses the genre of the sprawling family saga. Tracing four generations of an English family through both world wars, *The Burning Book* focuses on ordinary people struggling to exist in a world that hovers on the threshold of nuclear destruction. Gee weaves evocations of Hiroshima and Nagasaki into her narrative, imbuing the world of the novel with a sense of bleakness and impending doom. The uninspired, unfulfilled characters—lacking a sense of political and social consciousness—become victims of their own self-absorption and are ultimately annihilated.

Although some reviewers found the text difficult, *The Burning Book* received praise as well. Linda Taylor, writing in the *Times Literary Supplement,* deemed it "an odd kind of novel but a marvelously cogent anti-war statement." The *Contemporary Novelists* essayist noted, "As a nuclear warning the book certainly succeeds; and it succeeds as a work of literature as well." Especially impressed by Gee's descriptive powers, attention to detail, and skillful infusion of the work with a haunting sense of urgency, *New York Times Book Review* contributor Ronald De Feo observed, "At its

best, it is a wonderfully inventive saga of dreams and disillusionment." The reviewer added that *The Burning Book*'s "tragic ending is suggestively, almost poetically conveyed, and it is terribly affecting."

Gee's next novel, a touchingly humorous romance titled *Light Years,* chronicles a year in the lives of a middle-aged husband and wife following their breakup. The book's construction—fifty-five chapters divided into twelve sections—mirrors the year of their estrangement. During this time, each engages in a superficial affair, but the self-centered Harold and spoiled, rich Lottie are reunited by the novel's end. In a review for the *Spectator,* Christopher Hawtree theorized that "the effect of *Light Years* is to convey the gravitational forces which, however much they are impeded and however ill-matched the participants might appear, bring people together."

Some critics deemed the plot of *Light Years* overly contrived, but some praised the book as having vivid character portraits and effortless narrative technique. *Dictionary of Literary Biography*'s Henn remarked, "Though Harold and especially Lottie are problematic people, they are rounded and reasonably relatable. While the novel still possesses a complex structure, it is far easier to comprehend than the intricacies of her first novels." Roz Kaveney, writing in the *Times Literary Supplement,* concluded: "This is so fine a novel because so completely a planned and crafted one. . . . The book's posed philosophical view pile[s] up all of human possibility and perception as a barrier against the cold and the dark."

Grace is a thriller with an antinuclear theme; it was inspired by the murder in 1984 of antinuclear activist Hilda Murrell. Its primary characters are an unconventional eighty-five-year-old woman, Grace Stirling, who is a veteran supporter of liberal causes, and her niece Paula Timms, a writer who is involved in the antinuclear movement and is working on a book about Murrell. A British government agent is spying on them, even tailing them on trips. More than Murrell's murder, Henn noted, "the most significant crime in the context of the novel . . . is the global perpetuation of nuclear radiation through nuclear energy and armaments."

Henn thought the novel "occasionally stretches credibility" in pursuit of its political agenda. The *Contemporary Novelists* essayist, though, found *Grace* "an exciting and considerable advance in the art of Gee's novels," as "the threads of the story and the lives they describe gradually and skillfully converge and inter-mesh" while illuminating Gee's antinuclear theme, which is "fundamental to the story."

Where Are the Snows is about a wealthy, heedless, globe-trotting couple, Christopher and Alexandra Court (whose first names provide the title for the U.S. edition). They bring unhappiness to most of the people in their lives, including their son and daughter, who are teenagers when Christopher and Alexandra take off on an extended journey and grow to troubled adult-hood in their parents' absence. The Courts also bring unhappiness to each other, with Alexandra having an extramarital affair and Christopher shooting her lover. And despite all their travels, they miss their chance to see snow, which is vanishing because of global warming.

"The slow but steady eradication from the earth of snowfall mirrors the slow corruption of earthly and personal purity," explained Henn. A *Publishers Weekly* reviewer commented that some readers may find it hard to care about the Courts, but Henn remarked, "It is a measure of Gee's talent that readers are consis-tently concerned about the fates of her major charac-ters, despite the fact that they are almost always unlikable." The *Publishers Weekly* critic praised the novel overall, calling it "a memorable tale" written "in stylish prose."

In *Lost Children,* it is a child who leaves the parents behind to deal with the loss. Sixteen-year-old Zoe Bennett runs away from home, shocking her mother, Alma, who has always believed their relationship to be an uncommonly good one. The strain leads Alma to separate from her husband, Paul, and further distances her from their law-student son, Adam, to whom she has never been close. Alma goes into therapy "to ex-plore her childhood as a means of rediscovering the self she lost during marriage and motherhood," re-ported Mary Scott in *New Statesman and Society.* Therapy leads her to think she may have been sexu-ally abused in girlhood, by her father, her stepfather, or perhaps a stranger; she believes her mother let her down in some way but fails to recognize her own im-perfections as a mother to Adam and Zoe.

"The implication of the novel's title," noted Henn, "is that Adam and Zoe are not the novel's only lost chil-dren but that all of the characters could be considered

as such." Isobel Armstrong, writing in the *Times Liter-ary Supplement,* pointed out that the lost children in-clude "the children our past selves were" and "the actual children, unparented, deprived, frequently abused, who inhabit the urban London of our present." Henn found it typical of Gee that her "focus on indi-viduals takes place simultaneously with her investiga-tion of some breakdown of the social order—primarily homelessness," as numerous homeless people are camped near the London real estate office where Alma works. Gee presents the plight of these people against the background of the self-centered and materialistic attitudes of Alma's coworkers, whom Armstrong de-scribed as "small-time yuppies." Armstrong praised Gee's "brilliantly evoked" character portraits and her "cool, lucid writing," concluding that *Lost Children* is a "searching and ambitious novel."

In *The Ice People,* Gee deals with social issues through the science fiction genre. The novel is set in England the middle of the twenty-first century, when a new ice age is on its way. Also in this period, the services once provided by the government have been priva-tized; disease has devastated the population; class dis-tinctions are sharper than ever; most people are deeply apathetic about politics; and the sexes are largely seg-regated, voluntarily. For a time, the book's main char-acter and narrator, Saul, is an exception to the latter trend, living with a woman named Sarah. But Saul and Sarah eventually break up, and she moves to a women's community, bringing along their son, Luke. Saul then kidnaps Luke and takes him on a journey with the intended destination of Africa, a location at-tractive to many so-called ice people from northern lands.

The title also refers, however, to "the present chilly state of love," commented Eric Korn in the *Times Literary Supplement.* Gee "distributes the blame equi-tably" to both sexes, Korn reported, showing both Saul's and Sarah's flaws and frailties. He called the novel "stirring, witty, beautifully written" and "mor-dantly comic, unsparing, politically savvy, a beauti-fully clear and bracingly nasty vision," concluding, "Anyone who has ever been involved in human rela-tions must take it personally."

Race relations are the concern of *The White Family,* set in a working-class London neighborhood, once exclusively white but now attracting numerous new black and Asian residents, many of them from

CONTEMPORARY AUTHORS • New Revision Series, Volume 125

England's former colonies. The whites—including the Whites, the novel's central family—have been "shocked to find that the Empire had landed on their doorstep," Heather Clark explained in the *Times Literary Supplement.* The neighborhood's changing complexion brings varying responses from the members of the White family—park groundskeeper Alfred; his homemaker wife, May; and their three adult children. Racism brews in some of them, acceptance in others, and emotional barriers go up between them.

Gee uses multiple narrators, a device that generally "enriches our understanding of the Whites' predicament," Clark observed, although she thought the shifts occasionally distracting. She also found "much to admire in the way the novel both implicates and absolves the Whites of their transgressions," as "Gee moves skillfully between compassion and disgust." In London's *Sunday Times,* Margaret Walters wrote that "although Gee's novel adds up to a telling indictment of blind prejudice, she is too fine a writer to lapse into simple pessimism," with some characters "allowed happy or, rather, hopeful, endings." Walters summed up the book as "somberly perceptive" and Gee as "one of our most ambitious and challenging novelists."

BIOGRAPHICAL AND CRITICAL SOURCES:

BOOKS

Contemporary Novelists, 7th edition, St. James Press (Detroit, MI), 2001.
Dictionary of Literary Biography, Volume 207: *British Novelists since 1960, Third Series,* Gale (Detroit, MI), 1999, pp. 123-130.

PERIODICALS

Globe and Mail (Toronto), February 16, 1985.
New Statesman and Society, April 22, 1994, Mary Scott, review of *Lost Children,* p. 48.
New York Times Book Review, October 14, 1984.
Publishers Weekly, December 13, 1991, review of *Christopher and Alexandra,* p. 46.
Spectator, September 24, 1983, October 5, 1985.
Sunday Times (London), May 12, 2002, Margaret Walters, "Dark Visions of a Black and White World," p. 48.

Times Literary Supplement, July 17, 1981; September 23, 1983; October 4, 1985; April 29, 1994, Isobel Armstrong, "Bloody Parents," p. 20; October 2, 1998, Eric Korn, "Cold Comforts," p. 25; May 3, 2002, Heather Clark, "Empire on the Doorstep," p. 23.
Washington Post, May 2, 1986.*

*   *   *

GIBSON, William 1914-
(William Mass)

PERSONAL: Born November 13, 1914, in New York, NY; son of George Irving (a bank clerk) and Florence (Dore) Gibson; married Margaret Brenman (a psychoanalyst), September 6, 1940; children: Thomas, Daniel. *Education:* Attended College of City of New York (now City College of the City University of New York), 1930-32. *Politics:* Democrat.

ADDRESSES: Home—General Delivery, Stockbridge, MA 01262-9999. *Agent*—Flora Roberts, 157 West 57th St., New York, NY 10022.

CAREER: Author and playwright. Piano teacher at intervals in early writing days to supplement income. President and cofounder of Berkshire Theatre Festival, Stockbridge, MA, 1966—.

MEMBER: PEN, Authors League of America, Dramatists Guild.

AWARDS, HONORS: Harriet Monroe Memorial Prize, 1945, for group of poems published in *Poetry;* Topeka Civic Theatre Award, 1947, for *A Cry of Players;* Sylvania Award, 1957, for television play *The Miracle Worker;* Antoinette Perry Award Nomination for best play, 1958, for *Two for the Seesaw;* Antoinette Perry Award for best play, 1960, for *The Miracle Worker.*

WRITINGS:

PLAYS

I Lay in Zion (one-act play; produced at Topeka Civic Theatre, 1943), Samuel French (New York, NY), 1947.

William Gibson

(Under pseudonym William Mass) *The Ruby* (one-act lyrical drama), with libretto (based on Lord Dunsany's *A Night at an Inn*) by Norman Dello Joio, Ricordi, 1955.

The Miracle Worker (three-act; originally written as a television drama; produced by Columbia Broadcasting System for *Playhouse 90* in 1957 and by National Broadcasting Company in 1979; rewritten for stage and produced on Broadway at Playhouse Theatre, October 19, 1959; rewritten for screen and produced by United Artists in 1962; also see below), Knopf (New York, NY), 1957.

Dinny and the Witches [and] *The Miracle Worker* (the former produced off-Broadway at Cherry Lane Theatre, December 9, 1959; also see below), Atheneum (New York, NY), 1960.

Two for the Seesaw (three-act comedy; copyrighted in 1956 as *After the Verb to Love*; produced on Broadway at Booth Theatre, January 16, 1958; also see below), Samuel French (New York, NY), 1960.

Dinny and the Witches: A Frolic on Grave Matters, Dramatists Play Service, 1961.

(With Clifford Odets) *Golden Boy* (musical adaptation of Odets's original drama, with lyrics by Lee Adams, and music by Charles Strouse; first produced

on Broadway at Majestic Theatre, October 20, 1964), Atheneum (New York, NY), 1965.

A Cry of Players (three-act; produced at Topeka Civic Theatre, February, 1948; produced on Broadway at the Vivian Beaumont Theatre, November 14, 1968), Atheneum (New York, NY), 1969.

John and Abigail (three-act drama; produced at Berkshire Theatre Festival, 1969, later in Washington, DC, at Ford's Theatre, January 9, 1970), published as *American Primitive: The Words of John and Abigail Adams Put into a Sequence for the Theater, with Addenda in Rhyme,* Atheneum (New York, NY), 1972.

The Body and the Wheel (produced in Lenox, MA, at Pierce Chapel, April 5, 1974), Dramatists Play Service, 1975.

The Butterfingers Angel, Mary and Joseph, Herod the Nut, and the Slaughter of 12 Hit Carols in a Pear Tree (produced at Pierce Chapel, December, 1974), Dramatists Play Service, 1975.

Golda (produced on Broadway at the Morosco Theatre, November 14, 1977), Samuel French (New York, NY), 1977.

Goodly Creatures (produced in Washington, DC, at the Round House Theatre, January, 1980), Dramatists Play Service, 1990.

Monday after the Miracle (produced in Charleston, SC, at the Dock Street Theatre, May, 1982, later produced on Broadway at the Eugene O'Neill Theatre, December 14, 1982), Dramatists Play Service, 1990.

Handy Dandy (produced in New York, NY, 1984), Dramatists Play Service, 1986.

Raggedy Ann and Andy (musical; music and lyrics by Joe Raposo), first produced in Albany, NY, 1984, produced in New York City, 1986, as *Raggedy Ann.*

Golda's Balcony (one-act), produced in Lenox, MA, May 18, 2002.

OTHER

Winter Crook (poems), Oxford University Press (Oxford, England), 1948.

The Cobweb (novel), Knopf (New York, NY), 1954.

The Seesaw Log (a chronicle of the stage production, including the text of *Two for the Seesaw*), Knopf (New York, NY), 1959.

A Mass for the Dead (chronicle and poems), Atheneum (New York, NY), 1968.

A Season in Heaven (chronicle), Atheneum (New York, NY), 1974.

Shakespeare's Game (criticism), Atheneum (New York, NY), 1978.

ADAPTATIONS: The Cobweb was filmed by Metro-Goldwyn-Mayer, 1957; *Two for the Seesaw* was filmed by United Artists, 1962.

SIDELIGHTS: While William Gibson has published poetry, plays, fiction, and criticism, he is best known for his 1957 play *The Miracle Worker.* Originally written and performed as a television drama, and adapted in later years for both stage and screen, *The Miracle Worker* remains Gibson's most widely revived piece. It was refilmed for television in 1979 and also formed the basis for Gibson's 1982 play, *Monday after the Miracle,* which picks up the characters almost twenty years later. Writing in the *Dictionary of Literary Biography,* Stephen C. Coy called the drama "a classic American play—and television play, and film—the full stature of which has yet to be realized."

The story, which is based on real people and actual events, concerns the relationship between Helen Keller, a handicapped child who has been deaf and blind since infancy, and Annie Sullivan, the formerly blind teacher who has been called in to instruct her. When Annie arrives she finds that Helen has been utterly spoiled by well-intentioned parents who, in their sympathy, allow her to terrorize the household. Annie's efforts to civilize Helen and Helen's resistance result in a fierce, and frequently physical, struggle that forms the central conflict of the play. The "miracle" occurs when, after months of frustration, Annie is finally able to reach the child. Coy explained: "Just as the struggle appears to be lost, Helen starts to work the pump in the Keller yard and the miracle—her mind learning to name things—happens before the audience as she feels the water and the wet ground. Annie and others realize what is happening as Helen, possessed, runs about touching things and learning names, finally, to their great joy, 'Mother' and 'Papa.' The frenzy slows as Helen realizes there is something she needs to know, gets Annie to spell it for her, spells it back, and goes to spell it for her mother. It is the one word which more than any other describes the subject of *The Miracle Worker:* 'Teacher.'"

Praising the play's "youthfulness and vigor," *New York Times* reviewer Bosley Crowther described the tremendous concentration of energy apparent in the battle scenes between Helen and Annie: "The physical vitality and passion are absolutely intense as the nurse, played superbly by Anne Bancroft moves in and takes on the job of 'reaching the soul' of the youngster, played by Patty Duke. . . . When the child, who is supposed to be Helen Keller in her absolutely primitive childhood state, kicks and claws with the frenzy of a wild beast at the nurse who is supposed to be Annie Sullivan, the famous instructor of Miss Keller, it is a staggering attack. And when Annie hauls off and swats her or manhandles her into a chair and pushes food into her mouth to teach her habits, it is enough to make the viewer gasp and grunt."

The Broadway production of the play was so well-received that a film version with the same stars was made in 1962 and enjoyed similar success. Later revivals have not fared so well. When *The Miracle Worker* was filmed for television in 1979 (with Patty Duke playing Annie Sullivan), Tom Shales commented in the *Washington Post* that the only point in doing *The Miracle Worker* again "was to give Patty Duke Astin a chance on the other side of the food." His objections ranged from what he called "careless casting" to the inappropriateness (almost an insult, he called it) of making a television movie from a screenplay written for live television. For the writing itself, however, Shales had nothing but praise. "William Gibson's play . . . remains, even when not perfectly done, a nearly perfect joy, one of the most assuredly affirmative dramatic works to come out of the optimistic '50s."

Gibson's three-act play, *Two for the Seesaw,* which played on Broadway in 1958, starring Anne Bancroft and Henry Fonda, was a hit, giving momentum to the playwright's career. This "most adroit and refreshing dramatic duet," as Marya Mannes called it in the *Reporter,* revolves around the relationship of Jerry, a lawyer from Nebraska, and Gittel, a girl from the Bronx. Though Lionel Trilling suggested in the *Drama Review* that the play "challenges none of the vested interests, affronts none of the deep-rooted pieties of . . . [the] audience," he remarked that "even a modest comedy about a love affair may be more or less honest, as may any scene in the play, or any speech in a scene." Likening it to a best-selling novel, the *Nation's* Harold Clurman went on to describe the work as a "conventional tale" lacking concrete characters, but replete with jokes and clichés. When Gibson published the play as *The Seesaw Log,* he prefaced it with a chronicle of the more than two months of work that led up to its Broadway premiere. When the play was revived at the Marin Theatre in Mill Valley, California, in 2002, the director staged it as a period piece. Although *San Francisco Chronicle* critic Robert Hurwitt found the more than two-hour length unjustified for the plot and ill-suited to the modern theatergoer, he praised its undated emotional realism. "As much as its details demonstrate the degree to which things have changed since 1958," he added, "the emotional journeys of its characters haven't dated a bit."

In addition to *The Miracle Worker,* and *Two for the Seesaw,* Gibson wrote several other three-act biographical plays, including *Cry of Players,* about William Shakespeare and Anne Hathaway, and *John and Abigail,* about John and Abigail Adams, *Goodly Creatures,* about Anne Hutchinson, and *Golda,* about Israeli prime minister Golda Meir. In 1977 *Golda* appeared on Broadway, starring Anne Bancroft. The play portrays not only Meir's political role, but shows through flashbacks her childhood, life, and work with the Zionist movment. The original had a short and unsuccessful run, yet Gibson felt strongly enough about the work to return to it a quarter-century later. The octogenerian reworked what had been a play with a cast of more than twenty, to a one-act version titled *Golda's Balcony.* With the distance of time between the play and the historical events of the Yom Kippur War, during which the play takes place, *Golda's Balcony* fared much better. While during the original production, the personages and events were often in the news, in the reworked version subtle video projections of personages and events help viewers put the work into historical context. Noting that the play, "imparts a lot of information in its ninety minutes," *Variety*'s Marland Taylor found that "sometimes the transitions from Israel's history to her [Meir's] personal history are too abrupt," and the work seems rather like a lecture. Despite the fact that the play portrays only the Israeli viewpoint about the war, Neil Genzlinger described the play as "enlightening nonetheless" in his *New York Times* review. "Thanks to the vigor of Gibson's writing and actor Annette Miller's strong performance, *Golda's Balcony* is often involving and enlightening," concluded Taylor.

BIOGRAPHICAL AND CRITICAL SOURCES:

BOOKS

Contemporary Dramatists, 6th edition, St. James Press (Detroit, MI), 1999.

Contemporary Literary Criticism, Volume 23, Gale (Detroit, MI), 1983.

Dictionary of Literary Biography, Volume 7: *Twentieth-Century American Dramatists,* Gale (Detroit, MI), 1981.

Gibson, William, *The Seesaw Log,* Knopf (New York, NY), 1959.

PERIODICALS

America, November 10, 1990, p. 350.

Back Stage West, January 6, 2000, Terri Roberts, review of *The Miracle Worker,* p. 10.

Cosmopolitan, August, 1958.

Daily Variety, June 5, 2002, Marland Taylor, review of *Golda's Balcony,* p. 9.

Drama Review, May, 1960, Lionel Trilling, review of *Two for the Seesaw,* p. 17.

Los Angeles Times, October 19, 1982; May 13, 1999, Mark Chalon Smith, "Actors Carry *Miracle* in Costa Mesa," p. 6.

Nation, February 1, 1958, Harold Clurman, review of *Two for the Seesaw,* p. 107; December 2, 1968.

New England Theatre, spring, 1970.

New Leader, December 16, 1968.

New Republic, November 9, 1959, Robert Brustein, review of *The Miracle Worker,* p. 28.

Newsweek, March 16, 1959; July 27, 1970.

New York, November 5, 1990, p. 127.

New Yorker, November 23, 1968; November 5, 1990, p. 120.

New York Times, May 24, 1962; May 27, 1962; June 3, 1962; November 16, 1977; December 9, 1980; May 26, 1982; December 15, 1982; March 16, 2003, Shimon Peres, "Always a Lioness, Protecting Her Beloved Israel," p. 7(L); April 1, 2003, Neil Genzlinger, "A 1977 Golda Meir Gets into Shape," review of *Golda's Balcony,* p. E5.

New York Times Book Review, March 15, 1959, Harold Clurman, review of *Two for the Seesaw,* p. 5; April 14, 1968.

Poetry, August, 1948, James Hall, review of *Winter Crook,* pp. 278, 281.

Reporter, March 6, 1958, Marya Mannes, review of *Two for the Seesaw,* p. 36.

San Francisco Chronicle, May 23, 2002, Robert Hurwitt, "*Seesaw*'s Timeless Back-and-Forth; 1958 Broadway Hit Retains Relevance," p. D9.

Saturday Review, March 13, 1954, Charles Lee, review of "The Cobweb," p. 19; March 14, 1959, Henry Hewes, review of *The Seesaw Log,* p. 55; March 23, 1968.

Tulane Drama Review, May, 1960.
Variety, February 21, 1971; June 10, 2002, Marland Taylor, review of *Golda's Balcony,* p. 38.
Washington Post, October 13, 1979; January 20, 1980; January 26, 1980; November 27, 1981; December 3, 1981; October 3, 1982; October 14, 1982.

*   *   *

GLOVER, (David) Tony "Harp Dog" 1939-

PERSONAL: Surname sounds like "lover"; publishes under several variations of name listed above; born October 7, 1939, in Minneapolis, MN; son of Harold E. and Margaret (Hauser) Glover; married Karin (a dancer), April 3, 1961 (divorced, October, 1971). *Education:* Attended high school in Minneapolis, MN.

ADDRESSES: Office—Box 3689, Loring Station, Minneapolis, MN 55403.

CAREER:

Musician and author; member of trio Koerner, Ray & Glover. "Worked several years as offset pressman in mail advertising firm. Left to record and play gigs with Dave Ray and John Koerner; five albums on Electra label; appearances at Newport and Philadelphia folk festivals, etc. Somewhere near the end of the 60's, spent a year and a half as an all night DJ playing Moondog, Miles Davis, and Sonny Boy Williamson records and answering a lot of bizarre phone calls. Went to New York City on vacation, didn't come back for two years. In New York City, did mostly freelance music writing. Moved back to Minneapolis, tired of guerilla warfare necessary when going to the deli after dark. At present, writing mostly record reviews, working in a funky band called 'Nine Below Zero,' and doing some reunion recording and concerts with Koerner and Ray." Wrote and produced a television documentary on Koerner, Ray & Glover shown on Public Broadcasting System, 1986.

Albums include *Blues, Rags and Hollers,* 1963; *Lots More Blues, Rags and Hollers,* 1964; *The Folk Box,* 1964; *Snaker's Here,* 1965; *Spider Blues,* 1965; *The Return of Koerner, Ray & Glover,* 1965; *Good Old Koerner, Ray & Glover,* 1972; *Some American Folk Songs Like They Used To,* 1974; *Crossroads: White Blues in the Nineteen-Sixties,* 1984; *From the West Bank,* 1985; *Legends in Their Spare Time,* 1987; *Ashes in My Whiskey,* 1990; *Troubadours of the Folk Era,* 1993; *Picture Has Faded,* 1993; and *One Foot in the Groove,* 1996.

AWARDS, HONORS: "Won an overnight traveling case in talent show at a bar once;" has also won numerous musical awards, including "Best Folk Group," Minnesota Music Awards; elected to Minnesota Music Hall of Fame.

WRITINGS:

(Editor) Ron McElderry, *The Little Black Songbook,* Little Sandy Review Press, 1960.
(With Ted Sheilds) *That Ain't Quite What I Meant, Babe* (cartoons), "printed by Glover after hours at shop where he worked," 1963.
Mad Coast 1 (poems), privately printed ("since each page of every copy was created individually, this was produced only in a severely limited edition"), 1964.
(Under name Tony "Little Sun" Glover) *Blues Harp: An Instruction Method for Playing the Blues Harmonica,* Oak Publications (New York, NY), 1965.
(Under name Tony Glover, with Paul Nelson) *The Festival Songbook,* Amsco Music Publishing, 1972.
Blues Harp Songbook, Oak Publications (New York, NY), 1975.
Rock Hart, Oak Publications (New York, NY), 1981.
(With Scott Dirks and Ward Gaines) *Blues with a Feeling: The Little Walter Story,* Routledge (New York, NY), 2002.

Also published *Big Joe Blues,* a section of an autobiographical novel. Author of *Tribute* (to Sonny Boy Williamson; radio script), 1965; author of liner notes for "Get Together," by Sonny Terry, 1965, "Country Blues," by John Hammond, 1965, and for "Blues Harp" (to accompany the book). Contributor to *Little Sandy Review, Music Journal, Sing Out!, Folk Scene, Region, Twin Citian, Hullabaloo, Eye, Circus, Rock, Crawdaddy, Rolling Stone,* and *Creem.*

SIDELIGHTS: Tony "Harp Dog" Glover once told *CA:* "My major areas of interest are making music (blues, Indian, and electronic music). In writing about music I only write about what interests me and arouses my enthusiasm—which explains why I've only done one or two negative reviews—and also why, of late, my writing is slacking off some—it's pretty boring out there. Besides, I'd rather write and play music right now than write *about* it.

"In my writing, I'm interested in finding the spaces that nobody speaks of because they're too personal—but everybody needs to know that others feel as well. In my early life I was greatly influenced by Edgar Allan Poe . . . later I discovered that I was born ninety years (almost to the hour) after his death, and wonder if perhaps I'm not a reincarnation of his spirit—a feeling deepened by a visit to his house in Philadelphia.

"Wrote many gloomy Orson Welles-like vignettes in midnight hours, and wandered in AM alleys looking for something. Was a juvenile delinquent for a few years, ran with a minor gang, but quit because their society and concepts were as stifling as the ones they were rebelling against. At the age of sixteen I succeeded in staying drunk for a month and a half, but I don't have that much time or money nowadays."

"Somewhere along there found blues music of people like Sonny Boy Williamson, Muddy Waters, Jimmy Reed, Little Walter, etc., and got hung in learning how to play it on harp (harmonica). Had an R&B band for half a year. . . . Fell into the 'folk-music' scene." Indeed, the influential folk-blues trio of "Spider" John Koerner, Dave ("Snaker") Ray, and Glover (who billed himself as "Little Sun") played together for some two decades, cutting several albums and influencing such icons as John Lennon and The Doors. When the trio broke up, Glover continued to perform while branching out as an author. Koerner, Ray & Glover reunited several times, most recently for a 1996 recording session that led to the album *One Foot in the Groove.* Ray died in November, 2002.

As a writer of articles, album notes, and other material, Glover has countless publications to his credit. But his book output has been not been as prodigious; volumes tend to be published ten or twenty years apart. The impetus for his 1965 book, *Blues Harp: An Instruction Method for Playing the Blues Harmonica,* came from a public relations executive who "kept after me for a year or so, and finally convinced me that if I didn't do it, somebody who knew nothing about it . . .

would," as Glover was quoted on the *Island* Web site. "So I gave it a shot." The musician added that he strove to keep his instructions conversational, unlike "so many of the instruction methods around [that] were just basically boring and pedantic." *Blues Harp* became the standard-bearer of its topic, and, according to its author, has never been out of print.

In 2002 Glover cowrote a biography—the first, and only to date—on bluesman Little Walter. Born Marion Walter Jacobs in 1930, Little Walter revolutionized Chicago-style harmonica playing. He worked alongside Muddy Waters, taking the harmonica "to a place of prominence as an expressive, powerful, electrified lead instrument," in the words of *Library Journal* reviewer Bill Walker. In the pages of *Blues with a Feeling: The Little Walter Story,* Glover and his fellow musicians make the case that their subject "was to harmonica what Charlie Parker was to jazz saxophone." In a review for *Sing Out!,* Michael Cala praised the authors' efforts, calling the work an "exceptionally thorough and well-written history" highlighted by a "fine prose style."

BIOGRAPHICAL AND CRITICAL SOURCES:

BOOKS

Glover, Tony, with Scott Dirks and Ward Gaines, *Blues with a Feeling: The Little Walter Story,* Routledge (New York, NY), 2002.
The Face of Folk Music, Citadel Press, 1968.

PERIODICALS

Booklist, September 1, 2002, Mike Tribby, review of *Blues with a Feeling,* p. 38.
Insider, September, 1971.
Ivory Tower (University of Minnesota), June 1, 1964.
Library Journal, August, 2002, Bill Walker, review of *Blues with a Feeling,* p. 98.
Little Sandy Review, fall, 1964.
Sarasota Herald Tribune, January 3, 2003, Joel Welin, *Tradition of the Blues,* p. 3.
Sing Out!, July, 1964; winter, 2003, Michael Cala, review of *Blues with a Feeling,* p. 123.
Twin Citian, November, 1965.

*   *   *

GOLD, Herbert 1924-

PERSONAL: Born March 9, 1924, in Cleveland, OH; son of Samuel S. and Frieda (Frankel) Gold; married Edith Zubrin, April, 1948 (divorced, 1956); married Melissa Dilworth, January, 1968 (divorced, 1975); children: (first marriage) Ann, Judith; (second marriage) Nina, Ari, Ethan. *Education:* Columbia University, B.A., 1946, M.A., 1948; Sorbonne, University of Paris, licence-es-lettres, 1951.

ADDRESSES: Home—1051-A Broadway, San Francisco, CA 94133-4205.

CAREER: Full-time writer. Western Reserve University (now Case Western Reserve University), Cleveland, OH, lecturer in philosophy and literature, 1951-53; Wayne State University, Detroit, MI, member of English department faculty, 1954-56. University of California—Davis, regents professor, 1973. Visiting professor, Cornell University, 1958, University of California—Berkeley, 1963 and 1968, Harvard University, 1964, Stanford University, 1967, and University of California—Davis, 1974-79 and 1985. McGuffey Lecturer in English, Ohio University, 1971. *Military service:* U.S. Army Intelligence, 1943-46.

AWARDS, HONORS: Fulbright fellow at Sorbonne, University of Paris, 1950; Inter-American Cultural Relations grant to Haiti, 1954; *Hudson Review* fellow, 1956; Guggenheim fellow, 1957; Ohioana Book Award, 1957, for *The Man Who Was Not With-It;* National Institute of Arts and Letters grant in literature, 1958; Longview Foundation Award, 1959; Ford Foundation theatre fellow, 1960; California Literature Medal Award, 1968, for *Fathers: A Novel in the Form of a Memoir;* Commonwealth Club Award for best novel, 1982, for *Family: A Novel in the Form of a Memoir;* L.H.D., Baruch College of the City University of New York, 1988; Sherwood Anderson Prize for fiction, 1989.

Herbert Gold

WRITINGS:

NOVELS

Birth of a Hero, Viking (New York, NY), 1951.
The Prospect before Us, World Publishing (New York, NY), 1954, published as *Room Clerk,* New American Library (New York, NY), 1955.
The Man Who Was Not With-It, Little, Brown (Boston, MA), 1956, published as *The Wild Life,* Permabooks (New York, NY), 1957, with new introduction by author, Algonquin Books of Chapel Hill (Chapel Hill, NC), 1987.
The Optimist, Little, Brown (Boston, MA), 1959.
Therefore Be Bold, Dial (New York, NY), 1960.
Salt, Dial (New York, NY), 1963.
Fathers: A Novel in the Form of a Memoir, Random House (New York, NY), 1967, reprinted as *Fathers,* Donald I. Fine (New York, NY), 1991.
The Great American Jackpot, Random House (New York, NY), 1969.
Biafra Goodbye, Two Windows Press (San Francisco, CA), 1970.

My Last Two Thousand Years, Random House (New York, NY), 1972.

Swiftie the Magician, McGraw-Hill (New York, NY), 1974.

Waiting for Cordelia, Arbor House (New York, NY), 1977.

Slave Trade, Arbor House (New York, NY), 1979.

He/She, Arbor House (New York, NY), 1980.

Family: A Novel in the Form of a Memoir, Arbor House (New York, NY), 1981, reprinted as *Family,* Donald I. Fine (New York, NY), 1991.

True Love, Arbor House (New York, NY), 1982.

Mister White Eyes, Arbor House (New York, NY), 1984.

A Girl of Forty, Donald I. Fine (New York, NY), 1986.

Dreaming, Donald I. Fine (New York, NY), 1988.

She Took My Arm As If She Loved Me, St. Martin's Press (New York, NY), 1997.

Daughter Mine, Thomas Dunne (New York, NY), 2000.

STORY COLLECTIONS

(With R. V. Cassill and James B. Hall) *15 x 3,* New Directions (New York, NY), 1957.

Love & Like, Dial (New York, NY), 1960.

The Magic Will: Stories and Essays of a Decade, Random House (New York, NY), 1971, 2nd edition, Transaction Publishers (New Brunswick, NJ), 2002.

Stories of Misbegotten Love (bound with *Angel on My Shoulder and Other Stories* by Don Asher), Capra (Santa Barbara, CA), 1985.

Lovers & Cohorts: Twenty-seven Stories, Donald I. Fine (New York, NY), 1986.

NONFICTION

The Age of Happy Problems, Dial (New York, NY), 1962, published with a new preface by the author, Transaction Publishers (New Brunswick, NJ), 2002.

A Walk on the West Side: California on the Brink, Arbor House, (New York, NY) 1981.

Travels in San Francisco (memoirs), Arcade (New York, NY), 1990.

Best Nightmare on Earth: A Life in Haiti, introduction by Jan Morris, Prentice Hall (New York, NY), 1991, published as *Haiti: Best Nightmare on Earth,* with a new afterword by the author, Transaction Publishers (New Brunswick, NJ), 2000.

Bohemia: Where Art, Angst, Love, and Strong Coffee Meet, Simon & Schuster (New York, NY), 1993, published as *Bohemia: Digging the Roots of Cool,* Touchstone Books (New York, NY), 1994.

EDITOR

Fiction of the Fifties: A Decade of American Writing, Doubleday (Garden City, NY), 1959.

(With David L. Stevenson) *Stories of Modern America,* St. Martin's (New York, NY), 1961.

First Person Singular: Essays for the Sixties, Dial (New York, NY), 1963.

JUVENILE

The Young Prince and the Magic Cone, Doubleday (Garden City, NY), 1973.

Contributor to *The Living Novel,* edited by Granville Hicks, Macmillan (New York, NY), 1957; *Pardon Me, Sir, but Is My Eye Hurting Your Elbow?,* edited by Bob Booker and George Foster, Geis, 1968; and *San Francisco,* revised edition, edited by Herb Caen, Abrams (New York, NY), 1993. Also contributor to *O. Henry Prize Stories,* 1954. Contributor to periodicals, including *Atlantic, Playboy, New York Times Book Review, Hudson Review, Harper's, Esquire,* and *Partisan Review.*

ADAPTATIONS: *Salt* was adapted for television by Columbia Broadcasting System (CBS) and broadcast as *Threesome,* 1986.

SIDELIGHTS: Herbert Gold is known as a successful chronicler of life in modern America. His fiction and nonfiction are both marked by clearly evoked settings, well-drawn characters, and insightful presentations of personal relationships. Commenting on the realism of Gold's fiction, Robert G. Kaiser of the *Washington Post Book World* suggested that the author's books should be stored in a time capsule so that our descendants can see clearly how people of our time actually lived. Kaiser stated that Gold "is a gifted reporter, a writer whose characters' dilemmas are rooted in a precise cultural moment that [he] evokes supremely well." While some of Gold's work is set in his native midwest, much of his fiction takes place in California, where he has made his home for many years. He knows the state well, and "he manages as few do to get it down on paper," reported Bruce Cook in the *Detroit News.* Gold "is forever uncovering the latest totems and odd social byways of the Pacific shore," Peter Andrews noted in *New York Times Book Review,* "and writing about them with grace and humor."

In addition to his skill at evoking a California setting, Gold shows uncommon skill at portraying "the agonizing dynamics of contemporary male-female relationships," Landon asserted. The critic felt this was evident in the author's ongoing concern with the "breakdown of marriage as an American institution." In *Slave Trade,* for example, the detective Sid Kasdan is hired by an international group that supplies young Haitian boys to homosexual men in America and Europe. At first he works for the group, escorting the boys from Haiti to their buyers. But when he is to deliver a boy to a sadistic veterinarian with murderous plans, Kasdan balks. He frees the boy and takes him back to Haiti. Throughout his association with the slavers, Kasdan has been so obsessed with his ex-wife that he is insulated from the suffering around him. His own sorrow blinds him to the sorrow of others. But when he returns the boy to Haiti he finds that his former wife now works for the slavers. They kill the boy and at novel's end, Kasdan is negotiating with them for his own life. As Landon explained, Kasdan has been "a slave to the memory of his former wife [and] essentially a man paralyzed by divorce."

In *He/She,* Gold tells the story of an unnamed couple ("he" and "she") in the midst of a divorce. "She wants a life of 'unboredom,'" Anatole Broyard explained in the *New York Times,* "and her nameless husband wants their marriage to be 'a festival.'" His love for her is not the kind of love she needs. She is bored with him, but he doesn't know what the problem is. When she divorces him and lives with another man, he is heartbroken. She explains to him, Broyard wrote, "that everybody's heart is broken." But after a time they become lovers. "The book is about the tenacity of relationships," Larry McMurtry observed in the *New York Times Book Review,* "as expressed in the breakup of one marriage; the impersonal nature of the tenacity is underscored by the use of pronouns instead of names." Admitting that the premise of the novel is "a slender hinge on which to hang a narrative," Cyra McFadden of the *Chicago Tribune Book World* nonetheless found that "Gold makes of this marriage, and

what becomes of it, a book that is suspenseful, touching, and sometimes darkly funny."

Throughout his work Gold shows an understanding and sympathy for his characters and their problems. He expresses in *The Man Who Was Not With-It* "a deep compassion for human suffering and bewilderment," wrote W. L. Greesham in the *New York Times Book Review.* In *Lovers & Cohorts,* also in the *New York Times Book Review,* Hilma Wolitzer observed that Gold explores "very deftly" the "pain of love's dissolution" as well as the "particular agonies of the husband in a failed marriage." Erica Abeel, reviewing *A Girl of Forty* in the *Times,* noted that Gold is "especially astute about the prevarications of men when confronted with a loveable woman." But Gold's wisdom is not reserved solely for the agonies of men and marriage. Discussing *Fathers: A Novel in the Form of a Memoir,* Theodore Solotaroff in *Book Week* cited the strongest element in the novel as "Gold's feeling for his father." The author argues for perseverance in the face of life's hardships. As Ihab Hassan stated in *Radical Innocence: Studies in the Contemporary American Novel,* "The need to bounce with life, to take risks with its incompleteness, to celebrate the 'tin and hope' of human existence, knowing all the while that reality may be its own end . . . or, less frequently, that ambition contains its own death . . . these are the primary concerns of Herbert Gold."

These themes are explored by Gold in a variety of styles and settings and through a wide assortment of characters. *The Prospect before Us,* for example, concerns an old hotel for the destitute whose manager comes under fire for renting a room to a black woman. In *The Man Who Was Not With-It,* Gold writes of a carnival worker who is a drug addict. *Therefore Be Bold* tells the story of a young couple in 1950s Cleveland whose romance is doomed by her father's resistance. In *Fathers,* Gold draws upon his own family for inspiration, contrasting his father's generation of Jewish immigrants with his own generation. These diverse and sometimes unsavory characters come alive because Gold is particularly adept at accurately capturing their speech patterns, whatever their social backgrounds may be. "He has a sensitivity for the nuances of speech," Harry T. Moore observed in his *Contemporary American Novelists,* "and can frequently catch the precise accent, rhythms, and tone of dialogue and dialect." In *The Man Who Was Not With-It,* for example, Gold uses carnival jargon to tell his story. "He shows its tricks of insincerity, an important part of the story," Moore wrote, "but also displays its force in expressing the deepest feelings of the people who speak it." Discussing *The Prospect before Us* in *Literary Horizons: A Quarter Century of American Fiction,* Granville Hicks praised Gold's "mastery of a colloquial style. The dialogue is so perfect that it seems artless. . . . The effect is to immerse the reader in the garish world of [hotel manager] Harry Bowers."

A constant factor in all of Gold's work is "his love of wordplay," George Jensen wrote in the *Dictionary of Literary Biography.* Gold's wordplay, Jensen continued, "has been cited as his greatest accomplishment as a fiction writer and his greatest defect." This trait is a weakness, Jensen explained, because it "is too unusual and too present to ignore; the fate of his novels rests with the acceptance or rejection of his style." Hicks acknowledged Gold's Joycean style, seeing it as a means of attaining "greater freedom and freshness in the use of words, not for the sake of shocking the reader but in order to rouse him out of lethargy in order to compel him to see more clearly and feel more strongly."

In novels where the language of his characters is colorful, Gold's style seems to be most successful. David J. Gordon of *Yale Review* wrote that "Gold's virtues are more solidly present [in *Fathers*] than in his earlier novels. One reason may be that the constantly colorful idiom he seems to require is, in part, justified dramatically by the Yiddish-English speech of the parents. Another reason may be that his subject touches a deeper layer of feeling." In like terms, *The Man Who Was Not With-It,* with its carnival slang, gives Gold the opportunity to "handle colorful idiom," wrote Moore, who added, "It crackles. But the language isn't flashed just for its own sake. . . . Gold's tendency toward the bizarre in style exactly matches the subject matter in this book." Nicholas Delbanco also remarked on Gold's way with speech, noting in a review of *Dreaming* for the *New York Times Book Review* that "Gold's ear is excellent."

Elements of Gold's life also appear in several of his books—his divorce, childhood in Cleveland, and work as a hotel manager, for example— but Gold deals directly with his life only in three novels: *Fathers, My Last Two Thousand Years,* and *Family: A Novel in the Form of a Memoir.* The first of these focuses on Gold's relationship with his father and contrasts his father's

generation, and the many problems they overcame, with Gold's own generation, that had far fewer difficulties in life. *My Last Two Thousand Years* is an "autobiography-with-a-theme," as William Abrahams described it in the *Saturday Review of Education.* In it, Gold recounts his life with special emphasis on those moments of peak importance. *Family* concentrates on the women of the Gold family, as *Fathers* deals with the men.

Fathers traces the life of Gold's father, Samuel, from Czarist Russia to Cleveland, where he owned a grocery store for many years. The tension in the story arises from the conflict between the father, "a man of fact and commercial action, of will and property," as Robert Garis described him in the *Hudson Review,* and the son, whose values are nearly the opposite of his father's. Despite their differences, Gold is instructed by his father on how to enter into the adult world. Gold's own life finally begins to reflect his father's when it is disrupted by divorce. At that time, his father understands and helps him to overcome the pain. "Gold begins to learn," Jensen stated, "how to survive in an unstable world."

My Last Two Thousand Years is an exploration of Jewish history, with Gold relating the history of his people to his personal history, attempting to find his rightful place in the world. "The interests of *My Last Two Thousand Years,*" Alvin H. Rosenfeld wrote in *Midstream,* "are two-fold: as a critique of the literary life and with it most of the values of cultural Modernism, and as a discovery of a more central identity through an awakening to history." Thomas R. Edwards of the *New York Times Book Review* believed the autobiographical novel to be obsessed with "incidents that carry the theme of tribal discovery" rather than with the "necessary and interesting irrelevancies of a life." He does, however, find Gold's "account of his youth and early manhood . . . often quite wonderfully funny and poignant" and concluded that "Gold makes sense of his life."

As *Fathers* examines the men in Gold's family, *Family* looks at the women. It was titled *Family,* Gold explained to Cook, because "you can't call a book *Mothers* these days without being misunderstood." The novel, although essentially unstructured, revolves around Gold's mother, "as blazingly erratic and as trivial as a child's sparkler," Penelope Mesic noted in the *Chicago Tribune Book World.* Jerome Charyn pointed to Gold's mother as "the central force of the novel." Writing in the *New York Times Book Review,* Charyn reflected that *Family* "exists almost as pure song. . . . It is an homage to the loving and bullying women around [Gold]." When the novel's fact and fiction blend well, Mesic noted, they "produce a literary alloy with the strength of truth and lightness of fiction." Cook judged *Fathers, My Last Two Thousand Years,* and *Family*—all of which combine autobiography and fiction—as Gold's "three best novels."

In the 1980s, Gold began writing personal, nonfictional works about his travels throughout the world. *A Walk on the West Side: California on the Brink, Travels in San Francisco, Best Nightmare on Earth: A Life in Haiti,* and *Bohemia: Where Art, Angst, Love and Strong Coffee Meet* are autobiographical works about history and culture. In *Best Nightmare on Earth,* Gold's history of Haiti is inextricably linked with the personal experiences he had as a student in the early 1950s. Alex Raskin, writing in the *Los Angeles Times Book Review,* described that book as "travel writing of a high order, paralleling the author's own vulnerability with that of the land." Similarly, Gold's history of Bohemia, according to Brooke Allen in the *New York Times Book Review,* "is a very personal tour through late 20th century bohemia." However, even the author's nonfiction is rendered in a fictional style, as the *New York Times Book Review*'s Mark Danner observed in his review of *Best Nightmare on Earth:* "Mr. Gold writes like the novelist he is, roughing in scenes and characters with a few economical strokes."

Gold gave readers another novel with *She Took My Arm As If She Loved Me,* a hard-boiled detective novel that touched on his usual subjects of love lost and advancing age. His protagonist is Dan Kasdan, a philosophy teacher who has turned instead to working as a private investigator. Still in love with the woman he divorced many years ago, Dan decides to try to win her back. His attempts to do so involve him with Karim, a drug dealer and pornographer. The plot is "relatively weak," found Nancy Pearl in *Booklist,* yet it fades in importance next to "Gold's terrific ear for dialogue, his dead-on insights into the angst of growing up and growing old," and his artistry at evoking life in San Francisco. A *Publishers Weekly* writer was more concerned with the weak plot, stating that it weighed down the book despite the "small gems of insight, humor and local color" sprinkled throughout.

Judged more favorably by many critics was Gold's novel *Daughter Mine,* published in 2000. It is "free-wheeling in scope and unafraid of pathos," advised a *Publishers Weekly* writer. The plot concerns Dan Shaper, a sloppy, middle-aged bachelor who works as a courtroom translator. His life is shaken up when an attractive nineteen-year-old named Amanda arrives at his door, with the news that she is his daughter, the result of a brief tryst many years before. Amanda is now working in a bordello that passes itself off as a medical clinic, and her life is intertwined with that of D'Wayne, her boyfriend and pimp. *LosAngeles Times* critic Michael Harris also found the plot thin, but added that Gold renders his characters "with enormous gusto; they're so charming and raffish." Roger Harris, a contributor to the *Star-Ledger* added: "His specialty is humor, the kind that comes from interaction of characters. In this one, he displays fine technique not only with a clash between generations but between the hip and the square. It is all done very well and with great sympathy for everyone, including the grifters and semi-outlaws of San Francisco."

In McFadden's estimation, Gold's strengths as a fiction writer include "his talent for making high drama of ordinary events, ordinary experience." Bette Pesetsky, writing in the *New York Times Book Review,* cited his gifts as a "natural storyteller," including a "rhythmic dialogue" and a "voice that sustains." Kenneth Turan of the *Washington Post Book World* listed Gold's "ability as an observer of the social scene, his eye for cultural detail and nuance" as one of his strengths. Gold's "writing style, smooth, seductive and sly, carefully constructed to pull the reader along with a minimum of strain" is another of his assets, Turan concluded. Charyn saw Gold's "particular strength" as "the intimacy of detail that he establishes between himself and the reader. . . . In his very best work, . . . he establishes a sad but powerful voice, the wound of isolation, that is slowly dying within and around us." Cook described Gold, simply, as "one of the most gifted writers in America."

Gold once told *CA:* "When I first began to write, I thought I'd crack the egg and discover the secrets of the universe. Now I keep digging into the shell and discovering new nourishments. It's a game in dead earnest and it keeps me fed, surprised, and entertained. I'm doing the best I can to share the pleasure with readers. (Bottomless egg.)"

BIOGRAPHICAL AND CRITICAL SOURCES:

BOOKS

Allen, Walter, editor, *The Modern Novel in Britain and the United States,* Dutton (New York, NY), 1965.

Balakian, Nona and Charles Simmons, editors, *The Creative Present,* Doubleday (Garden City, NY), 1963.

Contemporary Fiction in America and England, 1950-1970, Gale (Detroit, MI), 1976.

Contemporary Literary Criticism, Gale (Detroit, MI), Volume 4, 1975, Volume 7, 1977, Volume 14, 1980, Volume 42, 1987.

Contemporary Novelists, St. James Press (Detroit, MI), 2001.

Dictionary of Literary Biography, Volume 2: *American Novelists since World War II,* Gale (Detroit, MI), 1978.

Dictionary of Literary Biography Yearbook: 1981, Gale (Detroit, MI), 1982.

Fiction!: Interviews with Northern California Novelists, Harcourt (New York, NY), 1976.

Hassan, Ihab, *Radical Innocence: Studies in the Contemporary American Novel,* Princeton University Press (Princeton, NJ), 1961.

Hicks, Granville, and Jack Alan Robbins, *Literary Horizons: A Quarter Century of American Fiction,* New York University Press (New York, NY), 1970.

Moore, Harry T., *Contemporary American Novelists,* Southern Illinois University Press (Carbondale, IL), 1964.

Nemerov, Howard, *Poetry and Fiction: Essays by Howard Nemerov,* Rutgers University Press (New Brunswick, NJ), 1963.

Newquist, Roy, *Counterpoint,* Simon & Schuster (New York, NY), 1964.

Solotaroff, Theodore, *The Red Hot Vacuum and Other Pieces on the Writing of the Sixties,* Atheneum (New York, NY), 1970.

Weinberg, Helen, *The New Novel in America: The Kafkan Mode in Contemporary Fiction,* Cornell University Press (Ithaca, NY), 1970.

Widmer, Kingsley, *The Literary Rebel,* Southern Illinois University Press (Carbondale, IL), 1965.

PERIODICALS

America, April 15, 1967.
Atlantic, April, 1956.

Best Sellers, June, 1979.

Booklist, March 15, 1993, Donna Seaman, review of *Bohemia: Where Art, Angst, Love and Strong Coffee Meet,* p. 1290; June 1, 1997, Nancy Pearl, review of *She Took My Arm As if She Loved Me,* p. 1656.

Books and Bookmen, February, 1968; October, 1974.
Book Week, April 9, 1967.
Chicago Tribune Book World, June 15, 1980; October 4, 1981.
Christian Science Monitor, March 23, 1967.
Columbia, summer, 1980.
Detroit News, April 12, 1981; June 14, 1981; September 27, 1981.
Figaro Litteraire, number 20, 1965.
Harper's, February, 1970; November, 1974.
Hudson Review, summer, 1967; winter, 1974-75.
Les Langues Modernes, number 58, 1964.
Library Journal, May 1, 1986, Marcia R. Hoffman, review of *Lovers & Cohorts: Twenty-seven Stories,* p. 131; August, 1986, Marcia R. Hoffman, review of *A Girl of Forty,* p. 169; November 15, 1989, Timothy L. Zindel, review of *Travels in San Francisco,* p. 101; February 15, 1991, Marlene M. Kuhl, review of *Best Nightmare on Earth: A Life in Haiti,* p. 213; March 1, 1993, William Gargan, review of *Bohemia,* p. 76; June 1, 1997, Mary Ellen Elsbernd, review of *She Took My Arm As If She Loved Me,* p. 146.

Life, April 7, 1967.
Listener, September 7, 1978.
Los Angeles Times, April 13, 1981; August 1, 2000, Michael Harris, review of *Daughter Mine,* p. E4.
Los Angeles Times Book Review, June 1, 1980; October 25, 1981; December 5, 1982; October 14, 1984; May 4, 1986, p. 3; April 17, 1988, p. 2; February 3, 1991, p. 6.
Midstream, April, 1975.
Nation, October 6, 1951; June 23, 1956; April 25, 1959; July 3, 1967; May 24, 1993, Dan Wakefield, review of *Bohemia,* p. 706.
National Observer, March 27, 1967; March 2, 1970.
New Leader, May 22, 1967.
New Republic, June 17, 1967.
Newsweek, March 27, 1967; January 26, 1970; October 16, 1972.
New Yorker, September 15, 1986, review of *A Girl of Forty,* p. 119.
New York Herald Tribune Book Review, March 27, 1960.

New York Review of Books, June 1, 1967; May 21, 1970.

New York Times, February 19, 1956; October 20, 1972; June 6, 1980; September 26, 1985.

New York Times Book Review, February 14, 1954; September 4, 1966; March 19, 1967; October 19, 1969; January 25, 1970; October 15, 1972; September 15, 1974; May 22, 1977; April 22, 1979; May 25, 1980; December 13, 1981; December 12, 1982; June 12, 1983, review of *True Love,* p. 37; November 11, 1984; April 20, 1986, Hilma Wolitzer, review of *Lovers & Cohorts,* p. 11; p. 11; August 10, 1986, p. 11; August 17, 1986, p. 32; July 26, 1987, Patricia T. O'Conner, review of *A Girl of Forty,* p. 24; March 27, 1988, p. 9; August 11, 1991, pp. 3, 18; April 11, 1993, p. 17; February 8, 1998, Emily Barton, review of *She Took My Arm As if She Loved Me,* p. 18.

Publishers Weekly, September 21, 1984, review of *Mister White Eyes,* p. 90; July 12, 1985, Genevieve Stuttaford, review of *San Francisco,* p. 43; August 30, 1985, review of *Stories of Misbegotten Love,* p. 418; February 14, 1986, Sybil Steinberg, review of *Lovers & Cohorts,* p. 70; June 6, 1986, Sybil Steinberg, review of *A Girl of Forty,* p. 57; August 1, 1986, Patrick Burnson, interview with Herbert Gold, p. 60; January 29, 1988, Sybil Steinberg, review of *Dreaming,* p. 416; December 22, 1989, Genevieve Stuttaford, review of *Travels in San Francisco,* p. 51; January 4, 1991, Genevieve Stuttaford, review of *Best Nightmare on Earth,* p. 63; February 8, 1993, review of *Bohemia,* p. 65; May 5, 1997, review of *She Took My Arm As If She Loved Me,* p. 198; May 29, 2000, review of *Daughter Mine,* p. 50.

San Francisco Chronicle, June 15, 1997, Brad Newsham, "Life in San Francisco Spills Out from a Table at Enrico's," p. 5.

Saturday Review, April 2, 1960; April 20, 1963; March 25, 1967; July 23, 1977.

Saturday Review of Education, November 11, 1972.

Spectator, August 12, 1978.

Star-Ledger (Newark, NJ), July 23, 2000, Roger Harris, review of *Daughter Mine,* p. 4.

Time, March 31, 1967; October 16, 1972; September 1, 1986, p. 85.

Times Literary Supplement, June 28, 1991, p. 24.

Virginia Quarterly Review, summer, 1970.

Vogue, April 1, 1967.

Washington Post Book World, June 3, 1979; June 15, 1980; January 8, 1983; February 4, 1990, p. 13.

Writer's Digest, September, 1972.

Yale Review, autumn, 1967.

*   *   *

GOLDEN, Arthur 1956-

PERSONAL: Born 1956, in Chattanooga, TN; married Trudy Legge, 1982; children: two. *Education:* Harvard College, B.A. (art history); Columbia University, M.A. (Japanese history), 1980; Boston University, M.A. (English), 1988. *Hobbies and other interests:* Classical guitar.

ADDRESSES: Home—P.O. Box 419, Brookline, MA 02446.

CAREER: Writer. Worked for an English-language magazine in Tokyo, 1980-82.

WRITINGS:

Memoirs of a Geisha, Knopf (New York, NY), 1997.

ADAPTATIONS: Memoirs of a Geisha was recorded as an audiobook, Random House (New York, NY), 1997. *Memoirs of a Geisha* has been translated into thirty-three languages, and rights were sold for an American film adaptation in 1997 to Red Wagon Productions.

WORK IN PROGRESS: A historical novel set in the United States.

SIDELIGHTS: Arthur Golden made a splash when he came on the literary scene in 1997 with the publication of his novel *Memoirs of a Geisha,* the fictional autobiography of a Japanese geisha during the 1920s and 1930s. A phenomenal best seller, this novel sold more than four million copies in English alone in a little over three years and has been translated into thirty-three languages. Many reviewers have praised the work for its portrayal of an obscure and little-understood part of Japanese culture and have marveled that a white American male should write such a work. *Newsweek* reviewer Jeff Giles called it "a faux autobiography ten years and 2,300 pages in the making. . . .

Arthur Golden

A few reservations aside, Golden has written a novel that's full of cliffhangers great and small, a novel that is never out of one's possession, a novel that refuses to stay shut." Film rights were sold to an American motion picture company, and work proceeded slowly on the project, which was still a work-in-progress in 2004.

Golden was raised in a literary family; his cousin Arthur Ochs Sulzberger is publisher of the *New York Times.* After earning a bachelor's degree in art history from Harvard University, a master's degree in Japanese history from Columbia University, and another master's degree in English from Boston University, Golden worked for an English-language magazine in Tokyo from 1980 to 1982. While in Japan, he met a man whose mother was a geisha and found the topic interesting. When Golden began toying with the idea of writing a novel, he remembered the intrigue he had felt about geishas and believed the topic would adapt well to a fictional treatment. Although an oft-taught tenet of writing is to write about topics the writer

knows, Golden decided it was "better to write about what sparks . . . [the] imagination," he told *Maclean's* writer Tanya Davies, "and the geisha district in Kyoto, Japan, sparked mine."

Golden is well-versed in the Japanese language, and even in Mandarin Chinese, so the language posed no barrier to his research. After conducting copious research about geishas in secondary sources, he embarked on the writing of a third-person novel that begins with the son of a geisha as a child. He discarded the novel when he decided that the geisha as the central character would be more interesting. Golden began his "second" novel after meeting Mineko Iwasaki, who had been a geisha during the 1960s and 1970s. From Iwasaki, whom he interviewed for several weeks, Golden learned details of geisha life that helped in the writing of the new version; but the second version, also in third-person, earned the epithet of "dry" from several of Golden's friends, who are professional writers. Not wanting to give up on a project with six years of effort invested, Golden rethought the novel, obsessing over it for a week. Finally he decided to make the leap to writing in first-person, which turned out to be the right move.

Even so, Golden knew that he had several cultural divides to bridge and that the success of his endeavor would be judged by how well he managed these issues: another and non-Western culture, another time period, and another gender. Even after deciding on the first-person voice and relying on his new research, Golden had to find a way to integrate the information needed by non-Japanese readers to understand the culture. The solution turned out to be placing his Japanese heroine in the West and employing the device of a fictional translator, as Golden explained at the Random House Web site: "The content is entirely fiction, although the historic facts of a geisha's life are accurate. The translator is also an invention. . . . I had to find a way to make it believable for Sayuri to annotate the story as she told it. . . . I wanted the reader to know from the beginning of the book that she is living in New York City, telling her story, looking back at her life . . . and talking to a Westerner. Under these circumstances, she would naturally annotate her story as she told it."

As Joanne Wilkinson wrote in *Booklist,* Golden "melds sparkling historical fiction with a compelling coming-of-age story." The work recounts the tale of young

Chiyo Sakamoto, born to a poor family in a Japanese fishing village. Following their mother's death during the depression years, their father sells nine-year-old Chiyo and her older sister Satsu. Satsu's fate is to become a prostitute, but the lovely Chiyo is bought by the madam of the Nitta okiya. Chiyo learns music, dance, and the tea ceremony, and wears the heavy costumes and makeup of the geisha. Her beauty soon surpasses that of the scheming Hatsumomo, until then the okiya's head geisha. Chiyo loses her virginity to a man who pays a record price in a bidding war.

Many reviewers discussed the author's ability to adequately portray the thoughts and feelings of a woman. "What is striking about the novel is Mr. Golden's creation of an utterly convincing narrator, a woman who is, at once, a traditional product of Japan's archaic gender relations and a spirited . . . heroine," wrote Michiko Kakutani in the *New York Times Book Review*. "Mr. Golden allows her to relate her story in chatty, colloquial terms that enable the reader to identify with her feelings of surprise, puzzlement and disgust at the rituals she must endure. . . . Mr. Golden gives us not only a richly sympathetic portrait of a woman, but also a finely observed picture of an anomalous and largely vanished world." Chiyo is tutored by Mameha, a renowned geisha, and becomes very successful during the 1930s and 1940s. As a professional, she takes a new name, Sayuri. After many men and years, she becomes mistress of the Chairman of an electrical supply company, whom she first met in the okiya; and he cares for her until his death. Golden has often been asked about the role of geisha in Japan as compared to the Western notion of the prostitute; he likens the geisha, to a mistress maintained by a single lover in Western culture.

Not all reviewers found Golden's characters convincing, however. While *New Leader* critic Gabriel Brownstein praised Golden's use of inanimate details, he found that his characters "fail to convey any emotional, psychological or historical complexities. His narrative is imposed on an exotic world rather than organic to it" and felt Sayuri's desire for the Chairman "is not demonstrated through the logic of the story either. She merely reiterates it in a series of widely spaced asides to the reader." Almost as if answering Brownstein's critique, Golden, commented in an *Amazon.com* interview: "I was not able . . . to really create a fully developed character in the Chairman. . . . Because my father and mother divorced when I was young, my

father moved away when I was seven or eight, died when I was thirteen, and for some reason I suppose it's emotionally toxic territory. And I just have a difficult time writing about it. And the Chairman was in many ways based upon my father. . . . When the Chairman was on the page, things were inert. I had so much trouble trying to create a believable person!"

Other reviewers also found fault with Golden's characterizations, including John David Morley, who wrote in *Working Woman* that Golden's "decision to write an autobiographically styled novel rather than a nonfiction portrait is most obviously justified in terms of empathy. . . . Unfortunately, Sayuri's personality seems so familiar it is almost generic. . . . What about the woman inside the sumptuous kimono, underneath the white mask?" Morley said the character Hatsumomo has "the potential one looks for and finds wanting in the heroine . . . with as many bad sides as Sayuri has good ones." Morley felt that if Golden "had been willing to develop this richer, more complex character, he might have been able to rouse the kind of empathy the novel needs—and perhaps one or two other qualities besides. Eroticism, for example." Morley said the book is much more successful with its facts, "filled as it is with colorful nuggets of information."

Much of the novel's verisimilitude results from Golden's use of detail, as Golden himself told Repps Hudson of the *St. Louis Post-Dispatch,* "Absolutely everything's in the details. The book will fail, at least by my standards, if you don't get the details right." Lindsley Cameron wrote of Sayuri in the *Yale Review:* "By the time she is living happily ever after at the Waldorf, the reader has learned quite a lot about geisha culture. . . . Many of these 'facts' are sartorial: not since reading the memoirs of that delightful seventeenth-century transvestite the Abbe de Choisy . . . have I encountered such drooling dwelling on the details of costume. The effect is piquant, something like reading soft-core pornography that keeps turning, as though in a dream, into the catalogue of a textile auction at Christie's." Brownstein also contended that Golden "is masterful at describing teahouses, hairdressers' shops and alleyways of Gion, the Geisha district of Kyoto. He excels, too, at teaching us about the way geisha put on makeup, the stages of their education and how they earn their living." "The meticulous research makes Gion come alive," wrote Hannah Beech in *Time International.* "Hatsumomo slathers on facial cream made of nightingale droppings, and geishas burn one-hour incense sticks to keep track of how much to bill per night. . . . Like a geisha who has mastered the art of illusion, Golden creates a cloistered floating world out of the engines of a modernizing Japan." Among the work's other enthusiasts was *Library Journal*'s Wilda Williams, who asserted that Golden "has brilliantly revealed the culture and traditions of an exotic world, closed to most Westerners," and a *Publishers Weekly* reviewer, who wrote, *Memoirs* is "rendered with stunning clarity. . . . Golden effortlessly spins the tale."

Memoirs of a Geisha sparked controversy in one arena. In 2000, after publication of the Japanese translation, former geisha Mineko Iwasaki brought suit against Golden for supposedly breaching her promised anonymity and for libeling her. "I spent seven to eight hours a day for two weeks talking to him, but he did not get anything right," Iwasaki complained to *U.S. News & World Report*'s Joseph L. Galloway. Because of the fictional memoir format, used in the West in such classic works as *Robinson Crusoe* and *Moll Flanders* and because of the author's acknowledgment of Iwasaki's help at the book's opening, Iwasaki contended that Japanese readers believe she has done everything the main character of the book has done. In 2002 Iwasaki published her own memoir, *Geisha of Gion*. Golden has continually maintained that although Iwasaki influenced his portrayal of Sayuri in *Memoirs of a Geisha*, the "character of Sayuri and her story are completely invented," as he wrote in the preface to *Memoirs of a Geisha*.

After *Memoirs of a Geisha*, Golden began work on another historical novel, this time to be set in the United States. As he told Hudson, "My pep talk to myself now is that I did this by permitting myself to take a risk and giving myself a real challenge and figuring out how to rise to it. My job now is to do exactly the same thing."

BIOGRAPHICAL AND CRITICAL SOURCES:

PERIODICALS

Booklist, September 1, 1997, Joanne Wilkinson, review of *Memoirs of a Geisha,* p. 7.

Commonweal, December 3, 1999, Robin Antepara, review of *Memoirs of a Geisha,* p. 25; April 1, 2000, Brad Hooper, review of *Memoirs of a Geisha,* p. 1442.

Daily Telegraph (London, England), August 4, 2001, Colin Joyce, "The Real Memoirs of a Geisha," p. 18.

Entertainment, January 23, 1998, p. 59; February 19, 1999, review of *Memoirs of a Geisha,* p. 128.

Globe and Mail (Toronto, Canada), April 17, 1999, review of *Memoirs of a Geisha,* p. D17.

Kirkus Reviews, August 15, 1997, review of *Memoirs of a Geisha,* pp. 1240-1241.

Kliatt Young Adult Paperback Book Guide, January, 1999, review of *Memoirs of a Geisha* (audio version), p. 46; March, 1999, review of *Memoirs of a Geisha* (audio version), p. 58.

Library Journal, August, 1997, Wilda Williams, review of *Memoirs of a Geisha,* p. 128; February 15, 1999, R. Kent Rasmussen, review of *Memoirs of a Geisha* (audio version), p. 200.

Los Angeles Times, November 30, 1997, review of *Memoirs of a Geisha,* p. 8; February 15, 1999, Elizabeth Mehren, "Geisha a Golden Moment for Author," p. NA; April 26, 2001, Elizabeth Mehren, "Geisha Charges Writer's Fiction Is Her Truth," p. E-1.

Maclean's, March 1, 1999, Tanya Davies, "A Crosscultural King of the Kimonos," p. 53.

New Leader, November 3, 1997, Gabriel Brownstein, review of *Memoirs of a Geisha,* p. 18.

Newsweek, October 13, 1997, Jeff Giles, review of *Memoirs of a Geisha,* p. 76.

New Yorker, September 29, 1997, review of *Memoirs of a Geisha,* pp. 82-83.

New York Times, January 7, 1999, Sheryl WuDunn, "A Japanese Version of *Geisha*? Well It May Sound Easy," p. E2; June 19, 2001, Calvin Sims, "A Geisha, a Successful Novel and a Lawsuit," p. E1.

New York Times Book Review, October 14, 1997, Michiko Kakutani, review of *Memoirs of a Geisha,* p. 32; February 14, 1999, review of *Memoirs of a Geisha* (audio version), p. 32.

People, December 1, 1997, Lan N. Nguyen, review of *Memoirs of a Geisha,* p. 49.

Publishers Weekly, December 16, 1996, review of *Memoirs of a Geisha,* p. 25; August 11, 1997, p. 255; July 28, 1997, review of *Memoirs of a Geisha,* p. 49; July 1, 2001, "Second Golden Signing at Knopf," p. 14.

Romance Reader, February 9, 1999, review of *Memoirs of a Geisha* p. ONL.

St. Louis Post-Dispatch (St. Louis, MO), February 22, 1999, Repps Hudson, "It's All in the Details," p. E1.

Sunday Times (London, England), April 29, 2001, Cherry Norton, "Betrayal of a Geisha," p. 14.

Time International, March 30, 1998, Hannah Beech, review of *Memoirs of a Geisha,* p. 49.

Times Literary Supplement, December 12, 1997, review of *Memoirs of a Geisha,* p. 21.

U.S. News & World Report, March 13, 2000, Joseph L. Galloway, "Protests of a Geisha," p. 12.

Wall Street Journal, April 25, 2001, "Former Geisha Sues Author, Random House over Book," p. B10.

Washington Post Book World, February 27, 1999, review of *Memoirs of a Geisha,* p. 7.

Working Woman, October 5, 1997, John David Moreley, review of *Memoirs of a Geisha.*

Yale Review, January, 1998, Lindsley Cameron, review of *Memoirs of a Geisha,* pp. 167-178.

ONLINE

Amazon, http://www.amazon.com/ (1998), "Interview with Arthur Golden."

BBC Books, http://www.bbc.co.uk/ (August 6, 2003), Ruth Green, "Arthur Golden."

Behind the Books, http://www.randomhouse.com/vintage/ (May 8, 2003), Arthur Golden, "A Conversation with Arthur Golden."

CNN, http://www.cnn.com/books/ (March 23, 1999), Miles O'Brien, "A Talk with Arthur Golden."

*   *   *

Bo Goldman

GOLDMAN, Bo 1932-

PERSONAL: Born September 10, 1932, in New York, NY; son of Julian (a Broadway producer and proprietor of retail stores) and Lillian (a hat model; maiden name, Levy) Goldman; married Mab Ashforth (a jewelry designer), January 2, 1954; children: Mia, Amy, Diana, Jesse, Serena, Justin. *Education:* Princeton University, B.A., 1953.

ADDRESSES: Home—1065 Greenfield Rd., St. Helena, CA 94574. *Office*—CAA, 9830 Wilshire Blvd., Beverly Hills, CA 90212-1804. *Agent*—Arnold Stiefel, 9200 Sunset Blvd., Los Angeles, CA 90069.

CAREER: Columbia Broadcasting System (CBS-TV), New York, NY, associate producer of television program *Playhouse 90,* 1958-60; National Educational Television (NET-TV; now WNET-TV), New York, NY, writer and producer of television program *NET Playhouse,* 1970-71, writer and producer of television program *Theatre in America,* 1972-74; screenwriter, 1974—. *Military service:* U.S. Army, 1954-56; became sergeant.

MEMBER: Writers Guild of America, Academy of Motion Picture Arts and Sciences, Dramatists Guild, American Society of Composers, Authors, and Publishers.

AWARDS, HONORS: Academy Award for best screenplay from Academy of Motion Picture Arts and Sciences, 1976, for *One Flew over the Cuckoo's Nest,* and 1981, for *Melvin and Howard;* screen award for best screenplay from Writers Guild of America, 1976, for *One Flew over the Cuckoo's Nest,* and 1981, for *Melvin and Howard*; Film Critics award, 1981, for *Melvin and Howard*; American Film Institute poll named *One Flew over the Cuckoo's Nest* among the ten best films of all time; Golden Globe Award for best screenplay, 1992, for *Scent of a Woman.*

WRITINGS:

SCREENPLAYS

(With Lawrence Hauben) *One Flew over the Cuckoo's Nest* (adapted from the novel of the same title by Ken Kesey), United Artists, 1974.

(With Bill Kerby) *The Rose,* Twentieth Century-Fox, 1979.

Melvin and Howard, Universal Pictures, 1980.

Shoot the Moon, Metro-Goldwyn-Mayer (MGM), 1982.

Little Nikita, Columbia/Tristar, 1988.

Scent of a Woman, Universal Pictures, 1992.

(With Ken Lipper, Paul Schrader, and Nicholas Pileggi) *City Hall,* Columbia Pictures, 1996.

(With Ron Osborn, Jeff Reno, and Kevin Wade) *Meet Joe Black,* Universal Pictures, 1998.

Imaging Nathan (also titled *Children of Angelsl*), Universal, 1999.

(With William D. Wittliff) *The Perfect Storm,* Warner, 2000.

Lyricist, with Glenn Paxton, of *First Impressions* (two-act musical; based on Jane Austen's novel *Pride and Prejudice*), first produced on Broadway at the Alvin Theatre, March, 1959, and with Glenn Paxton, of "Hurrah, Boys, Hurrah," a Civil War musical, as yet unpublished and unproduced. Contributor of articles to the *New York Times.*

SIDELIGHTS: Bo Goldman began his career as an associate producer for *Playhouse 90* on CBS-TV. When he turned to writing, first with lyrics for the 1959 Broadway musical *First Impressions,* little did he know what lay ahead. Goldman achieved commercial and critical success with his 1975 first motion picture screenplay, an adaptation of Ken Kesey's novel *One Flew over the Cuckoo's Nest,* for which he earned an Academy Award in 1976 for best screenplay. Goldman went on to create a handful of other motion pictures. In addition to the Academy Award-winning *Melvin*

and Howard, he wrote *Scent of a Woman, City Hall,* and *Meet Joe Black.* At the turn of the millennium, Goldman was one of the highest-paid screenwriters in Hollywood, earning a million dollars per film, and in demand as both a screenwriter and script doctor.

One Flew over the Cuckoo's Nest the film features Jack Nicholson in the role of McMurphy, a rebellious convict who feigns insanity in order to get transferred out of prison and into a mental hospital. Having outwitted the authorities, McMurphy becomes a psychiatric case study at the state mental institution, where he anticipates a comfortable stay. Instead, he encounters a formidable enemy in the character of Nurse Ratched, whose cold domination of the other patients provokes McMurphy's temper and fuels his rebellion. He becomes a liberating force in the ward, turning "daily group therapy sessions from a mass of groveling psychic surrender into a screaming strike for civil rights," observed *Newsweek* critic Jack Kroll. McMurphy's stunts—including a party he organizes, complete with prostitutes and liquor—come to an end when, in his final confrontation with Nurse Ratched, he nearly strangles the woman to death. A lobotomy is then performed on McMurphy, after which he dies at the hands of one his fellow patients who suffocates the hero in an act of mercy.

Evaluating Goldman's screen adaptation of Kesey's 1962 novel, *New Yorker*'s Pauline Kael wrote: "The movie is much less theatrical than the romantic, strong-arming book, yet it keeps you attentive, stimulated, up." Stanley Kauffmann remarked in the *New Republic* that "even Kesey didn't go as far as the film script does in its . . . implications that mental trouble is a kind of health, in its simplistic (and weary) allegory of the mental hospital as the world with the patients as the People struggling against Authority, the mental staff." Kroll disagreed, however, calling *Cuckoo's Nest* a "well-made film that flares at times into incandescence but lacks ultimately the novel's passion, insight and complexity."

Goldman followed *One Flew over the Cuckoo's Nest* with *The Rose,* his 1979 screenplay about an emotionally drained female performer who reacts against the pressures of fame in a series of impulsive—and ultimately self-destructive—acts. The film, according to the *New York Times*'s Janet Maslin, "takes the form of a crazy flashback": Rose kidnaps her chauffeur and parades through homosexual nightclubs and men's bathhouses, displaying what Maslin called "her feistiness," a quality that "emerges as one of [the character's] most lovable attributes." These incidents, however, signal the heroine's increasing sense of desperation, culminating in a suicidal heroin overdose. "For the first time in a backstage story we get a sense of just how physically tough the entertainment business really is," wrote Gene Siskel in the *Chicago Tribune.* "At its heart," the reviewer added, *The Rose* is "a routine show biz saga of the lonely life at the top of the heap. It perpetuates the myth that a successful female entertainer must be a hard woman who's unlucky in love." Maslin remarked that the film has "so many finely drawn episodes, so much brittle, raunchy humor. . . . *The Rose* has an earnest, affecting character at its core. Even at its most preposterous, it never feels like a fraud."

Goldman derived the premise for his 1980 screenplay, *Melvin and Howard,* from milkman Melvin Dummar's real-life claim that he rescued and befriended millionaire Howard Hughes, for which he was subsequently included in Hughes's will. The validity of the will was questioned, however, and it was never admitted to probate. The movie begins with Hughes racing his motorcycle across the Nevada desert. He has an accident, after which Dummar finds the injured man alongside the interstate. Unaware of the millionaire's identity, Dummar drives him to Las Vegas and eight years later, after Hughes's death, a will naming Dummar as beneficiary surfaces. According to *New Statesman* critic John Coleman, the film depicts Dummar as "a candid, largely uncomprehending but ever hopeful hick" in his plight as an average citizen struggling to live the American dream. "Goldman has tried to imagine what might have imprinted the encounter on Hughes's mind and persuaded him to become the silent benefactor" of Dummar—"a humble obscurity full of high hopes and prone to repeated failure," wrote Gary Arnold in the *Washington Post.* And, Kael proclaimed *Melvin and Howard* an "almost flawless act of sympathetic imagination," adding that the film's dialogue "is as near perfection as script dialogue gets—it's always funny, without any cackling."

Shoot the Moon, heralded by Kael as "a movie about separating that is perhaps the most revealing American movie of the era," contains touches of humor that recall Goldman's earlier screenplays. The 1982 film focuses on Faith and George Dunlap and the disintegration of their fifteen-year marriage. Buffeted between their parents' marital problems are the Dunlaps' four school-age daughters, who serve to illustrate not only the traumatic effects of the family situation, but who also provide levity—and what Kauffmann termed "emotional relief." *New York Times* reviewer Vincent Canby called *Shoot the Moon* a "domestic comedy of sometimes terrifying implications, not about dolts but intelligent, thinking beings." Kael also hailed it as "a modern movie in terms of its consciousness, and in its assumption that the members of the movie audience, like the readers of modern fiction, share in that consciousness." Moreover, *Rolling Stone*'s Michael Sragow lauded the work, dubbing it "the most complex, poetic, and moving study of an American marriage ever filmed."

Scent of a Woman, which *Entertainment Weekly*'s Owen Glieberman described as "an epic picaresque in the tradition of *Rain Man,*" with a "pleasingly literate script," follows the story of an aging and blind former military man, Frank Slade. Slade, played by Al Pacino, plans to commit suicide after enjoying a last fling, in the company of his aide, the prep school student Charley, who has been hired to assist him. On the other end of the spectrum, *Commonweal* reviewer Richard Alleva found the screenplay predictable, as Slade and Charley help each other resolve their conflicts. He dubbed the film simply a vehicle for Al Pacino, which in his view is "the fundamental reason why it's such a lousy script." Whatever its supposed flaws, the script garnered a Golden Globe award for Goldman and an Academy Award for Pacino.

Goldman was was one four writers to work on the screenplay of the 1996 motion picture *City Hall,* starring Al Pacino as New York mayor John Pappas. In what *Time*'s Richard Corliss described as a "cluttered drama that imagines a Faustian battle between Pappas and his deputy mayor Kevin Calhoun" (played by John Cusack), the action revolves around the political fallout of an accidental shooting of a six-year-old black boy during a shoot-out between police and a drug dealer. Several reviewers remarked that while the film had all the ingredients of success, it did not quite cohere. For example, *Newsweek* writer Jack Kroll suggested that the film suffers from "the classic Hollywood too-many-cooks disease" and cited lack of tension as the film's main flaw. "Goldman and [director] Becker are in love with moral ambiguity," Kroll contended; "they caress it rather than dramatize it." Calling *City Hall* "neither a nostalgic valentine to machine politics nor a truly incisive exploration of urban political power," *Cineaste*'s Leonard Quart determined it to be "an uneasy hybrid . . . [whose] ambitious evocation of urban political maneuverings and operations is subsumed by a convoluted, confusing political thriller with little dramatic tension or payoff." Quart continued, "It's a film which contains many strong, pointed scenes, both authentic and revelatory, about the nature of the political process. . . . But the film never quite comes together, being overall much more flaccid and conventional than its few powerful scenes and subtle, knowing depictions of what it means to be an urban politician." What tension that exists, according to *New Republic*'s Stanley Kauffmann, comes from "an attempt to explore political truths and obeisance to the attention span of today's audience." Kauffmann compared *City Hall* to the popular television drama *Law and Order,* and although he found the film mostly successful in its ability to draw in the viewer, he called the ending implausible.

The 1998 film *Meet Joe Black,* based loosely on the 1920s stage play *Death Takes a Holiday,* stars Brad Pitt as Death (a.k.a. Joe Black) and Anthony Hopkins as the media mogul whose time is up. When Joe falls in love with the mogul's daughter, the father gains the time he needs to put his media empire into safe care. *Meet Joe Black* was not a success at the box office, and several reviewers cited the film's excessive length and one-dimensional characters among its weaknesses. At *YourWorld,* Glenn Sequeira took a balanced approach in his criticism, remarking, "Some scenes were very powerful . . . other scenes cried out Monty Python." While Peter Travers of *Rolling Stone* quipped, "*Meet Joe Black* is a movie about death that stubbornly refuses to come to life," Sequeira concluded: "The movie has some merit, but would have benefited both from some consistency and judicious editing."

BIOGRAPHICAL AND CRITICAL SOURCES:

PERIODICALS

Chicago Tribune, November 9, 1979; February 13, 1981; February 9, 1982.

Cineaste, spring, 1996, Leonard Quart, review of *City Hall,* pp. 44-45.

Cinema (London, England), August, 1982.

City Limits (London, England), June 11, 1982, interview.

Commonweal, March 12, 1993, Richard Alleva, review of *Scent of a Woman,* pp. 12-13.

Cosmopolitan, February, 1993, Guy Flatley, review of *Scent of a Woman,* p. 14.

Entertainment, December 18, 1992, Owen Glieberman, review of *Scent of a Woman,* p. 42.

Film Comment, March-April, 1982.

Films (London, England), July, 1982.

Nation, November 29, 1975.

National Review, June 12, 1981; February 15, 1993, John Simon, review of *Scent of a Woman,* pp. 54-55.

New Republic, December 13, 1975; February 3, 1982; January 25, 1993, Stanley Kauffmann, review of *Scent of a Woman,* p. 29; March 18, 1996, Stanley Kauffmann, review of *City Hall,* p. 28; December 7, 1998, "Stanley Kauffman on Films: In the Midst of Life."

New Statesman, May 15, 1981.

Newsweek, November 24, 1975; January 25, 1982; December 28, 1992, David Ansen, review of *Scent of a Woman,* pp. 56-57; February 19, 1996, Jack Kroll, review of *City Hall,* p. 68.

New York, December 14, 1992, David Denby, review of *Scent of a Woman,* p. 89.

New Yorker, December 1, 1975; October 13, 1980; February 18, 1982; December 28, 1992, Terrence Rafferty, review of *Scent of a Woman,* pp. 198-199; February 19, 1996, Terrence Rafferty, review of *City Hall,* p. 99.

New York Times, November 20, 1975; November 25, 1975; December 21, 1975; November 7, 1979; May 20, 1981; January 22, 1982; May 20, 1983; March 18, 1988, Walter Goodman, review of *Little Nikita,* p. C26(L); December 23, 1992, Janet Maslin, review of *Scent of a Woman,* p. C9(L); February 25, 1993, Bernard Weinraub, "A Screenwriter Profits from His Years of Pain," p. C15(L); August 14, 1998, James Sterngold, "Death and Life," review of *Meet Joe Black,* p. E9; April 2, 1999, Janet Maslin, review of *Meet Joe Black,* p. E31; March 18, 2001, Jamie Malanowski, "Shaping Words into an Oscar: Six Writers Who Did," p. AR15(L).

People, April 18, 1988, Peter Travers, review of *Little Nikita,* p. 10.

Premiere, December, 1998, review of *Meet Joe Black,* p. 82.

Rolling Stone, March 18, 1982.

Saturday Review, January 10, 1976.

Stereo Review, July, 1999, Sol Louis Siegel, review of *Meet Joe Black,* p. 113.

Teen People, November, 1998, review of *Meet Joe Black,* p. 1.

Time, December 1, 1975; February 1, 1982; December 28, 1992, Richard Schickel and Richard Corliss, review of *Scent of a Woman,* p. 65; February 19, 1996, Richard Corliss, review of *City Hall,* p. 64.

Time South Pacific, March 22, 1999, "Death Be Not Proud," review of *Meet Joe Black,* p. 64.

Us, February, 1993, Lawrence Frascella, review of *Scent of a Woman,* pp. 89-90.

Variety, December 21, 1992, Todd McCarthy, review of *Scent of a Woman,* p. 61.

Wall Street Journal, January 7, 1993, Julie Salamon, review of *Scent of a Woman,* p. A12.

Washington Post, February 13, 1981; July 11, 1982.

ONLINE

Motion Picture Editors Guild Newsletter, http://www. editorsguild.com/ (September-October, 1995), "Helping Evolve the Script: An Interview with Bo Goldman."

Rolling Stone, http://www.rollingstone.com/ (August 8, 2003), Peter Travers, review of *Meet Joe Black.*

YourWorld, http://movies.yourworld.com/ (August 8, 2003), Glenn Sequeira, review of *Meet Joe Black.**

*   *   *

GOULD, Stephen Jay 1941-2002

PERSONAL: Born September 10, 1941, in New York, NY; died of cancer, May 20, 2002, in New York, NY; son of Leonard (a court reporter) and Eleanor (an artist; maiden name, Rosenberg) Gould; married Deborah Lee (an artist and writer), October 3, 1965; children: Jesse, Ethan. *Education:* Antioch College, A.B., 1963; Columbia University, Ph.D., 1967. *Hobbies and other interests:* Baseball.

CAREER: Antioch College, Yellow Springs, OH, instructor in geology, 1966; Harvard University, Cambridge, MA, assistant professor and assistant curator, 1967-71, associate professor and associate curator, 1971-73, professor of geology and curator of invertebrate paleontology at Museum of Comparative Zool-

Stephen Jay Gould

ogy, beginning 1973, Alexander Agassiz Professor of Zoology, beginning 1982. Member of advisory board, Children's Television Workshop, 1978-81, and *Nova* (television program), 1980-92.

MEMBER: American Association for the Advancement of Science, American Academy of Arts and Sciences, American Society of Naturalists (president, 1979-80), National Academy of Sciences, Paleontological Society (president, 1985-86), Society for the Study of Evolution (vice president, 1975; president, 1990), Society of Systematic Zoology, Society of Vertebrate Paleontology, History of Science Society, European Union of Geosciences (honorary foreign fellow), Society for the Study of Sports History, Royal Society of Edinburgh, Linnaean Society of London (foreign member), Sigma Xi.

AWARDS, HONORS: National Science Foundation, Woodrow Wilson, and Columbia University fellowships, 1963-67; Schuchert Award, Paleontological Society, 1975; National Magazine Award, 1980, for "This View of Life"; Notable Book citation, American Library Association, 1980, and National Book Award in science, 1981, both for *The Panda's Thumb: More Reflections in Natural History;* Scientist of the Year citation, *Discover,* 1981; National Book Critics Circle Award, and American Book Award nomination in science, both 1982, and outstanding book award, American Educational Research Association, 1983, all for *The Mismeasure of Man;* MacArthur Foundation Prize fellowship, 1981-86; medal of excellence, Columbia University, 1982; F. V. Haydn Medal, Philadelphia Academy of Natural Sciences, 1982; Joseph Priestley Award and Medal, Dickinson College, 1983; Neil Miner Award, National Association of Geology Teachers, 1983; silver medal, Zoological Society of London, 1984; Bradford Washburn Award and gold medal, Boston Museum of Science, 1984; distinguished service award, American Humanists Association, 1984; Tanner Lecturer, Cambridge University, 1984, and Stanford University, 1989; meritorious service award, American Association of Systematics Collections, 1984; Founders Council Award of Merit, Field Museum of Natural History, 1984; John and Samuel Bard Award, Bard College, 1984; Phi Beta Kappa Book Award in science, 1984, for *Hen's Teeth and Horse's Toes: Further Reflections in Natural History;* Sarah Josepha Hale Medal, 1986; creative arts award for nonfiction, Brandeis University, 1986; Terry Lecturer, Yale University, 1986; distinguished service award, American Geological Institute, 1986; Glenn T. Seaborg Award, International Platform Association, 1986; In Praise of Reason Award, Committee for the Scientific Investigation of Claims of the Paranormal, 1986; H. D. Vursell Award, American Academy and Institute of Arts and Letters, 1987; National Book Critics Circle Award nomination, 1987, for *Time's Arrow, Time's Cycle: Myth and Metaphor in the Discovery of Geological Time;* Anthropology in Media Award, American Anthropological Association, 1987; History of Geology Award, Geological Society of America, 1988; T. N. George Medal, University of Glasgow, 1989; Sue T. Friedman Medal, Geological Society of London, 1989; Distinguished Service Award, American Institute of Professional Geologists, 1989; fellow, Museum National d'Historie Naturelle (Paris, France), 1989; fellow, Royal Society of Edinburgh, 1990; City of Edinburgh Medal, 1990; Britannica Award and Gold Medal, 1990, for dissemination of public knowledge; Forkosch Award, Council on Democratic Humanism, and Phi Beta Kappa Book Award in Science, both 1990, and Pulitzer Prize finalist and Rhone-Poulenc Prize, both 1991, all for *Wonderful Life: The Burgess Shale and the Nature of History;* Iglesias Prize, 1991, for Italian translation of *The Mismeasure of Man;* Distinguished Service Award, National Association of Biology Teach-

ers, 1991; Golden Trilobite Award, Paleontological Society, 1992; Homer Smith Medal, New York University School of Medicine, 1992; University of California, Los Angeles medal, 1992; James T. Shea Award, National Association of Geology Teachers, 1992; Commonwealth Award in Interpretive Science, State of Massachusetts, 1993; J. P. McGovern Award and Medal in Science, Cosmos Club, 1993; St. Louis Libraries Literary Award, University of St. Louis, 1994; Gold Medal for Service to Zoology, Linnaean Society of London; Distinguished Service Medal, Teachers College, Columbia University. Recipient of numerous honorary degrees from colleges and universities.

WRITINGS:

NONFICTION

Ontogeny and Phylogeny, Belknap Press/Harvard University (Cambridge, MA), 1977.

Ever since Darwin: Reflections in Natural History (essays), Norton (New York, NY), 1977.

The Panda's Thumb: More Reflections in Natural History (essays), Norton (New York, NY), 1980.

(With Salvador Edward Juria and Sam Singer) *A View of Life,* Benjamin-Cummings (Menlo Park, CA), 1981.

The Mismeasure of Man, Norton (New York, NY), 1981, revised and expanded edition, 1996.

Hen's Teeth and Horse's Toes: Further Reflections in Natural History (essays), Norton (New York, NY), 1983.

The Flamingo's Smile: Reflections in Natural History (essays), Norton (New York, NY), 1985.

(With Rosamund Wolff Purcell) *Illuminations: A Bestiary,* Norton (New York, NY), 1986.

Time's Arrow, Time's Cycle: Myth and Metaphor in the Discovery of Geological Time, Harvard University Press (Cambridge, MA), 1987.

An Urchin in the Storm: Essays about Books and Ideas, Norton (New York, NY), 1987.

(With others) *Frederic Edwin Church,* National Gallery of Art (Washington, DC), 1989.

Wonderful Life: The Burgess Shale and the Nature of History, Norton (New York, NY), 1989.

The Individual in Darwin's World: The Second Edinburgh Medal Address, Edinburgh University Press (Edinburgh, Scotland), 1990.

Bully for Brontosaurus: Reflections in Natural History, Norton (New York, NY), 1991.

(With Rosamund Wolff Purcell) *Finders, Keepers: Eight Collectors,* Norton (New York, NY), 1992.

(Editor) *The Book of Life,* Norton (New York, NY), 1993.

Eight Little Piggies: Reflections in Natural History, Norton (New York, NY), 1993.

Dinosaur in a Haystack: Reflections in Natural History, Harmony Books (New York, NY), 1995.

Full House: The Spread of Excellence from Plato to Darwin, Harmony Books (New York, NY), 1996.

Questioning the Millennium: A Rationalist's Guide to a Precisely Arbitrary Countdown, Random House (New York, NY), 1997.

Leonardo's Mountain of Clams and the Diet of Worms: Essays on Natural History, Harmony (New York, NY), 1998.

(Contributor) *Melancholies of Knowledge: Literature in the Age of Science,* State University of New York Press, 1999.

Rocks of Ages: Science and Religion in the Fullness of Life, Ballantine (New York, NY), 1999.

(With Rosamond Wolff Purcell) *Crossing Over: Where Art and Science Meet,* Three Rivers Press (New York, NY), 2000.

The Lying Stones of Marrakech: Penultimate Reflections in Natural History, Harmony Books (New York, NY), 2000.

The Structure of Evolutionary Theory, Belknap Press/Harvard University Press (Cambridge, MA), 2002.

I Have Landed: The End of a Beginning in Natural History, Harmony Books (New York, NY), 2002.

The Hedgehog, the Fox, and the Magister's Pox: Mending the Gap between Science and the Humanities, Harmony Books (New York, NY), 2003.

Triumph and Tragedy in Mudville: A Lifelong Passion for Baseball, Norton (New York, NY), 2003.

Author of *An Evolutionary Microcosm: Pleistocene and Recent History of the Land Snail P. (Poecilozonites) in Bermuda,* &lsqbCambridge, MA], 1969. Also author, with Eric Lewin Altschuler, of *Bachanalia: The Essential Listener's Guide to Bach's "Well-Tempered Clavier."*

OTHER

(Editor, with Niles Eldredge) Ernst Mayr, *Systematics and the Origin of Species,* Columbia University Press (New York, NY), 1982.

(Editor, with Niles Eldredge) Theodosius Dobzhansky, *Genetics and the Origin of Species,* Columbia University Press (New York, NY), 1982.

(Author of foreword) Gary Larson, *The Far Side Gallery 3,* Andrews & McMeel (Fairway, KS), 1988.

(Editor) *Best American Essays,* Mariner Books, 2002.

Contributor to books, including *Models in Paleobiology,* edited by T. J. M. Schopf, Freeman, Cooper (San Francisco, CA), 1972; *The Evolutionary Synthesis: Perspectives on the Unification of Biology,* edited by Ernst Mayr, Harvard University Press (Cambridge, MA), 1980; *Darwin's Legacy: Nobel Conference XVIII, Gustavus Adolphus College, St. Peter, Minnesota,* edited by Charles L. Hamrum, Harper (New York, NY), 1983; *Between Home and Heaven: Contemporary American Landscape Photography,* National Museum of American Art (Washington, DC), 1992; and *Understanding Scientific Prose,* edited by Jack Selzer, University of Wisconsin Press (Madison, WI), 1993. Contributor to proceedings of the International Congress of Systematic and Evolutionary Biology Symposium, 1973; contributor to *Bulletin of the Museum of Comparative Zoology,* Harvard University, and contributor of numerous articles to scientific journals. Author of monthly column, "This View of Life," in *Natural History.*

General editor, *The History of Paleontology,* twenty volumes, Ayer, 1980; and *The Book of Life,* Norton (New York, NY), 1993. Associate editor, *Evolution,* 1970-72; member of editorial board, *Systematic Zoology,* 1970-72, *Paleobiology,* 1974-76, and *American Naturalist,* 1977-80; member of board of editors, *Science,* 1986-91.

SIDELIGHTS: Stephen Jay Gould, a Harvard University professor and evolutionary biologist, was renowned for his ability to translate difficult scientific theories into prose understandable to the layman. In his books and essays on natural history, Gould, a paleontologist and geologist by training, popularized his subjects without trivializing them, "simultaneously entertaining and teaching," according to James Gorman in the *New York Times Book Review.* With his dozen essay collections Gould won critical acclaim for bridging the gap between the advancing frontier of science and the literary world. With coauthor Rosamond Wolff Purcell, he addressed particularly the interface of art and science in the 2000 publication

Crossing Over: Where Art and Science Meet. "As witty as he is learned, Gould has a born essayist's ability to evoke the general out of fascinating particulars and to discuss important scientific questions for an audience of educated laymen without confusion or condescension," Gene Lyons commented in *Newsweek.* "What made Steve different was that he didn't make a cartoon out of science. He didn't talk down to people," Harvard professor Richard Lewontin told John Nichols of the *Nation.* "He communicated about science in a way that did not try to hide the complexities of the issues and that did not shy away from the political side of these issues. Steve's great talent was his ability to make sense of an issue at precisely the point when people needed that insight." Hallmarks of Gould's style include the use of metaphors and analogies from a variety of disciplines. Gould wrote a single draft on a typewriter, following a detailed outline, and editors soon learned not to touch his prose.

Gould's focus on the unexpected within nature reflects the worldview that permeates his entire body of work: that natural history is significantly altered by events out-of-the-ordinary and is largely revealed by examining its "imperfections." "Catastrophes contain continuities," explained Michael Neve in the *Times Literary Supplement.* "In fact Gould made it his business to see the oddities and small-scale disasters of the natural record as the actual historical evidence for taking evolution seriously, as a real event." Through imperfections, continued Neve, "we can . . . see how things have altered by looking at the way organic life is, as it were, cobbled together out of bits and pieces some of which work, but often only just." The thumb of the panda, highlighted in Gould's 1981 American Book Award-winning essay collection *The Panda's Thumb: More Reflections in Natural History,* particularly demonstrates this. Not really a thumb at all, the offshoot on the panda's paw is actually an enlarged wristbone that enables the animal to efficiently strip leaves from bamboo shoots. "If one were to design a panda from scratch, one would not adapt a wrist bone to do the job of a thumb," observed *Times Literary Supplement* reviewer D. M. Knight. An imperfection, the appendage "may have been fashioned by a simple genetic change, perhaps a single mutation affecting the timing and rate of growth."

Gould's writings also emphasize science as a "culturally embedded" discipline. "Science is not a heartless pursuit of objective information," he once told the *New York Times Book Review;* "it is a creative human activity." Raymond A. Sokolov, in the same publication, remarked that Gould's "method is at bottom, a kind of textual criticism of the language of earlier biologists, a historical analysis of their 'metaphors,' their concepts of the world." Gould frequently examines science as the output of individuals working within the confines of specific time periods and cultures. In a *New Yorker* review of *The Flamingo's Smile,* John Updike wrote of "Gould's evangelical sense of science as an advancing light, which gives him a vivid sympathy with thinkers in the dark." Updike continued: "Gould chastens us ungrateful beneficiaries of science with his affectionate and tactile sense of its strenuous progress, its worming forward through fragmentary revelations and obsolete debates, from relative darkness into relative light. Even those who were wrong win his gratitude." Sue M. Halpern noted in the *Nation:* "Gould is both a scientist and a humanist, not merely a scientist whose literary abilities enable him to build a narrow bridge between the two cultures in order to export the intellectual commodities of science to the other side. His writing portrays universal strivings, it expresses creativity and it reveals Gould to be a student of human nature as well as one of human affairs."

In his writing Gould also demonstrates instances where science, by factually "verifying" certain cultural prejudices, has been misused. *The Flamingo's Smile* contains several accounts of individuals victimized as a result of cultural prejudices used as scientific knowledge, such as the "Hottentot Venus," a black southern African woman whose anatomy was put on public display in nineteenth-century Europe, and Carrie Buck, an American woman who was legally sterilized in the 1920s because of a family history of mentally "unfit" individuals. And in his award-winning *Mismeasure of Man,* Gould focuses on the development of intelligence quotient (IQ) testing and debunks the work of scientists purporting to measure human intelligence objectively. "This book," writes Gould, "is about the abstraction of intelligence as a single entity, its location within the brain, its quantification as one number for each individual, and the use of these numbers to rank people in a single series of worthiness, invariably to find that oppressed or disadvantaged groups—races, classes or sexes—are innately inferior and deserve their status." Halpern pointed out that, "Implicit in Gould's writing is a binding premise: while the findings of science are themselves value-free, the uses to which they are put are not."

In a *London Review of Books* essay on *Hen's Teeth and Horse's Toes: Further Reflections in Natural History,* John Hedley Brooke summarized some of the major themes that appear in Gould's writings: "The 'fact' of evolution is 'proved' from those imperfections in living organisms which betray a history of descent. The self-styled 'scientific creationists' have no leg to stand on and are simply playing politics. Natural selection must not be construed as a perfecting principle in any strong sense of perfection. Neo-Darwinists who look to adaptive utility as the key to every explanation are as myopic as the natural theologians of the early 19th century who saw in the utility of every organ the stamp of its divine origin." Citing yet another recurrent theme, Brooke noted Gould's focus on "the extent to which the course of evolution has been constrained by the simple fact that organisms inherit a body structure and style of embryonic development which impose limits on the scope of transformation." This last principle was enhanced by Gould's field work with the Bahamian land snail genus *Cerion,* a group displaying a wide variety of shapes, in addition to a permanent growth record in its shell. "More orthodox evolutionists would assume that the many changes of form represent adaptations," noted James Gleick in the *New York Times Magazine.* "Gould denies it and finds explanations in the laws of growth. Snails grow the way they do because there are only so many ways a snail *can* grow."

Gould's *Wonderful Life: The Burgess Shale and the Nature of History* focuses on the fossil-rich remains discovered in a small area in the Canadian Rockies in 1909. The organisms preserved there display a much greater diversity than fossil sites from later eras, and their meaning has been hotly debated ever since their discovery. Gould chronicles the early studies of the Burgess Shale, then offers his own speculations on what the fossils reveal. In the process, he discredits the long-held notion that evolution is inevitably a progression toward higher and increasingly perfect life forms. Reviewing *Wonderful Life* in *New Statesman & Society,* Steven Rose related: "Far from being the mechanism of ordered transformation along a great chain of being towards adaptive perfection, evolution is a lottery in which winners and losers are determined by forces over which they have little control. Nearly everything is possible; what survives, including ourselves, confirms the truth that nothing in biology makes sense except in the context of history." High praise for *Wonderful Life* also came from Robin McKie, who wrote in the London *Observer* that

Gould's "book is written with such clarity and breathtaking leaps of imagination that it successfully moulds a mass of detail and arcane taxonomy into a lucid and highly entertaining whole." McKie took exception to Gould's contention that biologists have purposely presented evolution in anthropomorphic terms, yet McKie concluded that *"Wonderful Life* remains a masterly scientific explanation" of the Burgess Shale and evolution in general.

In essay collections such as *Eight Little Piggies: Reflections in Natural History, Bully for Brontosaurus: Reflections in Natural History,* and *Dinosaur in a Haystack: Reflections in Natural History,* Gould upheld the standards of accessibility and scientific integrity he set in earlier books. "What makes Gould so good?" Robert Kanigel asked in the *Washington Post Book World.* The critic went on to answer his own question: His essays transport readers "into a cozy little world where we are left in intimate touch with Gould's heart and mind. Gould is one part Harvard intellectual, nine parts curious little boy; that's one element of his distinctive appeal. For another, he has a commanding knowledge of his discipline, evolutionary biology, and the fields, like geology and paleontology, that flank it. He doesn't have to parade it around; but he has so much to draw upon, and does." Kanigel described Gould's characteristic technique: beginning with some odd fact and proceeding from there to sweeping insights as another special charm, along with his delight in interesting digressions. "This is a feast," declared Bryan C. Clarke in his *Nature* commentary on *Eight Little Piggies,* citing the work as "a lovely mixture of bizarre facts, nice arguments, clever insights into the workings of evolution and a quality of writing that can make your skin prickle."

While some reviewers have commented that Gould's writings display a repetition of key principles and themes—in critiquing *Hen's Teeth and Horse's Toes,* Brooke remarked that "the big implications may begin to sound familiar"—Gould earned consistent praise for the range of subjects through which he illustrates evolutionary principles. "Gould entices us to follow him on a multifaceted Darwinian hunt for answers to age-old questions about ourselves and the rest of the living world," commented John C. McLoughlin in the *Washington Post Book World.* "Like evolution itself, Gould explores possibilities—any that come to hand—and his range of interest is stupendous. . . . Throughout, he displays with force and elegance the power of evolutionary theory to link the phenomena of the living world as no other theory seems able." Steven Rose wrote in the *New York Times Book Review:* "Exploring the richness of living forms, Mr. Gould, and we, are constantly struck by the absurd ingenuity by which fundamentally inappropriate parts are pressed into new roles like toes that become hooves, or smell receptors that become the outer layer of the brain. Natural selection is not some grandiose planned event but a continual tinkering. . . . Gould's great strength is to recognize that, by demystifying nature in this way, he increases our wonder and our respect for the richness of life."

In a *New York Times Book Review* critique of *Full House: The Spread of Excellence from Plato to Darwin,* David Papineau stated that Gould's "central contention is that trends, in any area, should never be considered in isolation, but only as aspects of an overall range of variation (the full house of the title)." In terms of evolution, this means that the mechanism of natural selection does not always progress toward greater complexity; in fact, according to Gould, it is just as likely to run toward simplicity. Gould based this argument on "a very clear statistical insight. . . . The first is his own experience as a statistic, when he was a cancer patient. The second is an extended analysis of the disappearance of .400 batters in major league baseball," stated Lucy Horwitz in the *Boston Book Review,* who concluded that Gould's argument is "convincing" and "elegantly presented."

Questioning the Millennium focuses on three questions posed by Gould: "What does the millennium mean? When does a millennium arrive? Why are we interested in it and other divisions of time?" Gould uses "wit and style" to "launch an inquiry into the human 'fascination with numerical regularity'" and to seek this regularity "as one way of ordering a confusing world," according to *New York Times* contributor Michiko Kakutani. The critic also stated that the book "is not one of Mr. Gould's more important books, but . . . it beguiles and entertains, even as it teaches us to reconsider our preconceptions about the natural world."

After writing columns regularly over twenty-four years, in 2000 Gould served up a new selection of these short journalistic pieces in *The Lying Stones of Marrakech: Penultimate Reflections in Natural History,* in which he discusses the misconception of inevi-

table progress being made in scientific endeavors. Among the work's enthusiasts, *Booklist* reviewer Gilbert Taylor remarked that the work "evinces no dimming of Gould's humanistic brilliance," and *Audubon* critic Christopher Camuto dubbed them "elegant, complexly wrought essays." Gould's final essays for *Natural Science* were compiled into the 2002 work *I Have Landed: The End of a Beginning in Natural History,* which coincided with the publication of his major scholarly work *The Structure of Evolutionary Theory.* Included in *I Have Landed* are pieces of a slightly more personal nature, including a short essay titled "September 11, 2001." As a *Publishers Weekly* critic acknowledged, "Gould is at the peak of his abilities in this latest menagerie of wonders" for which, according to Gregg Sapp in *Library Journal,* his "many fans and foes alike should congratulate him."

Between 1999 and 2003, three works by Gould appeared that focus on the interstices of science and religion: *Rocks of Ages: Science and Religion in the Fullness of Life, Crossing Over,* and *The Hedgehog, the Fox, and the Magister's Pox: Mending the Gap between Science and the Humanities.* In the first, Gould explains what he perceives are the differences in subject matter, method, and intention between the disciplines of science and religion. Then he proposes what he terms "non-overlapping magisteria," that is, a "respectful non-interference—accompanied by intense dialogue between the two distinct subjects," which he dubbed NOMA. While *American Scientist's* Ursula Goodenough viewed this work as vintage Gould, with "graceful language flecked with occasional irreverence [and] wonderful anecdotes," she pointed out contradictions in his arguments. So too, in *Commentary* George Weigel pointed to Gould's failure to adequately deal with the common aspects of science and religions, "both of which aim to understand the truth of the human condition. To treat science and religion as 'utterly different' is convenient for certain kinds of scientists (deeply skeptical about religion but 'tolerant') and certain kinds of religious believers (tepid and/or intellectually insecure). But it does not help us think very seriously about either realm."

Unlike many of his contemporaries, Gould also warred constantly against what he considered "bad science," often ending up in the public spotlight, and he believed that paleontology as a science could add to the discussion of evolution. In his magnum opus, the 1,464-page study *The Structure of Evolutionary Theory,* he discusses how three principal tenets of Darwinism developed throughout modern works on evolutionary theory and, in the process, "presents Gould in all his incarnations: as a digressive historian, original thinker and cunning polemicist," to quote a *Publishers Weekly* reviewer. *Booklist*'s Donna Seaman admitted that "this astonishing feat of scholarship and creativity is intimidating at first glance," yet found that Gould's style makes it readable. On the other hand, Gregg Sapp, writing in *Library Journal,* dubbed *The Structure of Evolutionary Theory* both "indispensable" for collections on the subject and "bloated, redundant, and self-indulgent," the last because Gould wrote 250 pages about his own theory of evolution, known as punctuated equilibrium. Calling the work so full of "asides, digressions, polemics and hobbies that it is positively obese," an *Economist* reviewer found it both difficult to review and "enormously irritating." Yet the critic added, "it is also a book of great power, scope and learning In the end, its impressive features far outweigh its irritations." Also noting Gould's "remarkably undisciplined prose" was H. Allen Orr, who, writing in the *New Yorker,* suggested that "while Gould's popular essays are perhaps the most widely read texts in the history of biology, his magnum opus risks becoming one of the least." "What should be incisive analysis is intermittently swamped in highly creative persiflage," complained *Spectator* reviewer John R. G. Turner, who added, "Gould stands here to be judged not on his many literary merits but on the quality of his theory." Despite any perceived stylistic flaws, Orr deemed the first half of the work—the history of evolutionary theory—"particularly impressive."

Gould was a life-long baseball fan—a Yankee fan, in particular—an avidity that is amply evident in his posthumously published essay collection *Triumph and Tragedy in Mudville.* Compiled upon the suggestion of his friend Stephen King, the essays were written over the course of two decades and first appeared in a wide variety of periodicals ranging from the *New York Times* to *Vanity Fair.* While there is, therefore, some repetition of information in the book, in the opinion of *Booklist* reviewer GraceAnne A. DeCandido, the pieces are "uniformly wonderful." *Sports Illustrated* writer Charles Hirshberg pointed to the essay "Why No One Hits .400 Anymore" as the "book's most profound and challenging essay." In it Gould proposed that the lack of .400 hitters "is a sign of improvement, not decline" because modern players are better trained; thus, the difference between the best athletes and average players is slighter than it was in the past. While

Gould called this work "baseball scribblings," reviewers had a more respectful view, as in the case of a *Publishers Weekly* writer who dubbed *Triumph and Tragedy in Mudville* a "glorious testament to Gould's remarkable insights and passionate writing." Praising Gould's judgments of teams' and players' abilities, his assessments of books on the game, and actualities of the game itself as "smart, well-written, and eminently entertaining" was a *Kirkus Reviews* critic.

Gould passed away in May of 2002, after suffering from cancer for several years. In contemplating Gould's contribution to the field of paleontology, Orr suggested that it might not have so much to do with the evolutionary theory of snails or other organisms in the fossil record, but in his effect on his scientific colleagues. "Gould might well . . . represent something new in the historical strata of science: the first self-consciously revolutionary scientist—the first scientist who set out to create a revolution at least in part because he felt that the field just needed one." Orr explained, "Just as old and hopelessly constrained species can do nothing interesting unless they get periodically shaken, so old and hopelessly conservative paradigms can't give way to new science unless they receive a good swift kick now and then." Gould's legacy may be that he was a great punter.

BIOGRAPHICAL AND CRITICAL SOURCES:

PERIODICALS

America, May 24, 1986.

American Scientist, May-June, 1999, Ursula Goodenough, review of *Rocks of Ages: Science and Religion in the Fullness of Life,* pp. 264-265; May-June, 2003, Margaret Pizer, "The Steve Wars," p. 213.

Antioch Review, spring, 1978.

Asia Africa Intelligence Wire, January 26, 2003, "Vidal, Ehrenreich Stars of Essay Collection."

Audubon, March, 2000, Christopher Camuto, review of *The Lying Stones of Marrakech: Penultimate Reflections in Natural History,,* p. 156.

Book, March-April, 2003, Chris Barsanti, review of *Triumph and Tragedy in Mudville: A Lifelong Passion for Baseball,* p. 81.

Booklist, December 1, 1999, review of *Dinosaur in a Haystack* (audio version), p. 718; January 1, 2000, Gilbert Taylor, review of *The Lying Stones of Mar-*

rakech p. 832; December 1, 2000, Donna Seaman, review of *The Lying Stones of Marrakech,* p. 686; December 15, 2001, review of *The Structure of Evolutionary Theory,* p. 682; March 1, 2002, review of *I Have Landed: The End of a Beginning in Natural History,* p. 1050; December 15, 2002, Donna Seaman, review of *The Structure of Evolutionary Theory,* p. 682; February 15, 2003, GraceAnne A. DeCandido, review of *Triumph and Tragedy in Mudville,* p. 1031; April 1, 2003, Donna Seaman, review of *The Hedgehog, the Fox, and the Magister's Pox: Mending the Gap between Science and the Humanities,* p. 1354.

Boston Book Review, March 1, 1997.

Bulletin with Newsweek, May 15, 2001, Ashley Hay, review of *Crossing Over: Where Art and Science Meet,* p. 77.

Chicago Tribune, December 2, 1981; January 20, 1988.

Choice, March, 2000, F. M. Szasz, review of *Rocks of Ages,* p. 1312; July-August, 2002, F. S. Szalay, review of *The Structure of Evolutionary Theory,* p. 1985; November, 2002, J. Nabe, review of *I Have Landed,* p. 495.

Christian Century, June 2, 1999, review of *Rocks of Ages,* p. 624.

Christian Science Monitor, July 15, 1987; March 18, 1999, review of *Rocks of Ages,* p. 19.

Commentary, May, 1999, George Weigel, review of *Rocks of Ages,* p. 67.

Commonweal, April 23, 1999, review of *Rocks of Ages,* p. 29.

Detroit News, May 22, 1983.

Economist (UK), November 10, 2001, review of *Rocks of Ages,* p. 111.

Economist (US), May 16, 1987; November 10, 2001, review of *Rocks of Ages,* p. 77; December 7, 2002, review of *The Structure of Evolutionary Theory.*

Globe and Mail (Toronto, Ontario, Canada), July 24, 1999, review of *Rocks of Ages,* p. D14; March 23, 2002, review of *The Structure of Evolutionary Theory,* p. D3.

Journal of Chemical Education, June, 2002, Hal Harris, review of *The Lying Stones of Marrakech,* p. 651.

Kirkus Reviews, February 15, 2002, review of *I Have Landed,* p. 236; January 15, 2003, review of *The Hedgehog, the Fox, and the Magister's Pox,* p. 125, review of *Triumph and Tragedy in Mudville,* p. 125.

Kliatt, July, 1999, review of *Leonardo's Mountain of Clams and the Diet of Worms: Essays on Natural History* (audio version), p. 59; May, 2001, review of *Crossing Over,* p. 40; September, 2001, review of *The Lying Stones of Marrakech,* p. 42.

Library Journal, March 1, 1999, review of *Leonardo's Mountain of Clams and the Diet of Worms,* p. 47; February 15, 2000, Gregg Sapp, review of *The Lying Stones of Marrakech,* p. 193; February 15, 2002, Gregg Sapp, review of *The Structure of Evolutionary Theory,* pp. 174-175; April 15, 2002, Gregg Sapp, review of *I Have Landed,* p. 122; October 1, 2002, Denise J. Stankovics, review of *The Best American Essays 2002,* p. 94; February 1, 2003, Paul Kaplan and Robert C. Cotrrell, review of *Triumph and Tragedy in Mudville,* p. 90; March 1, 2003, Gregg Sapp, review of *The Hedgehog, the Fox, and the Magister's Pox,* p. 113.

Listener, June 11, 1987.

London Review of Books, December 1, 1983.

Los Angeles Times, June 2, 1987.

Los Angeles Times Book Review, July 17, 1983; November 29, 1987.

Magazine of Fantasy and Science Fiction, February, 1999, review of *Questioning the Millennium,* p. 35.

Nation, June 18, 1983; November 16, 1985; June 10, 2002, David Hawkes, review of *The Structure of Evolutionary Theory,* p. 29.

Natural History, January, 1988.

Nature, November 19, 1987; August 26, 1999, review of *Rocks of Ages,* p. 830; May 25, 2000, Henry Gee, review of *The Lying Stones of Marrakech,* p. 397.

New Criterion, October, 2002, Paul R. Gross, "The Apotheosis of Stephen Jay Gould," pp. 77-80.

New Republic, December 3, 1977; November 11, 1981; November 8, 1999, review of *Questioning the Millennium,* p. 76.

New Scientist, September 11, 1999, review of *Leonardo's Mountain of Clams and the Diet of Worms,* p. 53; May 12, 2001, review of *The Lying Stones of Marrakech,* p. 52.

New Statesman, February 19, 2001, review of *Rocks of Ages,* p. 49.

Newsweek, November 9, 1981; August 1, 1983.

New Yorker, December 30, 1985; September 30, 2002, H. Allen Orr, "The Descent of Gould."

New York Review of Books, June 1, 1978; February 19, 1981; October 22, 1981; May 28, 1987; October 18, 2001, Frederick Crews, review of *Rocks of Ages,* pp. 51-54; May 23, 2002, Tim Flannery, "A New Darwinism," reviews of *The Structures of Evolutionary Theory* and *I Have Landed,* pp. 52-54.

New York Times, October 17, 1987; November 11, 1997, p. E8.

New York Times Book Review, November 20, 1977; September 14, 1980; November 1, 1981; May 8, 1983; September 22, 1985; December 7, 1986; September 11, 1987; November 15, 1987; January 21, 1996, p. 9; September 22, 1996, p. 9; November 9, 1997, p. 9; March 17, 2002, review of *The Structure of Evolutionary Theory,* p. 11.

New York Times Magazine, November 20, 1983.

Observer (London, England), February 18, 1990, p. 57.

Odyssey, January, 2003, Barbara Krasner-Khait, "A Passion for Writing," pp. 24-25.

People Weekly, June 2, 1986.

Publishers Weekly, January 17, 2000, review of *The Lying Stones of Marrakech,* p. 49; February 11, 2002, review of *The Structure of Evolutionary Theory,* p. 179; April 1, 2002, review of *I Have Landed,* p. 64, "PW Talks with Stephen Jay Gould," p. 65; September 2, 2002, review of *The Best American Essays 2002,* pp. 65-66; February 17, 2003, review of *The Hedgehog, the Fox, and the Magister's Pox,* p. 63, review of *Triumph and Tragedy in Mudville,* p. 65.

Quarterly Review of Biology, June, 2000, Richard A. Watson, review of *Rocks of Ages,* p. 159; September, 2002, Kevin Padian, review of *The Book of Life,* pp. 318-319.

Rolling Stone, January 15, 1987.

Ruminator Review, spring, 2002, review of *The Structure of Evolutionary Theory,* p. 12.

Science, May, 1983; October 29, 1999, Craig B. Anderson, review of *Rocks of Ages,* p. 907; April 26, 2002, Douglas J. Futuyma, review of *The Structure of Evolutionary Theory,* pp. 661-663.

Science Books & Films, November, 1999, review of *Leonardo's Mountain of Clams and the Diet of Worms,* p. 249, reviews of *Leonardo's Mountain of Claims and the Diet of Worms* and *Wonderful Life* pp. 271-272.

Science News, July 20, 2002, *The Structure of Evolutionary Theory,* p. 47; August 10, 2002, review of *I Have Landed,* p. 95.

Scientist, June 10, 2002, Barry A. Palevitz, "Love Him or Hate Him, Stephen Jay Gould Made a Difference," pp. 12-13.

Spectator, November 24, 2001, review of *Rocks of Ages,* p. 44; June 29, 2002, John R. G. Turner, reviews of *The Structure of Evolutionary Theory* and *I Have Landed,* pp. 36-37.

Sports Illustrated, March 17, 2003, Charles Hirshberg, "Thinking Baseball: Renowned Scientist Stephen Jay Gould Was No Snob When He Focused His Intellect on His Favorite Game," p. R4.

Time, May 30, 1983; September 30, 1985.

Times Higher Education Supplement, April 6, 2001, Nick Petford, review of *The Lying Stones of Marrakech,* p. 26; June 21, 2002, Brian Charlesworth, review of *The Structure of Evolutionary Theory,* p. 36.

Times Literary Supplement, May 22, 1981; February 10, 1984; October 25, 1985; June 6, 1986; September 11-17, 1987; July 2, 1999, review of *Leonardo's Mountain of Clams and the Diet of Worms,* p. 28.

Tribune Books (Chicago, IL), November 30, 1980; June 26, 1983.

Voice Literary Supplement, June, 1987.

Wall Street Journal, March 29, 1999, review of *Rocks of Ages,* p. A24.

Washington Post Book World, November 8, 1981; May 8, 1983; September 29, 1985; April 26, 1987; April 14, 2002, review of *The Structure of Evolutionary Theory,* p. 4.

Whole Earth Review, spring, 2002, Lulu Winslow, review of *Crossing Over,* p. 85.

ONLINE

Salon.com, http://www.salon.com/ (May 20, 2002).

Unofficial Stephen Jay Gould Archive, http://www.stephenjaygould.org/ (May 8, 2003).

OBITUARIES:

PERIODICALS

Africa News Service, May 24, 2002.

Economist (US), May 25, 2002.

Financial Times, July 6, 2002, p. 5.

Nation, June 17, 2002, p. 6.

Newsweek, June 3, 2002, p. 59.

U.S. News & World Report, June 3, 2002, p. 15.

ONLINE

Popular-Science, http://www.popular-science.net/ (May 8, 2002).*

GOUREVITCH, Philip 1961-

PERSONAL: Born 1961. *Education:* Cornell University, B.A.; Columbia University, M.F.A. (fiction writing), 1992.

ADDRESSES: Office—c/o World Policy Institute, New School University, 66 Fifth Ave., 9th Floor, New York, NY 10011.

CAREER: Forward (newspaper), English edition, New York bureau chief, 1992-93, cultural editor, 1993-95, then contributing editor; *New Yorker,* New York, NY, staff writer; Yaddo (writers' colony), Saratoga Springs, NY, writer-in-residence. Appeared on television programs, including *The NewsHour with Jim Lehrer,* PBS, 1997. Affiliated with the Echoing Green Foundation and the United States Institute for Peace.

AWARDS, HONORS: National Magazine Award finalist, 1996, 1997; National Book Critics Circle Award for general nonfiction, 1999, Cornelius Ryan Award from the Overseas Book Club, Helen Bernstein Award from the New York Public Library, George Polk Book Award, London *Guardian* prize, and the *Los Angeles Times* Book Award, all for *We Wish to Inform You That Tomorrow We Will Be Killed with Our Families: Stories from Rwanda;* senior fellow, World Policy Institute.

WRITINGS:

We Wish to Inform You That Tomorrow We Will Be Killed with Our Families: Stories from Rwanda, Farrar, Straus (New York, NY), 1998.
A Cold Case, Farrar, Straus (New York, NY), 2001.
(Author of foreword) *Village of Waiting,* Farrar, Straus (New York, NY), 2001.

Contributor to periodicals, including *Commentary, Double Take, Forward, Granta, Harper's, New Yorker, New York Review of Books, New York Times Magazine, Outside, Southwest Review, Story,* and *Zoetrope.*

SIDELIGHTS: Though Philip Gourevitch had planned on becoming a fiction writer, his first book was an acclaimed work of political reportage. *We Wish to Inform You That Tomorrow We Will Be Killed with Our Fami-*

Philip Gourevitch

lies: Stories from Rwanda exposes the story of the 1994 genocide in Rwanda. During the massacre, large numbers of Rwanda's majority population, the Hutus, massacred an estimated 800,000 of the country's minority Tutsis and Tutsi sympathizers over a period of about 100 days. Disturbed by the dearth of information on the subject appearing in the Western press, which had heavily reported incidents of "ethnic cleansing" in Bosnia, Gourevitch traveled to Rwanda in 1995. He spent years researching the context and aftermath of the genocide. What he uncovered led to a book that shocked and shamed readers, provoking scrutiny about the United Nations' reluctance to intervene in time to avert the tragedy.

Critics found that one of the chief strengths of the book is its focus on individual lives. Gourevitch interviewed many witnesses and survivors, letting their voices carry their own powerful message. According to Africa correspondent Collette Braeckman in the *World Policy Journal,* Gourevitch "conjugates Rwanda in the singular. What his book mainly consists of are chronicles of individual Rwandan men and women. And in their particular destinies, he assembles the drama of a whole people." *Nation* contributor George Packer voiced similar praise, writing that Gourevitch is "at his very best when listening to ordinary Rwandans, especially the survivors, and trying to make sense of their stories. These voices haunt the book, and they haunt the reader afterward."

Gourevitch contends in *We Wish to Inform You* that representatives of the United Nations knew that the Rwandan genocide was imminent but chose not to intervene. He reports that as early as January, 1994, Kofi Annan, the chief of peacekeeping operations for the United Nations (and later the secretary-general of the United Nations), received warnings of a planned coup d'etat and Tutsi massacre, but he did not order peacekeeping forces into Rwanda. Later, the United States, despite evidence to the contrary, refused to admit that genocide was occurring in Africa. This indifference to the plight of Rwanda makes *We Wish to Inform You* "a burden on world conscience," in the words of Nigerian writer and Nobel laureate Wole Soyinka, writing in the *New York Times Book Review*.

Gourevitch "leaves all options open and does not give in to optimism. His purpose is to try to understand, not to judge or to predict events," observed Braeckman. In his review of *We Wish to Inform You* in the *Nation,* Packer admired Gourevitch's willingness to pose difficult questions, noting that their "resonance throughout his book shows a rare depth of ethical and philosophical inquiry in a work of political reportage." Soyinka praised the historical context that the book provides, stating that "no one explanation satisfies. Gourevitch assists us with antecedents but does not propose, and rightly so, any clear-cut answers." Angolan novelist Sousa Jamba wrote in the *New Statesman* that *We Wish to Inform You* was disappointing to him, because "it fails to probe into the darker forces behind the genocide." Jamba faulted Gourevitch for placing too little emphasis on the importance of ethnicity among Rwandans. While Gourevitch argues that these ethnic distinctions were imposed by European colonialists, Jamba criticized this approach for its failure to ask why Rwandans would embrace such "quasi-fascist theories of race." Nevertheless, Jamba admitted that the book "joins a long and distinguished list of attempts by Americans to understand Africa."

We Wish to Inform You takes its title from a Christian Tutsi congregation's futile letter to its pastor for help. The book received the National Book Critics Circle (NBCC) Award for general nonfiction as well as the Cornelius Ryan Award from the Overseas Book Club, the Helen Bernstein Award from the New York Public Library, the George Polk Book Award, and the *Los Angeles Times* Book Award. In awarding the prize, NBCC board member Steve G. Kellman praised the book as "vivid reportage, plangent elegy, and provocative meditation on evil and the fictions of an international community."

One of the many things that struck Gourevitch while he was writing *We Wish to Inform You* is how the perpetrators of the slaughter of thousands of people were able to justify these murders in their own minds. The Hutus felt they were entitled to kill the Tutsis, and so their consciences were not troubled by the genocide. Sometime later, Gourevitch came across the same mentality when he began to research a book about a double murder in New York City.

When Gourevitch first set out to interview district attorney investigator Andrew Rosenzweig, his intention was only to write an interesting profile about a man whose career as a criminal investigator was winding down toward retirement. But when Rosenzweig mentioned the case concerning Frankie Koehler's murder of two men, the writer could not get the story out of his mind. Back in 1970, Koehler got into an argument with two men at a restaurant. Feeling insulted by their remarks, Koehler decided to take his anger out by using a gun, killing both men. Although police quickly determined who the perpetrator was, Koehler managed to disappear, and for twenty-seven years no one knew what had happened to him. The case was considered closed until Rosenzweig, who happened to have known one of the murder victims, decided to conduct his own investigation. In 1997 he tracked Koehler down in San Francisco, where he was living under an assumed identity. Brought back to New York, Koehler was convicted of the crime. However, because the case had grown so cold, the prosecutor was only able to get Koehler sentenced to six to thirteen years.

Gourevitch became fascinated by the case and, even more so, by Koehler, Rosenzweig, and defense attorney Murray Richman. After conducting numerous interviews, he wrote the story down in *A Cold Case*. *A Cold Case* is not so much a murder mystery, or even a story about chasing down an elusive crook (Koehler is captured halfway through the book); it is a story about personalities. When interviewing Koehler, the author found him to be an intelligent, even likable character. "He's a man of considerable charm," he told Sage Stossel in *Atlantic Unbound*. "He's a seducer in a sense. He works his charms to try and persuade you to see things his way. He's clearly intelligent. . . . For him it was something of a treat to have the opportunity to sit down and talk in a quiet one-on-one way with somebody who was very interested in him—a subject which he seems to think is of universal interest—and also just to show off his intelligence and his thoughtfulness."

In their talks, Koehler reveals himself as someone who justifies his acts by saying that he is a product of his environment. "Where I come from," Koehler declares, "if you don't like somebody and they're really a scumbag, and they really bug you, you shoot them." Gourevitch, however, calls such reasoning patently false, pointing out that plenty of people grow up in tough New York neighborhoods without becoming killers. Oddly enough, Koehler also seems to have his own strange sense of morality in that he feels it is okay to kill someone who bugs you, but only a "scumbag" would kill for personal profit.

In addition to Koehler, the author finds Rosenzweig and Richman to be equally compelling characters. Rosenzweig is the moralist for whom "the truth is the truth," and Richman is an amoral charmer, who, while intelligent, has no problem being paid for defending people he knows are criminals. "Murray Richman," the author told Stossel, "is a fascinating man, because he's the unabashed, slightly comic, wisecracking kind of defense lawyer who makes remarks like 'I love murder—one less witness to worry about' that are inherently offensive and clearly outrageous, and also more than just schtick."

Gourevitch compares the three main players in *A Cold Case*'s drama to the movies about which they obsess: Koehler is fascinated by James Cagney, Rosenzweig by Gary Cooper in *High Noon*, and Richman by *Casablanca* because "it's all about life's ambiguities." Crit-

ics also found that the people in *A Cold Case* were easily typed, and Peter Slevin, writing in *Washington Monthly*, felt the comparison between the real people and movie characters to be "one of Gourevitch's great discoveries." However, Slevin also complained that *A Cold Case* is "not an ambitious book" because the author simply allows the principal actors to speak for themselves. "If Gourevitch had only dug deeper," Slevin felt, "everyone—including the accomplished author—might have had more to say." However, other reviewers were more pleased with the book as a character study. *Entertainment Weekly* critic Troy Patterson, for example, said that "the book's joys are not those of suspense and narrative tension but of character and narrative shape—the zigzagging through the lives of people you could say were out of Damon Runyon if they didn't inhabit our earth."

Although Gourevitch reveals Koehler to be an interesting person, what he does not do is excuse his acts in any way. As with *We Wish to Inform You*, in *A Cold Case* is a testimony to the author's desire for his audience not to forget the dead; he is, in a way, a speaker for the victims. As one *Publishers Weekly* contributor said in a review of *A Cold Case*, "Gourevitch has secured a place next to Rosenzweig in that lonely and all-important choir."

BIOGRAPHICAL AND CRITICAL SOURCES:

BOOKS

Gourevitch, Philip, *We Wish to Inform You That Tomorrow We Will Be Killed with Our Families: Stories from Rwanda*, Farrar, Straus, 1998.

PERIODICALS

Christian Century, February 27, 2002, Stephen R. Haynes, review of *We Wish to Inform You That Tomorrow We Will Be Killed with Our Families: Stories from Rwanda*, p. 30.

Contemporary Review, December, 1999, Tom Phillips, "Understanding Rwanda," p. 321.

Entertainment Weekly, October 23, 1998, p. 74; July 27, 2001, Troy Paterson, "Murders Ink: Journalist Philip Gourevitch's *A Cold Case* Transforms a Real Police Investigation into a Noirish Thriller," p. 64.

Foreign Affairs, March, 1999, p. 158.

Library Journal, September 1, 1998, review of *We Wish to Inform You,* p. 201; July, 1999, Michael Rogers and Norman Oder, "Gourevitch Wins NYPL Journalism Award," p. 24; May 15, 2001, Deirdre Bray, review of *A Cold Case,* p. 144.

Nation, November 16, 1998, George Packer, review of *We Wish to Inform You,* pp. 58, 60-62.

National Book Critics Circle Journal, April, 1999, pp. 2-3.

New Statesman, March 19, 1999, Sousa Jamba, review of *We Wish to Inform You,* pp. 44-45.

New York Times Book Review, October 4, 1998, Wole Soyinka, review of *We Wish to Inform You,* p. 11.

Publishers Weekly, August 17, 1998, review of *We Wish to Inform You,* p. 56; December 20, 1999, Jean Richardson, "American Wins 'Guardian' Prize," p. 15; May 21, 2001, review of *A Cold Case,* p. 88.

U.S. News & World Report, July 2, 2001, March Silver, "Speaking for the Dead," p. 48.

Washington Monthly, July, 2001, Peter Slevin, review of *A Cold Case,* p. 54.

World Policy Journal, winter, 1998, Collette Braeckman, review of *We Wish to Inform You,* pp. 99-104.

ONLINE

Atlantic Unbound, http://www.theatlantic.com/unbound/ (November 11, 2002), Sage Stossel, "A Tale of Two Murders."

Online NewsHour, http://www.pbs.org/newshour/ (January 7, 1999), "Remembering the 1994 Genocide."

World Policy Institute, http://www.worldpolicy.org/ (September 3, 1999).*

*   *   *

GREEN, Daryl D. 1966-
(Dewayne Green)

PERSONAL: Born February 5, 1966, in Shreveport, LA; son of Edward and Annette (Green) Elias; married Estraletta Andrews; children: Mario, Sharlita, Demetrius. *Ethnicity:* "Black." *Education:* Southern University A & M, B.S., 1989; Tusculum College, M.A., 1997. *Politics:* Independent. *Religion:* Baptist.

ADDRESSES: Office—Performance Management and Logistics Associates, P.O. Box 32733, Knoxville, TN 37930-2733; fax: 865-602-7702. *E-mail*—pmla@att.net.

CAREER: Tennessee Department of Energy, Oak Ridge, TN, program manager, 1989—, technology-development manager, 1997-2002; Performance Management and Logistics Associates, Knoxville, TN, president, 1997— .

MEMBER: Toastmaster International (Clinch River president), Blacks in Government (past president), Black Executive Exchange Program, Black Achievers, Knoxville Urban League, Pi Tau Sigma.

AWARDS, HONORS: Martin Luther King, Jr. Humanitarian Award, 1991; Community Service Award, Department of Energy, 1992; Pollution Prevention Award, Department of Energy, 1997.

WRITINGS:

My Cup Runneth Over: Setting Goals for Single Parents and Working Couples, Triangle Publications, 1998.

Awakening the Talents Within, Writers Club Press, 2001.

More Than a Conqueror, PMLA Press (Knoxville, TN), 2003.

Coauthor of the column "Family Vision" in the *Knoxville Enlightener,* 1998—; author of a nationally syndicated column distributed by National Newspaper Publishers Association, 2000—. Also author of works published under the name Dewayne Green.

ADAPTATIONS: The book *My Cup Runneth Over* was published as an audio book by Triangle Publications in 1999.

SIDELIGHTS: Daryl D. Green is the author of *My Cup Runneth Over: Setting Goals for Single Parents and Working Couples,* which he once described as a "'how-to' aimed at assisting families in setting goals for themselves." Green, who works as a program manager for the Tennessee Department of Energy, applied his organizational skills to his family life in order to establish goals and realize greater stability and optimism. "America is being destroyed from the inside out," Green commented. "Our children feel alienated in many of our families. Many couples are selfish and do not provide the healthy, nurturing environment for their children. . . . If our country is to be healed, we need to fix the problem at the very core—the family. Our children need hope. Hope is a very spiritual concept."

According to Jacqueline Brown, writing in the *Knoxville News-Sentinel,* Green also used the Bible to provide ideas for the family. This model, Brown noted, is only part of a large plan that includes the establishing of "a family mission statement" and the developing of "a plan to accomplish [family] goals." Green told the *Shreveport Sun* that *My Cup Runneth Over* "tells you how to give your family vision for life." He added, "Priorities are important to have in a family. They must have goals."

Green once told *CA:* "I'm a natural goal-setter. I read lots of self-help books to improve my learning and knowledge. I read 'how-to' books and textbooks just for the pleasure. I'm probably one of the few students in college who enjoyed reading his textbooks.

"I give God the credit for my writing ability. God directs my footsteps. This is definitely the case with *My Cup Runneth Over.* I felt this project was part of my destiny. I wrote *My Cup Runneth Over* in two months, found a publisher, and published it in ten months. I believe what has happened to me is not just chance. There are a lot of people that have more talent than I. However, most of them don't realize how important it is to take advantage of the opportunity given. I feel an obligation to use all of my talents and gifts in life."

Green later added: "Who or what particularly influences my work? I must admit I was heavily influenced by my schoolteachers, especially Maggie Green and Versia Jackson. My parents helped me to enjoy writing. I, however, am influenced by my environment. I write about how people are feeling in my community."

BIOGRAPHICAL AND CRITICAL SOURCES:

PERIODICALS

Knoxville News-Sentinel, March 18, 1998, article by Jacqueline Brown, p. N3.
Shreveport Sun, February 12, 1998.

*   *   *

GREEN, Dewayne
See GREEN, Daryl D.

*   *   *

GREEN, Martin (Burgess) 1927-

PERSONAL: Born September 21, 1927, in London, England; son of Joseph William Elias (a shopkeeper) and Hilda (Brewster) Green; married Carol Elizabeth Hurd, 1967; children: Martin Michael, Miriam. *Ethnicity:* "Caucasian." *Education:* St. John's College, Cambridge, B.A. (with honors), 1948, M.A., 1952; King's College, London, teacher's diploma, 1951; Sorbonne, University of Paris, certificate in French studies, 1952; University of Michigan, Ph.D., 1957. *Politics:* Labour. *Religion:* Roman Catholic.

ADDRESSES: Office—c/o Department of English, Tufts University, Medford, MA 02155.

CAREER: College Moderne, Fourmies, France, teacher,1951-52; Konya Koleji, Konya, Turkey, teacher, 1955-56; Wellesley College, Wellesley, MA, instructor in modern literature, 1957-61; Tufts University, Medford, MA, assistant professor of American literature, 1963-65; University of Birmingham, Birmingham, England, lecturer in American literature, 1965-68; Tufts University, Medford, MA, professor of English, 1968-94, professor emeritus, 1994—. *Military service:* Royal Air Force, 1948-50; became sergeant.

AWARDS, HONORS: Three Avery and Jules Hopwood Creative Writing Awards, University of Michigan, 1954.

WRITINGS:

Mirror for Anglo-Saxons, Harper (New York, NY), 1960.

Reappraisals, Hugh Evelyn (London, England), 1963, Norton (New York, NY), 1965.

Science and the Shabby Curate of Poetry, Norton (New York, NY), 1965.

The Problem of Boston, Norton (New York, NY), 1966.

Yeats's Blessings on von Hugel: Essays in Literature and Religion, Longmans, Green (London, England), 1967, Norton (New York, NY), 1968.

Cities of Light and Sons of the Morning, Little, Brown (Boston, MA), 1972.

The von Richthofen Sisters: The Triumphant and the Tragic Modes of Love—Else and Frieda von Richthofen, Otto Gross, Max Weber, and D. H. Lawrence in the Years 1870-1970, Basic Books (New York, NY), 1974, 2nd edition, University of New Mexico Press (Albuquerque, NM), 1988.

(Editor, with Philip C. Ritterbush) *Technology As Institutionally Related to Human Values,* Acropolis Books (Washington, DC), 1974.

Children of the Sun: A Narrative of "Decadence" in England after 1918, Basic Books (New York, NY), 1976, revised edition, Constable (London, England), 1977.

Transatlantic Patterns: Cultural Comparisons of England with America, Basic Books (New York, NY), 1977.

The Earth Again Redeemed: May 26 to July 1, 1984 (science fiction), Basic Books (New York, NY), 1977.

The Challenge of the Mahatmas (first book in "The Lust for Power" trilogy), Basic Books (New York, NY), 1978.

Dreams of Adventure, Deeds of Empire (second book in "The Lust for Power" trilogy), Basic Books (New York, NY), 1979.

Tolstoy and Gandhi: Men of Peace (third book in "The Lust for Power" trilogy), Basic Books (New York, NY), 1983.

The Great American Adventure, Beacon Press (Boston, MA), 1984.

The English Novel in the Twentieth Century: The Doom of Empire, Routledge & Kegan Paul (London, England), 1985, Pennsylvania State University Press (University Park, PA), 1987.

(With John Swan) *The Triumph of Pierrot: The Commedia dell'Arte and the Modern Imagination,* Macmillan (New York, NY), 1986.

The Origins of Non-Violence: Tolstoy and Gandhi in Their Historical Setting, Pennsylvania State University Press (University Park, PA), 1986.

Mountain of Truth: The Counterculture Begins—Ascona, 1900-1920, University Press of New England (Hanover, NH), 1986.

(Editor) Mahatma Gandhi, *Gandhi in India: In His Own Words,* University Press of New England (Hanover, NH), 1987.

New York 1913: The Armory Show and the Paterson Strike Pageant, Scribner (New York, NY), 1988.

The Mount Vernon Street Warrens: A Boston Story, 1860-1910, Scribner (New York, NY), 1989.

A Biography of John Buchan and His Sister Anna: The Personal Background of Their Literary Work, Edwin Mellen Press (Lewiston, NY), 1990.

The Robinson Crusoe Story, Pennsylvania State University Press (University Park, PA), 1990.

Seven Types of Adventure Tale: An Etiology of a Major Genre, Pennsylvania State University Press (University Park, PA), 1991.

Prophets of a New Age: The Politics of Hope from the Eighteenth through the Twenty-first Centuries, Scribner (New York, NY), 1992.

The Adventurous Male: Chapters in the History of the White Male Mind, Pennsylvania State University Press (University Park, PA), 1993.

Gandhi: A Voice of a New Age Revolution, Continuum Publishing (New York, NY), 1993.

Otto Gross, Freudian Psychoanalyst, 1877-1920: Literature and Ideas, Edwin Mellen Press (Lewiston, NY), 1999.

SIDELIGHTS: According to Jonathan Raban in the *New York Times Book Review,* Martin Green is a "merchant venturer in the commerce of ideas, a wickedly clever cultural historian at whose approach disciplinary frontiers seem to melt into thin air. He has the gift of making himself appear equally at home in literature, anthropology, social history, politics and gossip." Green, a British expatriate, has written several books on English cultural and social history, often using literary figures to illustrate his point.

In *Children of the Sun: A Narrative of "Decadence" in England after 1918,* Green explores the post-World War I cultural phenomenon of dandyism among the young, wealthy socialites and artists of the period. Focusing on such writers as Evelyn Waugh, Christopher Isherwood, and Harold Acton, Green sets out "to describe the imaginative life of English [high] culture after 1918 and to trace the prominence within it, the partial dominance over it, established by men of one intellectual temperament," as Gerry C. Gunnin quoted Green in his *World Literature Today* article. According to Hilton Kramer in his *New York Times Book Review* contribution, "Among much else that Mr. Green's book accomplishes, it gives us a new and vivid understanding of what the concept of the Establishment in England truly signified. . . . He has . . . written a very important book."

In *Transatlantic Patterns: Cultural Comparisons of England with America,* Green discusses the contemporary cultural differences between the two countries on the basis of their literature. Examining writers as diverse as Dorothy Sayers and John D. MacDonald, Norman Mailer and Doris Lessing, Green tries "to define the difference between England and America in terms of attitudes toward marriage, humor, detective stories, Marx and Freud. . . . What he is after is extremely subtle and pertinent—not cultural—caricature," explained Christopher Lehmann-Haupt of the *New York Times.* Lehmann-Haupt went on to say that this book "will not come as much of a surprise to anyone who has followed Mr. Green's lively and original intellectual career."

Green focuses on two revolutionary events in what Chicago *Tribune Books* critic Ron Grossman called a "masterly study of America's earliest rebels-with-a-cause" titled *New York 1913: The Armory Show and the Paterson Strike Pageant.* In February, 1913, Greenwich Villagers presented the first exhibition of modern art in the United States at the 69th Regiment Armory. For the first time, Americans encountered modern paintings by such artists as Matisse, Duchamp, and Picasso. A few months later some of these same revolutionaries helped demonstrate with striking textile workers of Paterson, New Jersey. Although neither of these events was a critical success, Green illustrates that "once upon a time in a certain place, revolutionary art and politics did appear to go hand in hand . . .," noted Lehmann-Haupt; "their leaders knew one another, being of the same class and sometimes sharing the rebellious culture of Greenwich Village. They were

saying no to certain things. . . . [Green] traces the tangled thread connecting the events and the people who figured prominently in them. . . . He makes us see what these people shared, where they came from and why they wanted to overthrow the old order in its various forms." In the opinion of Richard Snow for the *New York Times Book Review, New York 1913* is a "complex and intriguing book. . . . [It] is sometimes repetitive, and one may quail a bit at the outset when Susan Sontag's esthetic vocabulary is introduced to help clarify the analysis to follow. But the book is full of fascinating things, and alive with the vigor of the eloquent men and women who were so sure they were about to create a renaissance through the fusion of art and politics. It is greatly to Mr. Green's credit that he never patronizes them in their ardent certainties and that he is able to resurrect so sympathetically an era whose 'gay, inclusive, experimental spirit' seems as distant from us today as the Greenwich Village that fomented it."

Green once told *CA:* "I was taught, at Cambridge, by the literary critic, F. R. Leavis, who laid a heavy stress on the difference between criticism and scholarship. My first books were not much like his, but they were 'criticism' in that sense, and shaped by his teaching. My later books were shaped by a reaction against it. I came to aim at a more liberal serving of the imagination—scholarship as much as criticism—which involves crossing subject frontiers—implicitly defining imagination to cover history, sociology, psychology, et cetera. (Seeing likenesses between D. H. Lawrence and Max Weber was the major step.) To put it farcifully, I have been a nonfiction novelist.

"A risk involved in such a service of 'imagination' is falling into bland frivolity. Leavis's criticism began as a protest against that, and the danger will always be there. So I have kept my eye on the theme of violence-nonviolence as a guarantor of seriousness—a greater seriousness than criticism could ever be. But to keep my eye on it means to keep recurring to it, not steadily to stare at it and speak for it. These two poles, the serious and the playful, can be seen as complementing forms of intellectual conscience."

BIOGRAPHICAL AND CRITICAL SOURCES:

PERIODICALS

Globe and Mail (Toronto, Ontario, Canada), July 21, 1984.

New York Review of Books, April 15, 1976.

New York Times, June 29, 1977, Christopher Lehmann-Haupt, review of *Transatlantic Patterns: Cultural Comparisons of England with America;* June 11, 1986; December 8, 1988.

New York Times Book Review, January 25, 1976, Hilton Kramer, review of *Children of the Sun: A Narrative of "Decadence" in England after 1918;* August 7, 1977; May 27, 1979; August 28, 1983; June 29, 1986; July 13, 1986; December 11, 1988, Richard Snow, review of *New York 1913: The Armory Show and the Paterson Strike Pageant.*

Spectator, June 4, 1977.

Times Literary Supplement, July 18, 1980; February 22, 1985; February 6, 1987.

Tribune Books (Chicago, IL), January 18, 1989, Ron Grossman, review of *New York 1913.*

Washington Post Book World, November 27, 1988.

World Literature Today, spring, 1977, Gerry C. Gunnin, review of *Children of the Sun.*

*   *   *

GRIFFIN, Jill 1955-

PERSONAL: Born May 8, 1955, in Monroe, NC; married J. Mack Nunn (a chief financial officer). *Education:* University of South Carolina, B.S. (magna cum laude), M.B.A.

ADDRESSES: Home—1514 Preston Ave., Austin, TX 78703. *Office*—2729 Exposition Blvd., Austin, TX 78703. *Agent*—Jeff Herman Agency, New York, NY. *E-mail*—jill@loyaltysolutions.com.

CAREER: AmeriSuite Hotels, Austin, TX, director of marketing and sales, 1985-87; R. J. R. Nabisco, brand manager, 1979-85; University of Texas—Austin, Austin, TX, member of marketing faculty, 1988-90; Griffin Group, president, 1987—.

WRITINGS:

Power Packed Promotion, Marketing Resource Center, 1990.

Selling the Sizzle, Marketing Resource Center, 1993.

Customer Loyalty: How to Earn It, How to Keep It, Lexington Books (Lanham, MD), 1995, 2nd edition, 2002.

(With Michael W. Lowenstein) *Customer Winback: How to Recapture Lost Customers and Keep Them Loyal,* foreword by Don Peppers and Martha Rogers, Jossey-Bass (San Francisco, CA), 2001.

SIDELIGHTS: Texas-based marketing consultant Jill Griffin aims to help business owners generate repeat sales with her book *Customer Loyalty: How to Earn It, How to Keep It,* in which she focuses on the necessity of creating customer loyalty programs. Drawing on the examples of 165 businesses, Griffin discusses such topics as pricing, consumers' purchasing cycles, targeting potential repeat customers, regaining inactive customers, and creating a corporate culture that promotes customer loyalty. *Customer Loyalty* was chosen as a 1995 selection of the Fortune Book Club.

Growing up in the small town of Marshville, North Carolina, gave Griffin a first-hand perspective on customer loyalty. "By big city standards, our buying choices were limited, but we didn't know it," Griffin recalls in her introduction to *Customer Loyalty.* "Local businesses satisfied our needs and, in return won our loyalty." Griffin learned more about customer loyalty while employed as a brand manager for tobacco giant R. J. R. Nabisco, where she marketed Winston cigarettes.

Since leaving Nabisco, Griffin has taught college marketing courses and under the auspices of her company—The Griffin Group—has conducted seminars on loyalty marketing nationwide. She regularly works with a wide variety of clients, from the Fortune 500 to small businesses. Griffin's book, *Customer Winback: How to Recapture Lost Customers and Keep Them Loyal,* was a Soundview Executive Book Summaries selection in 2001.

BIOGRAPHICAL AND CRITICAL SOURCES:

BOOKS

Griffin, Jill, *Customer Loyalty: How to Earn It, How to Keep It,* Lexington Books (Lanham, MD), 1995.

PERIODICALS

American Statesman (Austin, TX), 1995.
Home News (Marshville, NC), February 2, 1995.

* * *

GROTH, A(loysius) Nicholas 1937-

PERSONAL: Born December 6, 1937, in Webster, MA; son of Aloysius Nestor and Sophie Mary (Karabash) Groth. *Ethnicity:* "Caucasian." *Education:* Boston University, B.A., 1959, M.A., 1960, Ph.D., 1972.

ADDRESSES: Home—7513 Pointview Cir., Orlando, FL 32836-6336; fax: 407-351-3148. *E-mail*—a.n. groth@att.net.

CAREER: Center for Diagnosis and Treatment of Sexually Dangerous Persons, Bridgewater, MA, psychologist, 1966-76; Whiting Forensic Institute, Middletown, CT, director, 1976-77; Harrington Memorial Hospital, Southbridge, MA, director of forensic mental health program, 1977-78; Connecticut Correctional Institution, Somers, CT, codirector of sex offender program, 1978-86; St. Joseph College Institute for Treatment and Control of Child Abuse, Hartford, CT, codirector, 1980-96; writer. Forensic Mental Health Associates, executive director, 1981-90; National Center for Prevention and Control of Rape, member of advisory board, 1981-85; consultant to Wyoming State Honor Farm.

MEMBER: American Association of Orthopsychiatry, American Psychology-Law Society, American Psychology Association, National Organization of Victim Assistance, Connecticut Psychology Association, Massachusetts Psychology Association.

WRITINGS:

(With H. Jean Birnbaum) *Men Who Rape: The Psychology of the Offender,* Plenum Press (New York, NY), 1979.

Anatomical Drawings for the Use in the Investigation and Intervention of Child Sexual Abuse, Forensic Mental Health Associates (Newton Center, MA), 1984.
(With A. W. Burgess, L. L. Holmstrom, and S. Sgroi) *Sexual Assault of Children and Adolescents,* D. C. Heath (Lexington, MA), 1978.
(With John M. Preble) *Male Victims of Same-Sex Abuse: Addressing Their Sexual Responses,* Sidran Press (Towson, MD), 2002.

Contributor to books, including *The Sexual Assault of Children and Adolescents,* Lexington Books (Lexington, MA), 1978; *Social Work and Child Sexual Abuse,* edited by Jon R. Conte and David A. Shore, Haworth Press, 1982; *The Sexual Aggressor: Current Perspectives on Treatment,* edited by J. G. Greer and I. R. Stuart, Van Nostrand Reinhold (New York, NY), 1983; *A Handbook of Clinical Intervention in Child Sexual Abuse,* edited by S. Sgroi, D. C. Heath (Lexington, MA), 1982, 2nd edition, Lexington Books (New York, NY), 1994; and *Vulnerable Populations,* Volume 2, edited by S. Sgroi, Lexington Books (Lexington, MA), 1989. Creator of videotapes on rape, sexual abuse, and working with offenders. Contributor to periodicals, including *Medical Aspects of Human Sexuality, International Journal of Offender Therapy and Comparative Criminology, Life, Criminal Justice and Behavior, New England Journal of Medicine, International Journal of Women's Studies, Crime and Delinquency, Journal of Prison Health, Social Science and Medicine,* and *Advocate.* Contributing editor, *Treatment for Sexual Aggressiveness News,* 1981.

SIDELIGHTS: A. Nicholas Groth is a psychologist who specializes in sexual abuse and is the author of several books related to that topic. Elizabeth Stark, in a *Psychology Today* article on incest, referred to Groth's studies on child molesters that uncovered exposure to childhood sexual abuse in 81 percent of sexual offenders (prisoners and mental patients). According to Stark, Groth distinguishes two types of sexual offenders: those who have never developed an adult perspective on sexuality and are thus fixated on sexual relations with children, and those who have regressed due to stress.

Among Groth's works is *Men Who Rape: The Psychology of the Offender,* in which he argues that rape is essentially what Dennis L. Peck, reviewing the book in

Contemporary Sociology, described as "a method for seeking social status, defining social identity, ventilating anger, and achieving power." This work, which Groth wrote in collaboration with H. Jean Birnbaum, analyzes the cases of more than 500 rapists and characterizes sexual offenders as unstable individuals who are often incapable of enduring the everyday pressures of contemporary life. In addition, explain Groth and Birnbaum, these rapists were often victims of childhood abuse and are often incapable of maintaining conventional sexual behavior. Peck, in his assessment of *Men Who Rape,* characterized the book as "a schol-arly exercise," and contended that it "should achieve a prominent position in the growing literature on [rape and rapists]."

BIOGRAPHICAL AND CRITICAL SOURCES:

PERIODICALS

Contemporary Sociology, November, 1981, Dennis L. Peck, review of *Men Who Rape: The Psychology of the Offender,* pp. 793-794.
Psychology Today, May, 1984, article by Elizabeth Stark, pp. 40-46.

H

HANSEN, Joseph 1923-
(Rose Brock, James Colton, James Coulton)

PERSONAL: Born July 19, 1923, in Aberdeen, SD; son of Henry Harold (operator of a shoe shop) and Alma (Rosebrock) Hansen; married Jane Bancroft (a teacher and translator), August 4, 1943; children: Barbara Bancroft. *Education:* Attended public schools in Aberdeen, SD, Minneapolis, MN, and Pasadena, CA, 1929-42.

ADDRESSES: Home—2638 Cullen St., Los Angeles, CA, 90034. *Agent*—Stuart Krichevsky, Sterling Lord Literistic, Inc., 1 Madison Ave., New York, NY 10010.

CAREER: Author and teacher. Member of editorial staff, *One,* beginning 1962; cofounder and staff member, *Tangents,* 1965-70; KPFK-FM, Los Angeles, CA, producer of radio show "Homosexuality Today," 1969. Teacher of fiction writing, Beyond Baroque Foundation, Venice, CA, 1975-76; affiliated with the University of California, Los Angeles, 1977-86. Member of advisory board, Wesleyan Writers Conference, 1989-91.

MEMBER: PEN, Mystery Writers of America, Private Eye Writers of America.

AWARDS, HONORS: National Endowment for the Arts grant, 1974; British Arts Council grant for lecture tour of Northumberland, 1975; nomination for best novel award, Private Eye Writers of America, 1983, for *Gravedigger;* nomination for best short story award, Mystery Writers of America, 1984, for "The Anderson Boy"; nomination for best short story award, Private Eye Writers of America, 1987, for "Merely Players"; honored for "outstanding literary contribution to the lesbian and gay communities," Out/Look Foundation, San Francisco, 1991; Lambda Literary Awards, 1992, for *Country of Old Men: The Last Dave Brandstetter Mystery,* and 1994, for *Living Upstairs.*

WRITINGS:

(As James Coulton) *Gard,* Award Books (New York, NY), 1969.

Fadeout, Harper, (New York, NY), 1970, Alyson Books (Los Angeles, CA), 2000.

(As Rose Brock) *Tarn House* (gothic novel), Avon (New York, NY), 1971.

Death Claims, Harper (New York, NY), 1973.

(As Rose Brock) *Longleaf* (gothic novel), Harper (New York, NY), 1974.

Troublemaker: A Dave Brandstetter Mystery, Harper (New York, NY), 1975, Alyson Books (Los Angeles, CA), 2002.

One Foot in the Boat (poetry), Momentum Press (Los Angeles, CA), 1977.

The Man Everybody Was Afraid Of, Holt (New York, NY), 1978.

Skinflick: A Dave Brandstetter Mystery, Holt (New York, NY), 1979.

The Dog and Other Stories (short stories), Momentum Press (Los Angeles, CA), 1979.

A Smile in His Lifetime, Holt (New York, NY), 1981.

Gravedigger: A Dave Brandstetter Mystery, Holt (New York, NY), 1982.

Backtrack, Countryman Press (Woodstock, VT), 1982.

Job's Year, Holt (New York, NY), 1983.

Nightwork, Holt (New York, NY), 1984.

Brandstetter and Others: Five Fictions (short stories), Countryman Press (Woodstock, VT), 1984.

Steps Going Down, Countryman Press (Woodstock, VT), 1985.

The Little Dog Laughed, Holt (New York, NY), 1986.

Early Graves: A Dave Brandstetter Mystery, Mysterious Press (New York, NY), 1987.

Bohannon's Book: Five Mysteries (short stories), Countryman Press (Woodstock, VT), 1988.

Obedience: A Dave Brandstetter Mystery, Mysterious Press (New York, NY), 1988.

The Boy Who Was Buried This Morning: A Dave Brandstetter Mystery, Viking (New York, NY), 1990.

A Country of Old Men: The Last David Brandstetter Mystery, Viking (New York, NY), 1991.

Living Upstairs, Dutton (New York, NY), 1993.

Bohannon's Country (short stories), Viking (New York, NY), 1993.

Jack of Hearts, Dutton (New York, NY), 1995.

Blood, Snow, and Classic Cars: Mystery Stories, Leyland Publications (San Francisco, CA), 2000.

Bohannon's Women: Mystery Stories, Five Star (Waterville, ME), 2002.

UNDER PSEUDONYM JAMES COLTON

Lost on Twilight Road, National Library (Fresno, CA), 1964.

Strange Marriage, Argyle Books (Los Angeles, CA), 1965.

The Corruptor and Other Stories (short stories), Greenleaf Classics (San Diego, CA), 1968.

Known Homosexual, Brandon House (Los Angeles, CA), 1968, revised edition published under name Joseph Hansen as *Stranger to Himself,* Major Books, 1977, published as *Pretty Boy Dead,* Gay Sunshine Press (San Francisco, CA), 1984.

Cocksure, Greenleaf Classics (San Diego, CA), 1969.

Hang-Up, Brandon House (Los Angeles, CA), 1969.

The Outward Side, Olympia (New York, NY), 1971.

Todd, Olympia (New York, NY), 1971.

Contributor to *The New Yorker Book of Poems,* Viking (New York, NY), 1974; *Literature of South Dakota,* University of South Dakota Press, 1976; *Year's Best Mystery and Suspense Stories, 1984,* Walker, 1985;

Murder, California Style, St. Martin's Press (New York, NY), 1987; *Mammoth Book of Private Eye Stories,* Carroll & Graf (New York, NY), 1988; *City Sleuths and Tough Guys,* Houghton Mifflin (Boston, MA), 1989; *Under the Gun,* Plume, 1990. Also contributor of poems and stories to numerous periodicals, including *Harper's, Atlantic, Saturday Review, New Yorker, South Dakota Review, Tangents, Bachy,* and *Transatlantic Review.*

Also editor of collections of essays, including *Dynamics of the Cuban Revolution: The Trotskyist View,* 1978, and *The Leninist Strategy of Party Building: The Debate on Guerrilla Warfare in Latin America,* 1982.

ADAPTATIONS: Four of Hansen's poems have been set to music by composer Richard Rodney Bennett in a work entitled *Vocalese,* first performed in London in 1983, and broadcast by the British Broadcasting Corporation.

SIDELIGHTS: "When I sat down to write *Fadeout* in 1967, I wanted to write a good, compelling whodunit, but I also wanted to right some wrongs," Joseph Hansen told the *St. James Guide to Crime and Mystery Writers.* He evidently succeeded on both counts. *Fadeout,* and Hansen's many subsequent works, represent a breakthrough in detective fiction: The author's popular series hero, Dave Brandstetter, is not only a hardboiled sleuth in the West Coast tradition, but also, according to a *Village Voice* writer, "one of the few practicing homosexuals in a genre where macho is sine qua non."

"It is fair and useful" to include a gay private eye in the genre, according to Charles Champlin, who asked in the *Los Angeles Times,* "Why should Mike Hammer have a monopoly on sexuality?" A *New York Times Book Review* writer added: "The author does not make a big thing out of Brandstetter's sexual habits. His affairs are treated as simply as the heterosexual affairs of other investigators." Hansen once told *CA,* "For years now my publishers have played down the homosexual element of my novels, preferring as I do that it be taken for granted."

A native of South Dakota, Hansen moved many times in his childhood as his family struggled to survive the Great Depression. Maturing into his teenage years, he admitted in a *Contemporary Authors Autobiography Series* (*CAAS*) article to being "the most completely asexual child who ever lived." In his early adulthood he identified his sexual orientation as homosexual. And while Hansen devoted his professional career, and much of his personal life, to gay issues, he also fell in love with and married Jane Bancroft, with whom he raised a daughter.

In Hansen's view, honed from a lifetime of writing and reading popular fiction, "almost all the folksay about homosexuals is false. So I had some fun turning cliches and stereotypes on their heads." Getting *Fadeout* published in the 1960s "took some doing," the author admitted. "Publishers were leery of my matter-of-fact, nonapologetic approach to a subject that the rule book said had to be treated sensationally or not at all." Finally, toward the end of 1969, Harper & Row accepted the manuscript. As Hansen took up the story in *CAAS,* on the day the news came, no one else was home to hear it. "I told our dog, Bantu, who lifted her head, wagged her tail once, lowered her chin . . . and went back to sleep. I told such of our snoozing cats as I could locate. Then I began ringing up anyone I figured there was a chance of reaching. This was the biggest and best news I would ever get in my life, and I simply had to tell someone, anyone. No one answered."

Once *Fadeout* hit the shelves, critics welcomed Brandstetter to the genre, noting that his creator's light touch regarding the detective's sexuality was a plus. A *Saturday Review* writer, for example, explained that while homosexuality is "integral" to the story, it is unobtrusive because it "is handled as a condition of life, never as a sensational element." Allen J. Hublin agreed, noting in the *New York Times Book Review* that the hero's sexual preference plays "so frontal a role" in the novel while remaining almost incidental because "Hansen portrays that other world sharply and without condescension."

For the most part, the later novels in the series garnered similar admiration from reviewers. According to T. J. Binyon in the *Times Literary Supplement,* Hansen has an "intelligent and sensitive style" that draws readers to plot and characters without eliciting prurient or prudish curiosity about Brandstetter's sex life. Hansen shows gay life "as entitled to its own privacies as any of the more shrill writers [of homosexual literature] do," concluded John C. Davis in the *New Republic.* Even in *Gravedigger,* in which the investigator's homosexuality "is pivotal to the relationships, the plot, and the solution," according to a *Washington Post Book World* writer, the author deals with it "honestly and tastefully and then only when it has a bearing on the story."

To *St. James Guide to Crime and Mystery Writers* essayist Newton Baird, Hansen's books are "strong in Southern California, particularly Los Angeles, atmosphere. Avid readers can enjoy the details regarding houses, cars, beverages, cooking, friends, enemies and out-of-the-ordinary people and events and find them, like all of Hansen's beautifully styled description and dialogue, a purposeful and meaningful part of characterization."

Hansen's style "is of the Ross Macdonald school—unsentimental, clinical," wrote a *New Republic* critic. While another *New York Times Book Review* writer, labeled it "objective" and commented that Hansen "is not one for much preaching." Hansen's novels move quickly, reviewers agree, and usually feature an "intricate, well-machined plot with a superb evocation of the California scene," as a *Times Literary Supplement* review noted. Commenting on *Skinflick* in the *Washington Post Book World,* Jean M. White believed that Hansen "tends to allow the psychos to run away with the plot" in this book, but nonetheless "he still writes crisply with a lean, spare prose that echoes Hammett, Chandler, and Macdonald."

Like White, other reviewers sometimes voiced criticism of a specific work while praising the Brandstetter series in general. Stephen Dobyns found the abundance of detail in *Nightwork* problematic, commenting in the *Washington Post* that Hansen's "keen sense of detail" is to be applauded, yet, in this work, it sometimes "creates decorative clutter." Appreciating the author's vivid evocation of the gay world and the strange characters that inhabit it—a much-noted feature of the mysteries—Robin M. Winks commented in the *New Republic* that in *Gravedigger* "the concern for the milieu gets in the way."

Critics in general attribute part of Hansen's success to the sensitivity and subtlety with which he addresses larger social issues through Brandstetter's views and activities. Several critics have pointed out that a social evil, such as political graft, pollution, or religious fraud, often lies at the heart of the investigator's cases.

The author also uses his fast-paced, whodunit genre to illuminate an aspect of society or human nature without making pointed "moral" judgments. Davis considered *Skinflick,* for example, to be as much about "the ways in which people twist their moralities to meet their needs" as about an investigator using his wits to win against the "bad guys." *Nightwork,* beyond being a sharp mystery, "has a more serious concern, which is simply how human beings treat each other," added Dobyns. The book's message, he felt, is that "one must treat one's fellow creatures with decency, respect and perhaps love."

The author's concern for how humans treat their fellow humans—and how they think about them—is addressed more fully in several novels outside the Brandstetter series. In *Backtrack,* Hansen "wanted to say something about the way parents cut their kids out of their own relationship, from selfishness," the author told Barbara A. Bannon in a *Publishers Weekly* interview. A mystery, the book features an eighteen-year-old protagonist who discovers aspects of his dead father's life that lead him to the novel's strange denouement—the boy waiting for a killer to come to him. Terry Teachout commented in the *National Review* that the story "lies well outside the canon of [the author's] popular David Brandstetter mystery series" and is, in fact, "a short, pithy *Bildungsroman* disguised as a suspense novel." While a *New Yorker* critic labeled it a "slight and often silly story," Callendar called it "a brilliant piece in which even flashbacks are handled convincingly." *Backtrack* "is enriched by the judicious artistic effects that Hansen obtains through the use of his striking style," Teachout claimed. Noting that it is not a happy book, Callendar expressed a fascination with its "sad, bitter ending," concluding that it is "a book that commands respect."

A Smile in His Lifetime concentrates on Whit Miller, a bisexual who finds himself growing apart from his wife and towards a purely homosexual existence. In the *Washington Post Book World,* Christopher Schlemering called it "a 'serious' change-of-pace novel" for Hansen. "The emotional landscape is bleak, lonely," explained Avery Corman in the *New York Times Book Review.* For Whit Miller, "sex does not buy happiness, nor do fame and money." Corman went on to comment that the author "has chosen a tough, staccato style for this novel, and it works against much of the emotional material, making it appear melodramatic. . . . Despite the lean quality of the

prose, the novel is weakened by the author's decision to tell us too much." Still, conceded Schlemering, the humor in the novel presents yet another aspect of Hansen's skill.

Hansen once told *CA* that he regards *Job's Year* as his "best and most important novel," and Stanley Johnson agreed in the *Oregonian,* writing, "It is clearly one of the most impressive novels" of 1983, one which invites "comparison with the very best of modern fiction." *Job's Year,* like *Backtrack* and *A Smile in His Lifetime,* concentrates on a man who reaches a point in life where the past impinges on his view of his present life. A homosexual actor returns to his family home to care for a dying sister. Characters and scenes from the past and present mix to present a novel that treads "the fine line between faith and modern existentialism," wrote Paul Levine. His *Los Angeles Times* review compared the work to "a walk along the tightropes between madness and sanity." The book works well, Levine felt, because "Hansen is at his best, moving from past to present, memories unlocked by a change of light, smell of perfume, feelings of love, lust, loneliness." A "quieter" book than *Backtrack* or *A Smile in His Lifetime, Job's Year* contains a subtlety similar to that which reviewers noted favorably in Hansen's treatment of Brandstetter's sexuality. Summarized Levine, "[The plot and characters are] brought to life with grace, style, and subtle surety."

Steps Going Down is another of Hansen's non-Brandstetter mysteries in which the former male prostitute Darryl Cutler becomes infatuated with an amoral youth who leads him to murder. Writing in the *New York Times Book Review,* Callendar described the novel as the "study of the disintegration of a human being." In spite of an ending which Callendar believed is manipulative, he praised the novel as "in its way a brilliant piece of work."

Returning to the Brandstetter series in 1986, Hansen published *The Little Dog Laughed,* which Margaret Cannon described in the *Globe and Mail* as "a novel as topical as tomorrow's news." In the book Hansen tells the tale of a Pulitzer Prize-winning journalist who may have been killed for the notes to the Central American story he is working on. Hansen's politics, Cannon wrote, are "no secret" and he makes his "contempt [known] for U.S. conservatives whose idea of support for democracy is support for guerrilla training at home and genocide abroad." Following in a similarly topical vein, *Early Graves* is another Brandstetter novel whose villain is a murderer whose victims are young homosexuals with AIDS. In the *New York Times Book Review,* Callendar wrote that while the book is "well-plotted and well-written," the "major emphasis of the book is about AIDS and the fear, even hysteria, it creates among otherwise rational people." *Time* contributor William A. Henry III wrote that *Early Graves* will "rank with the best" of the novels dealing with the impact of AIDS; John Gross called it "an unqualified success" in the *New York Times.*

Obedience finds Brandstetter on the brink of retirement, but called back to investigate a murder possibly committed by a Vietnam veteran living in a Vietnamese community. Cannon called *Obedience* "absolutely the best ever" Brandstetter book, and Gross wrote, "I do hope this isn't really Dave Brandstetter's last bow." It is not. Brandstetter solves another mystery with a political, socially-conscious slant in *The Boy Who Was Buried This Morning,* which involves, according to Marilyn Stasio of the *New York Times Book Review,* a "paramilitary outfit of crypto-fascists bent on purging a small California town of its minority residents."

In *A Country of Old Men: The Last David Brandstetter Mystery,* published in 1991, Hansen deals with both crime and mortality. Stasio noted that Brandstetter's health is failing, though his mind is keen, as he investigates a killing and the child who witnessed it. In the end, Stasio noted that although Brandstetter, with his cool, reserved, rational personality, may stay silent around "people who are hurting . . . he cares. . . . He has always cared a lot. And that's why we'll miss him."

Since ending the Brandstetter series, Hansen has written many short stories about the straight detective Hack Bohannon. *Bohannon's Country,* published in 1993, features three tales about the titled hero. A *Publishers Weekly* reviewer remarked that "Hansen is in top form, delighting readers with surprising, often risk-taking, fiction." *Bohannon's Women: Mystery Stories,* which followed in 2002, included five more stories about Hack. In this volume, Hack's wife, who had floated in and out of a coma in *Bohannon's Country,* is dead, and he is dating a woman named T. Hodges. Whitney Scott praised *Bohannon's Women* in *Booklist,* saying of Hansen's sleuth that "this appealing central figure and Hansen's sure, deft hand with both exterior and interior landscapes leave readers wishing for more."

Hansen once told *CAAS* in 1993 that, along with celebrating his fiftieth wedding anniversary, he planned a series of twelve novels about Nathan Reed, covering ages seventeen to seventy. "Unrealistic for a writer crowding seventy himself? I didn't think so. One of my reasons for ending the Dave Brandstetter series was to clear the time. I was going to be writing, anyway, for as long as I could sit up and think, and I wanted to give some shape to my own life and times."

BIOGRAPHICAL AND CRITICAL SOURCES:

BOOKS

Contemporary Authors Autobiography Series, Volume 17, Gale (Detroit, MI), 1993.
Contemporary Literary Criticism, Volume 38, Gale (Detroit, MI), 1986.
St. James Guide to Crime and Mystery Writers, 4th edition, St. James Press (Detroit, MI), 1996.

PERIODICALS

Armchair Detective, summer, 1984.
Booklist, May 1, 1993, Ray Olson, review of *Bohannon's Country,* p. 1573; July, 2002, Whitney Scott, review of *Bohannon's Women: Mystery Stories,* p. 1826.
Globe and Mail (Toronto, Ontario, Canada), May 19, 1984; February 28, 1987; August 5, 1989.
Kirkus Reviews, May 1, 2002, review of *Bohannon's Women,* p. 618.
Lambda Book Report, September-October, 1993, John L. Myers, review of *Bohannon's Country,* p. 37.
Library Journal, May 1, 1993, Rex E. Flett, review of *Bohannon's Country,* p. 121.
Listener, June 5, 1975; January 11, 1979.
Los Angeles Times, April 9, 1982; December 16, 1983.
Los Angeles Times Book Review, February 26, 1984; May 5, 1985.
National Review, May 28, 1982; December 24, 1982.
New Republic, April 12, 1980; May 30, 1981; August 2, 1982.
Newsweek, June 7, 1982.
New Yorker, November 5, 1979; February 7, 1983.
New York Times, December 4, 1987; December 2, 1988; June 3, 1990.

New York Times Book Review, September 20, 1970; January 21, 1973; December 2, 1973; December 28, 1975; November 4, 1979; October 12, 1980; June 28, 1981; September 20, 1981; May 30, 1982; January 16, 1983; April 8, 1984; January 19, 1986, p. 17; December 27, 1987, p. 13; June 3, 1990, p. 32; June 16, 1991, p. 21.

Oregonian, October 24, 1983.

Publishers Weekly, December 17, 1982; July 29, 1989, Penny Koganoff, review of *Bohannon's Book: Five Mysteries,* p. 216; March 29, 1993, review of *Bohannon's Country,* p. 38; June 28, 1993; December 5, 1994.

Saturday Review, September 26, 1970; February, 1973.

Time, November 4, 1985, pp. 83, 86; February 1, 1988, p. 66.

Times Literary Supplement, December 1, 1978; June 6, 1980; October 26, 1984.

Village Voice, December 15, 1975.

Washington Post Book World, September 21, 1975; October 21, 1979; November 16, 1980; June 7, 1981; April 18, 1982; October 16, 1983.

West Coast Review of Books, May, 1982; November, 1983.

Wilson Library Bulletin, December, 1993, Gail Pool, review of *Bohannon's Country,* p. 86.*

*   *   *

HAYNES, John Earl 1944-

PERSONAL: Born November 22, 1944, in Plant City, FL; son of John Milner (an educator) and Sarah Elizabeth (Farmer) Haynes; married Janette Marie Murray (an educator), December, 1971; children: Joshua, Amanda, William. *Ethnicity:* "American." *Education:* Florida State University, B.A. (magna cum laude), 1966; University of Minnesota—Twin Cities, M.A., 1968, Ph.D., 1978. *Religion:* Anglican Catholic.

ADDRESSES: Home—10041 Frederick Ave., Kensington, MD 20895. *Office*—Manuscript Division, Library of Congress, Washington, DC 20540-4780; fax: 202-707-6336. *E-mail*—jhay@loc.gov.

CAREER: Aide to the governor of Minnesota, 1971-77; U.S. Congress, Washington, DC, legislative aide, 1977-83; aide to the governor of Minnesota, 1983-87; Library of Congress, Washington, DC, twentieth-century political historian in Manuscript Division, 1987—. University of California—Berkeley, Bush leadership fellow, 1974; Central European University, lecturer, 2001; also speaker at other institutions and at scholarly conferences. International Council on Archives, historical advisor to International Computerization of the Comintern Archives project, 1998—; member of advisory board for H-US1918-45 list of H-Net discussion lists, 2000—. *Military service:* U.S. Army Reserve, 1979-90; became major.

MEMBER: Historians of American Communism (president, 1992-95), Phi Beta Kappa, Phi Alpha Theta.

AWARDS, HONORS: Woodrow Wilson fellow; Templeton Honor Roll, outstanding contemporary book, c. 1995, for *The Secret World of American Communism.*

WRITINGS:

Dubious Alliance: The Making of Minnesota's DFL Party, University of Minnesota Press (Minneapolis, MN), 1984.

Communism and Anti-Communism in the United States: An Annotated Guide to Historical Writings, Garland Publishing (New York, NY), 1987.

(With Harvey Klehr) *The American Communist Movement: Storming Heaven Itself,* Twayne Publishers (New York, NY), 1992.

(With Harvey Klehr and Fridrikh Igorevich Firsov) *The Secret World of American Communism* (Book-of-the-Month Club and History Book Club selections), Yale University Press (New Haven, CT), 1995.

Red Scare or Red Menace? American Communism and Anticommunism in the Cold War Era, Ivan R. Dee (Chicago, IL), 1996.

(With Harvey Klehr and Kyrill Mikhailovich Anderson) *The Soviet World of American Communism,* Yale University Press (New Haven, CT), 1998.

(Editor) *Calvin Coolidge and the Coolidge Era: Essays on the History of the 1920s,* Library of Congress (Washington, DC), 1998.

(With Harvey Klehr) *Venona: Decoding Soviet Espionage in America* (History Book Club selection), Yale University Press (New Haven, CT), 1999.

(With Harvey Klehr) *In Denial: Historians, Communism, and Espionage,* Encounter Books (San Francisco, CA), 2003.

Contributor to books, including *Minnesota in a Century of Change: The State and Its People since 1900*, edited by Clifford E. Clark, Minnesota Historical Society Press (Minneapolis, MN), 1989; contributor to encyclopedias. Contributor to periodicals, including *Public Historian, American Spectator, Problems of Post-Communism, New Republic, Heterodoxy, Film History, American Experiment Quarterly, Journal of Cold War Studies, Labour History Review,* and *Continuity.* Editor of *Historians of American Communism* (newsletter), 1982-2003; member of editorial board, *State and Local Government Review,* 1983-84, and *International Newsletter of Communist Studies;* member of editorial advisory board, *American Communist History,* 2002.

SIDELIGHTS: John Earl Haynes is a prominent scholar of the American communist movement. His books *The Secret World of American Communism* and *The Soviet World of American Communism* were the first to draw on documentation from official Soviet archive sources not previously available to those in the West.

In *The Secret World of American Communism,* Haynes and coauthors Harvey Klehr and Fridrikh Igorevich Firsov use documents found in the archives of the former Soviet Union to draw a more accurate picture of Soviet influence on the American communist movement than previously available. The authors found that, contrary to what American Communist Party members had maintained for decades, the party was an instrumental part of Soviet espionage operations, was heavily financed by the Soviet Union, and was implicated in the deaths or disappearances of many former members and political rivals. Furthermore, the evidence for these charges, noted Eric Breindel in the *National Review,* was found in "the Comintern archive and in the archive of the CPUSA [Communist Party of the United States of America]. Both collections are located in Moscow." "Documents now available in Russia," noted Arthur M. Schlesinger, Jr. in the *New Republic,* "prove beyond any question that the American party functioned as an instrument of Soviet espionage." As Mark Falcoff put it in *Commentary,* "Now, surviving members of the party and, even more, their tenured apologists, will be forced to make their case in the face of documentary evidence of a kind they never expected to confront."

Particularly damaging to American communists was the new evidence for the party's involvement in the murder of exiled Soviet leader Leon Trotsky in Mexico. Although, as Breindel noted, the book's "research serves largely to confirm much that had already been alleged," it does prove that Trotsky's murder was "a joint undertaking between the Soviet secret police and the U.S. Party's underground networks."

American communist involvement with the murder of Soviet dissidents is more fully documented in *The Soviet World of American Communism,* in which Haynes, Klehr and Kyrill M. Anderson present more documentation of Soviet influence on American communism, all of it drawn from official Soviet sources. A critic for *Booklist* pointed out the particular case of Lovett Fort-Whiteman, a black communist leader of the 1930s who disappeared when he went afoul of the party. He was, stated the critic, but "one of as many as a thousand accused Trotskyists that the American party turned over to Soviet police." A *Publishers Weekly* critic called *The Soviet World of American Communism* "another important volume for understanding the U.S., the U.S.S.R., and the 20th century."

Haynes once told *CA:* "I enjoy the study of history because it allows me to understand how and why human history happened the way it did. I enjoy writing about it because, once I have come to an understanding of how and why something came about, I want to tell others. I find writing about communism and anticommunism interesting because the conflict over communism was one of the defining events of the twentieth century."

BIOGRAPHICAL AND CRITICAL SOURCES:

PERIODICALS

Booklist, February 1, 1998, review of *The Soviet World of American Communism,* p. 883.
Commentary, June, 1995, Mark Falcoff, review of *The Secret World of American Communism,* p. 61.
Library Journal, February 15, 1998, p. 157.
Nation, June 12, 1995, p. 846.
National Review, June 12, 1995, Eric Breindel, review of *The Secret World of American Communism,* p. 63.
New Republic, May 29, 1995, Arthur M. Schlesinger, Jr., review of *The Secret World of American Communism,* p. 36.

Publishers Weekly, January 26, 1998, review of *The Soviet World of American Communism,* p. 77.
Society, November-December, 1996, p. 101.

ONLINE

John Earl Haynes: Historical Writings, http://www.johnearlhaynes.org/ (October 1, 2003).

*   *   *

HEDDERWICK, Mairi 1939-

PERSONAL: Born May 2, 1939, in Gourock, Renfrewshire, Scotland; daughter of Douglas Lindsay (an architect) and Margaret (Gallacher) Crawford; married Ronnie Hedderwick, June 24, 1962 (divorced); children: Mark, Tamara. *Ethnicity:* "Scots." *Education:* Edinburgh College of Art, Diploma of Art, 1962; Jordanhill College of Education (Glasgow, Scotland), art teaching certificate, 1963; primary teaching certificate, 1981; Stirling University, doctorate, 2003. *Hobbies and other interests:* House renovation, interior design.

ADDRESSES: Home—Scotland. *Agent*—Giles Gordon, Curtis Brown Agency, 37 Queensferry St., Edinburgh EH2 4QS, Scotland.

CAREER: Traveling art teacher in Mid Argyll, Scotland, 1962-64; crofter and mother, Isle of Coll, Scotland, 1964-69; Malin Workshop (art stationery, prints), Isle of Coll and Fort William, Scotland, artist, designer, and owner with husband, 1969-80; community cooperatives advisor in Highlands and Islands (based in Inverness), Scotland, 1986-89. Freelance writer, illustrator, and public speaker, 1980—.

AWARDS, HONORS: Souvenirs of Scotland Award, Scottish Design Centre, 1971 and 1974; Smarties Award finalist, for *Katie Morag and the Tiresome Ted,* 1986; Earthworm Award (with others), Friends of the Earth, 1993, for *Venus Peter Saves the Whale.*

WRITINGS:

SELF-ILLUSTRATED; FOR CHILDREN

Katie Morag Delivers the Mail (also see below), Bodley Head (London, England), Little, Brown (Boston, MA), 1984.

Katie Morag and the Two Grandmothers (also see below), Bodley Head (London, England), Little, Brown (Boston, MA), 1985.
Katie Morag and the Tiresome Ted (also see below), Bodley Head (London, England), Little, Brown (Boston, MA), 1986.
Katie Morag and the Big Boy Cousins (also see below), Bodley Head (London, England), Little, Brown (Boston, MA), 1987.
Peedie Peebles' Summer or Winter Book, Bodley Head (London, England), 1989, published as *P. D. Peebles' Summer or Winter Book,* Little, Brown (Boston, MA), 1989.
Katie Morag and the New Pier, Bodley Head (London, England), 1993.
Dreamy Robbie!, Oliver & Boyd (Harlow, England), 1993.
Robbie's First Day at School, Oliver & Boyd (Harlow, England), 1993.
Robbie's Trousers, Oliver & Boyd (Harlow, England), 1993.
Robbie and Grandpa, Oliver & Boyd (Harlow, England), 1994.
Robbie's Birthday, Oliver & Boyd (Harlow, England), 1994.
Peedie Peebles' Colour Book, Bodley Head (London, England), 1994, published as *Oh No, Peedie Peebles!,* Red Fox (London, England), 1997.
(Reteller) *The Tale of Carpenter MacPheigh: A Scottish Folk Tale,* Blackie (London, England), 1994.
Katie Morag and the Wedding, Bodley Head (London, England), 1995.
Katie Morag's Island Stories, (includes *Katie Morag Delivers the Mail, Katie Morag and the Two Grandmothers, Katie Morag and the Tiresome Ted,* and *Katie Morag and the Big Boy Cousins*), Bodley Head (London, England), 1995.
The Big Katie Morag Storybook, Bodley Head (London, England), 1996.
Katie Morag and the Grand Concert, Bodley Head (London, England), 1997.
The Second Katie Morag Storybook, Bodley Head (London, England), 1998.
Katie Morag's Rainy Day Book, Bodley Head (London, England), 1999.
Katie Morag and the Riddles, Bodley Head (London, England), 2001.
A Walk with Grannie, Hodder & Stoughton (London, England), 2003.

SELF-ILLUSTRATED; FOR ADULTS

Mairi Hedderwick's Views of Scotland, Famedram (Gartocharn, Scotland), 1981.

An Eye on the Hebrides: An Illustrated Journey, Canongate (Edinburgh, Scotland), 1989.

Highland Journey: A Sketching Tour of Scotland Retracing the Footsteps of Victorian Artist John T. Reid, Canongate (Edinburgh, Scotland), 1992.

Seachange: The Summer Voyage from East to West Scotland of the Anassa, Canongate (Edinburgh, Scotland), 1999.

ILLUSTRATOR

Rumer Godden, *The Old Woman Who Lived in a Vinegar Bottle,* Macmillan (London, England), Viking (New York, NY), 1972.

Jane Duncan, *Herself and Janet Reachfar,* Macmillan (London, England), 1975, published as *Brave Janet Reachfar,* Seabury Press (New York, NY), 1975, reprinted, Birlinn (Edinburgh, Scotland), 2003.

Jane Duncan, *Janet Reachfar and the Kelpie,* Macmillan (London, England), Seabury Press (New York, NY), 1976, reprinted, Birlinn (Edinburgh, Scotland), 2003.

E. R. Taylor, *The Gifts of the Tarns,* Collins (London, England), 1977.

Jane Duncan, *Janet Reachfar and Chickabird,* Macmillan (London, England), Seabury Press (New York, NY), 1978.

(With others) Enid Fairhead, editor, *The Book of Bedtime Stories,* Collins (London, England), 1979.

Wendy Body, *A Cat Called Rover; A Dog Called Smith,* Longman (Harlow, England), 1981.

Anne Wood and Ann Pilling, editors, *Our Best Stories,* Hodder & Stoughton (London, England), 1986.

Moira Miller, *Hamish and the Wee Witch,* Methuen (London, England), 1986.

Alexander Maclean, *The Haggis,* State Mutual Book & Periodical Service (Bridgehampton, NY), 1987.

Jamie Fleeman's Country Cookbook, State Mutual Book & Periodical Service (Bridgehampton, NY), 1987.

Alan Keegan, *Scotch in Miniature,* revised edition, State Mutual Book & Periodical Service (Bridgehampton, NY), 1987.

Moira Miller, *Hamish and the Fairy Gifts,* Methuen (London, England), 1988.

Moira Miller, *Meet Maggie McMuddle,* Methuen (London, England), 1990.

Beverley Mathias, editor, *The Spell Singers and Other Stories,* Blackie (London, England), 1990.

Christopher Rush, *Venus Peter Saves the Whale,* Canongate (Edinburgh, Scotland), Pelican (Gretna, LA), 1992.

Joan Lingard, *Hands Off Our School!,* Hamish Hamilton (London, England), 1992.

Tom Pow, *Callum's Big Day,* Inyx (Aberdour, Scotland), 2000.

Also illustrator of *Hamish and the Fairy Bairn,* 1989, and *A Kist of Whistles,* 1990, both written by Moira Miller.

ADAPTATIONS: Some of Hedderwick's works are in progress of being animated.

WORK IN PROGRESS: Katie Morag's Birthday Book; illustrations for *Hebridean Diary.*

SIDELIGHTS: Mairi Hedderwick, is, according to Ann Fotheringham in the Glasgow *Evening Times,* "one of Scotland's best-loved authors and illustrators." Her perceptive depictions of Scottish island life have found a wide audience in Great Britain, the United States, and Scandinavia. Hedderwick has illustrated works by other children's writers, but she is best known for her own picture books. Most of these feature Katie Morag, a youngster growing up on an island in the Hebrides. The author told *Horn Book:* "When I started creating the Katie Morag books, there were very few books about, and for, Scottish children by Scottish authors. This may sound a trifle chauvinistic, but it is pleasing to see that the major publishers are more aware of the demand. . . . I have been very lucky; I had little restriction put on my expression of my culture." Hedderwick, who is also a well-known travel writer, finds when she is touring for her adult books, that "Katie Morag is all people want to hear about," as the author told Fotheringham. "I know I can't stop writing about her." Hedderwick has second-generation readers now following the exploits of her plucky island lass, and the Morag tales have even been included in the school curriculum in England.

Hedderwick was born and raised in Scotland, the granddaughter of a missionary to Africa. Both her grandfather and her father painted, so her own artistic ambitions were encouraged at home and at school. Hedderwick told *Horn Book* that, although her economic circumstances were comfortable during childhood, she felt emotionally deprived. "I had a mother who did not show much affection," she said. "I do not have any memories of being held or cuddled by her. . . . I was an only child. My father was often ill with 'nerves', as it used to be called. He died when I was thirteen. That may be why I became a children's writer and illustrator—perhaps I am still trying to find that lost childhood."

As a youngster, Hedderwick discovered a book in which the children went to an island in the Hebrides. The description of that region's beauty filled her with a longing she never quite forgot. "I wanted with all my heart to go to that island and sail on that sea," she told *Horn Book*. First, however, came attendance at an all-girls' school in nearby Kilmacolm. As the school was both a day- and boarding-school, Hedderwick, a day student, experienced "snobbery and discrimination" from the girls who were boarding there, as she noted in an interview with a contributor to the *Scotsman* of Edinburgh. She had to travel by bus each day to catch a train for the school, and dressed in her school uniform, she also stood out among the working-class passengers. Caught between two worlds, she "did not like school very much," as she went on to observe in the *Scotsman*. "I was excruciatingly shy and, as I grew older, covered up this misery by appearing confident. This ploy was not in my interest and I came over as being superior." She did have some favorite teachers, however, including a piano instructor with whom she could relax. Art and music were her strongest subjects, but English was not a strong suit. She "had no confidence at all in writing," as she noted in the *Scotsman*. Neither was she much good at mathematics. At this time in her life, she wanted to be a missionary like her grandfather but soon that was displaced by her love of art.

Hedderwick attended Edinburgh College of Art from 1957 until 1961. "That was the first liberating experience of my life," she recalled for her *Scotsman* interview. "There was no snobbery whatsoever. It was a fantastic experience." Thereafter she earned a teaching certificate from Jordanhill College of Education and served as a traveling art teacher in several Scottish villages and married in 1962. For slightly more than a year she and her husband worked together on a dairy farm, then they moved to the Hebridean Isle of Coll. There they lived "in splendid isolation," as she noted in *Horn Book,* in an old farmhouse at the end of a beach. Hedderwick found they could support themselves by manufacturing postcards of Coll and neighboring islands better than struggling by working the croft.

"We started with a hand duplicator because there was no electricity on the island, and we made island map postcards of the West Coast," the author told *Horn Book*. "We churned out sixty-five thousand postcards in one season. . . . We expanded the range of stationery products and prints from my sketching tours on other islands and the mainland of Scotland. Our two small children had plenty of scrap paper to be creative with!"

When their two children became old enough to attend secondary school, Hedderwick and her husband reluctantly left Coll for the mainland town of Fort William. By that time, Hedderwick had begun to illustrate children's books by other authors. Her book illustrating career began with *The Old Woman Who Lived in a Vinegar Bottle* by Rumer Godden. Hedderwick was selected from a group of other beginning illustrators in a contest arranged by the well-known author Godden, who wanted to give new illustrators a hand up in the industry. Subsequently Hedderwick illustrated several "Janet Reachfar" books by Jane Duncan, including *Herself and Janet Reachfar, Janet Reachfar and the Kelpie,* and *Janet Reachfar and Chickabird*. As a contributor for *Children's Books and Their Creators* noted, "Hedderwick's impressionistic watercolors bring to life the Highlands farm setting of these warm family stories." These tales also gave Hedderwick experience in illustrating a sprightly young girl who lives surrounded by adults. With the death of Duncan, Hedderwick was encouraged to develop books of her own which feature just such a spunky young heroine. In the mid-1980s, now living in Inverness, Hedderwick began to write and illustrate her own books, featuring island-dwelling Katie Morag and her family.

The series began with *Katie Morag Delivers the Mail,* which introduces the red-haired protagonist and her family, who run the post office and shop on the Scottish island of Struay. The story is based on the life Hedderwick and her family lived on the island of Coll. The author/illustrator details very closely the island life and the life of young Katie Morag McColl. Removed from the mainland, the island has mail and goods delivered three times a week, weather permitting, and Katie's life is equally removed from the hurly-burly of the modern world. Katie's grandmother is usually dressed in dungarees and indulges in such unfeminine behavior as fixing the family tractor. Katie Morag is blessed—sometimes she feels cursed—with two grandmothers: one on the mainland whom she calls Granma and is appropriately grandmotherly and urbane, and one on the island, dubbed Grannie Island, who keeps young Katie in line.

Hedderwick's books chronicle life on Struay, and it is anything but dull or typical as Katie's mother runs the post office while her dad wins prizes for his baking and Grannie Island lumbers about in rubber boots and overalls and operates her croft on her own. Katie's adventures are further illustrated in *Katie Morag and the Two Grandmothers,* which brings to center stage the differences between these two relatives. In *Katie Morag and the Tiresome Ted,* the young girl takes out her frustrations and jealousy over the arrival of a new baby by repeatedly throwing her favorite teddy bear into the ocean. *Katie Morag and the Big Boy Cousins* introduces more of the extended family and their amazement with Katie's tomboyish behavior. In *Katie Morag and the New Pier,* the construction of a pier brings new guests to the island.

The "Katie Morag" books have been praised for their strong sense of place, their non-sexist role models, and their sensitive exploration of everyday life in Scotland. Reviewers have also commended Hedderwick for her artwork featured in the series. A critic for *Twentieth-Century Children's Writers* commented that "the success of the illustrations lies in the minute detail so beloved by children—the animals wreaking unseen havoc, the clutter of goods on the shelves of the shops, and the bustling, everyday life of the community."

Further tales of life on Struay are served up in *Katie Morag and the Wedding,* which again features Katie's two grandmothers. There is a wedding for one while the other temporarily reconnects with an estranged husband. "The charm of the story, however," noted Celia Gibbs in *School Librarian,* "is in the pictures." More of Katie's relations turn up in *Katie Morag and the Grand Concert,* in which identical twin uncles, Uncle Sven and Uncle Sean, who also happen to be world-famous musicians, visit the island and participate in a concert. Katie is also going to take part and practices a song endlessly. However, on the big night, Katie sees a friend sitting in the front, wearing the same dress as she. This throws her off momentarily, and she runs back stage where she finds that Uncle Sven who has lost his voice and is suffering similar distress. "Fans of Katie Morag will be delighted to see a new book in the series," thought Prue Goodwin in a *School Librarian* review of the title. Kate Kellaway, writing in the London *Observer,* called the same book "merry and vital," with illustrations "as much of a delight as ever." Similarly, Lindsey Fraser, writing in *Books for Keeps* about *Katie Morag and the Grand Concert,* felt that, "as in all Hedderwick's books, the illustrative detail is exquisite."

With her 2001 title, *Katie Morag and the Riddles,* Hedderwick presents her heroine at school and sick of having to help the younger children. She likes her time much better at home, where she dresses up in her mother's clothes and jewelry. But such delight is spoiled when Katie accidentally breaks one of her mother's necklaces; she tries to make up for this by putting out extra effort while at school. Her penance includes helping the other children to solve various riddles the teacher gives them. "The riddles are part of the fun of the story," wrote Wendy Axford in a *School Librarian* review of the title. Axford went on to praise the "delightful illustrations of island life."

Katie is also featured in story and poem collections, including *The Big Katie Morag Storybook* and *The Second Katie Morag Storybook.* In the first title, Katie is busy acting as mediator between her two grandmothers or becoming a friend to a seal, in a work that displays "the author's obvious love of the island," according to Marie Imeson, writing in *School Librarian.* A critic for *Publishers Weekly* commended Hedderwick's "cheerful, lively cartoon illustrations," as did a reviewer for *Junior Bookshelf,* who found them "superb." Writing in *Books for Keeps,* Gwynneth Bailey thought that *The Second Katie Morag Storybook* was "a magical collection of stories and poems to pore over."

More island fare is provided in *Katie Morag's Rainy Day Book,* as well as books for toddlers featuring Peedie Peebles, including *Peedie Peebles' Summer or Winter Book* and *Peedie Peebles' Colour Book.* Hedderwick also deals in non-series picture books, such as *The Tale of Carpenter MacPheigh: A Scottish Folk Tale,* and has continued to occasionally do illustrations for other authors, including her award-winning artwork for Christopher Rush's ecological parable, *Venus Peter Saves the Whale.*

"I'd like to think that all my work is more than pretty pictures," Hedderwick told *Horn Book.* "My children's books all have, at base, a moral message. That must be the missionary grandfather emerging from me. I would never lose the message of a story by hiding it behind a really gorgeous picture. For young children art appreciation is way down the line—the story and the characters are paramount." At the same time, the author notes, illustrations are crucial to the formation of young imaginations. "Illustrations in books are often the first place a small child sees and learns about what is beyond its own experience," she concluded. "That is a big responsibility!"

BIOGRAPHICAL AND CRITICAL SOURCES:

BOOKS

Kingman, Lee, and others, compilers, *Illustrators of Children's Books: 1967-1976,* Horn Book (Boston, MA), 1978.
St. James Guide to Children's Writers, 5th edition, St. James Press (Detroit, MI), 1999.
Silvey, Anita, editor, *Children's Books and Their Creators,* Houghton Mifflin (Boston, MA), 1995, p. 301.
Twentieth-Century Children's Writers, 3rd edition, St. James Press (Detroit, MI), 1989.

PERIODICALS

Booklist, June 1, 1992, p. 1766.
Books for Keeps, November, 1997, Lindsey Fraser, review of *Katie Morag and the Grand Concert,* p. 20; September, 1998, Gwynneth Bailey, review of *The Second Katie Morag Storybook,* p. 21; November, 1999, review of *Katie Morag and the Grand Concert,* p. 18.
Children's Literature in Education, Volume 22, number 1, 1991.
Evening Times (Glasgow, Scotland), June 12, 2003, Ann Fotheringham, "Katie Morag Up for More Mischief; Mairi Hedderwick," p. 26.
Horn Book, September-October, 1984, pp. 580-581; May-June, 1985, pp. 316-317; July-August, 1989, pp. 474-475; March-April, 1990, Mairi Hedderwick, "The Artist at Work: A Sense of Place," pp. 171-177.
Junior Bookshelf, December, 1996, review of *The Big Katie Morag Storybook,* pp. 252-253.

Library Journal, March 15, 2000, John Kenny, review of *Sea Change,* p. 117.
New York Times Book Review, February 15, 1987, p. 41.
Observer (London, England), July, 20, 1997, Kate Kellaway, review of *Katie Morag and the Grand Concert,* p. 18.
Publishers Weekly, April 29, 1988, p. 75; May 12, 1989, p. 289; November 25, 1996, review of *The Big Katie Morag Storybook,* p. 77.
School Librarian, May, 1995, Sybil Hannavy, review of *The Tale of Carpenter MacPheigh: A Scottish Folk Tale,* p. 59; August, 1995, Celia Gibbs, review of *Katie Morag and the Wedding,* p. 103; November, 1996, Marie Imeson, review of *The Big Katie Morag Storybook,* p. 146; November, 1997, Prue Goodwin, review of *Katie Morag and the Grand Concert,* p. 186; autumn, 1999, Liz Dubber, review of *Katie Morag's Rainy Day Book,* p. 130; autumn, 2001, Wendy Axford, review of *Katie Morag and the Riddles,* p. 131.
School Library Journal, October, 1984, p. 147; May, 1986, p. 75; December, 1986, p. 88; September, 1987, p. 163; July, 1989, p. 66.
Scotsman (Edinburgh, Scotland), April 16, 2003, "My Schooldays: Mairi Hedderwick Finally Finding Her True Voice," p. 13.
Sunday Times (London, England), November 7, 1994, Mairi Hedderwick, "Search for Grandfather's Soul," p. 4; March 19, 2001, Mairi Hedderwick, "Escape: Time Off," p. 10.
Times Educational Supplement, September 9, 1984, p. 20; September 2, 1994, p. 29; July 10, 1998, p. 13.*

*   *   *

HENISCH, Heinz K. 1922-
(Benjamin Spear)

PERSONAL: Born April 21, 1922, in Neudek, Germany; son of Leo (an attorney) and Fanny (Soicher) Henisch; married Bridget Ann Wilsher (a photo-historian and medievalist), February 6, 1960. *Education:* University of Bristol, B.Sc., 1940; University of Reading, B.Sc., 1942, Ph.D., 1949. *Hobbies and other interests:* Computers, music, photography.

ADDRESSES: Home and office—346 Hillcrest Ave., State College, PA 16803; fax: 814-238-3577.

CAREER: Royal Aircraft Establishment, Farnborough, England, junior scientific officer, 1942-46; University of Reading, Reading, England, lecturer in physics, 1948-62; Pennsylvania State University, University Park, PA, professor of physics, 1963-93, professor of the history of photography, 1974-93, research professor emeritus, 1993—, elected life fellow of Institute for the Arts and Humanistic Studies, also associate director of Materials Research Laboratory, 1968-75. Sylvania Electric Products, visiting scientist, 1955-56; Goucher College, Samuel Newton Taylor Lecturer, 1973; lecturer at colleges and universities in Austria, Czechoslovakia, England, France, Germany, Israel, Mexico, Peru, Romania, Switzerland, Taiwan, Venezuela, and throughout the United States, as well as on television. Central Pennsylvania Festival of the Arts, codirector of exhibition "Beauty in Science: Science in Art," 1973, 1974; Palmer Museum of Art, co-guest curator of a major photo-history exhibition at 1988; HUB Formal Gallery, University Park, PA, co-guest curator of an exhibition of Henisch's own photographs, "People, Places, Patterns," 1989. Holder of eight patents, all on various aspects of semiconductor technology. Tem-Pres Research, Inc., member of scientific advisory board, 1966-70; Volunteers in Technical Assistance, member. Pennsylvania State University Press, committee chair, 1973-75. Consultant to Philco Corp., Polaroid Corp., Energy Conversion Devices, Inc., and Carborundum Co.

MEMBER: American Physical Society (fellow), American Photographic Historical Society (fellow), Institute of Physics (England; fellow), Royal Photographic Society (fellow).

AWARDS, HONORS: Honorary fellow of A74 Group of Photographers, Warsaw, Poland, 1975; D.Sc., University of Reading, 1979; Rudolf and Hertha Benjamin Award, American Photographic Historical Society, 1996, for *The Painted Photograph, 1839-1914: Origins, Techniques, Aspirations.*

WRITINGS:

PHOTOGRAPHY BOOKS; WITH WIFE, B. A. HENISCH

Chipmunk Portrait, Carnation Press (State College, PA), 1970.

The Photographic Experience, Pennsylvania State University Press (University Park, PA), 1988.

The Photographic Experience, 1839-1914: Images and Attitudes, Pennsylvania State University Press (University Park, PA), 1994.

The Painted Photograph, 1839-1914: Origins, Techniques, Aspirations, Pennsylvania State University Press (University Park, PA), 1996.

Positive Pleasures; Early Photography and Humor, Pennsylvania State University Press (University Park, PA), 1998.

The Photographic World and Humour of Cuthbert Bede, Edwin Mellen Press (Lewiston, NY), 2002.

OTHER

Metal Rectifiers, Oxford University Press (Oxford, England), 1949.

(Editor) *Semiconductor Materials,* Butterworth (Woburn, MA), 1951.

Rectifying Semiconductor Contacts, Oxford University Press (Oxford, England), 1957.

Electroluminescence, Pergamon (Oxford, England), 1962.

(Editor, with others) *Silicon Carbide,* Pergamon (Oxford, England), 1969.

Crystal Growth in Gels, Pennsylvania State University Press (University Park, PA), 1970, paperback edition, Dover Press (New York, NY), 1997.

Semiconductor Contacts: An Approach to Ideas and Models, Oxford University Press (Oxford, England), 1984.

Crystals in Gels and Liesegang Rings, Cambridge University Press (New York, NY), 1988.

Periodic Precipitation: A Microcomputer Analysis of Transport and Reaction Processes in Diffusion Media, with Software Development, Pergamon (Oxford, England), 1990.

First Dance in Karlsbad (memoir), Carnation Press (State College, PA), 1993.

Editor of "International Series of Monographs on Semiconductors," Pergamon (Oxford, England), 1959-67. Author of nearly 150 research papers. Also contributor to journals of photo-history and related fields, sometimes under pseudonym Benjamin Spear. Founding editor, *Materials Research Bulletin,* 1968-93, and *History of Photography,* 1977-90; member of editorial board of *Journal of the Physics of Chemical Solids,*

1957—, *Journal of Solid State Electronics,* 1958—, *Physica Status Solidi,* 1961-63, *Penn State Studies,* 1963-66, and *Progress in Crystal Growth and Assessment.*

The book *Metal Rectifiers* was published in a Russian translation; *Electroluminescence* and *Crystal Growth in Gels* were both published in Japanese and Russian. Henisch's 1993 memoir has been translated into German and Czech.

WORK IN PROGRESS: Research on Victorian photographer James Robertson.

SIDELIGHTS: Heinz K. Henisch once told *CA* that he studies "science as an exercise in aesthetics, and science as literature."

Henisch updated *CA:* "Early in 1996, the considerable holdings of the *B. & H. Henisch Photo-History Collection* were transferred to the B. & H. Henisch Photo-History Collection Exhibit Room of the Pattee Library."

*　　*　　*

HERMAN, Didi 1961-

PERSONAL: Born April 18, 1961, in Toronto, Ontario, Canada. *Education:* University of Toronto, B.A.; York University, LL.B.; University of Warwick, Ph.D.

ADDRESSES: Office—Department of Law, University of Keele, Keele, Staffordshire ST5 5BG, England. *E-mail*—d.k.herman@keele.ac.uk.

CAREER: University of Keele, Keele, Staffordshire, England, began as reader, became professor of law and social change.

WRITINGS:

Rights of Passage, University of Toronto Press (Toronto, Ontario, Canada), 1994.

Legal Inversions: Lesbians, Gay Men, and the Politics of Law, Temple University Press (Philadelphia, PA), 1995.
The Antigay Agenda: Orthodox Vision and the Christian Right, University of Chicago Press (Chicago, IL), 1997.
(Editor, with Carl Stychin) *Law and Sexuality: The Global Arena,* University of Minnesota Press (Minneapolis MN), 2001.
Globalizing Family Values: The Christian Right in International Politics, University of Minnesota Press (Minneapolis, MN), 2003.

*　　*　　*

HEWLETT, Sylvia Ann 1946-

PERSONAL: Born 1946, in Wales; immigrated to United States; naturalized citizen in 1970s; married; children: four. *Education:* Cambridge University, B.A., 1967, M.A., 1971; London School of Economics and Political Science, Ph.D., 1973; additional study at Harvard University.

ADDRESSES: Office—Economic Policy Council, United Nations Association of the United States of America, 300 East 42nd St., New York, NY 10017.

CAREER: Barnard College, New York, NY, assistant professor of economics, 1974-81; United Nations Association of the United States of America, New York, NY, vice-president for economic studies and executive director of Economic Policy Council, 1981—. Research fellow at Girton College, Cambridge, 1972-74; graduate fellow at Harvard University.

WRITINGS:

The Cruel Dilemma of Development: Twentieth-Century Brazil, Basic Books (New York, NY), 1980.
(Editor, with Richard S. Weinert) *Brazil and Mexico: Patterns in Late Development,* Institute for the Study of Human Issues, 1982.
The Global Repercussions of U.S. Monetary and Fiscal Policy, Ballinger, 1984.
(With Alice S. Ilchman and John J. Sweeney) *Family and Work: Bridging the Gap,* Ballinger Publishing (Cambridge, MA), 1986.

Syliva Ann Hewlett

A Lesser Life: The Myth of Women's Liberation in America, Morrow (New York, NY), 1986.

When the Bough Breaks: The Cost of Neglecting Our Children, Basic Books (New York, NY), 1991.

(With Cornel West) *The War against Parents: What We Can Do for America's Beleaguered Moms and Dads,* Houghton Mifflin (Boston, MA), 1998.

Taking Parenting Public: The Case for a New Social Movement, Rowman & Littlefield (New York, NY), 2002.

Creating a Life: Professional Women and the Quest for Children, Miramax (New York, NY), 2002.

Baby Hunger: The New Battle for Motherhood, Atlantic Books (New York, NY), 2002.

After the Apple, Miramax (New York, NY), 2004.

Contributor of articles to periodicals.

SIDELIGHTS: Economist and author Sylvia Ann Hewlett sparked heated debate among American feminists with the publication of her 1986 book *A Lesser Life: The Myth of Women's Liberation in America.* At issue is Hewlett's charge that the U.S. women's movement is "anti-men, anti-children, and anti-motherhood" and has not worked effectively toward the economic betterment of women. Additionally, Hewlett claims, American feminist activists have ignored the needs of the majority of women, especially working mothers. She supports her arguments with statistics and cross-cultural studies that compare women's earning power and support services in the United States and in four Western industrialized nations.

Although she has been accused by many of writing a book that, according to Bronwyn Drainie of the Toronto *Globe and Mail,* "will fan the anti-liberationist flames and give the back-to-the-kitchen movement greater credibility," Hewlett maintains that she is a feminist. In *A Lesser Life* she recounts that as an assistant professor of economics at Barnard College during the 1970s, she unsuccessfully lobbied for maternity leave for faculty members. She contends that her outspoken activism—combined with her determination to have children—made her unpopular at the college and is the reason she was eventually denied tenure. She left Barnard in 1981 to serve as vice-president for economic studies at the United Nations Association, where she was also named director of the Economic Policy Council, a U.N. think tank that studies international economic matters. Her frustrations at trying to combine a career and a family during her years at Barnard and her findings as a member of the Economic Policy Council led her to write *A Lesser Life.*

Described by Florence Graves of *Common Cause Magazine* as "an impressive book" with "trenchant analysis and encyclopedic documentation," *A Lesser Life* presents a bleak view of the American woman's economic status. Despite nearly two decades of strong feminist activity, Hewlett reports, women's salaries are still only sixty-four percent of men's earnings—only one percent higher than they were in 1939. The wage earning gap between men and women in the four other nations she studied—France, Great Britain, Sweden, and Italy—is considerably narrower. Among her other findings: male high school graduates typically earn more money than female college graduates; only ten percent of U.S. working women earn more than twenty thousand dollars a year; and the majority of women work in service jobs that offer low pay and little advancement. Hewlett adds that ninety percent of U.S. women bear children and that seventy-three percent of those women hold jobs outside of the home. In the *New York Times* she concluded, "Unless we help women resolve their double burden as mothers and workers they are bound to remain second-class citizens."

Hewlett's contention that the U.S. feminist movement has done little to improve women's second-class status stems from her claim that the focus of the movement—that of attaining equality through the passage of the Equal Rights Amendment (ERA)—is misguided and is irrelevant to most American women. She asserts that American feminists, unlike their European counterparts, have largely ignored the needs of working mothers; rather than attempting to enact legislation that provides support services for working mothers, feminists have concentrated on becoming "clones of the male competitor." European feminists, Hewlett points out, joined forces with the unions in the early part of the twentieth century to pass laws that helped working mothers. As a result, women in Britain, France, Sweden, and Italy now enjoy greater benefits, including child care subsidies and family allowances. Furthermore, Hewlett notes, maternity leave is a guaranteed right in more than 117 nations, while in the United States sixty percent of women work without such a policy. She urges that the U.S. women's movement rearrange its priorities to focus on the working mother and suggests that women join forces with the unions to accomplish their goals. "The fact is," wrote Hewlett, women "need more than equality if they are to attain equal earning power in the marketplace."

Hewlett's book has drawn impassioned responses from many longtime feminists, some of whom have rallied in support of the author's ideas. Others, like writers Betty Friedan and Robin Morgan, assert that *A Lesser Life* obscures the gains made by the American feminist movement. They fear that Hewlett's criticisms unintentionally lend support to a growing trend of anti-feminism in the United States. Friedan, quoted in *Common Cause Magazine*, argued: "Women's liberation in America is not a myth. It's real that women's lives are better today. And it's not a lesser life. That title is simply playing to the backlash that is undermining the very things [Hewlett] enjoys." Friedan also took issue with Hewlett's criticism of the ERA and with her suggestion that women "need more than equality" to be successful in the workplace. The *New York Times* quoted Friedan as saying that the author "wants to go back to reactionary things like getting special protection for women. But these things are all wrong. . . . If these are asked for only as protection for women, it would give employers reason not to hire women, as they did before we demanded equality and forced them to open up more jobs and positions for women."

Robin Morgan of *Ms.* magazine claimed that "Hewlett's premise—that the U.S. [women's] Move-

ment is 'anti-motherhood'—is true in terms of fabricated media image but false in terms of reality." She added that the author's comparisons of women's movements in the United States and in Europe are "illuminating, but wobbly in context, and simplistic." Morgan argued that Hewlett does not take into account problems that are unique to the United States—such as ethnic diversity—that render such comparisons inaccurate and misleading.

Writing in the Toronto *Globe and Mail*, Drainie agreed that Hewlett's analysis has some flaws. Yet the reviewer judged the book "an exhilarating read. It's honest, well researched and passionate." Hewlett argues "persuasively" that American working mothers need more support services, noted Beryl Lieff Benderly in the *Washington Post Book World*, who added, "At the main task [Hewlett] sets herself . . . she succeeds very well indeed." And Joan Beck of the *Chicago Tribune Book World* credited Hewlett with raising some important issues and concluded: "The women's movement is still unfinished business. It's important to reassess what it has accomplished, see where it has gone astray and point out what still must be done. To that end, Hewlett's book does make an important contribution."

BIOGRAPHICAL AND CRITICAL SOURCES:

BOOKS

Hewlett, Sylvia Ann, *A Lesser Life: The Myth of Women's Liberation in America*, Morrow (New York, NY), 1986.

PERIODICALS

Atlantic Monthly, June, 2002, review of *Creating a Life: Professional Women and the Quest for Children*, pp. 108-110.
Chicago Tribune Book World, May 11, 1986.
Commentary, July-August, 2002, Lisa Schiffren, review of *Creating a Life*, p. 52.
Common Cause Magazine, May-June, 1986.
Globe and Mail, (Toronto, Ontario, Canada), June 21, 1986.
Journal of Marriage and the Family, February, 2003, Sylvia Yuen, review of *Taking Parenting Public: The Case for a New Social Movement*, pp. 267-268.

Los Angeles Times Book Review, March 30, 1986.

Ms., March, 1986.

Nation, May 13, 2002, Katha Pollitt, review of *Creating a Life,* p. 10.

New York Times, April 21, 1986; May 20, 2002, Warren St. John, review of *Creating a Life,* p. A1.

New York Times Book Review, March 30, 1986; April 5, 1987; June 9, 2002, Susan Chira, review of *Creating a Life,* p. 16.

Political Science Quarterly, winter, 1980-81.

Time, March 31, 1986.

Times Higher Education Supplement, September 6, 2002, Katrina Wishart, review of *Baby Hunger: The New Battle for Motherhood,* p. 32.

Times Literary Supplement, March 27, 1987.

Wall Street Journal, June 11, 2002, Carol Hymnowitz, review of *Creating a Life,* p. B1.

Washington Post Book World, April 6, 1986.*

*   *   *

Oscar Hijuelos

HIJUELOS, Oscar 1951-

PERSONAL: Surname is pronounced "E-way-los"; born August 24, 1951, in New York, NY; son of Pascual (a hotel worker) and Magdalena (a homemaker; maiden name, Torrens) Hijuelos; divorced. *Education:* City College of the City University of New York, B.A., 1975, M.A., 1976. *Religion:* Catholic. *Hobbies and other interests:* Pen-and-ink drawing, old maps, turn-of-the-century books and graphics, playing musical instruments, jazz ("I absolutely despise modern rock and roll").

ADDRESSES: Home—211 West 106th St., New York, NY 10025. *Office*—Hofstra University, English Department, 1000 Fulton Ave., Hempstead, NY 11550.

CAREER: Transportation Display, Inc., Winston Network, New York, NY, advertising media traffic manager, 1977-84; writer, 1984—; Hofstra University, Hempstead, NY, professor of English, 1989—.

MEMBER: International PEN.

AWARDS, HONORS: Outstanding Writer citation from Pushcart Press, 1978, for story "Columbus Discovering America"; Oscar Cintas fiction-writing grant, 1978-79; Bread Loaf Writers Conference scholarship, 1980; fiction-writing grant from Creative Artists Programs Service, 1982, and Ingram Merrill Foundation, 1983; Fellowship for Creative Writers award, National Endowment for the Arts, and American Academy in Rome Fellowship in Literature, American Academy and Institute of Arts and Letters, both 1985, both for *Our House in the Last World;* National Book Award nomination, National Book Critics Circle Prize nomination, and Pulitzer Prize for fiction, all 1990, all for *The Mambo Kings Play Songs of Love.*

WRITINGS:

Our House in the Last World, Persea Books (New York, NY), 1983.

The Mambo Kings Play Songs of Love, Farrar, Straus (New York, NY), 1989.

(Designer) *Iguana Dreams: New Latino Fiction,* HarperPerennial, 1992.

The Fourteen Sisters of Emilio Montez O'Brien, Farrar, Straus (New York, NY), 1993.

(Author of introduction) Lori M. Calson, editor, *Cool Salsa: Bilingual Poems on Growing Up Latino in the United States,* Holt (New York, NY), 1994.

Mr. Ives' Christmas, HarperCollins (New York, NY), 1995.

(Author of introduction) Dorothy and Thomas Hoobler, *The Cuban American Family Album,* Oxford University Press (New York, NY), 1996.

Empress of the Splendid Season (novel), HarperCollins (New York, NY), 1999.

A Simple Habana Melody: From When the World Was Good, HarperCollins (New York, NY), 2002.

Work represented in anthology *Best of Pushcart Press III,* Pushcart, 1978.

ADAPTATIONS: The Mambo Kings Play Songs of Love was adapted as the film *The Mambo Kings* in 1992; *Empress of the Splendid Season* was adapted for audiobook, 1999; *A Simple Habana Melody: From When the World Was Good* was adapted for audiobook, 2002.

SIDELIGHTS: Award-winning novelist Oscar Hijuelos turns the characters and experiences of his Cuban-American heritage into fictional works that have won both critical and popular praise. As Marie Arana-Ward explained in the *Washington Post Book World,* "Once in a great while a novelist emerges who is remarkable not for the particulars of his prose but for the breadth of his soul, the depth of his humanity, and for the precision of his gauge on the rising sensibilities of his time. . . . Hijuelos is one of these."

Hijuelos once explained to *CA* that his first novel, *Our House in the Last World,* "traces the lives of a Cuban family who came to the United States in the 1940s and follows them to the death of the father and subsequent near collapse of the family. In many ways a realistic novel, *Our House in the Last World* also reflects certain Latin attributes that are usually termed 'surreal' or 'magical.' Although I am quite Americanized, my book focuses on many of my feelings about identity and my 'Cubanness.' I intended for my book to commemorate at least a few aspects of the Cuban psyche (as I know it)."

Reviewing *Our House in the Last World* for the *New York Times Book Review,* Edith Milton affirmed that Hijuelos is concerned "with questions of identity and perspective," especially those concerning family. Hijuelos is "especially eloquent," lauded *Cleveland Plain Dealer* critic Bob Halliday, "in describing the emo-

tional storms" that transform the Santinio family of his novel as they "try to assimilate the rough realities of Spanish Harlem in terms of the values and personal identities they have inherited from their homeland." In an article for *American Literature,* Bridget M. Morgan stated: "Hijuelos compassionately depicts how each of the unequal participants in the American Dream is transformed by the process of assimilation." There is a "central tension," Milton explained, between the "lost, misremembered Eden [Cuba]" and the increasing squalor of the family's new life in their "last world"—New York. "Opportunity seems pure luck" to these well-intentioned immigrants, observed *Chicago Tribune Book World* reviewer Pat Aufderheide, and, in the absence of hope, each ultimately succumbs to the pressures that "work against the [American] dream of upward mobility." Hijuelos's "elegantly accessible style," Aufderheide stated, "combines innocence and insight" in creating the individual voices of his characters. Beyond that, noted the reviewer, there is a "feel for the way fear . . . pervades" the Santinios' lives. The characters and the "sheer energy" of the narrative are the book's strengths. Milton concluded that Hijuelos "never loses the syntax of magic, which transforms even the unspeakable into a sort of beauty." Critic Roy Hoffman in the *Philadelphia Inquirer* called *Our House in the Last World* a "vibrant, bitter and successful" story and compared Hijuelos to an "urban poet" who creates a "colorful clarity of life." Halliday likewise deemed the book to be a "wonderfully vivid and compassionate" first novel.

It was Hijuelos's Pulitzer Prize-winning second novel, *The Mambo Kings Play Songs of Love,* that moved him to the first rank of American novelists. Telling the story of two brothers, Cesar and Nestor Castillo, who leave their native Cuba and make careers as singers in the Spanish Harlem of the 1950s, the novel traces the brothers' rise to an appearance on the *I Love Lucy* television show before fading away from public attention again, like the mambo dance their band played.

The Mambo Kings, Cathleen McGuigan explained in *Newsweek,* "isn't conventionally plotted; it slides back and forth in time and meanders into dreams and fantasies." The novel is comprised of the dreams and fantasies of Cesar Castillo at the end of his career when he lives in a run-down hotel called the Splendour and drinks away his days. McGuigan noted that Cesar "is a classic portrait of machismo: he's in closest touch with his feelings when they originate below the waist."

But she acknowledged that "Hijuelos has a tender touch with his characters, and Cesar is more than a stereotype." Despite the novel's flaws, McGuigan found *The Mambo Kings Play Songs of Love* to be a "vibrant tragicomic novel." Joseph Coates in Chicago's *Tribune Books* found echoes of magical realism in the novel and felt that it "achieves the long backward look" of novels such as *One Hundred Years of Solitude,* "dealing as fully with the old worlds the migrants left as with the new ones they find." Writing in the *Washington Post Book World,* novelist Bob Shacochis also remarked upon Hijuelos's skilled contrasts between Cuban and American life, observing that "his *cu-bop* music scene gathers credibility as a grand metaphor for the splitting of a national family that took place [with the Cuban revolution] in 1959." Finally, Margo Jefferson of the *New York Times Book Review* observed that Hijuelos alternates "crisp narrative with opulent musings," achieving a "music of the heart."

Hijuelos's 1993 novel, *The Fourteen Sisters of Emilio Montez O'Brien,* takes a very different tack from its predecessor. Whereas *The Mambo Kings Play Songs of Love* is told by one male narrator, *The Fourteen Sisters of Emilio Montez O'Brien* is told from a number of female viewpoints and spans several generations in the life of a Cuban-Irish family living in Pennsylvania. Writing in *Time,* Janice E. Simpson praised the novel's warmth, suggesting that reading it "is like leafing through the pages of a treasured family album," but lamented that "the fate of the sisters is determined and defined by their relationships with men." *American Literature*'s Bridget Morgan felt that Hijuelos's work "is a celebration, even in its darkest moments, of the strength of love and family." "Hijuelos . . . displays a poetic exuberance in *The Fourteen Sisters of Emilio Montez O'Brien,*" stated George R. McMurray, in a *World Literature Today* review. Jane Mendelsohn, writing in the *London Review of Books,* generally admired the way Hijuelos characterizes his female characters, observing that "the novel skillfully chronicles the lives" of all the sisters and that Margarita, in particular, is an embodiment of the "women's movement . . . in the 20th century." At the same time, Mendelsohn faulted the novel for its sentimentality and concluded that there is "nothing of the glorious flame which set *The Mambo Kings* on fire." Nick Hornby in the *Times Literary Supplement* called the novel "at all times readable and diverting," but found that its many characters bog down its pacing. In contrast, Arana-Ward praised the story for its cel-

ebration of "human diversity and its promise of vitality," as well as for its compelling characters, who "hold us captive until the very last page."

With the short novel *Mr. Ives' Christmas,* Hijuelos steps away from his trademark theme of ethnic identity. Edward Ives, the book's chief protagonist, is a foundling of unknown background who is raised by nuns in a New York City orphanage. After several years pass, he is adopted by a man who inspires in Edward a deep and lasting love for Catholicism. When Edward enters adulthood, he works for a Madison Avenue advertising agency and is quite successful in his profession. He marries a wonderful woman, Annie MacGuire, they have a healthy son, Robert, and a younger daughter. Their lives proceed for nearly two decades in a seemingly perfect, secure routine. This peace is shattered, however, a few days before one Christmas, when seventeen-year-old Robert is killed by a hoodlum. Edward's belief in God and the Catholic faith is deeply shaken by this meaningless murder and the book traces how he comes to terms with Robert's death. Writing in *Booklist* Donna Seaman called *Mr. Ives' Christmas* a "sad and enchanting novel . . . of giving and of grace." In a *New York Times* article, Jack Miles felt that the novel is Hijuelos's "deepest and . . . best."

Empress of the Splendid Season, published in 1999, features a young woman of aristocratic Cuban descent who is banished from her home when her father discovers her romantic involvement with an older man. Lydia leaves Cuba for New York City, where she meets and marries Raul, another Cuban immigrant. Raul supports Lydia and their two children, Rico and Alicia, by working as a waiter in two restaurants, until he suffers a nearly fatal heart attack. Lydia must then go to work, and as she is not fluent in English, she decides to hire herself out as a housekeeper. The novel reveals not only Lydia's daily work, but her relationship to her clients. There is one whom she particularly likes—an international lawyer named Mr. Osprey, who intervenes in Rico's life when the boy is in trouble.

"While *Empress* does share similarities with Hijuelos's earlier work," wrote Joseph M. Viera in *American Writers,* "it nevertheless showcases the talents of a more mature, more seasoned author, as evidenced in the novel's compassionate narrative voice." London *Sunday Times* writer Phil Baker praised Hijuelos for his "lyrical . . . use of language" and his characterization of Lydia's inner life. "Hijuelos's achingly sweet novel captures beautifully the stateliness, strength and raw sensuality of Lydia España," said reviewer Barbara Mujica in an *Américas* article. Mujica concluded her review by saying: "Hijuelos transcends stereotypes and cliches, creating characters who speak to us on a profoundly human level."

Hijuelos introduces factual occurrences into his fictional rendition of *A Simple Habana Melody: From When the World Was Good*. Israel Levis's character is loosely based upon the life of Cuban composer Moises Simons, who brought the rumba rhythm to the United States with his 1930 song "The Peanut Vendor." In Levis's case, he writes a song called "Rosas Puras," basing it on a flower vendor's street call. His song becomes world famous due to a rendition by a Cuban songstress, Rita Valladares, whom Luis loves, unrequited, throughout his life. Hijuelos traces Levis's journeys from Cuba to Paris—where Cuban jazz musicians are highly welcome—to the Buchenwald concentration camp—he is mistaken for a Jew because of his relationship with a Jewish woman and because of his given name—and back to Cuba again.

Several reviewers commented on Hijuelos's novel. "This is a painfully sad novel about a sad man," wrote Mary Ann Horne in the *Orlando Sentinel*. She added, however, that "Hijuelos restrains his lyrical prose almost to the end of the book but sets it free as he sends Levis off to the afterlife." In the *Miami Herald* Fabiola Santiago commented: "*A Simple Habana Melody* is a love story to be enjoyed for its lyrical writing and desperately old-fashioned texture." Santiago found Valladares's character "too flatly portrayed," although she may have been "potentially more interesting . . . than Levis." "*Habana Melody* is . . . introspective, melancholy and sweetly elegiac," remarked Jerome Weeks in the *Dallas Morning News*.

New York Times critic Daniel Zalewski was less impressed by *A Simple Habana Melody*. The novel's "language . . . is consistently muted" in comparison to that of *The Mambo Kings Play Songs of Love*, Zalewski noted, continuing: "The result of all this linguistic tiptoeing is a melancholy, and sometimes wan, novel about the fruits and frustrations of repression." In a *St. Louis Post-Dispatch* review, Patricia Corrigan felt that Valladeres's character is insuf-

ficiently developed to warrant Levis's attachment to her. She also questioned the insertion of a small incident when Levis seems attracted to the physical appearance of a man: "the references to homosexual tendencies read as though tacked on." Yet, Corrigan added, "As always, Hijuelos's powers of description are masterful, even lyrical, and occasionally droll, sometimes all at once."

"This heartbreaking novel laments lost love while it helps us remember how love felt when we were young," commented *Booklist*'s Bill Ott of *A Simple Habana Melody*. Allan Turner, writing in the *Houston Chronicle*, opined that "Hijuelos perhaps resolves his novel a bit too neatly," but noted, however, that the novel's "bittersweet strains will resonate long after the last page is turned." A *Publishers Weekly* reviewer felt that the author "triumphs in capturing the sights and sounds of Habana at the edge of modernity," while a *Kirkus* reviewer dubbed the book a "masterpiece of history, music, wonder and sorrow." Francine Prose stated in an *O* review that "*A Simple Habana Melody* keeps us enthralled, then lingers in our minds."

BIOGRAPHICAL AND CRITICAL SOURCES:

BOOKS

American Literature, Gale (Detroit, MI), 1999.
American Writers, Supplement VIII, Gale (Detroit, MI), 1998.
Contemporary Hispanic Biography Volume 1, Gale (Detroit, MI), 2002.
Contemporary Literary Criticism, Volume 65, Gale (Detroit, MI), 1990.
Contemporary Novelists, 7th edition, St. James Press (Detroit, MI), 2001.
Dictionary of Literary Biography, Volume 145: *Modern Latin-American Fiction Writers, Second Series*, Gale (Detroit, MI), 1994.

PERIODICALS

Américas, July, 1999, Barbara Mujica, review of *Empress of the Splendid Season*, p. 62.
Americas Review, Volume 22, number 1-2, pp. 274-276.

Bloomsbury Review, May, 1990, p. 5.

Book, May-June, 1999, Patrick Markee, "Oscar Hijuelos and the Old Neighborhood."

Booklist, October 1, 1995, Donna Seaman, review of *Mr. Ives' Christmas;* August, 1999, review of *The Mambo Kings Play Songs of Love,* p. 2024; May 1, 2002, Bill Ott, review of *A Simple Habana Melody: From When the World Was Good,* p. 1445; January 1, 2003, review of *A Simple Habana Melody,* p. 792.

Boston Globe, November 18, 1990, p. 21.

Chicago Tribune, August 9, 1990, p. 1; January 3, 1993; May 30, 1993, sec. 6, p. 5; December 24, 1996.

Chicago Tribune Book World, July 17, 1983.

Christian Century, May 22, 1996, p. 581.

Dallas Morning News, July 3, 2002, Jerome Weeks, review of *A Simple Habana Melody.*

Entertainment Weekly, March 19, 1993, p. 57.

Hispanic, June, 2002, Fabiola Santiago, review of *A Simple Habana Melody,* p. 58.

Horn Book, May-June, 1995, p. 316.

Houston Chronicle, March 6, 1999, Joan Ann Zuniga, review of *Empress of the Splendid Season,* p. 41; June 23, 2002, Allan Turner, review of *A Simple Habana Melody,* p. 16.

Insight on the News, October 23, 1989, p. 56.

Kirkus Reviews, March 15, 2002, review of *A Simple Habana Melody,* p. 359.

Library Journal, January, 1999, review of *Empress of the Splendid Season,* p. 150; April 1, 2002, review of *The Mambo Kings Play Songs of Love,* p. 168; May 1, 2002, review of *a Simple Habana Melody,* p. 133.

London Review of Books, September 23, 1993, p. 23.

Los Angeles Times, April 16, 1990, p. 1.

Los Angeles Times Book Review, September 3, 1989, p. 1; March 14, 1993, pp. 3, 8; March 7, 1999, review of *Empress of the Splendid Season,* p. 3.

Los Angeles Times Magazine, April 18, 1993, pp. 22-28, 54.

Miami Herald, May 29, 2002, Fabiola Santiago, review of *A Simple Habana Melody.*

New Republic, March 22, 1993, pp. 38-41.

New Statesman, December 15, 1995, p. 64.

Newsweek, August 21, 1989, p. 60.

New York, March 1, 1993, p. 46.

New Yorker, March 29, 1993, p. 107; August 21, 1995, pp. 126-127.

New York Times, September 11, 1989, p. C17; April 1, 1993, p. C17.

New York Times Book Review, May 15, 1983; August 27, 1989, pp. 1, 30; March 7, 1993, p. 6; December 3, 1995, Jack Miles, review of *Mr. Ives' Christmas,* p. 9; February 5, 1999, Michiko Kakutani, review of *Empress of the Splendid Season,* p. E45; February 21, 1999, Verlyn Klinkenborg, review of *Empress of the Splendid Season,* p. 5; June 23, 2002, Daniel Zalewski, review of *A Simple Habana Melody,* p. 11; July 7, 2002, review of *A Simple Habana Melody,* p. 18.

O, June, 2002, Francine Prose, review of *A Simple Habana Melody,* p. 155.

Observer (London, England), July 25, 1993, p. 53; February 21, 1999, review of *Empress of the Splendid Season,* p. 13; December 19, 1999, review of *Empress of the Splendid Season,* p. 14.

Orlando Sentinel, July 31, 2002, Mary Ann Horne, review of *A Simple Habana Melody.*

People, April 5, 1993, p. 26.

Philadelphia Inquirer, July 17, 1983.

Publishers Weekly, July 21, 1989, pp. 42, 44; February 1, 1999, review of *Empress of the Splendid Season,* p. 35; May 20, 2002, review of *A Simple Habana Melody,* p. 46.

St. Louis Post-Dispatch, June 16, 2002, Patricia Corrigan, review of *A Simple Habana Melody,* p. F10.

Spectator, February 27, 1999, review of *Empress of the Splendid Season,* p. 37.

Sunday Times (London, England), December 12, 1999, Phil Baker, review of *Empress of the Splendid Season,* p. 45.

Time, August 14, 1989, p. 68; March 29, 1993, pp. 63, 65; March 15, 1999, review of *Empress of the Splendid Season,* p. 92.

Times Literary Supplement, August 6, 1993, p. 19; February 19, 1999, Henry Hitchings, review of *Empress of the Splendid Season,* p. 22.

Tribune Books (Chicago, IL), August 13, 1989, p. 6; January 3, 1993, p. 6.

U.S. Catholic, May, 1996, p. 46.

Village Voice, May 1, 1990, p. 85.

Wall Street Journal, February 5, 1999, Wendy Bounds, review of *Empress of the Splendid Season,* p. W10.

Washington Post Book World, August 20, 1989; March 14, 1993, pp. 1, 10; January 31, 1999, review of *Empress of the Splendid Season,* p. 5.

World Literature Today, winter, 1994, George R. McMurray, review of *The Fourteen Sisters of Emilio Montez O'Brien,* p. 127.*

HOOPES, Roy 1922-

PERSONAL: Born May 17, 1922, in Salt Lake City, UT; son of Roy H. (a lawyer) and Lydia Hoopes; married; wife's name Cora; children: Spencer, Sallie, Tommy. *Education:* George Washington University, A.B., 1946, M.A., 1949. *Politics:* Democrat.

ADDRESSES: Agent—c/o Author Mail, St. Martin's Press, 175 Fifth Ave., New York, NY 10010.

CAREER: U.S. Department of State, Washington, DC, research analyst, 1946-48; assistant world editor, *Pathfinder* (magazine), 1949-52; Time, Inc., New York, NY, general promotion manager of Time-Life International, 1952-53; managing editor of *High Fidelity*, 1953-56, and *Democratic Digest*, 1956-61; *National Geographic*, Washington, DC, editor and writer, 1963-65; *Washingtonian* (magazine), Washington, DC, associate editor, 1965-66; worked for U.S. Department of Health, Education, and Welfare, 1967-73, and *Newsday*, 1973-74; freelance writer, 1974—.

MEMBER: Oral History Association, National Press Club (Washington, DC).

AWARDS, HONORS: Edgar Award for *Cain: The Biography of James M. Cain.*

WRITINGS:

(Editor) *Wit from Overseas*, Avon (New York, NY), 1953.

(Editor) *Building Your Record Library*, McGraw-Hill (New York, NY), 1958.

(Editor) *The "High Fidelity" Reader*, Hanover House, 1958.

The Complete Peace Corps Guide, introduction by R. Sargent Shriver, Dial (New York, NY), 1961, 4th edition, 1968.

The Steel Crisis: 72 Hours That Shook the Nation, John Day (New York, NY), 1962.

What the President Does All Day, John Day (New York, NY), 1962.

(Editor) *State Colleges and Universities*, Luce, 1962.

A Report on Fallout in Your Food, New American Library (New York, NY), 1962.

(Editor) *The Peace Corps Experience*, preface by Hubert H. Humphrey, C. N. Potter (New York, NY), 1968.

Getting with Politics: A Young Person's Guide to Political Action, Delacorte (New York, NY), 1968.

What a United States Senator Does, John Day (New York, NY), 1970.

(With son, Spencer Hoopes) *What a Baseball Manager Does*, John Day (New York, NY), 1970.

What a United States Congressman Does, John Day (New York, NY), 1972.

What a Pro Football Coach Does, John Day (New York, NY), 1972.

What a State Governor Does, John Day (New York, NY), 1973.

What the President of the United States Does, Harper (New York, NY), 1974.

(With Erwin C. Hargrove) *The Presidency: A Question of Power*, Educational Associates, 1975.

Americans Remember the Home Front: An Oral Narrative, Hawthorn Books, 1977, Berkley (New York, NY), 2002.

Primaries and Conventions, F. Watts (New York, NY), 1978.

Political Campaigning, F. Watts (New York, NY), 1979.

The Changing Vice-Presidency, Crowell (New York, NY), 1981.

(Editor) James M. Cain, *The Baby in the Icebox and Other Short Fiction*, Holt (New York, NY), 1981.

Cain: The Biography of James M. Cain, Holt (New York, NY), 1982.

(With William Fry) *Paralegal Careers*, Enslow Publications (Hillsdale, NJ), 1984.

(Editor) *60 Years of Journalism,* Bowling Green University Popular Press (Bowling Green, OH), 1985.

Ralph Ingersoll: A Biography, Atheneum (New York, NY), 1985.

(Editor) *Career in C Major and Other Fiction,* McGraw-Hill (New York, NY), 1986.

(Coauthor) *Legal Careers and the Legal System,* Enslow Publishers (Hillsdale, NJ), 1988.

(Coauthor) *Everything You Need to Know about Building the Custom Home: How to Be Your Own General Contractor,* Taylor Publishing (Dallas, TX), 1990.

(Coauthor) *The Making of a Mormon Apostle: The Story of Rudger Clawson*, Madison Books (Lanham, MD), 1990.

(Editor) *The Life and Hard Times of the Late, Great Peter Potomac*, Potomac Press (Washington, DC), 1994.

When the Stars Went to War: Hollywood and World War II, Random House (New York, NY), 1994.
Our Man in Washington, Forge (New York, NY), 2000.
A Watergate Tape, Forge (New York, NY), 2002.

Contributor to newspapers and magazines. Author of weekly newspaper column for several years under undisclosed pseudonym.

SIDELIGHTS: Roy Hoopes is a biographer, historian, and novelist, and the author of numerous books in each genre. *Cain: The Biography of James M. Cain* is a "meticulously researched biography" of the famed novelist, wrote Nora Johnson in the *New York Times Book Review.* Cain wrote special memoirs for Hoopes to use in the book, and allowed himself to be interviewed extensively. Paul Piazza commented in the *Washington Post Book World,* that "a more detailed and comprehensive chronicle of a man's life can hardly be imagined."

The author of such bestsellers as *The Postman Always Rings Twice, Double Indemnity,* and *Mildred Pierce,* Cain wrote for over forty years, producing short stories, screenplays, newspaper articles, and novels. His subject matter was often considered shocking—murder, infidelity, and crime—and revealed the dark emotions of his characters. As Herbert Gold stated in the *Los Angeles Times Book Review,* "Cain's observation of America is far more accurate than that of John Dos Passos, more realistic than that of [Ernest] Hemingway, not dosed with pomp and poesy, as was Thomas Wolfe's. Yet, among these contemporaries, he was barely taken seriously." Johnson concluded that "one hopes this careful book will lead to a revival of interest in a writer who not only keeps the palms damp and the pages turning but whose work rings as true now as it did the day it was written."

Among Hoopes's other books are *When the Stars Went to War: Hollywood and World War II,* which examines what Hollywood celebrities did during World War II, including entertaining the troops and making war pictures. *Booklist*'s Ilene Cooper called it "a fascinating look at Hollywood at war."

BIOGRAPHICAL AND CRITICAL SOURCES:

PERIODICALS

American Heritage, July-August, 1995, review of *When the Stars Went to War: Hollywood and World War II,* p. 94.

American History Illustrated, November, 1986, review of *Ralph Ingersoll: A Biography,* p. 7; September-October, 1990, review of *The Making of a Mormon Apostle: The Story of Rudger Clawson,* p. 20.
Barron's, March 3, 1986, Edmund P. Klein, review of *Ralph Ingersoll,* p. 80.
Booklist, December 15, 1994, review of *When the Stars Went to War,* p. 727.
Chicago Tribune Book World, October 10, 1982.
Entertainment Weekly, February 10, 1995, D. A. Ball, review of *When the Stars Went to War,* p. 62.
Journal of American History, December, 1987, Christopher P. Wilson, review of *Ralph Ingersoll,* p. 1086.
Kirkus Reviews, March 15, 2002, review of *A Watergate Tape,* p. 370.
Library Journal, September 15, 1990, Bill Demo, review of *Everything You Need to Know about Building the Custom Home: How to Be Your Own General Contractor,* p. 70.
Los Angeles Times Book Review, July 25, 1982.
Nation, November 16, 1985, Casey Blake, review of *Ralph Ingersoll,* p. 515.
National Review, February 14, 1986, Arnold Beichman, review of *Ralph Ingersoll,* p. 50.
New York Times Book Review, November 28, 1982; November 17, 1985, Lester Bernstein, review of *Ralph Ingersoll,* p. 34.
Publishers Weekly, May 3, 1985, review of *Ralph Ingersoll,* p. 60; April 1, 2002, review of *A Watergate Tape,* p. 55.
Washington Post Book World, October 31, 1982.*

* * *

HOWARTH, Lesley 1952-

PERSONAL: Born December 29, 1952, in Bournemouth, England. *Education:* Attended Bournemouth College of Art and Croydon College of Art.

ADDRESSES: Home—Cornwall, England. *Agent*—c/o Author Mail, Puffin Publicity, 345 Hudson St., New York, NY 10014.

CAREER: Writer. Worked at market gardens and various other jobs.

Lesley Howarth

AWARDS, HONORS: Shortlisted for Whitbread Children's Book Award, 1993, for the *The Flower King;* winner, *Guardian* Children's Fiction Award, 1994, for *MapHead;* shortlisted for Writers' Guild Award, 1994; shortlisted for W. H. Smith Mind Boggling Books Award and *Young Telegraph* Book Award, all 1995, all for *MapHead;* Smarties Book Prize, 9-11 category, 1995, for *Weather Eye.*

WRITINGS:

CHILDREN'S BOOKS

The Flower King, Walker Books (London, England), 1993.

MapHead, Candlewick Press (Cambridge, MA), 1994.

Weather Eye, Candlewick Press (Cambridge, MA), 1995.

The Pits, Candlewick Press (Cambridge, MA), 1996.

Fort Biscuit, Candlewick Press (Cambridge, MA), 1996.

MapHead: The Return, Candlewick Press (Cambridge, MA), 1997.

Quirx: Welcome to Inner Space, Hodder & Stoughton (London, England), 1997.

Epix: Bad Rep, Mammoth, 1998.

Aliens for Dinner, Hodder & Stoughton (London, England), 1999.

Yamabusters!, Hodder & Stoughton (London, England), 1999.

Mister Spaceman, Walker Books (London, England), 1999.

Paulina, Walker Books (London, England), 1999.

The Squint, Walker Books (London, England), 1999.

No Accident, Barrington Stoke (London, England), 2000.

I Managed a Monster, Puffin (New York, NY), 2000.

Ultraviolet, Puffin (New York, NY), 2001.

Carwash, Puffin (New York, NY), 2002.

Dade County's Big Summer, Barrington Stoke (London, England), 2002.

Colossus, Oxford University Press (Oxford, England), 2004.

Drive, Puffin (New York, NY), 2004.

SIDELIGHTS: With her first young adult novel, *The Flower King,* English author Lesley Howarth made it to several shortlists for fiction awards. With her second book, *MapHead,* she served up a fictional brew that "one only occasionally happens upon," according to Robyn Sheahan in a cover story in *Magpies.* Sheahan went on to note that Howarth writes the sort of book that "is respectful of its readers' imaginative and intellectual capabilities, and which offers real insights into the difficult business of growing up."

Howarth herself was coming of age as a writer with these first published books and has since broadened her fictional universe to encompass not only a turn-of-the-century world filled with flowers and a modern country town with alien visitors in its midst, but also a wind farm in the near future in *Weather Eye,* and the chilly world of prehistory in *The Pits,* a story of an ice-age man told by a chatty ghost. These are all parts of Howarth and are indicative of the varied life she herself has led.

Born in Bournemouth, England, Howarth attended grammar school there and at the Bournemouth School for Girls. A self-confessed dreamer, she commented in an interview with Stephanie Nettell for *Magpies* that she puts her lack of success in school down to stubbornness and a "fierce strain of individualism: the more people told me to buckle down the less likely I was to do it." But she did develop a love for story at an early age; as an only child she created a rich interior life. "I'd live in a story, in its atmosphere, for days," she told Nettell, "and spent long hours plonking out stories on my Dad's typewriter." Growing up in the Westbourne district of Bournemouth, she was also in close proximity to the house where Robert Louis Stevenson lived while writing *Dr. Jekyll and Mr. Hyde* and *Kidnapped.* Howarth would sit in the garden of the house where Stevenson created those classics and marvel at how close the past was to her. Stevenson continues to be a major influence in her own writing—especially his sense of adventure and his ability to use "just the right word every time," as she explained to Nettell.

After marrying and moving to Cornwall, Howarth proceeded to write short stories and short screenplays which were submitted for a BBC video project. Though the films were not accepted, the process of writing them spurred Howarth into taking evening classes in creative writing. Soon her stories were expanding, turning into novels, and the voice she consistently wrote in was one directed at children. Finally, with three novels under her belt—none of them accepted by a publisher—she was able to place her fourth with the British publisher, Walker Books. This was "only the second unsolicited novel published by Walker," according to Kevin Steinberger in *Reading Time.* As Steinberger went on to point out, Howarth's varied background in work and family all play a large part in her fiction. This first young adult novel, *The Flower King,* is a "gentle turn-of-the century story," according to a *Magpies* reviewer, and some of the characters that she worked with in the retirement home find their way into the novel, as well as Howarth's experiences working in flower gardens. Shortlisted for both the Whitbread and *Guardian* children's fiction prizes, *The Flower King* won Howarth recognition and an agent.

For her second published novel, *MapHead,* Howarth adopted a science fiction format. Alien beings from the Subtle World, twelve-year-old MapHead and his father, Ran, come to Earth to search for the boy's mother, Kay. Before MapHead's birth, Ran saved his human mother from death by a lightning bolt, and she returned with him to the Subtle World where they had a baby. But pining for her home, Kay returned to Earth with no memory of her encounter with Ran nor of her son. Now MapHead—so-called because of his ability to project a map of the terrain on his face and bald head—needs to find his mother before he can enjoy the Dawn of Power. Under the names of Boothe and Powers, the son and father take up residence in a tomato glasshouse on Earth, and Boothe enrolls in the local school where he meets the boy who is his half-brother and will take him to find his mother. In the process, he and his half-brother, Kenny, become friends, and MapHead begins to fit in and know what it means to be loved. Meeting his mother, he experiences an internal integration that gives him power equal to his father's, but the actual process of his search has led him to this self-integration.

Told with humor and attention to detail, *MapHead* "is a sweet, tender, coming-of-age story . . . a marvelous read," according to Dorothy M. Broderick in *Voice of Youth Advocates,* and a "deliciously grotesque tale," according to John Peters in *School Library Journal.* Merri Monks in *Booklist* noted that "Howarth skillfully evokes the internal landscapes of a young man's emotions and imagination," while *Magpies'* Sheahan praised the novel's "felicitous turns of phrase," noting that it was "brimful with lyrical, luscious language; written with an intensity, a distillation of the senses." Though MapHead eventually leaves Earth without his mother, he has most definitely found himself: "Don't you know?" he asks toward the end of the book. "Can't you see? I'm not a little kid anymore. No one's got me, because I've got myself." In *Junior Bookshelf,* a reviewer concluded that "Lesley Howarth has mixed the imaginary and the real ingredients with great skill."

Howarth reintroduced MapHead and his adventures in a 1997 sequel, *MapHead: The Return,* in which the title character finds himself alone without his father for the first time and must return to Earth to find his destiny. In his loneliness MapHead misuses his powers, transferring his memories into the mind of his newfound friend, Jack Stamp, an action that has unintended consequences. *Voice of Youth Advocates* critic Roxy Ekstrom applauded the work, calling it a "great coming-of-age story that dwells on a respect for freedom, the desire for autonomy, and the fear of that independence." A reviewer in *Horn Book* also praised *MapHead: The Return,* stating, "Insightful characterization, concise prose, and sophisticated humor distinguish the fantasy." Steven Engelfried, writing in *School Library Journal,* remarked that MapHead's "deep concern for the humans he comes to love and his burning need to find his own place in the world are truly touching."

With increased recognition came the working hours of a full-time novelist. "I'm not interested in oral story-telling," Howarth told Steinberger for his *Reading Time* article. "For me the whole buzz is the word—the word making an effect on the page; that's what interests me." Normally Howarth does not begin her novels with a grand plan, but once in the story, she relishes in doing research and gathering more information than she'll ever need. "Then I let the stuff percolate for a long time," she told Steinberger. "You have to edge up to a story. . . . The whole essence of storywriting is to be excited. Once I get bored or find it a slog I decide to let it go."

Howarth's third novel is sometimes typified as an environmental story, though the author herself rejects the notion that she begins with a theme. For her, story is paramount and meaning follows story. With *Weather Eye,* Howarth was influenced both by an article about a near-death experience and by an apocalyptic feeling engendered in the novel by changing weather patterns. Thirteen-year-old Telly lives with her parents on a weather farm in Cornwall in 1999, just before the millennium. She helps her parents on this farm which generates electricity with huge windmills. All around the world unseasonal weather patterns are causing immense damage to property and life; in Cornwall strong winds have been blowing for days, and Telly is almost killed when struck on the head by a damaged turbine blade from one of the giant windmills. Telly feels she is imbued with special powers after this close scrape with death and resolves to do something to alter the human destructiveness responsible for the severe weather. Networking with youths around the world via computers, Telly, the Weather Eye, hopes to save the planet by redirecting energies. After many adventures and much hard work, a new turbine is brought on-line at the climax of the novel, just in time for the new millennium. Telly describes it, "wheeling into the twenty-first century. Dad has the right idea: 'Next century belongs to you lot. . . . I've a feeling you'll all make the best of it.'"

In a *Magpies* review of the novel, Steinberger noted that *Weather Eye* "may be read as a very reassuring 'environmental' novel but it is immediately a humorous, suspenseful, thoughtful narration. . . . It is a story for, and of, our times, but in Howarth's inimitable style." Other critics, including Maeve Visser Knoth in *Horn Book,* also commented on Howarth's humor: "The author . . . has written an unusual novel that will appeal to readers with its empowering theme and its strong element of humor." In *Junior Bookshelf,* a critic also remarked on Howarth's use of humor, saying "[Howarth's] vision of the world is essentially comic as well as profoundly moral." The reviewer went on to conclude that young readers "will read her book with joy and satisfaction because her children are drawn clearly and with humour as well as understanding."

Steinberger, in his *Reading Time* article on Howarth, noted that her use of idiom for both comic effects and depth of story set her apart from other writers. In *The Pits* she uses idiom to heightened effects. The book was inspired by news reports of the discovery of an iceman in the west of Austria and also by an article relating the discovery of an Ice Age pine chewing gum. This started Howarth looking for parallels between that time and ours and ended up with "a *West Side Story*-like gang rivalry set in Ice Age coastal Britain," according to Steinberger. The archaeologist Needcliff discovers Arf, the Iceman, a relic of a distant age, but his daughter, with him for the summer, wonders all the time what really made the Iceman tick. Such particulars are supplied by an adolescent ghost, Broddy Bronson, who was a pal of Arf. Broddy has been drifting around for some 9,000 years, picking up the speech and experiences of each succeeding age, and it is his voice—entered into the archaeologist's computer—that relates the story of Arf, and of Broddy. It is Broddy's distinctive idiom that gives life to the tale. There are parallels between Broddy's time and ours, especially the gang fighting and turf wars. There is also "much humor," according to a reviewer in *Magpies,* who went on to conclude that "*The Pits* is a great read. It rollicks along . . . and rejoices in telling an original story in an original way." Janice M. Del Negro, writing in the *Bulletin of the Center for Children's Books,* echoed this opinion of originality and commented that "what is most unusual about this book is that it works, and works remarkably well. Howarth creates a prehistoric world that is eminently credible, peopled by individuals with complex personalities."

In *Mister Spaceman* Howarth turns her attention to a contemporary teenager, Thomas Moon, who is doing badly in school because of his obsession with becoming an astronaut. Moon's interest in space leads him to do some strange things by way of "training": sleeping upright in a sleeping bag, eating only foods that come out of tubes, and wearing six tracksuits at the same time. His obsession also leads him to withdraw from his friends and family to spend all his time in the imaginative world of space travel. With the help of a teacher who knows how to ease Moon back into normal school life, things eventually work out for the best. "The crisis," explained Philip Pullman in the *Guardian,* "is resolved with great storytelling tact and craft, and the happy ending grows naturally out of the way things have been since the start of the story." Nicholas Tucker in the *Independent* found *Mister Spaceman* to be a "touching and above all a very funny story."

Carwash focuses on a group of English teens during one small-town summer. Luke has set up Loony Luke's Carwash, a one-man operation at a local car dealer. Luke is infatuated with his neighbor, Liv, who spends her time reading Jane Austen. Liv's sister, Sylvia, spends her days sitting high in a tree, surveying the goings-on below. Other characters include Matt Kramer, obsessed with cars, and Michael Paxman, a know-it-all. "Out of this Howarth weaves a backcloth of summertime incident that includes a teenage pregnancy, which is made part of a thread in the novel that sees some of the characters confronting the end of their childhood," Michael Thorn wrote in the *Scotsman.* "*Carwash* is an awesomely good read, with quickfire teenage dialogue that is utterly convincing." Christine Madden in the *Irish Times* found *Carwash* to be "an entertaining tangle of changing young lives for a perfect poolside holiday read."

Howarth, who complains that she is easily bored, has created in a short span of time, a most original group of works, full of adventure, humor, and meaning. Nicholas Tucker, writing in the *Independent,* maintained that she is "one of the best contemporary writers for the young, Howarth is still going from strength to strength." Howarth once told *CA:* "My primary motivation for writing is to have fun! Loads of people have influenced me, but my big heroes are Robert Louis Stevenson, Raymond Carver, Alan Bennett, Paul Jennings, and the authors of all the classic books I read as a child, the 'Penguin Modern Poets,' et cetera.

"My writing process is simple. I get excited about an idea, read a lot (but not too much) around it, then sit down in front of my word processor and begin. I set up the most exciting situation and the most believable, if quirky, characters that I can, then I let 'em roll and see what happens. Then I have to keep control over

the 'shape' of the story as it unfolds. I am never entirely sure it will all work out until I am almost through, but that's the excitement of it!

"What inspires me to write? It is the sheer excitement of reaching out to touch someone else with what I am excited about."

BIOGRAPHICAL AND CRITICAL SOURCES:

PERIODICALS

Booklist, October 1, 1994, Merri Monks, review of *MapHead,* p. 319; September 15, 1995, Chris Sherman, review of *Weather Eye,* p. 160.

Book Report, January-February, 1995, Jo Clarke, review of *MapHead,* p. 47; January-February, 1997, Judith Beavers, review of *The Pits,* p. 34.

Books for Keeps, November, 1993, p. 14; July, 1994, pp. 6, 28; July, 1995, p. 12; January, 1996, p. 11.

Bulletin of the Center for Children's Books, November, 1995, p. 93; December, 1996, Janice M. Del Negro, review of *The Pits,* pp. 138-139; March, 1998, p. 246.

Guardian, January 11, 2000, Philip Pullman, review of *Mister Spaceman.*

Horn Book, November-December, 1994, Anne Deifendeifer, review of *MapHead,* p. 732; March-April, 1996, Maeve Visser Knoth, review of *Weather Eye,* pp. 208-209; January-February, 1998, Anne Deifendeifer, review of *MapHead: The Return,* pp. 74-75.

Horn Book Guide, spring, 1995, p. 78; spring, 1996, p. 73.

Independent (London, England), November 6, 1999, Nicholas Tucker, review of *Mister Spaceman,* p. 11; December 12, 1999, Laurence Phelan, review of *Mister Spaceman,* p. 10; July 13, 2002, Nicholas Tucker, review of *Carwash,* p. 27.

Irish Times, July 6, 2002, Christine Madden, review of *Carwash,* p. 59.

Junior Bookshelf, August, 1994, review of *MapHead,* p. 145; June, 1995, review of *Weather Eye,* p. 108.

Kirkus Reviews, October 15, 1997, p. 1583.

Magpies, May, 1994, p. 24; July, 1994, Robyn Sheahan, review of *MapHead,* p. 4; July, 1995, Kevin Steinberger, review of *Weather Eye,* p. 25; May, 1996, Stephanie Nettell, "Know the Author: Lesley Howarth," pp. 18-21, and review of *The Pits,* p. 21.

Publishers Weekly, November 14, 1994, review of *MapHead,* p. 69.

Reading Time, May, 1996, Kevin Steinberger, "Lesley Howarth," p. 12.

School Library Journal, October, 1994, John Peters, review of *MapHead,* p. 124; November, 1995, Lyle Blake Smythers, review of *Weather Eye,* p. 100; January, 1998, Steven Engelfried, review of *MapHead: The Return,* p. 112.

Scotsman, June 29, 2002, Michael Thorn, review of *Carwash,* p. 10.

Times Educational Supplement, November 12, 1993, p. R12; December 24, 1993, p. 8.

U.S. News & World Report, December 5, 1994, Marc Silver, review of *MapHead,* p. 97

Voice of Youth Advocates, February, 1995, Dorothy M. Broderick, review of *MapHead,* p. 348; April, 1998, Roxy Ekstrom, review of *MapHead: The Return,* pp. 55-56.

ONLINE

English and Media Centre Web site, http://www. englishandmedia.co.uk/ (December 10, 2002), "Interview with Lesley Howarth."

Fantastic Fiction, http://books.fantasticfiction.co.uk/ (January 7, 2004).*

*   *   *

HOWE, Tina 1937-

PERSONAL: Born November 21, 1937, in New York, NY; daughter of Quincy (a broadcaster and writer) and Mary (an artist; maiden name, Post) Howe; married Norman Levy, 1961; children: Eben, Dara. *Education:* Sarah Lawrence College, B.A., 1959; graduate study at Chicago Teachers College, 1963-64, and Columbia University.

ADDRESSES: *Home*—New York, NY. *Agent*—Flora Roberts, 157 West 57th St., New York, NY 10019.

CAREER: Playwright and educator. New York University, New York, NY, adjunct professor, beginning 1983; Hunter College, City University of New York, visiting professor, beginning 1990.

AWARDS, HONORS: Rosamund Gilder Award for creative achievement, New Drama Forum, 1983; Rockefeller grant, 1983; Outer Critics Circle Award for best Off-Broadway play, 1983-84, for *Painting Churches;* Obie Award for distinguished playwrighting, 1983, for *Painting Churches, The Art of Dining,* and *Museum*; John Gassner Award, 1984; National Endowment for the Arts grant, 1984; Antoinette Perry Award nomination for best play, 1987, for *Coastal Disturbances;* honorary degree from Bowdoin College, 1988; Guggenheim fellowship, 1990; American Academy of Arts and Letters award in literature, 1993; Pulitzer Prize in Drama nomination, 1997, and New York Drama Critics Circle Award for best American play, 1998, both for *Pride's Crossing.*

WRITINGS:

PLAYS

Closing Time, produced in Bronxville, NY, 1959.

The Nest, produced in Provincetown, MA, 1969, produced off-Broadway, 1970.

Museum (produced in Los Angeles, CA, 1976, produced in New York, NY, 1977), Samuel French (New York, NY), 1979.

The Art of Dining (produced at New York Shakespeare Festival, 1979), Samuel French (New York, NY), 1980.

Appearances, produced in New York, NY, 1982.

Painting Churches (produced in New York, NY, 1983; produced in London, England, 1992), Samuel French (New York, NY), 1984.

Three Plays (includes *Museum, The Art of Dining,* and *Painting Churches*), Avon (New York, NY), 1984.

Coastal Disturbances (produced off-Broadway, 1986), Samuel French (New York, NY), 1987.

Coastal Disturbances: Four Plays (includes *Painting Churches, The Art of Dining,* and *Museum*), Theatre Communications Group (New York, NY), 1989.

Approaching Zanzibar (produced off-Broadway, 1989), Theatre Communications Group (New York, NY), 1989.

Swimming, produced in New York, NY), 1991.

One Shoe Off (produced on Broadway, 1993), Samuel French (New York, NY), 1993.

Approaching Zanzibar, and Other Plays (includes *Birth and After Birth* and *One Shoe Off*), Theatre Communications Group (New York, NY), 1995.

Pride's Crossing (two-act; produced in New York, NY, 1997), Theatre Communications Group (New York, NY), 1998.

Also author of *Teeth,* published in *Antaeus,* spring, 1991. *Birth and After Birth,* was originally published in *The New Women's Theatre,* Vintage (New York, NY), 1977.

ADAPTATIONS: A production of *Painting Churches* was adapted to videocassette, 1986.

WORK IN PROGRESS: A screenplay, *A Man's Place*; a play, *Realities,* to accompany "Appearances."

SIDELIGHTS: Noted playwright Tina Howe first became interested in penning dramas during her university years. While attending Sarah Lawrence College she wrote *Closing Time,* a work that focuses on the end of the world; the production was highly acclaimed among Sarah Lawrence students. Howe credits her college peers' approbation of her dramatic effort with sparking her desire to become a professional playwright. Upon graduation she traveled to Europe, and there became acquainted with the theater of the absurd when she saw a performance of *The Bald Soprano* by Eugene Ionesco. She thereafter felt an affinity for absurdist theater, and has since explored the theme of absurdity in realistic situations throughout her work. According to an *American Women Writers* essayist, "Howe's plays develop a rhythmic energy that carry them beyond the ordinary and into a heightened realism bordering on the fantastic or absurd, ending in a release: unexpected silliness [or] poignant ecstasy."

Museum, which was produced in New York in 1977 and features several characters wandering about a museum while commenting on art, was praised by *New Yorker*'s Edith Oliver as "an enchanting show." Oliver wrote: "The play is itself a collage of words and characters and action. . . . It has plenty of wit and humor, and no idea appears to be emphasized over any other."

Oliver was also impressed with Howe's *The Art of Dining.* She called the play, which concerns the struggles of a young couple to operate a restaurant in New Jersey, a "delightful little comedy." *The Art of Dining* resembles *Museum* in its vast array of charac-

ters and comedic incidents, and Oliver was entertained especially by a "sensationally awkward, nearsighted . . . young writer . . . , who, dining with her middleaged publisher, manages to spill a full plate of soup into her lap and on being furnished with a second plate drowns her lipstick in it." A writer for *Contemporary Dramatists* especially praised the characterization of Elizabeth Barrow Colt (the writer in the play) as "one of Howe's most brilliant creations."

In 1983 Howe was granted an Obie Award for distinguished playwriting for *Museum* and *The Art of Dining,* as well and for *Painting Churches.* This play, which is somewhat autobiographical, traces artist Mags Church's visit to her ageing parents' home in Boston. Mags's father, Gardner, once a prize-winning poet, is now in the beginning stages of senility, and his wife, Fanny, must bear the burden of this unwelcome illness. While Mags struggles to capture her parents in a portrait, she gradually learns to accept the inevitability of their decline. "Howe's quirky sense of humor and her distinctive verbal and visual idiom mark [this] work," stated a *Contemporary Dramatists* writer.

Coastal Disturbances was described as "a charming play, a landscape of the human heart in miniature" by *Nation* reviewer Moira Hodgson in discussing Howe's 1986 drama, which began as an off-Broadway production and later ran for 350 performances on Broadway. The piece, set on a private New England beach, examines the inner lives of the characters who visit the area during the final two weeks of summer. "Her characters . . . are vivid and recognizable," said Hodgson, noting also that "Howe is very good at dialogue." However, in a review for the *New Republic,* Robert Brustein felt that such a talented writer as Howe is capable of something much better than this "vapid and bloodless" piece. A *Contemporary Dramatists* critic commented that the setting of *Coastal Disturbances* "is as much metaphor as place."

Howe's next play, *Approaching Zanzibar,* reunited the playwright with friend, actress, and former Sarah Lawrence classmate Jane Alexander. In the play, which Alexander starred in, a family of four, seemingly on a cross-country vacation, are actually on their way to visit a dying aunt in Taos, New Mexico. Along the way, the family plays a geography game as a way to pass the time and to alleviate their feelings of anxiety about what awaits them at the end of their journey. Howe "has infused new energy into her work. . . .

[yet] sustained her gift for hinting at profound meanings in humdrum moments," remarked *Time* contributor William Henry III.

A Greek Revival farmhouse that is being invaded by huge trees which emerge through ceilings and floors and vegetables which sprout in any conveniently damp area is the setting for *One Shoe Off.* Inside this unusual dwelling, two married couples and a friend are struggling to have a dinner party. During the day these five characters explore the relative barrenness of their personal and professional lives against the lush background of the overgrown farmhouse. *One Shoe Off* was viewed by some critics as showing Howe's return to her absurdist roots, while a *Contemporary Dramatists* essayist cited it as "among Howe's most complex and rich works."

"Rarely has [Howe's] work exhibited [such] emotional depth and power," stated *Booklist* contributor Jack Helbig in regard to *Pride's Crossing,* produced in 1998. The play features ninety-year-old Mabel Tiding Bigelow, the first female athlete to swim across the English channel from the difficult direction of England to France. The play switches back and forth between memories of her younger days and her old age, to give the viewer insight into Mabel's complicated life. *Pride's Crossing* "moves fluidly from the present to the past," said Judy Richter in a *Back Stage West* review. Charles Isherwood noted in *Variety* that the play "is a lovely achievement for both Howe and The Old Globe Theater," and felt that the finale "is immensely moving. . . . a moment both sad and beautiful, a moment of great art."

Howe once told *CA:* "I find enormous pleasure in making playwriting as difficult as possible. I go out of my way to look for unlikely settings and situations; art museums, restaurants, fitting rooms, places that are basically predictable and uneventful. Nothing is more theatrical than putting the unexpected on stage. Because the theatre is a palace of dreams, the more original the spectacle, the better. I'm hopelessly drawn to digging out the flamboyant in everyday life."

BIOGRAPHICAL AND CRITICAL SOURCES:

BOOKS

American Women Writers, 2nd edition, Gale (Detroit, MI), 1995.

Betsko, Kathleen, and Rachel Koenig, editors, *Interviews with Contemporary Women Playwrights,* Beech Tree Books (New York, NY), 1987.
Contemporary Dramatists, 6th edition, St. James Press (Detroit, MI), 1999.
Contemporary Theatre, Film, and Television, Volume 15, Gale (Detroit, MI), 1996.

PERIODICALS

American Drama, spring, 1992, Kenneth E. Johnston, "Tina Howe and Feminine Discourse," pp. 15-25.
Back Stage West, September 2, 1999, Judy Richter, review of *Pride's Crossing,* p. 13; March 23, 2000, Zach Udko, review of *Painting Churches,* pp. 18-19.
Booklist, August, 1990, review of *Approaching Zanzibar,* p. 2147; October 15, 1998, Jack Helbig, review of *Pride's Crossing,* p. 387.
Christian Science Monitor, May 24, 1989, John Beaufort, review of *Approaching Zanzibar,* p. 10; April 27, 1993, Frank Scheck, review of *One Shoe Off,* p. 14.
Commonweal, January 13, 1984, Gerald Weales, review of *Painting Churches,* pp. 16-17.
Entertainment Weekly, February 13, 1998, Jess Cagle, review of *Pride's Crossing,* pp. 62-63.
Kliatt, winter, 1985, review of *Three Plays,* p. 29.
Library Journal, September 1, 1997, Ming-ming Shen Kuo, "Plays for Actresses," p. 183.
Nation, January 10, 1987, Moira Hodgson, review of *Coastal Disturbances,* pp. 24-26.
New Republic, January 5, 1987, Robert Brustein, review of *Coastal Disturbances,* pp. 26-27.
Newsday, December 7, 1997, Patrick Pacheo, review of *Pride's Crossing,* p. D17; December 8, 1997, Linda Winer, "Swimming into a Flood of Memories," p. B9.
New York, December 1, 1986, John Simon, review of *Coastal Disturbances,* pp. 148-149; March 30, 1987, John Simon, review of *Coastal Disturbances,* p. 97; May 15, 1989, John Simon, review of *Approaching Zanzibar,* pp. 124-125; May 3, 1993, John Simon, review of *One Shoe Off,* pp. 82-83; December 22, 1997, John Simon, review of *Pride's Crossing,* pp. 120-121.
New Yorker, March 6, 1978, December 17, 1979, May 24, 1982; December 1, 1986, Edith Oliver, review of *Coastal Disturbances,* p. 111; May 15, 1989, Edith Oliver, review of *Approaching Zanzibar,* p.

94; May 3, 1993, Edith Oliver, review of *One Shoe Off,* p. 99; January 5, 1998, John Lahr, review of *Pride's Crossing,* p. 79.

New York Times, April 10, 1970, February 28, 1978; December 7, 1979; February 18, 1983; November 20, 1986, Frank Rich, review of *Coastal Disturbances,* p. 22; January 7, 1987; May 19, 1986, John J. O'Connor, review of *Painting Churches,* p. 21; May 17, 1987, Walter Kerr, review of *Coastal Disturbances,* p. H43; May 5, 1989, Frank Rich, review of *Approaching Zanzibar,* p. B2; April 16, 1993, Frank Rich, review of *One Shoe Off,* p. B1; December 8, 1997, Ben Brantley, review of *Pride's Crossing,* p. B1; January 11, 1998, Vincent Canby, review of *Pride's Crossing,* p. AR5.

Theatre Crafts, May, 1985, Susan Lieberman, review of *Painting Churches,* pp. 18-20.

Theatre Journal, May, 1996, Helena M. White, review of *Birth and After Birth,* pp. 223-225.

Time, May 15, 1989, William A. Henry III, review of *Approaching Zanzibar,* p. 87; April 26, 1993, review of *One Shoe Off,* p. 71.

Variety, May 10, 1989, review of *Approaching Zanzibar,* p. 119; April 19, 1993, Jeremy Gerard, review of *One Shoe Off,* p. 53; September 25, 1995, Toby Zinman, review of *Birth and After Birth,* p. 105; February 10, 1997, Charles Isherwood, review of *Pride's Crossing,* p. 76.

Vogue, February, 1993, Sean Elder, "Who's Afraid of Tina Howe?," pp. 106-107.

Wall Street Journal, December 10, 1986, Sylviane Gold, review of *Coastal Disturbances,* p. 32E; May 12, 1989, Laurie Winer, review of *Approaching Zanzibar,* p. A10; December 10, 1997, Donald Lyons, review of *Pride's Crossing,* p. A20.

Washington Post, March 27, 1996, David Richards, review of *Birth and After Birth,* p. C1.*

* * *

HUTCHINS, Pat 1942-

PERSONAL: Born June 18, 1942, in Yorkshire, England; daughter of Edward (a soldier) and Lilian (Crawford) Goundry; married Laurence Hutchins (a film director), July 21, 1965; children: Morgan, Sam. *Education:* Attended Darlington School of Art, 1958-60, and Leeds College of Art, 1960-62.

ADDRESSES: Home—75 Flask Walk, London NW3 1ET, England. *E-mail*—pat@titch.net.

Pat Hutchins

CAREER: J. Walter Thompson (advertising agency), London, England, assistant art director, 1963-65; freelance writer and illustrator, 1965—.

AWARDS, HONORS: Kate Greenaway Award, Library Association (England), 1974, for *The Wind Blew.*

WRITINGS:

SELF-ILLUSTRATED; FOR CHILDREN

Rosie's Walk, Macmillan (New York, NY), 1968.

Tom and Sam, Macmillan (New York, NY), 1968.

The Surprise Party, Macmillan (New York, NY), 1969.

Clocks and More Clocks, Macmillan (New York, NY), 1970.

Changes, Changes, Macmillan (New York, NY), 1971.

Titch, Macmillan (New York, NY), 1971.

Goodnight, Owl, Macmillan (New York, NY), 1972.

The Wind Blew, Macmillan (New York, NY), 1974.

The Silver Christmas Tree, Macmillan (New York, NY), 1974.

Don't Forget the Bacon, Greenwillow (New York, NY), 1976.

The Best Train Set Ever, Greenwillow (New York, NY), 1978.

Happy Birthday, Sam, Greenwillow (New York, NY), 1978.

One-Eyed Jake, Greenwillow (New York, NY), 1979.

The Tale of Thomas Mead, Greenwillow (New York, NY), 1980.

One Hunter, Greenwillow (New York, NY), 1982.

You'll Soon Grow into Them, Titch, Greenwillow (New York, NY), 1983.

King Henry's Palace, Greenwillow (New York, NY), 1983.

The Very Worst Monster, Greenwillow (New York, NY), 1985.

The Doorbell Rang, Greenwillow (New York, NY), 1986.

Where's the Baby?, Greenwillow (New York, NY), 1988.

Which Witch Is Which?, Greenwillow (New York, NY), 1989.

What Game Shall We Play?, Greenwillow (New York, NY), 1990.

Tidy Titch, Greenwillow (New York, NY), 1991.

Silly Billy, Greenwillow (New York, NY), 1992.

My Best Friend, Greenwillow (New York, NY), 1992.

Little Pink Pig, Greenwillow (New York, NY), 1993.

Three Star Billy, Greenwillow (New York, NY), 1994.

Titch and Daisy, Greenwillow (New York, NY), 1996.

Shrinking Mouse, Greenwillow (New York, NY), 1997.

It's My Birthday!, Greenwillow (New York, NY), 1999.

Ten Red Apples, Greenwillow (New York, NY), 2000.

We're Going on a Picnic!, Greenwillow (New York, NY), 2001.

FOR CHILDREN; ILLUSTRATED BY HUSBAND, LAURENCE HUTCHINS

The House That Sailed Away, Greenwillow (New York, NY), 1975.

Follow That Bus, Greenwillow (New York, NY), 1977.

The Mona Lisa Mystery, Greenwillow (New York, NY), 1981.

The Curse of the Egyptian Mummy, Greenwillow (New York, NY), 1983.

Rats, Greenwillow (New York, NY), 1989.

Also creator of a 26-part stop-action puppet television series based on her Titch characters, released in England in 1997.

ADAPTATIONS: Clocks and More Clocks, Rosie's Walk, The Surprise Party, and *Changes, Changes* have all been made into filmstrips by Weston Woods.

SIDELIGHTS: Pat Hutchins is the author of many self-illustrated children's books. Her best-known character is Titch, a little boy, his best friend Daisy, and his cat, Tailcat. The Titch characters have appeared in a series of picture books for young readers and have also been adapted for television, with scripts written by Hutchins and directed by her husband, Laurence. According to the essayist for the *St. James Guide to Children's Writers,* Hutchins is "an excellent storyteller" whose "every picture book is a magnet for young listeners and readers."

Hutchins is especially noted for children's books that use humor in presenting sometimes complex situations. The essayist for the *St. James Guide to Children's Writers* noted that Hutchins's first picture book, *Rosie's Walk,* was particularly outstanding: "*Rosie's Walk* has a text of a mere thirty-six words. It is a picture book, of course, and its art work (which shows Rosie the hen going for a walk 'across the yard, around the pond . . . past the mill . . . under the beehives' and getting home in time for dinner) is strong and attractive. But it is neither the thirty-six words on their own nor the art work on its own that would entitle Hutchins to her entry: it is the brilliant interplay of the two, the assured use of dramatic irony. For young children listening to the story of Rosie, walking, will never hear a mention of the fox who, they can see from the pictures, is one step behind her, always tripped up (whether accidentally or intentionally is Hutchins's secret) by the strutting hen."

The Mona Lisa Mystery, also, is "superior children's fare . . . with enough humorous episodes to make readers of all ages laugh," Laurel Graeber stated in the *Christian Science Monitor.* While the critic believed that the mystery may present some vocabulary problems for younger readers, she nevertheless encouraged the reading of the book: "It's just too good to miss." Called "a major British illustrator/author" by *Chicago Tribune Book World* contributor Zena Sutherland, Hutchins presents a "convincing" blend of "fanciful and realistic elements" in *The Very Worst Monster,* a story of monster sibling rivalry. Calling the book "witty and whimsical," Toronto *Globe and Mail* writer Sandra Martin praised the author for "us[ing] the monster theme exquisitely and to gruesome advantage in dealing with the ultimate wicked sibling fantasy. [Hutchins] has a keen respect for children and an understanding for how they respond to situations." As Nancy Schmidtmann concluded in *School Library Journal,* "Hutchins is completely original in her treatment. . . . [*The Very Worst Monster* is] a monstrously wonderful addition to any picture book collection."

In the stories featuring the little boy Titch, Hutchins writes for a very young audience. In *Titch and Daisy,* for example, Titch goes to a birthday party only because he has been told that his friend Daisy will be there. When he arrives and cannot find her, Titch hides behind a sofa and in a cupboard, too shy to participate with the other children. But when he hides under the table, he finds that Daisy is also hiding there, just as scared of meeting strangers as he is. Hanna B. Zeiger of *Horn Book Magazine* found *Titch and Daisy* to be "a pleasant portrayal of young children's dilemma when facing a new situation."

Hutchins first based the character of Titch on her sons Morgan and Sam, who are now in their thirties. Taking the popular character from print to television was a challenge. In an article posted on the *Titch Web site,* Hutchins explained: "When I was writing the Titch books, the only other person involved was my editor. Suddenly I was co-operating with crowds—directors, animators, puppet makers, model makers, actors and commissioning editors." Puppets are made of each character and they are then filmed a frame at a time in different poses to make them seem to be moving. Hutchins explained in her article: "The puppets have to be sculpted in clay before the heads are cast in resin. The skeletons, or armatures, are made of special metals to high precision standards to withstand the variations in temperature that the puppets are subjected to, every day for nine months. Three puppets of each character are needed as the animators can be working on three different stages at any one time. The puppet maker worked from my original Titch drawings and it was wonderful witnessing Titch becoming three-dimensional."

Hutchins once told *CA:* "To me, the most important thing about a children's picture book is that it should be logical, not only the story, but the layout, too. To a very small child, an opened book is one page, not two—he doesn't see the gutter as a dividing line.

"I like to build my stories up, so the reader can understand what is happening and, in some cases, anticipate what is likely to happen on the next page. I think one can get quite complicated ideas across to small children as long as they are presented in a simple, satisfying way."

Hutchins added: "I was brought up in a small village in Yorkshire, the second youngest of seven children. As I loved drawing, I would wander round the countryside with my drawing book under my arm and my pet crow on my shoulder (he was too lazy to fly) and, while he searched for grubs, I sketched. Books were my other love, so it was inevitable that I would go to art school and study illustration.

"I am often asked if the experience of having children makes it easier to produce books for young children. As *Happy Birthday, Sam* was written specifically for my son Sam, and *Titch* for my son Morgan, I have to reply 'Yes.' But it is a tentative 'yes.'

"I still believe that the best experience of childhood is having been a child yourself and recognizing the emotional upheaval of 'growing up.' As I had five older brothers and sisters, I can remember how Titch, being the youngest, felt. Remembering the birth of my baby brother, my sympathies switch to Hazel, the little girl monster in *The Very Worst Monster,* who gives her baby brother away in a last, desperate effort to divert some attention from the baby to herself. Growing up can be painful, with all the real and imagined injustices it involves, and I try to write stories that are reassuring to the very young reader.

"I am also asked if I tested my stories on my children. I did once, and it didn't work. Morgan, who was 'into' space travel, said he liked the story, but why didn't I have a spaceship in it? Sam, who loved animals, said he liked it, too, but why didn't I have an elephant in it? As I didn't feel capable of writing a story about an elephant in a spaceship, my market research was short-lived.

"I feel that ultimately you write to satisfy yourself and hope that your readers will be satisfied with your offering, too."

BIOGRAPHICAL AND CRITICAL SOURCES:

BOOKS

Bader, Barbara, *A History of American Picture Books: From Noah's Ark to the Beast Within,* Macmillan (New York, NY), 1976.

St. James Guide to Children's Writers, 5th edition, St. James Press (Detroit, MI), 1999.

PERIODICALS

Booklist, April 15, 1996, Carolyn Phelan, review of *Titch and Daisy,* p. 1445; February 15, 1997, Ilene Cooper, review of *Shrinking Mouse,* p. 1026; June 1, 1999, Susan Dove Lempke, review of *It's My Birthday!,* p. 1842; May 1, 2000, John Peters, review of *Ten Red Apples,* p. 1678; March 1, 2002, Gillian Engberg, review of *We're Going on a Picnic!,* p. 1142.

Chicago Tribune Book World, June 9, 1985, Zena Sutherland, review of *The Very Worst Monster.*

Children's Literature Newsletter, July, 1996, Carol Hurst, "Pat Hutchins."

Christian Science Monitor, October 14, 1981, Laurel Graeber, review of *The Mona Lisa Mystery.*

Globe and Mail (Toronto, Ontario, Canada), March 30, 1985, Sandra Martin, review of *The Very Worst Monster.*

Horn Book Magazine, May-June, 1996, Hanna B. Zeiger, review of *Titch and Daisy,* p. 325; May-June, 1997, Marilyn Bousquin, review of *Shrinking Mouse,* p. 308.

New York Times Book Review, April 17, 1977; April 25, 1982.

Publishers Weekly, August 24, 1992, review of *Silly Billy!,* p. 79; April 5, 1993, review of *My Best Friend,* p. 76; October 3, 1994, review of *Three-Star Billy,* p. 68; February 24, 1997, review of *Shrinking Mouse,* p. 91; September 6, 1999, review of *Where's the Baby?,* p. 106; May 22, 2000, review of *Ten Red Apples,* p. 92; January 21, 2002, review of *We're Going on a Picnic!,* p. 89.

School Library Journal, May, 1985, Nancy Schmidt-mann, review of *The Very Worst Monster;* April, 1996, Carolyn Noah, review of *Titch and Daisy,* p. 110; April, 1997, Marianne Saccardi, review of *Shrinking Mouse,* p. 106; March, 1999, Gay Lynn Van Vleck, review of *It's My Birthday!,* p. 176; May, 2000, Beth Tegart, review of *Ten Red Apples,* p. 144; October, 2001, Teresa Bateman, review of audiocassette version of *The Doorbell Rang,* p. 88; March, 2002, Rosalyn Pierini, review of *We're Going on a Picnic!,* p. 190.

Teacher Librarian, June, 2000, Shirley Lewis, review of *Ten Red Apples,* p. 50.

Times Literary Supplement, March 27, 1981; May 24, 1985.

ONLINE

Titch Web site, http://www.titch.net/front.htm/ (December 5, 2002), Pat Hutchins, "The Making of Titch."

Young Writer Magazine Web site, http://www.mystworld.com/youngwriter/ (December 5, 2002), interview with Pat Hutchins.*

J

JAHN, (Joseph) Michael 1943-
(Mike Jahn)

PERSONAL: Born August 4, 1943, in Cincinnati, OH; son of Joseph C. (a newspaperman) and Anne (Loughlin) Jahn; married Catherine Knoll (a researcher), July 24, 1965; children: Evan R. *Education:* Adelphi University, B.A., 1965, graduate study, 1965-68; additional graduate study at Columbia University, 1967-68.

ADDRESSES: Office—Columbia University, New York, NY 10027. *Agent*—Meredith Bernstein, 2112 Broadway, Suite 503A, New York, NY 10023. *E-mail*—donovanbooks@hotmail.com.

CAREER: Moriches Bay Tide (weekly newspaper), Center Moriches, NY, news editor, 1964-65; *Newsday,* Long Island, NY, editorial assistant, 1965-66; *Long Island Advance* (weekly), Long Island, reporter and photographer, 1966; Columbia University, New York, NY, associate director for college relations, 1966-67; staff writer for Office of Public Information, 1967-68; freelance writer, 1968—; Columbia University, press officer, 1980—. Commentator on radio station WNEW-FM, 1969-70; lecturer, New School for Social Research, 1971.

MEMBER: American Association for the Advancement of Science, Mystery Writers of America.

AWARDS, HONORS: Edgar Allan Poe Award from Mystery Writers of America, 1977, for *The Quark Maneuver.*

WRITINGS:

UNDER NAME MIKE JAHN, EXCEPT WHERE INDICATED

Jim Morrison and the Doors: An Unauthorized Book, Grosset (New York, NY), 1969.

The Scene (novel), Geis, 1970.

Rock: From Elvis to the Rolling Stones, Quadrangle, 1973.

The Rockford Files: The Unfortunate Replacement, Popular Library, 1975.

The Invisible Man, Fawcett (New York, NY), 1975.

How to Make a Hit Record, Bradbury (New York, NY), 1976.

The Deadliest Game, Popular Library, 1976.

The Six Million Dollar Man: The Secret of Bigfoot Pass, Berkley Publishing (New York, NY), 1976.

Switch, Berkley Publishing (New York, NY), 1976.

The Six Million Dollar Man: Wine, Women, and War, Wingate, 1976.

The Quark Maneuver, Ballantine (New York, NY), 1977.

The Six Million Dollar Man: International Incidents, Berkley Publishing (New York, NY), 1977.

Killer on the Heights, Fawcett (New York, NY), 1977.

The Six Million Dollar Man: The Rescue of Athena, Wingate, 1978.

Thunder: The Mighty Stallion of the Hills, Grosset (New York, NY), 1978.

Thunder: Mighty Stallion to the Rescue, Grosset (New York, NY), 1978.

(Under name Michael Jahn) *Kingsley's Empire,* Fawcett (New York, NY), 1980.

(With Lewis Chesler and Elliot Blair) *The Olympian Strain,* Fawcett (New York, NY), 1980.

Shearwater, Hamlyn/American, 1980.
Armada, Fawcett (New York, NY), 1981.
Tambora, Fawcett (New York, NY), 1982.
Night Rituals: A Novel, Norton (New York, NY), 1982.
Death Games: A Novel, Norton (New York, NY), 1987.
City of God, St. Martin's Press (New York, NY), 1992.
Dragon: The Bruce Lee Story: A Novel (Based on a screenplay by Edward Khmara and John Raffo and Rob Cohen), Jove Books (New York, NY), 1993.

"BILL DONOVAN MYSTERY" SERIES

Murder at the Museum of Natural History: A Bill Donovan Mystery, St. Martin's (New York, NY), 1994.
Murder on Theater Row: A Bill Donovan Mystery, St. Martin's (New York, NY), 1997.
Murder on Fifth Avenue: A Bill Donovan Mystery, St. Martin's (New York, NY), 1998.
Murder in Central Park: A Bill Donovan Mystery, St. Martin's (New York, NY), 2000.
Murder on the Waterfront: A Bill Donovan Mystery, St. Martin's (New York, NY), 2001.
Murder in Coney Island, St. Martin's (New York, NY), 2003.

Also author of two novels in the "Black Sheep Squadron" series, 1979 and 1980. Author of columns, "New York Current," Bell-McClure Syndicate, 1968-70, "The Pop Side,"*Ingenue,* 1968-71, "Sounds of the Seventies," New York Times Syndicate, 1970-72, "New York Offbeat," New York Times Syndicate, 1972-73, "Jahn on Music,"*Cue,* 1972—, and "Music," *Gallery,* 1974—; rock music critic, *New York Times,* 1968-71; reviewer, *High Fidelity,* 1971—. Contributor to periodicals, including *Esquire, Vogue, Cosmopolition, New York Times Magazine,* and *Saturday Review.* Popular music editor, *Cue,* 1972-76.

SIDELIGHTS: Michael Jahn has penned many novels over the course of his career, including several novelizations of television series and films. One of his first independent works of fiction, however, *The Quark Maneuver,* garnered him the Edgar Award in 1977. Since the early 1990s, however, Jahn has been best known for his series of mystery novels featuring New York City locales and detective Bill Donovan. The first book in the series, *City of God,* takes place in the

Cathedral of St. John the Divine. The book also includes Donovan approaching marriage to a black fellow officer, Marcie Barnes. A *Publishers Weekly* reviewer of *City of God* noted that "Jahn shows sensitivity in depicting a biracial relationship, and he captures Manhattan's Upper West Side with gritty realism and touches of mordant humor."

Other settings Jahn has used include the theater district, the Museum of Natural History, and Central Park. *Murder at the Museum of Natural History,* which appeared in 1994, ends in a shootout among the dinosaur skeletons, and prompted another *Publishers Weekly* critic to remark that "Jahn's latest is suffused with a sense of place and a fitting irony." Discussing his 1997 novel, *Murder on Theater Row,* Marilyn Stasio in the *New York Times Book Review* reported that "the author knows his way around the theater and has sly fun sending up sacred cows." Robert A. Carter, reviewing the same novel in the *Houston Chronicle,* concluded: "It's another dandy piece of work from Michael Jahn, right on target." Similarly, David Pitt in *Booklist* praised Jahn's Donovan series for "its detailed look at New York," and called 2000's *Murder in Central Park* "a guaranteed hit with fans of the Donovan series and newcomers alike." Pitt also reviewed 2001's *Murder on the Waterfront* in *Booklist,* and while he did not like it as well as some others in the series, he remained willing to "recommend it confidently to anyone who likes mysteries set in the Big Apple."

BIOGRAPHICAL AND CRITICAL SOURCES:

BOOKS

Science Fiction and Fantasy Literature, 1975-1991, Gale (Detroit, MI), 1992.

PERIODICALS

Booklist, February 15, 2000, David Pitt, review of *Murder in Central Park,* p. 1088; August, 2001, David Pitt, review of *Murder on the Waterfront,* p. 2097.
Houston Chronicle, Robert A. Carter, "Sam Plays It Again, This Time Onstage," p. 23.
New York Times Book Review, March 16, 1997, Marilyn Stasio, review of *Murder on Theater Row,* p. 28.

Publishers Weekly, February 3, 1992, review of *City of God,* p. 66; October 10, 1994, review of *Murder at the Museum of Natural History,* p. 64.

ONLINE

Michael Jahn's New York, http://www.geocities.com/michaeljahn/ (November 9, 2003).*

*   *   *

JAHN, Mike
    See JAHN, (Joseph) Michael

*   *   *

JOHNSON, Spencer 1938-

PERSONAL: Born November 24, 1938, in Watertown, SD; son of J. O. (a designer) and Madeline (Sankey) Johnson; married Ann Donegan, June 21, 1968 (divorced, 1978); remarried; children: Cameron, Emerson. *Education:* University of Southern California, B.A. (psychology), 1963; Royal College of Surgeons (Ireland), M.D., 1968.

ADDRESSES: Office—Who Moved My Cheese?, 1775 West 2300 S., Suite B, Salt Lake City, UT 84119. *Agent*—Sterling International, 611 North Elmhurst Rd., Suite 226, Prospect Heights, IL 60070.

CAREER: Medtronic, Minneapolis, MN, director of medical communications, 1970-72; Value Communications, La Jolla, CA, chairman, 1974-77; University of California—San Diego, consultant to School of Medicine, 1977-79; Candle Communications, La Jolla, CA, chairman, beginning 1982; Institute for Inter-Disciplinary Studies, research physician; Center for the Study of the Person, consultant; Harvard Business School, leadership fellow.

WRITINGS:

(With Kenneth Blanchard) *One-Minute Manager,* Blanchard-Johnson (La Jolla, CA), 1981, Morrow (New York, NY), 1982.

The Precious Present, Celestial Arts (Millbrae, CA), 1981.

The One-Minute Father: The Quickest Way to Help Children Learn How to Like Themselves and Want to Behave Themselves, Morrow (New York, NY), 1983.

The One-Minute Mother: The Quickest Way to Help Children Learn How to Like Themselves and Want to Behave Themselves, Morrow (New York, NY), 1983.

The One-Minute Sales Person: The Quickest Way to More Sales with Less Stress, Morrow (New York, NY), 1984, 2002.

One Minute for Myself: A Small Investment, a Big Reward, Morrow (New York, NY), 1985.

The One-Minute Teacher: How to Teach Others to Teach Themselves, Morrow (New York, NY), 1986.

"Yes" or "No": The Guide to Better Decisions, HarperCollins (New York, NY), 1992.

Who Moved My Cheese?: An A-Mazing Way to Deal with Change in Your Work and in Your Life, Putnam (New York, NY), 1998.

Who Moved My Cheese? Little Nibbles of Cheese, Stark Books (Kansas City, MO), 2001.

Who Moved My Cheese? For Teens: An A-Mazing Way to Change and Win!, Putnam (New York, NY), 2002.

Who Moved My Cheese? For Kids: An A-Mazing Way to Change and Win!, Putnam (New York, NY), 2003.

The Present: The Gift That Makes You Happy and Successful at Work and in Life, Doubleday (New York, NY), 2003.

"VALUETALES" SERIES; FOR CHILDREN

The ValueTale of the Wright Brothers: The Value of Patience, illustrated by Steve Pileggi, Value Communications (La Jolla, CA), 1975, published as *The Value of Patience,* 1976.

The ValueTale of Elizabeth Fry: The Value of Kindness, illustrated by Steve Pileggi, Value Communications (La Jolla, CA), 1975, published as *The Value of Kindness,* 1976.

The ValueTale of Louis Pasteur: The Value of Believing in Yourself, illustrated by Steve Pileggi, Value Communications (La Jolla, CA), 1975, published as *The Value of Believing in Yourself,* 1976.

The Value of Humor: The Story of Will Rodgers, illustrated by Steve Pileggi, Value Communications (La Jolla, CA), 1976.

The Value of Courage: The Story of Jackie Robinson, illustrated by Steve Pileggi, Value Communications (La Jolla, CA), 1977.

The Value of Curiosity: The Story of Christopher Columbus, illustrated by Steve Pileggi, Value Communications (La Jolla, CA), 1977.

The Value of Imagination: The Story of Charles Dickens, illustrated by Steve Pileggi, Value Communications (La Jolla, CA), 1977.

The Value of Saving: The Story of Benjamin Franklin, illustrated by Steve Pileggi, Value Communications (La Jolla, CA), 1978.

The Value of Sharing: The Story of the Mayo Brothers, illustrated by Steve Pileggi, Value Communications (La Jolla, CA), 1978.

The Value of Honesty: The Story of Confucius, illustrated by Steve Pileggi, Value Communications (La Jolla, CA), 1979.

The Value of Understanding: The Story of Margaret Mead, illustrated by Steve Pileggi, Value Communications (La Jolla, CA), 1979.

The Value of Fantasy: The Story of Hans Christian Andersen, illustrated by Steve Pileggi, Value Communications (La Jolla, CA), 1979.

The Value of Dedication: The Story of Albert Schweitzer, illustrated by Steve Pileggi, Value Communications (La Jolla, CA), 1979.

Johnson's books have been translated into more than a dozen languages.

ADAPTATIONS: The One-Minute Father was released on audiocassette by Nightingale-Conant (Champaign, IL), 1983; *Who Moved My Cheese?* was recorded and released on audiocassette by Simon & Schuster Audio (New York, NY), 1999.

SIDELIGHTS: Until his *Who Moved My Cheese: An A-Mazing Way to Deal with Change in Your Work and in Your Life* became a nationwide bestseller, Dr. Spencer Johnson was best known for his 1981 business title, *The One-Minute Manager,* in which he and coauthor Kenneth Blanchard offered business leaders a three-pronged plan for success. All that changed when Johnson finally listened to Blanchard and wrote down an anecdote that Johnson had created about mice, men, and cheese. *Who Moved My Cheese,* which was at first sold through Johnson's own company and to business clients, gained a following among a wider audience. Since its 1998 debut with a major New York publisher,

the work has gone through eleven printings, selling more than eleven million copies within four years. Johnson later presented his parable about adaptability in separate versions for young adults and children, and provided ancillary materials for businesses through his *Who Moved My Cheese* Web site.

Who Moved My Cheese? features four characters who represent parts of a personality, live in a maze (read "life"), and look for cheese (read "whatever a person wants in life") to make themselves happy. Two of these characters are the mice Sniff and Scurry, and two are little people called Hem and Haw. When one day the cheese is moved to another part of the maze, the characters each react differently, some moving on, while others become stuck. After Johnson later told Blanchard about how he was using this paradigm to improve his own life, Blanchard told the "Cheese" story to business managers in his world-wide management seminars. After years of using the story, Blanchard insisted that Johnson put the tale on paper. Johnson did, and then he tested early versions on hundreds of friends and associates. "I listened to what people were saying they wanted in a book about dealing with change, and I've gotten to be very good at listening after twenty years of this," Johnson told Kate Fitzgerald of *Advertising Age.*

At first, *Who Moved My Cheese?* sold 500,000 copies without much notice, and then through word-of-mouth advertising, it became a runaway bestseller, landing on several best-seller lists, among them the *New York Times* and the *Wall Street Journal.* Leaders of companies purchased large quantities to give to their employees. Although Johnson wrote *Who Moved My Cheese?* with business people as his intended audience, it had great crossover appeal to general audiences because, as a *Planet IT* reviewer expressed it, "It's a simple parable that reveals profound truths about change." Readers have hardly been nonplussed, either liking or disliking the work. In a *Fortune* article, Johnson is quoted as saying: "A minority of readers hate the book—'hate' with a capital 'H.'" Yet "more impressive is that many of the book's biggest fans are hardheaded business people; they are reading it, recommending it, and using it at their companies," *Fortune's* Geoffrey Colvin wrote.

Adapting *Who Moved My Cheese?* for a young adult audience came next. "There was extensive teenage traffic on the book's Web site, and many who had read their parents' copies said that the book had made a big difference in their lives," Johnson told Sally Lodge of *Publishers Weekly*. "But they also said that they wished that the story could be told to relate to issues that concern kids their age." Although Johnson had no teenagers of his own, he thought about modern teenagers being the people whose lives change at a faster pace than anyone else's. So with the input of *Teen* magazine writer Cylin Busby, who gave Johnson insight into the issues that most concern modern teenagers, Johnson rewrote *Who Moved My Cheese?* with teens in mind, telling the same story with a more youth-oriented beginning and ending. Before sending it to a publisher, he tested it on this audience. "I passed the new book to many teenagers," he told Lodge, "and as I received feedback, I tweaked and added nuances to the teenage conversation that takes place in the book. I was constantly changing the dialogue." *Who Moved My Cheese? For Teens: An A-Mazing Way to Change and Win!*, geared to readers age ten and older, appeared in 2002. Writing in *Publishers Weekly*, a critic suggested that the book's theme about "anticipating, accepting, and using change to improve one's life" would be of use to teen readers.

A picture book version, *Who Moved My Cheese? For Kids: An A-Mazing Way to Change and Win!*, appeared in 2003. Though Johnson had not written any books for children since the mid-1970s, when he and illustrator Steve Pileggi put out the "ValueTales" series, Johnson told Lodge, that he "was really excited about writing for the picture-book audience again."

BIOGRAPHICAL AND CRITICAL SOURCES:

PERIODICALS

Advertising Age, March 26, 2001, Kate Fitzgerald, "Superstar Spencer Johnson," p. S6.
Booklist, February 15, 2001, Mary Frances Wilkens, review of *Who Moved My Cheese?: An A-Mazing Way to Deal with Change in Your Work and in Your Life* (audio version), p. 1164; December 1, 2002, Ilene Cooper, review of *Who Moved My Cheese? For Teens: An A-Mazing Way to Change and Win!*, p. 654.
Fortune, November 22, 1999, Geoffrey Colvin, "Behold the Power of Cheese," review of *Who Moved*

My Cheese?, p. 363; August 14, 2000, Geoffrey Colvin, "Who Moved My Cheese to Harvard?," p. 64.
Library Journal, October 15, 1999, Mark Guyer, review of *Who Moved My Cheese?* (audio version), p. 124.
Multicultural Review, July, 1992, Martin Goldberg, "Searching for Columbus," review of *The Value of Curiosity: The Story of Christopher Columbus*, pp. 10-12.
New York, January 24, 2000, Johanna Berkman, "Of Mice and Zen," review of *Who Moved My Cheese?*, p. 45.
New York Times, October 7, 1982.
People, December 13, 1982; May 1, 2000, Cynthia Sanz, "Pages," review of *Who Moved My Cheese?*, p. 41.
Planet IT, July 4, 2000, review of *Who Moved My Cheese?*.
Publishers Weekly, August 26, 1983; August 1, 1986, review of *The One-Minute Sales Person: The Quickest Way to More Sales with Less Stress*, p. 74; May 11, 1992, review of *"Yes" or "No": The Guide to Better Decisions*, p. 61; December 10, 2001, "Just Say Cheese," p. 18; September 30, 2002, Sally Lodge, "'Cheese' No Longer Stands Alone," pp. 28-29, and "New Cheese for Teens," review of *Who Moved My Cheese? For Teens*, p. 74; September 22, 2003, review of *The Present: The Gift That Makes You Happy and Successful at Work and in Life*, p. 100.
Reader's Digest, May, 2001, Max Alexander, "Who Moved My Cheese?" (interview), pp. 35-38.
San Diego Union/Tribune (San Diego, CA), August 20, 1982.
San Francisco Examiner, September 8, 1982.
School Library Journal, January, 2003, Jana R. Fine, review of *Who Moved My Cheese? For Teens*.
Washington Post, September 27, 1982.

ONLINE

Spencer Johnson Home Page, http://www.whomovedmycheese.com/ (March 11, 2003).
Sterling Speakers, http://www.sterlingspeakers.com/ (March 11, 2003).
Teenreads, http://www.teenreads.com/ (March 11, 2003), Carlie Kraft, review of *Who Moved My Cheese? For Teens*.*

K

KASABOV, Nikola K(irilov) 1948-

PERSONAL: Born August 12, 1948, in Svistov, Bulgaria; son of Kiril (a veterinarian) and Kapka (a teacher; maiden name, Mankova) Kasabov; married Diana Atanassova, October 3, 1971; children: Kapka, Assia (daughters). *Ethnicity:* "Bulgarian." *Education:* Technical University of Sofia, M.C., 1971, M.C., 1972, Ph.D., 1975. *Religion:* Christian. *Hobbies and other interests:* Playing the accordion, painting.

ADDRESSES: Home—47C Nihil Cres., Auckland, New Zealand. *Office*—Knowledge Engineering and Discovery Research Institute, Auckland University of Technology, Ronald Trotter House, Level 4, 581-585 Great South Rd., Penrose, Auckland, New Zealand; fax: +64-9-917-8501. *E-mail*—nik.kasabov@aut.ac.nz.

CAREER: Technical University of Sofia, Sofia, Bulgaria, began as lecturer, became senior lecturer, 1976-87, associate professor of computer science and director of International Graduate School in Artificial Intelligence, 1988-91; University of Otago, Dunedin, New Zealand, senior lecturer, 1992-95, associate professor, 1995-99, professor of information science, 1999-2002, director of Knowledge Engineering Laboratory, 1994-2002; Auckland University of Technology, Auckland, New Zealand, professor and chair of knowledge engineering and director of Knowledge Engineering and Discovery Research Institute, 2002—. University of Essex, senior lecturer, 1990-91. Asia-Pacific Neural Network Assembly, member of governing board, 1993—, president, 1997-98; leader of international conferences; holder of fifteen patents in the United States, England, France, Russia, and Bulgaria.

MEMBER: Royal Society of New Zealand (fellow), New Zealand Computer Society (fellow), Institute of Electrical and Electronics Engineers (senior member).

AWARDS, HONORS: Award for high achievement in patent work, Institute of Inventions, Sofia, Bulgaria, 1991; best paper award, European Meeting of Cybernetics and System Research, 1998; Silver Medal for contribution to science and technology, Royal Society of New Zealand, 2001.

WRITINGS:

(Editor) *1993 First New Zealand International Two-Stream Conference on Artificial Neural Networks and Expert Systems, November 24-26, 1993, Dunedin, New Zealand: Proceedings,* IEEE Computer Society Press (Washington, DC), 1993.

(Coeditor) *1995 Second New Zealand International Two-Stream Conference on Artificial Neural Networks and Expert Systems, November 20-23, 1995, Dunedin, New Zealand: Proceedings,* IEEE Computer Society Press (Washington, DC), 1995.

(With R. Romanski) *Computing,* Technika (Sofia, Bulgaria), 1995.

Foundations of Neural Networks, Fuzzy Systems, and Knowledge Engineering, MIT Press (Cambridge, MA), 1996.

(Editor, with S. Amari) *Brain-Line Computing and Intelligent Systems,* Springer Verlag (Singapore, China), 1997.

(Editor, with R. Kozma, and contributor) *Neuro-Fuzzy Techniques for Intelligent Systems,* Physica-Verlag (Heidelberg, Germany), 1998.

(Editor and contributor) *Future Directions for Intelligent Systems and Information Sciences: The Future of Speech and Image Technologies, Brain Computers, WWW, and Bioinformatics,* Physica-Verlag (Heidelberg, Germany), 2000.

Evolving Connectionist Systems: Methods and Applications in Bioinformatics, Brain Study, and Intelligent Machines, Springer Verlag (New York, NY), 2002.

Contributor to scientific books, including *Fuzzy Systems in Medicine,* edited by P. S. Szczepaniak, P. J. G. Lisboa, and J. Kacprzyk, Physica-Verlag (Heidelberg, Germany), 2000; *Neuro-Fuzzy Pattern Recognition,* edited by H. Bunke and A. Kandel, World Scientific Publishing (River Edge, NJ), 2000; and *Handbook of Brain Study and Neural Networks,* edited by M. Arbib, MIT Press (Cambridge, MA), 2002. Contributor of about eighty articles to periodicals, including *International Journal of Control and Cybernetics, Fuzzy Sets and Systems, Neural Networks, Journal of Advanced Computational Intelligence, Chemometrics and Intelligent Laboratory Systems, Neurocomputing, AI in Medicine, European Journal of Operation Research,* and *Genome Letters.* Member of editorial board of five international journals.

SIDELIGHTS: Nikola K. Kasabov once told *CA:* "I have been teaching graduate courses in neural networks, fuzzy systems, intelligent systems, and knowledge engineering for about twenty years. I find it fascinating to have an opportunity to pass my experience to other people, along with my latest research results. I produce advanced textbooks, which represent both 'classic' material and new research opportunities in artificial intelligence. My research focuses on contemporary issues in intelligent information systems that could inspire new researchers to join the field."

*　　*　　*

KETCH, Jack
　　See TIBBETTS, John C(arter)

L

LAPIERRE, Dominique 1931-

PERSONAL: Born July 30, 1931, in Chatelaillon, France; son of Jean (a diplomat) and Luce (Andreotti) Lapierre; married Aliette Spitzer, August 4, 1952; children: Alexandra. *Education:* Attended Institut des Sciences Politiques, Paris, 1951; Lafayette College, B.A., 1952. *Religion:* Catholic. *Hobbies and other interests:* Tennis, horseback riding.

ADDRESSES: Home and office—26 Avenue Kleber, 75116 Paris, France. *Agent*—Morton L. Janklow, 598 Madison Ave., New York, NY 10021.

CAREER: Paris Match (magazine), Paris, France, war correspondent in Korea, 1953, editor, 1954-67; writer, 1967—.

AWARDS, HONORS: Grand prize, Fondation des bourses de Zellidja, 1949, for a study on Mexico and the United States; Christopher Award, 1986, for *The City of Joy;* Christopher Award in books for adults category, 2003, for *Five Past Midnight in Bhopal.*

WRITINGS:

Un Dollar les mille kilometres (title means "A Dollar for One Thousand Kilometers"), Grasset (Paris, France), 1950.

Lune de miel autour de la terre, preface by Andre Maurois, Grasset (Paris, France), 1953, translation by Helen Beauclerk published as *Honeymoon around the World,* Secker & Warburg (London, England), 1957.

Dominique Lapierre

En Liberte sur les routes d'U.R.S.S. (title means "Freely on Soviet Highways"), Grasset (Paris, France), 1957.

Russie portes ouvertes (title means "Open Doors to Soviet Russia"), Editions Vie (Lausanne, Switzerland), 1957.

(With Stephane Groueff) *Les Caids de New York* (title means "The New York Bosses"), Julliard (Paris, France), 1958.

Chessman m'a dit (title means "Chessman Told Me"), Del Duca (Paris, France), 1960.

(With Stephane Groueff) *Les Ministres du crime* (title means "The Ministers of Crime"), Julliard, 1969.

The City of Joy, translated from the French by Kathryn Spink, Doubleday (New York, NY), 1985.

Beyond Love (Literary Guild selection), translated from the French by Kathryn Spink, Warner Books (New York, NY), 1991.

A Thousand Suns, Warner Books (New York, NY), 1999.

(With Javier Moro) *Il etait minuit cinq a Bhopal,* Laffont (Paris, France), 2001, translated from the French by Kathryn Spink, published as *Five past Midnight in Bhopal,* Warner Books (New York, NY), 2002.

WITH LARRY COLLINS

Paris brule-t-il?, Laffont (Paris, France), 1964, published as *Is Paris Burning?* (Literary Guild selection), Simon & Schuster (New York, NY), 1965.

Ou tu porteras mon deuil, Laffont (Paris, France), 1967, published as *Or I'll Dress You in Mourning* (Book-of-the-Month Club selection), Simon & Schuster (New York, NY), 1968.

O Jerusalem!, Laffont (Paris, France), 1971, reprinted, (Literary Guild selection), Simon & Schuster (New York, NY), 1988.

Cette nuit la liberte, Laffont, 1975, published as *Freedom at Midnight* (Literary Guild selection), Simon & Schuster (New York, NY), 1975.

Le Cinquieme Cavalier (novel), Laffont, 1980, published as *The Fifth Horseman* (Literary Guild selection), Simon & Schuster (New York, NY), 1980.

Mountbatten and the Partition of India, Vikas (New Delhi, India), 1982.

Mountbatten and Independent India, Vikas (New Delhi, India), 1983.

Also author of filmscript adaptation of *O Jerusalem!*

ADAPTATIONS: Is Paris Burning? was adapted for film and released by Paramount, 1965; *The City of Joy* was adapted for film and released by Tri-Star, 1992; Paramount holds the film option for *The Fifth Horseman.*

WORK IN PROGRESS: A new book; a film on Mother Teresa of Calcutta.

SIDELIGHTS: Dominique Lapierre told *CA:* "My main professional interest is to bring back to life great moments of our contemporary history. I am interested in the great modern epics of humanity. History has the reputation to be dull: It's not dull if only you devote enough time and sweat to bring it back to life. I consider myself a historian using the modern technique of investigative journalism. My books are as thoroughly and seriously researched as the most serious history books, and in this sense can be of use to professional, or rather, to 'scholarly' historians. But because of the dramatic nature of their subjects and their kaleidoscopic treatment, they are also very popular with the general public."

Many of Lapierre's books have indeed been immensely popular with the general public, reaching best-seller lists in Europe and the United States. The author is best known for his work with American writer Larry Collins; their collaborative titles include *Is Paris Burning?, O Jerusalem!,* and the novel *The Fifth Horseman.* A journalist who turned exclusively to full-length book projects in 1967, Lapierre is perhaps one of the most critically acclaimed and commercially successful authors in the field of historical documentary nonfiction.

In 1981, subsequent to the publication of *The Fifth Horseman,* Lapierre and his wife traveled to Calcutta, India, to visit a home they had sponsored for children of leprosy victims. During their stay in the city, Mother Teresa took the Lapierres to one of the world's worst slums, an area of Calcutta the name of which translates as "The City of Joy." Despite the fact that hordes of people living in the City of Joy subsisted on less than ten cents a day, Lapierre witnessed tremendous happiness and joy there. He decided to chronicle life in the slum from the points of view of three people: a Bengali peasant struggling to earn a living there, a Polish priest devoting his life to the poor, and an American doctor generously battling the area's many deadly diseases. Lapierre's book *The City of Joy* was published in 1985, a year later received the prestigious Christopher Award, and has sold more than seven million copies in thirty-one languages and editions, including five editions in Braille.

As Rumer Godden noted in the *New York Times Book Review, The City of Joy* "is about suffering, sorrow, cruelty and deprivation; about practices so hideous as almost to suspend belief, though they are shockingly true. It is about filth, rags, wounds, disease, even leprosy." Yet, wrote Godden, "the book is about other words that wonderfully leaven the whole: loyalty, kindness, tolerance, generosity, patience, endurance, acceptance, faith, even holiness. And it is about such love that we cannot pass by on the other side. In any case, it is too fascinating to let us do that." Godden also felt that the book is, in a sense, "too overwhelming. It tells so much that the mind becomes numbed, as happens in a famine or cyclone . . . when compassion ceases simply because the heart can take no more." In a *Washington Post Book World* review of *The City of Joy,* Elisabeth Bumiller expressed the opinion that Lapierre "has actually managed to describe the poor from their own point of view. This is a remarkable feat." Though Bumiller felt that the author "sometimes over-romanticizes the struggle of the poor . . . , diminishing their real pain and integrity," she nonetheless concluded: *"The City of Joy* is full of basic truths. Some of its moments may stay with a reader forever. . . . This book contains great lessons of resilience and dignity, and of what is really important when life is pared down to its essence. *The City of Joy* will make anyone a little richer for having read it."

Lapierre recently noted that he supports five homes for five hundred children of lepers in Calcutta, "along with a whole humanitarian action including dispensaries, schools, rehabilitation centers for lepers, irrigation programs, etc., funded with my royalties from *The City of Joy* and donations from my readers." Lapierre "calculates that he has spent $5 million on his small and largely unpublicized projects" designed to help the Indian people, wrote Barbara Crossette in the *New York Times.* Some of these assistance projects have been out of the ordinary, such as giving "poor village women small dowries to allow them to marry a bit above the lowest rungs of life," Crossette remarked.

In addition to the personal and individual difficulties suffered throughout India, Lapierre and writing collaborator Javier Moro are also keenly aware of the large-scale injustices that have been inflicted on the people of India—and at least one event that could easily be called an atrocity. In *Five past Midnight in Bhopal,* Lapierre and Moro recount in great detail the December 3, 1984 deaths of thousands of Bhopal residents—and the poisoning of more than half a million

others—in a chemical accident at Union Carbide's pesticide plant. Using a more novel-like structure, rather than a strict linear, historical account, Lapierre and Moro reconstruct decisions, events, and even dialogue that led up to the tragedy.

Most damning in Lapierre and Moro's account is that the accident could have been avoided. "But words such as 'accident' and 'tragedy' often imply a work of fate," wrote William K. Tabb in *OnEarth.* "More accurately, what happened that night was a result of [Union] Carbide's decision to cut back on necessary maintenance in order to save money at a plant that had, despite great opening fanfare, proven to be a financial disappointment." Originally intended to produce Sevin, an agricultural insecticide designed to bring dramatic improvements in India's crop production, the plant saw lower than anticipated profits. The company's "workers and management took shortcuts in equipping the Bhopal plant with modern safety features and in observing proper procedures for storing deadly methyl isocyanate" (MIC), a key ingredient in Sevin, wrote a *Kirkus Reviews* critic. Storage tanks lacked proper pressurization and refrigeration; alarm systems had been disconnected, and safety systems were nonfuctional. And one tank alone was overfilled with MIC, in violation of Union Carbide's own safety standards, containing too much of the deadly chemical "to allow for an emergency infusion of solvent to stop any runaway chemical reactions," Tabb wrote.

The result was a poisonous cloud that erupted from the Union Carbide plant at five minutes past midnight on December 3, 1984. It immediately suffused the slum areas of Bhopal surrounding the plant and traveled quickly outward. The death toll rose to as many as 30,000, and effects of the contamination are still seen in the health of the residents who were forced by circumstances to remain in the area. A settlement by Union Carbide resulted in payments of about $1,400 per victim, Tabb wrote, and Interpol warrants for the arrest of key figures at Union Carbide remain unserved.

"This account of one of the worst public health disasters of the past twenty years makes for uncomfortable, even scary reading, but it is simultaneously unputdownable," wrote Birte Twisselmann in the *British Medical Journal.* "The book thunders along, never losing any of its momentum, and the point at which it all 'goes up into the air' is tangible in its horror," remarked Twisselmann. John F. Riddick, writing in

Library Journal, called the book "a passionate, suspenseful, even vengeful account" of the event.

Even in the face of the tragedy and misery he has seen throughout India, Lapierre expresses optimism. Responding to a question during an interview in *Geographical* about what he enjoyed about the world, Lapierre replied, "Its extraordinary variety. I'm always looking for fifteen minutes more in every hour. You need ten incarnations to enjoy everything the world has to offer. I like the idea that the world never stops, that you are never bored."

BIOGRAPHICAL AND CRITICAL SOURCES:

PERIODICALS

Booklist, April 15, 2002, David Pitt, review of *Five past Midnight in Bhopal,* p. 1362.

British Medical Journal, September 7, 2002, Birte Twisselmann, review of *Five past Midnight in Bhopal,* p. 552.

Businessline, September 13, 2001, review of *Five past Midnight in Bhopal,* p. 1.

Far Eastern Economic Review, November 29, 2001, Shailaja Neelakantan, "Poison in the Night," pp. 76-77.

Geographical, September, 2000, interview with Dominique Lapierre, p. 114.

Guardian (Manchester, England), April 15, 2000, Hugo Young, "Words Were Not Enough," p. 22.

Kirkus Reviews, March 15, 2002, review of *Five past Midnight in Bhopal,* p. 385.

Kliatt, September, 2003, Katherine E. Gillen, review of *Five past Midnight in Bhopal,* pp. 39-40.

Library Journal, May 15, 2002, John F. Riddick, review of *Five past Midnight in Bhopal,* p. 109.

New York Times, August 22, 1999, Barbara Crossette, "In Calcutta, Writer's Joy Is in Deeds, Not Words," p. 16.

New York Times Book Review, November 3, 1985, Rumer Godden, review of *The City of Joy*; April 18, 1999, Ford Burkhart, review of *A Thousand Suns,* p. 20.

OnEarth, fall, 2002, William K. Tabb, review of *Five past Midnight in Bhopal,* pp. 37-39.

Publishers Weekly, February 1, 1999, review of *A Thousand Suns,* p. 67; April 22, 2002, review of *Five past Midnight in Bhopal,* p. 65.

Time, May 3, 1999, Jesse Birnbaum, review of *A Thousand Suns,* p. 78.

Times Literary Supplement, June 7, 2002, Toby Green, review of *Five past Midnight in Bhopal,* p. 30.

Washington Post Book World, October 27, 1985, Elisabeth Bumiller, review of *The City of Joy.*

ONLINE

City of Joy Web site, http://www.cityofjoyaid.org/ (November 14, 2003), biography of Dominique Lapierre.

Time Warner Bookmark Web site, http://www.twbook mark.com/ (November 14, 2003), biography of Dominique Lapierre.

Udayan Web site, http://www.udayan.org/lapierre.html/ (November 14, 2003), "Dominique Lapierre and *The City of Joy.*"*

*   *   *

LAREDO, Betty
See CODRESCU, Andrei

*   *   *

LESSNOFF, Michael 1940-

PERSONAL: Born January 23, 1940, in Glasgow, Scotland; son of Mark (a general practitioner of medicine) and Rae (Levitus) Lessnoff. *Ethnicity:* "Jewish." *Education:* University of Glasgow, M.A., 1963; Balliol College, Oxford, B.Phil., 1965. *Religion:* "Atheist." *Hobbies and other interests:* Art, science, literature, travel.

ADDRESSES: Home—58 White St., Glasgow G11 5EB, Scotland. *Office*—Department of Politics, University of Glasgow, Glasgow G12 8QQ, Scotland; fax 01-41-330-5071. *E-mail*—m.h.lessnoff@socsci.gla.ac.uk.

CAREER: University of Glasgow, Glasgow, Scotland, faculty member, 19666-86, reader in politics, 1986—.

MEMBER: Political Studies Association, Association of University Teachers.

WRITINGS:

The Structure of Social Science, Allen & Unwin (London, England), 1974.

Social Contract, Macmillan (New York, NY), 1986.

(Editor) *Social Contract Theory,* Basil Blackwell (Malden, MA), 1990.

The Spirit of Capitalism and the Protestant Ethic, Edward Elgar (Northampton, MA), 1994.

Political Philosophers of the Twentieth Century, Basil Blackwell (Malden, MA), 1998.

Ernest Gellner and Modernity, University of Wales Press (Cardiff, Wales), 2002.

WORK IN PROGRESS: Research on the relationship of modernity to science and religion.

SIDELIGHTS: Michael Lessnoff once told *CA:* "As a university teacher, research and writing are part of my job, which is undeniably one motivation for my writing. I am also keen to clarify ideas, expose nonsense, and deepen scholarship."

* * *

LUNDKVIST, (Nils) Artur 1906-1991

PERSONAL: Born March 3, 1906, in Oderljunga, Sweden; died, December 11, 1991; son of Nils (a farmer) and Charlotta Lundkvist; married Maria Wine (a writer), 1936. *Politics:* Socialist.

CAREER: Novelist, poet, and critic.

MEMBER: Mallarme Academy, Swedish Academy.

AWARDS, HONORS: Lenin Prize, 1958; Doblougska Priset, Swedish Academy, 1958; Golden Wreath Prize, Macedonia, Yugoslavia, 1978; various Swedish literary prizes.

WRITINGS:

Glöd, Bonnier (Stockholm, Sweden), 1928.

Naket Liv, Bonnier (Stockholm, Sweden), 1929.

Artur Lundkvist

(With others) *Fem Unga,* Bonnier (Stockholm, Sweden), 1929.

Jordisk prosa, Bonnier (Stockholm, Sweden), 1929.

Svart Stad, Bonnier (Stockholm, Sweden), 1930.

Altantvind (criticism), Bonnier (Stockholm), 1932.

Vit man, Bonnier (Stockholm, Sweden), 1932.

Negerkust, Bonnier (Stockholm, Sweden), 1933.

Floderna flyter mot havet, Tiden (Stockholm, Sweden), 1934.

Himmelsfärd, Bonnier (Stockholm, Sweden), 1935.

Nattens broar, Bonnier (Stockholm, Sweden), 1936.

Sirensång, Bonnier (Stockholm, Sweden), 1937.

Drakblod, Bonnier (Stockholm, Sweden), 1939.

Eldtema (poems), Bonnier (Stockholm, Sweden), 1939.

Ikarus' flykt (criticism), Bonnier (Stockholm, Sweden), 1939.

Tre amerikaner: Dreiser-Lewis-Anderson (criticism), Bonnier (Stockholm, Sweden), 1939.

Amerikas nya författare, Bonnier (Stockholm, Sweden), 1940.

Vandrarens träd, Bonnier (Stockholm, Sweden), 1941.

Korsväg, Bonnier (Stockholm, Sweden), 1942.

Dikter mellan djur och Gud, Bonnier (Stockholm, Sweden), 1944.

(Editor) *Twelve Modern Poets: An Anthology,* Continental (Stockholm, Sweden), 1946.

Skinn över sten (poems), Bonnier (Stockholm, Sweden), 1947.

Fotspaar i vattnet (poems; title means "Footprints in the Water"), Bonnier (Stockholm, Sweden), 1949.

Negerland (travel essays), Bonnier (Stockholm, Sweden), 1949.

Indiabrand (travel essays), Bonnier (Stockholm, Sweden), 1950.

Malinga (sketches), Bonnier (Stockholm, Sweden), 1952.

Vallmor från Taschkent; en resa i Sovjet-Unionen (travel essays), Bonnier (Stockholm, Sweden), 1952.

Spegel för dag och natt, Bonnier (Stockholm, Sweden), 1953.

Darunga eller Varginnans mjölk (essays; title means "Darunga; or, The She-Wolf's Milk") Bonnier (Stockholm, Sweden), 1954.

Liv som gräs (poems), Bonnier (Stockholm, Sweden), 1954.

Den förvandlande draken, Tiden (Stockholm, Sweden), 1955.

Vindrosor Moteld (poems; title means "Windroses Backfire"), Bonnier (Stockholm, Sweden), 1955.

Vindingevals (novel; title means "Vindinge Waltz"), Tiden (Stockholm, Sweden), 1956.

Vulkanisk Kontinent; en resa i Sydamerika (travel essays), Tiden (Stockholm, Sweden), 1957.

Ur en befolkad ensamhet (novel), Tiden (Stockholm, Sweden), 1958.

Komedi i Hägerskog (novel), Tiden (Stockholm, Sweden), 1959.

Utsikter över utländsk prosa (criticism), Bonnier (Stockholm, Sweden), 1959.

Berättelser för vilsekomna (short stories; title means "Stories for Lost Persons"), Tiden (Stockholm, Sweden), 1960.

Orians upplevelser (short stories; title means "Orian's Experiences"), Tiden (Stockholm, Sweden), 1960.

Det talande trädet (prose poems), Bonnier (Stockholm, Sweden), 1960.

Agadir (poem), Tiden (Stockholm, Sweden), 1961, translation by William Jay Smith and Leif Sjoeberg published by Ohio University Press (Athens, OH), 1979.

Ögonblick och vågor (poems), Bonnier (Stockholm, Sweden), 1962.

Drömmar i ovädrens tid (novel), Bonnier (Stockholm, Sweden), 1963.

Hägringar i handen: en resa i Israel (travel essays), Tiden (Stockholm, Sweden), 1964.

Texter i snön (poems), Bonnier (Stockholm, Sweden), 1964.

Så lever Kuba (travel essays), Tiden (Stockholm, Sweden), 1965.

Självporträtt av en drömmare med öpna ögon (autobiography; title means "Self-Portrait of a Dreamer with Open Eyes"), Bonnier (Stockholm, Sweden), 1966.

Buñuel (criticism), PAN/Norstedt (Stockholm, Sweden), 1967.

Moerkskogen (prose poems), Bonnier (Stockholm, Sweden), 1967.

Brottställen, Bonnier (Stockholm, Sweden), 1968.

Snapphanens liv och död (prose poem), Bonnier (Stockholm, Sweden), 1968.

Besvärjelser till tröst (poems), Bonnier (Stockholm, Sweden), 1969.

Utflykter med utländska författer (criticism), Aldus/Bonnier (Stockholm, Sweden), 1969.

Himlens vilja (novel), Bonnier (Stockholm, Sweden), 1970.

Långt borta, mycket nära (prose poems), Foerfattarfoerlaget (Goteborg, Sweden), 1970.

Antipoden (essays and stories), Bonnier (Stockholm, Sweden), 1971.

Tvivla, korsfarare! En sannolik beraettelse, Bonnier (Stockholm, Sweden), 1972.

Läsefrukter (criticism), Aldus/Bonnier (Stockholm, Sweden), 1973.

Lustgårdens demoni (prose poems), Bonnier (Stockholm, Sweden), 1973.

Fantasins slott och vardagens stenar (prose poems), Foerfattarfoerl, 1974.

Livet i oegat (poems), Bonnier (Stockholm, Sweden), 1974.

Livsälskare, svartmålare: en fantasi om Goya (novel), Bonnier (Stockholm, Sweden), 1974.

Världens härlighet/Elegi foer Pablo Neruda (prose poems), Bonnier (Stockholm, Sweden), 1975.

Krigarens dikt (poem), Bonnier (Stockholm, Sweden), 1976.

En gång i Nineve: berättelser i urval, Coeckelberghs (Stockholm, Sweden), 1977.

Flykten och överlevandet (prose poems), Bonnier (Stockholm, Sweden), 1977.

Fantasi med realism: om nutida utländsk skönlitteratur (criticism), LiberFörlag, 1979.

Utvandring till paradiset, Bonnier (Stockholm, Sweden), 1979.

Skrivet mot kvällen (prose poems; title means "Written toward Evening"), Bonnier (Stockholm, Sweden), 1980.

Babylon, Gudarnas Skoka (novel; title means "Baby-lon, Whore of the Gods"), Bonnier (Stockholm, Sweden), 1981.

Gustav Hedenvind-Eriksson, Norstedt (Stockholm, Sweden), 1982.

Sinnebilder (prose poems), Bonnier (Stockholm, Sweden), 1982.

The Talking Tree: Poems in Prose, translated by Diana W. Wormuth with Steven P. Sondrup, Brigham Young University Press (Provo, UT), 1982.

Gryningstrumpet och skymningsfloejt, Bonnier (Stockholm, Sweden), 1983.

Färdas i drömmen och föreställningen (prose poems), Bonnier (Stockholm, Sweden), 1984, translation by Ann B. Weissman and Annika Planck published as *Journeys in Dream and Imagination,* Four Walls Eight Windows (New York, NY), 1991.

Segling mot nya stjärnor: Artiklar om utländsk litteratur (criticism), Bonnier (Stockholm, Sweden), 1987.

Frändskaper: Essäer och urval, Arbetarkultur (Stockholm, Sweden), 1987.

De darrande löven: Nya afolyrismer, Trevi (Stockholm, Sweden), 1988.

Contributor of articles to numerous periodicals.

SIDELIGHTS: "Artur Lundkvist was one of the most prolific twentieth-century Swedish writers," Steven P. Sondrup wrote in the *Dictionary of Literary Biography.* "He wrote nearly ninety volumes of poetry, fiction, travel narratives, and essays and literally hundreds of articles and reviews for major Swedish newspapers and periodicals. As an influential member of the Swedish Academy and its Nobel Prize Committee for many years, he played an important role in bringing to the attention not only of Swedish but also international audiences some lesser-known writers of significant merit and interest. He was widely read in a variety of literary traditions but played an especially important role in introducing and championing Spanish-language authors (most notably, perhaps, Pablo Neruda) as well as an array of Anglophone writers—James Joyce, William Faulkner, Henry Miller, Patrick White, and Saul Bellow—through penetrating essays and sympathetic translations. His own literary works are extremely varied in subject, tone, style, and genre and compellingly illustrate the breadth of his literary genius. What unites the seemingly heterogeneous oeuvre, however, is that while it remains firmly anchored in the reality of daily life, Lundkvist always felt free to let his imagination soar unfettered around and above the material reality of this world. His fantasy, dreams, or imagination were never ends in themselves or fanciful games played for the sake of intellectual amusement but were grounded in the profoundly humanitarian belief that the human condition could be better. Though acutely aware of the dangers and vicissitudes facing mankind, Lundkvist maintained the hope that in the uncertainty of tomorrow something could be found that would improve the common lot."

Throughout his long and acclaimed career, Lundkvist wrote on many topics employing literary forms that often stretched the boundaries of established forms. His poetry has been particularly praised by critics. Magnus Eriksson, writing in *Scandinavian Studies,* found Lundkvist to be "one of Sweden's great modernist poets." In his book-length poem *Agadir,* Lundkvist recounted the 1960 earthquake in southern Morocco that killed forty thousand inhabitants of the city of Agadir. Lundkvist had been visiting Morocco at the time and survived the tragedy. His poem, Czeslaw Milosz maintained in *World Literature Today,* "is quite an extraordinary work. . . . *Agadir* is a descriptive poem, an attempt to be as faithful as possible to what really happened." *Skrivet mot kvallen* is a collection of prose poems and aphorisms from Lundkvist's later years. Steven P. Sondrup wrote in *World Literature Today,* "*Skrivet mot kvallen* is a product of great literary maturity and confidence, and although it would clearly be gratuitous to suggest his earlier works were only preparation for this volume, it is a work that is built on a foundation of vast experience as a writer and a human being." Lundkvist's *The Talking Tree: Poems in Prose* is a selection of eighty-two prose poems published between 1960 and 1977. James Larson in *World Literature Today* believed that "these prose poems are as characteristic of our time as the portraits, *caracteres* and maxims were of the *ancien regime.* I wish for them not a large but an appreciative audience."

In 1981, during a lecture, Lundkvist experienced a heart attack and was in a coma for sixty days. Although the prognosis was poor, Lundkvist recovered his faculties and even recalled the amazing variety of dreams he experienced while unconscious. Lundkvist recounts these hallucinatory adventures in *Färdas i drömmen och föreställningen* (translated as *Journeys in Dream and Imagination* in 1991). The critic for *Publishers Weekly* felt that in this book "Lundkvist writes movingly about fear of death, growing old and the redemptive power of art." According to Maxine Kumin, who reviewed the translation for the *New York Times Book Review,* these accounts "charm the casual reader, deeply engage the poet and captivate the harshest skeptic." "Subjects before which most poets quail, fearful of uttering banalities . . . evoke from Lundkvist an extraordinary metaphorical response," continued Kumin. "Lundkvist has made imaginative leaps that are truly breathtaking and startlingly apt. But more than anything, *Journeys in Dream and Imagination* is a tribute to human courage."

"The utopian vision at the heart of Lundkvist's oeuvre," Sondrup wrote in the *Dictionary of Literary Biography,* "is not the result of an acquired orientation or a cultivated aesthetic posture but emerges, rather, from the deep recesses of his personality. He saw his own work as the conjunction of the creative impulse and obsessive protest and his life as that of a romantic realism. The core of these descriptions consist not so much of a dualistic opposition as of two human tendencies that shape and animate each other and derive their power from their mutual illumination. Lundkvist, in this context, is neither a pessimist nor an optimist: his mature sense of concrete reality infuses his utopian desires, but his idealistic aspirations also play a role in his relationship with more mundane reality. A keen understanding of himself and his creative process warrants his description of himself as an open-eyed dreamer, as he relates in the title of his 1966 self-portrait."

BIOGRAPHICAL AND CRITICAL SOURCES:

BOOKS

Dictionary of Literary Biography, Volume 259: *Twentieth-Century Swedish Writers before World War II,* Gale (Detroit, MI), 2002.

Espmark, Kjell, *Livsdyrkaren Artur Lundkvist: Studier i hans lyrik till och med Vit man,* Bonnier (Stockholm, Sweden), 1964.

Lundkvist, Artur, *Journeys in Dream and Imagination,* translated by Ann B. Weissmann and Annika Planck, Four Walls Eight Windows (New York, NY), 1991.

Nordberg, Carl-Eric. *Det Skapande Ogat: En Fard Genom Artur Lundkvists Forfattarskap,* Bonnier (Stockholm, Sweden), 1981.

PERIODICALS

Books Abroad, Volume 50, number 2, 1976, Leif Sjöberg, "An Interview with Artur Lundkvist," pp. 329-336.

Hudson Review, summer, 1981.

New Mexico Quarterly, number 22, 1952, Richard B. Vowles, "From Pan to Panic: The Poetry of Artur Lundkvist," pp. 288-303.

New York Times, March 4, 1992.

New York Times Book Review, January 26, 1992, Maxine Kumin, "Death Is Nothing, Once It Has Arrived," p. 13.

Publishers Weekly, November 22, 1991, review of *Journeys in Dream and Imagination,* p. 44.

Scandinavian Studies, summer, 1994, Magnus Eriksson, "The Formation of an Artistic Identity: The Young Artur Lundkvist," p. 382.

Times Literary Supplement, September 25, 1992, p. 8.

World Literature Today, winter, 1977, p. 108; winter, 1978, p. 125; summer, 1980, Czeslaw Milosz, "Reflections on Artur Lundkvist's *Agadir,*" pp. 367-368; spring, 1981, Steven P. Soundrup, "Artur Lundkvist and Knowledge for Man's Sake," pp. 233-238; autumn, 1981, Steven P. Sondrup, review of *Skrivet mot kvällen,* p. 688; spring, 1983, Steven P. Sondrup, review of *Sinnebilder,* p. 306; summer, 1984, James Larson, review of *The Talking Tree: Poems in Prose,* pp. 430-431; spring 1988, p. 297; spring, 1994, W. Glyn Jones, review of *Färdas i drömmen och föreställningen,* p. 385.

OBITUARIES:

PERIODICALS

New York Times Biographical Service, December 13, 1991.*

M

MANLEY, Frank 1930-

PERSONAL: Born Francis A. Manley, November 13, 1930, in Scranton, PA; son of Aloysius F. and Kathryn (Needham) Manley; married Carolyn Holliday, March 14, 1952; children: Evelyn, Mary. *Education:* Emory University, B.A., 1952, M.A., 1953; Johns Hopkins University, Ph.D., 1959.

ADDRESSES: Agent—c/o Author Mail, 245 West 17th Street, 11th Floor, New York, NY 10011-5300.

CAREER: Yale University, New Haven, CT, started as instructor, became assistant professor, 1959-63; Emory University, Atlanta, GA, associate professor, then professor, 1964-2000, Charles Howard Candler Professor of Renaissance Literature, 1982-2000, Director of Creative Writing Program, 1990-2000; retired, 2000. *Military service:* U.S. Army, 1953-55, became specialist third class.

AWARDS, HONORS: Samuel S. Fels Foundation Fellowship, 1958-59; Guggenheim Foundation Fellowship, 1966-67, 1978-79; Translation Program Fellowship, National Endowment for the Humanities, 1981-1983; Distinguished Teaching Award, 1984; University Scholar and Teacher of the Year Award, 1989; Distinguished Alumnus Award, The Marist School, 1993; Creative Writing Fellowship in Fiction, National Endowment for the Arts, 1995-97; Devins Award for Poetry, for *Resultances;* co-winner of the Great American New Play Contest, Humana Festival, for *Two Masters.* The film version of *The Cockfighter* won first prize at the Santa Barbara Film Festival, 2003.

WRITINGS:

Resultances (poetry), University of Missouri Press (Columbia, MO), 1980.
Some Poems and Some Talk about Poetry, Floyd C. Watkins, University Press of Mississippi (Jackson, MS), 1985.
Two Masters: A Play in Two Parts, S. French (New York, NY), 1985.
Two Masters: Prior Engagements, S. Hunter (Atlanta, GA), 1987.
Within the Ribbons: Nine Stories, North Point Press (San Francisco, CA), 1989.
The Cockfighter (novel), Coffee House Press (Minneapolis, MN), 1998.
Among Prisoners (short stories), Coffee House Press (Minneapolis, MN), 2000.
The Emperors (poetry), Turtle Point Press (New York, NY), 2001.
True Hope (novel), Carroll & Graf (New York, NY), 2002.

EDITOR

John Donne, *The Anniversaries,* Johns Hopkins Press (Baltimore, MD), 1963.
(And translator, with Richard S. Sylvester), Richard Pace, *De Fructu qui ex Doctrina Percipitur,* Renaissance Society of America (New York, NY), 1966.
George Chapman, *All Fools,* University of Nebraska Press (Lincoln, NE), 1968.
(And author of notes and introduction, with Louis L. Martz) Sir Thomas More, *A Dialogue of Comfort against Tribulation,* Yale University Press (New Haven, CT), 1977.

(And translator, and author of notes and introduction), *Letter of Bugenhagen (Yale Edition of the Complete Works of St. Thomas More),* Yale University Press, (New Haven, CT), 1991.

Also author of the plays *The Evidence,* 1991, and *The Trap,* 1993.

ADAPTATIONS: The Cockfighter was adapted for stage and film.

SIDELIGHTS: "Frank Manley has emerged as one of the most promising new voices in modern Southern literature," wrote Sudip Bose of *Washington Post Book World* in 1998. Manley has won awards for his poetry and plays and has more recently earned critical attention with his fiction. In a review of his book *Among Prisoners,* a critic for *Kirkus Reviews* praised Manley as "one of the best storytellers now writing."

In his first fiction collection, *Within the Ribbons,* "Manley takes us deep into Flannery O'Connor territory," according to a reviewer for *Publishers Weekly.* The nine short stories have a religious theme and feature mainly female protagonists. "The Rain of Terror" tells of a poor couple who take in an escaped convict, hoping to profit from his stolen money, but realizing too late that this will cause disaster. "58 Babylon Dread Bean" follows a woman riding an escalator to ultimate grace. "Within the Ribbons" involves a realization in the life of a single, middle-aged woman given to her through a freak accident and a bridal bouquet. Other stories in the collection include "The Errand of Mercy," about a stroke victim who uses a Ouija board to communicate; "A Joy Forever," about two women coming to terms with their pasts; "The Concisest Tenant"; "The Baptism of Water"; "Chickamauga"; and "The Call of Nature." Beth Levine of *New York Times Book Review* noted, "Manley writes in a richly entertaining style that effectively incorporates the Southern tradition of oral storytelling." Sybil Steinberg, writing for *Publishers Weekly,* noted that what sets Manley apart from other Southern gothic-style writers "is an extraordinarily sensitive ear and a good humored, deep understanding of the people who inhabit his world."

Manley's 1998 novel, *The Cockfighter,* is the coming-of-age story of a twelve-year-old boy, named in the book only as Boy or Sonny. Jake, the boy's rough father, gives Sonny a gamecock to train for fighting, expecting Sonny to become a man through the process of learning the rituals of the sport. Sonny, however, wanting affection from his father and ashamed of his closeness with his mother, develops an unhealthy attachment to the gamecock, naming it Lion and thinking of it as a friend. When Lion is mauled by a competing gamecock, Sonny has to deal with the bird's death alone. David Murray wrote for the *New York Times* that Manley writes "with little passion but with carefully chosen detail" and went on to compare *The Cockfighter* to *God's Little Acre* by Erskine Caldwell, saying that though they are similar, *The Cockfighter* "acquires its own distinctive mythic fighter." Kay Hogan of the *Library Journal* praised the story, stating that despite the often violent content, "this is a sensitive portrayal of lost illusions and courage." Sudip Bose concluded, "There is much to admire here, especially in Manley's graceful prose . . . he captures perfectly the cadenced voices of these simple country people without ever patronizing them or rendering them as caricatures." *The Cockfighter* "could easily have fallen prey to the maudlin and familiar," wrote a critic from *Kirkus Reviews,* "but it rises soaringly above both, thanks to its author's wonderful timing, eye, ear—and heart."

Among Prisoners is a collection of eight short stories dealing with characters who are prisoners—either because they are literally prisoners or because they are trapped in their life situations and unable to escape. The narrator of "Thank God Almighty" is a convict who watches as the county commissioner continually breaks laws himself. In "Badass," a wife uncovers her prison-guard husband's four-decade-old lie about the murder of a black prisoner. The story "The Indian Way" revolves around a white man whose marriage to an older Native-American woman has broken. "The Housekeeper" and "What" both feature widows struggling with their isolation; in "The Evidence," truth becomes a type of prison when a man announces that he's been abducted by Bigfoot; and "Mr. Butterfuly" tells of a former soldier who is unsatisfied by his mail-order brides, of which he has had several. Only Uncle Bud, in a story titled after him, seems to find an escape from his prison. A reviewer in *Publisher's Weekly* commented about the book's many narrative voices: "Several [stories] feature lively, complex narrators who confess uneasy truths of their lives in monologue form." A critic for *Kirkus Reviews* called *Among Prisoners* a "fine second collection of eight emotionally charged stories."

True Hope, Manley's 2002 novel, "is a worthy successor to his first novel," proclaimed a writer for the *Economist.* A critic for *Kirkus Reviews* considered it "another poignant, psychologically probing tale from one of the brightest new lights of southern fiction." In the novel, Al Cantrell has just finished his jail sentence. His wife had died years before, and it was due to his grieving for her death that he set out on a downward spiral of alcohol and crime. Now a free man, though still struggling with his past, Cantrell moves in with his father-in-law, Tom. Tom gets Al a job working for a corrupt politician, but in the process of doing his dirty work for him, Tom ends up dying in an accident. Al, having started a relationship with Laurie, goes off with her to disastrous effect. A reviewer in *Publisher's Weekly* praised Al's narrative voice and concluded, "The gifted Manley . . . exhibits his formidable ability to evoke the lives of the down-and-out in the Deep South." Lawrence Rungren of *Library Journal* called it "a tough and tender tale," and a critic for *Kirkus Reviews* wrote that the themes of hope and resilience portrayed in Al's character "give a heat that fires all the characters, no matter how self-interested, with a common humanity and a flash of noble purpose." *True Hope,* according to Daniel Woodrell of *Washington Post Book World,* "is a humble novel, plain-spoken, quietly masterful in its rhythms and insights, sneaky humor and grace."

Along with his works of fiction, Manley is also the author and editor of several scholarly texts. His scholarship on Renaissance literature and his translation of the works of Thomas More have influenced his poetry.

BIOGRAPHICAL AND CRITICAL SOURCES:

PERIODICALS

Booklist, March 15, 1998, Joe Collins, review of *The Cockfighter,* p. 1202.

Christian Century, December 4, 2002, review of *The Emperors,* p. 31.

Economist (U.S.), June 8, 2002, "True Grit; New Fiction."

Kirkus Reviews, January 15, 1998, review of *The Cockfighter,* p. 73; December 15, 1999, review of *Among Prisoners,* p. 1906; April 1, 2002, review of *True Hope,* p. 445.

Library Journal, April 1, 1998, Kay Hogan, review of *The Cockfighter,* p. 124; January 2000, Joshua Cohen, review of *Among Prisoners,* p. 165; May 15, 2002, Lawrence Rungren, review of *True Hope.*

New York Times Book Review, August 20, 1989, Beth Levine, review of *Within the Ribbons,* p. 20; May 10, 1998, David Murray, review of *The Cockfighter,* p. 21.

Publishers Weekly, May 12, 1989, Sybil Steinberg, review of *Within the Ribbons,* p. 280; January 26, 1998, review of *The Cockfighter,* p. 70; December 6, 1999, review of *Among Prisoners,* p. 52; March 11, 2002, review of *True Hope,* p. 49.

Washington Post, July 26, 1989, Jonathan Yardley, review of *Within the Ribbons,* p. c2.

Washington Post Book World, May 10, 1998, Sudip Bose, review of *The Cockfighter,* p. 9; July 28, 2002, Daniel Woodrell, review of *True Hope,* p. T7.

ONLINE

Denver Post, http://denverpost.com/ (March 5, 2000), Jean Charbonneau, review of *Among Prisoners.*

*   *   *

MASON, Bobbie Ann 1940-

PERSONAL: Born May 1, 1940, in Mayfield, KY; daughter of Wilburn A. (a dairy farmer) and Christianna (Lee) Mason; married Roger B. Rawlings (a magazine editor and writer), April 12, 1969. *Education:* University of Kentucky, B.A., 1962; State University of New York at Binghamton, M.A., 1966; University of Connecticut, Ph.D., 1972.

ADDRESSES: Home—Lawrenceburg, KY. *Office*—University of Kentucky, Department of English, 1255 Patterson Office Tower 0027, Lexington, KY 40506. *Agent*—Amanda Urban, International Creative Management, 40 West 57th St., New York, NY 10019. *E-mail*—bamaso2@uky.edu.

CAREER: Writer. Mansfield State College, Mansfield, PA, assistant professor of English, 1972-79; University of Kentucky, Lexington, visiting writer-in-residence. *Mayfield Messenger,* Mayfield, KY, writer, 1960; Ideal Publishing Co., New York, NY, writer for magazines, including *Movie Stars, Movie Life,* and *T.V. Star Parade,* 1962-63.

Bobbie Ann Mason

AWARDS, HONORS: National Book Critics Circle Award nomination, American Book Award nomination, PEN-Faulkner Award for fiction nomination and Ernest Hemingway Foundation Award, all 1983, all for *Shiloh and Other Stories;* National Endowment for the Arts fellowship, 1983; Pennsylvania Arts Council grant, 1983; Guggenheim fellowship, 1984; American Academy and Institute of Arts and Letters Award, 1984; National Book Critics Circle Award nomination and Southern Book Award, both 1994, both for *Feather Crowns;* Pulitzer Prize for biography or autobiography nomination, 2000, for *Clear Springs: A Memoir;* Southern Book Award for fiction, Southern Book Critics Circle, both 2002, both for *Zigzagging down a Wild Trail.*

WRITINGS:

Nabokov's Garden: A Guide to "Ada," Ardis (Ann Arbor, MI), 1974.
The Girl Sleuth: A Feminist Guide to the Bobbsey Twins, Nancy Drew, and Their Sisters, Feminist Press (Old Westbury, NY), 1975.

Shiloh and Other Stories, Harper (New York, NY), 1982.
In Country (novel), Harper (New York, NY), 1985.
Spence + Lila (novel), Harper (New York, NY), 1988.
Love Life: Stories, Harper (New York, NY), 1989.
Feather Crowns (novel), Harper (New York, NY), 1993.
Midnight Magic: Selected Stories of Bobbie Ann Mason, Ecco Press (Hopewell, NJ), 1998.
Clear Springs: A Memoir, Random House (New York, NY), 1999.
Zigzagging down a Wild Trail (short stories), Random House (New York, NY), 2001.
Elvis Presley (nonfiction), Penguin, (New York, NY), 2003.

Contributor of short stories to anthologies, including *Best American Short Stories,* 1981 and 1983, *The Pushcart Prize,* 1983 and 1996, and *The O. Henry Awards,* 1986 and 1988. Contributor to numerous magazines, including *New Yorker, Atlantic,* and *Mother Jones;* frequent contributor to "The Talk of the Town" column, *New Yorker.*

ADAPTATIONS: In Country was filmed by Warner Brothers and directed by Norman Jewison in 1989.

SIDELIGHTS: The people and terrain of rural western Kentucky figure prominently in the fiction of Bobbie Ann Mason, a highly regarded novelist and short story writer. Herself a native Kentuckian, Mason has chronicled the changes wrought in her region by the introduction of such phenomena as television, shopping malls, popular music, and fast-food restaurants. Her characters often stand perplexed at the junction between traditionalism and modernity, between permanence and transience, between their own deep-seated need for individual expression and their obligations to family and home. As Meredith Sue Willis noted in the *Washington Post Book World,* Mason "has a reputation as a regional writer, but what she is really writing about is the numerous Americans whose dreams and goals have been uplifted and distorted by popular culture." According to David Quammen in the *New York Times Book Review,* "Loss and deprivation, the disappointment of pathetically modest hopes, are the themes Bobbie Ann Mason works and reworks. She portrays the disquieted lives of men and women not blessed with much money or education or luck, but cursed with enough sensitivity and imagination to suffer regrets." Mason has also written the autobiographical *Clear Springs: A Memoir,* which was a finalist for the Pulitzer Prize, and a short biography, *Elvis Presley.*

Mason's first volume of fiction, *Shiloh and Other Stories,* established her reputation as a rising voice in southern literature. Novelist Anne Tyler, for one, hailed her in the *New Republic* as "a full-fledged master of the short story." Most of the sixteen works in *Shiloh* originally appeared in the *New Yorker, Atlantic,* or other national magazines, a fact surprising to several critics who, like Anatole Broyard in the *New York Times Book Review,* labeled Mason's work "a regional literature that describes people and places almost unimaginably different from ourselves and the big cities in which we live." Explained Quammen: "Miss Mason writes almost exclusively about working-class and farm people coping with their muted frustrations in western Kentucky (south of Paducah, not far from Kentucky Lake, if that helps you), and the gap to be bridged empathically between her readership and her characters [is] therefore formidable. But formidable also is Miss Mason's talent, and her craftsmanship."

In an interview published in *Contemporary Literature,* Mason commented upon the fact that she seems to be read by an audience quite different from one in which her characters might find themselves. "I don't think I write fiction that's for a select group," she said. "I'm not sure a lot of people [in rural Kentucky] read my work. . . . I think a lot of people wouldn't *want* to read my work because they might find it too close to their lives. They're not interested in reading something that familiar; it would make them uncomfortable."

Most critics have attributed Mason's success to her vivid evocation of a region's physical and social geography. "As often as not," Gene Lyons reported in *Newsweek,* the author describes "a matter of town— paved roads, indoor plumbing, and above all, TV— having come to the boondocks with the force of an unannounced social revolution." In a similar vein, Emma Cobb commented in *Contemporary Southern Writers* that "along with giving voice to characters in language that reflects their backgrounds, Mason's work is important as a chronicle of the changing physical landscape of the contemporary South. Brand names and popular culture references infiltrate her characters' vocabularies as strip-malling, chain-store spreading, and convenience-promising change sweeps into previously isolated regions. Characters try to make their

way amid the changes . . . often unsure of how to proceed and struggling to articulate their feelings." While the language of Mason's characters reflects their rural background, her people do not fit the Hollywood stereotype of backwoods "hillbillies" content to let the rest of the world pass by. Tyler noted that they have "an earnest faith in progress; they are as quick to absorb new brand names as foreigners trying to learn the language of a strange country they've found themselves in." "It is especially poignant," she added, "that the characters are trying to deal with changes most of us already take for granted." Mason's Kentucky is a world in transition, with the old South fast becoming the new.

Mason often explores intensely personal events that lead to the acceptance of something new or the rejection—or loss—of something old. These adjustments in the characters' lives reflect a general uneasiness that pervades the cultural landscape; the forces of change and alienation are no less frightening because they are universal or unavoidable. The characters in Mason's fiction are caught between isolation and transience, and this struggle is reflected in their relationships, which are often emotionally and intellectually distant.

As a result, wrote *Time* critic R. Z. Sheppard, "Mason has an unwavering bead on the relationship between instincts and individual longings. Her women have ambitions but never get too far from the nest; her men have domestic moments but spend a lot of time on wheels." Mason's characters "exist in a psychological rather than a physical environment," Broyard similarly contended, "one that has been gutted—like an abandoned building—by the movement of American life. They fall between categories, occupy a place between nostalgia and apprehension. They live, without history or politics, a life more like a linoleum than a tapestry."

Other critics, while noting Mason's ability to evoke psychological states, have emphasized her skill at depicting the material details of her "linoleum" world. Tyler pointed out that readers know precisely what dishes constitute the characters' meals, what clothes hang in their closets, and what craft projects fill their spare time. Mason intones the brand names that are infiltrating her characters' vocabularies, and the exact titles of soap operas and popular songs provide an aural backdrop for the fiction's emotional dramas. Her characters' voices, according to Tyler, "ring through our living rooms." *Dictionary of Literary Biography* contributor John D. Kalb noted that "Mason is among the first to use seriously the so-called low art of popular culture as an important underpinning to her literature and the lives of her characters. While she portrays the encroaching impact of urban America on her rural occupants . . . she usually does so not as a criticism but as a means of providing an accurate and realistic depiction of the people within their changing environments. Her inclusion of these popular elements enhances the sense of meeting real people engaged in their everyday lives."

In her first novel, *In Country,* "Mason returns to this same geographical and spiritual milieu" as her short fiction, noted *New York Times* critic Michiko Kakutani, "and she returns, too, to her earlier themes: the dislocations wrought on ordinary, blue-collar lives by recent history—in this case, recent history in the form of the Vietnam War." Seventeen-year-old Samantha Hughes doesn't remember the war, but it has profoundly affected her life: her father died in Vietnam and her uncle Emmett, with whom she lives, still bears the emotional and physical scars of his service. In the summer after her high school graduation, Sam struggles to understand the war and learn about her father. "Ten years after the end of the Vietnam War," summarized Richard Eder in the *Los Angeles Times Book Review,* "in the most prosaic and magical way possible, she stubbornly undertakes the exorcism of a ghost that almost everything in our everyday life manages to bury." In the novel Mason demonstrates the same concern for particulars that distinguishes her short fiction, as *Christian Science Monitor* contributor Marilyn Gardner observed: "She displays an ear perfectly tuned to dialogue, an eye that catches every telling detail and quirky mannerism. Tiny, seemingly insignificant observations and revelations accumulate almost unnoticed until something trips them, turning them into literary grenades explosive with meaning."

Detroit Free Press writer Suzanne Yeager similarly believed that the author's details contribute to the authenticity of the novel. "Mason's narrative is so extraordinarily rich with the sounds, smells and colors of daily life in the '80s that Sam and her family and friends take on an almost eerie reality." As a result, the critic added, *In Country* "becomes less a novel and more a diary of the unspoken observations of ordinary America." Jonathan Yardley, however, faulted the novel for the "dreary familiarity" of its Vietnam themes. Writing in the *Washington Post Book World,*

he asserted that Mason "has failed to transform these essentially political questions into the stuff of fiction; none of her characters come to life, the novel's structure is awkward and its narrative herky-jerky, her prose wavers uncertainly between adult and teenaged voices." But other critics found Mason's work successful; *Chicago Tribune Book World* contributor Bruce Allen, for instance, said that the novel's "real triumph . . . is Mason's deep and honest portrayal of her two protagonists," especially Sam. "More than any other character in our recent fiction," the critic continued, Sam "is a real person who grows more and more real the better we come to know her—and the novel that affords us the opportunity to is, clearly, the year's most gratifying reading experience." "[Mason's] first novel, although it lacks the page-by-page abundance of her best stories," concluded Joel Conarroe in the *New York Times Book Review,* "is an exceptional achievement, at once humane, comic and moving."

Mason told *CA* that she had been most rewarded by the reaction real Vietnam veterans had to *In Country.* "It's been personally very gratifying to hear from them, to know that they took the trouble to write to me and tell me that the book meant something to them," she said. "Most of the Vietnam vets who wrote me didn't write at length; they just seemed to say thank you. It was very moving to hear from those people."

In *Spence + Lila,* Mason's second novel, Spence and Lila are a Kentucky farm couple who have been married for over forty years. Lila's upcoming surgery is forcing them to face the prospect of being separated for the first time since World War II. Also, as in her other work, Mason looks at the changes in the larger environment as well as those in her characters' lives—as Kalb put it, "the changes of attitudes and values in the modern world that has intruded in [an] isolated haven." "The chapters alternate between Spence's and Lila's point of view, and such resonances [in their thoughts] range freely through the past and present," described *Los Angeles Times Book Review* contributor Nancy Mairs. Despite the potential for sentimentality in the story, Mason "manages to avoid the gooey and patronizing muck that is usually described as heartwarming," remarked a *Time* reviewer. "Her account is funny and deft, with plenty of gristle." Likewise, in Kalb's opinion, "*Spence + Lila* is a novel about real love—not saccharine-sweet sentimentality, but the well-aged version of love between two people who have shared a long, sometimes difficult and trying, life together."

Newsweek writer Peter S. Prescott, however, found *Spence + Lila* a "gently tedious" book saved only by Mason's skillful writing. But Kakutani, although acknowledging that the book "suffers from a melodramatic predictability absent from Ms. Mason's earlier works," thought that the author treated her subject "without ever becoming sentimental or cliched." The critic went on to praise Mason's "lean stripped-down language" and "nearly pitch-perfect ear for the way her characters speak," and added, "Mainly, however, it's her sure-handed ability to evoke Spence and Lila's life together that lends their story such poignance and authenticity." *New York Times Book Review* contributor Frank Conroy likewise commended Mason's dialogue, but admitted that "one wishes she had risked a bit more in this book, taking us under the surface of things instead of lingering there so lovingly and relentlessly." "Awkward silence in the face of ideas and feelings is a common frailty," elaborated Mairs, "but it represents a limitation in *Spence + Lila,* constraining Mason to rush her story and keep to its surface. . . . If I perceive any defect in *Spence + Lila,*" the critic continued, "it's that this is a short novel which could well have been long." "As soon as [Mason's] characters open their mouths, they come to life and move to center stage," McCorkle similarly concluded. "If there is a weakness it would be the reader's desire to prolong their talk and actions before moving to an ending that is both touching and satisfying."

Despite the author's success with *In Country* and *Spence + Lila,* "Mason's strongest form may be neither the novel nor the story, but the story *collection,*" Lorrie Moore maintained in her *New York Times Book Review* assessment of *Love Life: Stories.* "It is there, picking up her pen every twenty pages to start anew, gathering layers through echo and overlap, that Ms. Mason depicts most richly a community of contemporary lives." While Kakutani remarked that "few of Ms. Mason's characters ever resolve their dilemmas—or if they do, their decisions take place . . . beyond the knowledge of the reader," she asserted that the stories "are not simply minimalist 'slice-of-life' exercises, but finely crafted tales that manage to invest inarticulate, small-town lives with dignity and intimations of meaning." Mason's "stories work like parables, small in scale and very wise, tales wistfully told by a masterful stylist whose voice rises purely from the heart of the country," stated Judith Freeman in the *Los Angeles Times Book Review.*

Reference Guide to Short Fiction contributor Laurie Clancy opined that this collection and *Shiloh* have shown Mason to be "a regional writer par excellence"; however, she cautioned, "the best of Mason's work has a gritty authenticity and dry humor, but at times the monotony and limitations of the figures she writes about seep into the prose as well." Mason, she observed, offers "little or no analysis of the characters' inner consciousness," and *New York Times Book Review* critic Michael Gorra remarked on this as well, in his review of *Midnight Magic: Selected Stories of Bobbie Ann Mason,* which republished several stories from *Shiloh* and *Love Life.* This collection, he contended, "demonstrates . . . Mason's narrow range—narrow in terms of the characters and situations on which she draws; narrow too in her reliance on a tight and impersonal third-person voice. . . . I admire Bobbie Ann Mason's craft, her precise eye, the vivid dialogue that stops just short of turning down the road toward local color. But after reading so much of her uninflected prose, I can't help longing for something a bit more full throated."

Mason's third novel marked a departure from her tendency to set her fiction in present times. *Feather Crowns* is set in turn-of-the-century Kentucky and tells the story of a farm wife named Christianna Wheeler who gives birth to quintuplets. Overnight the modest Wheeler tobacco farm becomes a mecca for the curious of every stripe as people flock to see—and hold—the tiny babies. As events unfold, Christie and her husband find themselves drawn away from home as a literal carnival sideshow attraction. The book is a meditation upon fame, self-determination, and the conflict between superstition and science. *New York Times Book Review* correspondent Jill McCorkle noted that in *Feather Crowns,* "Mason's attention to the microscopic detail of everyday life is, as always, riveting. . . . Along with the authentically colorful, often humorous dialogue, there are wonderful descriptions of churning and nursing and chopping dark-fire tobacco. And always there are subtle reminders of life's fragility, our uncertainty about what lies ahead." McCorkle concluded: "Thematically, *Feather Crowns* is a rich extension of Ms. Mason's other works. . . . The life of Christianna Wheeler and her babies is memorable and complete."

Mason told the *San Francisco Review of Books* that, far from being a diversion for her, *Feather Crowns* represented a new way of looking at her Kentucky culture, filtered through her grandmother's generation. "Right now it's hard to know what's going on in

America and where we're all going," she said. "It's gotten so complex, with so many people and our constant awareness of everybody globally, that it's bewildering. I think there must always be stages in history when we feel this way, but in order to get our bearings today we have to go back and get a clearer sense of where we came from and what formed us. To remember what is important. I think basically that is Christie's quest in the book. . . . It's about being faced with a bewildering set of circumstances. She tries to make sense of all of it and tries to rise above it and be herself, a survivor. I think that's also the challenge for us in this part of the twentieth century."

Women's Review of Books critic Michele Clark declared that in *Feather Crowns* Mason successfully depicts a moment of epiphany for its central character. "Christie Wheeler becomes empowered through her capacity to ask questions and her ability to experience each moment of daily life to its fullest," the critic stated. "And this long, satisfying novel offers readers who are willing to slow down the same chance to see ordinary life anew." In the *Los Angeles Times Book Review,* Lisa Alther called *Feather Crowns* "a brilliantly sustained and grimly humorous parable about fame in 20th-century America," adding: "Mason's stunning morality tale about the process by which . . . degradation can overtake innocent people who simply need cash or long for some excitement is extremely illuminating—and especially for anyone alive today who has ever pondered the ravages of our modern publicity juggernaut."

Having used her rural Kentucky background in fiction, Mason explored it autobiographically in *Clear Springs: A Memoir.* "She uses this memoir of growing up in the 1950s to provide a tantalizing glimpse into the origins of her fiction," noted Josephine Humphreys in the *New York Times Book Review.* "And in the process of taking a close look at her own beginnings, Mason gets to the heart of a whole generation—those of us born, roughly speaking, between Pearl Harbor and television. Behind us lay an old way, unchanged (we thought) for centuries; springing up before us was a world no one had predicted or imagined." Mason makes clear that the changes in her world—something she has explored so extensively in her fiction—are neither totally positive nor completely negative, as the old days were not idyllic. She observes that on their farm, her family had "independence, stability, authenticity . . . along with mind-numbing, backbreaking labor and crippling so-

cial isolation." Commented Humphreys: "Because Bobbie Ann Mason's language is spare and her eye unsparing, she's able to handle matters that ordinarily invite sentimentality or romanticism. She can write the hard truth about home, love, loss and the terrifying passage of time." Still, remarked a *Publishers Weekly* reviewer, Mason makes the book "a loving embrace" of her roots and "a richly textured portrait of a rapidly disappearing way of life."

Mason once told Mervyn Rothstein in the *New York Times:* "I basically consider myself an exile. . . . And I have been one for years. And that's what gives me the distance to look back to where I'm from and to be able to write about it with some kind of perceptiveness. . . . It seems to me that an exile has a rather peculiar sensibility—you're straddling a fence and you don't know which side you belong on." But Mason would later return to Kentucky, to live near Lexington. She has also returned to the University of Kentucky, where she was once a student, to become a writer-in-residence. When Mason published her next collection of short stories, *Zigzagging down a Wild Trail,* it also evidenced a change, with several of the eleven stories taking place outside of small-town Kentucky.

The collection earned commendations from reviewers for providing the sharp observations and precise detail that Mason is best known for. In the *Atlantic Monthly,* Bill Broun noted that "Mason almost zigzags out of her depth" in the few stories that strayed into unfamiliar thematic or geographic territory. Writing for *Library Journal,* Ann H. Fisher said the collection "reflects the sadder, wiser perspective of midlife" and concluded, "Only the kindest complaint applies: the stories end too soon." In a review for the *New York Times Book Review,* Walter Kirn was convinced that Mason had rescued the minimalist short story form from oblivion. Kirn felt that Mason's new stories responded to old criticisms that her work was marred by "detachment and simplemindedness." He explained, "Mason's people may still watch too much TV, drink to much beer and love too indiscriminately, but their limitations pain them. . . . they feel the pressures of the wider world and sense both its opportunities and perils."

As part of a series published by Penguin, Mason was asked to write a brief biography about the legendary singer Elvis Presley. In *Elvis Presley* Mason shows a special understanding of her subject, having grown up in roughly the same time and place as the singer, and having listened to him throughout his entire career. The biography includes familiar stories as well as the author's observations on topics including southern foods, the hiring of Colonel Tom Parker as Presley's manager because of his familiar horse-trading style, and the singer's struggle to be both a poor boy from Tupelo, Mississippi, and "the King" of rock and roll.

The biography was described by some reviewers as a good introduction for readers who were unfamiliar with the vast body of writings on the subject. Others judged that such a short biography failed to add to their understanding of Presley. In the *New York Times Book Review,* Eric P. Nash said the book was filled with "twice-told tales" and that it "does not account for the meaning of [Presley's] music or why a quarter-century after his death he remains a larger-than-life figure." Often, however, reviewers welcomed Mason's insight on Elvis Presley. Ellen Emry Heltzel wrote in the *Atlanta Journal-Constitution* that Mason had done "a superb job of honing pertinent facts into a plausible, well-told story." The idea that Presley had been "raised high in Highbrowland" interested *Los Angeles Times* writer Elaine Dundy, who reflected that Mason "knows firsthand how it felt to be a fan in hot-blooded youth; how it feels to be a fan for more than four decades."

BIOGRAPHICAL AND CRITICAL SOURCES:

BOOKS

Authors and Artists for Young Adults, Volume 5, Gale (Detroit, MI), 1989.
Contemporary Literary Criticism, Gale (Detroit, MI), Volume 28, 1984, Volume 43, 1987, Volume 82, 1994.
Contemporary Southern Writers, St. James Press (Detroit, MI), 1999.
Dictionary of Literary Biography, Volume 173: *American Novelists since World War II, Fifth Series,* Gale (Detroit, MI), 1996.
Dictionary of Literary Biography Yearbook: 1987, Gale (Detroit, MI), 1988.
Prenshaw, Peggy Whitman, editor, *Women Writers of the South,* University Press of Mississippi (Jackson, MS), 1984.
Reference Guide to Short Fiction, 2nd edition, St. James Press (Detroit, MI), 1999.

Short Story Criticism, Volume 4, Gale (Detroit, MI), 1990.
Wilhelm, Albert, *Bobbie Ann Mason: A Study of the Short Fiction,* Twayne, 1998.

PERIODICALS

Atlanta Journal-Constitution, January 24, 2003, Ellen Emry Heltzel, review of *Elvis Presley,* p. E1.
Atlantic Monthly, October, 2001, Bill Broun, review of *Zigzagging down A Wild Trail,* p. 130.
Chicago Tribune Book World, September 1, 1985, Bruce Allen, review of *In Country.*
Christian Science Monitor, September 6, 1985, Marilyn Gardner, review of *In Country.*
Contemporary Literature, winter, 1991, Bonnie Lyons, interview with Bobbie Ann Mason, pp. 449-470.
Detroit Free Press, October 13, 1985, Suzanne Yeager, review of *In Country.*
Library Journal June 1, 2001, Ann H. Fisher, review of *Zigzagging down a Wild Trail,* p. 220.
Los Angeles Times Book Review, September 22, 1985, Richard Eder, review of *In Country,* p. 3; June 19, 1988, Nancy Mairs, "A Well-Seasoned Love," p. 6; March 19, 1989, Judith Freeman, "Country Parables," p. 1; October 24, 1993, Lisa Alther, "Fame and Misfortune," pp. 2, 8; January 26, 2003, Elaine Dundy, "The Rich but Unhappy Life of a King," p. R8.
Nation, January 18, 1986, Mona Molarsky, review of *In Country,* p. 242.
New Republic, November 1, 1982, Anne Tyler, "Kentucky Cameos," p. 36.
Newsweek, November 15, 1982, Gene Lyons, review of *Shiloh and Other Stories,* p. 107; August 1, 1988, Peter S. Prescott, "Bored and Bred in Kentucky," p. 53.
New York Review of Books, November 7, 1985, Diane Johnson, review of *In Country,* p. 15.
New York Times, September 4, 1985, Michiko Kakutani, review of *In Country,* p. 23; May 15, 1988, Mervyn Rothstein, "Homegrown Fiction," p. 50; June 11, 1988, Michiko Kakutani, "Struggle and Hope in the New South," p. 13; March 3, 1989, Michiko Kakutani, review of *Love Life,* p. B4.
New York Times Book Review, November 21, 1982, David Quammen, review of *Shiloh and Other Stories,* p. 7; December 19, 1982, Anatole Broyard, "Country Fiction," p. 31; September 15, 1985, Joel Conarroe, review of *In Country,* p. 7; June 26, 1988, Frank Conroy, review of *Spence + Lila,* p. 7; March 12, 1989, Lorrie Moore, "What L'il

Abner Said," p. 7; September 26, 1993, Jill Mc-Corkle, "Her Sensational Babies," p. 7; August 9, 1998, Michael Gorra, "The New New South," p. 7; May 30, 1999, Josephine Humphreys, "Her Old Kentucky Home," p. 5; August 19, 2001, Walter Kirn, review of *Zigzagging down a Wild Trail,* p. 9; March 2, 2003, Eric P. Nash, review of *Elvis Presley,* p. 24.

Publishers Weekly, August 30, 1985, Wendy Smith, interview with Bobbie Ann Mason, p. 424; March 15, 1999, review of *Clear Springs,* p. 34; June 25, 2001, review of *Zigzagging down a Wild Trail,* p. 43.

San Francisco Review of Books, February-March, 1994, pp. 12-13.

Time, January 3, 1983, R. Z. Sheppard, review of *Shiloh and Other Stories,* p. 88; September 16, 1985, Paul Gray, review of *In Country,* p. 81; July 4, 1988, review of *Spence + Lila,* p. 71.

Tribune Books (Chicago), June 26, 1988, Michael Dorris, "Bonds of Love: Bobbie Ann Mason's Chronicle of Family Crisis Adds Up to an Affirmation of Life," p. 6; February 19, 1989, Jack Fuller, "Bobbie Ann Mason Sees Reality on Sale at Kmart," p. 1.

Washington Post Book World, September 8, 1985, Jonathan Yardley, review of *In Country*; March 26, 1989, Meredith Sue Willis, "Stories with a Sense of Place," p. 11.

Women's Review of Books, March, 1994, Michele Clark, review of *Feather Crowns,* p. 19.*

*   *   *

MASS, William
See GIBSON, William

*   *   *

MAYRÖCKER, Friedericke 1924-

PERSONAL: Surname listed in some sources as Mayroecker; born December 20, 1924, in Vienna, Austria. *Education:* Attended business school.

ADDRESSES: *Home*—Vienna, Austria. *Agent*—c/o Author Mail, Suhrkamp Verlag, Lindenstrasse 29-35, 60325 Frankfurt am Main, Germany.

CAREER: Poetry, playwright, novelist, and children's book author. Taught English in public schools in Vienna, 1946-97; freelance writer, 1969—.

MEMBER: Grazer Autorenversammlung, German Academy of Arts, Academy of Language and Literature.

AWARDS, HONORS: Theodor Körner Stiflungsvonds Förderungspreis, 1963; Ludwig von Ficker Gedächtnispreis, 1964; Hörspielpreis de Bundes der Kriegsblinden Deustschlands (with Ernst Jandle), 1968; Würdigungspreis des Bundesministeriums, 1973; Austrian State prize, 1976, 1987; Georg Trakl prize, 1977; Anton Wilgans prize, 1981; Greater Austrian State prize, 1982; Roswitha von Gandersheim prize, 1982; *Südwestfunk* prize, 1985; Hans Erich Nossack prize, 1989; Forum Stadtpark des Landes Steiermark manuscript prize, 1993; Friedrich Höderlinpreis, 1993; Bayerischen Akademie der Künste prize, 1996; Else Lasker-Schüer prize, 1996; Meersburger Drostepreis, 1997; George Buechner award, 2001.

WRITINGS:

Larifari: ein konfuses Buch, Bergland (Vienna, Austria), 1956.

Metaphorisch, Walther (Stuttgart, Germany), 1964.

Texte, Allerheiligenpresse (Innsbruck, Austria), 1966.

Tod durch Musen: Poetische Texte (title means "Death by the Muses"), Rowohlt (Reinbek, Germany), 1966.

Sägespäne für mein Herzbluten: 39 Gedichte, Rainer (Berlin, Germany), 1967, revised as *Sägespäne für mein Herzbluten und andere Gedichte,* 1973.

Minimonsters Traumlexikon: Texte in Prosa, Rowohlt (Reinbek, Germany), 1968.

Fantom Fan, Rowohlt (Reinbek, Germany), 1971.

(With Ernst Jandle) *Fünf Mann Menschen* (radio play; title means "Five Man Men"), Luchterhand (Darmstadt, Germany), 1971.

Sinclair Sofokles, der Baby-Saurier, Jugend und Volk (Vienna, Austria), 1971, translation by Renate Moore and Linda Hayward published as *Sinclair Sophocles, the Baby Dinosaur,* Random House (New York, NY), 1974.

Arie auf tönernen Füszen: Metaphysisches Theater (title means "Aria on Feet of Clay"), Luchterhand (Darmstadt, Germany), 1972.

Blaue Erleuchtungen: Erste Gedichte, Eremiten-Presse (Düsseldorf, Germany), 1973, reprinted, 1995, translation by Lesley Lendrum published as *In the Blue Mountain Evening,* illustrated by Heather Deenman, Morning Star (Edinburgh, Scotland), 1996.

Je ein umwölkter Gipfel: Erzählung, Luchterhand (Darmstadt, Germany), 1973, translation by Rosmarie Waldrop and Harriette Watts published as *With Each Clouded Peak,* Sun and Moon Press (Los Angeles, CA), 1998.

In langsamen Blitzen, Literarisches Colloquium (Berlin, Germany), 1974.

Augen wie Schaljapin bevor er starb, Vorarlberger Verlagsanstalt (Dornbirn, Austria), 1974.

Meine Träme, ein Flügelkleid, Fremiten-Presse (Düsseldorf, Germany), 1974.

Schriftungen oder Gerüchte aus dem Jenseits, Pfaffenweiler Presse (Pfaffenweiler, Germany), 1975.

(Author of text) *Graphik: Monographie mit einem Werkverzeichnis der Druckgraphik,* edited by Otto Breicha, Jugend und Volk (Vienna, Austria), 1975.

Das Licht in der Landschaft (title means "The Light in the Landscape"), Suhrkamp (Frankfurt am Main, Germany), 1975, reprinted, 1994.

(With Ernst Jandle) *Drei Hörspiele,* Sessler (Vienna, Austria), 1975.

Fast ein Frühling des Markus M., Suhrkamp (Frankfurt am Main, Germany), 1976.

Rot ist unten, Jugend und Volk (Vienna, Austria), 1977.

Heisze Hunde, Pfaffenweiler Presse (Pfaffenweiler, Germany), 1977.

Heiligenanstalt (title means "Saint's Asylum"), Suhrkamp (Frankfurt am Main, Germany), 1978, translated by Rosmarie Waldrop, Morning Star (Edinburgh, Scotland), 1992.

Lütt'koch, Herbstpresse (Vienna, Austria), 1978.

Schwarmgesang: Szenen für die poetische Bühne (radio plays; title means "Swarm Song"), Rainer (Berlin, Germany), 1978.

Tochter der Bahn, published with *Der Ureinwohner,* by Klaus Rinke, Premiten-Presse (Düsseldorf, Germany), 1979.

Ausgewählte Gedichte 1944-1978, Suhrkamp (Frankfurt am Main, Germany), 1979.

Friederike Mayröcker: ein Lesebuch, edited by Gisela Lindemann, Suhrkamp (Frankfurt am Main, Germany), 1979.

Pick mich auf mein Flügel (audiobook), Ohrbuck (Vienna, Germany), 1980.

(With Angelika Kaufmann) *Pegas, das Pferd,* Neugebauer (Salzburg, Austria), 1980, translation published as *Pegas, the Horse,* Neugebauer (London, England), 1982.

Die Abschiede (title means "The Farewells"), Suhrkamp (Frankfurt am Main, Germany), 1980.

Schwarze Romanzen: Ein Gedichtzyklus, Pfaffenweiler Presse (Pfaffenweiler, Germany), 1981.

(With Johann Kräftner) *Treppen,* Niederösterreichisches Pressehaus, 1981.

Bocca della Verita (radio play), Grasl (Baden, Germany), 1981.

Ich, der Rabe und der Mond: Ein Kinderbuch zum Lesen und Weiterzeichnen, Droschl (Graz, Austria), 1982.

Gute Nacht, guten Morgen: Gedichte 1978-1981, Suhrkamp (Frankfurt am Main, Germany), 1982.

Magische Blätter (also see below), Suhrkamp (Frankfurt am Main, Germany), 1983.

Im Nervensaal, Himmel am zwölften Mai, Herbstpresse (Vienna, Austria), 1983.

Das Anheben der Arme bei Feuersglut, edited by Heinz F. Schafroth, Reclam (Stuttgart, Germany), 1984.

Kockodan Samota, Odeon (Prague, Czechoslovakia), 1984.

Reise durch die Nacht, Suhrkamp (Frankfurt am Main, Germany), 1984, translation by Beth Bjorklund published as *Night Train,* Ariadne Press (Riverside, CA), 1992.

Rosengarten, Pfaffenweiler Presse (Pfaffenweiler, Germany), 1984.

(With Hubert Aratym) *Configurationen,* Sonderzahl (Vienna, Austria), 1985.

Das Herzzerreissende der Dinge, Suhrkamp (Frankfurt am Main, Germany), 1985.

Das Jahr Schnee, Volk & Welt (Berlin, Germany), 1985.

(With Bodo Hell) *Der Donner des Stillhaltens/ Larven, Schemen, Phantome,* Droschl (Graz, Austria), 1986.

Winterglück, Suhrkamp (Frankfurt am Main, Germany), 1986.

Blauer Streusand, Suhrkamp (Frankfurt am Main, Germany), 1987.

Magische Blätter II (also see below), Suhrkamp (Frankfurt am Main, Germany), 1987.

Mein Herz, mein Zimmer, mein Name (title means "My Heart, My Room, My Name"), Suhrkamp (Frankfurt am Main, Germany), 1988.

Jericho, Herbstpresse (Vienna, Austria), 1989.

Zittergaul: Gedichte, Otto Maier, Ravensburg, Austria), 1989.

Mein Träme, ein Flügelkleid, Eremitenpresse (Düsseldorf), 1989.

Materialien zum Wer Arno Schmidts (criticism), Text & kritik (Munich, German), 1989.

Umbra: der Schatten: das ungewisse Garten-Werk, illustrations by Linde Waber, Hora (Vienna, Austria), 1990.

Entfachung, D. Scherr (Vienna, Austria), 1990.

Stilleben, Suhrkamp (Frankfurt am Main), 1991.

(With Ingrid Wald) *Wald wiesen und anderes,* Freibord (Vienna, Austria), 1991.

Magische Blätter III (also see below), Suhrkamp (Frankfurt am Main, Germany), 1991.

Kinder Ka-Laender (juvenile), illustrated by Gerhard Jaschke, Freibord (Vienna, Austria), 1991.

ABC-thriller, Freibord (Vienna, Austria), 1992.

Das besessene Alter: Gedichte, 1986-1991, Suhrkamp (Frankfurt am Main, Germany), 1992.

(With Tone Fink) *Verfaulbett oder die Almlunge,* Thurnhof (Horn, Iceland), 1992.

(With Bodo Hell) *Gang durchs Dorf: Fingerzeig,* Bibliothek der Provinz, 1992.

Als es ist: Texte zur Kunst, Landessammlungen Rupertinum (Salzburg, Austria), 1992.

Phobie de Wäsche, Fundamental (Cologne, Germany), 1992.

Beblumen: (ein) mein Lieblingstod, Bibliothek der Provinz, 1992.

Blumenwerk: lädliches Journal/Deinzendorf, Bibliothek der Provinz, 1992.

Veritas: Lyrik und Prosa, 1950-1992, Reclam (Leipzig, Germany), 1993.

(With Daniela Riess-Beger) *Lebensveranstaltung: Erfindungen, Findungen, einer Sprache,* Dokumentationsstelle für neue österreichische literatur (Vienna, Austria), 1994.

Lection, Suhrkamp (Frankfurt am Main, Germany), 1994.

(With Silvia Kummer) *Feuerstein ungerieben,* Flutlicht (Vienna, Austria), 1995.

Den fliegenschrank aufegebrochen: bildgedichte, Kleinheinrich (Munster, Germany), 1995.

(And illustrator) *Kabinett Notizen, nach James Joyce: Für Linde Waber,* Thurnhof (Horn, Iceland), 1995.

Für H.C., Passagen (Vienna, Austria), 1996.

Notizen auf einem Kamel: Gedichte 1991-1996, Suhrkamp (Frankfurt am Main, Germany), 1996.

Das zu Sehende, das zu Hörende (radio play), Suhrkamp (Frankfurt am Main, Germany), 1997.

Gala des Messer auf einer Bettdecke, Wiener Bibliophilen-Gesellschaft (Vienna, Austria), 1997.

Brütt, oder, Die seufzenden Gärten, Suhrkamp (Frankfurt am Main, Germany), 1998.

Benachbarte Metalle: Ausgewählte Gedichte, Suhrkamp (Frankfurt am Main, Germany), 1998.

Magische Blätter V (also see below), Suhrkamp (Frankfurt am Main, Germany), 1999.

(Author of text) *Blättersitten: Fotos/Text,* photographs by Manfred Gruber, Haymon (Innsbruck, Austria), 1999.

Requieum für Ernst Jandl, Suhrkamp (Frankfurt am Main, Germany), 2001.

Peck Me Up, My Wing: Selections from the Work of Friederike Mayröcker (bilingual German and English), translated by Mary Burns, Smokeproof Press (Boulder, CO), 2000.

Gesammelte Prosa, Suhrkamp (Frankfurt am Main, Germany), 2001.

Magische Blätter I-V, Suhrkamp (Frankfurt am Main, Germany), 2001.

Contributor to books, including *Ein Gedichte und sein Autor,* edited by Walter Höllerer, Literarisches Colloquium, 1967; *Neues Hörspiel,* edited by Klaus Schöning, Suhrkamp, 1970, *Holzschnitte zu Hermann Hesse Siddhartha,* by Anton Watzl, Tusch, 1981; *Visuelle Dialogue zum Verhältnis von Weiblichkeit und Kunst,* Orlanda Frauenverlag, 1992; and *Spectaculum 53: Sechs moderne Theaterstücke,* Suhrkamp, 1992. Contributor to periodicals, including *Frankfurter Allemagneine Zeitung,* and *protokolle.*

Author's works have been translated into several languages, including Dutch and Spanish.

ADAPTATIONS: Many of Mayröcker's poems have been set to music. *Brütt, oder, Die seufzenden Gärten* was adapted as an audiobook, DerHör (Munich, Germany), 1998; translations of Mayröcker's poems by Margitt Lehbert have appeared in *Poetry.*

SIDELIGHTS: A prolific writer of both prose and poetry, Friederike Mayröcker is noted for her lack of concern with plot and character development in favor of a self-reflexive style absorbed with language and the creative process. Although Mayröcker's work is considered difficult, she gained prominence with 1980's *Die Abschiede* and has since garnered many awards in her native Austria. Mayröcker has collaborated with a number of writers, among them poet Ernst Jandle, a fellow member of the avant-garde Wiener Gruppe of the 1950s with whom she worked between 1954 and his death in 2000. Considered one of Austria's most noted authors, Mayröcker continues to draw critical praise for her focus on the means by which one maintains a unique identity within a society that has become dehumanized by technology and a pervasive popular culture that values materialism over creative substance. In reviewing the literary retrospective *Veritas: Lyrik und Prosa, 1950-1992* for *World Literature Today,* Rita Terras described reading a work by Mayröcker as entering "the world of a well-traveled, well-read, and well-informed modern intellectual." Discussing the overarching qualities the volume reveals, Beth Bjorklund added in her own review in the same journal that in *Veritas,* as in most of the author's work, "the 'problem of living,' cast as the problem of writing—i.e., creating a language commensurate with experience—is central."

Born in 1924, Mayröcker began writing at an early age. After college she taught English at a secondary school in Vienna before beginning her writing career in 1969. In addition to poetry and prose, she has authored a number of radio plays broadcast in her native Austria, among them *Fünf Mann Menschen* and *Schwarmgesang,* which, according to Robert Acker in the *Encyclopedia of World Literature,* "contain no recognizable plots or protagonists but instead explore the possibilities of acoustic and linguistic montage." She has also penned several children's books, including *Sinclair Sophocles, the Baby Dinosaur,* which a *Publishers Weekly* contributor praised as "a rich blend of comedy and wistfulness."

As Beth Bjorklund explained in an essay for the *Dictionary of Literary Biography,* Mayröcker's is an experimental writing that creates a "timeless amalgam" wherein "reality is portrayed as discontinuous, non-chronological, and open-ended. Her writing creates reality rather than reproducing it, and language is both its medium and its content. Traditional metaphorical use of language gives way to innovative techniques, including montage, evocation, assemblage, permutation, dislocation, word chains, phrasal leitmotifs, juxta-position, and repetition. The result is a network of associations in which all features of language—not only semantic meaning but also sounds, rhythms, and syntax—function as metaphor."

While Mayröcker's early work, such as that included in 1966's *Tod durch Musen,* was lyrical, by the early 1970s she had gained prominence as a unique and idiosyncratic writer. Her 1973 work *Je ein umwölkter Gipfel* is comprised of fragments of dialogue which relate her experiences on a visit to the United States, while 1980's *Die Abschiede* focuses on the end of a romantic relationship and the related images of "closure: evening, autumn, departure, desolation, decay, and death," according to Bjorklund. Becoming increasingly more accessible into the 1980s, books by Mayröcker such as *Reise durch die Nacht* weave together the author's familiar obsession with self and such themes as death, continuity, and the purpose of her life into a literary journey that *World Literature Today* contributor Robert Acker described as "accessible to the average reader." Noting that *Reise durch die Nacht* is, together with *Das Herzzerreissende der Dinge* part of an autobiographical trilogy, *Times Literary Supplement* contributor Jeremy Adler described the work as a "phastasmagoria of consciousness" comprised of dreams and "surreal transformations" that "testify to Mayröcker's most frequently quoted maxim: 'I have always avoided telling a story, that is, I can't see a story anywhere.'"

Among Mayröcker's works to be translated into English is *Heiligenanstalt,* first published in 1978 and translated by poet Rosmarie Waldrop in 1992. Containing fictional biographies of composers Bruckner, Chopin, Schumann, and Schubert, the work is an effort to "liberate" the life histories of these composers from their own time and "concentrate it upon [Mayröcker] . . . within the setting of her own world," according to *World Literature Today* contributor W. V. Blomster. While Blomster found the author's effort unsuccessful, in his appraisal of the English-language translation of *Heiligenanstalt* for the *Review of Contemporary Fiction,* Dennis Barone noted that in translator Rosmarie Waldrop's hands "the prose dances like fingerwork on keys."

The prose work *Mein Herz, mein Zimmer, mein Name* reflects what Bjorklund termed Mayröcker's "autobiographical tendency. . . . The theme of writing is central, as the author comments on the very text that is being written. The self-portrayal deals mainly with feelings about personal relationships and with the fear that time to pursue her 'obsession' (writing) is running out." Composed of a single sentence of dialogue directed at a woman named Rosa, the book at first appears to be what *World Literature Today* contributor Robert Acker described as "a wild jumble of words and ideas," although on closer examination Mayröcker employs structure by repeating certain phrases. Acker wrote that *Mein Herz, mein Zimmer, mein Name* is a search for self-meaning, noting that the text carries within it "a sense of a restless and breathless writing activity which obviously is absolutely essential for [Mayröcker] . . . to maintain her profession and to search for her own identity."

In addition to her booklength works, Mayröcker has also contributed essays and other writings to a number of journals, anthologies, and books issued by small presses in Austria, Germany, and elsewhere. Her major publisher, Suhrkamp, has issued several collections of these writings as *Magische Blätter,* the first published in 1983. Of the third volume in the series, Beth Bjorklund commented in *World Literature Today* that "many readers will recognize familiar themes and forms, as elements from imagination, memory, dream, thought, and emotion are brought together in an associative amalgam." Noting the importance of visual imagery and art that runs through the collected writings, Bjorklund added that these visuals are transformed from images into words, as Mayröcker characteristically "makes literature out of the raw materials of her life."

BIOGRAPHICAL AND CRITICAL SOURCES:

BOOKS

Daviau, Donald G., editor, *Major Figures of Contemporary Austrian Literature,* P. Lang (New York, NY), 1987, pp. 313-336.
Dictionary of Literary Biography, Volume 85: *Austrian Fiction Writers after 1914,* Gale (Detroit, MI), 1988, pp. 247-251.
Encyclopedia of World Literature in the Twentieth Century, St. James Press (Detroit, MI), 1999.
Schmidt, Siegfried J., editor, *Friederike Mayröcker,* Suhrkamp (Frankfurt am Main, Germany), 1984.

PERIODICALS

Bulletin of the Center for Children's Books, September, 1974, review of *Sinclair Sophocles, the Baby Dinosaur,* p. 13.

Kirkus Reviews, April 15, 1974, review of *Sinclair Sophocles, the Baby Dinosaur,* pp. 419-420.
Library Journal, September 15, 1974, Patricia Kurtz Bock, review of *Sinclair Sophocles, the Baby Dinosaur,* p. 2252.
Literatur und Kritik, number 142, 1980, pp. 106-110; numbers 165-166, 1982, pp. 73-78.
Poesis, Volume 5, 1984, pp. 48-67.
Publishers Weekly, February 25, 1974, review of *Sinclair Sophocles, the Baby Dinosaur,* p. 114.
Review of Contemporary Fiction, summer, 1995, Dennis Barone, review of *Heiligenanstalt,* p. 214.
Times Literary Supplement, January 14, 1972, review of *Fantom Fan,* p. 32; July 23, 1982, review of *Pegas, the Horse,* p. 792; July 4, 1986, Jeremy Adler, "From the Habitat of Knowledge," p. 738.
Wilson Library Bulletin, September, 1982, review of *Pegas, the Horse,* p. 59.
World Literature Today, summer, 1977, M. Goth, review of *Fast ein Früling des Markus M.,* p. 443; autumn, 1978, M. Goth, review of *Rot ist Unten,* pp. 628-629; spring, 1979, W. V. Blomster, review of *Heiligenanstalt,* p. 291; autumn, 1981, pp. 597-602; spring, 1983, Beth Bjorklund, review of *Gute Nacht, guten Morgen,* pp. 280-281; winter, 1986, R. Acker, review of *Reise durch die Nacht,* p. 106; autumn, 1987, Jerry Glenn, review of *Winterglück,* p. 622; winter, 1990, R. Acker, review of *Mein Herz, mein Zimmer, mein Name,* p. 109; spring, 1992, J. Glenn, review of *Stilleben,* p. 341; autumn, 1992, B. Bjorklund, review of *Magische Blätter III,* pp. 718-719; autumn, 1993, B. Bjorklund, review of *Das besessene Alter,* p. 816; summer, 1994, Rita Terras, review of *Veritas,* p. 562; summer, 1997, R. Terras, review of *Notizen auf Einem Kamel,* p. 583; winter, 1999, B. Bjorklund, review of *Das zu Sehende, das zu Hörende,* p. 141; winter, 2000, Susan Cocalis, review of *Brütt, oder, Die Seufzenden Garten,* p. 141; summer-autumn, 2001, Francis Michael Sharp, review of *Requiem für Ernst Jandl,* p. 188.*

*   *   *

MELNICK, Ralph 1946-

PERSONAL: Born September 14, 1946, in New York, NY; son of Lester (an electrician) and Evelyn (a homemaker) Melnick; married Rachel Shana Levy (a teacher of English as a second language), June 1, 1969; children: Joshua Jacob, Ross David. *Ethnicity:*

"Jewish." *Education:* New York University, B.A., 1968; Columbia University, M.S.L.S., 1970, M.A., 1974, M.Phil., 1975, Ph.D., 1977. *Politics:* "Independent and often outraged." *Religion:* Jewish.

ADDRESSES: Office—Williston Northampton School, 19 Payson Ave., Easthampton, MA 01027. *E-mail*—rmelnick@williston.com.

CAREER: New York City Department of Social Services, New York, NY, caseworker, 1970-71; Atlantic Counseling Center, counselor and supervisor of drug rehabilitation program, 1971; American Jewish Historical Society, Waltham, MA, archivist and librarian, 1971-72; Zionist Archives and Library, New York, NY, archivist and librarian, 1975-77; College of Charleston, Charleston, SC, head of special collections at library and lecturer in religion and history, 1977-84; Williston Northampton School, Easthampton, MA, library director and teacher of religion, 1984—. University of Massachusetts—Amherst, visiting professor of Judaic studies, 2002—. Avery Institute for African-American History and Culture, founding member of board of directors and curator of collections, 1980-84; American Jewish Historical Society, archivist and librarian, 1985-89; freelance archivist. *Wartime service:* "Conscientious objector."

MEMBER: Association for Jewish Studies, American Library Association, Phi Beta Kappa.

WRITINGS:

(Editor and contributor) *Columbia Encyclopedia,* 4th edition, Columbia University Press (New York, NY), 1974.

(Compiler) *The Wendell Mitchell Levi Library and Archives: A Catalog of Its Holdings,* College of Charleston Library Associates (Charleston, SC), 1979.

(Editor and contributor) Barbara Hughes, *Catalog of the Scientific Apparatus at the College of Charleston, 1800-1940,* College of Charleston Library Associates (Charleston, SC), 1980.

(Coauthor) *Guide for America: Holy Land Studies,* Volume I, Arno (New York, NY), 1980, Volume II, Praeger (New York, NY), 1982, Volume III, Praeger (New York, NY), 1984.

From Polemics to Apologetics: Jewish-Christian Rapprochement in Seventeenth-Century Amsterdam, Van Gorcum (Assen, Netherlands), 1981.

The Stolen Legacy of Anne Frank: Lillian Hellman, Meyer Levin, and the Staging of the Diary, Yale University Press (New Haven, CT), 1997.

The Life and Work of Ludwig Lewisohn, Wayne State University Press (Detroit, MI), Volume I: *A Touch of Wildness,* 1997, Volume II: *This Dark and Desperate Age,* 1998.

Justice Betrayed: A Double Killing in Old Santa Fe, University of New Mexico Press (Albuquerque, NM), 2002.

Contributor to books, including *Studies in American Jewish Literature,* Volume II, State University of New York Press (Albany, NY), 1983; and *Anne Frank: Myth and Reality,* edited by Alex Grobman, Martyrs Memorial and Holocaust Museum (Los Angeles, CA), 1997. Contributor to magazines, including *Journal of Religion, Library Journal, Studies in American Jewish Literature, Civil War History, Library Scene, South Carolina Historical,* and *Journal for the Study of Judaism in the Graeco-Roman Period.*

WORK IN PROGRESS: A biography of Senda Berenson, the founder of women's basketball; a study of the spiritual development of Anne Frank; a book on the political career of Raina Simons in revolutionary China.

SIDELIGHTS: Ralph Melnick once told *CA:* "I write primarily as a way of responding to what bothers me in the society around me, with the hope that some small bit of change may ultimately result from my efforts. The Lewisohn biography addressed issues of ethnic identity, regressive politics, and the life of the artist in America. The story of Meyer Levin's struggle to have his adaptation of Anne Frank's diary produced on the stage dealt with the suppression of free expression and the misuse of the Holocaust for ideological promotion. Thomas Johnson's legal lynching in Santa Fe is a sad tale of racism and the evils of capital punishment. My interest in Senda Berenson has grown out of her Jewish origins and her critique of athletics as outsized in America, which she noticed a century ago."

More recently he added: "The study of Raina Simons is an attempt to recapture a time when the passion for social and economic change was not yet dampened by the harsh recognition of ulterior motives by leaders on all sides. The examination of Anne Frank's spiritual development is an effort to restore to her the depth of perception that other, more shallow treatments have left behind."

"Finally," Melnick commented, "I write because it lends excitement, meaning, and deeply felt joy to my life."

*   *   *

MERCER, James L(ee) 1936-

PERSONAL: Born November 7, 1936, in Sayre, OK; son of Fred Elmo (an oil field worker) and Ora Lee (Davidson) Mercer; married Karolyn Lois Prince (an attorney), November 16, 1962, in Carson City, NV; children: Tara Lee Mercer Wales, James Lee Mercer, Jr. *Ethnicity:* "Caucasian." *Education:* Attended Sayre Junior College, 1959-60; University of Nevada, B.S., 1964, M.B.A., 1966; University of North Carolina, certificate in municipal administration, 1971; attended Syracuse University, 1973; Cornell University, diploma from Executive Development Program, 1979.

ADDRESSES: Office—Mercer Group, Inc., 551 West Cordova Rd., Suite 726, Santa Fe, NM 87505; fax: 505-466-1274. *E-mail*—mercer@mindspring.com.

CAREER: University of Nevada, Reno, NV, audio-visual technician, 1960-64; Pacific Telephone Co., Sacramento, CA, management trainee, 1965-66; General Dynamics Corp., Pomona, CA, production control supervisor, 1966-67; Litton Systems, Inc., Ingalls Shipbuilding Division, Pascagoula, MS, assistant to the vice president and general manager, and nuclear submarine project manager, 1967-70; City of Raleigh, NC, assistant city manager, 1970-73; Public Technology, Inc., Washington, DC, national program director, 1973-76; Battelle Memorial Institute, Atlanta, GA, general manager of southern operations, 1976-79; Korn/Ferry International (executive search firm), Atlanta, GA, vice president and partner, 1979-81; James Mercer and Associates, Inc. (management consultants), Atlanta, GA, chair, president, and chief executive officer, 1981-86; Georgia Institute of Technology, Atlanta, GA, senior research associate and director of Industrial Extension Division and Georgia Productiv-

ity Center, 1981-83; Coopers & Lybrand (certified public accountants), Atlanta, GA, director of governmental consulting, 1983-84; Wolfe and Associates, Inc. (management consultants), Atlanta, GA, regional vice president, 1984-86; Mercer, Slavin & Nevins, Inc. (management consultants), Atlanta, GA, president, chair, and chief executive officer, 1986-90; Mercer Group, Inc. (management consultants), Santa Fe, NM, president, chair, and chief executive officer, 1990—. Mississippi Gulf Coast Junior College, Gautier, MS, instructor in management, economics, and business communications, 1967-70; North Carolina State University, Raleigh, instructor, 1972-73; visiting lecturer at numerous universities; lecturer and seminar leader on subjects related to management and public administration; guest on numerous television programs. University of Nevada Foundation, founding member of board of directors, 1983-90; California Polytechnic State University, San Luis Obispo, member of advisory council of School of Business, 1980-90; member of advisory board for master of public administration program at University of South Carolina and College of Charleston, 1987-90. Taratec Corp., member of board of directors, 1985-96. Atlanta Chamber of Commerce, past member of executive steering committee; Raleigh Civic Center Study Commission, chair; Mordecai Square Historic Society, member of executive committee; consultant and industry expert advisor to numerous companies and organizations, including National Science Foundation, Southern Bell, Johnson Controls, and Charterhouse Group International. *Military service:* U.S. Navy, Submarine Service, 1955-59.

MEMBER: International City/County Management Association, International Personnel Management Association, Institute of Management Consultants (certified management consultant; member of board of directors; chapter vice president), Institute of Industrial Engineers (member of board of directors; past chapter president), American Society for Public Administration, Technology Transfer Society (past member of board of directors), Contract Services Association of America (member of board of directors, 1995—), National Council for Public-Private Partnerships, Georgia Municipal Association, University of Nevada Alumni Association (member of executive committee), Beta Gamma Sigma.

AWARDS, HONORS: Past President's Award, Mobile chapter, Institute of Industrial Engineers, 1970; George C. Franklin Memorial Award from North Carolina

League of Municipalities, 1971, for contributions in public administration; two service awards and key to city of Raleigh, N.C., 1973; named Kentucky Colonel, 1982; honored alumnus, College of Business Administration, University of Nevada, 1988.

WRITINGS:

(With Edwin H. Koester) *Public Management Systems,* American Management Association (Saranac Lake, NY), 1978.

(Editor, with Ronald J. Philips) *Public Technology: Key to Improved Government Productivity,* American Management Association (Saranac Lake, NY), 1981.

(Editor, with Jules J. Duga) *Technology and Productivity in Urban Government: The 1980s,* Battelle Press (Columbus, OH), 1981.

(With Susan W. Woolston and William V. Donaldson) *Managing Urban Government Services: Strategies, Tools, and Techniques for the Eighties,* American Management Association (Saranac Lake, NY), 1981.

Strategic Planning for Public Managers, Quorum Books (Westport, CT), 1990.

Public Management in Lean Years, Quorum Books (Westport, CT), 1992.

Public Employee Involvement Processes, Quorum Books (Westport, CT), 1997.

Contributor to books, including *Technological Innovation: The Experimental R & D Incentives Program,* edited by Donald E. Cunningham, John R. Craig, and Theodore W. Schlie, Westview Press (Boulder, CO), 1977; *Not Well Advised,* edited by Peter Szanton, Russell Sage Foundation (New York, NY), 1981; *Management Policy: Readings and Cases,* edited by Milton Leontiades, Random House (New York, NY), 1983; and *Local Government Innovation: Issues and Trends in Privatization and Managed Competition,* edited by Robin A. Johnson and Norman Walzer, Quorum Books (Westport, CT), 2000. Contributor of nearly 300 articles and reviews to government, business, and management journals, including *Harvard Business Review.* Author of *The Mercer Group Privatization Survey,* a periodic report on privatization and outsourcing practices in 120 local governments.

SIDELIGHTS: James L. Mercer once told *CA:* "My work has been primarily aimed at the field of public administration and at the private company executives who provide goods and services to that field. I have always tried to keep a vision of emerging trends and best practices in the private sector which can be of great value to the public sector. This has significantly influenced my writing and has been the general underpinning of most of it.

"My writing process has been to attempt to capture a subject in total that I wish to write about (such as strategic planning for public managers), and to increase my knowledge about that subject through reading and practice. Where possible, I have also developed and taught seminars and workshops on the subject so as to prove out my own concepts and thinking on it and to practice theories and concepts in more of a real world setting. Following that, I then separate the overall subject matter into component parts, write, edit and assemble those in a logical fashion and craft a book that gets across the points that I wish to express. I try to write in a style that is easily read and is interesting to the reader.

"The subjects that I have chosen to write about are those where I believe a need exists for a more effective approach to deal with change and to the way an enterprise is being managed. I have always received inspiration from the act of expressing my ideas and thoughts with the hope and realization that my work would be published and reviewed by a large number of people, some of whom might be positively influenced by it. It has been one of the ways that I have tried to make a difference in the way things happen, which I think is part of my responsibility as a human being. I have tried to establish high standards for this work and to make valuable contributions to the effort.

"In an era of downsizing, organizational flattening and transformation, merging, governmental devolution, world competition and concern for the environment, the need has continued to exist for the development and application of modern management practices to meet numerous demands.

"My primary motivation for writing has been to logically develop my own ideas about management, to share those ideas with others and to try to influence their thinking and actions to improve policy, strategy, organizations, processes and performance. I have always believed that the true mark of a professional is to share their ideas with others and, in so doing, give something back to the profession that they pursue. There is no more effective way to do this than to write about it, publish it and have it available for the utilization and critique of colleagues.

"I have devoted my career and my writings to bringing the practical benefits of science, technology, and business systems to bear on the high-priority needs of business, industry, state, and local governments. My future writings will continue to reflect this theme in an attempt to assist businesses and governments to develop strategy, to effectively deal with change, to become more efficient and to enable their functions and programs to be more cost-effective in the new millennium and beyond."

Mercer more recently added: "I also have a strong interest in writing a novel and have begun to develop one, but I find the writing style needed is much different from that of writing management books."

BIOGRAPHICAL AND CRITICAL SOURCES:

ONLINE

Mercer Group, Inc., http://www.mercergroupinc.com/ (September 11, 2003).

* * *

MILLS, Claudia 1954-

PERSONAL: Born August 21, 1954, in New York, NY; daughter of Charles Howard (a safety engineer) and Helen (a teacher; maiden name, Lederleitner) Mills; married Richard W. Wahl (a natural resources economist), October 19, 1985; children: Christopher Richard Wahl and Gregory Charles Wahl. *Education:* Wellesley College, B.A., 1976; Princeton University, M.A., 1979, Ph.D., 1991; University of Maryland, M.L.S., 1988.

ADDRESSES: Home—2575 Briarwood Dr., Boulder, CO, 80305. *Office*—Department of Philosophy, Campus P.O. Box 232, Boulder, CO 80309-0232. *E-mail*—Claudia.Mills@Colorado.edu.

CAREER: Four Winds Press, New York, NY, editorial secretary and production assistant, 1979-80; University of Maryland, College Park, editor at Institute for Philosophy and Public Policy, 1980-89, assistant professor of philosophy, 1991-92; University of Colorado, Boulder, assistant professor of philosophy, 1992—, associate chair of philosophy, 1999—, director of Summer Philosophy Institute of Colorado, 1995—. Judge in children's book grant program, Society of Children's Book Writers and Illustrators (SCBWI), 1992 and 1994; member of Book Award Committee, Children's Literature Association, 1994-96, chair of Book Award Committee, 1996-98; fiction judge for Golden Kite Award, SCBWI, 1996; correspondent, *Loose Leaf Book Company* radio series, 1999-2002.

MEMBER: Authors Guild, Authors League of America, Society of Children's Book Writers and Illustrators, Children's Book Guild of Washington, D.C. (president, 1986-87), Phi Beta Kappa, Colorado Authors League.

AWARDS, HONORS: Notable Children's Trade Book in the Field of Social Studies, National Council for the Social Studies/Children's Book Council, for *All the Living* and *Boardwalk with Hotel;* Children's Books of the Year, Library of Congress, 1986, for *The One and Only Cynthia Jane Thornton,* 1988, for *Cally's Enterprise,* 1991, for *Hannah on Her Way,* 1992, for *Dinah for President,* and 1998, for *Standing Up to Mr. O*; Recommended Reading List for Children, National Council of Christians and Jews, 1992, for *A Visit to Amy-Claire;* Books for the Teen Age, New York Public Library, 1996, Blue Ribbon List, *Bulletin for the Center of Children's Books,* and Top Hand Award for Young Adult Fiction, Colorado Authors League, all for *Dinah Forever;* Pick of the Lists, *American Bookseller,* 1997, for *One Small Lost Sheep;* Bank Street College of Education Best Children's Books of the Year selection, 1997, for *Losers, Inc.* and *One Small Lost Sheep,* 1998, for *Standing Up to Mr. O* and *Gus and Grandpa Show and Tell,* 1999, for *Gus and Grandpa and the Two-Wheeled Bike* and *You're a Brave Man, Julius Zimmerman,* and 2000, for *Gus and Grandpa at Show and Tell*; Top Hand Award for Young Adult Fiction, Colorado Author's League, 1997, for *Losers, Inc.*; Outstanding Acheivement Awards, Parents Guide to Children's Media, for *Gus and Grandpa Ride the Train, Gus and Grandpa at Show and Tell,* and *Gus and Grandpa and the Halloween Costume*; Oppenheim Toy Portfolio Gold Awards, for *Gus and Grandpa Show and Tell, Gus and Grandpa at Basketball,* and

Gus and Grandpa and the Halloween Costume; International Honor book, Society of School Librarians, 2000, for *You're a Brave Man, Julius Zimmerman*; Books for the Teen Age, New York Public Library, 2001, for *Lizzie at Last*; Notable Book citations, American Library Association, for *Gus and Grandpa at Basketball* and *7 × 9 = Trouble!*; Colorado Authors League Award and Blue Ribbon List, *Bulletin from the Center for Children's Books*, both for *7 × 9 = Trouble!*; Rebecca Caudill Young Readers' Book Award nominee, 2002, for *You're a Brave Man, Julius Zimmerman*.

WRITINGS:

YOUNG ADULT NOVELS

Luisa's American Dream, Four Winds (New York, NY), 1981.
At the Back of the Woods, Four Winds (New York, NY), 1982.
The Secret Carousel, Four Winds (New York, NY), 1983.
All the Living, Macmillan (New York, NY), 1983.
What about Annie?, Walker & Co. (New York, NY), 1985.
Boardwalk with Hotel, Macmillan (New York, NY), 1985.
The One and Only Cynthia Jane Thornton, Macmillan (New York, NY), 1986.
Melanie Magpie, Bantam (New York, NY), 1987.
Cally's Enterprise, Macmillan (New York, NY), 1988.
After Fifth Grade, the World!, Macmillan (New York, NY), 1989.
Dynamite Dinah, Macmillan (New York, NY), 1990.
Hannah on Her Way, Macmillan (New York, NY), 1991.
Dinah for President, Macmillan (New York, NY), 1992.
Dinah in Love, Macmillan (New York, NY), 1993.
Phoebe's Parade, Macmillan (New York, NY), 1994.
The Secret Life of Bethany Barrett, Macmillan (New York, NY), 1994.
Dinah Forever, Farrar, Straus, & Giroux (New York, NY), 1995.
Losers, Inc., Farrar, Straus, & Giroux (New York, NY), 1997.
Standing Up to Mr. O, Farrar, Straus, & Giroux (New York, NY), 1998.

You're a Brave Man, Julius Zimmerman, Farrar, Straus, & Giroux (New York, NY), 1999.
Lizzie at Last, Farrar, Straus, & Giroux (New York, NY), 2000.
Alex Ryan, Stop That!, Farrar, Straus, & Giroux (New York, NY), 2003.

PICTURE BOOKS

A Visit to Amy-Claire, illustrated by Sheila Hamanaka, Macmillan (New York, NY), 1992.
One Small Lost Sheep, illustrated by Walter Lyon Krudop, Farrar, Straus, & Giroux (New York, NY), 1997.
Ziggy's Blue-Ribbon Day, illustrated by R. W. Alley, Farrar, Straus, & Giroux (New York, NY), in press.

"GUS AND GRANDPA" SERIES; EASY READERS

Gus and Grandpa, illustrated by Catherine Stock, Farrar, Straus, & Giroux (New York, NY), 1997.
Gus and Grandpa and the Christmas Cookies, illustrated by Catherine Stock, Farrar, Straus, & Giroux (New York, NY), 1997.
Gus and Grandpa at the Hospital, illustrated by Catherine Stock, Farrar, Straus, & Giroux (New York, NY), 1998.
Gus and Grandpa Ride the Train, illustrated by Catherine Stock, Farrar, Straus, & Giroux (New York, NY), 1998.
Gus and Grandpa and the Two-Wheeled Bike, illustrated by Catherine Stock, Farrar, Straus, & Giroux (New York, NY), 1999.
Gus and Grandpa and Show-and-Tell, illustrated by Catherine Stock, Farrar, Straus, & Giroux (New York, NY), 2000.
Gus and Grandpa at Basketball, illustrated by Catherine Stock, Farrar, Straus, & Giroux (New York, NY), 2001.
Gus and Grandpa and the Halloween Costume, illustrated by Catherine Stock, Farrar, Straus, & Giroux (New York, NY), 2002.
Gus and Grandpa Go Fishing, illustrated by Catherine Stock, Farrar, Straus, & Giroux (New York, NY), 2003.
Gus and Grandpa and the Piano Lesson, illustrated by Catherine Stock, Farrar, Straus, & Giroux (New York, NY), 2004.

OTHER

(Editor, with Douglas MacLean) *Liberalism Reconsidered,* Rowman & Alanheld (Totowa, NJ), 1983.

(Editor, with Robert K. Fullinwider) *The Moral Foundations of Civil Rights,* Rowman & Littlefield (Totowa, NJ), 1986.

Values and Public Policy, edited by Robert J. Fogelin, Harcourt (Fort Worth, TX), 1992.

7 × 9 = Trouble! (chapter book), illustrated by G. Brian Karas, Farrar, Straus, & Giroux (New York, NY), 2002.

Perfectly Chelsea (chapter book), illustrated by Jacqueline Rogers, Farrar, Straus, & Giroux (New York, NY), 2004.

Also the author or editor of numerous professional publications in philosophy and public policy, as well as articles on children's literature for journals including *Children's Literature, Children's Literature Association Quarterly,* and *Children's Literature in Education.*

SIDELIGHTS: Claudia Mills has blended a career as a prolific children's author with that of a highly-regarded academic, an associate professor of philosophy at the University of Colorado who has specialized in practical ethics, ethical theory, and social philosophy. She is the author of a score of popular novels for middle-graders that introduce readers to spunky fifth- and sixth-grade girls and boys facing challenges on the way to growing up and learning about their personal identity. Often told with a dash of humor, Mills's stories feature protagonists who are outspoken and willful, such as the plucky Cynthia, the enterprising Cally, and the outgoing Dinah, who has appeared in four of Mills's books. Male protagonists also populate the Mills fictional universe, including twelve-year-old Julius Zimmerman whose mother is bent on improving him one summer, and seventh-grader Alex Ryan who loves being the center of attention. These are just two of the protagonists Mill serves up in her popular "West Creek Middle School" series, which began with the 1997 *Losers, Inc.* Mills maintains a lighthearted, though sometimes slow-paced, approach to her tales, while conveying important messages to her readers without being didactic, note critics. For younger readers, Mills has also produced numerous picture books, including the popular "Gus and Grandpa" series.

Born in New York City, Mills moved to North Plainfield, New Jersey, with her family before she began kindergarten. Possessing an active imagination, she played fantasy games with her younger sister, pretending to be in magical lands with names like Maloone, Socker, Bladen, and Moo. "My mother was an elementary school teacher who loved to write," Mills noted on her member's Web site of the Children's Book Guild. "When I was six years old, she gave me a blank notebook and told me that this was to be my poetry book. So I began to write poetry. This was the beginning of my life as a writer." In elementary school, the young Mills already had dreams of becoming an author and spent many hours writing poems and stories. Her first publishing success came as a surprise when her English teacher told her class to write a story. Mills did not think her effort was very good, but her teacher thought differently and sent it to the Junior Scholastic annual writing contest. It won first prize in the national competition. From this experience, Mills related in a *Junior Literary Guild* article, "I learned that it's hard to be a good judge of your own writing." When she was fourteen, Mills wrote an autobiography called "T Is for Tarzan," in which she talked about her experiences in the eighth grade. The manuscript was "the literary sensation of junior high school," she related. "I still draw heavily from my own life in my books, but at least now I change the names."

Electing to study philosophy in college, Mills attended Wellesley, where she earned a bachelor's degree. She continued on to a doctoral program at Princeton, but left the university before completing her Ph.D., a degree she would eventually earn ten years later at the same institution. "I didn't begin serious professional writing," Mills once told *CA*, ". . . until I left graduate school impulsively in mid-year to take a secretarial job at Four Winds Press. I occupied myself during the four-hour round-trip from Princeton [to New York City] by writing picture book and novel manuscripts, which I submitted to Four Winds Press under various pseudonyms. It was very easy—but so disheartening—to slip a rejected manuscript unobtrusively into my book bag.

"Finally a manuscript proved promising enough on a first skim for the editor to hand it over to me, her secretary, for a reader's report. I took the challenge and wrote an objective, candid report on my own manuscript, including suggestions for needed revisions. The editor forwarded to the author (me) her 'excellent reader's report,' and then I dutifully took my own suggestions in rewriting. I finally confessed my duplicity when the manuscript was completed. Fortunately, the editor had a keen sense of humor, and the manuscript was published as *At the Back of the Woods.*"

Mills's first book was not published until after she left Four Winds to take a job at the University of Maryland's Center for Philosophy and Public Policy in 1980. Her first three books, *Luisa's American Dream, At the Back of the Woods,* and *The Secret Carousel,* were all published by Four Winds, after which she moved on to other publishers, continuing to work with her "lifelong editor," Beverly Reingold, she explained to *CA.* Mills published *All the Living* in 1985, the same year she married her husband, Richard Wahl. Her fifth work, *What about Annie?,* was published by Walker & Co. as part of its American history series for young readers. This was a departure for Mills, who typically sets her books in the present. Taking place during the Great Depression, *What about Annie?* features thirteen-year-old Annie Bodansky, one of six children in a Catholic family living in Baltimore. Annie's father has just lost his job working for American Radiator, and his subsequent and severe emotional depression affects the entire family. When her father attempts suicide, Annie runs away from home in her friend Tim's airplane. When an emergency forces her to bail out of the plane, however, she returns home. The accident "contributes to her father's healing," according to Catherine Wood in *School Library Journal,* "but does not miraculously solve the family's many problems."

Family problems are also the subject of *Boardwalk with Hotel,* in which young Jessica Jarrell learns that her parents adopted her because they thought they could not have children of their own. Soon after adopting her, however, Jessica's mother gave birth to a son and a daughter, and now Jessica believes her parents do not love her as much as they do her younger siblings. Consequently she comes to hate and resent Brian and Julie and starts to fight with them. By the story's conclusion, Jessica learns that her parents love all three of their children, adopted or not. Although a *Bulletin of the Center for Children's Books* contributor complained that the story lacked "depth or momentum," Phyllis Graves commented in *School Library Journal* that many pre-teens "who vacillate between over-confidence and anxiety" will be able to sympathize with Jessica. Graves predicted that the book "should have wide appeal."

Creating less-than-perfect characters like Jessica, who are nonetheless sympathetic and appealing, is one of the hallmarks of Mills's books. As Phyllis Wilson put it in a *Booklist* review of *After Fifth Grade, the World!,* "Mills has a knack for creating plucky heroines whose armor has a believable tarnish." *The One and Only Cynthia Jane Thornton* features fifth-grader Cynthia, who resents the fact that her younger sister is stealing her spotlight by writing a book when Cynthia always felt that it was she who excelled at writing. In this work, Mills created a character who "can be small, petty, and jealous," as one *Booklist* contributor put it. However, the "flaws in Cynthia's personality are part of the book's allure." What Cynthia learns, and what the author shows her readers, is that a kid can be unique and special without necessarily being the best. She eventually gains perspective, with the help of her family, and obtains a better sense of self-worth. "Young readers will happily ride the roller coaster of emotions along with Cynthia," claimed *School Library Journal* critic Virginia Golodetz.

After Fifth Grade, the World! features another flawed young character, Heidi Ahlenslager. Heidi and her friend Lynette have a mean teacher, Mrs. Richardson, whose strict ways they set about trying to reform: first through kindness, then, when that does not work, through cruel pranks that wind up getting them both in trouble. Heidi has her good points (she's a bright student, energetic, and imaginative), but goes too far in her attacks against her teacher when she displays a caricature of Mrs. Richardson at a school assembly. After Heidi's attempts cause her to lose support from Lynette, her family, and the principal, she begins to understand the meaning of accepting others as they are. A *Publishers Weekly* critic praised the fact that Mills does not offer convenient solutions to Heidi's problems, such as having Mrs. Richardson lose her job or inexplicably metamorphose into a kinder person, and suggested that Mills should get an award "for writing realistically about the middle grades."

Parents can be less than perfect in Mills's stories, too, and in *Cally's Enterprise,* the author shows that adults can be guilty of trying to direct their children's lives, preventing them from finding their own identities. In this story, Cally Lippincott's parents control almost everything she does both in and out of school, including making her take classes in gymnastics and ballet that Cally does not enjoy. Through a business partnership with her friend Chuck Forster, however, Cally "grows in assertiveness . . . , finally challenging her parents' control over her schoolwork and extracurricular activities," as Mills herself wrote in a *Children's Literature in Education* article. A demanding teacher who insists her students do their homework without their parents' assistance also helps Cally when she finds she can write an excellent report all by herself. Though Susan Schuller, writing in *School Library Journal,* felt "the story line is fractured and the writing strained in its attempts at humor," a *Bulletin of the Center for Children's Books* contributor asserted: "It's nice to have a book about the desire for independence, so typical a development of the young teen years."

The problems of school popularity figure into several of Mills's later books. In *Hannah on Her Way,* Hannah Keddie is a smart and artistically inclined ten year old who is not too popular with the other kids because she still clings to her toy dolls and prefers wearing her hair in a braid rather than in one of the more fashionable, adult styles her friends like. So when Caitlin Crystal, a well-liked student who transferred to Hannah's school after flunking out of private school, makes friends with her, Hannah cannot believe it at first. But Caitlin helps Hannah in gym and gets her in with the popular girls at school, and Hannah starts to really like Caitlin. Trouble comes, however, when Caitlin asks Hannah to help her cheat on a math test. In the end, both girls learn from each other: Hannah grows up a little, and Caitlin learns something about integrity. *Hannah on Her Way* was praised by reviewers, who called the book an honest portrayal of contemporary girls. Phyllis G. Sidorsky, for example, writing in *School Library Journal,* said the story is "painfully true to life [and] is also humorous and heartwarming." "This book will be enjoyed not only by readers who themselves feel outshone by their classmates," commented Deborah Stevenson in *Bulletin of the Center for Children's Books,* "but also by Caities who are Hannahs at heart."

Like Hannah, sixth-grader Bethany Barrett has a problem with popularity, though from a somewhat different angle. In *The Secret Life of Bethany Barrett,* Bethany really likes a rather plain and unpopular girl at school named Jane. She is afraid that befriending Jane will cause her to lose friends. Bethany's problems do not end there, however. She has other worries, like her brother's speech problems, her concern that her older sister will let her boyfriend keep her out of going to Yale (thus devastating her parents' hopes), and the fact that the school authorities are looking for the author of a poem—which is Bethany—that was posted about the mean school librarian. While *School Library Journal* contributor Bonnie L. Raasch called *The Secret Life of Bethany Barrett* a "mundane addition to friendship/family stories," Stevenson asserted in another *Bulletin of the Center for Children's Books* review that "Mills has a knack for conveying the intensity of the pressures on the middle-grades crowd."

Since 1990, Mills has written a series of books featuring her character Dinah Seabrooke, including *Dynamite Dinah, Dinah for President, Dinah in Love,* and *Dinah Forever.* In typical Mills fashion, Dinah is a flamboyant girl with an artistic flair who has some lessons to learn about growing up, accepting others, and finding her place in the world. When the reader first meets Dinah in *Dynamite Dinah,* she is a ten year old who craves to be the center of attention, and she succeeds in various ways until a new baby brother comes into her life and her teacher tells her that she cannot be the star in the school play. But, just like Cynthia in Mills's earlier work, Dinah begins to understand that other people need attention too, and she becomes a little less self-absorbed, though "Mills is realistic enough to realize that people, especially Dinah, can only change so much," as a *Publishers Weekly* reviewer noted.

In *Dinah for President,* Dinah starts sixth grade at J. F. K. Middle School, where she has trouble with the fact that, surrounded by seventh and eighth graders, she is no longer the star of the school. Therefore, to get more attention, she runs for student president, basing her platform on urging the school to start a recycling program. At the same time, she develops a close friendship with the elderly Mrs. Briscoe, whom she is helping with work around the house, as well as reading to her from *The Wind in the Willows.* Critics have praised Mills's portrayal of how Dinah matures through these experiences, becoming more aware of the world around her and of the needs of other people. Dinah "is subtly transformed throughout the book," observed Jana R. Fine in *School Library Journal,* "from a self-absorbed girl to a young woman with a social conscience."

Mills's other books featuring Dinah move from the theme of respect and sympathy for others to the deeper problems of love and death. In *Dinah in Love,* Dinah begins to understand why boys can act so differently from girls when she considers asking Nick Tribble— her debate team rival—to the school sock hop. With some help from Mrs. Briscoe, Dinah learns why boys sometimes do immature things, like when Nick throws a pink bra on her head, and learns a little about the difficult art of courtship. *Dinah Forever* deals with the even more serious problem of death when Mrs. Briscoe, with whom Dinah has become very close friends, passes away, and Dinah struggles to convince herself that life has purpose and meaning. Both these books, critics felt, have appealing characters in entertaining story lines. Of *Dinah Forever,* Hazel Rochman said in *Booklist,* "Kids will enjoy the quarrels among friends and enemies, the romance, and the passionate ideas." Writing in *School Library Journal,* Cindy Darling Codell called *Dinah in Love* "nicely structured and gifted with interesting characters." "*Dinah in Love* and its companions," *Voice of Youth Advocates* critic Alice F. Stern asserted, "will be enjoyed by fans of [Lois] Lowry's Anastasia and [Phyllis Reynolds] Naylor's Alice."

With *Standing Up to Mr. O,* Mills presents another "school coming-of-age story for those who love a stimulating argument," according to *Booklist*'s Rochman. Mills takes on the theme of animal rights in this tale of twelve-year-old Maggie who begins to dread her biology class when it is time to dissect worms and other smaller animals. She is against killing on purpose, but her friends are divided on the issue. Complicating matters, Mr. O., her favorite teacher and something of a stand-in father, is the biology instructor and expects her to comply with class procedure. When Maggie resists, Mr. O. becomes angry with her, threatening to flunk her if she does not participate in the dissection. Things escalate even further when the instructor prevents her antidissection essay from winning an essay contest. Through all of this, Maggie learns hard lessons, primarily the need to "face her disappointment in others with moderation and compassion," as *Horn Book*'s Jennifer M. Brabander noted. Rochman similarly concluded that Maggie learns that occasionally in life, "People disappoint you, even your best friend lets you down, even your beloved mentor, and you go on." A critic for *Kirkus Reviews* had further praise for the middle-grade novel,

noting that "once again Mills renders the trials of a good kid in a sympathetic and believable style." Writing in the *Bulletin of the Center for Children's Books,* Stevenson similarly commented that "Mills does an excellent job of blending serious philosophical contemplation with middle-grades realities."

More "middle-grades realities" are served up in Mills's "West Creek Middle School" series, which was initiated with *Losers, Inc.* Ethan Winfield is twelve and figures that he is already a loser. So convinced is he, in fact, that he forms Losers, Inc., a club whose membership includes his buddy Julius, as unpopular and out of it as Ethan is. Ethan's self-esteem is not helped by the fact that his older brother, Peter, is perfect in everything he does; not only does he get straight A's, but he also excels at sports. Sudden motivation comes in the form of a beautiful new student teacher, Ms. Gunderson, who forces Ethan out of his love for being a loser. He even starts to work on a science project in order to impress her and takes on a hefty volume by Charles Dickens for his book report. The unpopular Lizzie gets a crush on him, and though he has been cruel to her in the past, along with the other kids, he is nice to her now just for Ms. Gunderson's sake, suffering the expected taunts from other children. Neither are things much better at home, and in the end, Ethan is not saved by some miraculous ending, but rather learns lessons about life and achieves new insights because of his own actions. "As usual, the author is particularly good at simple expression of complex characters and relationships," wrote Stevenson in a review for the *Bulletin of the Center for Children's Books.* Robert Lipsyte, writing in the *New York Times Book Review,* however, felt that Mills's take on middle-grade angst was less than realistic: "When the meanest kids in school come up with a plan to enter one of Lizzie's poems in a fake national contest, and when the outcome is totally benign, devoid even of nasty comedy, we know we are in a no-kid's land." Other reviewers, though, had more praise for the book. Rochman, writing in *Booklist,* felt that "Mills writes here with touching comedy about a boy's muddle at home and at school." A contributor for *Publishers Weekly* called the book "funny, lively, and hopeful," and "certain to strike a chord with the target audience."

Ethan's best friend Julius is next featured—"wittily and winningly," according to a *Publishers Weekly* contributor—in *You're a Brave Man, Julius Zimmerman.* Julius still feels like a loser, even though Ethan has suddenly found his own talents. With summer vacation coming up, Julius's mother decides to take things into her own hands and get her recalcitrant son in shape for the coming academic year. Such plans include a French class in the morning and a job babysitting in the afternoon. Through it all, Julius fears that he will once again disappoint his mother, but surprisingly he "ends up having a pretty decent time," according to *Horn Book*'s Brabander. Julius begins to see the world differently and even finds a girlfriend. Ilene Cooper, writing in *Booklist,* felt that "Mills relates all this with her usual amusing take on things and makes Julius an endearing hero." The *Publishers Weekly* reviewer went on to call the book an "often poignant comedy" that "as a whole rings satisfyingly true." Frederick McKissack, Jr., writing in the *Washington Post Book World,* praised Mills "for creating a character that is both credible and unconventional." McKissack concluded, "Boys as nurturers? Another good direction in which to move the genre."

Lizzie gets her own title in the series with *Lizzie at Last* and is "determined to shake off her reputation as a nerd," as a reviewer for *Publishers Weekly* commented. To this end, she dons stylish jeans and acts like she does not know the answers in math class. Even her poetry takes a backseat as she strives to fit in, but finally Lizzie comes to her senses and back to herself during a visit to the rare book room of a library. The same *Publishers Weekly* reviewer noted that "Mills delivers a timely message to middle graders confronted with peer pressure." Similarly, Patti Gonzales, writing in *School Library Journal,* observed that "readers will empathize with this appealing protagonist and delight in her accomplishments." *Horn Book*'s Brabander thought that "Mills excels at conveying the comforting news that everyone—popular or not—faces problems at school and at home," while *Booklist*'s Kay Weisman concluded that the novel was "a solid, upbeat choice for the middle grades."

In the fourth book in the "West Creek Middle School" series, Mills brings the class clown, Alex Ryan, to center stage in "a touching and funny read," according to Laura Reed in a review of *Alex Ryan, Stop That!* for *School Library Journal.* Alex is upset when his father becomes a chaperone for a school outing, as he often makes fun of his son. Additionally, Alex falls for Marcia Faitak, one of the cutest girls in seventh grade, and his efforts to get her attention only alienate her. Then, trying to make things up to her, he only manages to get the girl's leg broken. His subsequent rescue makes him a hero, but soon the truth comes out that he was responsible for the accident in the first place. *Booklist*'s Weisman predicted that with this latest installment, librarians should "expect requests for previous titles in this humorous series."

Writing for a slightly younger audience, Mills presents the difficulties of learning the multiplication tables in *7 × 9 = Trouble!,* a "lighthearted story," according to Marilyn Ackerman in *School Library Journal.* As Mills noted on the Children's Book Guild Web site, she wrote the book "because both my boys had to memorize all the times tables when they were in the third grade, and it was a big ordeal! I thought it might be an experience a lot of kids could relate to." Mills added another real-life incident to this tale, the time when a child's hamster escaped from a classroom and was found eating all the kindergarten snacks. In her novel, third-grader Wilson is having trouble learning the multiplication tables, while his younger brother, still in kindergarten, is already starting to remember them. Wilson desperately wants to pass his multiplication test, as his friends have, so he can win an ice-cream cone from his teacher. Ackerman called this chapter book "entertaining," and one that "youngsters will relate to." *Horn Book*'s Martha V. Parravano commented that "Mills has an unerring gift for identifying childhood challenges . . . and joys." And a critic for *Kirkus Reviews* found the book "an excellent selection for the new chapter book reader."

Mills further commented on the Children's Book Guild Web site that she has "always had another job while writing my books." Not only does she balance her work as a philosophy professor with her writing, but also her other "job" as mother to two sons. Writing, then, is more a "secret love" than labor for her. "Some writers say that they hate to write," Mills observed on the Farrar, Straus, & Giroux Web site. "I love to write. I write my books early in the morning, while the rest of my family is still sleeping. I get up at five a.m., fix myself a mug of hot chocolate or Earl Grey tea, and then curl up on the couch with my pad and pen." Mills writes all her first drafts by hand and usually composes about a page per day. "But page by page, day by day, on the couch at dawn, I've written many books now."

If Mills acknowledges that she has other jobs in addition to her writing, she also has more than one genre she writes in. Since the early 1990s, she has become well known as the author of beginning, independent-reader picture books. She has produced some stand-alone titles such as *One Small Lost Sheep,* about a young shepherd in Bethlehem who has lost a lamb. This Nativity tale "captures the mood with tenderness and warmth," according to Gail Hamilton, writing in *Canadian Materials,* and is "a beautiful tale," as Ursula Adams described it in *Children's Book Review Service.*

Much of Mills's picture book efforts, however, have gone into the numerous volumes in the "Gus and Grandpa" series, featuring seven-year-old Gus and his seventy-year-old grandpa. In the debut title, *Gus and Grandpa,* the two embark on adventures, like going shopping and losing their car in the parking lot, celebrating birthdays, and training a dog to do tricks. Reviewing that book in *Booklist,* Rochman praised the "simple, lovely words in short lines [that] will help beginning readers."

The duo makes sweets for themselves in *Gus and Grandpa and the Christmas Cookies,* but the neighbors have no idea about their cooking skills and supply the two with cookies galore at the holiday season. But never fear; Gus contributes the excess goodies to the local homeless shelter. *Booklist*'s Cooper thought that the book offers "a nice holiday-season feeling, making its point about giving in a fresh way."

Gus's grandfather has a heart attack in *Gus and Grandpa at the Hospital,* but Gus overcomes his fear at seeing his helpless relative when he realizes he can play with the automated bed. Finally, the grandfather comes home and the two are relieved that they will have more time together once again. Writing in *Booklist,* reviewer Elizabeth Drennan found this title "just as pleasant as the others" in the series.

Mills "seems to get better and better with each new book," wrote *Horn Book*'s Parravano in a review of *Gus and Grandpa and the Two-Wheeled Bike.* Once

again the grandfather displays his understanding when Gus is hesitant to surrender his training wheels. Gus gets inventive in *Gus and Grandpa and Show-and-Tell,* in which the young boy brings his grandfather to school for show-and-tell. Lisa Smith, writing in *School Library Journal,* felt that "the warm, loving relationship Gus and Grandpa share shines through."

Sports are featured in *Gus and Grandpa at Basketball,* in which the old man helps his grandson focus during basketball games. More critical praise met this title. Louis Lahana, reviewing the book in *School Library Journal,* noted that it was "filled with fast-paced action and a bit of humor," as well as being "rich with lessons in persistence, achievement, and family relationships." "Simple without being condescending, this will have huge appeal for new readers," predicted *Booklist* critic Rochman.

Grandpa's "wisdom and good sense come through for grandson Gus" in *Gus and Grandpa and the Halloween Costume,* according to *Booklist*'s Stephanie Zvirin. When Gus's parents disapprove of his Halloween outfit, he turns to his grandfather and his trunk of old clothes for help. Describing the book's ending as "satisfying," a *Kirkus Reviews* critic offered warm words for the way in which "Mills quietly shows Gus solving his own problem."

Mills has been praised for being able to portray the needs of modern children and present their difficulties in a realistic fashion. As she noted on the Farrar, Straus, & Giroux Web site, this is mostly an early morning affair. "Between five and seven a.m. every day, I return to fifth grade, or sixth grade, sometimes even seventh, and, between sips of cocoa or tea, I bring that world to life again. And I love doing it."

BIOGRAPHICAL AND CRITICAL SOURCES:

PERIODICALS

Booklist, September 1, 1985, pp. 66-67; January 1, 1987, review of *The One and Only Cynthia Jane Thornton,* p. 710; July, 1989, Phyllis Wilson, review of *After Fifth Grade, the World!,* p. 1906; May 15, 1991, p. 1799; November 15, 1993, p.

626; October 1, 1995, Hazel Rochman, review of *Dinah Forever,* p. 316; February 1, 1997, Hazel Rochman, review of *Gus and Grandpa,* p. 950; March 1, 1997, Hazel Rochman, review of *Losers, Inc.,* p. 1165; September 1, 1997, Susan Dove Lempke, review of *One Small Lost Sheep,* p. 140; September 15, 1997, Ilene Cooper, review of *Gus and Grandpa and the Christmas Cookies,* pp. 235-235; May 1, 1998, Kay Weisman, review of *Gus and Grandpa Ride the Train,* p. 1526; October 15, 1998, Hazel Rochman, review of *Standing Up to Mr. O,* p. 422; November 1, 1998, Elizabeth Drennan, review of *Gus and Grandpa at the Hospital,* p. 508; February 1, 1999, Stephanie Zvirin, review of *Gus and Grandpa and the Two-Wheeled Bike,* p. 975; October 15, 1999, Ilene Cooper, review of *You're a Brave Man, Julius Zimmerman,* p. 446; October 1, 2000, Kathy Broderick, review of *Gus and Grandpa and Show-and-Tell,* p. 352; November 1, 2000, Kay Weisman, review of *Lizzie at Last,* p. 540; November 15, 2001, Hazel Rochman, review of *Gus and Grandpa at Basketball,* p. 574; April 1, 2002, Julie Cummins, review of *7 × 9 = Trouble!,* p. 1328; September 1, 2002, Stephanie Zvirin, review of *Gus and Grandpa and the Halloween Costume,* p. 140; April 1, 2003, Kay Weisman, review of *Alex Ryan, Stop That!,* pp. 1397-1398.

Bulletin of the Center for Children's Books, May, 1985, Catherine Wood, review of *What about Annie?,* p. 93; November, 1985, review of *Boardwalk with Hotel;* March, 1987; April, 1988, review of *Cally's Enterprise,*; April, 1991, Deborah Stevenson, review of *Hannah on Her Way,* pp. 200-201; February, 1992, p. 164; April, 1992, pp. 217-218; December, 1993, p. 130; January, 1995, Deborah Stevenson, review of *The Secret Life of Bethany Barrett,* p. 173; April, 1997, Deborah Stevenson, review of *Losers, Inc.,* p. 290; October, 1998, Deborah Stevenson, review of *Standing Up to Mr. O,* p. 68.

Canadian Materials, February 27, 1998, Gail Hamilton, review of *One Small Lost Sheep.*

Children's Book Review Service, Ursula Adams, review of *One Small Lost Sheep,* p. 28.

Children's Literature in Education, September, 1990, Claudia Mills, "Capitalist Tools? Today's Entrepreneurial Novels for Children," pp. 189-197.

Horn Book, September-October, 1990, p. 603; August, 1992, p. 451; September-October, 1998, Jennifer M. Brabander, review of *Standing Up to Mr. O,* p. 613; March-April, 1999, Martha V. Parravano, review of *Gus and Grandpa and the Two-Wheeled Bike,* p. 211; September-October, 1999, Jennifer M. Brabander, review of *You're a Brave Man, Julius Zimmerman,* p. 614; November-December, 2000, Jennifer M. Brabander, review of *Lizzie at Last,* p. 760; November-December, 2001, Martha V. Parravano, review of *Gus and Grandpa at Basketball,* pp. 754-755; March-April, 2002, Martha V. Parravano, review of *7 × 9 = Trouble!,* p. 215.

Junior Literary Guild, April-September, 1988, review of *Cally's Enterprise.*

Kirkus Reviews, September 1, 1998, review of *Standing Up to Mr. O,* p. 1289; March 1, 2002, review of *7 × 9 = Trouble!,* p. 341; August 1, 2002, review of *Gus and Grandpa and the Halloween Costume,* p. 1138.

New York Times Book Review, June 8, 1997, Robert Lipsyte, review of *Losers, Inc.,* p. 27.

Publishers Weekly, April 28, 1989, review of *After Fifth Grade, the World!,* p. 81; March 30, 1990, review of *Dynamite Dinah,* p. 62; January 20, 1997, review of *Losers, Inc.,* p. 402; February 3, 1997, review of *Gus and Grandpa,* p. 107; July 26, 1999, review of *You're a Brave Man, Julius Zimmerman,* p. 91; October 7, 2000, review of *Lizzie at Last,* p. 96.

School Library Journal, May, 1985, Catherine Wood, review of *What about Annie?,* p. 93; September, 1985, Phyllis Graves, review of *Boardwalk with Hotel,* p. 137; December, 1986, Virginia Golodetz, review of *The One and Only Cynthia Jane Thornton,* p. 106; November, 1987, p. 106; April, 1989, p. 103; May, 1989, Susan Schuller, review of *Cally's Enterprise,* p. 99; July, 1990, pp. 77-78; May, 1991, Phyllis G. Sidorsky, review of *Hannah on Her Way,* p. 94; May, 1992, Jana R. Fine, review of *Dinah for President,* p. 114; June, 1992, p. 99; December, 1993, Cindy Darling Codell, review of *Dinah in Love,* p. 114; February, 1995, Bonnie L. Raasch, review of *The Secret Life of Bethany Barrett,* pp. 99-100; April, 1997, Susan W. Hunter, review of *Losers Inc.,* p. 138, Jody McCoy, review of *Gus and Grandpa,* p. 114; October, 1997, Jane Marino, review of *Gus and Grandpa and the Christmas Cookies,* pp. 42-43; May, 1998, Lisa Gangemi, review of *Gus and Grandpa Ride the Train,* pp. 121-122; September, 1998, Pamela K. Bomboy, review of *Gus and*

Grandpa at the Hospital, p. 177; December, 1998, Jennifer Ralston, review of *Standing Up to Mr. O,* p. 129; April, 1999, Maura Bresnahan, review of *Gus and Grandpa and the Two-Wheeled Bike,* p. 105; September, 1999, Terrie Dorio, review of *You're a Brave Man, Julius Zimmerman,* p. 277; August, 2000, Lisa Smith, review of *Gus and Grandpa and Show-and-Tell,* p. 160; November, 2000, Patti Gonzales, review of *Lizzie at Last,* p. 160; September, 2001, Louie Lahana, review of *Gus and Grandpa at Basketball,* p. 200; April, 2002, Marilyn Ackerman, review of *7 × 9 = Trouble!,* p. 118; April, 2003, Laura Reed, review of *Alex Ryan, Stop That!,* p. 165.

Voice of Youth Advocates, February, 1986, p. 386; April, 1994, Alice F. Stern, review of *Dinah in Love,* p. 29.

Washington Post Book World, December 12, 1999, Frederick McKissack, Jr., review of *You're a Brave Man, Julius Zimmerman,* p. 19.

ONLINE

Children's Book Guild, http://www.childrensbookguild.org/mills.htm/ (September 7, 2003), "Claudia Mills."

Claudia Mills Home Page, http://spot.colorado.edu/~cmills/ (July 2, 2003).

Farrar, Straus, & Giroux—Books for Young Readers, http://www.fsgkids.com/ (July 2, 2003), "Claudia Mills."

Rebecca Caudill Young Readers' Books Award, http://www.rebeccacaudill.org/ (July 2, 2003), "About the Author: Claudia Mills."

N

NAVA, Michael 1954-

PERSONAL: Born September 16, 1954, in Stockton, CA; son of Victoria Acuñ; companion of Don Romesburgh. *Ethnicity:* "Mexican; Yaqui." *Education:* Colorado College, B.A., 1976; Stanford University, J.D., 1981 *Religion:* Catholic. *Hobbies and other interests:* Baseball.

ADDRESSES: Home—San Francisco, CA. *Agent*—Charlotte Sheedy Literary Agency, 65 Bleeker Street, New York, NY 10012.

CAREER: Writer and lawyer. City of Los Angeles, CA, deputy city attorney, 1981-84; private practice of law in Los Angeles, 1984-86; California Court of Appeal, Los Angeles, research attorney, 1986-1995; California Supreme Court, San Francisco, CA, staff attorney, c. 1998—.

AWARDS, HONORS: Lambda Literary Award, for Best Small Press Publication, 1988; Lambda Literary Award, for Gay Men's Mystery, 1988, for *Goldenboy,* 1990, for *How Town,* 1993, for *The Hidden Law,* 1997, for *Death of Friends,* and 2002, for *Rag and Bone.*

WRITINGS:

(With Robert Dawidoff) *Created Equal: Why Gay Rights Matter to America* (nonfiction), St. Martin's Press (New York, NY), 1994.

(Editor) *Finale: Short Stories of Mystery and Suspense,* Alyson Publications (Boston, MA), 2002.

"HENRY RIOS" SERIES

The Little Death, Alyson Publications (Boston, MA), 1986, reprinted Alyson Books (Los Angeles, CA), 2001.

Goldenboy, Alyson Publications (Boston, MA), 1988.

How Town: A Novel of Suspense, Harper & Row (New York, NY), 1990.

The Hidden Law, HarperCollins (New York, NY), 1992.

The Death of Friends, Putnam (New York, NY), 1996.

The Burning Plain, Putnam (New York, NY), 1997.

Rag and Bone, Putnam (New York, NY), 2001.

Autobiographical essays have appeared in *Hometowns,* edited by John Preston, Dutton (New York, NY) 1990; *Member of the Family,* edited by John Preston, Dutton (New York, NY), 1992; *Common Ground: Reading and Writing about America's Cultures,* edited by Laurie G. Kirszner and Stephen R. Mandell, St. Martin's Press (New York, NY), 1994; *Friends and Lovers,* edited by John Preston, Dutton (New York, NY), 1994; *Wrestling with the Angel,* edited by Brian Bouldrey, Riverhead (New York, NY), 1995; and *Boys Like Us,* edited by Patrick Merla, Avon Books (New York, NY), 1996.

SIDELIGHTS: Over a period of fourteen years, Michael Nava—raised in Gardenland, the barrio of Sacramento—has published seven mystery novels in which the protagonist, Henry Rios, is—like the author himself—a California-based, gay, third-generation, Mexican-American attorney. In defending the defenseless, reformed alcoholic defense attorney Rios never forgets the pain and pleasure he experienced as a child growing up in the fictional neighborhood of Paradise Slough in the fictional town of Los Robles. The Rios novels have all received wide critical acclaim, been nominated for the Lambda Literary Award (five having won the Award), and been published internationally. Katherine Forrest wrote in her introduction to an interview with Nava for *Lambda Book Report:* "The seven-novel panorama of the life and times and trials—trials intensely personal as well as professional—of Henry Rios comprises the most distinguished and iconoclastic gay mystery series to grace the pages of American Literature. . . . Even the *New York Times,* hardly a bastion of support for our work in years past, has conceded that 'Michael Nava is one of our best.'"

While creating mysteries with professional challenges for the protagonist, Nava portrays personal challenges, as well—pain, loss, growth, and victory—through the character of Rios. In *The Hidden Law,* the forty-year-old Rios—already having struggled through alcoholism—must deal with the fact that Josh, his HIV-positive lover of five years, is leaving him for another man. "In direct and eloquent prose . . . [Nava writes] an intricate, satisfying novel," commented a reviewer for *Publishers Weekly.* In *Death of Friends,* an earthquake portends the personal and professional turmoil Rios finds himself in. Several friends die of AIDS, and he takes care of his former lover as he, too, dies of the disease. Professionally, he defends a "studly" young man accused of murdering his lover, a male married judge. "Nava has said he wants his writing to reflect the rich California environment he lives in: Multiethnic, multi-sexual, and multi-racial," wrote Lev Rapahel for *Lambda Book Report.* "He succeeded: Rios is Mexican-American, his ex-lover Josh is Jewish, Josh's doctor is Indian, one of the police officers investigating the murder is African-American, and the two judges are an Asian-American woman and a Latina." Rapahel called this a "smoothly told story that raises very serious questions about how society treats its gay citizens and how we treat each other—and ourselves." Ray Olson commented in *Booklist* that, in Rios, Nava has created "the ideal persona through whom to grasp the human meat of the issues (the closet, pornography, the power of social position) that the judge's murder raises. Like the other Rios mysteries, this is first and foremost a deeply moving novel."

Jim Marks explained in *The Lambda Book Report* that the title of *The Burning Plain* is taken from Dante's *Inferno* and the seventh circle of Hell where homosexuals must endure eternal torment. In Nava's novel, Hollywood is Dante's Hell. "From the opening lines painting the city in the bleakest of Dashiell Hammett prose, Nava lays bare a world in which morality has become almost literally pointless," explained Marks. "There is a terrible beauty in much of the writing by gay men about AIDS, and this opening scene will join their number." Rios, the protagonist, purchases a copy of Dante's classic, and we find him reading it through much of the novel, "almost as if he needs any guidebook that will help him navigate this horrible, strange terrain," commented Marks. After proving himself innocent of murdering a homosexual prostitute with whom he spent the evening before the brutal murder, Rios gets involved in the investigation of more brutal murders of gay men, and must deal with a gay-bashing policeman, an unsympathetic district attorney, and a conspiracy between Hollywood's rich and powerful. Most painful, however, is the long, drawn-out court battle with the grieving parents of his dead lover, Josh, over Josh's wish to be cremated. Josh's Jewish parents, recalling the Holocaust, are devastated when Rios wins the case, and Rios is devastated by their grief. "My sense is that Nava wrote this novel out of necessity," observed Marks. "Like Henry Rios in the opening court case, he knew that there could be no triumph in his portrait, and he pressed on knowing that he will surely be criticized for painting such a bleak picture of gay life. . . . But as Henry walks out of the cemetery where Josh's ashes are housed, I hope that readers are given at least a glimmer of redemption in the final image of a new rose placed by Josh's funeral urn."

In the seventh book in the "Henry Rios" series, *Rag and Bone,* Rios suffers a major heart attack and calls his estranged sister's name just before his heart stops beating. Upon being revived, he awakes to find her there and they ultimately become reunited. "The smooth integrated plot strands conspire to test and push Rios into reassessing everything, from the new love and the commitment it both promises and demands, to the news that his estranged sister Elena, had had a daughter, now grown and with a son of her own," explained a critic for *Publishers Weekly.* Vicky—the daughter Elena gave up for adoption and has never met, along with her ten-year-old son, Angel—lands at Elena's door. Vicky is running from an apparently abusive and addicted husband whom she ultimately kills. The case looks like self-defense but becomes much more complicated and dangerous. Henry heads Vicky's defense and cares for her troubled son, who reminds him of himself as a child. "A super plot, memorable characters, and touching prose makes this essential for fans," commented Rex Klett for *Library Journal.*

Michael Nava once told *CA*: "All any writer has to write about is his or her experience of the world. As a gay man—of Mexican descent, no less—my challenge as a writer is to convey the value of my experience without preaching or apologizing. Writing mysteries, I work with the familiar and am able to insert the unfamiliar." In *Gay & Lesbian Literature,* Patti Capel Swartz quoted Nava as saying: "I began writing mysteries because I identified, as a gay person, with a species of literature in which the protagonist is an outsider who embodies the virtues that society purports to value—like loyalty, decency, and compassion—but seldom demonstrates. For me, coming out as gay required an enormous act of self-compassion after which I could no longer be so intolerant of other kinds of difference or so rigid in my moral certainties. I think that if I were not homosexual, I would be an extremely intolerant person, so perhaps my being gay was a little joke God played on me to teach me tenderness."

As it turns out, *Rag and Bone* is to be Nava's last "Henry Rios" novel. In the first sentence of the Acknowledgments page, he writes: "This book brings to an end this series of mysteries and my career as a mystery writer." Explaining this decision in a review for *Publishers Weekly,* Charles Hix quoted Nava as saying: "I'm not interested in writing about being homosexual any more. . . . I'm older. I'm now 46. There are other more meaningful things to think about. I've returned to the Catholic Church. I'm a practicing Catholic again." Hix commented: "Nava believes gay fiction is losing resonance with its audience. 'Gay and lesbian young people, like their Generation X straight counterparts, don't read much. . . . Young people can see themselves on TV and in movies . . . there is not a need for the safe houses that gay bookstores used to represent. The missionary age is over. The bookstores did their job. Time moves on.'"

In his interview with Forrest, Nava remarked: "I have published eight books in fifteen years while also practicing law for all but three of those years. I have no intention of keeping up that pace anymore. When I finally do get around to writing another book, it will be in a more relaxed schedule and, frankly, I don't particularly care whether I'm published again. I've never enjoyed the public part of being a writer—book signings, interviews, dealing with the machinery of the publishing industry, that sort of thing—and I plan to drop out of sight now that this series is over. The only thing that matters to me is the writing. Everything else is just noise."

"What I've enjoyed most in Nava's mystery series is their somber, brooding quality; they have some affinities with the best of Georges Simenon's moody 'Maigret' novels," commented Rapahel. And Forrest noted: "If *Rag and Bone* is to be our farewell to Henry Rios, to the end of an era, we have much to be thankful for: these seven superb novels and an enduring literary legacy from Michael Nava no matter where his future writing endeavors may bring him."

BIOGRAPHICAL AND CRITICAL SOURCES:

BOOKS

Pendergast, Tom and Sara Pendergast, editors, *Gay and Lesbian Literature,* Volume 2, St. James Press (New York, NY), 1998.

PERIODICALS

Booklist, August 1996, Ray Olson, review of *The Death of Friends,* p. 1887; January 1, 1998, Emily Melton, review of *The Burning Plain,* p. 784; February 1, 2001, Ray Olson, review of *Rag and Bone,* p. 1042.

Entertainment Weekly, September 6, 1996, Suzanne Ruta, review of *The Death of Friends,* p. 7.

Gay & Lesbian Review, May 2001, Greg Herren, review of *Rag and Bone,* p. 42.

Lambda Book Report, September-October 1996, Lev Rapahel, review of *The Death of Friends,* p. 9; March 1998, Jim Marks, review of *The Burning Plain,* p. 14; March 2001, Katherine V. Forrest, "Adios Rios," interview with Michael Nava, p. 8.

Library Journal, February 1, 2001, Rex E. Klett, review of *Rag and Bone,* p. 127.

People Weekly, September 30, 1996, Pam Lambert, review of *The Death of Friends,* p. 33; February 2, 1998, J. A. Reed, review of *The Burning Plain,* p. 31.

Publishers Weekly, September 7, 1992, review of *The Hidden Law,* p. 82; July 8, 1996, review of *The Death of Friends,* p. 77; January 22, 2001, review of *Rag and Bone,* p. 306; April 23, 2001, Charles Hix, "Final Chapter," review of *Rag and Bone,* p. 31.

*   *   *

NORTON, Mary Beth 1943-

PERSONAL: Born March 25, 1943, in Ann Arbor, MI; daughter of Clark Frederic (a political science professor; a legislative assistant; and an employee for Congressional Research Services) and Mary (a professor; maiden name, Lunny) Norton. *Education:* University of Michigan, A.B., 1964; Harvard University, A.M., 1965, Ph.D., 1969. *Politics:* Democrat. *Religion:* Methodist.

ADDRESSES: Home—Ithaca, NY. *Office*—Department of History, 450 McGraw Hall, Cornell University, Ithaca, NY 14853-4601. *E-mail*—mbn1@cornell.edu.

CAREER: University of Connecticut, Storrs, assistant professor of history, 1969-71; Cornell University, Ithaca, NY, assistant professor, 1971-74, associate professor of American history, 1975-87, Mary Donlon Alger professor of American history, 1987—.

MEMBER: American Historical Association, Organization of American Historians, Society of American Historians, American Antiquarian Society, Berkshire Conference of Women Historians, Conference Group on Women's History, Coordinating Committee of Women in the Historical Profession, Phi Beta Kappa, Mortar Board, Phi Kappa Phi.

AWARDS, HONORS: Woodrow Wilson fellowship, 1964-65; Alan Nevins Prize of Society of American Historians, 1969, for best doctoral dissertation in American history; National Endowment for the Humanities Younger Humanists fellowship, 1974-75; Charles Warren Center fellowship, Harvard University, 1974-75; Shelby Cullom Davic Center fellowship, Princeton University, 1977-78; Berkshire prize for Best Book, Woman Historian, 1980, for *Liberty's Daughters: The Revolutionary Experience of American*

Women, 1750-1800; Alice and Edith Hamilton Prize, 1980; Douglass Adair Prize, 1980; Berkshire Conference prize, 1981; Rockefeller Foundation fellow, 1986-87; Society for Humanities fellow, Cornell University, 1989-90; John Simon Guggenheim Memorial Foundation fellow, 1993-94.

WRITINGS:

The British-Americans: The Loyalist Exiles in England, 1774-1789, Little, Brown (Boston, MA), 1972.

(Editor, with Carol Berkin) *Women of America: A History,* Houghton Mifflin (Boston, MA), 1979.

Liberty's Daughters: The Revolutionary Experience of American Women, 1750-1800, Little, Brown (Boston, MA), 1980, reprinted, Cornell University Press (Ithaca, NY), 1996.

(Coauthor) *A People and a Nation: A History of the United States,* Houghton Mifflin (Boston, MA), 1982, 6th revised edition, 2001, 6th brief edition, 2003.

(Editor, with Carol Groneman) *"To Toil the Livelong Day": America's Women at Work, 1780-1980,* Cornell University Press (Ithaca, NY), 1987.

(Editor, with Ruth M. Alexander) *Major Problems in American Women's History: Documents and Essays,* D. C. Heath (Lexington, MA), 1989, 3rd revised edition, Houghton Mifflin (Boston, MA), 2003.

(Editor, with Pamela Gerardi) *The American Historical Association's Guide to Historical Literature,* 3rd revised edition, Oxford University Press (New York, NY), 1995.

Founding Mothers & Fathers: Gendered Power and the Forming of American Society, Knopf (New York, NY), 1996.

In the Devil's Snare: The Salem Witchcraft Crisis of 1692, Knopf (New York, NY), 2002.

Contributor to *Women in the Age of the American Revolution,* edited by Ronald Hoffman and Peter Albert, 1989; *The Transformation of Early American History,* edited by James Henretta, and others, 1991; and *Learning History in America,* edited by Lloyd Kramer, and others, 1994. Also contributor to *History Today, William and Mary Quarterly, Signs,* and many other journals.

SIDELIGHTS: Historian Mary Beth Norton might well be called a "founding mother" of women historians in the United States and around the world. Norton was the first woman to be employed in Cornell University's history department; she has seen the annual Berkshire Conference of Women Historians (the "Little Berks") grow from a small group in the 1970s, to a group of up to sixty that meets every spring. In 1973, she attended the first Berkshire Conference on the History of Women, with three hundred other participants and has attended the three-year event ever since, watching it grow to more than three thousand participants from around the world. As a consequence of cochairing the program committee at the sixth conference in 1984, she and her cochair published seventeen of what they considered the best papers presented at the conference in the book *"To Toil the Livelong Day:" American Women at Work, 1780-1980*. Norton was also a founding member of the International Federation for Research in Women's History, established in 1985 and that now has affiliates in more than twenty countries.

Norton believes one of the reasons she became a scholar is that her parents were academics and encouraged her to pursue a Ph.D. The family moved in 1948 from Ann Arbor, where Norton was born, to Greencastle, Indiana, where her father taught political science and her mother taught Latin at DePauw University. "My childhood and adolescence revolved around DePauw," Norton told Roger Adelson during an interview for the *Historian,* noting that her family's routine was tied to the academic year. "The best thing about summers for me was that my father always taught summer school . . . after which he spent his summer earnings taking the family on vacations around the United States." They toured all forty-eight contiguous states and their capitals, many universities, Civil War battlefields, and the homes of presidents.

The young Norton was an avid reader and, after reading every book in the children's section of the Greencastle public library, she began "sneaking" into the adult section. Her first job was with the DePauw library making sure the books were in their correct positions. She chose the University of Michigan for her undergraduate work because both her parents went there. "The world opened up for me there in two ways. . . . First, I no longer felt as if I were a misfit, the way I had in high school where nobody else seemed to read as many books and nobody else thought history was interesting. As a member of the honors college, I met other people who were fascinated by what interested me. . . . The second . . . was through my involvement in national and campus

politics." She campaigned with the Young Democrats for John Kennedy in 1960 and said: "As a 'Kennedy girl' I met him when he came to the Michigan Union in October and first proposed the Peace Corps. The positive student response in Ann Arbor helped him decide to make the Peace Corps a major part of his presidential campaign."

Norton won a seat on the Michigan Student Government Council, became a delegate to several congresses of the National Student Association (NSA) and actively protested nuclear testing and supported civil rights. "However, I was frustrated by male NSAers who refused to let women take leadership roles. . . . Chairing meetings of the women's dorm . . . I wanted to chair some large NSA sessions, but was not allowed to by those in charge. This was one of my first experiences with sex discrimination," she told Adelson.

When it came time to apply to graduate school, the professor at Michigan in charge of Woodrow Wilson fellowship applications warned her that "girls" seldom won that fellowship. Distressed at coming up against her second real experience with sex discrimination, she applied for the fellowship anyway, and for the Fulbright—the only two national fellowships open to women. She won the Wilson and was offered a four-year fellowship at Harvard. Norton described researching a seminar paper on the Massachusetts' reactions to the Stamp Act. "One day . . . while reading a minor pamphlet by James Otis entitled: 'A Letter to a Noble Lord,' I had what I have since come to describe as a conversion experience. Otis seemed to reach out across the centuries, touch me on the shoulder, and say, 'Here's the eighteenth century and it's infinitely interesting.' I remember sitting there and wondering why I had never before thought of doing colonial history." Her Ph.D. dissertation, much of which was researched in England, won the Allan Nevins prize for the best-written dissertation in 1970, and was published in 1972 as *The British-Americans: The Loyalist Exiles in England, 1774-1789.*

She accepted a teaching position at the University of Connecticut, and began a long and illustrious career. During her two years there, she met Tom Paterson, who would later ask her to coauthor a new textbook on U.S. history. The publication of her dissertation caught the attention of a teacher at Cornell University, whom she had already met at an American Historical Association meeting. He offered her a position at Cornell teaching about the American Revolution. "I knew that Cornell had never had a woman in the history department," she told Adelson, "and doubted if I'd get the job." She did, and she has remained at Cornell ever since. Apart from her academic responsibilities and writings, she's served almost continuously on the faculty senate and was elected twice to the Board of Trustees.

It was not until she began her tenure at Cornell that she became interested in women's history. The university had a "female studies" program run primarily by graduate students. "During my first year at Cornell, along with everything else I was doing, I helped develop what has become one of the most successful women's studies programs in the country," she told Adelson. At the same time, she began reading U.S. women's history. She eventually returned to England to "reexamine Loyalist claims with the question of gender in mind. The information I had previously missed now leaped out at me," she told Adelson. The research culminated in her first women's history article, which was published in the *William and Mary Quarterly* in 1976 and inspired her first book, *Liberty's Daughters: The Revolutionary Experience of American Women, 1750-1800.*

Lawrence Stone in the *New York Times Book Review* said the book is a "remarkably thorough investigation," and that Norton's "exhaustive and fascinating documentation" supports her assessment of women's early steps toward equality. Gerda Lerner wrote in *Washington Post Book World* that "Norton's thoroughly researched evidence does not convincingly prove her thesis," yet admits that the book "makes a valuable addition to our knowledge of the lives, thoughts and activities of women in the revolutionary era." Marion Dearman of the *Los Angeles Times,* who also mentioned the author's "carefully documented" sources, concluded: "I strongly recommend this book. It is well and very interestingly written and full of quotable quotes, simultaneously painful and delightful to read."

Founding Mothers & Fathers: Gendered Power and the Forming of American Society was a finalist for the Pulitzer prize in history in 1997. The first in a proposed two-volume series, this volume analyzes fundamental changes that occurred between the early seventeenth and mid-eighteenth centuries in New England and the Chesapeake in relation to gender and power.

At this time, the prevailing worldview of family and state was patriarchal and, as Patricia Hassler explained in *Booklist,* "The head of the family held power parallel to that held by the head of state." Norton argues, however, that women also played crucial leadership roles, highlighting in particular religious dissenter Anne Hutchinson, ultimately excommunicated from Boston's church for preaching God's free gift of salvation, and Anne Eaton, wife of Connecticut's governor, whose regular religious meetings brought about her excommunication as a heretic. Kenneth A. Lockridge commented in the *Journal of Social History* that while Norton's argument "seems plausible . . . it really doesn't work." A critic for *Publishers Weekly* wrote: "This erudite study is full of intriguing lore on colonial neighbours, sexual gossip and men's political squabbles," and Patricia Hassler in *Booklist* called it "a scholarly, provocative read."

Before writing *In the Devil's Snare: The Salem Witchcraft Crisis of 1692,* Norton evaluated historical threads other scholars writing about the event had not. She analyzed cultural, social, and political events of the era, arguing, as a reviewer for *Kirkus Reviews* stated, that "massacres of colonists by the fearsome Wabanakis tribe during the Second Indian War and the colonial government's failure to effectively counter such killings were the main precipitators of the witchcraft trials." Michael Kenney wrote in the *Boston Globe,* "As Norton unequivocally puts it, 'The dramatic events of 1692 can only be fully understood by viewing them as intricately related to concurrent political and military affairs in northern New England.' The participants in these events, both the accusers and the accused, were living 'near the front lines of an armed conflict' which they knew as the Second Indian War (the first being King Philip's War of 1676). These wars, happening in quick succession, 'dramatically changed their circumstances for the worse. Flourishing communities were wiped out, and people and their property holdings destroyed.'" Norton discovers that ten accusers and confessors, and twenty-three accused, had personal ties to the war-torn frontier.

"Norton builds her case with the precision of a criminal prosecutor," wrote Kenney. "Her conclusion is forceful: 'Had the Second Indian War on the northeastern frontier somehow been avoided, the Essex County witchcraft crisis of 1692 would not have occurred. This is not to say the war caused the witchcraft crisis, but rather that the conflict created the conditions that caused the crisis to develop as rapidly and extensively as it did.'" Margaret Flanagan wrote in *Booklist:* "This meticulously researched narrative sheds new light on an old and ever-fascinating subject," while the critic for *Kirkus Reviews* commented: "[Norton's] fascinating new take on the crisis has particular relevance in our own era, when rumors of war and resurgent religious fervor again create a volatile cultural mix."

BIOGRAPHICAL AND CRITICAL SOURCES:

PERIODICALS

Atlantic Monthly, November, 2002, Benjamin Schwarz, review of *In the Devil's Snare: The Salem Witchcraft Crisis of 1692,* p. 109.

Booklist, April 15, 1996, Patricia Hassler, review of *Founding Mothers & Fathers: Gendered Power and the Forming of American Society,* p. 1400; August 2002, Margaret Flanagan, review of *In the Devil's Snare,* p. 1890.

Books & Culture, March-April, 2003, Thomas S. Kidd, "What Happened in Salem?," p. 35.

Christian Century, April 19, 2003, Kenneth P. Minkema, review of *In the Devil's Snare,* p. 37.

Historian, fall 1997, Roger Adelson, "Interview with Mary Beth Norton," p. 1

Journal of Social History, spring 1997, Kenneth A. Lockridge, review of *Founding Mothers & Fathers,* p. 783.

Kirkus Reviews, July 1, 2002, review of *In the Devil's Snare,* p. 938.

Los Angeles Times, July 31, 1980.

Newsweek, October 28, 2002, David Gates, review of *In the Devil's Snare,* p. 56.

New York Times Book Review, April 20, 1980; November 3, 2002, Jill Lepore, review of *In the Devil's Snare,* p. 12.

Publishers Weekly, February 5, 1996, review of *Founding Mothers & Fathers,* p. 73; July 1, 2002, review of *In the Devil's Snare,* p. 63.

Washington Post Book World, January 4, 1981.

Women's Review of Books, November, 2002, Sandra F. Van Burkleo, review of *In the Devil's Snare,* p. 14.

ONLINE

Borzoi Reader Online Web site, http://www.randomhouse.com/ (October 8, 2002) "From the Desk of Mary Beth Norton: Mary Beth Norton Tells the Story behind *In The Devil's Snare.*"

Boston Globe Web site, http://www.boston.com/ (October 1, 2002), Michael Kennedy, "Salem Caught in *Devil's Snare.*"

P

PARFENIE, Marie
    See CODRESCU, Andrei

* * *

PAXTON, John 1923-

PERSONAL: Born August 23, 1923; married Joan Thorne, 1950; children: Nicholas, Jonathy (daughter). *Ethnicity:* "English."

ADDRESSES: Home—Moss Cottage, Hardway, Bruton, Somerset BA10 0LN, England.

CAREER: Millfield School, Street, England, economics teacher and department head, 1952-63; *Statesman's Year-Book,* London, England, assistant editor, 1963-68, deputy editor, 1968-69, editor, 1969-90; writer, 1990—.

MEMBER: Society of Authors, West Country Writers' Association (chair, 1993-95).

WRITINGS:

(With A. E. Walsh) *Trade in the Common Market Countries,* Hutchinson (London, England), 1965.
(With A. E. Walsh) *The Structure and Development of the Common Market,* Hutchinson (London, England), 1968, Taplinger (New York, NY), 1969, 2nd edition published as *Into Europe: The Structure and Development of the Common Market,* 1972, 3rd edition published as *The Developing Common Market: The Structure of the EEC in Theory and in Practice,* Westview Press (Boulder, CO), 1976.
(With A. E. Walsh) *Trade and Industrial Resources of the Common Market and EFTA Countries: A Comparative Statistical Analysis,* Garnstone Press (London, England), 1970.
(With John Wroughton) *Smuggling,* Macmillan (London, England), 1971.
(Editor) *Dictionary of Abbreviations,* Rowman & Littlefield (Totowa, NJ), 1974, published as *The Penguin Dictionary of Abbreviations,* Penguin (New York, NY), 1989, also published as *Everyman's Dictionary of Abbreviations,* Dent (London, England), 1974, 2nd edition, 1986.
World Legislatures, Macmillan (New York, NY), 1974, St. Martin's Press (New York, NY), 1975.
(Editor, with Chris Cook) *European Political Facts, 1918-1973,* Macmillan (London, England), 1975, Facts on File (New York, NY), 1978, revised edition published as *European Political Facts, 1918-1990,* 1992, revised edition published as *European Political Facts, 1789-1996,* three volumes, Macmillan (New York, NY), 1997, revised edition published as *European Political Facts of the Twentieth Century,* 2001.
(With A. E. Walsh) *Competition Policy: European and International Trends and Practices,* St. Martin's Press (New York, NY), 1975.
(Editor) *The Statesman's Year-Book World Gazetteer,* St. Martin's Press (New York, NY), 1975, 4th edition, 1991.
The Developing Common Market, Macmillan (London, England), 1976.
A Dictionary of the European Communities, Macmillan (London, England), 1977, 2nd edition, 1982.

(Editor, with Chris Cook) *Commonwealth Political Facts,* Facts on File (New York, NY), 1979.

(Editor, with Sheila Fairfield) *A Calendar of Creative Man,* Facts on File (New York, NY), 1980.

(General editor) *New Illustrated Everyman's Encyclopaedia,* 1983.

Companion to Russian History, Facts on File (New York, NY), 1984.

Companion to the French Revolution, Facts on File (New York, NY), 1988.

(Editor) *The Statesman's Year-Book Historical Companion,* St. Martin's Press (New York, NY), 1988.

(With Geoffrey Payton) *The Penguin Dictionary of Proper Names,* Viking (New York, NY), 1991.

(With S. H. Steinberg) *Historical Tables, 58 B.C.-1990 A.D.,* 12th edition, Macmillan (London, England), 1991.

European Communities, American Bibliographical Center-Clio Press (Santa Barbara, CA), 1992.

Encyclopedia of Russian History, American Bibliographical Center-Clio Press (Santa Barbara, CA), 1993.

The Penguin Encyclopedia of Places, Penguin (New York, NY), 1998.

Calendar of World History, H. W. Wilson (Bronx, NY), 1998.

Imperial Russia: A Reference Handbook, St. Martin's Press (New York, NY), 2000.

A Dictionary of Financial Abbreviations, Taylor & Francis (London, England), 2002.

Leaders of Russia and the Soviet Union, Taylor & Francis (London, England), in press.

Contributor to periodicals.

R

RAELIN, Joseph A(lan) 1948-

PERSONAL: Born April 10, 1948, in Cambridge, MA; married Abby Dolin (a school psychologist), September 5, 1974; children: Jonathan, Jeremy. *Education:* University of Paris, certificate, 1969; Tufts University, B.A. (magna cum laude), 1970, Ed.M., 1971; Boston University, certificate of advanced graduate study, 1974; State University of New York—Buffalo, Ph.D., 1977.

ADDRESSES: Office—Department of Administrative Science, Boston College, 140 Commonwealth Ave., Chestnut Hill, MA 02167. *E-mail*—raelin@bc.edu.

CAREER: State University of New York—Buffalo, Buffalo, NY, research associate at Human Resource Institute, 1974-77; Boston College, Chestnut Hill, MA, assistant professor, 1977-82, associate professor, 1982-87, professor of administrative sciences, 1987—. Northeastern University, holder of Asa S. Knowles Chair of Practice-Oriented Education; president of his own consulting firm.

MEMBER: Academy of Management, Society for Organizational Learning, Beta Gamma Sigma.

AWARDS, HONORS: Grants from Alfred P. Sloan Foundation, 1978-79, Charles F. Kettering Foundation, 1979, W. E. Upjohn Institute for Employment Research, 1979-80, and National Science Foundation, 1980-82; award for "best paper in management education," John Wiley (publisher); recognition award for management and education development.

WRITINGS:

Building a Career, W. E. Upjohn Institute for Employment Research (Kalamazoo, MI), 1980.
The Salaried Professional, Praeger (New York, NY), 1984.
The Clash of Cultures: Managers and Professionals, Harvard Business School Press (Boston, MA), 1986.
Work-Based Learning: The New Frontier of Management Development, Addison-Wesley (Reading, MA), 1999.
Personal Career Development for Professionals, Beard Books, 2002.
Creating Leaderful Organizations: How to Bring Out Leadership in Everyone, Berrett-Koehler Books (San Francisco, CA), 2003.

Contributor of about eighty articles to professional journals.

SIDELIGHTS: Joseph A. Raelin told *CA:* "I have been working in two domains. First is the development of the field of work-based learning. Work-based learning considers how to make learning arise from work itself. Many of us, not only in academe, but in our work in continuing education, have become conditioned to a classroom model that separates theory from practice, making learning seem impractical or irrelevant. But what if we were to make our work-site an equally acceptable location for learning? In work-based learning, theory is expressly merged with practice, and knowledge is viewed concurrently with experience through reflection on work practices. Hence, it offers managers faced with the relentless pace of pervasive change an opportunity to overcome time pressures by reflecting upon and learning from the artistry of their actions.

"My other interest is in developing a new paradigm for leadership that I call 'leaderful practice.' Leaderful practice constitutes a direct challenge to the conventional view of leadership as 'being out in front.' In the twenty-first-century organization, we need to establish communities where everyone shares the experience of serving as a collaborative and compassionate leader, not sequentially, but concurrently and collectively. In other works, in leaderful practice leaders coexist at the same time and all together.

"My present work is tracing the links between the two research domains by applying and studying how practice-oriented learning methods might be used in leadership development to create a more collective, leaderful, and presumably more democratic form of leadership."

BIOGRAPHICAL AND CRITICAL SOURCES:

BOOKS

Bennett, S. J. and M. H. Snell, *Executive Chess,* New American Library (New York, NY), 1987.

PERIODICALS

Globe and Mail (Toronto, Ontario, Canada), July 4, 1987.
New York Times Book Review, December 14, 1986.

*   *   *

REEVE, Christopher 1952-

PERSONAL: Born September 25, 1952, in New York, NY; son of Franklin D'Olier (a poet and literary scholar) and Barbara (Johnson) Reeve; married Dana Morosini (a singer and actress), 1992; children: (with companion Gae Exton) Matthew, Alexandra, (second marriage) Will. *Education:* Cornell University, B.A., 1974; attended drama division of the Juilliard School.

Christopher Reeve

ADDRESSES: Home—Williamstown, MA; Bedford, NY. *Office*—C.R. Paralysis Foundation, 500 Morris Ave., Springfield, NJ 07081

CAREER: Actor, director, author. Appeared in regional theater, mid-1970s; cast as Ben Harper on the soap opera *Love of Life,* 1974-76; made first Broadway appearance with Katharine Hepburn in *A Matter of Gravity,* 1976. Movies and television films include *Gray Lady Down,* Universal Pictures, 1977; *Superman: The Movie,* Warner Bros., 1978; *Superman II,* Warner Bros., 1980; *Somewhere in Time,* Universal Pictures, 1980; *Monsignor,* 20th Century-Fox, 1982; *Deathtrap,* Warner Bros., 1982; *Superman III,* Warner Bros., 1983; *Bostonians,* 1984; *The Aviator,* United Artists, 1985; *Anna Karenina,* 1985; *Street Smart,* Cannon Films, 1987; *Superman IV: The Quest for Peace,* Warner Bros., 1987; *Switching Channels,* 1988; *Great Escape II: The Untold Story,* 1988; *The Rose and the Jackal,* 1990; *Bump in the Night,* RHI Entertainment, 1991; *Death Dreams,* ABC Video Enterprises, 1991; *Noises Off . . . ,* Touchstone Pictures, 1992; *Mortal Sins,* 1992; *Nightmare in the Daylight,* Saban/Scherick Productions, 1992; *Morning Glory,* Academy Entertainment, 1993; *The Sea Wolf,* Turner Pictures, 1993; *Re-*

mains of the Day, Columbia Pictures, 1993; *Speechless,* MGM, 1994; *Village of the Damned,* Universal Pictures, 1995; *Above Suspicion,* HBO, 1995; *Black Fox,* 1995; *Black Fox: The Price of Peace,* 1995; *Black Fox: Good Men and Bad,* 1995; *Nine,* 1996; *A Step toward Tomorrow,* 1996; and *Rear Window,* ABC, 1999. Also directed the television movie *In the Gloaming,* HBO, 1997. Notable television guest appearances include *The Muppet Show,* 1979, *Tales from the Crypt,* 1989, *Carol and Company,* 1990, *Road to Avonlea,* 1990, *The Carol Burnett Show,* 1991, *Frasier,* 1993, *The Unpleasant World of Penn and Teller,* 1994, and *Inside the Actors Studio,* 1994. Christopher Reeve Paralysis Foundation, chairman of the board, 1999—. Member of board of directors, Williamstown Theatre Festival, World T.E.A.M. Sports, TechHealth, and LIFE (Leaders in Furthering Education).

MEMBER: Creative Coalition (founder and co-president), National Organization on Disability (vice chairman), Funding First (member of executive committee).

AWARDS, HONORS: Special Obie Award and Walter Briehl Human Rights Foundation Award, both 1988; Grammy Award, 1998, for recording of *Still Me,* and Grammy Award nomination, 2003, for recording of *Nothing Is Impossible: Reflections on a New Life;* Golden Globe Award and Screen Actors Guild Award for Best Actor in a Television Movie or Miniseries, both 1999, both for *Rear Window.*

WRITINGS:

Still Me, Random House (New York, NY), 1998.
Nothing Is Impossible: Reflections on a New Life, Random House (New York, NY), 2002.

RECORDINGS

(Narrator) *Still Me* (recording), Simon & Schuster Audio (New York, NY), 1998.
(Narrator) *Nothing Is Impossible: Reflections on a New Life* (recording), Simon & Schuster Audio (New York, NY), 2002.

Also author of the story treatment for *Superman IV: The Quest for Peace,* 1987.

SIDELIGHTS: Actor Christopher Reeve, best known for his portrayal of the comic-book hero Superman in several films of the same name, became the focus of sympathetic media attention when a fall from his horse left him a quadriplegic. Reeve detailed his experiences in the 1998 memoir *Still Me.*

Reeve was born on September 25, 1952, in New York City to Franklin D'Olier Reeve and Barbara Johnson. When his parents divorced when he was four years old, Reeve moved with his younger brother Benjamin and his mother to Princeton, New Jersey. There Barbara met and married Tristam Johnson. As a child, Reeve spent time living with both parents. He went to public school for a short time before being enrolled at Princeton Day School, a private institution. By the time Reeve was eight years old, he began appearing in school plays and showed an affinity for music that led his parents to arrange piano lessons for him. Reeve also became involved in Princeton's professional theater, the McCarter Theater, where he would take any part available in his spare time. Feeling that he had lost his parents following their divorce, the one stable place in Reeve's life became the theater. When Reeve was nine years old, the McCarter Theater cast him in a Gilbert and Sullivan operetta.

Reeve continued to land parts in plays and at age fifteen received a summer apprenticeship to the Williamstown Theater Festival in Williamstown, Massachusetts. By the time Reeve hit his sixteenth birthday, he signed on with an agent. Following high school Reeve attended Cornell University, where he studied music and English but remained interested in theater. After completing his undergraduate studies at Cornell in the fall of 1974, Reeve was offered the chance to attend New York's Juilliard School under special circumstances. There he met comedian Robin Williams. The two became good friends and made a pact that if either made it in show business, they would help each other in a crisis. During Reeve's stay at Juilliard, he received further tutelage from John Houseman. After successful performances at London's Old Vic and the Comedie Francaise, Reeve returned stateside, where his first role in a television soap opera, *Love of Life,* led to a 1976 Broadway debut in *A Matter of Gravity,* in which he again received good notices playing opposite Katharine Hepburn.

In 1977, Reeve was offered an opportunity to audition for the role of Superman. He initially thought the role so silly, so beneath theater, he almost passed on the tryout. Reeve was chosen from a pool of over 200 hopefuls to play Superman. To get himself ready for the role once he was cast, Reeve entered a fitness program to whip himself into requisite shape. Reeve's charming humility breathed life into the comic book hero and his name became synonymous with Superman. The success of *Superman* resulted in three popular sequels, and Reeve appeared in seventeen other feature films. His performances in Merchant-Ivory's *Remains of the Day,* Sidney Lumet's *Deathtrap, Street Smart* with Morgan Freeman, and Broadway outings in Lanford Wilson's *Fifth of July* and *The Marriage of Figaro* illustrated his versatility to take on any role and make it his own.

Reeve's love of physical and artistic accomplishments led him to host numerous documentaries and television specials related to two of his passions, sailing and aviation. Reeve's love of sports included sailing, flying, skiing, scuba diving, and competitive horseback riding. Following the first *Superman* film, Reeve celebrated by sailing from Connecticut to Bermuda. Reeve also flew his own plane solo twice across the Atlantic. He had a great love of riding and owned a number of horses, including a twelve-year-old chestnut thoroughbred named Eastern Express. On Saturday, May 27th, 1995, Reeve was set to compete in the spring horse trials of the Commonwealth Dressage and Combined Training Association—a three-day event held on 200 sparsely wooded acres of the Commonwealth Park equestrian facility in Culpepper, Virginia.

During the event, Reeve steered Eastern Express toward a zigzagged, three-foot-high rail jump, the third of seventeen jumps they were to maneuver on the two-mile course. As Reeve and Eastern Express came to the jump, the horse suddenly stopped. Reeve had not anticipated the sudden halt, which threw him over the horse's body. Hitting his head on the rail fence, he landed on his forehead. Despite his safety equipment, the fall caused multiple fractures of the first and second cervical vertebrae and left him unable to move his limbs or to breathe without the use of a respirator. Many who had worked with him on Broadway or in films—including Katharine Hepburn, Jane Seymour, Margot Kidder, and Robin Williams—came forward publicly to show their support for Reeve.

When Reeve first awoke in the hospital after the accident and was told that he was a quadriplegic, he contemplated suicide. However, after seeing the faces of his wife and family, he reconsidered the alternatives and decided that even though his body must remain stationary, his mind did not share the same fate. Determined to help his own cause and that of 250,000 other paralyzed people in the United States, Reeve launched a one-man publicity and lobbying campaign that garnered impressive results. In 1999, Reeve became chairman of the board of the Christopher Reeve Paralysis Foundation (CRPF). The foundation, "a national, non-profit organization, supports research to develop effective treatments and a cure for paralysis caused by spinal cord injury and other central nervous system disorders. CRPF also allocates a portion of its resources to grants that improve the quality of life for people with disabilities," according to a statement posted at the organization's Web site. Since its inception, the CRPF has given some $30 million in research grants to neuroscientists.

In his autobiography *Still Me,* Reeve recollects his life prior to the riding accident, and writes of that fateful day in great detail. *Still Me* chronicles his long, difficult road to a semblance of recovery. A glimpse into his daily life, with its many indignities, is also matter-of-factly chronicled. More poignantly, Reeve also writes with clarity about the mental challenges and realizations that quadriplegia brings to its victims. "It's always a shock in the morning when you wake up and realize where you are," Reeve explained in the first chapter. "You think: This can't be my life: There's been a mistake."

Reviews of *Still Me* were positive. A reviewer in *Publishers Weekly* called it an "outspoken, wise and tremendously moving" work. In *Entertainment Weekly,* a contributor termed *Still Me* an "unflinching, compelling memoir," and declared that "Reeve's autobiography is distinguished not only by the dignified candor with which he describes his utterly changed world—that of a rich and famous movie star whose affluence and celebrity cannot buy the ability to hug his wife and three children—but also by his emotional directness." The magazine's reviewer found fault only with the title, deeming it "one of those plucky celeb-memoir titles . . . that [demean] the integrity of the text."

Reeve picks up his story in the memoir *Nothing Is Impossible: Reflections on a New Life,* focusing on the rehabilitation efforts he has been undergoing since the accident. Reeve works with Dr. John McDonald of the

Washington University School of Medicine, who believes that "electrical muscle stimulation combined with repetitive motion exercises might regenerate nervous-system cells," as Galina Espinoza noted in *People*. These efforts have resulted in Reeve regaining some movement in his feet and hands, feelings of pressure and of hot and cold, and the ability to move about in a pool. While *Nothing Is Impossible* recounts Reeve's experiences, "the focus of the book is the potential for all of us to transcend our limitations, both internal and external, and not just to accept difficulties and problems but to beat them," Maryam Naeem wrote in the *Student British Medical Journal*. Reviewing the audio edition of the book, in which Reeve himself reads the full text, the critic for *Publishers Weekly* praised it as "a uniquely powerful audio message of hope."

In March of 2003 Reeve underwent experimental surgery meant to prepare him for breathing independently of his ventilator. The surgeons inserted "four tiny electrodes in Reeve's diaphragm muscle and wired them to an external battery pack, which stimulates the muscle and sends air to the lungs," Joan Raymond explained in *Newsweek*. Reeve is now able to breathe on his own for some fifteen minutes every hour; in time, it is hoped that he will be freed from the ventilator entirely. Raymond wrote: "When doctors first removed the whooshing, hissing ventilator, [Reeve] found himself astonished by the simplest thing imaginable. 'All you could hear was me breathing. I haven't heard that sound since May 1995.'"

BIOGRAPHICAL AND CRITICAL SOURCES:

BOOKS

Encyclopedia of World Biography Supplement, Gale (Detroit, MI), 1998.
Newsmakers 1997, Gale (Detroit, MI), 1997.
Nickson, Chris, *Superhero: A Biography of Christopher Reeve,* St. Martin's (New York, NY), 1998.

PERIODICALS

Accent on Living, December, 1996, p. 30.
Booklist, July, 2002, review of *Nothing Is Impossible: Reflections on a New Life,* p. 1799.
Chicago Tribune, April 13, 1993; June 3, 1996.
Detroit Free Press, April 18, 1997, pp. D1, D7.
Entertainment Weekly, May 8, 1998, p. 66; June 2, 2000, Clarissa Cruz, "After the Fall: Ex-Superman Christopher Reeve Was Thrown from His Horse and Paralyzed Five Years Ago," p. 84.
Europe Intelligence Wire, March 13, 2003, "Reeve Undergoes Surgery to Recover Independent Breathing Abilities."
Good Housekeeping, August, 1997.
Kindred Spirit, spring, 2003, "Superman Improvement," p. 7.
Ladies Home Journal, April, 1996, p. 131.
Library Journal, February 1, 2003, Gordon Blackwell, review of audio edition of *Nothing Is Impossible,* p. 134.
McCall's, September, 1987; January, 1991.
Newsweek, April 21, 1997, p. 78; March 24, 2003, Joan Raymond, "Now for a Breath of Fresh Air," p. 67.
New York Times, April 11, 1996, p. C1; April 30, 1998, pp. E1, E4.
People, August 10, 1987, p. 8; August 7, 1995, p. 55; December 30, 1996; April 21, 1997, p. 19; September 23, 2002, Galina Espinoza, "Whispers of Hope: Lifting a Finger; Feeling a Son's Touch: For Christopher Reeve, Seemingly Simple Moments Add Up to a Medical Marvel," p. 78; March 31, 2003, "One Breath at a Time: An Experimental Procedure May Help Christopher Reeve Stay Off His Ventilator," p. 71.
Publishers Weekly, May 4, 1998, p. 200; November 4, 2002, review of *Nothing Is Impossible,* p. 25.
Saturday Evening Post, May-June, 2003, p. 14.
Student British Medical Journal, February, 2003, Maryam Naeem, review of *Nothing Is Impossible,* p. 39.
Time, August 26, 1996, pp. 40-52.

ONLINE

Christopher Reeve Paralysis Foundation Web site, http://www.apacure.com/ (April 28, 2003).

*   *   *

REEVE, F(ranklin) D('Olier) 1928-

PERSONAL: Born September 18, 1928, in Philadelphia, PA; son of Richard and Anne Reeve; married first wife Barbara (divorced, c. 1956); married Laura Stevenson, December 22, 1997; children: Christopher,

Benjamin, Alison, Brock, Mark, Katharine, Margaret. *Education:* Princeton University, A.B., 1950; Columbia University, Ph.D., 1958.

ADDRESSES: Home—P.O. Box 14, Wilmington, VT 05363. *E-mail*—lcsfdr@sover.net.

CAREER: Worked as longshoreman and truck driver; Columbia University, New York, NY, began as instructor, became assistant professor of Slavic languages, 1952-61; Wesleyan University, Middletown, CT, professor of Russian, 1962-66, professor of letters, 1968-2002, professor emeritus, 2002—. Exchange professor in the former U.S.S.R., 1961; visiting professor at Oxford University, 1964, Connecticut College, 1970, Yale University, beginning 1972, Columbia University, 1988, and Marlboro College, 1999. Pettee Memorial Library, member of board of trustees. *Exhibitions:* Exhibits include Poem Paintings at the Donnell Library in New York, 1985, and Via Dolorosa (poems; carbon and pencil drawings by Richard A. Clark) at Moonbrook Gallery, Rutland, VT, 1995.

AWARDS, HONORS: Ford Foundation Fellowship; literature award from American Academy-National Institute, 1970; PEN Syndicated Fiction Award, 1984 and 1986; Golden Rose Award, New England Poetry Society.

WRITINGS:

POETRY

The Stone Island: Six Poems, Salamander Press (London, England), 1964.
In the Silent Stones, Morrow (New York, NY), 1968.
The Blue Cat, Farrar, Straus & Giroux (New York, NY), 1972.
Concrete Music, Pyncheon House, 1992.
The Moon and Other Failures, Michigan State University Press (East Lansing, MI), 1999.
A World You Haven't Seen, Rattapallax Press (New York, NY), 2001.
The Urban Stampede, Michigan State University Press (East Landing, MI), 2002.
The Blue Boat on the St. Anne, Story Line Press (Ashland, OR), 2003.

FICTION

The Red Machines, Morrow (New York, NY), 1968, Azul Editions (Falls Church, VA), 1999.
Just over the Border, Morrow (New York, NY), 1969.
The Brother, Farrar, Straus & Giroux (New York, NY), 1971.
White Colors, Farrar, Straus & Giroux (New York, NY), 1973.
The White Swans, Ellis, 1978.
A Few Rounds of Old Maid, Azul Editions (Falls Church, VA), 1995.

CRITICISM

Aleksandr Blok: Between Image and Idea, Columbia University Press (New York, NY), 1962.
Robert Frost in Russia, Little, Brown (Boston, MA), 1964, reprinted, Zephyr Press, 2001.
On Some Scientific Concepts in Russian Poetry at the Turn of the Century, CAS, 1966.
The Russian Novel, McGraw-Hill (New York, NY), 1966.
The White Monk: An Essay on Dostoevsky and Melville, Vanderbilt University Press (Nashville, TN), 1989.

TRANSLATIONS

I. S. Turgenev, *Five Short Novels,* Bantam Books (New York, NY), 1961.
Anthology of Russian Plays, Vintage (New York, NY), Volume I, 1961, published as *Nineteenth-Century Russian Plays,* Norton (New York, NY), 1973, Volume II, 1963, published as *Twentieth-Century Russian Plays,* Norton (New York, NY), 1973.
Great Soviet Short Stories, Dell (New York, NY), 1963.
Contemporary Russian Drama, Pegasus (Fairview, NC), 1968.
A. I. Solzhenitsyn, *Nobel Lecture,* Farrar, Straus & Giroux (New York, NY), 1972.
(With W. J. Smith) Andre Voznesensky, *An Arrow in the Wall* (poetry), Holt (New York, NY), 1987.
Bella Akhmadulina, *The Garden* (poetry), Henry Holt (New York, NY), 1990.
Alexander Borshchagovsky, *The King and the Fool,* 2001.

Translator of introduction to *Six Short Stories by Tolstoy,* Dell (New York, NY), 1963; translator of *The Trouble with Reason,* a four-act comedy in verse by A. S. Griboyedov, published in *The Portable Nineteenth-Century Russian Reader,* edited by G. Gibian, Viking-Penguin (New York, NY), 1993.

PLAYS

The Three-Sided Cube, produced in Middletown, CT, and New London, CT, 1972.
Glass House (staged reading), performed in Williamstown, VA, 1980.
Electricity (staged reading), performed in New York, NY, 1981.
The Leak, produced at Vermont Theater Works, 1986.
Painted Apples, Playwrights & Players, 1995.

OTHER

(Editor, with Jay Meek) *After the Storm,* Maisonneuve Press (University Park, MD), 1992.
(Editor) *Winged Spirits,* with paintings by Jean Zaleski, Bayeux Arts (New York, NY), 1995.

Author of oratorios, including *Alycone* (modern oratorio for narrator, instruments, and voices), music by Thomas L. Read, performed in London, England, at Barbican Theater, 1998; and *The Urban Stampede* (modern oratorio for narrator, instruments, and voices), music by Andrew Gant, performed in London, England, at Barbican Theater, 2000.

Work represented in anthologies, including *September 11, 2001: American Writers Respond.* Contributor of poems, stories, articles, essays, and reviews to numerous periodicals, including *American Poetry Review, Atlantic, Hudson Review, Kenyon Review, Modern Poetry Studies, Nation, New Yorker, Poetry, Slavic Review,* and *Sewanee Review.* Founding editor of *Poetry Review,* 1982-84; member of advisory board, *Marlboro Review.*

WORK IN PROGRESS: The Puzzle Master, a modern oratorio, with music by Eric Chasalow; *My Sister Life, Man of Genius,* and *Rules of the Game,* works of fiction; *The Inconstant Translation,* a critical work.

SIDELIGHTS: F. D. Reeve told *CA:* "More and more I admire our bold, outspoken painters and poets—artists who stand up against our repressive government and cry for justice for all who suffer poverty and ethnic or racial humiliation. I admire the writer whose work presents society with images of freedom and whose life exemplifies awareness of moral obligation. And I have a grand time with everyone who laughs and makes us laugh, even ennobling us on our ridiculous hobby-horses."

*   *   *

RICHARDS, Hubert J. 1921-

PERSONAL: Born December 25, 1921, in Weilderstadt, Germany; son of Richard (a master butcher) and Bertha (a homemaker; maiden name, Lung) Richards; married Clare Milward (a teacher), December 22, 1975; children: Pedro and Blanca (adopted twins from Colombia). *Ethnicity:* "British." *Education:* Gregorian University, Rome, Italy, L.Th., 1946; Biblical Institute, Rome, L.S.S., 1949. *Religion:* Roman Catholic.

ADDRESSES: Home—59 Park Lane, Norwich NR2 3EF, England.

CAREER: Ordained Roman Catholic priest for Westminster diocese, 1946; St. Edmund's College, Ware, England, lecturer in scripture, 1949-65; Corpus Christi College, London, England, principal, 1965-72; research fellow at St. Edmund's House, Cambridge University, Cambridge, England, at Ecole Biblique, Jerusalem, Israel, and at King's College, University of London, London, England, between 1973 and 1975; released from priestly vows, 1975; University of East Anglia, Norwich, England, lecturer in religious studies, 1975-87; part-time lecturer, reviewer, publisher's editor, and author, 1987—. Lecturer in England, the United States, Canada, New Zealand, and Scandinavia on the biblical and theological problems facing teachers of religious education; broadcaster for British Broadcasting Corp. and Associated Television.

WRITINGS:

God Speaks to Us, Darton, Longman & Todd (London, England), 1963.

RICHARDS

(With Peter De Rosa) *Christ in Our World,* Chapman (London, England), 1965.

What the Spirit Says to the Churches, Chapman (London, England), 1965, P. J. Kennedy (New York, NY), 1966.

An ABC of the Bible, Chapman (London, England), 1967.

(Editor) *Forty Gospel Songs,* Chapman (London, England), 1969.

Ten Gospel Songs, Chapman (London, England), 1969.

Heart of a Rose (songs), Mayhew (Grand Rapids, MI), 1972.

The First Christmas: What Really Happened?, Fontana (London, England), 1973, 3rd edition, Twenty-Third Publications (Mystic, CT), 1986.

The Miracles of Jesus: What Really Happened?, Fontana (London, England), 1974, 3rd edition, Twenty-Third Publications (Mystic, CT), 1986.

The First Easter: What Really Happened?, Fontana (London, England), 1975, 3rd edition, Twenty-Third Publications (Mystic, CT), 1986.

St. Paul and His Epistles, Darton, Longman & Todd (London, England), 1979, published as *Reading Paul Today,* John Knox (Atlanta, GA), 1980, 2nd edition, St. Paul's Public, 1989.

Death and After: What Will Really Happen?, Fount (London, England), 1980, 3rd edition, Twenty-Third Publications (Mystic, CT), 1987.

Pilgrim to the Holy Land, McCrimmon, 1982, 4th edition, 1998.

The Gospel in Song, Mayhew (Grand Rapids, MI), 1983.

A Way of the Cross for Children, McCrimmon, 1986, 2nd edition, 1989.

A Carol Service for Children, McCrimmon, 1986.

The Our Father for Children, McCrimmon, 1987.

The Hail Mary for Children, McCrimmon, 1987.

The Rosary for Children, McCrimmon, 1988.

The Ten Commandments for Children, McCrimmon, 1988.

The Beatitudes for Children, McCrimmon, 1988.

The Parables for Children, McCrimmon, 1988.

The Sacraments for Children, McCrimmon, 1988.

Focus on the Bible, Mayhew (Grand Rapids, MI), 1989.

Some Parables for Children, McCrimmon, 1990.

The "I Confess" for Children, McCrimmon, 1990.

The Passover Meal, McCrimmon, 1990.

A Maundy Service for Children, McCrimmon, 1990.

The Mass for Children, McCrimmon, 1990.

The Creed for Children, McCrimmon, 1990.

The Gospel According to St. Paul, Liturgical Press (Collegeville, MN), 1991.

God's Diary, Twenty-Third Publications (Mystic, CT), 1991.

What Jesus Taught, Liturgical Press (Collegeville, MN), 1991.

What Christians Believe, Liturgical Press (Collegeville, MN), 1991.

Some Christian Prayers, Liturgical Press (Collegeville, MN), 1991.

Christus Natus Est, Mayhew (Grand Rapids, MI), 1992.

Tenebrae, Mayhew (Grand Rapids, MI), 1994.

Worship Anthology for Advent and Christmas, Mayhew (Grand Rapids, MI), 1994.

Worship Anthology for Lent and Easter, Mayhew (Grand Rapids, MI), 1994.

Pilgrim to Rome, McCrimmon, 1994.

Worship Anthology on the Beatitudes, Mayhew (Grand Rapids, MI), 1995.

Worship Anthology on the Creed, Mayhew (Grand Rapids, MI), 1995.

Processional Songs, Mayhew (Grand Rapids, MI), 1995.

Worship Anthology for Christian Festivals and Holydays, Mayhew (Grand Rapids, MI), 1997.

Quips and Quotes, Mayhew (Grand Rapids, MI), 1997.

Philosophy of Religion: A Beginner's Guide, Heinemann (Exeter, NH), 1998, 2nd edition, 2000.

An Anthology for the Church Year, Mayhew (Grand Rapids, MI), 1998.

Who's Who and What's What in the Bible, Mayhew (Grand Rapids, MI), 1999.

The Bible: What Does It Really Say?, Mayhew (Grand Rapids, MI), 1999.

Jesus: Who Did He Think He Was?, Mayhew (Grand Rapids, MI), 2000.

(With wife, Clare Richards) *Advent Adventures,* Mayhew (Grand Rapids, MI), 2000.

(With Clare Richards) *Lenten Journey,* Mayhew (Grand Rapids, MI), 2000.

Plain English Bible, Mayhew (Grand Rapids, MI), 2001.

More Quips and Quotes, Mayhew (Grand Rapids, MI), 2001.

1600 Quips and Quotes, Mayhew (Grand Rapids, MI), 2003.

WORK IN PROGRESS: Updating *Pilgrim to Rome,* retitled *Rome, for Pilgrims and Others: A Practical Guide.*

SIDELIGHTS: Hubert J. Richards once told *CA:*"My overwhelming interest at the moment is in the cultural relativity of *all* theological statements, including biblical ones. This has inevitably led me to ask awkward questions about the relationship between Christianity and other world religions. Have Christian claims been expressed too absolutely? If they have, can a 'relativized' Christianity survive? If they have not, can other religions survive?

"Our adoption of twin children from South America in 1980 has not made these questions less urgent, but more so. What do Christian faith statements actually mean? What is their cash value? Could you explain them faithfully in a way a child could understand? To teach children about religion is a far more demanding task than writing books of theology. Children, unlike theological readers, cannot be fooled."

* * *

RODRIGUEZ, Junius P. 1957-

PERSONAL: Born June 26, 1957, in Thibodaux, LA; son of Junius P., Sr. (a mechanic) and Mildred (a homemaker; maiden name, Degruise) Rodriguez. *Ethnicity:* "White." *Education:* Nicholls State University, B.A., 1979; Louisiana State University, M.A., 1987; Auburn University, Ph.D., 1992. *Politics:* Democrat. *Religion:* Roman Catholic. *Hobbies and other interests:* Travel, community service.

ADDRESSES: Home—707 South Vennum St., Eureka, IL 61530. *Office*—Eureka College, 300 College Ave., Eureka, IL 61530; fax: 309-467-6386. *E-mail*—jrodrig@eureka.edu.

CAREER: High school teacher in Mathews, LA, 1979-88; Eureka College, Eureka, IL, associate professor, 1992—. Member of parish council, Lafourche Parish, LA, 1980-84.

MEMBER: Southern Historical Association, Louisiana Historical Association.

AWARDS, HONORS: Helen Cleaver Distinguished Teaching Award, 1997.

WRITINGS:

(General editor) *The Historical Encyclopedia of World Slavery,* two volumes, American Bibliographical Center-Clio Press (Santa Barbara, CA), 1997.
The Chronology of World Slavery, American Bibliographical Center-Clio Press (Santa Barbara, CA), 1999.
The Louisiana Purchase: A Historical and Geographical Encyclopedia, American Bibliographical Center-Clio Press (Santa Barbara, CA), 2002.

WORK IN PROGRESS: An essay collection on abolitionists and higher education; research on slave revolts.

* * *

ROONEY, Andrew A(itken) 1919-

PERSONAL: Born January 14, 1919, in Albany, NY; son of Walter Scott and Ellinor (Reynolds) Rooney; married Marguerite Howard (a teacher), March 21, 1942; children: Ellen, Martha, Emily, Brian. *Education:* Attended Albany Academy and Colgate University, 1942. *Politics:* "Vacillating."

ADDRESSES: Office—CBS News, 524 West 57th St., New York, NY 10019. *Agent*—Public Affairs Publications, 250 West 57th St., Suite 1321, New York, NY 10107.

CAREER: Writer, primarily for television. Worked for Metro-Goldwyn-Mayer (MGM), Hollywood, CA, one year; freelance magazine writer, 1947-49; wrote material for Arthur Godfrey, 1949-55, Sam Levenson, Herb Shriner, Victor Borge, and for "Twentieth Century," and "Seven Lively Arts"; Columbia Broadcasting System (CBS) Inc., New York, NY, writer for CBS Radio's "The Garry Moore Show," 1959-65, writer and producer of television essays, documentaries, and specials for CBS News, 1962-70; worked for public television, 1970-71, and for American Broadcasting Companies, Inc. (ABC-TV), 1971-72; CBS News, writer, producer, and narrator of television essays, documentaries, and specials, 1972—, regular commentator on CBS News program *60 Minutes,* 1978—. *Military service:* U.S. Army, 1942-45, reporter for *Stars and Stripes;* became sergeant; received Air Medal and Bronze Star.

Andrew A. Rooney

The Fortunes of War: Four Great Battles of World War II, Little, Brown (Boston, MA), 1962.

A Few Minutes with Andy Rooney (includes "In Praise of New York City," "Mr. Rooney Goes to Washington," "Mr. Rooney Goes to Dinner," "Mr. Rooney Goes to Work," and "An Essay on War"), Atheneum (New York, NY), 1981.

And More by Andy Rooney (essays), Atheneum (New York, NY), 1982.

Pieces of My Mind, Atheneum (New York, NY), 1984.

The Most of Andy Rooney, Macmillan (New York, NY), 1986.

Word for Word, Putnam (New York, NY), 1986.

Not That You Asked . . . , Random House (New York, NY), 1989.

Sweet and Sour, Putnam (New York, NY), 1992.

My War, Times Books (New York, NY), 1995.

Sincerely, Andy Rooney, Public Affairs (New York, NY), 1999.

Common Nonsense, Public Affairs (New York, NY), 2002.

Years of Minutes, Public Affairs (New York, NY), 2003.

AWARDS, HONORS: Writers Guild of America Award for best television documentary, 1966, for "The Great Love Affair," 1968, for "Black History: Lost, Stolen, or Strayed," 1971, for "An Essay on War," 1975, for "Mr. Rooney Goes to Washington," 1976, for "Mr. Rooney Goes to Dinner," and 1979, for "Happiness: The Elusive Pursuit"; George Foster Peabody Award, University of Georgia, 1975, for "Mr. Rooney Goes to Washington"; Emmy Award, 1978, for "Who Owns What in America," and 1981 and 1982, for "A Few Minutes with Andy Rooney" on *60 Minutes.*

WRITINGS:

(With Oram C. Hutton) *Air Gunner,* Farrar & Rinehart (New York, NY), 1944.

(With Oram C. Hutton) *The Story of the "Stars and Stripes,"* Farrar & Rinehart (New York, NY), 1946.

(With Oram C. Hutton) *Conquerors' Peace: A Report to the American Stockholders,* Doubleday (New York, NY), 1947.

(Editor and author of notes and comment, with Dickson Hartwell) *Off the Record: The Best Stories of Foreign Correspondents,* collected by Overseas Press Club of America, Doubleday (New York, NY), 1952.

Author of television essays, documentaries, and specials for CBS-TV, including "An Essay on Doors"; "An Essay on Bridges"; (with Richard Ellison) "The Great Love Affair," broadcast 1966; "Hotels," broadcast June 28, 1966; "An Essay on Women," broadcast 1967; (with Perry Wolff) "Black History: Lost, Stolen, or Strayed," broadcast 1968; "In Praise of New York City," broadcast February 1, 1974; "Mr. Rooney Goes to Washington," broadcast January 26, 1975; "Mr. Rooney Goes to Dinner," broadcast April 20, 1976; "Mr. Rooney Goes to Work," broadcast July 5, 1977. Author of documentary "An Essay on War," broadcast by WNET-TV, 1971, as part of "The Great American Dream Machine" series. Coauthor of filmscript based on *The Story of the "Stars and Stripes,"* purchased by MGM. Writer, under name Andy Rooney, of column syndicated to over 250 newspapers by Tribune Co. Syndicate, 1979—. Contributor to periodicals.

SIDELIGHTS: Andrew A. Rooney, known to his many fans as "Andy," is "the homespun Homer whose celebrations of the commonplace and jeremiads against the degenerating twentieth century are cheered by forty million viewers of one of the nation's top-rated TV shows," wrote Elizabeth Peer in *Newsweek.* A longtime writer and producer for the Columbia Broadcasting System (CBS), Rooney became a regular essayist on the CBS newsmagazine *60 Minutes* in 1978 and has evolved into "a one-man institution," noted Anne Chamberlin in the *Washington Post Book World.* His observations on such everyday items as chairs, doors, jeans, and soap have not only appeared on television but also in a twice-weekly column syndicated to over 200 newspapers across the country. Moreover, many of these essays have been compiled into best-selling books. The multimedia success of these wry, down-to-earth editorials, stated Bruce Henstell in the *Los Angeles Times Book Review,* has made Rooney "the most listened-to curmudgeon in recent times."

Admitting in the *Detroit News* that it "makes me mad when people come up to me and don't know I lived before 1979," Rooney has been a writer all his working life. Rooney told *CA:* "I started dreaming of being a writer when I was about twelve. In college I did all the usual things and was editor of a literary-humor magazine." Rooney became a reporter for the armed forces' *Stars and Stripes* after being drafted into the army in 1941. "The army, in its ignorance, thought I knew something about being a newspaperman," Rooney told *CA.* "I didn't but I found out in three years with the army paper." He and colleague Oram C. "Bud" Hutton coauthored two books while serving their country during World War II and one after being discharged. *Air Gunner,* described by the late Edmund Wilson in the *New Yorker* as "an excellent piece of reporting," tells about the American boys who manned the guns on the flying fortresses over Europe, and *The Story of the "Stars and Stripes,"* published in 1946, discusses the development of the GI newspaper and its staff over the course of World War II. *Conquerors' Peace* reports the findings of a post-war tour of Europe by Rooney and Hutton, who not only examined the landscape, the American cemeteries, and the displaced persons problem, but also probed into the inhabitants' feelings about the war and the occupation troops.

Rooney's memories of World War II would also serve as the subject of a later book, the memoir *My War,* published in 1995. Recalling the war in Europe from the vantage of a wet-behind-the-ears reporter, Rooney recounts witnessing daylight bombing raids over Germany, troops landing on the beaches of Normandy, and the horrific remains of Nazi concentration camps discovered shortly before the war's end in 1945. While critics praised Rooney's readable narrative, some took exception to his efforts to construe the motives and strategies of military leaders such as generals Dwight

Eisenhower and George Patton. As Louis D. Rubin, Jr. commented in the *Washington Post Book World,* "Rooney's talents as an interpreter, as distinguished from a chronicler, of warfare are definitely on the flimsy side." However, John McDonough praised *My War* in his review for Chicago's *Tribune Books,* noting that "Rooney writes about the war he saw with wit, wisdom and a down-to-earth lack of sentimentality." The journalist recalls the opinions and emotions of his younger years candidly; although he had mixed feelings about serving in a foreign war—and had contemplated evading the draft as a conscientious objector—his skepticism about the reasons why Americans were fighting and dying overseas ended upon viewing the newly discovered Buchenwald concentration camp in April of 1945. As he wrote in *My War:* "I . . . stared in embarrassed silence, thinking about the doubts I'd had in college. I was ashamed of myself for ever having considered refusing to serve in the army. For the first time I knew for certain that any peace is not better than any war."

After being discharged from the army in August, 1945, Rooney went to Hollywood and cowrote the filmscript of *The Story of the "Stars and Stripes"* for Metro-Goldwyn-Mayer. After finishing the script as well as other assignments with Hutton, he became a freelance writer, publishing pieces in *Reader's Digest, Look, Life, Esquire,* and other magazines. But after spending six weeks on an article for *Harper's* and getting $350 for it, "I realized I was not going to make it as a magazine writer," Rooney told a *Time* reporter. From 1949 to 1955 Rooney was Arthur Godfrey's radio and television writer, "at a more comfortable $625 a week," according to the writer for *Time,* and he later crafted clever lines for such personalities as Victor Borge, Sam Levenson, and Herb Shriner.

Rooney began his long affiliation with CBS in 1959, when the network hired him to write for "The Garry Moore Show." "In 1949," Rooney told *CA,* "the freelance magazine-writing business started to seem like the wrong way to make a decent living. I looked for work at CBS News, did a few reports for them on a freelance basis, and ran into Arthur Godfrey on the elevator one day. I went to work for him the following Monday and it was a good thing because by then I needed the money again." Three years later, he teamed up with veteran newsman Harry Reasoner for the first in a series of television essays that focused mainly on such seemingly mundane subjects as bridges, doors, and hotels. During their six-year collaboration from 1962 to 1968, Rooney wrote the words and served as producer of the broadcasts, and Reasoner presented the reports on camera. Susan Slobojan of the *Detroit News* noted that in these specials, "observing life with both eyes open and tongue planted firmly in cheek became a sort of Rooney trademark." She cited the beginning of "An Essay on Women," produced in 1967, as indicative of his approach in which Rooney offers this disclaimer: "This broadcast was prepared by men, and makes no claim to be fair. Prejudice has saved us a great deal of time in preparation."

But Rooney did not take everything so lightly. In 1970, when CBS wanted to shorten his philosophical half-hour "An Essay on War," Rooney quit the network in protest and transferred to public television at lower pay. He then bought the essay from CBS to air on "The Great American Dream Machine" series, broadcast by New York's WNET-TV. Unable to use Reasoner's voice for his work, Rooney had to read it himself. "It was the only practical thing to do," he explained to *New York*'s Lewis Grossberger. "We didn't have a star on the 'Dream Machine.' Everybody did their own pieces. So I read it. It wasn't very well read, but the piece was good." Indeed, "An Essay on War" was good enough to win Rooney one of his six Writers Guild of America Awards; perhaps a more important consequence, however, was that it launched him on a career as an on-camera commentator.

Lured back to CBS in 1972, Rooney wrote, produced, and narrated a series of television reports on American life that, like many of his previous essays, "were characterized by the same droll, stubborn sensibility," observed Slobojan. The finest of these reports, according to a *Time* writer, "was probably 'In Praise of New York City,' a journalistic paean that anticipated parts of Woody Allen's 'Manhattan.'" In "Mr. Rooney Goes to Dinner," he examined numerous facets of eating out, noting among other things that a tassel on the menu "can add a couple of dollars per person" to the average bill.

"After traveling across the country and visiting more than a hundred factories and other places of business and after seeing a lot of people leaning on their shovels when they should have been shoveling and then hearing people testify that they don't work hard," he concluded in "Mr. Rooney Goes to Work," "I have still become convinced, to my great surprise, that Ameri-

cans *are* working their tails off." And in the best-known of these reports, "Mr. Rooney Goes to Washington," he wittily surmised that the federal bureaucracy is not "being run by evil people; it's being run by people like you and me. And you know how we have to be watched."

Rooney's reports won several awards and garnered much public attention, but his role at CBS was still somewhat ill-defined. "They have never known exactly what to do with me around here," he told Lewis Grossberger. Rooney felt there was a place for a short essay somewhere around the company, so he requested more air time. The network gave him a chance in 1978 as a summer replacement for the "Point Counterpoint" segment of the CBS newsmagazine *60 Minutes*. The move was so successful that "A Few Minutes with Andy Rooney" became a regular feature of the show that fall, alternating with the mini-debates of Shana Alexander and Jack Kilpatrick. One year later, Shana and Jack were gone for good, the frequency of Rooney's appearances increased, and Rooney's popularity soared. "Audiences began wondering where he'd been all these years," wrote Slobojan.

Since joining *60 Minutes,* Rooney has become a notable media figure. In addition to prompting comparisons with humorists E. B. White, James Thurber, and Art Buchwald, his deadpan delivery and acerbic wit have made him as popular as Mike Wallace and the rest of the *60 Minutes* crew. In addition, he has earned a total of four Emmy Awards in his capacity as commentator. Typically, Rooney dismisses their significance. "Awards are spinach," he told *CA*. "I like to get them but they don't mean anything. Everyone who has worked for very long in broadcasting wins a lot of them whether they're any good or not."

Paradoxically, Rooney's overwhelming success "derives largely from his persona as an ordinary guy," explained Michael Dirda in the *Washington Post Book World*. Described by a *Time* writer as "the Boswell of Stuff" and by CBS colleague Walter Cronkite as "Everyman, articulating all the frustrations with modern life that the rest of us Everymen . . . suffer with silence or mumbled oaths," Rooney told Slobojan he deliberately writes about "subjects of universal interest." "Rooney appreciates such things," noted Lewis Grossberger, "[because] he believes that the mundane is more important than commonly thought. The pencil, for instance, ultimately has a greater effect on our existence, he figures, than, say, the Vietnam war." Carolyn See maintained that Rooney's attention to the commonplace "puts the rest of those '60 Minutes' in perspective: Crooked union bosses may be one thing, but making good vanilla ice cream, or getting strung out on what shampoo to buy—these are the issues that should, and do, preoccupy America."

Rooney has tried not to let fame alter his normal habits. Asked about his attitude toward the giving of autographs, Rooney told *CA:* "I don't give autographs and it makes me feel foolish to be asked. Who'd want my name on a piece of paper? I just tell people 'I don't do that.' They seem to accept it. No one, by the way, ever says they want the autograph for themselves. It's for their wife or their son or their elderly mother."

Though Rooney does not think of himself as a humorist, his wry wit must ultimately be considered part of his appeal. "Rooney's humor is dry," noted Grossberger. "He doesn't do many jokes as such. Instead of 'Ha!' he goes for the 'Huh!'—that grunt of recognition and pleasure evoked when you hit somebody with a homely truth." The preface to *A Few Minutes with Andy Rooney* typifies the Rooney wit. Having expressed an uneasiness over the fact that a book by anyone on a popular television broadcast "will probably sell whether it's any good or not," he deftly admitted: "It wasn't hard to talk me into putting this book together. It is unsatisfactory for a writer to have his words said once and then disappear forever into the air. Seeing our names in print leads to the dream all of us have of immortality. You can't ask more from something than immortality and money next week."

Pieces of My Mind picked up where *And More by Andy Rooney* left off, culling the best of Rooney's essays from his syndicated newspaper columns. A proven formula, the book was warmly embraced by the public and genially reviewed by the press. "Rooney has mastered the art of simple, unassuming declaration," William Howarth asserted in his *Washington Post Book World* review of the collection. Though *Newsweek*'s Charles Leerhsen expressed a growing concern for what he calls Rooney's "intellectual laziness," Sue M. Halpern stated in the *New York Times Book Review* that "Mr. Rooney is not a trenchant analyst or a polished essayist, but to expect this of him is to fail to take his work on its own terms." Indeed, Rooney himself would be the first to agree. Asked by *CA* to comment on Don Hewitt's statement that Rooney is "to

today's television what H. L. Mencken was to newspapering many years ago," Rooney replied: "I like it but it's not true." He added: "Mencken was an intellectual. I'm not."

Word for Word, published in 1986, garnered a similar range of responses. "Those who missed the first three [volumes of Rooney's collected essays] can just take a seat anywhere," a *Time* reviewer advised, adding that "Rooney is always good company." Decrying the insensitivity he suggests Rooney reveals in his columns on bag ladies and homosexuals, Patrick K. Lackey of the *Washington Post* nevertheless praised Rooney's "genius for annoyance." Those critics with the most negative reaction to *Pieces of My Mind* still suggest that it may well be the medium as much as the message that lessens his appeal. "Rooney comes across better on television than he does in his book," Alfred Rushton claimed in the Toronto *Globe and Mail.* "After all, it's hard to translate a raised eyebrow, a snarled decibel or the special effects of a speeded-up camera to the page."

In 1989 Rooney took his business from Putnam to another publishing house after a controversy over Putnam's publication of a book about life after death. According to Edwin McDowell's column for the *New York Times,* Rooney "became so irate that he attacked [Joel Martin and Patricia Romanowski's *We Don't Die: George Anderson's Conversations with the Other Side*] in his syndicated newspaper column as 'irresponsible trash.'" Thus, Rooney's fifth collection of essays, *Not That You Asked Me . . .* was published by Random House in 1989.

Soon afterwards, however, Rooney became embroiled in another controversy that resulted in his brief suspension from *60 Minutes* and, temporarily at least, dampened public affection for him. Rooney was already under fire for a televised comment about homosexuals made in a 1989 year-end report when his comments in the *Advocate,* a magazine dedicated to speaking out for the homosexual community, were perceived as racist. Despite Rooney's denial of the offending remarks and his apology for the comment that had offended gay activists, CBS News president David Burke issued a three-month suspension of Rooney's *60 Minutes* contract.

Rescinded after just three weeks, the suspension nevertheless remained a source of speculation. For some, it was a virtual admission of Rooney's guilt. For Walter

Goodman of the *New York Times*, the suspension was a necessary appeasement of an angry public, whatever the case might actually have been: "By its treatment of Mr. Rooney, CBS is telling the whole nation, not just its black viewers, that television will make no slurs against any minority nor associate itself with anyone who might have made such a slur anywhere at any time, if the minority is of a size to cause it trouble." For still others, the suspension was an untimely mistake. "'There is a feeling that Burke should have at least stalled for time when the controversy broke,'" *Los Angeles Times* writer Jane Hall quoted an unidentified CBS employee as saying, "'[thus] allowing all sides to speak. . . . [Rooney] did not get his day in court.'"

Sincerely, Andy Rooney gathers together letters that Rooney has written to friends, family, enemies, television executives, and the general public over some fifty years. His usual acidic tone is present in what a *Publishers Weekly* reviewer described as "entertaining and witty, but also at times pontificating and arch" correspondence.

Common Nonsense is another collection of Rooney's brief essays, this time assembling some 150 of them on such topics as actor Jimmy Stewart, the beauty of old wooden barns, the lack of courtesy in modern life, the Catholic Church's pronouncements on sex, and the prevailing nature of advertising. Brad Hooper in *Booklist* described Rooney as being "more a humorous than an activist-type essayist, but we need all the humor we can get in this dysfunctional world." A critic for *Publishers Weekly* concluded: "His take on the annoyances and joys of humanity always hits home."

Rooney continues to bring his curmudgeonly brand of humorous commentary to one of America's most popular television shows. Speaking with Greta Van Susteren on her Fox News Channel television program *On the Record*, Rooney explained why he thought he was still such a popular television personality: "I'm very average, you know. I'm not a very special person. It's surprising how normal and everyday I am, and my reaction to things is normal. And I think people sense that. People come up to me on the street and say hello very easily as if—and I'm not a gracious, well-known person. I don't like it very much. . . . I would rather be an observer than to be observed. I'm not comfortable at all being on television. The money's good, but there isn't much else about it that I like."

For a complete interview with Rooney, see *Contemporary Authors New Revision Series*, Volume 9.

BIOGRAPHICAL AND CRITICAL SOURCES:

BOOKS

Rooney, Andrew A., *A Few Minutes with Andy Rooney*, Atheneum (New York, NY), 1981.
Rooney, Andrew A., *My War*, Times Books (New York, NY), 1995.

PERIODICALS

Accent on Living, fall, 1992, "Rooney Forces Us to Think," p. 38.
American History, July, 1995, review of *My War*, p. 54.
America's Intelligence Wire, March 4-6, 2003, Greta Van Susteren, "Interview with CBS News' Andy Rooney."
Booklist, April 15, 1995, Denise Perry Donavin, review of *My War*, p. 1450; October 15, 2002, Brad Hooper, review of *Common Nonsense*, p. 362; November 15, 2003, David Pitt, review of *Years of Minutes*, p. 547.
Detroit Free Press, January 19, 1983.
Detroit News, November 8, 1981.
Forbes, March 25, 1996, p. 30.
Globe and Mail (Toronto, Ontario, Canada), February 21, 1987.
Journalism History, summer, 2000, Michael D. Murray, review of *Sincerely, Andy Rooney*, p. 85.
Los Angeles Times, November 11, 1982; February 9, 1990; March 2, 1990.
Los Angeles Times Book Review, November 29, 1981; April 29, 1990, p. 14; May 20, 1990, p. 14.
Newsweek, December 6, 1982; October 15, 1984, p. 99.
New York, March 17, 1980.
New Yorker, October 21, 1944; February 16, 1946.
New York Times, October 29, 1944; February 17, 1946; May 25, 1947; March 22, 1989; February 13, 1990.
New York Times Book Review, December 19, 1982; October 7, 1984, p. 23, June 18, 1995, Tom Ferrell, review of *My War*, p. 20.

Publishers Weekly, April 17, 1995, review of *My War,* p. 45; November 29, 1999, review of *Sincerely, Andy Rooney,* p. 61; October 21, 2002, review of *Common Nonsense,* p. 62.

Rolling Stone, August 8, 1996, David Wild, "The Andy-Hero: In a Few Minutes, We Learn How Andy Rooney Has Survived 'Dateline,' Molly Ivins and Kurt Cobain," p. 65.

Saturday Review of Literature, February 23, 1946; July 26, 1947.

Television Quarterly, summer, 1996, Arthur Unger, "Andy Rooney of '60 Minutes': 'The Essence of Average?,'" p. 14.

Time, July 11, 1969; July 21, 1980; November 1, 1982; November 3, 1986.

Tribune Books (Chicago, IL), August 6, 1995, p. 3.

TV Guide, December 24, 1983.

Virginia Quarterly Review, spring, 1982.

Washington Post, November 8, 1982; January 5, 1987; February 8, 1990.

Washington Post Book World, December 20, 1981; October 14, 1984, p. 8; January 5, 1987; April 30, 1995, pp. 3, 12.

ONLINE

A Few Minutes with Andy Rooney Web site, http://www.cbsnews.com/ (April 28, 2003).*

*   *   *

ROONEY, Andy
See ROONEY, Andrew A(itken)

*   *   *

ROOT, Phyllis 1949-

PERSONAL: Born February 14, 1949, in Fort Wayne, IN; daughter of John Howard and Esther (Traut) Root; married James Elliot Hansa (a mason); children: Amelia Christin, Ellen Rose. *Ethnicity:* "American." *Education:* Valparaiso University, B.A., 1971. *Hobbies and other interests:* Canoeing, sailing, gardening, reading.

ADDRESSES: Home—3842 Bloomington Ave. S, Minneapolis, MN 55407. *E-mail*—rootx005@tc.umn.edu.

CAREER: Writer. Has worked as architectural drafter, costume seamstress, bicycle repair person, and administrative assistant. Vermont College, instructor in Master in Fine Arts in Writing for Children Program, 2002—.

MEMBER: Society of Children's Book Writers and Illustrators.

AWARDS, HONORS: Children's Books of the Year citation, Child Study Association of America, and Bologna International Children's Book Fair selection, both 1985, both for *Moon Tiger;* Minnesota Picture Book Award, 1997, for *Aunt Nancy and Old Man Trouble; Moon Tiger* and *Soup for Supper* were both Junior Library Guild selections; Best Books of the Year, *School Library Journal,* 1998, for *What Baby Wants;* Top Ten Easy Readers selection, *Booklist,* 2002, for *Mouse Has Fun,* and 2003, for *Mouse Goes Out; Boston Globe-Horn Book* Picture Book Award, 2003, for *Big Momma Makes the World.*

WRITINGS:

Hidden Places, illustrated by Daniel San Souci, Carnival Press (Milwaukee, WI), 1983.

(With Carol A. Marron) *Gretchen's Grandma,* illustrated by Deborah K. Ray, Carnival Press (Milwaukee, WI), 1983.

(With Carol A. Marron) *Just One of the Family,* illustrated by George Karn, Carnival Press (Milwaukee, WI), 1984.

(With Carol A. Marron) *No Place for a Pig,* illustrated by Nathan Y. Jarvis, Carnival Press (Milwaukee, WI), 1984.

My Cousin Charlie, illustrated by Pia Marella, Carnival Press (Milwaukee, WI), 1984.

Moon Tiger, illustrated by Ed Young, Holt (New York, NY), 1985.

Soup for Supper, illustrated by Sue Truesdell, Harper (New York, NY), 1986.

Great Basin, Carnival/Crestwood (Mankato, MN), 1988.

Glacier, Carnival/Crestwood (Mankato, MN), 1989.

Galapagos, Carnival/Crestwood (Mankato, MN), 1989.

The Old Red Rocking Chair, illustrated by John Sanford, Arcade (New York, NY), 1992.

The Listening Silence, illustrated by Dennis McDermott, Harper (New York, NY), 1992.

Coyote and the Magic Words, illustrated by Sandra Speidel, Lothrop (New York, NY), 1993.

Sam Who Was Swallowed by a Shark, illustrated by Axel Scheffler, Candlewick Press (Cambridge, MA), 1994.

Aunt Nancy and Old Man Trouble, illustrated by David Parkins, Candlewick Press (Cambridge, MA), 1996.

Mrs. Potter's Pig, illustrated by Russell Ayto, Candlewick Press (Cambridge, MA), 1996.

Contrary Bear, illustrated by Laura Cornell, HarperCollins/Laura Geringer Books (New York, NY), 1996.

One Windy Wednesday, illustrated by Helen Craig, Candlewick Press (Cambridge, MA), 1996.

Rosie's Fiddle, illustrated by Kevin O'Malley, Lothrop (New York, NY), 1997.

The Hungry Monster, illustrated by Sue Heap, Candlewick Press (Cambridge, MA), 1997.

Turnover Tuesday, illustrated by Helen Craig, Candlewick Press (Cambridge, MA), 1998.

What Baby Wants, illustrated by Jill Barton, Candlewick Press (Cambridge, MA), 1998.

One Duck Stuck: A Mucky Ducky Counting Book, illustrated by Jane Chapman, Candlewick Press (Cambridge, MA), 1998.

Aunt Nancy and Cousin Lazybones, illustrated by David Parkins, Candlewick Press (Cambridge, MA), 1998.

Grandmother Winter, illustrated by Beth Krommes, Houghton Mifflin (Boston, MA), 1999.

Hey, Tabby Cat! (contains "The Chase," "Hungry Cat," "Cat Bath," and "Bump! Thump!, Splat!"), illustrated by Katharine McEwen, Candlewick Press (Cambridge, MA), 2000.

All for the Newborn Baby, illustrated by Nicola Bayley, Candlewick Press (Cambridge, MA), 2000.

Kiss the Cow!, illustrated by Will Hillenbrand, Candlewick Press (Cambridge, MA), 2000.

Here Comes Tabby Cat (includes "Tabby Cat at Night," "Tabby Cat's Scarf," "Mouse Hunt," and "Where Is Tabby Cat?"), illustrated by Katharine McEwen, Candlewick Press (Cambridge, MA), 2000.

Meow Monday, illustrated by Helen Craig, Candlewick Press (Cambridge, MA), 2000.

Foggy Friday, illustrated by Helen Craig, Candlewick Press (Cambridge, MA), 2000.

Soggy Saturday, illustrated by Helen Craig, Candlewick Press (Cambridge, MA), 2001.

Rattletrap Car, illustrated by Jill Barton, Candlewick Press (Cambridge, MA), 2001.

(With Michelle Edwards) *What's That Noise?,* illustrated by Paul Meisel, Candlewick Press (Cambridge, MA), 2002.

Mouse Goes Out, illustrated by James Croft, Candlewick Press (Cambridge, MA), 2002.

Mouse Has Fun, illustrated by James Croft, Candlewick Press (Cambridge, MA), 2002.

Big Momma Makes the World, illustrated by Helen Oxenbury, Candlewick Press (Cambridge, MA), 2002.

Oliver Finds His Way, illustrated by Christopher Denise, Walker (New York, NY), 2002.

The Name Quilt, illustrated by Margot Apple, Farrar, Straus, & Giroux (New York, NY), 2003.

Ten Sleepy Sheep, illustrated by Susan Gaber, Candlewick Press (Cambridge, MA), 2004.

Baby Ducklings, illustrated by Petra Mathers, Candlewick Press (Cambridge, MA), 2004.

Baby Bunnies, illustrated by Petra Mathers, Candlewick Press (Cambridge, MA), 2004.

If You Want to See a Caribou, illustrated by Jim Meyer, Houghton Mifflin (Boston, MA), 2004.

ADAPTATIONS: Just One of the Family was recorded on cassette, Raintree (Milwaukee, WI), 1985.

WORK IN PROGRESS: Lucia and the Light.

SIDELIGHTS: The author of numerous works for young readers, Phyllis Root is perhaps best known for her picture books which celebrate intergenerational themes, Native-American traditions, tall tales, and the small, intimate moments of children. As Kelly Milner Halls noted in *Booklist,* Root "has carved a niche for herself by using homespun observations and the playful use of rural undertones." Working with illustrators such as Helen Craig, Paul Meisel, Jill Barton, Will Hillenbrand, and Helen Oxenbury, Root has created popular and award-winning titles such as *Windy Wednesday, Meow Monday, Soggy Saturday, What Baby Wants, The Rattletrap Car, Kiss the Cow,* and *Big Momma Makes the World.* Though Root began writing professionally in 1979, she has been writing for fun as long as she can remember. "I made up stories, poems, and songs," she once told *CA.* "In first grade, I wrote a poem about love and a dove, and in second grade, I won a class essay contest for my four-sentence story about the Sahara desert. In fifth grade, I had a remarkable and wonderful teacher, Mrs. Keller, who encouraged me to write. It was in her class that I decided I would be an 'authoress' when I grew up."

Family history has it that Root was born on the second floor of a parking lot in Fort Wayne, Indiana. As she noted on *Book Jackets,* "I grew up among lots of open space and fresh air." There were also "books, books, books," as she noted on the *Children's Literature Network* Web site. "My father says he remembers me reading in my high chair," Root further explained on the same site. "I used to make up stories in bed at night when I couldn't sleep and my parents had caught me with my book and flashlight. Of course, I was the heroine in all those stories." Root went on to college at Valparaiso University, earning a bachelor's degree in 1971; she did not begin writing professionally for another eight years, after taking course work in the tools of the writing trade, learning important book-writing skills, such as creating plots, settings, tension, and characters.

Since then, Root has written many well-regarded and award-winning children's books. One of her earliest books was *Gretchen's Grandma,* published in 1983, and cowritten with colleague Carol A. Marron. It tells the story of Gretchen and her Oma, or grandmother, who is visiting from Germany. At the beginning of the visit, the language barrier seems troublesome but is eventually overcome by pantomime and love. Ilene Cooper, writing for *Booklist,* described the tale as "a gentle story that could be used as [a] starting point for some preschool discussion."

Root's award-winning title *Moon Tiger,* published in 1985, was described by a *Bulletin of the Center for Children's Books* writer as "the stuff of which dreams are made," and by *School Library Journal* contributor Nancy Schmidtmann as a "heavenly treat." The story delves into a young girl's imagination and weaves her fantasy of being carried away by a magical tiger, who rescues her from having to care for her younger brother. Yet when the tiger offers to eat the boy, the sister declines, admitting that she might actually miss her brother after all.

The idea for Root's next book, *Soup for Supper,* published in 1986, came to her during a thunderstorm, as she once told *CA.* "I had gotten up to comfort my daughter Amelia, and remembered how, when I was a

child, my sister and I had sat on the bed with our parents, watching the lightning and rain. 'Don't let the thunder scare you,' they reassured us. 'It's just the noise potatoes make spilling out of the giant's cart.' Listening to the thunder with my own daughter, I suddenly saw the giant with his cart of vegetables and a wee small woman chasing after him. The next morning I wrote down the first draft of *Soup for Supper.*" The result is "an original story with a folkloric ring," as described by a *Bulletin of the Center for Children's Books* writer, which is "dandy [for] reading aloud because of the simple rhymes, name-calling, and sound effects." The wee small woman of Root's tale vigorously defends her garden against the Giant Rumbleton's attempts to plunder it. After an energetic confrontation, the two enemies discover a common culinary goal and become friends as together they make vegetable soup. Root even includes music for the giant's song at the end of the book.

In 1988 and 1989, Root wrote three books for a series based on natural wonders and National Parks, aimed at middle and upper elementary students. Root's contributions were *Galapagos, Great Basin,* and *Glacier,* each containing maps, large color pictures, and clear text written as an introduction to young armchair travelers.

In *The Old Red Rocking Chair,* published in 1991, a discarded rocking chair is rescued time and time again from the garbage by various eagle-eyed dump-pickers. Each new owner takes from the chair different pieces and discards the remains, until what was once a chair evolves into a blue footstool which is sold to its original oblivious owner at a garage sale. A *Publishers Weekly* critic wrote that "while the premise is hardly new . . . Root's cheerfulness and lucid logic propel the story."

Root's 1992 novel, *The Listening Silence,* draws on Native-American traditions, with a "strong, believable" heroine at the center of the action, according to Ruth S. Vose in *School Library Journal.* Kiri is a young, orphaned girl who is raised in a tribe where a healer recognizes Kiri's ability to send her spirit inside of other people and animals. Reluctant to use her power, Kiri goes on a vision quest to discover her true calling and eventually uses her gift to heal a young man she encounters. Vose praised the "smooth, lyrical, language" of the tale, while a *Kirkus Reviews* writer similarly hailed the "spare, carefully honed narration."

Much like J. R. R. Tolkien did in his classic *Lord of the Rings,* Root invents names for the woodland plants and animals, creating what Kathryn Pierson Jennings described in the *Bulletin of the Center for Children's Books* as "a fantasy culture . . . [which] is orderly and compelling and may inspire young creative writing students who need a more modest fantasy world than Tolkien."

Root's next book also employs elements of folklore, including the use of a coyote as the trickster, a common character in Native-American lore, and her character the Maker-of-all-things, who is similar to the Pueblo Thinking Woman (though Root only discovered this after writing the book). Root described *Coyote and the Magic Words* as "a story about storytelling, about how to create worlds with nothing more than our words." In the book, the Maker-of-all-things uses words to speak her creation into existence and grants her creatures the power to meet their own needs simply by speaking into existence what they want. But the Coyote grows bored with this easy way of life and begins to incite mischief using the magic words. To punish him, the Maker-of-all-things takes away the magic of the words, except the ones Coyote uses in storytelling. Karen Hutt, writing for *Booklist,* characterized the tale as "simple but satisfying," and a *Kirkus Reviews* critic observed that "Root's Coyote is appropriately childlike; her lively narration is well-honed and agreeably informal, just right for oral sharing."

Sam Who Was Swallowed by a Shark is Root's story of a rat who is determined to build a boat and sail the sea, despite the naysaying of his rat neighbors. When he finally accomplishes his goal and leaves, the neighbors assume the worst when they do not hear from him, although Sam is actually having the time of his life. A *Publishers Weekly* critic hailed Root's "understated prose" and "chipper dialogue," and noted that "the even pacing underlines [Sam's] quiet persistence and progress."

The "Aunt Nancy" of *Aunt Nancy and Old Man Trouble,* published in 1996, does not refer to the Aunt Nancy of the "Anansi" storytelling tradition; however Root's story, like many others she written, has a folklore flair to it. Using a down-home dialect, Root describes Aunt Nancy and the way she outsmarts Old Man Trouble when he dries up her well. When he shows up at her door and causes more mischief, Aunt Nancy just tells him it does not bother her because "I

just knowed it was my lucky day when I saw the spring dried up this morning. No more mud tracking up my floor. No more dampness aching in my bones." Old Man Trouble falls for it and restores the well before he leaves in one more attempt to squash Aunt Nancy's good spirits, not realizing he has been had. Deborah Stevenson of the *Bulletin of the Center for Children's Books* commented that this story of the "victory of the underestimated" is a "kid-pleasing version with some bite to it."

The same heroine was reprised in Root's 1998 *Aunt Nancy and Cousin Lazybones,* returning, as a *Publishers Weekly* reviewer put it, "to outwit a do-nothing relative in this spunky tale." Aunt Nancy is not looking forward to a visit from her Cousin Lazybones, for his laziness is legendary. Instead of going to get the water from the well, he simply sets a bucket outside and then hopes for rain. Aunt Nancy decides, however, to fight fire with fire; when she becomes as lazy as her cousin and much of the housework falls to him, he decides that it is time to cut his visit short. A *Publishers Weekly* reviewer further noted that "Root brings generous dollops of humor and homespun flavor to her folktale." Similar praise came from *Booklist*'s John Peters, who felt that "youngsters will delight in this battle of wits and look forward to Aunt Nancy's next visitor." *Horn Book*'s Lolly Robinson also commented that Root and her illustrator, David Parkins, "have created another original tall tale that sounds as though it's been told for years." Robinson further commended Root's "rhythmic" text, which "begs to be read aloud."

A *Publishers Weekly* writer called Root's 1996 book *Mrs. Potter's Pig* a "cheery tale of compromise." The story features Mrs. Potter, a neat freak who learns to appreciate the joy of mud when she has to rescue her dirt-loving daughter from a pigpen. After that, although Mrs. Potter still keeps a spotless house, she and her daughter enjoy regular romps in the pigpen.

The premise of *Contrary Bear,* a toy which is blamed for its owner's obstinate behavior, is described by another *Publishers Weekly* reviewer as made "fresh all over again" by Root's "knowing wit." Contrary Bear takes the rap for making loud train whistles during naptime and wanting a bigger piece of cake, but the last straw for Dad is when Contrary Bear splashes water all over the bathroom. Contrary Bear is relegated to the clothesline to dry and his penitent owner promises to help Contrary Bear "try harder to be good tomorrow."

Rosie's Fiddle is a "reworking of [an] American folktale [which] bursts with vitality and spunk," according to a *Kirkus Reviews* critic. Root's 1997 story features the devil himself in a fiddling contest with Rosie after he hears of her stellar fiddling reputation. After three rounds, Rosie fiddles the devil into a puff of smoke, wins his golden instrument, and saves her own soul from the devil's hands. A *Publishers Weekly* critic commented that "the folksy prose and stormy spreads convey the tale's intensity—the only thing missing is a bluegrass soundtrack." Janice M. Del Negro of the *Bulletin of the Center for Children's Books* also offered a favorable estimation of *Rosie's Fiddle,* asserting: "Root's adaptation of this traditional motif has a fine readaloud rhythm and a thoroughly satisfying progression as the devil gets his musical due."

Also in 1997, Root published *The Hungry Monster,* a picture book directed to the preschool set. When a hungry monster lands on Earth, his hunger cannot be satisfied until a little girl offers him a banana, peel and all. A *Kirkus Reviews* writer praised "this silly story that includes a dash of suspense," concluding that the author's economy of words makes it "a just-right readaloud for board-book graduates."

Root's ten-year-old daughter assisted with the text of *One Windy Wednesday,* a tale about a day so windy it blew the sound right out of the farm animals and into others. The lamb starts quacking, the ducks start mooing, and the cow starts oinking until Bonnie Bumble fixes everything by hitching the right animal to the right sound. Hazel Rochman, writing in *Booklist,* described *One Windy Wednesday* as a "simple, funny story." Helen Craig supplied the illustrations for this initial book, as well as for other books in the series that detail various days of the week. In *Turnover Tuesday,* Root and Craig team up again to tell of little Bonnie Bumble who herself starts literally turning over after making some plum turnovers. "Little children will get a giggle out of this," commented Ilene Cooper in *Booklist. Meow Monday* continues the fun, in which Bonnie finds that her pussy willow has actually sprouted some real pussycats. These furry bundles can only be calmed with milk from the milkweed plant. More praise greeted this addition to the series. Lynda Ritterman, writing in *School Library Journal,* commended the "winning combination of spare, well-chosen words and lively, crisp pacing." *Foggy Friday* finds Bonnie oversleeping when her faithful rooster forgets how to crow in the morning. In *Soggy Satur-*day, it has rained so hard that all the blue from the sky has washed off onto the animals on Bonnie's farm. A critic for *Kirkus Reviews* praised the "beguiling simplicity" of this book, while *Booklist's* Ilene Cooper noted that the same book was "simple yet amusing."

More rural settings are served up in *One Duck Stuck: A Mucky Ducky Counting Book,* featuring a poor fowl caught in the muck. This animal is helped in turn by varying numbers of fish, crickets, and frogs. Shirley Lewis, writing in *Teacher Librarian,* called it a "delightful picture book," and *Booklist's* Helen Rosenberg noted that it is "great fun and sure to become an instant favorite among the toddler crowd." *Kiss the Cow!,* illustrated by Will Hillenbrand, continues the farm setting in a tale about little Annalisa who watches her mother as she milks the cow. However, when she tries to reproduce her mother's procedure, she finds she can not make herself kiss the cow, Luella, on the nose. But without said kiss, the cow refuses to give milk. Her brothers and sisters are hungry, and finally the young girl bestows the kiss that brings the milk. Several reviewers commented positively on both text and illustrations. *Booklist's* Carolyn Phelan noted the "elements of folklore" in Root's narrative with its "satisfying folksy sound." Phelan also commended Hillenbrand's artwork that presents numerous scenes with "style and panache." Anne Knickerbocker, writing in *School Library Journal,* claimed that the book's "flowing language makes it a fun read-aloud," while a reviewer for *Horn Book* called the book "an original story of magic and mischief."

Babies are at the center of *What Baby Wants* and *All for the Newborn Baby.* In the latter work, Root presents a lullaby from the Nativity that a reviewer for *School Library Journal* found to be "a lovely book." Root collaborated with artist Jill Barton on *What Baby Wants,* a "farmyard tale of an implacable baby," as a contributor for *Publishers Weekly* described the book. The whole family goes into action when a mother has difficulty getting her crying baby to sleep. Each of the family members figures the baby needs something different; finally it is the younger brother who knows the trick. All baby wants is a big cuddle. *Booklist's* Stephanie Zvirin called this tale a "sweet, simple charmer." Root and Barton teamed up again for the 2001 *Rattletrap Car,* a cumulative story about the humorous mini-disasters that befall a family on their summertime trip to the lake in an old car. A critic for *Publishers Weekly* commented that "Root and Barton prove that they know how to convey mounting comic mayhem." *Booklist*'s Ilene Cooper had further praise for the title, noting that this is "a picture book that passes the fun test with flying fizz."

Taking inspiration from traditional sources, Root adapts a German fairy-tale character in *Grandmother Winter* and provides a new take on the creation story in *Big Momma Makes the World,* two picture books featuring strong female protagonists. The eponymous heroine of *Grandmother Winter* proves to be the harbinger of the cold season. All summer long she gathers the fallen feathers from her white geese; when autumn comes, she puts them all together into a feather comforter. Then, fluffing it up, the feathers fall, turning into snowflakes from the sky. A reviewer for *Horn Book* commended Root's "cadenced" and "lyrical" text in this folktale remake. Kay Weisman, writing in *Booklist,* also felt that the book would be "a wonderful choice for primary units on seasons or winter," and a reviewer for *Publishers Weekly* called it "a cozy mood-setter." *Big Momma Makes the World,* illustrated by Helen Oxenbury, on the other hand, is a "sassy creation myth that tweaks the first chapter of Genesis," according to a contributor for *Publishers Weekly.* In Root's rendition, Big Momma creates the world and surveys her creation with satisfaction and colloquial expressions. "Root infuses her tale with a joyful spirit, and her lyrical vernacular trips off the tongue," the critic for *Publishers Weekly* further commented. *Booklist*'s Cooper dubbed the tale "a raucous, joyous version of the creation story," while a critic for *Kirkus Reviews* called it a "paean to the Earth and to motherhood."

Root addresses some primal fears of children in two other titles. *What's That Noise?* is a "story of how imagination can run amok," according to Susan Marie Pitard in *School Library Journal.* Two little brothers hear noises in the night, and though at first frightened, they learn to control their fears by making up a silly song that classifies the various sounds. A contributor for *Kirkus Reviews* had positive words for the book, calling it a "reassuring take on a familiar theme." Similarly, in *Oliver Finds His Way,* Root explores the childhood fear of getting lost and the consequent relief in finding your way home again. Baby bear Oliver loses his way one warm day while his parents are busy. He follows a leaf as eddies of air carry it farther and farther away from his home, finally leading him into the shadowy woods. Eventually, the resilient bear is

able to find his way back again by calling out to his parents and then following the sound of their returning calls. A critic for *Publishers Weekly* praised both Root and her illustrator, Christopher Denise, for bringing "a fresh poignancy to the familiar theme." Likewise, Kathleen Simonetta, writing in *School Library Journal,* felt that the "happy ending . . . will leave readers smiling."

A grandmother full of memories and stories is at the center of *The Name Quilt,* in which a little girl elicits family tales from her grandmother each night by picking a name embroidered on the patchwork quilt on her bed. When the quilt is swept away by a fierce wind, the young girl is disconsolate. Finally her grandmother suggests they make a new quilt together, and this time the young girl's name is in the center of it. Mary Elam, writing in *School Library Journal,* noted that Root "stitches together generations, memories, and traditions in this tale of a much-loved family treasure."

The author has herself been "stitching" such tales together since the beginning of her writing career, crafting books that entertain and teach gentle lessons. Root once commented to *CA:* "My hope is to keep writing and to keep having stories to tell."

BIOGRAPHICAL AND CRITICAL SOURCES:

BOOKS

Root, Phyllis, *Aunt Nancy and Old Man Trouble,* illustrated by David Parkins, Candlewick Press (Cambridge, MA), 1996.
Root, Phyllis, *Contrary Bear,* illustrated by Laura Cornell, HarperCollins/Laura Geringer Books (New York, NY), 1996.

PERIODICALS

Booklist, January 1, 1984, Ilene Cooper, review of *Gretchen's Grandma,* p. 684; July, 1986, p. 1616; November 15, 1993, Karen Hutt, review of *Coyote and the Magic Words,* p. 633; October 15, 1996, Hazel Rochman, review of *One Windy Wednesday,* p. 437; April, 1998, Helen Rosenberg, review of *One Duck Stuck: A Mucky Ducky Counting Book,* p. 1333; September 15, 1998, Stephanie Zvirin, review of *What Baby Wants,* p. 240; October 15, 1998, Ilene Cooper, review of *Turnover Tuesday,* p. 429; November 15, 1998, John Peters, review of *Aunt Nancy and Cousin Lazybones,* p. 597; November 15, 1999, Kay Weisman, review of *Grandmother Winter,* p. 637; September 1, 2000, Gillian Engberg, review of *All for the Newborn Baby,* p. 134; November 15, 2000, Kelly Milner Halls, review of *Meow Monday* and *Foggy Friday,* p. 650, and Carolyn Phelan, review of *Kiss the Cow!,* p. 650; December 1, 2001, Ilene Cooper, review of *Soggy Saturday,* pp. 650-651; January 1, 2002, review of *Rattletrap Car,* p. 768; January 1, 2003, Ilene Cooper, review of *Big Momma Makes the World,* p. 88; March 15, 2003, Carolyn Phelan, review of *The Name Quilt,* p. 1333.

Bulletin of the Center for Children's Books, January, 1986, review of *Moon Tiger,* p. 95; July-August, 1986, review of *Soup for Supper,* p. 216; March, 1992, Kathryn Pierson Jennings, review of *The Listening Silence,* p. 191; March, 1996, Deborah Stevenson, review of *Aunt Nancy and Old Man Trouble,* p. 240; April, 1997, Janice M. Del Negro, review of *Rosie's Fiddle,* p. 293; December, 1998, Betsy Hearne, review of *Aunt Nancy and Cousin Lazybones,* p. 144; October, 1999, Fern Kory, review of *Grandmother Winter,* p. 66; February, 2001, Kate McDowell, review of *Foggy Friday* and *Meow Monday,* pp. 235-236.

Horn Book, September-October, 1996, pp. 585-587; January-February, 1999, Lolly Robinson, review of *Aunt Nancy and Cousin Lazybones,* p. 55; September-October, 1999, review of *Grandmother Winter,* p. 599; January-February, 2001, review of *Kiss the Cow!,* p. 85.

Kirkus Reviews, May 1, 1992, review of *The Listening Silence,* p. 616; September 1, 1993, review of *Coyote and the Magic Words,* p. 1151; May 15, 1996, p. 749; January 1, 1997, review of *The Hungry Monster,* p. 63; February 1, 1997, review of *Rosie's Fiddle,* p. 227; September 15, 2001, review of *Soggy Saturday,* p. 1366; July 1, 2002, review of *What's That Noise?,* p. 953; August 1, 2002, review of *Oliver Finds His Way,* p. 1141; January 15, 2003, review of *Big Momma Makes the World,* p. 146; March 1, 2003, review of *The Name Quilt,* p. 397.

Language Arts, March, 2003, review of *Rattletrap Car,* p. 317.

Publishers Weekly, May 18, 1992, review of *The Old Red Rocking Chair,* p. 68; May 30, 1994, review of *Sam Who Was Swallowed by a Shark,* pp. 55-

56; May 13, 1996, review of *Contrary Bear,* p. 75; June 10, 1996, review of *Mrs. Potter's Pig,* p. 99; November 4, 1996, p. 74; January 13, 1997, review of *Rosie's Fiddle,* pp. 75-76; May 4, 1998, review of *One Duck Stuck,* p. 211; September 14, 1998, review of *What Baby Wants,* p. 67; October 26, 1998, review of *Aunt Nancy and Cousin Lazybones,* p. 66; August 30, 1999, review of *Grandmother Winter,* p. 82; April 30, 2001, review of *Rattletrap Car,* p. 77; June 17, 2002, review of *What's That Noise?,* p. 64; August 19, 2002, review of *Oliver Finds His Way,* p. 87; November 25, 2002, review of *Big Momma Makes the World,* p. 66; January 13, 2003, review of *The Name Quilt,* p. 59.

School Library Journal, December, 1985, Nancy Schmidtmann, review of *Moon Tiger,* p. 81; May, 1986, p. 84; June, 1992, Ruth S. Vose, review of *The Listening Silence,* p. 125; January, 1994, p. 97; June, 1998, Heide Piehler, review of *One Duck Stuck,* pp. 118-119; September, 1998, Kathy M. Newby, review of *What Baby Wants,* p. 180; November 1, 1998, Gale W. Sherman, review of *Turnover Tuesday,* p. 94, and Barbara Elleman, review of *Aunt Nancy and Cousin Lazybones,* p. 94; September, 1999, Maryann H. Owens, review of *Grandmother Winter,* p. 201; August, 2000, Anne Knickerbocker, review of *Here Comes Tabby Cat,* p. 164; October, 2000, review of *All for the Newborn Baby,* p. 62; November, 2000, Lynda Ritterman, review of *Meow Monday,* p. 130; December, 2000, Anne Knickerbocker, review of *Kiss the Cow!,* p. 124; June, 2001, Adele Greenlee, review of *Rattletrap Car,* p. 128; December, 2001, Ann Cook, review of *Soggy Saturday,* p. 110; October, 2002, Kathy Simonetta, review of *Oliver Finds His Way,* p. 126; December, 2002, Susan Marie Pitard, review of *What's That Noise?,* p. 94; March, 2003, Laurie von Mehren, review of *Big Momma Makes the World,* p. 206; May, 2003, Mary Elam, review of *The Name Quilt,* p. 129.

Teacher Librarian, September, 1998, Shirley Lewis, review of *One Duck Stuck,* p. 47.

Times Educational Supplement, March 26, 1999, Ted Dewan, review of *What Baby Wants,* p. 23; February 23, 2001, Ted Dewan, review of *Kiss the Cow!,* pp. 19-20.

ONLINE

Book Jackets, http://www.bookjackets.com/ (September 8, 2003), "Phyllis Root."

Children's Literature Network, http://www.childrensliteraturenetwork.org/ (September 8, 2003), "Phyllis Root."

*   *   *

ROSENFELD, Dina 1962-

PERSONAL: Born November 6, 1962, in Pittsburgh, PA; daughter of Emil W. (a lawyer) and Rita (a teacher; maiden name, Perelman) Herman; married Shimon Rosenfeld (a lawyer), March 13, 1983; children: Eliyohu, Frumi, Dovid, Malka, Yosef, Mendel, Zalman. *Education:* Attended Beth Rivka Teachers' Seminary, 1979-81; attended Chatham College for Women, 1981-83. *Religion:* Jewish.

ADDRESSES: Home—555 Crown St., No. 2a, Brooklyn, NY 11213.

CAREER: Yeshiva Achei Tmimim, Pittsburgh, PA, preschool teacher, 1981-83; Beth Rivka Academy, Brooklyn, NY, preschool teacher, 1983-84; freelance writer and editor, 1984—.

WRITINGS:

The Very Best Place for a Penny, Merkos (Brooklyn, NY), 1984.
A Tree Full of Mitzvos, Merkos (Brooklyn, NY), 1985.
Tiny Treasures, Merkos (Brooklyn, NY), 1988.
A Chanukah Story for Night Number Three, Hachai (Brooklyn, NY), 1989.
All about Us, Hachai (Brooklyn, NY), 1989.
A Little Boy Named Avram, Hachai (Brooklyn, NY), 1989.
(Editor) Chana Sharfstein, *The Little Leaf,* Hachai (Brooklyn, NY), 1989.
Labels for Laibel, Hachai (Brooklyn, NY), 1990.
Kind Little Rivka, Hachai (Brooklyn, NY), 1991.
Hot on the Trail, Hachai (Brooklyn, NY), 1991.
Why the Moon Only Glows, Hachai (Brooklyn, NY), 1992.
Peanut Butter and Jelly for Shabbos, Hachai (Brooklyn, NY), 1995.
David the Little Shepherd, Hachai (Brooklyn, NY), 1996.
The Very Best Book, Hachai (Brooklyn, NY), 1997.

On the Ball, Hachai (Brooklyn, NY), 1998.
(Editor) Rikki Benenfeld, *I Go to School,* Hachai (Brooklyn, NY), 1998.
A Little Girl Named Miriam, Hachai (Brooklyn, NY), 2001.
(Editor) Ellen Emerman, *Is It Shabbos Yet?,* Hachai (Brooklyn, NY), 2001.
Get Well Soon, Hachai (Brooklyn, NY), 2001.
Where Does Food Come From?, Hachai (Brooklyn, NY), 2002.

Some of Rosenfeld's books have been translated into Russian, Portuguese, Italian, and German.

WORK IN PROGRESS: Avi's List: A Journal of Discovery about Smoking, a novel for middle school readers designed to educate them about the dangers of smoking.

SIDELIGHTS: Dina Rosenfeld once commented: "My books were born of necessity. As a preschool teacher in a Hebrew day school, I simply could not find age-appropriate materials for my three- to four-year-old students. The children loved stories from the Torah (the five books of Moses), with details from Jewish commentaries. However, so many more aspects of Jewish life, moral values, and holiday and Shabbat celebrations needed to be addressed.

"In Jewish philosophy, there's an important concept of elevating all objects to a higher level by performing mitzvos, good deeds, with them. Translating this to the level of a three-year-old, I wrote a book about a little penny that couldn't find the right place to live until he finally found happiness inside a charity box (*The Very Best Place for a Penny*).

"Again, using preschool curriculum as my guide, I wrote a book about parts of the body called *All about Us.* The Jewish twist is that each body part can be used to perform a mitzvah; for example, hands can be used to light candles for Shabbat, feet can run to the synagogue, a mouth is for smiling at a friend. The lack of quality literature in the traditional Jewish market continued to be my main motivation for writing these books. Instead of producing each to look or sound similar, I tried to fill the need for variety by working with different artists, different sizes and formats, and working in both poetry and prose.

"In the rhyming adventure of *Labels for Laibel,* the all-important topic of sharing is addressed with humor. When two brothers decide not to share anything, they learn that the world can only exist when people give freely to each other. In their next adventure, the two brothers go out of their way to do favors for a whole series of people they meet on a very hot, uncomfortable day (*Hot on the Trail*). Although the characters are Jewish, the values in these books are truly universal. The children in them are not perfect little people, but face the challenge of making moral choices.

"In a totally different series, "The Little Greats," I chose tales from Biblical times about great characters like Abraham, Rebecca, Miriam, and King David when they were small children. The intention was to enhance self-esteem in preschoolers, showing that they don't have to wait to grow up to make a difference. Even at a tender age, these great heroes and heroines of the Bible exhibited devotion, kindness, courage, and caring.

"When my oldest son was born, I left teaching and wrote at home. When he got old enough, I used him as my test audience. Now, he helps me use our new computer. He and his younger brothers and sisters continue to be my toughest critics. None of this would have happened without the blessings of the Lubavitcher Rebbe and the constant encouragement of my parents and my husband—as well as the very insightful editing of my mother. She first introduced me to classic children's literature and delights in the opportunity to combine artistic and literary quality with important Jewish content.

"It is gratifying that my books have recently been translated into Russian, Portuguese, Italian, and even German for children around the world to benefit from and enjoy. After all, a trip to the synagogue is once a week. A holiday celebration is once a year. But with an engaging Jewish book, a young child can learn to love and live Judaism every day at story time."

*   *   *

ROY, Donald H. 1944-

PERSONAL: Born July 29, 1944, in Hartford, CT; son of Donald H., Sr. (a laborer) and Madeline (a laborer; maiden name, Reynolds) Roy; married; wife's name Bernice Phyllis (divorced, August, 1996); children:

Daniel, Marisa. *Ethnicity:* "Anglo-French American." *Education:* Bard College, B.A., 1966; Georgetown University, M.A., 1970; University of Notre Dame, Ph.D., 1977. *Politics:* "Sloppy middle, radical centrist." *Religion:* Roman Catholic. *Hobbies and other interests:* Classical music.

ADDRESSES: Home—901 Colburn Ave., Apt. WD4, Big Rapids, MI 49307. *Office*—Department of Social Sciences, Ferris State University, Big Rapids, MI 49307. *E-mail*—droy@ferris.edu.

CAREER: Carroll College, Helena, MT, assistant professor of political science, 1978-82; Dallas Chamber of Commerce, Dallas, TX, director of research, 1984-87; Jefferson Community College, Louisville, KY, assistant professor of political science, 1987-89; Ferris State University, Big Rapids, MI, associate professor of political science, 1989—.

MEMBER: Amnesty International, Catholic League for Civil Rights, Michigan Conference of Political Scientists, Catholic League for Civil Rights.

WRITINGS:

Dialogues in American Politics, Kendall-Hunt (Dubuque, IA), 1993.
Public Policy Dialogues, University Press of America (Lanham, MD), 1994.
The Reuniting of America: Eleven Multicultural Dialogues, Peter Lang (New York, NY), 1996.
The Dialogic Resurgence of Public Intellectuals, Xlibris (Philadelphia, PA), 2001.

WORK IN PROGRESS: State and Local Government: Dialogues on Pivotal Issues, fifteen dialogues covering the full range of topical issues.

SIDELIGHTS: Donald H. Roy once told *CA:* "All kinds of people talk about 'dialoguing' but they only issue monologues. It is rare to find a dialogue. Dialogues don't decide; they provoke and stimulate even further dialogue.

"To date public policy issues primarily stir me to write, and dialogues are very useful as tools to focus attention on key, dividing arguments. I am influenced by normative political theorists who try to bridge the gap between theory and experts on one side and practice and ordinary people on the other side.

"My short public policy dialogues begin during the process of reading everything I can get my hands on concerning a hot topic. My dialogues go wherever the argument takes them. Whatever is topical and controversial is deserving of a fifteen-to-twenty-page dialogue. My larger dialogues will cover the role of the public intellectual, the conflict within modern liberalism, and religion's contribution to political theory. My plan is never to write a monologue."

S

SANDERS, Noah
   See BLOUNT, Roy (Alton), Jr.

*   *   *

SCHICK, Eleanor 1942-

PERSONAL: Born April 15, 1942, in New York, NY; daughter of William (a psychiatrist) and Bessie (a social worker; maiden name, Grossman) Schick; children: Laura, David. *Ethnicity:* "Jewish." *Education:* Studied modern dance at the 92nd St. "Y" and with Martha Graham, Alvin Ailey, and others. *Religion:* "Jewish." *Hobbies and other interests:* Dance.

ADDRESSES: *Home*—207 Aliso NE, Albuquerque, NM 87108.

CAREER: Author and illustrator of children's books. Writer in residence, Rio Grande Writing Project (a New Mexico site of the National Writing Project), 1986-96; speaker at schools and universities. Former professional dancer and member of Juilliard Dance Theatre and Tamiris-Nagrin Dance Company; has lectured and taught dance at Hofstra College, Bryn Mawr College, and Connecticut College.

WRITINGS:

Peter and Mr. Brandon, illustrated by Donald Carrick, Macmillan (New York, NY), 1973.

SELF-ILLUSTRATED

A Surprise in the Forest, Harper (New York, NY), 1964.
The Little School at Cottonwood Corners, Harper (New York, NY), 1965.
The Dancing School, Harper (New York, NY), 1966.
I'm Going to the Ocean!, Macmillan (New York, NY), 1966.
5A and 7B, Macmillan (New York, NY), 1967.
Katie Goes to Camp, Macmillan (New York, NY), 1968.
Jeanie Goes Riding, Macmillan (New York, NY), 1968.
City in the Summer, Macmillan (New York, NY), 1969.
Making Friends, Macmillan (New York, NY), 1969.
Peggy's New Brother, Macmillan (New York, NY), 1970.
City in the Winter, Macmillan (New York, NY), 1970.
Andy, Macmillan (New York, NY), 1971.
Student's Encounter Book for When a Jew Celebrates, Behrman House (New York, NY), 1973.
Peter and Mr. Brandon, illustrated by Donald Carrick, Macmillan (New York, NY), 1973.
City Green, Macmillan (New York, NY), 1974.
City Sun, Macmillan (New York, NY), 1974.
Neighborhood Knight, Greenwillow (New York, NY), 1976.
One Summer Night, Greenwillow (New York, NY), 1977.
Summer at Sea, Greenwillow (New York, NY), 1979.
Home Alone, Dial (New York, NY), 1980.
Rainy Sunday, Dial (New York, NY), 1981.
Joey on His Own, Dial (New York, NY), 1981.

A Piano for Julie, Greenwillow (New York, NY), 1984.

My Album, Greenwillow (New York, NY), 1984.

Art Lessons, Greenwillow (New York, NY), 1987.

I Have Another Language: The Language Is Dance, Macmillan (New York, NY), 1992.

(With Luci Tapahonso) *Navajo ABC: A Diné Alphabet Book,* Macmillan (New York, NY), 1995.

My Navajo Sister, Simon & Schuster (New York, NY), 1996.

Drawing Your Way through the Jewish Holidays, UAHC Press (New York, NY), 1997.

Navajo Wedding Day: A Diné Marriage Ceremony, Marshall Cavendish (New York, NY), 1999.

Mama, Marshall Cavendish (New York, NY), 2000.

I Am: I Am a Dancer, Marshall Cavendish (New York, NY), 2002.

ILLUSTRATOR

Jan Wahl, *Christmas in the Forest,* Macmillan (New York, NY), 1967.

Jeanne Whitehouse Peterson, *Sometimes I Dream Horses,* Harper (New York, NY), 1987.

Sheldon Zimmerman, *The Family Prayerbook,* Rossel Books (Dallas, TX), Volume 1: *Holidays and Festivals,* 1988, Volume 2: *The Fall Holidays,* 1989, Volume 3: *Shabbat,* 1989.

ADAPTATIONS: City in the Winter and *City in the Summer* have been made into filmstrips.

SIDELIGHTS: Eleanor Schick is a prolific writer and illustrator of children's books who focuses on the everyday comings and goings, the first-time experiences, and the daily routines that make up a child's life. Through her books, children have been introduced to the schoolroom, to sleep-away camp, to the arrival of a new sibling, a first trip to the store, the responsibilities of being a latch-key kid, and other milestones. Schick's style, both in writing and in illustration, has often been described as simple and realistic, covering territory familiar to young readers. It is a child's private world that Schick is interested in creating in her books. "Children always excite me," she once commented. "They are always reachable. They are always responsive when an adult makes it clear to them that he or she is interested in listening to them speak, or write, about what really happens in their lives, and how they feel about it."

One of Schick's earliest books, *The Little School at Cottonwood Corners,* addresses preschoolers' curiosity about what really goes on in a classroom. Elegy Meadows, clutching her teddy bear and visitor's pass in hand, takes a tour of the little school. She gets a look at the various rooms and activities of the kindergarten classes, and that night she confides to her teddy bear that she might like to go to the little school, too. Praising the informative detail of Schick's drawings, *Horn Book* contributor Virginia Haviland called the tale "refreshing real and childlike." Similarly, a *Bulletin of the Center for Children's Books* writer remarked that *Katie Goes to Camp* is "just long enough, simple and realistic, low-keyed and pleasant" in relating how a young girl deals with homesickness during her first sleep-away camp. And *Jeanie Goes Riding* "must strike a chord" in other young children awaiting their first trip on horseback, according to a *Times Literary Supplement* reviewer.

Many of Schick's books take place in an urban landscape, full of interesting buildings and peopled with characters of many races and cultures. Apartment dwellers may recognize the situation of Toby and Sandy in *5A and 7B;* each girl longs for a special friend, but the two only meet when a change in routine leads to a chance encounter. Although not dramatic, the story is "satisfying and useful," according to Ruth P. Bull in *Booklist,* especially for its "wonderfully detailed drawings." *City in the Summer* and *City in the Winter* both hinge on the effects of the weather on a young boy's daily existence: one tells of escaping the stifling heat of a city summer day with a trip to the beach at Coney Island; the other is the story of Jimmy's day with his grandmother when a blizzard forces the schools to close. Of the first, George A. Woods noted in the *New York Times Book Review* that it has the feel of a "documentary," making it "as if the city in summer had sat very still for its portrait." *City in the Winter* is "a most successful companion," Haviland observed in *Horn Book,* with the delicate drawings "just right for the little narrative."

The city serves as a setting for imaginative play in other books by Schick. When the other neighborhood children are too busy to play with him in the story *Andy,* the title character amuses himself around the city block by pretending to be a construction worker and cowboy, among other things. A *Booklist* reviewer praised the "simplicity and naturalness" with which Schick presents everyday play, as well as the "sharply detailed" drawings. Similarly, *Neighborhood Knight* is the tale of a young boy whose imagination turns his rundown apartment building into a castle, his mother into a queen, and his sister into a princess. His father, the king, has been "gone a long time." Schick once told *CA* that *Neighborhood Knight* is "truly about my son and is directly autobiographical." A critic described the story and illustrations in a *Publishers Weekly* review as "fine representations of the small boy's private world," while a *School Library Journal* critic noted that the realistic drawings "run in pleasant counterpoint" to the boy's imaginings. And in 1974's *City Green*, a young girl named Laura expresses her feelings through a collection of brief poems and observations about the little things in life that affect her and her younger brother, David. Schick's poems have the "same gentle ambience" as her other stories, Nancy Rosenberg observed in the *New York Times Book Review*, with text and pictures that are "sedate and affectionate."

Many of Schick's books deal with contemporary issues of urban society. *Home Alone* is the story of a latch-key kid learning about independence and responsibility, as he must come home to an empty house when his mother gets a full-time job. In *Joey on His Own*, a young boy goes out to the store by himself for the first time when his mother, who must stay at home with his feverish sister, sends him out for bread. On his way to the store, the city streets and buildings appear larger, taller, and more menacing than they ever have before. But in the end, Joey navigates the sidewalks and the supermarket successfully. "The narrative subtly conveys Joey's apprehension," Kate M. Flanagan observed in *Horn Book*, adding that the "clean, uncluttered" pencil drawings contain "a surprising amount of detail." A reviewer for *Publishers Weekly* likewise declared that young readers "will feel they're living Joey's anxieties and his exhilaration at mission completed," while a *School Library Journal* critic hailed Schick's drawings for using "perspective to canny advantage in reflecting Joey's shift in attitude."

In other works, Schick simply tells of how an ordinary, even dismal, situation can be lightened and brightened with a little creativity. In *One Summer Night*, Laura decides to play a record and dance instead of sleep, leading the entire neighborhood to dance along. Helen Gregory praised Schick's work in *School Library Journal* for combining "sensuous and dynamic" pictures

with a "simple but enjoyable story," while a *Publishers Weekly* reviewer called it "a lovely tale, with spirited pictures." Schick travels beyond the city for *Summer at the Sea*, where a young girl spends a happy, magical vacation before returning home. Containing "real emotional weight," as one *Kirkus Reviews* critic stated, this book will give children "a foretaste of what reading means not as a skill or a pastime but as total involvement." The story of how a girl enlivens a gray and dreary day, Schick's *Rainy Sunday* similarly demonstrates the power of the imagination. While a reviewer for the *Bulletin of the Center for Children's Books* found the book has "little action" and "no humor," Holly Willett noted in *Horn Book* that the "family's positive approach to a potentially disappointing day" makes for a "pleasant and comforting" work. And Susan Bolotin of the *New York Times Book Review* stated that this "quiet story" is made "brilliant" by Schick's use of colorful illustrations.

Schick has also communicated her love for the fine arts in her works, introducing children to music, art, and dance. In *A Piano for Julie*, a young girl listens to her father play the piano at her grandmother's house and wishes to learn how to play herself. *School Library Journal* contributor Kathy Piehl praised the author's text for creating "a soft verbal melody," while a *Kirkus Reviews* writer hailed Schick's gentle illustrations, calling the book "an exceptional here-and-now overall—with delicacy, involvement, and depth." *Art Lessons* similarly shows a young boy taking lessons in drawing from Adrianne, a neighboring artist. By showing the two talking about art, Schick takes a "provocative" approach in teaching children how to draw through "ideas instead of technique," commented a critic in *Publishers Weekly*. The way art can express emotion is also highlighted in *I Have Another Language: The Language Is Dance*, as a young girl prepares for her first dance recital. The girl's feelings before, during, and after her performance are "skillfully woven into her dance expression," Kay McPherson stated in *School Library Journal*. The author, a former dancer herself, "conveys the joy a dancer feels at successfully celebrating her emotions," Maeve Visser Knoth concluded in *Horn Book*, and Schick's pencil illustrations, with their creative use of line, shading, and perspective, "create the excitement and tension of a new situation."

A long-time resident of New York City, which set the backdrop for many of her urban picture books, Schick eventually moved to New Mexico, and desert landscapes and Native Americans fittingly became fodder for her stories and art. Beginning with *Navajo ABC: A Diné Alphabet Book,* Schick teamed up with Luci Tapahonso and created a children's book that introduces contemporary Navajo life to non-Native Americans. Most of the letters are paired with English words but the culture of T'aa Diné (how the Navajo call themselves) is emphasized throughout. *Booklist* reviewer Karen Hutt remarked that Schick and Tapahonso's approach, which underscores the particularities of Navajo language and culture, "is a welcome change from works that clump all Indians together."

This work was followed by *My Navajo Sister,* "a gentle story of boundless sisterhood," according to Claudia Cooper in *School Library Journal.* Here, a Navajo girl shares her life on the reservation with her friend, introducing the reader to the ways in which contemporary Navajos maintain their cultural heritage in everyday life while highlighting the affection shared by the girls. This is "a fine picture book to read aloud, particularly to children studying Native Americans," observed Carolyn Phelan in *Booklist.*

In *Navajo Wedding Day: A Diné Marriage Ceremony,* another book featuring a Native people of the Southwest, a girl guides the reader through all the preparations for celebrating a Navajo wedding. Although Julie Corsaro, who reviewed the book for *Booklist,* complained that "there's too much explanation of events" for the fictional framework to hold up well, this reviewer added that the scarcity of books on the life of contemporary Native Americans, and Schick's "realistically detailed colored-pencil drawings" help the book overcome this flaw. *School Library Journal* reviewer Darcy Schild, on the other hand, praised the writing as "clear and simple" and the illustrations as "beautiful and informative." *Navajo Wedding Day* is "a good choice for all collections," Schild concluded.

As Bolotin noted in the *New York Times Book Review,* Schick's work often "describes a child's emotional response to an all-too-real situation." This is especially true of *Mama,* a book that deals head-on with the death of its young protagonist's mother. Through first-person narrative and softly shaded watercolor illustrations, Schick "neither evades nor minimizes the feelings that a child in this situation might have," remarked Marian Drabkin in *School Library Journal.*

Schick herself is pleased that writers are listening to children more than they used to. "We write with more sensitivity to what children really do think, and see,

and feel," she once noted. "There is a true literature developing which speaks to children. It speaks to their thoughts, dreams, and yearnings. It addresses some of the experiences that they do have, which were not dealt with some fifteen or twenty years ago. I have witnessed, and surely been a part of, the development of 'children's books' from being vehicles of didactic adult teaching to a true literature which includes very deep and poetic expressions of childhood experience. This is very meaningful to me, and I feel deeply gratified to have been a part of this growth."

BIOGRAPHICAL AND CRITICAL SOURCES:

BOOKS

Schick, Eleanor, *Neighborhood Knight,* Greenwillow (New York, NY), 1976.

PERIODICALS

Booklist, May 15, 1967, Ruth P. Bull, review of *5A and 7B,* pp. 997-998; May 15, 1970, p. 1163; May 15, 1971, review of *Andy,* p. 800; April 1, 1984, p. 1122; September 15, 1987, p. 153; May 1, 1992, p. 1610; December 15, 1995, Karen Hutt, review of *Navajo ABC: A Diné Alphabet Book,* p. 706; December 1, 1996, Carolyn Phelan, review of *My Navajo Sister,* p. 669; April 15, 1999, Julie Corsaro, review of *Navajo Wedding Day: A Diné Marriage Ceremony,* p. 1537; February 15, 2000, Connie Fletcher, review of *Mama,* p. 1122.
Bulletin of the Center for Children's Books, November, 1965, p. 49; March, 1969, review of *Katie Goes to Camp,* pp. 117-118; October, 1970, p. 33; March, 1971, p. 114; July, 1981, review of *Rainy Sunday,* p. 217; June, 1982, p. 197.
Childhood Education, June, 1987, p. 364.
Christian Science Monitor, May 2, 1968, p. 83; November 12, 1970, p. 86; June 5, 1971, p. 21.
Horn Book, October, 1965, Virginia Haviland, review of *The Little School at Cottonwood Corners,* p. 495; February, 1971, Virginia Haviland, review of *City in the Winter,* p. 44; June, 1973, p. 261; June, 1976, p. 284; October, 1980, p. 516; June, 1981, Holly Willett, review of *Rainy Sunday,* p. 297; August, 1982, Kate M. Flanagan, review of *Joey on His Own,* p. 397; July, 1992, Maeve Visser Knoth, review of *I Have Another Language: The Language Is Dance,* pp. 446-447.

Horn Book Guide, spring, 1997, Debbie A. Reese, review of *My Navajo Sister,* p. 47; fall, 1999, Debbie A. Reese, review of *Navajo Wedding Day,* p. 284.

Kirkus Reviews, February 15, 1967, p. 194; March 15, 1970, p. 318; April 1, 1979, review of *Summer at the Sea,* p. 387; March 1, 1984, review of *A Piano for Julie;* August 15, 1987.

Language Arts, March, 1982, p. 269; October, 1982, p. 746.

New York Times Book Review, June 29, 1969, George A. Woods, review of *City in the Summer,* p. 26; October 26, 1969, p. 44; May 5, 1974, Nancy Rosenberg, "A Tree Grows in Print," review of *City Green,* p. 38; May 3, 1981, Susan Bolotin, review of *Rainy Sunday,* pp. 40-41.

Publishers Weekly, March 1, 1976, review of *Neighborhood Knight,* p. 94; March 14, 1977, review of *One Summer Night,* p. 95; April 16, 1982, review of *Joey on His Own,* p. 71; July 24, 1987, review of *Art Lessons,* p. 186; November 30, 1984, p. 92; March 9, 1992, p. 57; July 5, 1999, review of *Navajo ABC,* p. 73.

School Library Journal, May, 1976, review of *Neighborhood Knight,* p. 75; May, 1977, Helen Gregory, review of *One Summer Night,* p. 55; May, 1982, review of *Joey on His Own,* p. 80; May, 1984, Kathy Piehl, review of *A Piano for Julie,* p. 72; December, 1984, p. 76; November, 1987, p. 96; July, 1992, Kay McPherson, review of *I Have Another Language,* p. 64; December, 1995, Lisa Mitten, review of *Navajo ABC,* p. 100; December, 1996, Claudia Cooper, review of *My Navajo Sister,* p. 105; April, 1999, Darcy Schild, review of *Navajo Wedding Day,* p. 108; May, 2000, Marian Drabkin, review of *Mama,* p. 154; January, 2003, Dorian Chong, review of *I Am: I Am a Dancer,* p. 111.

Times Literary Supplement, December 4, 1969, review of *Jeanie Goes Riding,* p. 1392.

ONLINE

New Mexico Culture Net, http://www.nmcn.org/ artsorgs/writersguide/ (March 5, 2003), "Eleanor Schick."

SCHULTZ, Philip 1945-

PERSONAL: Born January 6, 1945, in Rochester, NY; son of Samuel B. and Lillian (Bernstein) Schultz; married Monica Banks (a sculptor), January, 1995; children: Eli, August. *Education:* Attended University of Louisville, 1963-65; San Francisco State University, B.A., 1967; University of Iowa, M.F.A., 1971. *Politics:* Democrat. *Religion:* Jewish.

ADDRESSES: Home—88 Osborne Lane, East Hampton, New York, NY 11937. *Office*—The Writers Studio, 78 Charles St. 2R, New York, NY 11937. *Agent*—Georges Borchardt, 136 East 57th St., New York, NY 10014. *E-mail*—gusbeny@optonline.net.

CAREER: San Francisco Department of Social Service, San Francisco, CA, clerk-typist, 1969-70; taught poetry in elementary schools in Michigan, 1971-72, Massachusetts, 1974-75, and New York, 1977-80; Kalamazoo College, Kalamazoo, MI, writer-in-residence, 1971-72; Newton College of the Sacred Heart, Newton, MA, lecturer in poetry, 1973-74; University of Massachusetts, Boston, lecturer in creative writing, 1973-75; New York University, New York, NY, lecturer in creative writing, 1978-88, founder and director of the creative writing program, 1984-88; founder, The Writers Studio, New York, NY, 1988—.

MEMBER: International PEN, Poetry Society of America, Writers Guild of America.

AWARDS, HONORS: Poetry award, *Kansas City Star,* 1971; Discovery-Nation Poetry award, 1976; Creative Arts Public Service fellow, New York Council on the Arts, 1976, 1980; National Book Award nomination, and American Academy of Arts and Letters award, both 1979, both for *Like Wings;* National Endowment for the Arts, fellow, 1980-81; Fulbright grant, 1983; Lamont Poetry Selection, Academy of American Poets, 1984, for *Deep within the Ravine;* fellowship, New York Foundation for the Arts, 1985; Academy of American Poets award; Levinson Prize, *Poetry* magazine, 1996.

WRITINGS:

POETRY

Like Wings, Viking (New York, NY), 1978.

Deep within the Ravine, Viking (New York, NY), 1984.

My Guardian Angel Stein (chapbook), 1986.

The Holy Worm of Praise, Harcourt (New York, NY), 2002.

Poems have appeared in the *New Yorker, Partisan Review, New Republic,* and the *Paris Review;* and in anthologies, including *New American Poets of the 90's,* Godine, 1991, and *100 Years of American Poetry,* 1996. Contributor of short stories to literary journals.

WORK IN PROGRESS: Living in the Past (book-length poem), for Harcourt; *First Person Persona.*

SIDELIGHTS: Philip Schultz's personal obsessions, his passions, his past, are the self-proclaimed stuff of his poems, a program that has been an extraordinarily successful one for him. He has received several prestigious awards and grants for his poetry, beginning with his first volume, *Like Wings,* which was nominated for a National Book Award and received an award from the American Academy of Arts and Letters. Beginning his career as an itinerant lecturer in poetry, Schultz was later ensconced at New York University, where he founded a new creative writing program in 1984. Leaving teaching in 1988, he established a private school, The Writers Studio, based upon the principles he developed while at NYU. A second verse collection, *Deep within the Ravine,* appeared at this time, and it was named the Lamont Poetry Selection for best second book of poetry of 1984. Richard Tillinghast reviewed *Deep within the Ravine* for the *New York Times Book Review.* He compared the humorous, conversational tone of many of Schultz's poems to bits in a stand-up comedy routine. Schultz "is at his best in familiar monologues—humorous and nostalgic, with an edge of irony, sadness and self-mockery. The pictures they paint are vivid and memorable," Tillinghast observed.

Fifteen years passed without another volume-length collection from Schultz. Then, in 2002, he published *The Holy Worm of Praise,* a collection that "confirms this poet's calling as an elegist," according to a contributor to *Publishers Weekly.* As in his earlier works, Schultz draws on his personal life for his material; here, there are poems about his parents as well as his literary influences, including Yehuda Amichai, Joseph Brodsky, John Cheever, and William Dickey. A *Publishers Weekly* critic, however, abjured Schultz's happier poems as too often exhibiting a tendency for "weak similes" and sentimentality, contending that the poet "is at his best in the gritty voice of a 'Prison Doctor.'" Though Stephen Whited, writing in *Book,* also found Schultz's most personal poems his least successful, he praised the author for not taking himself too seriously, for the care he lavishes on every line of every poem, and for the "delightful" personae he adopts in many of his poems. Schultz does not have all the answers, Whited concluded, "but he can be depended upon to ask all the important questions." Daniel L. Guillory writing in *Library Journal* called *The Holy Worm of Praise,* "one of the strongest collections of lyrics publised in the last decade."

Schultz once told *CA:* "I tend to write about my personal experience and how it affects and is affected by my times. My past, in particular, has proven to be a rich source of material. My father was born in Russia, and the street I grew up on—now a lost world—was filled with immigrants from several Eastern European countries. This culture offered a mysterious, if not bewildering, contrast to the American life I now lead. I write about those things which most obsess me, things I feel passionately about.

Schultz more recently told *CA:* "My first influences were paintings and painters; I spent hours pouring over art books in the library and bookstores. Van Gogh, Cezanne, Matisse—I loved their color and sense of design and, of course their passion. I drew throughout school (took art classes in graduate school) and was my high school cartoonist. To this day I envy painters and find painting and sculpturing a source of inspiration. I began writing, and wanting to be a writer, in my junior year of high school, and it was the fiction writers: Hemingway, Philip Roth, Bellows, and Walker Percy who inspired me. I also loved the sound of a well-designed first-person voice and strove to discover one that would do justice to the material I wanted to write about. I didn't begin reading poetry seriously until college, and then switched from fiction to poetry in graduate school at the Iowa Writer's Workshop. I always envied the fiction writer's narrative freedom, and have been working on long poems, wanting to recreate that sense of a self-made world in my work.

"I revise a great deal, and work, perhaps somewhat the way a painter does, applying layer after layer of ideas (sometimes in the manner of a collage), feelings and narrative incident onto the basic framework of a story I'm trying to tell. I rewrote "Souls over Harlem" thirty times or more over a six-year period, adding two stories onto the original: one of a crime committed in Harlem, personalizing it by identifying with both the criminal and the victims, and then adding my own story and that of a friend who committed suicide in 1972. One story became three, and the evolving structure allowed me to discuss ideas about race and innocence I'd been struggling with ever since I began writing. This process takes a long time to discover, but having worked on "Souls over Harlem" gave me the structure and fortitude to write an eighty-one page poem, "Living in the Dead." This poem is about the year leading up to a boy's bar mitzvah and the world of displaced people and immigrants he was surrounded by. This is material I've been working on, in one form or other, since I began writing. And I wrote it quickly (for me)—in little over a year.

"The most surprising thing I've learned as a writer is that I could be a painter and a fiction writer in my poetry by faithfully pursuing my instincts and taking those aspects I most loved and applying them to my poems. I love the surprises of narrative and the invention of the persona voice and the celebration and constant unfolding of color and form.

"I can't pick a favorite book because it's all an ongoing process and I don't really measure or compare the work in one to that of another; one book teaches me the necessary techniques to write the next. The one I'm working on presently insists on receiving special attention or it would never get written.

"I hope my work is strong enough to call attention to the stories I am telling. The world of the past is lost unless we reinvent it and our place in it. This is perhaps what all my work has been about—reinventing the past so that it didn't exist in vain. So that we don't."

BIOGRAPHICAL AND CRITICAL SOURCES:

PERIODICALS

American Poet, April, 1985, review of *Deep within the Ravine,* p. 43; spring, 2002, review of *The Holy Worm of Praise,* p. 61.

Book, July-August, 2002, Stephen Whited, review of *The Holy Worm of Praise,* p. 80.
Booklist, December 15, 1984, review of *Deep within the Ravine,* p. 555.
Book World, December 30, 1984, review of *Deep within the Ravine,* p. 6.
Coda, November-December, 1979.
Georgia Review, spring, 1985, review of *Deep within the Ravine,* 188.
Library Journal, September 1, 1984, review of *Deep within the Ravine,* p. 1677; July, 2002, Daniel L. Guillory, review of *The Holy Worm of Praise,* p. 86.
Los Angeles Times Book Review, January 6, 1985, review of *Deep within the Ravine,* p. 28.
Nation, December 22, 1984, review of *Deep within the Ravine,* p. 687.
New York Times Book Review, March 31, 1985, Richard Tillinghast, review of *Deep within the Ravine,* p. 14.
Publishers Weekly, September 7, 1984, review of *Deep within the Ravine,* p. 69; March 18, 2002, review of *The Holy Worm of Praise,* p. 93.
Virginia Quarterly Review, winter, 1985, review of *Deep within the Ravine,* p. 28.

ONLINE

Writers Studio, http://www.writerstudio.com/ (June 14, 2002), Frazier Russell, "An Interview with Philip Schultz."

*   *   *

SEULING, Barbara 1937-
(Carrie Austin; Bob Winn, a joint pseudonym)

PERSONAL: Surname pronounced "Soo-ling"; born July 22, 1937, in Brooklyn, NY; daughter of Kaspar Joseph (a postman) and Helen Veronica (a homemaker; maiden name, Gadie) Seuling. *Education:* Attended Hunter College (now Hunter College of the City University of New York), 1955-57, Columbia University, 1957-59, School of Visual Arts, and New School for Social Research; also studied art and illustration privately. *Hobbies and other interests:* Movies, travel, reading, music.

ADDRESSES: Home—New York, NY. *Agent*—Miriam Altshuler Literary Agency, RR #1, Box 5, 5 Old Post Road, Red Hook, NY 12571. *E-mail*—aplbrk@aol.com.

CAREER: Freelance writer and illustrator, 1968—. Has worked for an investment firm, for Columbia University, and at the General Electric Co. exhibit at the 1964 New York World's Fair. Dell Publishing Co., New York, NY, children's book editor, 1965-71; J. B. Lippincott Co., New York, NY, children's book editor, 1971-73. The Manuscript Workshop, Landgrove, VT, director, 1982—. Lecturer, teacher, and consultant on children's books and writing for children. Served as a consultant to the New York Foundling Hospital.

MEMBER: Society of Children's Book Writers and Illustrators (board of directors).

AWARDS, HONORS: Award from American Institute of Graphic Arts, 1979, for *The Teeny Tiny Woman: An Old English Ghost Story;* Christopher Award, 1979, for *The New York Kid's Book;* first place, Harold Marshall Solstad Prize, Cameron University Children's Short Story Competition, 1982.

WRITINGS:

"FREAKY FACTS" SERIES

Freaky Facts, Xerox Education Publications (Middletown, CT), 1972.

More Freaky Facts, Xerox Education Publications (Middletown, CT), 1973.

The Last Legal Spitball and Other Little-Known Facts about Sports, Doubleday (New York, NY), 1975.

You Can't Eat Peanuts in Church and Other Little-Known Laws, Doubleday (New York, NY), 1975.

The Loudest Screen Kiss and Other Little-Known Facts about the Movies, Doubleday (New York, NY), 1976.

The Last Cow on the White House Lawn and Other Little-Known Facts about the Presidency, Doubleday (New York, NY), 1978.

You Can't Count a Billion Dollars and Other Little-Known Facts about Money, Doubleday (New York, NY), 1979.

You Can't Show Kids in Underwear and Other Little-Known Facts about Television, Doubleday (New York, NY), 1982.

Elephants Can't Jump and Other Freaky Facts about Animals, Dutton/Lodestar (New York, NY), 1985.

You Can't Sneeze with Your Eyes Open and Other Freaky Facts about the Human Body, Dutton/Lodestar (New York, NY), 1986.

The Man in the Moon Is Upside Down in Argentina and Other Freaky Facts about Geography, Ivy Books/Ballantine (New York, NY), 1991.

Too Cold to Hatch a Dinosaur and Other Freaky Facts about Weather, Ivy Books/Ballantine (New York, NY), 1993.

OTHER NONFICTION

Abracadabra!: Creating Your Own Magic Show from Beginning to End, Messner (New York, NY), 1975.

(Editor and contributor) *The New York Kid's Book,* Doubleday (New York, NY), 1979.

Stay Safe, Play Safe: A Book about Safety Rules, illustrated by Kathy Allert, Golden Books (New York, NY), 1985.

(With Winnette Glasgow) *Fun Facts about People around the World,* illustrated by Leslie Connor, Xerox Education Publications (New York, NY), 1986.

It Is Illegal to Quack Like a Duck and Other Little-Known Laws, illustrated by Gwenn Seuling, Weekly Reader Books (Middletown, CT), 1987, published as *It Is Illegal to Quack Like a Duck and Other Freaky Laws,* Dutton/Lodestar (New York, NY), 1988.

Natural Disasters, Kidsbooks (Chicago, IL), 1994.

Bugs That Go Blam! And Other Creepy Crawly Trivia, Willowisp (Worthington, OH), 1995.

To Be a Writer: A Guide for Young People Who Want to Write and Publish, Twenty-First Century Books (New York, NY), 1997.

Where Do Ducks Go?, Harcourt (San Diego, CA), 1998.

Drip! Drop!: How Water Gets to Your Tap, illustrated by Nancy Tobin, Holiday House (New York, NY), 2000.

From Head to Toe: The Amazing Human Body and How It Works, illustrated by Edward Miller, Holiday House (New York, NY), 2002.

Flick a Switch: How Electricity Gets to Your Home, illustrated by Nancy Tobin, Holiday House (New York, NY), 2003.

PUZZLE AND ACTIVITY BOOKS

Monster Mix, Xerox Education Publications (Middletown, CT), 1975.

Monster Madness, Xerox Education Publications (Middletown, CT), 1976.

(With Winnette Glasgow) *Fun with Crafts,* Xerox Education Publications (Middletown, CT), 1976.

Dinosaur Puzzles, Xerox Education Publications (Middletown, CT), 1976.

Did You Know?, Xerox Education Publications (Middletown, CT), 1977.

Monster Puzzles, Xerox Education Publications (Middletown, CT), 1978.

(With Winnette Glasgow; under joint pseudonym Bob Winn), *Christmas Puzzles,* Scholastic (New York, NY), 1980.

Valentine Puzzles, Xerox Education Publications (Middletown, CT), 1980.

Space Monster Puzzles, Xerox Education Publications (Middletown, CT), 1980.

Goblins and Ghosts, Xerox Education Publications (Middletown, CT), 1980.

Scary Hairy Fun Book, Xerox Education Publications (Middletown, CT), 1981.

My Secrets, Xerox Education Publications (Middletown, CT), 1984.

FICTION; SELF-ILLUSTRATED

(Reteller) *The Teeny Tiny Woman: An Old English Ghost Tale,* Viking (New York, NY), 1976.

The Great Big Elephant and the Very Small Elephant, Crown (New York, NY), 1977.

The Triplets, Houghton Mifflin/Clarion (Boston, MA), 1980.

Just Me, Harcourt (New York, NY), 1982.

OTHER FICTION

What Kind of Family Is This? A Book about Stepfamilies, illustrated by Ellen Dolce, Golden Books (New York, NY), 1985.

I'm Not So Different: A Book about Handicaps, illustrated by Pat Schories, Golden Books (New York, NY), 1986.

Who's the Boss Here?: A Book about Parental Authority, illustrated by Eugenie, Golden Books (New York, NY), 1986.

Boo the Ghost Has a Party, Xerox Educational Publications (Middletown, CT), 1986.

Boo the Ghost and the Robbers, Xerox Educational Publications (Middletown, CT), 1987.

Boo the Ghost and the Magic Hat, Xerox Education Publications (Middletown, CT), 1988.

(Under pseudonym Carrie Austin) *Julie's Boy Problem* ("Party Line" series), Berkeley (New York, NY), 1990.

(Under pseudonym Carrie Austin) *Allie's Wild Surprise* ("Party Line" series), Berkeley (New York, NY), 1990.

Winter Lullaby, illustrated by Greg Newbold, Browndeer Press (San Diego, CA), 1998.

Spring Song, illustrated by Greg Newbold, Harcourt (San Diego, CA), 2001.

Whose House?, illustrated by Kay Chorao, Harcourt (San Diego, CA), 2004.

"ROBERT" SERIES; ILLUSTRATED BY PAUL BREWER

Oh No, It's Robert, Cricket Books (Chicago, IL), 1999.

Robert and the Attack of the Giant Tarantula, Scholastic (New York, NY), 1999.

Robert and the Great Pepperoni, Cricket Books (Chicago, IL), 2002.

Robert and the Weird and Wacky Facts, Cricket Books (Chicago, IL), 2002.

Robert and the Back-to-School Special, Cricket Books (Chicago, IL), 2002.

Robert and the Lemming Problem, Cricket Books (Chicago, IL), 2003.

Robert and the Three Wishes, Cricket Books (Chicago, IL), 2003.

Robert and the Great Escape, Cricket Books (Chicago, IL), 2003.

Robert and the Terrible Secret, Cricket Books (Chicago, IL), 2004.

FOR ADULTS

How to Write a Children's Book and Get It Published, Scribner (New York, NY), 1984, revised and expanded edition, 1991.

ILLUSTRATOR

Wilma Thompson, *That Barbara!,* Delacorte (New York, NY), 1969.

Nan Hayden Agle, *Tarr of Belway Smith,* Seabury Press (New York, NY), 1969.

Stella Pevsner, *Break a Leg!,* Crown (New York, NY), 1969.

Antonia Barber, *The Affair of the Rockerbye Baby,* Delacorte (New York, NY), 1970.

Stella Pevsner, *Footsteps on the Stairs,* Crown (New York, NY), 1970.

Moses L. Howard, *The Ostrich Chase,* Holt (New York, NY), 1974.

Melinda Green, *Bembelman's Bakery,* Parents' Magazine Press (New York, NY), 1978.

Contributor to books and periodicals for and about children, including *Cricket, Ladybug,* and *Once upon a Time.*

SIDELIGHTS: The author and illustrator of fiction, nonfiction, and picture books for young readers and the illustrator of works by such writers as Stella Pevsner and Antonia Barber, Barbara Seuling is well known for her "Freaky Facts" books, as well as for her "Robert" series about an elementary school boy and his humorous escapades in the classroom. The informational "Freaky Facts" books, organized thematically, provide middle graders with little-known facts, myths, and legends on such subjects as sports, law, money, television, geography, the weather, the human body, and the presidency. Reflecting the author's fascination with her subjects, the "Freaky Fact" books are generally considered both edifying and entertaining.

Seuling is also the author of individual volumes of middle-grade nonfiction on such topics as natural disasters, safety, and creating a magic show. In addition, she has written books on the art of writing and being published and has edited a popular guide to New York City for children. As the creator of picture books for preschoolers and early readers, Seuling is the author and illustrator of a well-received retelling of an English folktale; works that address such topics as friendship and individuality; and three stories about Boo, a ghost. For older children, she has written bibliotherapy titles on being handicapped, adjusting to a new step-family, and establishing personal independence with parents as well as two stories for middle graders published under the pseudonym of Carrie Austin. Seuling is also the creator of activity books on some of children's favorite subjects, such as monsters, ghosts, dinosaurs, crafts, and holidays.

"My early years," Seuling wrote in her essay in *Something about the Author Autobiography Series* (*SAAS*), "were the part of my childhood that left the deepest impression, and it is where I feel most connected." Born and raised in the Bensonhurst section of Brooklyn, New York, Seuling was the middle child and only girl in her family, which also includes two brothers. Her parents, Kaspar and Helen Seuling, were influential figures in Barbara's decision to create books for children. "My mother," Seuling said in *SAAS*, "passed on to me her love of reading, of fairy tales and mythology and stories in general. . . . While my mother filled my head with a love of books, it was my father who fostered the magic and wonder in our childhood, especially around the holidays." Her father, Seuling recalled in *SAAS*, "had a unique, witty [writing] style. I like to think I inherited some of my feeling for writing from him."

Growing up in the richly varied area of Bensonhurst, Seuling absorbed neighborhood life as well as the stories passed on by members of her family. "I didn't know then, of course," she recalled in *SAAS*, "that I was collecting details—the colors, the sounds, the language, the sights, the emotions, of my world—and that I would later use them as a writer and artist." She was also greatly influenced by the popular culture of the time: radio shows like "Gangbusters," "The Green Hornet," and "Inner Sanctum"; the comics; and movies, which, Seuling wrote in *SAAS*, "left a great impression on me, and it's no wonder that one of my freaky fact books—*The Loudest Screen Kiss and Other Little-Known Movie Facts*—is about them."

While Seuling was developing her love of story, she was also establishing her talent as an artist. "I showed talent for drawing as soon as I could hold a pencil," she recalled in *SAAS*. "For a long time, my talent for drawing became an important part of my identity. My family was close, but never showed affection openly. The praise and encouragement I received through my drawing, however, seemed to make up for that, giving me a sense of importance. All through my school years, my skill in drawing served as a kind of reminder to an otherwise not-very-confident youngster that I was really good at something." In addition to her interest in art, Seuling was developing a love of nature, fostered by the summers she spent outside of New York City. "These summers," she wrote, "instilled in me a deep love of the country and of space and time to explore and discover the natural world. They balanced my view so that I did not grow up thinking city life was the only life."

In grade school, Seuling was, she recalled, a "good student, if rather passive." In junior high, she experienced some difficulties, both social and academic—"I just wasn't ready for all the changes in my life, physical and social, happening all at once." However, she made some friends and learned to cope with her problem subjects, science and algebra. In addition, she was voted wittiest in her class, claiming, she once told *CA,* "I've been clowning around ever since." In the summer between junior high and high school, Seuling went to Indiana to live with one of her cousins, an experience that she feels helped her to gain self-confidence. "My trip to Indiana—seeing a slice of another way of life," she recalled, "set off something inside of me. . . . I didn't know what I wanted, but it seemed to be outside school, even outside Brooklyn. I began to question what I would do with my life, what I might accomplish. I wanted to see so much of the world, do so much, be *useful.*" By the time Seuling reached high school, there "was certainly none of the trauma that junior high had for me," she wrote in *SAAS.*

At fourteen, Seuling saw the movie *With a Song in My Heart,* the story of singer Jane Froman, who learned to walk again after surviving a plane crash that occurred while she was traveling as part of the USO. Froman's "strength and courage," wrote Seuling, "became my model for all that a person could be." Becoming a member of the Jane Froman fan club, Seuling met Froman in person and became friends with her. "It was through Jane," Seuling wrote, "that I began writing." Becoming the assistant editor of the Froman fan club journal, she wrote and illustrated stories and edited features. "I developed my love for editing at this point," she recalled in *SAAS,* "and while I still didn't think of myself as a writer, I was becoming one. I was, at that time, more confident in my abilities as an artist." The editor of the fan club journal, Winnette Glasgow, has remained Seuling's lifelong friend and has collaborated with her on several works.

Seuling attended night school at Hunter College in the Bronx while working at an insurance company during the day; at nineteen, she changed jobs and schools, taking a position at Columbia University, which offered free college credits as a benefit. She took a room with a single mother in exchange for part-time child-care help. Struggling with the balance of work and school, Seuling decided to take a full-time position as the office manager of an investment company. In charge of hiring temporary help, she hired Winnette Glasgow and Nancy Garden, a budding writer who later became a successful children's author. Seuling and Garden collaborated on a tale for young readers—"a long story about a bookworm," Seuling remembers—with Garden doing the text and Seuling the pictures. When the investment company went bankrupt, Seuling found a position at Dell Publishing Company as a secretary in the adult trade department; when Dell created a new department for children's books, Seuling transferred into it. Working with editor Lee Hoffman, she began to learn about the craft of editing and about the principles of successful writing for children. Seuling then became an assistant children's book editor and also began writing her own works. Her first book, *Freaky Facts,* was written for the Weekly Reader Book Club and published in paperback. *Freaky Facts* compiles hundreds of humorous and outrageous facts on a wide range of subjects, from, Seuling wrote in *SAAS,* "language and hair to animal behavior and diseases." This compilation, she continued, "came from my own love of the strange and fascinating. As a child I had devoured Ripley's *Believe It or Not* in the Sunday funnies and later on in paperback books. . . . I knew strange and funny facts would entertain kids, and I could illustrate them humorously as well. This little book began a long trail of fact books for me that has not stopped yet."

While creating her own books, Seuling continued to work at Dell with Lee Hoffman's successor, George Nicholson. "My association with children's books and publishing," she wrote in *SAAS,* "only whetted my appetite for illustrating. George liked some samples of my drawings that I showed him, and he gave me a middle-grade novel to illustrate. My illustrations were mentioned in a couple of reviews, and my career as an illustrator was started." Seuling showed Nicholson, who had moved from Dell to Viking, her first ideas for a version of the English folktale "The Teeny Tiny Woman." When she had completed the book, Nicholson accepted it for publication. *The Teeny Tiny Woman: An Old English Ghost Tale* is a picture book version of the ghost story in which a small woman in a miniature house finds a small bone on top of a tiny grave. When she gets home, the woman puts the bone in some soup and hears a voice saying, "Give me my bone." She does not give up the bone; instead, she tells the voice to take it. Seuling illustrates the tale in soft pencil with rosy overlays and incorporates hand-lettering into her drawings. A critic in *Publishers Weekly* noted that this "just-for-fun ghost story . . . is embellished with exuberant pictures," while a *School Library Journal* reviewer called *The Teeny Tiny Woman* "a fine new retelling . . . [The] gentle pencil drawings soften the scare so even the most timid beginning readers will enjoy this."

Seuling based her next picture book, *The Great Big Elephant and the Very Small Elephant,* on her friendship with Winnette Glasgow. Seuling describes this book, which is comprised of three gentle stories illustrated in inks and watercolors that stress the affection of her title characters for each other, as "a picture storybook about two friends who are opposite personalities and who see things differently but who ultimately get along by contributing what they each do best." A contributor in *Publishers Weekly* said that Seuling "tells and shows with equal skill in three stories of friendship. . . . Seuling has given beginners a funny, enduring, and altogether lovely book." *The Great Big Elephant* has been compared to Arnold Lobel's "Frog and Toad" books and James Marshall's "George and Martha" series. For example, a reviewer in the *Bulletin of the Center for Children's Books* said, "This hasn't the tenderness of the Lobel stories or the humor of the Marshall books, but it's adequate, both in writing style and as a testament to the give-and-take of friendship."

Two of Seuling's picture books published in the early 1980s have personal identity as their theme. In *The Triplets,* sisters Pattie, Mattie, and Hattie, who have been dressed and treated alike since birth, sequester themselves in their room and refuse to emerge until they are recognized as individuals. A contributor in *Kirkus Reviews* noted that the book contained "an obvious problem-solution contrivance, but there is some zip in the specific examples and in the author's simple two-color cartoons," while *Horn Book* reviewer Kate M. Flanagan noted the "guileless text" and thought that the illustrations of the "three round-faced triplets, though identical in appearance, exhibit subtle but distinct differences in facial expressions and mannerisms." In the easy reader *Just Me,* Seuling depicts a little girl who, over a three-day period, imagines herself as a horse (with hooves made by blocks on her feet), a dragon (with a jump rope for a tale), and a robot (with a box for a body); finally, she decides to just be herself when her supportive mother says, "I like you best of all." *Booklist* reviewer Judith Goldberger said, "With this unimposing set of first-person stories, Seuling shines a true yet carefully framed mirror on the younger reader," while a reviewer in *School Library Journal* noted that the "blend of real life and imagina-

tion in both text and pictures will strike a chord within any child who's ever . . . been sent to his room for refusing to go against dragon nature and 'be nice.'" In the piece she wrote for *SAAS,* Seuling said, "Of all I have written, the work I love best is in picture books. Picture books offer the greatest challenges and bring the most satisfaction. . . . Every word must count, so I have to choose my words carefully, and to hone and polish for the best effect. This has made me a better writer in all forms, not just in picture books."

While contributing books to other genres, Seuling continues to write and illustrate her nonfiction collections of arcane information. One of the earliest "Freaky Facts" titles, *You Can't Eat Peanuts in Church and Other Little-Known Laws,* is a collection of obscure and offbeat laws gathered from around the United States and illustrated in cartoon-like line drawings that underscore the incongruous nature of the laws; writing in *School Library Journal,* Linda Kochinski called *You Can't Eat Peanuts in Church* "[just] the ticket for upper elementary and junior high trivia buffs." Seuling's research for *The Last Cow on the White House Lawn and Other Little-Known Facts about the Presidency,* a collection of facts, firsts, and unique accomplishments, took the author to the Library of Congress, where she investigated the diaries and journals of presidents from George Washington to Jimmy Carter as well as their families and staffs. *Booklist* reviewer Denise M. Wilms claimed, "[This] historical hodgepodge is entertaining, to say the least," while a *Publishers Weekly* critic said, "Trivia fans have taken to Seuling's other books. . . . They may do the same for her new collection."

In *Elephants Can't Jump and Other Freaky Facts about Animals,* Seuling organizes her information in eleven categories such as eating habits, dwellings, and reproduction and enhances her facts with humorous line drawings. *Appraisal* reviewer Althea L. Phillips wrote, "The trivia enthusiasts with an interest in animals will devour this book," while Nancy Murphy, writing in the same publication, noted that Seuling provides "a fresh outlook on some familiar bits of knowledge." *School Library Journal* reviewer Mavis D. Arizzi commented, "These unusual bits of information just might inspire some students to do further research into the characteristics of various animals." With *You Can't Sneeze with Your Eyes Open and Other Freaky Facts about the Human Body,* Seuling covers, in the words of *Appraisal* reviewer Renee E. Blumenkrantz, "amusing and amazing facts" about the body in general, body systems and functions, the brain, birth, death, disease, medical practices, and unusual beliefs. *School Library Journal* reviewer Denise L. Moll said, "Like Seuling's other books . . . this one would be especially useful for book-talking or for suggesting for recreational reading." Writing in *Appraisal*, John R. Pancella observed, "The author is very good at this writing style."

Looking back on the "Freaky Facts" books, Seuling wrote, "I was fast becoming known for these books, and it worried me that I would be considered the Queen of Trivia instead of a bona fide writer of children's books, so I tried to steer away from them for a while. Every time I thought I had done my last freaky fact book, however, something came along to persuade me to do another one. . . . From the feedback I've received over the years . . . I'd say that these books, with their short readable bits of funny or fascinating information, have turned more than a few reluctant readers onto reading, and that pleases me enormously." Yet Seuling could not resist writing more fact books. At the turn of the millennium, she added such titles as *Drip! Drop!: How Water Gets to Your Tap, From Head to Toe: The Amazing Human Body and How It Works*, and *Flick a Switch: How Electricity Gets to Your Home*, to her roster of nonfiction treats.

Further works for younger children include the companion picture book titles *Winter Lullaby* and *Spring Song*, both illustrated by Greg Newbold. The pair celebrate the seasons through lyrical texts, using a question-and-answer format. In the first title, Seuling tells what happens as winter approaches, employing literary techniques such as "subtle alliteration and assonance as well as rhyme," which, according to Peg Solonika of *School Library Journal*, "work well for reading aloud." *Winter Lullaby* is "a picture-perfect conclusion to a frosty night," commented *Booklist* reviewer Ellen Mandel. Spring gets a similar treatment in *Spring Song*. Although "sometimes clumsy" in the view of a *Publishers Weekly* contributor, the text presents "a joyful introduction to the creatures of the woodland forest, mountain range, meadow, and marshland." Among the work's enthusiasts are Helen Foster of *School Library Journal*, who predicted that the picture "book will prompt lively discussion and conversation," and a *Kirkus Reviews* writer, who called *Spring Song* "a seasonal wake-up tune with nary a false note."

In 1999, Seuling launched her "Robert" series of easy readers, which, according to *Booklist*'s Todd Morning, are known for "a fast-moving plot, short chapters, and witty writing." Geared to readers in grades two through four, they also feature familiar characters and situations, such as the desire for a dog or for stress-free recognition from a teacher. Reviewing *Robert and the Back-to-School Special*, a *Kirkus Reviews* critic praised Seuling's command of a "tight plot and realistic situations," predicting that "young readers will identify with and root" for the young protagonist. Accompanying Seuling's humorous stories are pen-and-ink drawings by Paul Brewer, which "create satisfying visual interest," wrote Janie Schomberg in a *School Library Journal* review of *Robert and the Great Pepperoni*. Other reviewers saw much to like about the "Robert" books as well, including a *Kirkus Reviews* contributor, who appreciated the "familiar and comforting" and yet "goofy but believable situations" in *Robert and the Weird and Wacky Facts*. In her review of *Robert and the Great Pepperoni* for *Horn Book*, Betty Carter also cited Robert as a "familiar character" and praised Seuling's "tight plotting." Janice M. Del Negro, writing in the *Bulletin of the Center for Children's Books* about *Oh No, It's Robert*, complimented Seuling for her "easygoing humor," "conversational style," and "light hand with her messages." So too, Kay Weisman of *Booklist* found this work "a perfect choice for those looking for a humorous book." With *Robert and the Weird and Wacky Facts*, Seuling combined her long-held penchant for interesting tidbits and her likeable Robert character when Robert tries to enter a television trivia contest. "The Robert stories are instant winners," enthused *Horn Book*'s Betty Carter.

In addition to working as an author, illustrator, and editor, Seuling has been a teacher at the Bank Street College, the Manuscript Workshop, and the Institute for Children's Literature, among other places, and has become recognized as an authority on writing for children. She is eager to share her insight with would-be writers and in 1984 wrote *How to Write a Children's Book and Get It Published*, which she revised and expanded in the 1991 edition. Seuling explained her love of working in the juvenile literature field in *SAAS*: "I still try to do it all—write, illustrate, edit, and teach—sometimes to the point of frustration, because it's what I love to do. . . . I am pleased to have devoted my life to books for children, because I believe books will help young people to grow and think and see the world in all its variety." She once said, "My purpose is different for each book I create—to share an emotional experience, show some aspect of the world a little better, or more clearly; make it easier to get through a tough or stressful situation—and yet all this must be kept carefully hidden so that it doesn't frighten children away. So, on the surface, I want to make children laugh, to entertain them, tell them a good story, excite their interest. I feel fortunate to work at what I love so much—writing and illustrating children's books. Although it has never been easy, the rewards still outweigh the difficulties. Young people want to know more and more about the life around them, about people and relationships and feelings, and if we're truthful, we can support them in this quest for knowledge. Inevitably, it turns around, and we learn something from the kids."

Seuling concluded, "My advice to new writers is: be persistent. The saddest part of writing is the defeatism that is felt so early by writers. One's first work rarely gets published, but that is when our hopes and ideals are so high that they are easily dashed by rejection. It is a rough process, and if one can weather the first years, and keep writing in spite of the obstacles, the chances of success keep growing. A writer is a growing thing; we grow with each page we write, and therefore the more we write the more we learn and the better we become."

BIOGRAPHICAL AND CRITICAL SOURCES:

BOOKS

Seuling, Barbara, *Just Me,* Harcourt (San Diego, CA), 1982.
Something about the Author Autobiography Series, Volume 24, Gale (Detroit, MI), 1997, pp. 217-233.

PERIODICALS

Appraisal, fall, 1985, Nancy Murphy, review of *Elephants Can't Jump and Other Freaky Facts about Animals,* pp. 35-36, and Althea L. Phillips, review of *Elephants Can't Jump and Other Freaky Facts about Animals,* pp. 35; fall, 1987, Renee E. Blumenkrantz, review of *You Can't Sneeze with Your Eyes Open and Other Freaky Facts about the Human Body,* p. 49, and John R. Pancella, review of *You Can't Sneeze with Your Eyes Open and Other Freaky Facts about the Human Body,* pp. 49-50.

Booklist, October 1, 1975, p. 241; September 1, 1978, Denise M. Wilms, review of *The Last Cow on the White House Lawn and Other Little-Known Facts about the Presidency,* p. 53; May 1, 1982, p. 1163; June 15, 1982, Judith Goldberger, review of *Just Me,* p. 1372; February 15, 1985, p. 848; July, 1992, p. 1947; September 1, 1998, Ellen Mandel, review of *Winter Lullaby,* p. 123; July, 1999, Kay Weisman, review of *Oh No, It's Robert,* p. 1947; April 15, 2001, Carolyn Phelan, review of *Spring Song,* p. 1566; April 1, 2002, Todd Morning, review of *Robert and the Weird and Wacky Facts,* p. 1329; January 1, 2003, Carolyn Phelan, review of *Robert and the Back-to-School Special,* p. 893; April 1, 2003, Shelle Rosenfeld, review of *Robert and the Lemming Problem,* p. 1398.

Bulletin of the Center for Children's Books, July-August, 1975, p. 185; October, 1997, review of *The Great Big Elephant and the Very Small Elephant,* pp. 36-37; October, 1988, pp. 53-54; July, 1999, Janice M. Del Negro, review of *Oh No, It's Robert* p. 400.

Horn Book, August, 1976, Virginia Haviland, review of *The Teeny Tiny Woman: An Old English Ghost Tale,* pp. 591-592; April, 1980, Kate M. Flanagan, review of *The Triplets,* p. 400; January-February, 2002, Betty Carter, review of *Robert and the Great Pepperoni,* pp. 83-84; July-August, 2002, Betty Carter, review of *Robert and the Weird and Wacky Facts,* pp. 471-472.

Horn Book Guide, spring, 1999, Martha Sibert, review of *Winter Lullaby,* p. 16; fall, 2001, Danelle J. Ford, review of *Drip! Drop!: How Water Gets to Your Tap,* p. 382.

Kirkus Reviews, July 15, 1978, pp. 752-753; April 1, 1980, review of *Triplets,* p. 437; February 15, 2001, review of *Spring Song,* p. 265; March, 2002, review of *Robert and the Weird and Wacky Facts,* p. 246; August 15, 2002, review of *From Head to Toe: The Amazing Human Body and How It Works,* p. 1236; October 1, 2002, review of *Robert and the Back-to-School Special,* p. 1481.

Publishers Weekly, April 12, 1976, review of *The Teeny Tiny Woman,* p. 66; June 13, 1977, review of *The Great Big Elephant and the Very Small Elephant,* p. 108; May 15, 1978, review of *The Last Cow on the White House Lawn and Other Little-Known Facts about the Presidency,* p. 104; October 5, 1998, review of *Winter Lullaby,* p. 88; June 14,

1999, review of *Oh No, It's Robert,* p. 70; February 26, 2001, review of *Spring Song,* p. 84; September 6, 2002, review of *From Head to Toe,* p. 71.

School Library Journal, May, 1975, p. 73; October, 1975, Linda Kochinski, review of *You Can't Eat Peanuts in Church and Other Little-Known Laws,* p. 101; November, 1975, p. 83; May, 1976, review of *The Teeny Tiny Woman,* p. 75; September, 1977, p. 115; November, 1980, p. 67; May, 1982, review of *Just Me,* p. 80; August, 1982, p. 122; March, 1985, Mavis D. Arizzi, review of *Elephants Can't Jump and Other Freaky Facts about Animals,* p. 171; February, 1987, Denise L. Moll, review of *You Can't Sneeze with Your Eyes Open and Other Freaky Facts about the Human Body,* p. 84; September, 1998, Peg Solonika, review of *Winter Lullaby,* p. 198; July, 1999, Linda Beck, review of *Oh No, It's Robert,* p. 80; February, 2001, Ellen Heath, review of *Drip! Drop!,* p. 115; May, 2001, Helen Foster, review of *Spring Song,* p. 135; October, 2001, Janie Schomberg, review of *Robert and the Great Pepperoni,* p. 131; July, 2002, John Sigwald, review of *Robert and the Weird and Wacky Tales,* pp. 98-99; November, 2002, Dona Ratterree, review of *From Head to Toe,* p. 148.

Voice of Youth Advocates, October, 1997, p. 270.*

*   *   *

SMITH, Jonathan M(ark) 1957-

PERSONAL: Born November 6, 1957, in Stevens Point, WI; son of Delmont C. (a professor) and Jeannette R. M. (a librarian) Smith; married May 28, 1994; wife's name Ulrike M. *Ethnicity:* "White." *Education:* State University of New York—College at Geneseo, B.A., 1980; Syracuse University, M.A., 1987, Ph.D., 1991.

ADDRESSES: Office—Department of Geography, 800 Eller, Texas A & M University, College Station, TX 77843-3147; fax: 979-862-4487. *E-mail*—jmsmith@ tamu.edu.

CAREER: Texas A & M University, College Station, TX, visiting assistant professor, 1989-91, assistant professor, 1991-97, associate professor, 1997-2003, professor of geography, 2003—, member of executive steering committee of Center for Science and Technology Policy and Ethics, 1995—.

MEMBER: Association of American Geographers (chair of Cultural Geography Specialty Group, 1996-99), Society for Philosophy and Geography (cofounder).

WRITINGS:

(Editor, with Kenneth Foote, Peter Hugill, and Kent Matthewson, and contributor) *Re-Reading Cultural Geography,* University of Texas Press (Austin, TX), 1994.

(Editor, with Andrew Light, and contributor) *Space, Place, and Environmental Ethics: Philosophy and Geography I,* Rowman & Littlefield (Lanham, MD), 1996.

(Editor, with Andrew Light, and contributor) *The Production of Public Space: Philosophy and Geography II,* Rowman & Littlefield (Lanham, MD), 1998.

(Editor, with Andrew Light, and contributor) *The Philosophy of Place: Philosophy and Geography III,* Rowman & Littlefield (Lanham, MD), 1998.

(Coeditor and contributor) *Worldview Flux: Perplexed Values among Postmodern Peoples,* Lexington Books (Lexington, MA), 2000.

(Coeditor and contributor) *American Space/American Place,* Edinburgh University Press (Edinburgh, Scotland), 2002.

Contributor to books, including *Written Worlds: Discourse, Text, and Metaphor in the Representation of Landscapes,* edited by T. Barnes and J. Duncan, Routledge (London, England), 1991; *Place/Culture/ Representation,* edited by J. Duncan and D. Ley, Routledge (London, England), 1993; and *Concepts in Human Geography,* edited by Kent Matthewson, Carville Earle, and Martin Kenzer, Rowman & Littlefield (Lanham, MD), 1996. Contributor of articles and reviews to journals, including *Annals of the American Association of Geographers* and *Historical Methods.* Coeditor, *Philosophy and Geography;* newsletter editor, Society for Philosophy and Geography, 1994-97; member of editorial board, *Geographical Review,* 1998—; member of editorial advisory board, *Ecumene: Journal of Environment, Culture, Meaning,* 1993—.

SNYDER, Gary (Sherman) 1930-

PERSONAL: Born May 8, 1930, in San Francisco CA; son of Harold Alton and Lois (Wilkie) Snyder; married Alison Gass, 1950 (divorced, 1951); married Joanne Kyger (a poet), 1960 (divorced, 1964); married Masa Uehara, August 6, 1967 (divorced); married Carole Koda, April 28, 1991; children: (third marriage) Kai, Gen. *Education:* Reed College, B.A. (in anthropology and literature), 1951; attended Indiana University, 1951; University of California, Berkeley, graduate study in Oriental languages, 1953-56. *Politics:* Radical. *Religion:* Buddhist of the Mahayana-Vajrayana line.

ADDRESSES: Home—Kitkitdizze, NV. *Office*—c/o North Point Press, 850 Talbot Ave., Berkeley, CA 94706.

CAREER: Poet and translator, 1959—. Worked as seaman, logger, trail crew member, and forest lookout, 1948-56; lecturer at University of California, Berkeley, 1964-65; professor at University of California, Davis, 1985—. Visiting lecturer at numerous universities and writing workshops. Member of United Nations Conference on the Human Environment, 1972; former chair of California Arts Council.

MEMBER: American Academy and Institute of Arts and Letters.

AWARDS, HONORS: Scholarship from First Zen Institute of America, 1956, for study in Japan; National Institute and American Academy poetry award, 1966; Bollingen Foundation grant, 1966-67; Frank O'Hara Prize, 1967; Levinson Prize from *Poetry* magazine, 1968; Guggenheim fellowship, 1968-69; Pulitzer Prize in poetry, 1975, for *Turtle Island;* American Book Award, Before Columbus Foundation, 1984, for *Axe Handles.*

WRITINGS:

POETRY

Riprap (also see below), Origin Press (San Francisco, CA), 1959.

Gary Snyder

Myths & Texts, Totem Press (New York, NY), 1960, reprinted, New Directions (New York, NY), 1978.

Riprap & Cold Mountain Poems (the *Cold Mountain* poems are Snyder's translations of poems by Han-Shan), Four Seasons Foundation (San Francisco, CA), 1965, reprinted, 1977.

Six Sections from Mountains and Rivers without End, Four Seasons Foundation (San Francisco, CA), 1965, revised edition published as *Six Sections from Mountains and Rivers without End, Plus One,* 1970.

A Range of Poems (includes translations of the modern Japanese poet Miyazawa Kenji), Fulcrum (London, England), 1966.

Three Worlds, Three Realms, Six Roads, Griffin Press (Marlboro, VT), 1966.

The Back Country, Fulcrum (London, England), 1967, New Directions (New York, NY), 1968.

The Blue Sky, Phoenix Book Shop (New York, NY), 1969.

Regarding Wave, New Directions (New York, NY), 1970.

Manzanita, Kent State University Libraries (Kent, OH), 1971.

Piute Creek, State University College at Brockport (Brockport, NY), 1972.

The Fudo Trilogy: Spell against Demons, Smokey the Bear Sutra, The California Water Plan (also see below), illustrated by Michael Corr, Shaman Drum (Berkeley, CA), 1973.

Turtle Island, New Directions (New York, NY), 1974.

All in the Family, University of California Library, c. 1975.

Smokey the Bear Sutra (chapbook), 1976.

Songs for Gaia, illustrated by Corr, Copper Canyon (Port Townsend, WA), 1979.

Axe Handles, North Point Press (San Francisco, CA), 1983.

Good Wild Scared, Five Seasons Press (Madley, Hereford, England), 1984.

Left Out in the Rain: New Poems 1947-1986, North Point Press (San Francisco, CA), 1986.

The Fates of Rocks & Trees, James Linden (San Francisco, CA), 1986.

No Nature: New and Selected Poems, Pantheon (New York, NY), 1992.

North Pacific Lands & Waters, Brooding Heron Press (Waldron Island, WA), 1993.

Mountains and Rivers without End, Counterpoint (Washington, DC), 1996.

PROSE

Earth House Hold: Technical Notes and Queries to Fellow Dharma Revolutionaries (essays), New Directions (New York, NY), 1969.

(Contributor) *Ecology: Me,* Moving On, 1970.

The Old Ways: Six Essays, City Lights (San Francisco, CA), 1977.

On Bread & Poetry: A Panel Discussion between Gary Snyder, Lew Welch and Philip Whalen, edited by Donald M. Allen, Grey Fox (Bolinas, CA), 1977.

He Who Hunted Birds in His Father's Village (undergraduate thesis), preface by Nathaniel Tarn, Grey Fox (Bolinas, CA), 1979.

The Real Work: Interviews & Talks, 1964-1979, edited with introduction by Scott McLean, New Directions (New York, NY), 1980.

Passage through India (autobiography), Grey Fox (San Francisco, CA), 1983.

The Practice of the Wild, Farrar, Straus (New York, NY), 1990.

A Place in Space: Ethics, Aesthetics, and Watersheds (new and selected prose), Counterpoint (Washington, DC), 1995.

The Gary Snyder Reader: Prose, Poetry, and Translations, 1952-1998, Counterpoint (Washington, DC), 1999.

Look Out: A Selection of Writings, New Directions (New York, NY), 2002.

OTHER

The New Religion (sound recording), Big Sur Recordings, 1967.

Gary Snyder Reading His Poems in the Montpelier Room, Oct. 24, 1996, (sound recording) 1996.

A Place for Wayfaring: The Poetry and Prose of Gary Snyder / Patrick D. Murphy Oregon State University Press (Corvallis, OR), 2000.

(With Tom Killion and John Muir) *The High Sierra of California,* Heyday Books, 2002.

Contributor to anthologies, including *Contemporary American Poetry,* edited by Donald Hall, Penguin Books (New York, NY), 1962; *A Controversy of Poets,* edited by Paris Leary and Robert Kelly, Doubleday (New York, NY), 1965; and *Sustainable Poetry: Four American Ecopoets,* edited by Leonard M. Scigaj, University Press of Kentucky (Lexington, KY), 1999. Contributor to numerous periodicals, including *Janus, Evergreen Review, Black Mountain Review, Yugen, Chicago Review, Jabberwock, San Francisco Review, Big Table, Origin, Kulchur, Journal for the Protection of All Beings, Nation, City Lights Journal, Yale Literary Magazine, Beloit Poetry Journal,* and *Poetry.* The University of California, Davis, holds a collection of Snyder's manuscripts.

SIDELIGHTS: Gary Snyder is one of the rare modern poets who has bridged the gap between popular appeal and serious academic criticism. Snyder began his career in the 1950s as a noted member of the "Beat Generation," and since then he has explored a wide range of social and spiritual matters in both poetry and prose. Snyder's work blends physical reality—precise observations of nature—with inner insight received primarily through the practice of Zen Buddhism. *Southwest Review* essayist Abraham Rothberg noted that the poet "celebrates nature, the simple, the animal, the sexual, the tribal, the self. . . . He sees man as an indissoluble part of the natural environment, flourishing when he accepts and adapts to that natural heritage, creating a hell on earth and within himself when he is separated from it by his intellect and its technological and societal creations." While Snyder has gained the attention of readers as a spokesman for the preservation of the natural world and its earth-conscious cultures, he is not simply a "back-to-nature" poet with a facile message. In *American Poetry in the Twentieth Century,* Kenneth Rexroth observed that although Snyder proposes "a new ethic, a new esthetic, [and] a new life style," he is also "an accomplished technician who has learned from the poetry of several languages and who has developed a sure and flexible style capable of handling any material he wishes." According to Charles Altieri in *Enlarging the Temple: New Directions in American Poetry during the 1960s,* Snyder's achievement "is a considerable one. Judged simply in aesthetic terms, according to norms of precision, intelligence, imaginative play, and moments of deep resonance, he easily ranks among the best poets of his generation. Moreover, he manages to provide a fresh perspective on metaphysical themes, which he makes relevant and compelling."

Snyder's emphasis on metaphysics and his celebration of the natural order remove his work from the general tenor of Beat writing. *Dictionary of Literary Biography* contributor Dan McLeod explained that while authors such as Allen Ginsberg and Neal Cassady "represented in their different ways rather destructive responses to the alienation inherent in modern American technocracy, the example of Snyder's life and values offered a constructive, albeit underground, alternative to mainstream American culture." No less searing in his indictments of Western values than the other Beat writers, Snyder has proposed "a morality that is unharmful, that tends toward wholeness. An ethics not of the trigger or fist, but of the heart," to quote *New Republic* reviewer Timothy Baland. Snyder has looked to the Orient and to the beliefs of American Indians for positive responses to the world, and he has tempered his studies with stints of hard physical labor as a logger and trail builder. In the *Southwest Review,* Roger Jones called Snyder "one of the century's *healthiest* writers," a poet who "perceives man as completely situated within the schemes of natural order, and sees as a necessity man's awareness that he is as real and as whole as the world—a perception muddled by the metaphysical notion of the world as a mere stage for the enactment of our eternal destinies." Charles Molesworth elaborated on this premise in his work *Gary Snyder's Vision: Poetry and the Real Work.*

Molesworth saw Snyder as "a moral visionary who is neither a scourge nor a satirist; . . . he has spoken as a prophet whose 'tribe' is without definite national or cultural boundaries."

Altieri believed that Snyder's "articulation of a possible religious faith" independent of Western culture has greatly enhanced his popularity, especially among younger readers. If that is so, Snyder's themes have also been served by an accessible style, drawn from the examples of Japanese haiku and Chinese verse. In a book entitled *Gary Snyder,* Bob Steuding remarked that Snyder "has created a new kind of poetry that is direct, concrete, non-Romantic, and ecological. . . . Snyder's work will be remembered in its own right as the example of a new direction taken in American literature." *Nation* contributor Richard Tillinghast wrote: "In Snyder the stuff of the world 'content'— has always shone with a wonderful sense of earthiness and health. He has always had things to tell us, experiences to relate, a set of values to expound. . . . He has influenced a generation." McLeod found Snyder's "poetic fusion of Buddhist and tribal world views with ecological science" a "remarkable cross-cultural achievement—an utterly appropriate postmodernist expression of a post-industrial sensibility." Robert Mezey put it more simply in the *Western Humanities Review* when he concluded: "This missionary is really a joyful poet, and the gratitude and celebration at the heart of his view of life often overwhelm the necessity to teach and explain. So the teaching is done silently, which is the best way to do it."

Born and raised in the American West, Snyder lived close to nature from earliest childhood. Even at a very young age he was distressed by the wanton destruction of the Pacific Northwestern forests, and he began to study and respect the Indian cultures that "seemed to have some sense of how a life harmonious with nature might be lived," according to Rothberg. Snyder went to public schools in Seattle and Portland, and he augmented his education by reading about Indian lore and pioneer adventures. Wild regions continued to fascinate him as he matured; he became an expert mountain climber and learned back-country survival techniques. A visit to the Seattle Art Museum introduced him to Chinese landscape painting, and he developed an interest in the Orient as an example of a high civilization that had maintained its bonds to nature. After high school Snyder divided his time between studies at the prestigious Reed College—and later Indiana University and the University of California, Berkeley—and work as a lumberjack, trail maker, and firewatcher in the deep woods. The balance between physical labor and intellectual pursuits informs his earliest writing; McLeod felt that the unlikely juxtaposition makes Snyder either "the last of an old breed or the beginning of a new breed of backwoodsmen figures in American literature." In *Alone with America: Essays on the Art of Poetry in the United States since 1950,* Richard Howard described Snyder's youth as "the rapturous life of a cosmic bum."

In the autumn of 1952 Snyder moved to the San Francisco Bay area in order to study Oriental languages at Berkeley. He was already immersed in Zen Buddhism and had begun to write poetry about his work in the wilderness. McLeod contended that the four years Snyder spent in San Francisco "were of enormous importance to his . . . growth as a poet." He became part of a community of writers, including Philip Whalen, Allen Ginsberg, and Jack Kerouac, who would come to be known as the Beat Generation and who would be heralded as the forerunners of a counterculture revolution in literature. The literary fame of the Beat Generation was launched with a single event: a poetry reading in October of 1955 at San Francisco's Six Gallery. While it is Ginsberg's poem "Howl" that is best remembered from that evening, Snyder also participated, reading his poem "The Berry Feast."

If Snyder was influenced by his antisocial contemporaries, he also exerted an influence on them. Kerouac modeled his character Japhy Ryder in *The Dharma Bums* on Snyder, and the poet encouraged his friends to take an interest in Eastern philosophy as an antidote to the ills of the West. McLeod noted, however, that although "he is clearly one of its major figures, Snyder was out of town when the Beat movement was most alive on the American scene." Having been awarded a scholarship by the First Zen Institute of America, Snyder moved to Japan in 1956 and stayed abroad almost continuously for the next twelve years. Part of that time he lived in an ashram and devoted himself to strenuous Zen study and meditation. He also travelled extensively, visiting India and Indonesia, and even venturing as far as Istanbul on an oil tanker, the *Sappa Creek*. His first two poetry collections, *Riprap* and *Myths & Texts,* were published in 1959 and 1960. After returning to the United States, Snyder built his own house— along the Yuba River in the northern Sierra Nevada mountains— where he has lived since.

Snyder's early poems represent a vigorous attempt to achieve freedom from the "establishment" mores of urban America. *Sagetrieb* contributor Thomas Parkinson described the works as moments in which "action and contemplation become identical states of being, and both states of secular grace. From this fusion wisdom emerges, and it is not useless but timed to the event. The result is a terrible sanity, a literal clairvoyance, an innate decorum." The poems in *Riprap* and *Myths & Texts* are miniature narratives captured from the active working life of the author; Rothberg contended that in them Snyder wants "to be considered a poet of ordinary men, writing in a language shaped in their idiom." Audiences responded to Snyder's portrayals of the vigorous backwoods visionary whose joy flows from physical pursuits and contemplation of the wild world. In the *Los Angeles Times Book Review,* Schuyler Ingle wrote: "I could sense [Snyder] in his lines, all long-haired and denim-clad, laced-up hightop logger boots. He was an educated, curious man comfortable with his own sexuality." Rothberg too detects the education underlying the hardier roles. According to the critic, Snyder "cannot quite conceal the intellect or learning in his work, which everywhere reveals his considerable knowledge of anthropology, linguistics, Zen Buddhism, history, and other arcane lore."

Unquestionably, Snyder's involvement with Buddhism has been important to his poetry from the outset. As Julian Gitzen noted in *Critical Quarterly,* Snyder "was attracted to Buddhism because its teachings conformed to and re-enforced his native personality, interests and beliefs." Much of the poet's work "manifests a . . . movement out to an awareness of self in cosmos complemented by the perception of cosmos contained within the self," to quote Altieri. In *American Poetry since 1960: Some Critical Perspectives,* Alan Williamson also stated that Snyder's canon "suggests a process of meditation or spiritual exercise, clearing the path from temporal life to the moment of Enlightenment—the sudden dropping-away of the phenomenal world in the contemplation of the infinite and eternal, All and Nothingness." The aim, according to Parkinson, is "not to achieve harmony with nature but to create an inner harmony that equals to the natural external harmony." *Criticism* essayist Robert Kern declared that the resulting poems "are almost celebrations of those moments when the mind's resistances have been overcome and the difficult transition has been made from ordinary consciousness to a state in which the mind has dropped its symbolic burden of words, books, abstractions, even personal history and identity—whatever might stand in the way of a direct, unhampered perception of things."

The structure of Snyder's poetry is influenced by the intellectual dilemma of using language—the medium of rational discourse—to disclose deeper, extra-rational states of being. *Dictionary of Literary Biography* essayist Alex Batman observed that Snyder realizes mere words may be inadequate for the articulation of his discoveries. The poet overcomes this problem by producing verse "based on the Oriental haiku—sharp, uncomplicated images that, like many Oriental paintings, form sketches that the reader's imagination must fill in." Gitzen wrote: "Snyder's poems in general possess [an] air of spontaneity, almost as though they were hastily written notes for poems, rather than finished constructions. Such unpolished form harmonizes with the Zen aesthetic." The critic added, however, that spontaneous and simple though the works may seem, they are in fact "the result of conscious and painstaking effort." Batman likewise found Snyder's pieces "deceptively simple rather than superficially simplistic." Altieri commented that for the skeptic or half-believer, "the real miracle is the skill with which Snyder uses the aesthetic devices of lyrical poetry to sustain his religious claims. His basic achievement is his power to make his readers reflect on the ontological core of the lyrical vision by calling attention to the way it can be things or processes themselves, and not merely the elements of a poem, which mutually create one another's significance and suggest a unifying power producing, sustaining, and giving meaning to these relationships." Steuding concluded that the "Buddhist perception of oneness . . . creates a poetry of immediacy and startling originality."

Buddhism is by no means the sole departure point for Snyder's work, however. Well-versed in anthropology and the lore of so-called "primitive" cultures, the author reveres myth and ritual as essential demonstrations of man-in-nature and nature-in-man. In *The American West,* Thomas W. Pew, Jr. wrote: "Snyder, like a handful of other writers since Carl Jung, has discovered the similarities of myth, religion, and his own personal dream content as well as the product of his meditations and has fashioned that collective material into words that set off little explosions in our thought process and our own deeper memory." Harking back to the Stone Age, Snyder sees the poet as a shaman who acts as a medium for songs and chants

springing from the earth. McLeod explained: "The poet-shaman draws his songs from the [Earth] Mother Goddess and through the magic power of image, metaphor, music, and myth creates the artistic patterns that express the most deeply held knowledge and values of the community. Embodied in literary form, this knowledge and these values may survive and evolve, sustaining the group generation after generation." McLeod stated further that myth and ritual are for Snyder "far more than reflections of experience. . . . They are also a means whereby we can shape and control experience through the sympathetic magic inherent in the metaphysical connections that link myth and ritual to the quotidian world."

It is not surprising, therefore, that Snyder draws on the traditions of oral literature—chants, incantations, and songs—to communicate his experiences. *Denver Quarterly* contributor Kevin Oderman observed that the poet "writes out of a tradition of self-effacement, and his yearnings are for a communal poetry rooted in place." Scott McLean also addressed this idea in his introduction to Snyder's *The Real Work: Interviews & Talks, 1964-1979.* "All of Gary Snyder's study and work has been directed toward a poetry that would approach phenomena with a disciplined clarity that would then use the 'archaic' and the 'primitive' as models to once again see this poetry as woven through all the parts of our lives," McLean wrote. "Thus it draws its substance and forms from the broadest range of a people's day-to-day lives, enmeshed in the facts of work, the real trembling in joy and grief, thankfulness for good crops, the health of a child, the warmth of the lover's touch. Further, Snyder seeks to recover a poetry that could sing and thus relate us to: magpie, beaver, a mountain range, binding us to all these other lives, seeing our spiritual lives as bound up in the rounds of nature." McLean concluded that in terms of the human race's future, "Snyder's look toward the primitive may vouchsafe one of the only real alternative directions available." Addressing specifically the poetry, Jones admitted in *Southwest Review* that Snyder's shamanistic role is an important one for modern letters "as poetry seems to base itself less in sound than in the medium of print."

Many of Snyder's poems aim specifically at instilling an ecological consciousness in his audience. Jones observed that the poet advocates "peaceful stewardship, economy, responsibility with the world's resources, and, most importantly, sanity—all still within the capabilities of modern societies, and bound up in the perception of the world and its life-sources as a glorious whole." This theme pervades Snyder's 1974 Pulitzer Prize-winning volume, *Turtle Island,* a work in which the poet manages "to locate the self ecologically in its actions and interactions with its environment, to keep it anchored to its minute-by-minute manifestations in (and as a part of) the physical world," to quote Robert Kern in *Contemporary Literature.* According to Gitzen, Snyder assumes that "while man neither individually nor as a species is essential to nature . . . nature is essential to the existence of all men. Consideration for our own welfare demands that we abandon efforts to dominate nature and assume instead an awareness of our subjection to natural law. . . . Snyder repeatedly seeks to impress upon his readers the awesome immensity of space, time, energy, and matter working together to generate a destiny beyond the reach of human will." Some critics, such as *Partisan Review* contributor Robert Boyers, found Snyder's commitment "programmistic and facile," a simplistic evocation of the "noble savage" as hero. Others, including *New York Times Book Review* correspondent Herbert Leibowitz, applauded the poet's world view. "Snyder's sane housekeeping principles desperately need to become Government and corporate policy," Leibowitz wrote. "He is on the side of the gods."

"The curve of Snyder's career has been from the fact-like density of perceptual intensity to the harmonious patternmaking of the immanently mythic imagination," Molesworth stated. "Such a course of development has taken Snyder deeper and deeper into the workings of the political imagination as well." Snyder's more recent works reflect a growing concern for the environment and the plight of the American Indian as well as the new insights engendered by his domestic responsibilities. McLeod noted that a "shift from the examination of the self to the exercise of social responsibility is clearly reflected in the development of Snyder's writing which has moved from the still, almost purely meditative lyrics in *Riprap,* to the celebration of the human family as a vital part of a broad network of relationships linking all forms of life in *Regarding Wave,* to the eco-political poems and essays in *Turtle Island.*"*Axe Handles,* Snyder's 1983 collection, returns to the domestic environment—especially the relationship between father and sons—as a central motif. *Poetry* magazine reviewer Bruce Bawer contended that the work "conveys a luminous, poignant vision of a life afforded joy and strength by a recogni-

tion of the essential things which give it meaning. It is, to my tastes, Snyder's finest book."

Not all reviewers felt that Snyder's more recent poetry scales the heights he reached with *Turtle Island.* Reviewing *No Nature,* a collection of old and new poems published in 1992, David Barber commented in *Poetry* that "the vigor and output of Snyder's poetry has clearly been on the wane over the last twenty years. . . . The poet who was formerly adept at elucidating intimations now seems to be content with simply espousing positions." However, Richard Tillinghast, writing in the *New York Times Book Review,* claimed that Snyder possesses "a command of geology, anthropology and evolutionary biology unmatched among contemporary poets," adding that "there is an understated majesty about the ease with which Mr. Snyder puts the present into perspective." Both Tillinghast and Barber in particular commended Snyder's evocation of the subject of work. Noted Barber, "Few contemporary poets have written with such authentic incisiveness about the particulars of work and the rhythms of subsistence, and done so without succumbing to class-rooted righteousness or rural nostalgia."

One project that spanned much of the poet's career—a long poem, *Mountains and Rivers without End,* titled after a Chinese sideways scroll painting—was finally published in 1996 to glowing praise from critics. As Steuding claimed, "One finds directness and simplicity of statement, clarity and brilliance of mind, and profundity and depth of emotional range. In these instances, Snyder's is a poetry of incredible power and beauty." Similarly, a *Publishers Weekly* reviewer commented that *Mountains and Rivers without End* "is a major work by a venerable master of post-[World War II] American poetry." The poem is a conscious effort to recreate the social function of ancient epics: to tell a good story, while offering instruction in life by way of myth and history. Snyder's narrative is "less heroic in tone than Homer's," found Tom Clark in his *San Francisco Chronicle* review, but like classic works such as the *Odyssey, Mountains and Rivers without End* is "a universalizing, picaresque spiritual journey, the story not only of one man, but also of the human event on this planet," explained Clark. Ancient values are evoked and celebrated: fertility, the magic of animals, the power of dance, and the importance of tribal work. Snyder evokes an ancient civilization blessed by self-awareness, thriving in an unpolluted world. The narrative is "continually teetering perilously on the great divide between human and nonhuman worlds, demonstrating all over again the curiously ambivalent evenhandedness that has always created an interesting tension in his work," commented Clark. Conflicting desires to escape and redeem civilization form another part of the work, which show the poet in concrete landscapes of freeway and megalopolis. Taken as a whole, the poem celebrates "not only nature's exquisite delicacy and fragility but also its immense ruggedness, resilience and durability." Snyder's personal journey of several decades is reflected in the verses that took him so long to complete, and he commented to Jesse Hamlin in an interview for *San Francisco Chronicle* that those years were "a time of tremendous change, and yet I can see that the initial impulses with which I opened the work — which were curiosity and affection and respect for the whole natural world — naive in some ways as they were, were basically going in the right direction." He concluded: "I'm pleased with the poem," but he added: "I don't think in terms of masterpieces. . . . You do the work you do and you leave it for the world to judge where it fits. I did what I was impelled to do. It got me to the point where I could let go of it."

In addition to his many volumes of verse, Snyder has published books of prose essays and interviews that can be read "not only as partial explanation of the poetry but as the record of an evolving mind with extreme good sense in treating the problems of the world," according to Parkinson. Snyder's prose expands his sense of social purpose and reveals the series of interests and concerns that have sparked his creative writing. In *The Practice of the Wild,* published in 1990, Snyder muses on familiar topics such as environmental concerns, Native American culture, ecofeminism, language, and mythology. Praising the author's "exquisite craftsmanship and new maturity in style," Michael Strickland in the *Georgia Review* noted, "Any serious consideration of Snyder's work, whether critical text or classroom study, must now include *The Practice of the Wild.*" Environmental writer Bill McKibben expressed a similar view in the *New York Review of Books,* stating that the collection represents Snyder's "best prose work so far." Remarking on the author's wide-ranging skill, Parkinson suggested that Snyder is distinguished "not only as a poet but as a prose expositor—he has a gift for quiet, untroubled, accurate observation with occasional leaps to genuine eloquence. He has taken to himself a subject matter, complex, vast, and permanently interesting, a subject so compelling that it is not unreasonable to assert that he has become a center for a new set of cultural possibilities."

The Gary Snyder Reader: Prose, Poetry, and Translations, 1952-1988 was published in 1999, offering a rich selection of Snyder's work in one volume. Discussing the book in the *Seattle Times,* Richard Wallace remarked that many consider Snyder "one of the best poets to write about nature and wilderness since the early Chinese." The *Reader* presents poems, travel writings, letters, interviews, and portions from Snyder's prose works *Earth Household, The Practice of the Wild,* and *A Place in Space.* The prose selections clearly show "how fluid and original a thinker Snyder is," advised Wallace. He is not a "cranky wilderness freak" who believes man should keep nature completely pristine. He is in fact "much more revolutionary than that," looking for ways to deepen personal involvement in community, family, and nature. His philosophy is marked by repeated emphasis of the "witty and irritating idea that we are no smarter, and maybe less skilled, than our Paleolithic ancestors." But it is in his poetry that the writer truly shines, according to Wallace, as he lends his voice "to the ferocious energy of nonhuman beings. He has done it with a direct, masculine, and beautiful talent for more than four decades."

Critics and general readers alike have responded to Snyder's "new set of cultural possibilities." Steuding proposed that the writer's work "truly influences one who reads him thoroughly to 'see' in a startling new way. Presenting the vision of an integrated and unified world, this heroic poetic effort cannot but help to create a much needed change of consciousness." Robert Mezey noted that Snyder "has a compelling vision of our relationship with this living nature, which is our nature, what it is and what it must be if we/nature survive on this planet, and his art serves that vision unwaveringly." According to Halvard Johnson in the *Minnesota Review,* the "unique power and value of Snyder's poetry lies not simply in clearly articulated images or in complex patterns of sound and rhythm, but rather in the freedom, the openness of spirit that permits the poems simply to be what they are, what they can be. . . . They respond to the rhythms of the world." Molesworth offered perhaps the most succinct appraisal of Gary Snyder's poetic vision. "Snyder has built a place for the mind to stay and to imagine more far-reaching harmonies while preserving all the wealth of the past," Molesworth concluded. "This, of course, is the world of his books where he is willing and even eager to give us another world both more ideal and more real than our own. The rest of the work is ours."

In an essay published in *A Controversy of Poets,* Snyder offered his own assessment of his art. "As a poet," he wrote, "I hold the most archaic values on earth. They go back to the late Paleolithic: the fertility of the soil, the magic of animals, the power-vision in solitude, the terrifying initiation and rebirth; the love and ecstasy of the dance, the common work of the tribe. I try to hold both history and wilderness in mind, that my poems may approach the true measure of things and stand against the unbalance and ignorance of our times."

BIOGRAPHICAL AND CRITICAL SOURCES:

BOOKS

Allen, Donald M., editor, *The New American Poetry*, Grove (New York, NY), 1960.

Almon, Bert, *Gary Snyder*, Boise State University Press (Boise, ID), 1979.

Altieri, Charles, *Enlarging the Temple: New Directions in American Poetry during the 1960s*, Bucknell University Press (Lewisburg, PA), 1979.

American Nature Writers, Volume 2, Scribner (New York, NY), 1996.

Charters, Samuel, *Some Poems/Poets: Studies in American Underground Poetry since 1945*, Oyez, 1971.

Contemporary Literary Criticism, Gale (Detroit, MI), Volume 1, 1973, Volume 2, 1974, Volume 5, 1976, Volume 9, 1978, Volume 32, 1985.

Contemporary Poets, 7th edition, St. James Press (Detroit, MI), 2001.

Cook, Bruce, *The Beat Generation*, Scribner (New York, NY), 1971.

Dictionary of Literary Biography, Gale (Detroit, MI), Volume 5: *American Poets since World War II*, 1980; Volume 16: *The Beats: Literary Bohemians in Postwar America*, 1983; Volume 165: *American Poets since World War II*, second series, 1996; Volume 212: *Twentieth-Century American Western Writers*, Second Series, 1999; Volume 275: *Twentieth-Century American Nature Writers: Prose*, 2003.

Faas, Ekbert, editor, *Towards a New American Poetics: Essays & Interviews*, Black Sparrow Press, 1978.

Howard, Richard, *Alone with America: Essays on the Art of Poetry in the United States since 1950*, Atheneum, 1969.

Kherdian, David, *A Biographical Sketch and Descriptive Checklist of Gary Snyder*, Oyez, 1965.

Leary, Paris and Robert Kelly, editors, *A Controversy of Poets*, Doubleday (New York, NY), 1965.

McCord, Howard, *Some Notes to Gary Snyder's "Myths & Texts,"* Sand Dollar, 1971.

McNeill, Katherine, *Gary Snyder*, Phoenix (New York, NY), 1980.

Molesworth, Charles, *Gary Snyder's Vision: Poetry and the Real Work*, University of Missouri Press, 1983.

Rexroth, Kenneth, *Assays*, New Directions (New York, NY), 1961.

Rexroth, Kenneth, *American Poetry in the Twentieth Century*, Herder & Herder, 1971.

Schuler, Robert Jordan, *Journeys toward the Original Mind: The Long Poems of Gary Snyder*, Lang (New York, NY), 1994.

Shaw, Robert B., editor, *American Poetry since 1960: Some Critical Perspectives*, Dufour (Chester Springs, PA), 1974.

Sherman, Paul, *Repossessing and Renewing*, Louisiana State University Press (Baton Rouge, LA), 1976.

Snyder, Gary, *The Real Work: Interviews & Talks, 1964-1979*, edited and with introduction by Scott McLean, New Directions (New York, NY), 1980.

Steuding, Bob, *Gary Snyder*, Twayne (Boston, MA), 1976.

PERIODICALS

Alcheringa, autumn, 1972.

American Poetry Review, November, 1983.

American West, January-February, 1981; Volume 25; August, 1988, p. 30.

Austin American-Statesman, October 11, 2001, Mary Alice Davis, "The Gentle Message of a Poet," p. A17.

Beloit Poetry Journal, fall-winter, 1971-72.

Booklist, September 15, 1996, Ray Olson, review of *Mountains and Rivers without End*, p. 205; June 1, 1999, Ray Olson, review of *The Gary Snyder Reader: Prose, Poetry, and Translations, 1952-1998*.

Boundary II, Volume 4, 1976.

Colorado Quarterly, summer, 1968.

Contemporary Literature, spring, 1977; winter, 1998, Timothy G. Gray, "Semiotic Shepherds: Gary Snyder, Frank O'Hara, and the Embodiment of an Urban Pastoral," p. 523.

Critical Quarterly, winter, 1973.

Criticism, spring, 1977.

Denver Quarterly, fall, 1980.

Environment, December, 1996, Kenneth A. Ollif, review of *A Place in Space: Ethics, Aesthetics, and Watersheds,* p. 25.

Epoch: A Magazine of Contemporary Literature, fall, 1965.

Explicator, fall, 2001, M. Bennet Smith, review of *The Call of the Wild,* p. 47.

Far Point, Volume 4, 1970.

Georgia Review, summer, 1992, p. 382.

Holiday, March, 1966.

Iowa Review, summer, 1970.

Journal of Modern Literature, Volume 2, 1971-72; summer, 1999, Anthony Hunt, "Singing the Dyads: The Chinese Landscape Scroll and Gary Snyder's *Mountains and Rivers without End,*" p. 7.

Kansas Quarterly, spring, 1970.

Library Journal, July, 1999, Cynde Bloom Lahey, review of *The Gary Snyder Reader, 1952-1998,* p. 91.

Los Angeles Times, November 28, 1986.

Los Angeles Times Book Review, July 1, 1979; November 23, 1980; November 13, 1983; December 28, 1986.

Minnesota Review, fall, 1971.

Nation, September 1, 1969; November 19, 1983.

New Republic, April 4, 1970; March 24, 1997, Christopher Benfey, review of *Mountains and Rivers without End,* p. 38.

New Statesman, November 4, 1966.

New York Review of Books, January 22, 1976; April 11, 1991, p. 29.

New York Times Book Review, May 11, 1969; June 8, 1969; March 23, 1975; December 27, 1992, p. 2.

New York Times Magazine, October 6, 1996, p. 62.

Partisan Review, summer, 1969; winter, 1971-72.

Poetry, June, 197; June, 1972; September, 1984; June, 1994, p. 167.

Prairie Schooner, winter, 1960-61.

Progressive, November, 1995, p. 28.

Publishers Weekly, August 17, 1990, p. 62; August 10, 1992, p. 58; July 31, 1995, p. 62; August 26, 1996, p. 94; May 31, 1999, review of *The Gary Snyder Reader,* p. 87.

Sagetrieb, spring, 1984.

San Francisco Chronicle, September 1, 1996, Tom Clark, review of *Mountains and Rivers without End,* p. 1; Jesse Hamlin, interview with Gary Snyder, p. 30.

Saturday Review, October 11, 1969; April 3, 1971.

Seattle Times, July 11, 1999, Richard Wallace, review of *The Gary Snyder Reader, 1952-1998,* p. M9.

Sierra, March-April, 1997, Scott McLean, review of *Mountains and Rivers without End* and *A Place in Space,* p. 112.

Sixties, spring, 1962; spring, 1972.

Southern Review, summer, 1968.

Southwest Review, spring, 1971; winter, 1976; spring, 1982.

Spectator, December 25, 1971.

Sulfur 10, Volume 4, number 1, 1984.

Tamkang Review, spring, 1980.

Times Literary Supplement, December 24, 1971; May 30, 1980.

Village Voice, November 17, 1966; May 1, 1984.

Washington Post Book World, December 25, 1983.

Western American Literature, fall, 1968; spring, 1980; fall, 1980; spring, 1981.

Western Humanities Review, spring, 1975.

Whole Earth Review, winter, 1988, p. 22; spring, 1991, p. 80; spring, 1996, p. 7; summer, 1997, Rick Fields, review of *Mountains and Rivers without End,* p. 91; winter, 1997, review of *Turtle Island, A Place in Space,* and *The Practice of the Wild,* p. 59; fall, 2000, William Pitt Root, review of *The Gary Snyder Reader,* p. 98.

World Literature Today, summer, 1984; spring, 1997, Bernard F. Dick, review of *Mountains and Rivers without End,* p. 392.

Yale Review, July, 1997, Stephen Burt, review of *Mountains and Rivers without End,* p. 150.*

* * *

SONDHEIM, Stephen (Joshua) 1930-

PERSONAL: Born March 22, 1930, in New York, NY; son of Herbert (a dress manufacturer) and Janet (a fashion designer and interior decorator; maiden name, Fox; present name, Leshin) Sondheim. *Education:* Williams College, B.A. (magna cum laude), 1950; graduate study in music composition and theory with Milton Babbitt; studied privately with Oscar Hammerstein II.

ADDRESSES: Home—New York, NY. *Agent*—Sarah Douglas, Douglas & Kopelman Artists, 393 West 49th St., Suite No.5G, New York NY 10019.

CAREER: Composer and lyricist, 1956—. St. Catherine's College, Oxford, visiting professor of drama and musical theater and fellow, 1990. Appeared in television specials, including *June Moon,* Public Broadcasting Service (PBS-TV), 1974, and *Putting It Together—The Making of the Broadway Album,* Home Box Office, 1986. Appeared in episodes of television series *Great Performances,* including "Broadway Sings: The Music of Jule Styne," PBS-TV, 1987, and "Bernstein at 70," PBS-TV, 1989.

MEMBER: American Academy and Institute of Arts and Letters, American Society of Composers, Authors, and Publishers, Authors League of America, Writers Guild of America, Dramatists Guild (president, 1973-81).

AWARDS, HONORS: Hutchinson Prize, Williams College, 1950; Antoinette Perry ("Tony") Award nominations, 1958 (with Leonard Bernstein), for *West Side Story,* 1960 (with Jule Styne), for *Gypsy,* 1965 (with Richard Rodgers), for *Do I Hear a Waltz?,* 1976, for *Pacific Overtures,* 1982, for *Merrily We Roll Along,* and 1984, for *Sunday in the Park with George;* Tony Awards, 1963, for *A Funny Thing Happened on the Way to the Forum,* 1971, for best music and best lyrics in *Company,* 1972, for best score in *Follies,* 1979, for best score in *A Little Night Music,* 1979, for *Sweeney Todd: The Demon Barber of Fleet Street,* 1988, for best score in *Into the Woods,* 1994, for best score in *Passion,* and 2002, for best revival of a musical for *Into the Woods; Evening Standard* Drama Awards for best musical, 1959, for *Gypsy,* 1973, for *A Little Night Music,* 1987, for *Follies,* and 1989, for *Into the Woods;* New York Drama Critics' polls conducted by *Variety,* 1969-70, named best composer for *Company,* and 1970-71, named best composer and lyricist for *Follies;* Drama Desk Awards, 1969-70, for music and lyrics in *Company,* 1970-71, for music and lyrics in *Follies,* 1972-73, for music and lyrics in *A Little Night Music,* 1978-79, for music and lyrics in *Sweeney Todd,* 1981-82, for lyrics in *Merrily We Roll Along,* 1983-84, for lyrics in *Sunday in the Park with George,* and 1987-88, for lyrics and outstanding musical, for *Into the Woods;* New York Drama Critics' Circle Awards for best new musical, 1970, for *Company,* 1971, for *Follies,* 1973, for *A Little Night Music,* 1976, for *Pacific Overtures,* 1979, for *Sweeney Todd,* 1984, for *Sunday in the Park with George,* and 1988, for *Into the Woods;* Grammy Awards, National Academy of Recording Arts and Sciences, 1970, for best musical-cast album *Company,* 1973, for musical-cast album *A Little Night Music,* 1975, for song of the year "Send in the Clowns," 1979, for musical-cast album

Sweeney Todd, 1984, for musical-cast album *Sunday in the Park with George,* 1986, for musical-cast album *Follies in Concert,* and 1988, for musical-cast album *Into the Woods;* honorary doctorate, Williams College, 1971; Edgar Allan Poe Award (with Anthony Perkins), Mystery Writers of America, 1973, for best motion-picture screenplay, for *The Last of Sheila;* musical salute given by American Musical and Dramatic Academy and National Hemophilia Foundation at Shubert Theatre, 1973; Los Angeles Drama Critics' Circle Awards, 1974-75, for music and lyrics in *A Little Night Music,* and 1989, for original musical score in *Into the Woods;* Elizabeth Hull-Kate Warriner Award, Dramatists Guild, 1979, for *Sweeney Todd;* Brandeis University Creative Arts Award in theater arts, 1982; Unique Contribution Award, Drama League of New York, 1983, for initiating American Young Playwrights Festival; Common Wealth Award of Distinguished Service in dramatic arts, Bank of Delaware, 1984; Pulitzer Prize for drama, Columbia University Graduate School of Journalism, 1985, for *Sunday in the Park with George;* Laurence Olivier Award for musical of the year, Society of West End Theatre (England), 1988, for *Follies,* and 1991, for *Sunday in the Park with George;* named Lion of the Performing Arts, New York Public Library, 1989; Academy Award, Academy of Motion Picture Arts and Sciences, 1990, for best original song "Sooner or Later (I Always Get My Man)" from *Dick Tracy;* Golden Globe Award nominations, Hollywood Foreign Press Association, 1990, for original songs "Sooner or Later (I Always Get My Man)" and "What Can You Lose?" from *Dick Tracy;* National Medal of Arts Award, National Endowment for the Arts, 1992 (declined), and 1997; Kennedy Center Honor for Lifetime Achievement, 1993; Praemium Imperiale, Japan Art Association, 2000, for work in film and theater.

WRITINGS:

STAGE PRODUCTIONS

(Composer of incidental music) *The Girls of Summer,* produced at Longacre Theatre, New York, NY, 1956.

(Lyricist) *West Side Story* (also see below; produced in New York, NY, 1957), music by Leonard Bernstein, Random House (New York, NY), 1958, published in *Romeo and Juliet and West Side Story,* Dell (New York, NY), 1965.

(Lyricist) *Gypsy* (also see below; produced on Broadway, 1959), music by Jule Styne, Random House (New York, NY), 1960.

(Composer of incidental music) *Invitation to a March,* produced in New York, NY, 1960.

(Composer and lyricist) *A Funny Thing Happened on the Way to the Forum* (also see below; produced in New York, NY, 1962), Dodd (New York, NY), 1963, reprinted, Applause Theatre (Diamond Bar, CA), 1991.

(Composer and lyricist) *Anyone Can Whistle* (also see below; produced in New York, NY, 1964), Dodd (New York, NY), 1965.

(Lyricist) *Do I Hear a Waltz?* (also see below; produced in New York, NY, 1965), music by Richard Rodgers, Random House (New York, NY), 1966.

(Lyricist, with others) *Leonard Bernstein's Theatre Songs,* produced in New York, NY, 1965.

(Composer and lyricist) *Company* (also see below; produced in New York, NY, 1970), Random House (New York, NY), 1970, reprinted, Theatre Communications Group (New York, NY), 1995.

(Composer and lyricist) *Follies* (also see below; produced in New York, NY, 1971), Random House (New York, NY), 1971.

(Composer) *The Enclave,* produced in New York, NY, 1973.

(Composer and lyricist) *A Little Night Music* (also see below; produced in New York, NY, 1973), Dodd (New York, NY), 1974, reprinted, Applause Theater (New York, NY), 1991.

(Author of additional lyrics, with John LaTouche) *Candide* (revival; also see below), original lyrics by Richard Wilbur, music by Leonard Bernstein, produced in Brooklyn, NY, 1973-74, produced on Broadway, 1974.

(Composer and lyricist) *The Frogs,* produced at Yale Repertory Theatre, New Haven, CT, 1974, produced in Los Angeles, CA, 1983.

(Composer, with John Kander and Giuseppe Verdi) *Once in a Lifetime,* produced in New York, NY, 1975.

(Lyricist, with others) *By Bernstein,* produced in New York, NY, 1975.

(Composer and lyricist) *Pacific Overtures* (also see below; produced in New York, NY, 1976), Dodd (New York, NY), 1977, reprinted, Theatre Communications Group (New York, NY), 1991.

(Composer and lyricist) *Sweeney Todd: The Demon Barber of Fleet Street* (also see below; produced in New York, NY, 1979, produced as an opera, 1984), Dodd (New York, NY), 1979, reprinted, Applause Theater (New York, NY), 1991.

(Composer and lyricist, with others) *The Madwoman of Central Park West,* produced in New York, NY, 1979.

(Composer and lyricist) *Merrily We Roll Along* (also see below; produced in New York, NY, 1981), Theatre Communications Group (New York, NY), 1998.

(Composer and lyricist) *Sunday in the Park with George* (also see below; produced in workshop, 1983, produced in New York, NY, 1984-85), Dodd (New York, NY), 1986, reprinted, Applause Theater (New York, NY), 1991.

(Composer and lyricist) *Into the Woods* (also see below; produced in San Diego, CA, c. 1986, produced in New York, NY, 1987-89), Theatre Communications Group (New York, NY), 1989.

(Composer and lyricist, with others) *Jerome Robbins' Broadway,* produced in New York, NY, 1989-90.

(Composer and lyricist) *Assassins* (produced in New York, NY, 1991), Theatre Communications Group (New York, NY), 1991.

(With James Lapine) *Passion* (portions adapted from 1869 novel *Fosca* by Igino Tarchetti and 1981 film *Passione d'amore,* by Ettore Scola), Theatre Communications Group (New York, NY), 1994.

(With George Furth) *Getting away with Murder: A Comedy Thriller,* Theatre Communications Group (New York, NY), 1997.

(Composer and lyricist, with others) *Four by Sondheim, Wheeler, Lapine, Shevelove and Gelbart,* Applause Theatre (New York, NY), 2000.

(Composer and lyricist) *Follies,* Theatre Communications Group (New York, NY), 2001.

Composer, with Mary Rodgers, of song "The Boy from . . ." for *The Mad Show,* produced in New York, NY, 1966. Also provided music for *Twins,* produced in Detroit, MI, c. 1972.

Sondheim's compositions have been included in numerous stage productions, including *Sondheim: A Musical Tribute,* 1973; *Side by Side by Sondheim,* (also see below), 1976; *Marry Me a Little,* 1980; *Follies in Concert with New York Philharmonic,* 1985; *Julie Wilson: From Weill to Sondheim—A Concert,* 1987; *You're Gonna Love Tomorrow: A Stephen Sondheim Evening,* 1987; *Sondheim: A Celebration at Carnegie Hall,* 1992; and *Putting It Together,* 1993.

FILM SCORES

Stavisky (also see below), Cinemation, 1974.
(With Dave Grusin) *Reds,* Paramount, 1981.
(With others) *Dick Tracy,* Touchstone-Buena Vista, 1990.

Also author of music and lyrics for "The Madam's Song," in *The Seven-Percent Solution,* Universal, 1977.

TELEVISION PRODUCTIONS

(With others) *Topper* (television series), National Broadcasting Co. (NBC-TV), 1953.
The Last Word (television series), CBS-TV, 1957-59.
(Composer and lyricist, with Burt Shevelove) *The Fabulous '50s* (special), Columbia Broadcasting System (CBS-TV), 1960.
(Composer and lyricist) *Evening Primrose* (special), American Broadcasting Co. (ABC-TV), 1966.
(Composer and lyricist) *Annie, the Woman in the Life of a Man* (special), CBS-TV, 1970.
(Lyricist) *Candide,* for "Great Performances," PBS-TV, 1986.
(Composer) *Time Warner Presents the Earth Day Special,* ABC-TV, 1990.

Also author of lyrics to "Somewhere," included in *Putting It Together: The Making of the Broadway Album* (special), HBO, 1986, and song "The Saga of Lenny," included in "Bernstein at 70," "Great Performances," PBS-TV, 1989.

OTHER

(With Anthony Perkins) *The Last of Sheila,* Warner Bros., 1973.
(Author of introduction) Richard Lewine and Alfred Simon, *Songs of the American Theatre,* Dodd (New York, NY), 1973.
(Author of introduction) Hugh Fordin, *Getting to Know Him,* Random House (New York, NY), 1977.
The Hansen Treasury of Stephen Sondheim Songs, 1977.
The Stephen Sondheim Songbook, 1979.
All Sondheim, 1980.

Stephen Sondheim's Crossword Puzzles, Harper (New York, NY), 1980.
(Editor) *Lyrics by Oscar Hammerstein II,* revised edition, Hal Leonard Publishing, 1985.

Contributor to *Playwrights, Lyricists, Composers on Theatre,* edited by Otis L. Guernsey, Jr., Dodd (New York, NY), 1974. Contributor of crossword puzzles to *New York* magazine, 1968-69.

ADAPTATIONS: Into the Woods was adapted as a juvenile book by Hudson Talbott, Crown (New York, NY), 1988. Several of Sondheim's stage productions were adapted to film, including *West Side Story,* United Artists (UA), 1961; *Gypsy,* Warner Bros., 1962; *A Funny Thing Happened on the Way to the Forum,* UA, 1966; and *A Little Night Music,* New World, 1977. Recordings of Sondheim's music include *West Side Story,* 1957, film soundtrack, 1961; *Gypsy,* 1959; *A Funny Thing Happened on the Way to the Forum,* 1962; *Anyone Can Whistle,* 1964; *Do I Hear a Waltz?,* 1965; *Company,* 1970; *Follies,* 1971, as *Follies in Concert,* 1985; *A Little Night Music,* 1973; *Stavisky,* 1973; *Sondheim: A Musical Tribute,* 1973, released as *Sondheim Evening: A Musical Tribute,* 1990; *Pacific Overtures,* 1976; *Side by Side by Sondheim,* 1977; *Sweeney Todd: The Demon Barber of Fleet Street,* 1979; *Marry Me a Little,* 1981; *Merrily We Roll Along,* 1981; *Sunday in the Park with George,* 1984; *Music of Stephen Sondheim,* 1985; Barbra Streisand, *Broadway Album,* 1985; *Into the Woods,* 1988; *I'm Breathless,* 1990; *I Wish It So,* 1994; and *Stephen Sondheim: A Collector's Sondheim* (compilation of original cast recordings).

SIDELIGHTS: Stephen Sondheim's contributions to twentieth-century musical theater have been so significant that the *Dramatists Guild Literary Quarterly* designated its first ten years as the "Sondheim decade." "There can hardly have been an issue since," the editors commented, "when a work by Stephen Sondheim . . . wasn't a major attraction on the Broadway scene, and often more than one." Sondheim has indeed been instrumental in revolutionizing the stage musical. The composer's ability to incorporate a variety of musical styles into his scores caused T. E. Kalem of *Time* to claim after seeing a Sondheim production that the "entire score is an incredible display of musical virtuosity." Using music, Sondheim creates an attitude for the dramatic situation so that individual songs may push the drama along. Sometimes, unlike most of his predecessors, the composer strays from the traditional rhyming structure. Too, his lyrical cynicism and satire have moved musical comedy from the lighter and simpler shows of Rodgers and Hammerstein to what is termed "conceptual musicals."

Instead of escapism, Sondheim's conceptual musicals present serious concerns and dramatic subtexts. Each of the composer's works depends on one fundamental concept to act as a framework. One of the creators of the new, unromantic musical production, Sondheim has helped to place the musical on a more serious level than that of the traditional Broadway show. When Sondheim composes, it is a cooperative effort. "I go about starting a song first with the collaborators," he once divulged, "sometimes just with the book writer, sometimes with the director. We have long discussions and I take notes, just general notes, and then we decide what the song should be about, and I try to make a title." The composer, according to Sondheim, must stage numbers or draw "blueprints" so that the director or the choreographer may see the uses of a song.

For Sondheim, collaboration usually begins with the book and book writer from whom "you should steal." Since a good production sounds as though one writer is responsible for both the book and the score, the book writer and composer must work together if a play is to have texture. "Any book writer I work with knows what I'm going to do," explained Sondheim, "and I try to help him out wherever I can; that's the only way you make a piece, make a texture." "I keep hearing about people," he continued, "who write books and then give them to composers or composers who write scores and then get a book writer. I don't understand how that works."

Sondheim's first Broadway collaboration has an unusual history. At the age of twenty-five, the composer completed the music and lyrics for *Saturday Night,* a musical that never saw the Broadway stage owing to the death of its producer Lemuel Ayers. But *Saturday Night* still served Sondheim well. "It was my portfolio," he once explained, "and as a result of it I got *West Side Story.*" The story of the ugly life on a city street, with only glimpses of beauty and love, *West Side Story* is considered one of the masterpieces of the American theater. Beginning its first run in New York in 1957, *West Side Story* ran for 734 performances on Broadway. After an extended tour of the United States,

the play began a second Broadway run of 249 performances. In 1961 *West Side Story* was adapted into a motion picture that captured ten Academy Awards and became one of the greatest screen musicals in terms of commercial success.

Many critics have attributed much of *West Side Story*'s popularity to its musical score. In *The Complete Book of the American Musical Theatre,* David A. Ewen named the score as "one of the most powerful assets to this grim tragedy." Ewen cited "Maria," "I Feel Pretty," and "Somewhere" as "unforgettable lyrical episodes." Sondheim's comic songs, such as "America" and "Gee, Officer Krupke!," have also been applauded for their wittiness and their roles as satirical commentaries.

Sondheim's next production was *Gypsy,* a musical based on the autobiography of burlesque star Gypsy Rose Lee. Initially, Sondheim was contracted to write both the music and the lyrics for this show, but actress Ethel Merman felt uneasy with a little-known composer. So Jule Styne composed *Gypsy*'s music while Sondheim wrote the lyrics. Although the play is entertaining in the tradition of Broadway musicals, it is on a deeper level the story of universal human needs. One song from *Gypsy,* "Some People," is considered by several critics to be one of the best ever written.

An old-fashioned burlesque, *A Funny Thing Happened on the Way to the Forum,* followed *Gypsy.* Sondheim and playwrights Burt Shevelove and Larry Gelbart adapted *Forum* from the comedies of Plautus, a classical Roman playwright. The play is bawdy, rough-and-tumble, and fun. A low comedy of lechers and courtesans done in a combination of ancient Roman and American vaudeville techniques, *Forum* is paced with ambiguous meanings, risque connotations, and not-so-subtle innuendos. For instance, a slave carrying a piece of statuary is told by a matron: "Carry my bust with pride." Typically Sondheim, the score is saturated with humor. Some critics have cited "Everybody Ought to Have a Maid" as particularly amusing while "Lovely" has been suspected, at least by one critic, of being Sondheim's satire of his own song "Tonight." For *Forum,* unlike most of his previous plays, Sondheim wrote both the lyrics and the music. "With *Forum,*" a *Time* reviewer noted, "Sondheim finally proved that he, like Noel Coward, could indeed go it alone." *Forum* received a Tony Award as the season's best musical and in 1966 adapted for film and released by United Artists as a motion picture starring Zero Mostel, Jack Gilford, Phil Silvers, and Buster Keaton.

During 1970 and 1971 Sondheim produced two works in collaboration with Hal Prince and Michael Bennett that were considered to be "concept musicals." *Company* (1970) has no plot, but is a montage of observations about the institution of marriage. It depicts five married couples who hold a birthday party for a bachelor friend. As the play progresses, the observer realizes the amount of disharmony present within the marital relationships. *Company* garnered the New York Drama Critics Award and six Tony Awards, and completed a run of 690 performances.

1970's *Follies* focuses upon a reunion of two former showgirls from the fictional Weismann Follies who are about to witness the end of an era signified by the demolition of a once-renowned theater building. The play received seven Tony Awards and the Drama Critics Circle Award for best musical.

In 1973, when several critics worried that the Broadway musical had degenerated to an embarrassing state of high camp and rock music, Sondheim's *A Little Night Music* appeared, restoring faith in musical theater. Critics recognized *A Little Night Music* to be as spectacular as the great musicals that had gone before it, but also recognized its serious vein. Sondheim composed all the musical's songs in three-quarter time or multiples of that meter; this served as the play's concept and tied it together. Three-quarter time was the foundation to which the composer added a Greek chorus, canons, and fuguetos. Subtexts were injected into almost every song—most notably in "Every Day a Little Death," which allows a countess to express her feelings of loneliness as a philanderer's wife. In addition, Sondheim devoted himself to the "inner monologue song," which is a song, a *Time* critic explained, "in which characters sing of their deepest thoughts, but almost never to each other."

Though *A Little Night Music* addresses the standard musical-comedy subject—love—it "is a masquelike affair, tailor-made to fit Sondheim's flair for depicting confused people experiencing ambivalent thoughts and feelings," the *Time* reviewer assessed. Many of the songs illustrate ambivalence because Sondheim likes neurotic people. He once revealed: "I like troubled people. Not that I don't like squared-away people, but I *prefer* neurotic people. I like to hear rumblings beneath the surface." The show's cast of confused characters includes the giddy child-bride whose middle-aged husband takes up with his ex-mistress while his adolescent son has a crush on his new stepmother. Of course, the above-mentioned countess laments the sadness of her marriage to a straying husband, and a lusty chambermaid salutes carnal love through the play. Critically, *A Little Night Music* was a triumph. Many reviewers agreed that the strongest element in the play is Sondheim's score, which was compared to the work of musical greats such as Cole Porter and Lorenz Hart.

In 1976 Sondheim again collaborated with Hal Prince in the production of *Pacific Overtures,* a show that encompasses 120 years of Japanese history from 1856 to modern times. *Pacific Overtures* was performed by an entirely Asian, male cast and in order to achieve the correct sound, Sondheim used many Asian instruments in the orchestration. He also utilized elements of Japanese Kabuki theater, Haiku poetry, and Japanese pentatonic musical scales. *New York Times* reviewer Clive Barnes considered *Pacific Overtures* to be "very, very different."

Sondheim once again made his presence known on Broadway with *Sweeney Todd: The Demon Barber of Fleet Street.* He became interested in the play in 1973, related Mel Gussow of the *New York Times,* "when he saw a production of the melodrama at the Stratford East Theatre in England. He was captivated by it, although, as he said, 'I found it much more passionate and serious than the audience did.'" Composed as if it were an opera, *Sweeney Todd* is the story of a murderous barber who sends his victims downstairs to a pie shop where they become the secret ingredients in Mrs. Lovett's meat pies. By Sondheim's own admission, the play "has a creepy atmosphere." The main character, Todd, is out for revenge. Judge Turpin, who desired Todd's wife and daughter, shipped the barber off to Australia as punishment for a crime that he did not commit. Todd escapes and returns seeking vengeance. His attempt to kill the judge fails, causing his revenge to snowball into mass murder. In the end, Todd kills Turpin, but by then the barber, too, is doomed.

Sweeney Todd is about revenge. Harold Prince's production, however, mirrors the industrial age, its influences, and its effects. The play received numerous Drama Desk Awards and Tony Awards in 1979, including best score of a musical. In the opinion of director Harold Prince, the play's music is "the most melodic and romantic score that Steve has ever written. The music is soaring." Nearly eighty percent of the show is music, and musical motifs recur throughout the score to maintain the audience's emotional level. Sondheim even incorporated a musical clue, a theme associated with a character, into the score.

In 1984 Sondheim teamed up with artist-turned-dramatist James Lapine to create the musical *Sunday in the Park with George.* For Lapine and Sondheim, their first collaboration was a remarkable success, garnering the 1985 Pulitzer Prize for drama. Their feat was made even more unusual by the fact that *Sunday in the Park with George* is centered around an idea Clive Barnes deemed "audaciously ambitious" in the *New York Post.* "It is to show us the creation of a work of art, the formulation of an artistic style based on scientific principles, and to reveal, in passing, the struggles of an artist for recognition," Barnes explained.

"I write generally experimental, unexpected work," Sondheim told Samuel G. Freedman in the *New York Times;* he made that truth perhaps nowhere more evident than in *Sunday in the Park with George.* Conceptual rather than plot-driven, the play structures itself around two vignettes that are performed as two separate acts. The first follows French pointillist Georges Seurat in the evolution of his renowned painting *A Sunday Afternoon on the Island of La Grande Jatte.* The second is centered upon the artistic struggles of the American great-grandson of the artist, the "George" of the play's title, who pays homage to his ancestor's work through modern laser artistry.

Critical response to *Sunday in the Park with George* was divided. Many felt that the play confirmed the belief that the creative process is inherently undramatic. David Sterritt, in a review for the *Christian Science Monitor,* pointed to a conflict between the desire to depict art and the desire to depict an artist as the source for the play's failure. *Sunday in the Park with George,* he wrote, "hovers between the formal elegance of *La Grande Jatte* and the living, breathing, potentially fascinating life of Seurat himself—but partakes fully of neither." Other critics took exception to what they saw as the autobiographical note sounded by the play's theme: in the depiction of Seurat's rejection by art critics of his time, many felt, was

Sondheim's venting of his frustration at his own critical reception. "It is easy to see why Stephen Sondheim should have been attracted to the idea of creating a musical about Georges Seurat, whose career is a way of discussing some of the dilemmas that confront the contemporary artist," Howard Kissel observed in *Women's Wear Daily.* Kissel went on to object to what he saw as the "defensive" stance Sondheim reveals in songs like "Lesson #8," and to dismiss the notion that the play is avant garde. Instead, the critic expressed the opinion that *Sunday in the Park with George* is merely contrived.

Yet many critics were compelled by the play's premise and convinced of its status as a breakthrough for theater. "To say that this show breaks new ground is not enough; it also breaks new sky, new water, new flesh and new spirit," Jack Kroll proclaimed in *Newsweek.* Kroll not only approved of the material, but he celebrated the pairing of Lapine and Sondheim, declaring that over the course of the musical its creators "take us full circle, implying that there's still hope for vision in a high-tech world and that art and love may be two forms of the same energy . . . , in this show of beauty, wit, nobility and ardor, [that idea] makes this Sondheim's best work since . . . his classic collaborations with Harold Prince."

Not surprisingly, Lapine and Sondheim went on to collaborate on the 1986 musical *Into the Woods.* Again, their collaboration was richly rewarding. Winner of Tony awards for lyrics and outstanding musical, the play was a greater commercial success than *Sunday in the Park with George.* Essentially about the loss of innocence, the play explores the "grim" in the Brothers Grimm and in other tellers of children's tales. Turning fairytales like *Cinderella* and *Little Red Riding Hood* on their heads, the two acts of *Into the Woods* move from the happily to the unhappily ever after. Yet the musical ends on the surprisingly upbeat notes of the song "No One Is Alone," prompting some critics to complain that Sondheim had sold out to public demand for lighter material. Others, however, found the musical wholly appealing. "It is that joyous rarity," wrote Elizabeth L. Bland and William A. Henry III in a *Time* review, "a work of sophisticated artistic ambition and deep political purpose that affords nonstop pleasure."

In 1990 Sondheim earned his first Academy Award for the song "Sooner or Later (I Always Get My Man)," composed for the movie *Dick Tracy* and sung by

Madonna. From there, Sondheim went on to create a uniquely American show, *Assassins,* which showcases the assassins and would-be assassins of presidents of the United States. With characters such as John Wilkes Booth and Lynette "Squeaky" Fromme, the musical quickly earned the reputation of being Sondheim's darkest work to date. Undaunted, theater-goers lined up in droves for its sold-out run in 1991.

Two years later Sondheim received a prestigious lifetime achievement award from the Kennedy Center in Washington, D.C. In 1994 he answered with another award-winning musical, *Passion.* Based on an obscure Italian movie, the work features a love triangle between Fosca, an ugly, frail woman; Giorgio, a handsome Italian army officer; and Clara, Giorgio's beautiful mistress. After being assigned to a regiment in Parma, Italy, Giorgio meets the tormented Fosca. The two develop a rapport based on their mutual interest in literature, but their friendship quickly takes a new turn when Fosca declares her obsession and love for Giorgio. Repulsed by Fosca, Giorgio is nonetheless unable to rid her from his mind. Fosca pursues Giorgio relentlessly; when Giorgio finally admits that he too is in love with her, the two consummate their love. Fosca dies shortly thereafter, while Giorgio, on the verge of a nervous breakdown, is admitted to a hospital.

Audiences and critics alike had mixed reactions to *Passion. Nation* critic David Kaufman remarked, "A dark tale of an obsessive love that is cut short after it finally finds its perfect object, *Passion* is archetypal Sondheim in its content." Calling the work "passionless," Kaufman concluded that it "emerges as more of an elegant chamber piece than a full-scale musical." Similarly, Ben Brantley in the *New York Times* noted that *Passion* "isn't perfect. . . . There's an inhibited quality here that asks to be exploded and never is." But Robert Brustein of the *New Republic* declared the musical "Sondheim's deepest, most powerful work. . . . *Passion* is a triumph of rare and complex sensibility, fully imagined, fully realized." Despite its mixed reception, the show won several Tony awards, including best musical and, for Sondheim, best original music score.

In 2000, upon the occasion of his seventieth birthday, Sondheim granted an interview to *New York Times* magazine writer Frank Rich. When asked to critique his own work, Sondheim said: "Verbosity is the thing I have to fight most in the lyrics department. . . .

'Less is more' is a lesson learned with a difficulty." He later added: "I'm accused so often of not having melodic gifts, but I like the music I write. Harmony gives music its life, its emotional color, more than rhythm."

BIOGRAPHICAL AND CRITICAL SOURCES:

BOOKS

Contemporary Literary Criticism, Gale (Detroit, MI), Volume 30, 1984, Volume 39, 1986.
Contemporary Theatre, Film, and Television, Volume 11, Gale (Detroit, MI), 1993.
Encyclopedia of World Biography, 2nd edition, Gale (Detroit, MI), 1998.
Ewen, David A., *The Complete Book of the American Musical Theatre,* Holt (New York, NY), 1970.
Guernsey, Otis L., Jr., editor, *Playwrights, Lyricists, Composers on Theatre,* Dodd (New York, NY), 1974.
Lewine, Richard, and Alfred Simon, *Songs of the American Theatre,* Dodd (New York, NY), 1973.
Zadan, Craig, *Sondheim and Company,* Avon (New York, NY), 1976, 2nd edition, Da Capo Press (New York, NY), 1994.

PERIODICALS

America, December 12, 1987, p. 485.
American Spectator, March, 1988, pp. 28-29.
Atlantic Monthly, December, 1984, p. 121.
Chicago Tribune, June 5, 1979; October 14, 1983; May 3, 1984; April 29, 1985; December 7, 1986; December 14, 1986; November 6, 1987; June 12, 1988.
Chicago Tribune Book World, April 15, 1984.
Christian Science Monitor, May 3, 1984, p. 27.
Commonweal, January 15, 1988.
Daily News, September 27, 1957; April 6, 1964; April 27, 1970; February 26, 1973; March 2, 1979; February 15, 1980; May 3, 1984.
Globe and Mail (Toronto, Ontario, Canada), November 7, 1987.
Guardian (London, England), March 12, 2003, Mel Gussow, interview with Sondheim.
Harper's, April, 1979, pp. 71-74, 76, 78.
High Fidelity, August, 1979, pp. 80-81.
Insight, August 28, 1989, p. 59.
Journal American, September 27, 1957.

Journal of Popular Culture, winter, 1978, pp. 513-525.

Los Angeles Times, March 18, 1983; May 20, 1984, p. 3; November 26, 1984, pp. 1, 5; November 6, 1987; January 8, 1989, pp. 4-5, 75.

Maclean's, December 24, 1984, p. 41.

Musical Quarterly, April, 1980, pp. 309-314.

Nation, December 12, 1987, pp. 725-727; June 13, 1994, p. 843.

New Leader, December 28, 1987, pp. 18-19.

New Republic, June 18, 1984, pp. 25-26; December 21, 1987, pp. 28-30; April 3, 1989, pp. 28-29; January 1, 1990, pp. 27-28; August 1, 1994, p. 29.

New Statesman, August 7, 1987, pp. 23-24.

Newsweek, April 23, 1973, pp. 54-56, 61, 64; January 26, 1976, p. 59; May 2, 1977; March 12, 1979, pp. 101, 103; March 19, 1979; May 14, 1984, pp. 83-84; November 16, 1987, pp. 106-107; February 4, 1991, p. 72; June 22, 1992, p. 52.

New York, May 2, 1977; March 3, 1979; March 19, 1979; March 3, 1980; November 16, 1987, p. 109; October 2, 1989, p. 82; August 20, 1990, pp. 120, 124; February 4, 1991, p. 38.

New Yorker, August 11, 1975, pp. 74-76; May 2, 1977; March 12, 1979; November 16, 1987, pp. 147-148; February 11, 1991, pp. 68-69.

New York Post, March 19, 1965; January 12, 1976; April 19, 1977; March 2, 1979; February 15, 1980; May 3, 1984.

New York Times, January 12, 1976, p. 39; April 19, 1977; February 1, 1979; February 25, 1979; March 2, 1979, p. C3; June 2, 1979; February 14, 1980; March 14, 1981; November 17, 1981; December 13, 1981, pp. D3, D6; March 6, 1983; July 24, 1983; April 1, 1984; April 4, 1984; May 3, 1984, p. C21; May 13, 1984, pp. 7, 31; October 13, 1984; October 21, 1984; October 26, 1984; May 24, 1985; September 9, 1985; July 23, 1987; October 9, 1987; November 1, 1987; November 6, 1987; November 29, 1987; May 10, 1988; November 27, 1989, pp. C13, C15; January 22, 1990; September 30, 1990; November 7, 1990; February 3, 1991; June 20, 1996, p. B1.

New York Times Magazine, March 12, 2000, Frank Rich, interview with Stephen Sondheim.

Opera News, November, 1985, pp. 18, 20, 22.

People, September 23, 1985, p. 78; July 22, 1996, p. 23.

Saturday Review, May 1, 1971, pp. 16, 65.

Stereo Review, July, 1971, pp. 110-111; July, 1973, pp. 94-95.

Time, April 12, 1971, . 78; May 3, 1971; March 12, 1973; March 19, 1973; February 25, 1980; June 16, 1986, p. 90; November 16, 1987, pp. 96-97; December 7, 1987, pp. 80-82; September 25, 1989, p. 76; February 4, 1991, p. 62.

Times (London, England), May 5, 1984; July 11, 1987; July 23, 1987; August 2, 1989; January 28, 1991, p. 16.

U.S. News and World Report, February 1, 1988, pp. 52-54.

Variety, April 8, 1964, p. 80; November 19, 1975, pp. 64-65; April 20, 1977; February 20, 1980; November 22, 1989; February 4, 1991, p. 95.

Vogue, April, 1984, p. 85.

Washington Post, November 18, 1981; November 6, 1987.

Women's Wear Daily, April 27, 1970; April 5, 1971; February 26, 1973; March 2, 1979; May 3, 1984.

ONLINE

Songwriters Hall of Fame Web site, http://www.songwritershalloffame.org/ (June 2, 2003), "Stephen Sondheim."

Stephen Sondheim Official Web site, http://sondheim.com/ (November 21, 2003).*

*　　　*　　　*

SPARKS, Nicholas 1965-

PERSONAL: Born December 31, 1965, in Omaha, NE; son of Patrick Michael and Jill Emma Marie (Thoene) Sparks; married, 1989; wife's name Cathy; children: Miles Andrew, Ryan Cody, Landon, Lexie Danielle and Savannah Marin (twins). *Education:* University of Notre Dame, B.B.A., 1988. *Politics:* Independent. *Religion:* Roman Catholic.

ADDRESSES: Home—New Bern, NC. *Agent*—Theresa Park, Sanford Greenburger Associates, 55 Fifth Ave., New York, NY 10003.

CAREER: Writer. Also worked as real-estate appraiser, waiter, buyer and restorer of homes, business owner, and pharmaceutical company representative.

AWARDS, HONORS: Book of the year nomination, American Booksellers Association, 1997, for *The Notebook.*

Nicholas Sparks

WRITINGS:

NOVELS

(With Billy Mills) *Wokini: A Lakota Journey to Happiness and Self-Understanding,* Orion Books (New York, NY), 1990.

The Notebook, Warner Books (New York, NY), 1996.

Message in a Bottle, Warner Books (New York, NY), 1998.

A Walk to Remember, Warner Books (New York, NY), 1999.

The Rescue, Warner Books (New York, NY), 2000.

A Bend in the Road, Warner Books (New York, NY), 2001.

Nights in Rodanthe, Warner Books (New York, NY), 2002.

The Guardian, Warner Books (New York, NY), 2003.

The Wedding, Warner Books (New York, NY), 2003.

(With Micah Sparks) *Three Weeks with My Brother,* Warner Books (New York, NY), 2004.

Sparks's novels have been translated into over thirty-five languages.

ADAPTATIONS: Message in a Bottle was made into a 1999 film of the same title starring Kevin Costner, Robin Wright Penn, and Paul Newman and directed by Luis Mandoki; *A Walk to Remember* was made by Warner Bros. into a 2002 film of the same title starring Mandy Moore and Shane West; *The Notebook* was made into a film of the same title starring James Garner and Gena Rowlands; an adaptation of *The Rescue* was planned as a television series; *A Bend in the Road* was adapted for audiobook, 2002; *Nights in Rodanthe* was adapted for audiobook, 2003.

SIDELIGHTS: Nicholas Sparks's romance-heavy novels have spent weeks on the bestseller lists and have earned him a reputation as one of the few men to write successful love stories for a popular audience. His second foray, *Message in a Bottle,* became a 1999 motion picture starring Kevin Costner, while others have been optioned for the big screen as well. A film adaptation of Sparks's *A Walk to Remember* was released in 2002.

Sparks was born on the last day of 1965 and grew up in Minnesota and California. He was the valedictorian of his high-school class, and his prowess in track and field won him a full scholarship to the University of Notre Dame. There he broke a school record in the relay during his freshman year, but an injury sidelined him. Frustrated during his summer break, Sparks heeded his mother's advice and began writing to pass the time, and penned a horror novel he titled *The Passing,* which was never published. On spring break in 1988 he met a University of New Hampshire student who he promptly fell in love with, and who prompted his writing career to begin in earnest; Sparks wrote Cathy, who would eventually become his wife, a record 150 letters in a two-month span.

Sparks's second novel, "The Royal Murders," also went unpublished. His law school applications were also rejected, and so Sparks became a real-estate appraiser, waited tables, then bought and restored old homes. He began his own business, and then sold it to embark upon a career as a pharmaceutical sales representative. Minor publishing success came after he teamed with Billy Mills, the father of one of Sparks's ex-girlfriends, on the 1990 novel *Wokini: A Lakota Journey to Happiness and Self-Understanding.* Mills had won a gold medal in track in the 1964 Olympics, and was the inspiration for the film *Running Brave.* The novel centers upon a young Lakota Indian, David, who comes of age after the tragic loss of his sister.

In 1993 Sparks and his wife relocated to New Bern, North Carolina. The following year the final episode of the long-running television situation comedy *Cheers* spurred him once again to try his hand at a novel. "I didn't want another eleven years to go by without chasing my dreams," he told *People* writer Kim Hubbard. "I decided I'd give myself three more chances at writing." The result was his 1996 novel *The Notebook,* which Sparks based on the romance between his wife's maternal grandparents. They had been married for sixty years, and were too infirm to attend Sparks's 1989 wedding. The writer and his wife visited them the day after, and as Sparks recalled to the *People* interviewer, "I realized they were flirting with each other. There was still a hint of passion after sixty-two years of marriage. That stayed with me."

The plot of *The Notebook* is framed by two chapters set in the present day inside a nursing home, where an elderly man reads to a weeping woman. Flashing back to 1946 and rural North Carolina, the novel introduces a young war veteran named Noah, who recalls a thwarted teen romance in a riverfront town during the summer of 1932. He still thinks about Allie, whose wealthy parents disapproved of him, and how he wrote her letters she never answered. Allie is now engaged to an attorney, and one day she reads about Noah's recent purchase of an old plantation home in town with the intention of renovating it. She tells her fiancé that she is taking an antiques-hunting jaunt by herself, but instead visits Noah and tells him that she never received his letters. Allie returns again the next day, and when the pair are caught in a storm out on the water their passion is rekindled. Meanwhile, Allie's mother arrives at Noah's home carrying a bundle of unopened letters and tells her daughter to "follow your heart." The final chapter finds Noah concluding his notebook story to Allie, who suffers from a severe case of Alzheimer's disease, on their forty-ninth wedding anniversary.

When Sparks sent the manuscript to an agent, it was sold within two days for a million dollars, and a movie deal was signed that same week as well. Sparks and his debut became an overnight sensation, and many reviewers noted that the novel seemed to replicate the success of Robert James Waller's bestselling *The Bridges of Madison County.* Though critical assessments were sometimes less than kind, *The Notebook* spent 115 weeks on hardcover and paperback bestseller lists. *Booklist*'s Joanne Wilkinson called it "an upscale

Harlequin romance with great crossover appeal," but *Christian Century* writer Martha Whitmore Hickman asked: "Is it possible that, despite the medical prognosis, love can redeem some hours for those afflicted with Alzheimer's?"

Sparks kept his sales job for a time, surprised by the success of *The Notebook.* "I thought the book was pretty good when I wrote it," he told Hubbard in a *People* interview, "but I've gotten letters saying it was unforgettable. People—men, women, ministers—love this book." A film featuring James Garner, Ryan Gosley, Rachel McAdams, and Gena Rowlands was adapted from *The Notebook,* and Sparks himself went on to pen a sequel, *The Wedding,* in which Allie's daughter Jane experiences trouble in her thirty-year marriage with neglectful, work-consumed attorney Wilson Lewis. In *Booklist* Patty Engelmann dubbed *The Wedding* a "tender love story about a flawed hero trying to right his wrongs," while a *Publishers Weekly* reviewer praised Sparks for relating "a sweet story competently, without sinking too deeply into the mire of sentiment."

Sparks's next novel, *Message in a Bottle,* also spent months on the bestseller lists, including four weeks at the top. Inspired by the 1989 death of his mother in a horseback-riding accident, the 1998 work revolves around jaded Boston newspaper columnist and divorcee Theresa Osborne, who finds a letter in the sand of a Cape Cod beach one day. Its author is a man named Garrett, and the letter recounts a dream in which his lost love reappears. Theresa has spent the past three years trying to recover from her own failed marriage, and the letter ignites hope in her. She becomes obsessed with finding the writer and prints his letter in her column; she soon learns that it is one of many such missives found. Garrett turns out to be Garrett Blake, a diving instructor living in North Carolina. Theresa seeks Garrett out and learns that the woman to whom he is writing is his late wife, Catherine. "There are few surprises here as we watch the couple learn to love in Catherine's slowly waning shadow," a *Publishers Weekly* review observed. Pat Engelmann, writing in *Booklist,* termed the book "a deeply moving, beautifully written, and extremely romantic love story." *Message in a Bottle* was made into a film starring Kevin Costner, Robin Wright Penn, and Paul Newman.

First love is the theme of Sparks's third bestseller, *A Walk to Remember,* which the author penned as a way to deal with the premature death of a younger sister. The narrator of the 1999 novel is aging Landon Carter, who recalls his senior year of high school in Beaufort, North Carolina, in the late 1950s. Carter, the hedonistic son of a congressman, is senior class president and thus compelled to attend his homecoming dance. Scrambling to find a date, he asks drab Jamie Sullivan, the daughter of a Baptist minister. She agrees, but asks him to reciprocate and join her in a Christmas play scripted by her stern minister father. The two become unlikely friends, and Carter is moved by the play's theme, the elder Sullivan's love for his wife, Jamie's mother, and by Mrs. Sullivan's early death. Carter falls in love with Jamie, but learns of a tragic secret she harbors and is forced to make a life-altering decision. "Sparks," noted *Booklist* reviewer Engelmann, "proves once again that he is a master at pulling heartstrings," while a *Publishers Weekly* review noted that *A Walk to Remember* is "sure to wring yet more tears from willing readers' eyes." The novel was adapted as a film in 2002.

Sparks continued his success with *The Rescue,* published in 2000. Its focus is on the unlikely romance that develops between Denise Holton, a single mother in a small North Carolina town, and the rugged Taylor McAden. Once a teacher, Denise has fallen on hard times and must live with her mother in order to devote enough time to her son, Kyle, who has a language-processing disability. One night her car veers off the road, and McAden, a contractor who also serves as a volunteer fireman, rescues Denise and her son. A bond develops between the hero and the little boy, and Denise finds herself attracted to McAden romantically. However, the brooding hero is also hiding some deep psychic wounds and seems unable to forge a relationship. "The story here is mostly a pretext for the emotional assault that Sparks delivers, but when he manages to link affect to action, the result is cunningly crafted melodrama," remarked a *Publishers Weekly* reviewer. Engelmann, writing in *Booklist,* asserted that "all of Sparks's trademark elements—love, loss, and small-town life—are present in this terrific summer read."

Sparks's fifth novel, *A Bend in the Road,* is filled with the writer's characteristic elements. Teacher Sarah Andrews meets Miles Ryan when Miles's second-grade son, Jonah, develops a learning disability stemming from the child's grief over his mother's death. Miles, too, has been wounded by the hit-and-run ac-

cident that killed his high school sweetheart and wife, Missy. When Sarah enters their lives, she has already experienced a divorce from a husband who could not live with Sarah's inability to bear children. Miles and Sarah eventually fall in love, but their future is clouded by a secret connected with Missy's death. In a *Bookhaven* review, Amy Coffin described *A Bend in the Road* as "poignant."

Nights in Rodanthe, which appeared in 2002, quickly became a bestseller, heading the lists in the *Wall Street Journal, Publishers Weekly,* and *New York Times.* It tells the story of two middle-aged people who have experienced failure in love. Adrienne Willis, a forty-five year old, is the divorced mother of three children whose husband abandoned her for a younger, more attractive woman. Paul Flanner, a divorced workaholic surgeon, was unable to devote enough time to his wife and children to sustain either a successful marriage or family life. Adrienne and Paul meet in a bed-and-breakfast in the town of Rodanthe, North Carolina. A romance is enkindled over the next several days, and the two separate with the intention to continue an exploration of their love. Adrienne tells the story of their meeting—after a fourteen-year silence—to her daughter, Amanda, who is overcome with grief over the death of her own husband to the point that she is unable to properly attend to her young children's needs. As her mother's tale unfolds, so does the reason why Adrienne and Paul never married.

Nights in Rodanthe is "filled with a healthy dose of romance and emotion," commented Carol Fitzgerald in a *BookReporter* review. In *Kirkus Reviews* a critic felt that *Nights in Rodanthe* is a "harshly mechanical story" with a predictable plot, while in *Publishers Weekly* a reviewer remarked that "even fans may be irked" by the obvious twist in Sparks's characters' fates. Mary Frances Wilkens wrote in *Booklist* that the novel encapsulates a "beautiful love story." On his Web site, Sparks explained that he used middle-aged protagonists in the book "because so many family elements can come to play" between more mature men and women.

In 2003 Sparks departed from his typical romantic stories with *The Guardian,* a novel that also incorporates elements of a thriller. Young widow Julie Barenson finds herself romantically involved with two men. Richard Franklin, a smooth-talking, wealthy gentleman, treats Julie in a lavish fashion. She breaks off their relationship after a few dates, however, and begins to see her late husband's best friend, Mike Harris. Franklin, unhappy about her rejection of his suit, begins to interfere in Julie's personal life in sinister ways. In an interview with *BookReporter* Sparks revealed that he added a dark character like Franklin to his traditional romantic mix because "I wanted to write the type of novel that I hadn't written before . . . because I think it's important for my readers that they don't read the same book over and over."

Booklist writer Patty Engelmann called *The Guardian* a "tricky tale of romantic suspense" with a nail-biting conclusion. Although "the writing is lax at best. . . . this one will be another bestseller," predicted a *Publishers Weekly* critic. Calling *The Guardian* "undoubtedly his finest work," David Exum commented of Sparks's work in *BookReporter,* "It is pulse-pounding, breathtaking, suspenseful and intriguing."

BIOGRAPHICAL AND CRITICAL SOURCES:

PERIODICALS

Booklist, April 1, 1994, Pat Monaghan, review of *Wokini: A Lakota Journey to Happiness and Self-Understanding,* p. 1407; August, 1996, Joanne Wilkinson, review of *The Notebook,* p. 1856; October 15, 1997, Karen Harris, review of *The Notebook,* p. 424; February 15, 1998, Pat Engelmann, review of *Message in a Bottle,* p. 949; August, 1999, Patty Engelmann, review of *A Walk to Remember,* p. 1989; May 15, 2000, Nancy Paul, review of *A Walk to Remember,* p. 144; July, 2000, Patty Engelmann, review of *The Rescue,* p. 1976; January 1, 2002, review of audiobook version of *A Bend in the Road,* p. 875; January 1, 2003, Mary Frances Wilkens, review of audiobook version of *Nights in Rodanthe,* p. 920; March 1, 2003, Patty Engelmann, review of *The Guardian,* p. 1108; September 1, 2003, Patty Engelmann, review of *The Wedding,* p. 8.

Christian Century, December 17, 1997, Martha Whitmore Hickman, review of *The Notebook,* p. 1201.

Entertainment Weekly, April 24, 1998, Daneet Steffens, review of *Message in a Bottle,* p. 75; October 15, 1999, Clarissa Cruz, review of *A Walk to Remember,* p. 74; November 10, 2000, review of *The Rescue,* p. 82.

Good Housekeeping, February, 2001, Nicholas Sparks, excerpt from *The Rescue,* p. 157.

Kirkus Reviews, August 1, 2002, review of *Nights in Rodanthe,* p. 1072; March 1, 2003, review of *The Guardian,* p. 343.

Kliatt, January, 2002, review of audiobook version of *A Bend in the Road,* p. 39.

Library Journal, October 1, 1997, Nancy Paul, review of *The Notebook,* p. 147; September 1, 2000, Rebecca Sturm Kelm, review of *The Rescue,* p. 253.

New York Times Book Review, June 14, 1998, Sarah Harrison Smith, review of *Message in a Bottle,* p. 21.

People, November 25, 1996, Kim Hubbard, "Sentimental Journal," p. 165; March 24, 1997, Lan N. Nguyen, "Most Sappy Fella," p. 35; April 20, 1998, Cynthia Sanz, review of *Message in a Bottle,* p. 47; March 1, 1999, p. 126; November 29, 1999, review of *A Walk to Remember,* p. 63; October 23, 2000, review of *The Rescue,* p. 57; November 13, 2000, "Nicholas Sparks: Sexiest Author," p. 97; September 22, 2003, Daisy Maryles, review of *The Wedding,* p. 31; October 6, 2003, Allison Adato, "Writing through the Pain," p. 141.

Publishers Weekly, July 22, 1996, review of *The Notebook,* p. 224; November 4, 1996, review of *The Notebook,* p. 45; March 3, 1997, Paul Nathan, "Dream Deal," p. 22; February 16, 1998, review of *Message in a Bottle,* p. 201; June 1, 1998, review of *Message in a Bottle,* p. 34; August 23, 1999, review of *A Walk to Remember,* p. 42; October 18, 1999, "Making Sparks Fly," p. 22; January 10, 2000, John F. Baker, "The Ongoing Saga of Sparks," p. 16; August 14, 2000, review of *The Rescue,* p. 331; August 26, 2002, review of *Nights in Rodanthe,* p. 44; March 17, 2003, review of *The Guardian,* p. 52; August 11, 2003, review of *The Wedding,* p. 255.

ONLINE

Bookhaven, http://thebookhaven.homestead.com/ (August 1, 2003) Amy Coffin, review of *A Bend in the Road.*

BookReporter, http://www.bookreporter.com/ (June 2, 2003), Carol Fitzgerald, review of *Nights in Rodanthe;* interview with Sparks; David Exum, review of *The Guardian.*

Official Nicholas Sparks Web site, http://www.nicholassparks.com/ (January 15, 2004).

Gerald Spence

Time Warner Web site, http://www.twbookmark.com/ (June 2, 2003).*

*   *   *

SPAULDING, Douglas
    See BRADBURY, Ray (Douglas)

*   *   *

SPAULDING, Leonard
    See BRADBURY, Ray (Douglas)

*   *   *

SPEAR, Benjamin
    See HENISCH, Heinz K.

*   *   *

SPENCE, Gerald (Leonard) 1929-
    (Gerry Spence)

PERSONAL: Born January 8, 1929, in Laramie, WY; son of Gerald M. (a chemist) and Esther Sophie (a homemaker; maiden name, Pfleeger) Spence; married Anna Wilson, June 20, 1947 (divorced, 1969); married LaNelle Hampton Peterson Hawks (a designer), November 18, 1969; children: (first marriage) Kip, Kerry Spence Suendermann, Kent, Katy; Christopher Peterson Hawks, Brents Jefferson Hawks (stepsons). *Education:* University of Wyoming, B.S.L., 1949, LL.B. (magna cum laude), 1952.

ADDRESSES: Home—Jackson, WY. *Office*—Spence, Moriarity and Shockey, P.O. Box 548, Jackson, WY 83001. *E-mail*—gerry@gerryspence.com.

CAREER: Admitted to the Bar of Wyoming State, 1952, and the Bar of the U.S. Supreme Court; private practice of law, Riverton, WY, 1952-54; county and prosecuting attorney in Fremont County, WY, 1954-62; partner in private law firms in Riverton and Casper, WY, 1962-78; Spence, Moriarity and Shockey (law firm), Jackson, WY, senior partner, 1978-2002, partner, 2002—. Trial Lawyers College (nonprofit organization), founder and director; Lawyers and Advocates for Wyoming (nonprofit public interest law firm), founder; lecturer in trial advocacy for legal organizations and law schools. CNBC-TV, creator and host of the weekly program *The Gerry Spence Show,* 1995; guest on television programs, including *Larry King Live;* consultant on the O. J. Simpson trial to NBC-TV.

MEMBER: American Bar Association, Association of Trial Lawyers of America, National Association of Criminal Defense Lawyers, Wyoming Bar Association, Wyoming Trial Lawyers Association.

AWARDS, HONORS: LL.D., University of Wyoming, 1990.

WRITINGS:

UNDER NAME GERRY SPENCE

(With Anthony Polk) *Gunning for Justice,* Doubleday (New York, NY), 1982.

Of Murder and Madness: A True Story of Insanity and the Law, Doubleday (New York, NY), 1983.

Trial by Fire: The True Story of a Woman's Ordeal at the Hands of the Law, Morrow (New York, NY), 1986.

With Justice for None: Destroying an American Myth, Times Books (New York, NY), 1989.

From Freedom to Slavery: The Rebirth of Tyranny in America, St. Martin's Press (New York, NY), 1993.

How to Argue and Win Every Time: At Home, at Work, in Court, Everywhere, Every Day, St. Martin's Press (New York, NY), 1995.

The Making of a Country Lawyer (autobiography), St. Martin's Press (New York, NY), 1996.

(Author of foreword) Lou Jones, *Final Exposure: Portraits from Death Row,* Northeastern University Press (Boston, MA), 1996.

O. J.: The Last Word (Literary Guild selection), St. Martin's Press (New York, NY), 1997.

Give Me Liberty!: Freeing Ourselves in the Twenty-first Century, St. Martin's Press (New York, NY), 1998.

Gerry Spence's Wyoming: The Landscape: Photographs and Poetry, St. Martin's Press (New York, NY), 2000.

A Boy's Summer: Father and Son Together, St. Martin's Press (New York, NY), 2000.

Half-Moon and Empty Stars, Scribner (New York, NY), 2001.

Seven Simple Steps to Personal Freedom, St. Martin's Press (New York, NY), 2001.

WORK IN PROGRESS: The Lambs of Purgatory and *Dead End.*

SIDELIGHTS: Gerald Spence is a nationally known lawyer who has represented such high-profile clients as Randy Weaver, the children of Karen Silkwood, and Imelda Marcos.

Already a respected trial lawyer in his native Wyoming, Spence attained national prominence in 1979 when he won a multimillion dollar legal judgment on behalf of the children of Karen Silkwood. The suit, concerning Silkwood's contamination by radioactive plutonium in her job manufacturing fuel rods for nuclear reactors, is regarded as the most important nuclear power-related personal injury case to date.

Spence has since scored a number of other highly publicized victories in personal injury litigation. He won a record-setting $26.5 million decree against *Penthouse* magazine for a former Miss Wyoming. The batonist-beauty contestant claimed that the magazine's story of a Miss Wyoming whose sexual skills surpassed her baton-twirling talent was libelous. Considered a master of jury persuasion and the art of cross-examination, Spence is also an avocational poet and painter; he is, wrote David Noonan in *Esquire,* "a genuine Western renaissance man."

Spence began his career in trial advocacy as a prosecutor for Fremont County, Wyoming, a post he held for eight years. After an unsuccessful bid to become the Republican candidate for Congress in 1962, he joined a private law firm in the city of Riverton and represented insurance companies in personal injury trials. He compiled an extensive win record with an extremely aggressive courtroom style and litigated major cases in Colorado and other western states.

At age forty, however, Spence suffered a mid-life crisis and came to doubt the value of his work. "I just felt like I was going nowhere," he recalled to David Noonan. Spence describes that period in his book *Of Murder and Madness.* He lost an unprecedented three cases in a row and was passed over for appointment to a judgeship he had sought. He also repeatedly encountered people whose injury claims he had defeated in court, including an auto crash victim with a back condition whom, Spence admitted to *People*'s Cheryl McCall, "I arrogantly and unjustly beat" out of a compensation claim. "People said I had great skills, but what does it mean if you don't use them correctly?" he recalled asking himself.

So one afternoon in 1970 Spence abruptly severed all ties to some forty companies he had represented and pledged henceforth to advocate for "the little man" against corporations. "In America, corporations need us to survive, so they've enslaved our minds and our value systems," Spence observed to McCall. "But like dragons, corporations can be slain. I decided to be seen as the country lawyer, living in a small town, who could kill corporations in the courtroom." Spence does not consider himself a public interest or "movement" lawyer, noted *Esquire*'s Noonan, but he enjoys taking what he calls "double-barreled" cases—personal injury lawsuits that combine big fees and social significance. His strikingly successful track record has catapulted him into the ranks of the country's top lawyers and has given him the financial wherewithal to choose high-visibility cases he believes in, observed Noonan.

Observers of Spence's courtroom style attribute a good measure of this success to the Wyoming advocate's ability to hold sway with juries. "He comes off as so real that jurors trust him," Wyoming Supreme Court Chief Justice Robert Rose, a former Spence partner, remarked to *Time*'s Bennett H. Beach. "They have to decide which side to be on, and if he wants to be your friend, you can barely resist him." Spence himself thinks he owes his credibility to a gift for communicating in plain, simple English in the courtroom, conveying a sense of personal candor and respect for the jury. "I just talk Western," he explained to Noonan.

Spence further credits part of his success to the meticulous research and pre-trial case preparation his firm routinely practices, usually outspending the opposing side. He attributes his victory in the Silkwood case largely to his success in discrediting the defense's expert witnesses on cross-examination and to his ability to translate complex technical issues into human terms for the jury. Karen Silkwood, a union shop steward, died in 1974 in an automobile accident under mysterious circumstances. She was on her way to meet a journalist and a union official to discuss allegedly lax procedures in the manufacture and handling of plutonium at the Kerr-McGee Corporation's Cimarron, Oklahoma, plant. Silkwood herself had suffered plutonium contamination at the plant, and her survivors brought a negligence suit against the company. Spence won a $10.5 million damage award for Silkwood's estate—later appealed by Kerr-McGee—and for himself, praise from presiding federal judge Frank Theis as "the best cross-examiner I've ever heard." To David Noonan, Spence described the suit as perhaps "the most important case of all time, because it has to do with the survival of man, and there can't be anything more important than that."

Spence details the Silkwood trial in *Gunning for Justice,* along with two other of his most important cases. One of these found the customary defense attorney in the unlikely position of acting as unpaid special prosecutor for the state in the trial of a Wyoming man

charged with four murders. The victims included a close lawyer friend of Spence, killed with his wife and son when a dynamite bomb was hurled into their home. Though a lifelong opponent of capital punishment, Spence successfully sought the death penalty from the jury after the accused was charged with ordering from jail the contract murder of a key prosecution witness. The third case in the book involved Spence's successful defense of a Wyoming police officer accused of murdering an undercover narcotics agent. Reviewing *Gunning for Justice* for the *Los Angeles Times Book Review,* Morton Kamins commented that Spence "writes here with candor and flair about his up-and-down-and-up life—his roots, his love for the Wyoming landscape, his law career—admixed with full-blooded narratives of three complex and fascinating cases."

In his second book, *Of Murder and Madness,* Spence recounts his successful defense of an accused murderer on the premise of insanity due to socioeconomic circumstances. In what seemed an open-and-shut capital case, Spence's client, Joe Esquibel of Rawlins, Wyoming, had been charged with murdering his ex-wife in front of eight witnesses at the local welfare office. Spence originally took up Esquibel's defense, he writes, simply to amuse himself and test his legal prowess to win acquittal for a client "so obviously guilty that the public will demand he be hauled away without even a trial." In familiarizing himself with Esquibel's background and circumstances, however, Spence came up with the theory that a life of poverty, family deprivation, and ethnic discrimination had so twisted Esquibel's psyche as to render him incapable of distinguishing between right and wrong when he shot his ex-wife in a jealous rage. Though unable to find a single psychiatrist to buttress his argument in court during the first trial, Spence managed to convince the three different juries Esquibel faced over the course of seven years that his client was insane.

Reviewing *Of Murder and Madness* in the *New York Times Book Review,* Alan M. Dershowitz remarked, Spence "spins a wonderful yarn . . . speaks the folk language of the juror, and is as compelling as a country preacher." The *New York Times*'s Walter Goodman termed the author's autobiographical digressions an "exercise in self-dramatization," but added, "when it is in control, his prose can be evocative." Goodman drew attention to Spence's "convincing examples of the prejudice and exploitation suffered by Mexican-Americans in Wyoming and elsewhere."

Outside the courtroom, Spence told David Noonan, one of his main interests is the training of young lawyers in trial advocacy. He criticizes the legal education establishment, terming its leaders "the morticians of the profession." Spence's dream is to open a graduate school in trial law in the mountains of Wyoming to "unteach most of the things [students] learn in school," as he told Cheryl McCall. Specifically, he would concentrate on teaching direct, honest communication; the effective use of emotional energy; and the development of methods of resisting intimidation in the courtroom.

Spence realized that dream when he opened the nonprofit Trial Lawyers College in Dubois, Wyoming, where, as he told *CA,* "lawyers learn to try cases on behalf of the people." He also founded Lawyers and Advocates for Wyoming, a nonprofit public interest law firm. He continues to accept occasional cases that engage his interest and his passion for defending ordinary people against a system that he has called unjust. Spence also continues to write about what is wrong with the system and what might be done to correct it.

In *With Justice for None: Destroying an American Myth,* Spence argues that the American justice system protects the rich and powerful at the expense of the poor and disadvantaged. He criticizes the lawyers who concentrate on wealthy clients, the law schools that train them, and the judicial system itself. Spence offers potential solutions that, according to *Library Journal* reviewer Sally G. Waters, "range from idealistic to impractical." An *Atlantic* reviewer characterized them as "extensive and plausible" and described the book itself as "frequently witty and . . . enlivened by unexpected information and comparisons." Waters concluded: "Readers will find some good information about the legal system."

Another of Spence's explorations in American values is the book *From Freedom to Slavery: The Rebirth of Tyranny in America.* The author moves beyond the courtroom to puncture the notion that freedom is a reality in American society. He blames not only the corporate power-mongers and government bureaucrats who seem to be his favorite targets, but ordinary, individual citizens who naively relinquish their freedom in exchange for what they perceive will be increased personal security. Spence also recounts his defense of Randy Weaver, an Idaho man accused of firearms violations. During what has been called the Ruby Ridge incident, Weaver's teenaged son was killed by government agents who shot him in the back and his wife was killed with a shot to the head by an FBI sniper while she held the couple's infant daughter in her arms. Describing the book as "a blend of down-home anecdotes and populist political philosophy," Mary Carroll recommended it to *Booklist* readers as "an impassioned, accessible alternative to the [Ross] Perotista critique of American life-styles." To a *Publishers Weekly* reviewer, however, the lawyer's commentaries "sound more like impassioned court statements than well-structured arguments."

During the murder trial of football legend O. J. Simpson, Spence was a frequent legal commentator for NBC-TV and a variety of television talk shows. After the trial he wrote *O. J.: The Last Word,* "a compelling postmortem" according to *Library Journal* reviewer Phillip Young Blue. The book offers critical analyses of the prosecution team, the jury, and to a lesser extent the controversial Judge Ito. What separated this study from the spate of tomes that erupted into print after Simpson's acquittal, Ilene Cooper wrote in *Booklist,* was that the author "is more interested in speculating on what was going on in people's minds than he is in analyzing what the transcripts said." Spence avers that Simpson was indeed guilty of murder, but that the jury reached the proper verdict in light of the evidence admitted for examination. He also speculates that an opposite verdict could have occurred if alternative prosecution strategies had been employed—particularly if prosecuting attorneys had paid more careful attention to what Blue called "the sociology of race." A *Publishers Weekly* critic faulted *O. J.: The Last Word* for excessive speculation, but concluded that the author "seems an accurate reader of the scales of justice."

In 1996 Spence published *The Making of a Country Lawyer,* an autobiography covering his life up to the point where he abandoned his corporate clients and began his advocacy in the interest of the ordinary citizen. The chronicle discusses the author's personal background, from childhood in frontier Wyoming, through a wild youth, the suicide of his mother, his own substance abuse, and two colorful marriages. A critic for *Publishers Weekly* called it "a formidable autobiography, a striking evocation of . . . [Wyoming life, and] . . . a penetrating look into the heart of a youth." The volume is also, however, an account of the shaping of a lawyer, from law school through the early cases that prepared Spence for the high-profile career that lay ahead. *Booklist* reviewer Mary Carroll recommended the book: "Spence is an engaging story-teller with a gift for aphorism." Jerry E. Stephens reported in *Library Journal* that *The Making of a Country Lawyer* "is a masterful account of a great lawyer's life."

Spence shares the secret of his success in *How to Argue and Win Every Time: At Home, at Work, in Court, Everywhere, Every Day,* which has been translated into twenty-six languages and was on the *New York Times* bestseller list. According to Stephens, the core of the secret is "listen to the other person." Translated into what *Booklist* reviewer Gilbert Taylor called "the plain language of the real world," Spence offers advice about using the art of persuasion to one's own advantage at home and on the job, in love and in life. Taylor found the advice to be "pointedly sharp in essence" and recommended the self-help book as one that "rises above the herd."

Give Me Liberty!: Freeing Ourselves in the Twenty-first Century presents Spence's case that Americans are in slavery to a group of multinational corporations and an overly powerful federal government. After detailing the situation as he sees it, Spence then gives two dozen specific suggestions for freeing ourselves from tyranny. Mary Carroll in *Booklist* found the book to be "full of controversial, even outrageous, ideas and with something guaranteed to annoy almost everyone." Gregor A. Preston in *Library Journal* dubbed the book as "by turns bombastic, provocative, and tedious." A critic for *Publishers Weekly* praised Spence for "the ability to raise important social questions and attack rampant complacency while simultaneously recalling Ruby Ridge and Waco."

Spence turned to fiction with *Half-Moon and Empty Stars,* which a critic for *Publishers Weekly* described as "a masterful courtroom thriller and a haunting elegy for Native America." The story focuses on Charlie Retail, a Native American who witnessed the murder of his father years before. Unable to get justice in that case, Charlie has become embittered with the justice system. When one of the men who killed his father turns up dead himself, Charlie is the prime suspect and charged with the crime. C. D. Rogers in the *Florida Bar Journal* found that Spence "focuses on justice in the U.S. for the disadvantaged." Douglas C. Lord in *Library Journal* called the story "powerful and tragic."

BIOGRAPHICAL AND CRITICAL SOURCES:

BOOKS

Spence, Gerry, and Anthony Polk, *Gunning for Justice,* Doubleday (New York, NY), 1982.

Spence, Gerry, *Of Murder and Madness: A True Story of Insanity and the Law,* Doubleday (New York, NY), 1983.

Spence, Gerry, *The Making of a Country Lawyer,* St. Martin's Press (New York, NY), 1996.

Weaver, Randy and Sara, *The Federal Siege at Ruby Ridge: In Our Own Words,* Ruby Ridge, Inc., 1998.

PERIODICALS

Atlantic, June, 1989, review of *With Justice for None,* p. 97.

Barrister, May, 1984.

Booklist, July, 1993, pp. 1929-1930; September 1, 1993, p. 16; March 15, 1995, Gilbert Taylor, review of *How to Argue and Win Every Time,* p. 1283; September 1, 1996, Mary Carroll, review of *The Making of a Country Lawyer,* p. 5; October 1, 1997, Ilene Cooper, review of *O. J.: The Last Word,* p. 275; September 1, 1998, Mary Carroll, review of *Give Me Liberty!,* p. 5; May 1, 2000, John Rowen, review of *A Boy's Summer: Fathers and Sons Together,* p. 1632.

Christian Century, October 8, 1986, p. 867.

Esquire, May, 1981.

Florida Bar Journal, April, 2002, C. D. Rogers, review of *Half-Moon and Empty Stars,* p. 50.

Library Journal, April 1, 1989, Sally G. Waters, review of *With Justice for None,* p. 100; October 15, 1996, Jerry E. Stephens, review of *The Making of a Country Lawyer,* p. 68; November 1, 1997, Phillip Young Blue, review of *O. J.,* p. 102; October 1, 1998, Gregor A. Preston, review of *Give Me Liberty!,* p. 116; May 1, 2000, Douglas C. Lord, review of *A Boy's Summer,* p. 139; August, 2002, Douglas C. Lord, review of *Half-Moon and Empty Stars* audiobook edition, p. 170.

Los Angeles Times Book Review, October 24, 1982, Morton Kamins, review of *Gunning for Justice;* October 30, 1983.

National Review, March 18, 1983, pp. 332-333; December 28, 1984, pp. 41-44.

New York Times, March 14, 1984, Walter Goodman, review of *Of Murder and Madness.*

New York Times Book Review, March 18, 1984, Alan M. Dershowitz, review of *Of Murder and Madness.*

People, August 24, 1981.

Playboy, April, 1996, p. 122.

Publishers Weekly, May 31, 1993, p. 86; August 12, 1996, review of *The Making of a Country Lawyer,* p. 70; September 29, 1997, review of *O. J.,* p. 75; October 12, 1998, review of *Give Me Liberty!,* p. 65; May 28, 2001, review of *Half-Moon and Empty Stars,* p. 50.

Time, March 30, 1981.

Trial, May, 1998, Vincent J. Fuller, review of *O.J.,* p. 84.

ONLINE

Gerry Spence Home Page, http://www.gerryspence.com/ (June 18, 2003).

Ruby Ridge Updates Web site, http://www.ruby-ridge.com/ (June 18, 2003), excerpt of Chapter Two from Spence's *From Freedom to Slavery.*

Spence, Moriarty and Shockey Web site, http://www.smswy.com/ (June 18, 2003).

Trial Lawyers College Web site, http://www.triallawyerscollege.com/ (June 18, 2003).

*   *   *

SPENCE, Gerry
    See SPENCE, Gerald (Leonard)

*   *   *

SPILLANE, Frank Morrison 1918-
    (Mickey Spillane)

PERSONAL: Born March 9, 1918, in Brooklyn, NY; son of John Joseph (a bartender) and Catherine Anne Spillane; married Mary Ann Pearce, 1945 (divorced); married Sherri Malinou, November, 1965 (divorced); married Jane Rodgers Johnson, October, 1983; children: (first marriage) Kathy, Mark, Mike, Carolyn;

Frank Morrison Spillane

(third marriage; stepdaughters) Britt, Lisa. *Education:* Attended Kansas State College (now University). *Religion:* Jehovah Witness.

ADDRESSES: Home—Murrells Inlet, Myrtle Beach, SC. *Office*—c/o Author Mail, Simon & Schuster, 1230 Avenue of the Americas, New York, NY 10020.

CAREER: Writer of mystery and detective novels, short stories, books for children, comic books, and scripts for television and films. With producer Robert Fellows, formed an independent film company in Nashville, TN, called Spillane-Fellows Productions, which filmed features and television productions, 1969. Creator of television series *Mike Hammer,* 1984-87. Actor; has appeared in more than 110 commercials for Miller Lite Beer. *Military service:* U.S. Army Air Forces; taught cadets and flew fighter missions during World War II; became captain.

AWARDS, HONORS: Junior Literary Guild Award, 1979, for *The Day the Sea Rolled Back;* Lifetime

Achievement Award, 1983, and short story award, 1990, both from Private Eye Writers of America; Grand Master Award, Mystery Writers of America, 1995.

WRITINGS:

UNDER NAME MICKEY SPILLANE; CRIME NOVELS

I, the Jury (also see below), Dutton (New York, NY), 1947, reprinted, New American Library (New York, NY), 1973.

Vengeance Is Mine! (also see below), Dutton (New York, NY), 1950.

My Gun Is Quick (also see below), Dutton (New York, NY), 1950, reprinted, Signet (New York, NY), 1988.

The Big Kill (also see below), Dutton (New York, NY), 1951, reprinted, New English Library (London, England), 1984.

One Lonely Night, Dutton (New York, NY), 1951.

The Long Wait, Dutton (New York, NY), 1951, reprinted, New American Library (New York, NY), 1972.

Kiss Me, Deadly (also see below), Dutton (New York, NY), 1952.

The Deep, Dutton (New York, NY), 1961.

The Girl Hunters (also see below), Dutton (New York, NY), 1962.

Me, Hood!, Corgi (London), 1963, New American Library (New York, NY), 1969.

Day of the Guns, Dutton, 1964, reprinted, New American Library (New York, NY), 1981.

The Snake, Dutton (New York, NY), 1964.

The Flier, Corgi, 1964.

Bloody Sunrise, Dutton (New York, NY), 1965.

The Death Dealers, Dutton (New York, NY), 1965, reprinted, New American Library, 1981.

Killer Mine, Corgi, 1965.

The Twisted Thing, Dutton (New York, NY), 1966, published as *For Whom the Gods Would Destroy,* New American Library (New York, NY), 1971.

The By-Pass Control, Dutton (New York, NY), 1967.

The Delta Factor, Dutton (New York, NY), 1967.

Body Lovers, New American Library (New York, NY), 1967.

Killer Mine, New American Library (New York, NY), 1968.

Survival: Zero, Dutton (New York, NY), 1970.

Tough Guys, New American Library (New York, NY), 1970.

The Erection Set, Dutton (New York, NY), 1972.

The Last Cop Out, New American Library (New York, NY), 1973.

Mickey Spillane: Five Complete Mike Hammer Novels (contains *I, the Jury, Vengeance Is Mine!, My Gun Is Quick, The Big Kill,* and *Kiss Me, Deadly*), Avenel Books (New York, NY), 1987.

The Hammer Strikes Again: Five Complete Mike Hammer Novels (contains *One Lonely Night, The Snake, The Twisted Thing, The Body Lovers,* and *Survival: Zero*), Avenel Books (New York, NY), 1989.

The Killing Man, Dutton (New York, NY), 1989.

(Author of text) *Mikey Spillane's Mike Danger* (comic book series), Tekno Comics (Boca Raton, FL), 1995.

Black Alley, Dutton (New York, NY), 1996.

Together We Kill: The Uncollected Stories of Mickey Spillane, edited and with an introduction by Max Allan Collins, Five Star (Waterville, ME), 2001.

Something's Down There, Simon & Schuster (New York, NY), 2003.

Also author of *Return of the Hood.*

OTHER

(With Robert Fellows and Roy Rowland) *The Girl Hunters* (screenplay; based on Spillane's novel of the same title and starring Spillane in role of Mike Hammer), Colorama Features, 1963.

Vintage Spillane: A New Omnibus (short stories), W.H. Allen (London, England), 1974.

The Day the Sea Rolled Back (children's book), Windmill Books (New York, NY), 1979.

The Ship That Never Was (children's book), Bantam (New York, NY), 1982.

Tomorrow I Die (short stories), Mysterious Press, 1984.

(Editor, with Max Allan Collins) *Murder Is My Business,* Dutton (New York, NY), 1994.

(Editor, with Max Allan Collins) *A Century of Noir: Thirty-two Classic Crime Stories,* New American Library (New York, NY), 2002.

Also author of *The Shrinking Island.* Creator and writer of comic books, including *Mike Danger.* Author of several television and movie screenplays. Contributor of short stories to magazines.

ADAPTATIONS: I, the Jury was adapted to film in 1953 by United Artists; a remake of *I, the Jury* was filmed in 1981 by Twentieth Century-Fox; *The Long Wait* was filmed in 1954, *Kiss Me, Deadly* in 1955, and *My Gun Is Quick* in 1957, all by United Artists; *The Delta Factor* was filmed in 1970 by Colorama Features. *Mickey Spillane's Mike Hammer*, a television series based on Spillane's mystery novels and his character Mike Hammer, was produced by Revue Productions, distributed by MCA-TV, and premiered in 1958; another television series based on Spillane's writings, *Mike Hammer*, starring Stacy Keach, was produced and broadcast from 1984 to 1987. "That Hammer Guy" was produced on radio, 1953. Abridged recordings of *The Big Kill* and *My Gun Is Quick*, each read by Stacy Keach, were released as audio-cassettes by Simon & Schuster Audioworks (New York, NY), 1990.

SIDELIGHTS: Frank Morrison Spillane, who writes under the name Mickey Spillane, started his writing career in the early 1940s scripting comic books for Funnies, Inc. Spillane made the switch from comic books to novels in 1946 when, needing $1,000 to buy a parcel of land, he decided the easiest and quickest way to earn the money was to write a novel. Three weeks later, he sent the finished manuscript of *I, the Jury* to Dutton. Although the editorial committee questioned its good taste and literary merit, they felt the book would sell. *I, the Jury* did indeed sell—well over eight million copies have been sold to date. In addition to buying the property, Spillane was able to construct a house on the site as well. This book would be the start of a long and prolific career during which, as Julie Baumgold pointed out in *Esquire*, Spillane "sold two hundred million books and became the most widely read and fifth most translated writer in the world." All those books have made Spillane famous, wealthy, and a personality in his own right.

Spillane has no illusions about what he has accomplished through his books. As he explained to Baumgold, "I'm not an author, I'm a writer. . . . I can write a book in a few weeks, never rewrite, never read galleys. Bad reviews don't matter."

I, the Jury did sell, because it pleased the public, not because it won critical acclaim. Critics generally blasted the book's dark and seamy subject matter. These responses reflected the time in which the book was published, 1947, and the belief that the world

depicted in the book was only a small, dirty fringe on mainstream America, a fringe that Spillane was exploiting for its shock effect. Yet, as Frederic D. Schwarz, writing in *American Heritage*, noted, *I, the Jury* may represent one of the first signs of recognition of "the darker side of postwar America." Schwarz paired the July, 1947, publication of Spillane's first novel with an event that occurred on July 4 of that year. Hundreds of motorcyclists and their followers overwhelmed the town of Hollister, California, trashing it in a weekend of biker wildness. As Schwarz pointed out, "The incident formed the basis for a 1954 movie, *The Wild One*," starring Marlon Brando. Both the bikers' rampage and *I, the Jury*, according to Schwarz, "reflect a violent nature of the era." Spillane, who, Baumgold observed, lives under the motto "A Wild Man Proper," has always dismissed the charges of sensationalizing. As Schwarz quoted him, "I don't really go for sex and violence unless it's necessary."

Not only did *I, the Jury* introduce Spillane to the book-buying public, but it also gave birth to the character, Mike Hammer, a 6-foot, 190-pound, rough and tough private investigator. Spillane's next several novels recorded the action-packed adventures of Hammer as he drank, fought, and killed his way through solving mystery after mystery. While Hammer is not featured in all of Spillane's mysteries, he is undoubtedly the most popular of Spillane's leading men.

"Spillane is like eating takeout fried chicken: so much fun to consume, but you can feel those lowlife grease-induced zits rising before you've finished the first drumstick," noted Sally Eckhoff in the *Voice Literary Supplement*. "*My Gun Is Quick* is just the book to have with you on a Hamptons weekend or a stint at an exclusive art colony where everybody else is reading Huysmans. Guaranteed they leave you alone. But don't try to slide into *Me, Hood!* unless you want to permanently transform yourself into a snarling closet crimebuster. Any more of those seamed stockings, pawnshops, and stereotypical Irish gumshoes, and you'll be screaming for a Bergman movie to break your trance." In his 1951 review of *The Big Kill*, *New York Times* writer Anthony Boucher commented: "As rife with sexuality and sadism as any of his novels, based on a complete misunderstanding of law and on the wildest coincidence in detective fiction, it still can boast the absence of the hypocritical 'crusading' sentiments of Mike Hammer. For that reason, and for some slight ingenuity in its denouement, it may rank as the best Spillane—which is the faintest praise this department has ever bestowed."

In 1952 Spillane began a nine-year break from writing mystery novels. Some people have attributed this hiatus to his religious conversion to the sect of Jehovah's Witnesses, while others feel that Spillane earned enough money from his writings and by selling the film rights to several of his books to live comfortably, enjoying life in his new beach home on Murrells Inlet, located in Myrtle Beach, South Carolina. Although he stopped writing mysteries, Spillane wrote short stories for magazines and scripts for television and films. He also appeared on a number of television programs, often performing in parodies of his tough detective characters.

Spillane reappeared on the publishing scene in 1961 with his murder mystery *The Deep,* and in the following year Mike Hammer returned to fight crime in *The Girl Hunter.* The public was ecstatic—buying copies of the novel as soon as they were placed on the shelf, and reviewers seemed to soften their criticism somewhat at Hammer's return. Many of Spillane's later books also were somewhat praised by critics. For example, a reviewer for the *Times Literary Supplement* remarked: "Nasty as much of it is, [*The Deep*] has a genuine narrative grip; and there is a certain sociological conscience at work in the presentation of the street which has bred so much crime and an unusual perception in the portrait of an old Irish patrol officer." And Newgate Callendar commented in the *New York Times Book Review* that "editorials were written condemning [Spillane's novels], and preachers took to the pulpit. But things have changed, and one reads Spillane's . . . *The Erection Set* with almost a feeling of sentimental *deja vu.* The sex, sadism and assorted violence remain. Basically, what the Spillane books are about is the all-conquering hero myth. We all like to escape into a fantasy world to identify with the figure who is all-knowing, all-powerful, infinitely virile, sending off auras of threat in solar pulsations."

Spillane followed *The Erection Set* with *The Last Cop Out,* and then came another hiatus in his publication of crime novels. During this time, Spillane's publisher dared him to write a children's book. A number of editors at the company felt he could never change his style of writing in order to appeal or be acceptable to a much younger, more impressionable audience. Not one to back down from a challenge, Spillane produced

The Day the Sea Rolled Back in 1979 and, three years later, *The Ship That Never Was.* In general, reviewers have praised the books for their suspense and clean-cut high adventure.

In 1989 Spillane published his first Mike Hammer novel since 1970. In this return of Mike Hammer, *The Killing Man,* the detective returns to his office to find his secretary (and the unrecognized love of his life), Velda, unconscious on the floor and a dead man at his desk. True to form, Hammer sets out to bring the perpetrator to his own special brand of justice. Mickey Friedman, writing in the *New York Times Book Review,* maintained that "the book is a limp performance; the author makes no attempt to revitalize ingredients that are shopworn by now, and the book seems more like a ritual than a novel."

The year 1996 saw the publication of Spillane's thirteenth Mike Hammer novel, *Black Alley.* Hammer has just emerged from a coma, having been shot and put at the brink of death by gangsters. As with his first novel, *I, the Jury,* this book begins with the death of one of Hammer's military buddies. He sets off in search of his friend's murderer and billions in dirty mob money. The plot is familiar, but as a *Publishers Weekly* contributor wrote, "Spillane's hard-boiled hero has softened with time; he finally tells Velda how he really feels about her—but, on doctor's orders, he refrains from consummation." *Forbes* magazine's Steve Forbes found much to reward the reader in *Black Alley.* He observed, "The action never lets up as the tough, street-smart Hammer grapples with intense physical pain, revenue-hungry federal agents, cold-blooded gangsters, a recovering-alcoholic physician and a determined get-him-to-the-alter secretary."

Spillane's short fiction is showcased in *Together We Kill: The Uncollected Stories of Mickey Spillane.* Included in the collection are "The Night I Died," the only 1950s Mike Hammer story; "Together We Kill," a love story set in World War II; and "The Veiled Woman," a rare science fiction tale. The novella "Hot Cat" makes its first U.S. appearance in this volume. Wes Lukowsky, writing in *Booklist,* noted that collections such as this one often consist of "curiosities and rejects," but *Together We Kill* is not one of them. "Spillane's superviolent, no-frills approach to the genre is out of fashion today, but he remains a solid storyteller," Lukowsky remarked.

Spillane lends his first-hand knowledge of hard-boiled detective stories to *A Century of Noir: Thirty-two Clas-*

sic Crime Stories, edited with noted mystery writer Max Allan Collins. Described by Dick Adler in the *Chicago Tribune* as "a terrific collection of thirty-two hard-boiled crime stories," the book contains tales by genre luminaries such as John D. MacDonald, Evan Hunter, Lawrence Block, Sarah Paretsky, and Ross Macdonald. Also included is a tale by coeditor Collins and a Spillane story, "Tomorrow I Die," a "mordant novelette with a surprise ending," wrote Dick Lochte in the *Los Angeles Times.*

A new Spillane novel appeared in 2003. In *Something's Down There,* retired government spook Mako Hooker lives a leisurely retired life on Peolle Island in the Caribbean, fishing and boating with his fishing partner, Billy Bright. When a mysterious underwater creature begins attacking fishing boats, and functional World War II-era mines begin surfacing in the local troubled waters, Hooker finds himself reactivated by the government and charged with investigating the problems. Complicating matters is ex-mobster Anthony Pell, intent on gathering video evidence of the sea monster, and government agent Chana, a virulently hated old enemy of Hooker. A *Kirkus Reviews* critic declared that the book "ends with an unforgivably muffled finale that will leave an awful lot of readers wondering just what was down there." A *Publishers Weekly* reviewer, however, called the book an "entertaining island adventure" and "classic Spillane."

Neither a heavy drinker or smoker, Spillane doesn't manifest the stereotypical characteristics of his detective hero—he "even hates the city he sets the Hammer books in, New York," reported Peter Lennon in a profile of Spillane in the Manchester *Guardian.* Spillane even prefers mild oaths to dedicated swearing. "The final shock was that he has got religion in a big way. He is an active Jehovah's Witness who does house-to-house visits," Lennon wrote.

Spillane's work has often been noted as being simplistic and lacking in literary merit. At the height of his career in the 1950s and 1960s, "Spillane was considered the lowest of lowbrows," wrote Terry Teachout in *National Review,* "though he had some unlikely admirers, among them Kingsley Amis, who thought [Spillane] was a better writer than Dashiell Hammett or Raymond Chandler, and Ayn Rand, who said he was her favorite novelist since Victor Hugo." There are hints, however, that Rand was interested in more than Spillane's writing. Her letters to Spillane, reprinted in

Letters of Ayn Rand, suggest that at the very least, she was an unlikely ally who may have had romance in mind, observed John Meroney in the *Washington Post.* "When asked whether Ayn Rand had a crush on him, Spillane just smiles," Meroney wrote. "'I really liked her,' he says, noting that much of their camaraderie came from an 'us against them' view of the critics. 'They hate us, don't they?,' Spillane would say to her."

Critics notwithstanding, Spillane's audience has been very loyal to his Mike Hammer character and his other mystery novels. This loyalty and Spillane's ability to give his readers what they want accounts for hundreds of millions of books sold. It also accounts for the fact that seven of his books are still listed among the top fifteen all-time fiction best sellers published in the last fifty years. In 1984 Spillane shared these thoughts with the *Washington Post:* "I'm sixty-six. . . . If you're a singer, you lose your voice. A baseball player loses his arm. A writer gets more knowledge, and if he's good, the older he gets, the better he writes. They can't kill me. I still got potential." Or as Baumgold commented in *Esquire,* "Mickey Spillane still has a few good surprise endings left."

BIOGRAPHICAL AND CRITICAL SOURCES:

BOOKS

Collins, Max Allan, and James L. Traylor, *One Lonely Knight: Mickey Spillane's Mike Hammer,* Popular Press (Bowling Green, OH), 1984.

Contemporary Literary Criticism, Gale (Detroit), Volume 3, 1975, Volume 13, 1980.

St. James Guide to Crime and Mystery Writers, 4th edition, St. James Press (Detroit), 1996.

Van Dover, J. Kenneth, *Murder in the Millions: Erle Stanley Gardner, Mickey Spillane, and Ian Fleming,* Ungar (New York, NY), 1984.

PERIODICALS

American Heritage, July-August, 1997, Frederic D Schwarz, "Sex, Violence, and Motorcycles," p. 98.

Book, July-August, 2002, Allison Block, "Comfortable As an Old Gumshoe," p. 23.

Booklist, January 1, 2002, Wes Lukowsky, review of *Together We Kill: The Uncollected Stories of Mickey Spillane,* p. 820.

Chicago Sun-Times, Hillel Italie, "Mickey Spillane: Still Alive—and Writing," p. 7.

Chicago Tribune, May 5, 2002, Dick Adler, "Crimes, Questions, and Sleuths Old and New," p. 2.

Esquire, August, 1995, Julie Baumgold, "A Wild Man Proper," p. 132.

Forbes, December 16, 1996, Steve Forbes, review of *Black Alley,* p. 26.

Guardian (Manchester, England), July 23, 1999, Peter Lennon, profile of Mickey Spillane, p. 2.

Kirkus Reviews, February 1, 2002, review of *A Century of Noir: Thirty-two Classic Crime Stories,* p. 147; October 1, 2003, review of *Something's Down There,* p. 1198.

Los Angeles Times, May 8, 2002, Dick Lochte, "Mysteries: Guilt, Vengeance Come into Play for a Thrilling Read," p. E2.

National Review, October 1, 2001, Terry Teachout, "A Guy's Guy," pp. 50-52.

New York Times, November 11, 1951, Anthony Boucher, review of *The Big Kill.*

New York Times Book Review, February 27, 1972, Newgate Callendar, review of *The Erection Set*; October 15, 1989, Mickey Friedman, review of *The Killing Man,* p. 43.

Publishers Weekly, September 2, 1996, review of *Black Alley,* p. 11; October 6, 2003, review of *Something's Down There,* pp. 56-57.

Times Literary Supplement, November 10, 1961, review of *The Deep*; September 19, 1980.

Voice Literary Supplement, July, 1988, Sally Eckhoff, "Mysterious Pleasures: Sleaze Please," p. S13.

Washington Post, October 24, 1984 (interview); August 22, 2001, John Meroney, "Man of Mysteries: It'd Been Years since Spillane Pulled a Job. Could We Find Him? Yeah, It Was Easy," p. C1.

ONLINE

Pegasos Web site, http://www.kirjasto.sci.fi/ (November 14, 2003), profile of Mickey Spillane.

Unofficial Mickey Spillane Mike Hammer Web site, http://www.interlog.com/~roco/hammer.html/ (November 14, 2003).*

*   *   *

SPILLANE, Mickey
See SPILLANE, Frank Morrison

STAHL, Saul 1942-

PERSONAL: Born January 23, 1942, in Antwerp, Belgium; U.S. citizen; son of Mano Moses (a diamond broker) and Finkla (a nurse; maiden name, Schmidt) Stahl; married Susan Hogle (an occupational therapist), September 1, 1980; children: Dan Langdon, Lynne Elizabeth, Amy Joy. *Ethnicity:* "Caucasian." *Education:* Brooklyn College of the City University of New York, B.A., 1963; University of California—Berkeley, M.A., 1966; Western Michigan University, Ph.D., 1975. *Hobbies and other interests:* Dance, languages.

ADDRESSES: Home—Lawrence, KS. *Office*—Department of Mathematics, University of Kansas, Lawrence, KS 66045. *E-mail*—stahl@math.ukans.edu.

CAREER: U.S. Peace Corps, Washington, DC, volunteer high school and college teacher in Nepal, 1965-68; International Business Machines Co., Endicott, NY, systems programmer, 1969-73; Wright State University, Fairborn, OH, assistant professor of mathematics, 1975-77; University of Kansas, Lawrence, KS, professor of mathematics, 1977—.

MEMBER: American Mathematical Society, Mathematical Association of America.

AWARDS, HONORS: Carl B. Allendoerfer Award, Mathematical Association of America, 1986, for the article "The Other Coloring Theorem."

WRITINGS:

The Poincaré Half-Plane: A Gateway to Modern Geometry, Jones & Bartlett, 1993.

Introductory Modern Algebra: A Historical Approach, John Wiley (New York, NY), 1996.

A Gentle Introduction to Game Theory, American Mathematical Society (Providence, RI), 1999.

Real Analysis: A Historical Approach, John Wiley (New York, NY), 1999.

Geometry from Euclid to Knots, Prentice-Hall (Tappan, NJ), 2003.

Contributor to mathematics journals.

WORK IN PROGRESS: Research on topics in topology and geometry.

SIDELIGHTS: Saul Stahl once told *CA:* "I am writing the textbooks that I wish I had seen as an undergraduate student with a major in mathematics. To the extent possible, the exposition is informed, as Henri Poincaré suggested it should be, by the historical evolution of the subject matter. I avoid all unnecessary abstractions and make sure that the reader is provided with ample routine exercises and a sufficient number of challenging problems."

*   *   *

STEIN, Joseph 1912-

PERSONAL: Born May 30, 1912, in New York, NY; son of Charles and Emma (Rosenblum) Stein; married Sadie Singer (died, 1974); married Elisa Loti (a psychotherapist and former actress), 1976; children: Daniel, Harry, Joshua; stepchildren: John, Jenny Lyn. *Education:* City College (now City College of the City University of New York), B.S.S., 1935; Columbia University, M.S.W., 1937.

ADDRESSES: Office—1130 Park Avenue, New York, NY 10128; fax 212-410-3458. *Agent*—Paramuse Artists, 1414 Avenue of the Americas, New York, NY 10019.

CAREER: Playwright. Psychiatric social worker, 1939-45; writer for radio, television, and stage, beginning 1946.

MEMBER: Dramatists Guild (member of executive council), Authors League.

AWARDS, HONORS: Antoinette Perry Award nominations, for book of a musical, 1960, for *Take Me Along,* and for best musical, 1969, for *Zorba,* and 1987, for *Rags;* Antoinette Perry Award for best musical, New York Drama Critics Award, Newspaper Guild Award, all 1965, and Screen Writers Guild award, 1972, all for *Fiddler on the Roof;* Laurence Olivier award nomination, 1989, for *The Baker's Wife.*

WRITINGS:

PLAYS

(With Will Glickman) *Mrs. Gibbons' Boys* (three-act comedy; produced on Broadway, 1949), Samuel French (New York, NY), 1958.

Joseph Stein

Enter Laughing (two-act comedy; based on the autobiography by Carl Reiner; produced on Broadway, 1963; also see below), Samuel French (New York, NY), 1963, reprinted, 1984.
Before Dawn (adaptation of the play *A Ladies' Tailor* by Aleksandr Borshchagovsky), produced in New York, NY, 1985.

MUSICALS; AUTHOR OF LIBRETTO

(With Will Glickman) *Lend an Ear,* produced in New York, NY, 1948.
(With Will Glickman) *Alive and Kicking,* produced on Broadway, 1950.
(With Will Glickman) *Inside U.S.A.* produced in New York, NY, 1951.
(With Will Glickman) *Plain and Fancy* (produced on Broadway, 1955), Random House (New York, NY), 1955.
(With Will Glickman) *Mr. Wonderful* (produced on Broadway, 1956), Hart Stenographic Bureau (New York, NY), 1956.
(With Will Glickman) *The Body Beautiful* (produced on Broadway, 1958), Samuel French (New York, NY), 1958.

Juno (based on Sean O'Casey's play *Juno and the Paycock;* produced on Broadway, 1959), Hart Stenographic Bureau (New York, NY), 1959.

(With Robert Russell) *Take Me Along,* produced on Broadway, 1959.

Fiddler on the Roof (musical; based on short stories by Sholom Aleichem; produced on Broadway, 1964; also see below), Crown (New York, NY), 1965.

Zorba (based on Nikos Kazantzakis's book *Zorba the Greek;* produced on Broadway, 1968), music by John Kander, Random House (New York, NY), 1969.

(With Hugh Wheeler and others) *Irene,* produced on Broadway, 1973.

(With Stan Daniels) *So Long, 174th Street,* produced in New York, NY, 1976.

King of Hearts (based on the film of the same name), produced on Broadway, 1978.

(With Alan Jay Lerner) *Carmelina* (based on the film *Buona Sera, Mrs. Campbell*), produced on Broadway, 1979.

The Baker's Wife (based on a 1937 French film), produced in New York, 1985, produced in London, 1989.

Rags (musical), music by Charles Strouse, produced on Broadway, 1986.

Miracles, produced 1999.

Over and Over, produced in Washington, DC, 1999.

Author of scripts for radio shows, including *Raleigh's Room,* 1948-49, *Henry Morgan Show,* 1949-52, and *Kraft Music Hall;* and television shows, including *Your Show of Shows,* 1952-54, and *Sid Caesar Show,* 1954-55.

SCREENPLAYS; ADAPTED FROM HIS MUSICALS

Enter Laughing, Columbia, 1967.

Fiddler on the Roof, United Artists, 1971.

SIDELIGHTS: Playwright Joseph Stein began his career as a playwright on Broadway penning several popular comedies with fellow writer Will Glickman. His first musical, *Plain and Fancy,* took his career on a turn, however, when he found the genre suited him. *Mr. Wonderful,* a musical featuring a young Sammy Davis, followed, and although several subsequent plays did not fare well with New York critics, Stein is cred-

ited with the libretti for two of the most popular musicals of the mid-twentieth century: *Zorba* and the Tony Award-winning *Fiddler on the Roof.*

Stein once told *CA:* "I, in a career that spans four decades, have been connected with some of Broadway's biggest hits—*Fiddler on the Roof, Zorba, Enter Laughing, Take Me Along,* etc.—as well as some major disappointments, notably the musical *Rags.*

"My work deals largely with the relationships and emotional drives of basic, unsophisticated 'simple' people . . . —the Jews of the Russian 'shtetl' in *Fiddler on the Roof;* the Greek peasants of *Zorba;* the Amish of *Plain and Fancy;* the poor Dubliners of *Juno;* the immigrants of *Rags;* the French country folk of *The Baker's Wife*—their conflicts, their struggles, their romances. My tone is generally warm-hearted, affectionate and laced with humor.

"Ironically, both my major successes, *Fiddler on the Roof,* which continues to play all over the world, and perhaps my major disappointment, *Rags,* dealt with the Jewish experience, and in a sense, followed each other chronologically. As *Fiddler on the Roof* ended with the central characters leaving for America, *Rags* opens with the central characters arriving on these shores.

"Although *Fiddler on the Roof* had some difficulty getting produced (there was much concern that it would only appeal to a narrow ethnic audience) its subsequent history was most successful. *Rags,* on the other hand, was felled at the outset by a negative review by New York's principal critic. The cast, including its leading player, the opera star Teresa Stratas, were so enthusiastic about the show that they all offered to defer their salaries to keep it open, and after the closing curtain, they paraded down Broadway, together with the audience, chanting 'Keep *Rags* open!' But it was not to be; the producers had run out of funds.

"However, *Rags* was subsequently revived off-Broadway to a very favorable reaction, and it continues to play in regional theaters with considerable success."

BIOGRAPHICAL AND CRITICAL SOURCES:

BOOKS

Guernsey, Otis L., Jr., editor, *Broadway Song and Story: Playwrights/Lyricists/Composers Discuss Their Hits,* Dodd, Mead (New York, NY), 1986.

PERIODICALS

New York Times, April 10, 1979; April 22, 1979; March 25, 1985; August 17, 1986; August 22, 1986; September 21, 1986.
Washington Post, March 4, 1979; April 22, 1979.*

* * *

STOKER, R. Bryan 1962-

PERSONAL: Born March 8, 1962, in Hickory, NC; son of Roy D. (a district engineer) and Nancy D. (a bank officer) Stoker; married December 14, 1985; wife's name Sharyn D. (a programmer); children: Melissa L., Michelle B. *Ethnicity:* "White Caucasian." *Education:* North Carolina State University, B.S.E.E., 1984; Johns Hopkins University, M.S.E.E., 1987; California Coast University, M.B.A. and Ph.D., B.A., 1997. *Politics:* Republican. *Hobbies and other interests:* Investing, travel, martial arts, computers, fishing.

ADDRESSES: Home—Eldersburg, MD. *Office*— Lifestyle Publishing, 6685 Slacks Rd., Sykesville, MD 21784. *E-mail*—rbstoker@netzero.net.

CAREER: U.S. Department of Defense, Fort Meade, MD, technical director, 1984—. Lifestyle Publishing, Sykesville, MD, president, 1993—.

MEMBER: Theta Tau.

AWARDS, HONORS: Named master member of technical track, U.S. Department of Defense, 1998; ribbons from Toastmasters International.

WRITINGS:

Financial Freedom: A Wealth Manual for the Middle Class, Lifestyle Publishing (Sykesville, MD), 1994.
Growth and Income: How to Build a Mutual Fund Money Machine, Lifestyle Publishing (Sykesville, MD), 1999.
Money Secrets: How to Make . . . and Save . . . a Fortune for People Who Want More Money, Lifestyle Publishing (Sykesville, MD), 2003.

The Car Book: How to Save Big Money When You Buy, Sell, Drive, and Maintain Your New or Used Car . . . Including Free Money-Saving Internet Links, Lifestyle Publishing (Sykesville, MD), 2003.

SIDELIGHTS: R. Bryan Stoker once told *CA:* "I have been fascinated with personal finances and investing since I started working at age fourteen. The concept of making my money work harder than I do seemed like the only logical thing to do. Since then I have successfully invested in stocks, real estate, mutual funds, stock options, and commodity options. Although bonds do not really appeal to me, I have even owned a few of them. I have also created a handful of businesses, the first of which was a freelance house-painting business back in high school. Of course, the most recent is my publishing company, Lifestyle Publishing. In all cases, I have always had a full-time job, either as a student or an electronics engineer, at the same time.

"So, my primary motivation for writing about personal finance, investment, and retirement stems from my incessant desire to constantly research and create new ways to invest and to convey these new concepts to my readers. Eventually, I hope to create seminars on investment and personal financial planning as well. One special goal I would like to accomplish is to create a personal finance and investment course for graduating high school and/or college students, since this seems to be one of the biggest holes in the American education system.

"My first book, *Financial Freedom: A Wealth Manual for the Middle Class,* was inspired by a realization one night, about one o'clock in the morning, that most books present generic concepts for how to invest in one thing or another, or they discuss how you can become better with a 'more positive attitude' or whatever. However, none of the books I had read pulled everything together into more or less a life-plan. I attempted to do this in *Financial Freedom* by presenting some simple, 'can't fail' steps that anyone can take to get out from under the burden of the myths created by the financial and insurance industries. Once you have obtained your freedom, the book tells you how to boost your wealth tremendously and reduce your taxes at the same time.

"My second book for the consumer, *Growth and Income: How to Build a Mutual Fund Money Machine,* emerged from more than two years of research I conducted to obtain a master's degree and a doctorate in business administration. For my long dissertation, I examined a fairly unknown investment technique called 'dollar value averaging' and compared its performance to two other automatic-investment techniques: dollar cost averaging and asset allocation. This technique is very intriguing, because it truly does buy low and sell high, unlike dollar cost averaging. For my doctoral research, I determined when and in which type of markets value averaging outperformed or underperformed dollar cost averaging and asset allocation. I also investigated the impacts of several real world constraints, including income taxes, capital gains taxes, minimum investment requirements, volatility, long-term market trends, minimum number of exchanges, and more. The results were sometimes unexpected, and I incorporated them into a simple step-by-step plan that anyone can use almost without thinking. An exciting bonus I never expected, I created a new hybrid technique that really supercharges the performance of your investments. Once again, I tried to incorporate the rest of a life-plan by including sections on maximizing your retirement wealth and making it last longer than you do. *Growth and Income* even includes software, special reports, and another book at no extra cost."

BIOGRAPHICAL AND CRITICAL SOURCES:

ONLINE

Welcome to Lifestyle Publishing's Online Store, http://www.lifestylepublishing.com/ (October 2, 2003).

*   *   *

STONE, Oliver (William) 1946-

PERSONAL: Born September 15, 1946, in New York, NY; son of Louis (a stockbroker) and Jacqueline (Goddet) Stone; married Najwa Sarkis (an attaché), May 22, 1971 (divorced, 1977); married Elizabeth Burkit Cox (a film production assistant), June 7, 1981 (divorced, 1993); married; wife's name Chong; children: Sean, Michael, Tara. *Education:* Attended Yale University, 1965; New York University, B.F.A., 1971. *Religion:* Buddhist.

ADDRESSES: Home—Los Angeles, CA. *Office*—Ixtlan Productions, 201 Santa Monica Blvd., Ste. 610, Santa

Oliver Stone

Monica, CA 90401. *Agent*—Michael Menchel, Rick Nicita, Creative Artists Agency, 9830 Wilshire Blvd., Beverly Hills, CA 90212.

CAREER: Director, screenwriter and producer of motion pictures. Worked as teacher in Cholon, South Vietnam, 1965-66; wiper in Merchant Marines, 1966; taxi driver in New York, NY, 1971. Ixtlan Productions (film production company), founder, 1977. Has appeared in various motion pictures, including *Last Year in Vietnam,* 1970, *The Hand,* 1981, *Platoon,* 1986, *Wall Street,* 1987, *Born on the Fourth of July,* 1989, *The Doors,* 1991, *Dave,* Warner Bros., 1993, and *The Last Party,* Triton, 1991. Has also appeared in television movies and specials, including *Welcome Home,* HBO, 1987; *The Story of Hollywood,* TNT, 1988; *Firstworks,* TMC, 1988; *The New Hollywood,* NBC, 1990; *Naked Hollywood,* A & E, 1991; *Oliver Stone: Inside Out,* Showtime, 1992; *The Kennedy Assassinations: Coincidence or Conspiracy?,* syndicated, 1992; *Investigative Reports,* "Who Killed JFK? On the Trail of the Conspiracies," A & E, 1992; *Together for Our Children,* syndicated, 1993; *Nineteen Ninety-three: A Year at the Movies,* CNBC, 1993; and *Wild Palms,* 1993. Director of films, including *Seizure,* 1974, *Mad Man of Martin-*

ique, 1979, *The Hand,* 1981, *Salvador,* 1986, *Platoon,* 1986, *Wall Street,* 1987, *Talk Radio,* 1988, *Born on the Fourth of July,* 1989, *The Doors,* 1991, *JFK,* 1991, *Heaven and Earth,* 1993, *Natural Born Killers,* 1994, *Nixon,* 1995, *U-Turn,* 1997, and *Any Given Sunday,* 1999. *Military service:* U.S. Army, 1967-68; served in Vietnam; received Purple Heart with oak-leaf cluster and Bronze Star.

MEMBER: Academy of Motion Picture Arts and Sciences, Writers Guild of America, Directors Guild of America, Screen Writers Guild.

AWARDS, HONORS: Writers Guild of America Award for best dramatic adaptation, and Academy Award for best adapted screenplay, both 1979, both for *Midnight Express;* Directors Guild of America Award for outstanding feature film achievement, 1986, Academy Award and Golden Globe Award for best director, Academy Award nomination for best original screenplay, and Bulgarian Cinematography Diploma award, all 1987, and British Academy of Film and Television Arts (BAFTA) Award nomination for best director, 1988, all for *Platoon;* Academy Award nomination for best original screenplay, 1987, for *Salvador;* Filmmaker of the Year Award, Motion Picture Bookers Club, 1989; Bulgarian Cinematography Diploma award, Academy Awards for best director and best screenplay, Golden Globe Awards for best director and best screenplay, and Directors Guild of America Award for outstanding feature film achievement, all 1989, SANE Education Fund/Consider the Alternatives Peace Award, 1990, all for *Born on the Fourth of July;* Academy Award nominations for best director and best adapted screenplay, and Golden Globe Award nominations for best director and best screenplay, all 1992, all for *JFK;* Academy Award nomination for best screenplay, 1995, for *Nixon.*

WRITINGS:

SCREENPLAYS

(And director) *Seizure,* Cinerama, 1973.
Midnight Express (adapted from the autobiography by Billy Hayes), Columbia, 1978.
(And director) *The Hand* (adapted from the novel *The Lizard's Tail* by Marc Brandel), Orion Pictures, 1981.

(With John Milius) *Conan the Barbarian* (adapted from tales by Robert E. Howard), Universal, 1982.
Scarface (adapted from the 1932 film of the same title by Howard Hawks), Universal, 1983.
(With David Lee Henry) *Eight Million Ways to Die* (based on the novel by Lawrence Block), Tri-Star, 1985.
(With Michael Cimino) *Year of the Dragon* (based on the novel by Lawrence Block), Tri-Star, 1985.
(With Richard Boyle; and director and co-producer) *Salvador* (Hemdale, 1986), in *Oliver Stone's Platoon and Salvador,* Vintage (New York, NY), 1987.
(With Richard Boyle; and director) *Platoon* (Orion Pictures, 1986), in *Oliver Stone's Platoon and Salvador,* Vintage (New York, NY), 1987.
(With Stanley Weiser; and director) *Wall Street,* Twentieth Century-Fox, 1987.
(With Eric Bogosian; and director) *Talk Radio* (based on the play of the same title by Bogosian and *Talked to Death: The Life and Murder of Alan Berg* by Stephen Singular), Universal, 1988.
(With Ron Kovic; and director and co-producer) *Born on the Fourth of July* (based on the autobiography by Kovic), Universal, 1989.
(With J. Randall Johnson; and director) *The Doors,* Tri-Star, 1991.
(With Zachary Sklar; and director and co-producer) *JFK* (based on *On the Trail of the Assassins* by Jim Garrison and *Crossfire: The Plot That Killed Kennedy* by Jim Marrs; Warner Bros., 1991), published as *JFK: The Book of the Film: The Documented Screenplay,* Applause Books (New York, NY), 1992.
(With Bruce Wagner; and director) *Wild Palms* (television miniseries; based on the comic strip by Wagner), American Broadcasting Company, Inc., 1993.
(And director and co-producer) *Heaven and Earth* (based on the memoirs *When Heaven and Earth Changed Places* and *Child of War, Woman of Peace* by Le Ly Hayslip), Warner Bros., 1993.
(Author of introduction) Michael Singer, *Oliver Stone's Heaven and Earth: The Making of an Epic Motion Picture,* C. E. Tuttle (Boston, MA), 1993.
(With Richard Rutowski and David Veloz; and director) *Natural Born Killers* (based on a story by Quentin Tarantino), Warner Bros., 1994.
(With Stephen J. Rivele and Christopher Wilkinson; and director and co-producer) *Nixon,* Hollywood Pictures/Cinergi, 1995, published as *Nixon: An Oliver Stone Film,* edited by Eric Hamburg, Hyperion (New York, NY), 1995.

(With Alan Parker) *Evita* (based on the musical by Andrew Lloyd Webber and Tim Rice), Buena Vista, 1996.

(With Daniel Pyne and John Logan; and director) *Any Given Sunday,* 1999.

OTHER

A Child's Night Dream (novel), St. Martin's Press (New York, NY), 1997.

Oliver Stone: Interviews, University of Mississippi Press (Jackson, MS), 2001.

ADAPTATIONS: Midnight Express was filmed in 1978 by Columbia, directed by Alan Parker, starring John Hurt and Randy Quaid; *Conan the Barbarian* was filmed in 1982 by Universal, directed by John Milius, starring Arnold Schwarzenegger, James Earl Jones, and Max Von Sydow; *Scarface* was filmed in 1983 by Universal, directed by Brian DePalma, starring Al Pacino, Steven Bauer, Michelle Pfeiffer, Robert Loggia, F. Murray Abraham, and Mary Elizabeth Mastrantonio; *Eight Million Ways to Die* was filmed in 1985 by Tri-Star, directed by Hal Ashby, starring Jeff Bridges, Rosanna Arquette, and Andy Garcia; *Year of the Dragon* was filmed in 1985 by Tri-Star, directed by Michael Cimino, starring Mickey Rourke.

WORK IN PROGRESS: The film *Alexander,* directed and with a screenplay by Stone, was scheduled for release in November of 2004.

SIDELIGHTS: Film director and writer Oliver Stone was born in New York to an American stockbroker and his French wife. As a child, he led a privileged life: He had nannies, spent summers in France where he became fluent in French, and attended exclusive prep schools. His parents divorced when he was still in high school and Stone soon learned about his father's indebtedness, and that the values he had been taught were illusory. Stone enrolled at Yale University in 1965, but soon left to teach in Saigon, South Vietnam.

Arriving in Vietnam just as the first troops were entering the conflict, he left Saigon after only six months aboard a merchant tanker. Saigon had become a city without rules where shootouts were frequent and safety was hard to find. On his way across the Pacific, Stone began writing a novel to pass the time. He was unable to find a publisher for *A Child's Night Dream*—St. Martin's Press eventually published it in 1997—and this let-down, along with his father's condescension, led him to enlist in the U.S. Army. Stone was sent to Vietnam, where from 1967-68 as part of the Second Platoon of Bravo Company, 3rd Battalion, 25th Infantry, he was stationed near the Cambodian border and participated in the battle of Firebase Burt. He was wounded twice and transferred to the First Cavalry's motorized unit, later receiving the Bronze Star of Valor and the Purple Heart with First Oak Leaf Cluster. His tour ended in 1968, Stone reentered college at New York University where he studied under film director Martin Scorsese. He finished his B.F.A in 1971.

An acclaimed filmmaker, screenwriter, and producer, Stone is committed to exposing what he perceives as deceit and injustice in American history, resulting in such controversial films as *Born on the Fourth of July* and *JFK*. His films typically focus on individual survivors—"angel/creeps" in the argot of *Film Comment*'s Robert Horton—who possessed the characteristics needed to rise above a decaying society rife with violence, deceitfulness, and manipulation. Stone's films have consistently placed him at the center of controversy, inspired nationwide debate, garnered numerous prestigious awards, and, in the case of *JFK*, have even been the impetus for an act of congress.

Stone first gained critical attention with the screenplay for *Midnight Express,* a harrowing tale of an American's experiences in the Turkish penal system. Billy Hayes, who is captured at a Turkish airport while attempting to smuggle hashish, is sentenced to thirty years in prison where Turkish authorities routinely abuse and torture inmates. In the gruesome finale, Billy endures a beating from one of the guards who then prepares to sodomize the vulnerable prisoner. He escapes, dons the guard's uniform, and walks out of the prison.

Midnight Express set the tone for critical reaction to Stone's work, polarizing reviewers who have gone on to either laud or vehemently dismiss his work. Some reviewers faulted *Midnight Express* for its apparent condoning of violence, others viewed the film as evocative and socially relevant. *Newsweek* critic David Ansen decried the film's rendering of Hayes's experiences in Turkey, charging that "Billy's story has become a virtuoso horror show—an exercise in emotional manipulation designed not merely to arouse chills but to turn the audience into avengers." Ansen added that the film's "horror becomes histrionic, which is the last thing it must have been for the real Billy Hayes." Robert Edelman in *Films in Review,* however, argued that only "a person with a hard soul would fail to be moved by *Midnight Express.*" Edelman found that the film is not a mere horror show; rather, it reveals that "the quality of a society is based on how it determines what is crime and punishment, and how mercifully it metes out justice." *Midnight Express* garnered Stone his first Academy Award for best screenplay and established him as a powerful voice in contemporary film.

In 1981 Stone wrote and directed *The Hand,* a chilling tale of a cartoonist whose severed hand seems to respond to his jealousy and anger by stalking people who cause him distress. Vincent Canby, writing in the *New York Times,* hailed the work as "a suspense-horror film of unusual psychological intelligence and wit." Canby added: "Stone's screenplay is tightly written, precise and consistent in its methods, and seemingly perfectly realized" in performances by a cast that included Michael Caine. Canby concluded that *The Hand* showed Stone to be "a director of very real talent."

Critics were generally less impressed with *Conan the Barbarian,* the sword-and-sorcery epic Stone adapted with director John Milius from the works of novelist Robert E. Howard. The film follows Conan's experiences from the time of his mother's murder while she is protecting him as an infant to his development into a fearless, overwhelmingly muscle-bound barbarian seeking to avenge his mother's death. Kevin Thomas, writing in the *Los Angeles Times,* praised *Conan* for reviving "a beloved genre in all its innocent pleasures on a spectacular scale and with sophisticated style." While Thomas called the film "lively, witty entertainment," Vincent Canby was less impressed with *Conan,* deeming it "an extremely long, frequently incoherent, ineptly staged adventure-fantasy set in a prehistoric past." Canby was especially dismayed by the performance of body-builder Arnold Schwarzenegger as Conan, calling his performance at best, "good-humored." Canby added: "One has the impression that [*Conan*] cost a lot of money, though not all of it is on the screen. One is never unaware that one is watching a lot of extras trot around Spain wearing goathair jogging shorts and horns on their hats."

Stone's 1983 screenwriting effort, *Scarface,* is an adaptation of the legendary 1932 gangster film directed by

Howard Hawks. In Stone's version, the Depression-era, big-city environment of the original work is forsaken in favor of a more contemporary Miami suffering from a massive influx of Cuban immigrants. The title role of Tony was played by Al Pacino, who had earlier gained fame for his performances in Mario Puzo and Francis Ford Coppola's "Godfather" epics. The film contained sufficient violence to be threatened with an X rating from the Motion Picture Association of America (MPAA).

Reaction to *Scarface* was again mixed. Richard Corliss in a *Time* review of the film, argued that the film "lacks the generational sweep and moral ambiguity of the Corleone saga. At the end, Tony is as he was at the beginning: his development and degeneration are horrifyingly predictable; his Gotterdammerung death evokes not fear or pity, but numb relief." Canby, in a much more positive review of the film in the *New York Times,* found *Scarface* a film of "boldly original design." Canby concluded: "What goes up must always come down. When it comes down in *Scarface,* the crash is as terrifying as it is vivid and arresting."

Stone's next directorial project was the 1986 film *Salvador.* Cowritten with Richard Boyle, *Salvador* focuses on the reality of the civil war in El Salvador during 1980 through the eyes of Boyle, uncharitably described as "a foulmouthed photojournalist who has washed away his reputation in a flood of alcohol," by *Maclean's* reviewer Patricia Hluchy. David Denby, in a *New York* review of *Salvador,* lauded some of the film's cinematography, and added: "This kind of hair-trigger existential filmmaking—the atmosphere thick with loathing and violence—is not just good, it's great." Denby concluded, however, that there is "a wide streak of pop nihilism" in Stone's work. In a similarly mixed review, Roger Ebert of the *Chicago Sun-Times* commented: "*Salvador* is long and disjointed and tries to tell too many stories. . . . But the heart of the movie is fascinating. And the heart consists of . . . two losers set adrift in a world they never made, trying to play games by everybody else's rules."

In 1986 Stone directed *Platoon,* the first of his three films focusing on the Vietnam war that together are referred to as his "Vietnam trilogy." While *Platoon* deals with the day-to-day fears of the men slogging through the mud in the battlegrounds of Southeast Asia, 1989's *Born on the Fourth of July* follows one soldier returning stateside. Crippled for life from war-related injuries, veteran Ron Kovic's growing disillusionment with the beliefs in God, home, and country that he wore like a banner into battle are transformed by his experiences on U.S. soil into rebelliousness and open discontent. *Heaven and Earth* is the story of the war as told through the eyes of Le Ly Hayslip, a young woman who suffered at the hands of the Vietcong, U.S. troops in Saigon, and the residents of a California suburb by turns.

Stone's "Vietnam trilogy" was both highly praised and highly criticized. Ebert named *Platoon* "the best film of 1986," arguing that it serves as an exception to French filmmaker François Truffaut's classic edict that "it's not possible to make an anti-war movie," because all war movies in some sense "mak[e] combat look like fun." Pat Aufderheide in *Cineaste* noted the honesty of *Platoon* but faulted Stone for being overly sentimental. Larry Ceplair, also in *Cineaste,* called the film "nothing more than a B movie scenario from World War II jungle movies." *Platoon,* however, garnered Stone a Directors Guild of America Award, an Academy Award, and a Golden Globe Award for best director, and an Academy Award nomination for best screenplay.

Contrary to the response to many of Stone's films, critical reaction to *Born on the Fourth of July* was nearly universally positive. Denby praised Stone in *New York* for capturing "better than anyone before him, . . . the combined nightmarish and exhilarating quality of the 1966-1972 period," though he faulted Stone for being "overexplicit." Stuart Klawans, in a *Nation* review of the film, lauded Stone's honesty, arguing: "*Born on the Fourth of July* has the urgency of a truth told—or screamed—against a deafening Muzak of lies." Ebert named the film "one of the best movies of the year," describing it as one which "steps correctly in the opening moments and then never steps wrongly." Stone again was showered with awards for *Born on the Fourth of July,* including Academy Awards for best director and best screenplay, and Golden Globe Awards for best director and best screenplay.

Denby again praised Stone in *New York* for *Heaven and Earth,* which he admired for "moments of power and empathy." Ebert also found the film successful, though he credited some of this success to the "extraordinary performance" of leading actor Hiep Thi Le. Other critics disagreed. Stanley Kauffmann in the *New Republic* claimed: "From its thuddingly banal title

on," *Heaven and Earth* "is a laborious drag through material that ought to have been powerful, ought to have dramatized the other side of Stone's concerns about the Vietnam war, the story from the Vietnamese point of view." Anthony Lane in the *New Yorker* faulted the film as "a deeply unappealing mixture of fuzziness and brutality; each betrays Stone's reluctance, despite his pretensions as a purveyor of true grit, to face up to his subject."

Stone's 1987 film *Wall Street* focused on greed and corruption in New York during the 1980s. Bud Fox, an aspiring stockbroker, "bulls his way into the office of *Fortune* cover-boy Gordon Gekko, the hottest speculator and corporate raider in New York," summarized Denby in *New York.* Bud eventually faced the true nature of Gekko: moral corruption and an utter disdain for the working class. Denby commented: "*Wall Street* is exactly what I had hoped for—a sensationally entertaining melodrama about greed and corruption in New York, a movie that evoked the power of big money so strongly that you can savor it on your tongue like Stilton and port." Peter C. Newman in *Maclean's* called *Wall Street* "a flawed but powerful movie," and argued that Stone's attempt "to define Wall Street's gutter ethic . . . comes so close to succeeding that at times his film ventures dangerously close to being a documentary."

Stone collaborated with playwright Eric Bogosian for the film *Talk Radio.* Inspired in part by the murder of Alan Berg, a Denver talk-show host who was killed by white supremacists in 1984, and by Bogosian's stage play, *Talk Radio* recounts the final days in the life of Barry Champlain, an abusive radio talk-show host whose tirades and insults ultimately lead to his assassination. Denby called *Talk Radio* "without doubt one of the most complete expressions of paranoia ever put on film," praising Stone as a "master of unease and loathing." Denby faulted the film, however, for being "too overwrought to give much pleasure." Ebert gave the film four stars in the *Chicago Sun-Times,* admiring Bogosian's convincing performance, "especially . . . during a virtuoso, unsettling closing monologue, in which we think the camera is circling Bogosian—until we realize the camera and the actor are still, and the backgrounds are circling." The film was not universally praised, however. John Simon in the *National Review* preferred the stage play to the film which, he argued, "introduces pretentious excesses."

Stone focuses on the life of Jim Morrison for his feature *The Doors.* Lead singer of the rock group The Doors during the 1960s, Morrison became an icon of the period alongside contemporaries Jimi Hendrix and Janis Joplin. Robert Horton, in *Film Comment,* wrote: "*The Doors* is an Oliver Stone movie all the way, big and brave and foolish. It's broad, juicy, cheerless, by turns exhilarating and embarrassing, always ready, indeed eager, to let passion eclipse good judgment. Which is exactly what makes Oliver Stone so valuable these days." Ebert compared the film to "being stuck in a bar with an obnoxious drunk, when you're not drinking," though he praised the performance of actor Val Kilmer: "Because of Kilmer, and because of extraordinary location work with countless extras, the concert scenes in *The Doors* play with the authenticity of a documentary." Though ultimately faulting the film for redundancy and for portraying Morrison as a Christ-like figure "being crucified for his audience," Kauffmann in the *New Republic* commented: "Stone's directing excites with its hunger, its avidity, by the way he grabs a scene cinematically, squeezes it of its juice, and casts it aside—even if the scene itself is quiet."

With *JFK,* Stone found himself at the center of a red-hot media controversy. Although it was a position he had weathered several times in the past as a result of mixed responses to his hard-hitting cinematic projects, *JFK*—a draft of which was leaked to the press in 1991—succeeded in opening what many considered to be a national wound. Based on the oft-derided account of former New Orleans district attorney Jim Garrison, the film examines Garrison's investigation and conspiracy theory of the Kennedy assassination. Stone did not rely solely on Garrison's account, however. As Ebert explained: "The important point to make about *JFK* is that Stone does not subscribe to all of Garrison's theories, and indeed rewrites history to supply his Garrison character with material he could not have possessed at the time of these events." Many critics applauded Stone's willingness to question the ethics of American government in the film. David Ansen in *Newsweek* wrote: "Real political discourse has all but vanished from Hollywood filmmaking; above and beyond whether Stone's take on the assassination is right his film is a powerful, radical vision of America's drift toward covert government. What other filmmaker is even thinking about the uses and abuses of power?"

JFK also began a torrent of back-and-forth questions of factual accuracy between Stone and his detractors,

although most critics, despite arguing over the films veracity, admired the movie for its cinematic accomplishments. Kauffmann, for example, though concluding that the film "distorts facts in the assassination theory it presents," nonetheless wrote: "Cinematically, *JFK* is almost a complete success." Ebert, admitting that when the film is over viewers are not sure they understand "exactly what Stone's conclusions are," referred to the movie as "hypnotically watchable," and "a masterpiece of film assembly." In response to the accusation that the screenplay contains over one hundred lies and omissions of fact levied by Peter Collier in *American Spectator,* Stone wrote *CA:* "*JFK* is actually based on research documented in 340 research notes in the book of the film which was published by Applause Books. In addition, much of the information in the film about Clay Shaw and others has now been confirmed by new documents released under the JFK Records Act of 1992, which was passed by Congress in response to our film." Despite the whirlwind of controversy, *JFK* received Academy Award nominations for best director and best screenplay, and Golden Globe Award nominations for best director and best screenplay.

Stone's *Natural Born Killers,* based on a story by Quentin Tarantino, again placed the filmmaker at the center of controversy. The storyline—about the exploits of Mickey and Mallory Knox, a couple who began their relationship by killing both of young Mallory's parents and then embarking on a maniacal cross-country killing spree—led many critics to accuse Stone of gratuitous violence. Stone referred to the film as "a satire—a commentary on violence in America, on murder and what the American media makes of it," in an interview with Stuart Fischoff in *Psychology Today.* For Stone, violence is "as American as apple pie. I'm not saying we should run from it. There is nothing worse than television violence—people die so easily on TV! They just drop dead. If you're going to kill somebody, show the effect of the killing. Make it powerful, make it real, so that people really understand. Violence per se is a good dramatic tool. . . . It is a necessary conceit to give pity and terror. But it should be used sacredly. Violence should be sacred."

The extreme violence in *Natural Born Killers* was criticized by many critics. John Simon commented in a *National Review* piece, "Stone's narcissism and megalomania, like badly driven horses, run away with this gross, pretentious, and ultimately senseless movie.

Purporting to show how crime appeals to the American public, and how the media exploit it for the self-promotion and the public's cretinization, it is manifestly far too enamored of what it pretends to satirize, even if it knows how to do it." Other critics disagreed. Ebert rated the film four stars, and argued: "You do not see as much actual violence as you think you do in this movie; it's more the tone, the attitude, and breakneck pacing that gives you that impression. Stone is not making a geek show, with closeups of blood and guts. Like all good satirists, he knows that too much realism will weaken his effect." Ebert defended Stone against his critics by pointing to the opinion of the MPAA, which threatened to give the film an NC-17 rating. "I could point to a dozen more violent recent films that have left the MPAA unstirred, but Stone has touched a nerve here, because his film isn't about violence, it's about how we respond to violence, and that truly is shocking."

Stone returned to the arena of politics in 1995 with *Nixon.* The film, which traces the rise and fall of U.S. President Richard M. Nixon, again placed Stone in the center of controversy, as critics argued over the factual accuracy of the film while admiring many of the film's accomplishments. Joe Morgenstern, in a review of *Nixon* in the *Wall Street Journal,* claimed that Stone is "up to some dirty historical tricks once again." Morgenstern called the film a "bizarre, bloated and often fascinating psychobiography of our 37th president," while admiring the "gallery of terrific performances." Kauffmann in the *New Republic* came forth with a mixed review. While admiring especially the performance of Anthony Hopkins as Nixon, Kauffmann found that what is "missing is what Stone's best films have had: a subtext, a large theme evoked by the action on the screen." Ebert, however, called *Nixon* "one of the year's best films," admiring the empathetic portrayal of Nixon and the references in the film to Orson Welles's *Citizen Kane,* and noting in summation: "*Nixon* would be a great film even if there had been no Richard Nixon."

Stone once commented of his work as a director: "I consider my films first and foremost to be dramas about individuals in personal struggles and I consider myself to be a dramatist before I am a political filmmaker. I'm interested in alternative points of view."

BIOGRAPHICAL AND CRITICAL SOURCES:

PERIODICALS

American Spectator, April, 1992, pp. 28-31.
Chicago Sun-Times, April 25, 1986; December 30, 1986; December 11, 1987; December 21, 1988; December 20, 1989; March 1, 1991; December 20, 1991; December 24, 1993; August 26, 1994; December 20, 1995.
Cineaste, Volume 15, number 4, 1987.
Commonweal, May 3, 1991, pp. 294-296.
Film Comment, May-June, 1991, pp. 57-61; January-February, 1994, p. 26.
Film Quarterly, fall, 1990, pp. 44-47.
Films in Review, December, 1978, p. 635.
Hudson Review, autumn, 1987, pp. 458-464.
London Review of Books, February 13, 1992, pp. 6-8.
Los Angeles Times, May 14, 1982.
Maclean's, July 21, 1986, p. 50; December 28, 1987, p. 46.
Nation, January 1, 1990, pp. 28-30; March 25, 1991, pp. 388-391; May 24, 1993, pp. 713-715.
National Review, January 22, 1988, pp. 65-66; March 24, 1989, pp. 46-49; February 5, 1990, pp. 58-59; September 26, 1994, p. 72.
New Republic, January 4 & 11, 1988, pp. 24-25; February 13, 1989, p. 26; January 29, 1990, pp. 26-27; April 1, 1991, p. 28; January 27, 1992, pp. 26, 28; September 7 & 14, 1992, pp. 72-73; February 7, 1994, p. 26; October 3, 1994, p. 26; January 22, 1996.
Newsweek, October 16, 1978, pp. 76, 81; December 23, 1991, p. 50.
New York, March 24, 1986, pp. 86, 88-89; December 14, 1987, pp. 86-88; December 12, 1988, pp. 112, 114; December 18, 1989, pp. 101-102; February 17, 1992, pp. 44-47; January 10, 1994, p. 44.
New Yorker, July 28, 1986, pp. 77-80; January 22, 1990, pp. 122-124; January 17, 1994, p. 87.
New York Review of Books, February 17, 1994, pp. 22-24.
New York Times, April 24, 1981; May 15, 1981; May 15, 1982; December 9, 1983, p. C18.
Psychology Today, September-October, 1993, pp. 44-45, 64, 66-69.
Sight and Sound, spring, 1991, p. 7; August, 1993, pp. 60-61.
Time, October 16, 1978; December 5, 1983, pp. 96-97.

Wall Street Journal, December 21, 1995, p. A10.
Washington Post, May 14, 1982.
Wilson Library Bulletin, March, 1992, pp. 51-53.*

*   *   *

STOPPARD, Tom 1937-
(William Boot)

PERSONAL: Born Tomas Straussler, July 3, 1937, in Zlin (now Gottwaldov), Czechoslovakia; naturalized British citizen; son of Eugene Straussler (a physician) and Martha Stoppard; married Jose Ingle, 1965 (divorced, 1972); married Miriam Moore-Robinson (a physician), 1972 (divorced, 1992); children: (first marriage) Oliver, Barnaby; (second marriage) two sons. *Education:* Pocklington School, Yorkshire, A-levels, 1954.

ADDRESSES: Home—Chelsea Harbor, London, England. *Agent*—Peters, Fraser & Dunlop, The Chambers, 5th Floor, Chelsea Harbor, Lots Road, London SW10 0XF, England.

CAREER: Playwright, novelist, and radio and television script writer. *Western Daily Press,* Bristol, England, reporter and critic, 1958-60; *Evening World,* Bristol, reporter, 1958-60; freelance reporter, 1960-63. Director of play *Born Yesterday,* London, England, 1973; director of film *Rosencrantz and Guildenstern Are Dead,* 1991. Member of Royal National Theatre Board, 1989—.

MEMBER: Royal Society of Literature (fellow).

AWARDS, HONORS: Ford Foundation grant, 1964; John Whiting Award, Arts Council of Great Britain, 1967; London *Evening Standard* Drama Awards, 1967, for most promising playwright for *Rosencrantz and Guildenstern Are Dead,* 1972, for best play for *Jumpers,* 1974, for best comedy for *Travesties,* and 1983, for best play for *The Real Thing;* Prix Italia, 1968, for *Albert's Bridge*; Antoinette Perry Awards for best play, 1968, for *Rosencrantz and Guildenstern Are Dead,* 1976, for *Travesties,* and 1984, for *The Real Thing,* and nomination, 1995, for *Arcadia;* New York Drama Critics Circle Awards, 1968, for best play for *Rosen-*

Tom Stoppard

crantz and Guildenstern Are Dead, 1976, for best play *Travesties,* and 1984, for best foreign play *The Real Thing;* M.Lit., University of Bristol, 1976, Brunel University, 1979, University of Sussex, 1980; Commander, Order of the British Empire, 1978; Shakespeare Prize (Hamburg, Germany), 1979; Academy Award nomination, and Los Angeles Critics Circle Award for best original screenplay (with Terry Gilliam and Charles McKeown), both 1985, both for *Brazil;* Grand Prize, Venice Film Festival, 1990, for *Rosencrantz and Guildenstern Are Dead;* knighted by Queen Elizabeth II, 1997; Academy Award for best screenplay written directly for the screen, 1998, for *Shakespeare in Love;* inducted into Order of the Merit, 2000.

WRITINGS:

PLAYS

The Gamblers, produced in Bristol, England, 1965.
Tango (based on the play by Slawomir Mrozek; produced in London, England, 1966; produced on the West End, 1968), J. Cape (London, England), 1968.

Rosencrantz and Guildenstern Are Dead (three-act; also see below; first produced at Edinburgh Festival, 1966; produced on the West End, 1967; produced on Broadway, 1967), Samuel French (New York, NY), 1967.

Enter a Free Man (based on his teleplay *A Walk on the Water;* also see below; first produced on the West End, 1968; produced off-Broadway, 1974), Faber (London, England), 1968.

The Real Inspector Hound (one-act; first produced on the West End, 1968; produced off-Broadway with *After Magritte,* 1972), Samuel French (New York, NY), 1968.

Albert's Bridge [and] *If You're Glad I'll Be Frank* (based on his radio plays; also see below), produced in Edinburgh, 1969, produced in New York, NY, 1987.

After Magritte (one-act; first produced in London, England, 1970; produced off-Broadway with *The Real Inspector Hound,* 1972), Faber (London, England), 1971.

Dogg's Our Pet (also see below; produced in London, England, 1971), published in *Six of the Best,* Inter-Action Imprint, 1976.

Jumpers (first produced on the West End, 1972; produced in Washington, DC, 1974; produced on Broadway, 1974), Grove (New York, NY), 1972, revised edition, Faber (London, England), 1986.

The House of Bernarda Alba (based on the play by Federico García Lorca), produced in London, England, 1973.

Travesties (produced on the West End, 1974; produced on Broadway, 1974), Grove (New York, NY), 1975.

Dirty Linen and New-Found-Land (produced in London, England, 1976; produced on Broadway, 1977), Grove (New York, NY), 1976.

Every Good Boy Deserves Favor, music by Andre Previn, first produced in London, England, 1977, produced on the West End, 1978, produced in New York, NY, 1979.

Night and Day (produced on the West End, 1978; produced on Broadway, 1979), Grove (New York, NY), 1979, revised edition, Samuel French (New York, NY), 1980.

Dogg's Hamlet, Cahoot's Macbeth (double-bill of one-act plays; *Dogg's Hamlet* based on his play *Dogg's Our Pet;* produced in New York, NY, 1979), Faber (London, England), 1979.

Undiscovered Country (adapted from Arthur Schnitzler's *Das Weite Land;* produced on the West End, 1979; produced in Hartford, CT, 1981), Faber (London, England), 1980.

On the Razzle (adapted from Johann Nestroy's *Einen Jux will er sich Machen;* produced on the West End, 1981; produced in Los Angeles, CA, 1985), Faber (London, England), 1981.

The Real Thing (produced on the West End, 1982; produced on Broadway, 1984), Faber (London, England), 1982, revised edition, 1983.

Rough Crossing (adaptation of Ferenc Molnar's *The Play's the Thing;* produced in London, England, 1984; produced in New York, NY, 1990), Faber (London, England), 1985.

Dalliance (adapted from Arthur Schnitzler's *Liebelei),* produced in London, England, 1986.

(Translator) Vaclav Havel, *Largo Desolato,* Faber (London, England), 1987.

Hapgood (produced in New York, NY, 1988), Faber (London, England), 1988.

Artist Descending a Staircase (based on his radio play [also see below]; produced on the West End, 1988; produced on Broadway, 1989), Faber, 1990.

Arcadia, produced in London, England, 1994; produced on Broadway, 1995.

The Coast of Utopia (trilogy of plays), produced at the Royal National Theater, London, England, 2002.

Salvage: The Coast of Utopia Trilogy, Grove (New York, NY), 2003.

Shipwreck: The Coast of Utopia Trilogy, Grove (New York, NY), 2003.

Voyage: The Coast of Utopia Trilogy, Grove (New York, NY), 2003.

Also author of *Home and Dry* and *Riley.*

SCREENPLAYS

(With Thomas Wiseman) *The Romantic Englishwoman,* New World Pictures, 1975.

Despair (adapted from the novel by Vladimir Nabokov), New Line Cinema, 1978.

The Human Factor (adapted from the novel by Graham Greene), Metro-Goldwyn-Mayer (MGM), 1980.

(With Terry Gilliam and Charles McKeown) *Brazil,* Universal, 1985.

Empire of the Sun (adapted from the novel by J. G. Ballard), Warner Bros., 1987.

The Russia House (adapted from the novel by John le Carre), MGM/United Artists, 1989.

(And director) *Rosencrantz and Guildenstern Are Dead* (adapted from his play), Cinecom, 1991, published as *Rosencrantz and Guildenstern Are Dead: The Film,* Faber (London, England), 1991.

Billy Bathgate (adapted from the novel by E. L. Doctorow), Touchstone Pictures, 1991.

(With Marc Norman) *Shakespeare in Love,* Miramax, 1998.

FOR TELEVISION

A Walk on the Water, ITV Television, 1963, broadcast as *The Preservation of George Riley,* British Broadcasting Corporation (BBC-TV), 1964.

A Separate Peace (BBC-TV, 1966), Samuel French (New York, NY), 1977.

Teeth, BBC-TV, 1967.

Another Moon Called Earth, BBC-TV, 1967.

Neutral Ground, Thames Television, 1968.

The Engagement (based on his radio play *The Dissolution of Dominic Boot;* also see below), NBC-TV, 1970.

One Pair of Eyes, BBC-TV, 1972.

(With Clive Exton) *Eleventh House,* BBC-TV, 1975.

(With Clive Exton) *Boundaries,* BBC-TV, 1975.

Three Men in a Boat (based on the novel by Jerome K. Jerome), BBC-TV, 1975.

Professional Foul, BBC-TV, 1977, Public Broadcasting Service (PBS-TV), 1978.

Squaring the Circle: Poland, 1980-81 (BBC-TV, 1985), Faber (London, England), 1985.

RADIO PLAYS

The Dissolution of Dominic Boot, BBC-Radio, 1964.

"M" Is for Moon among Other Things, BBC-Radio, 1964.

If You're Glad I'll Be Frank (BBC-Radio, 1966), Faber (London, England), 1969.

Albert's Bridge, BBC-Radio, 1967.

Albert's Bridge [and] If You're Glad I'll Be Frank: Two Plays for Radio, Faber (London, England), 1969.

The Real Inspector Hound [and] After Magritte, Grove (New York, NY), 1970.

Where Are They Now?, BBC-Radio, 1970.

Artist Descending a Staircase, BBC-Radio, 1972.

Artist Descending a Staircase [and] Where Are They Now?: Two Plays for Radio, Faber (London, England), 1973.

Albert's Bridge, and Other Plays, Grove (New York, NY), 1977.

Every Good Boy Deserves Favor [and] Professional Foul, Grove (New York, NY), 1978.

The Dog It Was That Died, BBC-Radio, 1982.

The Dog It Was That Died, and Other Plays (contains *Teeth, Another Moon Called Earth, Neutral Ground, A Separate Peace, "M" Is for Moon among Other Things,* and *The Dissolution of Dominic Boot*), Faber (London, England), 1983.

Four Plays for Radio, Faber (London, England), 1984.

Dalliance [and] Undiscovered Country, Faber (London, England), 1986.

Stoppard: The Radio Plays 1964-1983, Faber (London, England), 1991.

In the Native State (BBC-Radio, 1991), revised edition published as *Indian Ink,* Faber (Boston, MA), 1995.

Also author of episodes of radio serials *The Dales,* 1964, and *A Student's Diary,* 1965.

OTHER

Lord Malquist and Mr. Moon (novel), Anthony Blond, 1966, Knopf (New York, NY), 1968.

(With Paul Delaney), *Tom Stoppard in Conversation,* University of Michigan Press (Ann Arbor, MI), 1994.

(With Mel Gussow) *Conversations with Stoppard,* Limelight (New York, NY), 1995.

(With Charles Rosen, Jonathan Miller, Garry Wills, and Geoffrey O'Brien) *Doing It: Five Performing Arts,* New York Review of Books (New York, NY), 2001.

(Translator from the Russian), Anton Chekhov, *The Seagull,* Faber (London, England), 2001.

Contributor of short stories to *Introduction 2,* 1964. Reviewer, sometimes under pseudonym William Boot, for *Scene,* 1962.

WORK IN PROGRESS: An original screenplay; negotiating to adapt Philip Pullman's award-winning trilogy *His Dark Materials* for New Line Cinema.

SIDELIGHTS: Tom Stoppard's plays revolutionized modern theatre with their uniquely comic combinations of verbal intricacy, complex structure, and philosophical themes. With such award-winning works as *Rosencrantz and Guildenstern Are Dead, Jumpers, Travesties,* and *The Real Thing* to his credit, Stoppard compares with "the masters of the comic tradition," Joan Fitzpatrick Dean wrote in *Tom Stoppard: Comedy As a Moral Matrix.* "Like the best comic dramatists, his gift for language and physical comedy fuses with an active perception of the excesses, eccentricities, and foibles of man." "Stoppard is that peculiar anomaly—a serious comic writer born in an age of tragicomedy and a renewed interest in theatrical realism," Enoch Brater summarized in *Essays on Contemporary British Drama.* "Such deviation from dramatic norms . . . marks his original signature on the contemporary English stage," the critic continued, for his "'high comedy of ideas' is a refreshing exception to the rule. Offering us 'a funny play,' Stoppard's world 'makes coherent, in terms of theatre, a fairly complicated intellectual argument.' That the argument is worth making, that it is constantly developing and sharpening its focus, and that it always seeks to engage an audience in a continuing dialogue, are the special characteristics of Stoppard's dramatic achievement. They are also the features which dignify and ultimately transform the comic tradition to which his work belongs."

"Stoppard's virtuosity was immediately apparent" in his first major dramatic work, *Rosencrantz and Guildenstern Are Dead,* Mel Gussow of the *New York Times* asserted. The play revisits Shakespeare's *Hamlet* through the eyes of the two players whose task of delivering Hamlet's death sentence prompts their own execution instead. Vaguely aware of the scheming at Elsinore and their own irrelevance to it, Rosencrantz and Guildenstern meander through the drama playing games of language and chance until, circumscribed by Shakespeare's script, they cease to exist. "In focusing on Shakespeare's minor characters Stoppard does not fill out their lives but rather extends their thinness," Anne Wright observed in her *Dictionary of Literary Biography* essay. By turning *Hamlet* "inside out" in this way, the play is "simultaneously frivolous in conception but dead serious in execution," Brater stated, and it addressed issues of existentialism reminiscent of Samuel Beckett's drama *Waiting for Godot.* The result, the critic added, "is not only a relaxed view of *Hamlet,* but a new kind of comic writing halfway between parody and travesty."

Also notable is the play's innovative use of language and Shakespeare's actual text. *Rosencrantz and Guil-denstern Are Dead* is interwoven with references to *Hamlet* as well as containing actual lines of the bard's verse; in addition, Stoppard packs the drama with "intricate word plays, colliding contradictions and verbal and visual puns," as Gussow described it. This "stylistic counterpoint of Shakespeare's poetry and rhetoric with the colloquial idiom of the linguistic games and music-hall patter" proves very effective, Wright commented. "Stoppard's lines pant with inner panic," a *Time* reviewer noted, as the title characters, according to *Village Voice*'s Michael Smith, ultimately "talk themselves out of existence." The play became one of Stoppard's most popular and acclaimed works; twenty years after its premiere, Gussow concluded, *Rosencrantz and Guildenstern* "remains an acrobatic display of linguistic pyrotechnics as well as a provocative existential comedy about life in limbo."

"With its dazzling feel for the duplicities and delights of language and its sense that modern consciousness is a gummed-up kaleidoscope that needs to be given a severe shake," Jack Kroll of *Newsweek* contended, *Rosencrantz and Guildenstern* established "the characteristic Stoppard effect." Stoppard's 1972 play *Jumpers* is a similar "montage of themes and techniques," said Wright, "by turns a whodunit, a farce of marital infidelity, and a philosophical inquiry." The inquiry is performed by George Moore, a professor of moral philosophy whose wife, Dottie, is suspected of both adultery and murder. The play is among Stoppard's most visually elaborate works, with a troupe of gymnastic philosophers, two lunar astronauts fighting over the only return berth to Earth, and sight gags such as an unfortunate accident involving George's pet hare and tortoise. The play also alternates between George's intellectual lectures and Dottie's music-hall numbers, creating further uncertainties. "The play ends with the murder unsolved, both the adultery and the existence of God unproved, one of the astronauts killed by the other, and another gymnast—the Archbishop of Canterbury—shot," Wright outlined.

"In *Jumpers,* much of the action and humor hinges on linguistic ambiguities and confusions," G. B. Crump wrote in *Contemporary Literature.* "These confusions mirror larger ambiguities present in the reality represented in the drama." As Brater elaborated, the play "never fixes moral philosophy and musical comedy in any stable order, hierarchy, or progression." The consequence, C. W. E. Bigsby related in *Contemporary Dramatists,* is that "the relativity of truth, man's apparent need to divert himself from painful realities, the failure of language to do more than parody conviction, the inability of the rational mind to adequately explain man to himself—all these coalesce in a play which unites the very best of Stoppard's characteristics as a playwright—a mastery of language, a clear sense of style and rhythm, and a wit which has both a verbal and visual dimension."

A *Times Literary Supplement* reviewer, however, believed that in *Jumpers* Stoppard's complex language overwhelms the drama: "Good intentions are swamped by words that get nowhere. No actor speaking this highly intellectual and convoluted jargon can talk and move at the same time. To be heard and understood, the actor must stand still and the stage around him must freeze." Thus, the critic continued, "the stage loses its scenic power, the word its resonance, and therefore, the playfulness of the 'play' is muted." In contrast, other critics found the playwright's linguistic intricacies suited to his sophisticated humor and ideas. Victor L. Cahn, for instance, stated in his *Beyond Absurdity: The Plays of Tom Stoppard* that Stoppard's "emphasis on variety of language" demonstrated his "belief in man's ability to communicate. He manages at the same time to make his language amusing, yet richly woven with ideas." "Stoppard is one of those rare writers who can move easily between treating language as an object in itself and making it totally transparent to meaning," Kroll likewise reported. In addition, this verbal ability allows Stoppard to successfully draw from and merge with the work of other writers; as Susan Rusinko claimed in *World Literature Today,* "His inventive puns, parodies, and pastiches brilliantly serve the cause of theatricality to the point that the original disappears with the wave of the word magician's wand."

Stoppard makes use of another dramatic adaptation in his second Tony Award-winner, *Travesties.* The play takes as its starting point the historical fact that Zurich in 1917 was inhabited by three revolutionaries: the communist leader Lenin, modernist writer James Joyce, and dadaist poet-critic Tristan Tzara. Their interactions are related through the recollections of Henry Carr, a minor British official who meets Lenin at the local library and the others during a production of Oscar Wilde's *The Importance of Being Earnest.* In a manner similar to that of *Rosencrantz and Guildenstern Are Dead,* Stoppard used plot line and characterization from Wilde's play to parallel and emphasize

events and characters in his own work; the play "races forward on Mr. Stoppard's verbal roller coaster, leaving one dizzy yet exhilarated by its sudden semantic twists, turns, dips, and loops," Wilborn Hampton remarked in the *New York Times*. The result, Wright asserted, is "a virtuoso piece, a 'travesty' of the style of each of its masters, including Joycean narrative and dadaist verse as well as Wildean wit. The parody extends to the discourse appropriate to Lenin, as the play incorporates lectures and polemical sequences."

"Multilayered, complex, intellectually astringent," Alan Rich declared in *New York,* "Stoppard's play bats about a remarkable number of important ideas," especially those concerning art, revolutionary politics, and the relationship between the two. Brater explained that "in terms of dramatic form [the play] is the culmination of Stoppard's attempt to 'marry' the play of ideas to comedy and farce. But in terms of theme the play demonstrates the author's increasing political consciousness." The critic continued: "In questioning the compatibility of the revolutionary and artistic temperaments, Stoppard for the first time makes politics a central issue in his work." But the playwright was able to deepen his examinations of more "serious" issues without sacrificing entertainment value or humor, as Alan Rich concluded: "The external brilliances in *Travesties,* its manic virtuosity of language, its diabolical manipulation of time and notion, cannot elude any visitor to Tom Stoppard's verbal prank. . . . It is thinking-man's theater that makes it a privilege to think."

Stoppard's political concerns come to the fore in *Every Good Boy Deserves Favor,* a piece for actors and orchestra set to the music of Andre Previn. Set in a prison hospital inhabited by lunatics and dissidents, *Every Good Boy Deserves Favor* "has the witty dialogue and clever plot that we associate with Stoppard's plays, and a sense of social concern that we didn't," *Los Angeles Times* critic Dan Sullivan recounted. Stoppard brings the musicians into the action of the play through the character of a madman who believes he conducts an imaginary orchestra; not only does the group respond to his direction, but one of the violinists doubles as his psychiatrist. The play's use of "irony, mixed identities, outrageous conceits (not to mention a full-scale symphony orchestra)," observed *Washington Post* contributor Michael Billington, distinguished it as "the work of a dazzling high-wire performer." In addition, the critic noted, *Every Good*

Boy is "a profoundly moral play about the brainwashing of political dissidents in Soviet mental hospitals."

John Simon, writing in *New York,* faulted the play for being "too clever by half," and added that the concept of a play for full orchestra seems forced and contrived. But Gussow posited that "the full orchestra and the enormous stage give the play a richness and even an opulence that embellishes the author's comic point of view." He continued: "So much of the comedy comes from the contrast between the small reality—two men in a tiny cell—and the enormity of the delusion." "Nothing if not imaginative, Stoppard's plot makes the orchestra an active, provocative participant in the story," Richard Christiansen wrote in the *Chicago Tribune.* Nevertheless, the critic advised, the play also stands "on its own as a moving and eloquent work, an occasional piece of quick wit and deep thoughtfulness."

With *Night and Day* Stoppard broaches another "public issue: the role of the press in what is commonly called the Western World," as James Lardner described it in the *Washington Post.* Set in an African nation beset by revolution, *Night and Day* looks at issues of censorship, politics, colonialism, and journalistic ethics through the character of a young, idealistic reporter. "There are theatergoers who will not sit still for a play that encompasses an intellectual debate, no matter how gracefully rendered," Lardner theorized. Indeed, some observers criticized the play for emphasizing ideas over characters; *New York Times* reviewer Walter Kerr, for instance, said that "virtually no effort is made during the evening to link up thought and events, arguments and action. The debate really takes place in a void." In contrast, Judith Martin believed that in *Night and Day* "it even seems as if the good lines were written for the play, rather than the play's having been written to display unrelated good cracks," as she wrote in the *Washington Post Weekend.* "This is a taut drama, dealing intelligently and with a degree of moral passion with a range of difficult issues," Wright concluded. "Moreover, despite its clear plea for freedom of speech and action, the play does not oversimplify the issues: *Night and Day* presents a genuine dramatic debate which confronts divergent and often contradictory attitudes."

Indeed, Stoppard's plays frequently demonstrated a "delight in contradiction and paradox," according to *New York Times* contributor Benedict Nightingale, with

"rebuttal constantly following argument, counter rebuttal following rebuttal, and no conclusion." Gussow explained in the *New York Times:* Stoppard "has always taken pride in his ability to refute himself endlessly, a practice especially well suited to dialogue. His interest is less in offering a judgment than in making light of other people's pretensions." A play such as *Jumpers,* for instance, takes various alternatives, "brings them together and lets them fight it out," London *Times* critic Irving Wardle summarized. The purpose of this war, stated Brater, is to confront the audience "with the recognizable dilemma of the man who, having read much, can't be sure of anything. The more possibilities Stoppard's marginal man allows for, the less he understands." Stoppard commented on the lack of firm conclusions in his work to Samuel G. Freedman in the *New York Times:* "If one had arrived at a definite answer, there wouldn't be a play to write about. . . . Most interesting questions . . . cannot be simply resolved." "Only a writer who cares deeply about convictions would dare to write plays to call his own convictions and those of others to account," Carl E. Rollyson, Jr. suggested in the *Dictionary of Literary Biography Yearbook.* Throughout his career, the critic continued, Stoppard "has been willing to test his principles and his lack of principles more directly and personally even as he has taken on profoundly difficult historical and political subjects that many artists of his stature would shy away from."

In the double-bill *Dogg's Hamlet, Cahoot's Macbeth,* for example, Stoppard "brilliantly harnessed his linguistic ingenuity to his passion for the cause of artistic freedom," Gerald M. Berkowitz noted in *Theatre Journal.* In the first half, *Dogg's Hamlet,* a group of schoolboys contort the English language by giving entirely new meanings to familiar words; their interactions with puzzled outsiders culminate in an abbreviated performance of *Hamlet.* The second play, *Cahoot's Macbeth,* presents an underground performance of Shakespeare that is interrupted by government censors; only by switching to "Dogg," the language of the first play, do the actors avoid arrest. Critics were split over the effectiveness of this double-bill; *Chicago Tribune* writer Sid Smith, for instance, found that the second play "promises more than it delivers, certainly more than a rehash of the first play's comedy." Berkowitz, however, thought that "Stoppard knows what he's doing," for instead of reducing "this serious play to the farcical level of the first," the switch to Dogg reinforced his message, which "strikes us with tremendous power: repressive societies fear artistic expression because it is a 'language' they don't share and thus can't control." As a result, the critic concluded, *Dogg's Hamlet, Cahoot's Macbeth* "may well be . . . [Stoppard's] most important play so far, and a harbinger of major works to come."

Berkowitz's words were prophetic, for in 1982 Stoppard premiered one of his most highly acclaimed dramas, *The Real Thing*. While the playwright returned to a favorite form, that of the play-within-a-play, his subject—"an imaginatively and uniquely theatrical exploration of the pain and the power of love," as Christiansen characterized it—surprised many critics. The opening reveals a man confronting his wife with evidence of her adultery; it soon becomes clear, however, that this encounter is only a scene in a play. "Reality" is much more complex, for the actors in the first scene are being betrayed by their spouses—the playwright and his mistress Annie, another actress. Henry is the successful author of witty, cerebral dramas of infidelity, but his own struggles with love, especially those in his sometimes-troubled marriage to Annie, prove more difficult and painful. Annie's romantic involvement with a young actor and professional involvement with the young revolutionary Brodie cause Henry to not only question his assumptions about love, but his opinions about the significance of writing. While the meaning of the "real thing" might seem a commonplace theme for Stoppard to examine, "home truths can be banal," Sullivan observed. "All that an author can do is to write a non-banal play around them, and this Stoppard has done."

Augmenting Stoppard's examination of romance and writing is a structure which scatters scenes from Henry's play throughout the show, thus forcing the audience to decide what is "real" and what is "drama." "The ingenious patterning helps to put the real thing into the same perspective as the artificial thing," Ronald Hayman suggested in the *Times Literary Supplement,* explaining that the playwright is clever in selecting "theatre people as his subject and to perch the action so spectacularly between their theatrical lives and their private lives." Thus "some of the play's intricacies defy full appreciation on a single viewing," *Washington Post* writer David Richards maintained, for the text is "intrinsically playful even as it deals with the delicate and obscure covenants that link men and women." But Frank Rich regarded the interchanges between "reality" and "drama" as "mannered digressions designed mainly to add literary gilding to

a conventional story." "But it's not cleverness for cleverness' sake," Richards countered. "Indeed, Stoppard is asking where theater leaves off and reality begins." Rollyson likewise asserted that this blurring of reality is Stoppard's intent: "Gradually their 'real' lives come to resemble their stage roles, but the point is that the theatricality of human lives is as 'real' as anything else about the nature of their existence."

The Real Thing "is an integrally designed piece whose content and form are inseparable," Frank Rich proposed. "The play is not only about how Henry learns to feel love, but also about how he learns to write about love." "Henry agonizes about being unable to write love scenes and complains that his credibility is hanging by a thread," Hayman elaborated, and the resulting dialogue "bristles wittily." Henry also learns, however, that the same words which provide him with his livelihood are insufficient to completely resolve real-life problems. Consequently, *The Real Thing* had a dramatic power created by "that tension between its glittering verbal surface and those dark, confused emotions beyond the reach of words," Richards wrote in another review. While the play "is every bit as clever as *Travesties* or *Jumpers*," the critic remarked in his first article, it also "recognizes the impotence of the intellect when confronted with the ambiguities of love." "Without blunting his wit," Catharine Hughes concluded in *America,* "Stoppard hints not of a new beginning—he does not require one—but a deepening of the talent that has been in evidence since New York audiences first encountered him in *Rosencrantz and Guildenstern Are Dead.*"

Stoppard's *Arcadia* juxtaposes three different time periods on one stage—the years 1809 and 1812 as well as present day—and combines such topics as mathematics and chaos theory, landscape gardening, and Lord Byron. In addition, noted Anne Barton in the *New York Review of Books,* "Arcadia constantly engages the imaginary in a dialogue with the historically true." Several reviewers noted the need for playgoers to review the printed text before seeing the play, seeing the play twice, or utilizing both methods to yield a better understanding of the complex story. In terms of staging and theatrics, however, "*Arcadia* is muted by comparison with most of Stoppard's previous work," found Barton. Barton praised the effort, hailing it as "wonderfully inventive and funny, full of the epigrams, puns and verbal pyrotechnics characteristic of this dramatist." Joseph Hynes, commenting in the *Virginia*

Quarterly Review, praised Stoppard's effort as "the wittiest, most movingly paradoxical, English dramatic language of this half-century."

Produced in 2002, Stoppard's anticipated *The Coast of Utopia* is a nine-hour look at the lives of some of Russia's revolutionary and liberal minds from the nineteenth century. Though not particularly impressed by the plays as a whole, an *American Theater* critic wrote that *Voyage* can possibly stand on its own and "can be seen to possess the emotional and physical sweep of Chekhov and Gorky." The reviewer considered *The Coast of Utopia* a grand undertaking and wrote that Stoppard and the trilogy are "brave enough to hint the fact that we may never reach the promised land [Utopia]." Herb Greer, a theater critic for *World and I,* acknowledged that Stoppard's work usually contains "wonderfully civilized humor." Ultimately however, Stoppard over-researched and over-thought his characters in *Voyage, Shipwreck,* and *Salvage.*

Stoppard's personal insights into his work were captured in *Conversations with Stoppard.* Spanning a twenty-year period, these conversations are the result of interviews Stoppard had with theatre critic Mel Gussow and focus primarily on the development of and influences on his work. Bevya Rosten in the *New York Times Book Review* remarked, "Gussow offers a chance to engage with the witty and quirky mind of a unique artist." Susan Rushinko, commenting in *World Literature Today,* noted that "Stoppard's remarks about his writing habits and sources of ideas for his plays are as freewheeling and as fascinating as the debates in his plays." Rushinko also remarked on Stoppard's confession of his "early admiration for Margaret Thatcher and Rupert Murdoch" as well as his sources of names for his characters. However, Jane Montgomery, in the *Times Literary Supplement,* found Gussow somewhat lax in his interviewing methods. "Gussow's interrogation is not probing . . . nor is his search for Stoppard's inner balance particularly contingent. His prepared questions often appear stilted in context, and he seems to rely chiefly on Stoppard's own graceful loquacity to steer the conversation." "On one level," Montgomery continued, "this is informative and interesting. . . . But just how many of [Stoppard's] 'apparent impromptus' were 'worked out beforehand' is the kind of interesting question Gussow will not, or cannot, address."

Stoppard's talents extend beyond writing for the stage; he is also noted for several highly literate screenplay adaptations, such as *Empire of the Sun, The Russia House,* and his own *Rosencrantz and Guildenstern Are Dead.* He has also distinguished himself as the creator of original works for radio, and he is "one of the writers who use the medium most imaginatively," Hayman stated in the *Times Literary Supplement,* for Stoppard "enjoys doing what can't be done on any other medium." The playwright makes the most of the exclusively aural medium, for in works such as *Albert's Bridge* and *If You're Glad I'll Be Frank* "what is left to the imagination gives the comedy its impetus," Gussow observed. As Rollyson explained, this strategy worked well because Stoppard "is under no constraint to hew to the facts or to balance his facility with words against the action or visualization for the stage and screen." In addition, Stoppard told Paul Donovan of the *Sunday Times Review,* "If you are dependent only on what people can hear, you can jerk things around in time and space, draw parallels and spin loops." The result, Rollyson concluded, is that "Stoppard has always worked well in radio and has produced for it some of his most innovative probings of human psychology."

Stoppard's use of various dramatic techniques, intricately worked into innovative forms, contributes greatly to the vitality of his plays. "He is a skilled craftsman," Wright said, "handling with great dexterity and precision plots of extreme ingenuity and intricacy. The plays are steeped in theatrical convention and stock comic situations, with mistaken identity, verbal misunderstandings, innuendo, and farcical incongruity." The playwright's use of traditional dramatic elements, contended Dean, reveals his "penchant for and skill in parodying popular dramatic genres. Like most contemporary playwrights, he has not contented himself with the confines of representational drama but has broken out of those constraints by revivifying the soliloquy, aside, song, and interior monologue." Despite his "free" use of various dramatic forms, Stoppard is able to superimpose an overall structure on his plays, Cahn declared: "Amid all the clutter and episodic action, a structure emerges, a tribute to the organizing powers of the playwright's rationality and his expectations of the audience's ability to grasp that structure." As the author related to Kroll, "Theater is an event, not a text. I respond to spectacle. Ambushing the audience is what theater is all about."

Part of Stoppard's "ambush" involves the way he shrewdly infuses his plays with sophisticated concepts.

As Billington described, Stoppard "can take a complex idea, deck it out in fancy dress and send it skipping and gambolling in front of large numbers of people," for the playwright has "a matchless ability to weave into a serious debate boffo laughs and knockdown zingers." This combination has led some critics to attempt to classify his works as either humorous or philosophical. Stoppard himself, however, believes that questions concerning the comic intent of his works are superfluous. "All along I thought of myself as writing entertainments, like *The Real Inspector Hound,* and plays of ideas like *Jumpers,*" he told Gussow. "The confusion arises because I treat plays of ideas in just about the same knockabout way as I treat the entertainments." He further explained to *Washington Post* interviewer Joseph McLellan: "The stuff I write tends to work itself out in comedy terms most of the time." But whatever degree of comedy or seriousness in Stoppard's approach, Nightingale concluded in the *New York Times,* he is consistent in the themes he examines: "All along he's confronted dauntingly large subjects, all along he's asked dauntingly intricate questions about them, and all along he's sought to touch the laugh glands as well as the intellect."

Various reviewers have attempted to analyze and define Stoppard's thematic concerns as he presents them within his plays. His ideas are often considered from an existentialist perspective and encompass such concepts as "the nature of perception, art, illusion and reality, the relativity of meaning, and the problematic status of truth," Wright declared. "Recurring themes include chance, choice, freedom, identity, memory, time, and death." Stoppard provided Tom Prideaux of *Look* with a simpler interpretation of his concerns: "One writes about human beings under stress— whether it is about losing one's trousers or being nailed to the cross." Cahn suggested, however, that Stoppard's works contains a "unifying element" by consistently demonstrating the playwright's "faith in man's mind." The critic elaborated: "He rejects the irrational, the reliance on emotion instead of intellect, the retreat from independent thought."

Stoppard's focus on human intellect and ideas has led some critics to fault his work as one-dimensional. Roger Scruton, for example, maintained in *Encounter* that "Stoppard is not a dramatist—he does not portray characters, who develop in relation to each other, and generate dialogue from their mutual constraints." "Stoppard has never been known for powerful charac-

terizations," DeVries similarly conceded. "People in his plays have usually taken a back seat to the ideas they articulate." However, the critic added, this "simple trade-off . . . has worked because of the compelling intelligence of the ideas." The playwright himself admitted to Gussow in the *New York Times:* "I'm a playwright interested in ideas and forced to invent characters to express those ideas." Other observers, however, refute the notion that Stoppard's work is wanting in depth. "I, for one, have never been disturbed by a lack of feeling or emotion in his plays," Wilson noted, "though it is true that he has often pursued a philosophical conundrum or turn of phrase at the expense of his characters." And still others believe Stoppard's philosophical investigations are a means of exploring the humanity of his characters. As Nightingale noted in the *New Statesman:* "What other dramatist worries so earnestly yet entertainingly about the moral nature both of ourselves and of the dark bewildering universe we glumly inhabit?"

Because Stoppard's wit "can hold its own with Oscar Wilde, G. B. Shaw and Noel Coward," Edwin Wilson commented in the *Wall Street Journal,* he is able to take his "fascination with ideas . . . and make them exciting." "Stoppard's special distinction is his linguistic and conceptual virtuosity," Gussow asserted in the *New York Times Magazine.* "One has to look back to Shaw and Wilde to find an English playwright who could so enlist the language as his companion in creativity. Others might finish ahead in terms of tragic vision or emotional commitment, but as a wordsmith Stoppard is supreme." Dean, who allies Stoppard with "the wittiest if not greatest writers of the English language," explained that "Stoppard indulges himself as well as his audience in the sheer pleasure of experiencing the density and richness of which the language is capable. Moreover, his attention to language results not only in humor but also in precision. As a means of considering the difficulty of communication as well as a comic vehicle, language is assiduously explored and exploited by Stoppard."

"There is plenty to indicate that if Stoppard had done no more than employ the drama as a vehicle for moral messages he would still have been a force in the theatre," Clive James suggested in *Encounter.* But, the critic continued, "Stoppard's heady dramatic designs impress us not as deliberately sophisticated variations on the reality we know but as simplified models of a greater reality—the inhuman cosmos which contains the human world. . . . If his speculative scope recalls modern physics, his linguistic rigour recalls modern philosophy. It is a potent combination whatever its validity." "If his plays endure," Dean claimed, "Stoppard's unique accomplishment may prove to be the theatrical treatment of the intellectual and artistic follies of our age." "In the past Stoppard has given us a new kind of comedy to capture the drama of contemporary ideas," Brater similarly stated. "Judging from the quality of his new work, there is no reason to suspect that this serious writer masquerading as a comedian has run out of ammunition. For style in Stoppard has always been a question of substance as well as technique. What he has found in his theater," the critic concluded, "is not only a special way of saying something, but something, at least, that needed very much to be said."

BIOGRAPHICAL AND CRITICAL SOURCES:

BOOKS

Bigsby, Christopher, and William Edgar, editors, *Writers and Their Work,* Longman (London, England), 1976.

Bock, Hedwig, and Albert Wertheim, editors, *Essays on Contemporary British Drama,* Hüber (Munich, Germany), 1981.

Brustein, Robert, *The Third Theatre,* Knopf (New York, NY), 1969.

Cahn, Victor L., *Beyond Absurdity: The Plays of Tom Stoppard,* Fairleigh Dickinson University Presses (Rutherford, NJ), 1979.

Contemporary Dramatists, St. James Press (London, England), 1982.

Contemporary Literary Criticism, Gale (Detroit, MI), Volume 1, 1973, Volume 3, 1975, Volume 4, 1975, Volume 5, 1976, Volume 8, 1978, Volume 15, 1980, Volume 29, 1984, Volume 34, 1985, Volume 63, 1991, Volume 91, 1996.

Dean, Joan Fitzpatrick, *Tom Stoppard: Comedy As a Moral Matrix,* University of Missouri Press (Columbia, MO), 1981.

Dictionary of Literary Biography, Volume 13: *British Dramatists since World War II,* Gale (Detroit, MI), 1982.

Dictionary of Literary Biography Yearbook: 1985, Gale (Detroit, MI), 1985.

Nadel, Ira, *Double Act: A Life of Tom Stoppard,* Methuen (London, England), 2002.

Schlueter, June, *Dramatic Closure: Reading the End,* Fairleigh Dickinson University Press (Rutherford, NJ), 1995.

Taylor, John Russell, *The Second Wave: British Drama for the Seventies,* Methuen (London, England), 1971.

PERIODICALS

America, February 18, 1984; January 29, 1994, p. 23.

American Theater, November, 2002, review of *The Coast of Utopia,* p. 40.

Atlantic, May, 1968.

Chicago Tribune, April 24, 1985; June 3, 1985; September 20, 1985; March 17, 1991.

Christian Science Monitor, April 25, 1974; November 6, 1975; December 6, 1982; January 11, 1984.

Commentary, December, 1967; June, 1974.

Commonweal, November 10, 1967.

Contemporary Literature, summer, 1979.

Drama, summer, 1968; fall, 1969; summer, 1972; winter, 1973; autumn, 1974.

Encounter, September, 1974; November, 1975; February, 1983.

Harper's Bazaar, March, 1995, p. 126.

Hudson Review, winter, 1967-68; summer, 1968.

Life, February 9, 1968.

Listener, April 11, 1968; April 18, 1968; June 20, 1974.

London, August, 1968; August-September, 1976.

Look, December 26, 1967; February 9, 1968.

Los Angeles Times, June 6, 1986; December 20, 1986; February 20, 1991.

Nation, November 6, 1967; May 11, 1974; May 18, 1974.

National Observer, October 23, 1967.

National Review, December 12, 1967; November 29, 1993, p. 71.

New Leader, September 21, 1992, p. 21.

New Republic, June 15, 1968; May 18, 1974; November 22, 1975; January 30, 1984.

New Statesman, June 14, 1974.

Newsweek, August 7, 1967; August 31, 1970; March 4, 1974; January 8, 1975; November 10, 1975; January 16, 1984; April 3, 1995, p. 64.

New York, March 11, 1974; May 13, 1974; August 26, 1974; November 17, 1975; August 13-20, 1979; July 26, 1993, p. 51; January 9, 1995, p. 36.

New Yorker, May 6, 1967; October 28, 1967; May 4, 1968; May 6, 1972; March 4, 1974; May 6, 1974; January 6, 1975; January 24, 1977.

New York Post, April 23, 1974; January 6, 1984.

New York Review of Books, June 8, 1995, p. 28.

New York Times, October 18, 1967; October 29, 1967; March 24, 1968; May 8, 1968; June 19, 1968; July 8, 1968; October 15, 1968; April 23, 1974; July 29, 1979; August 1, 1979; October 4, 1979; November 25, 1979; November 28, 1979; June 23, 1983; November 22, 1983; January 6, 1984; January 15, 1984; February 20, 1984; August 1, 1984; May 17, 1987; May 18, 1987; November 22, 1987; November 3, 1989; November 26, 1989; December 26, 1989; February 8, 1991.

New York Times Book Review, August 25, 1968; March 3, 1996, p. 19.

New York Times Magazine, January 1, 1984.

Observer (London, England), August 1, 1993.

Observer Review, April 16, 1967; December 17, 1967; June 23, 1968.

Playboy, May, 1968.

Plays and Players, July, 1970.

Publishers Weekly, February 12, 1996, p. 24.

Punch, April 19, 1967.

Reporter, November 16, 1967.

Saturday Review, August 26, 1972; January 8, 1977.

Show Business, April 25, 1974.

Spectator, June 22, 1974.

Stage, February 10, 1972.

Sunday Times Review, April 21, 1991.

Theatre Journal, March, 1980.

Time, October 27, 1967; August 9, 1968; March 11, 1974; May 6, 1974; June 20, 1983; August 24, 1992, p. 69; July 19, 1993, p. 60.

Times (London, England), November 18, 1982; April 3, 1985.

Times Literary Supplement, March 21, 1968; December 29, 1972; November 26, 1982; December 24, 1982; September 29, 1995, p. 23.

Times Saturday Review (London, England), June 29, 1991.

Transatlantic Review, summer, 1968.

Variety, November 22, p. 36.

Village Voice, May 4, 1967; October 26, 1967; May 2, 1974.

Virginia Quarterly Review, autumn, 1995, p. 642.

Vogue, November 15, 1967; April 15, 1968; December, 1994, p. 180.

Wall Street Journal, March 11, 1974; November 3, 1975; January 6, 1984.

Washington Post, May 11, 1969; June 25, 1969; July 9, 1969; August 29, 1978; November 26, 1978; January 12, 1984; May 23, 1985.

World and I, May, 2003, Herb Greer, review of *The Coast of Utopia,*, p. 228.

World Literature Today, winter, 1978; summer, 1986; spring, 1995, p. 369; winter, 1996, p. 193.*

*   *   *

STUHR(-ROMMEREIM), Rebecca (Ann) 1958-

PERSONAL: Born January 6, 1958, in Oakland, CA; daughter of Walter Martin (a theologian) and Barbara Jean (an artist and homemaker; maiden name, Gordon) Stuhr; married John Rommereim, January 1, 1979 (divorced, April 14, 1997); children: Helen Rachel, Martin Samuel Lee. *Ethnicity:* "Central/Northern European." *Education:* St. Olaf College, B.A., 1980; University of California—Berkeley, M.L.I.S., 1984. *Politics:* Democrat. *Religion:* Lutheran. *Hobbies and other interests:* Biking, gardening, music, reading.

ADDRESSES: Home—1418 Spencer St., Grinnell, IA 50112. *Office*—Burling Library, Grinnell College, 1111 Sixth Ave., Grinnell, IA 50112-1690; fax: 641-269-4283. *E-mail*—stuhrr@grinnell.edu.

CAREER: University of Kansas, Lawrence, reference librarian and German bibliographer, 1984-88; Grinnell College, Grinnell, IA, collection development and preservation librarian, 1988—. Flutist, performing Baroque and modern music, including the recording *Sonatas for Flute and Harpsichord,* Centaur Records, 1996, and *Benedetto Marcello: Flute Sonatas, Opus 2,* Centaur Records, 2003; gives music lessons. Iowa Conservation and Preservation Consortium, member of board of directors, 1990-2002.

MEMBER: American Library Association, Early Music America, Iowa Library Association.

WRITINGS:

Autobiographies by Americans of Color, 1980-1994: An Annotated Bibliography, Whitston (Troy, NY), 1997.

(With Deborah Iwabuchi) *Autobiographies by Americans of Color, 1995-2000: An Annotated Bibliography,* Whitston (Troy, NY), 2003.

Contributor to periodicals, including *Choice, Archival Products News,* and *Library Journal.*

WORK IN PROGRESS: Research on preservation in small colleges, computers in the classroom, and the Internet and society; continuing research on ethnic materials and autobiography.

SIDELIGHTS: Rebecca Stuhr once told *CA:* "As a librarian, I'm particularly concerned with representing and promoting the works of a broad spectrum of writers, especially those who have been excluded from the traditional canon. In compiling and annotating my bibliography, I wanted to bring attention to personal accounts of success, failure, exclusion, or painful and positive experience, so that people who had little or no experience of this would have a better sense of what it means to be the 'other,' and so that those whose experiences were similar could read about people like themselves, for inspiration or to gain a sense of not being alone. We *all* need to be able to put ourselves in other people's shoes."

*   *   *

STÜRMER, Michael 1938-

PERSONAL: Surname listed in some sources under Stuermer; born September 29, 1938, in Kassel, Germany; son of Bruno (a musical composer) and Ursula (Scherbening) Stürmer. *Education:* Attended London School of Economics and Political Science, London; University of Marburg, Ph.D., 1965; University of Darmstadt, habilitation, 1971.

ADDRESSES: Office—c/o Institut für Geschichte, Universität Erlangen-Nürnberg, Kochstrasse 4, 91054 Erlangen, Germany; fax: +49-91-31-852-5835; or c/o *Die Welt,* Axel Springerstrasse 65, D-10888 Berlin, Germany.

CAREER: University of Sussex, Brighton, Sussex, England, lecturer in European history, 1970-71; University of Erlangen-Nürnberg, Erlangen, Germany, professor of medieval and modern history, 1973-2003. Harvard University, research fellow, 1976-77; Institute for Advanced Study, Princeton, NJ, member, 1977-78; University of Toronto, visiting professor, 1983-84;

University of Paris, professor associate with the Sorbonne, 1984-85; Johns Hopkins School for Advanced International Studies, visiting professor in Bologna, Italy, 1985-86, 1998-99, and non-executive director of European Program; Research Institute for International Affairs, Ebenhausen/Isartal, Germany, director, 1988-98. J. P. Morgan Bank, member of German advisory council, 1990-2001; European Union Commission, advisor on common foreign and security policy, 1993-98.

MEMBER: International Institute for Strategic Studies.

AWARDS, HONORS: Officer, French Legion of Honor.

WRITINGS:

Das Ruhelose Reich: Deutschland, 1866-1918, [Berlin, Germany], 1983, 4th edition, 1994.
Scherben des Glücks: Klassizismus und Revolution, [Berlin, Germany], 1987.
Die Grenzen der Macht: Begegnung der Deutschen mit der Geschichte, [Berlin, Germany], 1992.
Striking the Balance: Sal. Oppenheim Jr. et Cie, a Family and a Bank, [London, England], 1994.
Die Reichsgründung, 4th edition, 1997.
(Editor, with Robert Blackwill) *Allies Divided: Transatlantic Policies for the Greater Middle East,* MIT Press (Cambridge, MA), 1997.
The German Century, 1998.

Columnist for *Frankfurter Allgemeine Zeitung,* 1984-94, *Neue Zürcher Zeitung,* 1994-98, *Financial Times,* and *Corriere della Sera;* chief correspondent for *Die Welt* and *Welt am Sonntag,* 1998—.

WORK IN PROGRESS: A study of the world without world order.

*   *   *

STYCHIN, Carl F. 1964-

PERSONAL: Born November 1, 1964, in Edmonton, Alberta, Canada. *Ethnicity:* "White Caucasian." *Education:* University of Alberta, B.A. (with distinction), 1985; University of Toronto, LL.B. (with honors), 1988; Columbia University, LL.M., 1992.

ADDRESSES: Home—37 B Mildmay Grove N, London N1 4RH, England. *Office*—School of Law, University of Reading, P.O. Box 217, Reading RG6 6AH, England; fax: 44-118-975-3280. *E-mail*—c.f.stychin@ reading.ac.uk.

CAREER: Osler, Hoskin & Harcourt, Toronto, Ontario, Canada, articling student at law, 1988-89; Supreme Court of Canada, Ottawa, Ontario, law clerk to Chief Justice Brian Dickson, 1989-90; University of Keele, Keele, Staffordshire, England, lecturer, 1992-96, senior lecturer in law, 1996-98; University of Reading, Reading, England, professor of law, 1998—. McGill University, visiting professor, 1996; University of Sydney, visiting Parsons Fellow, 1997.

MEMBER: Canadian Law and Society Association, Socio-Legal Studies Association, Society of Legal Scholars, Law and Society Association (United States).

AWARDS, HONORS: Grants from British Association of Canadian Studies, 1993, and British Academy, 1995 and 2001; prize from Oxford University Press and British Socio-Legal Studies Association, best book in socio-legal studies, 1996, for *Law's Desire: Sexuality and the Limits of Justice.*

WRITINGS:

(Editor, with Didi Herman, and coauthor of introduction) *Legal Inversions: Lesbians, Gay Men, and the Politics of Law,* Temple University Press (Philadelphia, PA), 1995.

Law's Desire: Sexuality and the Limits of Justice, Routledge (New York, NY), 1995.

A Nation by Rights: National Cultures, Sexual Identity Politics, and the Discourse of Rights, Temple University Press (Philadelphia, PA), 1998.

(Editor, with Didi Herman) *Law and Sexuality: The Global Arena,* University of Minnesota Press (Minneapolis, MN), 2001.

Governing Sexuality: The Changing Politics of Citizenship and Law Reform, Hart Publishing (Oxford, England), 2003.

Contributor to books, including *Outlooks: Lesbian and Gay Sexualities and Visual Cultures,* edited by Reina Lewis and Peter Horne, Routledge (London, England), 1996; and *Feminist Perspectives on Health Care Law,* edited by S. Sheldon and M. Thomson, Cavendish (London, England), 1998. Contributor of articles and reviews to professional journals, including *Feminist Legal Studies, Journal of Law and Society, Anglo-American Law Review, Canadian Journal of Law and Jurisprudence, Law and Sexuality, American Journal of Legal History,* and *Oxford Journal of Legal Studies.* Member of editorial board, *Social and Legal Studies,* 1996—.

T

TALLY, Ted 1952-

PERSONAL: Born April 9, 1952, in Winston-Salem, NC; son of David K. (a school administrator) and Dorothy E. (a teacher; maiden name, Spears) Tally; married Melinda Kahn (an art gallery director), December 11, 1977. *Education:* Yale University, B.A., 1974, M.F.A., 1977.

ADDRESSES: Home—New York, NY. *Agent*—Arlene Donovan, International Creative Management, 40 West 57th St., New York, NY 10019.

CAREER: Playwright and screenwriter, 1977—. Playwriting seminar instructor at Yale University, 1977-79; master artist-in-residence at Atlantic Center for the Arts, 1983.

MEMBER: Writer's Guild of America, Dramatists Guild, Playwrights Horizons (member of artistic board), Academy of Motion Picture Arts and Sciences.

AWARDS, HONORS: Yale University Kazan Award and Theron Rockwell Field Prize, both 1977, and *Drama-Logue* award, 1979, all for *Terra Nova;* Columbia Broadcasting System (CBS) Foundation playwriting fellowship, 1977; New York State Creative Artists Public Service grant, 1980; John Gassner Award, New York Outer Critics Circle, 1981, for *Coming Attractions;* National Endowment for the Arts grant, 1983-84; Obie Award, *Village Voice,* 1984, for *Terra Nova;* Guggenheim fellowship, 1985-86; Christopher Award, 1988, for *The Father Clements Story;* Academy Award for best screenplay based on material previously produced or published, 1991, for *Silence of the Lambs.*

Ted Tally

WRITINGS:

SCREENPLAYS

White Palace (adapted from the novel by Glenn Savan), Universal Pictures, 1990.

390

The Silence of the Lambs (adapted from the novel by Thomas Harris), Orion Pictures, 1990.

Before and After (adapted from the novel by Rosellen Brown), Buena Vista, 1996.

The Juror (adapted from the novel by George Dawes Green), Columbia Pictures, 1996.

All the Pretty Horses (adapted from the novel by Cormac McCarthy), Miramax Films, 2000.

Mission to Mars, Touchstone Pictures, 2000.

Red Dragon (adapted from the novel by Thomas Harris), Universal Pictures, 2002.

PLAYS

Terra Nova (two-act; first produced in New Haven, CT, 1977; produced off-Broadway, 1984), Doubleday (New York, NY), 1981.

Hooters (two-act; first produced off-Broadway, 1978), Dramatists Play Service (New York, NY), 1978.

Coming Attractions (one-act; first produced off-Broadway, 1980), Samuel French (New York, NY), 1982.

Silver Linings (revues), Dramatists Play Service (New York, NY), 1983.

Little Footsteps (two-act; first produced off-Broadway, 1986), Doubleday (New York, NY), 1986.

TELEVISION SCRIPTS

Hooters (adapted from author's play), Playboy Channel, 1983.

(With John Bruce) *Terra Nova* (adapted from author's play), British Broadcasting Corporation (BBC-TV), 1984.

(Contributor) *The Comedy Zone,* Columbia Broadcasting System (CBS-TV), 1984.

(With Arthur Heineman) *The Father Clements Story,* National Broadcasting Company (NBC-TV), 1987.

Works represented in anthologies, including *Plays from Playwrights Horizons,* 1987.

WORK IN PROGRESS: A film version of *Little Footsteps,* for release by Twentieth Century-Fox; a film version of Glenn Savan's novel *White Palace,* for release by Universal; *Free Spirit,* with A. J. Carothers, for TriStar.

SIDELIGHTS: Ted Tally's best-known play, *Terra Nova,* made its debut at the Yale Repertory Theater when its author was only twenty-five years old. A Yale drama school student who, according to a *People* magazine contributor, "was frankly hurt" that the university "rejected him as an actor," but "relieved to be accepted for his play-writing credits," Tally featured six of his classmates in his play's premiere performance. As Samuel G. Freedman reported in the *New York Times,* the set was built "out of scrap wood and yards of white muslin from Connecticut's tobacco fields." The audience, however, included New York producers and talent agents, and *Terra Nova* has since been performed off-Broadway and in countries all over the world, including Great Britain, Australia, and Japan. Tally's more recent efforts have been in a lighter vein than his darkly dramatic first success, and his comedic credits include *Hooters, Coming Attractions, Silver Linings,* and *Little Footsteps.* Tally has also supplemented his career with scriptwriting for film and television.

Terra Nova, named for the ship that bears its protagonist to the play's setting, is the story of Antarctic explorer Robert Falcon Scott. Describing himself in Tally's drama as a "footnote to history," Scott is remembered as the Englishman who came in second to Norwegian Roald Amundsen in the race to discover the South Pole. *Terra Nova* depicts Scott's expedition and its tragic end—the slow, torturous death of Scott and his men from exposure and hunger a mere eleven miles from safety—but as Frank Rich pointed out in the *New York Times,* "in a sense, there are three plays here." The historic action is intertwined with the psychological action of Scott's inner thought, and both are tied to the theme of Great Britain's decline as an empire. Though some critics, like Rich, felt that these different aspects do not successfully "converge in a single dramatic entity," others applauded the work. J. W. Lambert declared in *Drama* that "structurally the play is ingenious but not obtrusively so."

Terra Nova is often performed on a more-or-less completely white set. Speaking of the off-Broadway production at the American Place Theater, Rich affirmed that "the white stage serves as the terrain of both Antarctica and the hero's mind." Thus Scott's imagined conversations with his wife and with rival Amundsen are presented to the audience. Mrs. Scott appears on stage to reenact the couple's courtship and to add substance to the conflict in Scott's makeup between duty to country and duty to family. Amundsen's function is to force the hero to question the value of ideals—or, as James Harris put it in *Plays and Players,* to "chide him for being so sentimental as not to take dogs and eat them en route." Tally carefully blends his speculative interpretation of the explorer's psyche with illustrations of the horrible realities of the polar expedition. Many reviewers noted with David Richards the effectiveness of the scene in which Scott's daydreams of a triumphant banquet celebrating the expedition's return dissolve into despair. Richards, critiquing *Terra Nova* for the *Washington Post,* called the drama "an act of poetic conjuration" and described the banquet scene, with Scott and his men "spankingly attired in crisp tuxedoes," thus: "At the height of the festivities, the elegant crystal service is stripped away and the table is instantly transformed into the sled of death. The men are back in a freezing hell." Similarly, Rich praised the "startling images" the play created and cited as an example the scene in which "we see a celebratory group photograph taken at the Pole decompose into a vision of an entire civilization's imminent extinction."

Because *Terra Nova* is an "historical, heroic and narrative work," Freedman labeled it "a play that seems innovative in part by being such a throwback." But, combined with the scenes which take place in Scott's imagination, the more conventional storytelling nature of the play helps make it appeal more broadly. As Freedman explained, a "mix of traditional and modern elements" partially accounts for "the attraction of *Terra Nova* to so many . . . theaters." Freedman quoted Yale Repertory Theatre artistic director Robert Brustein when *Terra Nova* made its debut: "It wasn't going to alienate people who dislike experimental or avant-garde theater. And it wasn't going to alienate those who like experimental or avant-garde theater. It has a wide audience."

Tally's next play, *Hooters,* differs greatly from *Terra Nova.* A comedy taking its name from a slang term for female breasts, *Hooters* is set in 1972 and concerns two college freshmen vacationing on Cape Cod trying to pick up women. The freshmen, Ricky and Clint, meet two banktellers on holiday, Cheryl and Ronda. Cheryl is attractive and adventurous, Ronda is plain and reticent. Both women are older and more experienced than Ricky and Clint. In the *New York Times* Richard Eder described the boys' "meeting with Cheryl and Ronda" as having "the quality of two blind men

groping at two porcupines." *Hooters* has "a farcical structure and an endless supply of gags about pick-up rituals, about sexual role-playing, [and] about 'hooters' themselves," asserted Rich. He went on to affirm that "Tally, an intelligent writer, is not just interested in locker-room humor; he aspires to make some larger points about men and women in our supposedly liberated age," and praised as the play's best scene one in which Ricky and Clint confront the falseness of their own friendship. Eder applauded Tally's characterization of Cheryl, proclaiming her his "best creation." The reviewer declared: "She is a character with more than one dimension. . . . She loves her body, sex, men; and there is a real warmth and humor contending with her growing conviction that there is something more to life than to be used." John Simon in *New York* concluded the play's best features to be "the generally peppy, often genuinely droll, dialogue, and the consistently smile-producing interaction of the characters."

Tally's *Coming Attractions* also drew superlatives from Simon. Again reviewing for *New York,* the critic announced that the play contains "that most desiderated and least available commodity in our theater: purposeful satire." *Coming Attractions* spoofs the tendency on the part of Americans to make celebrities of notorious criminals. The musical comedy's protagonist, Lonnie Wayne Burke, begins as an incompetent thief holding four hostages. He is taken in hand by a theatrical agent who is down on his luck; with his guidance, Lonnie becomes a headline-grabbing mass murderer known as the "Halloween Killer." Then, as Rich reported, "like all American celebrities of the first rank, Lonnie is quickly rewarded with book contracts, movie deals, groupies, product tie-ins, nightclub appearances and magazine cover stories." Lonnie also appears on a television talk show in a scene almost universally applauded by critics—other guests include a Palestine Liberation Organization (PLO) terrorist-comedian who needs a translator to tell his jokes—and the host is a parody who "glides about in gold lame, fawning over his murderous guests with obscene abandon," chortled Rich. Simon rhapsodized over "several sequences as exquisitely roguish as anything you have ever delighted in," possibly among them the show's finale, which Rich described as "a singing-and-dancing television special saluting Lonnie's electric-chair execution." Simon concluded that *Coming Attractions* produces "the best kind of laughter there is—the thinking kind."

"Civilized, literate, mind-stretching entertainment" by "an authorial athlete as fit and playful as a fiddle" was the verdict Simon handed down on Tally's 1986 comedy, *Little Footsteps.* The play features Ben and Joanie, an upwardly mobile couple in their mid-thirties expecting their first baby. Both have doubts—Joanie is not sure she has chosen the right reasons to become pregnant, and Ben is uncertain that he can be as self-sacrificing as he feels a good parent should be. These doubts explode in marital fighting, and the couple separates. Act II begins with Joanie living with her parents and having the baby's christening party. In Rich's opinion, *Little Footsteps* is "merriest" in this act, which includes a "farcical game of hide-and-seek." Simon avowed that "the scene in which the wised-up Joanie tells a Ben bursting with paternal resolve what infant rearing is really like comes off as sustainedly riotous, verbally and visually, as anything the comic muse has granted a *farceur.*"

Tally has also expanded his talents from playwriting to become a screenwriter. Talking about his second career with Tim Appelo in an interview for *Entertainment Weekly,* he said that he was "never very good at making up plots." Able to adapt novels to film, Tally brought Thomas Harris's infamous serial killer, Hannibal Lecter, to life both in *Silence of the Lambs* and its prequel, *Red Dragon.* Tally took the opportunity of rewriting Harris's work to insert some of his own wit into the *Silence of the Lambs* script, and garnered an Academy Award in the process. In an interview on the *SydField* Web site, Tally explained that in adapting Harris's work, new characters had to be developed in order to preserve plot continuity. "You can't be a slave to the book. . . ," he explained. "You want it in your head but you don't want it oppressing you. After a while you reference your own story outline more than you do the novel. . . . [The screenplay] becomes about itself only. It starts to develop its own logic and its own meaning in writing."

Stanley Kaufmann, writing for the *New Republic,* found Tally's 1996 script for *The Juror* better than his work on *Silence of the Lambs.* The critic wrote that "the climax of *The Juror* is credible, at least within the credibility range of thriller endings." Breaking from thrillers, Tally also adapted Cormac McCarthy's western novel *All the Pretty Horses* for the screen. His work on *All the Pretty Horses* was noted by *Variety* critic Todd McCarthy, who wrote that Tally "respects the language and structure and is alert to the main themes pertaining to the essence of one's character, coming of age and Cole's search for a father figure."

BIOGRAPHICAL AND CRITICAL SOURCES:

BOOKS

Contemporary Literary Criticism, Volume 42, Gale (Detroit, MI), 1987.

Tally, Ted, *Coming Attractions,* Samuel French (New York, NY), 1982.

Tally, Ted, *Terra Nova,* Samuel French (New York, NY), 1981.

PERIODICALS

Drama, summer, 1979.

Entertainment Weekly, June 24, 1994, Tim Appelo, p. 64.

Nation, February 25, 1991, Stuart Klawans, review of *Silence of the Lambs,* p. 246.

New Republic, February 26, 1996, Stanley Kaufmann, review of *The Juror,* p. 28.

Newsweek, December 15, 1986.

New York, December 15, 1980; November 8, 1982; March 17, 1986.

New York Times, May 1, 1987; December 4, 1980; October 21, 1982; April 26, 1984; April 29, 1984; February 28, 1986.

People, October 1, 1979.

Plays and Players, June, 1980.

Variety, December 18, 2000, Tod McCarthy, review of *All the Pretty Horses,* p. 26.

Washington Post, April 7, 1982.

Yale Drama, summer, 1977.

ONLINE

SydField, http://www.sydfield.com/ (September, 2000), interview with Tally.*

*   *   *

TAMBIAH, S. J.
  See TAMBIAH, Stanley Jeyaraja

*   *   *

TAMBIAH, Stanley J.
  See TAMBIAH, Stanley Jeyaraja

TAMBIAH, Stanley Jeyaraja 1929-
(S. J. Tambiah; Stanley J. Tambiah)

PERSONAL: Born January 16, 1929, in Ceylon (now Sri Lanka); immigrated to the United States, 1973; son of Charles Rajakone (a lawyer) and Eliza Moothathamby Chellamma Tambiah; married Mary Wynne Huber (a finance research analyst), March 15, 1969; children: Jonathan Anand, Matthew Arjun. *Education:* University of Ceylon (now University of Sri Lanka), Peradeniya Campus, B.A., 1951; Cornell University, Ph.D., 1954.

ADDRESSES: Home—33 Arlington St., Cambridge, MA 02140. *Office*—Harvard University, William James 420, 33 Kirkland St., Cambridge, MA 02138. *E-mail*—Tambiah@wjh.harvard.edu.

CAREER: Lecturer at University of Ceylon (now University of Sri Lanka), 1955-60; UNESCO, Thailand, technical assistance expert, 1960-63; Cambridge University, Cambridge, England, Smuts fellow, 1963-64, Commonwealth fellow, St. John's College, 1963-64, lecturer, 1964-72, fellow, Clare Hall, 1965-70, fellow, tutor of graduate students, and director of studies in social anthropology, King's College, 1970-72; Center for Advanced Study in Behavioral Sciences, Palo Alto, CA, fellow, 1968-69; University of Chicago, Chicago, IL, professor of anthropology, 1973-76; professor at Harvard University, Cambridge, MA, and curator of South Asian ethnology at Harvard's Peabody Museum, 1976—. Malinowski memorial lecturer, London School of Economics and Political Science, London, England, 1968; Radcliffe-Brown memorial lecturer, British Academy, London, 1979; Radhakrishnan memorial lecturer, Oxford University, Oxford, England, 1982; Kingsley Martin memorial lecturer, Cambridge University, Cambridge, England, 1982; Lewis Henry Morgan lecturer, University of Rochester, Rochester, NY, 1984; American Ethnological Society distinguished lecturer, 1988; Daryll Forde memorial lecturer, University College, London, 1991; Hilldale lecturer, University of Wisconsin, 1996; Japanese Association Ethnology distinguished lecturer, 1997.

MEMBER: International Association of Buddhist Studies, American Academy of Arts and Sciences (fellow), American Anthropological Association, American Academy for the Study of Religion, Association for Asian Studies, Royal Anthropological Institute, National Research Council's Committee for International Conflict Resolution, British Academy (corresponding foreign fellow).

AWARDS, HONORS: Curl Bequest prize from Royal Anthropological Institute, 1964; Social Science Research Council of Great Britain grant, 1971; Rivers Memorial Medal from Royal Anthropological Institute, 1973; National Science Foundation grant, 1978; D.Litt. from Jaffna University, Sri Lanka, 1981; Guggenheim fellowship, 1982; honorary Doctor of Humane Letters, University of Chicago, 1991; Balzan Prize, 1997; Huxley Memorial Medal, Royal Anthropological Institute, 1997; Fukuoka International Academic Prize, 1998.

WRITINGS:

UNDER NAME S. J. TAMBIAH, EXCEPT AS NOTED

Buddhism and the Spirit Cults in Northeast Thailand, Cambridge University Press (New York, NY), 1970.

(With Jack Goody) *Bridewealth and Dowry,* Cambridge University Press (New York, NY), 1973.

World Conqueror and World Renouncer: A Study of Buddhism and Polity in Thailand against a Historical Background, Cambridge University Press (New York, NY), 1976.

A Performative Approach to Ritual, British Academy (London, England), 1981.

(As Stanley Jeyaraja Tambiah) *The Buddhist Saints of the Forest and the Cult of Amulets: A Study in Charisma, Hagiography, Sectarianism, and Millennial Buddhism,* Cambridge University Press (New York, NY), 1984.

(As Stanley Jeyaraja Tambiah) *Culture, Thought, and Social Action: An Anthropological Perspective,* Harvard University Press (Cambridge, MA), 1985.

Sri Lanka: Ethnic Fratricide and the Dismantling of Democracy, University of Chicago Press (Chicago, IL), 1986.

(As Stanley Jeyaraja Tambiah) *Magic, Science, Religion, and the Scope of Rationality,* Cambridge University Press (New York, NY), 1990.

(As Stanley Jeyaraja Tambiah) *Buddhism Betrayed?: Religion, Politics, and Violence in Sri Lanka,* University of Chicago Press (Chicago, IL), 1992.

(As Stanley J. Tambiah) *Leveling Crowds: Ethnonationalist Conflicts and Collective Violence in South Asia,* University of California Press (Berkeley, CA), 1996.

(As Stanley J. Tambiah) *Edmund Leach: An Anthropological Life,* Cambridge University Press (New York, NY), 2001.

SIDELIGHTS: Anthropologist Stanley Jeyaraja Tambiah is well known for his books on Thai Buddhism, *Buddhism and the Spirit Cults in Northeast Thailand, World Conqueror and World Renouncer: A Study of Buddhism and Polity in Thailand against a Historical Background,* and *The Buddhist Saints of the Forest and the Cult of Amulets: A Study in Charisma, Hagiography, Sectarianism, and Millennial Buddhism.* His later writings, however, explore different territory. Tambiah visited his native Sri Lanka in 1983, interested in learning more about the growing conflict between the Tamil and the Sinhalese minority groups; this trip was to have a great influence on his writing. "It was very traumatic for me. I felt that it was necessary for my own therapy to come to terms with what was happening there by writing something about it," Tambiah told Ken Gewertz of the *Harvard University Gazette.*

In the collection of essays *Culture, Thought, and Social Action: An Anthropological Perspective,* Tambiah examines "such seemingly arcane matters as the intricacies of Trobriand canoe building, the logic of Thai food prohibitions, and the nature of the Indian caste system," explained Roderick Stirrat of the *Times Literary Supplement.* Stirrat observed that the essays revolve around two themes: first, that rituals and symbolic activities, "universal features of human culture," must be judged not in terms of Western scientific thought but as "performative acts" that "achieve their goal through [their] imperative nature"; and second, that in a similar way all political formations must be viewed holistically, as "total phenomena." The reviewer found implicit in Tambiah's essays a rejection of much traditional Western thought, and though Stirrat noted that certain passages make for "very difficult reading," he nevertheless described the collection as "an important volume representing one of the ways in which modern anthropologists attempt to understand cultures, societies, and forms of life."

In his next book, Tambiah turned directly to the ethnic violence emerging in his native land. *Sri Lanka: Ethnic Fratricide and the Dismantling of Democracy* addresses the "sporadic—and ominously increasing—outbursts of racist pogroms" that plague that country,

wrote Paul Sieghart of the *Los Angeles Times Book Review.* Sri Lanka's Tamil minority, of which Tambiah himself is a member, is the target of violence perpetrated by a majority that "still believes that there really is such a thing as the 'Aryan race,'" the reviewer explained, "and that belonging to it is something to be proud of." Tambiah explores the problem from a variety of perspectives and proposes some solutions, making his book, in the reviewer's estimation, "excellent and thought-provoking."

Tambiah's *Buddhism Betrayed?: Religion, Politics, and Violence in Sri Lanka* continues with the discussion of ethnic violence, this time in a book aimed to educate the general reader. Some Buddhist groups took offense, and the book was banned in Sri Lanka. "Tambiah realizes that his own ethnic identity forces him to walk a fine line between objectivity and engagement, but he is willing to face this risk," noted Gewertz. Indeed, Tambiah feels that this "fine line" should be embraced as political and intellectual thought become globalized; "I must take a position both as an anthropologist and as a minority member," he told Gewertz. "This is a challenge today for Third World intellectuals."

Leveling Crowds: Ethnonationalist Conflicts and Collective Violence in South Asia encompasses a broader topic: Tambiah "attempts to synthesize the nature of the problem of collective violence in South Asia," summarized *Australian Journal of Anthropology* reviewer Rohan Bastin. Comparing the Sri Lankan violence with other ethnic conflicts in the broader area—namely, the Hindu/Sikh clashes in India and the Muhajir/Sindhi conflicts in Pakistan—Tambiah argues that South Asian nation-states have politicized ethnicity to the point where violence erupts far too frequently. "Particularly effective in discussing violence in Sri Lanka (he includes a personal first-hand account of the 1956 riots) and the anti-Sikh pogrom in India, Tambiah is less at ease in dealing with Pakistan and the Karachi imbroglio," commented James Chiriyankandath in the *Journal of Commonwealth and Comparative Politics.* Other critics, such as Neena Samota of the *Review of Politics,* found Tambiah's objective-yet-engaged stance to be provocatively effective. "The book is multidimensional," noted Samota. "Tambiah engages in an objective analysis of ethnonationalist conflict and proceeds to a subjective analysis of crowd psychology."

Tambiah has been the recipient of many awards, including the 1997 Balzan Prize "for his penetrating social-anthropological analysis of the contemporary central problems of ethnic violence manifested in South East Asia, as well as for his original studies on the dynamics of Buddhist society," according to the prize committee's citation.

BIOGRAPHICAL AND CRITICAL SOURCES:

PERIODICALS

American Anthropologist, June, 1991, review of *Magic, Science, Religion, and the Scope of Rationality*, p. 494; March, 1994, review of *Buddhism Betrayed?: Religion, Politics, and Violence in Sri Lanka*, p. 172.

American Ethnologist, May, 1994, review of *Magic, Science, Religion, and the Scope of Rationality*, p. 431; November, 1996, review of *Buddhism Betrayed?*, p. 905; February, 1999, review of *Leveling Crowds: Ethnonationalist Conflicts and Collective Violence in South Asia*, p. 248.

American Journal of Sociology, September, 1993, review of *Buddhism Betrayed?*, p. 531.

Australian Journal of Anthropology, December, 1997, Rohan Bastin, review of *Leveling Crowds*, pp. 359-361.

Choice, February, 1991, review of *Magic, Science, Religion, and the Scope of Rationality*, p. 970; February, 1995, review of *Buddhism Betrayed?*, p. 901; May, 1997, review of *Leveling Crowds*, p. 1585.

Come-All-Ye, spring, 1996, review of *Magic, Science, Religion, and the Scope of Rationality*, p. 13.

Contemporary Sociology, March, 1994, review of *Buddhism Betrayed?*, p. 261.

Current History, December, 1997, William W. Firam, Jr., review of *Leveling Crowds*, p. 443.

Isis, December, 1991, review of *Magic, Science, Religion, and the Scope of Rationality*, p. 728.

Journal of Asian Studies, May, 1991, review of *Magic, Science, Religion, and the Scope of Rationality*, p. 372.

Journal of Commonwealth and Comparative Politics, November, 1997, James Chiriyankandath, review of *Leveling Crowds*, pp. 127-129.

Journal of Religion, July, 1988, review of *Sri Lanka: Ethnic Fratricide and the Dismantling of Democracy*, p. 491; January, 1992, review of *Magic, Science, Religion, and the Scope of Rationality*, p. 161.

Journal of the American Academy of Religion, August, 1993, review of *Magic, Science, Religion, and the Scope of Rationality*, p. 619.

London Review of Books, May 23, 2002, Adam Kuper, "Clever, or Even Clever-Clever," review of *Edmund Leach: An Anthropological Life*, pp. 11-12.

Los Angeles Times Book Review, June 1, 1986; June 8, 1986.

Review of Politics, summer, 1997, Neena Samota, review of *Leveling Crowds*, pp. 618-620.

Reviews in Anthropology, January, 1991, review of *Sri Lanka: Ethnic Fratricide and the Dismantling of Democracy*, p. 297.

Sociology of Religion, spring, 1998, Joseph B. Tamney, review of *Leveling Crowds*, p. 98.

Times Literary Supplement, January 24, 1986; September 7, 1990, review of *Magic, Science, Religion, and the Scope of Rationality*, p. 951.

University Press Book News, September, 1990, review of *Magic, Science, Religion, and the Scope of Rationality*, p. 13; September, 1992, review of *Buddhism Betrayed?*, p. 6.

ONLINE

Harvard Anthropology Department Web site, http://www.wjh.harvard.edu/anthro/ (February 27, 2003), biography of Stanley J. Tambiah.

Harvard University Gazette Online, http://www.news.harvard.edu/gazette/ (October 23, 1997), Ken Gewertz, "Stanley Tambiah to Be Awarded Balzan Prize for Groundbreaking Work on Ethnic Violence"; (November 9, 2000), "British Academy Elects Tambiah."

National Academies Web site, http://www.nationalacademies.org/ (February 27, 2003), membership listing for Stanley J. Tambiah.

Tamil Tigers Web site, http://www.tamiltigers.net/eelambooks/ (February 27, 2003), Sachi Sri Kantha, review of *Buddhism Betrayed*.

University of California Press Web site, http://www.ucpress.edu/ (February 27, 2003), description and reviews of *Leveling Crowds*.*

*   *   *

TARANTINO, Quentin (Jerome) 1963-

PERSONAL: Born March 27, 1963, in Knoxville, TN; son of Tony (a musician) and Connie (a nurse and later a corporate executive) Tarantino.

Quentin Tarantino

ADDRESSES: Office—A Band Apart Productions, Capra Bldg. 112, 10202 West Washington Blvd., Culver City, CA 90232.

CAREER: Writer and filmmaker. Pussycat Theater, Torrance, CA, usher, early 1980s; Video Archives, Los Angeles, clerk, 1985-90; various film-related jobs, including production assistant on Dolph Lundgren exercise video, work at Cinetel Productions, bit part as Elvis impersonator on television show *Golden Girls,* 1990-92; screenwriter, filmmaker, director, producer, and actor, 1992—. Film and television roles include *Golden Girls* (television series), 1990; *Reservoir Dogs,* 1992; *Somebody to Love,* 1994; *Sleep with Me,* 1994; *Pulp Fiction,* 1994; *All-American Girl* (television series), 1994; *Four Rooms,* 1995; *Destiny Turns on the Radio,* 1995; *Desperado,* 1995; *Saturday Night Live*

(television series), 1995; *From Dusk 'till Dawn,* 1996; *Girl Six,* 1996; *Jackie Brown* (voice), 1997. Co-founder of A Band Apart Productions, 1991, Rolling Thunder distribution company (subsidiary of Miramax Pictures), 1995, and A Band Apart Records, 1997.

AWARDS, HONORS: All for *Pulp Fiction,* all 1994: Golden Palm, Cannes Film Festival; Academy Award for Best Screenplay Written Directly for the Screen (with Roger Avary); Best Director, National Board of Review; *Los Angeles Times* Film Critics Association Award; Best Director, Best Screenplay (with Avary), New York Film Critics Circle; Best Director and Best Screenplay (with Avary), Boston Society of Film Critics; Best Director and Best Screenplay (with Avary), Society of Texas Film Critics; Best Director and Best Screenplay (with Avary), National Society of Film Critics; Best Director and Best Screenplay (with Avary), Chicago Film Critics Association; Golden Globe Award for Best Screenplay (with Avary); Independent Spirit Award for Best Director and Best Screenplay (with Avary); British Academy of Film and Television Arts Award for Best Original Screenplay (with Avary); and MTV Movie Award for Best Movie.

WRITINGS:

SCREENPLAYS; AND DIRECTOR

Reservoir Dogs (Dog Eat Dog Productions/Miramax, 1992), published with *True Romance* (alsosee below) as *Reservoir Dogs and True Romance: Two Screenplays,* Grove Press (New York, NY), 1995.
True Romance, Morgan Creek/Warner Bros., 1993.
(Author of story) *Natural Born Killers,* Warner Bros., 1994.
(With Roger Avary) *Pulp Fiction* (Miramax, 1994), published as *Pulp Fiction: A Quentin Tarantino Screenplay,* Hyperion (New York, NY), 1994.
(Author of segment) "The Man from Hollywood," *Four Rooms,* A Band Apart/Miramax, 1995.
(Uncredited; with Michael Schiffer and Richard P. Henrick) *Crimson Tide,* Buena Vista, 1995.
(Uncredited; with David Weisberg and Douglas Cook) *The Rock,* Buena Vista, 1996.
(With Reb Braddock) *Curdled,* A Band Apart/Miramax, 1996.
(With Robert Kutzman) *From Dusk 'till Dawn,* Hyperion (New York, NY), 1995.

Jackie Brown (based on *Rum Punch* by Elmore Le-
onard; A Band Apart/Miramax, 1997), published
as *Jackie Brown: A Screenplay,* Hyperion (New
York, NY), 1997.
(Author of story) *From Dusk 'till Dawn: Texas Blood
Money,* Dimension Films, 1998.
Kill Bill, Vol. 1 (based on the author's novel; also see
below), Miramax, 2003.

Also uncredited author of *Past Midnight* (television
movie), 1992, and (with Julia Sweeney and Jim Emerson) *It's Pat,* 1994.

OTHER

Quentin Tarantino: Interviews, edited by Gerald Peary,
University Press of Mississippi (Jackson, MS),
1998.
(With Christopher Heard) *Ten Thousand Bullets: The
Cinematic Journey of John Woo,* Lone Eagle Press,
1999.
Quentin Tarantino: The Film Geek Files, edited by
Paul Woods, Plexus, 2000.
Kill Bill (novel), Talk/Miramax (New York, NY), 2003.

SIDELIGHTS: Few filmmakers have succeeded in
building a mystique, and indeed an entire cinematic
"world," to the degree achieved by Quentin Tarantino,
who first attracted critical attention with *Reservoir
Dogs* in 1992. In that film, Tarantino established aspects of his aesthetic that have continued to unfold
over subsequent motion pictures, most notably the
Tarantino-directed 1994 hit *Pulp Fiction* and the 1997
film *Jackie Brown,* which Tarantino also directed. The
filmmaker played roles in all three movies, each of
them successively smaller: from Mr. Brown in *Reservoir Dogs,* who in the opening scene delivers a memorable (and X-rated) exegesis on Madonna's 1985 hit
"Like a Virgin"; to Jimmie in *Pulp Fiction,* a man ir-
ritable over a messy dead body in the back seat of his
car; to a voice on an answering machine in *Jackie
Brown.* But along the way, even as the director's physical presence in his films has diminished, the characteristics of his art have propelled him to the status, as he
observed somewhat derisively in an interview with
New York Times Magazine, of "an adjective": "Every
third script out there," he said, "is described as
'Tarantino-esque.'"

Certain aspects characterize the Tarantino aesthetic,
and though not as visible in films where his touch appears uncredited, they are nonetheless there for the

discerning to see. One writer suggested, for instance,
that his contribution to the 1995 film *Crimson Tide*
could be summed up in two references to comic books
which, the reviewer implied, seemed out of character
when uttered by actor Denzel Washington. Comic
books play a significant part in Tarantino's onscreen
world, and numerous critics have likened his films to
"cartoons" in the way that they transform cinematic
violence—images that have become cliches through
ceaseless repetition in B-grade films—into a form of
postmodern humor. Tarantino himself, particularly during his five years as a clerk in a Los Angeles video
store, has absorbed a vast store of film history, making
his films almost encyclopedic in their references and
cross-references.

One is unlikely to find Bergman or Cocteau making
cameos in Tarantino's movies, however, although critics found in *Reservoir Dogs* suggestions both of Stanley Kubrick and Jean-Luc Godard. Rather, Tarantino's
interest is in pop culture, and his melding of this with
a modicum of more high-minded material has won
him the praise of numerous critics. There is little difference between Tarantino the screenwriter and Tarantino the man, as David Wild illustrated in a 1994 *Rolling Stone* profile. His home is a shrine to pop
paraphernalia, the flotsam and jetsam of twentieth-
century culture: "Along with items from his own movies," wrote Wild, "including the razor used in the infamous ear-slicing scene [in *Reservoir Dogs*], there's a
frighteningly lifelike head of B-movie diva Barbara
Steele, a pack of genuine *Texas Chainsaw* chili, a *Zorro*
knife given to him by Jennifer Beals, a Robert Vaughn
doll, cases by the dozen of bottled Pepsi, and what is
undoubtedly one of the world's most impressive collections of film- and TV-related board games."

Wild described Tarantino as a "chatterbox," a fitting
quality given the fact that, for all the blood and mayhem in them, his films are driven more by dialogue
than by action. Ron Rosenbaum in *Esquire* examined
the famous disagreement between Tarantino and director Oliver Stone over Stone's 1994 film *Natural Born
Killers.* Stone had so altered Tarantino's story that the
latter disclaimed all involvement in the resulting film
and even delayed release of *Pulp Fiction* in order to
further establish his distance. Rosenbaum portrayed
the difference between the two men's temperaments as
a "rival[ry of] sensibilities" not unlike that between
Ernest Hemingway and F. Scott Fitzgerald: "Mythic
Macho Outdoor Man of Nature versus Aesthete Ana-

lyst of Indoor Intrigue and Internal Self-Consciousness." Whereas Stone favors action, Rosenbaum noted, Tarantino's psyche finds its natural home with dialogue: "If you watch Tarantino's films, if you read his screenplays, all that writhing and stewing of images is not so much war as dance. 'To me, violence is a totally aesthetic subject,' he once said. 'Saying you don't like violence in movies is like saying you don't like dance sequences in movies.'"

Whereas Stone's characters are figures of action, Rosenbaum indicated, Tarantino's are talkers, and what they talk about—albeit while on the way to committing shocking acts, or after they have done so—are the subjects that fascinate the director. "The great defining moments in Tarantino films," Rosenbaum explained, "are almost always moments of literary criticism. The defining moment of *Reservoir Dogs,* . . . the scene that instantly distinguished it from all other violent gangster films ever made before, is the opening scene, in which his bank robbers are gathered around a breakfast table at a pancake house, deconstructing a Madonna song. . . . Oliver Stone, given that same group of murderous thugs, would have them facing off over urinals, comparing how long it took each to pee. Tarantino isn't afraid to depict his gangsters almost as if they were cultural-studies majors. And again, in *Pulp Fiction,* what's the defining moment? It's when Jules and Vincent (Samuel L. Jackson and John Travolta), two hit men, are analyzing the philosophical implications of the way brand names for burgers—designations of value—shift in different linguistic frameworks. In his heart, Quentin Tarantino is an English major."

Though violence, pop culture, and endless discussions are aspects of the Tarantino aesthetic, they are not the sum total of his world. Another facet of his work as a filmmaker is that he resurrects stars often perceived to be past their glory days. In the case of Travolta, who had enjoyed almost dizzying success in a number of roles during the 1970s, Tarantino's casting in *Pulp Fiction* resulted in a full-scale revival, making Travolta in the 1990s every bit the star he had been twenty years before. Similarly, the director cast Robert Forster and Pam Grier, both of whom had done little notable work in recent years, in *Jackie Brown.* Describing the onscreen romance between Forster and Grier, the latter whom Tarantino had admired for her roles in numerous 1970s "blaxploitation" films, Anthony Lane of the *New Yorker* wrote: Forster "is fifty-six, she is forty-four; when was the last time you went to the mov-

ies—let alone a Tarantino movie—and saw a fond, unironic, interracial kiss between a couple who are a hundred years old?"

Lane's larger point was that Tarantino seemed to have mellowed as his career progressed. He shocked audiences in *Reservoir Dogs* with a gruesome scene in which Mr. Blonde (Michael Madsen) cuts off a police officer's ear while the 1970s hit "Stuck in the Middle with You" plays in the background. Likewise, *Pulp Fiction* featured a brutal S-and-M male-on-male rape scene, along with a large body count; by contrast, *Jackie Brown,* though it offers gore aplenty, and half the cast are dead by the end of the film, is more character-driven and—in places, such as a long tracking shot in which Ordell (Jackson) shoots an employee—restrained for Tarantino. The director himself has suggested that, although the shocking violence may get him the most headlines, its purpose is to illustrate a larger absurdity: the very deification of such bloodshed in American film. Thus the violence itself is a part of pop culture, inseparable from the references to B-movies and comic books, and this attitude has helped gain him a reputation as a witty and sardonic filmmaker simultaneously spoofing and glorifying the detritus of twentieth-century mass media.

His postmodern approach—Tarantino himself eschews the high-blown term—has earned him not only widespread admiration among critics, but also the allegiance of numerous stars. Jackson has appeared in two of his films, as have Harvey Keitel and Tim Roth; likewise Travolta, Robert DeNiro, Uma Thurman, Bruce Willis, and Bridget Fonda have all played roles in Tarantino pictures. Keitel, a highly respected actor known for his interest in independent filmmaking, agreed to appear in *Reservoir Dogs* for a much smaller sum than his ordinary fee, simply because he believed in Tarantino's work.

The fact that Tarantino first emerged as an independent filmmaker is a final, and indeed crucial, element of his abiding success. He came from far outside the Hollywood establishment, gaining his knowledge of the movies not by going to film school—he is a high-school dropout—but by feeding a long-term addiction to movies themselves. As a youngster growing up in suburban Los Angeles, he haunted a theatre in the nearby town of Carson. It was a rough neighborhood, but "the theater . . . showed all the kung fu movies," Tarantino recalled, "and the Allied International movies like *The Van.*" As a teenager, he worked as an usher in a pornographic theatre and later spent five years as a minimum-wage employee in what he recalled as "the best video store in the Los Angeles area," Video Archives.

There he met Roger Avary, another future director—Tarantino would be executive producer on Avary's *Killing Zoe* in 1994—who later worked with Tarantino on the story for *Pulp Fiction.* Tarantino, Avary, and others constituted an informal film club: "I basically lived [at the video store] . . . for years," Tarantino told Wild. "We'd get off work, close up the store, then sit around and watch movies all night. Other times Roger, our friend Scott, and I would take a Friday and plot things out so we could see all four new movies we were interested in. We always took whatever we got paid and put it right back into the industry."

Eventually, however, Tarantino began to feel like the character Clarence in the 1993 film *True Romance,* who, as Wild noted, "was based on Tarantino's younger days living near the Los Angeles airport. 'All day long he just sees people taking off and leaving, and he's going nowhere. I'm not that guy anymore.'" How he ceased to be "that guy" is the stuff of independent-film legend, a story that has inspired ambitious filmmakers ever since. In 1990 Tarantino and Avary went to work with producer John Langley, a regular video-store customer, and moved to Hollywood. There they started to develop the all-important contacts—most notably with producer Lawrence Bender—necessary in the world of filmmaking, and they raised $1.5 million. In film terms it was a shoestring budget at best; but it was enough to make *Reservoir Dogs,* a film that grossed many times that sum.

The resulting work brought out cautionary statements from several reviewers—Terrence Rafferty of the *New Yorker,* for instance, described it as "stylized mayhem and playground machismo"—but audiences, and indeed even many critics, were captivated. The story itself, modeled on Stanley Kubrick's 1956 film *The Killing,* is simple: an aging crime boss and his son gather a group of criminals, designated by colors (e.g., Mr. Blonde, Mr. Pink) in order to protect their identities, and plan a jewelry-store heist. But one of them is a cop, and the robbery goes badly. The crime itself is not depicted, and much of the action takes place afterward in a warehouse where the robbers have gathered

to square off against one another in an attempt to find the traitor. The film plays tricks with time, shifting backward and forward, and as Manohla Dargis in *Art-Forum* observed, "The details [of the heist] surface only as retold by the robbers. . . . The effect is less the *Rashomon* point about rival truths than something akin to psychoanalysis: like the therapeutic process, *Reservoir Dogs* tells a story, is *about* telling stories, and depends on stories for its creation." As notable as the temporal tricks are the film's stylistic touches, which in retrospect appear as vintage Tarantino: the brutal violence against the 1970s soundtrack, the use of matching anonymous black suits by the color-designated robbers, and the long quasi-philosophical discussions which take place in the stage-like warehouse.

Tarantino, wrote Kenneth Turan in the *Los Angeles Times,* "has a gift for writing great bursts of caustic, quirky dialogue," and even Rafferty, in the middle of a largely negative review, conceded that "Tarantino is a director to watch." Turan was also critical of the film, wishing it was not so "determinedly one-dimensional, so in love with operatic violence at the expense of everything else"; nonetheless he too credited "the undeniable skill and elan that Tarantino brings to all this." Likewise, Stanley Kauffmann in the *New Republic* wrote that much of *Reservoir Dogs* "was difficult for me to watch"; he faulted the director's penchant for violence, while observing that "cinematically speaking, it's plainly the debut of a talent." Jonathan Romney, in the *New Statesman* expressed concern for the way the famous ear-cutting scene incites audiences to want to see the violence unfold, yet he called Tarantino "a young director whose *noir* literacy is evident in every detail."

Although concerned about the violence, most critics admired Tarantino's abilities as a promising new talent. In the case of *True Romance,* directed by Tony Scott (*Top Gun*) from a screenplay by Tarantino, reviewers were less positive. But with Tarantino once again in the director's chair for *Pulp Fiction,* positive reviews—and awards—poured in. As with *Reservoir Dogs,* the story alters time, ending just a few minutes after the point at which it begins, moving forward in between and then doubling back. However, *Pulp Fiction* is more complex than its predecessor. Whereas *Reservoir Dogs* takes place entirely in a world of men and features no female characters, *Pulp Fiction* involves at least as much male-female conflict as male-

male. In terms of structure it has several plots, most of them surrounding a drug lord named Marsellus Wallace (Ving Rhames). In the opening scene, a husband-and-wife crime team (Roth and Amanda Plummer) plan a stickup in a restaurant; then the action leaves them, not to return until the end of the movie some two and a half hours later. In between, there are subplots involving two hit men (Travolta and Jackson) employed by Marsellus; Marsellus's alluring wife (Thurman), who suffers a near-fatal heroin overdose while out on the town with Travolta; and a boxer (Willis) who double-crosses Marsellus and flees for his life, only to find himself in a position to save the man who wants to kill him. In the final scene, after dealing with Plummer and Roth, Jackson's character makes a decision to leave his life of crime; already the audience has seen a segment that takes place later in time, in which Travolta confronts the results of his own refusal to do so.

"The script," wrote Richard Alleva in *Commonweal*, "is put together with a jeweler's precision, and makes the writing of every American film I've seen in the past year . . . seem like so much child's play." In the *New Republic*, Kauffmann, who had expressed reservations about Tarantino's directorial debut two years earlier and still found cause for alarm in the new film's violence, nonetheless held that "*Pulp Fiction* is *Reservoir Dogs* rewarded." Peter Travers of *Rolling Stone* described the film as "ferocious fun without a trace of caution, complacency or political correctness to inhibit its 154 deliciously lurid minutes." David Denby in *New York*, admitting that "I can't say I was a fan of . . . *Reservoir Dogs*," observed that in *Pulp Fiction*, "Tarantino seems to be goosing the entire solemn history of action cinema. . . . In the roundelay of violence and comedy that is *Pulp Fiction*, he has hilariously summed up an immense genre and gloriously achieved his exit from it. Life beckons from beyond the video store."

Several reviewers, such as T. J. Binyon of the *Times Literary Supplement*, noted that although the film's title seems to relate to books, *Pulp Fiction* is more about movies than literature. With *Jackie Brown* three years later, Tarantino would make a step closer to literature by adapting an Elmore Leonard book; in the meantime, as he enjoyed the enormous fame and success that came in the wake of *Pulp Fiction*, he worked on a number of other projects. Along with three other directors, he contributed a segment to the film *Four*

Rooms and worked with Robert Rodriguez on *From Dusk 'till Dawn*. Jack Matthews of the *Los Angeles Times* described *From Dusk 'till Dawn* as "a film nerd's fever dream, a Frankenstein's monster of used movie parts" involving "a pair of murdering, bank-robbing brothers" who find themselves at "a topless biker bar in the middle of nowhere . . . [in a] chaotic, bloody, nonstop battle with ancient Aztec vampires."

Tarantino returns to more familiar territory with *Jackie Brown*, a film both more complex than *Pulp Fiction* in terms of character development and the double-crosses that move the plot forward, and less complex in its relatively linear use of time. The story centers on Jackie Brown (Grier), an underpaid flight attendant earning extra money by helping arms dealer Ordell (Jackson) launder money. But when she is caught, Ordell, fearing she will turn him over to the police, wants her eliminated. On this backbone of plot are attached numerous other subplots involving Ordell's airheaded girlfriend (Bridget Fonda), a henchman who has just gotten out of prison (DeNiro), the bail bondsman who comes to Jackie's rescue (Forster), and the federal agents who goad her into helping them (Michael Keaton and Michael Bowen). All her adversaries underestimate Jackie, as a sequence involving the transfer of a bag—the only tricky use of time in the movie, involving the replay of a scene from three points of view—serves to illustrate.

Todd McCarthy in *Variety* faulted Tarantino for taking too long to tell his story—like *Pulp Fiction*, Jackie Brown clocks in at approximately 150 minutes—but held that the "film takes its own sweet time setting its gears in motion, with the emphasis on sweet when it comes to amusingly establishing its characters." Turan in the *Los Angeles Times* warned that "those expecting Tarantino to pick up where he left off [in *Pulp Fiction*] will be disappointed in *Jackie Brown*. Instead of rearranging audience's sensibilities, he's taken the typically twisty plot of Leonard's *Rum Punch* and run it through his personal Mixmaster. The result is a raunchy doodle, a leisurely and easygoing diversion." Lane, in the *New Yorker*, quoted with approval an example of Tarantino's dialogue: when Ordell warns his girlfriend that smoking marijuana will "rob you of your ambition," she says, "Not if your ambition is to get high and watch TV." Travers in *Rolling Stone* wrote that Tarantino "score[s] a knockout. . . . Loaded with action, laughs, smart dialogue, and potent performances, *Jackie Brown* is most memorable for its unexpected feeling." Tarantino, Travers concluded, is charting new territory, and just as the film ends with Jackie "driving toward a life she can't define," listening to "a '70s song about busting out of ghettos"— Bobby Womack's "Across 110th Street"—so the film "crackles with the fear and exhilaration of moving on."

In 2003 Tarantino expanded his creative penchant into fiction writing with the novel *Kill Bill,* which was published almost simultaneously with the film he adapted from it. Starring Uma Thurman, Lucy Liu, and Vivica A. Fox, the film follows Thurman—playing The Bride—as she seeks revenge for the nightmare that occurred on her wedding day, when all in her wedding party were slaughtered. The only person to survive, the Bride, is revived from her coma after four years, and now dedicates herself to seeking out and defending herself against the five killers—Liu, Fox, Michael Madson, Daryl Hannah, and David Carradine—who massacred her friends and family. Drawing on everything from Japanese anime to 1960s Spaghetti Westerns, *Kill Bill, Vol. 1* contains more than the violence Tarantino fans have come to expect; however, that violence is somehow made less abhorrent by the film's otherworldly, graphic-novel look. While noting that some viewers will "instantly dismiss" *Kill Bill, Vol. 1* "as rubbish," *San Francisco Examiner* reviewer Jeffrey M. Anderson maintained that "Tarantino is the greatest American action director working today, and he shoots . . . [the film's] long and carefully choreographed fight scenes with a skill and clarity lacking in nearly every other recent American action film." Calling the film "just a funky, hermetic pulp bash," *Entertainment Weekly* contributor Owen Gleiberman added, "Each sequence in *Kill Bill* is like a detour that's more fun than the main road." Also commenting on the movie's surface quality, *Miami Herald* reviewer Rene Rodriguez noted that "for all its severed limbs and alarmingly large sprays of blood, *Kill Bill* is more of a vicious comedy than anything else. . . . We know so little [about the characters,] in fact, that this lively, energetic movie becomes a thin, disposable experience." However, Rodriguez concluded, the film "reminds you just how good a visual craftsman" Tarantino is. "There is such sheer cinematic joy in every one of *Kill Bill*'s blood-spattered frames . . . that the movie succeeds despite itself." Richard Corliss, recalling perhaps Tarantino's early remark equating film violence with dance, concluded his review of the film by noting: "Even the arcs of blood have the propulsion of crimson choreography. In this sense, *Kill Bill* is the greatest dance film since *West Side Story.*"

BIOGRAPHICAL AND CRITICAL SOURCES:

BOOKS

Bernard, Jimi, *Quentin Tarantino: The Man and His Movies,* HarperPerennial (New York, NY), 1995.
Clarkson, Wensley, *Quentin Tarantino: Shooting from the Hip,* Overlook Press (Woodstock, NY), 1995.
Dawson, Jeff, *Quentin Tarantino: The Cinema of Cool,* Applause (New York, NY), 1995.

PERIODICALS

ArtForum, November, 1992, p. 11; March, 1995, pp. 63-66.
Commonweal, October 22, 1993, p. 22; November 18, 1994, pp. 30-31.
Entertainment Weekly, October 17, 2003, Owen Gleiberman, review of *Kill Bill, Vol. 1.*
Esquire, December, 1997, p. 38.
Film Comment, January-February, 1996, pp. 83-88.
Literature-Film Quarterly, January, 1998, pp. 60-66.
Los Angeles Times, October 23, 1992, p. F1; September 10, 1993, p. F1; December 25, 1995, p. F12; January 19, 1996, p. F1; December 24, 1997, p. F2.
Miami Herald, October 10, 2003, Rene Rodriguez, review of *Kill Bill, Vol. 1.*
New Republic, November 23, 1992, pp. 30-31; November 14, 1994, pp. 26-27.
New Statesman, January 8, 1993, p. 34; October 8, 1994, p. 29.
Newsweek, October 13, 2003, p. 66.
New York, October 3, 1994, p. 96.
New Yorker, October 19, 1992, pp. 105-109; October 10, 1994, pp. 95-97; February 5, 1996, pp. 75-77; January 12, 1998, pp. 83-84.
New York Times Magazine, November 16, 1997, p. 112.
People, March 23, 1998, p. 130.
Rolling Stone, October 6, 1994, pp. 79-81; November 3, 1994, pp. 77-80; January 22, 1998, pp. 61-62.
San Francisco Examiner, October 10, 2003, Jeffrey M. Anderson, review of *Kill Bill, Vol. 1.*
Time, October 20, 2003, Richard Corliss, review of *Kill Bill, Vol. 1.*
Times Literary Supplement, November 11, 1994, p. 26.
Variety, December 22, 1997, pp. 57-58.*

TAYLOR, Cora (Lorraine) 1936-

PERSONAL: Born January 14, 1936, in Fort Qu'Apappelle, Saskatchewan, Canada; daughter of Harvey and Edith (Kalbfleisch) Traub; married Durward Thomas, 1953 (divorced); married Don Livingston, 1958 (divorced); married Russell Taylor (a physician), November, 1973; children: (first marriage) Granger, Wendy; (second marriage) Clancy, Sean. *Education:* University of Alberta, B.A. and teaching certificate, 1973. *Religion:* Anglican.

ADDRESSES: Home—#906, 10101 Saskatchewan Drive, Edmonton, Alberta T6E 4R6, Canada. *Agent*—c/o Author Mail, Coteau Books, #401, 2206 Dewdney Ave., Regina, Saskatchewan S4R 1H3, Canada.

CAREER: University of Alberta, University Hospital, Edmonton, medical secretary, 1964-68; Duffield School, Duffield, Alberta, Canada, teacher, 1973-75; writer, 1975—.

MEMBER: Canadian Authors Association (Alberta vice-president, 1980-86; national award chairman, 1987).

AWARDS, HONORS: Ross Annett Award, Alberta Writers Guild, Book of the Year Award, Canadian Library Association, and Canada Council Award, all 1985, all for *Julie;* Ruth Schwartz Book Award, Our Choice Award, Children's Book Center, and honorable mention for book-of-the-year award, Canadian Library Association, all 1988, all for *The Doll;* White Raven Award, International Youth Library, "notable book" citation, Canadian Library Association, both 1992, and nomination for Reading Cup, 1993, all for *Julie's Secret;* Arts Award, City of Edmonton, 1987; nomination for book-of-the-year award, Canadian Library Association, Ruth Schwartz Award, Silver Birch Award, and Mr. Christie Award, all 1995, all for *Summer of the Mad Monk.*

WRITINGS:

NOVELS FOR YOUNG ADULTS

Julie, Western Producer Prairie Books (Saskatoon, Saskatchewan, Canada), 1985.

Cora Taylor

The Doll, Western Producer Prairie Books (Saskatoon, Saskatchewan, Canada), 1987.

Julie's Secret, Western Producer Prairie Books (Saskatoon, Saskatchewan, Canada), 1991.

Ghost Voyages, Scholastic (Richmond Hill, Ontario, Canada), 1992.

The Summer of the Mad Monk, Greystone Books (Vancouver, British Columbia, Canada), 1994.

Vanishing Act, Red Deer College Press (Red Deer, Alberta, Canada), 1997.

On Wings of a Dragon, Fitzhenry & Whiteside (Toronto, Ontario, Canada), 2001.

Ghost Voyages II: The Matthew, Coteau Books (Regina, Saskatchewan, Canada), 2002.

Angelique: Buffalo Hunt, Penguin Books Canada (Toronto, Ontario, Canada), 2002.

OTHER

Parkland Spirit (musical play), 1980.

Dateline: Stony Plain (musical play), 1983.

Out on the Prairie: A Canadian Counting Book, North Winds Press (Markham, Ontario, Canada), 2002.

Theater critic for *Allied Arts Bulletin,* 1967. Contributor of articles and stories to periodicals, including *Chatelaine, Golden West, Heritage, Magpie,* and *Branching Out.* Editor of *Life Was a Bowl of Chokecherries,* 1980, and *Alberta Poetry Yearbook,* 1980-86.

SIDELIGHTS: Cora Taylor is a Canadian writer who has won acclaim with her novels for young adults. She began her career in 1985 with *Julie,* the story of a girl coming to terms with her extraordinary powers of premonition. David H. Jenkinson, writing in *Twentieth-Century Children's Writers,* called *Julie* "a haunting story of loneliness, in particular the isolation that can come from being different." Taylor's book secured awards from the Canadian Library Association and Canada Council, and it readily established her as an accomplished storyteller.

In 1987, Taylor followed *Julie* with *The Doll,* in which a young girl escapes from her troubled home life by using a magical doll that transports her into the past, where she lives as the daughter of westward pioneers. *The Doll* brought Taylor further honors, including a Ruth Schwartz Book Award and an Our Choice Award, and it served to confirm her status as a noteworthy writer of works for young adults.

Taylor next published *Julia's Secret,* a sequel to her debut volume. In the continuation, Julia uses her extrasensory powers to uncover a murder and solve a kidnapping. David H. Jenkinson, in his *Twentieth-Century Children's Writers* appraisal, deemed *Julia's Secret* "competently written," and he summarized it as an "action-adventure story."

Taylor continued to explore the supernatural in *Ghost Voyages,* wherein a young boy transports himself to the nautical settings represented on commemorative stamps, and *Vanishing Act,* in which an adolescent girl discovers a spell that renders her invisible. As in *Julia's Secret,* the heroine of *Vanishing Act* uses her amazing abilities to solve a crime.

Among Taylor's other works are *The Summer of the Mad Monk,* in which an adolescent boy comes to believe that a fellow villager is actually Rasputin, the legendary Russian monk, and *On Wings of a Dragon,* a fantasy wherein a girl uncovers evidence of treachery at a royal castle. Carolyn Cushman, writing in *Locus,* deemed *On Wings of a Dragon* "quirky," and Jennifer L. Branch, writing in *Resource Links,* affirmed that the book "soars with the beauty of the language."

BIOGRAPHICAL AND CRITICAL SOURCES:

BOOKS

St. James Guide to Children's Writers, 5th edition, St. James Press (Detroit, MI), 1999, pp. 1042-1043.
Twentieth-Century Children's Writers, 4th edition, St. James Press (Detroit, MI), 1995, pp. 940-941.

PERIODICALS

Locus, May, 2002, Carolyn Cushman, review of *On Wings of a Dragon,* p. 35.
Resource Links, December, 2001, Jennifer L. Branch, review of *On Wings of a Dragon;* October, 2002, Ann Abel, review of *Angelique: Buffalo Hunt,* p. 15; December, 2002, Laura Reilly, review of *Ghost Voyages II,* p. 34; February, 2003, Denise Parrott, review of *Out on the Prairie: A Canadian Counting Book,* p. 7.
Wind Speaker, December, 2002, Cheryl Petten, review of *Angelique: Buffalo Hunt,* p. 17.*

ONLINE

Canadian Society of Children's Authors, Illustrators, and Performers Web site, http://www.canscaip.org/ (August 21, 2003).
Official Cora Taylor Home Page, http://members.shaw. ca/mystery3/cindex1.html/ (August 21, 2003).*

*   *   *

THESEN, Sharon 1946-

PERSONAL: Born October 1, 1946, in Tisdale, Saskatchewan, Canada; daughter of Kelly and Dawn (Martin) Thesen; married Brian Fawcett, 1966 (divorced); married Peter Thompson (divorced); married Paul Mier; children: (first marriage) Jesse. *Ethnicity:* "Irish and Norwegian." *Education:* Simon Fraser University, B.A., 1970, M.A., 1974. *Politics:* "Left Libertarian." *Religion:* Roman Catholic. *Hobbies and other interests:* Books and writing, art, fashion, design, architecture, ecology, theology.

ADDRESSES: Home—755 South Crest Drive, Kelowna, British Columbia V1W4W7, Canada. *Office*—Department of English, Capilano College, 2055 Purcell, North Vancouver, British Columbia V7J 3H5, Canada. *E-mail*—sthesen@capcollege.bc.ca; sgthesen@telus.net.

CAREER: Educator and poet. Worked variously as a dental assistant, stenographer, cab driver, and record librarian in Canada, c. 1960s-70s; Capilano College, Vancouver, British Columbia, English instructor, 1975—.

MEMBER: Writers Union of Canada.

AWARDS, HONORS: Governor General's Literary Award, poetry, 1982, for *Selected Poems: The Vision Tree,* and nominee, 1984, 1987; BC 2000 Book Award, for *News and Smoke: Selected Poems*; Pat Lowther Memorial Award, 2001, for *A Pair of Scissors: Poems.*

WRITINGS:

POETRY

Artemis Hates Romance, Coach House Press (Toronto, Ontario, Canada), 1980.

Holding the Pose, Coach House Press (Toronto, Ontario, Canada), 1983.

Confabulations: Poems for Malcolm Lowry, Oolichan (Lantzville, British Columbia, Canada), 1984.

The Beginning of the Long Dash, Coach House Press (Toronto, Ontario, Canada), 1987.

The Pangs of Sunday, McClelland & Stewart (Toronto, Ontario, Canada), 1990.

Aurora, Coach House Press (Toronto, Ontario, Canada), 1995.

News and Smoke: Selected Poems, Talonbooks (Burnaby, British Columbia, Canada), 1999.

A Pair of Scissors: Poems, Anansi (Toronto, Ontario, Canada), 2000.

EDITOR

(And author of introduction) *Selected Poems: The Vision Tree,* by Phyllis Webb, Talonbooks (Vancouver, British Columbia, Canada), 1982.

The New Long Poem Anthology, Coach House Press (Toronto, Ontario, Canada), 1991, 2nd edition, Talonbooks (Vancouver, British Columbia, Canada), 2001.

(With Ralph Maud) *Charles Olson and Frances Boldereff: a Modern Correspondence,* University Press of New England (Lebanon, NH), 1999.

Contributor of poems to anthologies, including *Writing Right: Poetry by Canadian Women,* edited by Douglas Barbour and Marni L. Stanley, Longspoon Press (Edmonton, Alberta, Canada), 1982; *The Maple Laugh Forever: An Anthology of Comic Canadian Poetry,* edited by Douglas Barbour and Stephen Scobie, Hurtig, 1981; *The Oxford Book of Canadian Verse; Twenty Poets of the Eighties; Twentieth Century Poetry and Poetics,* 4th edition, edited by Gary Geddes; and *A Matter of Spirit,* edited by Susan McCaslin. Editor, *Iron,* 1966-71, and *Capilano Review,* 2002—.

SIDELIGHTS: In a critical review of *The New Long Poem Anthology,* edited by poet Sharon Thesen, Ann Diamond remarked in *Books in Canada* that she "was struck (again) by the Canadian preoccupation with 'emptiness,' 'uneventfulness,' and 'aloneness,' and by a certain earnest longwindedness in lyrically describing these states *ad infinitum.*" In the case of the poetry of Thesen, however, though there may be emptiness and aloneness, her world is hardly uneventful—nor is it dreary. "When I am writing and pause to think," Thesen once said, as quoted by Bruce Whitman in *Essays on Canadian Writing,* "the words I have already written have no history. . . . They are merely what went before, like the tracks of someone. They are signs, and they float, as it were, in an absolute present—a hall of mirrors in which I search for a true reflection or am amazed at the inventiveness of the distortions." Critics note that Thesen's poetry, which she has presented in a series of volumes beginning in the 1980s, has a similarly weightless and ineffable quality, mobile in its images and language, but far from insubstantial.

Thesen started out at Simon Fraser University in British Columbia, where she earned her M.A. with a thesis on Samuel Taylor Coleridge. She edited several literary publications, helped transcribe the works of other writers, and worked variously as a cab driver, record librarian, and dental assistant. Then, in 1980, she published *Artemis Hates Romance,* in which she complained (in "Usage") that "It's all been / said before, everyone knows that. / There are 31 stories, or 29, or 42, / everything is the same old story." Her line "31 . . . or 29 . . . or 42" stories seems to reflect on the universality of certain themes, and in "Jack and Jill" she explores some of the themes of failed and dysfunctional relationships, using as her vehicle two characters familiar to people in the English-speaking world from their earliest memories: "Jack fell down the hill / breaking his head on the stones of the earth / The stones of the earth / are the petrified heads of women / mouths agape." Judy Robinson, reviewing the collection for *Quill & Quire,* wrote that the poet's "gutsy approach to language is a challenge to experience the unexpected and frightening roles that may well be the future of man's interpersonal relations."

Clearly Thesen herself has plenty of stories in her, regardless of what she may have said in "Usage." She would later characterize her first three books as "mad," "sad," and "bad" in the *Malahat Review,* and *Artemis Hates Romance* certainly has anger in it, such as when she lashes at an ex-husband figure she refers to as "you slimy hogstool." Her emotions mellow into sadness in *Holding the Pose,* a quieter work; in *Confabulations: Poems for Malcolm Lowry,* "bad" might refer to the hell-scorched vision of her subject. Lowry, the troubled author of *Under the Volcano* and other works, spent his last days during the 1950s in Thesen's hometown of Vancouver, sometimes staring across the bay at a sign for Shell Oil with an *S* that on occasion did not get lighted—thus, he said, telling him where he was headed.

The implication of the title of *Confabulations* was that Thesen was trying to establish psychic identity with Lowry—something one reviewer pointed out might be a dangerous step to take. Further difficulty presents itself in the fact that, as Sherrill Grace observed in *Essays on Canadian Writing,* Thesen was far from the first to pay tribute to Lowry: before her there have been a string of writers beginning with Conrad Aiken (*Ushant*), as well as the filmmaker Donald Brittain, the visual artist Alberto Gironella, the actor Albert Finney (who starred in John Huston's 1986 film of *Under the Volcano*), the musician Graham Collier, and many others. Kathleen Moore in *Books in Canada*

held that Thesen had given it a good try without succeeding; but this book is not so much *about* Lowry as it is *for* him, as indicated in the title, and thus it was more difficult for critics to judge whether the author has achieved her objective. Through these poems, which—consistent with Thesen's underlying penchant to tell stories—together form a sort of biography of Lowry's soul, Thesen places the reader uncomfortably close to his pained reality. Using the Spanish word for "peeled," which Lowry had used in *Under the Volcano,* she writes: "Language the mask— /*pelado* — peeled— / now it takes me / up to a whole afternoon / to find the word / I need." With that mask of language pulled away, there is nothing but the solitary man in his haunted loneliness: "where I am it is dark."

With her next book, *The Beginning of the Long Dash,* Thesen turned to less heavy-hearted subjects. This time, in her words, she was "glad," and the title seems to indicate the anticipation preceding a race—though in fact it refers to the sound of the National Research Council Official Time Signal at the top of the hour on the radio in Vancouver. Nonetheless, the volume is full of a sense of anticipation—not necessarily all positive—of the future. In a witty indictment of modern life she writes, in the title poem, that "the five most compelling words / are *sex, free, cure, money,* and *baldness,* / a chain of conditions ranging from heaven to hell." Her poems critique the consumer culture— "there's nothing to eat / but images to hunger for"— but not in the usual well-worn and easy ways. In "Being Adults," for instance, there is "The doctor's BMW / etherized in the alley." Nor is she above having a little off-color fun, as in "The Landlord's Flower Beds," where a dog "gilds the landlord's tiger lilies" with a golden stream of urine.

Books in Canada reviewer Rosemary Sullivan noted Thesen's ability to create compelling titles, citing for example *The Pangs of Sunday;* another example is the title Thesen gave to her series of poems chronicling her time spent far away from home in Montreal: "Radio New France Radio." The meaning of the title *The Pangs of Sunday* comes from a line in *Northanger Abbey* by Jane Austen: after reminding the reader that she has already described the events of the preceding week in her characters' lives, Austen announces that "the pangs of Sunday only now remain to be described." As to why Thesen chose that title, few reviewers had much to say, but it seems to display her theme of moving toward the future, combined with a self-deprecating joke about what that future might hold for her and her work. Sullivan concluded a positive review of *The Pangs of Sunday* by citing Thesen's ability to retain readers' attention by (to use Sullivan's pun) keeping them "at-tension," looking inward, looking outward, looking forward and backward, but never allowing them to remain so complacent they do not see.

Among the other things about Thesen's career that *The Pangs of Sunday* shows is a sense of humor: in a poem from *Artemis Hates Romance* she notices that "Even the sky / looks like a 1955 social studies textbook / old & Atlantic / carrying bits of Nova Scotian / lake, the dust of Acadia." The persona in "Chicken in a Pensive Shell," preoccupied by matters other than this evening's dinner, finds herself confused: "I rest my case / on the kitchen counter where books / outnumber saucers & adjacent recipes / clash by night in pineapple shell / rowboats."

Susan Rudy Dorscht, reviewing Thesen's book alongside those of two others in *Essays on Canadian Writing,* found in *The Pangs of Sunday* the qualities that the other two works had promised but not delivered: "a self-consciously politicized poetry and a compositional strategy like that of jazz." As an example of an improvisational "jazz riff" in a Thesen poem, Dorscht quoted these lines: "The turning leaves / turn in a wind that rises / as if something warm, / invisible, and female just got up / from a nap and, half-dreaming, / walked to the kitchen / to make a cup of tea."

Five years after *The Pangs of Sunday* came *Aurora,* in 1995. Thesen proved in the title poem that, once again, she had a finger squarely on the pulse of modernity: "Everyone tied to phone or link. The risen cities / Of human splendor, cozy lounge, agencies, / Dog obedience school where two fall in love but there / Are complications not insurmountable. . . ." Jennifer Keene, in *Quill & Quire,* concluded that Thesen's "work is abidingly subtle and very moving." In contrast, Erin Moore, in *Books in Canada,* was ecstatic in her praise of the poet: "Reading *Aurora* reminds me fully of that first 'Thesen' experience," Moore wrote. "It is a book of gorgeous beauty, and it gives me those two things I crave: the familiar style of the beloved author, in this case the Thesen of wry whimsy and sadness . . . and, at the same time, a shift into new, sudden territory."

Thesen took a different literary path with the 1999 publication of *Charles Olson and Frances Boldereff: A*

Modern Correspondence. As coeditor with Ralph Maud, Thesen presented the three-year exchange of views between Boldereff, a typesetter, and Olson, author of *Call Me Ishmael,* a commentary on Herman Melville's *Moby Dick.* Boldereff had stumbled upon Olson's book while browsing the Melville section of her library, and was impressed enough to initiate correspondence with the writer who would go on to publish such classics as *The Kingfisher.* From 1947 to 1950, the letters between the two explored, among other topics, their mutual interest in poetry. The passages "include rehearsals of ideas and phrasing that later appear in [Olson's] essays and poems, as well as full drafts of essays and poems," according to *Mississippi Quarterly* reviewer Eleanor Berry. "They are copious and passionate, far-ranging in their concerns and references to readings, associative and sometime abrupt in their movements of thought, emphatically expressive their style, open . . . unconventional in syntax and punctuation—anticipating the characteristic prose style of [Olson's] essays."

Berry went on to say that one of the recurring themes of the letters was the state of American literature. Indeed, in the opening letter of the volume Boldereff praises *Call me Ishmael* as a "perfect book." "From the first," noted Berry, "Boldereff sees Olson as a writer with the capacity to redeem an America that has betrayed its promise. In an early letter she asks him to 'tell me about America—tell me how it is for you.'"

A *Seminary Co-Op Bookstore* reviewer called *Charles Olson and Frances Boldereff* "fascinating reading. . . . Here is Olson at the threshold of his career, still tentative, still feeling his way into his poetics . . . with someone equipped to understand him, sometimes better than he understood himself." The two maintained, through their letters and occasional face-to-face meetings, an intimate and complex bond, though both were married to others at the time. The two, according to Berry, "struggled to define the nature of their relationship, including the extent to which it depends on physical presence and sexual union. Immediately after their second meting, Olson writes her, 'The sense we are creating acts for men & women to come is very alive in me at the moment.'" Berry concluded that the correspondence makes "vivid the terrific difficulty faced by creative people in the United States of the mid-twentieth-century. . . . and will be of great value to those interested in matters of gender in postmodern American poetry."

Reviews of Thesen's works have generally been positive, except for occasional criticisms that she sometimes adopts a flippant tone in her first-person work. Overall, however, critics have found that her writing displays a deft precision of word and image. "Thesen moves through all our ordinary days making unusual, even startling connections," wrote Susan Schenk in *Contemporary Poets*. "Here is a poetry of careful observation, of precise statement; it challenges the way we see ourselves and see the world and ourselves in the world."

BIOGRAPHICAL AND CRITICAL SOURCES:

BOOKS

Contemporary Literary Criticism, Volume 56, Gale (Detroit, MI), 1989.
Contemporary Poets, St. James Press (Detroit, MI), 1996.

PERIODICALS

Books in Canada, March, 1985, p. 25; March, 1988, pp. 36-37; June-July, 1990, Rosemary Sullivan, review of *The Pangs of Sunday,* pp. 32-33; February, 1992, Ann Diamond, review of *The New Long Poem Anthology,* p. 53; September, 1995, Erin Moore, review of *Aurora,* pp. 31-32.
Canadian Book Review Annual, Volume 25, 2000, review of *News and Smoke: Selected Poems,* p. 214.
Canadian Forum, February, 1982, pp. 37-39; February, 1985, pp. 39-40.
Canadian Literature, spring, 2003, Ted Byrne, "The Genial Disconnects," pp. 191-192.
CM: A Reviewing Journal of Canadian Materials for Young People, July, 1990, p. 193.
Essays on Canadian Writing, summer, 1986, pp. 114-21; spring, 1987, pp. 18-23; spring, 1991, pp. 54-66; winter, 1992-93, pp. 48-54.
Globe and Mail (Toronto, Ontario, Canada), February 24, 2001, review of *News and Smoke,* p. D14.
Hungry Mind Review, spring, 1990, p. 44.
Mississippi Quarterly, spring, 2000, Eleanor Berry, review of *Charles Olson and Frances Boldereff: A Modern Correspondence,* p. 307.
Publishers Weekly, November 22, 1991, p. 48.

Quill & Quire, December, 1980, Judy Robinson, review of *Artemis Hates Romance,* p. 34; July, 1995, Jennifer Keene, review of *Aurora,* p. 52.
Resource Links, October, 2001, Ingrid Johnston, review of *A Pair of Scissors: Poems,* p. 58.
Sagetrieb, spring, 1988.

ONLINE

Danforth Review Web site, http://collection.nlc-bnc.ca/ (August 21, 2001), Aidan Baker, review of *News and Smoke.*
Seminary Co-Op Bookstore, http://www.semcoop.com/ (August 21, 2001), review of *Charles Olson and Frances Boldereff.*

*   *   *

THOMPSON, Emma 1959-

PERSONAL: Born April 15, 1959, in London, England; daughter of Eric (a director) and Phyllida (an actress) Thompson; married Kenneth Branagh (an actor, producer, and director), 1989 (divorced, 1994), companion of Greg Wise; children: one daughter, Gaia Romilly (with Wise). *Education:* Newnham College, Cambridge, studied English literature.

ADDRESSES: Agent—c/o Hamilton Asper Ltd., Ground Floor, 24 Hanway Street, London W1P 9DD, England.

CAREER: Actress for stage, television, and film. Began career as a performer with Cambridge University's Footlights revue. Stage appearances include *Me and My Girl,* 1985; *Look Back in Anger,* 1989; *A Midsummer Night's Dream,* 1990; and *King Lear,* 1990. Television appearances include *Fortunes of War,* 1988; "The Winslow Boy," 1990; *Cheers,* 1992; *Look Back in Anger,* 1993; "The Blue Boy," 1994; and *Wit,* 2001. Film appearances include *Henry V,* 1989; *The Tall Guy,* 1989; *Impromptu,* 1991; *Dead Again,* 1991; *Howard's End,* 1992; *Peter's Friends,* 1992; *Much Ado about Nothing,* 1993; *The Remains of the Day,* 1993; *In the Name of the Father,* 1993; *Junior,* 1995; *Carrington,* 1995; *Sense and Sensibility,* 1995; *The Winter Guest,* 1997; *Primary Colors,* 1998; *Judas Kiss,* 1998; *Maybe Baby,* 2000; *Treasure Planet,* 2002; and *Love Actually,* 2003.

Emma Thompson

MEMBER: Screen Actors Guild.

AWARDS, HONORS: British Academy of Film and Television Arts (BAFTA) Award for best actress, 1986, for *Fortunes of War;* New York Film Critics Circle Award for best actress, 1992, Academy Award for best actress, BAFTA Award for best actress, and Golden Globe Award for best actress in a drama, all 1993, all for *Howard's End;* Academy Award for best screenplay adaptation, 1995, for *Sense and Sensibility;* Humanitas Award for co-writing, 2001, for *Wit.*

WRITINGS:

Sense and Sensibility (screenplay; adapted from the novel by Jane Austen; Columbia, 1995), published in *The Sense and Sensibility Diaries and Screenplay: The Making of the Film Based on the Jane Austen Novel,* Newmarket Press (New York, NY), 1995.

Wit (teleplay), HBO Films, 2001.

SIDELIGHTS: Emma Thompson, a critically acclaimed and award-winning actress for film, stage, and television, wrote her first screenplay for Ang Lee's 1995 film adaptation of Jane Austen's classic novel *Sense and Sensibility,* in which Thompson also played the role of Elinor Dashwood. The Academy Award-winning screenplay, along with the journal Thompson kept during the production of the film, was published in 1995 as *The Sense and Sensibility Diaries and Screenplay: The Making of the Film Based on the Jane Austen Novel.* Stanley Kauffmann, in his *New Republic* review of the film, noted that Thompson "spent five years working intermittently on the script while she acted in seven films."

Remaining faithful to Austen's original story with only "very slight" alterations, Thompson's *Sense and Sensibility* screenplay "can easily be chided by maniacally zealous Austenites," observed Kauffmann, "but such folk probably should not go to films of Austen unless they want to sneer." Richard Schickel, writing for *Time,* found Thompson's adaptation "impeccable" and comparable to the romantic comedies of Frank Capra and Leo McCarey, adding that viewers "don't expect to find [this kind of joyous catharsis] in adaptations of classic literature" or "in modern movies." Dana Kennedy in *Entertainment Weekly* thought Thompson's adaptation "so crisp, merry, and timeless that it might inspire those who think of Austen as high school syllabus material to read the book." In his *Newsweek* review of the film, Jack Kroll called the screenplay "vigorous, faithful," and related Thompson's attitude toward critics who label Austen films as period pieces: "You don't think people are still concerned with marriage, money, romance, finding a partner? Jane Austen is a genius who appeals to any generation." Commenting on the actress's "restrained" performance in the role of Elinor, *New Yorker* cinema reviewer Terrence Rafferty remarked, "Thanks to Thompson's exertions—both as actress and screenwriter—the heroine's goodness never seems implausible, and Austen's quiet but insistent polemical fervor is never permitted to overtax the story's delicate comic structure." Janet Maslin summarized in her *New York Times* review of the film: "Thompson . . . proves as crisp and indispensably clever a screenwriter as she is a leading lady."

BIOGRAPHICAL AND CRITICAL SOURCES:

PERIODICALS

Entertainment Weekly, December 22, 1995, pp. 60-61.

New Republic, January 8, 1996, pp. 34-35.
Newsweek, December 18, 1995, pp. 66-68.
New Yorker, December 18, 1995, pp. 124-127.
New York Times, December 13, 1995, sec. C, pp. 15, 19.
People, February 12, 1996, pp. 38-39.
Time, December 18, 1995, pp. 72-74.*

*   *   *

TIBBETTS, John C(arter) 1946-
(Jack Ketch)

PERSONAL: Born October 6, 1946, in Leavenworth, KS; son of James C. (a printer) and Dorothy G. Tibbetts. *Education:* University of Kansas, B.A., 1969, M.A., 1975, Ph.D., 1979. *Hobbies and other interests:* Classical piano, collecting record albums and books (especially those by G. K. Chesterton and Robert Schumann), silent film (primarily those featuring Buster Keaton and Douglas Fairbanks, Sr.), illustrating for fantasy publications, American illustrators (Brandy-wine and Ash-Can schools), photography.

ADDRESSES: Home—1138 Indiana St., #1, Lawrence, KS 66044. *Office*—222 Oldfather Studios, Lawrence, KS 66045. *E-mail*—jtibbetts@ku.edu.

CAREER: KANU-FM Radio, Lawrence, KS, announcer, 1966-70; University of Kansas, Lawrence, instructor in film, 1973-78; Avila College, Kansas City, MO, instructor in film, beginning 1977. Freelance commercial artist. *Military service:* U.S. Army, Security Agency, German linguist, 1970-73.

MEMBER: Society of Cinema Studies, American Film Institute, National Film Society (member of board of governors).

WRITINGS:

(With James M. Welsh; self-illustrated) *His Majesty the American: The Cinema of Douglas Fairbanks, Sr.,* A. S. Barnes (South Brunswick, NJ), 1977.

(Editor) *Introduction to the Photoplay,* National Film Society (Shawnee Mission, KS), 1977.

The American Theatrical Film: Stages in Development, Bowling Green State University Press (Bowling Green, OH), 1985.

(Editor) *Dvorak in America, 1892-1895,* Amadeus Press (Portland, OR), 1993.

(With James M. Welsh) *The Encyclopedia of Novels into Film,* Facts on File (New York, NY), 1998.

(Editor, with James M. Welsh)*The Cinema of Tony Richardson: Essays and Interviews,* State University of New York Press (Albany, NY), 1999.

(With James M. Welsh) *Novels into Film: The Encyclopedia of Movies Adapted from Books,* Checkmark Books (New York, NY), 1999.

The Encyclopedia of Stage Plays into Film, Facts on File (New York, NY), 2001.

(With James M. Welsh) *The Encyclopedia of Filmmakers,* Facts on File (New York, NY), 2002.

(With James M. Welsh) *The Encyclopedia of Great Filmmakers,* Checkmark Books (New York, NY), 2002.

(With Chuck Berg and Tom Erskine) *The Encyclopedia of Orson Welles,* Facts on File (New York, NY), 2002.

(With James M. Welsh and Richard Vela) *Shakespeare into Film,* Checkmark Books (New York, NY), 2002.

Contributor of artwork and articles to film and literature journals. Editor (and contributor, sometimes under pseudonym Jack Ketch) of *American Classic Screen,* beginning 1977.

SIDELIGHTS: John C. Tibbetts is an author, educator, broadcaster, and pianist. He is an associate professor of film at the University of Kansas, and is the author or editor of several books on music and film.

In *Dvorak in America,* Tibbetts presents a collection of papers on the career of the composer Antonin Dvorak, focusing on the years he spent as director of the National Conservatory in New York from 1892 to 1895. In *Notes,* Thomas L. Riis wrote, "A potpourri of perspectives, it is a reader-friendly book, approachable by specialist and nonspecialist alike interested in exploring Dvorak's continuing impact."

Tibbetts and coauthor James M. Welsh, in *The Encyclopedia of Novels into Film,* describe 313 novels that have been adapted into film, as well as the films themselves. The authors also provide biographical sketches of selected authors, details of the novels' publication and of the films' production, and references for further reading.

In *The Encyclopedia of Stage Plays into Film,* Tibbetts and coauthor James M. Welsh provide a comprehensive work on stage plays that have been adapted into film. The volume is divided into three sections: Standard Dramatic Adaptations, Shakespearean Adaptations, and Musical Theatre Adaptations. Each entry includes a summary of the play, as well as a comparison to the film version. Photographs and line drawings bring notable performances to life, and lists of references for each play help readers locate critical comments about the plays and films.

Tibbetts studied art history, theater, photography, and film at the University of Kansas, and was the first person ever to earn an interdisciplinary Ph.D. from that institution. He has since hosted a television show in Kansas City, Missouri, and worked as a commentator for CBS Television and CNN. He is a regular contributor to the *Christian Science Monitor.*

Tibbetts once wrote: "Studying the rise of mass culture in the last century affords a fascinating glimpse into the ways people entertain themselves. Entertainment and art have so coalesced that they are at times quite indistinguishable, which challenges our own deeply rooted concepts of the nature of the art image as opposed to the mere transmission of information. The motion picture has always been for me an art form that pinwheels the observer off onto other tracks, historical, sociological, cultural, political, etc. It becomes *the* challenge to those aforementioned definitions of art and information. Thus it often confounds us to the extent that we are compelled to go further than the mere visual perception of a film; it becomes necessary to contemplate a different kind of literacy of the future—that of the image as well as the word.

"My own viewing experiences constitute a series of blinding encounters over the years, primarily with those events of *movement* and grand gesture, whether they be in my early years of viewing the films of Douglas Fairbanks and Buster Keaton, or, later, with the operatic works of Visconti and Ken Russell. These experiences have not been so very different from my other encounters with the important *writers* of my life—artists who also seemed to specialize in the leap-

ing gesture, the vibrant prose, and the imaginative vision. And I'm talking about the works of Charles Dickens, Ray Bradbury, G. K. Chesterton. Or take some of the composers who also are singularly self-propelled: Robert Schumann, Hector Berlioz, Carl Nielsen. Whether it's a film like Keaton's *Seven Chances,* Fairbanks's *The Gaucho,* or a book like Chesterton's *The Napoleon of Notting Hill,* or a composition like Schumann's *Davidsbundler Dances,* they all reveal the essentially modern predilection with flux and change, speed and device. These are art images that, as Strindberg noted in his preface to *A Dream Play,* constantly change, divide, and multiply.

"To enjoy and write about such things is to be caught up in this bewildering sense of constant shift. Each time I attempt to grapple with the aesthetic implications of the modern cultural image, it is like staking out a claim, albeit provisional, on an uncharted territory. Prospector-like, you work the territory, sifting and looking for the sensible and the significant. At times this is not easy, since our society is so flooded with mass-produced images to the extent that we are benumbed and desensitized. It is perhaps not so daring to write a book on mass marketers such as Doug Fairbanks and Max Steiner; it is not even so daring to attempt to delineate the social and cultural significances of such work; but it is a challenge to scan their work with a pretension toward calling it art. Indeed, it can be the height of pretention to apply aesthetic criteria toward it at all (and if so, whose criteria?).

"In the classes I have taught, I have found that the search for significance is itself problematic. Posit an interior meaning to *Hamlet* and no one can object to that act, but examine the films of Buster Keaton with an eye toward the twentieth century's preoccupation with man and machine, and eyes begin looking askance. We have refused to seriously examine our modern images for fear their entertainment values will diminish. My collaborator James Welsh and I tried to meet those fears with our book on Fairbanks. In a word, we both exerted the modern tendency to keep the bread buttered on both sides: to reveal an image's cultural and artistic significance, while firmly maintaining that image's role as entertainer.

"For me one of the nicest aspects of the above is that it enables one to creatively interpret modern images, whether they be visual, aural, or musical. There was once a time when the tenets of art seemed securely defined, as with the *Discourses* of Sir Joshua Reynolds late in the eighteenth century. Now we perhaps rarely admit of such definitions. Like the art images themselves, they are constantly subjected to fresh buffets, ongoing revisions, and new provisional definitions. To write about popular culture is, I think, to participate in this continual re-creation.

"So, while I continue to be entertained and delighted by the acrobatics of Fairbanks, the inner musings of Robert Schumann, the word-play of Chesterton, the baroque line of Visconti, etc., I am compelled at the same time to not let matters rest there. These things and others demand my own participation. So I write and will continue to write about that perplexing world of popular images all around me. And they are not images tucked away in a museum; they are clustered around us all, jostling for attention. What kind of attention we give them, and whether it will be an essentially enlightened attention, is a troubling issue. To feel that I am even on the road toward such resolution is enough justification for me.

"Perhaps it is more revealing than I care to admit to parenthetically note that my middle name is Carter. 'John Carter' was a fictional character from the wild imagination of Edgar Rice Burroughs. Carter was an earthling, a Confederate captain, who is miraculously transported to Mars. Through a series of books, he swashes and buckles away across the exotic landscapes, leaping with thirty-foot strides in the lesser gravity, on his way toward yet another rescue of his beloved princess, Deja Thoris. I grew up on these wonderful books, always conscious that my name had been given to me by Mr. Burroughs himself (and I have a letter from him to prove it). Perhaps that accounts for my seemingly innate tendencies to jump off roofs, over walls, and across streams whenever the chance affords itself. Maybe it even justifies the sense I often have of living in an exotic landscape peopled with creatures about whom I am constantly watchful. Certainly to wander among the popular images described above is in itself a visit to a strange planet that is curiously familiar but ultimately strange in its aspect."

BIOGRAPHICAL AND CRITICAL SOURCES:

PERIODICALS

American Reference Books Annual, 1999, review of *The Encyclopedia of Novels into Film,* p. 506.

Booklist, April 15, 1998, review of *The Encyclopedia of Novels into Film,* p. 1462.

Choice, December, 1993, review of *Dvorak in America, 1892-1895,* p. 614; June, 1998, review of *The Encyclopedia of Novels into Film,* p. 1682; December, 2001, review of *The Encyclopedia of Stage Plays into Film,* p. 662.

Entertainment Weekly, January 9, 1998, Megan Harlan, review of *The Encyclopedia of Novels into Film,* p. 64.

Library Journal, May 15, 1993, review of *Dvorak in America, 1892-1895,* p. 70; February 15, 1998, review of *The Encyclopedia of Novels into Film,* p. 134; June 1, 2002, Vivian Reed, review of *The Encyclopedia of Filmmakers,* p. 134.

Music and Letters, November, 1994, Karl Stapleton, review of *Dvorak in America, 1892-1895,* p. 622.

Notes, December, 1994, Thomas Riis, review of *Dvorak in America, 1892-1895,* p. 604.

Reference and Research Book News, May, 1998, review of *The Encyclopedia of Novels into Film,* p. 157; November, 2001, review of *The Encyclopedia of Stage Plays into Film,* p. 217.

Reference and User Services Quarterly, winter, 2001, Janell Carter, review of *The Encyclopedia of Stage Plays into Film,* p. 191.

School Library Journal, May, 1999, review of *The Encyclopedia of Novels into Film,* p. 162.

Young Adult Reference Book, September, 1998, p. 67.*

* * *

TIPTON, James (Sherwood) 1942-

PERSONAL: Born January 18, 1942, in Ashland, OH; son of James Robert (in business) and Ruth Loucetta (Burcher) Tipton; married Lynn Ellen Johnson (a teacher), September 5, 1965 (divorced); children: Jennifer Lynn, James Daniel. *Education:* Purdue University, B.A., 1964, M.A., 1968.

ADDRESSES: Home—1122 Aquarius Ave., Fruita, CO 81521. *E-mail*—jtpoet@aol.com.

CAREER: Kalamazoo College, Kalamazoo, MI, writer-in-residence, 1969-70; Alma College, Alma, MI, began as assistant professor, became associate professor of English, department chair and director of cultural affairs, 1970-83; stockbroker, 1983-94; High Desert

Honey Co., Glade Park, CO, owner and beekeeper, 1994—. Worked as investment consultant to Thomson, McKinnon & Kemper Securities, 1983-94. U.S. Department of Education, director of Young Michigan Writers project. Guest speaker at educational institutions, including Interlochen Arts Academy, Ohio State University, Adrian College, Western Michigan University, Bowling Green State University, and Poetry Center at San Francisco State University; presenter, Michigan Poetry in the Schools project.

MEMBER: Mesa County (CO) Friends of the Library.

AWARDS, HONORS: Bread Loaf scholar in poetry, 1969; grant from National Endowment for the Humanities, 1972; first prize, Birmingham, AL, Festival of the Arts, 1973, for story "Baby Jesus"; Michigan Council for the Arts grants, 1975, 1982; *The Giant Alphabet* named one of ten best poetry books of the year by *Bloomsbury Review*, 1987; Colorado Book Award in poetry, 1999, for *Letters from a Stranger: Poems.*

WRITINGS:

POETRY

Convent Pieces, Goliards Press, 1969.
Matters of Love, Cranium Press (San Francisco, CA), 1970.
Sentences, Cranium Press (San Francisco, CA), 1970.
Bittersweet, Cold Mountain Press (Austin, TX), 1975.
(Editor, with Herbert Scott and Conrad Hilberry, and contributor) *The Third Coast: Contemporary Michigan Poetry,* Wayne State University Press (Detroit, MI), 1976.
(Editor, with Robert Wegner, and contributor) *The Third Coast: Contemporary Michigan Fiction,* Wayne State University Press (Detroit, MI), 1982.
The Giant Alphabet, Leaping Mountain Press, 1987.
The Wizard of Is, Bread & Butter Press, 1995.
Letters from a Stranger: Poems, foreword by Isabel Allende, Conundrum Press (Crested Butte, CO), 1998.

Work anthologized in numerous publications, including *The Haiku Anthology,* Doubleday (New York, NY), 1974; *The Red Moon Anthology,* edited by Jim Kacian, Red Moon Press, 1998; *The Geography of Hope,* ed-

ited by David J. Rothman, Conundrum Press, 1998; *Bleeding Hearts,* edited by Michelle Lovric, Aurum (England), 1998, St. Martin's Press (New York, NY), 1999; and *Intimate Kisses: The Poetry of Sexual Pleasure,* edited by Wendy Maltz, New World Library (New York, NY), 2001. Contributor of poetry, short stories, translations, and reviews to literary journals and magazines, including *Crazy Horse, Satire Newsletter, Greenfield Review, American Tanka, Nation, Esquire, South Dakota Review, Carolina Quarterly, Contemporary Poetry,* and *Southern Humanities Review.*

*   *   *

TUCCI, Stanley 1960-

PERSONAL: Born November 11, 1960, in Peekskill (some sources say Katonah), NY; son of Stanley (a teacher) and Joan Tucci; married, April, 1995; wife's name Kate (a social worker); children: one son and one daughter (twins), two stepchildren. *Education:* Attended State University of New York at Purchase. *Hobbies and other interests:* Painting.

ADDRESSES: Office—First COID Press Productions, c/o Rysher Entertainment, 885 Second Ave., 30th Fl., New York, NY 10017. *Agent*—David Yocum, William Morris Agency, 151 South El Camino Drive, Beverly Hills, CA 90212-2775.

CAREER: Actor, director, and screenwriter. Director (with Campbell Scott), *Big Night,* Samuel Goldwyn, 1996; director and producer, *The Imposters* (also known as *Ship of Fools*), Twentieth Century-Fox, 1998; director and producer, *Joe Gould's Secret,* USA Films, 2000; executive producer, *The Mudge Boy,* 2003. Actor in films, including *Prizzi's Honor,* Twentieth Century-Fox, 1985; *Who's That Girl,* Warner Bros., 1987; *Monkey Shines: An Experiment in Fear* (also known as *Ella*), Orion, 1988; *Slaves of New York,* 1989; *The Feud,* 1989; *Quick Change,* 1990; *Men of Respect,* Central City, 1991; *Billy Bathgate,* Warner Bros., 1991; *The Public Eye,* Universal, 1992; *Beethoven,* Universal, 1992; *Prelude to a Kiss,* Twentieth Century-Fox, 1992; *In the Soup,* Cacous Films, 1992; *Undercover Blues* (also known as *Cloak and Diaper*), Metro-Goldwyn-Mayer, 1993; *The Pelican Brief,* Warner Bros., 1993; *Somebody to Love,* Initial/ Lumiere, 1994; *It Could Happen to You,* Tristar, 1994;

Stanley Tucci

Mrs. Parker and the Vicious Circle (also known as *Mrs. Parker and the Round Table*), Fine Line, 1994; *A Modern Affair* (also known as *Mr #247*), Nick of Time, 1995; *Captive* (also known as *Sex and the Other Man*) River One, 1995; *Jury Duty*, Tristar, 1995; *Kiss of Death*, Twentieth Century-Fox, 1995; *The Day Trippers*, Cine 360, 1996; (also director and screenwriter) *Big Night*, Samuel Goldwyn, 1996; *Montana*, 1997; *Life during Wartime*, 1997; *The Eighteenth Angel*, Rysher, 1997; *Deconstructing Harry*, Fine Line, 1997; *A Life Less Ordinary*, Twentieth Century-Fox, 1997; *Winchell*, HBO, 1998; (also director and producer) *The Imposters* (also known as *Ship of Fools*), Twentieth Century-Fox, 1998; and *A Midsummer Night's Dream*, Fox Searchlight, 1999; *Joe Gould's Secret*, USA Films, 2000; *Sidewalks of New York*, 2001, *America's Sweethearts*, 2001; *Road to Perdition*, 2002; *Maid in Manhattan*, 2002, *Big Trouble*, 2002, *The Core*, 2003, and *Robots*, 2005. Also appeared in *The Gun in Betty Lou's Handbag, Fear, Anxiety, and Depression*, and *Blaze*. Actor in television series, including *Crime Story*, NBC; *Miami Vice*, NBC; *The Equal-*

izer, CBS; *The Street*, syndicated; *Wiseguy*, CBS; *Thirtysomething*, ABC; *Revealing Evidence*, NBC; *Equal Justice*, ABC; *Lifestories*, NBC; *Urban Anxiety*, Fox; and *Murder One*, ABC. Actor on stage in Broadway productions, including *Execution of Justice, The Iceman Cometh, Brighton Beach Memoirs, The Misanthrope, The Queen of the Rebels*, and *Frankie and Johnny in the Clair de Lune;* appeared in off-Broadway productions, including *Scapin, Moon over Miami, Dalliance, Balm in Gilead, A Worker's Life, Merchant of Venice*, and *Romeo and Juliet.*

MEMBER: National Italian American Foundation.

AWARDS, HONORS: Emmy nomination for Outstanding Supporting Actor in a Drama Series, and Q Award for Best Supporting Actor in a Quality Drama Series, both 1996, both for role as Richard Cross on *Murder One;* Grand Special Prize nomination (with Campbell Scott), Deauville Film Festival Best First Film award (with Scott), New York Film Critics Circle Waldo Salt Screenwriting Award (with Joseph Tropiano), Sundance Film Festival Independent Spirit Award for Best First Screenplay (with Tropiano), Independent Spirit Award nominations for Best First Feature and Best Male Lead, National Board of Review Recognition of Excellence (with Scott), and Boston Society of Film Critics Best Screenplay and Best Director awards, all 1996, all for *Big Night; The Imposters* chosen as an official selection, Cannes Film Festival, 1998.

WRITINGS:

SCREENPLAYS

(With Joseph Tropiano) *Big Night*, Samuel Goldwyn, 1996.
The Imposters (also known as *Ship of Fools*), Twentieth Century-Fox, 1998.
(With Howard Rodman) *Joe Gould's Secret*, USA Films, 2000.

OTHER

(With Joan Tucci, Gianni Scappin, and Mimi Shanley Taft) *Cucina and Famiglia: Two Italian Families Share Their Stories, Recipes, and Traditions*, William Morrow (New York, NY), 1999.

SIDELIGHTS: Character actor Stanley Tucci grabbed the attention of the film industry when he cowrote, codirected, and costarred in the 1996 independent film *Big Night.* As Tucci explained in a *New York Times Magazine* article, he was tired of playing "the heavy—if not a goombah then some other kind of ethnic thug." So Tucci decided to write his own part—a leading part—and to direct his own film with the help of friends and relatives. His cousin, Joseph Tropiano, was his collaborator on the screenplay and actor Campbell Scott—Tucci's friend since high school—shared the job of directing the film. Describing *Big Night* in the *New York Times Magazine,* Eric Konigsberg wrote, "The film is whimsical, sentimental in places and deliberately paced. It is actor driven, in more ways than one: its appeal has as much to do with performance as with plot." As such, the four-million-dollar film was something of an anomaly but it nevertheless earned the admiration of many critics and movie-goers. The screenplay won Tucci and Tropiano several awards, including one from the Sundance Film Festival and another from the New York Film Critics Circle.

Big Night is the story of two brothers who immigrate to New Jersey from Italy during the 1950s. They open a small restaurant where the older brother, Primo, is the cook and the younger, Secundo, is the manager and host. The authentic, lovingly cooked food served by the restaurant goes unappreciated by its few customers and the brothers risk losing the business. A fellow Italian restaurateur—a man who has no culinary ethics but is hugely successful—promises to give the brothers a break by sending the famous singer Louis Prima to their restaurant for dinner, an event that is to be their "Big Night."

The autobiographical elements in *Big Night* were evident to Konigsberg when he visited with Tucci in his parents' home. His mother, Joan Tucci, threatened to defrost the last remaining timpano—a huge torte filled with a variety of ingredients—that she helped prepare for use in the film. Tucci so loves food that he became part owner of the Finch Tavern, in Westchester County, New York, near his home.

All of Tucci's various contributions to the film were commended. His performance as a director and as the character of Secundo—opposite Tony Shaloub's Primo—caused Terrence Rafferty to comment in the *New Yorker* that Tucci "has shaped the story into some-thing that functions as both a demonstration and a vindication of the sort of subtle, finely detailed character acting that he and Tony Shaloub have practiced in relative obscurity throughout their careers." Regarding Tucci's screenwriting efforts, Konigsberg remarked in the *New York Times Magazine,* "Tucci's strength as a screenwriter is his understanding that articulateness is a luxury of the confident; that most conversation is spilled in awkward rhythms and incomplete sentences. . . . meaning in *Big Night* is to be found in the blank spaces between what is said." And on a more general note, John Simon, in the *National Review,* wrote, "Even when the film runs out of steam, it maintains density of feeling: where it fails as art, it remains recognizable as life. And when it is derivative—as in the ridiculous nocturnal fight on the beach, which is pure Fellini—it borrows from the best sources, effectively."

Following *Big Night*'s release, Tucci began work on another film, a comedy titled *The Imposters* (originally titled *Ship of Fools*). This film starred actors from Tucci's personal group of friends, including Aidan Quinn, Elizabeth Bracco, Isabella Rossellini, Lili Taylor, Oliver Platt, Campbell Scott, and Steven Buscemi. The film, set aboard a cruise ship in the 1930s, featured two unsuccessful actors on the run after publicly embarrassing a well-known actor. After accidentally stowing away on the same ship as the actor they had criticized, the duo's attempts to avoid him lead them into a variety of strange circumstances and secrets in which their acting abilities are ultimately tested. Although *The Imposters* met with less critical and public acclaim, a reviewer in the *Wallflower Critical Guide* called it an "ambitious and valiant effort to recreate . . . classic screwball comedy." Jeff Giles of *Newsweek* wrote that the film "begins wonderfully but drifts farther and farther out to sea." Even though the *The Imposters* was not a commercial or critical success, through it Tucci clearly demonstrates his skills as a gifted actor, one reviewer noted.

Tucci's 2000 film, *Joe Gould's Secret,* is based on the life of bohemian Joe Gould. Born to a wealthy Bostonian family and educated at Harvard University, Gould rejected what was expected of him and became essentially a vagrant, while recording what he called "An Oral History of the United States." Gould met Joseph Mitchell by chance at a New York diner and the two struck up a friendship. Eventually, the relationship faded and Mitchell wrote two articles about Gould for the *New Yorker.*

While, like *The Imposters, Joe Gould's Secret* did not have the same box-office success as *Big Night,* Tucci nonetheless earned praise for his role as director and actor. Stuart Klawans in the *Nation* wrote: "Sleek and long-faced, Tucci carries himself down to [the dive bars of New York] with a slightly stiff modesty and emerges with decorum." Reviewing the film for the *Los Angeles Times,* Kenneth Turan called *Joe Gould's Secret* "a marvel of subtlety and restraint set in a carefully re-created 1940s and '50s Manhattan."

BIOGRAPHICAL AND CRITICAL SOURCES:

PERIODICALS

Cosmopolitan, April, 1995, p. 44; October, 1996, p. 120.

Detroit News, September 23, 1996.

Entertainment Weekly, April 21, 1995, pp. 36, 40; September 15, 1995, p. 92; September 20, 1996, pp. 20, 49; October 18, 1996, p. 92; December 27, 1996, p. 42; March 7, 1997, p. 17; April 25, 1997, p. 80.

Los Angeles Times, January 21, 2001, p. F1.

Nation, March 31, 1997, p. 35; April 24, 2000, p. 42.

National Catholic Reporter, November 8, 1996, p. 13; April 25, 1997, p. 14.

National Review, June 12, 1995, p. 71; December 9, 1996, pp. 65-66; June 2, 1997, p. 56.

Newsweek, April 11, 1988, p. 89; February 12, 1996, p. 81; March 31, 1997, p. 75.

New York, April 24, 1995, p. 68; September 25, 1995, p. 116; October 28, 1996, p. 124; April 21, 1997, p. 52.

New Yorker, December 11, 1989, p. 136; July 30, 1990, p. 78; October 19, 1992, p. 109; May 1, 1995, p. 93; September 23, 1996, pp. 100-103; March 24, 1997, p. 85.

New York Times Magazine, September 8, 1996, pp. 60-62.

People Weekly, August 1, 1988, p. 19; April 24, 1995, p. 18; October 2, 1995, p. 18; January 22, 1996, p. 57; October 7, 1996, p. 19.

Rolling Stone, May 4, 1995, p. 73; October 3, 1996, p. 78.

Time, May 1, 1995, p. 84; September 23, 1996, p. 72.

USA Weekend, December 5-7, 1997.

Variety, September 14, 1992, p. 50; January 25, 1993, p. 140; September 20, 1993, p. 27; October 24, 1994, p. 69.

Vogue, June 6, 1990, p. 46; September, 1996, p. 362; October, 1996, p. 212; February, 1997, p. 140.

ONLINE

Fox Searchlight, http://www.foxsearchlight.com/ (1998).*

U

UNSWORTH, Barry (Forster) 1930-

PERSONAL: Born August 10, 1930, in Durham, England; son of Michael (an insurance salesman) and Elsie (Forster) Unsworth; married Valerie Moor, May 15, 1959; children: Madeleine, Tania, Thomasina. *Education:* University of Manchester, B.A. (with honors), 1951.

ADDRESSES: Home—Umbria, Italy. *Agent*—Giles Gordon, Anthony Sheil Associates, Lauranpolku 1A 35, 01360 Vantaa 36, Finland.

CAREER: Norwood Technical College, London, England, lecturer in English, 1960; University of Athens, Athens, Greece, lecturer in English for British Council, 1960-63; Norwood Technical College, lecturer in English, 1963-65; University of Istanbul, Istanbul, Turkey, lecturer in English for British Council, beginning 1965; writer in residence, Liverpool University, 1984-85, and Lund University, Sweden, 1988; teacher at the University of Iowa's Writers' Workshop, 1999. *Military service:* British Army, Royal Corps of Signals, 1951-53, became second lieutenant.

MEMBER: Royal Society of Literature (fellow).

AWARDS, HONORS: Heinemann Award for Literature, Royal Society of Literature, 1974, for *Mooncrankers Gift;* Arts Council Creative Writing fellowship, Charlotte Mason College, Ambleside, Cumbria, 1978-79; Literary fellow, Universities of Durham and Newcastle, 1983-84; Booker Prize (joint winner), 1992, for *Sacred Hunger;* Litt.D., Manchester University, 1998.

Barry Unsworth

WRITINGS:

NOVELS

The Partnership, Hutchinson (London, England), 1966, Norton (New York, NY), 2001.
The Greeks Have a Word for It, Hutchinson (London, England), 1967.

417

The Hide, Gollancz (London, England), 1970, Norton (New York, NY), 1996.

Mooncrankers Gift, Allen Lane (London, England), 1973, Houghton Mifflin (Boston, MA), 1974.

The Big Day, M. Joseph (London, England), 1976, Mason/Charter (New York, NY), 1977.

Pascalis Island, M. Joseph (London, England), 1980, published as *The Idol Hunter,* Simon & Schuster (New York, NY), 1980.

The Rage of the Vulture, Granada (London, England), 1982, Houghton Mifflin (Boston, MA), 1983.

Stone Virgin, Hamish Hamilton (London, England), 1985, Houghton Mifflin (Boston, MA), 1986.

Sugar and Rum, Hamish Hamilton (London, England), 1988.

Sacred Hunger, Doubleday/Nan A. Talese (New York, NY), 1992.

Morality Play, Doubleday/Nan A. Talese (New York, NY), 1995.

After Hannibal, Hamish Hamilton (London, England), 1996, published as *Umbrian Mosaic,* Nan A. Talese (New York, NY), 1997.

Losing Nelson, Nan A. Talese (New York, NY), 1999.

The Songs of the Kings, Hamish Hamilton (London, England), 2002, Nan A. Talese (New York, NY), 2003.

Crete, National Geographic (Washington, DC), 2004.

OTHER

(With John Lennox Cook and Amorey Gethin) *The Students Book of English: A Complete Coursebook and Grammar to Advanced Intermediate Level,* Blackwell (Oxford, England), 1981.

Novels and Novelists in the 1990's, Random House (London, England), 1993.

Also author of television play, *The Stick Insect,* 1975.

ADAPTATIONS: A film adaptation of *Pascalis Island* was handled by Avenue Entertainment.

SIDELIGHTS: Barry Unsworth's novels have garnered him wide critical acclaim and recognition as one of the finest historical novelists writing in English. "Unsworth has explored his stated interest in 'moral complexities and ambiguities' in a wide variety of genres and settings," according to William F. Naufftus in the *Dictionary of Literary Biography.* "Several of his

books have been primarily comic or have mixed serious moral messages and tragic story lines with comic material. Half of his novels have been set, entirely or primarily, in Greece, Turkey, or Italy, often developing plotlines concerned with murder or political intrigue. Perhaps most significantly, he has participated in the recent rebirth of the British historical novel, dealing with periods as different as the late Middle Ages, the eighteenth century, and the last days of the Ottoman Empire but always providing messages clearly intended for modern times. The moral content of these messages often deals with the dangers posed to individuals by their own obsessive behavior. Another preoccupation of his work has been a broadly political concern for the fate of helpless 'subaltern' people (individuals or races) at the mercy of brutal power." Winner of Britain's prestigious Booker Prize in 1992, Unsworth has time-traveled in his fiction to such places as turn-of-the-century Constantinople in *The Rage of the Vulture,* to Renaissance Venice in *Stone Virgin,* to an eighteenth-century slave ship in *Sacred Hunger,* and to fourteenth-century Yorkshire in *Morality Play.* Amy Gamerman, interviewing Unsworth for the *Wall Street Journal,* found that "few contemporary writers have been as bold in mining history's provocative recesses for their fiction." Though Unsworth has been well regarded in England since the 1970s, it is only with his more recent novels that he has won international acclaim.

Sugar and Rum, published in 1988, is the story of a writer blocked in his attempts to write an historical novel on the slave trade. Unsworth's research for this novel led to his next work, as he explained in a *Wall Street Journal* interview: "I thought—well, couldn't I maybe do the novel that he was blocked about." The result was *Sacred Hunger. Sacred Hunger*'s central character is one Matthew Paris, a doctor who signs on as ship's surgeon on the maiden voyage of his uncle's slave-trading ship. The ship is captained by a man Paris describes as "an incarnation, really, of the profit motive," a man who throws a group of sick passengers—bound for sale into slavery—overboard because while there is no market for sick slaves, there is insurance compensation for lost cargo. The slaves and crew, partly at Paris's instigation, mutiny, killing the captain and setting up a would-be utopia in Florida where blacks and whites live, ostensibly, as equals. This paradise is itself eventually brought to ruin by the "sacred hunger" for money and power.

Critics have widely praised *Sacred Hunger*'s moral and philosophic aims and import. In the *Times Liter-*

ary Supplement, Mark Sanderson wrote that the author is, in this and other of his novels, "concerned with nothing less than the fall of man." He also stated that "the concepts of justice, liberty and duty are debated through the medium of a genuinely exciting historical adventure." Several critics, such as Adam Bradbury, writing in the *London Review of Books,* believed Unsworth's themes to be a commentary upon contemporary times: "It is hard to escape the impression that Unsworth is talking about the economic miracle with which we are supposed to have been blessed in the Eighties. But he is going further, chipping away at the fundamentals of capital trade with the question gradually emerging: would man, free and happy in a state of nature, still seek to accumulate wealth by enslaving others? Don't know, is the resounding reply."

Unsworth's next novel, *Morality Play,* concerns a young monk-errant in fourteenth- century England who joins a traveling troupe of actors. When the troupe's stock morality play, the "Play of Adam," fails to draw paying crowds, they decide to make current events—the murder of a local boy—the focus of the onstage drama. "It has been in my mind for years now that we can make plays from stories that happen in our lives," says the troupe's leader. "I believe this is the way that plays will be made in the times to come." Their choice thus prefigures the evolution of modern western drama.

At least one critic, Marc Romano writing for the *Boston Review,* found his credulity stretched too far by this novelistic strategy. "The historical shift from morality plays based on stock figures," Romano stated, "to modern drama based on psychological realism was a qualitative leap. . . . Psychological realism . . . asks its audience to draw its own conclusions. . . . That, in the end, *Morality Play* never manages to do—it is determined to tell modern readers about the history of drama, . . . even at the expense of its own credibility as a historical novel." Yet the *Los Angeles Times Book Review*'s critic, Charles Nicholl, had a more sanguine take on Unsworth's narrative intent. He contrasted the inn-yard stage with the jousts taking place on the feudal manor, where "knights and ladies play their parts in a performance that reinforces the hierarchies and assumptions of feudal society." "The play," Nicholl wrote, "does something different: it questions and explores, and . . . creates an area of comment and debate." Nicholl argued that Unsworth's intent in recapitulating the evolution of theatrical mod-

ernism is to tell a story "about the capacity of art . . . to create new meanings, and thereby new possibilities, in the lives of its audience."

Critics have taken particular note of Unsworth's historical evocation of the earthy, impoverished atmosphere in which much of *Morality Play* is staged, his "wintry scenes, hard-bitten lives etched against a background of frost and snow . . . the presence of hunger and plague; the daily oppression of feudal society," to quote Nicholl. And though Romano believed that the author "has the misfortune . . . of using history as a device rather than recreating it," Janet Burroway, in the *New York Times Book Review,* praised his subtlety in this regard: "Mr. Unsworth has the art to enter the sensibility of a period—its attitudes, assumptions and turns of phrase—so convincingly that he is able to suggest subtle yet essential parallels between an earlier era and our own."

In *Losing Nelson* Unsworth tells of Charles Cleasby, a Londoner with an overwhelming obsession with England's greatest naval hero, Lord Horatio Nelson. Cleasby enjoys reenacting Nelson's victorious battles using model ships in his basement and celebrates key days in Nelson's career as personal holidays. He also believes himself to be somehow psychologically "joined" to the eighteenth-century admiral. As Cleasby writes a biography of his hero, the lives of the two men become oddly entwined. "Paragraph by paragraph, Cleasby's sense of self shifts and dissolves," according to a critic for *Publishers Weekly.* "As he imagines Nelson's life," Ed Peaco wrote in the *Antioch Review,* "the novel sprouts an intensely dramatized parallel narrative—exciting sea battles, intriguing diplomacy, an alluring illicit affair." Edward B. St. John, reviewing the novel for *Library Journal,* believed that "Unsworth is in complete control of his material, effortlessly sustaining an almost unbearable level of tension that is suddenly resolved in an unusually effective surprise ending." Peaco found that "the ending is both ugly and beautiful, horrific yet strangely entertaining." Peter Bien in *World Literature Today* called *Losing Nelson* "a brilliant historical novel" and "a fascinating read both psychologically and historically, one that questions the very authenticity of history."

Speaking to Anson Lang of *BoldType Magazine,* Unsworth explained that he wrote *Losing Nelson* after trying to write a biography of the naval hero: "I was supposed to do a biography of Nelson. I was invited to do it, but I thought it was going to be too difficult. At least, living in rural Italy, there wasn't very good access to libraries or research facilities. And then, Nelson is a much-biographied figure. There have been about 200 biographies already. So there wasn't much prospect of doing something new in that way. In the end, I changed it into a Nelson novel."

In spite of his success as a novelist, Unsworth, in the *Wall Street Journal* interview, expressed a writer's dissatisfaction with his finished product: "The idea is so radiant and the conception so exciting, and somewhere the shadow falls between the idea and the execution. . . . I always feel that I did the best I could, I just didn't do proper justice to it." Unsworth's critics have tended to be less harsh. Writing in the *Pittsburgh Post-Gazette*, Bob Hoover maintained that "Unsworth is a hypnotic writer whose prose quietly snares the reader into a fully realized world." The London *Observer*'s Jonathan Keates, writing specifically of *Stone Virgin*, summed up the tenor of general critical response to Unsworth's recent novels: "The cumulative effect of such consistently sound storytelling is to remind us of an almost vanished art, to which Unsworth holds the enviable key."

BIOGRAPHICAL AND CRITICAL SOURCES:

BOOKS

Dictionary of Literary Biography, Volume 194: *British Novelists since 1960, Second Series,* Gale (Detroit, MI), 1998.

PERIODICALS

Antioch Review, spring, 2000, Ed Peaco, review of *Losing Nelson,* p. 241.
Atlanta Journal and Constitution, October 11, 1992, p. K13.
Book, March-April, 2003, Tom LeClair, review of *The Songs of the Kings,* p. 77.
Booklist, February 15, 2003, Brad Hooper, review of *The Songs of the Kings,* p. 1051.
Books, March, 1990, p. 21; March, 1992, p. 5; November, 1992, p. 18; January, 1993, pp. 15, 21.
Books and Bookmen, October, 1986, p. 37.

Book World, September 13, 1992, p. 2; November 1, 1992, p. 15; November 28, 1993, p. 12.
Boston Globe, August 9, 1992, p. B38.
Boston Review, February-March, 1996, p. 34.
British Book News, October, 1985, p. 624.
Chicago Tribune, August 9, 1992, p. 1.
Contemporary Review, October, 1985, p. 213; July, 1992, p. 43.
Kirkus Reviews, January 15, 1986, p. 88; May 15, 1992, p. 636; January 1, 2003, review of *The Songs of the Kings,* p. 24.
Library Journal, March 1, 1986, p. 110; July, 1992, p. 130; October 15, 1999, Edward B. St. John, review of *Losing Nelson,* p. 109; July, 2001, Caroline M. Hallsworth, review of *The Partnership,* p. 126.
Listener, September 19, 1985, p. 28; December 1, 1988, p. 33.
London Review of Books, June 11, 1992, p. 27.
Los Angeles Times Book Review, August 2, 1992, p. 3; November 12, 1995, p. 2.
New Criterion, May, 2000, Brooke Allen, "Meditations, Good and Bad," p. 63.
New Statesman, August 15, 1985, p. 28; August 8, 1986, p. 29.
New Statesman & Society, February 28, 1992, p. 45; October 16, 1992, Janet Barron, review of *Sacred Hunger,* p. 41.
Newsweek, January 28, 1983.
New Yorker, May 26, 1986, p. 106.
New York Times, November 20, 1980; February 7, 1983; December 23, 1992, p. C15.
New York Times Book Review, January 11, 1981; March 13, 1983; April 6, 1986, p. 27; August 28, 1988, p. 32; July 19, 1992, Thomas Flanagan, review of *Sacred Hunger,* p. 3, Susannah Hunnewell, "Utopia Then and Now," p. 23; December 12, 1993, p. 36; June 5, 1994, p. 60; November 12, 1995, Janet Burroway, review of *Morality Play,* p. 11; August 12, 2001, Tom Gilling, review of *The Partnership,* p. 13.
Observer (London, England), July 21, 1985, p. 22; July 27, 1986, p. 23; September 18, 1988, p. 43; September 13, 1992, p. 55; October 18, 1992, p. 59; November 22, 1992, p. 64; March 31, 1993, p. 62; May 30, 1993, p. 62.
Pittsburgh Post-Gazette, November 7, 1999, Bob Hoover, review of *Losing Nelson.*
Publishers Weekly, January 31, 1986, p. 363; May 11, 1992, p. 52; May 22, 1995, p. 55; August 21, 1995, p. 43; November 6, 1995, p. 60; August 23, 1999, review of *Losing Nelson,* p. 42; November 1,

1999, review of *Losing Nelson,* p. 47; June 25, 2001, review of *The Partnership,* p. 44; February 17, 2003, review of *The Songs of the Kings,* p. 57.

Punch, August 13, 1986, p. 45.

Spectator, August 24, 1985, p. 25; November 21, 1992, pp. 42-43; September 23, 1995, Harry Mount, review of *Morality Play;* August 24, 1996, review of *After Hannibal;* September 21, 2002, Penelope Lively, review of *The Songs of the Kings,* p. 47.

Stand, spring, 1990, p. 75.

Times (London, England), June 19, 1980; July 25, 1985; June 11, 1992, p. 4.

Times Educational Supplement, October 7, 1988, p. 34; April 3, 1992, p. 32.

Times Literary Supplement, August 30, 1985, p. 946; September 16, 1988, p. 1014; February 28, 1992, p. 23; September 8, 1995, Bernard O'Donoghue, review of *Morality Play.*

Tribune Books (Chicago, IL), August 9, 1992, p. 1; December 6, 1992, p. 13; November 14, 1993, p. 8.

USA Today, December 7, 1992, p. D6.

Wall Street Journal, December 5, 1995, p. A16.

Washington Post, January 24, 1981; September 13, 1992; October 14, 1992, p. C2.

Washington Post Book World, April 3, 1983.

World Literature Today, summer, 2000, Peter Bien, review of *Losing Nelson,* p. 598.

ONLINE

Bold Type Magazine, http://www.randomhouse.com/boldtype/ (October, 1999), Anson Lang, "Interview with Barry Unsworth."

Contemporary Writers Web site, http://www.contemporarywriters.com/ (January 18, 2003).

Salon.com, http://www.salon.com/ (May 28, 1999), Marion Lignana Rosenberg, review of *Sugar and Rum.**

*   *   *

URMUZ
See CODRESCU, Andrei

V

VERA, Yvonne 1964-

PERSONAL: Born September 19, 1964, in Bulawayo, Zimbabwe (then Southern Rhodesia); mother was a schoolteacher. *Education:* York University, B.A., M.A., Ph.D., 1995. *Hobbies and other interests:* Photography, film.

ADDRESSES: Office—National Gallery, Box 1993, Bulawayo, Zimbabwe. *Agent*—c/o Baobab Books, P.O. Box 1559, Harare, Zimbabwe. *E-mail*—sabona@ telconet.co.zw.

CAREER: Writer. Regional director of National Gallery of Zimbabwe, 1997—.

AWARDS, HONORS: Second Prize, Zimbabwean Publishers Literary Award for Fiction in English and special mention, Commonwealth Writers Prize for Africa Region, both 1994, both for *Nehanda;* Zimbabwean Publishers Literary Award for Fiction in English, Zimbabwean Book Publishers Association, 1995, for *Without a Name;* Commonwealth Writers Prize for Africa Region, 1997, and "The Voice of Africa" Swedish Literary Award, 1997, both for *Under the Tongue.*

WRITINGS:

Why Don't You Carve Other Animals (short stories), TSAR Publications (Toronto, Ontario, Canada), 1992.
Nehanda, Baobab (Harare, Zimbabwe), 1993.

Without a Name, Baobab (Harare, Zimbabwe), 1994, published as *Without a Name and Under the Tongue,* Farrar, Straus & Giroux, (New York, NY), 2002.
Under the Tongue, Baobab (Harare, Zimbabwe), 1997, published as *Without a Name and Under the Tongue,* Farrar, Straus & Giroux, (New York, NY), 2002.
Butterfly Burning, Baobab Books (Harare, Zimbabwe), 1998, Farrar, Straus & Giroux (New York, NY), 2000.
(Editor) *Opening Spaces: An Anthology of Contemporary African Women's Writings,* Heinemann (Portsmouth, NH), 1999.
The Stone Virgins, Farrar, Straus & Giroux (New York, NY), 2003.

SIDELIGHTS: Yvonne Vera is a Zimbabwean writer who has won acclaim for her fiction. She grew up in Bulawayo, one of the largest cities in Zimbabwe (then Rhodesia), and began writing as child. Educated at York University in Canada, she made the decision to move back to her hometown, where she accepted a position as director of Bulawayo's National Gallery. "I have always loved Bulawayo in a complete manner," she told *World and I* reviewer Charles R. Larson; "I hope to continue in this small town, with its gentle and unhurried pace." Vera's books, set in Zimbabwe, often address controversial issues pertaining to African women. "To the extent that women still experience the highest degree of social pressure and stigmatization in Zimbabwe, and that these various aberrations of human contact affect them the most, my writing is a critique of the weaknesses in my society," she explained to Larson. "The position of Women needs to be reexamined with greater determination and a forceful idea for change."

Vera's first publication, *Why Don't You Carve Other Animals,* contains fifteen tales set in Rhodesia during the turbulent 1970s, when that country was torn by conflict between the black majority and the ruling white minority. Many of the tales in *Why Don't You Carve Other Animals* are told from female perspectives.

Vera also probed racial issues in *Nehanda,* a novel published in 1993, concerning both the occupying English and the oppressed African natives. George P. Landow, writing for the *Postcolonial Web,* acknowledged Vera's contrasting of black and white cultures. Recalling an episode in which a priest attempts to convert a native to Christianity, Landow noted that Vera emphasizes the manner in which "each man comes from such a distinctly different intellectual and imaginative cosmos that supposedly identical, apparently shared ideas . . . mean very different things and resonate in different ways."

In 1994 Vera published *Without a Name,* a novel about Mazvita, a young native African woman struggling to survive during the downfall of Rhodesia and the consequent establishment of the Zimbabwean nation. Dissatisfied with life in the violent countryside, where guerrilla fighters vie with government forces for control, the pregnant Mazvita leaves her lover and heads for the city of Harare, where she hopes to find freedom and safety. In Harare, however, Mazvita merely discovers what Pamela J. Olubunmi Smith described in *World Literature Today* as the city's "own horrors and perils, its own warfare, unleashing false hope too readily, too soon." As a result of her perilous situation in the city, Mazvita kills her child and returns to her rural home. Smith described Vera's writing style as "terse, poetic, almost academic" and added that Vera's "metaphorical language [is] suggestive, suspenseful, [and] compelling." Smith described *Without a Name* as a "fine work of fiction."

Vera's next novel, *Under the Tongue,* is also about life in war-torn Rhodesia. *Mail and Guardian* writer Jane Rosenthal observed, "This novel, insofar as it has a plot at all, is about the rape of a ten-year-old girl by her father, returning from an absence during Zimbabwe's struggle for freedom from white-minority

rule." Noting the controversial nature of the novel's theme, Vera told Rosenthal, "We should possess the courage to examine ourselves, not always go back to the empire—look at our own weaknesses." Rosenthal called *Under the Tongue* an "intensely poetic novel" and "a book which somehow grows richer with each reading."

Butterfly Burning tells the story of young Phephelaphi and her lover, Fumbatha, who is twice her age. Phephelaphi is a free spirit, searching for fulfillment and independence; she enrolls in a nursing school, only to find out that her position there is jeopardized by the fact that she is pregnant. The girl gives herself an abortion—a scene that Larson called "one of the most harrowing that I have encountered in a work of fiction in many years"—with terrible consequences. A *Publishers Weekly* reviewer commented on Vera's "lyrical, metaphor-laden, symbolic prose" that weaves together the sad tale. *Booklist* contributor Gillian Engberg, noting that the structure is "more meditative than plot-based," called *Butterfly Burning* a "shocking yet beautiful book," and Ellen Flexman in *Library Journal* described it as "a rare work of beauty" that captures "the oft-tragic poetry of life."

Vera's novel *The Stone Virgins* is set in Zimbabwe in the 1980s after the war of liberation, and tells the story of two sisters, Thenjiwe and Nonceba, who are caught up in the freedom movement. Vera, with her characteristic sensitivity, writes of the conflict between personal and national histories. Weaver Press's description of the novel states: "In this gentle but fearless book, Yvonne Vera enables her reader to respond truthfully to the catastrophic depths of unspoken wars."

Vera also edited a collection of stories titled *Opening Spaces: An Anthology of Contemporary African Women's Writings.* Adele S. Newson-Horst stated in *World Literature Today* that Vera's selection reveals her to be "a writer's writer, a visionary whose understanding of continental African women's concerns, commonalities, and differences has the power to inspire the most disinterested of readers." Vera brings together a collection of writers whose stories address such issues as AIDS, abortion, international education, and the politics of feminism. "Yet there is nothing heavy-handed or stultifying in the presentation of ideas," noted Newson-Horst. "The total effect is electrifying."

Vera once told *CA:* "As a woman living in Zimbabwe, my life has had both charm and peril. The beauty of our landscape is stunning, the position of women in society tragic and perplexing. In my work, I have tried to celebrate both women and landscape, to explore the conflict, with all its magic and beauty, in ways that fulfill my every passion. In *Butterfly Burning,* my city Bulawayo is the focus, its thorn bushes, its city women, mesmerized and borne by the musicality of change and an oncoming liberation of souls. I love to have written it."

BIOGRAPHICAL AND CRITICAL SOURCES:

BOOKS

Contemporary Black Biography, Volume 32, Gale (Detroit, MI), 2002.

PERIODICALS

Booklist, August, 2000, Gillian Engberg, review of *Butterfly Burning,* p. 2117; February 15, 2002, Kristine Huntley, review of *Without a Name and Under the Tongue,* p. 994.
Kirkus Reviews, November 15, 2001, review of *Without a Name and Under the Tongue,* p. 1579.
Library Journal, September 15, 2000, Ellen Flexman, review of *Butterfly Burning,* p. 115; September 1, 2001, Reba Leiding, review of *Without a Name and Under the Tongue,* p. 237.
New York Times Book Review, March 17, 2002, review of *Without a Name and Under the Tongue.*

Publishers Weekly, August 28, 2000, review of *Butterfly Burning,* p. 58; December 24, 2001, review of *Without a Name and Under the Tongue,* pp. 40-41.
World and I, June, 1999, Charles R. Larson, review of *Butterfly Burning,* p. 282; November, 2001, Charles R. Larson, "Back to Bulawayo: Novelist Yvonne Vera's decision to leave Canada and return to her homeland of Zimbabwe," p. 263.
World Literature Today, autumn, 1993, p. 909; summer, 1996, p. 752; spring, 1999, review of *Under the Tongue,* p 382; winter, 2000, Adele S. Newson, review of *Butterfly Burning,* p. 230; summer, 2000, Adele S. Newson-Horst, review of *Opening Spaces: An Anthology of Contemporary African Women's Writings,* p. 565.

ONLINE

Complete Review, http://www.complete-review.com/ (March 13, 2003), reviews of *Under the Tongue, Without a Name, Butterfly Burning,* and *The Stone Virgins.*
Heinemann Web site, http://www.heinemann.com/ (March 13, 2003), biography of Yvonne Vera and review of *Opening Spaces.*
Mail and Guardian Online, http://www.mg.co.za/ (May 20, 1998), Jane Rosenthal, review of *Under the Tongue.*
Postcolonial Web, http://www.postcolonialweb.org/ (March 21, 2002), George P. Landow, "A Clash of Religions: Kaguvi Encounters the Christian Conception of an Afterlife."
Weaver Press Web site, http://www.weaverpresszimbabwe.com/ (March 13, 2003), description and reviews of *The Stone Virgins.**

W

WAYS, C. R.
See BLOUNT, Roy (Alton), Jr.

* * *

WEBB, Alex 1952-

PERSONAL: Born May 5, 1952, in San Francisco, CA; son of Dwight W. (an editor) and Nancy M. (a sculptor) Webb; married Susan O'Connor (marriage ended); married Rebecca Norris; children: (first marriage) Max. *Ethnicity:* "Caucasian." *Education:* Harvard University, B.A., 1974.

ADDRESSES: Home—319 Garfield Pl., Brooklyn, NY 11213. *Office*—Magnum Photos, 151 West 25th St., New York, NY 10001.

CAREER: Self-employed photographer, 1974—; associated with Magnum Photos, New York, NY, 1976—.

AWARDS, HONORS: Award from Overseas Press Club of America, 1980; grant, New York State Council on the Arts, 1986; Leopold Godowsky Award, 1988; grants, National Endowment for the Arts, 1990; and Hasselblad Foundation, 1998; Leica Medal of Excellence, 2000; David Octavius Hill Medal, 2002.

WRITINGS:

PHOTOGRAPHY COLLECTIONS

Hot Light/Half-Made Worlds, Thames & Hudson (New York, NY), 1986.

Under a Grudging Sun, Thames & Hudson (New York, NY), 1989.
From the Tropics, Comunidad de Madrid (Madrid, Spain), 1989.
From the Sunshine State: Photographs of Florida, Monacelli Press (New York, NY), 1996.
Amazon: From the Floodplains to the Clouds, Monacelli Press (New York, NY), 1998.
Crossings: Photographs from the U.S. Mexico Border, Monacelli Press (New York, NY), 2003.

Contributor to books, including *Police! A Precinct at Work,* by Sara Ann Friedman and David Jacobs, Harcourt Brace Jovanovich (New York, NY), 1975.

* * *

WIESEL, Elie(zer) 1928-

PERSONAL: Born September 30, 1928, in Sighet, Romania; immigrated to the United States, 1956, naturalized U.S. citizen, 1963; son of Shlomo (a grocer) and Sarah (Feig) Wiesel; married Marion Erster Rose, 1969; children: Shlomo Elisha. *Education:* Attended Sorbonne, University of Paris, 1948-51. *Religion:* Jewish.

ADDRESSES: Office—University Professors, Boston University, 745 Commonwealth Ave., Boston, MA 02215; and Elie Wiesel Foundation for Humanity, 529 Fifth Ave., Suite 1802, New York, NY 10017. *Agent*—Georges Borchardt, 136 East 57th St., New York, NY 10022.

Elie Wiesel

CAREER: Foreign correspondent at various times for *Yedioth Ahronoth,* Tel Aviv, Israel, *L'Arche,* Paris, France, and *Jewish Daily Forward,* New York, NY, 1949—; City College of the City University of New York, New York, NY, distinguished professor, 1972-76; Boston University, Boston, MA, Andrew Mellon professor in the humanities, 1976—, professor of philosophy, 1988—; cofounder with wife, Marion, of Elie Wiesel Foundation for Humanity, 1986—. Whitney Humanities Center, Yale University, New Haven, CT, Henry Luce visiting scholar in Humanities and Social Thought, 1982-83; Florida International University, Miami, distinguished visiting professor of literature and philosophy, 1982. Chair, United States President's Commission on the Holocaust, 1979-80, U.S. Holocaust Memorial Council, 1980-86. On advisory board of over seventy organizations.

MEMBER: Amnesty International, PEN, Writers Guild of America, Author's Guild, American Academy of Arts and Sciences (fellow), Jewish Academy of Arts and Sciences, European Academy of Arts and Sciences, Foreign Press Association (honorary lifetime member), Writers and Artists for Peace in the Middle East, Royal Norwegian Society of Sciences and Letters, Universal Academy of Cultures, Paris (founding president), Phi Beta Kappa.

AWARDS, HONORS: Prix Rivarol, 1963; Remembrance Award, 1965, for *The Town beyond the Wall* and all other writings; William and Janice Epstein Fiction Award, Jewish Book Council, 1965, for *The Town beyond the Wall;* Jewish Heritage Award, 1966, for excellence in literature; Prix Medicis, 1969, for *Le Mendiant de Jerusalem;* Prix Bordin, French Academy, 1972; Eleanor Roosevelt Memorial Award, 1972; American Liberties Medallion, American Jewish Committee, 1972; Frank and Ethel S. Cohen Award, Jewish Book Council, 1973, for *Souls on Fire;* Martin Luther King, Jr. Award, City College of the City University of New York, 1973; Faculty Distinguished Scholar Award, Hofstra University, 1973-74; Joseph Prize for Human Rights, Anti-Defamation League of B'nai B'rith, 1978; Zalman Shazar Award, State of Israel, 1979; Jabotinsky Medal, State of Israel, 1980; Prix Livre-International, 1980, and Prix des Bibliothecaires, 1981, both for *Le Testament d'un poete juif assassine;* Anatoly Scharansky Humanitarian Award, 1983; Congressional Gold Medal, 1985; humanitarian award, International League for Human Rights, 1985; Freedom Cup award, Women's League of Israel, 1986; Nobel Peace Prize, 1986; Medal of Libery Award, 1986; Special Christopher Book Award, 1987; achievement award, Artists and Writers for Peace in the Middle East, 1987; Profiles of Courage award, B'nai B'rith, 1987; Human Rights Law Award, International Human Rights Law Group, 1988; Presidential medal, Hofstra University, 1988; Human Rights Law award, International Human Rights Law Group, 1988; Bicentennial medal, Georgetown University, 1988; Janus Korczak Humanitarian award, NAHE, Kent State University, 1989; Count Sforza award in Philanthropy Interphil, 1989; Lily Edelman award for Excellence in Continuing Jewish Education, B'nai B'rith International, 1989; George Washington award, American Hungarian Foundation, 1989; Bicentennial medal, New York University, 1989; Humanitarian award Human Rights Campaign Fund, 1989; International Brotherhood award, C.O.R.E., 1990; Frank Weil award for distinguished contribution to the advancement of North American Jewish culture, Jewish Community Centers Association of North America, 1990; first Raoul Wallenberg medal, University of Michigan, 1990; Award of Highest Honor, Soka University, 1991; Facing History and Ourselves Humanity award, 1991; La Medaille de la Ville de Toulouse, 1991; Fifth Centennial

Christopher Columbus medal, City of Genoa, 1992; first Primo Levi award, 1992; Ellis Island Medal of Honor, 1992; Presidential Medal of Freedom Literature Arts award, National Foundation for Jewish Culture, 1992; Ellis Island Medal of Honor, 1992; Guardian of the Children award, AKIM USA, 1992; Bishop Francis J. Mugavero award for religious and racial harmony, Queens College, 1994; Golden Slipper Humanitarian award, 1994; Interfaith Council on the Holocaust Humanitarian award, 1994; Crystal award, Davos World Economic Forum, 1995; first Niebuhr award, Elmhurst College, 1995; President's Award, Quinnipiac College, 1996; Golden Plate Award, American Academy of Achievement, 1996; Lotos Medal of Merit, Lotos Club, 1996; Guardian of Zion Award, Bar-Ilan University, 1997; Canterbury Medalist, Beckett Fund for Religious Liberty, 1998; American Bar Association Annual Award, 1998; Rabbi Marc H. Tannenbaum Award for the Advancement of Interreligious Understanding, 1998; Yitzhak Rabin Peacemaker Award, Merrimack College, 1998; Aesop Prize, Children's Folklore Section, American Folklore Society, for *King Solomon and His Magic Ring,* 1999; Raoul Wallenberg International Humanitarian Award, American Jewish Joint Distribution Committee, 1999; Mathilde Schechter Award, Women's League for Conservative Judaism, 2000; Manhattan Award, National Arts Club, 2000; Benediction Medal, Delbarton School, 2001; Humanitarian of the Year Award, New York Society of Association Executives, 2002; Dean's Medal, Walsh School of Foreign Service, Georgetown University, 2002; Emma Lazarus Statue of Liberty Award, American Jewish Historical Society, 2002; Lifetime Visionary Award, Israeli Film Festival, New York, 2002; named Humanitarian of the Century, Council of Jewish Organizations; recipient of over 100 honorary degrees; honors established in his name: Elie Wiesel Award for Holocaust Research, University of Haifa; Elie Wiesel Chair in Holocaust Studies, Bar-Ilan University; Elie Wiesel Endowment Fund for Jewish Culture, University of Denver; Elie Wiesel Distinguished Service Award, University of Florida; Elie Wiesel Awards for Jewish Arts and Culture, B'nai B'rith Hillel Foundations; Elie Wiesel Chair in Judaic Studies, Connecticut College; Elie Wiesel Prize in Ethics, Elie Wiesel Foundation for Humanity.

WRITINGS:

Un Di Velt Hot Geshvign (title means "And the World Has Remained Silent"), [Buenos Aires], 1956, abridged French translation published as *La Nuit* (also see below), foreword by Francois Mauriac, Editions de Minuit (Paris, France), 1958, translation by Stella Rodway published as *Night* (also see below), Hill & Wang (New York, NY), 1960.

L'Aube (also see below), Editions du Seuil (Paris, France), 1961, translation by Frances Frenaye published as *Dawn* (also see below), Hill & Wang (New York, NY), 1961.

Le Jour (also see below), Editions du Seuil (Paris, France), 1961, translation by Anne Borchardt published as *The Accident* (also see below), Hill & Wang (New York, NY), 1962.

La Ville de la chance, Editions du Seuil (Paris, France), 1962, translation by Stephen Becker published as *The Town beyond the Wall,* Atheneum (New York, NY), 1964, new edition, Holt (New York, NY), 1967.

Les Portes de la foret, Editions du Seuil (Paris, France), 1964, translation by Frances Frenaye published as *The Gates of the Forest,* Holt (New York, NY), 1966.

Le Chant des morts, Editions du Seuil (Paris, France), 1966, translation published as *Legends of Our Time,* Holt (New York, NY), 1968.

The Jews of Silence: A Personal Report on Soviet Jewry (originally published in Hebrew as a series of articles for newspaper *Yedioth Ahronoth*), translation and afterword by Neal Kozodoy, Holt (New York, NY), 1966, 2nd edition, Vallentine, Mitchell, 1973.

Zalmen; ou, la Folie de Dieu (play), 1966, translation by Lily and Nathan Edelman published as *Zalmen; or, The Madness of God,* Holt (New York, NY), 1968.

Le Mendiant de Jerusalem, 1968, translation by the author and L. Edelman published as *A Beggar in Jerusalem,* Random House (New York, NY), 1970.

La Nuit, L'Aube, [and] *Le Jour,* Editions du Seuil (Paris, France), 1969, translation published as *Night, Dawn,* [and] *The Accident: Three Tales,* Hill & Wang (New York, NY), 1972, reprinted as *The Night Trilogy: Night, Dawn, The Accident,* Farrar, Straus (New York, NY), 1987, translation by Stella Rodway published as *Night, Dawn, Day,* Aronson (New York, NY), 1985.

Entre deux soleils, Editions du Seuil (Paris, France), 1970, translation by the author and L. Edelman published as *One Generation After,* Random House (New York, NY), 1970.

Celebration Hassidique: Portraits et legendes, Editions du Seuil (Paris, France), 1972, translation by wife, Marion Wiesel, published as *Souls on Fire:*

Portraits and Legends of Hasidic Masters, Random House (New York, NY), 1972.

Le Serment de Kolvillag, Editions du Seuil (Paris, France), 1973, translation by Marion Wiesel published as *The Oath,* Random House (New York, NY), 1973.

Ani maamin: A Song Lost and Found Again (cantata), music composed by Darius Milhaud, Random House (New York, NY), 1974.

Celebration Biblique: Portraits et legendes, Editions du Seuil (Paris, France), 1975, translation by Marion Wiesel published as *Messengers of God: Biblical Portraits and Legends,* Random House (New York, NY), 1976.

Un Juif aujourd'hui: Recits, essais, dialogues, Editions du Seuil (Paris, France), 1977, translation by Marion Wiesel published as *A Jew Today,* Random House (New York, NY), 1978.

(With others) *Dimensions of the Holocaust,* Indiana University Press (Bloomington, IN), 1977.

Four Hasidic Masters and Their Struggle against Melancholy, University of Notre Dame Press (Notre Dame, IN), 1978.

Le Proces de Shamgorod tel qu'il se deroula le 25 fevrier 1649: Piece en trois actes, Editions du Seuil (Paris, France), 1979, translation by Marion Wiesel published as *The Trial of God (As It Was Held on February 25, 1649, in Shamgorod): A Play in Three Acts,* Random House (New York, NY), 1979, reprinted, Schocken Books (New York, NY), 1995.

Images from the Bible, illustrated with paintings by Shalom of Safed, Overlook Press (New York, NY), 1980.

Le Testament d'un poete Juif assassine, Editions du Seuil (Paris, France), 1980, translation by Marion Wiesel published as *The Testament,* Simon & Schuster (New York, NY), 1981.

Five Biblical Portraits, University of Notre Dame Press (Notre Dame, IN), 1981.

Somewhere a Master, Simon & Schuster (New York, NY), 1982, reprinted as *Somewhere a Master: Further Tales of the Hasidic Masters,* Summit Books (New York, NY), 1984.

Paroles d'etranger, Editions du Seuil (Paris, France), 1982.

The Golem: The Story of a Legend As Told by Elie Wiesel (fiction), illustrated by Mark Podwal, Summit Books (New York, NY), 1983.

Le Cinquieme Fils, Grasset (Paris, France), 1983, translation by M. Wiesel published as *The Fifth Son,* Summit Books (New York, NY), 1985.

Against Silence: The Voice and Vision of Elie Wiesel, three volumes, edited by Irving Abrahamson, Holocaust Library, 1985.

Signes d'exode, Grasset (Paris, France), 1985.

Job ou Dieu dans la tempete, Grasset (Paris, France), 1986.

Le Crepuscule au loin, Grasset (Paris, France), 1987, translation by Marion Wiesel published as *Twilight,* Summit Books (New York, NY), 1988, reprinted, Schocken Books (New York, NY), 1995.

(With Albert H. Friedlander) *The Six Days of Destruction,* Paulist Press (Mahwah, NJ), 1989.

L'Oublie: Roman, Editions du Seuil (Paris, France), 1989.

(With Philippe-Michael de Saint-Cheron) *Evil and Exile,* translated by Jon Rothschild, University of Notre Dame Press (Notre Dame, IN), 1990.

From the Kingdom of Memory: Reminiscences, Summit Books (New York, NY), 1990.

The Forgotten (novel), translated by Stephen Becker, Summit Books (New York, NY), 1992.

(With Salomon Malka) *Monsieur Chouchani: L'Enigme d'un maitre du XX siecle: Entretiens avec Elie Wiesel, suivis d'une enquete,* J. C. Lattes (Paris, France), 1994.

Tous les fleuves vont a la mer: Memoires, Editions du Seuil (Paris, France), 1994, published as *All Rivers Run to the Sea: Memoirs,* Knopf (New York, NY), 1995.

(With Francois Mitterrand) *Memoire a deux voix,* Jacob (Paris, France), 1995, published as *Memoir in Two Voices,* Arcade (New York, NY), 1996.

Das Gegenteil von Gleichgueltigkeit ist Erinnerung: Versuche zu Elie Wiesel, edited by Dagmar Mensink and Reinhold Boschki, Matthias-Gruenewald-Verlag (Mainz, Germany), 1995.

Jorge Semprun, *Semprun, Wiesel: Se taire est impossible,* Editions Mille et une nuits (Paris, France), 1995.

(Author of foreword) Robert Krell and Marc I. Sherman, editors, *Medical and Psychological Effects of Concentration Camps on Holocaust Survivors,* Transaction Publishers (New Brunswick, NJ), 1997.

Ethics and Memory, with a preface by Wolf Lepenies, W. de Gruyter (New York, NY), 1997.

Celebration prophetique: Portraits et legendes, Editions du Seuil (Paris, France), 1998.

Alan Rosen, editor, *Celebrating Elie Wiesel: Stories, Essays, Reflections,* University of Notre Dame Press (Notre Dame, IN), 1998.

King Solomon and His Magic Ring, paintings by Mark Podwal, Greenwillow Books (New York, NY), 1999.

Ekkehard Schuster and Reinhold Boschert-Kimmig, *Hope against Hope: Johann Baptist Metz and Elie Wiesel Speak Out on the Holocaust,* translated by J. Matthew Ashley, Paulist Press (New York, NY), 1999.

And the Sea Is Never Full: Memoirs, 1969—, translated from the French by Marion Wiesel, Knopf (New York, NY), 1999.

(With Richard D. Heffner) *Conversations with Elie Wiesel,* edited by Thomas J. Vinciguerra, Schocken Books (New York, NY), 2001.

The Judges, Knopf (New York, NY), 2002.

After the Darkness, Schocken Books (New York, NY), 2002.

Elie Wiesel: Conversations, edited by Robert Franciosi, University of Mississippi Press (Jackson, MS), 2002.

Also author of *A Song for Hope,* 1987, and *The Nobel Speech,* 1987.

Contributor to numerous periodicals.

SIDELIGHTS: In the spring of 1944, the Nazis entered the Transylvanian village of Sighet, Romania, until then a relatively safe and peaceful enclave in the middle of a war-torn continent. Arriving with orders to exterminate an estimated 600,000 Jews in six weeks or less, Adolf Eichmann, chief of the Gestapo's Jewish section, began making arrangements for a mass deportation program. Among those forced to leave their homes was fifteen-year-old Elie Wiesel, the only son of a grocer and his wife. A serious and devoted student of the Talmud and the mystical teachings of Hasidism and the Cabala, the young man had always assumed he would spend his entire life in Sighet, quietly contemplating the religious texts and helping out in the family's store from time to time. Instead, along with his father, mother, and three sisters, Wiesel was herded onto a train bound for Birkenau, the reception center for the infamous death camp Auschwitz.

For reasons he still finds impossible to comprehend, Wiesel survived Birkenau and later Auschwitz and Buna and Buchenwald; his father, mother, and youngest sister did not (he did not learn until after the war that his older sisters also survived). With nothing and no one in Sighet for him to go back to, Wiesel boarded a train for Belgium with four hundred other orphans who, like him, had no reason or desire to return to their former homes. On orders of General Charles de Gaulle, head of the French provisional government after World War II, the train was diverted to France, where border officials asked the children to raise their hands if they wanted to become French citizens. As Wiesel (who at that time neither spoke nor understood French) recalled in the *Washington Post,* "A lot of them did. They thought they were going to get bread or something; they would reach out for anything. I didn't, so I remained stateless."

Wiesel chose to stay in France for a while, settling first in Normandy and later in Paris, doing whatever he could to earn a living: tutoring, directing a choir, translating. Eventually he began working as a reporter for various French and Jewish publications. But he could not quite bring himself to write about what he had seen and felt at Auschwitz and Buchenwald. Doubtful of his—or of anyone's—ability to convey the horrible truth without diminishing it, Wiesel vowed never to make the attempt.

The young journalist's self-imposed silence came to an end in the mid-1950s, however, after he met and interviewed the Nobel Prize-winning novelist Francois Mauriac. Deeply moved upon learning of Wiesel's tragic youth, Mauriac urged him to speak out and tell the world of his experiences, to "bear witness" for the millions of men, women, and children whom death, and not despair, had silenced. The result was *Night,* the story of a teen-age boy plagued with guilt for having survived the camps and devastated by the realization that the God he had once worshipped so devoutly allowed his people to be destroyed. For the most part autobiographical, it was, stated Richard M. Elman in the *New Republic,* "a document as well as a work of literature—journalism which emerged, coincidentally, as a work of art."

Described by the *Nation*'s Daniel Stern as "undoubtedly the single most powerful literary relic of the holocaust," *Night* is the first in a series of nonfiction books and autobiographical novels this "lyricist of lamentation" has written that deal, either directly or indirectly, with the Holocaust. "He sees the present always refracted through the prism of these earlier days," commented James Finn in the *New Republic.* The *New York Times*'s Thomas Lask agreed, stating:

"For [more than] twenty-five years, Elie Wiesel has been in one form or another a witness to the range, bestiality, and completeness of the destruction of European Jewry by the Germans. . . . Auschwitz informs everything he writes—novels, legends, dialogues. He is not belligerent about it, only unyielding. Nothing he can say measures up to the enormity of what he saw, what others endured." Writing in *Nonfiction Classics for Students,* Kelly Winters explained that Wiesel tells his story in *Night* using simple, direct statements: "The story is told in an extremely understated, tight style. Wiesel does not tell the reader what to think; he simply presents events as plainly as possible and lets them speak for themselves. The events, such as the mass killing of babies who are thrown into a flaming furnace, or the hanging of children, are so horrifying that Wiesel does not need to belabor them or to express his own terror or anger directly; his taut style and emotional restraint make them even more believable and frightening."

Other novels by Wiesel about the Jewish experience during and after the Holocaust include *Dawn* and *The Accident,* which were later published together with *Night* in *The Night Trilogy: Night, Dawn, The Accident.* Like *Night,* the other two books in the trilogy have concentration camp survivors as their central characters. *Dawn* concerns the experiences of one survivor just after World War II who joins the Jewish underground efforts to form an independent Israeli state; and *The Accident* is about a man who discovers that his collision with an automobile was actually caused by his subconscious, guilt-ridden desire to commit suicide. "Wiesel's writings after *Night* have been attempts to reclaim faith in language, in humanity, in God, and in himself," explained Jane Elizabeth Dougherty in an essay for *Novels for Students.* "In *Night,* faith seems an incredible burden, a hindrance to survival, and yet it remains the only way in which the Jews can survive the horrors of the Holocaust. In the context of the concentration camp universe, Wiesel suggests that the only thing more dangerous than faith is disbelief."

In two of Wiesel's later novels, *The Testament* and *The Fifth Son,* the author also explores the effects of the Holocaust on the next generation of Jews. Some critics, such as *Globe and Mail* contributor Bronwyn Drainie, have questioned the validity of the author's belief that children of Holocaust survivors would be "as morally galvanized by the Nazi nightmare as the survivors themselves." But, asserted Richard F. Shepard in the *New York Times,* even if the feelings of these children cannot be generalized, "the author does make all of us 'children' of that generation, all of us who were not there, in the sense that he outlines for us the burdens of guilt, of revenge, of despair."

Indeed, the Holocaust and the Jewish religious and philosophical tradition involve experiences and beliefs shared by a great many people, including other writers. But as Kenneth Turan declared in the *Washington Post Book World,* Elie Wiesel has become "much more than just a writer. He is a symbol, a banner, and a beacon, perhaps *the* survivor of the Holocaust. . . . He seems to own the horror of the death camps, or, rather, the horror owns him." But it is a moral and spiritual, not a physical, horror that obsesses Wiesel and obliges him to compose what Dan Isaac of the *Nation* called "an angry message to God, filled with both insane rage and stoical acceptance; calculated to stir God's wrath, but careful not to trigger an apocalypse." Explained Isaac's *Nation* colleague Laurence Goldstein: "For Elie Wiesel memory is an instrument of revelation. Each word he uses to document the past transforms both the work and the memory into an act of faith. The writings of Elie Wiesel are a journey into the past blackened by the Nazi death camps where the charred souls of its victims possess the sum of guilt and endurance that mark the progress of man. It is a compulsive, fevered, single-minded search among the ashes for a spark that can be thrust before the silent eyes of God himself."

Unlike those who dwell primarily on the physical horror, then, Wiesel writes from the perspective of a passionately religious man whose faith has been profoundly shaken by what he has witnessed. As Goldstein remarked, "He must rediscover himself. . . . Although he has not lost God, he must create out of the pain and numbness a new experience that will keep his God from vanishing among the unforgettable faces of the thousands whose bodies he saw." According to Maurice Friedman of *Commonweal,* Wiesel is, in fact, "the most moving embodiment of the Modern Job": a man who questions—in books that "form one unified outcry, one sustained protest, one sobbing and singing prayer"—why the just must suffer while the wicked flourish. This debate with God is one of the central themes of what a *Newsweek* critic referred to as Wiesel's "God-tormented, God-intoxicated" fiction.

In addition to his intense preoccupation with ancient Jewish philosophy, mythology, and history, Wiesel displays a certain affinity with modern French existentialists, an affinity Josephine Knopp believed is a direct consequence of the Holocaust. Wrote Knopp in *Contemporary Literature:* "To the young Wiesel the notion of an 'absurd' universe would have been a completely alien one. . . . The traditional Jewish view holds that life's structure and meaning are fully explained and indeed derive from the divinely granted Torah. . . . Against this background the reality of Auschwitz confronts the Jew with a dilemma, an 'absurdity' which cannot be dismissed easily and which stubbornly refuses to dissipate of its own accord. . . . The only possible response that remains within the framework of Judaism is denunciation of God and a demand that He fulfill His contractual obligation [to protect those who worship Him]. This is the religious and moral context within which Wiesel attempts to apprehend and assimilate the events of the Holocaust. [He seeks] to reconcile Auschwitz with Judaism, to confront and perhaps wring meaning from the absurd." In a more recent novel, *Twilight,* Wiesel explores this absurdity—in this case, he goes so far as to call it madness—of the universe. Again, the protagonist is a Jew, who begins to wonder, as *New York Times* reviewer John Gross explained, whether "it is mad to go on believing in God. Or perhaps . . . it is God who is mad: who else but a mad God could have created such a world?"

The strong emphasis on Jewish tradition and Jewish suffering in Wiesel's works does not mean that he speaks only to and for Jews. In fact, maintained Robert McAfee Brown in *Christian Century,* "writing out of the particularity of his own Jewishness . . . is how [Wiesel] touches universal chords. He does not write about 'the human condition,' but about 'the Jewish condition.' Correction: in writing about the Jewish condition, he thereby writes about the human condition. For the human condition is not generalized existence; it is a huge, crazy-quilt sum of particularized existences all woven together."

To Stern, this time commenting in the *Washington Post Book World,* it seemed that "Wiesel has taken the Jew as his metaphor—and his reality—in order to unite a moral and aesthetic vision in terms of all men." Manes Sperber of the *New York Times Book Review* expressed a similar view, stating that "Wiesel is one of the few writers who, without any plaintiveness, has succeeded in revealing in the Jewish tragedy those features by which it has become again and again a paradigm of the human condition."

According to Michael J. Bandler in the *Christian Science Monitor,* Wiesel conveys his angry message to God "with a force and stylistic drive that leaves the reader stunned." Concise and uncluttered, yet infused with a highly emotional biblical mysticism, the author's prose "gleams again and again with the metaphor of the poet," wrote Clifford A. Ridley in the *National Observer.* Though it "never abandons its tender intimacy," reported Sperber, "[Wiesel's] voice comes from far away in space and time. It is the voice of the Talmudic teachers of Jerusalem and Babylon; of medieval mystics; of Rabbi Nachman of Bratzlav whose tales have inspired generations of Hasidim and so many writers." As Lask observed, "[Wiesel] has made the form of the telling his own. The surreal and the supernatural combine abrasively with the harsh fact; the parable, the rabbinic tale support and sometimes substitute for narrative. The written law and oral tradition support, explain and expand the twentieth-century event." Goldstein, noting the author's "remarkably compassionate tone," declared that "he writes with that possessive reverence for language that celebrates, as much as describes, experience. The written word becomes a powerful assertion, the triumph of life over death and indifference. . . . Words carved on gravestones, legend torn from the pit where millions of broken bodies lie. This is the inheritance which Elie Wiesel brings to us. His voice claims us with its urgency. His vision lights the mystery of human endurance."

Several critics, however, felt Wiesel's prose does not quite live up to the demands of his subject. Jeffrey Burke, for example, commenting in the *New York Times Book Review,* stated that the author occasionally "slips into triteness or purple prose or redundancy," and a reviewer for the *New Yorker* found that Wiesel becomes "nearly delirious" in his intensity. *Newsweek's* Geoffrey Wolff believed that Wiesel's work at times "suffers from unnecessary confusions, linguistic cliches, dense and purple thickets, and false mystifications. Ideas tend to hobble about . . . on stilts. . . . The language, seeking to transport us to another world, collapses beneath the weight of its burden much too often." Burke concluded: "No one can or would deny the seriousness and necessity of Elie Wiesel's role as witness. . . . It is natural that such a mission would remain uppermost in the writer's mind, but that the requirements of art should proportionately diminish in significance is not an acceptable corollary. [Wiesel tends] to sacrifice the demands of craft to those of conscience."

In defense of Wiesel, Turan stated that "his is a deliberate, elegant style, consciously elevated and poetic, and if he occasionally tries to pack too much into a sentence, to jam it too full of significance and meaning, it is an error easy to forgive." Elman, this time writing in the *New York Times Book Review,* also found that "some of Wiesel's existentialist parables are deeply flawed by an opacity of language and construction, which may confirm that 'the event was so heavy with horror . . . that words could not really contain it.' But Wiesel's work is not diminished by his failure to make his shattering theme—God's betrayal of man—consistently explicit." Thus, according to Jonathan Brent in the *Chicago Tribune Book World,* Wiesel is "the type of writer distinguished by his subject rather than his handling of it. . . . Such writers must be read not for themselves but for the knowledge they transmit of events, personalities, and social conditions outside their fiction itself. They do not master their material esthetically, but remain faithful to it; and this constitutes the principal value of their work."

Few agree with these assessments of Wiesel's stylistic abilities, but many support Brent's conclusion that the author is almost compulsively faithful to his subject. As Lawrence L. Langer observed in the *Washington Post Book World:* "Although Elie Wiesel has announced many times in recent years that he is finished with the Holocaust as a subject for public discourse, it is clear . . . that the Holocaust has not yet finished with him. Almost from his first volume to his last, his writing has been an act of homage, a ritual of remembrance in response to a dreadful challenge 'to unite the language of man with the silence of the dead'. . . . If Elie Wiesel returns compulsively to the ruins of the Holocaust world, it is not because he has nothing new to say. . . . [It is simply that] the man he did not become besieges his imagination and compels him to confirm his appointments with the past that holds him prisoner."

Wiesel expresses what *Commonweal*'s Irving Halpern called "the anguish of a survivor who is unable to exorcise the past or to live with lucidity and grace in the present" in the book *Night,* his first attempt to bear witness for the dead. Wiesel wrote: "Never shall I forget that night, the first night in camp, which has turned my life into one long night, seven times cursed and seven times sealed. Never shall I forget that smoke. Never shall I forget the little faces of the children, whose bodies I saw turned into wreaths of smoke beneath a silent blue sky. Never shall I forget those flames which consumed my Faith forever. Never shall I forget that nocturnal silence which deprived me, for all eternity, of the desire to live. Never shall I forget those moments which murdered my God and my soul and turned my dreams to dust. Never shall I forget these things, even if I am condemned to live as long as God Himself. Never."

Concern that the truths of the Holocaust, and memories in general, might in time be forgotten has often fueled Wiesel's writing. In comparing his many works, Wiesel remarked to *Publishers Weekly* interviewer Elizabeth Devereaux, "What do they have in common? Their commitment to memory. What is the opposite of memory? Alzheimer's disease. I began to research this topic and I discovered that this is the worst disease, that every intellectual is afraid of this disease, not just because it is incurable, which is true of other diseases, too. But here the identity is being abolished." From this realization Wiesel created *The Forgotten,* a novel in which a Holocaust survivor fears he is losing his memories to an unnamed ailment. He beseeches his son to listen and remember as he recounts the events of his life. The dutiful son embarks for Romania to recover the details of his father's experience, including the death of his family at the hands of the Nazis and his role as an Eastern European partisan and freedom fighter for the establishment of Israel. Though Wiesel told Devereaux that this novel is "less autobiographical" than his others, *The Forgotten* contains recognizable allusions to his own life and work in references to the one-word titles of his first three novels and similarities between the father's childhood village and Wiesel's own. As Frederick Busch observed in the *New York Times Book Review,* Wiesel "intends to warn us that many of the survivors of the Holocaust are dying, that the cruel truth of the war against the Jews might one day be lost or clouded." Citing the author's "characteristic blend of petition, contemplative discourse, and devotion to Jewish tradition," Jonathan Dorfman wrote in a *Chicago Tribune* review, "*The Forgotten* is ample proof that . . . Wiesel remains a writer of significance and high merit."

The novel *The Judges* is a moral fable that deals with issues of justice and truth. An airplane is forced to land unexpectedly due to bad weather. Once on the ground, five of the passengers are taken captive by a strange figure who calls himself "the Judge." In a series of probing, intimate questions, the Judge forces the prisoners to face their own deepest selves, their beliefs and values. A *Publishers Weekly* critic explained that "each character, caught in the facts of his or her past and oriented toward future projects, must confront a present threat that crystallizes their existences." "Courageous and profoundly philosophical," Patrick Sullivan wrote in the *Library Journal,* "this novel skillfully explores moral questions that have never been more relevant."

Wiesel produced the first volume of his projected two-volume personal memoirs with *All Rivers Run to the Sea,* spanning the years from his childhood to the 1960s. He begins by recollecting the haunting premonition of a well-known rabbi which foretold the young Wiesel's future greatness, though it predicted that neither Wiesel nor his mother would live to know of his acclaim. In the reminiscence and anecdote that follows, Wiesel revisits his early village life, postwar orphanage and education in France, initiation as a professional journalist, and involvement in events surrounding the birth of Israel. As James E. Young noted in the *New Leader,* Wiesel devotes only twenty pages of the book to his concentration camp experiences. "Wiesel's memoir is not about what happened during those eleven months," Young wrote, "but about how they shaped his life afterward, how they have been remembered, how he has lived in their shadow." Despite Wiesel's confessed over-sensitivity to criticism and painful episodes of self-doubt, critics noted that his memoir reveals little about the author's personal life that is not evident in his previous works. Daphne Merkin wrote in the *New York Times Book Review,* "If the reader finishes this book with an impression that the public and private Elie Wiesel seem to dance around each other without ever really connecting, the author has foreseen this: 'Some see their work as a commentary on their life; for others it is the other way around. I count myself among the latter. Consider this account, then, as a kind of commentary.'" Wiesel concluded, as quoted by Vivian Gornick in the *Nation:* "The aim of the literature I call testimony is to disturb. I disturb the believer because I dare to put questions to God. I disturb the miscreant because I refuse to break with the religious and mystical universe that has shaped my own. Most of all, I disturb those who are comfortably settled within a system—be it political, psychological, or theological."

And the Sea Is Never Full continues Wiesel's life story since 1969. His activities as an activist promoting the memory of the Holocaust and of spreading the word

about human rights violations in the Soviet Union are covered in great detail. As Pierre L. Horn noted in *World Literature Today,* "The emphasis is on Wiesel the public figure rather than the private man." Alvin H. Rosenfeld, writing in the *New Leader,* explained that "while this is a book of often vivid autobiographical reflection, it is also something more—an anguished probing of the links between memory and traumatic event, memory and justice, memory and the quest for a common morality." A critic for *Publishers Weekly* stated: "Wiesel's writing is as fluid and evocative as ever, and his storytelling skills turn the events of his own life into a powerful series of morality plays."

In 1996 *Memoir in Two Voices,* which Wiesel coauthored with his friend, former French president Francois Mitterrand, was published. The volume offers a glimpse into the life of the former leader, who served as France's president from 1981 to 1995; the topics covered are driven by Wiesel's questions, which are intended to elicit explanations from Mitterrand. The book was characterized by a *Publishers Weekly* reviewer as containing insights into Mitterrand's personal life that were "as fascinating for their revelations as they [were] for their silences," indicating that the book did not probe as deeply into the mind of the French leader as the critic would have liked. Bonnie Smothers, reviewing *Memoir in Two Voices* for *Booklist,* assessed the section of the book in which Wiesel questions Mitterrand about the leader's knowledge of the Nazis' treatment of Jews during World War II as providing "a very enlightening exchange" between the two authors, and called the volume as a whole "a very special book, powerful at times, always provoking the reader's inner thoughts."

Many years after *Night,* Wiesel is still torn between words and silence. "You must speak," he told a *People* interviewer, "but how can you, when the full story is beyond language?" Furthermore, he once remarked in the *Washington Post,* "there is the fear of not being believed, . . . the fear that the experience will be reduced, made into something acceptable, perhaps forgotten." But as he went on to explain in *People:* "We [survivors] believe that if we survived, we must do something with our lives. The first task is to tell the tale." In short, concluded Wiesel, "The only way to stop the next holocaust—the nuclear holocaust—is to remember the last one. If the Jews were singled out then, in the next one we are all victims." For his enduring efforts to keep the memory of the Holocaust alive so that such a tragedy would not repeat itself ever again, Wiesel was awarded the Nobel Peace Prize in 1986. In a *New York Times* article on the event, James M. Markham quoted Egil Aarvik, chair of the Norwegian Nobel Committee: "Wiesel is a messenger to mankind. . . . His message is one of peace, atonement and human dignity. His belief that the forces fighting evil in the world can be victorious is a hardwon belief . . . repeated and deepened through the works of a great author." Speaking of Wiesel's fiction, Albert H. Friedlander in *Contemporary World Writers* concluded: "Each new book by Wiesel is filled with the concern for humanity which earned him the Nobel Peace prize. Each book is a letter addressed both to humanity and God. When one understands this, one begins to understand Elie Wiesel and his message."

BIOGRAPHICAL AND CRITICAL SOURCES:

BOOKS

Authors and Artists for Young Adults, Volume 7, Gale (Detroit, MI), 1991.

Authors in the News, Volume 1, Gale (Detroit, MI), 1976.

Berenbaum, Michael, *Elie Wiesel: God, the Holocaust, and the Children of Israel,* Behrman House, 1994.

Cohen, Myriam B., *Elie Wiesel: Variations sur le Silence,* Rumeur des ages, 1988.

Contemporary Authors Autobiography Series, Volume 4, Gale (Detroit, MI), 1986.

Contemporary Issues Criticism, Volume 1, Gale (Detroit, MI), 1982.

Contemporary Literary Criticism, Gale (Detroit, MI), Volume 3, 1975, Volume 5, 1976, Volume 11, 1979, Volume 37, 1986.

Contemporary World Writers, 2nd edition, St. James Press (Detroit, MI), 1993.

Davis, Colin, *Elie Wiesel's Secretive Texts,* University Press of Florida Press (Gainesville, FL), 1994.

Dictionary of Literary Biography, Volume 83: *French Novelists since 1960,* Gale (Detroit, MI), 1989.

Dictionary of Literary Biography Yearbook: 1987, Gale (Detroit, MI), 1988.

Lazo, Caroline Evensen, *Elie Wiesel,* Macmillan (New York, NY), 1994.

Newsmakers 1998, Gale (Detroit, MI), 1998.

Nonfiction Classics for Students, Volume 4, Gale (Detroit, MI), 2002.

Novels for Students, Gale (Detroit, MI), 1998.

Pariser, Michael, *Elie Wiesel: Bearing Witness,* Millbrook Press, 1994.

Rosenfeld, Alvin, *Confronting the Holocaust,* Indiana University Press (Bloomington, IN), 1978.

Schuman, Michael, *Elie Wiesel: Voice from the Holocaust,* Enslow (Springfield, NJ), 1994.

Sibelman, Simon P., *Silence in the Novels of Elie Wiesel,* St. Martin's Press (New York, NY), 1995.

Stern, Ellen Norman, *Elie Wiesel: A Voice for Humanity,* Jewish Publication Society (Philadelphia, PA), 1996.

Wiesel, Elie, *Night,* translated by Stella Rodway, Hill & Wang (New York, NY), 1960.

PERIODICALS

America, November 19, 1988.

Atlantic, November, 1968.

Best Sellers, March 15, 1970; May, 1981.

Booklist, February 15, 1994, p. 1100; September 1, 1995, p. 96; July, 1996, Bonnie Smothers, review of *Memoir in Two Voices,* p. 1798.

Book Week, May 29, 1966.

Chicago Tribune Book World, October 29, 1978; March 29, 1981; May 3, 1992.

Christian Century, January 18, 1961; June 17, 1970; June 3, 1981.

Christian Science Monitor, November 21, 1968; February 19, 1970; November 22, 1978.

Commentary, June, 1996, p. 64.

Commonweal, December 9, 1960; January 6, 1961; March 13, 1964; October 14, 1966.

Contemporary Literature, spring, 1974.

Detroit Free Press, April 12, 1992.

Detroit News, April 4, 1992.

Globe and Mail (Toronto, Ontario, Canada), April 20, 1985; August 6, 1988.

Library Journal, February 15, 1994, p. 202; December, 1995, p. 120; June 1, 2002, Patrick Sullivan, review of *The Judges,* p. 198.

London Times, September 3, 1981.

Los Angeles Times Book Review, June 19, 1988.

Nation, October 17, 1966; February 24, 1969; March 16, 1970; January 5, 1974; December 25, 1995, p. 839.

National Observer, February 2, 1970.

National Review, June 12, 1981.

New Choices, December-January, 1993, p. 64.

New Leader, December 30, 1968; June 15, 1981; December 18, 1995, p. 17; December 13, 1999, Alvin H. Rosenfeld, review of *And the Sea Is Never Full,* p. 13.

New Republic, July 5, 1964; December 14, 1968.

Newsweek, May 25, 1964; February 9, 1970.

New York, December 11, 1995, p. 72.

New Yorker, March 18, 1961; January 9, 1965; August 20, 1966; July 6, 1970; July 12, 1976.

New York Herald Tribune Lively Arts, January 1, 1961; April 30, 1961.

New York Review of Books, July 28, 1966; January 2, 1969; May 7, 1970.

New York Times, December 15, 1970; March 10, 1972; April 3, 1981; April 16, 1984; March 21, 1985; October 15, 1986; June 10, 1988; December 5, 1995, p. B2.

New York Times Book Review, July 16, 1961; April 15, 1962; July 5, 1964; January 21, 1979; April 12, 1981; August 15, 1982; April 30, 1989; April 19, 1992, p. 8; December 17, 1995, p. 7.

People, October 22, 1979.

Publishers Weekly, April 6, 1992; October 16, 1995, p. 49; October 23, 1995, p. 33; January 15, 1996, p. 320; May 20, 1996, p. 245; November 8, 1999, review of *And the Sea Is Never Full,* p. 53; July 15, 2002, review of *The Judges,* p. 55.

Saturday Review, December 17, 1960; July 8, 1961; July 25, 1964; May 28, 1966; October 19, 1968; January 31, 1970; November 21, 1970.

Tikkun, July-August, 1999, "An Interview with Elie Wiesel," pp. 33-35.

Time, March 16, 1970; May 8, 1972; July 12, 1976; December 25, 1978; April 20, 1981.

Times Literary Supplement, August 19, 1960; November 20, 1981; June 6, 1986.

TV Guide, February 15, 1969.

Washington Post, October 26, 1968; February 6, 1970; November 15, 1986; November 4, 1989.

Washington Post Book World, October 20, 1968; January 18, 1970; August 8, 1976; October 29, 1978; April 12, 1981; May 29, 1988.

World Literature Today, summer, 2000, Pierre L. Horn, review of *And the Sea Is Never Full,* p. 630; summer-autumn, 2002, Pierre L. Horn, review of *Conversations with Elie Wiesel,* p. 101.

ONLINE

Elie Wiesel Foundation for Humanity Web site, http://www.eliewieselfoundation.org/ (June 25, 2003).

*   *   *

WINN, Bob
  See SEULING, Barbara

WU, Yenna 1957-

PERSONAL: Born 1957, in Kaohsiung, Taiwan; U.S. citizen. *Ethnicity:* "Pacific Islander." *Education:* National Taiwan University, B.A., 1978; University of California—Los Angeles, M.A., 1981; Harvard University, Ph.D., 1986.

ADDRESSES: Office—Department of Comparative Literature and Foreign Languages, University of California—Riverside, Riverside, CA 92521-0321; fax: 909-787-2160. *E-mail*—yenna.wu@ucr.edu.

CAREER: University of Vermont, Burlington, VT, assistant professor and director of Chinese Language Program, 1986-92; University of California—Riverside, Riverside, CA, assistant professor, 1992-96, associate professor, 1996-99, professor of Chinese, 1999—, director of Asian Languages and Civilization Program, 2002—.

AWARDS, HONORS: Geraldine R. Dodge Foundation scholar at Middlebury College, 1986; grants from Pacific Cultural Foundation, 1990-91, 1994.

WRITINGS:

(Translator into Chinese) Knut Hamsun, *E* (title means "Hunger"), Chi-wen Publishing (Taipei, Taiwan), 1982.

(Translator) *The Lioness Roars: Shrew Stories from Late Imperial China,* Cornell University Press (Ithaca, NY), 1995.

The Chinese Virago: A Literary Theme, Council on East Asian Studies, Harvard University (Cambridge, MA), 1995.

(With Philip F. Williams) *Chinese the Easy Way,,* Barron's (Hauppage, NY) 1999.

Ameliorative Satire and the Seventeeth-Century Chinese Novel, Xingshi Yinyuan Zhuan—Marriage As Retribution, Awakening the World, Edwin Mellen (Lewiston, NY), 1999.

(Editor, with Philip F. Williams, and contributor) *Zhongguo funü yu wenxue lunji* (title means "Critical Essays on Chinese Women and Literature"), Daw Shiang Publishing (Taipei, Taiwan), Volume 1, 1999, Volume 2, 2001.

(With Philip F. Williams) *The Great Wall of Confinement: The Chinese Prison Camp through Contemporary Fiction and Reportage,* University of California Press (Berkeley, CA), in press.

Contributor to books, including *The Columbia History of Chinese Literature, The Oxford Guide to Literature in English Translation, Encyclopedia of the Novel,* and *The Indiana Companion to Traditional Chinese Literature.* Contributor to numerous journals, including *American Journal of Chinese Studies, Chinese Culture, Asia Major, Harvard Journal of Asiatic Studies, Journal of the Chinese Language Teachers Association, Tamkang Review: Quarterly of Comparative Studies between Chinese and Foreign Literatures,* and *Chinese Literature: Essays, Articles, Reviews.*

Y

YAFFE, Alan
    See YORINKS, Arthur

*   *   *

YAZDANFAR, Farzin 1953-

PERSONAL: Born November 27, 1953, in Tehran, Iran; naturalized U.S. citizen; son of Muhammad-Amin (a government employee) and Farah (a bank clerk; maiden name, Shafiee) Yazdanfar. *Ethnicity:* "Persian." *Education:* National University of Iran, B.A. (economics), 1975; College of Translation, Tehran, Iran, B.A. (translation), 1976; University of Michigan, M.A. (applied economics), 1977, M.A. (Near Eastern studies), 1986; attended University of Stockholm, 1980.

ADDRESSES: Home—233 East Erie St., Apt. 2207, Chicago, IL 60611. *Office*—Richard J. Daley College, 7500 South Pulaski Rd., Chicago, IL 60652. *E-mail*—yazdanfar@yahoo.com.

CAREER: University of Chicago, Chicago, IL, Persian bibliographer, 1994-96; Richard J. Daley College, Chicago, instructor in English as a second language, 1986—.

AWARDS, HONORS: Translation award, 1984.

WRITINGS:

(Editor, with John Green) *Walnut Sapling on Masih's Grave, and Other Stories by Iranian Women,* Heinemann (Portsmouth, NH), 1993.

(Editor, translator, and coauthor of introduction) *In a Voice of Their Own: A Collection of Stories by Iranian Women Written since the Revolution of 1979,* Mazda Publishers (Costa Mesa, CA), 1996.
The Downhearted (short stories), Ibex Publishers (Bethesda, MD), 1999.
(Compiler and translator) *Loneliness, the Thin Skin of Porcelain: A Collection of Fourteen Short Stories,* Simorgh Publishers (Mission Viejo, CA), 2003.

Contributor of English and Persian translations to periodicals.

SIDELIGHTS: Farzin Yazdanfar once told *CA:* "I have been interested in the concerns of Iranian women, and Iranian women writers in particular, since the revolution of 1979 and the establishment of the Islamic Republic in Iran. I have coedited and cotranslated two collections of short stories by Iranian women authors. In the first collection, the stories cover a period from 1945 to 1989. The second collection includes stories written by more than a dozen Iranian women during the last eighteen or nineteen years. I am also interested in writing scholarly articles about the history of Iranian women in this century and the role of women writers in modern Persian literature. My primary goal is to introduce the post-revolutionary Iranian women fiction writers and their rapidly growing contributions to the western reader."

*   *   *

YORINKS, Arthur 1953-
    (Alan Yaffe)

PERSONAL: Born August 21, 1953, in Roslyn, NY; son of Alexander (a mechanical engineer) and Shirley (a fashion illustrator; maiden name, Kron) Yorinks; married Adrienne Berg (an artist and illustrator), October 23, 1983. *Education:* Attended New School for Social Research and Hofstra New College, 1971. *Hobbies and other interests:* Opera, theater, dogs, visiting art museums.

ADDRESSES: Home—New York, NY. *Agent*—c/o Hyperion, 77 West 66th St., 11th Fl., New York, NY 10023.

CAREER: Author and illustrator of children's books; writer for opera, ballet, film, and theater. American Mime Theatre, New York, NY, writer, teacher, and performer, 1969-79; Cornell University, Ithaca, NY, instructor in theater arts, 1972-79; New Works Project, New York, NY, associate director, beginning 1977; Moving Theatre, New York, NY, founder, artistic director, 1979; The Night Kitchen (a national children's theater), New York, NY, cofounder and associate artistic director, 1990—.

AWARDS, HONORS: Best Books of the Year selections, *School Library Journal,* 1980, for *Louis the Fish,* 1988, for *Bravo, Minski,* 1989, for *Oh, Brother,* and 1990, for *Ugh;* Children's Editor's Choice, *Booklist,* 1984, for *It Happened in Pinsk;* Notable Book selection, American Library Association (ALA), 1986, Little Archer Award, Department of Library and Learning Resources, University of Wisconsin—Oshkosh, 1988, and Kentucky Bluegrass Award, 1988, all for *Hey, Al;* Ten Best Books of the Year selection, *Redbook,* and Notable Book selection, ALA, both 1988, both for *Company's Coming.*

WRITINGS:

Sid and Sol, illustrated by Richard Egielski, Farrar, Straus (New York, NY), 1977.

(Under pseudonym Alan Yaffe) *The Magic Meatballs,* illustrated by Karen B. Anderson, Dial (New York, NY), 1979.

Louis the Fish, illustrated by Richard Egielski, Farrar, Straus (New York, NY), 1980.

It Happened in Pinsk, illustrated by Richard Egielski, Farrar, Straus (New York, NY), 1983.

Hey, Al, illustrated by Richard Egielski, Farrar, Straus (New York, NY), 1986.

Bravo, Minski, illustrated by Richard Egielski, Farrar, Straus (New York, NY), 1988.

Company's Coming, illustrated by David Small, Crown (New York, NY), 1988.

Oh, Brother, illustrated by Richard Egielski, Farrar, Straus (New York, NY), 1989.

Ugh, illustrated by Richard Egielski, Farrar, Straus (New York, NY), 1990.

Christmas in July, illustrated by Richard Egielski, HarperCollins (New York, NY), 1991.

Whitefish Will Rides Again!, illustrated by Mort Drucker, HarperCollins (New York, NY), 1994.

The Miami Giant, illustrated by Maurice Sendak, HarperCollins (New York, NY), 1995.

Frank and Joey Go to Work (based on *So, Sue Me*), illustrated by Maurice Sendak, HarperFestival (New York, NY), 1996.

Frank and Joey Eat Lunch (based on *So, Sue Me*), illustrated by Maurice Sendak, HarperFestival (New York, NY), 1996.

Tomatoes from Mars, illustrated by Mort Drucker, HarperCollins (New York, NY), 1999.

Harry and Lulu, illustrated by Martin Matje, Hyperion (New York, NY), 1999.

The Alphabet Atlas, illustrated by Adrienne Yorinks, letter art by Jeanyee Wong, Winslow Press (Delray Beach, FL), 1999.

The Flying Latke, illustrated by William Steig, photo illustrations by Paul Colin and author, Simon & Schuster (New York, NY), 1999.

The Floating Cow and Other Stories, Arthur A. Levine (New York, NY), 2000.

Company's Going, illustrated by David Small, Hyperion (New York, NY), 2001.

(Self-illustrated) *Everybody Sleeps,* Winslow Press (Delray Beach, FL), 2002.

Quack!: To the Moon and Home Again, illustrated by Adrienne Yorinks, Abrams (New York, NY), 2003.

Matzoh Balls!: The Story of Passover, illustrated by Paul Cohen, Simon & Schuster (New York, NY), 2003.

Monsters in Space, ("Seven Little Monsters" series; based on the characters by Maurice Sendak), illustrated by Raymond Jafelice, Hyperion (New York, NY), 2003.

We Love You, Mama, ("Seven Little Monsters" series; based on the characters by Maurice Sendak), illustrated by Raymond Jafelice, Hyperion (New York, NY), 2003.

Harry and Lulu in the Himalayas, illustrated by Martin Matje, Hyperion (New York, NY), in press.

ONE-ACT PLAYS

Six, produced in New York, NY, at Hunter College Playhouse, November, 1973.

The Horse, produced in New York, NY, at Cornelia Street Cafe, November, 1978.

Crackers, produced in New York, NY, at Theatre of the Open Eye, June, 1979.

The King, produced in New York, NY, at South Street Theatre, July, 1980.

Kissers, produced in New York, NY, at South Street Theatre, July, 1980.

Piece for a Small Cafe, produced in New York, NY, at Cornelia Street Cafe, February, 1981.

Piece for a Larger Cafe, produced in New York, NY, at Cornelia Street Cafe, April, 1982.

So, Sue Me (also see above), produced in Washington, DC, at the Kennedy Center, September, 1993.

It's Alive!, produced in New York, NY, at Tribeca Performing Arts Center, 1994.

OPERA LIBRETTOS

Leipziger Kerzenspiel, produced at Mt. Holyoke College, 1984.

The Juniper Tree, music by Philip Glass and Robert Moran, Dunvagen Music (New York, NY), 1985, produced at the American Repertory Theater, Boston, MA, 1985.

(Adapter, with Philip Glass) *The Fall of the House of Usher,* produced at American Repertory Theater, Boston, MA, May, 1988.

OTHER

Sid and Sol (screenplay; adapted from his book of the same name), Four Penny Productions, 1982.

Story by Arthur Yorinks, Pictures by Richard Egielski (video), Farrar, Straus (New York, NY), 1987.

Also author of a full-length story ballet commissioned by the Hartford Ballet; author of a screenplay, "Making Scents," developed by A & M Films; author, with

film director Michael Powell, of screenplay *Usher;* and coauthor, with Maurice Sendak, of the text for the dance *A Selection.*

ADAPTATIONS: Louis the Fish was produced as an episode of *Reading Rainbow,* PBS-TV, 1983. *Louis the Fish* and *Sid and Sol* have both been adapted into cassette with hardcover book sets by Random House; *Hey, Al,* was adapted for videocassette by Spoken Arts (Holmes, NY), 2001.

SIDELIGHTS: Author of two dozen picture books and numerous stage plays, Arthur Yorinks is known for his outrageous and sometimes surreal stories which are frequently accompanied by the carefully composed, realistic illustrations of Richard Egielski, David Small, and Maurice Sendak. From *Sid and Sol,* in which a small man stands up to a formidable giant, to *Company's Coming* and its 2001 sequel, *Company's Going,* in which a woman graciously invites aliens to dinner, Yorinks's bizarre tales are told with deadpan humor that delights readers. According to Alice Miller Bregman in the *New York Times Book Review,* the "genius" of Yorinks's "understated texts . . . is that he knows what's truly important to youngsters."

The plots of some of Yorinks's stories demonstrate the futility of complaining, wishing to be someone else, or envying the possessions of others. Other tales stress the importance of tolerance and flexibility. While such morals are easily grasped by children, some critics assert that the best work of Yorinks and Egielski features irony and dark humor that mature readers will appreciate. In books like *Louis the Fish* and *Hey, Al,* insisted Bill Ott in the *New York Times Book Review,* adults will experience the "rare pleasure of finding a perverse subtext trapped in the straitjacket of 'positive moral values.'" For example, according to Ott, *It Happened in Pinsk* demonstrates that "life is one long complaint."

While children may recognize Yorinks as a favorite author, writing picture books is just one of his many talents. He has written several one-act plays which have been produced in New York City. Two of his opera librettos, combined with the music of the famous minimalist composer Philip Glass, were produced at the American Repertory Theater in Boston, Massachusetts. Yorinks has studied piano, ballet, and acting, performs as a mime, and acts. Yorinks also teaches acting, founding The Moving Theatre in 1979, and, in 1990, a national children's theater with the renowned picture-book author and illustrator Maurice Sendak.

"It seems I've always been involved in some form of the arts," Yorinks once told *CA.* For seven years of his childhood, Yorinks formally trained as a classical pianist with Robert Bedford. From Bedford, he "learned a great deal of what it means to be an artist." Yorinks's mother, a fashion illustrator, was also influential; "I think it was through those early years of watching and drawing with my mother that pictures became very important to me," Yorinks once explained to *CA.*

With an illustrator friend, Michael DePaolo, Yorinks began to create comic books in junior high school. Later, in high school, he became interested in the picture book genre. He once remarked, "Discovering Tomi Ungerer, William Steig, particularly Maurice Sendak, was a turning point. I was already a young adult, and I saw clearly that their books weren't just kids books. They were for everyone. They had such depth and excitement and had everything I was interested in—drama, pictures, rhythm, music."

Yorinks began to write his own picture books and, at the age of sixteen, "summoned all the courage I had and did something that was to have an *enormous* effect" on his "life and work," Yorinks once explained in. "I showed up at Maurice Sendak's door unannounced. . . . It was presumptuous of me, bordering on obnoxious, but my way of learning was always to talk to people I considered among the best at what they did. . . . I walked up to Maurice's door, and as I was about to ring the bell, I lost my nerve. Just as I turned to leave, the door opened and a man (Sendak? I wasn't even certain it was him) said, 'Can I help you?'

"'Would you like to see some of my stories?,' I blurted out.

"'Well,' he said in a slightly flustered voice, 'send them to me.'

"I had them with me and I simply handed him my bundle. To have my work read and commented on by Maurice Sendak was a dream come true." The two

ultimately became friends, and have collaborated not only on picture books, but also on stage productions. Yorinks once admitted, "Maurice has been a big help and a constant inspiration. I still think he is the contemporary standard for picture books and children's literature in general."

After graduating from high school, as he once related, Yorinks began to explore and develop his many interests. "I became involved in theater by studying ballet and acting and ended up at the American Mime Theatre. For ten years I wrote plays, performed, and taught with the theatre company. Looking back, this was excellent training for picture books. In a mime play, there is no dialogue. The spectacle is all images. Plot, relationships, passage of time are all communicated through action and the 'pictures' made by the performers. In a real sense, the actors *are* the pictures. The scripts I wrote were blocks of prose—this happens, then this happens, then this. I had to deal with character, situation, place and narrative without describing anything. This, as I was to learn, was pretty much the best way to write picture books."

In the late 1970s, one of Sendak's suggestions led to another turning point in Yorinks's career. As Yorinks once elaborated: "I had sold a manuscript to a publisher, but as yet they hadn't found an illustrator, a situation which was to drag on for years before it fell apart altogether. I was miserable, as this was my first book, and it was sitting there, crying out for pictures. One day I was talking with Sendak, who told me that he'd had a student at Parsons who would be terrific for my work. His name was Richard (Sendak was not able to remember his last name)."

Yorinks went to Parsons to find Richard, whom Sendak had described, and found him standing by an elevator. "I was shy, but *desperate,* so I tapped him on the shoulder and said, 'Richard.' He turned around and looked at me as if I was about to pick his pocket!" After Yorinks told Egielski how he'd recognized him and explained the purpose of his visit, the pair reviewed Egielski's portfolio. "I had never seen work like his. . . . Maurice was absolutely right about Richard Egielski being the perfect illustrator for my stories."

According to George Shannon in a *School Library Journal* review of *Louis the Fish,* "Yorinks and Egielski work together as if they were one." Yorinks once described his working relationship with Egielski: "By the time I show Richard a story, it's almost finished. It may need some fine tuning, but essentially it's all there. If he likes it, we talk—generally quite briefly—about how I came up with the story, what inspired it, what I was reading at the time I wrote it. I never have any kind of image of what the book should look like or what the pictures should feel like. The real fun for me is having to wait while Richard does his storyboard. When he shows it to me, it's like Christmas. All of a sudden I see things I never would have thought of in conjunction with the story. They were buried—apparently without my being conscious of them—in the text."

Yorinks's collaboration with Egielski allows him to live up to his principles of book creation. According to Yorinks, he has "dedicated" himself to the picture book "art form in the tradition of those artists who look upon the picture book as a medium where the marriage of words and pictures is all important, and the seam that binds them together is all but invisible. Too many picture books of today have sorry texts used only as vehicles for a set of pictures, like a description attached to a portfolio. That is not what I believe picture books should be. It is a serious art form, most exact. And it is with the responsibility of any artistic pursuit that Richard Egielski . . . and I approach each new work."

Yorinks and Egielski's first project was published in 1977. *Sid and Sol* features a giant, Sol, who threatens the world with his mighty power. World leaders advertise for a giant killer, and the only person to respond is Sid. Despite his small size, Sid accomplishes his task by convincing the giant to build a tall tower and climb it. When the giant falls to his death, the Grand Canyon is created. Welcoming Yorinks and Egielski in the *New York Times Book Review,* Maurice Sendak rejoiced in the duo's "deft and exciting collaboration," and praised Yorinks's "gorgeous writing" and "cool audacity to mix purest nonsense with cockeyed fact."

In the wake of the success of *Sid and Sol,* Yorinks and Egielski published *Louis the Fish,* a story inspired by Austro-Czech writer Franz Kafka's *The Metamorphosis,* in which a man wakes to find himself transformed into an insect. In the opinion of Ott, *Louis the Fish* provides "irony in its purest form" as it sends a message: "No matter what we have, it's not what we want." Although Louis comes from a family of butch-

ers and is a butcher himself, he hates meat. He thinks of nothing but fish and then, finally, is transformed into a happy salmon with silvery scales and big lips. Flashbacks recall Louis's human life, in which he was surrounded by meat. According to Shannon, *Louis the Fish* is "an exciting tale" in which "no words are wasted."

Yorinks once noted that his next book, *It Happened in Pinsk,* "grew out of his reverence for [Russian writer Nikolai] Gogol, and particularly my love for his story 'The Nose' in which one morning a man wakes up without his nose. As is my habit, when I have read and loved a work by a given author, I read everything he's done, as well as biographies of him. . . . When Richard and I talked about my story, I mentioned Gogol and my infatuation with pre-revolutionary Russia. I would have loved to have opened my piece with a two- or three-page description of Nevsky Avenue—something I couldn't do in a picture book.

"Richard's double-page spread more than satisfied the craving I had to have the street described. It's very filmic, as though the camera was coming from a great distance at a very slow pace, lighting one image after another, after another. You get many tantalizing hints about what is going to happen in the book from this one illustration. . . . I'm not permitted to explain the text in detail, but as Richard echoed the text in his visuals, nothing was lost—in fact, much was gained."

According to Ott in the *New York Times Book Review,* the protagonist of *It Happened in Pinsk* is characterized "as the perennially dissatisfied modern man." Although Irv Irving has a nice wife, fine clothes, and good food, he is sure he would rather be someone else—a wrestler, a tycoon, a widow with a mansion. One day at breakfast he notices that his head is missing. Irv's wife fashions him a head from a pillowcase and some socks, and he wanders the city in search of his head. His substitute head gets him into much trouble as he is mistaken for various scoundrels. The story is resolved after Irv states his acceptance of his identity and finds his head. Marguerite Feitlowitz praised *It Happened in Pinsk* in a *New York Times Book Review,* commenting that Yorinks's and Egielski's "work is unusual, vivacious, hilarious and touching."

For Yorinks and Egielski's next work, *Hey, Al,* Egielski received one of the picture book genre's most prestigious awards, the Caldecott Medal. In this story, Al, a janitor, and his loyal dog, Eddie, are visited by a huge purple bird offering to take them to paradise. They eagerly accept the bird's invitation—they have had enough of Al's cleaning job and their small New York apartment. Al and Eddie enjoy the beautiful and bountiful island in the sky until they begin to grow beaks and feathers and realize that the price of paradise is to become a bird. They return to their safe apartment, molt, and happily paint their room yellow. Kenneth Marantz suggested in *School Library Journal* that the "theme" of *Hey, Al* is "be happy with who you are," or "there's no free lunch." In the opinion of *New York Times Book Review* contributor Judith Viorst, *Hey, Al* delivers a moral about "even the humblest home" with "warmth and wit and imagination." Reviewing the 2001 video recording of *Hey, Al*, Marilyn Hersh, writing in *School Library Journal*, found the story "delightful," and further noted that "everything about this tender, morality based fantasy is expertly executed."

Bravo, Minski features a child prodigy whose life has, as a critic for *Kirkus Reviews* observed, "inescapable parallels" to that of classical composer Wolfgang Amadeus Mozart. Minski, however, is a great scientist, discovering gravity and electricity. As the inventor of aspirin, automobiles, airplanes, eyeglasses, light bulbs, and telephones, he becomes famous. Scientists like Leonardo da Vinci and Albert Einstein anachronistically show up in the eighteenth century to pay tribute to the boy. Nevertheless, the young scientist's dream is to sing—he works diligently until he creates a formula to make him an artist with a "heavenly" voice. One of the messages in this book, according to *Washington Post* reviewer Selma G. Lanes, is to "follow your own enthusiasms." Aside from the message, as Patricia Dooley observed in *School Library Journal*, the "deadpan illogicality and gay absurdity" of *Bravo, Minski* "should leave children giddy."

Yorinks's "tongue-in-cheek tone," as Betsy Hearne of *Bulletin of the Center for Children's Books* called it, coupled with Egielski's "satirical . . . softly rounded shapes and absurdly deadpan characters" prove a winning combination in *Oh, Brother*. In this story, the constant fighting of twin twentieth-century English brothers, Milton and Morris, sets the course of their life. On a voyage with their parents, the twins explore the forbidden hold and, as they fight over a skyrocket, destroy the ship. The boys survive the wreck, land in New York City, and live in orphanages before going to work in the circus. There, they wash elephants and

even get a chance to work on the flying trapezes. Once again, however, their fighting causes them trouble, and they are fired. When they attempt to earn a living by selling apples, they get in an argument and waste the apples by throwing them at each other.

Finally, when the boys resort to thievery, their pickpocketing attempt is foiled. Their intended victim, Nathan, takes the boys home to live with him and serve as his apprentice tailors. Although they learn reluctantly, they become excellent tailors and even grow to love Nathan. When he dies, they secretly pretend to be his cousins and continue his work so well that they receive an invitation to meet the Queen of England. In her court, they are recognized by their parents (the Queen's gardener and nanny), who survived the shipwreck; the family is happily reunited, and Milton and Morris become the personal tailors of the Prince of Wales. Writing in *School Library Journal*, Linda Boyles concluded that adults will "appreciate Yorinks's wry humor, while kids are sure to enjoy the antics of the obnoxious twins." Cathleen Schine asserted in the *New York Times Book Review* that *Oh, Brother* is Yorinks and Egielski's "finest work to date," a book which demonstrates that childhood is "not just another time but another world."

Ugh is set "Many, many, many, many, many, many years ago," in a prehistoric landscape. In this tale, the Cinderella-like Ugh is forced to do all the cavework while his sisters and brothers play and watch dinosaurs eat trees. Ugh secretly invents a bicycle, and accidentally rides it into a group of world leaders. Thinking he will be punished, Ugh hides. The leaders recognize the importance of the invention, however, and vow that the inventor will be king. Just as the prince found Cinderella, Ugh is found to be the inventor and is crowned king with a saber-tooth crown. Disturbed by their inability to claim the invention as their own, Ugh's brothers and sisters jump into the ocean, where a whale devours them. *School Library Journal* reviewer Karen James thought that the "pidgin English" used "to indicate a primitive peoples' language" might offend some readers, but Hearne of the *Bulletin of the Center for Children's Books* concluded that *Ugh* is the "real winner" among the Yorinks-Egielski books. She asked, "Who wouldn't want to *hear* . . . this uniquely American tall tale of material success?"

Christmas in July begins when Santa takes his pants to the cleaners. The cleaners accidentally return Santa's pants to the wrong person, a wealthy man named Rich

Rump. Santa follows Rich Rump to his home in New York City, where he is forced to beg for pants. The police arrest him for loitering, and Santa is sentenced to six months in jail. Upon his release, Santa learns that his absence at Christmas had terrible effects on the world. Fortunately, he sees Rich Rump, now poor, trying to unload his pants on the streets. Rich Rump gives Santa the pants, Rudolph and the other reindeer arrive with Santa's sleigh, and Santa takes off to bring Christmas to the world—in July. According to a critic for *School Library Journal,* the "phrasing is clever" and the "pacing is quick." Roger Sutton of *Bulletin of the Center for Children's Books* commented that the "dry and sly" humor is not successful "in disguising the fact that this book is an old-fashioned Christmas heartwarmer."

Yorinks has worked with illustrators other than Egielski on a number of books, and since 1991, has turned to illustrators such as Maurice Sendak, Mort Drucker, David Small, and to his wife, Adrienne Yorinks, for artwork. *Company's Coming,* illustrated by Small, is, in the words of a *Kirkus Reviews* critic, "deliciously funny." Shirley and Moe are outside preparing for a visit from some cousins when Shirley notices a "barbecue" that turns out to be a flying saucer. When helmeted aliens that look like cockroaches emerge from the saucer, they ask for a bathroom and get an invitation to Shirley's party. Unlike Shirley, Moe is not a gracious host—he telephones the FBI, which alerts the Pentagon, and the Pentagon mobilizes the army, air force, and the marines.

By the time the aliens return for dinner, the armed forces are in position and invade the dinner party. Nevertheless, once everyone realizes that the present the aliens have brought Shirley and Moe is a blender, and not a bomb, everyone sits down for a spaghetti dinner. *School Library Journal* contributor David Gale thought that children would be delighted by Yorinks's "dry humor" and "deadpan telling" of a tale about "faulty assumptions and over-reacting." "Yorinks's dialogue is as well timed as the best comedy act," wrote Bregman in the *New York Times Book Review.*

Yorinks and Small reprised the unexpected alien guests in the 2001 title, *Company's Going,* a book, according to *Horn Book* reviewer Martha V. Parravano, that "is, if anything, funnier than the first, and less preachy as well." In this tale, the friendly aliens request that Moe and Shirley cater their sister's wedding. Only problem

is, the wedding is taking place on Nextoo, a planet that is, of course, *next to* Uranus. Moe and Shirley are doubtful, but finally agree. When they arrive on Nextoo, however, the locals react negatively to these Earthly aliens—whom they mistake for Martians—and zap the couple with a ray gun. The bride-to-be is disconsolate, with the wedding seemingly ruined. But all ends happily, as Moe and Shirley recover—now cured of their arthritis—and cook up a mess of meatballs and then dance the night away. Parravano lauded the "broadly humorous, blithely innocent story," but *Booklist*'s Michael Cart was not as impressed. For him, "the humor seems a bit forced." A *Publishers Weekly* reviewer, however, found the sequel a "droll follow-up to *Company's Coming,*" and concluded that "this comical collaboration makes a very good company." More praise came from Deborah Stevenson, who noted in a *Bulletin of the Center for Children's Books* review that "youngsters more inclined towards E.T. than Buck Rogers will be ready to take off with this."

Yorinks worked with illustrator Drucker for *Whitefish Will Rides Again!* Whitefish Will, readers learn at the beginning of the book, is "just about the best danged sheriff that ever lived." Having put away the cattle rustlers that plagued his town, Sheriff Will has nothing left to do but tend to his flock of roosters and play the harmonica. Yet when Bart and his band of bad guys ride into town, Will saves the day with his trusty harmonica. "No question 'bout it," wrote a critic for *Publishers Weekly,* "kids gonna love this one."

The pair teamed up again for the 1999 title, *Tomatoes from Mars,* in which the aforementioned tomatoes land on Minneapolis, Minnesota, and then proceed to drop all over the United States and the rest of the Earth, as well. When the red fruits stain not only the Statue of Liberty, but also Mount Rushmore and the White House, wise minds know something must be done. Strange Dr. Shtickle steps up to the plate and belts a homerun with his discovery that a dollop of salad dressing will send the tomatoes back to where they came. Not as well received as the duo's earlier effort, this collaborative effort was found to have "less-than-clever results," by a critic for *Kirkus Reviews.* Similarly, a contributor for *Publishers Weekly* felt that "this shtick doesn't quite cut the mustard."

Beginning in 1990, Yorinks began working with Sendak to create The Night Kitchen, a national children's theater. Their goal was to provide quality children's plays and operas, rather than the simplified performances of adult theater which are usually the norm. The two have extended that collaborative effort into other plays and dance theater, as well as to books. *The Miami Giant* follows the adventures of an Italian explorer, Giuseepe Giaweeni, who sets out for China and discovers Miami instead. There he finds a tribe of giants who dance gleefully; Giaweeni convinces the head of the tribe, Joe Mishbooker, to come back to Europe with him where he will surely become a star. In the event, theatergoers are not so enthusiastic; Joe eventually returns to Miami, and the intrepid explorer ends up discovering Boca.

Adapting the stage production of Yorinks's play *So, Sue Me* to board book format, Sendak and the author also collaborated on *Frank and Joey Go to Work* and *Frank and Joey Eat Lunch*. The two construction workers of the title get into some "simple—and funny—trouble" in this pair of books, according to *Horn Book*'s Sutton, discussing both works. Joey drops Frank's huge sandwich off the building site, to land on a passerby in *Frank and Joey Eat Lunch*, while Joey loses his boots and pants when he steps in fresh cement in *Go to Work*. Elizabeth Bush lauded the "classic beefy guy/dweeby guy comedy team" in a review of both titles for the *Bulletin of the Center for Children's Books*.

In *Harry and Lulu*, Yorinks paired with illustrator Martin Matje to create "an odd twist on the usual fantasy of a child who believes a toy is real," according to *School Library Journal*'s Kate McClelland. Lulu is pining for a dog, and when her parents give her a stuffed poodle instead, the little girl delivers a first-class tantrum. Later that night, however, Lulu discovers that her little red poodle named Harry can talk, telling Lulu he is going back to his native France. She decides to follow along, and walking down the street, they end up in Paris in the morning. There the clever poodle saves Lulu from a cab, and she returns the favor, saving him when he falls in the Seine. Returning to Lulu's home, the two have become best of friends. A critic for *Kirkus Reviews*, while noting that this story is not quite a "*Velveteen Rabbit* for the '90s," did find that the tale "captures a child in several deeply recognizable moments." *Booklist*'s Ilene Cooper felt that the artwork "suits the tale perfectly," and further noted that *Harry and Lulu* was "an insouciant yet sweet story."

In *The Flying Latke*, Yorinks pairs with William Steig for a Hanukkah tale of a very different sort. An argu-

ment over the make of the car that cut off two uncles earlier in the day results in a food fight on the first night of Hanukkah, during which a latke gets tossed so hard that it goes ballistic. Flying out over the New Jersey Turnpike, it is mistaken for a flying saucer by the air force. When the uncles' attempts to tell the world the truth of this latke/UFO fail, they are besieged by reporters and virtually imprisoned in their own home for the next eight days. During this time the family is forced to survive on the remaining latkes, a real Hanukkah miracle. Danny, the young boy of the family, narrates this tale in a manner that "has the roll and rhythm of a family story punctuated by bits of Yiddish and schtick," according to Janice M. Del Negro, writing in *Bulletin of the Center for Children's Books*. Del Negro concluded, "To say that this is a tale made to be read aloud would be an understatement of colossal proportions." Similarly, Teri Markson, writing in *School Library Journal*, felt this "is a very funny story that simply begs to be read aloud after the menorah is lit and the latkes are just a grease spot on a plate."

Yorinks has also collaborated with his fabric-artist wife, Adrienne, on *The Alphabet Atlas* and *Quack!: To the Moon and Home Again*, two books with simplified text. Fabric from the twenty-five nations included in the alphabet book provides the illustrations, along with a calligraphic rendition of each letter. A critic for *Kirkus Reviews* had praise for the artwork, noting that "this alphabet of countries makes a magnificent showcase for Adrienne Yorinks's textile art."

In *Quack!*, a duck goes off to the moon after viewing the object from afar through his telescope. Plagued by a bout of homesickness, however, the duck eventually parachutes back to Earth. The tale is told in English as well as in the one-word duck language, Quack. Again, the story features fabric collages by Adrienne Yorinks. A contributor for *Publishers Weekly* found the result "fine feathered fun," while *School Library Journal* critic Kristin de Lacoste predicted, "Although this is an odd duck of a book, very young children will love saying the word quack over and over again."

Yorinks believes that creating picture books for children is a serious responsibility. "Children's first books are often picture books," he once remarked. "From picture books, children get their first inkling about literature and visual art. The importance of picture books is therefore profound. The stories and images adults make for children may well say more about a given society than anything else. Children deserve the best we can offer—authentic and uncompromising art."

BIOGRAPHICAL AND CRITICAL SOURCES:

BOOKS

Children's Books and Their Creators, edited by Anita Silvey, Houghton Mifflin (Boston, MA), 1995.

Children's Literature Review, Volume 20, Gale (Detroit, MI), 1990, pp. 213-218.

Continuum Encyclopedia of Children's Literature, edited by Bernice E. Cullinan and Diane G. Person, Continuum International (New York, NY), 2001, p. 839.

Lanes, Selma G., *The Art of Maurice Sendak,* edited by Robert Morton, Abrams (New York, NY), 1980, pp. 251-270.

St. James Guide to Children's Writers, 5th edition, edited by Sara Pendergast and Tom Pendergast, St. James Press (Detroit, MI), 1999.

Yorinks, Arthur, *Ugh,* illustrated by Richard Egielski, Farrar, Straus (New York, NY), 1990.

Yorinks, Arthur, *Whitefish Will Rides Again!,* illustrated by Mort Drucker, HarperCollins (New York, NY), 1994.

PERIODICALS

Avenue, October, 1994, p. 13.

Bookcase, April, 1995, p. 16.

Booklist, October 1, 1979; December 15, 1988, p. 716; April 1, 1999, Ilene Cooper, review of *Harry and Lulu,* p. 1409; January 1, 2002, Michael Cart, review of *Company's Going,* pp. 868-869; April 1, 2003, Julie Cummins, review of *Quack!: To the Moon and Home Again,* p. 1404.

Bulletin of the Center for Children's Books, February, 1981, p. 124; November, 1989, Betsy Hearne, review of *Oh, Brother,* p. 74; November, 1990, Betsy Hearne, review of *Ugh,* p. 75; Roger Sutton, November, 1991, review of *Christmas in July,* p. 80; February, 1997, Elizabeth Bush, review of *Frank and Joey Go to Work* and *Frank and Joey Eat Lunch,* p. 228; November, 1999, Janice M. Del Negro, review of *The Flying Latke,* p. 112; January, 2002, Deborah Stevenson, review of *Company's Going,* p. 189.

Horn Book, January-February, 1996, Mary M. Burns, review of *The Miami Giant,* pp. 70-71; January-February, 1997, Roger Sutton, review of *Frank and Joey Go to Work* and *Frank and Joey Eat Lunch,* p. 53; January-February, 2002, Martha V. Parravano, review of *Company's Going,* pp. 74-75.

Kirkus Reviews, December 1, 1977, p. 1265; November 15, 1980, p. 1463; January 15, 1988, review of *Company's Coming,* p. 130; October 15, 1988, review of *Bravo, Minski,* p. 1536; March 15, 1999, review of *Harry and Lulu,* p. 459; May 15, 1999, review of *The Alphabet Atlas,* p. 807; October 15, 1999, review of *Tomatoes from Mars,* p. 1654; January 1, 2003, review of *Quack!,* p. 68.

Los Angeles Times, October 14, 1979.

New York Times, October 23, 1994; October, 28, 1994.

New York Times Book Review, December 10, 1978, Maurice Sendak, "The Giant and the Runt," p. 72; December 18, 1983, Marguerite Feitlowitz, review of *It Happened in Pinsk,* p. 20; January 11, 1987, Judith Viorst, review of *Hey, Al,* p. 38; January 10, 1988, Bill Ott, "A Convention of Grousers," p. 37; May 8, 1988, Alice Miller Bregman, "Dinner Guests from Outer Space," p. 38; May 13, 1990, Cathleen Schine, review of *Oh, Brother,* p. 30.

Publishers Weekly, November 11, 1988, p. 54; July 11, 1994, review of *Whitefish Will Rides Again!,* p. 77; March 29, 1999, review of *Harry and Lulu,* p. 103; September 27, 1999, review of *The Flying Latke,* p. 52; October 18, 1999, review of *Tomatoes from Mars,* p. 81; November 5, 2001, review of *Company's Going,* p. 68; January 6, 2003, review of *Quack!,* p. 57.

Reporter Dispatch, October 17, 1994.

School Library Journal, November, 1980, George Shannon, review of *Louis the Fish,* p. 68; March, 1987, Kenneth Marantz, review of *Hey, Al,* pp. 151-152; February, 1988, David Gale, review of *Company's Coming,* p. 66; December, 1988, Patricia Dooley, review of *Bravo Minski,* pp. 95-96; December, 1989, Linda Boyles, review of *Oh, Brother,* p. 92; December, 1990, Karen James, review of *Ugh,* p. 91; October, 1991, review of *Christmas in July,* p. 35; January, 1998, review of *Oh, Brother,* p. 43; May, 1999, Kate McClelland, review of *Harry and Lulu,* pp. 101-102; July, 1999, Linda Greengrass, review of *The Alphabet Atlas,* p. 91; October, 1999, Teri Markson, review of *The Flying Latke,* p. 72; January, 2000, Margaret Bush, review of *Tomatoes from Mars,* p. 114; June, 2001, Marilyn Hersh, review of *Hey, Al* (videocassette), p. 64; February, 2002, Grace Oliff, review of *Company's Going,* p. 116; April, 2003, Kristin de Lacoste, review of *Quack!,* p. 144.

Teaching K-8, November-December, 1991.

Time, July 26, 1999, Terry Teachout, "A Selection: Pilobolus Dance Theatre," p. 76.

Tribune Books (Chicago, IL), January 25, 1987, p. 4.

Washington Post, September 21, 1993.

Washington Post Book World, February 15, 1987, p. 13; November 6, 1988, Selma G. Lanes, "Lookin' Real Good," p. 14.*